Indian Foreign Policy

FOREIGN SERVICE INSTITUTE, NEW DELHI

Indian Foreign Policy

Challenges and Opportunities

FOREWORD:

Pranab Mukherjee

Minister of External Affairs, New Delhi

EDITORS:

Atish Sinha

Dean, FSI, New Delhi

Madhup Mohta

Director, FSI, New Delhi

ACADEMIC FOUNDATION
NEW DELHI

First published in 2007

by : ACADEMIC FOUNDATION

4772-73 / 23 Bharat Ram Road, (23 Ansari Road),
Darya Ganj, New Delhi - 110 002 (India).
Tel : 23245001 / 02 / 03 / 04.
Fax : +91-11-23245005.
E-mail : academic@vsnl.com
www.academicfoundation.com

Published in collaboration with
Foreign Service Institute, New Delhi.

Cataloging in Publication Data--DK
Courtesy: D.K. Agencies (P) Ltd. <docinfo@dkagencies.com>

Indian foreign policy : challenges and opportunities/
editors, Atish Sinha, Madhup Mohta ;
foreword by Pranab Mukherjee.

p.   cm.
Contributed articles.
Includes bibliographical references.
ISBN-13 : 978-81-7188-593-4
ISBN-10 : 81-7188-593-4

1. India--Foreign relations--1984- 2. National security
--India. 3. Nuclear weapons--Government policy--India.
4. India--Foreign economic relations.   I. Sinha, Atish.
II. Mohta, Madhup.

DDC 327.54   22

Designed and typeset by Italics India, New Delhi.
Printed and bound in India.

10 9 8 7 6 5 4 3 2 1

We may talk about international goodwill and mean what we say. We may talk about peace and freedom and earnestly mean what we say. But in the ultimate analysis, a government functions for the good of the country it governs and no government dare do anything which in the short or long run is manifestly to the disadvantage of that country.

— *Jawaharlal Nehru*

CONTENTS

Foreign economic policy

Heritage, culture and diplomacy

Contributors to this volume

Rajendra M. Abhyankar, Director, Centre for West Asian Studies, Jamia Millia Islamia, New Delhi. Formerly career diplomat, he has been Ambassador to the EU, Belgium, Luxembourg, Syria, Turkey, and Cyprus. He has also served as Secretary, Ministry of External Affairs, Government of India.

Talmiz Ahmad, career diplomat since 1974; he has been Ambassador to Saudi Arabia and Oman; Additional Secretary (International Cooperation) in the Ministry of Petroleum and Natural Gas (2005-06), Government of India. Since April 2006, Director-General of the Indian Council of World Affairs (ICWA).

Hamid Ansari is Chairperson of the National Commission for Minorities and a former Permanent Representative to the UN and Ambassador to Iran and Saudi Arabia. He has been Vice-Chancellor of the Aligarh Muslim University, Member of the National Security Advisory Board and Distinguished Fellow at the Observer Research Foundation.

Ishrat Aziz, formerly career diplomat, served in Baghdad, Rabat, Beirut, San Francisco. He has been Ambassador to UAE, Saudi Arabia, Brazil, and Tunisia.

K. Shankar Bajpai, presently Chairman of the Delhi Policy Group. Formerly career diplomat, he has been Secretary, Ministry of External Affairs; Government of India's Representative in Sikkim; Ambassador to the Netherlands, Pakistan, China and the US. Subsequently, he has also been Visiting Professor at the University of California, Berkeley and Professor at the Brandeis University.

Harsh Bhasin, currently Visiting Professor of International Relations at the State University of New York, Stony Brook (USA). Formerly career diplomat, he has been envoy to South Africa, Botswana and Denmark; besides assignments in Hong Kong, Beijing, Washington, New York, Kuala Lumpur and Kathmandu.

Sanjay Bhattacharyya, career diplomat since 1987, served in Beijing, Brussels, Hong Kong and Headquarters. He studied Economics in St. Stephen's College and Delhi School of Economics and Chinese at Chinese University, Hong Kong.

Prem K. Budhwar, formerly career diplomat, served in Moscow, Hong Kong, Hanoi, Hamburg, Bonn; Ambassador to Ethiopia, Brazil, High Commissioner to Canada.

Anuradha M. Chenoy, is Professor, School of International Studies (SIS), Jawaharlal Nehru University, New Delhi; Chairperson and Director of Russian and Central Asian Studies, SIS. Her books include: *The Making of New Russia; Militarism and Women in South Asia* and *Human Security: Concept and Implications,* co-authored with Shahrbanou Tadjbakhsh.

A.K. Damodaran, formerly career diplomat, has served in Colombo, Prague, Bonn, Berlin, Beijing and Moscow. He has been Ambassador to Sweden, Italy; Visiting Professor, Centre for Diplomatic Studies, Jawaharlal Nehru University.

Chandrashekhar Dasgupta, formerly career diplomat, has served in Mexico, Italy, Bangladesh, United Kingdom; at Permanent Mission in New York. He has been High Commissioner to Singapore, Tanzania; Ambassador to China and the European Union. Currently Distinguished Fellow, The Energy and Resources Institute (TERI). Dasgupta is the author of *War and Diplomacy in Kashmir 1947-48.*

Muchkund Dubey, is currently President, Council for Social Development and Vice Chairman, Planning Commission of Sikkim. Formerly, Foreign Secretary; Professor, Jawaharlal Nehru University; High Commissioner to Bangladesh and Permanent Representative to UN Organisations in Geneva. He has authored several books and contributed chapters to various books and articles in reputed national and foreign journals. Professor Emeritus, Foreign Service Institute, New Delhi.

Chinmaya R. Gharekhan, formerly career diplomat, served in Egypt, Democratic Republic of the Congo, Laos, Vietnam, former Yugoslavia. He has a quarter century of dealing with the United Nations in various capacities; Permanent Representative to the United Nations in Geneva and New York and Under Secretary General in the United Nations Secretariat.

Arundhati Ghose, formerly career diplomat, served in various posts in Bangladesh, Europe and the Indian delegations to the UN in Paris and New York. Till 1997, Permanent Representative to UN offices in Geneva and Conference on Disarmament. She has been Ambassador to South Korea and Egypt; served on UNSG's Disarmament Advisory Board (1998-2001); member of CSCAP Study Group on Countering the Proliferation of Weapons of Mass Destruction in the Asia Pacific. Currently, Member, UN Committee on Economic, Social and Cultural Rights.

Baladas Ghoshal, Visiting Professor, Department of Intercultural Studies, Nagoya City University, Japan. Formerly, Professor and Chairman, Centre for South, Central, South-East Asian and South-West Pacific Studies, Jawaharlal Nehru University, New Delhi. He was also a Consultant to the United Nations Support Facility for Indonesian Recovery (UNSFIR) in Jakarta in 2003. He reads, writes and speaks Malay and Bahasa Indonesia and is currently working on Radical Islam and Regional Security in South-East Asia.

Ranjit Gupta, formerly career diplomat, served in Cairo, New York (PMI), Gangtok, Jeddah, Frankfurt and Kathmandu; successively India's Ambassador to Yemen (North), Venezuela, Oman, Thailand, Spain, and Head of the non-official Office in Taiwan. Currently Visiting Fellow, Institute of Chinese Studies, New Delhi.

Abid Hussain, a distinguished Economist and Diplomat; Member of the Planning Commission; India's Ambassador to USA (1991-1993); Member of the International Panel on Democracy and Development of UNESCO. Professor Emeritus, Foreign Service Institute, New Delhi.

S. Jaishankar, career diplomat since 1977; served in Tokyo, Washington, Moscow, Colombo, Budapest; Ambassador to Czech Republic; presently Joint Secretary (Americas), closely involved in the India-United States civil nuclear negotiations.

Nagendra Nath Jha, formerly career diplomat, served in Vienna, Permanent Mission in New York, Kathmandu; Ambassador to Ireland, Turkey, Kuwait; High Commissioner to Colombo.

Afsir Karim, Maj. Gen (Retd.), specialist on issues related to terrorism and internal conflicts; published a number of books on the subject: *Counter Terrorism: The Pakistan Factor* (1991); *Transnational Terrorism: Danger in the South* (1993). Currently, editor of *Aakrosh*, a journal on Terrorism and Internal Conflicts.

I.P. Khosla, formerly career diplomat, Secretary, Ministry of External Affairs, served in several assignments, mainly in the neighbouring countries, in Myanmar and successively, India's Representative to Bhutan and then High Commissioner to Bangladesh, also Ambassador to Afghanistan.

Krishan Kumar, career diplomat since 1984, served in Egypt, Saudi Arabia, Mozambique, Japan, Jordan, France, presently Deputy Chief of Mission in Brasilia.

Mohan Kumar, career diplomat since 1981, served in Permanent Mission of India in Geneva and as Deputy High Commissioner to Sri Lanka (2001-2005). Currently, Joint Secretary, in charge of relations with Bangladesh, Sri Lanka, Maldives and Myanmar.

Nagesh Kumar, Director-General of RIS (Research and Information System for Developing Countries, New Delhi). Previously served the UN University, Maastricht, and has been a consultant to the World Bank, ADB, UNCTAD, UNIDO, UN-ESCAP, and ILO. He is the recipient of the Exim Bank's first international trade research award and is a GDN Research Medal winner.

Dilip Lahiri, formerly career diplomat, he has been Ambassador to France, Spain; served in Bangladesh; Permanent Mission in New York; at Headquarters coordinating UN matters, and Dean, Foreign Service Institute. He has published articles on India's nuclear and security policy, and edited Foreign Service Institute's book on India's Foreign Policy for the 21st century.

Mani Singh Mamik, Commodore, a retired naval aviator; alumni of NDA, DSSC Wellington; holds MSc. and Ph.D. (Effectiveness of Sea Based Nuclear Weapons in International Relations) from University of Madras. He has served as Deputy Director General Defence Planning Staff; OSD to the Chief of Naval Staff for Strategic Affairs and also as faculty of DSSC, Wellington.

Dalip Mehta, formerly career diplomat; Ambassador to Bhutan and the Central Asian Republics of Uzbekistan, Tajikistan and Turkmenistan; Secretary in the Ministry of External Affairs, Government of India and Dean, Foreign Service Institute, New Delhi till 2002. Dalip Mehta is a Trustee of the Dalai Lama's Foundation for Universal Responsibility and a Director of the India-Bhutan Foundation.

Jagat Singh Mehta, formerly career diplomat (1947-1980), Charge d'affaires, China (1963-1966); High Commissioner, Tanzania (1970-1974); Foreign Secretary, (1976-1979). He was involved in Negotiations on (i) Sino-Indian Boundary Question (1960); (ii) Compensation for Indians expelled from Uganda (1975); (iii) Comprehensive normalisation with Pakistan (1976); (iv) Salal Hydel Project (1976); (v) Withdrawal of Farakka from UN and Finalising Agreement (1977); and (viii) Separating Trade and Transit Treaties with Nepal (1978). He was Associate at Harvard (1969 and 1980) and Fellow at Woodrow Wilson Centre, Washington (1981). His publications include: *Militarization in the Third World* (1985); *The March of Folly in Afghanistan* (2002); and *Negotiating for India* (2006).

Raja Menon, Rear Admiral (Retd.), was Indian Navy career officer till 1994. Subsequently, he authored three books: *Sea Power and India's Security; A Nuclear Strategy for India,* and *Weapons of Mass Destruction: Options for India.* He headed the Naval Headquarters group that recently wrote the Indian Navy's New Maritime Strategy. He is currently the Chairman of the Task Force on Net Assessment and Simulation in the National Security Council.

C. Raja Mohan, Foreign Policy Analyst, with a Masters Degree in Nuclear Physics and Ph. D. in International Relations, was Professor of South Asian Studies, Jawaharlal Nehru University, New Delhi. Currently the Strategic Affairs Editor of the Indian Express. His publications include: *Crossing the Rubicon, The Shaping of India's New Foreign Policy and Impossible Allies: Nuclear India, United States and the Global Order.*

Madhup Mohta, graduated in Medicine from All India Institute of Medical Sciences. Career diplomat since 1986, he served in Hong Kong, Nepal and Thailand; Director, Indian Council of Cultural Relations; and presently, Director, Foreign Service Institute, New Delhi. Well known poet. Has edited many magazines and books.

Deb Mukharji, formerly career diplomat, has served in Berne, Islamabad, Bonn, San Francisco. He was High Commissioner to Nigeria, Bangladesh and Ambassador to Nepal.

G. Parthasarathy, formerly career diplomat; served in Moscow, Washington DC; Official Spokesman of the Ministry of External Affairs; Joint Secretary, Prime Minister's Office; Ambassador to Myanmar; and High Commissioner to Cyprus, Australia, Pakistan.

Hardeep Puri, career diplomat since 1974, served in Tokyo, Geneva, Colombo; Deputy High Commissioner in London, Permanent Representative to the UN in Geneva. He has been Ambassador to Brasilia since 2005.

Lakshmi Puri, career diplomat since 1974, served in Tokyo, Geneva, Colombo; Ambassador to Budapest. Since 2002, on deputation as Director, Division on International Trade and Goods and Services and Commodities, UNCTAD, Geneva.

C. V. Ranganathan, formerly career diplomat, served in Permanent Mission in New York, Bonn; Deputy Chief of Mission in Moscow; and Ambassador to Ethiopia, China and France.

Krishna V. Rajan, formerly career diplomat, served as Advisor to the Minister of External Affairs; Secretary, Ministry of External Affairs; Ambassador to Algeria and Nepal. Served in diplomatic assignments in Washington DC and Paris. Presently, Member, National Security Advisory Board.

Sunanda K. Datta-Ray, now Senior Research Fellow at Singapore's Institute of Southeast Asian Studies, was Editor, The Statesman (Calcutta and Delhi); Visiting Fellow, Corpus Christi College, Oxford; Editor-in-Residence, East-West Center, Honolulu. He has practiced and taught journalism in Britain, India, the US and Singapore for nearly 50 years.

Shyam Saran, Special Envoy, Prime Minister's Office; formerly Foreign Secretary; Ambassador to Nepal, Indonesia, Myanmar; High Commissioner in Mauritius; and also served in Tokyo, Beijing; Permanent Mission of India, Geneva.

Navtej Sarna, career diplomat since 1980, MEA's Official Spokesman. He has served in Russia, Poland, Bhutan, Iran, USA and Geneva. He is the author of *We Weren't Lovers Like That, The Book of Nanak, Folk Tales of Poland.*

Aftab Seth, formerly career diplomat, served as Ambassador to Greece, Vietnam, Japan. During 2004-2006, Professor and Director of Global Security Research Institute, Keio University (2004-2006). Presently, Chairman, International Advisory Committee.

J.C. Sharma, formerly career diplomat; Secretary, Ministry of External Affairs; Member Secretary of the High Level Committee on Indian Diaspora. He has made significant contribution in formulation of India's policy towards its Diaspora; organised first and second Pravasi Bhartiya Divas. He has headed Indian Consulates in Vancouver and Chicago and the Embassies in Cambodia and Vietnam.

Gurjit Singh, career diplomat since 1980, Ambassador to Ethiopia, Djibouti and Representative of India to the African Union; served in Tokyo, Colombo, Nairobi and Rome. He has published *The Abalone Factor–An Overview of India-Japan Business Relations* in 1997 which won the Bimal Sanyal Award for Research by the Foreign Service Institute.

Jasjit Singh, Air Commodore (Retd.) is currently Director, Centre for Strategic and International Studies, New Delhi. Author and editor of more than three dozen books including *Air Power in Modern Warfare* (1985); *Non-provocative Defence* (1989); *Security of Third World Countries* (1993); *India's Defence Spending* (2000), and *Nuclear Deterrence & Diplomacy* (2004). Member of the National Security Advisory Board.

Atish Sinha, career diplomat since 1970; served in Bangladesh, USA, Thailand, Kuwait, Nepal, Canada, Nigeria. Presently Dean, Foreign Service Institute.

Krishnan Srinivasan, formerly career diplomat, High Commissioner to Zambia, Nigeria and Bangladesh; Ambassador to Netherlands; Foreign Secretary (1994-95); Commonwealth Deputy Secretary-General (1995-2002); Fellow of Wolfson College, Cambridge and School of Advanced Studies, London (2002-2005); Fellow of Maulana Azad Institute for Asian Studies, Kolkata (2006-2007); and Visiting Professor, ASCI, Hyderabad from 2005.

P. Stobdan, served in Central Asia as the Director of the Indian Cultural Centre, Almaty, Kazakhstan; Joint Director, National Security Council Secretariat (NSCS); Senior Fellow, Institute for Defence Studies and Analyses (IDSA), New Delhi; currently Director of the

20

Indian foreign policy: challenges and opportunities

Centre for Strategic and Regional Studies (CSRS), University of Jammu.

K. Subrahmanyam, Strategic and Foreign Affairs Analyst; Convener of the first National Security Advisory Board; Chairman of Global Strategic Task Force. Formerly, Director, Institute for Defence Studies & Analyses (IDSA), New Delhi and Secretary, Defence Production, Ministry of Defence.

Navdeep Suri, career diplomat since 1983; served in Cairo, Damascus, Washington DC, Dar-es-Salaam, London, and at Headquarters as Joint Secretary (Africa). Presently, Consul General in Johannesburg.

Pavan K. Varma, career diplomat since 1976; served in Sofia, Bucharest, Permanent Mission in New York; Director, Nehru Cultural Centre, Moscow and The Nehru Centre, London; Official Spokesman, Ministry of External Affairs. Well known author of many books including bestselling *Being Indian*. Presently Director General, Indian Council for Cultural Relations.

प्रणब मुखर्जी
PRANAB MUKHERJEE

विदेश मंत्री, भारत
MINISTER OF EXTERNAL AFFAIRS
INDIA

FOREWORD

India's Strategic Perspective

India's strategic perspectives have been moulded by its civilizational memory, its sense of geography, its composite culture and geopolitical realities.

India has always been an open society, receiving and assimilating major influences from outside its geographical boundaries, like Islam and Christianity, and disseminating its composite cultural influences outward. The Indian civilization, along with the Arab, Persian and Sinic civilisations influenced many parts of Asia. India has also been a land of intellectual and spiritual activity, giving birth to the great religions—Hinduism, Buddhism, Jainism and Sikhism.

Since the 17th Century, India's relations with the outside world underwent a fundamental reorientation. European maritime domination of the Indian Ocean changed the very nature of political, trade and cultural ties between India and its regional maritime partners to the east and the west. Further north, in mainland Asia, it introduced relationships of domination and rivalry between imperial powers, where earlier only local powers had played out their dynastic destinies. Independent India was faced with legacy in some ways negative and disruptive.

Several developments in the 20th Century affected India's traditional relationships with its neighbourhood. Perhaps the most fateful was the partition of India. It can be argued that the first half of the 20th Century was certainly an aberration in the evolution of India's historical and traditional relationship with the outside world. The historical experience of the British East India Company, and imperialism in general, left India suspicious of foreign trade.

While colonialism upstaged our traditional links, the Cold War delayed their restoration. The fall of the Berlin Wall and the end of the Cold War has, in recent years, provided us an opportunity to rediscover our traditional and historical linkages that had become weak during the Cold War years, and to pursue our interests in a wider and increasingly integrated manner.

In recent years, India has attracted worldwide attention for its economic growth, inclusive and beneficial to all sections of society. However, future economic growth will depend on a secure and stable environment and India's own ability to integrate with the global economy.

The first priority in our nation building endeavour is countering terrorism. In most parts of the world, terrorism is perpetrated by non-state actors. However, in India, militants and terrorists are also sponsored and aided by agencies from across India's borders.

Secondly, since Independence, India has had to fight three wars on its western and northern borders and it continues to face a proxy war from across its western border. Its unresolved territorial and boundary issues with neighbours persist.

Thirdly, India has been placed in an arc of proliferation activity running from east to west, with the linkages between proliferation of weapons of mass destruction and terrorism, which have become evident in recent years, being of great concern to our security.

Fourthly, the unstable political fabric of states in India's neighbourhood is a source of great anxiety. This is a risk to the stable and peaceful environment that India seeks for its own steady economic growth.

Fifthly, India sits astride the Indian Ocean. The security of the entire region from East Africa to South-East Asia is increasingly challenged by the rising incidence of violent conflict, growing fundamentalism and terrorism. It is also affected by trafficking in arms, drugs and human beings as well as piracy. Sixty thousand ships carry merchandise and energy from the Gulf to East Asia, through the Straits of Malacca, every year. Therefore, maritime security is a major preoccupation for India as it is for other littoral states in the Indian Ocean.

Sixthly, with the Indian economy set on a higher growth trajectory, its demand for energy is, and will be, increasing rapidly. In this context, energy security and security of sea lanes of communication, on which India's trade is dependent, assume significance.

In order to meet the challenges that India faces, it has been focussing on inclusive economic development, strengthening of its defence to deter aggression, ensuring stability and peace in its neighbourhood, developing friendly and mutually beneficial ties in its extended neighbourhood like West, Central and South-East Asia and establishing strategic partnerships with all the major actors in the world, particularly the United States, European Union, Russia, China and Japan. In order to deepen its engagement with Asia-Pacific and ASEAN, it is also pursuing its 'Look East Policy'.

India's nuclear deterrence is a measure of self-defence in a hostile and nuclearised environment. Its nuclear doctrine emphasises no first use, non-use against non-nuclear weapon states, a voluntary moratorium on testing and credible minimum deterrence. India has been, and remains, a staunch advocate of nuclear disarmament and it has had an impeccable track record in the area of non-proliferation.

This volume on "Indian Foreign Policy: Challenges and Opportunities" was already with the publishers when I returned to start my second innings at the Ministry of External Affairs. I understand from the Dean of the Foreign Service Institute that the views of the distinguished authors, diplomats, foreign affairs and strategic analysts and of academicians and serving officers in the Ministry do not necessarily reflect the policy of the Ministry of External Affairs. The volume provides a range of viewpoints which we need to study and analyse to shape foreign policy in the years to come.

I have been highlighting in my addresses, at Harvard University recently and elsewhere, the need to focus our attention and determine the challenges and opportunities that face Indian foreign policy. This book encapsulates thought-provoking articles on the entire gamut of foreign policy issues. I am confident that it would encourage much discussion and debate on the direction that Indian foreign policy should take in the years ahead. I therefore commend and dedicate this volume to all students and scholars of Indian foreign policy.

(Pranab Mukherjee)

Introduction

1

Foreign policy considerations

Atish Sinha

The burgeoning size and growth of the Indian economy is drawing so much attention in the world's psyche and in the international arena, that whether there is commensurate enhancement of India's political influence and military power is not being studied and analysed in the proper perspective. Given the subcontinental geography and years of history witness to invasions and incursions through the thousands of miles of land and sea frontiers, a suitable perspective might view India isolated amongst the large economies of the world, faced with an unfavourable environment outside its boundaries, and not possessing the aggressive politico-military power projection to protect and sustain peaceful national development.

In the coming decades, the largest economies in the world should comprise the United States, China, Japan, India, the European Union and the Russian Federation. Of these India stands out alone outside the cover of defence alliances or the military tradition of countries, which have owed their national developments during the 19th and 20th centuries to the strength of military machines, and in authoritarian regimes as the political arm of the ruling power. Industrial development in India progressed only after Independence and in the tradition of the non-violent ethos of the freedom struggle, and indeed of the peace-loving citizens of democratic India, military industrial complexes, as established in the other large economies, were not even contemplated.

India after Independence was not fully prepared for the inter-play of global forces, politico-military, ideological rivalries, extra-territorial ambitions of aggressive authoritarian Powers, erupting right on India's boundaries, threatening young India's peace and security. During the decades of Jawaharlal Nehru's charismatic presence on the international stage, Indian foreign policy was enthused by and in turn inspired the struggles against colonialism and apartheid, the Non-Aligned Movement, the developing countries and their socioeconomic strategies.

The security environment in the neighbourhood, to the North-West and to the North, should have inexorably re-structured India's foreign policy considerations to global realities. In fact, in the early sixties, confronted by the stark reality of military aggression and detonation of nuclear devices in its neighbourhood, national political will in a non-violent democratic ethos was not manifesting strongly, taking cover in the argument that economic resources were not adequate to compete with the military industrial complexes being built up in other countries, even as close as in India's neighbourhood.

"The means by which to maintain one's own state is to arm oneself with one's own weapons, treat one's subjects well and be friends with one's neighbours" (N. Machiavelli from *Pensieri II*).

Indira Gandhi's strong and decisive leadership recognised the priorities in foreign policy even though the national economy was not buoyant to bolster the enormous security and defence initiatives she took in the seventies. In the next decade, the eighties, the momentum of modernising defence capabilities, not only for the land forces, but also for the air force and the navy, was sustained at the same time as landmark foreign policy initiatives towards an environment conducive to peaceful development of relations with neighbours was the distinctive feature of Rajiv Gandhi's dynamic diplomacy.

It is a matter of inescapable interest that when Indian foreign policy began at last to look beyond the compulsions—political, strategic, economic and commercial—of the neighbourhood, the world began to enlarge its area of interaction with India's smaller South Asian neighbours and their problems of socio-political and economic development. The interest of outside Powers in South Asia had been for years an issue of great security sensitivity in subcontinental India's traditional sphere of influence. And yet globalisation and European Union's increasing international role playing activity, alongwith the United States, saw their continuing engagement in, for instance, Nepal and Sri Lanka, in peace talks, and internal political democratic processes, international aid flows and even reports of arms supplies. The spectre of failing States in the neighbourhood is of more serious direct concern to India than to Western States. In fact, the South Asian Association of Regional Cooperation is a very important framework for all the South Asian countries to benefit in mutual prosperity, and to share with India the gains of India's massive economic growth and development.

At the same time, international terrorist activities and the existence of terrorist havens along the long land boundaries, not only in the North-West but also in the North-East, have become so formidable a prospect that defence and foreign policy interests have never been so dramatically inter-twined, exerting tremendous pressure on Indian diplomacy in bilateral relations with South Asian neighbours.

"Strength is of three kinds: power of deliberation is intellectual strength; the possession of a prosperous treasury and a strong army is the strength of sovereignty; and martial power is physical strength" (*Arthasastra* of Kautilya, Book VI, "The Source of Sovereign States", Ch 2.19).

The security environment in the neighbourhood is not only endangered by the existence of nuclear weapon States in the North-West and in the North but also of the hostile presence of non-State actors, militants, religious fundamentalists, acquiring, holding and having access to nuclear explosive devices. Facing the reality of this nuclear terrorist environment, foreign policy cannot but strategise with defence policy. Though India is not part of the first session, in Rabat, of the Global Initiative to Combat Nuclear Terrorism, following the St. Petersburg Summit, the threat to India from all sources and forms of terrorism is as severe, if not more, than that of any other country or alliance anywhere in the world.

The prevailing world power dynamics in which the United States is the dominant actor has brought into play the initiatives taken by India and the United States to enlarge the very extensive areas of bilateral interaction to include civil nuclear cooperation. This facilitates for India access to technology to supplement the advanced scientific, technological and engineering expertise and infrastructure, amongst the largest in the world of which India is proud. As civil nuclear cooperation involves the Nuclear Suppliers Group, India has to demonstrate to NSG member countries, with many of whom, like the Russian Federation, India has long years of time-tested friendship, the perfect sense of high responsibility, which is the hallmark of India's policy towards nuclear non-proliferation

In spite of the dramatic strides made in political and economic cooperation between India and the United States and with the European Union, the developing country priorities of over-riding importance to India are still being resisted by the advanced countries. The United Nations which in its early years had a composite agenda for economic development lost the initiative and control to the World Trade Organization, the World Bank and the International Monetary Fund, which are now controlled by the industrially advanced States, either because of their trading power or by virtue of their voting rights as in the World Bank and the IMF. It is in this overall context that foreign policy has the challenge of promoting strategic partnerships that enable for mutual satisfaction in the political, economic as well as in the development and world trade fields.

Even though it took longer than necessary for moving beyond the immediate neighbourhood in the decade of economic liberalisation and globalisation, the Look East policy has been very successful indeed, bringing the Association of South East Asian Nations and East Asia so close to India as to have seen four India-ASEAN Summits, as well as India's participation last year in the first East Asia Summit. It is as well a matter of proactive foreign policy that Japan and India have also moved to not only closer economic cooperation but also politically strategic partnership in the evolving Asian dynamics.

In West Asia however, the immense fund of goodwill for Indian foreign policy in the Arab world, an incontrovertible fact till the end of the 20th century, is now no longer perceived by the Arabs as an interminable feature of Indian diplomacy. This is because of the Arab perception that India is no longer as visible or perceptible when there are crises in Iraq, or in Palestine, or in Lebanon, or when a crisis situation is confronting Iran. In the Arab world, there is an expectation for India to define its role and this is as much a challenge for Indian diplomacy as for the Arab world to recognise the dynamics of democratic India's foreign policy.

The directional content of Indian foreign policy in Africa, as also in Latin America, is also a challenge for Indian diplomacy and demanding when compared with the international role played by other major powers. India's aspirations for being a Permanent Member of the United Nations Security Council are not flying with the Indian flag on the African continent which has more than 50 countries, while the Indian flag flies in resident diplomatic missions in less than half of this number. On the other hand all other major Powers–China, Russian Federation, France, United Kingdom and the United States have each of them resident diplomatic missions in more than 40 countries of the African continent. In 1978, the Estimates Committee of the Parliament of India, in its report on the functioning of the Ministry of External Affairs, recommended establishment of resident diplomatic missions in as many countries as possible, as it was considered by the Estimates Committee that India's interests: political, economic, commercial, cultural cannot be effectively promoted and advanced by Indian Embassy officers visiting once or twice a year from another neighbouring country. As a result of these recommendations, a number of Indian diplomatic missions were established in Africa, as in other continents in the 1980s. However, in later years these missions were closed because of budgetary constraints, which did not take into account the declining overall bilateral multilateral impact of diplomatic representation overseas.

At a time when India is not only giving priority to engagement with every member State of the United Nations, conforming with its aspirations to be a Permanent Member of the Security Council, as well as to find sources of mineral resources and trade avenues overseas, it is a matter for foreign policy consideration that in the last 10 years there have been only a few high-level visits from India to Africa, and that only to South Africa and Mauritius. During the last four years, high-level visits from China have also covered West Africa, Nigeria, and Angola which are major oil producing countries. The last bilateral visit from India to Nigeria, which is the largest oil producing country in Africa, was made by Prime Minister Jawaharlal Nehru more than 40 years ago. International high profile diplomacy is also the noteworthy feature of the China-African Leader Summit in Beijing in the first week of November 2006; not as Chairman of an international grouping like EU, NAM or CHOGM, China hosted a Summit of 40 Heads of the Government/State.

In Latin America also, the first high-level visit in 30 years was made by the Prime Minister to Brazil for the IBSA Summit in

September 2006. The President of China during the last two years has travelled to Argentina, Brazil, Chile, Cuba and Mexico. Chinese total trade turnover with South America is USD 60 billion and Chinese investment in Latin America, though only USD 6.5 billion through 2004 equals half of Chinese foreign investment overseas. India's overall trade with Latin America is USD 3 billion while the Indian investment of USD 3 billion has been made by Indian private enterprises. In Africa, Chinese trade turnover is USD 40 billion compared to India's trade in 2005 at USD 9 billion. In the first year of this millennium, India purchased more Nigerian crude than Saudi crude. China, which is the world's second largest oil consumer, as also the world's second largest importer of crude, imported from Angola more crude oil than from Saudi Arabia since the beginning of this year. By way of strategic diversification of energy sources, during President Clinton's visit to Nigeria in 2000, one of the objectives of the visit was to enhance America's share of crude oil imports from Nigeria from 12 per cent to 17 per cent. (The United States as is known is the world's largest consumer, as well as the world's largest importer of crude.) The visit to Nigeria by President Bush in 2003 was also reported to have as an objective to increase the import of crude oil from Nigeria up to 25 per cent. During these years of the first decade of the New Millennium, the Presidents and Prime Ministers of Australia, Canada, UK, France, Germany, Japan have all made bilateral visits to Nigeria. While visiting Nigeria in December for the 2003 Commonwealth Summit, Atal Bihari Vajpayee observed that the Ministry of External Affairs should study why Africa's biggest democracy was not visited for more than 40 years by the Prime Minister of the world's largest democracy.

There are many issues and considerations in the realm of foreign policymaking, which seldom come up for debate or discussion. In the pages that follow many distinguished diplomats and strategic analysts have deliberated with much insight on many nuances of policymaking and implementation. Some questions have been answered by those that made policy, and some questions have been raised for implementing policy in the years to come.

2

An enquiry into India's international identity: the next great power?

Madhup Mohta

Since the turn of the millennium, the single most important phenomenon that has been witnessed in India is the way Indians see themselves. This assertion of a new identity has also been accompanied by a clear perceptible shift in the way outsiders see India. The reasons for both lie in the qualitative change in the Indian demography. India now constitutes more than a billion people, a population fast catching up with that of China. India has one of the youngest populations in the world, with a plurality of its citizens born after independence (in 1947). This demographic shift in the character of the population has given rise to a new political, economic and linguistic elite, thrown up by the democratic process. The generation nurtured in a slew of religious and colonial cocktails that brewed in India over the last two centuries is no longer dominant. The administration in India is now effectively run by modern minded decision makers who do not suffer from personal memories of the pain of Partition, are not traumatised by the humiliating face-off with China in 1962, and most importantly, are fiercely committed to democracy and human rights. The democratic process has expanded slowly, but surely, over the last 60 odd years, to bring the entire population of India into the democratic mainstream. The political ambition and the vision of those that administer New Delhi, is no longer clouded by a few strongmen from Hindi heartland surrounding New Delhi. A robust Press, and the power of Television and Cinema, have catapulted India into arguably the world's foremost information society. Not only the indices relating to health and education are rising rapidly, the underlying socio-economic revolution has also created the so-called 'great Indian middle class', which provides the mainstay for movements for democracy, human rights and economic growth with distributive justice. Today's India is radically different from that conveyed in images of yesteryears that still abound in many parts of the world. The significant event that compelled the world to sit up and take notice of the new brand India, were the series of nuclear explosions in 1998, that provided the manifest justification for the Indian foreign policy establishment to declare "we have set the stage to reclaim our rightful inheritance as a great power".

India as a global power

The debate about India as a global power has since spilled beyond the drawing rooms in Lutyen's Delhi and the corridors of Mumbai's corporate houses, and has become a subject of discussion in universities, financial institutions, strategy sessions of multinational corporations and television talk-shows across the world. One can hardly open a newspaper today without reading about India emerging as a 'global power'. Those sections in India, which seriously believe in India's destiny as a global power, point to the attention being paid at the highest political level in the industrially advanced as well as developed countries to strengthening and upgrading relations with India. Encouraged by unprecedented global attention, there is a strong articulation and lobbying for India's inclusion as a Permanent Member of the United Nation's Security Council. An interesting phenomenon that never ceases to amuse serious practitioners of the art of diplomacy, is the attempt to develop 'scientific indices' to measure global power potential and to try and measure India's 'actual power' for comparative analyses, and to determine India's standing *vis-à-vis* the rest of the world. Needless to say, while such indices serve well as hypothetical models for development of political theories and as a very interesting tool to help university students understand the place of India in the global scheme of things, they contribute very

little to a geopolitical understanding of real issues and challenges ·
that present themselves to the Indian Nation and the State, in the
contemporary world. It is important to understand the dynamics
of the current international milieu in the context of the challenges
the contemporary political and economic developments present to
Indian decision makers, and then evaluate whether India is or can
be a global power.

It is universally recognised and accepted that we live in a
unipolar world with a fringe of multipolarity, in which the politics
and economy of the United States of America sets the global agenda,
obliging important political players on the global scene, including
India, to constantly react and re-adjust policies to stay in the race.
There are any numbers of multinational corporations that constantly
monitor the US policies and try to keep on the right side of the
US administration to ensure that they are not at the receiving end
of the economic fall-out of developments in the United States. US
pervasiveness has reduced many of the Bretton Woods institutions
to an informal extension of the US Administration. There are other
international non-governmental organisations that derive
sustenance from various departments of the United States
Government and work in tandem with US policy makers. This is
the subliminal argument which underlines the syntax and the tenor
of phrases to the effect that, "United States will help make India a
global power."

Most Indians understand the intent of such pronouncements,
but are secure in the knowledge that only the youthful Indian
intelligentsia, which harbours in its multitudes the substantial body
of the best scientific and technological brains in the world, will
transform India into a great power, if and when such a thing may
happen. Away from the glib debates in international fora, the Indian
policy establishment is conscious of the fact that the 'Scientific
Indian' is working hand in hand with the 'Scientific American' and
indeed his counterparts in other technology power houses like
Germany, Japan, UK, Canada, France, Australia and Russia to evolve
state of the art technologies, which will radically re-structure the
realities of tomorrow's world. If the US administration is keen to

foster, just as India, the notion that India and US are 'natural allies', it is because there is a realisation among American policy makers that a robust India-US partnership can help develop new technologies direly needed by the world at a significantly faster pace if both the countries synergise and harness their pool of scientific talent.

Given the dynamics of a rapidly changing international landscape, where political and economic alignments change with every critical event, such as the Iraq War, the Middle East crisis or the recent development in Nepal and other countries of South Asia, the conventional measure of a great power has become redundant and is in fact misleading. This is particularly true in case of India because it leads uninformed public opinion to underestimate the comprehensive national strength India has acquired in recent years, and will continue to harness through diplomatic apparatus, besides peaceful management of developing the human resources of more than a billion people. However, India's unambiguous and demonstrable ability to keep others from imposing their will on her, eminently qualifies India to be regarded as an emerging global power. An assessment of whether India is a truly global power or is likely to become one in the foreseeable future or whether it shall be perpetually in pursuit of that hypothetical goal will require a serious examination of India's real and possible potential in the context of the influence of established global powers in a number of political, social and economic aspects.

Does India have the political attributes of a global power?

India is a stable democratic polity. It has a constitutional system of government which has been tried and tested over about 60 years since independence. The Constitution of India has demonstrated unambiguously that it is workable and viable. The changes of government through a robust electoral process are clear signs of a healthy democracy. India is a 'Union of States' and the Constitution provides for bi-cameral legislatures, both at the Centre and in the states. While the Lower House is directly elected, the members of the Upper House at the Centre are elected through indirect elections, by state legislatures. The system of elections is monitored by an independent Constitutional body, the Election Commission. Like any other Parliamentary democracy, there have been calls for reforms. Most of these demands have been sought to be justified on ground that changes in legislative structure are needed so that socioeconomic *status quo* is not perpetuated. The political process both at the centre and states is sufficiently robust to resolve these issues through a political and democratic dialogue. The effectiveness of legislatures has increased considerably after live telecast of Parliamentary proceedings was started. Public and media scrutiny is an important instrument of monitoring performance of legislatures and that of individual legislators. Legislative institutions in India are among the best in the world and have encouraged many other countries to emulate legislative practices of India.

The judiciary, though not as powerful as in countries like the United States, is independent. The Supreme Court and High Courts are known for their judicial prudence and enjoy an appeal across the country. The judicial system at lower levels is undergoing a rapid transformation with the induction of knowledge based technologies and is expected to become fairly responsive when the process of modernisation is complete. The executive has the disadvantage of being a generalised bureaucracy, which lacks specialisation in many key areas of governance. This problem is particularly perceptible in departments, which deal with matters relating to science, technology and economic affairs. The process of reform is being implemented in both the Central and State Governments through induction of knowledge based technologies. However, this is a critical area of governance where the progress is clearly unsatisfactory, particularly in the State Governments. The process of liberalisation has started taking roots across the country and various institutions of the executive have no choice but to reform in unison with a rapidly progressing information society.

It can safely be said that the Indian polity is sufficiently stable to withstand pulls and pressures of the 'revolution of rising expectations' sweeping India. This includes the increasingly infrequent, but at times alarming acts of religious or ethnic fanaticism, the caste and class clashes, besides law and order problems on account of frequent strikes in a diminishing public sector. Once the process of modernisation of the executive is complete, India would surely be in a position to carry off the mantle of a truly great global power.

Does India have the ability to prevent domination by an external power?

Since its inception in an independent India in 1947, the Indian foreign policy establishment has acquired the reputation of being pontificating and too moralistic in the articulation of its foreign policy. The policy of non-alignment was perceived to be convoluted by a number of global players, until the rationale for the policy weakened with the end of the Cold War. This historical phase necessitated a fundamental shift in foreign policy formulation and the paradigms that guided the process. Bereft of traditional moorings, the Indian policy makers had no choice but to fall back on the concept of extension of enlightened national interest as the basis of foreign policy. This process was helped by the fact that the foreign policy establishment had expanded to include decision makers from across the country, rather than a small princely or cosmopolitan elite. This change also ushered in an unprecedented expansion in the area of foreign policy activism. The disproportionate focus on our relationship with Pakistan, China, Russia, UK and USA and other established actors on the Indian foreign policy radar declined. A new set of priorities emerged, which included our relationship with neighbouring countries in South and South-East Asia and an effort to open up serious dialogues with a number of other regions with which India's interaction was hitherto minimalist. This set of countries include among others, Japan, South Korea, Australia, Singapore, South Africa, Nigeria, Kenya, Brazil, Canada, Israel, Saudi Arabia and a number of West European countries.

This broad basing of relations has ensured that, today, India has the ability to resist domination by any single power that has the capacity to crowd out others, and which may use aggressive measures to threaten Indian interests or India's relations with not only the States in India's immediate neighbourhood but also with friendly powers outside the Indian subcontinent. Needless to say, even in the backdrop of a rapidly improving relationship with the United States and China, India has been able to ensure that her relationship with other countries does not become a victim of the process of engagement with these two important powers. Our continued good relationship with traditionally friendly powers like Iran, Cuba and indeed all sections of Iraqi society is an example of India's ability to maintain relations with countries that may be out of favour with the global superpowers.

Foreign policy priorities notwithstanding, an economically resurgent India has also acquired the military wherewithal to ensure that countries like Pakistan and China, with which India has territorial disputes, are not in a position of advantage militarily, which could have a negative impact on the conduct of our policy *vis-à-vis* these countries. The increased interface with US has ensured that US is no longer seen as an adversarial power. Our cooperation with US in Afghanistan and Nepal, and indeed in many UN peacekeeping missions across the world, are examples of the change.

Does India have the ability to eliminate the threats posed by terrorism?

India has demonstrable technological ability to counter threats posed by State sponsors of terrorism which may seek to use violence against innocents to attain political objectives, and more generally, the dangers posed by terrorism and religious extremism in a free society. However, India has a poor track record in implementation of these resources. The hijack of IC-814 from Nepal that ended in negotiating with the Taliban regime in Afghanistan is a classical example. The sorry surrender at Kandhar has provoked serious introspection. Efforts have been made to reduce the role of individual decisionmaking and crystalise a set of institutional responses to potential crises in future. However, the effectiveness of these new instruments is yet to be tested. Also, India is yet to acquire the ability to act in the interest of Indian expatriates across the worlds, which are potential targets for terrorism inspired by Talibanised Islam and racism, as also in those countries where there is a history of despotic regimes persecuting a section of their society on grounds of their Indian ethnicity. Our ability to clear out terrorist bases in

Bhutan has been demonstrated. But then, Bhutan is a friendly country. Our ability to contain terrorism sponsored through Bangladesh and Pakistan will be a critical test, and if we are able to contain this, it will act as a strong signal that India is beginning to be a global power.

Does India have the ability to prevent the spread of weapons of mass destruction?

India is not a signatory to the Non-Proliferation Treaty, nor is it expected to sign on the dotted line except as a nuclear weapons state. India's commitments to non-proliferation derive from its commitment to the IAEA Charter in respect of nuclear technology and other multilateral treaties in respect of chemical, biological and conventional weapons. The rules of the game cannot be relaxed to admit India as a Nuclear Weapons State into the NPT without upsetting other potential aspirants. The recently signed US-India Nuclear Deal is a conscious effort by US to keep India engaged and to persuade it to follow conventional rules of non-proliferation.

The US Administration and indeed other members of the Nuclear Supplier Group realise that unless the international community puts in place mechanisms to keep a uranium deficient India provided with nuclear fuel, the Indian nuclear establishment will have no choice but to seriously embark on a long delayed programme for construction of advanced heavy water reactors, which would be able to utilise thorium, a radioactive element found in abundance in India. The thorium based technologies in India are more than a decade away. India has the technological wherewithal to focus on development of advanced heavy water reactors (AHWRs) that will use the U-233 produced in stage 2, encased in a thorium blanket, to generate about two-thirds of these reactors' output from the thorium casing itself. Since fast neutron reactors are designed to produce more plutonium than they consume, and since India has enormous reserves of thorium, the stage 3 facilities currently being planned would not only meet India's energy requirements but keep it supplied with more plutonium than it would ever need. There is a realisation in US that India would indeed do so unless there are sufficient guarantees of abundant enriched uranium fuel for existing reactors based on universally used technologies. Since US has abundant supplies of uranium, it could easily provide India's nuclear energy programmes with the necessary uranium fuels. In return, India has offered to open its civilian nuclear reactors to international inspection. While the arrangement has ended the nuclear apartheid to which India was subjected over the last four decades, the success of the US-India deal would lie in the efficacy and honesty of its implementation. If US obligations are not met, it is likely to provoke a reaction in India with vociferous demands for pursuing the 'thorium route' with full vigour. Needless to say, embarking on a technological process unique to India will present India with non-proliferation challenges not witnessed before. If the US commitments enable India to remain tied down to the existing technologies, the task of abiding with the existing rules of non-proliferation would be easier.

Although India has not signed the NPT, it has a spotless track record in non-proliferation. Although India's neighbourhood is volatile in respect of proliferation concerns, it is difficult to foresee any problems arising on account of India's pursuit of a highly ambitious civilian nuclear energy programme. India has the technological ability, to ensure that WMDs do not proliferate in areas of its strategic concern. India, however, seems to lack the political will to do so and therefore, has no choice but to cooperate with other responsible nuclear powers in the matter.

Does India have the ability to protect and enforce human rights and civil rights?

The world is rapidly moving to a stage where the utility of war as an instrument of politics is becoming a near impossibility, and, at best, an undesirable option. The advent of the information revolution and growth of mass media has helped propel and sustain the quest for democracy, enforce the rights of minorities, address the aboriginal rights concerns in former colonies, protect the rights of women and children, particularly in terms of prevention of exploitation and human trafficking, and, last but not the least, promote freedom of speech. A global recognition of these rights has ushered in an era, where one country after another is moving towards enhanced democracy.

Since the Indian Constitution obliges the government to promote democracy and civil rights, support for such rights in other countries is a natural element of India's foreign policy. Accordingly, India has supported democratic movements across the world, the most recent example being India's support for the assertion of people's rights in Nepal. India is also likely to be engaged in providing moral and material support to political reconstruction of Nepal. India has also used its diplomatic influence with other countries in the region to persuade Governments to recognise and respect the rights of aboriginal populations and minorities. India's support for protection of the rights of the minority Tamils in Sri Lanka, for religious and ethnic minorities in Bangladesh and for restoration of democracy in Pakistan are pointers in this direction. Farther away, India has been constructively engaged in restoration of democracy in Fiji, Trinidad and Tobago, former Yugoslavia, and Cambodia, and has been supportive of restoration of the democratic process in a number of countries in Middle East and Africa. India's support for establishment of democratic rights and preservation of human rights is likely to become and remain a very important element of its foreign policy in the years to come. On a more practical plane, India has been advising a number of countries on actual processes of conducting free and fair elections, as also providing through Indian aid, equipments like voting machines and ballot boxes, as well as training of personnel. Such policies are likely to be implemented with greater vigour in the years to come.

Does India have the ability to safeguard environment through sustainable development?

The transformation of India from an impoverished economy to a fairly developed one has entailed assimilation of technologies for environmental friendly sustainable economic development. A number of countries in Africa, Latin America and Asia look forward to benefiting from the Indian experience. With enhanced economic ability, India is now ideally placed to share its experience with other countries in this field. India is an active economic partner with a number of developing countries under the aegis of the South-South Cooperation Programmes, the G-15 process, SAARC, the Ganga-Mekong Economic Cooperation, BIMSTEC, EAC and SADC. In years to come, India is likely to make enhanced budgetary allocations for both bilateral and multilateral economic cooperation with developing countries through its economic, scientific and technological aid programmes like ITEC. If India is to acquire the status of a global power, India will have to enhance its bilateral aid to developing countries significantly, besides providing quick assistance in the event of natural disasters like earthquakes, famines, floods and tsunami.

Does India have the ability to contribute to global economic development?

The primary reason for India being a favourite with the international community is the fact that it is seen as a large unsaturated potential market as also an ideal place for safe investments with yields much higher than those in developed industrial economies. India's newfound status of a nuclear weapons power has created sufficient confidence across the globe that it is politically stable and is immune from military adventurism on part of powers inimical to India. Added to this perception is the realisation that after China, India is the most promising emerging market. This has brought large-scale foreign direct investment into India, a process that will only grow in years to come. India's large scale requirements for investments in infrastructure sector including roads, power, ports and also the immense possibilities of safe investments with high yields in Indian real estate, manufacturing, pharmaceutical and information and technology sectors, has made India a hot favorite with international institutional investors. Not surprisingly, therefore, India today has one of the highest reserves of hard currency denominated foreign exchange reserves. Domestic savings have also grown. The synergised effect of this dual process is to be seen in an average annual growth exceeding 8.5 per cent in the gross domestic product over the last few years. In the last quarter of the financial year 2005-06, the growth rates exceeded 9 per cent, a clear sign that if the present set of policies continues

India will soon achieve growth rates consistently higher than those of the Chinese economy. While much of the fruits of economic development are likely to be absorbed by the Indian middle class, a trickle down effect is likely to ensure both a rise in the standard of living among rural poor as well as their joining the ranks of the burgeoning middle classes. The spiralling result of this process is likely to see higher literacy rates and universal access to health and education over the next decade. India has substantial surpluses for export and has a demonstrable ability to advance the diffusion of the economic development with the intent of spreading peace through prosperity, the expansion of the liberal economic order that increases trade in goods, services and technology worldwide.

India is determined to make SAFTA a reality as soon as possible. India has also entered into free trade area agreements with countries like Sri Lanka and Thailand. Similar agreements are within the realm of possibility with India's tried and tested economic partners like Qatar and Oman. More countries in the littoral of the Indian Ocean could be added to the basket of free trade area in near future. Many US academics have been known to toy with the idea of a US-India free trade area. The idea is at once exciting and full of promise, but a lot would need to be done to make it a reality, given the divergence between short-term and medium-term objectives of US and Indian economies.

Regardless, India has a clear responsibility to share its newfound economic prosperity with its neighbours in South Asia. Bilateral economic cooperation with Bhutan, particularly in the power sector, is a clear example of what such cooperation can do to transform the economy of a small country. The possibility of economic cooperation with China, Iran, Saudi Arabia and Pakistan, holds tremendous promise but the success of such partnerships is uncertain on account of existing territorial disputes with Pakistan and China, and the inability of Saudi Arabia and Iranian elite to forge relations with India independent of their perspective of Pakistan as an Islamic country. The potential for economic cooperation with Central Asia and Africa is immense but is unlikely to yield spectacular results due to lack of access and physical distance from India.

The fact that India is already the world's fourth largest economy when measured in terms of gross domestic product, calculated on purchasing power parity basis, and among the world's five largest economies, ahead of France and Britain, when calculated in US dollar terms, is a clear sign that the Indian economic miracle has arrived and is here to stay. The confidence in the Indian economy is likely to become an increasingly important instrument of India's foreign policy in the years to come.

Does India have the ability to secure its trade rules?

If India is to expand its area of diplomatic influence and also acquire a proven ability to influence political and economic events in its sphere of strategic importance, she will need to acquire the means to protecting the internationally recognised global trade links, especially the sea lanes through which flow goods and services critical to the international economy. India will also have to contribute significantly towards prevention of undesirable commerce such as drug trafficking, human smuggling and trade in arms. As India is located in one of the most heavily populated regions of the world, with more than its share of socioeconomic strife, the concern relating to the arms and drugs nexus and illegal immigration, both into India and from India, is real. India will need to equip its intelligence agencies and the concerned law and order enforcement agencies with new knowledge based technologies including biometric identification systems and space based intelligence. If India is to discharge the responsibilities expected of a great power, India will also have to establish a large number of new ports to facilitate exports directly to key markets in Africa, South-East Asia, Europe and US. It will have to continue to vigorously follow the 'open skies' policy and encourage both the public and private sector airlines to forge strategic partnerships with airlines in the Middle East where the fuel costs are less, and those operating in regions like South-East Asia, Europe and North America, where the bulk of global passenger and goods traffic ends or originates, (so that Indian Airlines can also acquire an economy of scale). Modernisation of airports in India is also an imperative. These are goals which can easily be achieved over a decade or so.

Does India have the ability to ensure its energy security?

Ensuring energy security is India's single most important economic concern and is likely to undo her dreams of being a global power. India is debilitated in a great measure by low domestic petroleum reserves and is required to import the bulk of its natural gas and crude oil requirements, a serious drain on its economy. Of late, the state and private sector oil companies are exploring for oil in the countries in Central Asia, Middle East and Africa. But these are humble beginnings and it could well take almost a decade for such initiatives to start yielding desirable results in meeting India's crude oil requirements.

India has about 120,000 MW of installed capacity for electricity production, with an ability to produce about 70 per cent of installed capacity. This implies that India is able to produce only half of its realistic demand for 150,000 MW. During the last financial year, the shortfall in energy requirements was about 40 per cent of the total demand and peaking shortage was about 15 per cent. The shortages of such magnitude have a crippling effect not only on a day-to-day life but also on the potential for economic growth in the country.

There are opportunities for India to set up a number of thermal power stations using a mixture of domestic and imported coal as fuel. This should not be difficult, given India's large coal reserves. There is also the untapped potential for installation of about 50,000 MW in the hydro power sector. The problem, however, is of long gestation periods, invariably attended by cost over runs. The solution lies in corporatising the management of hydropower production with the government keeping away from the execution of such projects even while providing the private sector with security and assistance in the form of large scale credit and capital flows required for hydro projects. Bilateral cooperation with Nepal can help meet the demand for another 50,000 MW of electricity.

The nuclear power sector is in a dismal state both in terms of promise and performance largely because India does not have adequate enriched uranium, badly needed for operating its civilian reactors. The recent India-US deal would help. However, to make the nuclear power sector more advanced, it is imperative that while the reactors meant for military use are retained with the Atomic Energy Commission, those reactors, which are intended for production of nuclear power for civilian use, should be privatised and handed over to non-government agencies. This will not only bring a measure of economic efficiency in the management of nuclear power sector but will also bring the Indian civilian nuclear programme out from a cloak of absolute secrecy, to greater public scrutiny and create an informed opinion about the performance of the atomic energy sector in the country. It is obvious that in the absence of such scrutiny, our civilian atomic energy programme has lagged behind by at least four decades. Not only is nuclear power production uneconomical, we have consistently failed to address the shortcomings and mismanagement resulting from secrecy. The Indian leadership was not even aware of the extent of the problem until the realisation that India did not have sufficient enriched uranium fuel to keep its existing reactors functional, let alone build new reactors, in the run up to the US-India deal. This factor constrained India's negotiating ability.

The cherished ideal of production of about 300,000 GW of electricity from nuclear technologies using thorium fuel is more than a decade away. While such a reality would be a real panacea for India's energy security, it is unlikely that current management practices in the atomic energy sector will bring this objective to an early realisation. Clearly, there is a need to have a more transparent management of the civilian nuclear energy sector, open to public and Parliamentary scrutiny, which would only be possible if the management of nuclear reactors for military purposes and civilian energy processes is segregated—the latter preferably being privatised.

Does India have the ability to ensure a favourable international information order?

In the age of an information and communication revolution, both the quality and quantity of information is a key determinant in decisionmaking. While India is an undisputed leader in information technology, India lags significantly behind the rest of the world when we measure the quotient of information availability to general public, with access to computers and internet confined to a few million in a country which has a billion people. More importantly, the development of computer software technology in Hindi and other Indian languages lags woefully behind that in English, leading to a situation where a majority of Indian citizens do not have access to either the same quality, or the quantity of reliable information as those in developed countries. This situation will need to be addressed.

From a foreign policy perspective, it is more important to ensure that we have the ability to provide correct information about India to the rest of the world. This task is easier. Assimilation of knowledge based tools in governance, including e-governance and e-commerce is a clear sign that we are moving in the right direction. Similarly, information technology is now also being integrated into other areas, which touch the life of Indians, as well as of the international community in its interface with India or Indians. The revolution in the television industry and the miraculous growth of Indian cinema and its influence across the world has contributed significantly towards making India an international favourite. Images of India can now be found across the globe, and the information available about India is more accurate and reliable than it was 10 years ago.

The information revolution has also helped India address the cultural needs of the Indian diaspora abroad. We have also been able to contribute in a significant measure to preserve the universal heritage of mankind including ancient monuments and manuscripts as also foster a sustained dialogue with other civilisations, old and new. India's expertise in information technology and its application in all aspects of life are likely to be of enormous significance that will contribute towards making India a global power. The demand for Indian software personnel in key economies of the world is growing, as is the appreciation for their contribution to the growth of new technologies in countries like the United States of America. It has also led to significant outsourcing of projects from developed countries into India which has contributed both to income generation and implementation and assimilation of new IT skills in the Indian economy.

Does India have the ability to integrate its diaspora?

People of Indian origin constitute one of the single most important ethnic groups in the world, besides China. Notwithstanding the fact that ethnicities of Indian origin are quite diverse with a number of ethnic, linguistic and regional groups masquerading as a pan Indian group in countries outside India, this has been the problem faced by the Government of India in integrating the Indian diaspora with the mother country. However, over the last 60 years, just as a pan Indian identity is being forged in India, a sense of pan Indian cultural identity is also emerging within Indian diaspora abroad. The growth in the means of communication and transportation over the years, both in India and in the countries with a large presence of the Indian diaspora, has added to the government's ability to address the political, economic and cultural needs of Indians overseas. This process is likely to grow, with the government taking on greater responsibilities for Indians overseas.

The people of Indian origin abroad are likely to enjoy greater political powers through participation in Indian polity as also in being able to engage with the mother country through investments and technology transfer on account of specialised schemes tailored for them. It is important to note that the bulk of remittances from overseas Indians come from the more economically disadvantaged sections like skilled and unskilled labour and not the affluent sections. This migrant labour is seasonal and tries to maintain familiar emotional and cultural links with India. However, the process of liberalisation of the Indian economy has now created a potential for economically well-off Indians overseas to participate in the great Indian economic experience. It is, therefore, not surprising that a very large number of investments in corporate India come from affluent Indian origin people abroad. Such investments not only provide adequate returns but also help the

Indians overseas in gaining a sense of security and connection with the motherland in case of instability or other problems relating to political and social rights in their country of residence.

Opportunities and challenges for Indian foreign policy in its emergence as a great global power

Clearly, India has the potential to be a global power. Does India have the vision and the will to be a global power? At the time of independence in 1947, the leaders of the Independence movement had targeted the year 2000 as the date for realising their vision to be a great global power. This vision guided India's Five Year Plans under the Mahalanobis model, when economic development followed socialistic pattern with a centralised public sector at the commanding heights of the economy. It is with the advent of the nineties that economic liberalisation started taking roots. But for the vision of the political leadership, the domestic opposition to economic reforms would have ensured that the process collapses even before it could kick-start. There is now, a broad political consensus among the mainstream political parties that the process of economic reforms is irreversible. India's rise towards the great power status shall be based on the edifice of the economic reforms, which have been pursued relentlessly over the last decade.

India is almost a decade behind China in carrying out economic and technological reforms in its polity. It is evident that any blueprint to be followed for India's emergence as a great power will have to take into account the fact that India must catch up with China, both in terms of internal reform process as also the ability to project such power outside India. Just as China, in its pursuit to replace US as a pre-eminent global power, continues to implement economic and foreign policy reforms, India must ensure that it simulates the Chinese success and is not left behind on account of the tendency to acquiesce in *status quo* or lack of political will to pursue the reform process.

India's security

While the newly acquired nuclear weapons state status provides a deterrent to potential adversaries, it is not a credible deterrent. It is obvious to any discerning observer that use of nuclear weapons in a potential India-Pakistan war is not a policy option either for India or Pakistan. The fact that India and Pakistan share a coastline, a shared boundary with heavily populated areas on both sides of the border, and waters of as many as six major rivers, any India-Pakistan war with use of nuclear weapons will result in total destruction of Pakistan and partial destruction of major Indian cities like Delhi, Bombay and Ahmedabad on account of radioactive fallout. It is unlikely that any responsible and sane regime, either in Pakistan or India will toy with the idea of nuclear engagement with the other country. This scenario necessitates that credible confidence-building measures be put in place between the two countries. The final outcome of these measures is likely to no different from the results obtained in Europe after the end of the Second World War. These are freezing of borders at the existing Line of Control along the entire India-Pakistan Border, opening of the border with gradual withdrawal of the ground based armed forces and conversion of the international border into a soft border which permits free trade and transit to general population on both sides of the border. Conscious of these imperatives, the political leadership of two countries has initiated a process of confidence building measures. It should be possible for both countries to convert the entire India-Pakistan border into a soft border over the next decade.

The criticality of the nuclear deterrent *vis-à-vis* China, the only other country with which India has had an armed conflict, is more important. An increasingly powerful China is known to harness the so called 'Middle Kingdom Complex', an important determinant of its foreign policy. If India is unable to match China militarily, including the reach of its air force, navy and ballistic missile Systems, and keep up with the economic strides being made by China i.e. about 10 per cent annual growth in GDP, China is unlikely to take India seriously. The only guarantee of stable India-China relations is a credible perception in China that India is equal to China, both militarily and as an economy. If this realisation does not sink with the Chinese leadership, the tendency on part of the Chinese Government to keep pinpricking India is unlikely to subside. Over the next decade or so, the blueprint for development of Indian Army, Navy, Air Force, and its missile based defence and nuclear weapons are clear i.e. to seek parity with China. This is a task in which a robust Indo-US relationship can help.

Development of India's space programme

Development of any military technology gradually results in its commercialisation and its assimilation in a nation's economy. Indian policy makers have erred seriously in keeping its communication, nuclear and space related technologies confined to the state sector. This has prevented the economy to benefit from indigenously developed technologies. There is a need to enable the non-state sector of Indian economy to share and benefit from technologies developed for India's defence establishments. This alone can guarantee that optimum technologies are assimilated in rest of Indian economy. Since space research is one of the pioneering area in which India has a technological edge, it requires attention at the highest level. India also needs to ensure that non-state section of Indian economy also get an opportunity to participate in India's space research programme. Sharing of technologies available to state sector with the mainstream economy can transform India and immensely help India becomes a great power by 2020.

The road ahead

If India is able to sustain the pace of economic reforms, augment energy security, modernise its defence forces with greater attention to navy and the air force, and induction of ICBMs and nuclear weapons, at par with China, energise its space research programme to yield optimum results (in terms of its contribution to general economy), sustain the rate of infrastructure development, enhance economic linkages with and assistance to neighbouring countries and countries in the littoral of the Indian Ocean, and carry out internal constitutional and administrative reforms to ensure distributive justice, India is likely to become an established global power by the year 2020.

India's global profile

3

India and global politics
Jagat Singh Mehta

1946: intimation of the future

In 1946, in Fulton, Missouri, at the request of President Truman, Winston Churchill—just eight months out of office—tolled the bell of the war-time non-ideological alliance by pronouncing that Europe was already divided by "an Iron Curtain in twain" with the Soviet Union imposing Communism on the Eastern half and posing a threat to the democracies of the West. A few months later, Stalin, in what resembled an 'election' speech, resuscitated the old ideological antagonism against the capitalist West which had been muted during the war against Hitler's Germany. It was in the context of this ominous confrontation that, on the 7th September, only a few days after becoming Vice-Chairman of the Governor General's Council—the first stage in the transfer of power in the subcontinent—that Nehru announced that India would refrain from joining either of the emerging blocs.[1] He seemed to be echoing George Washington's declaration in 1776 to keep away from "entangling alliances", but Nehru's thinking contained the grandeur of a far more comprehensive vision to international politics: "Peace and freedom were indivisible; denial of freedom anywhere must endanger it elsewhere, as it would lead to conflict and war." He further extrapolated on the inevitability of

---

1. See Jawaharlal Nehru, *India's Foreign Policy: Selected Speeches*: September 1946-April 1961, Publication Division, Government of India, p. 2.

decolonisation, implied respect for all 'other nationalisms' and pledged crusading against racism and tyranny everywhere. The full text is worth scrutiny. Just over one year after Hiroshima and Nagasaki, he seemed not in awe of nuclear weapons; in fact, he implied that development was the key to real security, and hinted at One World, a kind of anticipation of globalisation coming along with independence. He sent greetings to the peoples of USA and Soviet Union and said he would work for friendly and cooperative relations amongst all nations.[2]

Nehru's principled declaration becomes even more significant by what followed only three months later. On the 3rd December 1946, when Nehru, Jinnah and Sardar Baldev Singh, accompanying the then Viceroy Lord Wavell, were flying to London to meet Clement Attlee, the British Prime Minister in an attempt to avert partition, Dean Acheson, the Acting US Secretary of State, issued a *suo motto* press statement stating: "We feel most strongly that it will be in the interest of India, as well as the whole world, for its leaders to grasp the opportunity for a stable and peaceful India. The United States has long taken a sympathetic interest in the progressive realisation of India's political destiny. We have expressed in tangible form our confidence in the ability of the Indian leaders to make vital decisions that lie immediately ahead, with full awareness that their actions at this moment in history, may directly affect world peace and prosperity for generations to come." The assertion and faith in India's role in world politics was made when Acheson could not but be aware of the developing ideological bipolarity.

On the 6th December 1946, the Constituent Assembly of India commenced its deliberations. Jinnah and the Muslim League boycotted the Assembly but the first resolution of the Assembly declared, "India will be a sovereign Democratic Republic". Acheson must have sensed that independent India was going to be democratic, but there was no premonition of Partition. No similar statement expressing the crucial importance of India for world peace was made by USSR or France or any other power. It was a full six decades later, when President Bush declared in New Delhi on 3rd

---

2. *ibid.*

March 2006, "India and USA together could transform the world... India was a global power and Indian democracy would set an example for the world." In the years between 1946 and 2006, the vision of India's international role had got clouded and its importance was never unambiguously and gratuitously reiterated.

In fact, the story of India-US relations has been encapsulated by Dennis Kux under the title, *Estranged Democracies*.[3] Why such voluntarily expressed hopes in 1946 when the Cold War was on the horizon? Why was it obscured after only two months and why revived with seeming sincerity only 60 years later with decades of hesitations and reservations in between?

The process of estrangement

Dean Acheson's statement in 1946 had no compulsions; the Bush affirmation in 2006 could have been limited to measured politesse and traditional diplomatic circumspection. Relations between India and US have gone through ups and downs, and even plummeted to deliberate hostility in 1971 when India faced at least a psychological gunboat diplomacy just when 10 million refugees had come into India after facing tyrannical brutalities, India intervened only when the aspirations for an independent Bangladesh carried proof of free and fair democratic manifestation.

All professionals know that prepared speeches, including at banquets, joint communiqués and well-crafted declarations carry varying degrees of exaggerations; they are often concessions to temporary circumstances or flattering responses to hospitality but frequently succeed in deceiving analysts and observers. American Presidents like Eisenhower, Carter and Clinton and other visiting dignitaries have indulged in hyperbolic tributes to India, specially its commitment to democracy. Our Prime Ministers when visiting Washington have also made extravagant affirmations underlying shared faith, and solidarity with the USA, but these were also concessions to the occasion, not necessarily seriously meant. The rediscovery of strong commonality between India and the US in

---

3. Kux, Dennis (1993). *India and the United States: Estranged Democracies 1941-1991*, NDU Press and Sage.

2006 highlights one of great avoidable tragedies of the 20th Century. Though the two countries still have serious differences, as indeed they did in 1946, but distilling lessons from this protracted oscillating experience, may provide guideposts for the new century.

The one word answer to this whole story of misperceptions is, of course, 'partition'. At the very moment of fulfilment of more than half-a-century of aspirations to self-government, the subcontinent was divided, overlooking the permanent logic of geography, many centuries of a unique pluralist civilisation and an enmeshed ethnicity. But there was another reason. The process of negotiations of the transfer of power in the subcontinent coincided exactly with the unexpected domestic developments in the US which distracted it from what Acheson had confidently hoped was the significance of India's emergence on the world stage and its importance for world peace for future generations.

The full opportunity costs of 'divide and quit' have never been exhaustively examined; reunification in the subcontinent of the partitions of 1947 and 1971 cannot and should not be contemplated but an analysis could provide the scaffolding of policy for the 21st Century. Two mighty modern forces, both inexorable, came into serious conflict by accidental juxtaposition in the first half of the 1947 and changed the course of history, inflicting unforeseen penalties for the Indian subcontinent. Centrifugality resulted in decolonisation and diffusion of power to new identities like nation states and centripetality spurred by the accelerated march of technology resulted in new international ideological and military compulsions and globalisation of political awareness. Reading between the lines, Nehru was dimly aware of both these forces in his 7th September 1946 statement but in the 100 odd days between February 20 and June 5, 1947, centrifugality of decolonisation and centripetality of ideology (and the strategic alarm it caused) and the consequential polarisation through alliances artificially compartmentalised decisionmaking. The Dumbarton Oaks Conference 1944 (where the future shape of the world body to succeed the defunct League of Nations was considered), the Yalta Conference of Roosevelt, Stalin and Churchill (1945) (where they decided on their respective domains of responsibilities) and the San Francisco Charter of the UN (1945), even though recognising the conflicting divergent ideas, envisioned an integrated system for world security. Alas Roosevelt, the chief motivator passed away in April 1945. On 20th February 1947 British Prime Minister announced to the House of Commons the appointment of Mountbatten as successor to Wavell and the transfer of power to "responsible Indian hands" would take place not later than June 1948. No political party in India thought the June 1948 deadline was too far away. At Yalta, Churchill had insisted on the right to 'superintend' the Mediterranean in order to remain in control of the lifeline to the Empire. On the 21st February, the same British government, through its embassy in Washington DC, informed the State Department that it was not possible for the HMG to keep its obligation to sustain the governments of Greece and Turkey where insurgency or instability was suspected to be supported by Kremlin. The USA saw it as part of the Soviet inspired Communist expansionism. The USA might have taken over the burden in Greece and Turkey more readily even if the Democratic Party had not suffered reverses in the mid-term Congressional elections of November 1946.

The developments in Europe with 'an iron curtain' partitioning the culturally united continent, the future importance of democratic India would not have been ignored by the USA but for an isolationist Republican majority wanting to return to pre-war isolationist normalcy. The Truman doctrine of Containment announced on 12th March was the result of unexpected British abdication, which led to the single-minded preoccupation of the administration to persuade the Congress to vote aid, for the first time in peace. It required two months of hard lobbying supported by exaggerated alarm about the menace of a Universalist ideology, commanded by a mighty land power to get the US Congress to agree to $400m aid for Greece and Turkey and to take over the British vacated commitment. The Marshall Plan for Europe was announced in the Harvard commencement speech on 5th June but, meanwhile, on the 3rd June, just 2 days earlier, Lord Mountbatten had already announced that the transfer of power will take place not to one India but to two dominions and not in June 1948 but on 15 August 1947. It was simply an unforeseen coincidence that the Truman doctrine of Containment overlapped in the same 100 odd days when the fate of India pledged to be a sovereign democratic Republic was on the anvil. Centrifugality and centripetality by happenstance coincided with disastrous consequences, which only got exposed with the end of the Cold War in the nineteen-eighties and nineties.

Containment started the process of irrational centripetality — the subordination and conformity of the foreign, defence and even economic policies under the leadership of USA on the one hand and the USSR on the other. It made non-alignment, which in principle was prophetic, tied to the presumption of the permanence of bipolarity. The exact coincidence of partition and partition precipitating intra-subcontinental tensions, distorted secularism and the enlightened aims in people's welfare, which the struggle for self-rule had projected — not only by leaders of the Indian National Congress but also by Jinnah of the Muslim League. At the moment of triumph, most of the leaders in Congress became myopic in their impatience for power. Only Mahatma Gandhi and Maulana Azad were against the division and no one — neither the British, nor the successors in India and Pakistan — foresaw the horrendous holocaust, which followed. With a little reflection, they could have anticipated that India and Pakistan would be drawn in and get enmeshed with the Great power strategic bipolarity, and so weaken the very expectations of self-government for all communities.

The militarisation, the intelligence activism and the four India-Pakistan conflicts all deflected both India and Pakistan from development which was implicit in their constructive nationalism. The bifurcation of a united landmass not only enfeebled the kinetic energy of successor governments, but it led to a psychological re-dependence on an outside power. The centrifugality of decolonisation and centrepetality of globalisation and interdependence were always inexorable, but the precise overlap in those 103 days has been the root cause for compounding the most fatal tragedy of the 20th Century.

The British must, of course, carry a disproportionate share of the consequences for this tragic misjudgement. The British alone were participant in both developments in noting the Iron Curtain and in activating Containment on the one hand and hurriedly catalysing the division of the Indian Empire—the jewel in the Imperial crown—on the other. The British were still intoxicated with the confidence of their role in international affairs and presumed that its pre-war global position and authority could be preserved by deliberately compartmentalising the two processes. The British Foreign Secretary, Ernie Bevin, had informally even asked advice of Stalin, "What to do in India?" Apparently, the old Marshall simply shrugged his shoulders, but it is of interest that in the spring of 1947 Washington was deliberately kept in the dark about the transfer of power discussions in the subcontinent. One imagines that even the Labour government had not forgotten the sharp wartime differences between Franklin Roosevelt and Winston Churchill, which had left a deep down suspicion in London that the US wanted to takeover at least economically the sinews of the old Empire and displace the inherited British advantage in the Gulf, in Iran, and except in Saudi Arabia, maintain control over much of the "wells of power".[4]

It may also be mentioned that a third parallel development with enormous future importance for Asia and the world was wholly overlooked. In the vast literature on the transfer of power in South Asia and its interaction with the Cold War, the parallel development in China finds little mention. After two decades of civil war, the People's Liberation Army of China was defeating the Kuo-min-tang army of Chiang-Kai-shek, overrunning the mainland China. The People's Republic of China was going to be proclaimed on 1st October 1949, a little more than two years after the subcontinental transfer of power. It incidentally reinforces my speculation that if the date of independence had not been advanced from June 1948 to August 1947, the linkage with developments in China might not have been ignored. But for the exact coincidence and the myopic preoccupation

---

4.   Caroe, Olaf (2000). *The Pathans*, Kegam Paul, London.

in Washington, the impatience to power of most leaders of the Indian Congress and Lord Mountbatten's nervous anxiety at communal riots in Calcutta, the date of transfer in the subcontinent would not have been advanced. United States would have preferred—as was implicit in Dean Acheson's statement of December 1946—a democratic India to face united Communist China, which even before final victory had announced that it would get allied to Stalin's Soviet Union.

New opportunities

The challenge for India in the new century is to escape the bequeathed hold of the 20th Century falsehoods. In a democratically governed country, this is more difficult, but statesmanship must not shirk from focussing on the economic, social and opportunity penalties inflicted by misperceptions traceable to the simultaneity of centrifugality and centrepetality in the subcontinent's political history. We must acknowledge—as we have been reluctant to do—that it led to the emasculation of the vision of self-government projected in 1946.

We cannot say to what extent the misjudgements delayed the economic 'take-offs' of the countries of the subcontinent but the responsibility must be shared by both the great powers and the newly independent ones. The momentum of Nehru's declared "non-entanglement" with blocs did, however, command respect on many issues: it helped to consolidate peace in Korea and ensure the right to the prisoners-of-war to choose their destinations; it supported nationalism and independence in Indo-China (1954) and played a pioneering role in the UN and its Trusteeship Council for the fulfilment of the aspirations to independence in many countries in Asia and Africa and round the world; it helped in launching the Afro-Asian conference in Bandung 1955. It was India's responsible idealism that persuaded an old imperialist like Churchill to consecrate Nehru in 1955 as the "Light of Asia".[5] In 1956 India was in a courageous minority in the Users' conference following the nationalisation of the Suez. For many years, India was the first

---

5. Gopal, S. (ed.), (1986). *Selected Works of Jawaharlal Nehru*, Vol-II, OUP; New Delhi.

choice in UN peacekeeping operations, notably in Lebanon (1957) and the Congo (1960). Our officers and our Generals won laurels for objectivity in Indo-China, Cyprus, Namibia, Yugoslavia, Iraq, West Africa, etc.

On the nuclear question

The splitting of the atom may have been the greatest breakthrough in science. Atomic fission gave the world both nuclear weapons and non-pollutant potential of constructive power. But Clauswitzian aphorism that war was politics by other means has been deeply embedded in the minds of decision-makers with little realisation that it has become out-of-date. Hiroshima for a while held forth the promise of incomparable command of destructive power but that has proved to a delusion. The parents of the first nuclear bombs, intellectual giants like Oppenheimer and Sakharov were alarmed at seeing 'death' in the indiscriminate loss of civilian life, but those conditioned by military history, saw the weapons of mass destruction (WMDs) as providing absolute condign power and ultimate national prestige.

A near revolution may be underway in the utility of military power. While it gave hypothetical confidence to the possessor, it has not frightened any adversary; indeed it has been paralysed from effective use. Beginning with the Cuban Missile crisis in the sixties but culminating in the eighties and nineties, the realisation is growing that nuclear weapons were wholly different from conventional weapons. It took decades to recognise by strategists, generals and defence ministers that nuclear weapons could not be used positively; their use risked suicidal destruction; the confidence in possessing them did not seem to even frighten the adversary or avert conventional defeat.[6, 7] It became clear to incisive minds, alas too slowly, that the obsession of anxiety and state level paranoia only increased the chances of an accidental nuclear conflagration. In a monograph written at Harvard (1970), I had speculated that

6. Schell, Jonathan (1998). *The Gift of Time: The Case for Abolishing Nuclear Weapons*, Henry Holt & Company, New York.

7. The Canberra Commission.

nuclear weapons gave an overriding community of interests between nuclear adversaries. It invited polite approbation but no credibility.[8] Much late, out of that crucible of nightmarish fear emerged the Helsinki declaration of Presidents Reagan and Gorbachev that "Nuclear wars should never be started as they can never be won." The superpowers chiefs worry now is not each other's capability but nuclear irresponsibility by rogue nations and terrorist groups.

Nehru was the first statesman to warn against the hazards of nuclear radiation. He had requested for a scientific analysis of the effects of nuclear explosions;[9] he pointedly reiterated his pleading for disarmament in the speech at the first Non-alignment Conference in Belgrade (1961). The Partial Test Ban Treaty was a belated response to the international dangers from accidental triggering as nearly happened in the Cuban missile crisis. My own guess is, had Nehru lived, he would have authorised signing the Non-Proliferation Treaty (NPT) in 1969 and then joined in protest against the privileged military licence for the Five for their moral inconsistency. In fact, India with Pakistan and Israel alone remain non-signatories. The overwhelming majority, however, renounced the military option and signed the NPT. There is a current false smugness at having arrested proliferation of WMDs, but for decades the nuclear Five have ignored the pledge to disarmament contained in article VI of the Treaty.

The wholly artificial difference between responsible and non-responsible powers cannot last for ever. Who knows how many others (apart from North Korea and Iran) have been whetted with surreptitious ambitions at nuclear weapon capability. India in its approach straddled contrary impulses. On the one hand, some wanted India to be the sixth weapon power but on the other hand, others felt we should not be out of step with the majority who renounced (atleast publicly) the reliance on nuclear weapons. In fact, it was one of the first occasions when on a general question of international relations, we took position justifying exceptionalism.

---

8. Fellows papers 1969-70. Center for International Affairs, Harvard.

9. See Dr. D.S. Kothari (1958). *Nuclear Explosions and Their Effects* with a Foreword by Jawaharlal Nehru, Publications Division, Ministry of Information and Broadcasting, Government of India.

The notion that nuclear weapons was the passport to Great power status had, however, strong appeal; in India it led to an underground peaceful nuclear test in 1974 and after 24 years of internal debate weighing the pros and cons on non-proliferation, a series of tests were authorised in 1998 and this was followed by similar testing in Pakistan. The tests led to UN sanctions but they neither paralysed the Indian economy nor significantly added to the national prestige of India.

The utility of nuclear weapons now poses a dilemma for the world. The confidence in deterrence is being eroded as it is seen as based on the subjective notion that the decision-maker of an adversary might go berserk. In a knowledge-free politically aroused centrifugal world, the spirit of NPT is bound to be challenged. While India has scrupulously refrained from proliferation, A.Q. Khan of Pakistan has shamelessly sold know-how to North Korea, Libya and Iran. Iran and others in secrecy have violated its own voluntary commitment to the agreed obligation to the NPT, but all these examples have exposed the moral double-standards of USA and the other approved 'weapon powers'.

Let me make a diversion by referring to the address of Prof. Thomas Schelling, the winner of the Nobel Prize for Economics in 2005. He stated, "The most spectacular event of the past half-a-century is one that did not occur. We have enjoyed sixty years without nuclear explosions exploded in anger." Quoting from McGeorge Bundy, *Danger and Survival*, he recalled that in 1953, John Foster Dulles, then Eisenhower's Secretary of State, had strongly pleaded that the taboo between conventional and nuclear weapons be superceded and the moral restraint on the use of nuclear weapons be removed; the plea was not endorsed and over the years the distinction has got reinforced. Schelling speaking in 2005 goes on to wonder whether this anti-nuclear instinct was not confined to Western countries. He rhetorically asks would it inhibit India and Pakistan, North Korea, China or Iran? I find this anxiety carries ominous implication without any justification. After all, Hiroshima and Nagasaki were perpetrated by the USA. In Kargil (1999), in response to aggressive surreptitious intrusions over very difficult high mountainous terrain, there was moral restraint in the non-use of nuclear weapons by India. There was no nuclear based defiance by Pakistan at the Clinton injunction for complete withdrawal to the LOC, including by the so called freedom fighters. It only confirms the non-utility of nuclear weapons. The illusion of psychological utility and influence continues, but this must be weighed to quote Professor Schelling again, "the restraining effect of a nearly universal attitude that has been cultivated through universal abstinence for sixty years."[10]

Technology globalisation

Globalisation, which gave the world unprecedented affluence, has also given the disaffected, power of defiance and stumped the military prowess of the most powerful states as in Vietnam and Chechnya. In 1979, the Chinese also suffered unexpected setbacks at the determination of the defenders when it attacked Vietnam. The real eye-opener has been for the US in Iraq. After a spectacular military victory in 2003, it found that instead of welcome for pulling down the brutal regime of Saddam Hussein (and his statue), there has been unending suicidal crescendo against the most powerful military machinery in the world. The communication revolution and globalisation of trade and investment has, of course, contributed immeasurably to improving world's living conditions; it has removed much drudgery. The gallop of technology has exceeded any other period of history, but the comprehension by the decision-makers of its implications remained on a slow trot. The multi-pronged technological advance ignited political consciousness of the poor, including of those living in isolated hamlets and tribal forests. While we, the educated, working in the political establishment continued to believe that the illiterate were docilely inoculated against protesting capacity and assumed that the traditional fatalistic acquiescence of the handicapped will not turn violent; in fact, this quiescent multitude is now aroused.

---

10. Center for International Affairs, Harvard, Spring 2006.

Technology has facilitated satellite intelligence, strengthened military alliances and vertical bipolarity of the advanced nations led by USA and erstwhile USSR, but technology has also sharpened the challenge to complacent old social structures. The improved dissemination of worldwide knowledge whetted expectations and impatience amongst the disaffected. The determination to demand greater equity in distributional justice by two-thirds of the marginalised in the world has made terrorism the real 21st Century threat to most governments. The double edged nature of technological advance, as it affects national security in the nuclear age, will demand reorienting political, economic, social priorities, including rethinking of defence priority and weapon armouries.

India has now shown that the positive use of nuclear energy is more urgent. It has modified its earlier absolutist position against the privileged exemption for select nuclear weapon powers. The obligation inherent in the treaty of not testing or exporting weapons knowhow has been unilaterally accepted. Even though nuclear apartheid persists but with priority for development, international safeguards applying on 14 of our reactors—as for reactors of all the other signatories—have now been accepted. There is implicit recognition that military power translated into hegemonism has suffered atrophy unknown in history. Nehru's concept of political equality of nationalism is now surreptitiously being 'vindicated'.

Military alliances reinforced centripetality and vertical solidarity round national security, but the information revolution is leading to a growing horizontal bipolarity of common interests of the disaffected—a sort of trans-border coalition around internal anger and grievances. All governments have stakes of responsibility for internal stability and are baffled by the internationalisation of protests fuelled from across borders, which are enlarging porous chinks of frontiers. While in the 19th Century, empires could be built and sustained by isolating gentle or oppressive coercion, in the 20th Century, this compartmentalised control stands perforated. There were fanatics trained in Afghanistan in the attack on the twin Towers and Pentagon in the USA; the cassettes of Osama-bin-Laden are broadcast round the world. Pakistani militants, no doubt unknown to their government, are suspected to be involved in Sinkiang and the underground bombings in London; Algerians and Moroccans are amongst the protesters in France and all over Europe. In other words, despite technology and international deployment of intelligence agents, terrorist cells with international linkages are now a feature of our times. Sovereignty is being bypassed not just by international investment bankers but also by terrorism. Anti-Americanism and Islamaphobia are all manifestations of this unforeseen horizontal bipolarity.

It has crystallised into a sort of clash of civilisations, faiths and cultures, which recall the crusades, the Crescent consolidating victory of the sword over many countries; the Cross followed imperial conquests in the expansion of European power. Governmental decision-makers must be worried that this can cast a shadow on modernisation, economic progress, urbanisation and the imperative for a salad bowl of diversity in a dynamic state. While in India, internationalised terrorism has had comparatively limited impact, but militants based in Pakistan or Bangladesh cannot be presumed to be inactive. But there are 175 districts within India which, in different degrees are under the influence of Naxalites defying law and order enforcement and this started long before religion motivated militancy.

This 21st Century jolt flow out of the internationalisation of information. This century with its easier travel and perceptions has also facilitated migrations for employment and heightened mal-distribution of growth benefits—nationally and internationally. It has resulted in aggressive protest against deliberate or suspected discrimination. Population pressures on natural resources, global warming, the threat of environmental destruction almost justifies in despairing for the future of the planet. But the Green and environmental movements, the saving of flora and fauna including whales and vultures have become international concerns. Earlier, there was imperial presence of tariff concessions within the British dominions and colonies but that was decided by centrepetality ordered in London to facilitate intra-empire trade. The present global interdependence—financial, technological and commercial—is based on technological progress, which mocks the political independence implicit in the Westphalian notion of sovereignty. One World remains an impossible dream but diplomacy does face a new challenge, which compels modification of the old precept 'my country right or wrong'. Great and superpowers must consciously guard against arrogant manifestations of neo-imperialism. This is a mismatch or call it mismanagement of centrifugality and centrepetality in the 21st Century. It only confirms Régis Debray when he wrote, "History advances in disguises: we are never contemporaneous with the present." Statesmanship, however, demands adjustment to contemporaneity and the moulding of the past so that it is in tune with the future.

India and the US: the 21st century

The political failure of American 'neo-imperialism' however, brought about a positive change in the subcontinent. Anti-Americanism suddenly overtrumped 60 years of anti-Indianism in Pakistan and unearthed the long-concealed reality that geography is more powerful in both countries than the embedded emotional sediments of recent history. In the face of the spectre of near despair, one can detect the seeds of cautious optimism and the possibility of the quest for principled return of the foreign policy in both countries to maximising people's welfare.

Guideposts for foreign policy in the 21st century

In the light of all this, there are specific ingredients to provide guideposts for foreign policy of India in the 21st Century. These can be encapsulated briefly:

Stooping to win back the trust of our neighbours

The recognition of past failures in diplomacy with our neighbours could undo suspicions of hegemonistic propensities and assist in restoring confidence and trust in India. In Sri Lanka, we have recovered from the adverse consequences of an impetuous intervention, but it will require a careful balancing between sympathy for the Tamil minority and a credible support for the integrity of the country. India has a particular stake in the viability of Nepal and Bangladesh.

Why not aim to de-nuclearise South Asia?

Our diplomacy must remain sensitised to rationalising relations with Pakistan, but it will necessarily be a long haul as it involves erasing embedded memories. We can optimise our future and build confidence in the 21st Century India by dismantling the legacy of old paranoia. Siachen and Sir Creek, if solved, will boost confidence building. Both countries therefore should aim to renounce the nuclear weapon option as Libya has done. Except in the nervous breakdown scenario, meteorology will always inhibit the use of nuclear bombs against each other as the consequence could be suicidal. Pakistan must abandon the nuclear supply relationship— both imports and exports—with all countries, specially with China as we have done, at least by implication with the other weapon powers by accepting IAEA safeguard on two-thirds of our reactors and committing ourselves to 'no test' and 'no first strike'.

Develop SAARC and SAFTA

We should no longer be squeamish about SAARC discussing political issues. Our strength is our democratic openness. SAARC would and should benefit our neighbours but the improvement in their purchasing power will correspondingly be of advantage to India. The progress of SAARC and its subsidiary SAFTA will, however, remain halting if the old political inhibitions continue.

Enlarge concentric regionalism in BIMSTEC, ASEAN and Central Asia

We have often overlooked that our own progress as well as that of our neighbours can only be by simultaneous development of all of them; geography and economics must enlarge the definition of our region. Stability in Afghanistan, and ensuring energy supply from Iran and Turkmenistan, in other words, revise the definition of South Asia. We should maximally vigorate trading concessions and developmental relations not just with Myanmar, BIMSTEC and ASEAN but eventually with Asia itself. Development and assistance to Central Asia can improve dramatically. India is a large industrial country and will get additional advantage by shorter communication with the bigger region, but we have to chisel and sensitise our diplomacy.

Independent mutuality with all the great powers

As an emerging world power, we should husband the growing functional relations and technological cooperation with the US, Europe, Japan and Russia. On balance, globalisation and outsourcing accelerates our advantage but it implies reciprocal openness with other developed countries for greater international trade.

With China both functional complementarity and rivalry

We should continue to improve functional relations with China. Consistent with our own political system, we should emulate China's economic pragmatism. A *de jure* border settlement with China is desirable but it must not be a precondition to improving functional relations with the country. In the long run, India-China relations are both complementary and of rivalry. Let us not hesitate to acknowledge that China has gained ground in South Asia but it has been by diplomatic attrition of India rather than by military operations or ideological propaganda. With geographical proximity and our own economic progress, India should be able to offer more to Pakistan, Nepal, Bhutan, Bangladesh and Sri Lanka than a distant country like China. Our functional relations can be reinforced by commonality or affinity of cultures, but diplomacy alone can balance China's military superiority and economic advantage.

Solidarity with West Asian governments and the people

With the Gulf countries, India is reaping the benefit of emigration, bringing high skills and strong work ethics even at the expense of humiliating disabilities, discrimination and denial of basic human rights. Such political denial has been suffered by millions for the advantage of economic benefit of remittances, which would have invited protests elsewhere. In West Asia, we have traditional, cultural connections, reinforced by geographical proximity, which go beyond dependence on energy imports. It is important that in Palestine, Iraq and Iran, we do not get identified with the US or even with the West European policies. With improved relations with Pakistan, we should not appear to be merely out-competing with our neighbour, nor need we abandon our established functional cooperation with Israel.

Our developmental experience made available to Africa and fellow developing countries

For Africa, Asia and the many developing or poor countries of the world, our greatest asset is our developmental experience. With President Nyerere in the seventies, when Tanzania was one of the highest recipients of per capita aid in the world, I made a dent for India by stating that India's advantage was our inability to hide our failures; we could teach what mistakes to avoid! However, our training establishments, higher educational and professional institutions, modern medical facilities match world standards and are available in English at a fraction of costs. India is a true magnet for management degrees, IIT and other specialised skills. We come second only to US in the treatment of complex diseases and surgery and provide better nursing and aftercare facilities.

India should be seen as supportive of UN and multilateralism

India pioneered decolonisation. (China never bothered about protesting the phenomena of European Imperialism in other parts of Asia, Africa and the world.) Multilateralism has, therefore, always suited India; the reservations which we have had of the UN because of the aberrations on Kashmir, should no more come in the way of more wholehearted support for the international peace-keeping system. As stated earlier, exceptionalism for India—be it on the proliferation of nuclear weapons, reservations on the jurisdiction of the International Criminal Court or the Convention against anti-personnel mines—have done only harm to our international standing. India will be judged whether we stand by the 21st Century application of Nehruvian internationalism i.e. international principles rising above narrow nationalism. At the time of writing this chapter in 2006, no large or middle-sized developing country is as much on the ascendancy in upholding multilateralism in the solution of world problems as India; the old myopia could militate against our rising reputation and standing. Of course, we deserve to be a permanent member of the UN Security Council but, in my view, we have expanded too much diplomatic capital on what realistically has built-in procedural and political odds against a lonely triumph. It is worth remembering that when India was consecrated the Light of Asia and was pre-eminent in the developing world, we did not have a veto. It was because India of Gandhiji had the highest moral standing—not because we were economically and militarily in the big power league.

Combining sophistication in diplomacy but always navigating by the North Star of principled internationalism

India is comparatively well placed to steer through the 21st Century by diplomatic realism but without abandoning principled international morality. This can apply to transparency in environmental and human rights rectitude (though not in augmenting global warming), Third World poverty alleviation, generally easing trade barriers, promoting NGOs cooperation and a hundred other ways to enhance the logic of one global village. We are far from One World which Nehru dreamt of, but more than most countries, we can draw strength on the plurality of India's civilisation and moderate, if not resolve, the looming possibilities of tensions and terrorism, which are now hovering over the world.

India as a self-confident partner in the league of responsible powers

Finally, let it be acknowledged that US and India have many unique similarities. We were the first and the second to throw away the British imperialism; both nurtured civilisational values of plurality and salad bowl ideals of citizenship. But for different reasons both, however, abdicated the original ideals. India, however, is groping to recapture the strength which flowed from its cherished ideals. Unless US dramatically corrects course, US may be on the decline. Even so, for the next 50 years the US would still be the most powerful country in the world. India can be a fuller partner to US but also simultaneously with Russia, Europe, Japan and even China. India has to better manage the web of multiple partnerships than we did in the first 50 years of our freedom. The time for total identification and ideological or developmental imitation or becoming active partner in strategic alliances as in the Cold War is over.

India can exemplify the middle ground blending of democracy, defence and development but must better manage centrifugality and centripetality

When the US is perceived as trying to impose democracy, India should only remain true to its own democratic functioning and not seriously join in advocacy much less in imposing our model abroad. International law is best safeguarded by principled adherence and practice of national independence. We should show faith in furthering conflict resolution through diplomacy. India does not need any off-shore umpires even 'facilitators' like the US in furthering bilateral relations with its neighbours. Beyond our strategic proximity, we should be seen again as committed to principled internationalism. As the Prime Minister told the Harvard alumnae in Delhi, India must hold to the liberal 'Middle' ground and not be buffeted by the international illiberal 'Right' or the extreme 'Left', both of which are prisoners of the past and often articulate old prejudices and are victims of the hypnosis of history.

4

Engaging with the world

K. Shankar Bajpai

It is now common for observers and analysts of world affairs to include the rise of India as one of the new phenomena that count in any serious assessment of the forces already at work or likely to be so. To many Indians this is a long overdue recognition of capabilities that have always been ours. The truth is that while we have been more influential in the past than most outsiders have been prepared to acknowledge, we have not really played the role we could have or that our more easily self-satisfied compatriots like to think we have been doing. It is the main thesis of this essay that we have neglected to develop either the conceptual or the mechanical apparatus needed to cope with the role of power in world affairs, and that unless we do so, urgently and extensively, we cannot be as effective as our size, situation and resources, not least the talents of our people, ought to have made us long since.

We are in fact in the curious position of being looked upon by others as one of the more significant players on the international stage while we ourselves have yet to grow into a suitable awareness both of the nature of that role and of the capabilities required to play it. As our Prime Minister has often observed, we lack an adequate grounding in the broad strategic thinking without which no state can manage its interests effectively, specially a state rightly considered to be a major power. Not that we have lacked for tall claims of having being such a power from the start; certainly, we have been active enough from that start even to the point of being called 'international busy-bodies'. But my submission is that, that kind of involvement in world affairs was extremely limited, both in approach and in effect; we lacked a hard-headed understanding of the way the world works and the ways in which we have to work with and in it.

This rise of India has been increasingly attracting the world's attention for nearly two decades, and under different home governments. The procession of state leaders, businessmen and political analysts who have been visiting us, is only an outward manifestation of the extent to which India has begun to count in their approaches to their own country's international interests. Unquestionably, the way our economy has broken through into the world's horizons is the single most significant cause, but realisation of our military capabilities, paradoxically noticed more because of the nuclear tests which earned us such denunciations, is not far behind. And buttressing these two basic developments have been the perception of our techno-scientific strength and the view that we have achieved that miracle, virtually unknown in the decolonised states, a stable system of government. In short, we are now seen as a state that can carry influence beyond its borders, and must be reckoned with, in regard to a growing number of issues.

Even a random selection of some of the salient issues requiring the world's attention brings this out: the security of the Persian Gulf, or of energy supply generally, or the stability of Central Asia, the changing power equations of East Asia, the safe openness of sea lanes, the spread of terrorism, the dangers of religious extremism, the proliferation of WMDs, or such non-traditional challenges to international order as HIV-AIDS or global warming—take any such major issue and India has both great interests involved and great contributions to make.

But it is instructive to remember that we have been here before. Soon after independence, Prime Minister Nehru pointed out a similar situation:

"Look at the map. If you have to consider any question affecting the Middle East, India inevitably comes into the picture. If you have to consider any question concerning South-East Asia, you cannot do without India. So also with the far East. ...whatever regions you may have in mind, the importance of India cannot be ignored. ......So the point I wish the House to remember is this: first of all the emergence of India in world affairs is something of major consequence in world history. We... in the Government are men of relatively small stature. But it has been given to us to work at a time when India is growing into a great giant again. So, because of that, in spite of our own smallness, we have to work for great causes and perhaps elevate ourselves in the process."

When Panditji so addressed our Constituent Assembly on March 8, 1949, we seemed to have the opportunity of being a major international player very much as we have today, of being "a great giant," albeit in very different circumstances. International affairs were then dominated by the established powers, and we were an unknown entity. Yet others as well as we ourselves felt we would really count. And in objective terms we were far more powerful than is even now realised. We had one of the world's five largest armies, ranked tenth in industrial capacity; despite the terrors and strains of partition we had a strong administrative structure, a pool of exceptional talent and, incidentally, no foreign exchange shortages. True, we were new to international affairs, but it was a less complex world and, oddly enough, proportionately speaking we had a better fund of knowledge available for policy making and for public debate than we do today. We had another advantage we may prefer not to acknowledge: expecting us to exercise our capabilities in the same way as others did, the world assessed us as stronger than we allowed ourselves to be, not knowing our self-imposed constraints.

And the world did turn to us for important work: from Korea to Gaza, from Indo-China to the Congo, whenever an international crisis needed international cooling down, India was asked to provide both individuals and forces. And as the Cold War took over the global arena to become the central fact of international life, India was constantly in the lead, both to reduce the possibilities of world war and to help structure a new world order. Yet, without belittling in the slightest what we tried for and indeed what we contributed, we must acknowledge that we did not become of that "major consequence in world history", much less that "great giant" which we expected and which our inherent capabilities ought to have made us. And the reason lies in our difficulty in coming to terms with the role of power in world affairs.

To substantiate that view, I must get back to certain basics. What are the elements in history, personal and national experience, culture and view of life, that shape a people's view of the world? Without getting too involved in that complicated subject, I will just draw attention to a few major influences that worked on us in those formative years. First must be put our inwardness. Both as a people and as a state, we have throughout history been a world unto ourselves. The evidence of extended trading links and of repeated invasions does nothing to contradict this fact. Angkor Wat and Borobudur bear enduring witness to the power of our thought and of our peoples to be felt beyond our borders but it was never a case of an Indian state exerting imperium abroad. Hegel's famous observation that: "India as a wished-for land has been a major principle of history" underlines how others have sought us out, how we have been acted upon by others, in contrast to acting outwards ourselves. From being only an object of power, our British rulers made us a base of power, which enabled them to exercise their control from Suez to Singapore and indeed, farther East. We of course considered that part of the era of imperialism, which we opposed; and as we assumed charge of our destinies, our historic isolationism resumed charge of our approach to the world. Let me offer one illustration. In the late fifties, as Britain withdrew from the Persian Gulf area, they relinquished Gwadar which, though on the coast of Baluchistan, was for some reason administered from Muscat and Oman. The latter enquired if we would like to buy the place. We would not even think of the possibility. We also, more famously, agreed to withdraw the rupee as the currency of the region; with the Gulf region's oil development, it was doubtless only a matter of time before the rupee would cease to be relevant there. Doubtless, too, if we had followed up on the Gwadar possibility, it would have been withdrawn, what with Pakistan protesting and its Baghdad Pact members helping it; but the point to note is that we were not even prepared to think in such terms, the strategic significance of acquiring Gwadar simply would not enter our minds. Two other formative influences, reinforcing this inwardness, arose from our freedom movement: anti-imperialism and pacifism, meaning both non-violence and an innate inclination to work for peace. I do not think we should ever claim to be holier than others in these respects; the needs of the state drove us to the use of force soon enough—Junagadh, Hyderabad, Kashmir, later on Goa, were cited gleefully by our critics as mocking what we professed, but apart from the justifications of necessity, these cases in no way lessened the very profound beliefs that power, especially military power, was the cause of evil. It took our humiliation of 1962 to drive home the inescapability of developing our military capabilities, but no conceptual thinking on security strategies developed to inform our policy making. We continued in particular to believe that imperialism and its reliance on power was the cause of the world's troubles. Both the annals of the Congress Party going back to the 1930s and the pronouncements of leaders across our entire political spectrum after independence, provide ample evidence of our abhorrence of power politics, and even of the concept of balance of power, from which it was all too easy to condemn power as such.

This mistrust of power strengthened one of the principal concerns of our early foreign policy: anti-colonialism. Eager to consolidate our own independence, we also believed in the independence of other subjugated peoples, and working for the end of colonial rule everywhere was one of our prime objectives.

One component of 'the intellectual prism' through which we viewed the world is rarely mentioned but is nonetheless important, and that is Socialism. No one growing up under colonial rule could fail to be a socialist in some degree or another; not only were the theories based on Marxist thought anti-imperialist, it was among the world's socialists that we found such friends as the cause of independence could turn to. Moreover, for those living through the thirties, with the twin disasters of the economic crash of 1929 and the rise of Fascism, Socialism offered the most appealing answers, morally and intellectually, even romantically, thanks to the heroes of the Spanish Civil War. Marxism reinforced our suspicions about the Western powers, which we associated with imperial ambition and its hand-maiden, a grasping capitalism; it also provided a readymade frame of reference, such as we otherwise lacked, within which to evaluate international developments. Coupled with the fact that no Indian had exercised power at strategic levels for centuries, it severely limited the evolution of our national perspectives.

Circumstances attendant on our emergence into the world as an independent player also came into play. The coming of our freedom coincided with two events of huge importance: the end of World War II, and the beginning of the nuclear age. The horrors of the former underlined the over-riding necessity of avoiding the horrors the latter could lead to. A brief spell of idealism pervaded the world, with hopes arising everywhere that a new world order could be created, depending not on the enforcement capabilities of the world's great powers, who had constantly shown that their own selfish interests took precedence over world order, not to mention peace, but on multilateral cooperation based on equality, mutual benefit, equity and international law.

In short, everything conspired to amalgamate our instinctive proclivities : our historical aloofness from the world, abhorrence of imperialism and what we saw as an emerging neo-colonialism, the aversion to power politics, the primacy of consolidating freedom at home and supporting it abroad, the moral and philosophical tenets of our independence movement, the situation in the world we were entering—all this encouraged us to believe that the world needed a new approach to handling its inter-relationships and that we in India could offer the new approach.

Please note the one thing missing in this thinking: the realisation that until a new way was found, the old ways had to be dealt with on their own terms. We also failed—one might say we positively refused—to realise both that we were stronger than we allowed to be, and that we were so situated geographically that we needed to develop that strength in order to establish as well as protect our interests.

Panditji had said " Look at the map." How many of us have ever done so? We have more neighbours than all but a handful of countries—seven by land and three by sea, but how conscious are we that we have them, much less what they signify? Jungles, mountains, deserts, oceans connect or separate them; Buddhism, Islam, Hinduism, Communism animate them; we must deal with military dictatorships, monarchies, Marxist democracy, happily a real democracy. The geographical and political complexity is exceptional, requiring knowledge, skill and flexibility we hardly ever allow for. I wonder how many of us go through a year without ever hearing about Myanmar; do we realise that the last major attempt to invade India was through that country, whose strategic importance for us cannot be over-stated? And how many of us still think of China as some distant land you fly 2,000 miles east to enter from Hong Kong, rather than the country with whom we have the longest land frontier?

Above all, we are one of the world's great crossroads. Our interests in West Asia are relatively well known, and those with South-East Asia happily at last becoming so; we are less aware that our Northern borders make developments in Central Asia of direct interest to us; and of course the great waters on three sides of us make us and the Indian Ocean mutually important. I fear, however, that few of us—fewer even, alas, of our policy makers or those who shape our public discussions—ever heeded Panditji's injunction.

It has in recent years become increasingly fashionable to blame Jawaharlal Nehru for just about everything that is wrong with us or has gone wrong for us. His contributions to our potential greatness, material and intellectual, and his own greatness as a human being and as a leader, put such modish carping to shame; certainly they need no defence from me. No doubt, he made mistakes, of judgement and of policy, but if we look at most of what we might now wish had been otherwise, it will be evident that it was not so much that he was in error, but that the rest of us did not grasp the infinite nuances that shaped his approaches. Crude oversimplifications became our guiding concepts. His vision that we should "work for great causes" became an excuse for us to concentrate on the major international problems of the day, to the detriment of the strategic thinking about our national interests. And far from "elevating ourselves", I fear we have become ever more parochial in our thinking and smaller in our behaviour.

Today, the world's expectations, but above all our own obligations to our country and peoples, call loudly and imperatively for us to shed notions and attitudes that are out of date or otherwise irrelevant. I am reminded of George Kennan's admonition to America:

> "If we are to regard ourselves as a grown-up nation—and anything else would henceforth be mortally dangerous—... we must...put away childish things .... the first to go (being) our self-idealisation, and the search for absolutes in world affairs: absolute security, absolute amity, absolute harmony."

Kennan adapted St.Paul: "When I was a child, I spoke... understood... thought as a child; but when I became a man, I put away childish things.". Our discard-list might be different—certainly including sentimentality and wishful-thinking—but the basic lesson remains the same: for nations, as for human beings, different stages of life, or circumstances, demand increasing maturity. Today's India is as different from that of independence as today's world is from that of the Cold War. Have our speech, understanding, thought— our whole behaviour, as a people and as a state, matured accordingly?

The capabilities we have developed, which are attracting this attention of the world to India as a key player for tomorrow, behove us to grow out of our yesterdays. The weaknesses that are keeping so many of our people beyond the benefits of our progress, and even beyond the reach of hope, are an appalling reflection on all that we still need to do, but they cannot be overcome by pity or idealism, howsoever admirable those virtues may be in themselves. Nor should they be allowed to distract us from realising that, despite the weaknesses, we have acquired great strengths, and are no longer one of the disadvantaged countries, waiting for the world's pity or idealism to come to our aid. It passes all understanding how we are still conditioned in our approaches to the world by slogans of non-alignment, third-world solidarity, anti-imperialism and the like. Even at the best of times, these were substitutes for thought; now they stifle thought.

Consider the most persistent of these slogans: non-alignment. There are a number of countries in the world that continue to find comfort in both the concept and the grouping. As a rhetorical instrument for helping our ties with these countries, obeisance to the movement may be harmless, even marginally useful, but as a guide to foreign policy it is positively malign. Let us remember that non-alignment never was and never could be a policy: it was an attitude, a way of approach, a basis for developing policies. Nasser and Tito, two of the original founding triumvirate, could not bring the real philosopher of the idea to join their efforts to make it a grouping. For Jawaharlal Nehru, the independence of a nation included above all independence of thinking: he resisted the attempt to constitute a bloc, or create an organisation, because he feared, alas, all too rightly, that it would not suit his purpose of making us think for ourselves but would impose positions on us—the very negation of the independence which he hoped to strengthen. Unfortunately, he lived only for one session, in Belgrade, after which non-alignment was hijacked to serve the national objectives of almost everyone but ourselves. It is time for us to serve our own national objectives.

I do not for a moment overlook the facts that might appear to controvert what I am urging here. Over half a century has seen us confront the most serious challenges to our territorial integrity and to our very nationhood; yet here we are, with all but a sliver of our territory intact, our nationhood consolidated, with a history of respect for our international activities and our standing in the world higher than ever. Surely, we have been doing things right for all that to be the case; what is there to cavil at? I do not go so far as to say that we have achieved all this despite ourselves, but I do maintain that we owe more to circumstances that have favoured us than we are willing to acknowledge, much less learn from. Furthermore, we now face opportunities as well as difficulties for which all our past achievements still leave us less adequately equipped than we can afford to be.

To be better equipped, we must first develop both the concepts and the mechanics for using state power for state purposes. By power is meant neither more nor less than the capacity to move others towards doing, and even thinking, what they might not otherwise envisage or be inclined to. We in India unfortunately lack both a body of experience in the use of the power of a state for the purposes of a state, and a body of thought devoted to such use. Everyone thinks of Kautilya, but the most important point to note about him is that he was two thousand years ago-and unique: he left no school, nor did anyone develop any kind of political or strategic thinking which still inform the policymaking of countries belonging to other major civilisations. To make matters worse, as already mentioned, the century-plus of colonial rule left us without any practitioners of power at any significant level. To this day, most people who have power seem unable to rise above *patwari*-power, meaning, its use, for essentially limited and personal purposes — giving or obtaining a licence here, a school admission there, a job, a protection, a favour of one kind or another. Unfortunately, moreover, from our initial aversion to developing the instruments of force, we have come to rely on force to the detriment if not the exclusion of other instruments of power. This is most evident in domestic matters, where we let a problem simmer up till it boils over, when no solution remains possible without at least using some force to begin with. But in the affairs of the world at large, we neither use the instruments of power nor allow for the way others use them. I don't suppose many people read Thucydides these days; a pity, for there is much to learn there, particularly in the Melian Dialogues. Athens was asserting itself, and tried to get the independent island of Melos to go along with it. In the course of the negotiations, arguing to avoid the Athenian take-over on various grounds, the Melian delegation finally invoked the question of justice. The Athenian reply is a classic guide to our much abhorred but wholly inescapable bugbear, power politics: "Surely we both know that in these matters the question of justice only arises when the equation of power is equal; for the rest, the strong take what they can and the weak yield what they must."

It is not a nice thought, and goes against the whole grain of our national upbringing and hopes of a better world, but it is a reality we can ignore only at our peril. Nor is it a negation of the moral principles we must all seek to strengthen in the world. As G.S. Bajpai said in a lecture on the balance of power,

> "We should never make the mistake of assuming that the rightness of a cause can even eventually ensure its success. We live in a world of power. Power exercised without regard to morality is a crime against humanity; but morality cannot prevail without the backing of power."

Let me re-emphasise that force is far from being the only means of exerting power. I do not want to get into the controversy over soft-power, whether there is such a thing effective apart from hard-power. But there can be no doubt that there is a whole range of instruments available in statecraft; the power of ideas is manifest; less obvious are the powers of anticipation, positioning and maneuvering; the power of persuasion and reasoning; all that is nowadays much talked about, the power of knowledge; not least, the power of being considered a power, of respect and the image of knowing what you are about and of the capability to succeed. The world today believes we have all that; it also recognises that we have interests beyond our borders. In this respect, as in many others; the world looks like being ahead of us. We have to wake up both to our capabilities and the challenges of using them as a constructive power in the evolution of tomorrow's world. When told that nuclear fission had been achieved in the deserts of Los Alamos, Einstein's comment was: "everything has now changed-except our ways of thinking." We need to change our ways of thinking.

First, we have to start thinking of ourselves as a source of power, not as a victim that must ward off power. Secondly, we must think afresh of where our interests lie. Third, we must develop our capabilities for shaping events, not merely reacting to them. In a sense, we as a state must emulate what our business entrepreneurs have started doing: after decades of inwardness, of deliberate self-limitation to small horizons, our businessmen are not only successfully competing with the world's best, they are building up their activities in the world. India needs to engage with the world in similar fashion.

Our first area of attention ought to be our neighbourhood. It is not easy to be by far the largest state in any region: one inherently arouses fear, resentments, extreme touchiness among adjacent peoples. India is by no means alone in that situation, nor in being unable to go too far in being generous as the 'big brother'. Smaller states naturally wish to feel confidence in a big neighbour, that its power will not be used to intimidate them. It is obviously an asset to diplomacy to help our neighbours develop such confidence; even in wider circles, it is important to be seen as what we are, a force for stability, not hegemonism. But big countries also have interests, with limits on what they can concede. There are also limits on influence: the greatest power in the world has for decades been unable to do anything effective about the intractable difficulties with a small island just off its land-mass. But certainly, other big states have devoted more constant and purposeful attention to neighbours, and have enjoyed the help of large bodies of opinion and of interest working for better relations with the 'big brother.' We do fortunately have such advantage in a couple of countries, but need to develop more with others.

Let us look again at some of the other leading issues mentioned earlier as being of vital interest to us. Islam and oil, are only the most obvious reasons why West Asia is important for us; we also have some three million of our citizens at work there, and the peoples there and here get on with each other more easily than with other parts of the world. We have not till now applied our minds to the ways in which we can be useful in easing some of the infinitely complex problems of the region, or whether indeed we have any role to play in the stability-promoting possibilities there. Central Asia is more distant and less immediately relevant, but its long-term significance requires positioning ourselves today to be helpful there tomorrow. We have finally for a decade or so tried to build up interaction with South-East Asia, but it is no secret that countries in that region have been disappointed in us and look for greater attention. Just beyond, in regard to East Asia, we have been less active, and no doubt on questions such as North Korea or Taiwan there is virtually nothing we can do, but in regard to the changing power equations in the region, we are looked upon by all concerned, as of major significance.

To shed the euphemisms, we are talking about the rise of China. It goes without saying that healthy cooperation between India and China is our preferred purpose; that it has been developing well is a measure of the benefits both sides can derive from it. We do have the great unsettled question of our boundary, which presents some fairly intractable difficulties; it is good that tranquility prevails and possibilities of settlement are being seriously probed. Meanwhile, in a fine case of practical statesmanship which ought to serve as an example to some of our other neighbours, both sides have decided to build up relations even as the major difference between us remains unsettled. But nor can India afford to ignore some worrying aspects of Chinese policies. China's incalculably vital help to Pakistan in developing nuclear weapons capabilities we are told is a thing of the past; but apart from having achieved its purpose of plaguing us for all eternity, it cannot alas be taken as finished and done with. The development of naval facilities by and for China in Myanmar and Gwadar, also, we are asked to consider innocuous, intended for China's broader interests; the fact remains that they could pose serious problems for us. Above all, no one can be sure how benevolent China's growing power will prove in its applications to Asia as a whole. Clearly, it is no part of India's interests to let mistrust, much less confrontation, return to Sino-Indian relations; equally, it is in nobody's interest to see China dominate Asia.

What we would all like to think is now at last our real engagement with the world will require a highly sophisticated handling of many such complex combinations of pros and cons. One more illustration is telling. Nothing is more topical or more complex, than our relations with Iran. With its hugely important strategic situation, its equally important potential as an economic, especially an energy, partner for us, not to mention the extremely skilful talents of its peoples, Iran obviously is a country we should also seek good relations with; and again, as in the case of China; we are fortunate that Delhi has for well over a decade sought steady betterment. But in regard to Iran, as to some other issues where sentiments tend to take over, it is also common among us to bring in cultural and historical links. These surely are more double-edged. That so much of our language, music and literature, ways of living and behaving, even our food, come from Persian influences, and *vice versa*, demands respect and strengthening. No less notable is the place Persia or Iran holds in the minds and feelings of many of our peoples. I am less sure about our inclination to call it a great friend; not only under previous regimes but ever since the revolution, there is too much on record that does not fit such a rosy image. But what is truly mystifying is the degree to which opinion makers in India, especially political parties which are supposedly concerned more about India's interests than those of other countries, have sought to mobilise support for Iran's nuclear programme without the slightest attention to its being inconsistent with India's vital interest in non-proliferation.

Of various irrelevancies cited, what betrays precisely the mind-set we have to be rid of is the appeal for third-world solidarity. Apart from what I have urged about India no longer being a third-world country, we might reflect that all the countries normally referred to by that term have signed the NPT, opposed India's going nuclear—as did Iran—and oppose Iran's doing so. What solidarity is referred to? Worse still, parties constantly championing secularism not only cite India and Iran's Shia links but blatantly sought to arouse our Muslim population. Iran is important, and we certainly do not want to be antagonistic, but this is another example of how we will increasingly have to sort out conflicting pressures and pursue policies that reconcile our own conflicting interests, in this case good relations and non-proliferation.

The more we engage with the world, the more such dilemmas and balancing acts will face us. A skilful diplomacy will need the vital reinforcement of a large body of informed strategic thinkers, of area and subject experts, and a reasoned public debate. Above all, in the Kennan-St.Paul sense, we must grow up. Let us respect but adapt the wisdom and the values of our older traditions but let us also learn from the experience of our own lifetime. A diplomat in a South-East Asian country told me a couple of years ago: "Now when we consider every morning the decisions we have to take, we no longer ask ourselves even what will Washington think; we wonder what will Beijing think, We are waiting for the day when we can add the same question about Delhi." If we can update and upgrade both the concepts and the mechanisms of our interactions with the world, what Delhi thinks will count more and more.

The body of this essay was developed for the 2006 Prem Bhatia Memorial Lecture; I am grateful to the Trustees for letting me reproduce much of it.

5

India and the changing balance of power

Chandrashekhar Dasgupta

Predicting political trends has something in common with monsoon forecasting. Both are necessary exercises, since they enable us to position ourselves more advantageously in facing the future. Both exercises are also liable to prove inaccurate, involving as they do a large number of variable factors. It is, therefore, not only becoming but also prudent for an analyst to lay no more than a modest claim to accuracy in making any forecast of long-term international political developments.

It is in this spirit that we approach the daunting but necessary task of anticipating the changes that are likely to occur in the global distribution of power over the next several decades and the implications of these developments for India. We shall first look at the current balance of power and identify its principal features. In particular, we shall examine the extent to which the current global order may accurately be described as 'unipolar'. In the next section, we shall examine the directions in which the balance is likely to evolve during, say, the next half century. Aggregate and per capita GDP projections provide a useful indication of a country's long-run power potential. We shall look at differential growth rates and demographic trends in major countries in order to assess their future power potential. In the concluding section, we shall consider some of the implications of the changing balance of power for India's foreign policy.

A unipolar world

The current international order may be described, with a large measure of accuracy, as unipolar. With the disintegration of the Soviet Union in December 1991, the United States became the sole superpower on the international stage. In terms of military-political power, it has n.. equal or even near equal. The United States has an unmatched capability to project its military power to any part of the globe. It possesses the world's most sophisticated and powerful nuclear armoury. The extent of its military lead over all other powers can be gauged from the fact that its defence expenditure in 2003 exceeded the combined total of the next 15 biggest defence spenders. Its determination to maintain its unquestioned lead in defence technology is reflected in the fact that, in 2003, it spent more on military R&D than the combined total of the next 6 major spenders.

From an historical angle, there is nothing unique in a power enjoying primacy within an international states system. In different historical periods, Spain, France, Britain and Germany have each been the leading power in the European states system (which evolved in the 20th Century into a truly global system). The unique feature of the current international scene is not US primacy *per se* but the extent of the lead that the US enjoys over any other power. In past eras, states tended to combine in alliances or pacts in order to restrain the most powerful nation in a 'balance of power' system. At present, however, the extent of the politico-military lead that the US enjoys over all other powers is so large that it cannot be countervailed by any combination of other powers. For the first time in many centuries, the balance of power mechanism has ceased to operate. This is the unique feature of the current international order.

Despite this feature, it is necessary to qualify the characterisation of the contemporary global order as unipolar. If we look exclusively at the economic dimension of power, the global order is not unipolar. The European Union is equal, or comparable, to the United States in the economic domain. Even before the expansion of its membership from 15 to 25 countries, the European Union had a combined Gross National Income approaching that of the United

States (US$ 8,170.5 billion in 2001, compared to US$ 9,780.8 billion for the US). In international trade, the European Union carries as much weight as the United States. Thus, in 2002, its merchandise exports amounted to US$ 939.8 billion, compared to the United States' US$ 639.9 billion; while its merchandise imports stood at US$ 933.1 billion, *versus* US$ 1,202 billion for the United States. Brussels carries as much influence in the WTO as Washington. In the multilateral financial institutions—the World Bank and the IMF—the role of the European Union is broadly comparable to that of the United States. Though the US dollar still remains the world's preferred reserve currency, this position may be challenged in the near future by the euro. The combined foreign aid budget of the member states of the European Union significantly exceeds that of the United States. Finally, the total population of the 25 countries of the European Union (around 450 million) is about 50 per cent larger than that of the United States.

In many respects, Japan is also a comparable economic power. Japan's per capita income is almost equal to the US', reflecting its position as a global leader in technology. However, its Gross National Income is very much smaller since its population (around 130 million) is less than half the size of the US population. Japan's Gross National Income and trade volume (as also population) are larger than those of any individual EU country but are much smaller than those of the European Union as a group. Since the European Union follows a single policy in trade issues, it carries somewhat greater weight than Japan in this field.

Thus, the global distribution of economic power is much more diffused than is the case with military-political power. The current global power structure resembles an irregular pyramid, with a political face resting on a much narrower base than its economic face. The United States is at the apex but the slope is much more gentle on the economic side than on the political side. Viewing power in composite terms, the United States must be regarded as the only superpower in today's world.

Towards a polycentric global order

The power balance described in the preceding section does not, of course, rest in a state of static equilibrium. As we noted earlier, long-term economic and demographic trends influence the rise and fall of states. GDP and per capita income projections are particularly useful indicators of a country's power potential. Growth rates in developed countries mainly depend upon new advances in technology and productivity or an expanding work force. Growth rates, therefore, tend to be low. There can be exceptions to this general rule. A developed country whose economy has been shattered by war (e.g. Germany and Japan in 1945), or by political upheaval (e.g. Russia after 1992), can speedily rehabilitate its economy. In general, however, developing countries can achieve more rapid growth (provided political and social conditions are auspicious) because they can quickly adopt already existing advanced technologies. However, as they catch up with the developed countries and approach the technological frontier, their growth rates will also decline. Growth prospects will also be influenced by demographic trends, which determine the size of the work force.

The GDP projections employed here are drawn from a widely cited Goldman Sachs study[1]. Among other studies that have employed the BRICs report projections is the US National Intelligence Council's 2004 report, *Mapping the Global Future*. It should be noted that the BRICs GDP projections are based on currency conversions at exchange rates. An alternative projection, based on GDP at Purchasing Power Parity rates, has been offered by Arvind Virmani[2]. The Virmani projections suggest that China and India would catch up with the US in terms of power potential at an earlier date than indicated by exchange rate based GDP projections. For reasons that need not detain us here, we believe that GDP at exchange rates is a better indicator of a country's international imprint for most, but not all, purposes. We have, employed the BRICs projections but have also cited some of Virmani's conclusions

---

1. Wilson, Dominic and Roopa Purushothaman (2003). "Dreaming With BRICs: The Path to 2050", *Global Economics Paper No: 99*, October.

2. Virmani, Arvind (2005). *A Tripolar Century: USA, China and India*, ICRIER, March.

for purposes of comparison, since any projection depicts only a plausible scenario.

After these preliminary observations, let us turn to the prospects of the major existing and potential global powers.

European Union

As we have seen, the European Union (EU) is today the only player at the global level that can already match the United States in at least one of the dimensions of power. In global trade and aid, it is in every respect an equal of the United States. With progressive unification of the policies of its member states in other economic areas, such as finance and environment, the influence of the European Union in these areas will expand. The euro, for example, is likely to emerge as an international reserve currency comparable to the dollar.

The European Union is, however, a unique creature: it functions like a federal state in international commercial issues while, in other areas, it operates as a regional association seeking to coordinate the independent national policies of member states to the extent possible. This asymmetry in the functions of the EU is reflected in the global power structure, which does not display unipolar characteristics in the trade domain, where the EU has a single policy, but is unipolar in all other areas. The crucial question, therefore, is how far the process of European unification will extend, particularly in the areas of foreign and defence policies.

Europeans are divided between the advocates of a Federal Europe that would follow a single foreign and security policy, and the defenders of a Europe of Nations, in which each European state continues to follow its own independent national foreign and security policy. The former envisage a future Federal Europe that plays the role of a superpower and an equal of the United States. The latter are anxious to preserve the sovereignty of their nation states and are apprehensive about the possibility that a Federal Europe may be dominated by a Franco-German axis. For the present, the latter approach appears to be dominant. Indeed, it has been reinforced with the recent entry into the EU of central European countries with lively memories of German and Russian domination.

In view of the lack of consensus about the future of Europe, the European Union has moved toward political integration through modest and incremental steps, without defining the final objective in clear terms. Its Common Foreign and Security Policy (CFSP) is an attempt at coordinating policies of member states, wherever possible. Since CFSP positions must be adopted unanimously, they tend to reflect the lowest common denominator in the policies of member states. The scope of the CFSP is thus limited to questions where EU member states have more or less identical views, or where differences can be papered over through skilful drafting. Despite this major limitation, the European Union has, indeed, made some progress in regard to CFSP. It maintains regular diplomatic interaction with foreign states and has occasionally emerged as a major player on a specific issue (as in the current case of Iran's nuclear programme). On balance, however, the major European powers—such as France, Britain and Germany—are far more influential in their individual capacity than the European Union as a group. In the area of foreign and security policy, it may be said of the European Union that the whole is smaller than some of its parts!

The EU has also made some modest progress in respect of a European Security and Defence policy (ESDP) since 1999, when it decided to develop an "autonomous capacity to take decisions, and where NATO as a whole is not engaged, to launch and conduct EU-led military operations in response to international crises." The ESDP is subject to the same limitations as CFSP and, in addition, is severely constrained by its relationship to NATO. The core issue of territorial defence falls outside the mandate of CSDP, being reserved for NATO. Moreover, despite claims to autonomy, ESDP operations cannot be launched independently of NATO. Determined to prevent the emergence of a truly independent EU military capability, the United States successfully insisted (with support from many European countries) that Turkey and other European members of NATO must be fully involved in ESDP decisionmaking and, moreover, that there should be no 'duplication of assets' with NATO. In other words, ESDP decisionmaking involves not only the EU but also other NATO countries, nor can they be launched without the use of NATO—controlled assets, particularly intelligence, planning and command and control capabilities. Washington has ensured that the nascent EU defence capability is subordinated to NATO and is thus, incapable of evolving into a truly independent EU military capability.

The rejection of the so-called EU Constitution by the French and Dutch electorates in 2005 suggest that there is no enthusiasm for EU political integration even in countries that have traditionally been leaders in the European project. Moreover, the rapid expansion in EU membership has added to the difficulties of forging consensus on common foreign and security policy. For these reasons, we may rule out the emergence of a Federal Europe in the next decade and federation will remain a highly unlikely prospect for at least another decade beyond the next. Over a longer time horizon—say, 2050—a Federal Europe is a possible but uncertain prospect. We may conclude that, as a result of deepening economic integration, the European Union will see a steady enhancement of its economic power but it is unlikely to challenge American military and political primacy, at least before the mid-century.

Russia

Can Russia re-emerge as a superpower? From a geopolitical as also a demographic viewpoint, the Russian Federation is a much smaller entity than the former Soviet Union. Nevertheless, it still possesses great assets in its pool of outstanding scientists and engineers; its vast mineral resources (in particular, oil and natural gas); and its shrunken but still impressive nuclear armoury. Over the past few years, assisted to no small extent by a sharp rise in the price of its oil exports, Russia has finally begun to lift itself out of the economic tailspin and institutional chaos into which it descended in the 1990s.

Certain features of Russia's national assets deserve notice. Russia's pool of scientific and technological manpower has always been concentrated in defence-related industries. After the collapse of the Warsaw Pact, Russia's economic contraction and the sharp fall in the defence budget, the domestic market alone is no longer sufficiently large to sustain defence R&D on the scale required of a first rank power. In such important areas as aircraft and armour, export markets—in particular the large Indian and Chinese markets—are crucially important for the maintenance of cutting edge R&D and an up-to-date Russian defence industry. Cooperation in defence technology is, perhaps, the most important dimension of Indo-Russian, as well as Sino-Russian, relations today.

As one of the world's biggest energy suppliers, Russia wields an influence that is disproportionately large in relation to its GDP and foreign trade figures. Russia is the second largest producer and exporter of petroleum (after Saudi Arabia). It is also the world's largest exporter of natural gas. Russia's relations with the European Union are influenced by the mutual interdependency arising from the fact that it supplies around a quarter of the latter's requirements of natural gas. Similar links of interdependence will be established with neighbouring China, which is set to emerge as a major market for Russian natural gas. Geographical factors currently preclude construction of gas pipelines to India but, with its rapidly rising demand, India could in the near future become a major customer for liquefied natural gas (LNG).

Current trends in Russia display both positive and negative features. On the positive side, as we have already noted, there are encouraging signs of an economic resurgence. This allows Moscow to pursue a somewhat more assertive foreign policy (for example, in the Iran nuclear issue). High levels of education, a skilled work force, a large pool of scientists and engineers, and bountiful natural resources provide favourable conditions for rapid rehabilitation of the economy. It should be noted, however, that the recent economic revival has been largely driven by a sharp increase in petroleum prices and growth prospects will remain dependent upon the vagaries of the international oil market, unless Russia is able to diversify its exports.

On the negative side, the first and foremost item is the declining demographic trend. The Russian Federation came into existence with a much smaller population than the former Soviet Union and even this reduced population (around 144.5 million in 2003) shows a marked downward trend. Demographic statistics reveal not only a low birth rate but also rising mortality rates resulting from the collapse of medical services. The critical question is whether Russia's future population will be sufficiently large to sustain the role of an economic and military superpower. Because of its much smaller population, the size of the Russian economy today, measured in terms of GDP, (US$ 764 billion in 2005) is smaller than that of India (US$ 785 billion), not to mention China (US$ 2.2 trillion). Unless current demographic trends are sharply reversed, Russia's declining population and work force will be unable to support an economy sufficiently large to meet the requirements of a superpower.

Second, there has been a significant decline in the prospects of a revival of Russia's influence around its periphery. NATO has expanded to incorporate not only former Warsaw Pact countries but also the former Soviet Baltic republics. Two other former Soviet republics, Ukraine and Georgia, are new applicants for NATO membership. As a result of the incorporation of Poland and the Baltic republics in the western alliance, the great Russian naval base of Kaliningrad has become an enclave surrounded by NATO territories. Ukraine's application for NATO membership raises serious questions about the future of Sevastopol, the other great ice-free Russian naval base in Europe. It will also result in severing the close links between the Russian and Ukrainian defence industries and a restructuring of Russian defence production to compensate for the loss of Ukrainian facilities.

Furthermore, NATO's Partnership for Peace agreements with the former Soviet republics of Central Asia, the Caspian and the Caucasus have undermined Russian primacy in its 'near abroad'. In the energy sector, the western powers, led by the United States, have successfully contested Russia's monopoly over the transportation and distribution of the oil and natural gas production of the former Soviet republics of Central Asia and the Caspian region. These commodities have traditionally been marketed through pipelines lying across Russian territory. Western companies are now building alternative pipelines, bypassing Russia, to transport Central Asian and Caspian gas and oil to European markets. One of the great success stories of US foreign policy relates to the rising influence of the western powers in the geopolitical as well as geoeconomic space vacated by the former Soviet Union.

Demography will probably determine the ceiling of Russia's power potential. The BRICs study indicates that, by 2050, Russia might have a per capita income of almost US$ 50,000, roughly on par with France and Germany. Russia at mid-century would thus be a prosperous country, with a modern economy and armed forces. However, its GDP (reflecting its shrinking population) would be smaller than Brazil's, less than a quarter of India's, and around a sixth of the US' GDP forces. Such a Russia might be a great power but not a full superpower. It would be unable to match the United States, though it might be able to play the role of a balancer by aligning itself with China or, just conceivably, with a Franco-German combination.

Japan

The demographic factor also limits Japan's power potential. It has already resulted in an erosion of Japan's established role as the leading economic power in East Asia. Though it far surpasses China in levels of technology and living standards, its more populous neighbour has overtaken it as a global trading entity. Moreover, Japan's lead over China in respect of other economic indicators (such as GDP, levels of technology, etc.) are shrinking on account of the wide disparity in the growth figures of the two countries. Japan's current (2005) GDP stands at US$ 4.5 trillion, far ahead of China's US$ 2.2 trillion. According to the BRICs report projections, however, China will catch up with Japan in terms of GDP around 2015. By 2025, China's GDP will be almost double that of Japan and, by mid-century, it will be almost seven times larger. Japan will, therefore, probably see a fairly rapid erosion in its role as an economic power, relative to neighbouring China.

However, Japan is re-inventing itself as a major military and political power. Its post-World War II constitution debars Japan from maintaining "land, sea and air forces, as well as other war potential". However, this constitutional provision has been imaginatively reinterpreted on successive occasions, commencing from 1954, when it was interpreted as permitting the maintenance of ground, maritime and air self-defence forces in order to "preserve peace and independence of the nation and maintain internal security." In 1992, it was decided to employ them abroad specifically for UN peacekeeping operations. In 2001, as a response to 9/11, the self-defence force was authorised to support the US and other countries in combating terrorism — implying a widening of its overseas role. In 2003, the requirement for a UN mandate was dropped when Japanese units were sent to Iraq for "humanitarian assistance and reconstruction". Defence expenditure was initially kept down to 1 per cent of GDP; however, it showed a rapid increase in absolute terms on account of the spectacular growth rates of the Japanese economy till the late 1980s. When growth rates faltered, the 1 per cent ceiling was breached in 1987. Japan now has a huge defence budget of around US$ 50 billion, enabling it to maintain a 240,000 strong self-defence force armed with the latest conventional weapons.

The evolution of Japan's defence policy reflects changes in the regional security environment — in particular, China's growing military power, North Korea's new missile and nuclear capabilities, and the likelihood of a gradual reduction in US military commitments in East Asia. We may expect to see a continuing expansion of Japan's military role, in the context of further regional developments and US responses. A crucial question, to which no clear answer is currently available, is whether Japan will 'go nuclear', shedding its deep aversion to nuclear weapons. Much will depend on North Korean developments and on the credibility of a US nuclear umbrella in the context of China's growing strategic capabilities.

In short, Japan is set to strike a more 'normal' balance between its economic and military roles. It has already ceased to be a military lightweight. The rate of expansion of its defence capability will be strongly influenced by the regional security environment and the state of Sino-Japanese relations. At the same time, there will be a steady erosion of Japan's economic influence, compared to China.

The gap between Japan and the USA in terms of both GDP and per capita income levels is expected to widen during this century. In 2005, Japan's GDP was US$ 4.5 trillion—around 40 per cent of the US GDP of US$ 12.5 trillion. Its per capita income is only a little lower than the American level. By 2050, however, the projections suggest that Japan's GDP will be less than 20 per cent of the United States', and its per capita income significantly lower than the US figure (US$ 66,805 against US$ 83,710).

The US lead over Japan may thus be expected to widen considerably over the next half century. Even though Japan will remain one of the global leaders in technology (well ahead of China), its population and GDP will probably be insufficiently large to maintain a power base comparable to that of the United States or even China. Japan, like Russia, lacks the demographic base required of a superpower, even though its advanced civilian and military technology and level of development will ensure for it an influential role in regional and global affairs.

China

The spectacular performance of the Chinese economy following the reforms introduced by Deng Xiaopeng has raised China from the level of a low-income country (with a per capita income level comparable to that of India in the 1980s), to the level of a lower middle-income country (in the World Bank classification based on per capita GNI). With a population of 1.2 billion, China's GDP in 2005 amounted to the impressive figure of US$ 2.2 trillion. It was exceeded only by the USA (US$ 12.5 trillion), Japan (US$ 4.5 trillion and Germany (US$ 2.8 trillion). Like other Far Eastern economies, China has followed an export-led development strategy but it differs from the others in its much heavier reliance on foreign investment inflows and MNC participation. Both factors have led to a relatively high degree of interdependence with major trade and investment partners. China overtook Japan in 2004 in terms of volume of foreign trade. Because of the size and competitiveness of the Chinese economy, other countries follow its exchange rate policy with close interest. During the East Asian economic crisis, China's policy of maintaining the stability of the Chinese RMB contributed to regional recovery. More recently, the United States, which has a huge trade deficit with China, has been pressing the latter to revalue its currency. In short, China has already emerged as one of the world's leading economic powers, in the areas of trade as well as finance. It has also made impressive progress in select areas of technology but it still lags behind the major industrial powers in this respect.

Though the primary focus in the past two decades has been on economic development, military modernisation has followed in the wake of the economy. Moreover, the transformation of China's communications infrastructure—roads, railways, civil aviation and telecommunications—is a huge force multiplier, enabling China to rapidly induct and maintain much larger force levels at any point on its borders.

By maintaining a balance between economic and military development, China has been able to avoid overstretching its resources in the quest for power.

China has registered some advance in respect of the legal system and freedom of expression, but political reform in general is proceeding at a much more deliberate pace than economic growth. Virtually every section of Chinese society has benefited from economic reform but the benefits have been distributed very unevenly between individuals; between the urban and the rural populations; and between the coastal and the interior provinces. The authorities are seeking to reduce these imbalances but there are increasing public protests against perceived injustices. Some observers have questioned whether China will be able to maintain political stability during the transition period. The record of the Chinese leadership since the 1980s suggests that it is likely to succeed in sequencing economic and political reforms without precipitating instability. Nevertheless, we cannot rule out the possibility that

China's rise might be temporarily interrupted by an outbreak of political disorder.

Barring such a setback, China is expected to maintain high but declining growth rates over the next two decades. Growth rates will taper off as China progressively closes the technology gap with the most advanced economies. According to the BRICs projections, China's growth rate may fall to 5 per cent by 2020. Nevertheless, by 2041, China will become the world's largest economy overtaking the US. (In Virmani's projections, based on PPP, China emerges as the world's largest economy as early as in 2014.) In terms of per capita GDP, however, China will lag far behind the USA, Japan or Western Europe even at mid-century. Thus, its projected per capita GDP in 2050 would be less than two-fifths that of the USA (at exchange rates). To sum up, by mid-century, China will probably be a prosperous country with per capita income levels comparable to current (2006) Western levels, but it would still trail behind the most advanced countries in terms of technology and per capita income.

Taking into account the overall size of the economy as well as its relative technological level, China may be reasonably expected to emerge as a near equal of the United States by mid-century, if not somewhat earlier. (Virmani predicts that China's power potential will equal that of the US by 2045.) Well before then, it will probably have overtaken all other powers; and its foreign, defence, commercial and financial policies are likely to have a global footprint larger than that of any other country, except the US.

India

After a late start, the other Asian mega state, India, has also achieved high growth rates for more than a decade. If the growth is sustained, India will enter the ranks of the lower middle-income countries early in the next decade (in 2011-12, according to the BRICs report). India's current growth rates are lower than China's but this is likely to be reversed in the next decade (in 2013, according to the same source) as China's development slows down. India would become an upper middle-income country by 2030, and a high-income country (in terms of today's criteria) by 2043-44, trailing China by about 15 years in the first case and 10 years in the latter. The BRICs report indicates that, even at mid-century, India's per capita GDP would remain lower than the current (2006) levels in the leading industrial countries. Though rising rapidly, India's per capita GDP would remain much smaller than those of the western countries, or even China well beyond 2050, according to these projections. Because of India's demographic profile, the size of its workforce is expected to continue increasing long after the trend is reversed in China, making it possible for India to sustain growth rates above 5 per cent even after 2050, and to catch up with China in the latter half of the century.

Turning to the total size of the economy, the BRICs study suggests that India's GDP would overtake Japan's by 2032, making it the world's third largest economy, after USA and China (or the fourth largest, if the EU is regarded as a single economic unit). In Virmani's projections, based on GDP calculated on a PPP basis, this would occur as early as by 2008; and, by 2040, India's GDP (PPP) will equal the US'.

A unique feature of India's development is the extent to which it has been led by exports of services, particularly IT and IT-enabled services. This tends to create a greater degree of interdependence between partner countries than commodity exports of the same value. India has an impressive potential for expanding exports of services in new sectors (e.g. R&D, medical, legal and educational).

India's decisionmaking procedures are generally based on consensual politics. Thus, in contrast to China, it does not face a significant risk that its development may be disrupted by a political breakdown. In India's case, the major risk is that, from time to time, populist temptations have tended to undermine the global competitiveness of its economy, through promotion of such policies as reservations for the small-scale sector, or for specified social groups. Populist policies exact a price in terms of growth rates and slow down India's emergence as a major global power. In general, the risk of a sudden interruption of development trends is much smaller in the case of India, than of China. The pattern of development is less spectacular but more stable.

There are promising prospects of India's emergence as a leading global power in the next half century or so. China will probably complete this transition at an earlier date. China is a rising great power; India an emerging one. This has policy implications, as we shall see in the concluding section.

The diffusion of power

To sum up, the rise of the two Asian mega states, China and India, will lead to the most profound changes in the balance of power during this century. Because of size of their population (and thus, their GDP), they will become major global powers long before they catch up with the US, Japan or EU in terms of per capita income or technological levels.

If the EU were to evolve into a federal state, it would become a superpower almost overnight but this is an uncertain and, at best, a distant prospect. It is much more likely that the EU will remain an association of nation states whose leading members—France, Germany and UK—will continue to play a much more important role than the EU as a group. No European power will, however, be sufficiently large and populous to challenge the United States and their power potential is likely to fall behind that of China— and, later, India—during the next three decades. The demographic factor will operate even more decisively in the cases of Japan and Russia. Nevertheless, because of their technological advancement, all these countries will remain major global powers.

In this brief survey, we have been unable to examine the prospects of several other countries which will play an important regional and possibly, global role. Countries like Italy and Spain in Europe, Brazil and Mexico in Latin America, Indonesia and Korea in Asia, or South Africa and Nigeria in Africa are all likely to make important contributions in shaping regional and even global events.

Thus, the two principal characteristics of the emerging global order are, first, the rise of new superpowers in Asia and, second, a much wider diffusion of power between a large number of states.

The United States is likely to retain its position at the apex of the global power pyramid for at least the next half century. China may be expected to emerge as a near equal well before 2050. India may follow in the second half of the century. Germany, France, Russia and Japan will remain major powers for the foreseeable future. Other powers such as Brazil, Italy, Spain, South Africa, Korea and Indonesia will also have important roles to play. The global power pyramid will thus gradually develop a gentler slope and wider base.

Relations between the major states will be influenced by the pattern of global economic integration in this century. Two developments are noteworthy. First, in the colonial period, globalisation took the form of a 'vertical' economic integration between the imperial state and its colonies. The main trade flows involved the export of raw materials from the colonies to the imperial state and the reverse flow of manufactured goods to the colonies. The current pattern of global economic integration is 'horizontal', in the sense that the major trade and investment flows take place between major economies, creating greater mutual interdependence between these economies. Second, during the Cold War era, a parallel international economic system emerged in the socialist bloc, with its own rules governing trade and investment flows. The collapse of the COMECON paved the way for the integration of all major economies in a single global regime. Both these developments tend to create greater economic interdependence between the major powers. Side by side with economic rivalry, there is the sense that a serious reverse in another major economy is likely to have an adverse fall-out for other major economies. Economic interdependence tends to soften or moderate political conflicts (but does not, of course, eliminate them).

During the Cold War, relations between the two leading powers were characterised by contest as well as cooperation, with the former being the defining characteristic. The world was described as bipolar. The metaphor was fitting, in the sense that there were only two superpowers, that the two 'poles' opposed each other, and that each 'pole' had a magnetic attraction for numerous allies. The emerging global order will feature multiple major powers but it cannot be presumed that their interests will mainly be in conflict with one another's, or that each of the major powers will form a pact or bloc of its own. It would thus seem more appropriate to describe the emerging international order as 'polycentric', rather than 'multipolar'.

India and the emerging polycentric order

Do these projections have any implications for our current foreign policy? Can they help us to anticipate problems or to position ourselves advantageously in order to meet emerging challenges or new opportunities? It would seem reasonable to draw the following conclusions from our analysis:

- The projections indicate that the United States will remain the most powerful state for at least another quarter century (Virmani) and, more probably, well into the latter part of the 21st Century. In either case, for the time horizon relevant to policymaking, American preeminence is a given factor. No other state can assist India's rise to the same extent as the United States. Relations with Washington must, therefore, be accorded top priority in our foreign policy. Indo-US ties have shown rapid development in all areas since 1999 (when Washington unambiguously condemned Pakistan's Kargil adventure). The momentum must be kept up in Indo-US relations. We should seek opportunities for cooperation wherever our interests coincide, forming a partnership with the United States on a case-by-case basis (as distinct from an alliance, which commits a country in advance to provide automatic support to the ally). We should also resist the temptation to take up cudgels on behalf of others, where US policies do not directly affect our national interests, bearing in mind our foreign policy priorities.

- India-China relations are based on mutual friendship and cooperation. The two countries are friendly neighbours and there is no reason to doubt that China reciprocates India's commitment to resolve all bilateral issues through peaceful negotiation. China's principal security concerns appear to lie in the east (Taiwanese separatism, rise of Japanese defence capability, and the role of the US Seventh Fleet), rather than the south. China's rise poses no 'threat' to India's security; it does, however, pose a challenge. While China's intentions are peaceful, long-term planning must also take into account China's capabilities. In the long run, intentions can change on account of domestic or international factors. If a political upheaval or breakdown were to occur in China (an unlikely contingency but one that cannot be ruled out altogether), Chinese intentions might become unpredictable. A collapse of China's political stability would thus carry risks for its neighbours. Secondly, history shows that the intentions and policies of states can change when a big shift occurs in the balance of power. For these reasons, it would be prudent for India to ensure that there is no major widening in the gap between our defence capabilities and China's during the transition period.

- The triangular relationship between the United States and the two ascendant Asian mega states, China and India, will assume increasing importance during this century. China's rise will progressively erode the US role in the Asia-Pacific region as well as its preeminence in global affairs. Against this background, there is a growing appreciation in America of the fact that India's rise will be a stabilising factor in the Asia-Pacific region, expanding the range of economic and diplomatic policy options available to other states in the region. It is important to note that this appreciation is based on changing power equations, not on any expectation that India will depart from its independent foreign policy.

- The rise of the two Asian mega states rests on solid domestic foundations; neither can be 'contained' by external forces. Some western analysts have speculated about a possible 'containment' policy directed against China. Should such a development take shape in future, India should take no part in it. By the same token, China should refrain from adopting a negative attitude in issues concerning India's rise, such as its nuclear status or its claim to a permanent seat on the UN Security Council.

- India's dialogue with the European Union will acquire greater depth and content *pari passu* with the incremental growth of the EU's international role. Moves to expand the euro zone and the scope of CFSP initiatives are two current developments that merit special attention. However, since a Federal Europe is at best a distant and uncertain prospect, the great nation states of West Europe — UK, France and Germany — will remain our principal regional interlocutors in political and security issues for the foreseeable future. It should be noted that closer cooperation with Western Europe would be facilitated by the development of Indo-US ties. From an overall perspective, the two developments are mutually complementary, not competitive.

- Though demographic trends work to their long-term disadvantage, both Russia and Japan will remain major powers and important partners for India. Russia has long been important to us as a supplier of sophisticated defence equipment and technology. India's foreign policy should also fully recognise the role Russia can play in promoting our energy security. The next few decades will see a sharp rise in the global demand for oil and gas and an intensification of international competition in these markets. Ensuring our energy security requires not only access to markets but also diversification of sources of supply in order to avoid overdependence on a single region. Russia, the world's largest exporter of gas and second largest oil exporter, offers great possibilities.

- Japan is steadily re-emerging as a major political and military power. Because of memories of Japanese occupation, this development has aroused a certain measure of suspicion in the Far East and, to a lesser extent, South-East Asia. History, however, casts no cloud over Indo-Japanese relations, making it easy for us to maintain normal political and military exchanges. The political dimension in Indo-Japanese relations will grow in parallel with the expansion of Japan's global political role. In developing political and military closer ties with Japan, India will, of course, steer clear from bilateral controversies involving Japan and other regional countries.

• India's policies towards countries such as Brazil, Indonesia and South Africa should factor in their rising influence in regional and international affairs. In addition, the quest for energy security will require prioritisation of relations with oil exporting countries not only in Asia but also Africa and Latin America. More generally, the expansion of India's overseas trade will impart new depth to our relations with many distant countries with which our relations are currently confined largely to an exchange of ceremonial assurances of goodwill.

6

Present dimensions of the Indian foreign policy

Shyam Saran

The end of the Cold War, the accelerating process of globalisation and the emergence of transnational challenges have become the defining features of contemporary international relations. India's foreign policy has had to adapt to this rapidly changing international environment.

Our foreign policy has also had to contend with remarkable changes within India itself. For more than a decade and a half, India has been engaged in a thoroughgoing reform and liberalisation of its economy. Its engagement with the rest of the world has increased dramatically. It has become more than ever important to ensure for India a peaceful and supportive international environment, an environment which contributes to our developmental goals.

While meeting these challenges, India has maintained a remarkable continuity in the fundamental tenets of its policy. The core of this continuity is to ensure autonomy in our decisionmaking. It is to ensure independence of thought and action. This was and remains the essence of our adherence to the principle of non-alignment. It is also the basis of our commitment to the *Panchsheel*, or the five principles of peaceful co-existence, which India and China jointly advocated in the early 1950s, and still believe to be relevant in contemporary international relations.

There are other key elements of continuity as well. These include maintenance of friendly relations with all countries, resolution of conflicts through peaceful means and equity in the conduct of international relations. There is a solemn commitment to pursue an independent foreign policy, promote multipolarity in world relations and oppose unilateralism.

In pursuing her national interests and in seeking an appropriate role in the global political and economic order, India has consciously promoted multipolarity in international relations. The corollary to this approach is to strengthen multilateral institutions and mechanisms. We believe that such an approach is indispensable in addressing global challenges, such as terrorism, proliferation of weapons of mass destruction, pandemics like HIV/AIDS or avian flu, and drug-trafficking. Such an approach is also helpful in pooling together the scientific and technical achievements and collective wisdom of peoples around the world in overcoming the scourge of poverty, disease and the environmental degradation of our planet. No one country or even a group of countries, however rich and powerful, can hope to tackle these challenges on their own.

There is a need to evolve a new paradigm of cooperation relevant to the emerging multipolar world in which global threats demand global responses. India has actively pursued the strengthening of multilateral institutions, in particular the United Nations. We are committed to the comprehensive reform of the United Nations, including its Security Council, so that the concerns and aspirations of the majority of the UN membership are adequately reflected and multilateralism becomes an effective tool for addressing global challenges.

It is obvious that in any reform of the United Nations, the restructuring of its Security Council must be a priority. India believes that the Security Council must, in its composition, reflect the contemporary geopolitical realities and not those of 1945. Its actions must be representative, legitimate and effective and its methods of work and decisionmaking processes more democratic, transparent and responsive. We believe that India, with its large population, dynamic economy, long history of contribution to international peacekeeping and other regional and international causes, deserves to be a permanent member of the UN Security Council. At the same time, we also realise that there is resistance to change among several powerful countries. However, this is the first time in many years that a certain momentum has been built up for a comprehensive reform of the UN, which should not be allowed to wither away.

A basic tenet of India's foreign policy since Independence has been the pursuit of global nuclear disarmament. We believe that general and complete disarmament, including nuclear disarmament must remain on the international agenda. It must be a key objective of the United Nations. India's status as a Nuclear Weapon State does not diminish its commitment to the objective of a nuclear weapon-free world. Aspiring for a non-violent world order, through global, verifiable and non-discriminatory nuclear disarmament continues to be an important plank of our nuclear policy, which is characterised by restraint, responsibility, transparency, predictability and a defensive orientation. As a responsible nuclear power with impeccable credentials on non-proliferation, we have earned increasing international recognition as a partner against proliferation. We hope to work more closely with our Chinese friends on this front, too.

It is said that the logic of geography is unrelenting. Proximity is the most difficult and testing among diplomatic challenges a country faces. We have, therefore, committed ourselves to giving the highest priority to closer political, economic and other ties with our neighbours in South Asia. We have a vision of South Asia, unshackled from historical divisions and bound together in collective pursuit of peace and prosperity. We remain convinced that, on the foundations of its ancient civilisational and commercial interlinkages, South Asia can work together to emerge as a major powerhouse of economic creativity and enterprise. For that to happen, it is essential that we unlock the potential of South Asia by dismantling the existing barriers that restrict the movement of people, goods and investment within and across the region. It is with this perspective that we have extended our hand of friendship and cooperation to all our neighbours and proactively addressed whatever differences we may have, including with Pakistan. We look at the SAARC process as a stimulus to strengthen cross-border economic linkages, through initiatives such as South Asian Free Trade Agreement, by drawing upon the complementarities among different parts of our region. We are encouraged by a growing perception among our neighbours in South Asia that a prosperous and economically vibrant India is an asset and opportunity for them. We encourage them to take advantage of India's strengths and reap both economic and political benefits as a result, since it is our belief that India's national security interests are better served if our neighbours evolve as viable states with moderate and stable political and social environment and robust economies.

We regard the concept of neighbourhood as one of widening concentric circles, around a central axis of historical and cultural commonalties. In this, we see India's destiny interlinked with that of Asia. From this point of view, developing relations with Asian countries is one of our priorities, while pursuing a cooperative architecture of pan-Asian regionalism is a key area of focus of our foreign policy. Geography imparts a unique position to India in the geo-politics of the Asian continent, with our footprint reaching well beyond South Asia and our interests straddling across different sub-categories of Asia—be it East Asia, West Asia, Central Asia, South Asia or South-East Asia. To those who harbour any scepticism about this fact, it would suffice to remind that we share one of the longest land borders in the world with China, that Central Asia verges on our northern frontiers, that we have land and maritime borders with three South-East Asian countries, that our Andaman and Nicobar Islands are just over a hundred kilometres from Indonesia, and that our exclusive economic zone spans waters from the Persian Gulf to the Straits of Malacca. It is this geopolitical reality and our conviction that enhanced regional cooperation is mutually advantageous, which sustain our enthusiasm to participate in endeavours for regional integration, ranging from South Asian Association of Regional Cooperation to East Asia Summit and Shanghai Cooperation Organisation.

We believe that in our march towards economic progress, Asia in general and East Asia in particular, has been a natural partner. A common thread joins us. We stand to share the opportunities thrown open by the region's increasing economic integration, just as we face the common threats of proliferation of weapons of mass destruction, terrorism, energy shortage, piracy and others. The Tsunami disaster has also brought home the point, in a tragic way, of how much we share our destiny in the region.

It was in this context that more than a decade ago, we launched the 'Look East' policy, which is now a vital part of India's foreign policy. More than an external economic policy or a political slogan, the 'Look East' policy was a strategic shift in India's vision of the world and her place in the evolving global economy. It was also a manifestation of our belief that developments in East Asia are of direct consequence to India's security and development. We are therefore, actively engaged in creating a bond of friendship and cooperation with East Asia that has a strong economic foundation and a cooperative paradigm of positive interconnectedness of security interests.

India's relationship with China is a key component of our 'Look East' policy. There is a strong consensus in India on improving and developing our relations with China. Together with China, we have taken a number of positive measures to improve the quality of our relations across a wide range of areas, without allowing the existing differences to affect the overall development of our ties. Despite our differences on the boundary issue, peace and tranquility has been maintained in the India-China border areas, which is by no means a minor achievement. We have an active defence exchange programme and an elaborate matrix of confidence building measures that have helped promote greater trust between our two armed forces. We have a range of dialogue mechanisms through which we are increasingly able to understand and appreciate each other's point of view and address outstanding issues.

There are many who look at India-China relations with the old mindset of 'balance of power' or 'conflict of interests' and see Asia as a theatre of competition between these two countries. Such theories are outdated in today's fast-emerging dynamics of Asia's quest for peace and prosperity and its interconnectedness. So are perceptions in some quarters that India and China seek to contain each other. To the protagonists of such theories, I would only like to say that India and China, as two continental-size economies and political entities, are too big to contain each other or be contained by any other country.

Today, India and China are engaged in a positive way to expand their commonalities with extensive dealings in bilateral, regional and multilateral forums. Indeed, the determination of our two countries to qualitatively elevate our ties by establishing a 'strategic and cooperative partnership for peace and prosperity' reflects our shared conviction that India-China relations have now acquired a long-term, global and strategic character and hence, must be treated as such. Our rapidly growing trade and economic ties are a testimony that we are not just passively bound by our common neighbourhood, but are constantly interacting through a positive and meaningful agenda of collaboration. That from a meagre few hundred million dollars in the beginning of 1990s, our trade was expected to surpass US$ 18 billion last year should only underline the enormous potential for mutual reward that lies in store if our two countries cooperate. We are determined to take this process further ahead.

The simultaneous emergence of India and China as Asian and global powers in fact, makes it imperative for them to be sensitive to each other's interests and aspirations. The prevailing global paradigm of cooperation among major powers also demands from the two countries that they work together to mutually support their rightful place in the comity of nations. We in India believe that there is enough space and opportunity in Asia and beyond for the two countries to grow.

With regard to the resolution of the boundary question, we are committed to carrying forward the process of exploring a political settlement through the mechanism of special representatives. We acknowledge the complexity of this longstanding issue but remain confident that a mutually acceptable solution can be reached if both sides show willingness to take bold and pragmatic decisions, accommodating each other's vital interests. As we move forward through negotiations, it is important for us to look at the boundary question from the long-term and strategic perspective of India-China relations, rather than as a mere territorial issue. There is a historic opportunity in front of us to settle this outstanding issue that we should not miss.

If we look at the emerging scenario in Asia there is no doubt about a major realignment of forces taking place in our continent. Besides the emergence of India and China as two economic powerhouses in this region, there is Japan, the second largest economy in the world, which will retain an influential role in Asia's political and economic future, and with whom our relations are developing on the foundations of 'global partnership' with a strong economic and strategic thrust. With ASEAN as well, our partnership is steadily expanding and deepening. We believe that the ASEAN holds the potential to become the fulcrum of economic integration in our region.

The future of Asia is in reality the sum of the success of each of these components and the strength of their interlinkages. The key to ensuring long-term security and stable equilibrium in Asia lies in the collective ability of Asian countries to build mutual economic stakes in one another. It is with this conviction that we espouse a vision of an Asian Economic Community. It can be a neighbourhood of peace and shared prosperity in which people, goods, services and ideas can travel with ease across borders. It may perhaps take the form of a dynamic, open and inclusive Pan-Asian Free Trade Area that could offer a third pole of the global economy after the European Union and NAFTA and would, in all certainty, open up new growth avenues for our economies. This will not be easy, but India is willing to associate with other likeminded countries to make it happen. The recently concluded East Asia Summit has laid the foundations for a cooperative architecture in Asia on an unprecedented scale and we hope, will potentially launch the process towards the possible creation of an East Asian

Community. We would be happy to work closely with China towards progressive realisation of such an East Asian Community and eventually, a larger Asian Economic Community.

It is true that India-US relationship has acquired remarkable maturity and dynamism in recent years. A number of independent developments, have created the climate for this transformation, including the end of the Cold War, India's emergence as a dynamic economic force and an objective assessment of the strategic implications of a world dominated by knowledge-driven societies. During the visit of Prime Minister Dr. Manmohan Singh to the US in July 2005, both sides agreed that India-US relations are moving beyond a bilateral partnership towards a global partnership, which is anchored not only on common values but also on common interests. The visit served to highlight the strategic dimension of India's relationship with the US and underlined our common interest in combating terrorism, proliferation of weapons of mass destruction and enhancing global peace. There has been a convergence of views on strategic and security issues and on opportunities that exist for the India-US cooperation in defence, science and technology, health, trade, space, energy and environment. There is also a growing US recognition of India's central and enhanced role in international institutions and processes. The US's economic and political stakes in the growth of the Indian economy and its integration with the global market have provided impetus to the India-US cooperation in a way that meaningfully addresses constraints on India's growth, including the deficits of energy and infrastructure.

India has also embarked on strengthening her multi-faceted relationship with Russia, with whom her traditional strategic partnership has been renewed. Recent high-level visits, including that of President Putin to India and the visits of our President and Prime Minister to Moscow within the last a little over one year, have added great impetus to this process. We are also encouraged by the emerging contours of the trilateral cooperation between China, Russia and India.

We have also moved forward in rejuvenating our relations with the European Union through our new 'strategic partnership'. There is a growing recognition of India as an indispensable partner within the EU. Indeed, the EU is as reflective as India is of a multilingual, multireligious and multicultural society. Our shared values and beliefs in democracy, human rights, pluralism, independent media, and rule of law make India and the EU natural partners as well as factors of stability in the present world order.

India remains committed to pursuing an independent foreign policy that best serves her national interests and accords with her expected role in the emerging global political and economic order. This policy seeks to promote multipolarity in international relations and to strengthen forces of multilateralism that help protect the interests of the developing countries and reinforce geo-strategic stability in the region and the world at large. To this end, we have sought to build on our traditional links with Africa and to cultivate stronger bonds with the Latin American countries. We believe that as two largest developing countries, India and China can together lend greater voice to the aspirations of the developing world and help the developing countries harness the positive forces of economic globalisation. We should continue to work towards shaping a coalition of the developing world.

Today, India is on the cutting edge of economic, technological and developmental transformation of significant dimensions. She is regarded as a factor of stability, a model of secularism and plurality and as an economic power that is destined to play a greater role in international affairs. In keeping with this changing image of India, we have adopted a foreign policy, which has a clear focus, a sense of maturity and responsibility, and a vision to make India strong and prosperous in the 21st Century. As we do so, we remain steadfast to the core ideals of India's foreign policy, which were laid down by our first Prime Minister Jawaharlal Nehru and which have guided us since our Independence. At the same time, we also remain vigilant to the new demands and compulsions imposed upon us by a rapidly transforming world around us. We are confident of our capacity and capability as a nation to respond successfully to these newly emerging challenges and opportunities. We also remain confident that India would continue its journey towards a destiny that was eloquently articulated by Pandit Nehru in 1947, a destiny in which India "attains her rightful place in the world and makes her full and willing contribution to the promotion of world peace and welfare of mankind".

Edited version of Address delivered at Shangai Institute of International Studies, Shanghai, January 2006.

India's international priorities and multilateral institutions

7

Non-aligned movement and its future

A.K. Damodaran

I

Any discussion of the future prospects for non-alignment in the 21st Century has to take into account the long history and the pre-history of the movement during the last three centuries—that is, the age of European expansionism out into all the continents of the planet and the responses to it by different peoples, regions and nation states. Unless we do that, there is always the temptation to write premature epitaphs on what was after all a specific phenomenon in time in the second half of the 20th Century. If, on the other hand, we see modern non-alignment against the background of neutrality in war and peace as practised by various countries in the 19th and the 20th Century we will be able to explain to ourselves the rationale behind the movement, the popular urges in various countries which led to its emergence and the challenges it faced in a rapidly changing international environment.

Neutrality as an instrument of policy has been familiar enough down to the ages. The refusal to identify oneself with any one nation or its policies which one cannot control, can be easily understood. Perhaps, the most interesting example of neutrality during the year of peace would be the attitude of the United States towards Europe and the other hemisphere itself during the 19th Century. The founders of the American Constitution were all products of the European civilisation and familiar with the experiences of Europe in intra-continental warfare and the necessary consequences of its geographical separation in Britain's own policy. The English Channel had, then, made all the difference; and in the 19th Century, the Atlantic Ocean made the neutrality in peace of the United States easy enough to conceive and practice. It is not necessary to go into actual events but the attitude of the new American state towards the problems of cooperation and confrontation with Europe and Britain were articulated by George Washington in his farewell address and by Thomas Jefferson in his first inaugural address. There are echoes of these speeches in Nehru's famous broadcast in September 1946 after assuming charge as Head of the Interim Government. Phrases like "entangling alliances" are there in these early explorations into the future policy of the new Indian State. It is important to note this because Nehru was one of the few seminal thinkers in the first formulations of non-alignment with its emphasis on detachment from the cold war and the need for the solidarity of the colonised territories and the need to be involved with the world outside in their lonely pilgrimage after Independence towards economic self-sufficiency and genuine democracy. This is not mere Indian chauvinism. Nehru happened to be in the right place at the right moment in the evolution of the post-war world. He was also, because of purely personal preference, sensitive to history and the need for explaining the mysteries of history to oneself, to one's little daughter, and so on, to his countrymen.

To understand non-alignment, we have to go back to the history of imperialism and colonialism in the 19th and 20th Centuries. The dominance of the British Empire in all corners of the world was already a fact in the 19th Century, then came the 'Europeanisation of Imperialism' with France, Italy, and Germany establishing new colonies in Asia and Africa. Two subsidiary empires, the Dutch, the Portuguese, had already existed in the early centuries after the Renaissance, Enlightenment and the discovery of the world by European soldiers and sailors. The Dutch and Portuguese imperialisms are important enough by themselves but in our perspective they are adjuncts to the British conquest of the America, Asia and Africa. The response of the new US state to European conflicts, particularly the French Revolution and the Napoleonic wars, was based on geographical isolation and the consequent strategic security in that technological epoch. There is something inevitable about the link between US isolationism during the Civil War, for instance, and the earlier careful formulation of the Manroe doctrine. These are all minor developments in the pre-history of non-alignment, but only by understanding the motivations of the statesmen who formulated these policies shall we begin to understand the motivations behind non-alignment in various countries in the second half of the 20th Century.

It is a matter of interesting historical irony that the United States, in its earlier periods of development, provides useful hints to understanding non-alignment, precisely at a time when that country was becoming a dominant force on earth and because of that, was hostile to the idea of non-alignment as a national policy of the newly independent countries. The US attitude towards Europe and Britain during the First World War is an interesting enough evolution of policy from isolationism to total involvement by the time the war was over. In the beginning, it was neutral between the Western Allies and Germany. Later, it became totally identified with Britain and France and played a powerful and influential role in the formulation of the Treaty of Versailles and the founding of the League of Nations. There are, of course, other subsidiary elements here like the empathy between the two English speaking nations; but the United States and Latin America do provide examples of first, neutrality, and then slow involvement in the European conflict. It should also be remembered that, during this period, Washington was also beginning its own minor excursions into colonialism in the Philippines and the Caribbean. This is also the period when Tzarist Russia embarked on its own Eurasian colonialism and Turkey developed into a major imperial power and Japan emerged as a potential imperial power in its neighbourhood.

The period between the two wars shows the emergence of new political and social developments in a rapidly contracting world, the most important of which was, of course, the Soviet Revolution and the emergence of Japan as a powerful new entity. The former colonies of Germany in Africa and the Ottoman Empire in Asia produced a wholly new class of smaller states, unsure of themselves, and tentatively inching forward towards a respectable position in the world outside. At the same time, the freedom movements in countries like India and Egypt became an important factor. The emergence of Fascism in Italy and Nazism in Germany, and the slide towards the Second World War made it necessary for the defenders of the *status quo* in the global world order to find new methods of alignment. Arrangements, short of alliances, were discovered. The uncomfortable reactions of the European nation states to the Spanish Civil War demonstrated the inadequacy of the League of Nations to tackle major national crises. A good example of a major power trying to negotiate peace in difficult situation is the Munich Pact. All this led to the Second World War and, the late entry, it is important to note, of Russia, the United States, and Japan into the global conflict. And all this led to the United Nations and the post-World War dilemmas. During the thirties, when Communism, Fascism, and Nazism, were challenging the older conservative empires, the anti-colonial movement in most metropolises began to develop new strengths and explore new directions. The Brussels Conference against imperialism in 1927 is important in this connection. The activities of the Indian National Congress under Gandhiji led to the awareness of the sufferings of the colonised people all over the world. This was particularly true of Britain where the India league played an important role in communication and propaganda. The neo-imperialistic activities of Italy in Ethiopia made it imperative for the people in the colonies to understand the synergy between various imperialist powers in Europe and Asia and also in Africa. The writings of Jawaharlal Nehru in the thirties give us some indication of this new awareness.

The end of the Second World War witnessed four or five simultaneous developments: (a) the constitution of the United Nations as a world grouping with special powers retained by the Big Five in the Security Council, (b) the completion of India's

Freedom Movement and the creation of truly national governments in Delhi and Karachi, (c) the activities of the anti-colonial forces in Burma, Indonesia and Indo-China, and finally, (d) the emergence of the Cold War within two years after the end of the hostilities.

This was the background to the appearance in the world scene of anti-colonialism, a new solidarity of the newly liberated countries and their reluctance to be identified totally with either party in the Cold War which led to non-alignment as we know it today.

II

The first two decades after the Second World War witnessed the emergence of Non-alignment as not merely the policy of some individual countries but also as a movement of many post-colonial developing nations trying to find their way in the jungle of world capitalism. It is not a coincidence that Jawaharlal Nehru was then at his peak as a political activist, both on the national scene and at the global level. He became the *de facto* ruler of India in late 1946 and passed away in 1964. The early years of non-alignment as a concept and as an idea are inevitably associated with Jawaharlal Nehru's activities as the Prime Minister of India.

The Asian Relations Conference in April 1947, a few months before India officially became independent, marks the beginning of this new awareness in the poorer countries. It is no coincidence that this tentative attempt at solidarity included the 'would be independent' countries, like Indonesia and member countries of the Soviet Union like Uzbekistan. Asia had, however, a large number of regions absent from the conference. In spite of these shortcomings, Nehru and his colleagues succeeded in issuing a manifesto of anti-colonialism and economic independence. This inevitably led to the next major event in the post-war decade, the Bandung Conference of Afro-Asian Countries in which China and India played a major role. The Bandung Conference took place against the heady optimism of Panchsheel or the five principles of mutual co-existence formulated by Indian and Chinese statesmen. At a personal level, Nehru and Chou-En-Lai dominated the scene apart from, of course, the central figure of Sukarno, the Head of the host State. Many important views were expressed by the member countries in the Conference. But there was no immediate plan for holding a next Afro-Asian Conference. A paradigm shift took place in world politics in 1961 when, instead of another Afro-Asian Conference, an Intercontinental Non-alignment Meeting was held in Belgrade. Here again, India played an important role; even though it should not be forgotten that to Nehru, non-alignment was primarily the national policy of his country and not necessarily the basis of global movement. This distinction is important. As was mentioned earlier, Nehru was very much influenced by the sample of the American Revolution in the nineties of the 18th Century. There is no doubt that there is some conscious or unconscious semantic influence on Nehru's thinking in the references to "entangling alliances" and "too much attachment" to any single nation. 'Non-attachment' was practised by the United States during the 19th Century both because of geographical isolation and the technological limitations of an evolving nation state. Jawaharlal Nehru had definitely non-attachment at the back of his mind when the idea of non-alignment occurred to him, just as, in an entirely different context, the celebrated phrase "tryst with destiny" was suggested by Roosvelt's "Rendezvous with Destiny" a lover of English poetry at all times, he would have noticed that Roosevelt was himself inspired by the poem "I have a Rendezvous with Death" written by the American soldier, Alan Seegar, who died in the First World War.

These literary details are not entirely irrelevant. They help us to understand the Non-Aligned Movement as it developed during the 50s. Here of course, there is no doubt that an equally important role was played by President Nasser of Egypt and Marshal Tito of Yugoslavia. Slowly, from Bandung to Belgrade, from 1955 to 1961, the idea of autonomy, non-alignment, or independence, began to take on an inter-continental complexion in which some countries of Latin America began to be interested. It should not be forgotten that was also the period when the British Commonwealth developed into a genuine world organisation with independence being given to many Caribbean and African nations, but not all. France also was beginning to react to the forces of anti-colonialism in her far-flung empire. There was, however, conscious resistance in the sixties from other imperialist nations particularly Belgium and Portugal. The centrality of India in the formulation of the non-aligned ideology can be best seen in G.H Jansen's book *From Afro-Asia to Non-alignment*. The Non-alignment Conference did not make any dramatic policy statements except, perhaps, on disarmament, both nuclear and conventional. The idea of a periodic conference to express these new nations of state activity took some time to develop. The Cairo Conference in 1964 was successful in a limited sense and the absence of the fact that no conference was held in 1967, in Lusaka; in 1973, in Algiers; very important conferences were held in which Yugoslavia and Egypt played important roles, and Indonesia was a changed nation since 1965 after the failed coup attempt of the Communist Party, the PKI in that country. The decade of the sixties also saw the emergence of two high profile ideological issues which provided the Non-aligned Conferences and the movement between conferences with a useful ideological platform. The first was the anti-apartheid which, during the fifties and the sixties, became an important world problem in which major nation states like France and Britain, Britain and America played an important role and where the Soviet Union and China on the other side of the ideological divide gave powerful support to the Anti-apartheid Movement. The anti-apartheid problem in South Africa was also connected with the gradual changes in British and Belgian Central Africa. The Lusaka Conference is important from this point of view. It focussed attention on the remaining colonial questions, most of them in Africa. At the same time, outside Africa, Cuba was becoming a force to reckon with, in the Western hemisphere as a trendsetter in socialist ideology. This was also the period when the World Socialist Movement became more active with its central inspiration from the European Socialist Democratic Countries and Burma. It is also no coincidence that the Israel-Palestine issue became the central piece of the Cold War during the late sixties. In all this, non-aligned countries played an important role in the United Nations, in the General Assembly and, in the various political committees.

This is important to note because slowly, UN General Assembly was becoming an available platform for both anti-colonialism and non-alignment. The Summit conferences were only periodic but the activities in New York and Geneva were continuous. To complete the picture we should also remember that, apart from the United Nations, the Commonwealth also played an important role in influencing global change. Here again, India's contribution was significant. The Cold War was at its height during these years and a major change took place in the early seventies when China detached itself formally from the Soviet Camp and established a new understanding with the United States after the Nixon visit in 1972. There are, in retrospect, some important developments in the Cold War between 1945 and 1991. Many Soviet satellite countries in East Europe began to play a mildly dissentient role, most importantly Romania, Hungry and Czechoslovakia during a tragically brief interlude. At the same time, in the Western camp there had always been dissident voices. All these new ideas crystallised in a common approach towards global economic problems. The Algeria summit in 1973 came out with a new demand for a new world economic order. At a time when technical, political imperialism was no longer there, it was important to worry about the economic reality of world capitalism and underdevelopment in the majority of countries in Africa, Asia and Latin America. Interestingly enough, Mao-Zedong contributed a great deal to this Afro-Asian-Latin American consciousness on strategic and economic matters. This need not be exaggerated but is mentioned here only to point out the various centres of dissidence in the two warring camps, and outside in the Scandinavian countries, Cuba and the newly independent countries of Indo-China whose struggle for survival in these years was so much connected with the global ideological confrontation.

During the seventies and the eighties we have a repletion of the old problems of apartheid and Palestine and new emphasis on global economic equality. The 1976 conference in Colombo repeated these familiar approaches but also added the new information order. By this time, the Portuguese and Belgian empires had become things of the past with nightmarish legacies in Central Africa. The Conference in Cuba in 1979 was an important landmark in the NAM's consistent opposition to military, political, economic domination by a few powers over the rest of the world. The anti-colonial movement continued to flourish outside the NAM as clearly demonstrated in the liberation of Zimbabwe in 1981 which was exclusively a Commonwealth affair. Then the eighties saw a completion of decolonisation in British Africa. The Havana Conference is also memorable for the withdrawal of Burma, an original founding member of the movement, from NAM. These details are important to recall now when we are discussing the future of the movement. There were many hiccups, many hesitations, some withdrawals and some new entries like Pakistan, for example. The uncertainty of the movement in the eighties was best demonstrated by the postponement of the scheduled conference from Baghdad in 1982 to New Delhi in 1983. There is no doubt that the New Delhi conference was certainly a mega event both from the point of view of publicity and ideological formulations. The ineffectiveness of the movement in crucial areas, when member countries were involved in war with each other, became also clear during this conference and the subsequent year. There was nothing the conference could or did do to help in solving the Iran-Iraq conflict. There was also very little it could do in sorting out the problems of Cambodia in Indo-China. More and more it became clear that the Non-Aligned Movement owed its very existence to the necessity for propaganda, lobbying and pressure tactics in the United Nations. The movement continued to have its very limited but very purposeful role in emphasising global priorities. This was most clearly demonstrated in Rajiv Gandhi's Six-Nation Disarmament Initiative in the late eighties. By the end of the eighties major changes had begun to take place in Eastern Europe and the Soviet Union. A new Commonwealth of Independent States emerged from the disintegration of the USSR. In China, while the ruling party exercised control with anew authority after the Tiananmen Square incident in 1989, the economic situation was transformed by Deng Hsiao Ping's new policies. It was in this context that different states in the world had to look at the new realities and react to them in a constructive manner rather than continue in old, familiar directions. The end of the Cold War meant that some of the basic premises of the policies of the founders of the Non-Aligned Movement were no longer there. The question remains as to whether in the new situation today, 16 years after the end of the Cold War with many of the problems of poverty, exploitation still there and new emerging power groups, it is necessary for the developing countries in the world to continue to act together in all the forums possible, progress in the United Nation, in the Commonwealth, the Commonwealth of the Independent States, the Organization of American States and other regional and sub-regional groupings. In such a situation ideological and intellectual inputs are essential. That is why, in retrospect, one contribution of the 1983 summit in New Delhi is vital. It founded a research institute for the study of these problems in the RIS—The Research and Information System for Non-aligned and Developing Countries. Any discussion of the future agenda of non-alignment will have to take into account such institutions.

III

It is now 15 years since the end of the Cold War between the two great military blocs and also the two major powers in the world system, the US and the USSR. This period has brought about, not surprisingly, dramatic changes. Immediately after the dissolution of the Soviet Union we had a number of new medium-sized states entering the United Nations system as sovereign entities. We had confusion and chaos within Russia which are being slowly sorted out only in the last 5 or 6 years after President Vladimir Putin came into power. Some of the earlier prognostications after the disintegration of the Soviet Union have proved to be wrong, particularly the highly excited optimistic interpretation of the new historical context as representing the end of history and ideology. Many changes have taken place within the former Soviet Union in which there are inevitable echos of the Cold War. The attempts under US influence to have new 'democratic' changes of regime in many post-Soviet Republics of Central Asia and Caucasus have not really led to any revival of Cold War hostilities. There is a great deal of interaction and understanding today between Moscow and Washington in spite of their differences about the role of NATO and the future of individual Balkan states. The capacity of the global economic system to intervene in the economy of Russia and the other members of the Commonwealth of Independent States is a major aspect of the new globalisation. In fact, the discussion of prospects, political and economic, of any individual country anywhere in the world cannot but take into account the impact of globalisation. This is true of the two new powerful nations of the 21st Century , China and India both because of their economic power and their political stability. Then, there is the continuing prosperity of the countries in East Asia and South-East Asia in the ASEAN, and, also Japan. In the other continents also, there are developments like the emergence of South Africa as an important actor on the world stage and Brazil, Mexico and Argentina in Latin America as active players among the nations of the world. These are the newcomers but the old stalwarts are still there, a rejuvenated and strengthened European Union, Japan and the West Asian countries with their religious identity and energy capacity driving from oil resources.

It is in such a changed world that we have to examine the possibilities of a meaningful role for the non-aligned philosophy and the Non-Aligned Movement. Many of the premises on which the development of this ideology in the second half of the 20th Century took place may no longer exist, but some of the most important preconditions are still very much there, the most important of which is the yet undemocratic nature of the United Nations system and the necessity to fight external exploitation in weak domestic economies by fully utilising the available resources within the UN, that is, the General Assembly and various specialised agencies. All this would indicate that there is still very much scope for activities within the state system and outside it. Here, we come to one central aspect of the Non-Aligned Movement. It acted as a non-authoritative 'non-official' opposition to the decisions of the great powers and particularly the Security Council. In other words, to use a phrase which has now become common in international discussions, the Non-Aligned Movement represents a 'civic society' of nation states in the world system of Great Power dominance. Much of the action in the vital areas of international trade, aid, environment and food production for the masses, has to take place within the system, but also outside the system. The powerful popular opposition to several global decisions on environment, climate change, trade re-arrangements etc. in many recent conferences of the WTO and other organisation in Seattle, Hong Kong, Cancun and other venues of global negotiations has also to be taken into account when we discuss the role of the Non-aligned Movement in the first half of the 21st Century. It is by no means self-sufficient and effective by itself; it has to be supplemented by popular movements within the big metropolitan powers, the new entrants to the high table like China and India, and also the large majority of the weaker nations.

All this has to be seen against the background of the last four years since the September 11, 2001 attacks on the World Trade Center. This period has seen many important developments which are still unresolved. Most of them are related to the indifferent success of the US action against the majority of the world opinion in Iraq. Here, we come to a basic factor, the emergence of new terrorist groups with a certain religious colour. During the last 8 or 10 years, it has been a convenient policy for successful politicians in the United States and some other countries to blame for everything Islamic fundamentalism. There is no doubt that there is a connection between the two but there have been non-Islamic or extra-Islamic, or intra-Islamic terrorist activities in recent world history, in Oklahoma in the United States, in the LTTE movement in Sri Lanka, in the Sunni-Shia violence in Iraq and in the terrible holocaust of Cambodia. What is common to all this is not Islam but the multiplier effect of modern communications and advertisement in exaggerating differences. Osama Bin Laden is not the inventor but the invention of history. This is important for us in India to remember because we have successfully resisted any attempt to divide our multilingual, multireligious society. Any attempt to understand the complexities of the modern world should also take into account the exponential growth of information technology with its consequences on the employment situation in the metropolitan countries in America and Europe. We have also to consider the huge increase in the movement of peoples by legal and illegal migration from Eastern to Western Europe, from South Asia to Europe and Canada, Europe and the United States, and the thrust of the Hispanic population from the south to the United states.

All these problems have to be sorted out. We have some extremely efficient existing instruments. But are they complete by themselves or can they be assisted or supplemented by conferences, parades, movements and other types of mass action? It is here that the Non-Aligned Movement appears to have a genuine future in the next decade or two. Continuing its activities in the General Assembly and other UN organisations the non-aligned countries cannot only point out the infirmities in the present system but politely and firmly fight against them. As was noted earlier, the Non-Aligned movement as such has had a certain meaningful role in the last 60 years as a powerful enough pressure group. In this period of transition such a grouping and such an ideology have a certain inevitable importance. It would be easy enough to dismiss the Non-aligned Conferences as ultimately irrelevant. But a Summit Conference is important because it utilises the modern advertising methods to the maximum possible extent. In the 20th Century there are many such organisations, effective in different ways, the New Commonwealth; the Organisation of States in Latin America and African Union, Organization of Islamic Conference (OIC) and the Arab League; and the new organisations which are coming up in Asia and the pacific. It is along with these countries that the Non-aligned Movement will be able to function effectively. There is certainly no reason to stop its activities now.

Much more important than the movement is the ideology as preached and practised by various countries within each regional and political system. It is here that India has a meaningful role to play in the coming uncertain years; and it is here that the part played by India and Nehru during the first years of Afro-Asia and non-alignment seems genuinely relevant, in retrospect. Here, India has a decisive contribution to make in keeping the movement alive through its conferences and the pressure groups active within the United Nations, the WHO, the WTO, the FAO and the UNESCO. To be effective in these activities at all levels in various venues, the Non-Aligned Movement will have to continue to position itself against the indifference, scorn and opposition from the arrogant masters of the present system. It is by any means a daunting experience but also an exciting one.

8

Reform of the UN system and India

Muchkund Dubey

I. UN Reform: main features and brief history

Reform is an essential ingredient in the process of the evolution of any institution, be it local, national, regional or international like the United Nations. Reform is an inevitable process of readjustment, repositioning, renewal and reinvigoration of an institution. Every institution, in order to survive and remain relevant to contemporary reality, must reform itself from time to time. It must discard outmoded methods of functioning and usher in new ones in their place. It must restructure its organisation, role, functions and agenda. For an international organisation like UN, it is also important to adjust to the emerging power equations and power play in the international arena.

The United Nations has been under continuous scrutiny and a number of major and minor efforts have been made to improve its functioning and to adapt the organisation to changing times and requirements.[1] On the social and economic side, the item, 'restructuring of the role and function of the Economic and Social Council' (ECOSOC) has been on the agenda of the Council for decades. According to one study, the United Nations technical

---

1. South Centre (1997). *For a Strong and Democratic United Nations; A South Perspective on UN Reform;* Zed Books Ltd., London and New York, p.56.

cooperation machinery has gone through major reorganisations six times between 1958-59 to 1992-93.[2] Another study has found that during the 50-year period between 1945 and 1995, major reforms in the UN have been carried out at roughly eight years interval.[3]

Reforms in the UN have been invariably driven by major developed countries which have always taken the initiatives in this behalf. These have put the developing countries on the defensive. All that the developing countries have managed to do is to react to the proposals of developed countries and to minimise the damage to their interests. The developing countries have never been on the offensive on the reform front and they seldom have had blueprints of their own for reforming the United Nations.

The reform offensive on the part of developed countries has been well planned and orchestrated, with well-defined objectives and longer term perspective. They have used reforms on a continuous basis and relentlessly to pursue their interests. As the authors of the book, *Renewing the United Nations System*, have put it, "UN civil servants have scarcely put some newly decreed reforms into operation before having to cope with a new wave of outside management consultants bent on another round of reforms."[4] Major developed countries have used all the leverages at their disposal— bilateral pressures of all kinds, use of economic and political clouts, threats of denial of funds to the UN, withholding their contributions to UN budgets—to force their reform proposals on other member states. For the developing countries, the reform overkills mounted by major developed countries have become a charade, apart from being a continuing threat to their position and interests in the United Nations.

Reform proposals put forward by developed countries are ostensibly designed to achieve the standard goals of an efficient institution—rationalisation, coordination, avoiding duplication, modernising management, improving competence and efficiency,

---

2. *ibid.*, p. 57.

3. Childers, Erskine and Brian Urquhart (1994). *Renewing the United Nations System,* Dag Hammarskjold Foundation, Uppsala, Sweden, p.34.

4. *ibid.*, p.34.

and reducing cost and reaping of comparative advantage.[5] However, more often than not, the real purpose has been to maintain the *status quo* in international economic relations, eliminate pluralism and stem dissent inconvenient to them, tighten their control over UN institutions, and restrict the democratic functioning of the organisation. At times, reforms spearheaded by developed countries have been intended to chop off structures the functioning of which is not perceived by them to be in keeping with their interests; and get rid of individuals whom they find inconvenient because they question policies followed by them, and putting in their place their own persons.

There are very few examples in human history where reforms have been used to bring about outcomes which are exactly the opposite of the noble purpose implicit in the term, reform. The overall outcome of UN reforms has been the general enfeebling of the organisation, brought about mainly by dismantling its capacity to deliver public goods to the international community and transferring its roles and functions to institutions which major developed countries control by virtue of their voting power. Reforms have also been used to dilute the pluralistic and democratic character of the UN. Moreover, they have resulted in the proliferation of bodies and institutions to control, monitor, and do internal surveillance at the cost of those designed to harmonise policies, negotiate agreements and find common grounds on substantive issues of global concern. Yet another outcome of reforms has been to reduce the UN activities in the development field largely to the provisioning of technical assistance based on voluntary contributions by these countries and, more recently, drawing upon sporadic and profit-driven charities of multinational corporations.

Over a period of time, the developing countries have accepted the *fait accompli* brought about by major developed countries through reforms. They do not see any possibility of reversing the trend and, therefore, they have not taken any initiative in this direction. Of course, theoretically, they have the votes to reverse

---

5. South Centre (1992). *Enhancing the Economic Role of the United Nations*, October, Geneva, p.4.

the process. But they are realistic enough to realise that they cannot impose changes on developed countries by the strength of their votes. They are also aware that the United Nations cannot function in any meaningful manner without the support of major developed countries. This is particularly so after the drastic decline in assessed budgets for financing UN activities and the commensurate increase in dependence on voluntary contributions. By their voting power, the developing countries can call a conference but without the support of the developed countries, they cannot ensure its success. They can get a new institution created, but they alone cannot ensure that it will function effectively. Besides, votes in the UN cannot be used for legislating changes in the trade, aid and other economic policies of major developed countries.

There have been very few instances when reforms were intended to enhance UN's capacity to cope with new challenges and create new institutions and make additional resources available for this purpose. It was only during the golden era of UN development cooperation between the late 1950s and the beginning of the 1970s, that new institutions like UNDP, UNCTAD, UNIDO and UNEP were created to enable the UN system to do full justice to its mandate in the Charter and deal adequately and in a systematic manner with emerging global issues. But this was not a part of agreed reform of the United Nations system; this was the consequence of years of relentless pressure by the developing countries and tactical concessions by developed countries.

UN reforms have been carried out at regular intervals since the mid-1950s. Most of these reforms have related to organisational structure, content, policies and method of carrying out operational activities. One of the important sets of reform in UN operational activities was carried out in 1971, based largely on the recommendations in a report known as the *Capacity Study*, submitted in 1970 by Sir Robert Jackson. The main feature of this reform was the introduction of five-year country programming based on an indicative planning figure (IPF) of resources to be made available for programming for each member country. Another major reform which involved the amendment of the Charter, was carried out in

1963 when the number of the non-permanent members in the Security Council was increased from 6 to 10, thus increasing the total strength of the Council from 11 to 15. The total number of votes required for a decision by the Council was increased from 7 to 9.

The period after the Cold War witnessed three waves of reform of the UN system. The first wave came immediately after the end of the Cold War. In the early 1990s, expectations regarding the strengthening of multilateralism ran very high. It was widely believed that the changes brought about by the end of the Cold War and by globalisation called for a thoroughgoing reform of the UN system. The end of the Cold War saw the revival of the role of the UN in the security field. The number of peacekeeping operations undertaken during 2-3 years after the Cold War increased many fold. The general expectation was that there would be further increase in such operations in the coming years, and the question was whether the United Nations was equipped to discharge this fast expanding role in the security field. In an unprecedented move, the Security Council held its first meeting at the level of Heads of State and Government at the end of January 1992, to consider this and related issues. The Summit leaders assembled at the Security Council invited the Secretary-General of the United Nations to prepare an "analysis and recommendations on ways of strengthening and making more efficient within the framework and provisions of the Charter, the capacity of the United Nations for preventive diplomacy, for peacemaking and for peacekeeping".[6]

In pursuance of this invitation, the Secretary-General submitted his report on 17 June, 1992.[7] Some of the important recommendations made in this report were: greater reliance on and wider acceptance of the jurisdiction of the International Court of Justice, the creation of 'peace enforcement units', increasing the level of funding of the Working Capital Fund to finance peacekeeping

---

6. *Document S/23500*, Statement of the President of the Council.

7. United Nations (1992). *An Agenda for Peace: Preventive Diplomacy, Peacemaking and Peacekeeping: Report of the Secretary-General*, United Nations Document A/47/277, June 17.

operations and the establishment of a United Nations Peace Endowment Fund with an initial target of one billion dollars. As it happened, soon after the submission of this report, major powers lost interest in enhancing the capacity of the UN in the security field. Consequently, none of these recommendations of the Secretary-General were given serious consideration.

The demand for strengthening the UN's capacity of conflict management in the post-Cold War period, was accompanied by a demand for a thoroughgoing reform of the role and functions of the UN in the economic and social spheres. The initiatives in this regard came mainly from developed countries. The campaign was spearheaded by the Nordic countries, joined by other major developed countries with their own proposals. The Nordic proposals were based mainly on the findings and recommendations of the Nordic UN Project which was completed in 1991 with the publication of the report: *United Nations in Development: Reform Issues in the Economic and Social Fields—A Nordic Perspective.* The focus of reforms proposed in this report was on the operational activities of the United Nations. One of the main arguments in this report was that the then existing system of voluntary funding was not satisfactory as it involved inequitable burden-sharing. Therefore, the major reform proposal put forward in this report was that the future funding of UN operational activities should have three components:

(i)   a token sum of assessed contributions;

(ii) negotiated pledges which should provide the bulk of the resources for operational activities; and

(iii) voluntary funding.

Some of the other reform proposals made by the Nordic and other developed countries during 1989-1991 were:

(i)   reducing the size of the governing bodies of various programmes and funds for technical cooperation;

(ii) equal representation of donor and recipient countries in these governing bodies; and

(iii) introducing the principle of consensus in decisionmaking in these bodies, thereby giving to donor countries an informal veto.

This initiative of developed countries for reform put the developing countries on the defensive. They requested the South Centre, a think tank located in Geneva to study all these proposals and suggest what should be the response of the developing countries. The report prepared by the South Centre[8] in response to the request of the developing countries dealt with some of the conceptual aspects of the proposals of developed countries, suggested possible response to these proposals and made suggestions of its own for restoring to the United Nations its Charter functions in the economic and social fields. The developing countries did not put forward proposals of their own based on the recommendation in this report. They, however, used the facts and arguments in the report to counter the move of the developed countries. As a result, the latter decided not to pursue their proposals and rest content with some minor changes in the system. Thus once again, all that the developing countries could achieve was damage control.

The second wave of reform followed soon after the first wave, on the eve of the 50th anniversary of the establishment of the United Nations. It was hoped that the 50th anniversary in 1995 would be the most opportune moment to start a thoroughgoing reform of the multilateral system under the United Nations. A number of high level discussions were held both within the United Nations and outside, to delineate the contours of the desired changes in the UN system. Several commissions and expert groups were set up to study the entire gamut of issues relating to UN reform and to make appropriate recommendations.

Unfortunately, none of the recommendations made in these reports for introducing reforms of a substantive and structural nature in the multilateral system was given serious consideration in any of the forums of the United Nations. Instead, one witnessed the continuation of the process of reform of an administrative and

---

8. The report was subsequently published by the South Centre under the title *Enhancing the Economic Role of the United Nations*.

financial character, all driven by developed countries, for further weakening the United Nations and reshaping it after the image of their interest.

The third and the last wave of reform started in 2003 with the constitution by the UN Secretary-General of a 'High-Level Panel on Threats, Challenges and Change' and concluded in September 2005, with the adoption by the General Assembly of resolution 60/ 1 under the title "World Summit Outcome". The main impetus to the third wave of reform was provided by the unprecedented terrorist attacks in the United States on September 11, 2001, and the consequent launching by the US of a global war on terrorism, and the US attack on Iraq in March 2003. The former event highlighted the need for identifying new threats to security and devising novel means of dealing with them. In the run up to the latter event, the United States and its allies challenged, totally unjustifiably, the very *raison d'être* of the United Nations and declared it "impotent", because of the inability of the Security Council to authorise use of force against Iraq. In the event, the United States bypassed the United Nations and launched military operations against Iraq in collaboration with 'a coalition of the willing'. Several questions arose at that time: Could the UN have acted otherwise? What changes in the UN Charter must be made to authorise military action in such events in order to retain the relevance of the UN to the United States and its allies? Answers to these questions became the most important motivation driving the reform move of the year 2003. Of course, for public consumption and for the sake of being correct, other objectives of reform were also included in the terms of reference of the high-level panel.

This gives rise to another question of a fundamental nature: Should the reform of the UN be realistic or idealistic? If it is to be realistic, then it must take into account the current power equations in international relations. One of its major objectives should be to keep major powers engaged and involved in the United Nations. To achieve this purpose, the reform package must be acceptable to them.

A realistic reform package will reek with all kinds of compromises. It may go against the objectives and principles of the United Nations and may militate against its underlying values. Besides, its outcome will remain uncertain till the end. And when the outcome emerges, it will be a matter of accident rather than something planned deliberately on the basis of a set of criteria and commonly shared objectives. Besides, such a reform package will be like a house built on sand. It will collapse each time there is a change in the world power equation or any component of the package is found too inconvenient by a major power.

Idealistic reform, on the other hand, will be anchored in the commonly shared human values and the most evolved set of international laws, underlying the United Nations. It is very unlikely that there would ever be a complete agreement on an idealistic reform package. But the very articulation of such a package and its availability will serve as a mirror to the member states, of the true image of the United Nations. And, even a partial agreement on it will help in preserving the basic character of the United Nations and mark a progress towards reaching a higher order of international relations.

An attempt is made in the third section of this chapter to delineate an idealistic reform package. This is preceded in the next section, by an analysis of the value system on which the United Nations is based, a recapitulation of some of the original principles, purposes, objectives and functions of the United Nations and an analytical account of the derogations that have taken place from these values, objectives and principles and the substantial curtailment, dilution and distortion of the role and functions of the United Nations that have occurred during the last few decades, particularly from the early 1980s.

II. Multilateralism besieged

Multilateralism is not an option but a necessity—indeed an inevitability—for the international community. It is the product of an evolutionary process. It represents a progress from a lower order of organising human society to a higher order. Any retreat from multilateralism amounts to lapsing into chaos in international life, where hegemony of power prevails as was the case in the not too distant past and before the establishment of the United Nations.

The United Nations represents the highest level of excellence in the evolution of multilateralism. It is based on the twin pillars of a body of the most up-to-date international laws and the framework of commonly shared human values. These values consists of those which have been cherished by humankind through time immemorial, like peace, harmony, cooperation and solidarity derived from the awareness of common humanity; and those which have evolved through the more recent strivings of humankind, like fundamental freedoms, basic human rights, equity and justice.

Some of the basic principles of international law on which the UN is founded are the sovereign equality of states (Article 2.1), non-intervention in the domestic jurisdiction of states except as laid down in the enforcement measures in Chapter VII (Article 2.7), non-use of force (Article 2.4), and the right of self-defence in the event of an armed attack (Article 51).

Any deviation from this body of international law or the commonly shared human values amounts to a retreat into the dark ages and paves the ground for the dominance by the powerful and the mighty. Unilateralism is a blatant form of such a retreat; so is the long discredited concept of pre-emptive use of force in self-defence.

The United Nations was created not only to prevent another Second World War nor a Third World War, but to 'save the succeeding generations from the scourge of war' (that is, all wars). One of the means by which the UN was meant to set about accomplishing this task was to try to root out causes of war through its activities in the economic, social, cultural and human rights fields. The Charter contains extensive provisions in this regard. Furthermore, the United Nations established for this purpose a whole network of institutions which includes its Specialized Agencies, Regional Economic Commissions and other organisations and specialised institutions subsequently created by the General Assembly and the Economic and Social Council. The UNESCO Constitution describes this overall purpose of the Charter in a fundamental way. It says: "Since wars begin in the minds of men, it is in the minds of men that the defences of peace must be constructed."

Visionaries and savants have for long aspired to 'one world'. Mahatma Gandhi had said, "I would not want to live in a world that was not one world." They all saw the UN as the harbinger of such a world. At least in the economic and social field, from the mid-1950s until the early 1970s, the UN acted as a global authority, laying down norms and standards, setting targets and creating new frameworks and structures.

Multilateralism under the United Nations was conceived and structured as a central overarching authority, both in the military and non-military fields of security, both in the 'hard' and 'soft' sense of the term. In the 'hard' security field, the Charter left no scope for the functioning of a rival instrumentality for the prevention of "threats to peace, breaches of peace and acts of aggression". UN was envisaged as the sole authority for determining the existence of such threats and acts and for taking measures for circumventing them. The Charter envisages no alternative source of authority in this domain, and no non-Charter response to threats to international security. Thus, preventive or peace enforcement action unilaterally by nations, by 'a coalition of the willing' or by an outside institution like NATO, is not permitted under the Charter.

Action outside the UN is permitted only as an exercise of "the inherent right of individual and collective self-defence", and that too only in the event of an armed attack. Even such actions should be immediately reported to the Security Council, which has the authority to act on its own in such events "in order to maintain or restore international peace and security".

Though in Chapter VIII, the Charter recognises the role of regional arrangements or agencies for dealing with matters relating to the maintenance of international peace and security, it makes it clear that such arrangements or agencies and their activities must be "consistent with the Purposes and Principles of the United Nations". It is also made clear that such arrangements will not in any way impair the Security Council's own overriding jurisdiction over matters of international peace and security, that the Security Council at all stages will be kept informed of such activities and actions and that no enforcement action under such arrangements will be taken without the authorisation of the Council.

In the social, economic, cultural and human rights fields, the role assigned to the UN is equally overarching and central. The Charter leaves no doubt that the UN "represents the planetary system" or the authoritative central piece of the international system in the economic, social, cultural and human rights fields. Some of the provisions in the Charter conferring upon the United Nations such an overarching role are in Articles 1, 13, 55, 57 to 59 and 62 to 64. According to Article 1, the UN is "to be a centre for harmonising the actions of nations" in the attainment of common ends in the economic, social, cultural and humanitarian areas. Articles 13 and 55 assign to the United Nations the responsibility of promoting international cooperation in these areas. Article 57 provides that "the various Specialized Agencies shall be brought into relationship with the United Nations". It should be noted that the term used is "shall be". This means that these Agencies do not have the choice of opting out of such a relationship. Article 58 provides that the UN "shall make recommendations for the coordination of the policies and activities of the Specialized Agencies". Article 59 empowers the UN "to initiate negotiations for the creation of any new specialized agencies required for the accomplishment of the purposes set forth in Article 55". Article 64 provides for the UN to receive reports from Specialized Agencies on a regular basis, including reports on how they are implementing its recommendations. These Articles of the Charter leave no doubt about the centrality of the role of the United Nations *vis-à-vis* the Specialized Agencies. And this role extends to all Specialized Agencies, including the IMF, the World Bank and WTO.

Unfortunately, the UN has not fully lived up to the expectations of its founders either in the area of peacekeeping or in the economic, social and cultural and human rights fields. Some of the Charter provisions are yet to be operationalised. The full potentialities of some others remain to be harnessed. And the most serious of all, there has been derogation from some of the key provisions of the Charter both in the actions by member governments as well as the manner in which they have been applied.

Most of the UN decisions, particularly those in the economic field, have remained unimplemented. And in the security field, for the greater part of its life, the UN has remained paralysed. Furthermore, the developing countries increasingly perceive the multilateral system as an instrument for imposing unequal treaties on them and being generally biased against their interests. They have also seen that important decisions affecting the international community as a whole, and in particular the developing countries, are taken outside the UN, in groupings like the G-8 and through defence mechanisms like NATO.

Part of the disillusionment from the UN is simply misinformed. Part of it arises from unfulfilled, unrealistic and unwarranted expectations from the UN. But, by far the largest part of disillusionment is due to the lack of political will on the part of countries which really matter, to allow the UN to discharge its functions on key issues on the global agenda and their refusal to make available adequate resources to the UN for this purpose.

In spite of these limitations, the UN has a distinguished and unique record of achievements to its credit. These include: bringing about decolonisation and an end to apartheid; evolving commonly shared human values and principles of international law; bringing into being a prodigious corpus of norms and standards governing international relations; facilitating and promoting, through its analysis and studies, a shared understanding of the multitude of problems confronting humankind; convening global conferences on such diverse issues as disarmament, sustainable development, social development, desertification, water, population, food, gender equality etc., which have succeeded in focussing attention on and arousing worldwide awareness of these issues and formulating norms, principles, guidelines and plans of action for dealing with them. The UN has also provided a prestigious and the only available global platform and forum to the downtrodden, exploited and marginalised nations of the world, to challenge the *status quo* and to seek justice, equity and basic human rights. One also cannot ignore the indispensable services rendered by the UN system and the Specialized Agencies in providing global public goods in the areas of their activities—putting in place and maintaining the international civil aviation order, postal order, telecommunications order, meterological order, maritime order, promoting health and controlling epidemics, advancing food security, etc.

The period between the mid-1950s and the mid-1970s can legitimately be regarded as the golden era of international cooperation under the United Nations in the economic field. That was a period when most of the creative and far-reaching ideas like the general system of preferences (GSP), integrated programme for commodities including the commodity fund, compensatory financing, supplementary financing, special drawing rights and debt amelioration and forgiveness were advanced and agreed upon within the United Nations. The follow-up action on several of them was taken by Specialized Agencies, particularly the IMF and the World Bank.

Unfortunately this success turned out to be the bane of the United Nations. Major powers thought that the UN had gone too far in the direction of challenging the global *status quo* and some of the underlying premises of the world order which they favoured, and that this process must be stopped in the track. There then ensued a trend of decline in multilateralism under the United Nations. Beginning towards the end of the 1970s, major powers launched a deliberate, well-planned and concerted campaign to besmear the reputation of United Nations and disenfranchise it of the economic functions entrusted to it under the Charter. Their mission was largely completed by the beginning of the 1990s, but the process is still continuing, as these countries, relying on their political, economic and institutional clout, attempt to reshape the United Nations comprehensively after their own image, and as an instrument for serving their national interest.

During the period of a decade and a half, the UN Agenda in the economic field was changed beyond recognition, the mode of discourse in the UN forums was drastically altered and the core competence of the secretariats of the UN organisations substantially whittled down. Among others, the economically advanced countries have succeeded in putting themselves outside the pale of UN scrutiny and surveillance . They have diligently kept the UN at arm's length from their domestic and regional affairs and the implications of these for the international community and in particular the developing countries. The UN has been declared by these countries, incompetent to deal with its Charter functions in the realms of money, finance, trade, external indebtedness and development strategy. These functions have been transferred to the IMF, World Bank and WTO—the troika which the major economic powers, by virtue of their voting power or the power of retaliation in the case of WTO, dominate and use as instrument for advancing their interests. The UN is now considered to be competent to deal only with disaster relief, post-war rehabilitation and construction and humanitarian issues. It is only supposed to pick up the pieces after a war and do fire-fighting during peace time.

Today, discussions in the UN are confined to domestic economic and social problems of developing countries and their internal governance. Among domestic policies, there is almost an exclusive concentration on how developing countries can give greater play to free market forces, how to be friendly to foreign investors, liberalise the external sectors of their economies, privatise economic activities and whittle down the role of the State.

There is also a sea change in the UN's mode of functioning. Instead of being a negotiating forum for undertaking legally or morally binding commitments, the UN has become a debating society where mostly non-consequential speeches are pronounced and where experts are called upon to give lectures to delegates in specially convened meetings like the special segments of the various sessions of the Economic and Social Council. UN has ceased to be a forum for negotiations on hard core economic issues. The negotiating forum has shifted principally to the WTO, and to the IMF and the World Bank.

The major powers have adopted a series of devices to bring the UN to its present unenviable state. They have launched a false, misguided and misinformed campaign against the efficiency and the integrity of the United Nations. They derided and went back on the whole body of consensus that had been achieved in the development field during the sixties and the early seventies, to all of which they were willing partners.

The second device used by them for weakening the UN has been to keep the UN organisation on the brink of financial bankruptcy by withholding dues and by applying budgetary squeeze in the form of the so-called zero nominal growth in budget. As a result, the core capabilities of the UN organisations have more or less been dismantled and their global regulatory and norm-setting activities vastly curtailed. The major powers' determination to keep the UN perpetually crippled and under their control is also borne out by the fact that they have summarily dismissed all proposals for providing predictable and autonomous sources of financing to the UN and for enhancing its peacekeeping capabilities.

A major factor responsible for the loss of autonomy of the United Nations and the distortion of its priorities, has been the growing voluntarisation of the funding of its activities, i.e., the progressive replacement of funding through the assessed budget by funding through voluntary contributions. The major powers have used this device to impose their priorities on the UN organisations, and to take full control of its budgeting, accounting and administrative apparatus.

The organisations of the UN system, except the UNDP, had, until the mid-1970s, retained a sufficient degree of autonomy because of the essentially assessed system of the funding of their activities. Until the end of the 1960s, assessed contributions provided 80 to 90 per cent of the finances of these organisations. However, since the mid-1970s there has been a trend of an increasing voluntarisation of their funding. The process has now come to a stage where the earlier proportion between assessed and voluntary financing is reversed. Voluntary contributions now account for 60-80 per cent of the funding of the UN Specialized Agencies and the

Regional Economic Commissions. As a result, all UN organisations have become donor dependent.

In the security field, the UN remained paralysed throughout the Cold War period because of the lack of unanimity among the P-5 as a result of the division of the world into two rival power blocs. Its role in the area of preventive diplomacy, peacemaking and peacekeeping was revived for a brief period after the end of the Cold War from 1989 to 1992. This gave rise to the hope that the end of the Cold War would witness a paradigm shift towards the full assertion of genuine multilateralism. It has been witnessed in history that each great divide which often came at the end of a prolonged war, was followed by an effort to organise the world order on the basis of a new paradigm. The end of the Cold War was undoubtedly a great divide in history and the new paradigm following it could not but have been an effective, democratic and dynamic multilateralism under the United Nations. But that opportunity was sadly squandered. None of the major recommendations made at that time designed to give real clout to the UN, was given serious consideration.

Just when the United Nations seemed to be doing justice to its Charter functions relating to the maintenance of peace and security, the major powers stepped in and once again marginalised the UN in this most vital and visible sphere of its functioning. They forced the UN to withdraw from some peacekeeping operations. They utilised NATO to carry out some major preventive and enforcement operations. In the case of Kosovo, they simply bypassed the UN and carried out military operations without being so authorised by the Security Council. With the attack on Iraq, the descent towards anarchy and chaos in the world order was further precipitated. This caused concern even among some prominent major powers, like France, Germany and Russia. They have now started talking about restoration of multilateralism. So, the crisis before the UN is not that there is no consensus on the nature of the threats to security or on the methods to meet these threats. Nor is the crisis about the failure of the UN to adjust to the existing global power structure; for, it should be the global powers that should adjust to the body of international law and commonly shared human values underpinning the UN. The real crisis is that the more powerful among the member states now want to go back on this body of international law and on the common values and are bent upon perpetuating the obvious inequities and imbalances in the rules and regimes which govern international relations. The crisis does not so much lie in occasional paralysis in decisionmaking, but in the built-in system of unequal decisionmaking and decisions under pressure based on the exploitation of the vulnerability of the weaker member states. The crisis lies in imposing on weaker nations unequal treaties and asking them to do what the powerful nations themselves are unprepared to do (as in the case of bringing down agriculture protection). The crisis does not lie in the alleged irrelevance or inflexibility of the UN, but in its disenfranchisement, in undermining its role as the central authority and nucleus of the multilateral system, in keeping it at the brink of bankruptcy and in the ever expanding voluntarisation of its funding. Nor is the crisis one of inefficiency, prolificacy or the alleged burgeoning bureaucracy of the UN system. These problems in some measures or the other beset all institutions—national, bilateral or multilateral. There are also facts to prove that several of these allegations are highly exaggerated.[9] Moreover, there are always ways of tiding over these problems to the extent that they really exist. These should be tackled on their merits and not made the excuse for berating or weakening multilateralism under the UN.

III. Strengthening the United Nations

The challenge facing the reformers of the UN is not just tinkering with its structures, functions, methods and rules and regulations. The challenge is to reverse the ongoing trend of the systematic undermining of the legitimacy of the United Nations,

---

9. "The image of the UN system as an intractably large and reform-defying bureaucracy is a myth of distance, ideological denigration and media distortion. The number of its distinct institutions is less than in a small government. The staff of the system worldwide is no larger than the civil servants in one city of a medium-sized country" (Childers and Urquhart, *op. cit.* 1994).

and whittling down its role and functions under the Charter and dismantling its capacity. The challenge is one of renewing and strengthening the multilateral system. Proposals for the renewal of the multilateral system should be based on a set of principles and shared objectives and not of expediency or practicability in terms of their acceptability to a particular member state or a group of them.

Here are some basic principles and criteria that must guide and govern a strengthened United Nations.

Adherence to international law and commonly shared human values

This, among others, would imply that there can be no retreat to either unilateralism or new hegemonism. There can be no enforcement measure to restore peace outside the United Nations by an individual nation or a so-called coalition of the willing. This would also imply that no entity except the United Nations has the right to take preventive action and that preventive war for individual or collective self-defence, can be waged only when attacked.

Establishment of the position of the UN as the centrepiece of the multilateral system

True to the provisions of the Charter, the UN must be recognised as the central authority in the multilateral system, whose role cannot be usurped by any rival or alternative organisation. This rules out any notion of 'multilateralism *a la carte*'. To counterpoise to the UN, bilateralism and regionalism outside the UN system or the private sector or the transnational corporations, is a traversty of the basic tenets of the UN Charter and retreat from multilateralism. Re-establishing the UN as the centrepiece of the UN multilateral system would call for the following:

(i) The association agreements with the IMF and the World Bank should be revised in order to bring them in line with those concluded with other Specialized Agencies.

(ii) WTO should be brought under association with the UN according to Article 57 of the Charter.

(iii) Functions of the UN in the economic field provided for in the Charter, but now largely transferred to IMF, World Bank and WTO, should be restored. The United Nations should once again be the forum for analysing and discussing global economic issues like money, finance, trade, external indebtedness, harmonising member states' policies, recommending policies and strategies for international cooperation in these areas, and negotiating specific agreements and global regimes as appropriate. It should bring under its surveillance and make appropriate recommendations on the development strategies and macroeconomic policies of all its member states, including the developed ones.

(iv) The United Nations must have a say in determining the shape and structure of the emerging international financial architecture which is becoming more discretionary and less regulatory and rule-based. In this scheme of things, the IMF and the World Bank will be left with no effective power or means to play any role of intervention or intermediation in the international monetary and financial systems. They are not going to have the resources or liquidity to be able to play such a role. Bailing-out operations in moments of financial crises, will not be left to the discretion of the creditor countries, which are likely to be predominantly motivated by political considerations in deciding to intervene. There must be an opportunity to discuss these issues within the UN with a view to making suitable recommendations before it is too late.

(v) The Economic and Social Council should be made the forum for discussing the coordination of the global macroeconomic policies of member states. The major developed countries, of course, are free to have their own mechanism of coordination under G-8. But this cannot be a substitute for such a mechanism at the global level. Instead of making developing countries petitioners in the Court of G-8, the G-8 countries should come to the universal UN forum to coordinate their economic policies with those of the other member states.

(vi) There is a widespread criticism of the ECOSOC as it functions today. Its authority and prestige as a principal organ of the UN stands vastly diminished. There is a general feeling that it has failed to discharge its Charter responsibility to coordinate the activities of and provide policy guidelines to the organisations of the UN system in the economic, social, cultural and human rights fields and that it has ceased to be an effective forum for deliberation and decisionmaking on global economic and social issues. It has, therefore, been proposed that the ECOSOC should be replaced by an Economic Security Council[10] with the mandate to:

- Continuously assess the overall state of the world economy and the interaction between major policy areas.

- Provide a long-term strategic policy framework in order to promote stable, balanced and sustained development.

- Secure consistency between the policy goals of the major international organisations, particularly the World Bank, IMF and the WTO.

- Give political leadership and promote consensus on international economic issues.

These are precisely the responsibilities entrusted to the ECOSOC under the Charter. The major economic powers as part of a deliberate policy have prevented the ECOSOC from discharging its responsibilities. There is no reason to believe that the mere establishment of an Economic Security Council will bring about a change in the situation. The real issue is not simply to re-designate an existing institution, but to undo the damage that has been done

10. Commission on Global Governance (1995). "Our Global Neighbourhood", *The Report of the Commission on Global Governance*, Oxford University Press, pp. 155-156.

to the UN system over the past 25 years. The only way in which UN authority in the economic ànd social field can be re-established is to restore to it its Charter functions and endow it with adequate resources and power to discharge these functions. The problems besetting the UN in this area are not institutional but political. These problems will bedevil the proposed Economic Security Council also as long as there is no change in the attitude of the major powers towards the UN And if the political will is there, there is no reason why the ECOSOC should not be able to discharge its stated functions.

Furthermore, the mere addition of the word 'security' does not make any difference unless there is also a provision to enable the UN to enforce its decisions in the economic field, as there is in the security field under Chapter VII of the Charter. No member state even in its wildest dream is thinking of vesting the Economic Security Council with such an authority.

(vii) There can be no lasting peace without disarmament. The UN, therefore, cannot afford to allow its disarmament agenda to remain suspended. Making progress in this area is a *raison d'être* of the United Nations. The UN disarmament agenda should be revived on an urgent basis and in this the highest priority should be attached to the elimination of nuclear and other weapons of mass destruction. In the report, *Our Global Neighbourhood*, it is recommended that the international community should reaffirm its commitment to eliminate nuclear weapons and should adopt a 10 to 15 years programme to achieve this goal.[11]

New mandate and enhanced capability in the area of human security

Taking into account the changes that have taken place in the world recently, the mandates of the UN organisations should be considerably expanded and their capabilities vastly enhanced in

---

11. *ibid.*, pp. 340-341.

order to enable them to play a positive pro-active leadership role in the area of human security. There is also clearly a need for a changed approach and priority for dealing with global economic issues. The following measures are suggested in this regard:

(i) Equity and justice in the international trading, monetary and financial systems and structures should be introduced and some of the grossly unequal treaties like TRIPS and rules emanating from the World Bank, IMF and the WTO should be rectified.

(ii) The capability of the UN organisations should be enhanced to enable them to undertake activities designed to provide, particularly to developing countries, global public benefits, like protection of the global environment, controlling trans-boundary health hazards, developing and disseminating new knowledge, technology and information and contributing to the maintenance of financial stability. For this purpose, the UN system should undertake global projects in the areas of energy, environment, knowledge and information, health, etc.

(iii) There is a glaring lacuna in the UN, in the virtual absence of analysis, discussion and negotiations on regulation and guidelines on the operation of the transnational corporations as key actors on the world scene and in the globalisation process. Earlier, institutions and structures created for this purpose have either been wound up or rendered ineffective. This situation needs to be remedied, preferably by creating a new specialised agency or a separate UN body to deal with the complex and crucial issues in this area.

Democratisation of the UN structure and of the way of its functioning

The democratic character of the UN organisations should be promoted and enhanced in a conscious, earnest and systematic manner. This will, first of all, call for the transformation of those structures of the UN system which are not sufficiently democratic.

Expansion of the membership of the Security Council

The first priority in this regard should be to the expansion of the membership of the Security Council. The ongoing long drawn out process of the expansion of both the permanent and non-permanent membership of the Security Council should be quickly brought to final conclusion and decision. This is needed to ensure that the decisionmaking process in the Security Council reflects the vastly enhanced membership of the United Nations and thus acquires greater legitimacy. Moreover, an expansion of the membership will make it much more difficult for getting decisions in the Security Council taken under bilateral pressure or other means of coercion.

There is, by and large, a consensus on increasing the number of both permanent and non-permanent members of the Council. An important issue in this connection is whether the new permanent members should be conferred veto rights. If the UN is to move towards further democratisation then the obvious choice is not to confer such rights on the new permanent members and phase out the veto rights of the existing permanent members. The recommendation on this subject of the Commission on Global Governance is exactly along this line. They have recommended against conferring veto rights on the five standing members (equivalent to permanent members) to be brought to the Security Council, They have further suggested that the voting rights of the existing permanent members should be phased out after a full review of the issue of the membership of the Security Council 10 years later. In the meantime, these permanent members should reach an agreement among themselves to forego the use of veto power except in circumstances of an exceptional or overriding nature.[12]

The Independent Working Group on the Future of the United Nations has also suggested the inclusion in the Security Council of five more permanent members, but with the power of veto. They have, however, recommended that the veto power of all the

12. *ibid.*, p. 345.

permanent members should be applicable only to peacekeeping and enforcement measures.[13]

Democratising decisionmaking in the IMF and the World Bank

Democratisation of the UN system will also call for changing the decisionmaking process in the IMF and the World Bank. There should be a change in the quota structure of the Fund and the Bank so as to bring about a greater quota dispersal among member states. In addition to the quotas, other criteria should be introduced for determining the voting strength of member countries and making it possible for developing member countries to have a greater say and influence in the decisionmaking process in these institutions.

Bringing in culture of democracy in the functioning of the United Nations

Democratisation is not only a matter of structure, but also of culture. The spirit and culture of democracy must be reflected in the member states' commitment to engage in dialogue and debate, discouraging isolationism, accepting decisions reached democratically, promoting and respecting the rule of law in international relations and in maintaining a general spirit of solidarity, cooperation and community. This will also mean not shutting out the consideration or applying the so-called sunset clause on the discussion of issues of concern and interest to a large number of countries.

Hearing the voice of the people

A more inclusive participation in UN deliberations and decision-making is an indispensable part of the process of the democratisation of the UN organisations. Ensuring a more effective participation by non-State actors, in particular civil society organisations (CSOs) will no doubt impart a new dimension and speed to this process. The CSOs have already forced their way into the system. The task now is to bring their formidable knowledge, experience and commitment to bear more closely and formally on the policy and

---

13. "The United Nations in its Second Half Century", *The Report of the Independent Working Group on the Future of the United Nations*, Yale University Press, 1995, p.16.

decisionmaking process in the UN system. A suggestion to achieve this purpose is to create a global forum of the CSOs that should meet for a day or two prior to the annual session of the General Assembly. It is of particular importance to ensure fuller participation in this forum, and in the deliberations of the UN system in general, of CSOs from developing countries, that are marginalised and under-represented in these forums. Another suggestion made to provide for people's participation in the UN system, is to create a People's Assembly as a deliberative body complementing the General Assembly. This will be an assembly of parliamentarians consisting of representatives elected by existing national legislatures of member governments. Subsequently, a World Parliament, directly elected by the people in the style of the European Parliament, could be created.[14]

Addressing the role of the private sector

There is no doubt that the private sector, particularly transnational corporations, have emerged as a major force in the world economy and, by virtue of that, in world politics too. They can, no doubt, bring a great deal to the UN system, particularly in the form of expertise, experience, networking, technology and financial resources. However, because of their overwhelming power and influence, their method of operation and their basic motivations, they have added to rather than provided a solution to the problems confronting the United Nations, for example, in the areas of biodiversity, agriculture, food security and health. Their commitment to the objectives, purposes and values of the UN remains, at best, uncertain. They are accountable neither to the UN organisations nor to member governments. Their own governance leaves much to be desired. Historically, they are known to have actively worked for the imposition of inequitable and exploitative WTO agreements (like that of the TRIPS) on developing countries. They have also managed to keep themselves safely outside the regimes and disciplines that have recently been created in the international trading and financial system, and in the area of environment and

---

14. Commission on Global Governance (1995), *op. cit.*, p.257.

sustainable development. They have accepted no commitment, restraint or accountability under these regimes. Finally, their operation is guided almost entirely by profit motives; social purposes do not enter into, or figure only symbolically in their calculus of profit-making.

Therefore, one need not have any great expectations from their voluntary association with the UN system. In fact, one should approach such association with great circumspection. Their association should be sought in highly selected areas on the basis of clearly laid down ground rules and in a framework of total transparency.

Dispersal of power and decentralisation

Dispersal of power and decentralisation is a very important aspect of democracy. As originally conceived and operationalised, the UN system is fairly decentralised. It was decentralised sectorally through the dispensation of the autonomous functioning of its Specialized Agencies, and regionally through the functioning of the Regional Economic Commissions. There was no provision or scope for a detailed or day-to-day control of the operation of the Specialized Agencies. The UN responsibility *vis-à-vis* these agencies was confined to the provisions in Articles 57-59 and 62-64 of the Charter. The Regional Economic Commissions, though under greater control of the UN than the Specialized Agencies, functioned more or less autonomously. By virtue of this, they, particularly the Economic Commission for Latin America and Economic Commission for Europe, pioneered many ideas and strategies that have left an indelible mark on the history of international economic relations. The creation of UNCTAD and of UNIDO within the framework of the UN General Assembly, was also meant to achieve the same goal of decentralisation and dispersal of power, and to provide the developing countries with additional fora in which to work towards evolving international development strategies and policies.

Unfortunately, the Specialized Agencies, the Regional Economic Commissions as well as UNCTAD and UNIDO have, mainly because of the increasing voluntarisation of their funding, virtually lost their autonomy to the key donor countries. They have become the instruments for carrying out technical cooperation activities preferred by and on behalf of donor countries. If the process of the voluntarisation of their funding is reversed and they are then adequately funded through the UN regular budget, these organisations and bodies can once again resume their role as the fountainhead of new ideas and approaches and can start functioning as the bulwark of a fairly decentralised UN system. This will also go a long way towards the dispersal of power and influence, away from the Fund, Bank and WTO.

An important step towards decentralisation is to recognise member governments' sovereignty and autonomy of decision-making and action, on matters relating to economic and social development. It is now widely accepted that member countries and their governments alone should be the owners of their development policies and strategies and arbiters of their economic destiny. This alone can ensure both the soundness and appropriateness of such policies and strategies and their implementation without giving rise to resentment or conflict. In this context, it will be useful, among others, to revisit some of the important changes introduced in the UN system in the 1960s and 1970s to devolve power and functions to the regional and national levels, particularly through country programming of technical assistance, government execution of projects, and the decentralisation of the formulation, appraisal and approval of UN projects and programmes, at the country level.

Enhancing the UN capabilities

Enhancing the capabilities of the United Nations is of crucial importance to enable the organisation to discharge adequately and effectively its Charter functions and any new mandate that may be given to it. Among these, by far the most important are those related to the financial resources at the disposal of the United Nations, the policies related to its budget and financing, and the wherewithal for carrying out its peacemaking and peacekeeping functions.

Financing of UN organisations

In the financing of UN organisations, the member states should have zero tolerance for any deliberate withholding of payment of dues to the organisation. The Charter provision in this regard, including the denial of vote, should be strictly applied.

Second, it is time to terminate the prolonged financial blackmail against the UN. The organisations of the UN system must be allowed to breath freely by lifting the embargo on any increase in their budgets, and by considering their programmes on merit rather than within the straitjacket of the budget embargo.

Third, the UN must be given access to new and predictably recurring sources for financing its activities. There is a whole array of proposals in this regard. A proposal for levying an international tax for financing UN activities was first made in the mid-1960s in a report of the Committee for Development Planning. This was also included among the recommendations adopted by the 1972 UN Conference on Human Environment. Since then, a number of other proposals, particularly for levying taxes on the use of global commons, have been made by different committees, commissions and experts. Among these is the proposal put forward by James Tobin, the Noble Laureate in Economics for imposing a tax (known as Tobin Tax) on capital transactions for speculative purposes, with the objective of both limiting such speculative transactions and for raising resources for the organisations of the UN system. More recently, the Monterrey Conference on the Financing of Development also called for further study of proposals providing to UN new and predictably recurring resources. The Commission on Global Governance recommended more than 10 years ago: "It is time for the evolution of a consensus on the concept of global taxation for serving the needs of the global neighbourhood."[15] Unfortunately, none of these proposals has so far been seriously considered at the inter-governmental level within the forum of the United Nations. It is time to consider them on an urgent basis with

---

15. *ibid.*, p.344.

a view to reaching agreement on at least one or two of them and put them into operation expeditiously.

Finally, the process of the voluntarisation of the funding of the UN organisations should stop and the earlier practice of the bulk of the finances of these organisations coming from assessed contributions should be restored. Assessed budget method of financing is squarely rooted in democratic principle. On the other hand, voluntary contributions detract from the democratic character of the UN.

Enhancing the UN capacity to mount peacemaking and peacekeeping operations

Financing of peacekeeping operations

Enhancing the UN capacity to mount operations under Chapters VI and VII of the Charter calls for the acceptance of several of the proposals on the financing of such operations made in the report, *An Agenda for Peace*. The two most prominent among them are: (i) increasing the Working Capital Fund to a level of US$ 250 million and endorsing the principle that the Fund should constitute approximately 25 per cent of the annual assessment under the regular budget; and (ii) the establishment of a United Nations Peace Endowment Fund, with an initial target of US$ 1 billion.

A rapid deployment force for the UN

There is also a very strong case for approving and operationalising the proposal made in the *Agenda for Peace* for creating peace enforcement units for the United Nations. This proposal has also been made by a number of committees and commissions on UN reforms. In the report of the Commission on Global Governance, these units are called UN Volunteer Force whereas the Independent Working Group on the Future of the United Nations calls it a Rapid Reaction Force. The strength of such a force has been estimated to be about 10,000 personnel, involving an expenditure ranging between 300 and 500 million dollars. This modest figure will be an amount well spent, because it has the potentiality of pre-empting situations in which the UN may be called upon to take preventive or peacekeeping operations involving the deployment of forces and hence the expenditure of resources on a much larger scale.

Undertaking negotiations under Article 43

If the UN is going to be entrusted with all preventive and peacekeeping operations, then it will be necessary, as recommended in the *An Agenda for Peace*, for the UN to initiate negotiations with member states in order to arrive at the "special agreement" envisaged in Article 43 of the Charter. Such an agreement will provide for Member States making armed forces, assistance and facilities available to the Security Council for the purpose stated in Article 42, not only on an *ad hoc* but on a permanent basis.

The International Court of Justice (ICJ)

For any system of global governance to be effective, there must be specific and strong provisions for dispute settlement and dispensation of justice at the international level. The founders of the United Nations were, therefore, very wise to include in the UN Charter the Statute of the International Court of Justice. The ICJ was accorded the status of a principal organ of the UN Unfortunately, for a variety of reasons, the potentialities of the ICJ have remained largely unutilised. In any scheme of the strengthening of the UN, it is essential to include measures for fully utilising the potentialities of the ICJ not only in the area of peacemaking and peacekeeping but also in the broader field of improving international relations and cooperation and imparting stability to the international system. Some of the measures that can be taken in this regard are:

- All member states should accept the general jurisdiction of the ICJ without any reservation.

- In cases where it is not possible due to binding national laws which cannot be amended in the short and medium-run, states should agree bilaterally or multilaterally to a comprehensive listing of matters they are willing to submit to the Court and they should withdraw their reservations to the Court's jurisdiction in the dispute settlement clauses of multilateral treaties.

- The Secretary-General should be authorised to take advantage of the provisions in the Charter relating to the advisory competence of the Court, and turn to the Court more frequently for seeking advisory opinion on important matters pending or remaining unresolved in the United Nations.

- Similarly, the Security Council, under Articles 36 and 37 of the Charter, should start fully utilising its power to recommend to the member states the submission of disputes to the ICJ.

IV. The third wave of UN reforms

Report of the high-level panel

The most recent initiative for reforming the UN system was taken with great fanfare and in an atmosphere of very high expectations. A High-Level Panel on Threats, Challenges and Change was set up towards the end of 2003. After almost a year-long deliberations, which included a number of regional consultations, the Panel submitted its well-publicised report in December, 2004. It then followed the attempt to sell its main findings and recommendations with an evangelical zeal, in which the UN Secretary-General was an active participant. In fact, there are few instances in the UN history when such a high voltage effort was mounted to mobilise international support for an expert panel's recommendations.

The principal findings and recommendations of the Panel were leaked out to the international media long before the submission of its report. Some very distinguished members of the Panel wrote signed articles highlighting these findings and recommendations. The UN Secretary-General himself took space in the London Economist to write a signed article. After the submission of the report, high level informal consultations among delegates were organised in New York to develop a consensus on the Report's main recommendations. Moreover, seminars were organised in prestigious academic and research institutions to mobilise the support of the movers and shakers of ideas and policies in leading countries of the world.

After a few months, the UN Secretary-General submitted his own report based on the report of the High-Level Panel under the title *In Larger Freedom: Towards Development, Security and Human Rights for All*. The Secretary-General's report was considered at a Summit level session of the UN General Assembly convened to review progress made in the implementation of the UN Millennium Declaration adopted by the Assembly in 2000. After protracted negotiations which commenced even before the commencement of its session, the Assembly adopted Resolution 60/1 of 16 September, 2005, as the outcome of the last round of the effort to reform the United Nations.

The High Level Panel's as well as the Secretary-General's reports are an attempt to make the UN acceptable to the establishment and public opinion in the countries representing major powers. These reports are aimed at obliging the UN to adjust itself to the underlying power reality in the world. The High Level Panel Report reflects the long standing agenda of major powers to dilute the objectives and functions of the organisation in order to use it as an instrument for advancing their national interest.

The Report looks at the UN as a security system. Development is brought in only as a means to address the environment which, according to the authors of the Report, breeds threat to security. Elimination or reduction of poverty, diseases, illiteracy, etc. are important not on the ground of their own merits but because they constitute a threat to security. It is significant that all the threats identified in the Report, like poverty, diseases, terrorism, transnational crimes, large scale violations of human rights, proliferation of weapons of mass destruction, etc. emanate from developing countries.

The Report totally ignores the systemic problem besetting the organisation of the UN system in the economic and social fields. The UN organisations and bodies which mainly suffer from these problems, like UNCTAD, UNIDO, UNEP, the Regional Economic Commissions, and the Specialized Agencies do not even find a mention in the Report. There is only a mention of the World Bank and the IMF, and of WHO in the context of the threat to security posed by pandemic diseases. The deepening crisis in which these organisations find themselves and the systemic maladies affecting them are not touched upon in the Report.

The Report takes the enfeeblement of the UN and the erosion of its functions and role as a *fait accompli* about which nothing can be done. In fact it makes out a case for the international community to get reconciled to the vast erosion that has taken place in the functions, role and authority of United Nations in the economic field during the last 25 years. The Report states: "...decisionmaking on international economic matters, particularly in the areas of finance and trade has long left the United Nations and no amount of constitutional reform will bring it back."[16] It further says, "historical developments in the governance of the multilateral system have limited the capacity of that body to influence international policies in trade, finance and investment."[17] This is not an accurate description of what happened in the UN. The erosion of the functions of the United Nations in the economic field and their transfer to the IMF, World Bank and the WTO, started not in the distant past in history, but systematically only from the beginning of the 1980s. This did not happen by itself due to objective historical factors; this was brought about by conscious and well planned policy and strategy.

The Report confines the development agenda of the United Nations to the Millennium Development Goals which are addressed mainly to developing countries and which concern mainly the development policies of these countries. It almost completely ignores the structural problems besetting the world economy and international economic relations—in short, the entire agenda of the North-South dialogue which took place till almost the end of the 1970s. These structural problems include external indebtedness, agricultural protectionism, various forms of neo-protectionism, the

---

16. United Nations (2004). "A More Secure World: Our Shared Responsibility", *Report of the Secretary-General's High-level Panel on Threats, Challenges and Change*; New York, p.86.

17. *ibid.*, p.88.

vagaries of international financial markets, monopolistic practices of transnational corporations, pre-emption of the bio-resources and other vital natural resources of the developing countries, and inequity and imbalances in the international financial, monetary and trading systems. These have been and will continue to be the real threats to international peace and security. The United Nations system was designed, among others, to meet these threats. In the system of collective security recommended by the Report, there will be a decisive shift away from these fundamental concerns.

The Report suggests the establishment of institutions and creation of capacity which will tilt the balance of the United Nations towards the security side at the cost of its activities on the economic and social side, and towards further expanding the role of the Security Council at the cost of the other organs of the organisation.

The Report recommends the creation of institutions and capacities in the UN Secretariat and acceptance of doctrines which will enable major powers to intervene in the domestic affairs of developing countries almost at their will, to take punitive actions against them if they do not conform to their design of the world order, and to use the UN machinery to take action to deal with threats that emanate mainly from developing countries.

Lip service to nuclear disarmament

The Report pays only lip service to nuclear disarmament and concentrates almost exclusively on the prevention of the proliferation of weapons of mass destruction. There is no recommendation in the Report that the nuclear weapon powers should subscribe to the objective of a nuclear weapon free world, that they should agree to a deadline for achieving this objective, and that they should immediately resume negotiations for this purpose. In this respect, there is very little to separate the Secretary-General's Report from the Panel's Report.

No recommendation on enhancing UN's own resources and capacity

There is hardly anything in the Report by way of recommendations for enhancing UN's own resources and capacity.

Instead, the Report suggests outsourcing of what United Nations is supposed to do on its own and by its own resources. For example, on peacekeeping, the Report recommends an increasing resort to the utilisation of the military capacity of major powers and their organisation, NATO. The Report suggests outsourcing to think tanks outside the UN, of studies and research that the UN is supposed to do.

Expanded G-20 at leader's level

Even on the question of discussing inter-relationship between global macro-economic variables, the Report recommends going outside the UN and entrusting this task to an enlarged G-20, a group of Finance Ministers of developed countries, which is an offshoot of G-7. G-20 is not only outside the UN but in the strict formal sense, even outside the World Bank and the IMF. It is completely dominated by G-7 (now G-8) and any discussion in it with the participation of selected representatives of developing countries at the leaders' level as suggested in the Report, would be used for securing a broader consensus for G-7 generated ideas and initiatives.

The UN Charter vests the function of addressing the critical inter-linkages between trade, finance, money, environment etc., with the ECOSOC, and not with an elite group outside the UN. Therefore, the most appropriate forum for discussing these inter-relationships at the Summit level is the ECOSOC.

Use of force under Article 51 to prevent imminent threat to security

The Report has mercifully excluded from the scope of Article 51 of the UN Charter, the preventive use of force in individual or collective self-defence. This came as a setback to the United States and its allies which wanted to legitimise their recent use of force in Iraq, on the ground of preventing the so-called threat to their security. However, in an attempt to make its report more acceptable to the US and its allies, the Panel recommended the use of force in self-defence under Article 51, in the event of 'imminent' or 'proximate' threat to national security. The justification given in the Panel's Report for this extension of the scope of action under Article 51 is that it is "according to long established international law" or customary international law. This is apparently untenable, because treaty law must prevail upon a customary international law and the treaty law as enshrined in the UN Charter, clearly provides that member states can use force in the exercise of their right of self-defence under Article 51 only "if an armed attack occurs." The extension of the scope of Article 51 as suggested by the Panel, is the thin end of the wedge to permit preventive attack in self-defence. The term 'imminent' can be interpreted flexibly enough to justify preventive attack.

The Secretary-General in his report, endorses this recommendation. In support, he advances the argument that lawyers have long recognised that Article 51 covers both "an imminent attack as well as one that has already happened." It is a total, if not deliberate, misreading of Article 51. The words used in Article 51 are "if an armed attack occurs." These words can by no stretch of imagination be interpreted to include 'an imminent attack'.

Responsibility to protect

The Panel endorses what it calls "the emerging norm that there is a collective international 'responsibility to protect', exercisable by the Security Council authorising military intervention as a last resort in the event of genocide and other large scale killings, ethnic cleansing or serious violation of international humanitarian law which sovereign governments have proved powerless or unwilling to prevent." This extension of the mandate of the Security Council relating to the authorisation of military intervention by it is not tenable in international law. The so-called norm of collective international 'responsibility to protect' is still under dispute. This norm is also susceptible to being used selectively and discriminatory, depending upon the political convenience and national interest of the dominant nation or nations. If all the situations mentioned in the Report like large scale killings, ethnic cleansing, violation of international humanitarian law, etc. are to qualify for military action by the Security Council, then it will mean a *carte blanche* sanction for intervention in the domestic affairs of member states. Moreover, judgements with regard to what constitutes a failed state or sovereign governments which have proved powerless or unwilling to protect, are bound to be subjective and under the influence of a variety of extraneous factors. It would, therefore, be preferable to authorise military intervention in such situations by declaring them as a threat to international peace and security as provided in Article 39 of the Charter. The violation of humanitarian law need not always turn out to be such a threat. For, there can be a whole spectrum of such violations the vast majority of which would be well below the threshold of being declared as threat to international peace and security.

The Secretary-General also endorses the Panel's recommendation for the acceptance of the notion of the international 'responsibility to protect', though he has dropped some of the controversial circumstances like violation of humanitarian laws in which such a responsibility can be exercised.

Expansion of the membership of the Security Council

The Panel recommends two models for the enlargement of the membership of the Security Council. According to the first, six permanent members and three non-permanent members should be added to the Council, bringing its total strength to 24. According to the second model also, the membership of the Security Council should be expanded to 24 by the addition of 9 members. Of these, 8 should be elected on a four-year renewable term and the other additional member should be elected only on a two-year non-renewable term. The Panel has recommended that the new permanent members should not be conferred the power to veto. It very rightly justifies this recommendation on the ground that "the institution of veto has an anachronistic character that is unsuitable for the institution of an increasingly democratic age." However, the Panel has made an exception to this principle by suggesting that the existing permanent members should retain their veto power. This has been justified on the ground that there is no "practical way of changing the existing members' veto power." We have already pointed out that a number of other panels on UN reform have suggested the phasing out of the veto of the current permanent members.

The Secretary-General in his report commends for the consideration of the member states, the two options put forward in the High-level Panel Report.

Greater involvement of those who contribute most

As regards the criteria for election to the Security Council, the Panel has made the extraordinary recommendation that a major criterion for election should be contributions to the regular budget of the United Nations and voluntary contributions of funds for carrying out peacekeeping and other UN activities. More specifically, the Panel has recommended that the General Assembly should now "elect Security Council members by giving preference for permanent or longer term seats to those States that are among the top three financial contributors in their relevant regional area, or the top three troop contributors from their regional area to United Nations peacekeeping missions." This will ensure "greater involvement in Security Council decisionmaking by those who contribute most."

This recommendation of the Panel is based on a complete misreading of Article 23 of the Charter and of the basis on which financial contributions are made to the United Nations. Financial contributions to the UN regular budget are made on the basis of a set of criteria relating to the capacity to pay. This contribution, which constitute a treaty obligation, are based on the principle of equity. The assumption is that no country pays more or no country pays less. All the countries pay equally based on the capacity to pay and, therefore, the question of rewarding those who pay more in absolute term but equal in relative term, does not arise. The authors of the report, *Renewing the United Nations System* have specifically recommended: "Member Govts. using arguments based on the notion of 'contributing most' and 'more' to the UN should cease to do so. Such argument is antithetical to the Charter as well as to the basic concept of democratic revenue raising.

"It has provoked difficulty in providing their due share in the countries where such language circulates and dangerous tension in the UN body politic" (page 209).

And so far as the voluntary contributions are concerned, there is no provision in the Charter for making such contributions. Such contributions benefit both who give them and those who receive them. There is also a reasonably valid point of view that those who give this kind of contribution benefit more than those who receive.

Apart from the illegality of this recommendation, its acceptance would have the effect of detracting from the principle of sovereign equality of member states enshrined in the Charter, eroding the democratic character of the UN, and introducing further hierarchy in the Security Council membership by giving greater say to militarily and economically powerful countries.

The Secretary-General also supports the recommendation of the High-level Panel regarding increasing the involvement in decision-making of those who contribute most to the United Nations financially, militarily and diplomatically, specifically in terms of contributions to the United Nations' assessed budget, participation in mandated peace operations, contributions to voluntary activities of the United Nations in the area of security and development, and diplomatic activities in support of the United Nations objectives and mandates.[18]

Peacebuilding commission

The Panel has recommended that the Security Council should establish under it a peacebuilding commission with the avowed objective of helping and avoiding state collapse or slide to war and assisting member states in their transition from war to peace. The Panel has suggested that the proposed commission should be able to identify countries which are under stress and under the risk of sliding towards state collapse; organise proactive assistance for preventing such an eventuality; and assist in planning for transition from conflict to post-conflict.

---

18. United Nations (2005). "In Larger Freedom: Towards Development, Security and Human Rights for All", *Report by Secretary-General of the United Nations*, New York.

The recommendation of the Panel has the effect of institutionalising continuing intervention in the domestic affairs of the developing member states of the United Nations. Under the mandate of identifying countries which are under stress and risk of sliding towards state collapse, any developing country can be kept under surveillance.

The act of identification is bound to be subjective and political factors, particularly the strategic and other interests of major powers, are likely to play a decisive role. In fact, this recommendation amounts to creating a new trusteeship system in the UN, not to assist in the emergence of colonial countries into independence as was the mandate of the UN Trusteeship Council, but as a means of bringing independent sovereign states from the developing world under a new form of colonisation.

In view of these considerations, it was indeed wise on the part of the UN Secretary-General, in his Report, to have deleted from the terms of the proposed Commission, the objective of helping to avoid a state collapse or slide to war. The Secretary-General's Report confines the function of the commission to helping and assisting member states in their transition from war to peace. It is with this limited mandate that the United Nations General Assembly has now established the Commission (vide General Assembly Resolution A/60/L40). The Commission has been envisaged as an inter-governmental advisory body which would martial resources and advise on and propose integrated strategies for post-conflict and peacebuilding recovery. It will have no early warning function.

The Commission has been set up by a joint resolution adopted both by the Security Council and the General Assembly. Along with a decision to establish the Commission, a decision has also been taken to establish a peacebuilding support office and a peacebuilding fund. Burundi and Sierra Leone are the first two countries to have been placed on the agenda of the Commission. Their inclusion on the agenda was recommended by the Security Council and these countries have themselves agreed to it.

It is problematic whether without tackling the issue of resources for the United Nations in a fundamental way, even this limited mandate for which the Commission has been created, can be fulfilled. The practice so far of United Nations' assistance to countries afflicted by war and conflict, has been to make an appeal to the IMF, World Bank and donor countries for providing resources, as UN's own resources for this purpose are very limited and, being of a voluntary nature, subject to the whims of the legislative and public opinion of major donor countries. So far as the international financial institutions are concerned, experience shows that adequate resources have never been forthcoming from them and whatever resources come, are subject to onerous and multifarious conditionalities. Therefore, the creation of yet another institution in the United Nations is not going to be of great help in assisting countries in their transition from war to peace. The assistance will continue to be inadequate, sporadic and designed to serve the strategic and other interests of major powers.

Moreover, peacebuilding, above all, calls for the resumption of the process of development. This calls for not only foreign assistance but also policy measures to be adopted by the war-ravaged countries as well as changes in those policies of major powers which adversely affect the development prospects of these countries. The effectiveness of the Peacebuilding Commission will also depend a great deal on the extent to which these policies of developed countries are brought on the agenda of the organisations of the UN system with a view to bringing about the desired changes in them.

Human Rights Council

The Panel regards the protection of human rights as "one of the central missions of the United Nations."[19] It has used some harsh words on the manner in which the Commission on Human Rights has been functioning. It has stated, "the Commission cannot be credible if it is seen to be maintaining double standards in addressing human rights concerns."[20] However, the solution to the problem suggested by the Panel, is rather facile. The central part of the Panel's recommendation for reforming the human rights mechanism

---

19. United Nations, *op. cit.*, (2004), p.88.

20. *ibid.*, p.89.

is to make it universal. It is difficult to see how this itself would have led to the removal of the malfunctioning of the Commission. In fact, the results could have been just the reverse, as it would have made it much more difficult for a decision to be taken in a Commission of universal membership.

The Secretary-General's Report puts human rights on a very high pedestal in the UN system. At two places in the Report, the Secretary-General suggests the eventual creation of a Principal Organ of the United Nations on Human Rights. However, as an interim measure he suggests the creation of a smaller Human Right Council to replace the then existing Commission on Human Rights. In order to make the proposed Human Rights Council more effective than the Human Rights Commission, the Secretary-General suggests that the Council be elected by the General Assembly (and not by the Economic and Social Council as was the case with the Human Rights Commission) by two-thirds majority of the members present and voting in the Assembly. A new Human Rights Commission, constituted largely on the basis of the Secretary-General's recommendations is now in place.

UN secretary-general's report

The Report of the Secretary-General steers clear of some of the highly controversial and contentious concepts and suggestions in the High-level Panel's Report. For example, the Secretary-General's Report does not endorse the idea that the UN system is basically a security system. It lays considerable emphasis on the UN's role in the economic, social, cultural and humanitarian fields. The very title of the Secretary-General's Report constitute a denial of the false assumption made by the Panel regarding the true nature of the UN system. The balance is restored further by quoting Charter provisions relating to development and by a more extensive discussion of the issues of development.

Secretary-General's Report also leaves out a number of the suggestions made by the High-level Panel, for the creation of new bodies to strengthen the Security Council at the cost of the other permanent organs of the United Nations. Among others, the Report drops the idea advanced by the High-level Panel, of discussing inter-relationship between the major variables of the world economy, in an expanded G-20 at the Summit level; and instead suggests that the ECOSOC should serve as the high-level development cooperation forum, meeting bi-annually for this purpose.

In spite of the above positive aspects, the overall thrust of the Secretary-General's Report is not very different from that of the Report of the High-level Panel. Like the Panel's Report, the underlying purpose behind the Secretary-General's Report is also to make the United Nations acceptable to the major powers, particularly the United States. It is, therefore, not surprising that the reform agenda in the Secretary-General's Report is essentially that of these powers.

Like the Panel's Report, the Secretary-General's Report also completely ignores the systemic problems confronting the UN system. It also ignores the structural problems of the world economy and international economic relations. It makes no effort to restore to the United Nations the functions it has lost to the World Bank, IMF and the WTO. Though a lot of space has been devoted to economic issues in the Secretary-General's Report, there are no specific suggestion or idea which represents an advance from the position reached years ago. For example, on the financing for development, all that the Secretary-General's Report does is to refer to the Monterrey consensus.

Besides, like the High-level Panel, the Secretary-General asserts that the MDGs now serve as a common policy framework for the entire UN system and indeed for the broader international development community. The MDGs have virtually replaced the earlier development consensus and the traditional issues of North-South dialogue.

World summit outcome: the general assembly resolution 60/1

In the negotiations on the reform package at the last session of the General Assembly, the developing countries were once again on the defensive. They had not placed before the General Assembly any blueprint or agenda of their own to strengthen multilateralism and reverse the trend of the all round decline and decay of the United Nation's system. Since they were negotiating on an agenda designed essentially to make the UN more palatable to major powers, they saw their main task to be one of damage control. In this they succeeded in some measure. They managed to prevent the inclusion in the final text of any reference to 'imminent attack' as a justification for the use of force in self-defence under Article 51. They also succeeded in keeping out of the text any reference to the proposal by both the Panel and the Secretary-General to involve in the decisionmaking in the Security Council, those who contributed most to the organisation financially, militarily and diplomatically.

The developing countries, however, had to concede their ground on one or two very important issues in order for the General Assembly to reach a consensus. The most important concession is the endorsement, in the resolution, of the concept of international community's 'responsibility to protect' populations from genocides, war crimes, ethnic cleansing, etc. It has been accepted in the resolution that in such situations, the Security Council can take action including military action. It has also, by implication, been accepted that such action can be taken in the event "national authorities are manifestly failing to protect their population ...". The above stipulation has, however, been qualified to some extent. Instead of stating that the international community has the 'responsibility to protect', the text says that it has the responsibility to 'help to protect'. The text also provides for the Security Council to take collective action in such situations on a 'case-by-case' basis. This carries the implication that it cannot act on the strength of any presumed new criterion or principle.

The developing countries have also gone along with the Secretary-General's proposal for establishing a Peacebuilding Commission and a Human Rights Council. The idea of a Peacebuilding Commission in any case had mustered the support of a majority of the developing countries, particularly from Africa, even before the commencement of the General Assembly, because these countries saw in it an opportunity to receive more aid.

There is a distinct attempt in the text to dilute the dominant status accorded to the MDGs in the United Nations system. The text states that other goals and objectives agreed at major UN conferences and summits are also important. In one of the paragraphs there is a reference to "internationally agreed goals and objectives, including the Millennium Development Goals."

The resolution is studiously silent on some of the important issues which figured in the negotiations. This is perhaps because of lack of agreement among the developing countries themselves on these issues. For example, the resolution is completely silent on nuclear disarmament. It is also highly circumspect in approaching any consensus on any of the different approaches and choices suggested for expanding the membership of the Security Council. The Resolution only commits the member states to continue their efforts to achieve a decision on this issue.

Overall, the outcome of the latest round of the effort to reform the UN system is rather meagre and limited. It falls far short of the high expectations aroused during the course of the consideration of this subject over the last three years. All that the Secretary-General and optimists are claiming as achievements are the establishment of the Peacebuilding Commission, Human Rights Council, the Democracy Fund and the Peacebuilding Fund. However, the major powers have not taken the agreement reached in the Resolution as the last word. They are still pursuing their inexhaustible agenda for reforms and the US has threatened to withhold its contributions to the UN in case more reforms of its choice are not carried out.

V. India's role in UN reforms

India's role in UN reforms has, to a large extent, depended on India's general attitude towards the United Nations. This general attitude has undergone change over time; and so has India's earnestness and zeal for and its active role in reforming the UN.

India started with an idealistic approach towards the United Nations. The UN was viewed as the chosen instrumentality of humankind for preserving and advancing peace, fostering cooperation and promoting economic development and progress. Pt. Jawaharlal Nehru who, more than any one else, shaped and piloted India's foreign policy in the early post-independence period, perceived the UN as the embryonic form of a world government. In several of his speeches and broadcasts extending up to the last year of his life in 1964, he articulated the dream of building a world government on the foundations of the United Nations. He took initiatives in the UN whenever he perceived an imminent threat to peace and security, particularly during one of the peak periods of the Cold War in the early 1960s and following the resumption of nuclear tests in 1954.

Soon after Nehru's death, India's idealistic view of the UN started yielding ground to a realistic view of the world body. In the later years of his stewardship of India's foreign policy, Nehru started getting disillusioned of the UN and moderated his high hopes from the organisation. Of course, the experience of the UN's handling of the Kashmir issue was an eye opener. At the same time, Nehru was greatly concerned about the arms race among the major powers, particularly the nuclear arms race. Even then he did not lose faith in UN, but he thought that halting the nuclear arms race and general disarmament was a precondition for the UN to develop into a world government.

In spite of this general shift towards a realistic view of the UN, India continued to persist with its idealistic approach so far as UN activities in the economic field were concerned. India continued to take initiatives, and even assume a leadership role, in strengthening and expanding the United Nations to enable it to discharge its role as a purveyor of developments in the world economy and international economic relations, for maintaining surveillance over the macroeconomic policies of major economic powers, for setting norms, standards, rules and regulations and for laying down principles governing international economic relations and devising frameworks for undertaking commitments and being accountable for their implementation. The most comprehensive among such frameworks was the International Development Strategies adopted by the UN for the 1970s. If UN activities and achievements in all these areas are viewed in totality, it will appear that in the economic realm the UN was functioning as though it was a world government.

This golden period of UN development cooperation came to an end by the mid-1970s when ensued the process of the decline of the UN. By that time, India's realistic approach to UN acquired greater salience. Like other developing countries, India also got reconciled to the trend of the continuing erosion of the role and functions of the UN.

In adopting such a realistic approach, India was very much influenced by its domestic situation, its position in the South Asian region and the general political condition prevailing in the region, in which India's relationship with Pakistan was a key factor. Because of its military, economic and technological superiority in the region, India believed that its interest in the region would be best served by bilateralism rather than through multilateralism under the United Nations.

The presence of a hostile neighbour, that is Pakistan, with which India has fought three declared wars, one undeclared war and a long proxy war which is still continuing, has also considerably influenced India's attitude towards the United Nations. Pakistan has made the solution of the Kashmir problem a precondition for having normal relations with India and has not given up resort to force as a means of solving this problem. Till recently, Pakistan was insisting that the only way to solve the problem was to implement the past UN resolutions on Kashmir. Pakistan has also a record of wanting to get the UN involved at the slightest of provocation on the line of control or in the Indian State of Jammu and Kashmir. This situation has been an important factor accounting for India's preference for bilateralism and aversion to UN activism in the region.

Finally, the problems that India has been facing in maintaining domestic peace and harmony have also shaped its attitude towards UN. These problems include rise of ethnic aspiration often taking the form of violence and insurgencies, providing adequate security and equitable economic opportunities to the minorities and mitigating the sufferings of the marginalised groups. There have been complaints of violations of human rights in the manner in which some of these problems have sometimes been sought to be solved. India regards these problems as falling within its domestic jurisdiction and does not want to be accountable in this regard to any outside body or agency, including the United Nations. That is the reason why India, for a long time, was not in favour of strengthening the human rights machinery of the United Nations. It also took India a long time in acceding to the Convention on Civil and Political Rights and that on Economic, Social and Cultural Rights. That is also one of the reasons why India has never agreed to the notion of self-determination of a part of a sovereign territory and has insisted that this concept applies only to territories under foreign occupation. The conditions prevailing in the region also explain at least in part India's non-acceptance of the full jurisdiction of the world court.

Regional factors partly account for India's strong traditional opposition to the concept of intervention in the domestic affair of the member states of the UN on the humanitarian ground. India had no doubt accepted the *fait accompli* in this regard and had gone along with UN's involvement in domestic affairs on a case-by-case basis. But it never accepted the principle of UN intervention on humanitarian ground. This position has apparently changed with India's endorsement of the General Assembly Resolution of 60/1 of September 2005, which provides a legal basis to the concept of 'responsibility to protect'. India was obliged to accept the resolution because of the concerted effort by major powers and the UN Secretary-General to build a consensus on it and because a majority of the developing countries were unwilling or unable to take a strong position against it.

Regional and domestic situations are also largely responsible for India not being inclined to favour proposals intended to enhance the capacity of the United Nations to intervene in different parts of the world. India, therefore, had reservations on the proposal for the creation of a rapid deployment force for the United Nations.

Since this proposal never came to the stage of a formal debate in the UN, India did not have to express its reservations publicly. However, the fact that it never made public statement in favour of it, speaks volume about its apprehensions regarding it.

Nor has India shown any great enthusiasm for strengthening the UN capacity by giving it access to new predictable sources of financing. It never came out openly in favour of any form of international taxation. Indian representatives never took a strong stand in support of the Tobin Tax because of the Finance Ministry's objection to it on the totally mistaken and unwarranted ground that it would discourage the flow of private capital. In taking this view, the Finance Ministry apparently ignored that the proposed tax was confined to speculative transactions of capital for making quick bucks, and did not apply to its flow for investment purposes and that incentives for capital to flow are driven by other powerful factors which can easily overcome the nominal tax proposed by Professor James Tobin, on speculative flows of capital.

India also did not show any enthusiasm for the proposal made from several quarters, to put a ceiling on an individual member's contribution to the assessed budgets of the UN organisations at 10 to 12 per cent of the total budget and call upon medium economic powers like India, to enhance their contributions to these budgets in order to compensate for the loss of revenue resulting from the imposition of the ceiling.

India in collaboration with other developing countries played an active role in stalling the moves of developed countries during the 1960s and the early 1970s, for UN reforms designed mainly to curtail some programmes and shift activities covered under the regular budget, to financing by voluntary contributions. During this period, India and other developing countries also succeeded in creating new organisations within the UN and thereby vastly expanding its activities.

From the mid-1970s onwards, the resistance of the developing countries to the reform offensive of developed countries started wavering. This was largely because of the significantly increased vulnerability of these countries, particularly following the twin crises of debt and development of the early 1980s. Soon thereafter, these countries started coming, one by one, under the surveillance of the IMF and World Bank under the structural adjustment programmes imposed on them. They then started going along with UN reforms pressed forward by major developed countries. India was no exception to this trend, even though it was less vulnerable than most other developing countries. In fact, India joined and played an active role in some of the panels established by the UN Secretary-General for discussing reform proposals and proposing reform packages. Sensing that there was no alternative, India did not want to get isolated and, therefore, joined the mainstream, in the drive for UN reforms.

One of the important moves of developed countries in the early 1980s was to curtail the negotiations role of the principal economic bodies of the UN. To this end, they suggested that the final outcome of discussion in a UN forum should take the form of Chairperson's summary instead of being a negotiated text. The developing countries including India, got reconciled to this position as well as to the trend of the voluntarisation of UN funding. In a situation of extreme economic distress, the majority of the developing countries attached great importance to UN assistance for development, irrespective of the form—whether through assessed budgets or as voluntary contributions—in which the assistance came.

After the end of the Cold War, reform proposals once again came to the top of the UN agenda. One of the most important among these proposals was the expansion of the membership of the Security Council. India did not take any major initiatives nor did it present any blueprint of its own on UN reforms, in an attempt to reverse the negative trends of the 1980s and regain the ground lost during that period. From the early 1990s onwards, India's sole objective in the context of the new wave of reforms, was to become a permanent member of the Security Council. A comprehensive offensive was launched for this purpose both within the UN as well as bilaterally. Inclusion in the joint statements issued at the end of the visits of Indian leaders to foreign countries and *vice versa*, of an assurance to support India's candidature for the permanent membership of the Security Council, became an index of the success of those visits. For over a decade and a half, India went on collecting such testimonials which by now must amount to an impressive number.

Preparatory to and during the last summit session of the General Assembly, India single-mindedly pursued its objective of getting a decision favourable to it, taken by the General Assembly on the question of the expansion of the membership of the Security Council. Its exclusive concentration was to get a broadest possible consensus on a possible GA resolution on the subject. In the process, India completely ignored the other proposals for reform suggested by the Secretary-General. In any event, India was not among the frontline states opposing those proposals, most of which were not in the interest of developing countries. This was because India did not want to alienate major developed countries which were pushing for these reforms, nor the Secretary-General whom they were using as their instrument for this purpose, nor the vast number of developing countries which had fallen in for some of the proposals. For fulfilling its ambition for a permanent seat in the Security Council, India needed the support of all these countries as well as of the Secretary-General. Thus, India failed in a historic moment to discharge its responsibility for halting and reversing the long continuing decline of multilateralism under the UN.

As it happened, India's ambition to become a permanent member of the Security Council remained unfulfilled. This was not because of anything wrong with the strategy India adopted for pursuing its candidature. India's strategy to go in for a vote in the General Assembly on the basis of a resolution which ruled out rotation of the seats of permanent members and which provided for decision to be taken by voting in the General Assembly and not by regional groups, offered the best if not the only chance of its becoming a Permanent Member. This will remain the best route in future also. It is only through this route that India can capitalise on the support it has garnered for its permanent membership of the Security Council. However, there was no need for India to have become a prisoner of its pursuit for the permanent membership of the Security

Council. There was no compelling reason for India to have willfully spurned whatever chances there were for India to contribute to the resurrection of the UN at the present critical juncture by proposing the kind of reforms outlined in section III of this chapter.

Bibliography

"An Agenda for Democratisation", 1996, a report submitted by the UN Secretary-General.

Dubey, Muchkund (2005). "Multilateralism Besieged", *Indian Journal of International Law*, Vol.45 No.2, April-June, New Delhi.

————. (2005). "Comments" on the *Report of the High-Level Panel on Threats, Challenges and Change, What UN for the 21st Century? A New North-South Divide*; South Centre, Geneva, June.

————. (2005). "Comments" on the *Report of the High-Level Panel on Threats, Challenges and Change*, also in *Reforming the United Nations for Peace and Security*, Yale Center for the Study of Globalization, March.

9

India and the United Nations

Chinmaya R. Gharekhan

"Over the decades, India has made an enormous contribution to the United Nations, through the efforts of its Government, and the work of Indian scholars, soldiers and international civil servants. India's has been one of the most eloquent voices helping the United Nations to shape its agenda on behalf of the developing world. And the experience and professionalism of its armed forces has proved invaluable, time and again, in UN peacekeeping operations—in which over a hundred Indian soldiers have given their lives." (UN Secretary-General Kofi Annan).

Much of the impetus for the creation of the United Nations Organisation came from the President of the United States Franklin D. Roosevelt in 1941, even before the United States formally entered the Second World War. The United Nations was conceived of as the successor to the League of Nations, although the League was formally dissolved only on 18 April, 1946 whereas the United Nations officially came into existence on 24 October, 1945. The League of Nations, which was established following the end of First World War in 1919, had the same basic objective as the United Nations, namely, to maintain international peace and stability. The resolution adopted at the final plenary meeting of the 21st session of the League's General Assembly explicitly recognised that the Charter of the United Nations had created an international organsation "for purposes of the same nature as those for which the League of Nations was established." The principal reason for the failure of the League was the refusal of the United States Senate to approve US membership in the League. This was due to strong isolationist sentiment and partisan politics in the country at that time. The opponents of the League strongly objected to Article 10 of the League Covenant which committed member states to protect the territorial integrity of all other member states against external aggression. Many American Congressmen felt that this article would oblige the United States to participate in wars which might be morally and ethically indefensible. The absence of the United States, together with the absence of the Soviet Union which did not join the League until 1932, crippled the League from its inception.

Another significant weakness in the Covenant of the League was the requirement of unanimity, with a few exceptions, for decisions in both the Council and the Assembly. Every member of the Council had veto power. Amendments to the Covenant required ratification by all the members of the Council as well as by a majority of the members of the Assembly. The provision regarding the composition of its Council was another factor contributing to its inefficient functioning. The Covenant provided that the Council was to be composed of the representatives of the 'Principal Allied and Associated Powers'—USA, the British Empire, France, Italy and Japan—the so-called permanent members, and four other members of the League who were selected by the Assembly from time to time. The Council, however, could be enlarged in both categories by the Council with the approval of the majority of the Assembly. The membership of the Council, consequently, fluctuated frequently. The number of permanent members, for example, increased from four in 1920 to six in 1934-35 and declined to two at the end of 1939.

The Allied powers began discussing the creation of a new world organisation well before the Second World War ended. The origin of the United Nations can be traced to the Atlantic Charter, which was a joint declaration issued by President Roosevelt and British Prime Minister Winston Churchill in August 1941. In January 1942, shortly after the United States entered the war, the governments of the US, Soviet Union, UK and China formalised the Atlantic Charter proposal. They, along with 22 other states, agreed to join forces against the Axis powers (Germany, Japan and Italy) and committed themselves to the establishment of United Nations after the war. Following a series of meetings among themselves, during the course of which they agreed on the broad framework of the future organisation, including the all important right of veto for themselves, the San Francisco Conference was held from April 25 until June 26, 1945. Delegations from 50 countries attended the conference. It might be of interest to point out that US and UK had to make an important concession to the Soviet Union. Stalin at first asked for seats for all 16 Soviet socialist republics, but was granted seats for Ukraine and Byelorussia as a compromise. United States had countered Stalin's radical proposal with a demand to allow all 50 American states into the United Nations! There was also difficulty regarding the seating of Argentina; Soviet Union strongly opposed Argentina's membership on the ground that Argentina had supported the Axis during the war. The other Latin American states refused to support Ukraine and Byelorussia unless Argentina was admitted.

Learning from President Wilson's experience, the Roosevelt Administration had undertaken a wide range of consultations with the Congress and the media. As a result, the Senate approved the Charter in July 1945 by a vote of 89 to 2 with 5 abstentions.

The Indian delegation to the San Francisco Conference was led by Sir C.P. Ramaswamy Mudaliar and included Sir Firoz Khan Noon and Sir V.T. Krishnamachari. The Indian delegation seems to have played a fairly active role during the discussion of the various provisions of the Charter including the Articles dealing with the composition and voting procedures for the Security Council. Its suggestion regarding the method for selection of the non-permanent members was somewhat strange. It proposed that the General Assembly should 'appoint' rather than 'elect' the six non-permanent members; the proposal found no takers. However, the criteria that the Indian delegation put forward for choosing the non-permanent members were sound and should be valid while considering addition to the category of permanent members in future. These were— relative population, industrial and economic capacity, contribution in armed forces, etc. The Indian delegation also suggested that, in addition to the six full non-permanent members, the General Assembly should also appoint six other states as observers who would participate in the deliberations of the Security Council, but without the right to vote. This suggestion too was not accepted. Sir Ramaswamy Mudaliar had spoken against the veto provision. However, he said that it was better to have an imperfect organisation than none at all. He went on to add that there should be no illusion with the thought that the United Nations could prevent wars between the great nations or between small nations, if the great powers were divided in their sympathies. He proved to be prophetic.

It was a miracle that agreement was reached on the Charter within a period of merely three months. If a similar exercise had to be undertaken today, even three years would not be enough. The San Francisco Conference succeeded, perhaps beyond the expectations of its sponsors, because it was held at a time when the Second World War was still in progress and because of an overwhelming desire among the peoples of the world to create an organisation which they hoped would avoid a third world war. The United Nations certainly has not let the international community down as far as this particular desire is concerned.

India became a founding member of the new Organisation well before it became a sovereign, independent state in August 1947. The Indian Government of the day had apparently decided to play an active role in the United Nations right from the first day of India's independence. Thus, for example, Mr. S. Sen, India's first Representative to the United Nations, conveyed to the American delegation in September 1947 India's disappointment at not having been included in the American slate for any office. The Indian delegation at one time even thought that Mrs. Vijayalakshmi Pandit could emerge as a compromise candidate for the President of the General Assembly, since there was a bitter contest between Brazil and Australia for the honour. More significantly, India put forward its candidature for election to the Security Council in 1947. At that time, the present system of well-defined geographical groups was not in place. India and Ukraine contested one seat. The vote went through as many as seven ballots in one single day, September 30,

1947. Ukraine scored better than India on all seven ballots, but fell short of the required 2/3rd majority. The deadlock was broken only on November 13, 1947 when India decided to withdraw her candidature. The Latin Americans supported Ukraine because they were miffed at Mrs. Pandit's criticism of Argentina on the question of Spain. Mrs. Pandit had also felt that the deadlock between India and Ukraine was not healthy for the work of the General Assembly.

When the General Assembly of the United Nations held its first plenary meeting in London on 10 January, 1946, there was an understandable atmosphere of mutual congratulations and a sense of achievement among the delegates. That, however, did not prevent the Soviet Union from insisting on presenting a candidate of its choice to become the President of the General Assembly, in opposition to the candidate proposed by Western countries. Mr. Spaak, the Foreign Minister of Belgium was proposed by the Western delegates. Mr. Gromyko, the Foreign Minister of the Soviet Union, proposed the name of Mr. Lie, the Foreign Minister of Norway. The matter could not be resolved through consultations and had to be settled by a secret ballot. Mr. Spaak got elected.

The assembled leaders made eloquent speeches and pledged their countries to work for the success of the new Organisation. Mr. Attlle, the British Prime Minister stated: "I have intense faith that we shall make the United Nations Organisation a success ... I think too that at the present time, the ordinary men and women in every nation have a greater realization of what is at stake. To make this Organisation a living reality, we must enlist the support, not only of Governments but of the masses of the people throughout the world. We desire to assert the pre-eminence of right over might and the general good against selfish and sectional aims."

The American Secretary of State, Mr. Byrnes, affirmed: "The functioning of the United Nations will depend not merely upon the words of its Charter or the rules of procedure we adopt here or upon the individuals we elect to hold office. It will depend upon the support it receives from the Governments and the peoples of the nations which have created it and which must sustain it. If the United Nations lives in the minds and hearts of our peoples, it will be able to adapt itself to the changing needs of a changing world and it will endure. If it lacks broad popular support, no Charter, however perfect, will save it."

Mr. Byrnes went on: "It is argued that the great States may abuse the rights given to them under the Charter. There are risks in any human undertaking. But I have confidence that the great states will respect their obligations." He quoted the following extract from President Truman's opening address at the San Francisco Conference: "While these great states have a special responsibility to enforce the peace, their responsibility is based upon the obligations resting upon all states, large and small, not to use force in international relations, except in the defence of law. The responsibility of great states is to serve and not to dominate the world." Mr. Byrnes added: "Great states, as well as small states, must come to view their power as a sacred trust to be exercised not for selfish purposes but for the good of all peoples." It is relevant to recall these words in the present international situation for the benefit of the countries whose representatives presented these sentiments.

India, too, approached its membership in the new Organisation with a sense of commitment and idealism. Sir Ramaswamy Mudaliar spoke with sincerity and conviction. "There have been cynics, there are cynics, pessimists, men who always foretell disaster, who even now, here and there, with bated breath perhaps, are speaking and thinking in terms of the possible futility of establishing an organisation like this. Let us ignore them, for when in the world, when in honest history, has a pessimist or cynic been able to do anything constructive or helpful for himself or for mankind? Let us put them aside, not indeed in a spirit of foolish optimism and having our head in the clouds and our feet in the air, but standing firmly on the ground, realising that the most realistic of all things is that peace is indivisible, realising that the most fruitful of all notions is that aggression never pays. Let us in that spirit try to organise and work this great United Nations and its organs so that humanity in the future, our children and our children's children yet unborn, may have the blessings of peace and of progress."

Sir Ramaswamy Mudaliar was particularly eloquent on the subject of atom bomb: "But if I may be permitted to say this, I should like to voice one thought that has been repeating itself in my brain. Time and again, ever since I heard of atomic energy and of the bomb that destroyed Hiroshima and Nagasaki, I have asked myself, and I ask myself again: Are we not being too much upset with this problem of atomic energy? Are we not forgetting something fundamental when we pay so much attention to the conditions that have been created, undoubtedly very difficult conditions, namely, the possibility of the world itself being wiped out, civilization being lost for ever, through the misuse of atomic energy? Standing here in this hall, consecrated by a great faith, speaking from a platform from which evil has been violently and boldly deprecated, I find it difficult to believe that all the horrors that have been predicted about the misuse of the atomic bomb are as great, or will come about, as has been suggested. To listen to some it would look as if a vital change, a change beyond all calculation, has been brought about by the discovery of atomic energy. Can atomic energy, if I may say so with great respect, bomb out the Sermon on the Mount or the Ten Commandments? Can the best designed U-boat sink the Holy Koran? Can the most heroic human torpedo put out of existence the most ancient of eastern scriptures, the Gita and the Kural? Is there anything that has been devised, or that could be devised which would obliterate forever the teachings of Buddha or the great tenets of Confucius? Are we not likely to lose all sense of proportion, even when we regard the main horror of the misuse of atomic energy, and when we fail to realize that beyond all these things there is a Power which looks upon people and upon nations and which, in its own inscrutable way, carries out its purposes for all eternity and to all eternity?"

It was partly because of the idealistic faith in the United Nations, and partly or perhaps largely because of the pressure of the then British Governor General of India, Lord Louis Mountbatten, that the Government of India decided to refer the issue of Pakistan's aggression against India in Jammu & Kashmir to the Security Council on 31st December 1947. By then India had been an independent nation for only 4½ months. Pakistan's aggression, initiated through the tribesmen of the North West Frontier Province, began in October. The Maharaja of the State of Jammu and Kashmir acceded to the Indian Union on 26 October. He appealed to India for help against the Pakistani aggression. According to most Indian military observers, India would have succeeded in throwing Pakistan's regular and irregular forces out of the whole of Jammu and Kashmir, had India not agreed to the cease fire demanded by the Security Council.

Be that as it may, the Indian Government, particularly Prime Minister Nehru, realised soon enough that it was futile to expect fairness or justice from the United Nations. It became obvious that the Security Council was a strictly political body and that decisions were taken by its members on the basis of their perspective of their national interest and not on the merits of any particular case. Even before referring the matter to the Security Council, Mr. Nehru had contemplated direct intervention across the international border into Pakistan in the exercise of the right of self defence guaranteed under Article 51 of the Charter. He had shared this particular thought with the British Prime Minister Mr. Attlee who lost no time in discouraging Mr. Nehru from pursuing the course of action being considered by him. In a message to Mr. Nehru on 29 December, 1947 Mr. Attlee wrote: "May I say in all frankness that I am gravely disturbed by your assumption that India would be within her rights in international law if she were to move forces into Pakistan in self defence. I doubt whether this is in fact correct juridically and, I am positive, it would be fatal from every other point of view. It would, in my opinion, place India definitely in the wrong in the eyes of the world; and I can assure you, from our experience on international bodies, that it would gravely prejudice India's case before UNO, if, after having appealed to the Security Council, she were to take unilateral action of this kind." Having in mind the humiliation suffered by British forces in the Afghan wars of the 19th Century, Mr. Attlee went on to offer a profound bit of advice to Mr. Nehru: "From our experience here, I think you are very optimistic in concluding that your proposed military action would bring about a speedy solution. On the contrary, all military history goes to show how difficult it is to deal with the tribes of the North West Frontier even when one is operating from secure bases." In the end, India did not pursue this particular option, primarily on the advice of the British Commander-in-Chief of Indian Army, in whose assessment Indian Army was not in a strong enough position to undertake such an operation.

India's contribution to peacekeeping

In spite of a sense of disillusionment with the United Nations in the early years of our independence, India never lost faith in the Organisation. India was committed to strengthening the United Nations and its capacity for the achievement of its purposes and principles as enshrined in the Charter. Since the paramount objective behind the establishment of the UN was, and remains, the maintenance of international peace and stability, India spared no efforts in contributing to its activities in this area. Time and again, India has risked the lives of its soldiers in peacekeeping operations of the United Nations, not for any strategic gain, but in the service of an ideal. India's ideal was and, remains, strengthening the world body, and international peace and security. More than 85,000 Indian troops, military observers and civilian police officers have participated in 42 out of the 60 peacekeeping missions established since the inception of the UN. 116 Indian soldiers have made the supreme sacrifice while serving with the UN and have been awarded the Dag Hammarskjoeld Medals. Indian troops have taken part in some of the most difficult operations. The professional excellence of the Indian troops has won universal admiration. India's most significant contribution has been towards peace and stability in Africa and Asia. It has demonstrated its unique capacity of sustaining large troop commitments over prolonged periods. Presently, India is ranked as one of the largest troop contributors to the UN. India has also offered one brigade of troops to the UN Standby Arrangements.

It is of interest to note that the Charter itself makes no mention of the concept of peacekeeping. The practice to deploy peacekeeping personnel in conflict situations emerged during the initial years of the United Nations which coincided with the commencement of the Cold War. The UN operation in Korea in the early 1950s, which was led by the United States of America, was a major military undertaking. Besides participating militarily in the form a medical unit, India provided a Custodian Force of more than 6,000 personnel for the Neutral Nations Repatriation Commission headed by Lt. General K.S. Thimayya. India also contributed to the preservation of peace in the Middle East. India provided an Infantry Battalion to the United Nations Emergency Force (UNEF); over a period of 11 years, from 1956 to 1967, more than 12,000 Indian troops took part in UNEF.

Even before achieving its independence from Belgium on 30 June, 1960, the Republic of Congo was faced with secessionist threats. The success of UNEF led the Security Council to agree to a request by the Congo in 1960 for assistance in ending secession and reunifying the country. The UN operation in Congo was unique in many ways. It was for the first time that the UN undertook an operation in an intra-state, rather than an inter-state conflict. The operation was successful in upholding the national unity and territorial integrity of the Congo. India's contribution to it was vital. 39 Indians lost their lives in the operation.

In recent times, one of the biggest peace keeping operations which was completed successfully was the UN operation in Cambodia. India provided an Infantry Battalion, military observers and a field ambulance unit. The UN operation in Somalia was one of the most difficult and challenging operations ever attempted by the UN. The Indian contingent, consisting of one brigade with stand-alone capacity had operational responsibility for 1/3rd of Somalia. In addition to preserving peace, the Indian contingent won the hearts and minds of the Somali people with its wide range of socially useful activities such as construction of wells, schools and mosques, running mobile dispensaries and relief camps as well as providing humanitarian relief to a large number of Somalis and their livestock. India provided an Infantry Battalion to the UN Assistance Mission to Rwanda which was not able to accomplish its objectives mainly because of the negative attitude of some major powers. India also made available sizeable contingents for UN operations in Mozambique, Angola, Liberia, Sierra Leone etc. India is once again actively engaged in helping UN operations in the Middle East by providing an Infantry Battalion to the UN Interim Force in Lebanon (UNIFIL). Currently, India is also participating in the UN Mission in Ethiopia and Eritrea (UNMEE). Recent peace keeping operations have tended to be multidimensional and include police monitors and election observers. India has contributed personnel in both these areas to UN operations in Cambodia, Mozambique, Angola, Bosnia, Western Sahara and Kosovo. India did not send troops to the UN Protection Force (UNPROFOR) in former Yugoslavia, but the first force Commander and Civilian Head of UNPROFOR, was Lt. General Satish Nambiar of India. Major General I.J. Rikhye served as Military Adviser to the Secretary General from 1960 to 1969.

India has considerable experience in demining activities and has made significant contribution to the demining work in Mozambique, Somalia, Angola and Cambodia.

The focus of attention and effort of the United Nations for the first three decades of its existence was devoted to dealing with 3 D's—decolonisation, disarmament and development.

Struggle against racism and colonialism

Long before India achieved independence in August 1947, the leaders of its nationalist movement, in particular Jawaharlal Nehru, had come to the conclusion that freedom, like peace, was indivisible. It was inevitable, therefore, for India to give a very high priority to the struggle against colonialism and racism as a member of the United Nations.

The purposes of the UN Charter include promotion and encouragement of the respect for human rights and for fundamental freedoms for all without distinction as to race, sex, language or religion. India was in the forefront of the struggle against colonialism, apartheid and racial discrimination. Mahatma Gandhi's struggle against injustice based on racial considerations had begun in South Africa where he spent 21 years fighting racism before returning to India. It was natural that India was the first country to raise the question of the discriminatory treatment of South Africans of Indian descent at the very first session of the UN General Assembly in 1946. It took 45 years of sustained domestic struggle in South Africa combined with international pressure, in which India played a leading role, for the apartheid regime of South Africa to repeal the laws that formed the legal basis of the hated system in 1991. South Africa's first non-racial general election was held in April 1994.

India's independence in 1947 was the harbinger of the emancipation of a large number of countries from colonial rule. The provisions of the UN Charter relating to Non-self Governing Territories were given a new thrust when the General Assembly adopted the historic Resolution 1514 (XV) in 1960 on the Declaration on the Granting of Independence to Colonial Countries and Peoples. This Declaration solemnly proclaimed the necessity of bringing a speedy and unconditional end to colonialism in all its forms and manifestations. In 1961, the General Assembly established a Special Committee on the implementation of the Declaration with the mandate to study, investigate and take action to put an end to colonialism. Mr. C.S. Jha was elected as the first Chairman of the Special Committee which came to be known as the Committee of 24, since it had 24 members. The Special Committee was eminently successful in largely achieving its mission. It conducted hearings and gave opportunity and hope to peoples around the world suffering under colonialism. A large number of individuals who appeared before the Committee as petitioners went on to become the leaders of their countries such as Julius Nyerere (Tanzania), Kenneth Kaunda (Zambia), Sam Nujoma (Namibia), Kwame Nkrumah (Ghana), Sekou Toure (Guinea), etc. Because of the close ties that India had established with these leaders during their freedom struggles, India was able to enjoy excellent relations with them.

One of the territories which had to be liberated from colonial rule was the tiny Portuguese enclave of Goa in India. Years of patient diplomatic efforts failed to persuade the dictatorial regime of Salazar in Lisbon to give up Goa and allow it to unite with India. Finally, in December 1961, the Indian Army, in a brief operation, rescued Goa from Portuguese rule and unified it with India. India's action was deplored by the US and some Western countries, but applauded by the rest of the world. India's Permanent Representative, C.S. Jha, famously stated in the Security Council on December 8, 1961: "It must be realized that this is a colonial question. It is a question of getting rid of the last vestiges of colonialism in India. That is a matter of faith with us. Whatever anyone else may think, Charter or no Charter, Council or no Council, that is our basic faith which we cannot afford to give up at any cost."

Disarmament

Since Independence, India has consistently pursued the objective of global disarmament based on the principles of universality, non-discrimination and effective compliance. Given the horrific destructive capacity of nuclear weapons, India has always believed that a world free of nuclear weapons would enhance both global security and India's own national security. Thus, India has always advocated that the highest priority be given to nuclear disarmament as a first step towards general and complete disarmament.

India is fully committed to the goal of curbing nuclear proliferation in all its aspects. It was at India's initiative that the item 'non-proliferation of nuclear weapons' was included in the agenda of the UN in 1964. In 1965, India along with other like-minded countries submitted a joint memorandum towards achieving a solution to the problem of proliferation; it included the conclusion of an international nuclear non-proliferation treaty. However, the NPT as it emerged from these negotiations, was flawed and discriminatory, seeking to create a permanent division between the nuclear 'haves' and 'have-nots'. It would be pertinent here to record the contribution made by Shri V.C. Trivedi who was India's Ambassador in Berne and concurrently entrusted with the responsibility of leading the Indian delegation at the crucial and complex negotiations on the conclusion of Non-Proliferation Treaty. It was Mr. Trivedi who brought out the discriminatory nature of the proposed Treaty and who first differentiated between 'vertical and horizontal proliferation' which provided the legitimate and widely recognised rationale for India's decision not to become a party to the NPT.

As early as 1948, India called for limiting the use of atomic energy for peaceful purposes only, and the elimination of atomic weapons from national armaments. India was the first country to call for an end to all nuclear testing in 1954. This was followed in subsequent decades by many other initiatives, for example, on the Partial Test Ban Treaty, and the call for international negotiations on nuclear non-proliferation. In 1978, India proposed negotiations for an international convention that would prohibit the use or threat of use of nuclear weapons. Another initiative in 1982 called for a 'nuclear freeze'—i.e. prohibition on the production of fissile material for weapons, production of nuclear weapons, and related delivery systems. At the special sessions of the United Nations General Assembly on disarmament, India put forward a number of serious proposals including Prime Minister Rajiv Gandhi's proposal in 1988 for a Comprehensive Plan for total elimination of weapons of mass destruction in a phased manner. It was a matter of regret that the proposals made by India along with several other countries did not receive a positive response and instead, a limited and distorted non-proliferation agenda, meant above all to perpetuate nuclear weapons, was shaped.

India was compelled by considerations of national security to establish and adopt a policy of keeping its nuclear option open while it continued to work for global nuclear disarmament. India's nuclear capability was demonstrated in 1974 when it detonated a peaceful nuclear explosive. India exercised an unparalleled restraint in not weaponising its nuclear capability. It is relevant to recall that during this period, when India voluntarily desisted from testing, over 35,000 nuclear weapons were developed through a series of tests by states possessing nuclear weapons. This had happened even as Article VI of the Non-Proliferation Treaty committed the Nuclear Weapons States, party to the NPT, to take steps in good faith for nuclear disarmament. In 1996, India was obliged to stand apart on the

Comprehensive Test Ban Treaty—CTBT—after having been actively engaged in the negotiations for two and a half years, because the issues of non-proliferation, global disarmament and India's concerns about her security and strategic autonomy were ignored.

India's continued commitment to nuclear disarmament and non-proliferation is clear from the voluntary measures announced by it after undertaking a limited series of underground nuclear tests in 1998. India remains committed to its voluntary moratorium on testing. India has declared that it will maintain a minimum credible nuclear deterrent and will not engage in an arms race. India has declared a no-first use doctrine. India is willing to strengthen this commitment by undertaking bilateral agreements as well as by engaging in discussions for a global no-first use agreement. India believes that a global no-first use agreement would be the first step towards the delegitimization of nuclear weapons. India is the only state possessing nuclear weapons to unambiguously call for a Convention to ban and eliminate nuclear weapons just as the Biological Weapons Convention and the Chemical Weapons Convention have banned the other two categories of weapons of mass destruction.

Nuclear disarmament and non-proliferation

In 1996, India along with the members of the Group of 21 countries submitted to the Conference on Disarmament (CD) a Programme of Action calling for a phased elimination of nuclear weapons (1996-2020). India has indicated its commitment to the establishment of an ad hoc committee in the Conference on Disarmament in Geneva to negotiate global nuclear disarmament. India is also the only state with nuclear weapons, which responded positively to certain aspects of the 8-nation initiative on disarmament, entitled *Towards a Nuclear Weapon Free World*, put forward in June 1998 by Brazil, Canada, Egypt, Ireland, Mexico, New Zealand, South Africa and Sweden. At the Non-aligned Summit in Durban, at India's initiative, the Non-Aligned Movement agreed that an international conference should be held, preferably in 1999, with the objective of arriving at an agreement, before the end of the millennium, on a phased programme for the complete elimination of all nuclear weapons. The call for the elimination of nuclear weapons has been reiterated by the Prime Ministers of India in their addresses to the UN General Assembly. India remains committed to cooperating with like-minded states to attain this goal. India also introduced a resolution at the 53rd Session of the General Assembly calling for reducing nuclear danger by de-alerting nuclear weapons.

Development

One of the fundamental purposes of the United Nations, enshrined in its Charter, is to "promote higher standard of living, full employment, and conditions of economic and social progress and development" (Article 53). Since its establishment 60 years ago, the UN has devoted its attention and resources to achieving these objectives. The UN concern with the development of developing countries or the least developed countries (LDCs) acquired urgency and momentum with the sharp increase in its membership as a result of the process of decolonisation in the decade of 1960s. With developing countries in a majority, the articulation of their concerns about economic development became items of high priority on the UN agenda.

Eminent Indians were associated with this process. Particular mention should be made of the contribution of Professor D.R. Gadgil and Dr. V.K.R.V. Rao. Professor Gadgil was associated with the estimation of the official development assistance required by the developing countries. He chaired the group of experts whose efforts triggered the negotiations that led to the acceptance of the norm of 1 per cent of national income of developed countries to be transferred to developing countries. Of this 1 per cent, 0.7 per cent was expected to constitute official development assistance. Dr. Rao was Chairman of the Sub-Commission on Economic Development which made a proposal called Special United Nations Fund for Economic Development (SUNFED), a conceptual forerunner of what finally took shape as United Nations Development Programme (UNDP) in the United Nations and as International Development Agency (IDA), the soft lending agency of the World Bank, an institution of which India was a major beneficiary until recent times.

The debates in the United Nations on developmental issues led to the promulgation of successive development decades, starting with the decade of 1961-1970 as the first development decade. The 1990s was the fourth and last such decade. Indian delegates played active and energetic roles in the formulation of the strategies for the development decades. A candid assessment of the development decades leads one to conclude that they did not make any material difference to the lives of people in developing countries. There were some successes in creating consciousness among developed countries about the problems and handicaps of developing countries. However, the target of 0.7 per cent of the national income of developed countries to be channeled into the official development assistance is nowhere near fulfillment except by the Scandinavian countries. It was, in fact, not realistic on the part of the developing countries to set such an ambitious target. Most developing countries lacked the capability to absorb and judiciously deploy such large resources for the alleviation of poverty of their peoples. During the Cold War period, there was perhaps some incentive for the rich countries to provide development assistance. As the former Secretary-General Dr. Boutros Ghali observed in his report entitled *An Agenda for Development*: "The competition for influence during the Cold War stimulated interest in development. The motives were not always altruistic, but countries seeking to develop could benefit from that interest. Today the competition to bring development to the poorest countries has ended. Many donors have grown weary of the task. Many of the poor are dispirited. Development is in crisis."

Developing countries now realise that they have to concentrate more on the reform of their domestic economic policies, restructure their economies, depend less on official aid and attract more foreign private capital. The post-Cold War situation has changed the earlier format of North-South issues. Nonetheless, the rhetoric about reducing poverty and ushering a more equitable world economic order continues. At the Millennium Summit in New York in September 2000, world leaders signed the UN Millennium Declaration pledging to meet time-bound and measurable targets to reduce deprivation by 2015. The Summit adopted eight Millennium Development Goals (MDGs).

In addition to adopting resolutions and declarations, the United Nations has a specific programme to extend assistance to developing countries to promote developmnt, reduce child mortality, combat HIV/AIDS, promote gender equality, empower women, etc. The UN system's annual expenditure for development programmes, excluding international financial institutions, exceeds US$ 10 billion. The largest of these programme is UNDP. India is one of the largest contributors to the core resources of UNDP as well as one of its major beneficiaries.

Reform of the United Nations

Any organisation, particularly if it is big and multinational in composition, has to continually adapt its structure as well as working methods in response to changing circumstances and global environment. The United Nations is no exception. Attempts to reform the United Nations have been made from time to time ever since its inception. Reform is a process and not an event.

The impetus for the current movement for UN reform came from the events of September 11, 2001 in New York and Washington DC. The President of the United States, in an address to the UN General Assembly a few days later, questioned the continued relevance of the United Nations in the changed circumstances. He said if the UN was to remain relevant, it had to respond to the threats and challenges facing the international community in the 21st Century. The Secretary-General established a High Level Panel on Threats, Challenges and Change which submitted its report in December 2004. The Panel examined the threats and challenges under six broad clusters—economic and social, inter-state conflict, internal conflict, nuclear, biological and chemical weapons, terrorism and trans-national organised crime. The Panel made over 100 recommendations. The Secretary-General presented his own report entitled *In Larger Freedom* in March 2005. In his own words, he limited himself: "To items on which I believe action is both vital and achievable in the coming months. These are reforms that are within reach—reforms that are actionable."

The High-Level Panel dealt at some length with the issue of terrorism. While some countries, especially India, have been the victims of terrorism for nearly two decades, the international community had to wait until the horrendous events of September 11, 2001 to focus its attention on this menace. There is no universal agreement even on what constitutes terrorism. The High-Level Panel suggested that terrorism would consist of any action if it is intended to cause death or serious bodily harm to civilians or non-combatants with the purpose of intimidating a population or compelling a Government or an international organisation to do or abstain from doing any act. The Secretary-General strongly urged world leaders to unite behind this definition of terrorism and to conclude a Comprehensive Convention on Terrorism. Regrettably, there was no consensus on the definition of terrorism at the World Summit in New York in 2005. Some countries insist that 'freedom fighters' should be exempted from this definition. However, there is now general acceptance that no action, whatever the cause, can justify killing or harming innocent civilians. India concurs with this concept.

The General Assembly has already implemented two important reform proposals. A Peace-Building Commission has been set up to help countries emerging after a prolonged internal conflict during the course of which they would have suffered immense damage to infrastructure besides human lives. India, by virtue of it being among the five largest troop contributing countries, would be a permanent member of the Peace Building Commission.

The other, significant reform adopted in the spring of 2006 is the formation of the Human Rights Council. Protection and promotion of human rights is one of the most important functions of the United Nations. Since adopting the Universal Declaration of Human Rights on 10th December, 1948, the United Nations has helped enact more than 80 comprehensive agreements on political, civil, economic, social and cultural rights. The United Nations has endeavoured to prevent genocide, combat torture and eliminate all forms of discrimination based on race, gender, religion or belief.

India took an active part in the drafting of the Universal Declaration on Human Rights. Dr. Hansa Mehta, a Gandhian social worker and leading educationist, led the Indian delegation and made significant contribution in the drafting of the Declaration. India is a signatory to the six core human rights covenants. Until recently, the United Nations machinery in the field of human rights consisted of the Commission on Human Rights (CHR) and the UN High Commissioner for Human Rights. During the Cold War era, the CHR frequently got bogged down in East-West confrontation. Each bloc sought to exploit the CHR in its ideological confrontation with the other. The non-aligned and developing countries, for their part, perceived the CHR as an instrument for the developed countries of the west to put pressure on them. This is not to deny that some developing countries indeed had a deplorable human rights record which they tried, often successfully, thanks to solidarity among them, from being discussed at the CHR. The new Human Rights Council has replaced the CHR. It is somewhat smaller in size than CHR—46 members as opposed to 53 in the CHR. The principal element of reform lies in the procedure for electing members of the Council. For the CHR, elections took place in the Economic and Social Council (ECOSOC). Thus, the CHR was a subsidiary organ of ECOSOC which had 54 members. The new Council will be elected directly by the General Assembly and the candidate countries must obtain absolute majority, i.e. majority of the total membership of the General Assembly, instead of a simple majority of members present and voting. Among all the countries which had to contest elections to the new Council, India obtained the highest number of votes.

Reform of the security council

The focus of the international community, however, was on the reform of the Security Council. At the time of the foundation of the United Nations, the Security Council had 11 members, 5 permanent and 6 non-permanent members elected for a 2 years' term. Even at that time, there was a proposal to fix the membership of the Security Council at 15, but it was not approved. The Security Council membership was increased to 15 in 1967. The additional members were all in the category of non-permanent members. The last few years have witnessed a sustained movement to enlarge the membership of the Council in both categories, permanent and non-permanent. The rationale for expanding the Council commands wide acceptance. There is a consensus that the Security Council must adequately reflect both the vast increase in the membership of the Organisation, i.e. from 51 in 1945 to 192 at present as well as the altered geopolitical and economic realities of the contemporary world.

In spite of India's disillusionment with the Security Council, India maintained its strong attachment to the United Nations. India sought membership of the Security Council as a non-permanent member at regular intervals. Until 1992, India served seven two-year terms on the Security Council at an average interval of six years. In 1996, however, India and Japan clashed for one seat on the Security Council. Japan won overwhelmingly by a margin of over 100 votes. Since then, India has not put forward its candidature for a non-permanent seat. It has been argued that since India is seeking permanent membership of the Security Council, it should not waste its energy on contesting a non-permanent seat.

In early 2005, India, Brazil, Germany and Japan formed an informal group which came to be known as G-4. These four countries were and are aspirants for permanent membership in the Security Council. The G-4 prepared a draft resolution in June 2005 proposing six additional permanent seats. Their efforts were fairly successful in that their draft resolution attracted nearly 35 co-sponsors, including France, a permanent member. However, there was a major weakness in their effort. They failed to win over the African group to their cause. The Africans supported the idea of expanding the membership in both categories but there was deep dissension within their ranks. Africa, like Latin America, does not have a single permanent member in the Security Council. Since there are more than twice as many African members in the UN as Latin American members, Africa demanded two permanent seats. This was conceded by G-4 and generally recognised as reasonable by others. There are, however, more than two countries in Africa who claim to be fully entitled to permanent membership. The

Africans have also been insisting as a matter of principle that the new permanent members should have the same rights and obligations as the existing permanent members. In other words, they are demanding veto rights for the new permanent members. No country, not even the Africans, have any illusion that the current five permanent members would ever agree to extend the veto privilege to anyone outside their exclusive club. The P-5, in fact, would prefer not to have any additional permanent member even without veto rights.

The campaign for expanding Security Council membership had gathered a great deal of momentum during the first half of 2006. Since then, some of the momentum has dissipated. Even the G-4 has had problems preserving unity among themselves. Japan, in particular, came to the conclusion that it stood the best chance of pushing its candidature if it disengaged from G-4. Japan was possibly encouraged in following an independent path by American statements to the effect that the United States would support Japan's candidature. Of late, Japan seems to have realised that, in fact, there was no possibility of it getting an endorsement of the General Assembly unless the aspirations of other groups were met at the same time. The campaign for reform of the Security Council will and must continue.

Conclusion

The peoples of the world, in whose name the United Nations has been founded, had great expectations of the Organisation. They believed in their simplicity and naive faith that the United Nations was an ideal, a perfect institution. They thought that their United Nations would right all wrongs, remove all injustices from the world, protect human rights of all, promote economic and social well-being especially among the deprived sections of humankind and, most importantly, promote or restore international peace and stability. The record of the United Nations in all these sectors is a mixed one. All its members profess deep commitment to the United Nations Charter. From time to time, the United Nations suffers from a loss of credibility in public opinion. In the decade of 1980s, the phrase 'retreat from multilateralism' was much in vogue. The military intervention by the United States and others in Iraq in the spring of 2003 had an extremely damaging impact on the credibility of the United Nations. According to a study conducted by the Pew Research Centre after the Iraq War, positive views for the United Nations dropped by 37 percentage points in Britain, 33 in Germany and 28 in France. Majorities were negative about the United Nations in Jordan, Italy, Lebanon, Brazil, Pakistan, Russia etc. In an unusual note of agreement, 63 per cent Israelis and 78 per cent Palestinians were negative about the United Nations. As of the time of writing this article, the image of the United Nations has taken another severe beating, following Israel's military intervention in Lebanon after the kidnapping of two of its soldiers by Hizbullah on July 12. Governments and peoples around the world have been shocked at the masterly inactivity of the Security Council and its failure to call for cessation of hostilities and ceasefire, even after more than three weeks of brutal warfare.

A less credible United Nations, however, does not necessarily mean a less relevant United Nations. The truth of the matter is that no country is prepared to give primacy to its commitment to the United Nations at the cost of its national interests. Membership in the multinational organisation does not prevent any nation from pursuing what it decides, unilaterally, to be its national interests. With all its faults and imperfections, the international community is better off with the United Nations than it would be without it. It has become a cliché to say that if there were no United Nations, one would have to be invented. The hard reality is that it would be impossible to invent a new United Nations in today's world. Sir Ramaswamy Mudaliar was right: "It is better to have an imperfect Organisation than none at all."

10

India and the Commonwealth
A legacy and an opportunity
Krishnan Srinivasan

Introduction

What is the Commonwealth? A well-kept secret, some might say! It can be admitted at the outset that its public profile, even by the standards of contemporary international organisations, is not high.

The Commonwealth is a voluntary association of independent states united by common purposes, and functions with a common language, English. With a staff of about 280 in London and a budget of about Pounds Sterling 35 million a year, the Commonwealth provides to its members various services covering political and economic consensus; trade, debt and investment advice; and demand-driven, cost, conditionality and repayment-free technical assistance.

The British Commonwealth started as a consultative group between the six 'white' self-governing dominions of the Empire in the early part of the 20th Century—Australia, Canada, Ireland, New Zealand, South Africa, and the United Kingdom; and turned out to be so durable that it now comprises 53 countries ranging in size from the micro-state Tuvalu with a population of 10,000 to India with a population of over one billion. Obviously, all member countries see different kinds of benefit accruing from their membership of the Commonwealth, but what is apparent is that since its numbers had grown from a handful to 54,[1] the association retains a considerable allure. Of countries clearly eligible for membership, only Ireland and Burma (now Myanmar) have stayed out of the modern Commonwealth. Burma never joined it and Ireland, only a few days before the 1949 Nehru formula, left the Commonwealth on the issue of allegiance to the Crown. Fiji, Pakistan and South Africa, who left the association in various ways and for various reasons, have all restored their membership at the earliest opportunity. So one day may Zimbabwe. The total population of the Commonwealth is nearly one-third of the world's population, but now including only six per cent from the developed countries of Anglo-Saxon origin. The change from a monoethnic to a multiracial association is therefore self-evident. Britain is without doubt the key-stone member of the Commonwealth, and the historical *raison d'être*, although in 1949 the Commonwealth lost the adjective 'British' and in 1965 the setting up of the Commonwealth Secretariat served to diminish Britain's influence even further;— that was in fact the objective of its establishment. Up to that time, Britain's Commonwealth Relations Office had been responsible for the convening, organisation, and record-keeping of meetings, a role which was then taken over by the neutral Secretariat consisting of officials from across the wide racial spectrum of the new Commonwealth. Because of the growing indifference over the years of the British government and public, despite London being the main contributor (to the tune of 30 per cent) to Commonwealth budgets, the Commonwealth's heartbeat is no longer in the United Kingdom but is perhaps to be found among the smaller countries of the association. This is somewhat ironic, since when the first independent small state, Cyprus, wanted to join the Commonwealth in the early 1960s, it was opposed by countries like Canada, who preferred a two-tier Commonwealth—the inner tier of influential countries, and an outer tier of weaker and smaller states with something equivalent to observer status. In the end, however, the principle of the sovereign equality of states prevailed. Small

---

1. Fifty-four is the highest number reached in Commonwealth membership. The number is now 53 with the withdrawal of Zimbabwe in 2003.

countries, with a population of one and a half million or less, a somewhat arbitrary Commonwealth definition of 'small', are now a majority in the membership.

There are six monarchies in the Commonwealth, and the British monarch is by common consent the symbol of the community, though the number of republics is almost double that of the realms of which the Queen is still the Head of State. The Commonwealth is a continuing bond between the independent ex-colonies and the former metropolitan country, but it is one that is apparently worth emulating if one looks at the background to the French Union, the Indonesian-Dutch Union, the Organisation Internationale de la Francophonie (OIF) or the Community of Portuguese Speaking People (CPLP). The Commonwealth has been the inspiration for t..ose bodies, but is very different from the Francophonie and the Lusophonie in three ways; it is bigger in size; it does not propagate language or culture; and it makes no presumption of a central role for the former imperial metropolitan country.

The Commonwealth is the only intergovernmental group that survived the Second World War, having begun long ago in a formal sense in the 1920s, and with Prime Ministers Conferences going back even further to the end of the 19th Century. Fifty-seven years on from the London Declaration of 1949, the Commonwealth is one of the biggest non-regional groupings in the world, with its members sharing common ideals and subscribing to a current orthodoxy to which all the members present their policies as broadly conforming. The Commonwealth has no written constitution and makes its decisions by consultation, convention and consensus. And yet despite, or probably because of, this feature, it has survived over the years. The lack of "tying up" that Pandit Jawaharlal Nehru referred to in 1956 is still there. No one could justifiably claim that Commonwealth members are uniformly perfect in their good governance and value-systems, but the Commonwealth has principles which all members are ready to profess and like to appear to be practising. Moral suasion and peer pressure in the Commonwealth are the main instruments at the disposal of the organisation.

The Commonwealth is not all about big government machines. It has a wide civil society network of NGOs, and makes awards for sportsmen, scientists, writers, poets, musicians and artists. The Commonwealth brings people together, though it has to be accepted that the vast majority of Commonwealth citizens belong to the Commonwealth without being aware of it. It has become a comfortable pair of old shoes that we take for granted, though the Commonwealth accounts for 5 out of 10 of the world's fastest growing economies, approximately 20 per cent of world exports and 14 per cent of the world's GDP, and members conduct 20 per cent of their trade and investment relations with each other.

There is no great virtue in today's world in performing good works anonymously, but that is the fate of organisations like the Commonwealth which remain unsung because the benefits and achievements of the association are on a modest scale and are largely taken for granted. There can be an argument about the relevance of the Commonwealth in the world today, how it may be losing its way, and whether it should or should not exist—and these aspects should certainly be debated, as they should indeed in regard to every international organisation to which India belongs—but that is a debate for another day. Let us for the moment consider the Commonwealth at its own self-estimation, and examine the cost-benefit ratio in this organisation for Indian membership.

Of the 1.8 billion people in the Commonwealth, 1.1 billion—that is 60 per cent—are located in India alone. Apart from this, the next two most populated members are Bangladesh and Pakistan. The centre of the Commonwealth's demographic gravity is therefore squarely in South Asia. But what has the Commonwealth contributed to India and *vice versa*?

Early beginnings

After the Second World War, Britain had an agenda for the Commonwealth. Britain could only match its two big partners in world affairs, the United States and the Soviet Union, by creating a Commonwealth third force. Britain aspired to be at the hub of three interlocking circles; the Commonwealth, the Atlantic Alliance, and Europe. Empire and the Commonwealth provided a hope of the same vitality in peace as previously shown in war, and were regarded as a possible key to Britain's future international status. Wartime cooperation between the United Kingdom and the dominions had led to notions of Commonwealth solidarity and the challenge was to make the new post-war Commonwealth a close-knit unit with a common foreign policy and integrated defence, transforming the hitherto informal partnership into a cooperating bloc of associated states. There was also the need to reconcile the position of the Crown and the question of allegiance, so far the entrenched principle, with the expressed desire of some new aspirants for membership like India and Burma to acquire republican status. Finally, there was the task of absorbing the new members without breaking up the traditional practice of informal consultation and cooperation which was a characteristic of the Imperial Conferences and Prime Ministers' Meetings.

The Second World War had destroyed the old patterns of politics in the Indian sub-continent and Burma. The United Kingdom could not reassert its power through garrisons and administrators due to its acute shortage of manpower, a need to curtail foreign expenditure, and crises elsewhere such as in Palestine. As a result, it had neither the will nor the means. Viceroy Curzon had said, "as long as we rule India, we are the greatest power in the world. If we lose it, we shall drop straight away to a third rate power."[2] With the transfer of power to India and Pakistan, the strategic core of the Empire, along with three quarters of its population, were indeed gone.

Before Independence, Jawaharlal Nehru was disconcerted by unsolicited proposals from London about Privy Council appeals, designs for a flag, and so forth, and before he became India's first Prime Minister, he informally advised Mountbatten that emotionally and psychologically, India could not be a member of the Commonwealth. This reflected the displeasure of many members of the Indian National Congress Party at any continuing connection

---

2. Dilks, David (1969). *Curzon in India*, Vol. 1, Rupert Hart-Davis, London, p. 113.

with Britain because of London's plans for partition. Pleas by Attlee and Mountbatten to steer Nehru away from a republican path were unavailing, and the British Cabinet had to fight opposition from their own legal and foreign office officials who persisted in insisting on the traditional principle of allegiance to the Crown as a pre-requisite for Commonwealth membership.

But India was always to be an exception because of the emotional factor of the Indo-British relationship. Britain feared that an India outside the Commonwealth might build an anti-western bloc of Asian States, whereas inside the association, there was the asset of India as a large creditor, a trading partner and a zone of stability in a continent where communism was seen as threatening alarming incursions. In March 1948, Attlee wrote to Nehru arguing that joining the Commonwealth would mean adherence to certain values, democratic institutions, the rule of law and toleration, making up a 'way of life', which led to a sense of community. Such a philosophical and idealistic approach appealed to Nehru, though his specific ideas of the value of the Commonwealth connection to India were naturally rather different; to offset the factor of the Soviet Union which was unpredictable and initially hostile, to counter-balance growing dependence on the USA, and to deny Pakistan the advantage of an Indian refusal. Within his Congress Party Nehru argued that there were advantages for India in membership; that it would promote world peace, and that it did not imply alignment with any military bloc or any sacrifice of full independence. Nehru was to say in 1948, "... there is great scope for the Commonwealth ... its very strength lies in its flexibility and its complete freedom."

In 1947, the British government declined to allow Burma to become a republic and seek Commonwealth membership, and in 1948, no attempt was made to prevail on republican Ireland to remain in the Commonwealth. But Mountbatten said when he arrived in India as Viceroy that keeping India in the Commonwealth was "the single most important problem", and Britain relaxed the criteria remarkably quickly for India. Acceptance of India's republican status was a self-conscious and deliberate act by London for the preservation of British influence. Many leaders of India's pre-war and wartime national movement had expected independent India not to join the Commonwealth, but India's leaders were prepared to trust in Pandit Nehru's judgement in international affairs.

The modern Commonwealth

In 1949, India was to become a republic the following year, and it is hard to imagine today, nearly six decades later, that the matter of allegiance to the British Crown could have been such a passionate issue with the public and politicians, especially from the old dominions, as to threaten to abort the creation of a new multiethnic association of nations. And it was not only, for the South Asians, a question of fealty. There were the highly sensitive issues of de-colonisation and sovereignty. Would India, less than two years independent, wish to remain in a group which to some political circles still smacked of empire and neo-colonialism? And there was another important factor. The world at that time was beginning to coalesce into two major contesting blocs, militarily, politically and ideologically. At the Prime Ministers' Meeting of 1949, India was the only country out of the eight which was not ideologically aligned to the West in the context of the looming Cold War. This situation was to continue for nearly a decade until Ghana joined the association. It could not have been very comfortable for India, confabulating with the others in the armchairs of No. 10 Downing Street. The old white dominion members considered a two-tier Commonwealth, the first-tier in which security and sensitive issues would be freely discussed; and a second, comprising the less reliable companions. The project did not fly, though it is a fact then as now, that Australia, Canada, New Zealand and the United Kingdom consult closely in separate discussions to which the non-white members are not privy.

1949 was the year which future historians may well describe as a turning point, when the glow of victory in the Second World War, towards which India had contributed so massively in men and material, was replaced by the 40-year Cold War. NATO was launched in Washington in April that year. The Soviet Union detonated its first atomic device and ended the American monopoly.

On 1 October, Mao Zedong proclaimed the People's Republic of China. In April 1949 another, and somewhat more benevolent, event occurred; the Commonwealth ceased to be the 'British Commonwealth', and the eight members, the United Kingdom, Canada, Australia, New Zealand, South Africa, India, Pakistan and Sri Lanka (then Ceylon) declared themselves to be free and equal members of the Commonwealth of Nations, the British Commonwealth and the Commonwealth. All three formulations were used in the London Declaration, and Attlee told members of the House of Commons to use whichever one they liked best. The modern Commonwealth came into being, and this membership remained constant until Ghana joined it in 1957.

The Final Communiqué of the Commonwealth Prime Ministers in 1949, of only one printed page – unlike the verbosity of today— came to be known as the London Declaration. It specifically referred to India's intention to become a sovereign independent republic, to continue its full membership of the Commonwealth, and its acceptance of King George VI as the symbol of the free association of the member nations and as such the head of the Commonwealth. The issue of India as a republican member of the Commonwealth was in fact the sole subject of discussion at that meeting of the Prime Ministers. In a broadcast on his return to India, Jawaharlal Nehru sought to counter possible criticism by saying that he had "looked to the interests of India, for that is my first duty." And in a speech to the Constituent Assembly, he spoke of the need to touch upon the world problems "in a friendly way and with a touch of healing; and the fact that we have begun this new type of association with a touch of healing will be good for us, good for certain other countries, and I think, good for the world." The Constituent Assembly then endorsed the London Declaration by an overwhelming majority. In the event, Commonwealth membership proved to be compatible, even complementary, with what was soon to be enunciated as India's independent and non-aligned foreign policy.

Cooperation between Pandit Nehru and British Prime Minister Clement Attlee had produced a splendid irony relating to the British

Crown's role in the new Commonwealth and an improbable but fascinating solution—though King George VI confided to Attlee that he hoped there would not be many more republics in the Commonwealth! And during a state dinner the King leaned over and quipped to Nehru, "Mr. Nehru, you have reduced me to an as such!" Nehru's flexibility can be credited with the creation of an entire international organisation. Nehru was no monarchist; yet he sent a telegram on the death of the King in February 1952 to Queen Elizabeth when she was still on safari in Kenya, felicitating her on her accession and describing her as the head of the Commonwealth, thereby finessing the issue of the King's successor and her connection with the Commonwealth even before his colleagues, the other Commonwealth Prime Ministers, were to assemble a year later to consider the implications of the King's death.

The Suez Crisis in 1956 took place, to say the least, with negligible Commonwealth consultation by Britain, and voices were again raised in India to leave the Commonwealth. A resolution presented by Shri Mazumdar of the Communist Party in the Rajya Sabha in December 1956, declaring membership of the Commonwealth to be incompatible with the five principles of peaceful co-existence, was defeated. Pandit Nehru said in concluding the debate that "while normally I would have opposed such a resolution [to leave the Commonwealth], in the present circumstances I would oppose it still more. Are we helping the cause of peace or not? I am sure that every kind of contact we have with other countries, whether it is through the Commonwealth or any other, helps the cause of peace ... I am for everything that brings us together without tying us up in any way. The Commonwealth is no tying up of any kind. What is tying up is all this array of alliances from the Warsaw Pact to NATO, from the Baghdad Pact to SEATO. The whole world is full of these knots. We want to unravel them, to open them out, so that people may live their lives without fear."

As the membership of the Commonwealth grew larger with the achievement of independence of more former colonies, agreement through consensus on political issues became ever more difficult. It was clear to realists that the modern Commonwealth could not aspire to be a 'third force' as a counterweight to the United States or the Soviet Union. It could not also be a military alliance; there were in fact few military agreements between the United Kingdom and its former colonies. Nor could it be an economic bloc—the Sterling Area and Commonwealth preferences were under ever-increasing strain and had become rapidly diminishing assets. If it was to be successful, the modern Commonwealth would have to remain a political consultative association, the members of which had decided on balance that it was better to face the problems of the complex post-war world together in consultation rather than separately. In other words, it was a practical concert of convenience, even if at times prone to rhetoric and self-congratulation mixed with a degree of surprise and satisfaction that the organisation had not only survived but had expanded in membership and scope of activity over the decades.

Not everyone could accept that the Commonwealth was not a military pact. Libyan leader Muammar Gaddafi summoned the Indian diplomatic envoy in Libya,[3] in 1971 to castigate the Commonwealth over the emergence of Bangladesh, describing the association as a military alliance which had as its goal the break-up of world Islam. Twenty-five years and more later, the Commonwealth had a role to play discreetly and tangentially behind the scenes to help the same Col. Gaddafi find a way out of United Nations sanctions against Libya over the Pan-American airliner explosion in 1988 over Lockerbie in Scotland.

The question of a multiracial partnership was neither specifically raised nor was especially appealing to the old dominions. All of them felt misgivings about the company of the three Asian newcomers, but they realised that the Commonwealth's importance would sharply decline if India was not of its number. India was key, because it was in the best position to rock the boat, and it chose not to do so. In that sense, Nehru, who as Indian Prime Minister attended every single Commonwealth Prime Ministers' Meeting in his lifetime, personified the informal collegial ways of the new Commonwealth. Despite obvious British pre-eminence at

---

3.   The author.

that time, and Nehru's disinclination to be assertive in that forum, the presence of the Indian Prime Minister in its meetings held the modern Commonwealth together and gave it credibility. "It was perhaps in the Commonwealth setting," recalled senior British civil servant Joe Garner, "that Nehru performed at his best."[4] From being the jewel in the Crown, India became the jewel in the Commonwealth. For its part, Britain sought to minimise confrontation with India over international issues, not only because of India's importance in the organisation but on account of the substantial Indian communities in the colonies.

Nehru died in 1964. One year later the Commonwealth Secretariat came into existence, at the instigation of Ghana leading the African members and Canada. Nehru did not approve of a Secretariat, for much the same reasons that he had always opposed a Secretariat for the Non-Aligned Movement. He valued the Commonwealth for its informality, its conviviality, and its absence of bureaucracy. Although the modern Commonwealth was a British creation for British interests, Nehru had emerged as a true supporter of the multiethnic Commonwealth, and used his influence to encourage Britain to apply the formula of self-government and Commonwealth membership elsewhere in the Empire. India remaining in the Commonwealth of its own accord was the greatest achievement of the modern Commonwealth, and balm to the British mood after the war. The apparently seamless continuity between the Empire and the Commonwealth blunted anti-colonial sentiments both in Britain and abroad. During and after Suez, Nehru was, in the Commonwealth's first major crisis, its saviour. To Britain's relief, despite recurrent tensions between the South Asian members, both India and Pakistan chose to remain in the Commonwealth, and Britain's special ties with them were safeguarded. "It was India, the pioneer of modern Asian nationalism," wrote the Commonwealth journal of international affairs, *The Round Table*, "who established the *bona fides* of the new Commonwealth based less on blood than on will."[5]

---

4. Garner, J. (1978). *The Commonwealth Office 1925-68*, Heinemann, London, p. 280.

5. *The Round Table*, Volume 50, 1959-60, p. 371.

Decolonisation and the campaign against racism

From 1948 to 1957 the membership of Commonwealth conferences had remained static. In January 1957, the British colonial Empire in Africa was at its fullest extent; by December 1967, nothing of it remained except Swaziland and the seemingly inte·rminable problem of rebel Rhodesia. French President de Gaulle's offer in 1960 of full independence to West and Equatorial Africa and the chaos of Congo's independence aftermath had a profound influence on Britain, and led to a complete turnaround in policy. Independence had to be granted urgently if London was to keep any control over the proceedings.

By 1961, there was a non-European majority in the Commonwealth conferences. The Africans were united and strident and the Commonwealth gave them an international platform for the first time. In the past, Britain had sought to influence the Commonwealth; now the Commonwealth was openly seeking to influence Britain. The Commonwealth had become largely a third world forum and issues relating to racism and white minority rule in Africa became the main agenda throughout the three decades from 1960 to 1990. There was large-scale non-white immigration into Britain, the widespread erosion of democracy in Africa, and the 15 year long problem of Rhodesian intransigence from 1965 to 1980. Republics now outnumbered the monarchies. By the end of 1968, the role of sterling as a reserve currency had effectively ended and the 1960s also marked the decreasing importance of Commonwealth preference, which was of no significance for the new members, and no country wished to lay itself open to reprisals from growing markets in USA, Japan or Europe. London was no longer even *primus inter pares*. In every region of the world Britain found that moving to a less formal kind of superior status proved unworkable. This presupposed the existence of a world-wide British system, but Britain lacked the economic and military strength needed to hold its own against the competition of other world powers. During this period, Britain's interest in the Commonwealth diminished sharply as it increasingly saw its future prospects as a major participant in a unified and industrialised Western Europe.

It was during this period of the British Commonwealth's steep decline, when African issues dominated the association, that the Prime Ministerships of Indira Gandhi and Rajiv Gandhi took place. Indira Gandhi attended four Commonwealth summits during her long period in office, and hosted the most important Commonwealth meeting ever to take place in India, the summit of 1983, but she was not believed to have any particular attachment to the organisation. Rajiv Gandhi however, was rather committed to the association; in his comparatively short tenure of five years he participated in two summits in 1985 and 1987, as well as the Commonwealth review meeting on South Africa in London in 1986. He may well have been disposed to attend his third summit in Malaysia in 1989, but by then his resignation was imminent.

The Rhodesian problem had been resolved in the Commonwealth by the time Rajiv Gandhi became Prime Minister, but the South African apartheid-based white minority government remained an affront to the world's conscience. This was not a classical decolonisation issue, because South Africa was a sovereign independent republic. But Britain was trapped in its historical past and in its perceived economic and strategic needs of the present and future. On the issue of sanctions, Margaret Thatcher was adamantly opposed to them while the rest of the membership was equally adamantly in favour. It was over South Africa that Rajiv Gandhi shone in the Commonwealth limelight. He did much to bring the focus of the world's attention to the racially discriminatory policies of the Pretoria regime. If his grandfather had been the first to bring the issue of racialism in South Africa before the United Nations, so Rajiv Gandhi bent himself to the task of sharpening the opposition to racism in the Commonwealth. A seven-member Eminent Persons Group, including Rajiv Gandhi's nominee, the Congress veteran Swaran Singh, was set up in 1985 to promote a process of dialogue in South Africa, and it submitted its report in the following year. At the London meeting to review this report, Rajiv Gandhi was often prevailed upon by the rest of the Commonwealth leaders to be an informal go-between to Mrs. Thatcher, perhaps because few of them relished the prospect of confrontation with her, or perhaps, as they plausibly argued, because she was likely to give more attention to a young and personable gentleman. Of course, in the case of Mrs. Thatcher, the lady was not for turning, and at the ensuing Commonwealth summit in 1987, she entered four negative reservations in five paragraphs on proposed action against South Africa. But it is clear who had the last word, though Rajiv Gandhi was not to live to see the fruits of his energies.

The Commonwealth after the Cold War

In the 1990s, the Commonwealth tried to develop a post-Cold War platform of good governance and human rights that would be generated and enforced among its members through encouragement, penalties and peer pressure. But it has proved difficult for the organisation to play any role of substance with this new agenda because the member states bring to various issues their different starting points, interests and capacities, resulting in a common minimum programme for operational unity. The Commonwealth has held together a disparate membership, notwithstanding a certain similarity of legacies, by virtue of informality and some element of fudge. As the writer, Virginia Crowe shrewdly observed, "to turn the Commonwealth from being a club to wielding a club is not appropriate."[6] It is obvious that the Commonwealth will never achieve unanimity on any fellow-member's domestic situation, especially when such issues are far from resolved in the international community at large.

It was possible for *The Times* editorial of June 2, 1953 to pronounce that "the only certain threat to Commonwealth unity would arise if a member deliberately pursued a policy ... that put her outside the traditions of civilized conduct", but it soon became impossible to argue that parliamentary and other democratic institutions in themselves constituted a sufficiently strong bond to hold the Commonwealth together. Or even less, that the existence of the Commonwealth by itself guaranteed a continuation of the

---

6. Crowe, Virginia (1997). *The Commonwealth in a Changing World*, Bernan Associates, p. 23.

common values supposedly shared among its original members. It is equally impossible to assert that these common values now pervade the various societies of Commonwealth membership, or to imagine that the degree of common culture that the much smaller Commonwealth displayed until the late 1950s could remain constant. In practice, laudable institutions such as a free press, the rule of law and parliamentary democracy will continue to exist in several former colonies, irrespective of their relations with Britain or the future of the Commonwealth.

The democracy agenda which the Commonwealth has adopted gives it an ability to bring peer-group coercion to bear when its members choose to exercise it, and this can be valuable for India in exerting pressure on member states with large Indian populations, such as Fiji, and on Pakistan when it suits New Delhi. Nevertheless, in general, the association suffers from the indifference of its larger and more powerful member states and accordingly a deficit in leadership.

India and the Commonwealth

As a founding member of the modern Commonwealth and with 60 per cent of the organisation's total population, India should be able to exercise great leverage and influence over the Commonwealth's entire scope of activity. India is attached to the Commonwealth for several reasons. It is not an association which deals in bilateral disputes between member countries and there are several examples of these—India and Pakistan, Namibia and Botswana, Solomon Islands and Papua New Guinea, Nigeria and Cameroon—and there is a convention that there is no exercise of Commonwealth mediation or 'good offices' without the specific agreement of the parties concerned. This is very much in line with India's thinking in the context of its relations with its neighbours.

There is also no intrusion in the internal affairs of member countries. The Memorandum which set up the Commonwealth Secretariat in 1965 explicitly states "... the Commonwealth is not a formal organization. It does not encroach on the sovereignty of individual members. Nor does it require its members to seek to reach collective decisions or to take united action." In this respect, it is quite unlike the United Nations. Save in exceptional cases, where there are serious and persistent violations of the principles of democracy and human rights, rather vaguely defined, the Commonwealth does not seek to pronounce on the internal affairs of any member country without its approval. Of course, that approval has sometimes been given—though not in the recent case of Zimbabwe, which led to that country's withdrawal from the organisation. In the past decade, the Commonwealth has played a good offices role in the affairs of Bangladesh, trying to resolve the problems between the Awami League and the BNP; and in Sri Lanka trying to build a negotiating bridge between the Government and the LTTE. In other continents, the Commonwealth intervened in St. Kitts & Nevis, on the separatist tendencies of Nevis; in Guyana, between the two main political parties; in Papua New Guinea, on the separatist movement in Bougainville; in Tanzania to resolve the disputes between the two major Zanzibari parties, the CCM and CUF; and in the Solomon Islands, to resolve the problems between Guadalcanal and Malaita. In some of these interventions, but significantly not in South Asia, the Commonwealth has registered reasonable success.

All the major communities of persons of Indian origin outside India are in Commonwealth countries with one single exception, the USA. In about half the member countries, India has no resident diplomatic mission. This makes the Commonwealth an attractive alternative channel of contacts through which the Indian Government can reach out, not only to persons of Indian origin abroad, but also to the governments of the countries where India has no resident representation. Due to the considerable network of governmental, non-governmental and professional organisations, scope exists for making rewarding contacts and promoting the Indian national interest. The Commonwealth provides a forum in which national positions and national candidatures—including for the United Nations Security Council—can be promoted internationally.

India is among the top half-dozen contributors to the budgets of the Commonwealth. However, the aggregate expenditure for all this is small—a total of about $ 2 million, of which around one-third is delivered in non-convertible Indian rupees. As in the United Nations, the person who pays the piper tends to call the tune. Despite this contribution, India is in net credit with the Commonwealth, though all the revenues may not accrue to the national exchequer. This is because India provides 15-20 per cent of the consultants and experts recruited to serve under the Commonwealth technical assistance programme (the second after Britain), and lies fourth in the number of persons trained each year by the Commonwealth, apart from being the first in providing facilities and venues for Commonwealth training programmes.

The four-yearly Commonwealth Games are one of the few international athletic meetings—regrettably perhaps the only one— where India is among the top 10 medal winners. Twenty-five per cent of India's total trade is with other Commonwealth countries. The Commonwealth is the only political organisation in the world in which India automatically attracts a leadership role despite rarely taking any lead or initiative. India's impact on the important milestones in the Commonwealth, the creation of the Secretariat in 1965, the Singapore Declaration of 1971, the Harare Declaration of 1991, and the setting up of the Ministerial Action Group in 1995, to deal with good governance and human rights violations, has however been limited, largely because of the absence of the Indian Prime Minister from various summits. Rajiv Gandhi had perceived the utility of the Commonwealth in promoting the anti-apartheid cause in South Africa and his differences with Margaret Thatcher are among the more interesting aspects in the records of the summits. But since 1991, India has been represented at seven summits only, thrice by the prime minister, and at a conclave meant for heads of government, a deputy can make little impression.

The Commonwealth changed dramatically with the decline of Britain's pre-eminence after Suez, the setting up of a Secretariat, and the start of four decades when African issues predominated to the near exclusion of other matters. But after the death of Jawaharlal

Nehru, India had also changed, and the interest that Nehru had taken in the Commonwealth, especially as a continuing link with Britain, was not shared by any of his successors. Pandit Nehru attended every single Commonwealth Prime Ministers meeting of his time personally. In fact, he attended 10 such meetings between 1948 and 1962, more than twice as many as any other Indian Prime Minister.

The Commonwealth is a body in which membership confers benefits, but inevitably some derive more benefits than others. The chief patrons will always be the principal beneficiaries. "Frankness compels one to admit," writes the historian Peter Lyon, "that many informed and influential Indians regard the Commonwealth as a rather puny affair, dispensing small change internationally and not significantly punching above its weight."[7] This is a singular irony considering that 50 years ago India had itself been a crucial partner in the creation of the modern Commonwealth, a legacy of the statesmanship of Pandit Nehru.

This attitude could stem from a misconception that the Commonwealth is a hangover from dominion status, a theory Nehru had countered 50 years ago. Despite being a founding member and its huge preponderance in terms of its population, India has never held the post of Commonwealth Secretary-General, though there was one candidature put forward in 1979, for which the campaign was badly conceived and even worse executed by New Delhi, with the result that the contest never even went to the vote. In over 40 years, it has held the position of deputy Secretary-General only twice. New Delhi has hosted a Commonwealth summit only once, in 1983, and since the next two summits are already spoken for, the next earliest opportunity will arise only in 2011.

It may be instructive to compare the attitude of India to the Commonwealth, where history has endowed it a leadership role, with India's attitude to the United Nations and the Non-Aligned Movement. The Commonwealth, of course has no Security Council, no Chapter VII, no enforcement machinery and no peacekeeping

---

7. Correspondence with the author.

operations. It may therefore be argued that there is little in common between these organisations, but the national interest has surely to be to promote and project India's image and influence; to participate in shaping the great issues of our times for the global commons; and to create the world as we would have it in our vision. It is doubtful whether Indian Prime Ministers have missed any Non-aligned summit, or even a United Nations General Assembly in recent years. Apart from the set pieces, one of the reasons for attendance would certainly be to make personal contacts with other world leaders. The Commonwealth summits are still very much the affairs of heads of governments themselves. The Retreat for heads only, which has become such a feature of the SAARC and G-15 summits, is in fact an aspect borrowed from the Commonwealth which started this practice in 1973. And above all, in the Commonwealth, when India speaks, everyone listens. This is by no means the case in the UN or NAM. For sure, every international organisation goes through a cycle of ups and downs, and this is not a plea for less attention to other international organisations of which India is a participant, but for more attention to the Commonwealth. With greater understanding of what the Commonwealth means to India and what India means to the Commonwealth, we can look forward to better times; to fresh involvement, impetus and initiatives in the early years of the new Millennium.

Regional foreign policy

11

India and its neighbours

Shyam Saran

It is said that the logic of geography is unrelenting and proximity is the most difficult and testing among diplomatic challenges a country faces. Frontiers with neighbours are where domestic concerns intersect with external relationships. This is where domestic and foreign policies become inextricable and demand sensitive handling. It should come as no surprise therefore, that in defining one's vital national and security interests, a country's neighbourhood enjoys a place of unquestioned primacy.

The intertwining of domestic and external interests has acquired a new intensity in this new millennium. Technological change is bringing in its wake a more globalised world where nation states and national boundaries can no longer provide the untrammelled autonomy that is associated with national sovereignty. While globalisation has brought many benefits and opportunities for development and for the enrichment of our lives, there are also fears of losing one's identity and of being overwhelmed by powerful and technologically advanced societies. We are faced with the emergence of sub-nationalism and ethnic exclusivity even while a more interconnected world requires mutual understanding and tolerance. South Asia is not immune to these global trends and this forms the backdrop to the challenge we face in formulating our policies with regard to our neighbours.

South Asia is a compact unit, of subcontinental proportions, but occupying an easily identifiable geographical space, enjoying a broad cultural unity and a wide range of intra-regional economic complementarities. There were mighty empires in our history that straddled this subcontinent and the experience of colonialism more recently, reinforced the legacy of interconnectedness and affinity. Then came the trauma of partition, the growth of assertive nationalism, the drift away from democratic freedoms in some countries of our neighbourhood and the impact of global strategic and ideological rivalries, turning our subcontinent into a region of division and conflict, engendering a sense of siege both among States in our periphery and in India itself. The subcontinent is now home to several independent and sovereign states and this is a compelling political reality.

As a flourishing democracy, India would certainly welcome more democracy in its neighbourhood, but that too is something that we may encourage and promote; it is not something that we can impose upon others. We must also recognise, regrettable though this may be, that the countries of South Asia, while occupying the same geographical space, do not have a shared security perception and, hence, a common security doctrine. This is different from EU or ASEAN. In South Asia, at least some of the States perceive security threats as arising from within the region.

Keeping in mind this reality, India's approach to SAARC was the only one logically sustainable, that countries in South Asia set aside differing political and security perceptions for the time being, and focus attention on economic cooperation.

India's expectation was that the very dynamic of establishing cross-border economic linkages, drawing upon the complementaries that existed among different parts of tha SAARC region would eventually help overcome the mutual distrust and suspicion which prevents us from evolving a shared security perception. This remains India's hope today, even though the record of SAARC in this respect, has been hardly inspiring. The fact is that SAARC is still largely a consultative body, which has shied away from undertaking even a single collaborative project in its 20 years of existence. In fact, there is deep resistance to doing anything that could be collaborative. On the other hand, some members of SAARC actively seek association with countries outside the region or with regional or international organisations, in a barely disguised effort to 'counterbalance' India within the Association or to project SAARC as some kind of a regional dispute settlement mechanism.

It should be clear to any observer that India would not like to see a SAARC in which some of its members perceive it as a vehicle primarily to countervail India or to seek to limit its room for manoeuvre. There has to be a minimal consensual basis on which to pursue cooperation under SAARC, and that is the willingness to promote cross-border linkages, building upon intra-regional economic complementarities and acknowledging and encouraging the obvious cultural affinities that bind our people together. If there continues to be a resistance to such linkages within the region, even while seeking to promote linkages outside the region, if the thrust of initiatives of some of the members is seen to be patently hostile to India or motivated by a desire to contain India in some way, SAARC would continue to lack substance and energy.

India already has a set of bilateral relationships with its neighbours, which vary in both political and economic intensity. What can SAARC offer as an additionality to this set of relationships? Clearly, the creation of a free market of 1.3 billion people, with rising purchasing power, can be a significant additionality for all SAARC members. Currently, intra-regional trade accounts for only 5 per cent of SAARC's total foreign trade and this needs to be addressed. But the mere lowering of tariffs and pruning of negative lists do not add up to a true free market. The political lines dividing South Asia have also severed the transport and communication linkages among member countries. The road, rail and waterway links that bound the different sub-regions of the sub-continent into a vast interconnected web of economic and commercial links, still remain severed. Transit routes, which would have created mutual dependencies and mutual benefit, have fallen prey to narrow political calculations. Unless we are ready to restore these cross-border linkages and transportation arteries throughout our region, SAFTA would remain a limping shadow of its true potential.

India is today one of the most dynamic and fastest growing economies of the world. It constitutes not only a vast and growing market, but also a competitive source of technologies and knowledge-based services. Countries across the globe are beginning to see India as an indispensable economic partner and seeking mutually rewarding economic and commercial links with the Indian economy. Should not India's neighbours also seek to share in the prospects for mutual prosperity India offers to them? Do countries in India's neighbourhood envisage their own security and development in cooperation with India or in hostility to India or by seeking to isolate themselves from India against the logic of our geography? Some neighbours have taken advantage of India's strengths and are reaping both economic and political benefits as a result. Others are not. If globalisation implies that no country can develop in an autarchic environment, is this not true even more for countries within a region? If SAARC is to evolve into an organisation relevant to the aspirations of the peoples of South Asia, then these questions will need deep reflection and honest answers.

The challenge for Indian diplomacy lies in convincing India's neighbours that India is an opportunity not a threat, that far from being besieged by India, they have a vast, productive hinterland that would give their economies far greater opportunities for growth than if they were to rely on their domestic markets alone.

It is true that as the largest country in the region and its strongest economy, India has a greater responsibility to encourage the SAARC process. In the free markets that India has already established with Sri Lanka, Nepal and Bhutan, it has already accepted the principle of non-reciprocity. India is prepared to do more to throw open the Indian markets to all the neighbours. India is prepared to invest capital in rebuilding and upgrading cross-border infrastructure with each one of them. In a word, India is prepared to make her neighbours full stakeholders in India's economic destiny and, through such cooperation, in creating a truly vibrant and globally competitive South Asian Economic Community.

However, while India is ready and willing to accept this regional economic partnership and open up her markets to all her neighbours, India expects that they demonstrate sensitivity to Indian concerns. These vital concerns relate to allowing the use of their territories for cross-border terrorism and hostile activity against India, for example, by insurgent and secessionist groups. As countries engaged in the task of economic cooperation, we South Asian neighbours need to create a positive and constructive environment by avoiding hostile propaganda and intemperate statements. India cannot and will not ignore such conduct and will take whatever steps are necessary to safeguard its interests.

India would like the whole of South Asia to emerge as a community of flourishing democracies. India believes that democracy would provide a more enduring and broad-based foundation for an edifice of peace and cooperation in the subcontinent. Half a century of political experience in South Asia has provided a clear lesson that while expediency may yield short term advantage, it also leads to a harmful corrosion of core values of respect for pluralism and human rights. The interests of the people of South Asia sharing a common history and destiny, requires that members of SAARC remain alert to the possible dangers implicit in attempts to extinguish a democratic order or yield space to extremist and communal forces.

While democracy remains India's abiding conviction, the importance of India's neighbourhood requires that the Indian Government remain engaged with whichever government is exercising authority in any country in the neighbourhood. Indian sympathies will always be with democratic and secular forces. India will promote people to people interaction and build upon the obvious cultural affinities that bind South Asian peoples together. There is a need to go beyond governments and engage the peoples of South Asia to create a compact of peace and harmony throughout the region. To remain relevant, SAARC must begin to function as an effective vehicle to facilitate such contacts, bringing scholars, artists, scientists, youth and sportsmen together in regular events.

India is fully aware that its destiny is inseparable from what happens in its neighbourhood. For sustained economic development in India and the welfare of Indian people we need a peaceful and tranquil periphery. We also believe that the establishment of a peaceful neighbourhood is integrally linked to economic development in our neighbouring countries, an objective that would be best served by India giving access to its neighbours to its huge and growing market. Economic integration in the subcontinent must restore the natural flow of goods, peoples and ideas that characterised our shared space as South Asians, and which now stands interrupted due to political divisions.

India has always sought to reassure its neighbours that it respects their independence and sovereignty. What it regards as unhelpful is the display of narrow nationalism based on hostility towards India that often becomes a cover for failure to deliver on promises made to their own peoples. This inhibits the development of normal relations, including economic cooperation, and prevents our region from emerging as a region of both political stability and economic dynamism.

The people of South Asia are one of the most talented and creative people anywhere in the world. They have won honours for their motherland in distant climes. If these creative energies of over 1.3 billion people were pooled together what heights could we not achieve? There is, therefore, a need to make a new compact among the countries of South Asia, and to exorcise the ghosts of the past and join hands together across borders to unleash the immense energies of our peoples in a shared pursuit of collective prosperity. The destiny of South Asian peoples deserves nothing less.

Edited version of the Address delivered at India International Centre, February 2005.

12

SAARC: looking ahead

I.P. Khosla

Introduction

Successful regional cooperation requires two kinds of conditions to be fulfilled. The first are the necessary ones, which are more pre-conditions than simple conditions; there are only three and without any of these regional cooperation has little chance of success. The second are the sufficient ones; there are many of these, but all need not be fulfilled. If some of them are, then regional cooperation can go forward successfully.

The first necessary pre-condition is that war, or, more broadly, the promotion or use of violence or the threat of it, will be abjured by all the participating states in their mutual relations. This then becomes what Karl Deutsch called a pluralistic security community, one where "there is real assurance that the members of that community will not fight each other physically, but will settle their disputes in some other way."[1] The second is tightly linked to the first; it is that states accept each other's sovereignty and legitimacy, since the questioning of a states existence or right of control over its territory and citizens is the most general cause of violent conflict. The third is a mutual dispute settlement system that inspires trust among the participating states; the assurance that where there are

---

1. Deutsch, Karl *et al.*, (1957). *Political Community and the North Atlantic Area*, Princeton University Press, Princeton, p.5.

mutual differences the states concerned will be obliged to make a serious and sustained effort to resolve them, and to make compromises as part of this effort.

Sufficient conditions may emerge from endogenous causes or from exogenous ones. The endogenous ones are a shared geographic space, a shared culture, a shared history and a shared economics in the sense that the resources and produce of different parts of the region complement each other in such a way that trading can be seen to be obviously beneficial. But it is important to recognise that all this sharing is a matter of perception; it is difficult to pinpoint an objective reality which can convince all concerned that geography or culture or history is shared. Exogenous causes may be a common threat which is the most frequently cited, or common interests in relation to some external situation like negotiations at a multilateral forum; in other words any situation arising external to the region in which all the member states of the region have a reason for cooperation or common action.

Necessary preconditions

The three necessary preconditions illustrate the issues of peace and justice that have been at the heart of contemporary international relations theory and practice. States may be willing to renounce violence in their mutual dealings; but if one state questions the elements of sovereignty of another, such as its borders and its right to exercise control within the borders, or, as has happened, its very right to exist, this willingness cannot be taken seriously. Further, disputes and differences of other kinds do exist; if a state believes that such a renunciation will be used to perpetuate injustice, it will be tempted to go back on it. This, therefore, means more than a generalised agreement, such as is to be found in the first paragraph of the preamble to the SAARC Charter, on "nonuse of force and noninterference in the internal affairs of other States and peaceful settlement of all disputes." It requires a specific regional agreement renouncing the use of force, accepting the legitimacy of each state, as well as mechanisms for the pacific settlement of disputes that are spelt out in some detail.

Three examples may be given to illustrate the way this has been attempted, though this is not necessarily to suggest that this could be emulated in South Asia.

The first is from West Europe, where regional cooperation originated. What is now the European Union has provided the inspiration and example to other regions, especially the innovative ideas of Robert Schuman and Jean Monnet. It demonstrated that regional cooperation can benefit all the participating states and generated the theories of federalism, functionalism, neo-functionalism and the communication model, that scholars and statesmen elsewhere used to support their own regionalism. In a Europe that had seen seven centuries of recurrent war this could only be done by building on a firm foundation of peace—the European Coal and Steel Community. Under a plan drawn up by Robert Schuman, the then French Foreign Minister, it was decided in April 1951 that six countries—the Benelux, France, Italy and West Germany—would place their entire steel and coal industries under a fully empowered and autonomous High Authority. In effect, since these were the essential materials required for it, none of the signatories would be able to run an independent armaments industry; the very means of war were placed under joint control. Jean Monnet, a campaigner for federalism in Europe as the road to peace, became the first Chairman of the High Authority. From the outset the preservation of peace has been the main guiding principle for European unity. So political aims came first and the economic measures, like the Rome Treaty of 1957 to lower trade barriers, were a means to political ends. As Walter Hallstein, the then President of the European Commission said in 1961, "We are not in business to promote tariff preferences, or to ... form a larger market to make us richer, or a trading bloc to further our commercial interest. We are not in business at all; we are in politics."[2]

For the settlement of disputes and differences all members of the European Union as also the wider membership of the Council of

2. Quoted in Palmer, Norman D. and Howard C. Perkins (1969). *International Relations: The World Community in Transition,* Scientific Book Agency, Calcutta, p.423.

Europe agreed under the European Convention for the Peaceful Settlement of Disputes of April 1958 to settle by peaceful means any disputes which may arise between them; such disputes 'shall' be submitted by the parties to the International Court of Justice or for conciliation or for arbitration; and in each case details are specified as to how to go about it.

The second is from Africa. Under the 1963 Charter of the Organization of African Unity (OAU) the signatories committed themselves, Article 3(4), to the peaceful settlement of disputes by negotiation, mediation, conciliation or arbitration. The basis was the acceptance of the right of each state to exist within its borders as inherited from the colonial era, despite the many questions that were raised at the time about this. It was also decided to ensure this by establishing, under Article 19, a Commission for this purpose. In succeeding years the Commission never became functional; the peacekeeping efforts of the OAU had a somewhat mixed record of success; and its efforts to mediate in the Chad conflict and in the dispute between Algeria and Morocco over the Western Sahara—this was a questioning of sovereignty—almost led to the disintegration of the organisation itself. Eventually the Assembly of Heads of Government or *ad hoc* committees formed by it became the main organs when disputes needed to be managed. But the Charter does illustrate that as soon as the majority of African states gained independence and thought about a regional organisation, they committed themselves to peace, the principle of sovereignty and to the peaceful settlement of disputes.

The third is from South-East Asia. ASEAN, the Association of South-East Asian Nations, was launched in 1967, but little progress was made until the first summit held in February 1976 in Bali. There a Treaty of Amity and Cooperation in South-East Asia was signed in which, under Article 2, it was agreed that in their relations with one another, the parties will renounce the threat of use of force and will settle their differences or disputes by peaceful means. For this purpose it was agreed in Chapter IV of the Treaty to constitute a High Council at Ministerial level; which would, if direct negotiations between the parties failed to produce a solution, recommend other steps like good offices or mediation or even constitute itself as a committee of mediation, inquiry or conciliation. This did not really work. Chapter IV of the Treaty was never invoked. The High Council was not finalised; even its rules of procedure were agreed only in July 2001, and under these the Council cannot initiate action; it has to be approached by one or more parties to the dispute and has to seek written confirmation from all the parties concerned that they agree to the application of its procedures for resolution.

The important point here is that, as in the case of the OAU, there is the consciousness that a supreme commitment to peace is the first and necessary precondition for regional cooperation; and that mechanisms should exist for peaceful settlement of disputes and differences. And in South-East Asia this has happened, though not in the way envisaged in February 1976. The Indonesian policy of Konfrontasi towards Malaysia, 1963-1966, still left memories in 1976; there was the Philippines claim to Sabah; the tension filled separation of Singapore from Malaya in 1965, and the ongoing differences about the islands in the South China Sea. "Nonetheless, ASEAN countries over the years displayed tremendous success in resolving intra-group conflicts and/or minimising their damaging impact on the process of regional cooperation through effective measures of conflict management."[3]

Arrangements for the promotion of peace, sovereignty and justice need not always be based on written treaties or agreements, but those in the region must believe they will work.

South Asia and the necessary preconditions

In South Asia neither of these three necessary preconditions have been fulfilled so far.

India would be prepared to enter into a commitment to settle all differences exclusively by peaceful means, and has done so with some of the smaller neighbours who reciprocated. Bilateral treaties with Bhutan (August 1949) and with Nepal (July 1950) commit

3. Sabur, A.K.M. Abdus (2003). "Management of Intra-group Conflicts in SAARC: The Relevance of ASEAN Experiences", *South Asian Survey*, Vol.10, No.1, January-June, p.86.

the signatories to perpetual or everlasting peace. A treaty with Bangladesh (March 1972, lapsed after completing its 25 year validity) did the same; though it can be surmised that, given the present state of our relations Bangladesh would not be ready to sign a similar treaty today. Though there is no formal treaty on the subject with Sri Lanka, bilateral relations have been on the same basis.

Pakistan has not been able to make this commitment; and in the foreseeable future will not do so. Declarations of peaceful intent have to be seen in the context of Pakistan's questioning of the sovereignty of India where Kashmir is concerned. Pakistan's approach can be summarised by saying that if political differences and disputes are not solved, there cannot be durable peace. This is the meaning of the statement made by the Pakistan Prime Minister at the SAARC summit in Colombo, 1998, that "without an environment of peace, security and stability, efforts towards mutually beneficial regional cooperation will have limited success. SAARC cannot and must not remain indifferent to or pretend to be oblivious of the differences and tensions between its members."[4] So the sequence is clear: first solve the political differences, which means the Kashmir question, then there will be an environment of peace and then regional cooperation can be successful.

The statements made by Pakistani leaders have developed nuances in the last two years; thus Prime Minister Shaukat Aziz is reported[5] to have 'reiterated' in July 2005 Pakistan's commitment to resolve the Kashmir and other disputes through peaceful means and that only peace could bring political stability and economic prosperity (used interchangeably with regional cooperation) to South Asia. Some months later, on 30 March 2006, the Pakistan Ministry of Foreign Affairs issued a press release saying that a British delegation was told a solution of Kashmir was 'essential' to bring durable peace in South Asia. So it is sometimes that peace will come first, and at other times that disputes should be settled first. In any

---

4. A considered view from Pakistan is in Husain, Ross Masood (2003). "New Directions for SAARC: A View from Pakistan", *South Asian Survey*, Vol.10, No.1, January-June, and for the quote see p.63.

5. *www.dailytimes.com.pk*, see the report dated July 29, 2005.

case the argument of Pakistan is consistent: that regional cooperation can go forward only if the disputes are settled. The first impediment to the progress of SAARC, as PM Shaukat Aziz told the SAARC summit in Dhaka in November 2005, is "the political disputes and tensions in the region ... we need to move towards conflict resolution."

There are three factors at work here, and signs of the influence of all three on the policy of Bangladesh are occasionally to be seen.

The first goes back to the roots of partition. An important root was the fear of majoritarianism among many of India's Muslims, specially in the North. Congress governments formed in eight states from July 1937 to October 1939 refused to treat with the Muslim League except on terms that would imply the demise of the latter; the incidents of persecution of Muslims and their culture which took place during this period went almost unpunished, increasing their bitterness and making them more willing to listen to arguments that only if they were treated as a separate and equal nation would they be able to get justice. And it led to the Lahore resolution, proposed by a Bengali and at a time when the movement for Pakistan was strongest in that part of India. Even in the months after August 1947 senior Indian leaders commented that soon India and Pakistan would be one again, reinforcing the fear of majoritarianism. Allama Iqbal had gone further than the quest for parity; in his demand to a separate state he dreamed of the Indian Muslims establishing an empire equal to the great empires of Persia and of the Arabs. This vision also surfaces from time to time in Pakistan, as in the Pakistani attack of September 1965, when probings in the Rann of Kutch in May that year, seemed to show that India had no will to fight. Repeated failures on the military front may have corrected the vision somewhat.

The second lies in their domestic situation. Hostility to India helps the military retain its grip on the levers of power. It is only the military, as the then head of the army's Command and Staff College wrote, that can ensure "India will be cut to its proper size and dimension."[6] The promotion of *jehadi* groups is part of this policy, a part that has not been abandoned despite the recent thaw in India-Pakistan relations. Note that traces of this can be found in Bangladesh also. The military has also used its prolonged rule in Pakistan to gain a dominating role in the economy. Foundations linked to the military such as the Fauji Foundation (army), the Bahria Foundation (navy) and the Shaheen Foundation (air force) are among the largest business conglomerates in the country. The political temper in Pakistan is such that a military coup is greeted with a collective sigh of relief, as happened recently in October 1999; and the judicial system has endorsed each coup.

Third, external involvement has reinforced the Pakistani belief that nothing is lost by a policy of hostility to India. When US military aid to Pakistan began in 1954 the latter had made no secret that its search was for military parity with India and that the arms could be used only against India, not for any communist state, the ostensible reason given within the US to its legislators and public opinion. US officials knew this but went along, for their global concerns were more important than the way a particular consignee used arms aid. In the years to follow the military leadership in Pakistan has developed manipulative skills in securing external backing even when the circumstances appear particularly unpropitious. When Pakistan helped to create, train and install in Kabul a movement, the Taliban, responsible in large part for 9/11, it would have been reasonable to believe that the friendship with the US was over. However, skilled manipulation ensured that it grew stronger, with President Bush declaring Pakistan a "major non-NATO ally" on June 16, 2004, thus conferring a special status on US-Pakistan military ties and giving the military in the latter the reassurance they required.[7] Through the years the military,

---

6. Major General M. Amin Khan Burki, Foreword to Lt. Col. Javed Hassan, *India: A Study in Profile*, Services Book Club, Rawalpindi, 1990, p.ii, quoted by Haqqani, Husain (2005). *Pakistan, Between Mosque and Military*, Vanguard Books, Lahore, p.268.

7. Public Law 104-164, enacted in July 1996, added a new section 517 to the Foreign Assistance Act of 1961 (P.L. 87-195) governing the designation of major non-NATO allies. The new section granted the President the authority to name new countries to be MNNAs. The President's designations of new MNNAs take effect 30 days after the Congress is notified in writing.

nuclear and missile aid Pakistan has received from North Korea, Iran, China and other countries have over the years caused trouble for the US, but it has not affected its friendship with that country. And in China there is an ally that would encourage the policy of hostility and supply the arms needed for the purpose.

In regard to the third necessary precondition India's firm 'bilateralism only' approach has consistently opposed any regional or other multilateral role in resolving differences with neighbours. This is because the important ones, and only the important ones could retard regional cooperation, are political. As Hans Morgenthau approvingly quoted Jawaharlal Nehru in his classic *Politics Among Nations*, "great political questions ... are not handed over in this way to arbitrators from foreign countries or any country."[8] There is little chance that in the foreseeable future this policy will change, and India took the lead in ensuring that, as inserted into Article X of the SAARC Charter, all decisions at all levels shall be taken unanimously, and that bilateral and contentious issues shall be excluded from the deliberations. As in almost every other aspect of regional organisations, comparison with other regions is invalid. In Europe, to give one example, value systems based on a foundation of Roman law have permeated deeply and there are today no differences that arise from the questioning of sovereignty or attempts to change the *status quo*. A legal or at least quasi-judicial approach to dispute settlement is therefore possible. In ASEAN there is the ASEAN way of conflict control and management, informal, based on personal relations between the leaders, characterised by understanding, sensitivity, and tolerance. As the Vietnamese Foreign Minister told at a US-ASEAN Partnership Conference in September 2000, to cite just one example, "our Association's fundamental principles and the ASEAN way, first and foremost, the principles of consensus and non-interference into each others internal affairs, continue to be preserved and upheld;" again the desire to change the *status quo* unilaterally has been held under control.

---

8. Morgenthau, Hans J. (1966). *Politics Among Nations*, Scientific Book Agency, Calcutta, p.431.

Neither of these could be relevant for South Asia since the starting point is Pakistan's eagerness unilaterally to change the *status quo*, the keenness of Bangladesh to help in this effort, and the somewhat fluctuating policies of the next two (in size), Nepal and Sri Lanka. From the official Pakistan viewpoint SAARC is largely another opportunity to promote its case on the Kashmir question.

In sum, the necessary preconditions for successful regional cooperation do not exist in South Asia and are not likely to exist in the early future.

The sufficient conditions: geography

We have next to examine whether sufficient preconditions exist, whether these sufficiencies are there in plenty and whether there is hope that this plenty will help create the necessary ones.

Sufficient conditions can emerge from a shared past and from a current sense of togetherness; the first is, of course, helpful in creating the second. In South Asia there is apparently an abundance of the first, in geography, as well as in history.

From ancient times, when the *Vishnu Purana* wrote: "The country that lies north of the ocean and south of the snowy mountains is called Bharat; there dwell the descendants of Bharata;"[9] going on to Babur who equally recognized this in writing: "The country of Hindustan is extensive, full of men, and full of produce. On the east, south and even on the west, it ends at the great enclosing ocean. On the north it has mountains which connect with those of Hindu-Kush, Kafiristan and Kashmir;"[10] to the present, when it is no longer called Bharat or Hindustan but South Asia, as Foreign Secretary Shyam Saran said on 14th February 2005 in a speech on India and its neighbours at the India International Centre, Delhi, "South Asia is a compact unit, of sub-continental proportions, but occupying an easily identifiable geographical space, enjoying a broad

---

9. *Vishnu Purana*, II, 3.1.

10. *Babur Nama*, translated from the original Turki text by Annette Susannah Beveridge, Oriental Books Reprint, 1979, pp. 480-481.

cultural unity and a wide range of intra-regional economic complementarities" and he went on to talk of the empires and the era of colonialism that "reinforced the legacy of interconnectedness and affinity" and the need to "restore the natural flow of goods, people and ideas that characterized our shared space as South Asians."

This argument has been used by Indian spokesmen to urge greater connectivity. At the 13th SAARC summit, for instance, Prime Minister Manmohan Singh said, "We are clearly witnessing nothing short of an Asian resurgence based on the rebuilding of the pre-colonial arteries of trade and commerce that created a distinct Asian identity in the first place ... ancient roads criss-cross the sub-continent and then link up with the sea posts that were the gateways to the rest of the world. So we must reconnect the countries of the subcontinent ... and reconnect the subcontinent to the larger Asian neighbourhood."

It is, however, equally true that among India's smaller neighbours there is no apparent current sense of togetherness to match this. Pakistan and Bangladesh in particular, but also Nepal and Sri Lanka, have been at pains to create a sense of their separate geographic identity. Pakistanis emphasise the separateness of the Indus as a geographic region with links to the Islamic world westwards. Many Nepalese consider their Himalayan Kingdom to be geographically clearly separated from India and a link between India and China, not part of the Indian subcontinent. To give another example, Sri Lankan historians underline that the geographic separation of the island from India is "just as important a factor in the island's historical evolution, as the obvious proximity to the subcontinent."[11]

There is also the undeniable fact that geography has only since about 1970 come to know of a region called South Asia, which for years thereafter was thought of as a name needing a place more than a place needing a name. During the centuries before that, there

---

11. This is from the standard text on Sri Lankan history: Silva, K.M.De (2005). *A History of Sri Lanka*, Penguin Books, New Delhi, p.1.

was the unity of Hindustan, or, later, the Indies, and later still, India, all of which included Afghanistan and Myanmar. This was gradually broken as borders were mapped and demarcated to separate Nepal and Bhutan, then Afghanistan and Myanmar and Sri Lanka, and finally Pakistan and Bangladesh. From this perspective India's neighbours find it difficult to endorse proposals that could in any sense hint at the recreation of past unity; their idea is to promote cooperation, the cooperation of equals, and since it was the colonial period that brought all of them into their present existence, the suggestion about the rebuilding of pre-colonial arteries of trade and commerce is regarded with some, often unspoken, suspicion.

As for the practical implications in the matter of connectivity, it does not look as if, at any time soon, Pakistan or Bangladesh will give India the right to use their territory for transit to Afghanistan or to the East, respectively.

History and culture

As to history, books written and statements made in India underline the unity of the region. Most notably Jawaharlal Nehru wrote "a dream of unity has occupied the mind of India since the dawn of civilization". That unity was not imposed from outside, a reference to the idea that without British rule there would have been no unity; it was something deeper, within every Indian, from the Pathan to the Kashmiri to "the Tamils, the Andhras, the Oriyas, the Assamese ... all have been throughout these ages distinctively Indian."[12] This general sentiment, in acceptably attenuated form, was incorporated into the SAARC Charter, in which the preamble reaffirms that the member states of the South Asian region are bound by ties of history and culture; a theme reiterated at the very first summit, Dhaka, December 1985, whose declaration said regional cooperation was the logical response to the formidable challenges faced by their countries because of the "many common values rooted in their social, ethnic, cultural and historical traditions". Succeeding summit declarations went back to the same theme, as in Bangalore,

---

12. Nehru, Jawaharlal (1956). *The Discovery of India*, Meridian Books, London, p.49.

November 1986, which said, "South Asia had been linked by age-old cultural, social and historical traditions." More recently the Prime Minister of India informed the SAARC summit in Islamabad, January 2004, that "many of us have a shared history" and that "our forefathers fought side by side, transcending religious, regional and linguistic differences against a common colonial oppressor in our first war of independence in 1857." And the last summit at Dhaka, November 2005, noted, "SAARC is based on the sound foundation of shared values, beliefs and aspirations."[13]

It is more difficult, but not impossible, to find spokesmen from other member states of SAARC emphasising the same theme, as for instance the Prime Minister of Bangladesh on a recent (March 2006) visit to Delhi saying India and Bangladesh were "bound by a common history, shared values of democracy, tolerance and an ethos rooted in pluralistic and moderate traditions."[14] President Chandrika Kumaratunga of Sri Lanka has voiced similar sentiments, that "India is our immediate neighbour, with whom we have been inextricably bound by ties, the origin of which have long been lost in the mist of time."[15]

By and large, just as India has emphasised unity in diversity within the subcontinent, the neighbours have emphasised diversity in unity, or the "immense diversity within a very broad contour of unity."[16] As against the unities of a shared culture that is the product of a joint history, three things have been pointed out.

First, there were, according to some scholars, more disunities than unities in the history of the region. As against the syncretic trends of religion, typified by Sufism, the periods of communal hostilities are cited such as the time of Aurangzeb. As against the

---

13. Texts of the SAARC summit declarations and of the statements made by heads of delegations at those summits can be accessed at the SAARC secretariat website *www.saarc-sec.org*, and in the various issues of *South Asian Survey*.

14. As reported in The Hindu, Delhi, March 22, 2006

15. Quoted by DeVotta, Neil (2004). "Ethnic Nationalism and Indo-Sri Lanka Relations", *South Asian Journal*, No. 6, October-December, p.100.

16. The phrase used in one of the few books on South Asian history, culture and political economy, and the very first written jointly by an Indian and a Pakistani: Sugata Bose and Ayesha Jalal, *Modern South Asia*, Routledge, London, 2001, p.4.

unities of language based, say, on the single source for all of them in Sanskrit, the reorganisation of states in India or the problems in Sri Lanka are cited. An eminent scholar of the region says that the "history of South Asia is the history of the violent and protracted clash of these different streams of civilization that had found their way into the subcontinent,"[17] though also of cohabitation.

Second, there is no doubt about the efforts by the neighbours, sometimes determined, at other times less enthusiastic, to widen as much as possible the differences between their cultures and that of India. The view is expressed that these differences are original and fundamental, as for instance "some essential and primordial differences between Pakistan and India" so that the partition was due more to cultural and economic differences than to the communal factor.[18] In Sri Lanka the intimate connection between the land, the race and the religion is stressed so that an identity quite distinct from the Indian emerges. This spills over into the tale from the chronicle Mahavamsa in which the Sinhala Duttagamani battles the evil Tamil usurper Elara; this is the one cited and recited at all levels rather than those tales from the chronicles, and there are many such, which refer to the commonalities. Many Sinhalese today believe they are in a minority, that is, if one takes together all the Tamils of India and Sri Lanka, and would, accordingly, have to fight that much harder to assert their separate culture and identity. Even in Nepal many are convinced that theirs is a different and superior kind of Hinduism, less rigid, than that found in India; the difference is compounded by the cultural mix of Indo-Aryan in the Terai or southern belt, and the Mongoloid stock of the regions bordering Tibet, with their respective distinctions of social pattern, caste structure and religion. Further, the Nepalese are proud of the independence they never wholly lost in contrast to India.

---

17. Gunatillake, Godfrey (2001). "The Cultural Dimensions of the South Asian Community", *South Asian Survey*, Vol.8, No.1, January-June, p.109.

18. See Ahsan, Aitzaz (2005). "Why Pakistan is not a Democracy", in David Page, (ed.), *Divided by Democracy*, Roli Books, New Delhi, pp. 78-79.

The point is that whereas Indian spokesmen emphasise the commonalities our neighbours emphasise the opposite.

In this reality history is fashioned by present self-definition or "the past is always practiced in the present, not because the past imposes itself, but because subjects in the present fashion the past in the practice of their social identity"[19]: where India talks of unity in the subcontinent, the neighbours think 'homogenisation', which they translate into 'hegemonisation', so they emphasise dehomogenisation which equals dehegemonisation.

Third, a common culture may be a help in cooperating, but it may not; where there is conflict of interests it may encourage actual conflict when one side thinks it knows enough about the other due to a common culture to be able to exploit weaknesses, as has actually happened between Pakistan and India. The Arab nation has a common language and culture and largely a common religion; none of this has helped cooperation or even prevent intra-Arab war. Europe has a common religion and a common Graeco-Roman culture; in May 1910 the sovereigns of Europe gathered in London for the funeral of King Edward VII. Among them was the German Kaiser, who was a member of the British royal family, which in turn was related to all the other rulers who were there, including Russia, Austria, Belgium, Italy; there could hardly be more to common culture than belonging to the same geographic space, the same history and culture, even the same family; but a year later all of them were at war. It is true that cultural commonality is not a hindrance to cooperation; history does not show that it is necessarily a help.

Economic cooperation

Economic cooperation is an important aspect of SAARC. Five out of the eight objectives of the Association set out in Article 1 of the Charter are about this, including the first three, about promoting the welfare of the people, economic growth and collective self-reliance. The first SAARC summit reaffirmed the "fundamental goal was to accelerate the process of economic and social

---

19. Friedman, Jonathan (1996). *Cultural Identity and Global Process*, Sage Publications, London, p.141.

development in their respective countries."[20] And every summit has reiterated this goal.

There are just three ways in which regional cooperation can contribute to these goals.

One is by learning from each other, what the 13th SAARC summit called "exchange of best practices in various fields."[21] This had been an ongoing exercise on a sporadic and selective basis even before the Charter was signed; thereafter it has become more regular and intensified. There is reference below to the frequency of regional South Asian meetings; an important function of such meetings is the promotion of this learning process.

The second is by working together on the international stage. Then the collective weight of the South Asian economies will enhance their bargaining power, making for better terms in trade and financial negotiations and, therefore the promotion of welfare and the acceleration of economic growth. Since India accounts for 75 per cent of the international weight of the region there would be more gains for the neighbours, less for India. Even so, experience has shown that, with rare exceptions, the SAARC member states have been able to coordinate their viewpoints on international economic negotiations and thereby gain bargaining strength, specially as a nodal point for the developing countries as a whole. This will become more important if the region can take advantage of Article XXIV of GATT 1994, which provides that in free trade areas the member states can discriminate in favour of other members in their trading regimes.

It is the third way, however, which is expected to produce the biggest results: economic integration or the elimination of economic barriers so as to restore the natural flow of goods, investment and other economic factors, the making of the region into a single economic space or, as the 11th SAARC summit (Kathmandu, January 2002) decided, and this was reiterated at subsequent summits, "a phased and planned process eventually leading to a South Asian

---

20. Declaration of the First Summit, Dhaka, 1985, para 4.

21. See the Declaration of the Summit, para 5.

Economic Union", what a leading South Asian economist called "a bold and far-reaching vision."[22]

From the purely historical angle there are two opposing views on whether the restoration of the pre-1947 economic links will actually lead to a greater flow of goods and capital. One is that this was a coherent economic region, with free trade and travel, complementarities in production and consumption, so it should be quite a simple matter to restore the old links. The other is that the South Asian economies at that time were "geared to produce to suit the requirements of the colonial regime for nearly two hundred years ... and there is little evidence to maintain that there were massive trade flows within the region."[23] It is, in any case quite apparently true that too much has happened during the last 60 years or so to be able to envisage that just going back to the past is a simple and feasible option. Each country has adopted its own regulations in the matter of tariff and non-tariff barriers; has liberalised at its own pace; adopted its own standards in port and customs procedures, quality control, weights and measures and a host of other things that need to be standardised; transport and banking and communication links have been cut—it is now cheaper, sitting in Calcutta or Dhaka to buy goods from Singapore than from Dhaka or Calcutta. A one step reversion to economic union is just not a practical option.

The next step is to consider whether the lowering or elimination of trade barriers increases the flow of goods, which would, of course, contribute to the economic goals of SAARC. It obviously should, since the foundation of international economic theory is specialised production. However, in other parts of the world the impact has been mixed. The World Bank, in its annual *World Development Indicators*, publishes statistics on global links, which show that neither in the European Union nor in ASEAN was there any increase in intra-regional trade as compared to trade with the rest

---

22. Sobhan, Rehman (2005). "The Twelfth SAARC Summit: Charting a Road Map for South Asian Cooperation", *South Asian Survey*, Vol. 12, No.1, January-June, p.4.

23. Kelegama, Saman (1999). "SAARC—From Association to Community: A Small Country Perspective", *South Asian Survey*, Vol.6, No. 2, July-December, p.263.

of the world after trade barriers were abolished. In Mercosur, on the other hand, there was, though commentators have said this was the result of informal pressures exercised on companies. In South Asia the example is often given of the Indo-Sri Lanka free trade agreement (ISFTA). Praise for it has referred to the dramatic increase in trade between the two, particularly of exports from Sri Lanka, but even this does not stand up to detailed scrutiny, for that increase was largely in items not native to Sri Lanka, in other words things like copper, edible oil, aluminium and electrical machinery, which were being imported from elsewhere, were diverted through the island to avoid the payment of import duties, which only benefited the traders. Furthermore, as far as India is concerned, the most rapid increase has in the last decade and a half been, and is expected to continue to be, in services exports, which are not affected by tariff cuts.

Next we can consider whether an expansion of trade, which is the result of greater specialisation, promotes growth and welfare. Since trade will extend the production possibility frontier, growth will benefit. However, if we look at economic dynamics then, if this is an important reason for growth, a growing economy should have a fas·er rate of growth of international trade, and this is a basic assumption of the neo-liberal economists. But in South Asia experience has been varied. In the case of India the growth of trade was faster than that of GDP by nearly 7 per cent p·er annum in the period 1990-2003. But in the case of Pakistan it grew slower, nearly 1 per cent per annum slower. Looking further afield there are countries in which it grew faster and others in which it didn't. And it needs to be remembered that rapid growth in conditions of autarchy was known before 1990 and globalisation, as for example, in the Soviet Union, which recorded growth rates of over 8 per cent per annum for the 20-year period 1954-1974. In other words the expansion of trade need not lead to economic growth, and there could be more important reasons for growth than the expansion of trade.[24]

---

24. Statistics taken from *World Development Indicators*, 2005, The World Bank, Washington, pp. 322-324. The figures for trade, less growth are regularly included to show the way trade led growth operates, an integral feature of neo-liberal economic thinking.

Even if trade expands significantly within South Asia, and we assume that this will have a positive effect on growth, this cannot be a significant positive effect. Intra-regional trade is less than 5 per cent of the region's trade with the rest of the world; it expanded from 2.36 per cent in 1990 to 2.46 per cent in 2003. The figure was much less in 1990, 1.5 per cent, in the case of India, but had grown to 3.32 per cent by 2003. In the absence of significant possibilities for comparative advantage it will not expand much. It has been remarked by an eminent regional economist that the South Asian region "has an almost identical pattern of comparative advantage in some products and that there is no strong complementarity in the bilateral trade structures ...", and the possibilities of rapid growth in regional trade are limited.[25]

As for welfare the effects of trade are to benefit the factors of production in the specialised product and to harm the others. If, as a result of lower trade barriers India exports engineering goods to Pakistan then those employed in that industry there will lose. There is, however, the possibility that the gaining factor will be the one whose welfare is most in need of improvement, or that the government will use the gain in total product to take redistributive measures. There has also been a three year debate between economists like Jagdish Bhagwati and those in US administration mainstream, on the one hand, and others like Nobel laureate Paul Samuelson, on the other, with the latter questioning the contention that the overall gains would necessarily be larger than the losses if trade expands. In short, we do not know whether the growth of trade is good for welfare.

To sum up there would no doubt be benefits in expanding trade in South Asia, which provides a factor for sufficiency, but it is not a strong one. From the viewpoint of the economists the Charter puts altogether too much responsibility onto regional cooperation in expecting it to promote the welfare of the people, accelerate economic growth and strengthen collective self-reliance.

---

25. Kemal, A.R. (2004). "SAFTA and Economic Cooperation", *South Asian Journal*, October-December, p.24.

So far it has been seen that, looking at geography, history, culture and economics, there is a sufficiency of conditions for successful regional cooperation, but the perceptions of the smaller members of SAARC as also a few objective considerations have weakened the practical implementation of this.

External factors

We may next examine the kind of external factors that might supplement this sufficiency and the ways in which the exact opposite happens in the region; so much so that whatever positive sufficiencies exist in other areas, are perhaps more than nullified.

The existence of a common external threat has, it is said, contributed to the initiation and rapid progress of regional cooperation in Europe (the threat from the Soviet Union) and Southeast Asia (the threat from China). In South Asia, on the contrary, Pakistan would welcome the intervention of an external power hostile to India; Bangladesh too, perhaps somewhat less enthusiastically, would do the same. It is until quite recently that Nepal and Sri Lanka rejoiced in initiating the kind of external relationships that India saw as threatening. Soon after the Chinese aggression on India, Sri Lanka embarked on a tight rope walk diplomatic venture on the India-China dispute, which to India seemed to lean too far in the direction of the latter; by 1963 it had concluded a bilateral maritime agreement with China conferring reciprocal most favoured nation treatment in relation to sea borne traffic, clearly a provocation. Within a few years (1971) it provided landing facilities to Pakistani aircraft carrying (in fact if not declared) troops to the East, seen by India as a direct military threat. Moves to lease Trincomalee harbour to US interests and an offer to host a Voice of America station at the time were seen in India as the calculated pursuit of a policy of nibbling away at India's security interests. Today this is not so, but a wise Indian policy analyst will not be able to pretend that the pendulum is never going to swing back.

Nepal, too, has used its relations with China to nibble at India's security interests. In April 1960, as the exchanges on the border question between India and China were getting difficult, the two of them signed a treaty of peace and friendship. By October 1961, just as the exchanges between India and China were getting quite acerbic, Nepal and China signed a boundary treaty; the desire of both was to show that India was being obdurate. Then, when Marshal Chen Yi of China visited Nepal in October 1962 he said, to much approbation from Nepalese officials, "in case any foreign army makes a foolhardy attempt to attack Nepal ... China will side with the Nepalese people."[26] The construction of the Kathmandu-Kodari highway, opened for traffic in December 1964, and reportedly strong enough to carry heavy armour, seemed to show that this was not idle talk. There were similarly grave provocations in later years.

Again, the situation looks different today, but when the King of Nepal offered in Dhaka at the November 2005 SAARC summit that "Nepal serves as a transit point between India and China, the two largest emerging markets in the world" he was underlining also the options available in geopolitical terms.

SAARC achievements

Despite all the above SAARC has some real achievements to its credit, at the heart of which is a gradual internalisation among a steadily growing circle in all the member states of the need to meet, meet again and keep on meeting. That there has been no SAARC project so far, and nothing much otherwise either except meetings, can be taken, not as a reflection of how slowly regional cooperation has moved, but of the fact that the necessary pre-conditions have not been met so far.

At the political level there have so far been 13 summits, almost 30 regular and special sessions of the Council of Ministers, which is at Foreign Minister level, and 3 dozen ministerial meetings covering specific areas like commerce, women and children, the environment, youth, poverty alleviation, housing, agriculture, terrorism, culture and health. It has now been accepted by all

26. Thapliyal, Sangeeta (1998). *Mutual Security, The Case of India-Nepal*, Lancer Publishers, New Delhi, p.89.

member states that Ministers concerned will have a SAARC meeting on the sidelines of global meetings such as the annual Asian Development Bank and World Bank/IMF, as well as the World Trade Organization. It is clear after the 13th summit that the number of ministerial meetings will increase. In 1992 an Association of SAARC Speakers and Members of Parliament was formed which meets once a year to talk about parliamentary matters, but also about politics and economics and other subjects of common interest. Separately, in collaboration with the International Centre for Peace Initiatives, the Parliamentarians for Global Action and the International Peace Academy parliamentarians from the region have attended workshops in peacemaking.[27]

At the official and technical levels there have, of course, been many more meetings. The Standing Committee comprising the Foreign Secretaries of the seven has had over three dozen regular and special meetings so far. To this should be added the meetings of other Secretaries to government in specific areas of cooperation, of the legal advisers, of the heads of the police agencies, the governors of the Central Banks, and the various committees to oversee the working of the SAARC agreements, and of the regional centres, of which there are five and the decision now is to increase them to eight. The SAARC Audiovisual Exchange Programme or SAVE, is to show regional programmes regularly on national television. The Integrated Programme of Action is a key component of regional cooperation and includes fields as diverse as agriculture and rural development, transport and communications, the environment, education, culture and sports, health and population and tourism. A large number of the official level meetings are conducted under the auspices of the IPA.

There are a number of SAARC agreements and conventions: one of the first to be signed (1987) was the Regional Convention on the Suppression of Terrorism aimed at the prevention and elimination of terrorism from the region; the same year an agreement on establishing a food security reserve was signed, which

---

27. For more details see: Futehally, Ilmas (2001). "Conflict Management and Confidence-Building Measures in South Asia", in *South Asia 2010, Challenges and Opportunities*, Konark Publisher, Delhi, p.233.

was aimed at regional and sub-regional collective self-reliance with respect to food security; there is a Convention on Narcotic Drugs and Psychotropic Substances aimed at eliminating drug trafficking; one on Preventing and Combating the Trafficking in Women and Children for Prostitution and another for the Promotion of Child Welfare. These have been never been used, even if ratified; the enabling legislation is not in place or the will to use it is not there, but they do give rise to meetings.

The most important is the agreement on a free trade area, or SAFTA (signed January 2004), which envisages that, apart from the removal of all quantitative restrictions on mutual trade, tariffs will be brought down in two steps to 0-5 per cent throughout the region in three stages: by the non-least developed states for the least developed, within 3 years of coming into force; by the non-least developed for their own category, in 7 years, and by the least developed for the latter, in 10 years. This should, as the Dhaka summit declaration of November 2005 noted, "mark an important milestone on the road to a South Asian Economic Union."[28] There is, however, a caveat to this; from Pakistan there is so far no commitment that they will give MFN treatment to Indian exports; and from Bangladesh no firm commitment that India will enjoy the terms agreed under SAFTA. Two further points need to be made. Sri Lanka seems to have lost interest in the SAFTA; they have a free trade regime with India and with Pakistan and that is all they were interested in; Pakistan and Bangladesh are engaged in talks on a bilateral free trade agreement, which casts some doubt on their commitment to SAFTA. However, all these doubts and problems will only be clarified once the SAFTA is in operation.

Further to promote meetings at both official and non-official levels there are the SAARC years; since 1989 each year has been designated SAARC year of something: the girl child (1990), youth (1994), poverty eradication (1995) and tourism (2005) are some examples. And there are SAARC decades: of the girl child (1991-2000); and of the rights of the child (2001-2010). There are also the

---

28. Para 14 of the Declaration.

SAARC centres, such as the Documentation Centre located in Delhi, the Agricultural Information Centre in Dhaka and the Cultural Centre in Kandy and their governing bodies which meet regularly.

And if one takes all the officially sponsored workshops and training courses, the symposia and seminars, the technical committees and governing bodies of regional centres then, according to the information on the SAARC secretariat website, there was a total of 134 meetings in just one year, 2004. Given the five-day week and the fact that many meetings continue for more than one day, this means that, on average, SAARC is in meeting everyday.

The existence of the secretariat in itself, helps in the general objective, for here is a group of people whose only aim is to promote regional cooperation, despite the fact that they have been given little power to initiate any action.

Outside government there are as many if not more meetings of SAARC formal or informal bodies and groups. There are the professional bodies like the South Asia Media Association, established in December 1991, which includes the leading editors, journalists, filmmakers, media activists and artists of the region. There is also a South Asia Editors Forum with the participation of regional language editors. Beyond this there is the SAARC Chamber of Commerce, which meets regularly to get business people together, organises trade fairs and other special events. In India several chambers of commerce have separate sections to handle SAARC affairs, including the Confederation of Indian Industry, the Federation of Indian Chambers of Commerce and Industry and the PHD Chamber of Commerce. Then there is SAARC Law for the lawyers, a SAARC Federation of Accountants, and other groups for architects, management development, town planners, cardiologists, dermatologists, radiologists and Surgical Care Societies, to mention just a few of the many bodies that exist, are registered and meet from time to time.

Again outside government, and growing in importance are meetings arranged by the NGOs and civil society organisations, what is often called people to people contact. In recent years official level SAARC has given more importance to this. Summits have agreed on the contribution of these contacts. The first summit emphasised "the greater involvement of their peoples" in regional cooperation. And subsequent summits have reiterated and fleshed out the pledge to enhance people to people contact. The 13th summit, for the first time, went a little further in saying "that the Association should broaden its engagement with the civil society organizations, professional groups, and entrepreneurs" as well as to encourage greater people to people contact.

To give some idea of what is being done we may cite the South Asia Women's Forum, the South Asia Peoples Action Network, the South Asia People's Ecology Network, the Independent Group for South Asian Cooperation, the Regional Centre for Strategic Studies, or the Coalition for Action on South Asian Cooperation. One estimate[29] is that "there are more than forty dialogue channels currently operating in South Asia," but this estimate was made in 1996; there would be many more now. There are too many to list since such a list should include writers and artists, those who organise film festivals, which are held annually, alumni associations, fora for peace and for democracy and for many other purposes, some of which get funding for one or two meetings and then no more or remain active for longer, the point being that it is considered worthwhile for those who consider such events that South Asia should be their focus.

All these meetings heighten the awareness of South Asian cooperation as a desirable objective, lead to a stronger commitment, regardless of political persuasion, to promote this end among political circles, officials, and others outside, and even help in the initiation of a South Asian identity which could attenuate the primacy of the political which has been at the core of the problem of South Asian cooperation. Alternatives are explored, public discussion is influenced and there is a growing consciousness that there is a region called South Asia, in which there should be peace and cooperation. They also establish over time the kind of personal rapport, which ensures that learning from each other as well as

---

29. Behera, Navnita Chadha, Paul M. Evans and Gowher Rizvi (1997). *Beyond Boundaries*, University of Toronto-York University, p.4. This is a report on non-official dialogues in South Asia.

working together, say, in international fora, are facilitated. The success of micro-credit in Bangladesh or of legal aid in Pakistan is now not only widely known in the region but also emulated.

But it cannot be said that, with all that has happened at the official and non-official levels they have succeeded yet in overcoming the obstacle created by the lack of necessary preconditions for regional cooperation to be a success.

Conclusion: looking ahead

Looking ahead there are four levels to be considered.

Firstly the bilateral. Economic cooperation at the bilateral level is not a substitute (hence does not jeopardise) but can be an example for regional cooperation. Thus relations with Bhutan have served as a model. India's aid has focussed on human development and concentrated on the largest natural resource, hydropower, in which Bhutan has a potential of 30,000 MW (24,000 MW has actually been identified). Cooperation in developing this resource has been smooth. The bilateral free trade agreement with Sri Lanka has also been exemplary, despite not conforming to the economist's vision of what a free trade agreement should do. It has reduced the latter's deficit in trade with India while leading to a rapid growth in total trade figures, so that now a Comprehensive Economic Partnership Agreement is under negotiation. We can today say that India-Sri Lanka relations are a model for the bilateral network that could emerge in the region.

Secondly the regional. At this level the creation or expansion of a sufficiency of conditions for successful regional cooperation signifies the development of a collective South Asian identity.

This means two things. First, that each SAARC member state must see every other member state as a cooperative partner; a non-India-centric network of connections (but not excluding India, of course) should develop between every state and every other state, i.e. across the entire region. The frequent regional meetings, official, non-official and at various levels, have helped in this but an acceleration of these and of the economic and cultural programmes is needed. Second, that the member states should identify with the region. It is they who own the meaning of the concept of South Asian identity, and it is they who have to develop it. Political economy can provide some suggestions about necessary and sufficient conditions for regional cooperation, but not the details of the route to be taken.

So far there has been a heavy dependence on meanings imported from Europe or South-East Asia. It is hard to come across a speech or piece of writing on regional cooperation without some reference to the way South Asia has fallen behind this region or that, usually Europe and South-East Asia, in trade or investment or visa liberalisation and so on. Different regions have developed their own meanings, which are unique to those regions and not suitable for South Asia. In no other region in the world, to give just the most obvious instance, do summits and minister level meetings alternate so regularly with conflict and high tension confrontation along one border and frequent bursts of tension along another; nor is there any other region in which a 15 year campaign of terrorism sponsored by one member state against another (with some help, perhaps passive, from one and perhaps two others) has travelled parallel to the promotion of regional cooperation. So we must be able to distinguish what can be learned from other regions and what cannot. Irrelevant imitation has been responsible for some at least of the problems encountered in South Asian cooperation.

In South Asia the search has to be for the expansion of sufficient conditions in such a way that the necessary ones are created alongside: that war or violence are no longer regarded as a possibility; the basic parameters of sovereignty are accepted; and acceptable means for dispute settlement are found.

The decision to invite Afghanistan to be a member of SAARC, would take this forward.

The third level is the Asian. Here it is likely that SAARC will become one of a large set of emerging regional cooperation arrangements.[30]

---

30. There is already a large body literature on Asian Cooperation. See, notably, Kumar, Nagesh (ed.), (2004). *Towards an Asian Community: Vision of New Asia*, RIS-ISEAS, Singapore.

There has been much flexibility in the initiation of regional cooperation arrangements. In fact there are seven kinds of flexibility: in the combination of countries, of which some examples have been given here; in the sectors covered, since it is not necessary that trade and investment be a part of all the arrangements, they can cover health, education, environment, or others, jointly or severally; in the depth of cooperation, in other words the extent to which it covers the sector or sectors selected; in the stake-holders, which may include government, the private sector, civil society, aid donors, the MNCs and these in any permutation or combination; in the issues which may range from the traditional economic ones to human rights, security, terrorism or others; in the kinds of institutions to be built, whether intergovernmental or supra-national or just for monitoring; in the values to be incorporated, democracy, pluralism, a liberal economy, since these are increasingly being insisted upon by the developed countries at least and will come to occupy a more important part in Asian cooperation agreements; and in the kinds of things which are to be done, whether only meetings as has been the case with SAARC, or projects, the promotion of joint ventures and so on.

India played a significant role in sponsoring and is a member of BIMSTEC, which started with Bangladesh, India, Myanmar, Sri Lanka and Thailand. The first summit was held in July 2004. There the organisation admitted Nepal and Bhutan and was renamed the Bay of Bengal Initiative for Multi-Sectoral Technical and Economic Cooperation. A framework agreement for a free trade area was signed with the aim of implementation by 2017. A BIMSTEC Chamber of Commerce was also established.

There is also the IOR-ARC, or Indian Ocean Rim Association for Regional Cooperation, formally launched in 1997, with the aim of promoting sustainable growth, economic cooperation and liberalisation through the enhanced flow of goods, services investment and technology among the member countries. It now has 19 members; China, France, Japan and the UK are dialogue partners. And there is the Mekong Ganga Cooperation or MGC, launched at India's initiative in November 2000, partly to promote culture and education, but also for economic cooperation between India and the other members—Cambodia, Laos, Myanmar, Thailand and Vietnam.

It goes further. As Prime Minister Manmohan Singh pointed out in December 2005, "India has concluded a framework agreement on comprehensive economic cooperation with ASEAN in 2003 and with Singapore more recently;"[31] a framework agreement for a free trade area with Thailand was signed in June 2005; others are on the anvil with Malaysia, Indonesia, the Republic of Korea, even China and these "are milestones on the road to the eventual creation of an Asian Economic Community, or the 'arc of prosperity' that I envisage to become a reality in the early part of the 21st Century."[32] As for SAARC, he had pointed out at the 13th Summit in Dhaka, November 2005 that it is important we assess SAARC in the larger context of Asian resurgence and be a part of it. In consonance with this the last two years in particular have seen a proliferation of studies lauding the idea of an Asian Economic Community and even an Asian Economic Union, with the smaller regional ventures, which then qualify as sub-regional cooperation, being seen as building blocks.

This is a coin with two sides. One side has the prospect that SAARC will complement several other initiatives already in the making; depending on how active it can become it will take a larger or smaller role in this large enterprise. The other side is that if the necessary preconditions are not met, then it could be bypassed as other arrangements overtake it and render it out of date.

Finally, there is the global level. There are three relevant aspects to this. First, India (and every SAARC member state) has a deep and continuing interest in the markets of the developed world; its two largest customers are the EU and the US. Statistics showing the expansion of intra-Asian trade notwithstanding, this fact is not going to go away soon. In this sense, rhetoric aside, the Asian

---

31. Signed June 2005.

32. Prime Minister of India, Keynote address at Special Dialogue of ASEAN Business Advisory Council, December 12, 2005, Kuala Lumpur.

economies are competitors. The 13th SAARC Summit decided that China and Japan would be invited as observers; India had earlier made known its view that it would be opposed to such a move, but agreed with some reluctance in the face of pressure from Pakistan, Bangladesh and even Nepal. Soon thereafter the senior officials agreed that the USA and the Republic of Korea would be invited likewise; the European Union has shown some interest and if it applies it would also receive the same welcome. There may be some political fallout of this, but the concrete results may well be in the commercial and economic sphere, as these major markets are going to be an increasing focus of SAARC as an institution.

Second, India needs also to engage with developing countries outside Asia. The India-Brazil-South Africa Dialogue Forum is one example, the first meeting of the trilateral commission having been held in New Delhi at Foreign Minister level in March 2004, where a plan of action was drawn up. This is likely to evolve into further ventures of cooperation between India and Mercosur as well as SACU.[33] There are others like TEAM-9, which brings together India and eight West African countries to seek ways of cooperation at government, institutional and private sector levels.

Third, globalisation also means a general expansion of world trade, and the commitments already made at the World Trade Organization by the different SAARC member states are not far behind what has been agreed under SAFTA or any of the earlier regional trade agreements. This is a general point; regional trading agreements are growing in numbers, but the advantage of these, as compared with the regimes being developed by the WTO, are not as substantial as once thought.

---

33. Mercosur, a regional cooperation organisation with Argentina, Brazil, Paraguay, and Uruguay, started in 1991; Chile and Bolivia joined as associates in 1996. This is widely regarded as a successful regional trading system. SACU is the South African Customs Union.

13

India and the Persian Gulf

Hamid Ansari

I

Locating the Gulf in relation to India is an exercise in geography and history. Widely used words, expressions and proverbs in the region are reflective of the vintage, and depth, of the Gulf's relations with India.[1] Down the ages, these contacts were embedded in a trading relationship that, of necessity, went beyond a mere exchange of commodities. Traders carried information and perceptions, and even assessments. Their contacts generated curiosity and led to acquisition of knowledge. The annals of cultural history demonstrate this in ample measure. In the trading metropolis of Makkah the name of a locality, Jabal Hindi, suggests the presence in pre-Islamic times of a resident Indian community. Families with an Indian ancestor are to be found all over the coastal areas of the Gulf, in cities like Buraydah and Uniyzah in the interior of the Arabian peninsula, and in Makkah, Madinah and Jeddah.

The 19th Century traveller Burckhardt gave an accurate description of the Indian business presence in Makkah:

"Trade is carried out by means of brokers, many of whom are Indians: in general, the community of Indians is the wealthiest

---

1. The uses of the proper noun 'Hind', and its derivatives, establish the affinity and the admiration that early residents of the Arabian peninsula had for India. The Arabic words for engineering (*handesa*) and sword made of Indian steel (*muhannad*) testify to the areas of excellence in mathematics and technology. The historian Tabari reports an equally telling legend: "The land with the sweetest smell on earth is the land of India"—*The History of Al-Tabari* (New York 1989), Volume I, p. 291.

in Mecca. They are in direct communication with all the harbors of Hindustan and they can often afford to undersell their competitors. Many of them...are stationary here , while others are constantly travelling backward and forward between India and Hijaz. They retain their native language , which they teach to their children, and also many merchants of Mecca superficially, so that most of the latter understand, at least, the Hindustani numerals and the most ordinary phrases in buying and selling...They are shrewd traders, and an overmatch, sometimes, even for the Arabians...[2]"

The Persian Gulf region is India's proximate neighbourhood. The distance from Mumbai to Dubai is 1000 nautical miles and to Basra 1500. For this reason and since the advent of European rule in Asia, control of the Gulf was in strategic terms considered essential for the defence of colonial possessions in India. The first to comprehend this were the Portuguese who, on the discovery of the sea route to India, added a new title for the King of Portugal: 'Lord of the Conquest, Navigation and Commerce, of India, Ethiopia, Arabia and Persia." The great Portuguese fortress at Hormuz dominated the Persian Gulf for over a century. The British, who followed them as the dominant power, did likewise through the suppression of local rulers and compelling them to sign treaties of submission in 1820, 1839 and 1853. The doctrine of supremacy was formally proclaimed by the Viceroy of India at Sharjah in November 1903: "The peace of these waters must be maintained; your independence will continue to be upheld; and the influence of the British Government must remain supreme."[3] In 1928, the Committee on Imperial Defence in London concluded that "no foreign power must be allowed to establish a naval base or a fortified post in the Gulf or air undertakings within striking distance of it."[4] This dispensation lasted till the British withdrawal from the Gulf on November 30, 1970. The initial US reaction to this was to insist that the "vacuum left by the British withdrawal... be filled

---

2. Burckhardt, John Lewis. *Travels in Arabia* (1829) pp. 190-191.

3. Lorimer, J.G. *Gazeteer of the Persian Gulf, Oman and Central Arabia* (Calcutta 1915), Volume I Part II, p. 39.

4. Morsy Abdullah, Mohammad. *The United Arab Emirates: A Modern History* (London 1978) p. 43.

by a local power friendly to us;"[5] later developments were to ensure a robust US presence that continues to this day.[6]

Until the end of the British rule in India, the administrative control of the British posts on the Persian Gulf littoral was entrusted to the Viceroy of India. The Reserve Bank of India was the currency issuing authority even to a later date. At the popular level, and for those who could afford it, Bombay and surrounding areas were the destination of choice for recreation and medical treatment; the ownership of some of the waterfront properties on the Marine Drive testifies to it and so does the living memory of the older generation. On the Indian side, some trading families established themselves in Muscat, Bahrain, Kuwait and Basra.

The Persian Gulf was thus a familiar region for independent India. Did it also mean that it was fertile soil for trading activity, and for the cultivation of political influence?

II

A survey of the geopolitical landscape of the Gulf littoral in the 1947-1960 period reveals that it was a British lake whose shore areas in the shape of local principalities were in treaty relationship with Great Britain and obliged to conduct external relations through the Resident in Bahrain and his Agents in other places. Iran, the biggest of the littoral states was under strong Western influence and its incapacity to chart out an independent course was demonstrated during the Mosaddeq episode.[7] The same was true of Iraq till the Revolution of July 1958. Saudi Arabia too, despite high level visits from both sides in 1955-56 as well as its decision

---

5. Kissinger, Henry (1979). *White House Years*, p. 1264, Boston.

6. Palmer, Michael A. (1992). *Guardians of the Gulf: A History of America's Expanding Role in the Persian Gulf 1833-1992*, pp. 87-88, 106, 122, 243-245, New York.

7. India's position on the nationalisation of the British-owned Anglo Iranian Oil Company in Iran was that "while the principle of nationalisation must be accepted (the) oil dispute between United Kingdom and Iran should be settled by peaceful means" and that India was "reluctant to interfere", Telegrams of May 25 and November 22, 1951 to V.K. Krishna Menon, *Selected Works of Jawaharlal Nehru*, Second Series, Volume 16, Part I, p. 449 and Volume 17, p. 547 (New Delhi, 1994 and 1995).

to avoid Western military alliances, retained its Western-camp orientation.

It has been argued, with justice, that four considerations governed Indian policy in the Gulf and West Asian region in that early period: (a) the historical links with the region (b) the Israel factor and the fact that "a certain principle was involved in extending support to the Arabs which India could not discard or forget about without compromising its own position and interests" (c) quest for oil (d) the continuing struggle with Pakistan for support among West Asian and Gulf states and the effort here was to neutralise positions if outright support was not forthcoming. "The policy tried to combine principle with practical considerations and was a mix of all the four aspects."[8]

The beginning of mutually beneficial economic cooperation with Iran, despite differences of perception on each other's worldview, can be traced back to the early 1960s. The agreement to purchase Iranian crude, and to build a joint venture refinery with Iran was signed in March 1965. Four years later, in January 1969, the Shah of Iran on a visit to India spoke of "unlimited possibilities" and wide scope of economic cooperation. Pursuant to the agreements arrived at, Iran agreed to buy railway wagons from India and to supply ammonia to India. Bilateral relations were severely tested at the time of the Bangladesh crisis in 1971 but were revived with considerable intensity once the Shah was satisfied that "India had no interest in working for the dismemberment what remained of Pakistan."[9] As a result , economic cooperation flourished in the 1972-1979 period.

With Iraq, and after the Revolution of 1958, the convergence of views facilitated cooperation in different fields; this included training of the pilots of the Iraqi air force and deputation to Iraq of a considerable number of Indian experts in different fields. In October 1972, Iraq agreed in principle to give crude oil to India on long-term credit.[10]

---

8. Dutt, V.P. (1984). *India's Foreign Policy*, pp. 306-307 and 327-328, New Delhi.

9. *ibid.*, p. 318 and 314-322.

10. *ibid.*, pp. 322-327.

The spurt in oil prices in 1972-73, and the apprehension of scarcity of crude supply, 'catapulted' the Gulf region to the front rank of strategic concerns and propelled India to reinvigorate traditional relations and develop new ones. New agreements were signed with all the suppliers in the Gulf littoral and efforts were made to off-set the cost of oil imports through more intensive commercial exchanges. A new vitality in relations with Saudi Arabia, Kuwait and the United Arab Emirates was one outcome of this effort. The inflow of wealth made it possible for all these countries to embark on ambitious programmes of infrastructure development and this added a new element in the bilateral relationships; Indian manpower thus emerged as a major factor and a principal earner of the much needed foreign exchange for the country.

The Revolution in Iran in 1979, disturbed the strategic balance in the Persian Gulf region and upset regional and global calculations. India overcame this crisis with considerable ease and established a reasonably good relationship with revolutionary Iran. In September 1980, Iraq decided to attack Iran and initiate a war that was to last for eight years. Pressures of a war economy in both countries slackened the pace of bilateral economic cooperation with the outside world. India also had to develop a carefully balanced diplomatic position relating to this dispute.

Iraq's attack on Kuwait in 1990, once again disturbed the strategic picture in the Gulf and resulted in great hardship to the Indian community in Kuwait. After the war of 1991, the US policy of Dual Containment of Iraq and Iran and the UN regime of sanctions against Iraq left India with no choice but to focus the totality of its attention on cultivation in full vigour of political and economic relations with the countries of the Gulf Cooperation Council.

III

A study of India's relations with the countries of the Persian Gulf littoral shows, there is no history of bilateral disputes.

Differences of perception relating to the global and regional issues did however arise from time to time. These, on the global plane, pertained to India's policy of non-alignment, to India's objection to membership of military alliances, to India's friendship with the Soviet Union and to some aspects of India's domestic economic policy. There were, in addition, Pakistan-specific issues like Jammu and Kashmir, Indian Muslims, the East Pakistan situation resulting in the War of 1971, and questions relating to these that surfaced in the deliberations of the OIC since its inception in 1969. The approach of the individual states to these questions impacted in some measure on the bilateral relations; in no case, however, was it allowed to override bilateral considerations and do serious or irreparable damage. The Indian response was to counter Pakistani moves, and to sustain a level of bilateral relations that would assist in the process. This also resulted in some duality of approach: "Muslim countries, while temporising on the Kashmir issue, and taking an impartial stand at the bilateral level with India, were collectively supportive of Pakistani position on Jammu and Kashmir. Such support found expression in OIC resolutions, in deliberations at the UN in New York and Geneva and in the meetings of the Human Rights Commission" (in the 1990s).[11]

Changes in the global and regional situation at the end of the Cold War impacted favourably on India's relations with the GCC states. The misunderstanding caused by the Indian position at the time of the start of the Kuwait crisis in 1990, motivated principally by desire to save and evacuate the Indian nationals in Kuwait, were quickly put aside; so was New Delhi's decision to establish diplomatic relations with Israel. The liberalisation of the Indian economy, and the new opportunities it offered, were cautiously welcomed by the Gulf business communities.

Relations with Iran, after having touched a low point in 1989-1990, were carefully nurtured and restored to normalcy. In this new approach, the focus of both governments was "on complementarities

---

11. Dixit, J.N. (1998). *Across Borders: Fifty Years of India's Foreign Policy*, pp. 248-249, New Delhi.

of interests and concerns."[12] The relationship touched a high water-mark in January 2003, when President Khatami was the chief Guest for the Republic Day.

The imperatives of a relationship with the Gulf states today, and in the foreseeable future, can be identified with a fair degree of precision. The entire region is within the security parameter of India and the operating radius of the Indian Navy, is the principal source of imported hydrocarbon energy supplies, is the principal destination for manpower exports that provides employment to 3.5 million Indian nationals whose remittances exceed US$ 7 billion per annum, is a major trading partner with overall trade of over US$ 18 billion, is an increasingly important destination for Indian projects and IT services, and has an India-friendly and Indian-friendly orientation and desirous of enhancing its political, economic and technological interaction with India.

For each of these reasons, political stability and sustained economic vibrancy in all parts of the Gulf are in India's interest. For the same reason, political and economic dislocation, induced by domestic or external factors, is not in the interest of India since such dislocations would have an adverse impact on the Indian economy and the wellbeing of a large number of Indian citizens. Some aspects of the policy approach were spelt out by Prime Minister Manmohan Singh in January 2005:

> "Besides energy imports, there is also ample potential for India to evolve broader long-term economic relations with the region. This could include expanding our contacts with the Gulf Cooperation Council and other regional bodies into an enduring institutional relationship. We could also examine a more proactive strategy of seeking investments from West Asia, given India's emergence as an exciting and safe destination for foreign direct investment."[13]

---

12. Dixit, J.N. (1996). *My South Block Years: Memoirs of a Foreign Secretary,* p. 151, New Delhi. He makes the point (p. 153) that "in overall terms Iran will always remain a cardinal factor affecting our Asian policies." This became evident at the time of sending Indian assistance to the Northern Alliance in Afghanistan.

13. Speech at Jamia Millia Islamia, inaugurating the Centre for West Asian Studies, January 29, 2005.

Nothing reflects better the policy that India seeks to develop towards the states of the Persian Gulf littoral than three documents that have taken shape since 2003. These are:

- The New Delhi Declaration and the Memorandum of Understanding on Road Map to Strategic Cooperation of January 25, 2003 between Iran and India,
- The Mumbai Declaration on the First GCC—India Industrial Conference of February 18, 2004, and
- The New Delhi Declaration of January 27, 2006 by Saudi Arabia and India.

These reflect shared perceptions and their contents therefore need to be carefully analysed.

The New Delhi Declaration with Iran built upon the Tehran Declaration of April 2001. The two sides affirmed that "their growing strategic convergence needs to be underpinned with a strong economic relationship, including greater trade and investment flows." They identified "a complementarity of interest in the energy sector," expressed satisfaction over "the operationalisation of the North-South transit arrangement," spoke of the decision to "explore opportunities of cooperation in defence in agreed areas, including training and exchange of visits," and announced the resolve of the two countries "to exploit the full potential of the bilateral relationship." Six other agreements were signed on the occasion, including one on cooperation in science and technology.

The Mumbai Declaration with the GCC was preceded, in September 2003, by the initiation of a political dialogue when the foreign ministers of India and the GCC states met together for the first time. The Mumbai conference endorsed the GCC-India Framework Agreement for Economic Cooperation, focussed on four priority areas of trade, investment, industrial cooperation and transfer of technology. It welcomed the intention of the two sides to explore the possibility of an India-GCC Free Trade Area.

The India-Saudi Arabia Declaration stressed the desire to develop "a broad strategic vision," recognised "the inter-linkage of stability and security of the Gulf region and the Indian sub-continent" and identified areas in which bilateral cooperation would be developed. The latter included a Memorandum of Understanding on combating crime and fighting the menace of terrorism, drug trafficking and money laundering. The Declaration committed itself to the institution of a "strategic energy partnership" that would cover (a) reliable, stable and increased volume of crude to India through 'evergreen' long-term contracts (b) cooperation in joint ventures, in both public and private sectors, in the upstream and downstream oil and gas sectors in India and Saudi Arabia as well as in third countries (c) Saudi investment in oil refining, marketing and storage in India, subject to commercial viability (d) setting up of Indo-Saudi ventures for gas-based fertiliser plants in Saudi Arabia. It was also decided that the two countries would seek to develop cooperation in the field of technology, particularly information and communication technology, agriculture, biotechnology and non-conventional energy technologies.

The Second GCC-India Industrial Conference at Muscat in March 2006, carried the process of convergence further by identifying six major areas for joint ventures—industry, energy, petrochemicals, information and communication technology (ICT), biotechnology and tourism. Speaking in the conference, Commerce and Industry Minister Kamal Nath underlined the immense strategic relevance of the Gulf for India and said it is "part and parcel of India's economic neighbourhood." He said India hoped that by 2007 a Comprehensive Economic Cooperation Agreement covering Services and Investments, instead of 'a mere FTA', would be in place.

The three documents are reflective of a mutual impulse to cooperate. For India, countries in the Gulf are of prime economic, political and strategic importance and are second largest trading partners after the US with the trade turnover of around US $ 20 billion annually. Two-thirds of India's oil imports are from this region, which not only has the advantage of geographical proximity, but the quality of crude oil suits the Indian refineries. Cooperation in the energy sector has been the hallmark of the ties with most of these countries and India is one of the biggest markets for energy products of these countries in the years to come.

The growing awareness of India in the GCC states is based on the realisation that by 2010 India (a) would be the fourth largest economy in terms of PPP and the fourth largest consumer of energy in the world (b) will be a major technology and knowledge-based economy (c) with its renewed interest in the Gulf, driven by necessity, ambition and opportunity and by expanded security perspective, will be ready to contribute to the stability of the Gulf region by sharing its experience in maritime security and military training and in combating terrorism.[14] Each of these would be supplemented by GCC's realisation, on realistic forward projections, that its centrality in the global economy would be enhanced in the coming two decades with the GDP increasing three or four folds over the 2005 level and the economy considerably diversified on account of income from services and tourism. The liquidity thus generated would seek investment opportunities, particularly in Asian markets that would include India in increasing measure.

The liberalisation of Indian economy has already yielded substantial benefits to the Gulf countries. According to the Ministry of Commerce, Government of India, GCC exports to India increased from $ 3252.05 million in fiscal year 2003-2004 to an estimated $ 6900.80 million in 2004-2005. Indian Exports to GCC countries during the same period increased from $ 7067.07 million to 9536.69 million. UAE has the distinction of being the largest trading partner of India in the GCC followed by Saudi Arabia, Qatar, Kuwait, Bahrain and Oman. The GCC's biggest export to India is crude oil. The main product groups imported from India to GCC are agro products, textiles and garments, precious stones, building materials, plastic products, engineering goods, process plant and electrical

---

14. Sager, Abdulaziz. "Strategic Roadmap for robust Saudi-India ties". *http://corp.gulfinthemedia.com/ gulf_media/view_editorial_en.php?id=1684,* January 22, 2006. Also, Jamil Ziabi: "The Saudi Invasion", Al-Hayat, April 18, 2006. The latter comments on the visit of the Saudi Crown Prince to some Asian countries within months of the Saudi King's visit to China, India, Malaysia and Pakistan and argues that "the Kingdom is aware that the world is not only confined to the West but there is a balanced world in the East...A world that moves, innovates and produces just as the people of the West do. The difference lies in the 'calm' political and economic voice in the East as opposed to 'the high voice' in the West".

equipment, manmade filaments/staple fibre, food products and miscellaneous goods.

The Indian economy's quest for 'massive doses of investment in every conceivable area' was underlined by the Prime Minister on the occasion of the Saudi King's visit to New Delhi in January 2006:

> "Our requirement of foreign investment are particularly large in the field of power, telecommunications, roads, ports and housing sectors. Investment needs for the power and telecom sectors alone are estimated at over $ 100 billion over the next five years! Transport infrastructure, including airports and railways, will require another $ 55 billion over the next ten years. I therefore invite the business community of the Kingdom of Saudi Arabia to take advantage of these opportunities to further establish mutually beneficial joint venture projects."[15]

The message, and the new areas cooperation and investment identified in the Indo-Saudi Joint Declaration of January 27, 2006 is valid in equal measure for investors in other GCC counties.

India's economic relationship with Iran is undergoing a change in view of the ever-changing international economic environment, which has impact on both the countries and taking into account Iran's capabilities in the industrial sector. India's total trade for the year 2004-2005 with Iran was of the value of $ 1610.59 million, with exports accounting for $ 1213.70 million and imports for $ 396.89 million. The political climate relating to Iran remains a constraining factor, preventing the realisation of the potential visualised in the Declaration of 2003. In the case of Iraq, the disturbed conditions there prevent revival of normal economic exchanges.

The import structure of the Gulf countries is undergoing change as they move towards diversification. The region imports products from agriculture to software, from healthcare to the defence equipments, agricultural products, construction materials, telecommunication equipment, pharmaceuticals, biotechnology and services.

---

15. Speech at the inauguration of the Saudi Exhibition, January 25, 2006.

The Gulf economies are expanding service sectors like education, tourism, construction, infrastructure, finance and business, pharmaceuticals and healthcare. These offer considerable business potential to India:

- Education: The policy of gradual replacement of expatriates with the local workforce has opened up a new segment for education and training. The growing number of young people in the labour market and the obligations on the private sector to employ them is leading to exponential growth of organisations, both government and private, now offering business-related training courses, either in-house or at specialised institutions. The marketplace is becoming competitive and extremely price conscious. The increase in the number of GCC university student numbers makes the university sector a key area where many foreign universities are starting Gulf campuses. This is particularly true of the technical education sector.

- Tourism: The Gulf States are stepping up investment in tourist industry to make the region one of the world's prime travel destinations. Following the lead of Dubai, Qatar has planned to invest $ 20 billion over the next eight years in a new airport, new hotels, museums, golf courses and other leisure facilities. The master plan for tourism aims to increase tourist numbers from 400,000 to one million in 2010. (One optimistic projection puts the number of tourists to the Gulf at 150 million in 2030.) Oman intends to increase tourism earnings from 0.8 per cent to 5 per cent of GDP in the next 15 years by developing new beach resorts built along the 1,700 km coastline. Abu Dhabi is developing the Al Ain oasis as a tourist destination, while Sharjah is going to work on targeting shopping and cultural visitors with 24 museums and 100 art galleries. Kuwait too has plans to build more hotels, and Iran (in addition to cultural tourism) is exploring the prospects of developing holiday facilities on Kish Island. Iraq's potential for cultural tourism, once normalcy returns, is very considerable. Even Saudi

Arabia has taken steps to encourage tourism, apart from upgrading facilities for pilgrims whose numbers are going up year by year and whose contribution to the economy of the Hejaz is significant.

• Construction Services: Given the revenue levels and projected expansion, a rise in construction levels is inevitable. The policy to engage private sector in infrastructure developments open new opportunities for service suppliers including accommodation for construction workers.

• Financial Services: Prospects have improved with the liberalisation of investment regime. Given the new income levels, there will be an enhanced demand for new financial services and financial products. An unexplored area (for India) is Islamic banking.

• Business Services: The growing application of electronics in business will have bourgeoning impact on market for trade and investment in IT related services.

• Insurance and Banking: Insurance is emerging as lucrative market since large projects need to cover against risks. Furthermore, and as the local labour regulations are rationalised, the demand for employee compensation and medical insurance will inevitably surface. Though local regulations generally prohibit foreign insurance companies from life insurance business, gradually health insurance is beginning to be open to foreign companies. Similarly, the region will become a good destination for retail banking.

• Healthcare Services: With, on average, pharmaceutical expenditure running at US$ 58 per capita in 2005—and growing—the Gulf States represent valuable and strong markets. According to one estimate the market is to be approximately US$ 2.0 billion in 2005. With rapidly increasing population, all GCC markets are dependent on imports of pharmaceutical. The UAE, which has a domestic manufacturing capacity, exports the bulk of its production within the Gulf region. Saudi Arabia is the largest Gulf States market for pharmaceuticals, valued at US$ 1.2 billion in 2005. Much of that market is supplied by Western countries.

The Indian workforce in the GCC states is an important ingredient of the relationship. The break up, country-wise,[16] is as follows:

Table 13.1
Indian Workforce in GCC States: Country-wise

Bahrain	130,000
Iran	800
Iraq	1,600
Kuwait	295,000
Oman	312,000
Qatar	131,000
Saudi Arabia	1,500,000
UAE	950,000

Indians constitute the largest expatriate workforce in the region. The estimates that there are about 3.2 to 3.5 million Indians are working in the region. Their annual remittances amount to around $ 7 billion. Though the bulk of the Indian expatriates are in semi- and low-skilled segments of the market, of late the profile has been undergoing change. In Dubai, for instance, "a rough estimate would put 25 per cent of the Indian working population in the category of unskilled workers, 50 per cent semi-skilled/skilled workers and the remaining 25 per cent constitute professionals and businessmen." In most other places, however, the unskilled, semi-skilled and non-professional white workers would constitute between 90 and 95 per cent of the total numbers.

---

16. Ministry of Overseas Indian Affairs, Government of India. The figures are for December 2001. They include Persons of Indian Origin (PIOs) in Iraq (50), Kuwait (1000), Oman (1000), Qatar (1000) and UAE (50,000). These are at best estimates and do not include PIOs in Saudi Arabia.

For about a decade now, GCC countries have debated the social and economic impact of large expatriate workforces.[17] Their manpower requirement is a result of demographic realities, societal attitudes to manual labour, and the imperatives of globalisation and its requirements of skills. Policy adjustments aimed at satisfying, on the one hand, the requirements of the economy (principally controlled by the private sector) and on the other, the need to create greater job opportunities for their citizens, are underway though at varying pace in different states.

Gulf countries are now, gradually, enforcing minimum educational requirements on the expatriate workforce. This would affect Indian workers adversely. In addition, workers in the semi-skilled category, are exploited both by the labour recruiting agencies in India and by the employers in the Gulf countries where they confront a number of problems that cause a great deal of hardship. These include an inadequate and incomplete database with the Government of India, the presence of a large number of 'illegal or irregular' workers having no jobs and no valid visas, the presence of a large and recurring number of workers whose contracts have been violated in regard to salaries, living conditions, leave and terminal benefits, and lack of funds with Indian diplomatic missions in the region to cover emergency expenses. To aggravate matters, Gulf returnees lack institutional means to rehabilitate themselves in society. Indian communities in the Gulf also complain that despite their large remittances of foreign exchange, the Government pays greater attention to the requirements of the NRI communities in the Western world.

Given the changing perceptions of the GCC states with regard to workforce of foreign origin, it would be prudent to initiate detailed studies to assess the likely impact of proposed changes on the Indian workforce and its implications for foreign exchange remittances.

---

17. This concern, about the Indian numbers, surfaced in an earlier period also though in a different context. The King-Crane Commission, sent by the US President in 1919 to make an assessment of the post-war situation in Syria-Palestine and Iraq, cautioned against the British policy of sending Indian immigrants to Iraq: "the Iraqis feel very strongly the menace particularly of Indian immigration, even though that immigration should be confined to Moslems. They dread the admixture of another people of entirely different race and customs, as threatening their Arabic civilisation"—George Antonius: *The Arab Awakening* (London 1938), Appendix H, p. 458.

Energy: India meets its growing demand for petroleum crude and products from nearly 30 different countries but it is the Gulf region, which accounts more than half of it. Saudi Arabia, Iran, UAE, Kuwait are the major energy partners of India.

The energy relations between India and the region are moving beyond the sale-purchase format. The stakes are in consolidating the energy trade with investment tie-ups to ensure both the supply and demand security. With the energy sector moving to the mode of liberalisation, the potentials of synergy of the mutual interest are enormous. Arab Gulf countries' engagement with Indian energy sector is not very significant.

Given the political will, and the identified opportunities, India's trade and economic cooperation with the GCC countries is now set to grow rapidly. The same however, cannot be said about Iraq and Iran where security or political considerations would, in the immediate future, hamper commercial interaction.

IV

Some circles in the GCC states have urged that India should take greater interest in security arrangements in the Gulf. Specific ideas on this remain to be spelt out. In the immediate future, Indian interests would be better served by capacity-building to demonstrate capability and by letting the debate on this subject to unfold within the region and globally.

India also needs to remain prepared for situations and contingencies that may arise in the Gulf region. These may relate to internal political developments or to externally induced situations. Some of these can be factored into normal planning, others will remain in the 'wild card' category. Both would have impact on Indian communities in the Gulf countries and on India in strategic, political and commercial terms. By the same logic, and given the intense competition that is likely to surface relating to the energy resources of the Gulf littoral, the possibility of a divergence or clash of interests with other principal regional or global players, cannot be ruled out. In such situations, the complementary of interests and the intensity and depth of bilateral relationships, could emerge as the critical factor. For this reason, and for many others, India's Gulf relations at the official and public levels need to be invested with content and goodwill on a continuing basis.

14

India and West Asia/North Africa

Ishrat Aziz

Introduction

While a new Gulf Division was created two decades ago due to the growing importance of the Gulf countries, following the oil boom and the rapidly expanding expatriate Indian communities in Saudi Arabia, Kuwait, UAE, Bahrain, Qatar and Oman, and the resultant workload, we cannot completely separate the Gulf and the WANA, when talking of our interests in the region. For a proper perspective about our interests in WANA, I have included data for the Gulf also. Occasionally, there has been some overlap, again for the same reason. For the rest, I have avoided unnecessary intrusions into the Gulf region.

Based on my experience and reading, my view is that the policies of India as well as WANA countries, in their mutual relationship were based more on secular consideration of geopolitical and economic interests and less on ideology and religion. The trump card was always self-interest, which of course is as it should be in the matter of relations between nations.

Some of my views may be contrary to the prevailing impressions, but I have tried very objectively to weigh and assess the facts that I know, including many that I have learnt in the course of my reading since my retirement. Objectivity, of course, depends

The statistics given in the article are from *Time Almanac 2005*, various published sources, and the internet. Since they have been rounded off, the figures are approximations.

partly on intentions and partly on knowledge. While one can try to be objective, one's views sometimes can be erroneous due to lack of knowledge of facts on one's part. I hold no final opinions and am always open to knowledge-based criticism and correction. Indeed, I welcome them.

Geopolitical importance of WANA

With the exception of our immediate neighbourhood, geopolitically and economically, West Asia and North Africa (WANA) is the most important area for our diplomacy today.

Consisting of approximately 20 countries (including those in the Gulf) WANA region, starting about a thousand miles from the shores of India, stretches westward until the Atlantic Ocean. Mostly arid desert, its total area would be about 5 million square miles or more than 8 per cent of the world's land mass. This vast swath of land has a length of approximately 4 thousand miles, with an average width mostly of 1250 miles. It lies more or less on the same parallels as India–10 to 30° North.

The total population of WANA countries is approximately 300 million, with a total GDP of $ 1400 billion and per capita GDP of $ 4600. For the sake of comparison: the world's average per capita GDP is $ 8200 and that of India $ 2800.

More than 60 per cent of this population is in WANA countries of the Mediterranean rim, e.g., Morocco, Algeria, Tunisia, Libya, Egypt, Lebanon and Syria.

Located in the same region, Israel, has an area of 8020 square miles, a population of 6.9 million (including about 1.35 million Palestinians); a total GDP of $130 billion and a per capita income of $20,000.

Geopolitically, the facts to be borne in mind are: the richest oil and gas bearing areas, indispensable to world's economies fall within this region; vital waterways like the Straits of Hormuz (gateway to the Gulf), Babel Mandab (entrance to the Red Sea from Indian Ocean), the Suez Canal, and the Straits of Gibraltar, all fall within this region.

The Gulf and the Red Sea are more or less surrounded by the WANA countries. Besides, half of Mediterranean Sea rim consists of WANA countries, and they constitute the vital underbelly of Europe.

For us, apart from its importance as an indispensable source of our galloping energy needs, its geo-strategic significance arises from the navigational routes and air corridors through this region for our trade, travel, and other links to Europe and beyond. Suez Canal cuts the distance by sea to Europe and UK by nearly 4500 miles. Avoiding this vital crossroad has significant economic costs.

The presence in the Gulf today of 3.5 million Indians because of employment opportunities, following the oil boom of the seventies, is also a very important consideration in our relationship with the region.

Two words used in connection with this region–Arabism and Islam, need a little clarification. Frequent and uncritical use of these words creates the impression of homogeneity, uniformity and unity of people in this region. The reality is much more diverse and complex. There are many races and innumerable tribes scattered over this vast region, the two most well known ethnic groups being the Berbers in North Africa and the Kurds in Iraq and Syria. (The latter are to be found in significant numbers in Iran and Turkey, resulting in a political problem in the region.)

Throughout history, especially during the Abbaside Caliphate from 8th to 13th centuries, people from Turkey and Central Asia came and settled in many of these countries especially in Iraq, Jordan, Syria and even distant Tunisia and Algeria in significant numbers.

The conqueror of Spain, Tariq ibn Zyad (8th Century AD) was a Berber; Salahaddin Ayyubi (12th Century AD) who re-conquered Jerusalem during the crusades was a Kurd, and more recently King Faruk of Egypt was an Albanian. Many non-Arabs from Central Asia, Iran and Spain made significant contributions in science, astronomy, medicine, philosophy, religious thought, etc., during the heydays of Islamic civilisation. In more recent years, Christian Arabs have made significant contributions to Arabic language and liberation and Arab nationalism.

Amongst the most unifying factors is the Arabic language, which is cherished by both Muslims and Christians. Despite some variations in the spoken regional dialects, the standard written Arabic is the same in all countries from the Gulf to the Atlantic. Any literate person, whether in Bahrain or Morocco can read and understand a book or a newspaper published in any Arab country and follow a news bulletin transmitted by radio or TV anywhere in WANA. At the same time, Kurds and Berbers have their own languages, which they speak, besides Arabic.

Though most of the people in the region follow Sunni Islam, there are significant number of adherents of other faiths also–Shias in Iraq, Lebanon and Bahrain; Christians (of many different churches) in Egypt, Sudan, Lebanon, Syria and Iraq; and Druze in Lebanon, Syria and Israel.

A closer look also reveals differences between various countries of the region due to boundary disputes, conflicting economic interests, security considerations and sharing of river waters. Often within the same country various groups have difference of interests.

The situation in WANA is not so different from that prevailing in Latin America. Despite commonalty of language and religion, both regions are divided into many countries. An emotional bond between the peoples has not prevented conflicts of interest. A sound foreign policy must be sensitive to these differences and craft a bilateral and customised approach with respect to each country.

Conscious of the geopolitical importance of WANA, India established strong diplomatic presence in the region first in West Asia and then in North Africa as French colonial rule ended and Morocco, Tunisia and Algeria emerged as independent countries. The only region, where relative to our interests, we were tardy in establishing our diplomatic presence was the Gulf.

India's foreign policy goals in WANA

India gave considerable importance to WANA region in view of its geopolitical importance.

It was important for India to see a resolution of the Arab-Israeli problem as it impacted on our interests in the region. Since it did not have an Embassy in Israel, India's efforts in this direction were made mostly through the diplomacy at the UN. The basic goal was a peace settlement, which recognised Israel's right to exist in peace and security in the region. The reasons for lack of progress are many and complex, but the most important was the delay on the part of Arab States in recognising the realities, and instead, focussing on the legalities. By the time they recognised them, the realities had become much more adverse from their point of view. In the meantime, many opportunities were missed. For its part, Israel being in a strong position, always insisted on direct and bilateral negotiations for a peace settlement without third party involvement. For Arab countries, this approach was unacceptable, as this would be tantamount to recognition of Israel.

Another important foreign policy goal of India was to prevent Islamisation of the Kashmir issue by Pakistan in the WANA countries. Pakistan's efforts had to be consistently and vigorously countered. It consumed a lot of our energy and resources, but there was no choice, because WANA was an important arena of contest, as far as Kashmir issue was concerned.

For the rest, our goals in the region were the usual ones— strengthening of bilateral relations, promotion of trade and economic cooperation. As for economic relations, the lack of progress was less due to efforts to promote economic relations and more because neither side had that much to offer to the other. Consequently, agreements and MoUs were signed, joint commissions were created, without enough to show as concrete results. Our own anaemic economic performance with less emphasis on global competitive trading and more on import substitution could not be the basis for expanding exchange of goods and services.

Fundamentals of India's WANA policy

Before proceeding further, it might be appropriate to examine the validity of a few broad criticisms of India's WANA policies.

It is often implied and sometimes stated that India's policy in West Asia was pro-Arab and anti-Israel, because of the large Muslim population in India, and that the establishment of full diplomatic relations with Israel was unduly delayed due to this same reason.

There is very little concrete evidence to show that India's Middle East policy was fundamentally influenced by the Indian Muslim factor. On the other hand, there is a lot of evidence to show that it was all along guided by our very significant secular geopolitical and economic interests in WANA. The issues that are important to Muslims are here in India and not in far away WANA; nor are they very different to the issues important to others in India, *viz.*, food, clothing, shelter, medicines, security, justice and dignity. In no election was the Muslim vote influenced in any significant way by India's WANA policy. There is no organised Muslim lobby impacting India's foreign policy decisions, the way Israeli, Irish, Greek, Indian and a number of other lobbies do, in the US.

Israel, created by the UN resolution in 1948, was recognised by India in 1950. After that, we all along made it amply clear, that Israel had a right to exist in the region. We also accepted its *de facto* 1948 borders. Israel was permitted to establish a Consulate in Bombay. Our decision to establish full diplomatic relations was taken at the right time in 1992. By then a number of developments had taken place. In 1989, Palestinian National Council had recognised Israel's right to exist; Jordan had withdrawn its claim to sovereignty over West Bank and Gaza, thus clearing the way for a Palestinian State in those areas. Secret contacts between PLO and Israel had resulted in the Madrid peace process. With the disintegration of Soviet Union, US had emerged as the sole superpower and establishment of relations with Israel had many spin-off benefits for Indo-US relations. Time was appropriate for full diplomatic relations and we did so without hesitation or delay.

Another criticism often made is that India tended to see its relationship with the countries of WANA region, through the ideological prism—non-aligned *versus* aligned, progressives *versus* the conservatives, excessively favouring the former and unnecessarily cold shouldering the latter. It would have been, the argument goes beneficial much more for India if it had based its policy on self-interest and pursued it on a bilateral basis.

Actually, India's WANA policies were all along based on pragmatic pursuit of self-interest and we were never unwilling to strengthen bilateral ties, to the exclusion of other considerations, with any country, if there was scope for it.

First of all, for India, non-alignment was not a moral dogma, but a practical means to secure national interests. Its purpose was to enable India to avoid harmful external entanglements, so that India could focus on economic development and attain its full stature and role in world affairs. It was dictated by the external reality of a world divided into two hostile camps and the breadth of India's internal political spectrum. Joining one side or other would have had internal repercussions. At the same time, we maintained close political relations with Soviet Union to protect our interests.

Why India was not entirely successful in maintaining peaceful relations with all nations, avoiding conflicts and achieving the goal of high economic growth, is a vast subject in itself. But there should be no doubt that India pursued non-alignment for reasons of self-interest, and never knowingly sacrificed the latter for the former.

It also happened that the progressive, non-aligned and secular countries, with whom we had high profile relationship, in the 1950s, the '60s and the '70s, eg. Egypt, Iraq, Algeria, etc., were also major players in WANA. Close interaction with them was also good diplomacy, besides being good non-alignment. Relations with the non-aligned progressives were recalibrated as the circumstances changed in the eighties and the nineties.

As for relations with 'conservatives' it is not that we cold shouldered their initiatives for better relations with us. There was divergence of interests and perceptions, which could not be ignored. There was little scope for bilateral economic exchanges. Hence, lack of solid substance in our relationship with them.

The most important point overlooked by proponents of the *mantra* of bilateralism is that bilateralism cannot be pursued successfully without strong political and economic clout. Bilateralism is best pursued when others need you. With its recent political and economic success, India is much better placed to pursue bilateralism today.

At the popular level, there is the impression that there was an asymmetry between our position on the Arab-Israeli problem and Arab stand on the Kashmir issue and our problems with Pakistan. It is generally believed that our support to the Arabs on the Palestinian issue was stronger than their understanding of our position on Kashmir and problems with Pakistan.

The most objective way to sum up would be that the stand all sides took was conditioned by the parameters of their interests and realities not by ideologies. Certainly, there was no element of altruism anywhere.

We supported the legitimate rights of the Arabs and Palestinians, but this support was defined by our recognition of the right of Israel to be in the region and lead a normal existence. We could not go beyond this point.

It is hard to define the Arab position on Kashmir and Pakistan in relation to India because of the multiplicity of countries involved and also over the years their position has evolved, relatively speaking in favour of a better appreciation of our views, mainly because of changed circumstances. Without a detailed analysis of each country's position, which is excluded by the space available for this chapter, wrong impressions could be created about the position of WANA countries on Kashmir and Pakistan. So it is best not to attempt it.

But here are a few general statements based on my experience and study.

The stand of these countries on Kashmir and Pakistan was dictated more by considerations of their secular geopolitical interests than religious considerations. On Kashmir, in official discussions and statements, these countries, including the so-called conservative regimes, emphasised UN resolutions and not religious considerations. As for their relations with Pakistan, the attitude of many Middle East countries was influenced by geopolitical considerations. While needing India's understanding and support they also needed Pakistan for the same purpose. In fact, Pakistan could be more uninhibited and vocal on Palestine issue because it did not recognise Israel. In their own way, these countries in their policy towards India and Pakistan tried to balance their conflicting interests.

Foreign policy represents the net result of all factors and the religious factor cannot be ignored; but overemphasis on religious factor distorts assessments and foreign policy decisions. The emerging self-confident India can build mutually beneficial relations with WANA countries, based on secular considerations of common political, economic and security interests.

One important subject with regard to WANA countries is the factor of religion in their foreign policy decisions. In concrete terms, it was very limited. Even conservative regimes based their foreign policy on secular considerations of political, economic and security interests, and developed relations accordingly.

Pakistan's sustained efforts to capitalise on the religious link and Islamise the Kashmir issue, even in conservative countries, had limited success in concrete terms. The WANA countries had little to do with the internationalisation of the Kashmir issue in the fifties and the early sixties, which was done by certain big powers for their own global interests in the context of the Cold War.

It is impossible to generalise about the position of 20 WANA countries over the decades. Their positions were not identical and each country had its own nuance. Most countries showed reluctance to make statements on the issue. Statements made were often in the context of some bilateral visit or a crisis. Left to themselves they generally remained clear of the issue.

The common denominator in the statement of these countries was that the issue should be resolved in accordance with the UN resolutions. Sometimes to make it more pointed, reference to UN Resolution 1948 and 'in accordance with the wishes of the people' was specified.

Since the early nineties, the position of WANA countries has evolved. There are decreasing references to UN Security Council resolutions in their public utterances; instead the advice is to solve the Kashmir problem peacefully in accordance with Simla

Agreement or bilateral talks. This change has come about due to many global developments but most of all because of the threat of terrorism that those countries are facing. The success of India's democratic political model, as a solution to the problem of many identities living in one polity has also helped in changing attitudes to the Kashmir issue.

Overall, I think, we overestimated the interest and involvement of these countries in the Kashmir issue and expended more resources and time on the subject, in these countries, than was necessary.

Since objectivity is essential for sound policy, it would be instructive to compile an exhaustive tally of all public statements by WANA countries, as well as their voting record in UNSC and other international fora, on the Kashmir issue and see how facts square up with impressions, and how the stand of WANA countries compares with the stand of other countries in other regions.

Recent developments and their implications

Israeli-Palestinian issue

By building a security wall, separating the Israelis and Palestinians, the Israeli leadership is attempting a unilateral solution of the Palestinian problem. Since Biblical Israel, consisting of West Bank and Gaza, in addition to pre-1967 territories, cannot become a Jewish State, because of the presence of 46 per cent Palestinian population, increasing at a rate of 3.4 per cent as against Jewish population increase rate of 1.3 per cent, even leaders like Ariel Sharon realised that the only way to maintain the Jewish character of Israel was to withdraw from Palestinian areas of Gaza and West Bank and reduce the percentage of Palestinian population in Israel.

The seeds of the present complications were sown because of the unrealistic policy following the victory of June 1967 war, to create facts on the ground and finally, *fait accompli* by establishment of settlements in occupied territories.

Apart from being contrary to international law, UN Resolutions, the declarations of many multilateral organisations and the position of individual governments, it was an unrealistic and short-sighted policy. It was a mistake to imagine that the establishment of settlements, would change the demographic profile of West Bank and Gaza, and result in assimilation of those territories into one Biblical Israel.

While Israel has failed in its goal to integrate West Bank and Gaza, those settlements have created an intractable obstacle in the way of the establishment of a viable Palestinian State in those areas, as part of the two State solution, to the Arab-Israeli problem.

To understand the situation better, a closer look at the ground reality is essential.[1]

Palestine under the British Mandate before the establishment of Israel, had an area of 10,422 square miles.

Israel (without West Bank and Gaza) has an area of 8020 square miles, a population of about 6.9 million of which 5.55 million (80%) are Jews and 1.35 million (20%) Palestinians.

West Bank with an area of 2263 square miles has a population of 2.35 million and Gaza with an area of about 139 square miles has a population of 1.3 million. Together they have an area of 2402 square miles and a total population of 3.6 million.

In addition, there are 155,000 Israeli settlers in West Bank and 164,000 in East Jerusalem. All the 5000 settlers in Gaza were withdrawn recently.

If we add up everything and look at the total picture, Israel and the territories of West Bank and Gaza together, we find 10.5 million people living in an area of 10,422 square miles of which 5.6 million (54%) are Jews and 4.9 million (46%) Palestinians. The most significant fact is, however, the demographic trend. While the Arab population in West Bank and Gaza is increasing at the rate of 3.4 per cent per annum, the Jewish population is increasing only at the rate of 1.3 per cent. At this rate, the Palestinians will become a majority within a few years.

---

1. The Israeli population data is based on Israeli Central Bureau of Statistics figures, and the Palestinian population data is based on USAID figures as given on the internet.

Hence, the decision of Israel to withdraw from West Bank and Gaza, to maintain its Jewish character.

A few more facts will put things in perspective. The 1948 UN Resolution, which created Israel, by partitioning Palestine, envisaged its establishment on 55 per cent of the British Mandate Palestine, with the remaining 45 per cent of the territory to constitute the Palestine State.

The Arab States rejected the UN Partition plan and in the war between Israel and the Arab States, that ensued, the Arab armies lost. At the end of the war, Israel had expanded its territory from 55 per cent allocated to it under the UN Resolution, to 78 per cent.

As the winner of the 1967 War, Israel occupied West Bank and Gaza (besides Egyptian Sinai and Syrian Golan Heights), thus extending its control to the whole of what Arabs call Palestine and the Israelis consider Biblical Israel.

The Israeli military victory immediately raised the question of what to do about West Bank and Gaza. After some hesitation and debate the policy of establishing Jewish settlements in West Bank and Gaza was launched, which many Israelis hoped would lead to the integration of these territories and the establishment of Biblical Israel. In the process, the insurmountable difficulties of changing the Arab character of West Bank and Gaza, as well as the potential of long-term complications of permitting Jewish settlements in these territories were not seriously addressed. The extremist fringe had its own illusions.

More than 30 years after the commencement of the settlements, the position is that there are approximately 315,000 Israelis in East Jerusalem and West Bank, in about 90 settlements, of greatly varying sizes.

Fortunately, of the 315,000 settlers, 164,000 are in East Jerusalem, which is geographically contiguous to Israel, making a solution of these settlements easier. The real problem are the 160,000 settlers scattered deep inside the West Bank, in a large number of settlements. To create a viable Palestinian State, without dismantling these Jewish settlements is to square the circle.

The latest Israeli move is to build a wall separating Israeli settlements from the Palestinian areas of West Bank after reducing the number of settlements through consolidation (it has already withdrawn from Gaza).

Israel started the construction of the wall on security grounds but most people believe that, it intends to make the wall the permanent boundary between Israel and the Palestinians by 2010, and thus impose a unilateral solution.

The wall, it appears, will enclose large areas of Palestinian territory, and perhaps as much as 45 per cent of the existing West Bank may become a part of Israel as a result. Consequently, on completion of the wall, only 1350 square miles of territory or only 12-13 per cent of the British Mandate Palestine, would be available for the Palestinian State of more than 3.6 million Palestinians. But that is not all.

West Bank and the Gaza, the constituents of the proposed Palestinian State are already separated by Israeli territory and maintaining links between the two is a problem. Moreover, the Israeli settlements in West Bank and Gaza will be linked with corridors slicing the Palestinian territory in separate pieces. It is hard to see how a viable Palestinian State can be formed out of these separate pieces of territory.

So, what is the future of such a unilateral solution? The question of morality and legality apart, on grounds of practicability this move is unworkable. It will be a unilateral imposition and will last only as long as there is power to impose it. But power is nobody's permanent prerogative. Moreover, such an exercise of power on the unwilling does not come without costs.

Such unilateralism will not only be rejected by the Palestinians but will also be unacceptable to the Arabs. The region will remain in ferment and forces of extremism and destabilisation will be strengthened.

For its long-term economic health, Israel needs to integrate Palestinian manpower into its economy. The construction of the wall and increased segregation will hinder such integration.

Without a genuine across-the-board peace settlement, Israel will have to maintain deliberately high defence expenditure and remain excessively dependent on US financial aid.

The emergence of Hamas on a political platform is a significant development for the region. Having people's mandate, it is well placed to take a bold initiative. Hamas could strengthen its diplomatic position and international standing by categorically committing itself to 'full peace for full withdrawal'. Such a move will clear the way for Hamas for a genuine peace offensive. And the sooner Hamas does it, the greater the dividends it will earn.

India's interests would best be served by upholding international legality and commitment to a just and fair solution to the Palestinian problem, based on two state solution with a viable Palestinian State on West Bank and Gaza. India has significant interests in Israel and extensive interests in WANA countries. Our policy must therefore be balanced accordingly.

Iraq

Three years into the US military action there is no sign of the situation in Iraq stabilising. Indeed by all indications, the prospects of stabilisation in Iraq are growing less, not more. Recently, US Secretary of State Condoleezza Rice, admitted to many technical mistakes (reportedly a thousand) in Iraq. Unfortunately for our interests in the region, as well as beyond, it is a strategic mistake and requires strategic correction. Tactical tinkering will not do; without a strategic correction, the situation will have a sticky end.

First of all, it is incomprehensible that with the examples of their own experience in Vietnam, the French in Algeria, the Egyptians in Yemen, the Soviets in Afghanistan and Israelis in South Lebanon, the Americans should have launched a similar misadventure in Iraq.

The shifting explanations given by US leadership justifying military operations against Iraq are mystifying. None of them stands up to scrutiny. No convincing proof of links between Saddam and Al Qaeda was given or found. No solid evidence of possession of weapons of mass destruction by Iraq was given before the war, and none was produced after the military takeover of Iraq. Regime change has certainly been achieved but it is hard to see how the Iraqis are, or will be better off, with the developing civil war scenario.

If the Iraqi operation was intended to assert US strength as the only superpower and shape the region according to its interests, in this vital area, then it has only exposed the limits of US power.

If the Iraqi operation was about planting the tree of democracy in Iraq, whose seeds will disperse and spread democracy in the region, then the way it was sought to be achieved, showed the approach of a construction engineer, not the sensitivity of a social reformer. The idea of introducing democracy through military operation is so unrealistic that it should not have been even contemplated. The examples of Japan and Germany are irrelevant because of differences in circumstances.

New figures constantly appear about the cost of the war to the US economy and it is hard to make realistic forecasts. One estimate is that the ultimate cost of the war, direct and indirect, over the years would be 2 trillion dollars. But the way things are going, this figure will more likely be revised upward rather than downward. This war, combined with the cost of global fight against terrorism is a significant financial burden for the US already beset with massive trade imbalance (more than 600 billion dollars per annum), budgetary deficit, looming social security deficit, ballooning healthcare costs and a host of social, urban and environmental problems.

Whatever the reasons for the war and whatever it costs, one thing is fairly predictable. Iraq cannot be controlled and pacified with a military force of 130,000 soldiers. It is too small a force for a country the physical size of Iraq and its population of 25 million. Some top army men had warned that the number of soldiers required for effective control of Iraq would be around 300,000, but they were overruled. If we carefully study such misadventures in the past, even three hundred thousand soldiers are inadequate for the task.

If US withdraws without stabilising Iraq (and it is hard to see how US can stabilise the situation there) it will leave behind a country wracked by violence, strife and potential for civil war and destabilisation of the region.

Equally, US withdrawal, which is seen as having been forced upon it by pressure, will be seen as a victory for extremists. Such a perception about the extremists, after their success in Afghanistan about a decade and a half ago will send up their prestige and following manifold. Ironically, this would be the very opposite of what President Bush had set out to do in Afghanistan and Iraq after 9/11.

President Bush is talking of staying the course in Iraq for years to come. He has hinted that his successor will have to deal with the question of when and how to withdraw from Iraq. But staying the course helps only when things are getting better, or likely to do so shortly, and not getting worse.

America is caught in a war it cannot win nor afford to lose. Going by the past examples of Vietnam, Afghanistan, etc. countries caught in such a dilemma have chosen to de-escalate and wind up their involvement in the quagmire. Will America repeat the Vietnam model in Iraq? Perhaps even the Americans cannot answer that question definitively, now.

India is facing a particularly difficult situation because of what is happening in Iraq. The Gulf, Iraq and Iran constitute a region that is important for India. But it is hard to see what role India can play given the present US position that while tactical mistakes have been made in Iraq, the strategic decision was right.

Keeping in view the likely outcome of the Iraqi imbroglio, it would be best not to get involved in this strategic mistake in any way. However, we should be prepared for constructive engagement should there be a clear indication of change of approach by the US in favour of a strategic correction. Until then, we must refrain from anything that can compromise our option for such a role later.

Meanwhile, through quiet and firm diplomacy, India should try to prevent the potentially disastrous escalation of this conflict into the neighbouring Iran and Syria. The developments in Iraq are even more important for the future of the region than those in the West Bank and Gaza.

Democracy and WANA

America's declared goal of introducing democracy not only in Iraq but in many other countries in the region, raises many questions, besides eyebrows.

Undoubtedly, there are clear signs of urge in these societies for more consultative governance, fairer and more broad-based economic opportunities and personal freedom. There is growing realisation that in this rapidly globalising world and borderless communication, there is need for reforms. The leadership in these countries is aware of the need for adjustment and some efforts in this direction are being made. It is a sensitive situation.

With regard to Western attempts to spread democracy, a few points need to be emphasised.

First of all, democracy can be encouraged from outside, but not imposed. An intrusive approach can backfire and bring down the old order without putting the new one in its place.

American efforts at introducing democracy in the region will face opposition, because US motives for trying to do so are suspect in the eyes of the people. Nurturing democracy in the region will require patience and sustained effort for which Americans have yet to show enough aptitude.

In the 1990s, the electoral success of FIS (Islamic Salvation Front) in Algeria and of Hamas now in West Bank and Gaza shows the nature of challenges that will have to be faced in introducing democracy in the region.

Can the mandate given by the people to a party be cancelled, on the ground that the people have elected the wrong persons? Who is to decide and on what basis? The mandate of FIS in Algeria was cancelled on the ground that their outlook is anti-democratic and that once they come to power they will act anti-democratically and abolish democracy altogether. Can outsiders prognosticate and prejudge what elected representatives will do?

Governance and responsibility have a sobering and chastening effect. One can come to power on the basis of ideology, but decision-making as government requires a broader approach, with ability to balance and reconcile conflicting claims. In this globalising and contracting world, no regime can pursue extremist policies which will isolate it, damage its interests and hurt its people.

Voters elect leaders less for their ideology and more because of their belief, that those they are electing are better suited to solve their problems, which are the same everywhere, eg., food, clothing, shelter, healthcare, education, security, justice, etc., than the present position holders. The elected representatives who fail to show progress in these respects are shown the door at the next opportunity.

The best way to defeat fundamentalists would be to do so in open and democratic competition. Their support comes from the incumbency factor *viz.*, the corruption and incompetence of those in power. If after coming to power, fundamentalists fail to fulfil the needs of the voters, they will lose their appeal and ground support.

It will be in India's interests to deal with democratically elected leaders, so long as they go by the norms of responsible governance, irrespective of the ideology that brought them to power. If Hamas is willing for a just and peaceful settlement, based on the concept of two States—an Arab and a Jewish—living side by side, it should be actively engaged. Ostracising Hamas will only complicate an already difficult situation and persuade people in the region, that behind the façade of democracy, the West wants to install regimes subservient to its interests.

As a democracy, India must follow the logic of democracy and pursue its own independent line with Hamas, consistent with its interests.

European Union and WANA

An important and far-reaching development in the WANA region is the growth of ties between European Union and Mediterranean rim WANA countries, eg., Morocco, Algeria, Tunisia, Egypt, Israel, Lebanon, Syria, Jordan and Palestine, following the Barcelona Declaration of 1995. In addition to these 9 countries, the

Barcelona Declaration covers 3 other countries—Cyprus, Malta and Turkey, collectively referred to as Med-12.

Because of the economic and strategic importance of the area, EU (in its earlier incarnation as European Community) had tried to strengthen ties with the region through European Community's Global Mediterranean Policy, launched in 1972 and the Euro-Arab Dialogue established by the European Community in the aftermath of the 1973 oil shock. Both initiatives aimed at improving relations with the Arab world through promotion of economic and cultural ties.

These initiatives, which were limited in scope did not yield significant substantive results, mainly because throughout the seventies and the eighties, West Asia was racked by crisis and turmoil, e.g., expulsion of Egypt from the Arab League following the Camp David Agreement; Intifada in the West Bank; Iraq-Iran War of 1981-1988 and the Kuwait Crisis of 1990-91. Such a continuous stream of crises, called for fire-fighting rather than long-term ambitious initiatives.

But by 1995, with Israeli-PLO dialogue creating hopes of better days ahead for Middle East, time seemed appropriate for a bold and comprehensive initiative.

The Barcelona Declaration envisages partnership between EU and Med-12, broadly in three areas.

The first is partnership in political and security relations. In this regard, the participants have identified peace, stability and security in the Mediterranean region as common asset that they pledge to promote and strengthen. Accordingly, they declared their commitment to the following principles and objectives: respect for human rights and fundamental liberties (including freedoms of expression, thought and association), the equal rights of people and the right of self-determination; non-interference in each others affairs; dispute settlement by peaceful means; greater cooperation in the fight against terrorism; stronger regional security through adherence to and compliance with, international agreements in such areas as non-proliferation of nuclear, chemical and biological weapons; and a Middle East free of weapons of mass destruction (nuclear, chemical and biological) as well as their delivery systems.

The second part of the Declaration calls for an economic and financial partnership to achieve three important objectives: intensified efforts for social and economic development, improvement of individual's living conditions by raising employment and reducing economic gap with the Euro-Mediterranean region and promotion of cooperation and regional economic integration. The main vehicle for achieving this partnership is the establishment of a free-trade area, involving progressive elimination of tariff trade barriers. The plan also includes an increase in EU's financial assistance to Med-12 countries.

The third area covered by the Declaration is partnership in social, cultural and human affairs. This will involve cooperation in the fields of education and training; social development; migration; media; cultural exchanges; youth programmes and fight against terrorism, international crimes, corruption, racism and xenophobia.

While the primary goals of Europe in the Mediterranean rim countries are political and security related, the vehicle for achieving them is economic integration of the region. The basic strategy is to enhance security through shared prosperity. Every indication is that it is a serious initiative and significant progress has been achieved in the area of economic cooperation.

Under the umbrella of the Barcelona process, the EU has entered into bilateral trade agreements with Tunisia (1995), Morocco (1996), the Palestinian Authority (1997), Jordan (1997), Egypt (2001), Lebanon (2002), Algeria (2002) and Syria (2004).

Even more significant is the fact that EU is the largest trading partner for many of these countries: Tunisia 74.4 per cent; Algeria 62.4 per cent; Morocco 62.2 per cent; Syria 49.5 per cent; Lebanon 39.6 per cent; Egypt 30 per cent; Jordan 23.7 per cent and Palestine 9.6 per cent.

EU is also putting money where its mouth is. It has provided significant financial assistance for modernisation and industrialisation programmes allocating Euros 5.3 billion for the period 1996-2000 and Euros 5.5 billion for the period 2001-2005. Most of this assistance went to Egypt, Morocco, Tunisia and Palestine.

The growing economic integration is expected to lead to closer political and security cooperation between EU and these countries. EU's strategy seems to be that economic prosperity in this region will reduce terrorism and the pressure of immigration from these countries to Europe. The presence of 10 to 12 million immigrants from these countries into Europe is a major concern of EU. Stability in the region will also enhance security of EU's oil and gas supplies from Libya and Algeria, which are important for Europe for its energy needs.

The size of the common market that will emerge from this economic integration process can be imagined from a few facts. The present population of the Med-12, including Turkey, is about 260 million, with a total GDP of 1.4 trillion dollars. The figures for EU are: Total population 450 million and total GDP about 12 trillion dollars.

The gravitational effect of such a large economic market will not remain confined to only Mediterranean rim countries but would extend right up to the Gulf. It will significantly alter the landscape in the region.

For us, this will have political as well as economic implications. Since this area, especially the Gulf, is important for us, we will have to strengthen our relationship with this area through focussed and sustained effort. The emerging scenario of greater prosperity could provide us with expanded economic opportunities especially joint ventures in North Africa for exports to Europe.

Terrorism

The phenomenon of terrorism has got so linked with WANA countries that it is essential to deal with it in some detail.

First of all, there is a general reluctance by societies facing terrorism, to admit, at least publicly, that there are causes for terrorism, as if such an admission would be tantamount to accepting that there is some justification for terrorism. Such an attitude will not help in eradicating terrorism, nor is the admission that there are causes, a justification for terrorism. As a matter of fact, nowhere is terrorism justified today, because there are peaceful avenues available, which can better achieve their goals than violence. This is particularly true of terrorism in democratic societies.

The relationship of religion with terrorism is another tangled issue that needs to be looked into carefully and objectively. What cannot be overemphasised is that the most fundamental reasons for terrorism are political, social and economic, not religious.

If terrorism has its roots in religion, then how can we explain the wide spectrum of terrorism cutting across religious lines, eg., terrorism in Northern Ireland, in Spain, in Latin America, in Sri Lanka, even in Palestine during British Mandate, and a host of other cases.

In all cases, the common thread is deep-rooted political, social and economic malaise. Terrorism's real foundations are laid by deep sense of frustration, resentment and humiliation due to the perception, some times justified and sometimes not, of unjust political, social and economic circumstances.

Often those, who lead terrorist movements, use religion or an ideology to tap the frustrations of the people for their goals. Religion and ideology are used to motivate the people. Religion becomes the vehicle of terrorism without being its true cause. Religion and ideology have their appeal because, instead of evolutionary gradualism of democracy they promise instant total solution. Of course, it is an abuse of religion and contrary to religious teachings.

That force has to be used against terrorists cannot be seriously contested. But force alone will not solve the problem of violence and terrorism. Irrespective of public postures, the causes of terrorism will have to be addressed and corrective actions taken. A two-pronged strategy of the carrot and the stick will be far more effective than the force-alone approach. Addressing the causes of terrorism will reduce support for terrorists and make it easier to isolate and deal with them.

With the phenomena of terrorism and violence having become global, our struggle against terrorism is getting a wider understanding. Many of the countries in WANA are also facing the growing problem of terrorism and violence. India and a number of WANA countries, including those in the Gulf are increasing mutual cooperation for combating this common menace.

India's success in managing its political, social and economic affairs through the long haul of democracy, freedom and equality, is getting increasing attention globally. The importance of such an approach in constructively combating terrorism is also being increasingly recognised by the insightful. We could enhance the profile of our public diplomacy in this respect. As our political and economic success strengthens, we can convince many more that, slow and steady path of democracy rather than the quick leap of violence is answer to their problems, that ballots succeed where bullets fail. For ourselves, we will always have to bear in mind that others will not go by the preachings they hear but the practices they see.

Organisation of Islamic Conference

In view of our political and economic success in recent years, and our future interests, time has come to review our relationship with OIC, which counts amongst its membership of 55 countries, with a population of 1.3 billion. Recently, King Abdullah had reportedly expressed the view that India, like Russia, should have an observer status. While considering India's relations with WANA, it would be appropriate to deal with OIC, because it was in WANA that OIC was born, its Secretariat is located in Jeddah and more than one-third of its membership is from WANA.

For more than three decades our relationship with OIC has been clouded by the manner in which India was first invited to the Islamic Summit Conference in 1969 and then excluded. The full account of what happened in Rabat at the first Islamic Summit Conference will soon be available. Ambassador Gurbachan Singh in Morocco in 1969, has recorded his recollection of the events, which would soon be published. Here only a few details may be mentioned.

The invitation to India was proposed by the Late King Faisal and seconded by the late King Hassan of Morocco. No country objected, and invitation to India was issued on 23rd September morning. The same evening India participated in one session of the Conference. Next day, Yahya Khan, on getting reports of strong adverse reaction in Pakistan against his handling of the matter in letting India be invited, refused to participate further in the Conference, if India continued to attend.

Efforts were made to persuade India to voluntarily abstain from the Conference, as otherwise the Conference would break up. Heads of delegations of four countries jointly approached the leader of the Indian delegation, the late Shri Fakhruddin Ali Ahmad for this purpose. Saudi Arabia, the sponsor of the invitation to India, did not in any way associate itself with these diplomatic efforts. India of course, refused to accept such a suggestion.

The basic position may be summed up as follows: While almost all the countries disagreed with Pakistan's attitude in threatening to boycott the Conference, if India continued to attend it, no country was willing to stand up for us, and leave the Conference, if India was excluded. No country agreed with Pakistan's attitude, but neither did any country effectively oppose Pakistan. This was certainly unfair to India if not unfriendly. Of course, there is no doubt that if some countries had walked out of the Conference because of Pakistan's attitude on India's participation, the Conference would have suffered a serious blow and probably broken up in confusion.

All this is old history. The question is how should we look at OIC today and what relationship with it is dictated by our interests.

First, it can be very convincingly argued that India's decision to express strong interest in being associated with Islamic Summit Conference in 1969 was not based on careful reflection. India would have been at odds with the agenda and direction of the Organisation at that time. Countries like Iraq and Syria had not participated in the first Islamic Summit for similar reasons.

Perhaps equally ill-considered was the decision to rush a high-level delegation to the Conference, when it was more than half way through. India had been formally invited, and a locally constituted delegation consisting of the Ambassador, a Second Secretary and a prominent Muslim personality had attended the delegation. The speech of the leader of the delegation is a part of the minutes of the Conference. Legally, India had become a member of the OIC, something which has never been formally cancelled. At least, India has never been informed to that effect. Given the circumstances, we could and should have waited for a subsequent meeting of the OIC to send a well-prepared high-level delegation in time, rather half way through a Conference.

Today, 36 years later, the circumstances have changed. Its unsuccessful diplomatic experience of Iraq-Iran war, Iraq's occupation of Kuwait and a host of other issues, have induced a degree of realism in OIC's view of its role in international relations. Moreover, terrorism is a major global issue consuming the energies of many of the OIC countries today.

Meanwhile, India's political success in managing a pluralistic society and combining economic success with democracy, have given our way of doing things credibility. Our view that Kashmir issue should be resolved peacefully through bilateral contacts has gained wider acceptance.

Given all these developments, it is time perhaps to have a more cordial, constructive and structured interaction with OIC. More formal relationship with OIC is likely to give us an opportunity to conduct more effective public diplomacy at OIC Conferences with various OIC member countries on matters of mutual interest. It can also further strengthen our relations with many WANA countries, especially in the Gulf.

In the absence of any formal initiative from the OIC, one should avoid hypothetical ideas and suggestions about the nature of relationship with OIC. At the same time, India can suitably make it clear, that it is willing to have relations with any organisation conducting itself according to norms of diplomatic intercourse, based on mutuality of interests. Time has come to not act on the basis of past emotions but future calculations, to approach the issue with the self-confidence of the strong, not the sensitivities of the weak.

India's economic interests and WANA

Since policies follow interests, here is a basic data about our trade and economic relations with WANA (including the Gulf Cooperation Council countries) and Israel.

Our both-way trade with WANA (including Gulf) is US $ 19 billion per annum, imports $ 7.8 billion and exports $ 11.2 billion. The bulk of our trade is with GCC countries: Exports 9.5 billion and imports 6.9 billion.

Additionally, the value of remittances from 3.5 million Indian expatriates in the Gulf is estimated to be around $ 7 billion.

The total quantity of our oil imports from the Gulf (including Iran) is about 470 million barrels per annum or 66 per cent of our total imports of 705 million barrels. Our total oil consumption currently is about 990 million barrels per annum.

In the absence of information about contracted price, no value on the quantity of our oil imports is being put, though at the notional price of $ 60 per barrel, the value of 470 million barrels of oil comes to $ 28.2 billion.

A few points may be underlined here:

Considering that 3.5 million Indians in the Gulf support their families back home, probably 12 million men, women and children in India, depend for the economic wellbeing on remittance.

Secondly, in view of our growing oil consumption estimated at 6-7 per cent per annum, and our depleting indigenous oil production, our oil import from the Gulf could triple from about 470 million barrels per annum to about 1400 million barrels per annum by 2030.

Finally, our share of WANA countries' trade (excluding the Gulf) being still relatively small, there is significant potential for expansion.

Our total trade with Israel for the year 2005 reportedly was US $ 3 billion both ways. It is projected to grow to US $ 5 billion by 2008. These figures exclude military purchases which according to one newspaper report are about $ 2 billion.

Sixty per cent of our trade with Israel consists of import, cutting and polishing and re-export of diamonds. The rest consists mainly of high tech economic exchanges for which Israel is an important and stable source.

Our economic relationship with Israel has been increasing at a very fast pace since relations were established in 1992. Considering that Israeli GDP is about $ 130 billion, at some point the growth of trade relationship will slow down and level off. Even so, because of the nature of our exchanges, with emphasis on high-tech trade, Israel will remain an important economic partner.

Conclusion

Historically on a familiar wicket in WANA, India's economic and political success in recent years has opened new possibilities for strengthening ties with the countries of the region.

Geographically, the Gulf is our most natural and cost effective supplier of oil and gas for our expanding economy. We are also a very suitable economic partner for these countries for joint ventures, especially in oil refining, petrochemicals, fertilisers and other petroleum based industries because of our growing need for these products. We should leverage our geographical serendipity in relation to Gulf more effectively for this purpose.

The growing threat of terrorism has affected many of the WANA countries and there is increasing sign of drive for cooperation to tackle this problem. For results, sustained efforts and regular contacts will be required.

As for issues like the Israeli-Palestinian problem, the developing situation in Iraq and US attempts at introducing democracy are concerned, we must follow an active but independent policy dictated by our long-term interest in the region.

With regard to OIC, we must base our relationship on pragmatic considerations of our growing interests in the WANA countries, especially the Gulf, without the emotional distortions of the past.

We should enhance the profile of our public diplomacy in the region in an unobtrusive manner, based on growing recognition of our success in managing social and political pluralism and achieving economic growth.

WANA is one of the most important regions for us, geopolitically and should be the focus of commensurate attention on our part.

15

India's West Asia policy: search for a middle ground

Rajendra M. Abhyankar[1]

The setting

The importance of West Asia to India is seen from the fact that three of the first decisions on foreign policy related to West Asia: our support to the Khilafat Movement; India's stand in the UN Special Committee on Palestine (UNSCOP) in 1947 and the decision on how we were going to deal with Israel. These decisions can be seen in the context of the Partition of India which had left a larger Muslim community within India than went to Pakistan. The importance of the region, particularly Mecca and Medina in fulfilling the spiritual and religious needs of India's Muslim population could not be underestimated. These early decisions by the Government of India regarding our policy towards West Asia illustrate the counter pressures which have always led India to search for a middle ground in its policy towards the region. They also illustrate the considerations which come into play even today in India's policy towards the region.

1. I was greatly assisted in preparing this paper by Dr. H.A. Nazmi and Dr. Sujata A. Cheema, both lecturers and colleagues at the Centre for West Asian Studies, Jamia Millia Islamia. This paper has benefited greatly from the ideas presented at the National Conference on West Asia organised by the Centre for West Asian Studies, Jamia Millia Islamia, New Delhi, August 20-21, 2006.

The active support of the Indian National Congress to the Khilafat Movement, which called for the restoration of the Caliphate in Turkey, was perhaps the first foreign policy statement on West Asia. It was an early demonstration of the effect of domestic politics on foreign policy. The Caliphate was abolished by Mustafa Kamal Ataturk and was not restored despite protests from Muslims all over the world. The decision of the Congress to take up the Khilafat cause (as a factor for Hindu-Muslim unity in the subcontinent) signalled for India the role of Islam as a significant factor in foreign policy. It is another matter that the funds collected by the Khilafat Movement to support the Caliphate reached Turkey after the abolition of the Caliphate, and in his wisdom, Ataturk used the funds for constructing the first building of the Turkish Grand National Assembly.

In 1947, as a member of the United Nations Special Committee on Palestine (UNSCOP), India proposed a minority plan which called for the establishment of a federal Palestine with internal autonomy for the Jewish population. When the UN General Assembly voted for the majority plan providing for the creation of two states—Arab and Jewish—in Palestine, India joined the Arab and Islamic countries in opposing the partition of Palestine and proposed a federal state with two autonomous areas. Nearly 60 years later today that solution may evolve being the only viable solution to this continuing problem. India was also against Israel's membership of the UN pointing out that it could not recognise an Israel which had been achieved through the force of arms and not through negotiations. While reflecting on the events of the time, K.M. Panikkar, Indian diplomat and statesman, who played an important role in shaping the contours of India's West Asia policy, remarked, "on the question of Jewish State in Palestine, however, my sympathies were not at all with the Zionists. The Indian attitude has always been friendly to the Arabs. Having just come out of its own partition, India's dissenting note recommended a single federal state with appropriate autonomy for the two communities while sympathizing with the claims of the Jews...I thought that this demand for a State based on religious exclusivism was in the first instance likely to revive Islamic fanaticism and, second, was unjust to the Palestinian Arabs."[2]

Yet the establishment of the State of Israel had created a new political reality in West Asia. To begin with, India did not want to recognise Israel as an independent State, despite repeated requests from the latter. Jawaharlal Nehru explained thus: "the Government of India have received a request from the State of Israel for recognition. We propose to take no action in this matter at present. India can play no effective part in this conflict at the present stage either diplomatically or otherwise."[3] It is believed that Maulana Abul Kalam Azad prevailed on Nehru to delay the proposed step relating to Israel as it would be misread by the Muslim community which had yet to get over the trauma of partition. It was only in September 1950, that Prime Minister Nehru agreed to grant Israel *de jure* recognition while refusing to establish full diplomatic relations. The decision to recognise Israel emerged from the consideration that "continuing non-recognition is not only inconsistent with the overall relationship but even limits the effectiveness of Government of India's role as a possible intermediary between Israel and Arab States."[4] Whether India can, or should, play such a role remains moot even today.

By according formal recognition to Israel, "India acknowledged Israel's right to exist...recognized the desirability of solving the Arab-Israeli dispute without resort to threats of annihilation and provocations by the Arabs, but India also expressed its disapproval of Israeli military retaliations and Israel's appropriations of additional Arab territory and its alteration of the flow of River Jordan's water." It was Nehru's view that the policy on Israel was "not a matter of high principle, but it is based on how we could best serve and be helpful in that area." For Nehru the "Zionist movement was the child of British imperialism" and in his famous *Glimpses of World*

2. Panikkar, K.M. (1955). *In Two Chinas: Memoirs of a Diplomat*, London, p.12.

3. Quoted in Parthasarathy, G. (ed.) (1985). *Jawaharlal Nehru, Letters to Chief Ministers 1947-64*, Volume 1, London, p.128.

4. Mishra, K.P. (1966). *India's Policy of Recognition of States and Governments*, Allied Publishers, Bombay, p.58

History, he observed "the story of Palestine ever since has been one of conflict between Arabs and Jews, with the British Government siding with one or the other as occasion demanded, but generally supporting the Jews."[5] In 1947, India's Representative to the UN stated that the British wanted the establishment of a Jewish State for political and strategic reasons in total disregard of the principle of self-determination.

The Palestinian question has engaged Indian leaders since the national movement. It was Mahatma Gandhi who in the early 1920s first spoke of Indian support to the Palestinian cause which after independence translated itself into the staunch support that India gave to the PLO and to the creation of Palestinian State. India and West Asian countries have had a history of struggle against colonialism. Despite a lack of joint struggle against foreign domination, India's principled opposition to imperialism and leadership of the Non-Aligned Movement was greatly appreciated in the region and strengthened its historical ties with the Arab countries. This support goes back to 1936, when the Congress Working Committee sent its greetings to the Palestinian Arabs and observed September 27, 1936, as Palestine Day in order to show their solidarity with the Palestinian people.[6] Consequently, one of the cardinal points of the Non-Aligned Movement founded by Nehru, Nasser and Tito was the support for an independent Palestinian State. India was the first country to recognise Yasser Arafat as the President of the Palestinian State in 1980. India's support to the Palestinians has been total and it mattered greatly in bringing the entire membership of the Non-Aligned Movement to focus on the Palestinian issue.

Indian leaders also saw a sharp contradiction between the goals of the Zionist movement and the Indian freedom movement, specially the issue of partitioning countries on religious grounds.[7] The Zionists made several attempts to elicit Mahatma Gandhi's "powerful

---

5. Nehru, Jawaharlal (1988). *Glimpses of World History*, New Delhi, p.763.

6. *ibid.*

7. Kumar, Dinesh (2001). *India and Israel: Dawn of a New Era*, Jewish Institute of West Defence.

moral support" without any success.[8] Gandhi and other nationalists argued that the consent of the Arab inhabitants was essential for the creation of a Jewish national home in Palestine. While being sympathetic towards the Jews they were unwilling to endorse the Zionist demands.

India's pro-Arab stance received a setback at the Rabat Conference in September 1969 which was convened by the Arab leaders to condemn Israel for the burning of the Al-aqsa Mosque in occupied East Jerusalem. The Indian delegation led by Fakhruddin Ahmed was not allowed to participate in the Conference at the instance of Pakistan. Pakistan's use of the Islamic dimension became most evident thereafter in the subsequent meetings of the Islamic Conference Organisation. Nevertheless, India continued to support the cause of the Arabs, specially the Palestinians, at world forums. During the Arab-Israeli War of 1973, India supported the Arabs and blamed Israel for the existence of the conflict in the region. India endorsed the PLO's bid for Observer status at the UN in 1974 and became the first non-Arab country to extend formal diplomatic accreditation to the PLO representative. India was also the first non-Arab country to recognise Yasser Arafat as the President of Palestine. The basic reason behind India's support for the cause of the Palestinian Arabs has been the anti-colonial character of the movement which had been the principle of India's own struggle for independence. Another important factor was the identity of interests between the secular stream within the Arabs, represented by the PLO and the Arab Ba'ath Socialist Party, with India's ingrained secular polity. India gave tacit support to Arab leaders who were launching military operations against Islamic-oriented groups represented by the Muslim Brotherhood, *Ikhawan muslimeen.* It was another matter that none of the Arab leaders represented anything approximating the kind of democracy that India had. However, India has never been an exporter of its democratic choices.

Indian position on the Palestinian issue has not changed greatly since the 1980s. K.K. Tiwari, the Indian Minister of State for

---

8. Jansen, G.H. (1991). "Relations with Israel would be Immoral", *Times of India,* September 10.

External Affairs, observed in 1988 that "the fundamental issues involved in the peace process were the attaining by the Palestinian people of their inalienable right to self-determination and the recognition that all States in the region, including the States of Palestine and Israel and other neighbours, have the right to live in peace and security within internationally recognized borders." This statement was read by some as the Government's willingness to reassess the whole situation in West Asia and as an attempt to rectify the tilt in its pro-Arab policy.

From the Indian perspective, West Asia must be seen as our extended neighbourhood which means that Indian understanding of the region has to be responsive to its sensitivities. As Girijesh Pant said, "For India, West Asia is the region to augment its power rather than to display or assert its power ...The thrust of India's West Asia policy and diplomacy thus has to be geared towards mobilizing resources–political, strategic, economic and cultural– from the region to contribute in its emergence as global power. While India's recent economic success has made this, possible at the political level, Indian policy makers need to recognize that West Asian sensitivities have been offended and hurt by aggresive US intervention in the region. Indian policy has to be shaped in consonance with regional concerns. This does not mean that Indian policy has to be hostage to West Asian expectations but to underline that rise of India as a global player critically hinges upon its clout in its extended neighbourhood. In defining an Indian perspective it needs to locate itself within the geo-politics of a rising Asia in order to alter the current discourse on global affairs."[9]

From an early concentration on looking at the region through the Islamic prism, Indian policy considerations have evolved in the last 50 years. The prism has shown other dimensions of the relationship: the oil-rich countries of the Gulf particularly Iran and Iraq became increasingly important for India in the 1960s and 1970s and remain so for our energy security; from the 1980s, the region

---

9. Pant, Girijesh (2006). "Imagining West Asia beyond the Neocon Construct: Defining an Indian Perspective", Paper presented at *National Conference on West Asia*, Centre for West Asian Studies, Jamia Millia Islamia, August 21-22.

became a source of employment for Indian workers who today number 3.5 million, and correspondingly a source for huge remittances which today are about $ 12 billion annually. Yet throughout this period the relationship remained one-sided. It is only in the new Millennium that for the first time the relationship between India and West Asia has become truly two-dimensional: these countries are ready to see India as a partner—both economic and strategic. This change has been possible entirely due to India's economic success and recognition as an emerging global player.

The considerations which guided our policy in these years remain valid even though the political, economic and social matrix in the region has changed:

- friendly relations with the Arabs particularly the Palestinians;
- desire to play an effective role in the region, even as a possible intermediary;
- oppose both religious exclusivism and religious fanaticism while being aware of the spiritual and religious needs of India's Muslim community;
- develop economic and trade ties.

Recent developments

The attrition and degradation from the eight year long Iraq-Iran War affected only the belligerents directly. It suited all the major powers, and even some minor, that it continued endlessly. India, like the other non-aligned countries, took a neutral position being a friend to both and unable to choose. It lost equally since both Iraq and Iran were major suppliers of crude; although in Iraq India's financial exposure on construction contracts was of the order of $ 3 billion when the War broke out. India was able to weather the consequences albeit at a high cost. Indian debt of the order of $ 2 billion due to the deferred payment scheme that was put in place after the Iran-Iraq War still remains outstanding.

The Iraqi invasion of Kuwait on 2 August 1990, on the other hand, was as much a loss of innocence for the region as for India.

It forced choices on every Arab leader and shattered the assiduously cultivated image of Arab unity and solidarity. It also led to belligerent military action by US and European forces on a scale not seen since the Second World War. The political uncertainty that Saddam Hussein created had a profound effect on the Western assessment of future security of energy resources. The consequent establishment of US military bases in Saudi Arabia to secure the oil wells became the catalyst for extremist Islamic forces led by Osama Bin Laden to target the Saudi regime. The fact that Bin Laden had cohorts of well-trained and committed cadres from the Afghanistan War fuelled his campaign against the West in general and the presence of foreign troops in the holy land of Mecca and Medina. The need to choose whether to join the US-led Coalition's invasion force against Iraq in January 1991 put many an Arab leaders at variance with their people. This was most visible in countries like Syria, Egypt, Jordan and Saudi Arabia. The fact that the political systems in those countries did not provide an opportunity for the people to express their frustration and anger exacerbated the situation.

Political developments in the region since 2000, the most provocative act being the 9/11 attack on the World Trade Center, changed the face of the region warranting an assessment of how they have affected India's historical, political and economic space. It would be appropriate, at this point, to enumerate the major tendencies which characterise the West Asian region in order to understand how India has responded to them:

- The use of terror as an instrument of political negotiation: The increasing use of violence by extremist Islamic groups to express their frustration and inability to change the existing political order in West Asia is now a recurring feature of political discourse. The multiplicity of groups forming part of the al-Qaeda or its clones in various countries has introduced 'non-state' actors as a factor in international relations and forced the international community to define and combat terror on a global scale. For India, with its two decade experience of cross-border terrorism the War on Terror did not start after 9/11, it became 'global' after it.

- As events, and particularly terror attacks, have unfolded it has become evident that even though its origins can be traced in West Asia, the al-Qaeda network has managed to recruit nationals from every country using Islam as the binding factor. Furthermore, the connection between the al-Qaeda and the Taliban has meant that the investigation of every terrorist attack in the world since 2000, has a common thread running to the Afghanistan-Pakistan border area.

- The obverse has been the targeting of all Muslims to the great detriment of a major world religion. It has provoked the international community to think of a dialogue amongst different civilisations and cultures and to look for paradigms of political and cultural diversity and inclusion.

- The realisation on the part of the rulers in the region that they need to reach out to their people by including them in the political processes in their countries. The experience since the Gulf War I has shown various attempts to encourage limited opposition groups, co-opt the opposition through nominated seats in the Parliament; and holding of sub-national and national level elections. The over-arching theme in all these attempts at 'democracy' has been the fear of the rulers to losing political power. As a result, these efforts have been self-serving, unpopular and truncated. What is more, it has provoked others to embark on a democratisation mission for the region. The US intention to create a Greater Middle East is a part of this dynamic. In contra-position, wherever free elections were held, as in Turkey, Iraq and Palestine, Islamic-oriented parties have gained office demonstrating the growing salience of the Islamic stream in Arab political thought to the detriment of the secular, nationalist stream represented among others by the PLO, the Arab Ba'ath Socialist Party and the secular Turkish political parties.

- The failure of the UN and the international community to find a solution to the longstanding Arab-Israeli issue with UNSC Resolutions 242 and 338—the well-accepted 'land-for-peace' formula—still on the books. The Middle East Peace Process followed by the Oslo Process failed to meet the aspirations of either side. The *Intifada* of 2000, virtually put paid to these efforts engendering the Quartet process—yet another attempt to take the issue forward. It now remains at an impasse after Israel's unilateral withdrawal from Gaza. The last years of Yasser Arafat—when he was cut off by Israel and the US—and his passing has changed the situation dramatically: neither is PLO the unquestioned representative of the Palestinians, nor is Israel prepared to accept a government led by Hamas. There is an increasing conviction amongst the Arabs that United States is no longer the honest broker that they expected it to be. These series of efforts to find a solution have however established, first, that only a solution to the vexed Arab-Israeli issue will end strife and frustration in the region; second, the acceptance that there will have to be two states—Palestine and Israel—living together within secure borders; and third, that the US is still the only power with leverage to bring about a solution.

- The inviolability of Israel in the region under the aegis of the United States: US policies in the region are perceived as Israel-centric and seen reflected both within the UN and on-the-ground. This conclusion was inescapable most recently during the Israeli missile attack in Gaza and the aggression on Lebanon when the US neither called for restraint nor stopped the conflict until it was too late even for Israel to get much credit from its adventure. Furthermore, the unwritten edict which makes it taboo to mention Israeli nuclear weapons while giving no quarter to Iraq and Iran on the presumption that they either possess or seek to build them has increased the anti-US sentiment in the region.

- The US invasion of Iraq in March 2003 was a defining moment in the history of the region. Three years since the fall of Baghdad on 8 April 2003, there is neither any sign of closure nor have any of its goals been achieved. If anything, it has proved that any imposition of an idea is unlikely to succeed unless it comes from the people of the region itself. It has also demonstrated that so long as oil remains the motive force of industry, the region will continue to be the focus of political and security interest of regional and great powers. The massive and unending violence has led to a huge number of Iraqi deaths, the destruction of existing economic infrastructure, misery and deprivation for a proud people and the shattering of social and religious peace in this cradle of the three eastern religions. Finally, it has made mockery of the conception of Iraq as the spearhead of the democratic upsurge in the region.

- It has become equally clear that notwithstanding the phenomenal oil wealth of the region its people are not seen as partners in its use or in reaping its benefit; neither have they been empowered to participate in the tremendous gains that the world has seen from scientific research and development, particularly information technology. It is only in the last three years that governments in the region have launched programmes to meet the rising expectation for higher education and employment from the increasing proportion of youth in the demographic profile of the region.

The listing of some of the major developments above is intended to highlight those which will continue to impact West Asia till 2015 and beyond. They form the backdrop to looking at the possible course of India's policy in the region.

India's response

It will be seen that the developments which have defined the shape of the region in the recent past have necessarily centred on US policy *vis-à-vis* Palestine, Israel, Iraq and Saudi Arabia. Iran has impinged on developments in all these countries yet itself remains without a *denouement* so far as its relations with the US are concerned. It has also been a time when India's relations with the US have diversified and gained depth without necessarily meeting all our concerns. It can be expected that these relations will depend crucially on India's continuing economic success and ability to assume a greater international role in the future. So far as West Asia is concerned, India's interest will continue to be at variance with the US primarily due to our long historical and cultural link with the region and because India's security directly depends on developments there. In searching for convergence, India's dilemma will be to strike a balance between its historical interests and the growing demands of its relations with the US and the other great powers.

It will be useful to consider India's policy towards Israel, Palestine and Iraq as it best illustrates the factors which have, and will continue to, determine our policy towards the region. These three ongoing foreign policy issues have received maximum national exposure in the recent past and have brought to the fore considerations which apply equally to our relations with other countries in West Asia. They also show the complex linkages between the political, cultural, security and economic dimensions in the region making it difficult to deal in isolation with a single country. In that sense West Asia is relatively a more homogenous region because of the commonality of both religion and language and common cultural traditions.

Israel

India initiated a few direct and indirect contacts with Israel mainly in the field of technology in the late 1980s. In December 1991, India voted in favour of UNGA Resolution 46/86 which rescinded its November 1975 Resolution equating Zionism with racism. This was seen as the first considered indication of change in India's policy towards Israel. There are also reports to suggest that the absence of diplomatic relations did not inhibit India from seeking Israeli assistance during the Sino-Indian conflict in 1962 and the Indo-Pakistani wars in 1965 and 1971 when it obtained a limited quantity of small arms and ammunition from Israel.

With the change in the international balance of power after the 1991 Gulf War and the disintegration of the Soviet Union, India and Israel finally found the opportunity to normalise their relations. There were various factors that played a significant role in this regard.

First, the end of the Cold War and other events during that time compelled India to take a renewed look at the region. The Kuwaiti Crisis and the subsequent successful intervention of the US in Iraq, with the support of Moscow, facilitated the two formal rivals to converge on various pressing international issues, including those in West Asia. While the Soviet Union showed positive indications that it would recognise Israel, the US began talking to the PLO. In addition, the PLO itself in its Conference in Algiers in 1998, recognised Israel's right to exist and the possibility of a peaceful solution to the Palestinian-Israeli conflict. These events necessitated a change in India's position on establishment of diplomatic relations with Israel and on the Arab-Israeli conflict.

Second, repeated pro-Pakistan OIC Resolutions on Kashmir with the consistent criticism of India on the Kashmir issue and on the Muslim community in India, both at the behest of Pakistan, would have also played a role. Israel's support to India on Kashmir came into stark focus. As J.N. Dixit writes, "despite our consistent and principled support to the Arab cause in Palestine and despite our distance from, and the absence of diplomatic relations with Israel, the country remained supportive of India on issues relating to the latter's territorial integrity and on Jammu and Kashmir."

Third, after the Madrid Peace Conference of October 1991, the argument of annoying friendly Arab States and Muslims at home lost relevance as the Arabs, including the PLO, began negotiating peace with Israel. In this context, India too wanted to be involved in the historic process having the potential to alter the political dynamics of the region. It was felt that "using quiet and unobtrusive diplomacy India could smoothen the bumpy and halting transition of the occupied West Bank and Gaza to full Palestinian Statehood."[10] Echoing this sentiment, J.N. Dixit[11] commented "in the post-Gulf War period, the West Asian scene has

---

10. Agwani, M.S. (1994). "India and West Asia", World Focus, Vol. 15, Nos. 11 and 12, November-December.

11. J.N. Dixit quoted in Pasha, A.K. (1993). "India and Israel Growing Cooperation", World Focus, Vol. 14, No. 8, August.

changed and the strait-jacket adversarial relations between Israel and Arab countries have started fading. If India did not remain in the mainstream of these activities, then it would have shown lack of political judgment."

In the early 1990s, the growing stridency of Islamic fundamentalist movements and terrorist activities in Kashmir worsened the domestic and the regional security environment of India, and some saw a common cause with Israel. The main opposition party BJP kept the pressure on the government to normalise relations with Israel.

Another important consideration for India to normalise ties with Israel was that the latter's expertise in agriculture, science and technology, and defence could be utilised to great benefit.

With the establishment of formal diplomatic relations with Israel, there were many rounds of talks and exchanges on military and defence-related matters. Despite this cooperation, India hesitated to buy weapons from Israel. However, during the Kargil Crisis (1999), Israel responded positively to Indian requests for military equipment and ammunition in the face of US pressure to implement an arms embargo on India. It opened a new chapter in the arms trade between the two countries. India is today Israel's largest arms market, displacing Turkey, with Israel becoming India's biggest arms supplier.

The major West Asian players have not made India's growing relations with Israel an issue even though press opinion in these countries keeps the issue in focus. An important reason for this has been India's economic success in recent years. For example, Saudi Arabia and other countries in the Gulf have been actively seeking political and economic ties with India. India has also been seeking close economic ties with the Gulf countries and negotiations for an FTA with the GCC are in progress. Due to longstanding political relations, the large Muslim community in India, geographic proximity, dependence on petroleum resources and labour migration to the region, it is unlikely that India will abandon its close ties with the Arab world, even as it deepens its relations with Israel.

Even the Palestinian leadership, especially that of President Mahmoud Abbas, have argued that its ties with the Jewish State should enable India to play a more active role in the region.

Egypt, however, is an exception and continues to express reservations, misgivings and opposition over India-Israel ties. One reason for this is to deflect attention from the untenability of Egypt's own commitments under its peace treaty with Israel after the *Intifada* of 2002. It also diverts the focus from its ongoing intelligence cooperation with Israel. India and Iran also do not see eye to eye on the former's relations with Israel. The differences of perceptions on Iran between India and Israel are fundamental. Iran enjoys a rare consensus in India and since the early 1990s every Indian Government has placed a high priority on strengthening its ties with Tehran. India is unlikely to share Israeli apprehensions over neither Iranian radicalism nor Israel of India's concern over China. A number of factors such as India's need to counter Pakistan's influence in the Islamic world, the increasing geopolitical importance of Central Asia, and the need to strengthen economic and commercial ties have led to a growing convergence in India-Iran interests in the post-Cold War period.

India and Israel are nuclear states existing in hostile security environments, which makes the nuclear programme strategically important for their national defence and security. There may be common nuclear interests between the two countries but there is no nuclear cooperation between them. Both countries are non-NPT nuclear weapon powers although they have never cooperated in changing the parameters of the international non-proliferation regime to take it beyond the NPT framework. This is evidently because of Israel's intention to not attract any attention to its nuclear weapon capability.

The Iranian puzzle also brings in the American dimension that has both positive and negative implications for Indo-Israeli relations. The US played a pivotal role in ending Israel's diplomatic isolation and has stood by Israel within the UN and outside it. Despite the fact of Israeli nuclear capability, the United States has kept mum on it and has kept the distance between India and Pakistan on the one hand and Israel on the other. Given its dependence on Washington for political support, technological assistance and economic largesse, Israel's ability to pursue any major defence deals with the outside world, including India, depends squarely on Washington. As Israeli defence exports to India are being conducted under the watchful eyes of the United States, the ties between India and Israel will also be constrained by the extent to which the US wants this engagement to expand.

Another dimension in the Israel-US-India relationship was introduced by the statement of Brajesh Mishra, then National Security Adviser, speaking before an American Jewish Committee (AJC) audience on 8 May 2003. He said that "India, the United States and Israel have some fundamental similarities. We are all democracies, sharing a common vision of pluralism, tolerance and equal opportunity. Strong India-US relations and India-Israel relations have a natural logic." This was a far cry from the charge of "religious exclusivism" made by K.M. Panikkar in the 1950s. Predictably, this was interpreted as an India-Israel-US triangle aimed at Islam and Islamic countries. Such thinking was the obverse side of fundamentalist Islamic literature put out by the terrorist groups in Kashmir and elsewhere citing US, Israel and India as the three enemies of the religion. The more pragmatic explanation would be India's intention to keep the US on board in pursuing its military ties with Israel. US has generally approved high-tech military exports from Israel to India, but has been reluctant to give its nod to systems involving American technology or financial input, as for example the Arrow anti-missile system. US acquiescence to Israel's selling advance weapons systems to India would be inversely proportional to the US desire to strengthen the US-India strategic relationship in the context of its relations with Pakistan. Yet the question remains moot whether US desire to counter-balance a rising China would nudge India and Israel to work together.

Until 2000, Israel's single-minded focus in developing, diversifying and strengthening relations with India outweighed its assessment of Pakistan. Israel has always seen Pakistan as one of the important countries in the Islamic world and seeking regular relations when possible, has been a goal of its foreign policy. It was only after a level of confidence was acquired by Israel in its relations with India towards the beginning of this millennium that Israel made determined attempts for an opening towards Pakistan. On its part, one of the fallouts of 9/11 and the growing US dependence on Pakistan in the global war on terror was to push Pakistan in moving towards Israel. Since 2003, a certain *entente cordiale* between Israel and Pakistan has emerged. Israel has moved away from the paradigm of exclusive relations which were a common feature of the bipolar world. In justifying the erosion of the so-called special relationship with India, Israel has tended to quote the thaw in India-Pakistan relations and the existence of a unipolar world in which international relations should not be seen as a 'zero-zero-sum' game. An important consequence of this has been the gradual shift in Israel's policy *vis-à-vis* Kashmir. In the early 1990s, immediately after normalisation, Israel maintained Kashmir to be an integral part of India and that Pakistan would have to vacate from those parts it had occupied in 1947. It is ironic that this position was in direct contrast to Israel's own policy of continued occupation of Palestine. The extent of the dilution of Israel's position can be judged from the fact that the Delhi Declaration issued at the end of Prime Minister Sharon's visit in 2003, did not carry any reference to the Israeli position on Kashmir. India preferred to hold Israel to its earlier position rather than have it diluted in that Declaration. India has shown a certain degree of ambivalence towards Israel's growing ties with Pakistan and this issue is no longer taken up in bilateral discussions. Should Israeli ties with Pakistan attain a strategic dimension they would prove greatly negative to India-Israel relations. As is clear, India's burgeoning ties with Israel, particularly in defence exchanges, are based on mutual benefit and cannot be wished away. There may be a change of rhetoric but not of substance despite changes of government.

Palestine

As mentioned above, India became the first non-Arab State to recognise the Palestine Liberation Organization(PLO), as the "sole legitimate representative of the Palestinian people" and allowed it to open its office in New Delhi in January 1975. The PLO Office in New Delhi was accorded full diplomatic recognition in March 1980. India accorded recognition to the State of Palestine in November 1988 and the PLO Office in New Delhi started functioning as the Embassy of the State of Palestine. In the wake of establishment of the Palestinian National Authority (PNA), India opened its Representative Office in Gaza on 25 June 1996 for ensuring effective coordination with the PNA. That Office was shifted to Ramallah in 2002, after Yasser Arafat shifted his base there. India has extended its consistent and unwavering support on the Palestinian issue. It shares the perception that the question of Palestine is at the core of the Arab-Israeli conflict. India supports the legitimate right of the Palestinian people to a State and the imperative need for a just, comprehensive and lasting peace in the region based on UNSC Resolutions 242 and 338 and the principle of 'land for peace'.

India has supported the Middle East Peace Process (MEPP) from its beginning in 1991 and was part of the defunct multilateral track of the MEPP. When it was in operation, India participated in the meetings of the four Working Groups on regional economic development, arms control and regional security and environment and water resources. India voted in favour of UNGA Resolution No. 52/250 of 7 July 1998 conferring upon Palestine, in its capacity as Observer, additional rights and privileges of participation in the sessions and work of the General Assembly and the international conferences convened under the auspices of the UNGA or other organisations of the UN. India has voiced concern at various times at the stalling of the MEPP maintaining that the momentum of the Declaration of Principles and Oslo Accords in 1993 has not been maintained. India welcomed the Wye River Memorandum signed between Israel and PLO on 23 October 1998. India also welcomed the Sharm-el-Sheik Agreement between Israel and PLO concluded on September 19, 1999.

The Palestinian issue impinges directly on Indo-Israeli relations. The Palestinian cause remains popular in India and it cannot ignore the sentiments of its substantial Muslim populace that overwhelmingly regards Israel's policy towards the Palestinians as totally unjustifiable. Fear of alienating Muslim population was one of the major factors which constrained India from normalising its relations with Israel for decades. Before 1992, India had made this normalisation contingent upon the resolution of the Palestinian issue. In 1992, India decided to de-link the two in accordance with what much of the world was already doing. India's position then was that it would normalise relations with Israel in tandem with the Peace Process. This policy continued even after the Oslo Accord results had broken down. While there was rapid progress in India-Israel relations, they were no longer in tandem with what was happening *vis-à-vis* Palestine. It was quite clear that the two had got disconnected for reasons of pragmatism and self-interest. India also took a less strident position against Israel in the UN forums much to the chagrin of the Palestinians and made considerable attempts to moderate anti-Israeli resolutions at the NAM meetings in Durban and elsewhere.

The outbreak of the Al-Aqsa *intifada* in September 2002, gave strength to India's earlier positions on Israel which remains so till today. It was also realised by India that despite having vital political, economic and cultural interests in West Asia, it was still not seen as a player in the Peace Process. India's role in the MEPP was confined only to the multilateral track since in 1991 it did not have diplomatic relations with Israel. On the other hand, China which had a much lower profile in West Asia at the time, was given Observer status largely due to its permanent membership of the Security Council. When the Quartet process was unveiled, once again India's role was not recognised, although China remained an Observer and had by then considerably increased its profile in the region. While there was a degree of ambivalence on India's part on whether or not to participate and increase India's profile in the Peace Process (largely due to the apprehension that its *quid pro quo* could provoke activism on Kashmir by the countries in the region), on the side of the Palestinians there was nothing more than lip service to seeking India's active role in the Peace Process. On the other hand, neither did Israel propose India for a role in the Quartet process. It appeared that while the Palestinians were paying lip service to continue the widespread support it had amongst the Indian public, the Israelis were talking of India's role only in order to advance its own interests in India. The result has been that the Palestinian issue has become emotive from time to time by exploiting the Muslim sentiment in the country without any corresponding benefits, in foreign policy terms, for India. Yet to a large extent it has created a favourable environment in the Arab countries, especially the Gulf, for Indians to live and work there. At the same time, in a larger sense, the situation in the region particularly the Gulf, has also changed enough for support on the Palestinian issue to be no longer seen as a touchstone for bilateral, political and economic relations.

This issue came to the fore in recent times during the visit of Prime Minister Sharon to India in 2003. It focussed on the differences in nuance that existed on India's West Asia policy between the NDA Government and the Congress. Although Prime Minister Sharon met the then Leader of Opposition Sonia Gandhi, it did not receive much coverage in the Indian media. When the Congress-led UPA Government came to power in July 2004, they had taken a strongly pro-Palestinian position in their common platform. Although relations with Israel have continued to grow, particularly in the defence area, India has maintained a distance at the political level from Israel. The manner in which India responded to the Israeli withdrawal from the Gaza Strip added weight to such a perception. Israel's unilateral withdrawal was seen as a major development in the Arab-Israeli conflict, although India reacted to it nearly three weeks after the event. In doing so, it welcomed the removal of Israeli settlements from the Gaza Strip and northern West Bank but hoped that it would be the beginning of a process that will culminate in a mutually acceptable negotiated settlement in accordance with the Roadmap and the relevant UN Security Council resolutions. In parenthesis, Pakistan used the fact of the withdrawal to organise a public meeting between the Foreign Ministers of the two countries in Ankara on 1 September 2005.

The divisions that came up during the later years of President Arafat, where he was losing support both from the principal Arab states and from within the Palestinian population also placed India in a difficult position. The resurgence of Hamas and its eventually forming the Government in the PNA has meant a dramatic change in the dynamics of the Israeli-Palestinian issue. It has meant the waning of the secular nationalist stream in Palestine and the dominance of the Islamic-oriented Hamas. It has also posed the same dilemma to the other countries in the region and the non-recognition of the Hamas Government by the US and Israel has led to an impasse in further progress on the goal of creating two States living with secure borders.

India has continued its moral, material and technical support to the Palestinian people. It has pledged funds for construction of a library-cum-activity centre at the Palestinian Technical College in Deir-al Balah and one at the Al-Azhar University in Gaza. It has also welcomed Palestinian students under the ICCR scholarship programmes as well as provided specialised training in security to Palestinian officers.

Iraq

Iraq has been an important part of India's foreign policy before Independence. India continued to maintain diplomatic relations with Iraq even after the US invasion of the country.

Indo-Iraqi relations commenced at the end of the Second World War. Jawaharlal Nehru and Maulana Abul Kalam Azad established the initial cooperative relationship with the monarchy in Iraq between 1946 and 1955. The overthrow of King Faisal II in July 1950, did not adversely affect Indo-Iraq relations because successive Iraqi governments right until March 2003 looked to India, as the leader of the non-aligned group, for support and legitimacy. India did not take sides in the periodic confrontations which affected Iraq's relations with Egypt, Syria, and Jordan, and with Iran. Indo-Iraq relations were animated by sensitivity and respect for each other's political and security concerns, complementarily of economic interests and similarity of views on global issues.

In the Arab world, Iraq was one of the few countries which remained a steadfast friend largely due to a 'strategic decision'[12] by

---

12. As told to the author in July 2002.

President Saddam Hussein after his state visit to India in 1974. It also marked the beginning of strong party-level contacts between the Indian National Congress and the ABSP. Iraq was a country of high priority in India's policy towards the region. All of India's interests in the region came to bear on India's relations with Iraq:

- In line with its Arab Ba'ath ideology, Iraq strictly separated the authority of state from the religious authority and considered itself secular. Iraq was part of the Mesopotamian basin which had nurtured the three major Western religions–Islam, Christianity and Judaism–and had an in-grown tradition of tolerance. These were appealing to India with its secular ethos.

- Indian troops used by the British since the Mesopotamian Campaign had brought to the Iraqi people a view of India and Indians as a friend. This was one reason for US pressure on India to send troops to join the Coalition forces after the Invasion of 2003.

- At the political level, Iraq was an important member of the Non-aligned Movement and the proximity of Saddam Hussein's regime ensured Iraq's support on Kashmir at the OIC and other international forums. It helped to shore up India's case and influence other OIC countries.

- Iraq became India's major economic partner in the region: till Gulf War II, Iraq was a major supplier of crude; Indian companies received contracts valued at $ 3 billion during Iraq's development boom in the 1980s; Indian experts, doctors, nurses and other professionals were employed by the Iraqi government to run and beef up its services. It is estimated that about 100,000 Indians were working in Iraq till the invasion on Kuwait in 1990. India also became a major source of consumer goods and intermediate range technologies to Iraq.

- As much as Saudi Arabia is important for Indian Muslims to fulfil their religious obligations, so also Iraq has had a longstanding religious connection with India. Starting with the theology scholarships bestowed by the erstwhile Begums of Awadh in the 18th Century, Shia scholars and pilgrims from India continue to visit Najaf and Karbala even today.

- India was the source of some defence supplies to Iraq in the 1980s and Indian defence teams trained Iraqi armed forces, particularly its air force. Iraq had also made unsuccessful attempts in the late 1970s to seek nuclear technology from India.

Some distance appeared to have developed in our bilateral relations during the long Iran-Iraq War (1980-1988) because India did not take side with either belligerent in this conflict. India was committed equally to maintaining good relations with both the government of Saddam Hussein and the Government of Iran. The then Foreign Minister, Mr. Narasimha Rao was a member of the Non-aligned Goodwill Mission to mediate the conflict. India also bailed out Iraq when a majority of NAM members were not willing to go to Baghdad for the 1983 Non-aligned Summit scheduled in Baghdad. However, Iraq's invasion of Kuwait in 1990, resulted in a disruption in Indo-Iraqi relations. Indian public opinion reacted adversely to Iraq invading a fellow Muslim, and more importantly, a fellow non-aligned country. On the other hand, Indian government gave priority to the safety of the large number of Indians working in Kuwait and in Iraq and even in other Gulf countries because of the perception that the conflict may spread. Indian government's policy was thus, at variance with its public opinion. While Indian Foreign Minister Gujral focussed his attention on demand of the Indian diaspora, Indian political circles and media remained critical of the Iraqi Government and demanded that Iraq vacate its aggression on Kuwait. Yet India made no official statement criticising Iraq. The situation was repeated in April 2003, when US invaded Iraq even though the government was composed of a different coalition of political parties.

Following Gulf War I, India opposed omnibus and prolonged sanctions imposed against Iraq by the United Nations on grounds that the primary sufferers were the common people of Iraq. India's position was that the wellbeing of the people of Iraq was the primary concern. India was equally opposed to the pernicious and intrusive role played by the UN Inspectors in determining Iraq's chemical, biological and missile weapons capacities. The UN official in overall charge of the inspection regime Richard Butler succeeded in his brief to keep the Iraqi Government under continuous pressure raising a chorus of opposition in the UN. There was also reason to believe that US weapons inspectors were simultaneously working for its Intelligence agencies. At the height of the resulting crisis, the UN Secretary-General was forced to appoint a senior Indian diplomat[13] as the Supervising Authority of the Inspection team in Baghdad removing Mr. Butler from the scene. India continued to argue against the continuation of sanctions and for bringing back Iraq into the mainstream of international relations.

During the Oil-for-Food Programme which became operational in 1996, India found its economic space further restricted due to the cornering of the implementation mechanism by the members of the 661 Committee. The highly restricted interpretation of goods and services allowed under the OF Programme reinforced the belief that the Programme was working in a partisan manner. Between the end of Gulf War I in January 1991 and the operation of the OF Programme, India had offered a line of credit of Rs. 250 million for the export of items which would meet the massive humanitarian requirements of the Iraqi people. Despite the goods being within the permitted categories, and formal discussions with the 661 Committee, it did not allow India to export. It is only now after the UN Investigation into the OF Programme that the corrupt and partisan character of the Programme has been revealed. It can be said that the gainers from the OFP were the companies who were able to export the goods and services by the intermediary agencies and Saddam Hussein and his *nomenclatura*. By showering largesse through oil titles he sought to build favourable lobbies in the chanceries and parliaments in the world. It can be said that this effort was not without recompense as it kept Iraq in the public eye the world over even if it could not stave off the US invasion.

---

13. Prakash Shah, former Indian Ambassador to the UN.

However, that was more because of the bypassing of the UN by the US once it had decided that it had a sufficient case to attack. The folly of that decision has become evident now as the situation in Iraq continues to deteriorate. With both its premises having been disproved–the existence of weapons of mass destruction and the link between al Qaeda and the Saddam Hussein regime–the US goal of securing Iraqi oil becomes explicit. No amount of veneer of fostering democracy is able to mask the tragic situation in Iraq today:

- the unending spiral of violence with nearly half a million Iraqis killed or seriously wounded as well as a good number of US casualties, coupled with the stories coming out of Abu Ghraib and Ramadi;

- conditions of civil war with private militias combating a weak, untrained and ineffectual Iraqi army;

- the failure of successive elections to bring in the willing participation of the groups, ethnic, religious and political, to come together, coupled with the exacerbation of tension between the Sunnis and Shias on the one hand and between the Arabs and Kurds on the other;

- the inability of any meaningful economic reconstruction to take place given conditions of heightened insecurity, and the degradation of the economic and social infrastructure below the level even before the war;

- the consolidation of Kurdish power in North Iraq and the beginning of a Shia-dominated province in the south; coupled with a hostile Sunni population which feels usurped from political power;

- the presence of nearly 100,000 US troops in Iraq and 18 military bases without any exit strategy for handing over sovereignty to the Iraqi people.

The US Invasion of Iraq once again presented India with difficult choices. On the one hand was mounting US pressure to send 15000 troops to join the US-led Coalition Forces, and on the other, a highly critical public opinion cutting across the political spectrum opposing any involvement in Iraq. Once again the government chose to seek the middle ground. The All Party Meeting of Party Leaders in Parliament was able to pass a Resolution in Parliament stating that India will go to Iraq only under UN auspices, including the sending of its troops. Yet the government was successful in ensuring that the word 'condemn' did not figure in the Resolution. It tied government's hands leaving it no option to further India's interest with either the US or Iraq. It is ironic that this pyrrhic victory was achieved on 8 April 2003, the day Baghdad fell to the US Army which had not received UN approval. It was no surprise therefore that on the eve of the invasion, the US Ambassador in New Delhi was able to claim that US and Indian positions were the same.

The Indian government remained muted in its criticism of Washington's unilateral action against Iraq stating that 'military action lacks justification' and was 'avoidable'. The reasons for the government's soft-pedalling the issue was in the expectation of further deepening the US-India strategic relationship and to retain Washington's support over Kashmir. It was however, clear that while the costs for sending Indian troops to North Iraq would have to be met by the exchequer, they would still be under US command and control. There was no clear response to the question of how Indian casualties in Iraq were to be explained to the Indian people. Furthermore, there was no guarantee that it would assure US support for India's bid for permanent membership of the UN Security Council. On the other hand, there was a strong probability that Indian troops could end up in conflagration either with the Turkish Brigade stationed north of Erbil or the Iraqi Army or the *Peshmerga* of the PUK and KDP, the two Kurdish political parties.

Nevertheless, India sought to retain its presence in Iraq by becoming the first non-oil developing country to contribute $ 10 million to the UN Fund, thereby earning the right to sit on the Iraq Donor's Committee. It also committed $ 20 million bilaterally for the reconstruction of Iraq. India's plans to refurbish a maternity hospital in Najaf had to be given up at an advanced stage due to the inability to deal with the security parameters of the project. The UPA government in July 2004 decided that no Indians would be sent to Iraq for any activity, reconstruction or military. After the kidnap of seven Indian truck drivers by Iraqi insurgents and their release after an agonising wait, India virtually stepped out of the Iraq imbroglio. Despite India's long experience with constitutional democracy and its processes we did not contribute to Iraq's fledgling democratic experiment under UN auspices. Neither have our companies been able to re-establish themselves in a country with which they have had considerable experience. The giving up of the Ba'ath ideology and the re-assertion by the Shias of their majority status has meant the passing of political power to Islamic parties like DAWA and SCIRI. India's salience has waned on the political front as well. It remains moot whether by taking distinct positions on the choices which confronted us in Iraq we would have done better. By taking the middle path we have been able to save ourselves from being identified with the occupying power in that country. Such identification would have served us badly in the region in the future.

Conclusion

India still has considerable political capital in West Asia built up over the Nehru years. The re-defining of this capital would be the challenge of our West Asian policy in the years to come. India's security depends on three pillars: Iran, Iraq and Saudi Arabia. All three are in an unsettled state at this time. It will be seen from the case studies above that in defining an Indian role in West Asia a number of considerations not directly in the realm of foreign policy come into play. The immutable considerations—all domestic—that have weighed heavily on our policy are the presence of the second largest Muslim community in the world; the dependence of our country on West Asia's energy resources; and the remittances from the Indian diaspora in the Gulf. These will continue to determine the parameters of our policy in the future also. To this have to be added new determinants: India's economic success which has created a growing market for energy and other natural resources from West Asia and a secure destination for its investment; India's role in a rejuvenated group of developing countries as seen in the WTO negotiations; India as a paradigm for democratic and cultural pluralism; and India's firm opposition to terrorism in any form.

In this background it is possible to list some cardinal points on which India's policy on West Asia should be based:

- India will always support secular, democratic and plural societies in West Asia while finding a *modus vivendi* to do business with the parties in power in order to maintain its traditional friendship with the countries of the region. Its continuing interest in the Palestine issue must be translated into constructive engagement.

- India's primary goal has to be the safeguarding of the security in the Gulf, and to this end, enhancing its relations with Saudi Arabia, Iraq and Iran in a 'non-zero sum' approach. It would mean developing cooperative maritime security arrangements with all the Gulf countries. It would also require close contact with these countries in combating terrorism and the linked nexus of arms smuggling, money laundering and drugs.

- India's relations with Israel have acquired a depth and diversity which cannot be rolled back. This has happened because Israel has been able to meet crucial Indian needs in the field of defence, agriculture and technology. The relation has to be seen in the context of the imperative of any Indian government to assure the security of one billion people. Our experience has shown, as in Kargil, that despite usurious costs Israel has shown itself to be a reliable partner. India does not need to be defensive on this score especially since the importance of this relationship cuts across party lines. It is a situation which needs advocacy both within the country and the region.

- India by the weight of its historical relations with and its current economic success has to carve a role leveraging its growing market and talent pool and the natural and financial resources of the region. While the Gulf countries, including Iraq and Iran are the most susceptible to this approach, it is equally possible with countries like Egypt and the other countries in the Maghreb like Libya and Morocco. Maximising economic and trade interactions will provide the ballast for closer and more balanced overall relations. As stated above the rise of India hinges on its clout in its proximate neighbourhood.

• India's goal will be to develop a two-dimensional relation with the countries of the region. Recent indications of West Asian countries 'looking East' towards India need to be capitalised upon. India's future lies in its increasing recognition as a rising Asian economic power.

• India's model of a secular and democratic polity and its commitment to ensuring minority rights has a great attraction in today's West Asia where religious and cultural differences amongst the diverse ethnicities have been exposed. In this context, India needs to develop a new channel of interaction through civil society organisations as a means to foster exchange of views on common social and economic problems. Some trends in this direction with Saudi Arabia and Iran are already noticeable. Development of cultural relations will have to be a major plank of India's policy towards West Asia.

• India will have to carefully calibrate its relations with the region in such a way that its policy parameters remain inviolable amidst pressures of its growing relations with the great powers, particularly the US. A regular dialogue with the US and EU on developments in West Asia would provide a tool to understand the parameters on both sides.

• A number of minorities in the region like the Kurds who have found a voice, in the churning that the region has undergone, hold India in high esteem. A subsidiary goal of Indian policy in the region has to be to encourage these communities within the framework of the constitutional structure in the countries in which they live.

In sum, the overall thrust of India's policy in West Asia is to develop relations in such a way that the region truly becomes a part of our immediate neighbourhood. This will mean going beyond the limits which are set by the existence of the waters of the Gulf.

16

India's 'Look East' policy

Ranjit Gupta

Jawaharlal Nehru wrote, prophetically, in his book, *The Discovery of India*, in 1944: "The Pacific is likely to take the place of the Atlantic in the future as the nerve center of the world. Though not directly a Pacific state, India will inevitably exercise an important influence there. India will also develop as the center of economic and political activity in the Indian Ocean area, in South-East Asia, right up to the Middle East. Her position gives an economic and strategic importance in a part of the world which is going to develop in the future." He further wrote, "India will have to play a very great part in security problems of Asia and the Indian Ocean, more especially of the Middle East and South-East Asia" and added, "India is the pivot around which these problems will have to be considered." India's 'Look East' Policy is about the unfolding of this vision in contemporary times, albeit after India had virtually marginalised itself from being considered a meaningful factor in the region during the Cold War.

'Rising China' has been the most significant strategic feature of the post Cold War world. Conventional wisdom suggests that China is the primary reason why the 21st Century will be the century of the Asia Pacific. The evolving geopolitical scenario in the Asia Pacific region will inevitably revolve around China. Ambassador K. Kesavapany, an eminent Singaporean diplomat-scholar, has written in a monograph entitled *India's Tryst With Asia* published earlier this year: "In seeking to deal with China, other countries have to understand its culture, history and mentality. Traditionally, China perceived itself as the Middle Kingdom, surrounded by less culturally advanced countries. China would receive their tribute in exchange for Chinese recognition of their legitimacy and subordinate status... China's Middle Kingdom mentality may persist in some quarters and it is useful to remember this point." The phraseology used by Deng Xiaoping to describe China's attack on Vietnam, "to teach Vietnam a lesson"—is cited as an example. "China is an ancient civilisation urgently pursuing modernisation ...a wounded civilisation trying to recover from 150 years of humiliation .... (When) it regains full strength and a multi dimensional—not just economic – power, then the Dragon will be fully awake and probably shake up the world...Once it is highly developed, it is unlikely to be like Japan, an economic giant and political pigmy. Rather, it is possible that China would aspire to be a co-hegemon with the US (which leaves open the question) whether the US would be willing to share global domination with it." This brings us to another and equally significant strategic factor. The US has shaped, if not largely determined, the geopolitical contours of the Asia-Pacific region since World War II and it has very clearly indicated in its National Security Strategy documents of September 2002 and February 2006, that it fully intends to maintain this ability and is gearing up to meet any challenge in this regard. China is more than implicitly identified as posing the main challenge. Thus, the fundamental catalyst of international relations during the first half of the 21st Century will be the contest between US efforts to maintain its current global and regional predominance and China's attempts to challenge this, motivated mainly by its ambition to resurrect its traditional and historical 'Middle Kingdom' position of preeminence in this region.

This article considers India's 'Look East' Policy in a futuristic perspective in the context of the evolving strategic and geopolitical scenario in the region, the broad framework of which has been outlined in the preceding paragraph. However, revisiting the background of the evolution of the relationship between India and the region east of India is an absolutely unavoidable and vitally important prior necessity. India's future role in the region—both 'challenges' and 'opportunities'—can only be visualised in the context of this background.

The first step in the formulation of coherent and effective policy is to define objectives with clarity and precision. The broad overall objective is fairly straightforward. The 21st Century is going to be the century of the Asia Pacific—India must be a meaningful player in the region. An equally important step is to have a realistic appreciation of potential hurdles in achieving the objectives. India must be cognizant of certain limitations on India's potential role in the region because it is "not directly a Pacific state" as Nehru had acknowledged. These limiting factors are part of the 'challenges' that India would face in carving an appropriate role for itself in the region. These may be summarised as follows:

- Geographical: There is long held perception in countries of East and South-East Asia that Asia consists of countries from Japan to Thailand (even Myanmar is a recent addition to their configuration of Asia) including the archipelagic member countries of ASEAN. India being a 'distant and mysterious land' remains a widespread regional thought syndrome. Indeed, even in the West, in discourse relating to strategic issues and in high business circles the definition of Asia basically refers to East and South-East Asia and does not normally include India. Several regional countries have used this definition, as one amongst many factors, to seek to keep India out of regional affairs and entities and succeeded, for example, in the case of APEC and ASEM and almost succeeded in the case of the first East Asian summit.

- Historical: Countries of the region have interacted intensively and continuously with each other for millennia. They have interacted quite significantly with the Western world for the past two centuries. They are familiar with each other and with issues of common concern, even when these issues divide them rather than bring them together. In the distant past, India too had enduring and deep civilisational and economic links with South-East Asia and consequently, significant elements of Indian culture became a valuable and

integral part of the culture of most South-East Asian
countries. However, in modern times, two centuries of
Western colonialism snapped India's linkages with the
region. With India's independence, there was a burst of
activity seeking to revive the old relationships. India became
actively involved in independence movements and decolonisation processes in South-East Asia, initially with
Indonesia and Burma, then Malaya and later, with Vietnam.
The Asian Relations Conference convened in 1946, the Special
Conference on Indonesia in 1949, and later, the Bandung
Conference in 1955 sought to lay the foundations of an
Asian renaissance with India's proactive involvement with
this region. However, the evolving dynamics of Cold War
politics and India's increasingly insular economic policies
ensured that this happy beginning was replaced by a
progressively more strained relationship with the region.
Thus, the fact is that modern India's substantive relationship
and interaction with the region is virtually a post-
independence phenomenon, and even that has been largely
rather patchy when not indifferent or worse. This has served
to psychologically and metaphorically enhance the 'distance'
between India and the region.

- Political: As far as East Asia is concerned, the North Korean
nuclear issue and the Taiwan issue are usually regarded as
the main flashpoints and causes of regional tension and
possible sources of conflict. India has never been involved
in any intraregional or interregional discussions relating
to these issues. The third important regional issue, of
competing territorial claims in the South China Sea, straddles
East and South-East Asia and again India has not been
involved. These issues of great importance to countries of
the region do not *prima facie* appear to be of direct relevance
to India. However, there was one issue in which India was
actively involved: the standoff between Vietnam and ASEAN
in the 1970s and 1980s, first in the context of the Vietnam
War, and later, in the context of Vietnam's intervention in

Cambodia. The Vietnam issue, particularly in its second incarnation, contributed directly to the normalisation of the very difficult relationship that countries of South-East Asia had with China since the establishment of the PRC. On the other hand, the Vietnam issue caused a very sharp deterioration in India's relations with ASEAN. Though Vietnam is no longer an issue, the mindset that motivated India's policies in the region remains a perceptional question mark. Beyond these mainly regional considerations, experts who have studied Indo-ASEAN relations in depth, and officials who have handled such relations, have consistently underlined that India's ability to nurture and manage a stable, peaceful and prospering South Asia would be a very important factor in shaping South-East Asian perceptions in particular, and East Asian perceptions as well, about India's capabilities in playing a role in Asia. India's poor relations with Pakistan in particular and other South Asian countries in general, have in the past been a severely constraining factor in India's ability to command respect in Asia.

• Economic: Despite strongly antagonistic relationships between East Asian countries throughout history, contemporary trade, investment and people oriented economic links amongst East Asian countries, amongst South-East Asian countries and between East Asian and South-East Asian countries have become exceedingly close and are becoming deeper by the day. Indeed, the fact is that their economies are on the verge of becoming parts of a single large economy. Despite the very impressive development of economic relations between India and these countries in the past few years, the reality is that it is going to take India quite some time to develop anywhere near the same depth, range and quality of economic linkages with these countries as they have amongst themselves. Some statistics exhibit the enormous gulf. Approximate trade figures 2005: China-Japan US $ 184 billion; India-Japan US

$ 7 billion; China-ASEAN US $ 100 billion; India-ASEAN US $ 15 billion; China-South Korea US $ 112 billion; India-South Korea US $ 7 billion; China-Taiwan US $ 90 billion; India-Taiwan US $ 2.4 billion; China-US 285 US $ billion; India-US 21 US $ billion; China-India US $ 18 billion. China has become the leading trade partner of Japan, Korea and Taiwan and within the next 2-3 years at most, would become so of the countries of the region too. China has consistently had an overall trade surplus, whereas India has trade deficits. From 1991, when India embarked upon economic reform and integrating its economy more with the global economy, till 2004, India received FDI of US $ 38.37 billion as compared to China receiving US $ 513.58 billion. FDI as per cent of GDP is around 0.7 per cent in India's case and about 3.3 per cent in China's case. Investments from India to ASEAN countries during 1995-2001 came to US $ 225 million; and, from ASEAN countries to India from 1996-2001 the figure was US $ 2.1 billion. The figures for China's investment in ASEAN countries till 2001 were US $ 1.1 billion and from ASEAN to China US $ 26.2 billion. Investment flows since 2001 to date have increased noticeably both in respect of India and China but the growth rate for China is much higher. Taiwan, Hong Kong, US, South Korea and Japan are the top five foreign investors in China. Investment from Hong Kong and Taiwan into India is miniscule and though it is much higher from US, Japan and Korea the figures do not remotely compare with those for China. China was the most helpful country during the Asian financial crisis of 1996-1997, whereas India could not offer any assistance. Thus, a comparison of *inter se* economic linkages amongst these countries and between India and these countries presents a particularly lopsided picture. In the contemporary world, economic linkages have become the main drivers of relationships and therefore India has an enormously huge task ahead of it, particularly when compared to China.

- Institutional: Kesavapany has written that since India was made a full Dialogue Partner of ASEAN in December 1995, 14 bilateral ASEAN-India mechanisms have been established. China was accorded full Dialogue Partner status in June 1996 and since then 27 China-ASEAN institutional mechanisms have been established. By way of additional comparison it may be mentioned that 33 such mechanisms exist in respect of Japan even though the dialogue relationship is much older, having been established in 1977. The Sino-ASEAN mechanisms are the most active and productive amongst all these mechanisms. China's role during the Asian financial crisis contributed directly to the establishment of the ASEAN+3 mechanism. This aggregation remains the regional 'High Table' and after their Finance Ministers met in Hyderabad on the sidelines of the Asian Development Bank Annual Meeting on May 5, 2006, the Korean Deputy PM, who chaired the meeting, declared that "nothing has been decided about inclusion of India."

It is axiomatic that India can play a role in the region only to the extent that countries of the region and countries that exercise influence in the region perceive that India's involvement in or with the region is relevant to their needs and concerns. Therefore, these 'challenges' circumscribe the scope of India's ability to take initiatives; it is much more up to the countries playing roles in the region to involve India. Through the 'Look East' Policy, India signalled its interest and desire in reengaging with the region. To that extent this policy represented India's first step on the path to overcome these 'challenges'.

It would be desirable to recall the scenario that existed when the 'Look East' Policy was initiated. The disintegration of the Soviet Union and the collapse of its Communist empire marked the end of the Cold War. A dramatically changing global scenario started emerging with new equations and new relationships clearly on the horizon. The US became the sole global superpower. A rising China emerged as an increasingly significant player in East Asia. Japan entered a period of economic recession and was under severe US criticism for its hands-off attitude in the first Gulf War and thus, uncertain and confused about how to handle its relations with ASEAN, China and the US. ASEAN countries had dramatically transformed their economies by opening up to each other, to Japan, then to Taiwan and Korea, and finally to China to establish strong economic linkages, consciously setting aside and overcoming mutual historical animosities, for the greater benefit and prosperity of all. A country's economic strength, vibrancy, policies and linkages with other countries were manifestly becoming the preeminent drivers of regional relationships. In the context of the constantly enlarging shadow of an increasingly self confident China looming over them, ASEAN countries came up with the strategy of engaging China by forging increasingly closer economic relations with it and by encouraging it to become involved in an increasing web of regional institutional linkages; at the same time they sought to reinforce, bilaterally and otherwise, their security and defence relationships with the US in particular and other Western countries. ASEAN had tried to engage India earlier but had not been successful. Meanwhile, India lost its only friend of international strategic consequence, the Soviet Union, and found itself marginalised from the global mainstream in both the economic and political domains with its relationships in this region in particularly poor shape. India was also on the verge of financial and economic collapse.

The 'Look East' Policy represented the Indian response to this new and changing strategic milieu in the region.

What was the 'Look East' Policy? India's new and revamped approach towards the region east of India was dubbed the 'Look East' Policy. This was the brainchild of the then new Prime Minister Narasimha Rao. The first signal of the desire to change policy was the innovative and unorthodox choice of a technocrat as Finance Minister, Dr. Manmohan Singh. He was not a politician; not even a member of the Congress Party; however, he was an internationally known economist. Speaking at the 16th Asia Society Corporate Conference in Mumbai on March 18th 2006, Prime Minster Manmohan Singh said, "I must pay tribute to our East and South-

East Asian neighbors for shaping our own thinking on globalisation and the means to deal with it. Some of you might recall that in 1992 our Government launched India's 'Look East' Policy. This was not merely an external economic policy, it was also a strategic shift in India's vision of the world and India's place in the evolving global economy. Most of all it was about reaching out to our civilisational Asian neighbours in the region. I have always viewed India's destiny as being interlinked with that of Asia and more so South-East Asia."

In just two decades—the 1970s and 1980s—South-East Asia had witnessed a miraculous economic transformation despite regional conflict, mutual disputes, and very different political orientations of the region's major players, thus underlining the preeminent importance of the economic factor. ASEAN's economic performance attracted the world's attention and the world's major countries felt prompted to step up their interaction and engagement with it. The region provided a model for emulation for India. In the context of these changing circumstances, India felt the need to substantively reorient its foreign and economic policies. With the initiation of economic liberalisation and reforms, India began its transition from building a self-reliant socialist society to building a modern economy based on free market principles and to start opening up its potentially huge market to freer international trade and investment. This heralded the era of seeking to integrate the Indian economy with the global economy. It also resulted in a new emphasis on economic issues in the making of foreign policy. If one factor can be singled out and described as the most important contributory factor to, and segment of the 'Look East' Policy, it would be the economic factor. The example of ASEAN countries proved to be the great motivator. The second and equally significant component was that the 'Look East' Policy was ASEAN oriented. ASEAN has since been the key and the gateway.

India's supportive and cooperative approach in ensuring a political settlement in Cambodia leading to the success of the Paris Conference of 1991, helped lay the foundation for a new political relationship between ASEAN and India. India's new Foreign and

Finance Ministers, Madhavsingh Solanki and Dr. Manmohan Singh visited a number of ASEAN countries in 1991-92 with the latter remarking: "We thought that if we had to market New India, we have to begin with Singapore." These new Indian policy orientations represented a conscious change from the past. It was evident that India's reengagement with the region this time around was on the basis of pragmatism, a predominantly economic focus and devoid of preachy ideological preconceptions. The dynamics of Cold War politics had seriously hurt India's relationships with South-East Asian countries. The end of the Cold War removed this major impediment to the development of a close and substantive relationship. Both sides began acknowledging that inhibitions of the past no longer existed. This is what ASEAN had been waiting for. The new orientations of India's economic policies attracted positive attention in ASEAN countries. Lee Kuan Yew had introduced Prime Minister Narasimha Rao to the audience before he delivered the Singapore Lecture in 1994 as the leader who launched fundamental changes in India as Deng Xiaoping had done in China. Prime Minister Goh Tok Chong of Singapore paid his first official visit to India in 1994 and on his return said "I recognised the potential of the country; I returned to Singapore determined to spark off an India Fever. Although many doubted India's commitment to economic openness I never lost faith in India."

India's 'Look East' Policy was welcomed because it dovetailed very well with ASEAN's fundamental strategic requirements. The fact is that ASEAN had always wanted India to be involved in the region but it was India that had been reluctant and rejected ASEAN's overtures while continuing to pursue policies which ensured estrangement. The establishment of ASEAN in 1967, though given the veneer of regional economic cooperation, was primarily motivated by the perceived threat posed by Mao's China which had actively induced and supported insurgencies by Communists and other rebel groups throughout South-East Asia. Ali Alatas, the Indonesian Foreign Minister wrote: "The truth is that politics attended ASEAN at its birth. It was the convergence in political outlook among the five original members, their shared convictions on national priority objectives and on how best to secure these objectives in the evolving strategic environment of East Asia which impelled them to form ASEAN." As Kesavapany has remarked: "India was then seen as the counterweight to Communist China." Mainly because of this motivation; partly because of the background of the region's contrasting historical interaction and experiences with India and China; and reinforced by concerns arising out of China's aggression against India in 1962, when discussions were initiated in the early 1960s for the formation of ASEAN, India was considered a natural potential founder member and sounded out, but India chose other policy paths. Despite the very considerably strained relationship between India and ASEAN, mainly due to India's strong and consistent support to Vietnam, in an attempt to preempt Indian recognition of the Vietnam installed Heng Samrin regime in Cambodia and in a conscious effort to dilute India's perceived special relationships with the Soviet Union and Vietnam, the two countries that the then ASEAN considered as enemies, ASEAN suggested discussions in the context of India being considered as a potential dialogue partner in 1980. India once again declined the invitation. By that time, ASEAN and China had developed a strongly shared common strategic objective in South-East Asia and were working very closely together in the context of the Cambodian issue; indeed, for all practical purposes there was a trilateral partnership between ASEAN, China and the US. Yet China was not invited to become a dialogue partner. (Japan as well as the US had already been made Dialogue Partners in 1977.)

What messages had ASEAN been conveying? There were two messages—the first message was that ASEAN countries harboured a sense of apprehension of future Chinese intentions in this region; the second message was that despite India's policies being perceived as hostile, ASEAN did not have suspicions that India had ulterior ambitions of its own in this region. India was viewed as providing an insurance policy to ASEAN countries being overwhelmed by China. This line of thinking finally led to India being accepted as a partner and to the continuous upgradation of the relationship with India since then.

ASEAN responded favourably to the 'Look East' Policy through the decision to accord sectoral dialogue partner status to India in 1992. Once India had taken the initiative, it is the ASEAN that deserves greater credit for taking the relationship with India forward to the heights that it has scaled in just over a decade. It is particularly noteworthy that ASEAN's decision to accord full dialogue partner status to India in 1995 at the ASEAN summit in Thailand was made without India being given any prior indications whatsoever. Thus, again, for the third time, ASEAN had taken the initiative. The decision had been partly precipitated by increasing exasperation with China's aggressive rhetoric and actions in 1994-1995. Kesavapany has noted "in April 1995, at the ASEAN-China meeting in Hangzhou, Beijing realised the full depth of ASEAN's unhappiness over Chinese policies and moves in the South China Sea." When this decision was formally conveyed to the Indian Ambassador in Bangkok he was specifically told that though ASEAN countries were quite unhappy about India's past attitude towards ASEAN and its policies towards South-East Asia and disappointed at the tardy pace of substantive interaction and lack of focussed interest even after India was made a sectoral dialogue partner, ASEAN had nevertheless decided to upgrade India's status in the expectation that India will be more proactive in the future. India was duly accepted as a full and normal member of ARF in the first meeting thereafter in 1996.

India attended an ASEAN PMC for the first time in June 1996 and India's representative, External Affairs Minister, I.K.Gujral, highlighting the importance of ASEAN's decision to make India a full dialogue partner, spoke of "ASEAN's farsighted assessment about political and strategic convergence, acceleration of economic relations and their future potential, and complementarities in areas that were hitherto not evident or remained unexploited." He saw the decision "as a step forward and as a move from a derivative to a direct relationship, so that there are no distortions, no misperceptions, no ignorance and no intermediation." He pledged to pursue "our ASEAN engagement at the bilateral as well as multilateral levels and deepen our understanding of and interaction with the individual countries as well as with ASEAN institutions and mechanisms."

Though there was considerable unhappiness and even strong criticism from some ASEAN countries in regard to India's nuclear tests, this was not allowed to stand in the way of this relationship continuing to be nurtured. The ARF statement of July 1998, 'deplored' rather than condemned India's nuclear tests. In reality, though this could hardly be publicly articulated, India's nuclear status added to the credibility of India's power potential and hence to India's balancing role. In the year 2000, ASEAN was pleased that India announced that it accepts the Protocol of the South-East Asia Nuclear Weapons Free Zone (Seanwfz) even though as a non-member of the NPT it could not formally accede to it. Finally, India was accepted as a summit level partner (on par with China, Japan and Korea) with the first summit being held in Cambodia in November 2002. In his speech at the first India-ASEAN summit in 2002, Singapore Prime Minister Goh Chok Tong referred to India and China being the two wings of the ASEAN aircraft. This metaphor has since become common currency in the region.

Delivering the Annual Singapore Lecture in April 2002, Prime Minister Vajpayee had noted "India's belonging to the Asia Pacific community is a geographical fact and a political reality" and described the region as "one of the focal points of India's foreign policy, strategic concerns and economic interests." Prof. S. Jayakumar, Foreign Minister of Singapore, welcoming External Affairs Minister Jaswant Singh in Singapore in June 2002, remarked "whatever the new equilibrium or security architecture or geopolitical balance that eventually emerges, India will be a part of it….. India's strategic importance cannot be overlooked. India's strategic engagement with South-East Asia will evolve as the broader political and strategic context in which South and South-East Asia are embedded also evolves."

Four India-ASEAN summits have since taken place. A Framework Agreement on Comprehensive Economic Cooperation (for establishing a FTA in a time frame of 10 years) was concluded in 2003; an ASEAN India Joint Declaration for Cooperation to Combat International Terrorism has been issued; India acceded to ASEAN's Treaty of Amity and Cooperation in 2003; an Agreement on India-ASEAN Partnership for Peace, Progress and Shared Prosperity was signed in November 2004. Trade between India and ASEAN has increased from US $ 2.3 billion in 1992 to US $ 15 billion in 2005. These constitute important landmarks of the developing Indo-ASEAN relationship. The icing on the cake was, India being invited to participate along with China, Japan and South Korea (as well as Australia and New Zealand) in the first East Asian summit in December 2005 in Kuala Lumpur despite China's reservations. With this invitation, ASEAN has confirmed that it welcomes India as a full and equal player in the region.

China had conveyed its unhappiness and displeasure to ASEAN countries in no uncertain terms about its decision to give India full dialogue partner status in December 1995 (a status which China was granted only in June 1996 despite China's more substantive involvement with ASEAN since 1991 when it was made a consultative partner). China has been unhappy about the growing linkages between ASEAN and India Since then. The latest manifestation has been China's strong reservations about India being invited to the first East Asian summit.

ASEAN announced at its summit in November 2004 that the first East Asian Summit would be held in end 2005, but due to lack of consensus the list of participants was only finally announced in July 2005 at the ASEAN Foreign Minister's meeting in Laos. This included India, Australia and New Zealand in addition to ASEAN+3. This was only because of the sustained efforts of Singapore in particular and strong support extended by Indonesia, Japan and Vietnam. A few quotations are relevant. Supporting the potential of Indian participation, Gọh Tok Chong said in a speech in Singapore in January 2005, "It would be shortsighted and self defeating for ASEAN to choose a direction that cuts itself off from a dynamic India." In a speech before the Singapore Parliament on March 4, 2005, the Singapore Foreign Minister said, "Singapore supports the inclusion of India, Australia and New Zealand in the East Asia summit. Their inclusion will keep ASEAN at the center and put it beyond doubt that ASEAN are externally oriented and inclusive." In April 2005, the ASEAN Foreign Ministers laid down three criteria for participation in the summit and at the end of the meeting, the Singapore Foreign Minister stated, "India obviously qualifies on all three counts and it will be included in the first EAS." The Minister further said that ASEAN alone will decide the future membership of subsequent summits, "to ensure that ASEAN remains in the driver's seat of the EAS process."

It should be evident from this account that ASEAN has repeatedly exhibited in the clearest possible manner that it wants and welcomes India as an active player in the region.

With India's economy showing impressive growth rates and policies of welcoming foreign investment being put in place, engagement between the dynamic economies of South-East Asia and new opportunities in India has started in earnest and has grown in a very satisfactory manner throughout the past decade; expanding trade and investment linkages, free trade arrangements, subregional economic cooperation mechanisms, energy ties, etc., are some of the manifestations of a rapidly growing, mutually beneficial, symbiotic economic partnership. The initiative for most of these developments have been taken by ASEAN or individual member countries of ASEAN, for example, Thailand in regard to BIMSTEC. Though economic linkages with India do not at present remotely compare with the extremely strong economic ties that ASEAN has developed with China, the Indian economy is bounding ahead and India is clearly on its way to also becoming an economic superpower. Every month sees new strategic alliances between the leading global companies and India. Indeed, international economic and financial analysts are waxing eloquent about India's many comparative advantages. India's demography—average age of 26 compared to China's 33 could potentially be an enormous advantage because as Lee Kuan Yew pointed out "there is no precedence for any country to grow old before it has grown rich." Thus, India increasingly offers ASEAN countries more than a balancing option to economic over- dependence on China. George Yeo, Singapore's Trade and Industry Minister, said in February 2004, at a CII meeting in Bangalore, "We in South-East Asia have no wish to become an adjunct to China's economy." Beyond this overall economic relationship, there has been a sea change in all aspects of the bilateral relationships marked by increasingly frequent exchanges of high level visits. The excellent multifaceted relationship that India and Thailand have today, could not have even been imagined a decade ago; the relationship with Myanmar has been transformed dramatically with growing cooperation in the energy and transport sectors and particularly, in the very sensitive field of national security; the relationship with Singapore represents a true strategic alliance even if it is not formally consecrated as such. India-Vietnam relations have always been specially close and warm. Relations with the two other Indo-China countries—Cambodia and Laos have always been cordial too and the Mekong-Ganga Cooperation project, brings these three countries, Myanmar and Thailand into an India initiated sub-regional cooperation arrangement. India-Indonesia relations have been witnessing renewed warmth. Despite some reservations that Malaysia has harboured in regard to closer Indian involvement with ASEAN and the region, the overall economic and commercial relationship is excellent and bilateral ties are very good. Cooperation in the security, military and defense fields with ASEAN countries is also developing very satisfactorily. Defense training is an important aspect of expanding defense cooperation and India has been paying special attention to ASEAN countries as can be gauged by the fact that in contrast to the past, out of a total of 300 seats allocated to foreign countries in 2001-2002, 130 were allotted to ASEAN countries; 137 out of 301 in 2002-2003; and, 82 out of 151 in 2003-2004. Finally, it merits mention that most countries of the region support India's permanent membership of the UN Security Council.

All this clearly indicates that ASEAN countries, individually and collectively, consciously desire to build a strong relationship with India.

India and South-East Asian countries are pluralistic, free and open societies in which spirituality and religion have a very significant role. Strong cultural connectivity is another bonding factor. India has the world's second largest Islamic population and is manifestly the bastion of moderate Islam and the Indian experience is of great relevance to South-East Asia. There are no contentious issues between India and South-East Asia and there is much that they share. India does not carry any negative historical baggage *vis-à-vis* the region. India has no territorial claims or ambitions in the region and does not have any bilateral disputes with any country of the region. India does not need or want military alliances or bases in the region. Despite India itself being a major victim of the tsunami disaster, India's immediate, unselfish and efficient response in the context of the tsunami's devastating effects in the region, won widespread acclaim throughout the region. Maritime security in its multifarious dimensions is particularly important for countries of South-East Asia. It is equally important for India and indeed for China, Korea and Japan. This is a field in which few countries are positioned to offer as meaningful and mutually beneficial cooperation as India can and growing manifestations of this have become increasingly evident in recent years. The establishment of the Far Eastern Naval Command in July 2001 in the Andaman Islands and its upgrading to a Tri-Services Command last year, is an indication of progressively increasing Indian interest in security issues of the region. India is now in the forefront of regional cooperative joint naval patrol efforts in the Malacca Straits.

Interests of the major powers—India, China, Japan, Russia and the US—will intersect more and more in East Asia as we move further into the 21st Century. Since its inception, ASEAN has been and will remain a significant player in the Asia Pacific region. It is imperatively important for ASEAN to have excellent relations with all these powers so that it is not overly susceptible to pressures from any one of them. From a realistic and rational perspective, in the context both of the historical background and the inevitability of China becoming an economic and military superpower, South-East Asia has reason to be wary of China more than of any of the others. For all its involvement with the region, the US is an 'outsider'; the balance of power is still in favour of the US, but the balance of influence has already begun to shift in China's favour. The power gap between the US and China, both in the economic and military contexts, will steadily narrow. India has land and maritime boundaries with ASEAN—with Myanmar, Indonesia and Thailand. It has a lengthy border with China. Due to its population, size, economic and military potential, geographical proximity, cultural bonds, soft power attributes, etc. looking decades ahead, India will increasingly be the country that could provide ASEAN countries the needed regional counterbalance to China. In contrast to the other four countries, India had been marginally involved in and with the region till the mid-1990s. Once India had given the right signals, ASEAN was happy, indeed keen, to draw India in. For these reasons, the China factor has been a very important consideration in ASEAN's view of its relationship with India from the beginning. However, it would be entirely incorrect to infer that ASEAN seeks to develop its relations with India at the cost of its relationship with China. Indeed, ASEAN consciously wants an India which does not have hostile or antagonistic relations with other players in the region— China, the US or Japan. The primary reason for ASEAN's interest in India is because it would contribute to providing and maintaining regional balance and stability. It would not have served ASEAN's purposes if India had conflictual relations with China. Involving India then would be inviting increased fractiousness and tension into the region. ASEAN does not seek to pit one against the other. Indeed, ASEAN countries are very pleased about and have warmly welcomed improving relations between the two countries.

The China factor is definitely a consideration in any country's interaction with and involvement in the region for the simple reason that China is the largest and potentially the most powerful country and economic hub of the region. This is a reality. However, China *per se* was neither the main motivation for nor the major cause of India embarking upon its 'Look East' Policy. The 'Look East' Policy is not being pursued on any conscious assumptions of a looming, overt India-China rivalry in South-East Asia. India's Minister for External Affairs, Yashwant Sinha, had said during the first India ASEAN Summit in 2002 that: "mutuality of interests alone determined the ASEAN-India dynamic" adding that there is no intention "to upset Beijing's strategic applecart." Speaking to the press in October 2003 he said, "But even if we had not taken the China factor into consideration, ASEAN countries would do that." India recognises that both countries, China and India, will remain actively involved and engaged with the region and seek to promote their respective interests in a spirit of healthy competition but without confrontation.

Minister of External Affairs, Yashwant Sinha, in a lecture at Harvard University in October 2003 had said: "The other aspect of ...the 'Look East' Policy is the movement away from exclusive focus on economic issues in Phase One to a broader agenda that involves security cooperation, including joint operations to protect sea lanes and pooling resources in the war against terror. The military contacts and joint exercises that India launched with ASEAN states on a low key basis in the early 1990s are now expanding into full fledged cooperation." India's Defence Minister, Pranab Mukherjee, delivering the Valedictory Address at the Asian Security Conference in New Delhi, in January 2005 said "India's strategic perspective *vis-à-vis* East Asia is based on two fundamental principles. First, the maintenance of an equitable strategic balance and prevention of regional rivalries from destabilizing the region...Second and more importantly, India would like to engage all players both bilaterally and collectively through institutions like the ASEAN Regional Forum. Towards this end, India has initiated a security dialogue to constructively engage all the major players in the region." In this context, the Defence Minister drew pointed attention to the fact that "the two fundamental aspects that will have a significant bearing on the East Asian security are: the degree of US regional commitment and the texture of its relations with China." Goh Chok Tong, speaking at the official launch of the Institute of South Asian Studies in Singapore, in January 2005, had said: "With India's rise, it will be increasingly less tenable to regard South Asia and East Asia as distinct strategic theatres interacting only at the margins. US-China-Japan relations will still be important, but a new grand strategic triangle of US-China-India relations will be superimposed upon it.... Reconceptualising East Asia holistically is of strategic importance...It would be shortsighted and self defeating for ASEAN to choose a direction that cuts itself off from a dynamic India." Singapore Prime Minister, Lee Hsien Loong speaking at the 11th International Conference on the Future of Asia in Tokyo said on May 25, 2005 said: "First we need to integrate China into the regional economy in an orderly, win-win manner. Second, we need to strengthen cooperation among the other economies in East Asia. Third, East Asia must stay outward looking, and without becoming closed and protectionist. Fourthly, economic integration must be underpinned by a stable security environment. Within Asia, India is a key player which is opening up to the world, and which can potentially play as large a role as China. For ASEAN, India is an additional engine of growth." Senior Minister Goh Chok Tong speaking at the Asia Society Conference on June 9, 2005 in Bangkok said, "East Asia will be multipolar: China, Japan and India will be poles. Relationships between them have been historically uneasy... Adjustments, as they grew and redefine their roles, will not be easy or comfortable. Great power competition and rivalry are facts of life ... The South-East Asian experience shows that the construction of a broad framework to manage and contain differences cannot be left to market forces ... Allow(ing) the participation of India, Australia and New Zealand in the first East Asia Summit,(was) a wise decision to keep East Asian regionalism inclusive, open and forward looking. It would be a mistake to define the summit agenda too narrowly, it should deal with the widest possible range of issues and confront sensitive security concerns ... The role of the US in East Asian regionalism cannot be excluded ... The US should be an integral part of the overall architecture."

With ASEAN having ensured India's integration into the Asia Pacific region, in the future the 'Look East' Policy would relate to India's involvement with the Asia Pacific region as a whole in the context of the considerations mentioned in the various remarks quoted above and in particular, in the light of the considerations detailed in the next paragraph.

The main factors that will shape the evolving strategic scenario in the Asia Pacific region and India's involvement with it may be summarised as follows:

- For the past three decades, East Asia has been the world's most dynamic region, posting astonishingly high economic growth rates on a consistent basis in a historically unprecedented socioeconomic and political transformation involving hundreds of millions of people. Japan is currently the world's second largest economy after the US. China is expected to overtake Japan in 2016 and equal the US by 2042. India is expected to become the world's third largest economy by 2030-2035. Thus, three Asian countries will be amongst the world's top four economies well before the middle of this century. This factor was persuasively used to ensure that India was invited to participate in the first East Asian summit and virtually guarantees that India will have a significant role in the Asia Pacific region.

- Though India embarked on economic and foreign policy reorientations in the early 1990s, it is really in the past five years—first 5 years of the 21st Century—that the world has started unambiguously recognising that India is an economic giant in the making. 'Rising China' was the big story during the last two decades of the 20th Century and remains a front-page story. But 'Rising India' is the new big story. As India's economy continues to grow at the current impressive rates and more, so will India's attractiveness for the world. ASEAN's attitude towards India was a precursor of globally changing attitudes. The world in general and the US and Japan in particular, have drastically reoriented their policies towards India. China's changing attitude towards India is almost entirely induced by the dramatic change in global attitudes towards India, as a consequence of India's impressive new economic credentials. These changing relationships with India will ensure that India will be amongst the major players in the evolving strategic balance in East Asia.

- Global strategic commentators have been obsessed for over a decade with the implications of a 'rising China' and more recently with a 'rising India'. Not enough attention has been given to the political and military unshackling of Japan and its endeavour, strongly encouraged by the United States, to become a 'normal' country. The emergence of a 'normal' politically assertive, militarily powerful Japan is bound to have an enormous impact on the emerging strategic calculus in the region. Changing US policies towards India heralded an utterly dramatic transformation in Indo-Japanese relations beginning with Prime Minister Yoshiro Mori's visit to India in the year 2000, when India and Japan agreed to establish a 'Global Partnership for the 21st Century'. This initiated a spate of important high level visits culminating in Premier Koizumi's visit in 2005. At the end of that visit, a Joint Statement was issued entitled "Japan India Partnership in a New Asian Era: Strategic Orientation of Japan India Global Partnership". Except with the US, this is the only other instance of the phrase 'global partnership' being used in the context of Japan's relations with a foreign country. Thus, Japan would clearly like India to be a big league player in the region. Japanese commentators increasingly talk of synergising Japan's reinvigorated relationship with ASEAN with its emerging relationship with India.

- The US-Japan military alliance has been the cornerstone of the US role in East Asia. This US-Japanese relationship ensured the security of a defeated and pulverised Japan, acted as a bulwark against China's territorial expansion in the region and reassured Japan's neighbours and the broader region against a reassertion of Japanese militarism. This helped create the milieu that has enabled the spectacular economic rise of the region. Parallel with the rise of China's economic, military and political profile and influence in the region, there has been a concomitant and continuing strengthening and deepening of the military alliance between the United States and Japan. The original focus of military cooperation arrangements was the defence of Japan but the ambit has been progressively expanded to include 'surrounding waters and airspace', 'adjacent areas', 'areas surrounding Japan'. In the post 9/11 scenario, in an unprecedented development, for the first time since World War II, elements of Japanese Self-Defence Forces were dispatched to a combat zone: to the Indian Ocean extending logistic support to US operations in Afghanistan and in Iraq. The Joint Statement of the US-Japan Security Consultative Committee consisting of the US Secretaries of State and Defense and their Japanese counterparts issued in February 2005, contained a specific reference to Taiwan for the first time ever. China is extremely sensitive about external involvement in the Taiwan issue. The region's strategic community, well versed in the nuances of East Asian vocabulary, understands the immense significance of this reference. Japan has joined the US in the development of ballistic missile defence (BMD) and its ultimate deployment. The most recent Japanese National Defence Policy Outline of 2005 specifically mentions China's military buildup as an issue of concern for the first time. Japan is witnessing a conspicuous rise in public manifestation of rising nationalist sentiment typified by Prime Minister Koizumi's visits to the Yasukuni Shrine and increasing support for scrapping of the pacifist Article 9 of the Constitution. All these developments are taking place at a time when Sino-Japanese relations seem to have dipped to their lowest point, since the days of Japanese occupation of parts of China in the 1930s and 1940s.

• During the past three years in particular, the US-India relationship has been developing with exceptional warmth. The US has repeatedly and publicly proclaimed at the highest levels, its intention of helping India become a great power in the 21st Century. A quotation from the US Quadrennial Defense Review, released on February 6, 2006 is relevant. "India is emerging as a great power and a key strategic partner. On July 18, 2005 the President and the Indian Prime Minister declared their resolve to transform the US-India relationship into a global partnership that will provide leadership in areas of mutual concern and interest. Shared values as long-standing, multiethnic democracies provide the foundation for continued and increased strategic cooperation and represent an important opportunity for our two countries." On the other hand, references to China in the Review underline continuing and deepening US concerns about China's intentions, policies and military capabilities. The Bush-Manmohan Singh Joint Statement of March 2, 2006, constitutes a truly historic landmark in Indo-US relations. It represents a policy reorientation of unprecedented and monumental proportions for the US— President Bush's visit to India is as much a watershed as the Nixon visit to China in 1972 in the context of future US strategy and involvement in Asia. The US has made no effort to conceal its belief that India could have a vital role in the context of US's intentions of remaining fully involved in the Asia Pacific. Prime Minister, Manmohan Singh, speaking at a conference on March 18, 2006 which had 'India's New Priorities, Asia's New Realities' as the theme, said, "Cooperation between them (Asian countries) and America is no less essential than cooperation between themselves. In that context, the strengthening of ties between India and America is, I believe, a major positive development for Asia as a whole." Thus, India is clearly suggesting that the US should continue to have an important role in Asia in the future and India could be a partner.

- Russia clearly has important stakes in the region. It is involved in the six-party talks to resolve the potentially dangerous North Korean nuclear issue. It has become China's largest arms supplier and strategic ally. They are working together in the Shanghai Cooperation Organisation to diminish if not eliminate US presence and influence in Central Asia. They are working together to mitigate Western pressures on Iran. Russia is becoming an increasing source of oil and gas supplies for both China and Japan. Russia has an unresolved territorial dispute with Japan. There are indications that it may be invited to attend the next East Asia summit. When Russia broke up, it lost significant chunks of its non-Russian population and now has a predominantly Western, 'Christian' personality. Its current cozy relationship with China seems to be dictated by tactical considerations, due to the need for priority attention to counter American hegemony. In the longer term there could be problems as the sparsely populated, resource rich Russian far east regions will inevitably attract the predatory attention of resource hungry China. In the light of all these considerations, many seemingly contradictory, the nature of its future role remains nebulous. There is a robust partnership between India and Russia and there is no reason for any clash or divergence of interest between them in any part of Asia and to that extent India should be well disposed towards Russian involvement in Asian affairs and *vice versa*.

• The Taiwan factor. Taiwan is a globally significant economic power with the world's third largest foreign exchange reserves; is the world's sixth largest foreign investor including being the largest single foreign investor in China; is the world's 15th ranked trading nation and the world's 17th largest economy. It is a high-tech superpower particularly in the IT hardware sector. It has a per capita income of more than US $ 17000 and a literacy rate of 97 per cent with very impressive capabilities in higher education and applied research. Taiwan has significant military capability with an excellent indigenous high-tech foundation. Thus, Taiwan's reunification with China would very significantly boost China's already strong economic, financial, technological and military capabilities. Beyond Taiwan's intrinsic strengths, Taiwan's location is an enormously important strategic factor. A significant proportion of global trade to China, South Korea and Japan and oil traffic from Middle East passes through the South China Sea and through the Taiwan Strait and Bashi Channel. Taiwan is located astride these two vital sea lanes. Taiwan is in physical possession of the largest island in the Spratleys in the South China Sea and of Pratas island, which controls the Sea's northeast exit. In the past two decades, China has increasingly and stridently asserted that all the islands in the South China Sea are an integral part of China making the Sea virtually a Chinese lake. The South China Sea is also believed to contain significant oil and gas deposits. Therefore, Taiwan's reunification with China would enable China to virtually take control of the South China Sea, ensconce itself in South-East Asia's belly, have a stranglehold on vitally important sea lanes, and become a maritime power in the Pacific Ocean to which it has no direct access at present. Thus, reunification is likely to further burnish China's credentials as the partner of choice for other regional countries, impacting adversely on their ability to make strategic choices with the potential to seriously erode US relationships and consequently its capabilities in the region. While discussing Taiwan, it may be mentioned that India was the only country in the region, which did not have any kind of a relationship with Taiwan. Motivated by economic considerations, the 'Look East' Policy led India and Taiwan to set up unofficial relations in 1995. In contrast to all other countries, India's self-imposed restrictions on interaction with Taiwan remain a major impediment to realising the very considerable economic potential of the relationship.

- In the past 2-3 years, the political and military relationship between the United States and South Korea has been under increasing strain. There are distinct indications of a closer relationship with China as well as of more assertive autonomy in policy relating to North Korea. Indeed, reunification in 5 to 10 years is a distinct possibility and if this happens there will be clear consequences for the regional balance of power. Meanwhile, *en passant*, it merits mention that the most spectacular early economic results of the 'Look East' Policy had come, surprisingly, from South Korea. Korea's initial responses in the early 1990s were the most encouraging. With the signing of the US $ 12 billion steel project last year, South Korea has become Asia's largest foreign investor in India. Both sides feel upbeat about the future.

In the ultimate analysis, all the above-mentioned factors will play out in the context of China's involvement with and impact upon the region. With India's rise, India's involvement with and impact upon the region will attract China's increasing attention. Therefore, evolving Sino-Indian relations may well become the pivotal contributory factor of the strategic future of the Asia-Pacific region.

From India's perspective, India's involvement with the region east of India extending to Japan will always be influenced by the centrality of its relationship with ASEAN. ASEAN has been and will remain the gateway. ASEAN provides the connectivity and is the unavoidable essential bridge. The US desires a unipolar world and a multipolar Asia; China desires a multipolar world and a unipolar Asia; India and ASEAN would like a multipolar world and a multipolar Asia. Neither ASEAN nor India represents any threat to either China or to the US. Neither ASEAN nor India wishes to join an alliance with the US against China. Nor do they want to join any alliance, which seeks to challenge the US. It is important for both India and South-East Asia to maintain strategic autonomy. ASEAN has become an important pole in East Asia's strategic configuration. ASEAN countries and India are positioned to forge a true strategic partnership to enable both, to withstand pressures from the US and China to take sides in the looming Sino-US contest on the one hand and to act as a bridge between them on the other. For the future, these are likely to be the objectives of India's 'Look East' Policy.

It would be evident from the foregoing account that more than any startling policy initiatives that India has taken beyond perceptively adjusting to new and emerging realities, it is India's rising economic profile, ASEAN's proactive attitude *vis-à-vis* India, the consequences of China's rise and the changing relationships between major powers that are the factors that have created opportunities for India in the region. For all practical purposes, ASEAN, Japan and the US have given a resoundingly positive answer in favour of India's active involvement in the region; South Korea and Taiwan are very favourably disposed to India's greater involvement; the robust partnership with Russia remains a positive factor for Indian involvement with the region. If India's role in the region is to be sustained and meaningful, India will have to move away from abstract idealism to conscious pragmatism, from past tendencies of advocacy of populist 'Third World' causes to the focussed promotion of its own national interests, from rhetoric to action in shaping of the domestic economic environment to benefit fully from the global marketplace, and adopt a much more proactive approach in implementing agreements and understandings that have been arrived at. Prime Minister Manmohan Singh unveiled a vision of an Asian Economic Community at the first East Asian Summit and has been pushing India's full economic integration with the rest of Asia—a "Pan-Asian FTA could be the future of Asia." This was the main theme of his keynote address to the Asian Development Bank Annual meeting in Hyderabad on May 5, 2006. This effort is likely to be the centrepiece of the evolving 'Look East' Policy. An Asia on the EU pattern could well be the best solution to the very large number of disputes and problems within the region.

In any consideration of India's relations with South-East Asia, the role played by Singapore deserves special mention. Ever since its separation from Malaysia and emergence as an independent country in 1965, Singapore has displayed a uniquely friendly attitude towards India. Prime Minister Lee Kuan Yew visited India in 1966, 1970 and 1971 and again in 1988. From the beginning, Singapore was very keen to develop a strong defence relationship with India. Though India was reticent then, the defence relationship has been growing strongly through the 1990s; joint naval exercises have regularly been held for more than 10 years; joint armour-artillery exercises and joint air force exercises have also been held in recent years. Similar exercises have not been conducted with China. A Defence Cooperation Agreement was signed by the two Defence Ministers in October 2003. A landmark Comprehensive Economic Cooperation Agreement was signed in June 2005 and Singapore has been India's largest and fastest growing trade partner within ASEAN. Kesavapany has reported that George Yeo, Singapore's Foreign Minister, speaking in Parliament on March 4, 2005, described bilateral relations with India as "almost a love affair", an unusual phrase to use; certainly far beyond anything similar used to refer to its relationship with China. Beyond this strong bilateral relationship, Singapore has played a pivotal role in all landmark ASEAN decisions relating to India, starting from the mid-1960s when ASEAN was probing India's possible membership; again in 1980 and in 1992; it was a Singapore initiative, very strongly pressed, that led to the decision in 1995 to grant India full dialogue partner status; again in 1996 in the context of ARF, in 2001 in the context of the first ASEAN–India Summit which was held in 2002 and finally, the extremely important role it played in ensuring Indian participation in the first East Asian Summit.

Seventy-five per cent of Singapore's population is ethnic Chinese. It is widely considered to be a 'Chinese' state. For this reason, Singapore has consciously striven not to be perceived as China's agent in South-East Asia. It has consistently emphasised that its China policy is founded on economic opportunity and not on ethnic affinity. Singapore very deliberately chose to be the last amongst the original ASEAN members to establish diplomatic relations with China, only in 1990, after Indonesia had done so. Yet, Singapore has been in the forefront of seeking to integrate China into its broader neighbourhood. Universally considered a wise and astute elder statesman, Lee Kuan Yew has been the architect of Singapore's foreign policy and its China policy in particular. There is no world statesman or leader, today or in the past, who knows China as intimately as Lee Kuan Yew; no one has interacted as intensively with its leadership as he has, given that he has paid three dozen visits to China since his first visit in

May 1976. (Since the Taiwan issue is the most sensitive issue as far as China is concerned, it may be relevant to note that Lee Kuan Yew has paid 30 visits to Taiwan in the same time frame and interacted as intensively with Taiwan's leaders; and that the present Singapore Prime Minister very consciously and deliberately paid a three day visit to Taiwan on the eve of his assumption of office in 2005 to personally assess and understand Taiwan's China policy. It may be mentioned that the Singapore Army has been training in Taiwan ever since its inception, with the first Chiefs of Singapore's Air Force and Navy being Taiwanese officers — India was requested but declined.) No country's leadership is as well informed about China as Singapore's is. Singapore claims excellent relationships with all four major Powers–China, India, Japan and the US. For all these reasons, Singapore's assessments of China and Chinese policies and motivations are perhaps the most objective and thus, most valuable. It has always expressed its views with refreshing candour and an unmatched clarity in strategic thinking relating to the potential role of major powers in the Asia Pacific region. This is part of the reason why there is a heavy emphasis on using Singapore sources to substantiate the main themes of the article.

Even as India's relationships with South-East and East Asia have been transformed fairly dramatically and positively, the situation in India's neighbourhood continues to be a source of great, if not increasing, anxiety and worry. The internal situation in virtually each of India's South Asian neighbours has been steadily deteriorating and the dangerous prospect of their becoming failing states is increasing. There is little or no change in the inimical policies that Pakistan and Bangladesh continue to pursue *vis-à-vis* India, particularly insofar as the terrorism aspects are concerned. The military relationships between these countries and China are deepening and expanding ceaselessly. The Taliban is reemerging as a substantive force in Afghanistan. Nepal is in a state of chaos. Sri Lanka seems poised to drift back into civil war. Not only does all this represent an increasing external security threat but this could severely undermine India's own internal stability also. The security situation in the Northeast could become much worse in the future than it was ever in the past if the demographic aggression from Bangladesh continues to be ignored. Developments in the sub-continent could cause renewed strain in Sino-Indian and Indo-US relationships. All this could gravely undermine India's ability to play its due role in East Asia, South-East Asia and West Asia, regions which are of absolutely vital importance to India's future prosperity and stability.

17

India and broader economic integration in Asia

An agenda for the East Asia Summit

Nagesh Kumar

Introduction

In the context of emergence of strong regional trade blocs in Europe, North America, South America, parts of Africa over the past decade, the relevance of evolving a broader pan-Asian grouping has been attracting a lot of attention. It had been argued that with more than half of world trade being conducted on a preferential basis rather than on most-favoured nation (MFN) basis the threat of trade diversion from Asia was becoming increasingly potent. Different Asian leaders and statesmen had spoken of the importance of broader regional cooperation in Asia asserting the Asian identity. Prime Minister Dr. Manmohan Singh has given a vision of an Asian Economic Community which seems to be the way forward for Asian economic integration that could not only respond to the global trend towards regionalism but also become an engine of growth for Asia expediting the realisation of the Asian dream. In that context, the launch of a new forum of East Asia Summit in December 2005 combining 16 major and most dynamic economic economies of Asia creates new possibilities for launching such broader scheme of regional community building in Asia.

Against that background, this chapter discusses the relevance of broader regional economic cooperation in Asia, an agenda for the East Asia Summit and the relevance and role of India in these initiatives. Section 2 summarises the emerging patterns with respect to regional economic cooperation in Asia and relevance of a broader approach to economic integration. Section 3 presents a possible approach to regional integration and Section 4 summarises the potential and gains of such integration. Section 5 discusses the relevance of India for East Asian economic integration. Section 6 concludes the chapter with some remarks on the agenda of the East Asia Summits.

Regional economic cooperation in Asia

Having been the faithful adherents of multilateralism till nearly the turn of the millennium, Asian countries have been slow to respond to the global trend of regionalism. Successful experiences with regional economic integration in the industrialised countries since the mid-1980s in Europe and North America have also prompted South-East and South Asian countries to adopt economic integration strategies. For instance, ASEAN in 1992 decided to set up the ASEAN Free Trade Area (AFTA). Similarly, SAARC agreed to create in 2004 a SAARC Free Trade Agreement (SAFTA) to be implemented over 10 years. Another notable initiative in Asia is BIMSTEC (Bay of Bengal Initiative for Multisectoral Techno-economic Cooperation) involving five South Asian countries *viz.* Bangladesh, Bhutan, India, Nepal, and Sri Lanka and two South-East Asian countries *viz.* Myanmar and Thailand. Hence, it is seen as a bridge between South and South-East Asia. BIMSTEC also adopted a Framework Agreement for an FTA to be implemented within 10 years at its first Summit held in Bangkok in July 2004. The regionalism in the West also led Japan reviewing its trade policy and putting due emphasis on regional economic integration.

The East Asian Crisis of 1997 also highlighted the importance of regional economic cooperation. The ASEAN countries expedited the programme of implementation of ASEAN Free Trade Area (AFTA) and moved on to further deepen the economic integration. The crisis also led to launch of several regional initiatives such as the Chiang-Mai Initiative, which involves ASEAN+3 (Japan, China, and

South Korea) countries. Besides this, the ASEAN's policy of engaging key Asian countries namely Japan, China, India and South Korea as dialogue partners have provided much needed cohesion in the Asian region as is clear from the numerous schemes of regional and bilateral free trade arrangements that are at different levels of implementation. China, Japan, and India are all engaged in negotiations of free trade arrangements with ASEAN and South Korea considering one. The annual Summits of ASEAN and its dialogue partners have also facilitated to a large number of bilateral FTAs between individual ASEAN countries and their dialogue partners as well as between the dialogue partners themselves. At the moment there are a number of such bilateral FTAs at different stages of study or formation such as Japan-Singapore FTA (2002) and Japan-Philippines, Japan-Malaysia, Japan-Thailand, China-Thailand, China-Malaysia, India-Singapore, India-Thailand, India-China, India-South Korea, India-Japan, India-Malaysia, Japan-China-South Korea, among others.

However, it can be argued that the subregional or bilateral attempts at regional cooperation that have been initiated such as those under the framework of ASEAN and SAARC or the dialogue partners while desirable are unlikely to exploit the full potential of the regional economic integration in Asia and hence are sub-optimal. This is because the extent of complementarities are limited at the subregional levels because of similar factor endowments and economic structures within a neighbourhood. It is clear from the fact that trade of ASEAN or SAARC countries with the East Asian countries is much larger than their intra-subregional trade. It is for this reason that the success achieved so far from the subregional or bilateral attempts at cooperation have so far been meagre. At the broader Asian level, on the other hand, the diversities in the levels of economic development and capabilities are quite wide thus providing for more extensive and mutually beneficial linkages. The diversity in economic structure provides its own indigenous capacity and markets for dynamic industrial restructuring within the region on the basis of 'flying geese' patterns. Hence, Asia needs an overarching Asia-wide scheme of economic integration to fully exploit the full potential of efficiency-seeking industrial restructuring or to exploit the synergies that exist in the region. Among other factors the twin scourges of SARS and terrorism have also promoted East Asian regionalism.[1]

The Asian region has a distinct Asian identity shaped by history and cultural exchanges over several centuries. There have been vibrant flows of goods and services as well as labour and capital amongst Asian countries sustained over several centuries. In the ancient time, the famed silk routes provided the channels for such exchanges. Marco Polo's tales are just one of many such descriptions. During the 19th Century, the colonial powers provided the framework for extensive and liberal trade within Asia in goods and services as well as massive movements of labour and capital. Assisted by Japan's rise, trade was brisk. Even during the first half of the 20th Century the intra-regional trade ratio was over 50 per cent. These trade and investment flows were disrupted by political and military factors during the colonial period and in the post-war Asia. Along with the trade there was a vibrant exchange of ideas. Chinese scholars visited India and *visa versa*. Ideological influences spread across the nations binding them in ties of religion. Hinduism and with it the art of governance of Chanakya found its way across to much of Indonesia, Malaysia and Thailand. The sweep of Buddhism is well known. Religion has been a strong unifying factor, for with the religious beliefs comes a way of life and as religious influence spread so did the cultural ties. Pagan, Borobudur and Angkor Wat are only but a small testimony to the vast trading and cultural network that Asia had in ancient times.[2]

There is now growing recognition in Asia of the importance of regional economic integration[3] for generating growth impulses from within, especially in the wake of the East Asian crisis. Voices emanating from different parts of the region in support of pan-Asian cooperation and integration are ample proof of the growing

---

1. See Eric Teo (2005a).

2. See Shankar (2004) for more details.

3. See the writings of Yamazawa (1998, 2001a, 2001b), Alatas (2001), Shinawatra (2001), among others, for arguments for closer economic cooperation in Asia.

recognition of the importance of Asian economic integration. At the initiative of Prime Minister, Dr. Thaksin Shinawatra, of Thailand, the Asian Cooperation Dialogue (ACD) was launched on 18-19 June 2002 at Cha-Am, Thailand. Similarly the Chinese President Jiang Zemin had launched the Boao Forum for Asia in 2001 at Boao, in Hainan province of China, as a pan-Asian economic forum. The Prime Minister, Dr. Manmohan Singh, of India has been making case for an Asian Economic Community combining Japan, ASEAN countries, China, India and South Korea as an "arc of advantage across which there will would be large-scale movement of people, capital, ideas and creativity....Such a community would release enormous creative energies of our people." The East Asian Summit (EAS) held on 14 December 2005 in Kuala Lumpur, a new forum for dialogue on regional issues has been created. Bringing together 16 of Asia-Pacific major economies *viz.* ASEAN, Japan, China, South Korea, India and Australia and New Zealand, EAS could be an important platform for launching a broader Asian grouping in future.

An approach to broader Asian economic integration

Keeping in mind the experiences of regional economic integration from other regions, a practical approach to regionalisation in Asia would be a phased one, as outlined below.

The approach towards the process of broader regional economic integration has to be take into consideration the process of cohesion in Asia brought about by ASEAN. As argued earlier, ASEAN has helped to bring together four major economies of Asia as its annual summit-level dialogues partners *viz.* Japan, China, South Korea and India. These countries meet annually at the ASEAN summits, in ASEAN+1 summits besides an ASEAN+3 (Japan, China and Korea) summit. It has been observed that ASEAN+1 approaches have become more attractive compared to ASEAN+3 as is clear from the FTAs being evolved by China, Japan, India and Korea with ASEAN.[4] FTAs between Japan, Korea and China and those between India-

---

4. See Bonapace (2005).

China, India-Korea and India-Japan are being studied. In other words, ASEAN and the four dialogue partners namely Japan, ASEAN, China, India and Korea (JACIK) countries are all engaged in evolving FTAs between their different pairs. Through this complex web of FTAs a virtual JACIK or an East Asian FTA is emerging. However, these bilateral or sub-regional FTAs do not allow full exploitation of potential of regional economic integration that exists in view of substantial complementarities arising from diversity in the factor endowments and levels of development. Hence, a vision for the Asian economic integration is to begin by coalescing these multiple FTAs between JACIK countries into an overarching East Asian RTA.[5] A broader overarching framework alone will allow optimal utilisation of Asia's resources and synergies for their mutual common benefit.

The East Asian RTA combining JACIK economies could become a core of an East Asian Community which could be expanded later to include other Asian countries into an Asian Economic Community. This approach is supported by a number of Asian leaders including the former Singapore Prime Minister Lee and the Indian Prime Minister.[6] President Arroyo of the Philippines has observed, "the emerging ASEAN+3+India ... will be a formidable regional grouping that can negotiate then with the European Union, the Americas, Africa and such regional groupings."[7]

Combining 14 of the largest and fastest growing economies of Asia with vast complementarities, East Asian or JACIK trade bloc is a potential third pole of the world economy. For instance, they combine between them a population of three billion or a half of the world population (Table 17.1). In terms of purchasing power parity, the JACIK grouping will have the gross national income of

---

5. The JACIK approach to Asian economic integration was first proposed by RIS in 2002, see Kumar (2002), RIS (2003). Among experts who have favoured such an approach include Wei (2004), Yao (2005), Bonapace (2005) and Rowley (2004).

6. See for instance, address of Singapore's Mentor Minister, Lee Kuan Yew at the Foreign Correspondents Association of Singapore reported in *The Straits Times*, 22 December 2004. Prime Minister Dr. Manmohan Singh has envisioned an Asian Economic Community evolved using a building bloc approach to begin with Japan, ASEAN, China, India and Korea at the Laos Summit in November 2004.

7. See speech delivered at the ASEAN Business Summit, Vientiane, Laos, 28 November 2004.

Table 17.1

*Proposed East Asian or JACIK Community in Relation to
European Union and NAFTA in 2003*

(billion US $)

Parameter	EU	NAFTA	JACIK (14)	EAS Participants (JACIK-AN 16)
Gross National Income, PPP (in Purchasing Power Parity)	10137	12847	16058	16716
% of World Total	20.14	25.53	31.91	33.22
GDP	10505	12431	7262	8198
% of World Total	29.37	34.76	21.24	22.92
Exports (2002)	3523	1486	1657	1757
% of World Total	46.50	19.62	21.88	23.20
International Reserves	285	170	1657	1757
Population (million)	381	425	3065	3089
% of World Total	6.12	6.83	49.27	49.65

Source: RIS based on World Bank, *World Development Indicators 2005*, CD-ROM; IMF, *International Financial Statistics 2004*.

$ 16 trillion, much larger than either NAFTA or EU. JACIK's exports will add up to $ 1.66 trillion compared to $ 1.48 trillion of NAFTA. The combined official reserves of the JACIK economies at $ 1.6 trillion in 2003 are much larger than those of the US and the EU put together. In fact, the latest estimates suggest that foreign exchange holdings of JACIK countries are more than US$ 2 trillion. Therefore, the region would have sufficiently large market and financial resources to support and sustain expedited development of the region's economies.

Combining both China and India, the two most populous emerging economies of Asia that are projected to emerge as the two of the three largest economies of the world with their rapid growth in the next 3-4 decades, JACIK is likely to be the centre of gravity of the world economy. Alternatively, the EAS participating countries that include in addition to JACIK, Australia and New Zealand i.e. JACIK-AN could be a possible core of an East Asian FTA.

Gains from East Asian or JACIK economic integration

The studies conducted by RIS have found considerable evidence of complementarities between the JACIK countries' production and trade structures.[8] Formation of an RTA may help in exploitation of these complementarities for mutual advantage. RIS studies conducted in computable general equilibrium (CGE) model framework have shown that a trade liberalisation in the framework of an RTA in JACIK could produce efficiency gains worth US$ 210 billion representing more than three per cent of combined GDP of JACIK economies (Table 17.2). What is more, all the JACIK countries benefit from integration. Interestingly, the welfare of even the rest of the world also improves by US$ 109 billion suggesting that Asian economic integration will be Pareto optimal.

Table 17.2

Welfare Gains from Economic Integration in East Asia or JACIK

Trade, Investment and Mobility of Skilled Workers	Welfare Gains	
	in US$ million	Percentage change in welfare
Japan	150695	3.55
Korea	14076	3.25
China-HK	16328	1.65
ASEAN (5)	19405	
India	9937	2.5
JACIK	210441	3.14
Rest of the world	109916	
World	320357	

Source: RIS Simulations. See Mohanty *et al.*, (2004) for details.

The above findings have been corroborated by a recent study conducted by the Asian Development Bank.[9] Using GTAP 6 database with a version of World Bank's Linkage model, the ADB team generated projections of income and trade to 2025 for different scenarios to examine the relative relevance of regional integration *vis-à-vis* global trade liberalisation. The findings suggest that

8. See Sinha-Roy (2004).

9. Douglas, Roland-Holst and Zhai, 2005.

"regional trade and integration offer Asia great potential for rapid and sustained growth." ADB study finds that much of Asia's benefits from global trade liberalisation can be realised by regional initiative alone. Significantly, they find that combined gains from removing tariff and structural barriers to Asian trade far outweigh those of global tariff abolition. Hence, regionalism should be very high priority for Asia. ADB study also finds that regional integration can promote Asian economic convergence, raising average growth rates and benefiting poorer countries. In particular, greater regional integration will propagate commercial linkages and transfer the stimulus of Asia's rapid growth economies, particularly China and India, to their neighbours. The Asian economic integration increases trade and incomes for the rest of the world. Hence it is a win-win for the region and the world!

Other economic and strategic gains from broader economic cooperation in Asia

Trade and investment cooperation among the JACIK economies can be fruitfully complemented by monetary and financial cooperation, cooperation for energy security and in core technologies as summarised below.

Mobilising Asian foreign exchange reserves for Asian development

Combined foreign exchange reserves of JACIK countries now add up to nearly US $ 2 trillion and comprise the bulk of such reserves in the world. It has been argued that these funds have been invested in low yielding US treasury bonds and are able to contribute to the Asian development more meaningfully. There is a growing consensus that Asia needs a regional institution for mobilising these resources for its own development besides for achieving stability of real effective exchange rates and for an orderly response to external shocks.[10] Studies have shown that there is growing macroeconomic interdependence between Japan, Korea and ASEAN. Such interdependence is likely to include China and India,

---

10. See Wolf (2004), among many others.

besides Australia and New Zealand with ongoing reforms, liberalisation and market opening.[11]

RIS has developed a proposal of a Reserve Bank of Asia. It is argued that even a moderate proportion say five per cent of combined JACIK reserves i.e. US $ 100 billion will be adequate to make a beginning with the Reserve Bank of Asia.[12] An institution with a reserve of US $ 100 billion at its disposal, it can create an Asian monetary unit of account[13] or an Asian SDR. The Asian SDR or an Asian currency unit (ACU) can be used increasingly as a unit of account and as reserve asset in the region.[14] Besides providing a mechanism for exchange rate stability, and facilitating trade transactions within the region, the Asian SDR can also provide a channel for funding development of regional public goods and other huge infrastructure development projects without putting pressure on the government budgets in the member countries.[15] On the basis of such a reserve, an instrument like an Asian SDR can be created and used to finance infrastructure and IT investments in the region. The borrowers could be regional companies (such as Channel Tunnel Company for the UK and France) jointly owned by governments and private sector in the region. Similarly, there is also substantial potential of bond market development in Asia and some steps have been taken in that regard.[16] This will help in creating demand for the underutilised construction capacity in parts of Asia as observed earlier. Among other possibilities for monetary and financial cooperation in Asia are to develop an Asian Bond Market for which a couple of initiatives have been taken, or to set up an Asian Investment Bank for facilitating infrastructure financing, and cooperation between the national exim banks of the region.[17]

---

11. See Kawai (2004).

12. See RIS (2003a).

13. See Kawai, *op.cit.*

14. See RIS (2006), also see Kumar (2006).

15. See Agarwala (2004).

16. See presentation by Ambassador M. Xuto at the *High-level Conference on Asian Economic Integration* organised by RIS in Tokyo, 18-19 November 2004.

17. See Rajan (2006) for more details.

Cooperation for energy security

Major countries of Asia namely Japan, China, India, Korea among others are highly dependent upon oil and gas imports and could benefit by mutual cooperation in the area. The regional cooperation in the area of energy could cover, for instance, to ensure security and sustainability of energy supply, overseeing efficient utilisation of natural energy resource in the region, rational management of energy demand, with due consideration of the environment, establishing policy framework and implementation modalities for setting up of energy networks in the region such as region-wide oil or gas grids, and coordinate, manage and monitor the implementation of such a network. One of the target areas of Asian energy cooperation could be to build an Asian Strategic Petroleum Reserve (SPR) and to create an Asian Emergency Response System. An Asian SPR would be like a global energy security insurance policy. The Asian SPR would be a safeguard against OPEC's ability to raise oil prices and would prevent any market failure, by enabling governments to provide supply liquidity in an emergency situation. Asian countries have some ongoing cooperation in the area as joint exploration or oil equity sharing by Japanese, Korean, Chinese and Indian oil companies in exploration projects in third countries within the region such as in Myanmar and Vietnam and outside the region as in Sudan. Japan, Korea, China and India have begun to coordinate their positions in their negotiations with OPEC with respect to Asian premium that is being charged by the Middle East countries on their supplies to Asian countries.[18] The cooperation could also extend to cover the joint patrolling of the sea-lanes through which the bulk of the oil and gas supplies for the region pass through such as Malacca Straits to prevent piracy. Finally, JACIK countries could contemplate building an Asian gas/oil pipeline connecting them. Asian energy ministers have met in January 2005 and in December 2005 in New Delhi to advance cooperation in this area.[19] Subsequently, India and China agreed to cooperate in the area of energy security.

---

18. See Ito *et al.,* (2005) for more details.

19. India hosted a Meeting of Asian Energy Ministers in New Delhi in early 2005 to discuss issues of mutual concern. See *New Asia Monitor*, January 2005 for details.

Global governance, peace and security

Regional economic integration is also likely to strengthen Asia's role in global economic governance. Although Asian countries hold two-thirds of world's foreign exchange reserves, the decisionmaking powers in the Bretton Woods institutions, for instance, is dominated by the Western countries. By forming credible schemes of regional economic integration, Asia will be able to seek its due place in the global economic governance and contribute to building a more democratic and multipolar world economy. Asian economic integration by increasing the interdependence of countries in the region will ensure peace and stability. That is why Prime Minister Dr. Manmohan Singh has argued that the Asian economic community would constitute an "arc of advantage and prosperity and stability and closer economic integration" and would release enormous creative energies of its people.

Relevance of India for the East Asian economic integration

India's economic integration with East Asia can be a win-win for the economic integration in Asia for the following reasons:

Imparting its own dynamism to the grouping

With a US $ 700 billion economy growing at 7-8 per cent per annum and even faster growing and sizeable (300 million strong) middle class, India brings its own dynamism to the emerging Asian regionalism. With foreign exchange reserves of over US $ 140 billion, one of the best performing stock market in Asia,[20] low rates of inflation, market determined exchange rates, abundant human capital and entrepreneurial resources, rapidly growing industry and services, prudently managed financial system,[21] India is attracting attention for its strong macro-fundamentals. India has now been

---

20. India's capital markets are highly developed with world-class electronic settlement system and rapidly improving corporate governance systems. Over 6000 companies are listed on India's stock exchanges next only to NYSE. India topped the MSCI index for Asian countries in terms of stock market returns for September-December 2004 period as reported in *The Financial Express*, 17 December 2004.

21. Ratio of non-performing assets to GDP is just 3 per cent compared to China's 41 per cent, Japan's 11 per cent and Thailand's 9 per cent.

ranked among the top three investment destinations in the world by AT Kearney in terms of FDI Confidence Index recently.[22] Recent studies by Goldman Sachs indicate that India is poised to emerge the third largest economy in the world by 2032. 'India has the potential to show the fastest growth over the next 30 and 50 years'.[23] Another study by IMF finds India poised to sustain about 7 per cent growth rates for over next 30-40 years with very few downside risks.[24] According to IMF, India is contributing nearly 10 per cent of the global growth and 20 per cent of Asian growth.[25] With the growing economic integration of the Indian economy, this growth is spilling over to the other economies as well. With two major dynamos *viz.* China and India propelling regional growth, the Asian dream will be realised faster.[26]

With booming demand for infrastructure investments that are projected to be over US $ 500, India can help neutralise any loss of demand in Asia resulting from US trying to curb its mounting trade deficit. Malaysian companies, among others, have already won substantial projects in roads construction in open competitive bidding. Booming middle class in the country is increasingly becoming a source of final consumption with rising income levels. India, for instance, has emerged a major market for high spending tourists from a number of countries in East Asia.

Growing integration of India with East Asia

As a part of the Look East Policy, India has consciously integrated its economy with East Asia since the early 1990s. With this, the share of East Asia in India's trade is approaching nearly a third thus making it a more important trade partner compared to the EU or the United States. India's trade with China grew by nearly

---

22. http://www.atkearney.com/shared_res/pdf/FDICIOct_2004_S.pdf.

23. See Goldman Sachs BRICs study (2003).

24. An IMF Working Paper (04/118) projects India's growth rate in 2025 at 7 per cent "with more upside potential than downside risks."

25. See "Is India becoming an Engine for Global Growth?" in IMF (2005) *World Economic Outlook*, September 2005: 36-7.

26. Kesavapany (2005) has used the metaphor of dynamo: "One can ask why we should deny ourselves the benefits to be derived from one of the two major dynamos propelling regional growth."

75 per cent in 2004 to surpass US $ 13 billion. Her trade with Korea grew by 48 per cent in 2003. ASEAN-India trade has grown by over 30 per cent over the past couple of years and is projected to cross US$ 30 billion by 2007. As India's tariff levels become more closely aligned to those of East Asia, recent sharp growth in merchandise trade is expected to continue. India has autonomously brought down applied tariffs drastically since 1991. In the Budget 2005/06, the peak tariffs were brought down from 20 per cent to 15 per cent. Because of economic growth and ambitious unilateral trade liberalisation, India's imports have grown by 27 per cent a year on average over the past three years and crossed US$ 100 billion in 2004/05.

To further strengthen her economic links with East Asian countries India is evolving FTAs with ASEAN and +3 countries. India signed a Framework Agreement on Comprehensive Economic Cooperation with ASEAN at the Bali Summit involving an FTAs to be implemented in 10 years.[27] This is complemented by bilateral agreements signed with Thailand and Singapore. India is currently studying an FTA with China, Japan, Korea and Malaysia. With FTAs either under negotiation or under study with ASEAN, Japan, China, and Korea, it is very much part of the growing web of FTAs linking the East Asian countries.

Growing synergies and integration with
East Asian production networks

India's strengths in software and services fruitfully complement the hardware and manufacturing prowess of East Asia and together could produce a formidable strategic combination. With the growing recognition of these complementary strengths by corporations, India is increasingly getting linked with the East Asian production networks. These links may not be very substantial in value terms as yet but are certainly critical as they generally relate to more knowledge intensive parts of the value-chain such as software development, R&D, engineering and designing, and high quality

---

27. See Kumar, Sen and Asher (2006) for a detailed treatment of the India-ASEAN partnership.

manufacturing. Indeed East Asian companies have begun to exploit India's strengths in R&D, software and design by locating their global R&D centres in India. For instance, Samsung's R&D centre in India, recently announced successful development of a hybrid mobile phone that works across GSM and CDMA environments. China's Huawei Technologies, like many others, employs hundreds of engineers doing chip design or embedded software development in Bangalore. Hyundai uses its Indian operations as a sourcing base for compact cars. Toyota is sourcing engines from its Indian plant for South-East Asian markets. Furthermore, these production networks not only include those belonging to Japanese or Korean companies but also those being developed by Indian enterprises. For instance, Daewoo Trucks has become linked with the production chain of Tata Motors with its acquisition by the latter. Several Indian companies have also begun to take advantage of cheaper manufacturing costs for hardware in China and other East Asian countries by rationalising their production. The trend is likely to be more firmly entrenched as the emerging free trade arrangements between India and East Asian countries come into effect.

Win-win opportunities for trade in services

India ranks 19th in world exports and imports of commercial services ahead of any ASEAN country.[28] India is increasingly playing a role in two-way flow in education services, among others. Many Indian students study in rest of Asia, while Indian schools (two are already operating in Singapore) and universities are venturing in South-East Asia. India is also expanding collaboration with Malaysia beyond just medical education. India's world-class technical and management institutions are being recognised in the rest of Asia as well. Its media and entertainment industry is influencing audiences in Asia as well as the rest of the world, and 'Bollywood' is now a global brand.[29]

---

28. *International Trade Statistics 2003* by WTO.

29. Asher and Sen (2005).

Complementary demographic trends

There are complementarities in demographic trends of East Asia and India. Just as East Asia is about to enter into a phase of demographic burden, implying lower share of working age population, and higher median age of workers, India is entering a demographic gift phase, with higher share of working age population. Through IT, an India integrated into Asia could help address East Asia's demographic challenges.[30]

Geographical contiguity, shared history and culture

India shares land boundaries with China and Myanmar and maritime boundaries with Thailand and Indonesia. India's geographical contiguity with East Asia was highlighted vividly by the ASEAN-India Car Rally organised in November 2004 in conjunction with the ASEAN Summit. India has deep age-old civilisational links with a number of East Asian countries. As noted Thai journalist Kavi Chongkittavorn has argued, "India feels much more East Asian because of its cultural influence and aspirations in the ASEAN region, than for example, Mongolia."[31] Even in the modern history, Pandit Nehru, India's first Prime Minister spoke about the need for Asian regionalism 50 years ago and substantiated his vision with Pancha Sila, the Five Principles of Coexistence subsequently adopted at the Bandung Conference that still remain the cornerstone of India's foreign policy.

India as a bridge to South, West and Central Asia for East Asia

With its excellent trading and transport links and emerging preferential trading arrangements with South Asian countries, GCC and West Asian countries India could act as a bridge for East Asia for the markets in South, West and Central Asian countries.

India as a balancing force in East Asia

It can be argued that India's participation in the grouping will make it more balanced and less susceptible to domination by any

---

30. *ibid.*

31. See *New Asia Monitor*, October 2004, p.6.

particular large country. As Keizo Takemi, Member, National Diet, Japan has argued, India is needed for maintaining a balance in East Asia given the huge influence of China.[32] Noted Singapore diplomat K. Kesavapany has observed, "any such group without India in it will seem unbalanced, as though one leg of the table is missing".[33]

Growing popular support for East Asia-India economic integration

Growing economic integration of East Asia and India and its potential is catching people's imagination. A survey conducted by the World Economic Forum and Taylor Nelson Sofres at the World Economic Forum's New Asian Leaders (NALs) Retreat held in Seoul in June 2003, covering all participants and invitees and other Asia-based global leaders for tomorrow revealed that over 37 per cent of new Asian leaders view an extended Asia—ASEAN+4, including China, Japan, India, and Korea–as the most desirable model of economic integration, with only 26.8 per cent preferring ASEAN+3.[34] Former Singapore Prime Minister and Minister Mentor Lee Kuan Yew has argued, "India should join in, as there is nothing to be lost. It will expand the market, force more specialisation, division of labour, and India has some thing to contribute in economic, political, diplomatic as well as the security field. So I believe it is to the advantage of the ASEAN countries that any such East Asian Community should include India."

India-East Asia integration, a win-win for Asia:
Evidence from CGE simulations

The foregoing discussion underscores the mutually beneficial nature of India's economic integration with East Asia in an East Asian Community. This is also borne out from the CGE simulations conducted to examine the potential gains from Asian economic integration when these were repeated after dropping India from JACIK. The simulation results as summarised in Table 17.3 clearly bring out that welfare gains for each participant in JACIK are much

---

32. See *New Asia Monitor*, October 2004, p.7.

33. Kesavapany (2005).

34. The World Economic Forum, Press Release, June 18, 2003.

higher than in a framework excluding India. Significantly, India's participation increases the welfare gains for other participants by US$ 48 billion this is far higher than India's welfare gain of US$ 8.9 billion. The explanation for considerable improvement in welfare gains with the inclusion of India is possibly the complementary strengths that India brings to the grouping in terms of services and software dimension to East Asia's strengths in manufacturing and hardware thus improving the competitiveness of other East Asian countries besides its dynamism, as summarised above. Obviously India's inclusion is welfare enhancing for all the partners and is a win-win for Asia.

Table 17.3

Relative Welfare Gains from Economic Integration in JACIK and ASEAN+3

	Estimated Welfare Gains in US$ million		Gains from India's Inclusion
	JACIK	ASEAN+3	
Japan	150695	124065	26630
Korea	14076	11683	2392
China-HK	16328	10810	5517
ASEAN (5)	19405	14585	4821
India	9937	972	8965
Asia	210441	162115	48326

Source: RIS simulations.

Concluding remarks

To sum up the above discussion, it is clear that there is great interest in Asia to build on growing functional economic integration and emerging web of FTAs linking ASEAN and its Summit-level dialogue partners namely Japan, China, India and South Korea and possibly with Australia and New Zealand into an inclusive East Asian Community which could eventually grow into a broader Asian Economic Community. By bringing together all these countries on a single platform, the East Asia Summit launched in December 2005 in Kuala Lumpur, a new valuable forum for working together to realise the Asian dream by promoting broader regional economic integration.

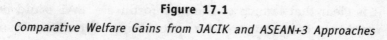

Figure 17.1

Comparative Welfare Gains from JACIK and ASEAN+3 Approaches

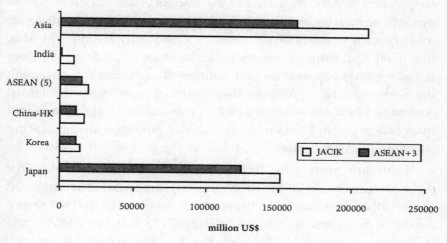

Source: Table 17.3.

Being the maiden summit and a brief duration of just few hours, not much concrete action was expected of the Kuala Lumpur Summit. However, it managed to take a landmark decision to create a "forum for dialogue on broad, strategic, political and economic issues of common interest and concern with the aim of promoting peace, stability and economic prosperity in East Asia." The leaders recognised the interdependence of their economies and "shared interest in achieving peace, security and prosperity in East Asia." They sought to enhance cooperation and strengthen the bonds of friendship between them and felt that the "EAS could play a significant role in community building in the region." They also affirmed EAS as an open, inclusive, transparent and outward looking forum. Among the areas of cooperation they considered important include, promoting development, financial stability, energy security, economic integration, poverty alleviation, narrowing the development gap in East Asia through technology transfer and infrastructure development, capacity building and good governance. The EAS leaders agreed to meet on an annual basis back-to-back with the ASEAN summit and continue their dialogue.

It is clear that launch of the new forum i.e. EAS could be of far-reaching consequence for promoting broader regional cooperation in Asia. By giving to the leaders of the largest and most dynamic economies of Asia a much needed annual forum for dialogue it is expected to facilitate the cause of community building in Asia. It is likely that future summits will take steps towards concretising Asian regional cooperation in a number of areas thereby hastening the reemergence of Asia as the centre of gravity of the world economy. RIS studies summarised in this chapter have shown that integration of these economies has the potential of generating substantial welfare gains for Asia and the rest of the world.

Therefore, among the first priorities for the forthcoming East Asia summits could be to create a framework for regional cooperation in trade and investment among the participating countries by coalescing various ongoing FTAs between ASEAN and its dialogue partners and between the dialogue partners. Even with 16 EAS partners to begin with it will cover half of world's population, nearly a quarter of world's output and trade and two thirds of world's foreign exchange reserves. By providing a seamless market to the EAS (or Asian) businesses and industry such an arrangement will help in efficiency-seeking restructuring of Asian industry and could emerge as an engine of growth.

The East Asian arrangement should target to liberalise regional trade and investment regimes in a phased manner by 2020 with provisions for safeguards for sensitive products, special and differential treatment for countries at different levels of development and dispute resolution. The agricultural trade liberalisation should be attempted on a separate track from that of industrial goods to allow supremacy to considerations of food security and livelihood issues.

Care must be taken in designing the programmes of regional economic integration in such a manner that they keep equity, employment generation and necessary social transformation and social safety nets for the vulnerable sections of the society at their heart so that it represents regionalism with an 'Asian Face'. By balancing the interests of efficiency and equity, the Asian arrangement could well emerge as a role model for trade liberalisation in multilateral as well as regional contexts in the whole world.

An Asian Monetary Architecture of EAS countries could be another priority for pooling reserves and creation of an Asian Currency Unit (ACU) as a unit of account for facilitating intra-regional trade and exchange rate stability within the region. Energy security should also be high on the agenda. The Fourth High-Level Conference on Asian Economic Integration organised by RIS and the Institute of South-East Asian Studies, Singapore in New Delhi in November 2005 found a case for launching an Asian Energy Forum as an Asian counterpart of International Energy Agency to pursue regional cooperation including Asian strategic energy reserve, a pan-Asian gas grid, development of Asian energy market, among other areas. They could also begin creating institutional infrastructure for scientific and technological cooperation in Asia to exploit the synergies for mutual benefit. The EAS could also create forums for annual meetings of Ministers of Trade and Industry, Finance and Energy of EAS countries besides the annual summits to carry the agenda of regional economic integration forward besides a discussion of Asian cooperation and participation in global governance. These initiatives should be effectively supported by networks of think tanks of EAS countries which could brainstorm on the policy challenges for regional economic integration and provide a road map for the official processes. It may be desirable that different networks of think tanks such as the New Asia Forum coordinated by RIS and NEAT (Network of East Asian Think-Tanks), ACD Think Tank Network, ASEAN-India Network of Think Tanks, among other such think tanks, coordinate their work agenda to assist the policy process in a more effective manner. Finally, EAS could take initiatives for greater people-to-people exchanges, cultural interactions and educational and media exchanges for allowing an Asian identity or 'Asianness' or 'One Asia' to take hold.[35]

---

35. See RIS and ISEAS (2006) for a Report of the High-Level Conference.

The cause of evolving a framework for broader regional cooperation in Asia as proposed above has received a shot in arm with the recent announcements made by Japanese Minister of Economy, Trade and Industry Toshihiro Nikai. Mr. Nikai has proposed creation of a Comprehensive Economic Partnership Arrangement in East Asia combining the 16 countries that participated in EAS. The Nikai's proposals include regional trade liberalisation for strengthening the regional production networking in Asia by providing one economic space and making the region more attractive for investment by evolving common rules for trade in services, investment, etc. and fostering sectoral cooperation. Nikai proposals are quite consistent with the vision of Prime Minister Dr. Manmohan Singh when he called for a Pan-Asian FTA combining all the EAS members at the first EAS in December 2005 as a way forward towards building an Asian Economic Community as an 'arc of advantage'. A comprehensive arrangement covering all the EAS member countries that could be subsequently expanded to cover other Asian countries is perhaps what Dr. Singh had in mind when he gave a call for it.

Therefore, the Indian and Japanese positions on the issue of broader Asian integration are quite converging. In fact the two nations "committed themselves to work together to promote the vision of an Asian Economic Community" as proposed by India during the visit of Prime Minister Koizumi to India during April 2005. The proposed East Asian Comprehensive Economic Partnership Arrangement could be a major building bloc of the proposed East Asian Community or an eventual Asian Economic Community.

To conclude, launch of EAS as a forum for dialogue between Asian leaders represents a landmark development in the direction of regional cooperation in Asia. In the coming years, it will hopefully prove to be an important vehicle for charting the agenda for broader regional cooperation and integration for realising the Asian dream! India needs to work together with Japan and other EAS partners to take it forward.

Bibliography

ADB (2005). *Asian Economic Cooperation and Integration: Progress, Prospects and Challenges*, Manila: Asian Development Bank.

Agarwala, Ramgopal (2002). "Towards and Asian Economic Community: Monetary and Financial Cooperation", *RIS Discussion* Paper #33, New Delhi: Research and Information System for Developing Countries.

————. (2004). "Reserve Bank of Asia: An Institutional Framework for Regional and Monetary Cooperation in Asia", in Nagesh Kumar ed. *Towards and Asian Economic Community: Vision of a New Asia*, New Delhi and Singapore: RIS and ISEAS: 177-203.

Asher, Mukul and Sadhna Srivastava (2004). "India and the Asian Economic Community", in Nagesh Kumar ed. *Towards and Asian Economic Community: Vision of a New Asia*, New Delhi and Singapore: RIS and ISEAS: 91-108.

Asher, Mukul and Rahul Sen (2005). "India's Integration with East Asia: Win-Win for Asia", *RIS Discussion Paper* #93, New Delhi: Research and Information System for Developing Countries.

Alatas, Ali (2001). *"ASEAN Plus Three" Equals Peace Plus Prosperity*, No. 2, Singapore: Institute of South-East Asian Studies.

Bergsten, Fred (2000). "Towards a Tripartite World", *The Economist*, July 15: 20-22.

Bonapace, Tiziana (2005). "Regional Trade and Investment Architecture in Asia-Pacific: Emerging Trends and Imperatives", *RIS Discussion Paper* #92, New Delhi: Research and Information System for Developing Countries.

Brooks, Douglas, David Roland-Holst and Fan Zhai (2005). Growth, Trade and Integration: Long-term Scenarios of Developing Asia, Manila: Asian Development Bank, July.

ESCAP (1994). "Infrastructure Development as Key to Economic Growth and Regional Economic Cooperation", *Economic and Social Commission for Asia and the Pacific*, New York: UN.

Ito, Kokichi, Li Zhidong and Ryoichi Komiyama (2005). "Asian Energy Outlook to 2020: Trends, Patterns and Imperative of Regional Cooperation", *RIS Discussion Paper* # 93.

JBIC (2000). "Special Issue: Infrastructure for Development in the 21st Century", *JBIC Review, No. 3, Japan Bank for International Cooperation*, Tokyo, Japan.

Kawai, Masahiro (2004). Prospects for Monetary Cooperation in Asia: ASEAN+3 and Beyond, Presentation at the High-level Conference on Asian Economic Integration: Vision of a New Asia, organised by RIS, Tokyo, 18-19 November 2004 (*www.ris.org.in*).

Kesavapany, K. (2005). "A New Regional Architecture: Building the Asian Community", public lecture delivered, New Delhi, March 31, excerpted in *New Asia Monitor*, April 2005: p1.

Kondo, Masanori (2006). "Japan and an Asian Economic Community", *RIS Discussion Paper* #106, New Delhi: Research and Information System for Developing Countries.

Kumar, Nagesh (1998). "Multinational Enterprises, Regional Economic Integration, and Export-Platform Production in the Host Countries: An Empirical Analysis for the US and Japanese Corporations", *Weltwirtschaftliches Archiv*, 134(3): 450-483.

————. (2001). "Flying Geese Theory and Japanese Foreign Direct Investment in South Asia: Trends Explanations and Future Prospects," *Journal of International Economic Studies*, 15: 179-192.

————. (2002). "Towards an Asian Economic Community: Relevance of India", *RIS Discussion Paper* #34.

————. (2004). editor, *Towards and Asian Economic Community: Vision of a New Asia*, New Delhi and Singapore: RIS and ISEAS.

————. (2005). *Towards a Broader Asian Community: Agenda for the East Asia Summit*, New Delhi: RIS Discussion Paper #100.

————. (2006). "Asian Currency Unit minus Indian Rupee?" *Financial Express*, April 25.

Kumar, Nagesh, Rahul Sen and Mukul Asher (editors) (2006). *India-ASEAN Economic Relations: Meeting the Challenges of Globalization*, New Delhi and Singapore: RIS and ISEAS.

Madison, Angus (2000). *The World Economy: A Millennial Perspective*, OECD.

Mohanty S.K. *et al.*, (2004). "Implications of Economic Cooperation Among JACIK Economies: A CGE Modelling Approach", in Nagesh Kumar (ed.), *Towards and Asian Economic Community: Vision of a New Asia*, New Delhi and Singapore: RIS and ISEAS: 109-122.

Pleskovic and Nicholas Stern (eds.) (2000). *Annual Bank Conference Development Economics*, The World Bank, Washington, D.C.

Rajan, Ramkishen S. (2006). "Monetary and Financial Cooperation in Asia: Emerging Trends and Prospects," New Delhi: *RIS Discussion Paper* # 107.

RIS, (2002). *South Asia Development & Cooperation Report 2001/02*, New Delhi: Research and Information System.

————. (2003). *Towards an Asian Economic Community*, RIS Policy Brief #1.

————. (2003a). "Reserve Bank of Asia: Institutional Framework for Regional Monetary and Financial Cooperation," RIS Policy Brief # 3.

————. (2004). *South Asia Development and Cooperation Report 2004*, New Delhi: RIS.

————. (2005). *Towards and Asian Economic Community: An Agenda for the East Asia Summit—Reflections from Asian Think-tanks Dialogue on Broader Asian Economic Integration*, New Delhi and Singapore: RIS and ISEAS.

————. (2006) "The Case for an Asian Clearing Union: Need for a Broad-based Approach", *RIS Policy Brief* # 23.

RIS and ISEAS (2006). *Towards an Asian Economic Community: An Agenda for the East Asia Summit*. New Delhi and Singapore: RIS and ISEAS.

Rowley, Anthony (2004). "Asian Integration needs and overarching framework", *The Business Times, Online Edition,* January 7, excerpted in *New Asia Monitor,* March 2004, p.6.

Shankar, Vineeta (2004). "Towards and Asian Economic Community: Exploring the Past", in Nagesh Kumar (ed.) *Towards and Asian Economic Community: Vision of a New Asia,* New Delhi and Singapore: RIS and ISEAS: 13-42.

Shinawatra, Thaksin (2001). "Asian Cooperation Dialogue", Speech Delivered in New Delhi, November 28, excerpted in *RIS Digest*, December 2001: 3-5.

Sinha-Roy, S. *et al.*, (2004). "Complementarities and Potential of Intra-regional Transfers of Investments, Technology and Skills in Asia", in Nagesh Kumar (ed.) *Towards and Asian Economic Community: Vision of a New Asia,* New Delhi and Singapore: RIS and ISEAS: 123-155.

Teo, Eric Chu Cheow (2005a). "Strategic Relevance of Asian Economic Integration," *RIS Discussion Paper* #90. New Delhi: Research and Information System for Developing Countries.

————. (2005b). "Towards an Asian Economic Community: A Strategic Perspective," at the 3rd High-Level Conference on Asian Economic Integration, held in Taiyuan, Shanxi, China, September, RIS, New Delhi.

Wei, Li (2004). "A Road to Common Prosperity: Relevance of an FTA between India and China", in Nagesh Kumar ed. *Towards and Asian Economic Community: Vision of a New Asia,* New Delhi and Singapore: RIS and ISEAS: 75-90.

Wolf, Martin (2004). "Asia Needs the Freedom of Its Monetary Fund", *Financial Times*, May 19, excerpted in *New Asia Monitor,* July 2004: p6.

World Bank (2000). *Trade Blocs*, The World Bank Policy Research Report, New York: Oxford University Press.

Yamazawa, Ippei (1998). "How to Get Over the Asian Currency Crisis: A Proposal for an East Asian Stable Currency Group", *Discussion Paper No.6*, APEC Study Centre, Columbia University.

————. (1999). "APEC After Ten Years: How Much Has Been Achieved in Liberalization and Facilitation", in *Towards APEC's Second Decade: Challenges, Opportunities and Priorities*, APEC Study Centre.

————. (2001a). "Asia-Pacific Regionalism and Japan's Strategy", *Japan Review of Internal Affairs*, pp. 203-221.

————. (2001b). "How will Asia and Japan Survive the Globalization Challenge?" *Asahi Shimbun*, October 2, 2001.

Yao, Chao Cheng (2005). "China's Role in the Asian Economic Unification Process", *RIS Discussion Paper* #89.

18

Rediscovering *Suvarnabhumi*: India and South-East Asia

Sunanda K. Datta-Ray

It was Her Royal Highness Maha Chakri Sirindhorn of Thailand who warned me not to speak of Indian influence in South-East Asia. The acceptable term, said the scholar princess, learned in Pali and Sanskrit and with a Masters degree in Oriental epigraphy, was Indic. Presumably, the academic alternative signifies an abstraction, a cultural entity, that need not be synonymous with the political, economic and demographic reality of Asia's second most populous country. The fact that many South-East Asians prefer it suggests a certain sensitivity about India itself. Living and travelling in the region, it sometimes seemed to me that academics, diplomats and even tourists from the West were not averse to encouraging that reservation.

It may not be politically correct any longer to assert with A.L. Basham that "the whole of South-East Asia received most of its culture from India."

But, South-East Asia is where in ancient times India met China. Hence, Indo-China. Race and religion, culture and lifestyle speak of that synthesis. South-East Asia is also where the interaction of modern India and China, the world's two most populous nations, both nuclear-armed, might help to balance the global polity by shaping an Asian Economic Community of the future. The expectation is that it will consist in its initial phase of five strong units combining to form a core group that regional thinkers have dubbed JACIK—Japan, ASEAN (the Association of South-East Asian Nations), China, India and Korea. JACIK will provide a third focal point in addition to the United States (US) and the European Union (EU). ASEAN, representing 10 nations forged in the Indochinese crucible, has been designated to help with the birth. Its commitment to the concept of *musyawarah dan muafakar* (consultation and consensus) makes Asean admirably suitable for the role of midwife.

Indo-China's individual ethnic groups began to be differentiated linguistically and culturally over the broad span of territory from central China's Yangtse Valley to the Indonesian islands only about 10,000 years ago. It was largely because of their desire to open land communications with India that successive Chinese dynasties in later historic times, especially the Han emperors, sought to absorb the province of Yunnan bordering today's Myanmar. Yunan's Sino-Thai Nan-chao state contributed to the spread of Buddhism, as well as to the more diffuse acculturation of the region to the Indian arts and sciences until Kublai Khan's conquest in 1253. The Maurya kings traded with South-East Asia in the 3rd Century before Christ. The most famous of them, Asoka, sent monks to preach Buddhism. In 78 AD Prince Aji Caka established the first known kingdom of Java Dwipa and took Sanskrit and the Pallava script to Sulu in what is now the Philippines. Sanskrit was the region's official language by the 4th Century AD.

The Srivijaya empire spread out from Sumatra—Swarna Dwipa—for six centuries until Java's Majapahit kings, also Hindu, overwhelmed it. Hindu art languished with the rise of Theravada Buddhism. Then the tide of Islam swept over the region, leaving it with three Muslim states—Indonesia, Malaysia and Brunei—and three others—the Philippines, Thailand and Singapore—with a substantial Muslim minority. Hinduism, Buddhism and Islam, three of the world's four great religions, went to Indo-China from India which has the world's third largest congregation of Muslims today. The merchants and missionaries who took Islam from India were responsible for Indonesia's distinctive blend of Sufi mysticism.

Lee Kuan Yew, Singapore's first prime minister, thought of contemporary India as a player in this multicultural world before India itself did so. India did not—in a phrase that has since become fashionable—'look east' until economic necessity forced P.V. Narasimha Rao to do so. Wisely, Manmohan Singh chose Singapore in October 1991 as the first foreign venue for an exposition of his fiscal reforms. That was at least partly a consequence of a stopover a couple of months earlier by Madhavsinh Solanki, who briefly held the external affairs portfolio, and his meeting with Goh Chok Tong, who had succeeded Lee Kuan Yew as prime minister. Goh pledged to generate what he called "a mild India fever" and "a second wing" (China being the first) in Singapore's foreign policy. This interest was in many respects the motor that drove India's other initiatives in Indo-China.

A nation that seeks to play a part in world affairs needs strategic depth and geographic space for manoeuvre. Despite historical links and powerful contemporary pulls, central and western Asia are less accessible to India for this purpose than the lands that lie to its east where today's political and economic compulsions reinforce historical kinship. Ties are driven now by felt needs, not external obligations. Many Asian countries face separatist ethnic or religious movements. All have to cope with the threat of terrorism. Water is in short supply in some parts of Asia and floods inundate others. Illegal migration, cross-border crime, piracy on the high seas and pandemics like severe acute respiratory syndrome (Sars) and avian flu are common dangers. So is environmental degradation. The quest for a higher standard of living—assured jobs, improved housing, medicare, more education facilities, better retirement benefits and a social welfare net—unites the region. India is historically familiar with the countries of East and South-East Asia; sublimally, they know each other; and with a few exceptions, they boast similar parliamentary forms of governance driven by reformist agendas.

But despite shared interests and pressing challenges, however, it would be difficult to push relations to their optimum level and achieve the goal of an integrated Asian community without peeling off Indo-China's layers of ignorance, indifference or resistance to history's legacy. While the present mostly unconscious denial of the past may not seriously impede meaningful interaction, a proper awareness of the linkage would enrich the partnership that is the purpose of the new thrust in collective and bilateral diplomacy.

ASEAN invited India to join as a sectoral dialogue partner the year after Manmohan Singh's visit to Singapore. Full dialogue partnership followed in 1995, and in 1996 India became a member of the ASEAN Regional Forum (ARF) which was Asia's first attempt at a conflict resolution machinery. This marked a significant milestone in mutual acceptance. For, when someone had asked about India at the time of the ARF's founding in 1993, a regional spokesman answered that it was the ASEAN—not Asian—Regional Forum. But perceptions changed under geopolitical as well as economic pressures, and later in 1996 India attended the first post-ministerial conference of the Asean and ARF.

Cooperative subregional and bilateral links are a healthy parallel development though, admittedly, still a long way from fruition. The 1994 border trade agreement with Myanmar began what Inder Kumar Gujral called "constructive involvement" to take care of vital national interests—border trade, hostile activity and, above all, oil and gas—without abandoning political principles. The Indian Ocean Regional Cooperation conference in Mauritius the following year signified growing concern for sealanes, maritime security and the wealth of the ocean bed. India's 2003 Free Trade Agreement (FTA) with Thailand covering goods, services and investment, 84 items in all, was a major watershed. But the most exhaustive arrangement, finalised on June 29, 2005 after 13 rounds of negotiations, was the landmark Comprehensive Economic Cooperation Agreement (Ceca)—India's first ever—with Singapore, encompassing trade in goods and services, investment protection, banking and work visas.

Calling Ceca "a historic agreement," Manmohan Singh predicted that it would take "economic relations to a new plane." India was already Singapore's 14th largest trading partner in 2004, with bilateral trade nearly tripling during the previous decade. It increased by almost half in the last 12 months of the negotiations, making

India Singapore's fastest growing trading partner. India's exports to Singapore grew faster in 2004-2005 than exports to any other country. Indian companies are flocking to set up shop in Singapore where many young Indian technologists now seek their future. But that only highlights the need for more FTAs and Cecas, and effective institutional arrangements to facilitate the transfer of skills and technology to countries like Vietnam, Cambodia and Laos with which India has always had cordial political ties without much economic content. Also for mutual legal assistance, extradition treaties and joint policing on land and at sea.

At the subregional level, India, Thailand, Sri Lanka and Bangladesh signed an economic cooperation agreement in Bangkok in 1997. Myanmar's addition expanded it to form the Bangladesh, India, Myanmar, Sri Lanka, Thailand Economic Cooperation (Bimstec) forum in December of that year. It was a neat acronym, but Bimstec was later cumbersomely renamed Bay of Bengal Initiative for Multisectoral Technical and Economic Cooperation, a mouthful that defies felicitous reduction. Another potentially important initiative was the agreement that India, Thailand, Laos, Cambodia, Myanmar and Vietnam signed in Vientiane in 2000 to set up the Mekong Ganga Cooperation project. The trilateral India-Bangladesh-Myanmar agreement to lay an oil pipeline, signed in Yangon in January 2005, promises to take subregional cooperation to a new height at which it might also act as a solvent for security concerns.

These developments testify to the gradual disappearance of many of the factors that kept India and South-East Asia apart in recent centuries, bearing out Lord Palmerston's famous dictum that only a nation's interests, not its friends, are "eternal and perpetual". India and Indo-China had ceased to share interests or feel any sense of interdependence even before the age of Western imperialism. The rise of the European powers and the indelible stamp of colonial rule, whether of Britain, France, the Netherlands, Portugal or, in the case of the Philippines, Spain and the US, on Asian thought and structures further underlined estrangement. Looking to the colonial metropole for inspiration and resources, Asian societies had little time for other Asian peoples grappling with similar challenges.

The Cold War and its legacy exercised a further divisive and stultifying influence on perceptions. Asia's resurgence generated its own rivalries and tensions. So, later, did the rise of militant Islam. Local settler communities of Indian origin should logically have been able to facilitate better contact with the mother country (as ethnic Indian residents of Britain and the US are doing) but were often caught in a time warp or lacked. Enmeshed in internal and regional problems and hamstrung by the Hindu rate of growth, India could not offer them much. Some ethnic Indians chose, therefore, in the flush of newfound prosperity to make a point of distancing themselves from all their forefathers had left behind. But there are many others like the elderly Sikh with children scattered in Australia and the US who said to me after Pokhran II that though he had made Malaysia his home and would never return, anything that made India stronger also strengthened his and his family's position wherever they lived. The diaspora can be a catalyst for dynamic diplomacy in the east too, helping to realise Jawaharlal Nehru's vision, glimpsed during his wartime captivity in Ahmednagar Fort, of India "as the centre of economic and political activity in the Indian Ocean area, in South-East Asia and right up to the Middle East."

To some extent Nehru's view reflected British strategic thinking which saw Aden in the west and Singapore in the east as marking the perimeter of India's security glacis. But he also argued that geography gives India "an economic and strategic importance in a part of the world which is going to develop rapidly in the future." Not that many Indians shared the first prime minister's sense of destiny. Pranab Mukherjee, who combined the external affairs portfolio with the deputy chairmanship of the Planning Commission, rightly complained at the time of the first Asia-Europe meeting in Bangkok in March 1996 that Asia without India was like *Hamlet* without the prince of Denmark. But the spurt of interest that found expression in the Asian Relations Conference even before the dawn of independence hardly inspired any kind of sustained national commitment.

All the same, it was an epochal event in March-April of 1947, flowing from Nehru's South-East Asian tour the previous March when Aung San, the Burmese leader who was later assassinated, broached the idea of both a South Asian federation and a wider Asian union. Vietnam's Ho Chi Minh had spoken of a "pan-Asian community" in September 1945. Indonesia's Soekarno and King Norodom Sihanouk of Cambodia were two other regional leaders whose Asian vision extended beyond their own geographical confines. The much smaller conference—only a handful of nations participated—on Indonesia that Nehru convoked in January 1949 had an even more romantic origin. In 1947, long before he became chief minister of Orissa, the flamboyant Biju Patnaik responded to Nehru's request by piloting his own aircraft to Indonesia to rescue the vice president, Mohammad Hatta, and the prime minister, Sutan Sjahrir, from the Dutch and flying them to New Delhi for consultations. Soekarno subsequently made Patnaik an honorary *Bumiputra*.

Nehru's attempt to galvanise opinion against a sudden Dutch military attack on the infant Indonesian republic fuelled intense rumours of an emerging Asian bloc and aroused tremendous anxiety in the West. Washington feared both that Moscow would exploit such a group and that a direct American attempt "to prevent its formation would probably be ineffective and would certainly intensify anti-US sentiment in Asia." So, obliging Asians like President Elpidio Quirino of the Philippines and his representative, Carlos P. Romulo, were lobbied discreetly to scuttle the conference. Whatever the outcome for Indonesia, the gathering allowed Nehru to declare that it was "natural that the free countries of Asia should begin to think of a more permanent arrangement than this conference for effective mutual consultation and concerted effort in the pursuit of common aims."

Though Bandung—the next step in 1955—was officially an Afro-Asian event, it also honoured and invoked, citing Nehru and Soekarno, the "spirit of Asia." It prepared the ground for the non-aligned movement to be launched six years later, and for the adoption in statecraft of the ancient Hindu and Buddhist concept of *Panchsheel*, the five principles of peaceful co-existence, that, called Pancasila, is still Indonesia's governing creed. Conference participants came from far beyond the region but the conference itself was a major event for South, South-East and East Asia. It marked a diplomatic debut for 23 Asian (out of 29) participating governments, Zhou Enlai's China among them. Anthony Eden's American-instigated suggestion that the Chinese should be excluded had no effect on Nehru. When Bandung was revisited in 2005, decolonisation, especially in Africa, had swollen the 29 original participants to 105.

It would be unrealistic to pretend that the 1947 and 1949 conferences or even the first Bandung meeting revived any memories in India—or in Indo-China—of the vanished glories of *Suvarnabhumi*, the Farther India of historians. Amnesia about colonial episodes is more explicable; nevertheless, it bears recalling that in 1819 when Stamford Raffles set up the trading outpost of Singapore in a corner of the Riau sultanate, he predicted that it "bids fair to be the next port to Calcutta." The British governed Singapore from Calcutta for 48 years until an agitation by expatriate businessmen resulted in administrative responsibility being transferred to the Colonial Office in London in 1867. Supporting the move, Britain's *Times* newspaper asked rhetorically, "What has Singapore to do with India?" Those 48 years have left so little resonance in India (or Singapore) that Lee Hsien Loong, Goh Chok Tong's successor as prime minister, surprised everyone by asking India for copies of the administrative records of the period.

When Indira Gandhi visited Singapore in May 1968, Lee Kuan Yew repeated the suggestion that had earlier taken him to Delhi— that India should take an "active interest in the security, political stability and economic development" of South-East Asia. It was a crucial time in the region's history. The Cold War was at its height. Vietnam had become a battleground of interests and ideologies. What China was to call its "peaceful rise" had already begun to create ripples throughout Nanyang, the Chinese name for South-East Asia. Britain had only recently announced the withdrawal of its forces from east of Suez. India seemed the obvious candidate to fill the vacuum and safeguard stability. But it was not to be. Mrs. Gandhi advised self-reliance. With trouble brewing in what was still East Pakistan, India did not have the capability to extend itself beyond the subcontinent. The option of doing so soon ended with the Five-Power Defence Arangement being signed in 1971.

The neglect of an earlier opportunity was less pardonable. Tom Abraham, India's first high commissioner to Singapore, has recorded with chagrin that when Singapore parted company with Malaysia, Lee Kuan Yew failed in his efforts to obtain Indian help to train his embryonic defence forces. Only when Egypt followed India did Singapore turn to Israel. That was in 1965 when India's was also the first name that came to Lee Kuan Yew's lips when he was asked if his city-state, rudely thrust on the world's stage, would seek diplomatic relations with other countries. India's ready recognition ensured the support of the Afro-Asian community, including its Muslim members.

Lee Kuan Yew described Nehru as "the first of the Afro-Asians" while *Asia* magazine called Lee "the first recognisable voice of Asia since Mr Nehru." But their Asias were not the same. Loy Henderson, American ambassador to India from 1948 to 1951, defined Nehru's "primary foreign policy objectives" as the "eventual exclusion" of "all Western military power and what he would consider as Western political and economic pressures" from the mainland and waters of Asia. Despite his early flirtation with socialism, Lee Kuan Yew thought Singapore's viability lay in cooperating with the West. Nevertheless, the younger Chinese Singaporean had tremendous respect for the veteran Indian's efforts at nation-building. As he told an Uppsala University seminar, Nehru's India was the only Third World country that had made "any appreciable progress towards the industrial society, with the erection of steel mills, hydro-electric dams, as the infrastructure of the modern industrial state." Disillusionment set in when, in Lee Kuan Yew's view, Nehru failed to refashion Indian society in his own liberal secular image.

Simultaneously, Singapore's growing prosperity and the quality of Indian manufactures, especially of consumer goods—largely because of the emphasis on import substitution—meant a setback for economic ties that the British colonial umbrella had fostered. Older Singaporeans learnt their school lessons from Indian-printed textbooks. Usha fans, Godrej safes, Tata trucks and Calcutta-made manhole covers were a feature of the landscape they grew up in. Gradually, these were not—to put it bluntly—good enough for people who could afford to buy the best from Europe and America. What was true of goods applied also to services. Singapore sought Air India's technical and manpower cooperation when launching its own national airline. Tatas formally set up in 1973 the very first Technical Training Institute in collaboration with the government "to train tool-makers, precision machinists and skilled craftsmen that were crucial to Singapore's industrialisation at the time." As industrialisation acquired a more sophisticated definition, experts were imported from the US and Europe. Television and air-conditioning sounded the death-knell of long evenings watching Bombay's Hindi romances in crowded tents.

But it sometimes seemed as if India and South-East Asia remained joined at the hip even as they drifted apart. A word (*kshatriya* for soldier in Bahasa—itself a giveaway—Indonesia), a concept (Malaysia's *bumiputra*), or a spectacle like a red and sweating Chinese in a *dhoti*, his torso smeared with saffron powder, treading the smouldering coals of the annual fire-walking ritual at Singapore's Sri Mariamman temple bring back to life a remote glimmer of Farther India. A sad modern touch is a solitary unknown Indian face among the grim rows of victims of Pol Pot's Killing Fields in Cambodia. The connection is most alive in Thailand where Thai passersby will stop to make a deep obeisance at a wayside Vishnu shrine in Bangkok.

Thailand's old name, Siam, was coined by Khmers, hereditary enemies of Thais, to denote their darker complexion, *shyam*. Princess Sirindhorn's father's honorific of Rama IX indicates mythic lineage from the legendary god-king of the *Ramayana*. Versions of the *Ramayana* or *Ramakien*, as it is called locally, constitute popular theatre in several South-East Asian countries, including Muslim Indonesia. There is a story, probably apocryphal, of an Indonesian dignitary entertaining a visiting Indian notable with a rendering in flat leather puppets (Wayang Kulit) of the *Ramayana*, and saying disingenuously at the end, "I believe you have something like this in your country too?"

Another story has it that Jaswant Singh, as External Affairs Minister, was waxing eloquent about Balinese culture and the Sanskrit resonance of Megawati Soekarnoputri's name when Paul D. Wolfowitz, the American Deputy Secretary of State for Defence, who had served as ambassador to Indonesia, repeated Tagore's observation in Java, "I see India everywhere but I find it nowhere." According to Princess Sirindhorn, most Thais believe that the Buddha was born in Thailand.

Ayudhya is for them a local kingdom that rose in the 14th Century, blossomed into an empire and survived until the 17th and from which the royal family still derives its title. At a wayside halt en route to the new bridge that spans the river Kwai and the Death Railway of stark memory were further signs of India: three white-gowned men with their long hair drawn into buns in the style of South Indian Shaivites. They were the Dhavichat, Brahmins who had been imported from India a thousand years ago. Some 4,000 of them were identified in the 15th Century. Going by surnames, six clans survive under the Dev Muni, as the chief Hindu priest is styled. Around 1960, King Bhumibol Adulyadej revived the ceremony of Brahmins offering three *panungs*—of which more follows—to the Lord of the First Ploughing and Sowing at the annual Royal Ploughing Ceremony.

My first glimpse of the garment that is variously known throughout South-East Asia as *panung, pha han nyao, pha chong kaben* and *sampot* and which we call a *dhoti* was in Jakarta's Freedom Square where the massive figure of a muscular barebodied man, festooned with ornaments as in princely illustrations from the *Mahabharata*, draped in a short *dhoti*, rides a chariot drawn by six galloping horses. I learnt later that this warlike brave, poised with bow and arrow, was Arjuna Wijaya, archer of the Pandava brothers, and that the scene was taken from what is known in Bahasa Indonesia as Bharata Yuda War. Even devout Muslims believe that the figure opens a door to the spiritual world. Another statue went up only about four years ago in Vientiane, capital of Laos, officially the Lao People's Democratic Republic, whose communist revolutionaries overthrew their last king in 1973 and established a republic. But even the radical Laotians decided to celebrate the establishment of the 14th Century kingdom of Lane Xang and honour its founder, King Fu Ngum, who ascended the throne in 1353, with a 4.3-metre figure round whose ample loins are also wound the folds of a *dhoti*, its pleated end tucked between the massive stone thighs.

The only time I have seen someone so dressed in real life was on the carpeted stairs of Bangkok's Chitralda Palace where a smart royal guard stood stiffly at attention. His dazzling white jacket reached to the top of a deep blue knee-length silk *dhoti* that looked for all the world like knee breeches, Europe's old court dress. Indeed, I had assumed that was what the Francophone King Norodom Sihanouk was wearing in an old formal portrait. But, no, it was the abbreviated *dhoti* that is still the ceremonial nether garment for the kings of Thailand and Cambodia, as it used to be of Laos too, and also for less exalted men on special occasions. Mine was not the only mistake. The *Bombay Gazette* thought King Chulalongkorn (Rama V) of Thailand wore "a greyish silk pair of half knickerbockers and grey stockings" during the royal visit to India in 1872 when, in fact, the monarch, his five brothers and their enormous suite all wore *dhotis*. A photographer in Phnom Penh told me that he was married in a *sampot*.

I like to think of Myanmar's *longyi* and the Malay *sarong* as versions of the same attire. Also the lengths of cloth in which my son and I had to conceal our trousers to enter a temple in Bali. They are the sartorial markers of what was once and can be again *Suvarnabhumi*. Wherever they are worn is forever Farther India. The garment bears out Ananda Coomaraswamy's view that "the further we go back in (Asia's) history, the nearer we come to a common cultural type; the further we advance, the greater the differentiation."

Elements of commonalty extend from India beyond South-East Asia to China, the Korean peninsula and Japan. Take the example of the single-tusked elephant-headed Ganesa, *Vighnakarta*, creator of obstacles, *Vighnaharta*, remover of obstacles. The treasures of Japan's 9th Century Daigo-ji temple include a splendid scroll painting of Ganesa standing imperiously on a mountaintop. Another Ganesa from China's T'ang dynasty can be seen in the Cleveland museum in the US. Seventh Century Pallava colonists are credited with the terracotta Ganesa, reclining at royal ease, excavated in Kedah in Malaysia. Ganesa icons exist from Turkestan to the Philippines. He has been found in Borneo, and is still worshipped in Bali. The pot-bellied, roly-poly deity has been so thoroughly internalised that some Western writers call him the "Indonesian god of wisdom." Unseen hands always place flowers at his feet in the West Cell of the magnificent 9th Century Prambanam temple complex near Yogyakarta. You can buy stone and metal Ganesas throughout Java and, indeed, everywhere in the Orient. If the elephant-god has turned out to be the most durable of Indian divinities, it is at least partly because a pragmatic people respond more readily to the bestower of success than to the abstruse philosophy of other Hindu deities.

The enlarged 16-nation East Asia Summit (EAS) brings all these strands together. Its first meeting, an historic occasion held in Kuala Lumpur on December 14, 2005, announced that the new group would be a "forum for dialogue on broad strategic, political and economic issues of common interest and concern, and with the aim of promoting peace, stability and economic prosperity in East Asia." The leaders' statement also described the EAS as an "open, inclusive, transparent and outward-looking forum, in which we strive to strengthen global norms and universally recognised values, with Asean as the driving force working in partnership with other participants." The summit would be "convened regularly," would be hosted and chaired by an Asean member, and would be held "back to back with the annual Asean summit."

This emphasis on ASEAN is a reminder that modern India has reached East Asia by way of South-East Asia. ASEAN took the initiative at its meeting in Phnom Penh in 2002 and invited India to be a summit partner. Three documents were signed at the next year's Bali summit—the Instrument of Accession to the Treaty of

Amity and Cooperation in South-East Asia, a framework agreement on Comprehensive Economic Cooperation between Asean and India, and, finally, the Asean-India Joint Declaration for Cooperation to Combat International Terrorism. Then came the Vientiane summit in November 2004 when the Asean-India Partnership for Peace, Progress and Shared Prosperity and the Plan of Action to implement it were finalised.

The ASEAN+3 (China, Japan and South Korea) group had been set up in 1997. It involved annual meetings of the 13 leaders, and many meetings of ministers and officials in areas including politics and security, trade, labour, agriculture and forestry, tourism, energy and environment. A significant element in its activities was the development of regional financial cooperation, which included the inauguration of Asian Bond Funds (to mobilise capital for investment) and a series of 'currency swap' arrangements designed to avoid any repetition of the financial crisis that crippled many regional economies in 1997. The ASEAN+3 leaders commissioned studies and reports to explore bases for further East Asian cooperation which, in turn, encouraged proposals for an expanded summit.

The stage was set for Gloria Arroyo, president of the Philippines, to call on ASEAN to "embrace China, Japan, South Korea and India" in a larger grouping that would "hold its own" in future negotiations with the US, Europe or other emerging entities. In the event, and with Malaysia's prime minister, Abdullah Ahmad Badawi, in the chair, Australia and New Zealand were also invited to join India, by then interlocked with ASEAN at many levels, in the birth of a 'new Asia' free of narrow ethnic or geographic labels.

It would be unrealistic to pretend that integration and community-building have been accomplished or that it has been smooth sailing even to come this far. Just as ASEAN members differed on fleshing out details of the East Asian community, notably on defining its future membership and organisational modalities, they also differed on the non-regional nations to be inducted. While most controversies were resolved in the *musyawarah dan muafakar* spirit, differences persist on structure and chairmanship and on relations with the US, described as "the most influential non-Asian East Asian participant." Being wary about institutional arrangements that might drive a wedge between itself and the region, and enable China (as the US fears) to consolidate its own influence, the US has sought other entries into East Asia ever since the Asia-Pacific Economic Cooperation (APEC) forum—from which India remains excluded—was established in 1989. ASEAN, which by common consent drives the EAS, will no doubt address these questions and the fear that the centre of gravity will shift to the bigger and more powerful members.

The EAS is still not a formalised organisation but a loose cooperative framework based on conferences and dialogue. It faces many challenges. The very wide differences in the character and level of economic development (for example, between Japan and Laos) makes cooperation programmes extremely difficult. Political differences between China and Japan that hark back to the Second World War and the territorial dispute between China and India are thought to prevent the emergence of a clear central leadership or of any consensus. The relationship between the EAS and existing cooperation dialogues, particularly ASEAN+3, is somewhat hazy. Membership is another issue. If Australia and New Zealand can join, why not Russia? Vladimir Putin attended the first summit as an observer.

Some Asians see American cooperation as essential if the EAS is not to be just another talking shop where leaders meet, declarations are made, but little community building is achieved. There is a feeling that agendas are not substantive enough and that there is insufficient follow-up action. The ARF could probably assert itself more in trying to resolve regional disputes.

These are dangers that confront all multilateral organisations. What makes Asia's collective search for 'political space' different is the trauma of 1997; Apec's inability to maintain the momentum towards trade liberalisation it had in the mid-1990s; and the salutary examples of the EU and the North American Free Trade Agreement (NAFTA). China's dynamic growth has stimulated a rise in the importance of regional trade. It has also persuaded smaller regional powers of the need to enlist the cooperation of India's increasing strategic and economic weight, its industrial and technological strength and military power.

The EAS is an important further step toward dialogue in a part of the world that does have strong motivations for cooperation, but which will not necessarily follow the institution-building models pursued by Europe and America. Asian regionalism is taking a different route where cooperation does not preclude bilateral competition or even disputes. With its diplomacy steeped in the subtleties of *musyawarah dan muafakar,* ASEAN is expected to manage the rise of two new powers without confrontation.

Lee Hsien Loong's comment on the Kuala Lumpur inaugural bears recalling. "You don't always get spectacular fireworks, big decisions and major changes in policy," he said. "But step by step, each time you meet, you are cultivating ground, keeping it fertile, maintaining relationships and dealing with problems before they arise, before they become serious." India's brush with H5N1 in early 2006 vests retrospective significance in the summit's specific declaration on avian flu and commitment to report all outbreaks rapidly and transparently, and to take steps to ensure that the disease does not infect humans.

Other issues that the EAS discussed at Kuala Lumpur included denuclearisation of the Korean peninsula, terrorism, sustainable development, the Doha round of World Trade Organization negotiations and its own role as a complement to existing cooperation dialogues in the process of community building. With their ancient interlinked histories, the 16 nations had no difficulty in recognising that the clue to all else lies in confidence-building. That must be the first step towards more substantial collaboration.

Once the process of integration is consolidated and some gains of integration are visible, JACIK can consider opening its doors to other regional nations with the aim of eventually creating an Asian Economic Community on the lines of the EU's predecessor. The indicators are promising. Japan is already the world's second largest economy. JACIK includes 13 other of the world's largest and fastest growing economies with vast complementarities. India and China account for nearly three billion people—half the world's population—with the number of consumers growing by leaps and bounds. JACIK's gross national product of $ 16 trillion, adjusted in terms of purchasing power parity, is more than that of NAFTA or the EU. Exports add up to $ 1.66 trillion compared to NAFTA's $ 1.48 trillion. At $ 1.6 trillion, the combined official reserves were much larger in 2003 than those of the US and the EU put together.

India's 'look east' policy does not have to be explained any longer. East Asia already accounts for one-third of India's trade. Trade with China went up by nearly 75 per cent in 2004 to stand at more than $ 13 billion. Trade with South Korea increased by 48 per cent, and that with Asean by more than 30 per cent. There is no reason why the 2007 target of $ 30 billion for India-ASEAN trade should not be fulfilled. There has been a sharp growth in merchandise trade since Indian tariff levels were closely aligned to those of ASEAN, and Palaniappan Chidambaram's 2005-2006 Budget brought peak tariffs down from 20 per cent to 15 per cent. The US still remains the single most important country for India but a viable Asian community will also have a beneficial effect on burgeoning Indo-US ties.

Many barriers are dissolving. In 1992, Goh Chok Tong expressed concern about India's naval expansion. A year later, he accepted it as a natural concomitant of a long coastline and an extensive exclusive economic zone. The once prevalent feeling that Asia began with Myanmar, in other words, the notion that an entire continent is identified with a specific ethnic type—what I have elsewhere called Chopsticks Asia—is disappearing. So is the perception of a Japanese foreign ministry official who once confessed to me that he did not regard as Asian any country that had not belonged to the wartime Co-Prosperity Sphere. But resistance is not always so easily defined or detected. When I wrote in Singapore about ubiquitous versions of the *dhoti*, a reader responded that South-East Asia had a vigorous indigenous culture before the advent of Indian influence.

There was a persistent canard, too, that the harsh chemicals that Indian restorers had allegedly used on the Saivite temples of Angkor Wat had damaged some of the magnificent carvings. An outraged Cambodian movingly rebutted the allegation. "India gave us our gods," he retorted angrily. "Would they destroy their own gift, especially when these happen to be the deities they themselves still worship?" More prosaically, he pointed out accidental flaws in the work of teams of restorers, and the fresh contract that had been awarded to the Archaeological Survey of India.

Attitudinal adjustments have to be made in India too where the phenomenal rise of East and South-East Asia did not initially seem credible. Even now, not everyone can resist the temptation to explain away these miracles of hard work, astute planning and shrewd alliances as fortuitous. Only the other day a Calcutta lawyer asked me if Singapore had an underground railway 'like ours'. I resisted the temptation to reply, "No, not at all like ours. It's bright, attractive, shining clean and chillingly air-conditioned, and the stations are glittering shopping malls." Hamish Macdonald of the *Far Eastern Economic Review* recalls the passenger next to him on, I think, a Delhi-Mumbai flight resenting India being compared with an "under-developed" country like South Korea.

Few, however, match the superior disdain of an administrative service officer who habitually refers to the Straits of Malacca, linking Asia with Europe and conduit of 40 per cent of the world's trade, as the "Straits of Mleccha" to indicate that only the outcasts of Hindu society found refuge in the lands of South-East Asia. I hasten to add that such bigotry is an increasingly minority position nowadays. Going by advertisements all over the country for houses and holidays, Singapore is obviously the hallmark of excellence. But the compliment does not extend to the rest of the region. And the belief persists among many who lack visual experience that China's growth figures are fudged.

Manmohan Singh, however, laces realism into romance. As when, noting the 'look east' policy's 'strong economic rationale and commercial content' he added, "We wish to look east because of the centuries of interactions between us." Scholars have pointed out that the voyages of those centuries were not inspired only by the urge for adventure or religious proselytisation or imperial conquest.

As Kautilya's *Arthasastra*, the Pali *Niddesa*, the *Jatakas* and other works bear out, the names reveal a commercial motive. *Suvarnabhumi* is the land of gold, *Karpur Dvipa*, the isle of camphor, and *Yava Dvipa*, the isle of barley. Trade was the spur. Culture and colonisation followed in the wake of commerce. An ancient Tamil inscription describes the "Corporation of the Fifteen Hundred" as a band of "brave men, born to wander over many countries ever since the beginning of the Krita age, penetrating the regions of the six continents by land and water routes, and dealing in various articles such as horses, elephants, precious stones, perfumes and drugs, either wholesale or in retail." Oriya women still pray for the safe return of their menfolk, laden with gold ornaments from *Suvarnabhumi*, when they cast adrift symbolic boats on the banks of the Mahanadi river during the annual Bali Yatra festival.

The prospect of a seamless market is again the major incentive. But the discourse with Asia also involves energy, investment, communications, education, specialised skills, security, sports and recreation, disaster management and much else. In fact, the EAS is potentially far more than the sum total of bilateral relations with each of the other 15 members. At one level, it can be seen as enabling India to rise above a troubled neighbourhood whose development is held back by Pakistan's instability and intransigence, terrorism, the Kashmir problem, civil strife in Nepal, civil war in Sri Lanka, and Bangladesh's growing Islamic militancy. At another, it holds out for India the promise of an equal dialogue with its global peers and a launching pad for the status it feels is its due. Both demand, of course, sustained and more uniform growth in India. Foreign policy, like charity, begins at home.

There can be no going back in time even when this is achieved. Farther India must remain in history and memory, but there is no reason why *Suvarnabhumi*, as a metaphor for prosperity, should not recreate itself, and India help in the recreation, to embrace a wider region. The 21st Century was long ago dubbed the Asian Century. South-East Asia's ignorance of its ties with India is certainly a drawback in realising that vision but not as great as India's about its own stirring past when Indian merchants and mariners, maharajas and mandarins (*mantris*) left their footprints in abundant profusion. Correct that omission and through *Suvarnabhumi* "the Wonder that was India" (returning to Basham) can be again.

19

India and Central Asia

P. Stobdan

The situation in Central Asia has undergone a sweeping change since the 9/11. The region has become a pivotal theatre for war against terrorism that enhanced its importance internationally. Since its reappearance, many suitors have been engaged in reshaping the region while also seeking affinity, proximity and political legitimacy. The five states (Kazakhstan, Kyrgyzstan, Uzbekistan, Tajikistan and Turkmenistan) however have been undergoing painful and complex nation-building processes, which are far from completed. Their inherent shortcomings include both political and socioeconomic structures that continue to remain frozen in a Soviet past. The underlying weaknesses of these countries therefore have made the world outside, including India to shore up their independence and provide assistance to enable them to develop into stable modernising countries. However, any major transitions in changing the basic nature of the region and its polity would require a generational change.

Internal dynamics

Central Asia's main problems are primarily within. The post-Soviet political formations, especially the loyalty of population is getting rest not with national but along regional or tribal-clan identities. With the collapse of the communist structure, people not sufficiently prepared for democracy instead returned to traditional clan-based polity. Among them, Uzbekistan relatively enjoys a stronger national consciousness, attributed mainly to Uzbek settled lifestyle, whereas nomadic Kazakhs, Kyrgyz and Turkmens cling to tribal loyalties. The internal power struggles, particularly in the smaller states are therefore increasingly assuming violent forms, putting in doubt their survivability—unless governments are able to address the domestic issues seriously. The recent developments in Kyrgyzstan (March 24, 2005) and the Andijan crisis in Uzbekistan (May 13, 2005) have shown the intricate power play among various internal and external forces challenging central authorities, particularly, the inter and intra clan dynamics and regional power brokers, including the criminal network shaping the domestic trends.

Kyrgyzstan has been undergoing its worst crisis since independence. The sharp division and disparity between the 'southern Kyrgyz' and 'northern Kyrgyz' has posed threat to country's unity. Following on the heels of regime change in other CIS states like Ukraine and Georgia, Kyrgyzstan became the first in the region to witness a change in power through a popular vote through its own 'coloured' revolution in March 2005. Earlier, Kyrgyzstan has been credited with the greatest progress in market reforms and democratisation. Much of the country's economy has been privatized; media was free; political parties held seats in the parliament. Gradually, however, political reform got stalled, media was subjected to harassment and dissidents were jailed. The ousted President, Askar Akayev tried to resist rapid change saying that democracy must be an 'organic growth' from within a nation and not to be exported like Communist revolution was exported from outside. However, public upsurge in Bishkek, which saw uncontrollable violence and looting, unexpectedly enforced the regime change resulting in Akayev fleeing the country. Among critical factors that brought down Akayev included, popular dissatisfaction and pent-up frustration, resulting from pervasive corruption, persistent poverty, and pathetic governance. Besides, the hard aspects of economic weakness and security dilemma faced by the country had compounded the crisis.

In Kazakhstan political system is also determined by power play among major *jhuz* or hordes (senior, middle and junior). But despite the vertically divided tribal structure the country managed to launch early economic reforms and managed to contain causes for major dissent. Kazakhstan's President Nazarbayev blamed Akayev's neglect of socioeconomic factors and lax security measures—though Kazak situation resembled that of Kyrgyzstan. Nazarbayev seemed to have learnt lessons from the Bishkek events and ensured that the presidential election held in December 2005 went smooth. He was reelected for another seven years term with landslide majority. Kazakhstan is more prosperous and less religious oriented that makes demand for change less urgent, but newly emerging business class is increasingly striving for political power as a means for protecting its interests.

In Uzbekistan, President Islam Karimov has managed to co-opt regional clans in power structure, but he has been facing stiff challenge from rising Islamic forces. Karimov has been saying that Central Asian states could not demolish their old Soviet houses until they were able to build new democratic ones. Uzbekistan enjoys a strong national consciousness but the country faces strong challenges from Islamic forces through violent means. As a result, opposition groups and media remain suppressed. Karimov is more inclined to opt for a Putin type of solution as his successor. He is preparing young, western-minded elite to take up country's managerial positions.

Tajikistan is nearly bankrupt and yet to fully recover from the civil war that plagued the country immediately after its independence. Almost a million Tajiks seasonally travel to Russia to earn living. The country has many shortcomings including lack of resources as compared to others. It is yet to evolve a comprehensive political or economic strategy to find long-term solutions. The existing power-sharing agreement of 1997 between president Rahmonov and the Islamic groups represented by the United Tajik Opposition (UTO) remains fragile. The northern region of Sogd, home to 40 per cent of the country's population and 70 per cent of its industry remains alienated and the UTO threatens the possibility of a resumption of civil war, as stated by its leader Sayed Abdullo Nuri.

Turkmenistan remains increasingly isolated and closed. President Niyazov has suppressed or exiled political opposition and evolved a cult of personality for himself. The country's educational system is being destroyed, and in spite of natural gas wealth, its economic situation is in shambles. Opposition to Niyazov's rule is turning violent. The country is experiencing a boom of new opposition movements and parties, mostly based on regional clan or tribal loyalties. Niyazov's possible fall from power could, therefore, bring violent confrontations in Turkmenistan.

Islamic resurgence

Central Asia has been witnessing revival of Islam since independence. Although majority of Central Asian Muslims follow conventional and moderate Islamic practices, many extremist religious groups such as the Hizb-ut-Tahrir (HuT), the Islamic Movement of Uzbekistan (IMU) have made a strong presence in the region and are able to create major upheavals from time to time. Both IMU and HuT suffered setbacks after the 9/11, but they are regaining strength posing serious challenge to the regimes. The Ferghana Valley, which is the hub of poverty and religious conservatism, is already beginning to shape the events. Ethnic Uzbeks in the Ferghana Valley who are relatively more Islamic than the nomadic Kyrgyz played significant role in fuelling domestic opposition in Kyrgyzstan. The shift of power has already taken place from predominantly Russian speaking north to the southern Kyrgyz clans. President Kurmanbek Bakiyev belongs to South Kyrgyzstan.

However, in general, Islamic movements in Central Asia remains externally fuelled and an Afghanistan related phenomenon. The members of Uzbekistan-based outfit Mazhab-e-Tahrir (Harkat) and others continue get succor from Pakistan. The governments in the region have been seeking Pakistan's support in locating a group of suspected extremists allegedly received training in Pakistan.

Ironically, in Central Asia, any hopes for democratic transformation also remains mutated into anxiety about the spread of Islamic radicalism. The Afghan experience underscores the possibility of fundamentalism thriving in an uncertain political environment. Many people both inside and outside the region, therefore, believe that weakening of the present regimes will turn the region into a safe haven for international terrorists. Russians have long been cautioning against possible rise of the Taliban type militia fomenting trouble in Central Asia. At the same time many believe that democratic process may ultimately weaken appeal for HuT. Western analysts also hold the view that though widespread conditions to breed 'extremist' ideologies are absent in Central Asia, the hard-line policies of Uzbekistan and Kyrgyzstan have helped to swell the ranks of HuT and IMU.

The Kyrgyz situation also exposed the strength of criminal network, connected to drug trade unleashing upheavals in the region. The colossal production of narcotics in Afghanistan and Kyrgyzstan's Chuu Valley are fuelling the strength of drug barons and mafia power and their role in shaping the domestic policies.

Another disturbing aspect in the region is the interstate rivalry over supply of water, gas, dispute over territory and resources. Some of them have water while others have energy, but the states have not been able to evolve a mechanism for proper regional cooperation. The inter-ethnic problems in and around Osh region could easily spark renewed hostility between Uzbeks and Kyrgyz as it happened in the 1990s. Ethnic tensions have hampered regional cooperation and developing transportation links to the world outside.

Clearly, the internal contradictions also get manifested in their external outlooks. For example, all states, excepting Turkmenistan, tend to follow the 'multi-vector' approach to foreign policy—maintaining cordial relations with major powers while extracting concessions for them in the bargain. This essentially underlines the internal political underpinning faced by young states, which neither had political institutions nor leadership to deal with such multiple challenges. Akayev's fall and Karimov's actions have exposed the play of a double/triple game by the regimes, involving the US, Russia and China—playing major powers against each other in the 'multidirectional foreign policy.' But external powers are currently opting not to risk destabilising the regimes, as they see no better alternative to them. While the political groups are divided and fractious; the Islamists are unacceptable to the West. As a result, the regimes have been willing to work with all sides, favouring one or the other according to their calculations to sustain their continued rule for the moment. However, in the recent past the regimes feared Western intervention rather than Islamic rebels challenging their authorities. The events in 2005 have forced local regimes to accuse western powers of engineering upsurge in the region. In fact, the rigged-election in Kyrgyzstan apparently helped the US consultants infuse popular discontent into a potent movement through their sponsored NGOs.

Central Asia's balance of record since independence, therefore, could be termed as mixed. The states have largely failed to meet the challenges facing them—including political and economic transition. The internal fissures including ethnic and regional tensions, persistent squabbles amongst regional clans impeded political cohesiveness and stability. On the other hand, they have managed to retain a degree of independence while conflicts have not been allowed to precipitate into direct confrontation. A greater awareness among the countries is growing for cooperative efforts to address the common challenges facing them. The above regional scenario, therefore, indicates that Uzbekistan and Kazakhstan are better placed to overcome these difficulties with relative success, and are likely to further strengthen their positions as leading regional powers of Central Asia, whereas the situation in the three smaller states of Kyrgyzstan, Tajikistan and Turkmenistan is less hopeful. All in all, the region is likely to remain fluid in its orientation and its underlying problems would remain unaddressed for a long time.

External power game

There has been a general propensity to view Central Asia as an object of interest and contention in a zero-sum game. Therefore, region has become a recurring subject of geopolitical and economic interest for most of the actors involved. Key to this is the region's geostrategic centrality, entailing major powers seeking military presence and a share in energy resources.

The US interests in Central Asia has been shaped by the danger of Afghanistan and Central Asia potentially becoming breeding grounds for international terrorists. But, its interests also preceded the 9/11 while trying to help them to take reform measures necessary for long-term prosperity and stability. In fact, until recently, US engagement was viewed by others as complementing rather than competing for interests, particularly in the context of containing region's deteriorating economic and security situation. To a large extent military intervention, particularly NATO's presence in the region as also in Afghanistan enjoyed international legitimacy as it suited the interests of others as well.

Since July 2005, Russia together with China has been doing everything possible to blunt the US influence in the region.[1] Their assertion *vis-à-vis* US also came against the backdrop of the crises in Kyrgyzstan (March 2005) and Uzbekistan (May 2005). Moscow and Beijing supported Tashkent's accusation that the events were engineered by the US and Western sponsored NGOs. This provided the Shanghai Cooperation Organization (SCO) an opportunity to issue deadline in July last to quit on the US airbase in the region. Tashkent especially told Washington to leave its Karshi-Khanabad (K2) airbase in 180 days.[2] Since then, Russian military has already returned to its old garrisons in Kyrgyzstan and Tajikistan. Following the US military withdrawal from K2 Moscow quickly secured a military agreement with Uzbekistan as a major ally, while China, by committing $6 billion in aid, has rescued Uzbekistan from its difficulties since the Western support ended after the Andijan crisis.[3] The balance of power has already tilted against the US, partly

---

1. On July 5, the SCO issued a declaration calling for the US to set a timeline for its withdrawal of military forces from the region. See *Kommersant-Daily*, July 5, 2005.

2. On 29 July, Uzbek President Islam Karimov informed the US that it has 180 days to vacate the K2 airbase.

3. Uzbek President Islam Karimov visited China in May end 2005. It was his first trip abroad since the bloody crackdown on protesters in Andijan. Beijing announced that it 'strongly' backs Uzbekistan's response to the events of 13 May. *People's Daily* and *http://www.rferl.org/featuresarticle/2005/5/8AEC6277-B0A6-450A-8E08-CBCE0B4688B2*.

due to Washington's cancellation of foreign aid on the basis of human rights violations and, more fundamentally, because US investment had not come up to expectations. With SCO asserting, such international cooperative mechanisms will slowly weaken and Central Asia—by the end of this decade—could once again become a flashpoint among major powers, particularly because of its energy reserves. A subtle form of competition is already seen among Japan, South Korea and China; China and India; Russia and the West. The US wants Central Asian oil and gas to flow to Japan rather than to China. China works extra to keep Russia on the board through the SCO.

China is dealing diligently with the unfolding events in Central Asia. Beijing, in the recent years, has enhanced both its military postures in the region under the SCO framework. Earlier, China had successfully coerced three Central Asian states (Kazakhstan, Kyrgyzstan, Tajikistan) into border deals in its favour. But now Beijing is using SCO as a linchpin for its energy policy. Following the Chinese giant CNOOC's failed attempt at acquiring Unocal in 2005, Beijing is on the lookout for major takeover targets in Kazakhstan. Recently commissioned 988 kilometre long Atasu-Alashankou pipeline will pump 10 million tonnes of Kazakh crude to China every year. Kazakhstan and China have also mulled cross-border gas pipeline connection. The sale of PetroKazakhstan to China in 2005 was technically a commercial deal, but geopolitics certainly factored pushing India's ONGC away. China is going to win many more upstream opportunities in Kazakhstan in the longer term. However, it is too early to predict what kind of shape China SCO will take. In the past Central Asians ignored China's concerns following the 9/11 as they went along with the US decision on strategic matters. Suspicion about China is a strong factor in Central Asia. If the region's political outlook undergoes a change, nationalists will have a different perception about China, especially when China's Turkestan is yet to be liberated.

China remains cautious about the events unfolding in Central Asia and their implications on its strategic interests. The Uighurs are on both sides of the frontier and any democratic change would inevitably encourage Uighur activism against China's interests. The US would certainly view this as an opportunity to play up the Uighur case on the ground of democracy and human rights.

As stated earlier, Russia, after the initial disquiet, is now finding more reasons to return to Central Asia. Russia's military reinforcement is primarily designed to deliver a sobering message to terrorists, as well as an attempt to blunt NATO's expansion. In recent years, Moscow has quietly regained control over the region's key sectors including oil, space, minerals and the defence industry. Russia has also joined a purely Central Asian grouping the Central Asian Cooperation Organization (CACO). It is clear that Russia will always remain important for the region due to geography, history and economy.

Outside the region, notably Japan, EU and US, which lack access to the region, seek deepening of regional integration within by committing investment and aid for developing infrastructure, transport and energy networks. The idea is to lessen dependence on exports and instead create a regional market. Japan has also recently agreed to boost political and economic contacts in the region under a new Central Asia-Japan formula. More interestingly, the recent US decision to club Central Asia with the Bureau of South Asian Affairs certainly reflects its new geopolitical thinking. It indicates that US will pursue a policy of disentangling Central Asia from the Russian and Chinese fold and instead work towards reviving the historic links between Central and South Asia. The focal point of this is to locate Afghanistan in an enduring regional framework. It may also create a constructive basis for Indo-Pak cooperation. US officials expect India to be the linchpin of this policy and work for mitigating the SCO's influence.[4] The US unveiling of a strategic partnership with Kabul and its support for

---

4. India has important role in Central Asia (*rediff.com*), *http://specials.rediff.com/news/2006/mar/29sld1.htm.* Ambassador Richard Boucher, who replaced Christina Rocca as the new Assistant Secretary of State for South and Central Asian Affairs, said the expanded bureau with the addition of Central Asia, has opened up new opportunities and that India has a "very important role to play" in this region.

Afghanistan's entry[5] into the SAARC plus Washington's own desire for an observer status in the SAARC points to the beginning of a new interlocking process underway.[6] However, critical to this would be Pakistan's willingness to offer transit facilities. General Musharraf has been talking about Pakistan's potential role of a transnational transport bridge. Islamabad is beginning to see the benefits, both economic and political, of playing bridge role in reshaping the landscape involving South Asia, Afghanistan and Central Asia. Similarly, Hamid Karzai too advocates a tripolar structure for economic cooperation and to access Central Asia.[7] All three stand to gain especially by stimulating the energy field.

India and Central Asia

The developments stated above indicate that a number of 'outside' powers have entrenched themselves in and around Central Asia, which, without doubt, is part of India's zone of strategic interest. This reconfiguration in the region, particularly against the backdrop of growing external military forays, should form a compelling reason for India to reclaim its geopolitical rights and responsibilities in Central Asia. However, India has not been able to make significant inroads into this vital region. Central Asia had a considerable impact on the polity and economy all through Indian history. In the ancient past Central Asia was known in ancient India as 'Uttara Kuru'. Much of India's own political history was shaped by events in Central Asia. The region was always a staging ground for invasions into India. Its description in the military context is amply found in Indian history textbooks as also the origin of Indian strategic thought has had their genesis in Central Asian dynamics. Conversely, Central Asia was a bridge for promoting Indian commerce and culture across Asia. Trade routes linking ancient 'Uttara Paath' to the Silk Route also carried Indian

---

5. Afghanistan was admitted in SAARC on November 14 2005. Besides, China and Japan got 'observer status' to the SAARC.

6. In May 2005, a Strategic Partnership between the United States and Afghanistan was signed.

7. Afghan President Hamid Karzai during his visit to New Delhi on April 9-10 called for a tripolar structure for economic cooperation, *Hindustan Times*, 10 April 2005.

religion, philosophy and science beyond to inner and Eastern Asia.[8] This aspect has been grossly ignored while formulating any perspective for India's policy towards the region.

British India's security and frontier trade policy with East Turkistan and Afghanistan is well known. People of Central Asian Republics always looked towards India with fondness even while they were under Russian dominance or even when they became part of the Soviet system. Most Indians traditionally viewed this vast stretch of land under the USSR as a positive historical phenomenon—an ideal experiment in building a multinational state, transcending the provisional identities. The benign environment sustained by the Soviets in Central Asia was perceived, therefore, as having enduring security implications for India. However, in recent years, Central Asia, in its reordered geopolitical form, has emerged as a field of continuing interest and concern in India, particularly in the context of its strategic relevance to India's economy and security.

At the same time, Central Asia's core characteristic as an actor on the world stage as displayed during the Timurid period (14th Century) no longer exists. The region remained a backwater of world politics, a pawn of the great powers for a long time, as such there is no case for Central Asia regaining the Timurian dominance of power—the region finds itself in a stage of revivalism both in terms of external interest and internal potentials. The dynamisms evolving in the region would inevitably have implications far beyond what one might have imagined a decade ago. As described earlier, there are already signs of geopolitical actions being applied in this direction, though the stage is not yet getting set for a clash of major power interests. But owing to the persisting rhetoric,

---

8. In ancient Indian literature the land beyond the Himalayas from Pamir up to Arctic was described as Uttara Kuru. Radha Kumud Mookerji citing Vedic literature mentions about countries Uttara Kuru and Uttara Madra, the ruler of which was known as Virat. See *Fundamental Unity of India*, Hindustan Cellulose & Paper Co. Ltd., Bombay, 1954. Also see B.B. Kumar, *Central Asia: The Indian Links, Dialogue, Vol. 3*. No. 4 April-June 2002.

probably intended, perhaps its inevitability cannot be just wished away.

Indo-Central Asian relations

The Soviet disintegration created fresh opportunities, with new states also looking towards India for political and economic sustenance. By opening missions in the five capitals, India initially strove to build political/economic influence and provided substantive development aid and technical support to the five states. Several Prime Ministerial visits took place since early 1990s and instituted cooperation agreements in diverse fields. India evolved its 'extended neighbourhood' policy for Central Asia, but somehow it could not transcend its nostalgia for the Soviet times. But more than that it was the geographical inaccessibility compounded by Pakistan's hostility and the Afghan instability that hampered India's ability to make a major dent into Central Asia. Pakistani diplomacy throughout 1990s was aimed at averting India's reach to Central Asia. India, therefore, had to tread with caution lest the spread of Islamic fundamentalism. The rise of the Taliban seriously undermined India's quest for a closer cooperation with the region.

While India has been able to build strong bilateral relations with each Central Asian nation based on cultural and political goodwill— they have failed to get translated into any substantive and meaningful partnership. India initially supported a number of regional initiatives including India-Iran-Turkmenistan tripartite railway-line project which provided Central Asia a direct land route access to the Persian Gulf.[9] This rail link, commissioned in 1997, for various reasons did not bear full fruition. The region was also seen as important for India's energy security. India's ONGC Videsh Limited (OVL) has been bidding for energy contracts in Central Asia without success. Notwithstanding strong commitments made pursuant to the high-level discussions, India is yet to achieve a significant stake in the region's strategic mineral and energy

---

9.   Stobdan, P. (1998). "Regional Issues in Central Asia: Implications for South Asia", *South Asian Survey*, Vol. 5, No. 2, Sage Publications, New Delhi.

resource. As a result, India's commercial progress with central Asia has been slow with total trade amounting only about $ 230 million.

The failure of the bid for PetroKazakhstan by OVL-Mittal combine in 2005 only reinforced the impression that India lacks a clearly defined Central Asia policy and an overall strategic intent.[10] Obviously, there have been many impediments including lack of interest for the region at the highest political level in India; as a result Central Asian leaders over the years have remained cool towards India. In the initial years, these leaders looked towards India for support and in fact they had made India as their first destination. But Indian leadership failed to respond and therefore did not meet their expectations. For example, Nazarbayev did show interest towards India. His wife, Sara Nazarbayev, visits Bangalore at least a dozen times a year. He has been keen to give India oil fields and wanted Indian support for creating a techno park in Almaty. But the Indian side failed to nudge him in securing interests. Indian leaders have generally never been munificent towards the Central Asian leaders. From the beginning the chemistry between then Prime Minister P.V. Narasimha Rao and President Nazarbayev never worked well. In 1992, Nazarbayev cut short his visit to Delhi and instead went to Islamabad where he received most friendly reception. Similarly, Central Asian leaders found 'meditative' Prime Minister Vajpayee to be unimpressive,[11] while in stark contrast, Pakistani leaders displayed genuine enthusiasm, brotherly attitude and above all greater warmth for them. Some of these nuances seemed to have left negative imprints for cementing closer Indo-Central Asian relationship. Moreover, there is also the aspect of Central Asians avoidance of competing with Russia when it comes to India. They have also learnt to maintain a neutral position on the Indo-Pak disputes.

---

10. Read, P. Stobdan, "Central Asia and India's Security", *Strategic Analysis*, Vol 28, No. 1, January-March 2004.

11. For impression of Kazakh Foreign Minister, Kassymzhomart Tokaev, during his meeting with Atal Behari Vajpayee in August 1999, read Tokaev's book *Meeting the Challenges—Memoirs of Kazakhstan's Foreign Minister*, Global Scholarship Publication, New York, 2004.

The way forward

India has been grossly and perhaps consciously overlooking its interests in Central Asia, which traditionally formed a 'buffer zone' against external aggression. India has already paid prices for this in the case of Afghanistan, Tibet, Myanmar and Xinjiang. Regional complexities are likely to undergo major change with major powers stepping in and around India's northern flanks. As an emerging power, India ought to be taking note of the fast changing strategic scenario and clearly define and devise a meaningful response along the following lines:

1. A rising and confident India should launch a new policy initiative in the framework of Central Asia plus India to raise the current level of bilateralism to a greater regional dialogue on an institutionalised basis. This must be qualitatively a new step. While the cultural and technical exchanges and similar image-building activities must continue, India must look at the hard reality to concretise its multifaceted goals. The new policy outlook could do well if India evolves an independent cause with Central Asia without tagging it much with its Russia or Iran policy. India needs to recognise the hard reality of envisioning a partnership with China, Pakistan and Afghanistan to access Central Asia. Such an approach will complement India's economic integration process with South, West and Southeast Asia. Besides, it will generate regional stability and promote closer India-Central Asia cooperation in regional and international fora.

2. The policy outlook should seek to offer a new orientation of what India could offer to Central Asia while articulating persuasively: i) the techno-economic-security potential of India, which could be accessed in a cooperative, mutually beneficial partnership; ii) India's modernising and stabilising influence, its liberal-democratic values, building civil societies, managing pluralistic structure and ethno-religious harmony; iii) the need for an inter-dependent 'energy community' of suppliers and consumers, as their desire for diversifying energy export routes corresponds with India's

quest for diversifying imports; iv) willingness for a partnership in setting up downstream production facilities instead of exporting raw materials out of the region through expensive pipelines; v) India for them will also be a countervailing factor *vis-à-vis* China.

3. Central Asia plus India dialogue process would complement the objectives of other organisations like the SCO, the Eurasian Economic Community (EEC), the Central Asian Cooperation Organization (CACO), the Central Asian Regional Economic Cooperation (CAREC) and others. This will complement the wider Asian economic integration process currently underway through the multilateral institutions of cooperation.

4. While India may complement the objectives of others, it could also play a positive role in moderating their aims. The SCO, for example, is indubitably expanding beyond Central Asia, but it may face several challenges ahead, such as: i) the SCO's current popularity is mainly related to shared perception on internal insecurity (threat to regimes); ii) the atmosphere of lurking suspicion may grow with Pakistan and Iran joining as observers; iii) Iran's future, Pakistan's role and the Afghan instability could pose several challenges to SCO; iv) Pakistan's proliferation activities and WMD possibly falling into the hands of fundamentalists could cause serious concern; v) fervent anti-US stance will impede the SCO, and if it shapes into any politico-military alliance, some members could opt out; vi) prospect for a strong opposition upsurge in Uzbekistan in the medium term, with the Western support, should not be ruled out. India's engagement with the Uzbek regime requires a closer attention.

5. India's initiative could provide an abstemious effect on the region, but to be realistic, India cannot match the leverages enjoyed by Russia and China, which are more intrinsic in terms of security interest, ideological convergence and economic complementary. However, India stands to gain a

greater say in the SCO by addressing particularly the security issues including terrorism. India will have a greater role to ensure that the SCO does not shape into a military bloc, which is detrimental to regional peace and security.

6. India's initiative must factor the regional underpinnings. It must include rebuilding of Afghanistan. The improvement in the Kazakh-Uzbek relations is a positive sign and it should help India to pursue a substantive goal in the region. Afghanistan's entry[12] into the CAREC, SAARC, and creation of SCO-Afghanistan Contact Group would have positive influence for stabilising Afghanistan.[13]

7. India's initiative must also include the factor of impeding any possible role by US or Pakistan to ever become arbitrator of future changes, singly or jointly, in Central Asia, particularly in (a) restricting the SCO's influence, (b) infusing Islamic fundamentalist tendencies for the long term containment of Russian, Indian or Chinese influence. NATO's entry into Afghanistan, which is rather in proximity to Jammu & Kashmir, is another factor that needs monitoring. While India foresees no real differences with US policy in the region, it calls for continuous caution that America refrains from establishing cohabitation with the Islamic forces.

8. Central Asia plus India initiative needs to be framed in a broader context and should be consonant with India's Pakistan and China policy. The exposure of Jammu and Kashmir to Central Asia must become part India's initiatives. This can be done by restoring the old frontier diplomacy beyond the Himalayas. India needs to factor Xinjiang Ugyur Autonomous Region (XUAR) in India's Central Asia calculus. XUAR is centrally located in the Eurasian continent. It has border with Kazakhstan, Russia, Mongolia, Kyrgyzstan,

---

12. The Central Asia Regional Economic Cooperation (CAREC) Program is an ADB-supported initiative to encourage economic cooperation in Central Asia that began in 1997. Afghanistan participated in CAREC meeting in Bishkek in November 2005, *http://www.mof.gov.af/english/CAREC.htm*.

13. Protocol on establishment of SCO-Afghanistan contact group was signed on November 4, 2005 in Beijing, *http://www.sectsco.org/news_detail.asp?id=649&LanguageID=2*.

Tajikistan, Pakistan, Afghanistan and India. XUAR directly borders with the Jammu & Kashmir. In fact, India was a legitimate Central Asian player until 1950s. Until 1954, India was an active player and its Consulate in Kashgar actively conducted trade across Ladakh-Xinjiang frontier. The SCO and also China's 'go-West' mentality is transforming the region as a major hub of trans-Eurasian connectivity and cooperation. India should aim at joining this network and make Jammu & Kashmir a springboard for its entry into the region.[14] The process could inevitably spur economic prosperity, as well as help diminish the current level of political standoff in the state.

9. The Governor of XUAR, during his visit to India (2004) proposed to start flights from Urumchi to Delhi.[15] The matter needs be pursued further to improve India's air connectivity with the landlocked Central Asia.

10. While Uzbekistan, undoubtedly, is the key to Central Asia's overall regional dynamics; it is Kazakhstan and its potentials that should deserve India's immediate attention. The country, largest in Central Asia, is of key interest to every major world power. It has emerged as the most prosperous, most stable, most secular (despite Muslim majority population), most free economy and most democratic in the entire post-Soviet space. Kazakhstan's potential oil reserves are on par with Kuwait that will make it the world's major alternative energy supplier in the next 10 years. It has 35 billion barrels of oil reserves (twice as much as the North Sea) and its projected reserves are 100-110 billion barrels by 2015 (would be in world's top 3). The country is already a global economic force and has attracted foreign investments of $ 42 billion so far. It is already a leading oil producer and exporter. The per

14. Stobdan, P. (2005). "India-China Cooperation in Central Asia: Evolving a Look-North Policy", *Security and Society*, Centre for Strategic and Regional Studies, University of Jammu, Vol. 2, Number 1, Summer.

15. The Governor of Xinjiang, Ismail Tiliwaldi visited India in October 2004 to discuss the feasibility of laying a natural gas pipeline from Xinjiang to India. Tiliwaldi expressed interest in a land link with India. India and Xinjiang have identified four areas for potential cooperation—agriculture and food processing, traditional medicine and herbs, energy and oil production, and tourism.

capita GDP is expected to increase to $ 9,000 by 2012 and likely to double roughly every seven years that will allow Kazakhstan to overtake the levels of many wealthy countries.[16] The country is a factor of regional stability. Its Constitution proclaims adherence to democratic and secular system, rule of law and rights to individual freedom. It shares a strong affinity with India in recognising ideological, political, linguistic and ethnic diversity. It promotes harmony among over 100 nationalities.

11. During the past few years, bilateral relations between India and Kazakhstan have acquired a dynamic character with the increase in economic, political and cultural contacts. Kazakhstan shares close affinity with India in terms of political and economic commitment, shared values of secularism, democracy and plural structure. Both share full commitment to fight against terrorism and the Joint Working Group (JWG) on counter-terrorism could form the basis for cooperation in the SCO. Nazarbayev's plans for regional integration are similar to those of India, as well as in conformity with the process currently underway in Asia for the creation of the Asian Union. All these shared values plus the imperative for cooperation in energy field should become the cornerstone of India's partnership with Kazakhstan.

12. Similarly, prospect for cooperation in defence is enormous. India has already made a significant achievement in building interlocking interests with military industrial complexes such as Dastan (Kyrgyzstan) and KiroMashzavod (Kazakhstan) and Uzbek Aviation Company. Indian airbase at Ayni in Tajikistan operating since 2002 obviously added a new dimension to the quality of defence cooperation with Tajikistan. Serious efforts are needed to build a vision for long-term defence cooperation with these countries. One

16. Since the start of 2006, Nazarbayev has spoken repeatedly about his aim to transform Kazakhstan into one of the "50 most competitive, dynamically developing countries in the world" within the next decade-RIA Novosti, Astana, 21 November, 2005.

major problem that would remain relates to future R&D programmes of those equipments. Secondly, India's cooperation with states does not have a strategic component, for instance *vis-à-vis* China. Therefore, defence cooperation with these countries should involve comprehensive strategy with the eventual goal of serving India's long-term strategy.

13. India needs to review its cultural diplomacy. Some of the activities conducted in the region by Indian cultural centres are redundant and do not serve any purposeful objectives. The objective of these centres should be oriented to promote as well as acquire deeper understanding of the region and engage in areas, which would have long-term benefits for India.

14. India's air connectivity to landlocked Central Asia needs to be improved. The air traffic between the region and India has notably increased. It is time that we encourage private airliners to fly Central Asian capitals.

15. India's security concerns are inextricably linked with turbulence in the region though there are no discernible evidences to suggest that instability in Central Asia having any major repercussions to India. However, any possible future linkages between energy resources and Islamic forces may pose threats to India. This means that the region will engage India's security concerns for a long time. Events in the aftermath of 9/11 have assumed critical importance with wide ranging security ramifications for India. It needs to be noted that Pakistan over the years has successfully used terrorism as an instrument to push its agenda. As a result, Pakistan remains a strong factor in the foreign policies of all the Central Asian states. The Governments of the region have lately become acquiescent to Islamabad, particularly in the context of mounting threat they face from terrorism. There are certainly many obstacles for India to move in the region and therefore, it would require much more than the diplomatic channel and make extra efforts to push its interests. Moreover, Pakistan always had an ambitious

programme for the region, which lost steam due to its
inherent shortcomings. However, Pakistan still has the will,
driven by its hostility with India, to undermine its interests
in the region. After a brief lull fundamentalist outfits seem
to be regaining strength.

16. India needs to counter these portents with strategic foresight.
    Kazakhstan, Kyrgyzstan and Tajikistan like India share long
    borders with China. These countries, in the recent years,
    have resolved their longstanding territorial disputes with
    China. Besides learning from their experiences on border
    negotiations, it would be also pertinent to factor these three
    Central Asian states in its China policy.

17. India's lack of understanding of the regional complexities
    should entail steps for instituting closer cooperation and
    dialogues with Central Asian states at National Security
    Council level. It is understood that NSCs of these countries
    hold importance in the decisionmaking structures and are
    controlled directly by the Presidents of these states.

18. From the viewpoint of policy implications, Uzbekistan, home
    for half of Central Asian population and as the hub of
    Islamic culture, would remain as the epicentre for future
    change in the region. Karimov has so far failed to distinguish
    between nationalism and Islamism. As a result, even the
    peaceful form of Islam has suffered under his policies.
    Moreover, the country borders with each Central Asian
    states, like India in South Asia, and as such suffers from
    intrinsic regional problems. Therefore, Uzbekistan would
    remain as the most unpredictable and problematic areas of
    great power conflict and would require close watching.

19. Islam would remain as most critical factor for future change
    in Central Asia. The strength of HuT and others appear to
    be growing that could only be possible with the domestic
    support and participation. However, it needs to be
    underlined from Indian viewpoint that both Islamists and
    nationalists in Central Asia have not shown so far any
    antipathy towards India. Contrarily, the nostalgia for India

among majority traditional people runs far deeper than the Communists who share no clear commitments other than seek their own interests. It is important therefore to bear in mind that India is not in a position to infuriate majority population or groups in the region. Instead, India needs to build up meaningful contacts with all sections based on its cultural and historical relationship. Least India can do is to learn from its lessons in Afghanistan.

20

India and the European Union: non-associable to strategic partner

Rajendra M. Abhyankar

The setting

Every millennium comes with its own challenges and opportunities which determine the direction of the international system. The last millennium recalls Charles Dickens in *A Tale of Two Cities*, "it was the best of times, it was the worst of times. We were heading for heaven, we were heading for hell." It was a century of contradictions.

It saw two World Wars and over a hundred regional, bilateral and internal civil conflicts, some of which still continue; yet the determination of the international community to ban the scourge of wars through the only weapon it had—the United Nations. The use of only two atom bombs at Hiroshima and Nagasaki despite the earth-shaking discovery of nuclear power; yet the destruction and loss of life turned the world against the use of its devastating power. It saw the full course of the Cold War with the two superpowers ranged against each other ideologically and militarily; yet it gave birth to the largest number of independent states in the history of humankind. It saw democracy becoming the preferred choice for aggregating individual choices; yet the virtues of democracy being exploited for narrow, sectarian and violent aims. It saw greater regulation of the world's financial and trading systems; yet provoked voices to protect the dispossessed and the deprived. It saw the *mantras* of free market and unbridled capitalism gaining respectability; yet recognised the imperative to focus on the rights of the individual and his economic well-being.

As we start the new millennium it would be well to see where we stand and where we may go. The last five years since 2000 have seen:

- the ever-present threat of nuclear war and total annihilation, yet success in developing sophisticated nuclear weapons and delivery systems which could still 'limit' destruction;

- the world dominated by one hyper-power, yet a belief in multipolarity with a large number of major and regional powers each with its own sphere of influence;

- the international system dependent on a United Nations increasingly controlled by the five permanent members;

- UN resolutions becoming an existentialist crutch for a large number of its member-states, yet the UN powerless in combating the malefic acts of non-state actors;

- the erosion of the Westphalia concept of sovereignty and a movement towards shared sovereignty emphasising security of the individual rather than the nation-state;

- the globalisation of transnational crime, disease and technological systems leading to a fluidity of settled borders;

- an ever-expanding role of science and technology in the life of the nation and of the individual, particularly in the exploitation of the earth, its space and waters;

- the anticipated clash of civilisations narrowing down to a clash of religions, yet a recognition of the diversity of the human condition;

- a growing conviction that human well-being improves in an open, democratic and transparent system of governance;

- the inevitability of economic globalisation and interdependency, yet paradoxically recourse to regional trading arrangements so as to make the global trading system equitable;

- energy—its security and variety of sources—becoming the single over-arching determinant of a nation's progress; and
- the freeing of knowledge through the Internet.

During the last century, the world's population grew from 1.7 billion in 1900 to 6.1 billion in 2000 majority of which was in the relatively poorer countries. This exacerbated the tendencies listed above which would have to be confronted in the coming century. They provide the context in which we would need to evaluate the future of the relations between India and the European Union.

Historical overview

India has always had longstanding relations in diverse fields with the countries of Europe even though the status of those countries, and of India itself, has changed over time. For the purpose of this chapter, we will look at India's relations with Europe from the Cold War onwards, and that too with that part of Europe which then was part of the 'free world' and now is, or will be, part of the European Union. It was India's spiritual and material wealth which first attracted Europeans; its latter-day equivalents, our prowess in information technology and our massive market, attracts them even today.

The desire to end all wars in Europe after the end of the Second World War provoked Jean Monet to propose the idea of 'a united Europe' by setting up common institutions for Europe as a whole and the eventual surrender of national sovereignty to a supranational European government. It was the only successful experiment of turning bitter foes into longlasting friends. The end of the Cold War and the splintering of Europe into many more nations, 49 at current count, each aspiring to become part of the single European entity has reinforced the *raison d'être* of a united Europe.

The European Economic Community (EEC) came into being in 1957 along with the European Coal and Steel Community (ECSC) and Euratom following the Treaty of Rome. India accredited its first Ambassador to the EEC in 1963 starting a formal relationship with this new entity. It was understood that this was not at the cost of, or would replace, India's growing bilateral relations with individual member-states, like Germany, France, Italy, Netherlands, Belgium and Luxembourg. The same principle was maintained as the EEC expanded from 6 to 15, and then to 25 in 2004; and transformed itself into the European Union (EU) after the Single Act of 1987, with unequivocal emphasis on the principle of subsidiarity, citizenship of the Union and respect for fundamental rights.

In recognising the EEC, India would appear to have prepared itself for the forthcoming break with its colonial past. UK's accession to the EEC in 1973 left India bereft of the imperial preferences which had hitherto determined our trading relationship with our largest partner. It dictated the imperative need to develop a new relationship with the European grouping. The Joint Declaration of Intent (JDI) between the UK and the EEC stated that solutions to the problems arising for the Commonwealth countries due to the expiry of trade preferences would be dealt with. The brevity of the JDI conveyed the fact that this issue was not a major negotiating point in the accession talks. It was a far cry from the arrangements for trade and aid that France was able to extract from the ECC for its erstwhile African colonies. In the event the parties to the JDI were more occupied with working through the details of UK's entry than with the residual problems affecting countries like India. It was also interesting that none of the other member-states who had a colonial past in India did much to alleviate India's pain. India was seen as Britain's baby and it was up to the British to act in its favour.

India's initial attempt was to explore the possibility of an Association Agreement with the EEC on the lines of those with the countries of the Mediterranean basin and later with the ACP countries. India's effort failed since the European Commission (EC) had classified all countries in South Asia as 'non-associable'—a most unfortunate choice of words. This at a time when two significant developments were taking place: first, the negotiation of the Lome Convention which would give wide-ranging trade preferences to the ACP countries, including subsidies for their agricultural products; and second, the formulation of the EEC's Generalised

System of Preferences (GSP). The idea of generalised trade preferences for developing countries had taken root following the Second UNCTAD Conference in New Delhi in 1968. It was not altruism which dictated this move by the developed countries, but a hard-headed reason to rejuvenate their economic ties with erstwhile colonies. India's decision to carve out a totally new path with the EEC was entirely due to the genius of Dr. K.B. Lall, then India's Ambassador to the EEC. The Commercial Cooperation Agreement (CCA) which he devised became a precursor for similar Agreements with all other South Asian countries. It took the EEC's GSP as the starting point and added the dimensions of trade development and trade promotion. It was based on sovereign equality between the two entities and restructured India-EEC relations in a way in which it would not conflict with India's bilateral relations with the member-states.

The first CCA signed in 1973 set up a Joint Commission as the primary forum for all interaction between the two entities. The CCA was expanded between 1973 and 1993 to include economic cooperation and investment in keeping with the changing needs and priorities of the relationship. The India-EEC Trade Centre, set up in the early 1980s and funded in the initial years by the EEC, to promote Indian exports was a novel idea during its time. India-EEC trade continued to show an upward trend during this period with the EEC accounting for about 20 per cent of India's total trade turnover.

In 1994, India and the EEC adopted their first Political Declaration which highlighted their adherence to the common ideals of democracy and diversity. The political dimension which it introduced was an explicit recognition of India's changing profile in South Asia and of the success of its economic direction following the reform programme. It was not an unmixed blessing. EEC's greater interest in India was seen from its statements on developments within India, and on India-Pakistan issues. It encouraged a tendency to place India into an India-Pakistan box. India was then seen as a large democratic, yet an anarchic country mired internally in its poverty and externally in the perennial Kashmir issue.

The EU saw India's economic liberalisation process as a welcome development, which needed to be strengthened and encouraged. India's consistent GDP growth of 6-7 per cent annually from 1997 onwards demonstrated the success and irrevocability of India's economic liberalisation process. It brought about a much greater interaction with the EU from 1993 through its economic cooperation and development cooperation windows. The intention to engage India more intensively also had a strong underlying streak of capping India's nuclear programme. The EU shared the US assessment that after the 1998 nuclear tests by India and Pakistan, the subcontinent had become 'the most dangerous place on earth'. India's self-imposed moratorium on further testing, no-first-use policy and the strict ban on export of nuclear materials was not sufficient to convince the EU of India's good intentions. Surprisingly, even the remarkably restrained way in which India handled the Kargil conflict despite heavy losses of life could not change their perception.

India and the EU held their first Political Summit in Lisbon in 2000. From now on the thrust was to be political but the content would remain economic. It was a watershed in the evolution of the relationship. The Lisbon Summit also noted that there was a broad consensus amongst member-states to positively engage India through dialogue in all areas of common interests and concerns. It decided to hold annual summits alternately in New Delhi and in the Capital of the EU Presidency. It was also agreed that the Ministerial EU-India Troika—with the Indian External Affairs Minister, and on the EU side, the Foreign Minister of the country of Presidency, the External Relations Commissioner and the Special Representative for Foreign and Defence Policy—would meet before the Summit, so also the Joint Commission. The India-EU Round Table for Civil Society interaction would also meet in a way to feed into the Political Summit.

From the mid-1990s the EC had taken the initiative to prepare a blueprint for a Substantially Enhanced Partnership with India.

It was a long overdue acknowledgement that India had become an increasingly significant political and economic player on the global stage. The success of Indians in Silicon Valley, the rapidly increasing middle class numbering almost 350 million, and the consistently high rate of growth forced a re-look at relations with India. The US led the field and others, including the EU, were quick to follow. Chris Patten, the then External Relations Commissioner, remarking on this development noted that "if there is a natural partner for Europe in South Asia, then surely it is India." While their common goal in strengthening the EU's Common Foreign, Security and Defence Policy (FSDP) was still at a distance the FSDP provided an additional dimension to the exercise of their bilateral foreign policy *vis-à-vis* India. EU created an agenda and policy niche in areas, like human rights and humanitarian law, democracy and adherence to core UN Conventions, and mainstreaming labour and environment standards. Its development cooperation assistance and economic cooperation programmes became useful instruments to pursue this policy. The issues that EU takes up would often cause embarrassment and irritation if taken up bilaterally. The EU exercises this 'soft power' assiduously not only in relation to India but other interlocutors as well.

Since Lisbon, six summits have been held—the last in New Delhi on 7 September 2005. The Summit is the highest level body in the India-EU relationship bringing together all the threads connecting the major European institutions:

- the India-EU Ministerial Troika with the EU Council of Ministers and the Presiency;
- the Joint Commission, the Sub-Commissions and the Expert Groups with the European Commission;
- the India-EU Round Table for Civil Society with the European Economic and Social Commission; and
- the Resolutions and Reports of the South Asia Delegation in the European Parliament.

It can thus be seen that the institutional architecture for sustaining the relationship is multi-tiered and in fact appears to err on the side of access. However, given the complicated decision-making process of the EU with the participation of 25 member-states, there would appear to be no alternative.

The fifth Summit at The Hague approved the strategic partnership (SP) between India and the EU. It had taken a little over 30 years for India to ascend from a 'non-associable' to a 'strategic partner'. India became one of only six entities—US, Canada, Japan, Russia and China—to have such a relationship. The EU's initiatives for Strategic Partnerships are based on Javier Solana's paper on European Security of December 2000 which was essentially provoked by the perception of Europe's declining role in international affairs, dissonance in the trans-Atlantic relationship, and the EU's inability to evolve a common foreign, defence and security policy. To a large extent, events leading to, during and after US invasion of Iraq were responsible. But the seeds were sown much earlier. The thrust of this strategy is to emphasise multilateralism, and in that context, to reassert a European role, that 'we are stronger when we act together'. While re-emphasising the transatlantic relationship, it seeks to bring about an effective and balanced partnership with the US through strategic partnerships with Russia, Japan, China, Canada and India.

The sixth Summit approved the Joint Action Plan (JAP), which will set the pace and direction of the partnership in the new millennium. Along with the Political Declaration, the JAP contains the joint Vision of the two sides for the next 15 years. The JAP covers the entire gamut of bilateral interaction and no institution on either side is excluded. Yet the success of the SP will depend on how each side visualises its goals and the relative importance of each to the other. A comparative study of the content of all EU's strategic partners shows that in the case of the others EU's motivation was based entirely on the 'ground realities' of its relationship, while in India's case it is based on its potential. The JAP is expected to turn this promise into reality.

The difference in emphasis in the way in which India and the EU approach their strategic partnership is well illustrated by two recent pieces on the relationship. Christofe Jaffrelot[1] *inter alia* highlights:

1. Multicultural cooperation: a stress on conflict prevention, anti-terrorism, non-proliferation, promotion of democracy and defence of human rights.

2. Strengthening sectoral economic dialogue and jointly drafted regulatory policies.

3. Cooperation to allow India attain MDGs.

On the other hand, O.P Sharma[2] summarises the major strategic partnership objectives as:

1. Strengthening dialogue and consultation mechanism.

2. Deepening political dialogue.

3. Enhancing economic policy dialogue and cooperation.

4. Developing trade and investment.

The difference in perspectives can be seen clearly. While the former emphasises areas which have traditionally been seen as intrusive by the Indian side, the latter emphasises an equality of the relationship. I have brought out this contrast to show that the unfolding of the strategic partnership pre-supposes a change of mindsets on both sides, and a good deal of compromise on traditionally held agendas. Whether this would happen in the coming decades is a function of the importance of India and the EU in each other's evolving world view. In my view, a strategic partnership pre-supposes that it is a relationship at a higher level than the normal intercourse between any two entities. To break it down further, such a relationship would:

- be based on sovereign equality, and for the larger good of their peoples, approximating towards the Pareto's condition of making everyone better off without making even one worse off. The ultimate goal of any relationship has to be the welfare, security and well-being of the peoples involved;

---

1. Jaffrelot, Christofe (2006). "India and the EU: The Charade of a Strategic Partnership", *EIAS Bulletin* February-March.

2. O.P. Sharma "India, the European Union and the World Trade Organisation—An Indian View".

- assume cooperation in international fora, even on issues on which the partners differ;

- assume that positions taken on any issue bilaterally would be reflected multilaterally;

- not be subject to the vicissitudes of the relationship of either partner with any third party;

- assume that any critical statement by one partner of the other would be made after a full process of consultation;

- invite participation by the partner in any event organised by the other in which the former has an interest.

Admittedly these principles would be difficult to follow in practice, yet they show the larger goal to which a strategic partnership should aspire.

It is equally interesting to compare the content of EU's strategic partnership with India with that of its other partners. The content in each case depends on the present state of the relationship and its future possibilities. As stated above, EU's relationship with its other partners[3] were forced by the 'ground realities'—both historic and emerging. EU's oldest strategic partner is the US and the transatlantic relationship will remain strong. All others were initiated in the century with India being the last so far. It reflects the EU's view of the likely shift in the world's economic focus towards Asia—considering that three out of six partners are Asian— and the dominant role that the Asian strategic partners are expected to play as this century unfolds. It is also worth noting that of the six, three are UNSC permanent members while two—India and Japan—are aspirants. Within the EU itself are the other two P-5 members and Germany, another aspirant. Clearly the EU sees these strategic partnerships as reinforcing multipolarity, which for the EU is a cardinal pillar of the international system.

The relationship with India is entirely based on its potential for the future which places it in the big league. From Euro 4.4 billion in 1980, India-EU trade turnover was Euro 33 billion in 2004, and

---

3. USA (1995), Japan (2001), China (2003), Russia (2004) and Canada (2004).

the Indian economy was valued at US $ 3.36 trillion. It is interesting to list the major items which are present in the other partnerships but are omitted from India's:

- while acknowledging India's centrality and regional role in South Asia, it ignores India's equally important relations with ASEAN, North, West, Central and East Asia;

- the area of defence/military cooperation does not find a mention even though India has the third largest active army in the world and the largest para-military force numbering one million. It is also a non-NPT nuclear power and one of the largest importers of defence material;

- despite India's strong interest in combating counter-terrorism, it has a relatively weak formulation on cooperation in this sector;

- no mention of cooperation in non-proliferation despite India's impeccable record in this area;

- no reference to encouraging investment flows into India especially through the European Investment Bank.

It is possible that in the implementation of the JAP additional areas for inclusion or strengthening will be thrown up. An examination of the way this special relationship has evolved since the Lisbon Summit will highlight the areas of strength and weakness in the future. Views on the performance so far are diametrically opposed. Christophe Jaffrelot states that, "it is on the political level—involving both diplomatic and strategic objectives—that the EU-India relations appear most bogged down".[4] On the other hand, Charles Grant asserts that there is no way that the EU can afford to ignore India since over the next half century, India will grow faster than any large national economy (based on a report by Goldman Sachs). By 2050 it will be the world's third largest economy (behind China and US) but around four times bigger than each of the next three: Japan, Brazil, Russia.[5]

---

4. *op. cit.*

5. Grant, Charles (2006). "India and the EU: Strategic Partners?" *CER Bulletin*, Issue 46, February-March.

Bases for cooperation and conflict

The European Union represents the only example in the world since the Second World War where bitter and long-standing enemies have shed past rancor and come together to jointly build a prosperous and peaceful life for their peoples. It remains a work-in-progress, especially after the rejection of the new Constitution by France and Netherlands in 2005. What is more, a referendum in the UK will always be in doubt. This has also meant that progress towards a unified foreign, defence and security policy has been delayed, as also the appointment of an EU Foreign Minister. Although the EU continues to function on the basis of the Maastricht Treaty, the question of a new unified Constitution will have to be tackled in the future. It is only when all the member-states, particularly UK, France, Germany and Poland, are ready to surrender the larger part of their national sovereignty to this supra-national entity that a unified Constitution will become possible. That all EU member-states are neither in the Euro-zone nor the Schengen area illustrates the difficulty. The 'national pillar' to which a large number of issues are imputed will have to reduce in its salience. At present, between 30-70 per cent of the decisions that affect the man in the street are made in Brussels and not in the national capitals.

Economic prosperity in Europe would be an important determinant of whether the EU would eventually integrate internally. Currently barring the UK major European economies have not performed well and there is a perception that the European social model has failed. The continuing tensions arising from the alienation of immigrant minorities in major European countries, majority of whom are Muslim and those arising from the mobility of nationals from the new entrants has also had a deleterious effect on the economy. Another factor which would hold back integration and progress is the anticipated enlargement to include Bulgaria, Romania and Turkey. These factors make it necessary for the EU to consider a period of consolidation during which the present relationships both within its member-states and with the strategic partners become settled and are able to contribute to an upward economic spiral based on comparative advantage and mutual benefit. There is no doubt that the pace of further integration within the EU will correspondingly increase its influence on world events, even if the focus is on Asia in this century. "Whatever assertions there may be about the world having become unipolar with United States of America as the central prism, the accompanying reality is that there are other centres of political and economic importance—Europe collectively is such a centre."[6] This statement will continue to hold equally valid in the future.

Their common adherence to democracy and pluralism at home, and multilateralism abroad, has provided a sound basis for the India-EU relationship. India's status as the world's fastest growing major economy has improved its standing on the world political stage. On its part, India's political moves are increasingly being influenced by economic imperatives. The strength of their strategic partnership will depend on whether India reaches the high level of expectation of its economic performance, and hence its political importance, in this century. Only then would India become, and be seen, as an equal partner in this relationship. It would be well at this point to list factors which could impede India's resurgence to highlight areas which would benefit from India-EU cooperation:

- High cost of democracy: With India's tremendous diversity, democracy is necessarily a delay-involving system and more often than not the decision taken is the lowest common denominator—a huge tax on the economy.

- Disputes: India has long-standing disputes with Pakistan and China. The present trend towards settling them would hopefully be reinforced. At the same time, India's peripheries, and all its neighbours, are presently disturbed. Furthermore, the linking of leftist movements within India and with the Maoist group in Nepal is alarming.

- Lack of international representation: India's absence from the UN Security Council goes against its historic role in

---

6.   J.N.Dixit; *cf*: Grant, *ibid.*

the UN system, its claim on the basis of every existing criteria, and its potential as a major global player.

- Poverty: Despite continuing economic prosperity, 260 million still remain below the poverty line. This is a contributory factor in the resurgence of leftist militant groups in India's heartland.

- Social infrastructure: The capacity of roads, power grid, water, communication, housing and education is inadequate to meet even current needs.

- Disorganisation: Stemming from bad governance and excessive red-tape.

- Unemployment: Remains high. At the same time 90 per cent of India's labour force of 432 million is in the unorganised sector without any coverage for health and providence.

- Energy dependence: India is critically dependent on imported hydrocarbons for its continued development at least until renewable sources of energy can meet the demand. India currently imports 70 per cent of its energy requirements.

The above factors highlight crucial areas for India-EU cooperation to forge a meaningful and beneficial partnership. Its success would ultimately depend on the strength of the vision and the political will of the leadership on both sides. It would also depend on the relative importance of India and the EU in the international system as it evolves. The dramatic, yet tragic, events in the first five years of this millennium have called into question the assumptions on which the international order was based. These events have shown that the international community is groping with answers to the fundamental questions that it has thrown up *inter alia* concerning democracy and political participation, terrorism and non-state actors, economic progress and poverty alleviation, nuclear energy and proliferation, state sovereignty and human security. An important reason which led to the virtual break-up of the international economic and political order has been the realisation that the individual—his rights, duties and well-being— must be better represented in governance and become central to international, regional and national action. This would be the only way in which peace and prosperity in the world can be ensured in the future. In such a scenario their common adherence to democratic institutions and an inclusive society make India and the EU natural partners as well as rallying points in a re-structured international system. The strength of both entities will come from their 'soft power'. The EU already uses its 'soft power' to establish itself as an entity and to introduce itself into current political and economic situations in the world. India, on its part, has increasingly perceived that its 'soft power' which stems from its ethos of secularism, tolerance and democracy has made it a paradigm in today's world.

On the economic front as well, the EU with its 450 million consumers and the fourth largest GNP of Euro 10 trillion will remain a major destination for India's trade, and source for inward foreign investment. In realisation of this potential, it is as well that the two sides have decided to explore the possibility of an India-EU free trade arrangement which will not only go beyond trade, but also beyond the eventual outcome of the Doha Development Round. Europe's industrial strength can be of immense benefit to power India's dynamic growth particularly in infrastructure projects, environmental protection and civilian use of nuclear energy. Similarly, cooperation in science and technology, particularly in high-tech and frontier technology areas like space applications and remote sensing, information society technologies and biotechnology, would become important components of the India-EU relationship. Indian participation as a full partner in both the Galileo Satellite Navigation Project and the International Thermo-nuclear Energy Reactor (ITER) project attests to the potential of this partnership as also European participation in Chandrayaan, India's first lunar mission. EU's special scholarship window for India under its Erasmus Mundus programme could ensure that Indian professional talent would be available to mitigate the problems of EU's ageing population and contribute to the Lisbon Agenda on competitiveness.

Notwithstanding the positive forecast of future opportunities, the relationship remains vitiated by old mindsets. The two entities need to focus on their strengths in order to meet the challenges ahead. If the EU feels that India does not take its political ambitions seriously, India feels that there is a good deal of 'talking down' on the part of the EU and, more often than not, EU's views are seen as intrusive. Similarly, while India is currently focussing strongly on two areas–United States and East Asia—EU's Sino-centrism becomes responsible for it hardly figuring on the Indian radar screen. EU's visibility in India has also suffered because of the fact that major EU member-states, like UK, France and Germany, have substantial bilateral relations with India even in areas where common European policies are agreed. Europe does not present a united front *vis-à-vis* India. At the same time, on important issues that concern India like a level playing field for its professionals, civil nuclear energy cooperation and the policies of the Nuclear Suppliers Group or cross-border acquisitions, the EU is wont to invoke the 'national pillar' in order to frustrate forward-looking decisions. The various dimensions of the India-EU relationship have been largely determined by the national interests or preferences of its member-states. In this context, some of the major challenges which will continue into the coming century are:

(i)   Non-proliferation: The India-US civil nuclear energy cooperation Agreement was expected to open the possibility of going beyond the NPT framework in combating proliferation. India has sought to project itself as a part of the solution and not of the problem. On the other hand, the EU still speaks in NPT terms and its member-states who are also members of the NSG have yet to concede the possibility of civil nuclear energy cooperation with India. The fact that both India and the EU share equal concerns on energy security and the EU has unmatched and current experience in manufacture of nuclear power generators has not weighed with the decisionmakers. As J.N. Dixit has said, "Although the controversies of 1998 and 1999—when India tested its nuclear weapons—have died down, there are reservations about India's nuclear weaponisation in Europe."[7]

(ii) India's permanent membership of UNSC: Despite a strong momentum in 2005 on the possibility of a *via media* for the G-4 countries—India, Japan, Germany and Brazil – the effort was frustrated. An important reason for this was the inability of the EU to support India's candidature. While both France and UK were supportive of India, and Germany was a co-aspirant, the lack of agreement within the EU on how to deal with the question of a 'European seat' had a negative influence on India's candidature also. The *denouement* of this issue is still to come.

(iii) Management of international trade: The Doha Development Round has run into difficulties stemming from India's articulation of the position of others, like China, Brazil and South Africa, that nothing more can be done to improve market access for imports of manufactured products until and unless the EU (and US) do more to open up their markets to import of agricultural products. Its linkage with progress in trade in services and world trade rules is also a factor. While EU and India have worked together to bring forward better offers by all major participants, in the spirit of their strategic partnership, they may well look at a bilateral trading arrangement in the future.

(iv) Continuing differences between the EU and India on issues like support to the International Criminal Court and the Ottawa Convention against Anti-Personal Mines as well as on joint action to promote democracy in the world. Furthermore, the EU tendency to mainstream core humanitarian and labour conventions through its trade, economic and development cooperation windows.

(v) EU's continuing proclivity to see India through an India-Pakistan or a South Asian prism not only militates against

---

7. J.N. Dixit, *cf*: Grant, *ibid*.

India's own wide-ranging world interests but also does disservice to an emerging relationship.

It is, therefore, no surprise that there is at this time the absence of a strong political will on both sides to move their relations on a higher plane. This has been reflected on the Indian side by the need to align itself, as much as possible, with the only hyper-power in the world. On the European side, its obsession with China has made it overlook its concerns on democracy, human rights and diversity which it projects to its other partners. It is up to the political leaderships on both sides to work their way through these challenges in order to unshackle the positive agenda.

Conclusions

The India-EU strategic partnership comes at a time when both are searching for a stable role as a major player in international affairs. But it also comes at a time when the international community is looking at ways to make the international system more democratic and representative. It also come at a time when globalisation has imposed the imperative to make the individual the focus of action at the national, regional and international level. There is also a fatigue with the operation of a system with one pre-eminent power and effective multilateralism has become attractive once again. There is no doubt that it will reassert itself in the future. In this context EU and India working together have the potential to determine the course of world events. Hard power will not win wars any more and a world war is unthinkable. In such a scenario, EU and India can harness their soft power for the good of their people. It will be up to the acumen of the leaders and policy makers in the two entities to develop a niche for themselves in the fast-changing world.

21

IBSA summit

Hardeep Puri and Krishan Kumar

The first IBSA Summit, which brought together Prime Minister of India Dr. Manmohan Singh, President of Brazil Mr. Luiz Inacio Lula da Silva and President of South Africa Mr. Thabo Mbeki in Brasilia on September 13, 2006, signifies the coming of age of the India-Brazil-South Africa (IBSA) Dialogue Forum. The historic meeting was an endorsement at the highest political level by the three countries of their desire to forge multifaceted links at a trilateral level with a view to facilitating the realisation of their developmental aspirations. The Summit of the three leaders was also an affirmation of the fact that the IBSA Dialogue Forum, conceived in 2003, as a major exercise in transformational diplomacy, had assumed concrete reality. All three leaders alluded to the landmark nature of the meeting.

The IBSA experiment derives its strength from the underlying commonalities, bringing together as it does, three countries with multicultural societies and vibrant democracies located in three different continents. Their major South-South initiative brings together open societies with rapidly growing economies, each possessing specific industrial and technological capabilities.

It is the democratic ethos of the political system of the three countries as well as the transparent, open and bottoms-up nature of their societies which sets this unique gathering apart from other international groupings of developing countries. At a hypothetical level, it would have been possible for the founding fathers of IBSA Dialogue Forum to consider other countries as potential members. The developing status of their economies and the desire to uplift the living standards of their people as well as to share, and benefit from, economic, commercial, scientific and technological exchanges would have vested them with some of the desirable attributes of membership. The names of other large countries in Asia, Africa and Latin America naturally came up in this regard. However, the critical touchstone was the nature of the polity and whether it represented the democratic yearnings of their people and whether the state apparatus was designed to be for the people, of the people and by the people. It was no doubt important to ensure that the member countries were embarked on a path of economic liberalisation. But even more significantly that this path was being charted in a democratic framework.

In addition, it is possible to contend that a bold experiment naturally beset with challenges, should not be embarked upon with a wide membership which naturally brings into play centrifugal tendencies. A core nucleus of only three countries, each a major player in its region, each located in a different continent, each imbued with multicultural ethos and each firmly anchored in the free world with a stable network of democratic institutional mechanisms, amply reflected the common vision of the founding fathers.

Any new organisation inevitably faces both inner challenges and outer scepticism. It is natural, therefore, that IBSA Dialogue Forum, particularly given the unique nature of its composition and the boldness of its vision, was viewed with doubts about its future. Sceptics and critics were hesitant about its agenda, tentative about its chances of success and were even critical of its coming into existence at a time when the global trade and developmental agenda was faced with myriad obstacles. It was posited that three countries, located thousands of kilometres apart from each other, with tenuous political ties and limited commercial and economic interaction shared little to lay the foundations of an enduring international political body.

In the three years since June 2003, when the idea of IBSA as a trilateral initiative germinated, it has come a long way in establishing itself as a growing network which brings the governments, business communities and their peoples to work towards a collaborative and cooperative approach to the developmental challenges confronting them.

Since the Brasilia Declaration of June 2003, three meetings of the Trilateral Commission headed by Foreign Ministers have been held, with a fourth one to be hosted by India in the first quarter of 2007. Seven Focal Points meetings have provided a fora for the senior officials of the three countries to conduct in-depth review of the progress achieved at periodical intervals and formulate work plans to further strengthen and intensify the budding trilateral relationship. Twelve Working Groups have been set up in diverse fields encompassing areas like agriculture, energy, defence, education, health, science and technology, culture, social development, transport and tourism. As a result of the intensive deliberations and consultations, IBSA has agreed upon MoUs in the fields of maritime transport, civil aviation, higher education, health and agriculture.

Significantly, IBSA funding facility for developmental projects with set capital contribution of US$ 1 million from each country has also become operational. A notable feature of the fund is that its mandate is not confined merely to undertaking projects in the three countries but to extending a helping hand to any developing country. Indeed, the ongoing projects on developing agriculture and livestock in Guinea Bissau and waste collection in Haiti, are eloquent testimonies to the shared commitment of the three countries to further South-South cooperation by evolving institutional mechanisms from the perspective of the South to enhance technological cooperation, alleviate poverty and mainstream the developing world perspective in the current discourse on development.

Against this rapid and considerable progress achieved by IBSA in its infancy years, the holding of the first Summit represents the take-off of the South-South initiative. The Joint Declaration issued at the end of the deliberations of the three leaders was a comprehensive document, which reflected the shared vision of the three developing democracies to contribute their might to their regional and global endeavours. The heads of state and government reaffirmed their commitment to the promotion of peace, security and sustainable economic and social development in the world and in their respective regions. They also reaffirmed their commitment to multilateralism, reform of the UN and successful conclusion of the Doha round in the WTO with the development dimension at the core of its outcome. The comprehensive document noted that the three democracies shared similar views regarding the promotion of economic growth, eradication of poverty and protection of environment.

On global issues of concern, the leaders reiterated their commitment to the goal of complete elimination of the nuclear weapons and emphasised the necessity to start negotiations on a phased programme for the complete elimination of nuclear weapons in a comprehensive, non-discriminatory and verifiable manner within a specified framework of time. They also reaffirmed the inalienable right of all states to the peaceful application of nuclear energy, consistent with their international legal obligation. They agreed to explore avenues for cooperation in the peaceful uses of nuclear energy under appropriate IAEA safeguards. It was also agreed that international civilian nuclear cooperation could be enhanced in the future through mutually acceptable, forward-looking approaches amongst countries committed to non-proliferation and nuclear disarmament objectives.

The first summit concluded with the signing of five trilateral agreements in the areas of biofuels, information society, agriculture, maritime transport and trade facilitation. The MoU on establishing a Trilateral Task Team on Biofuels seeks to have a close cooperation among the three countries for augmenting biofuels production and consumption worldwide with a view to establishing a world market for biofuels, particularly for ethanol and biodiesel. In concrete terms, it proposes to establish a task team under the aegis of IBSA Working Group on Energy.

The framework for Cooperation on the Information Society seeks to promote cooperation on information society and development. It considers ICT as an essential tool for job creation, economic growth and poverty eradication. The fields of cooperation encompass digital inclusion, e-governance and ICT for development, with provision for establishing a joint committee.

An effort has been made to establish a framework to strengthen cooperation in the field of agriculture among the three countries and work jointly to ensure that the results of R&D are shared. The areas of cooperation are research and capacity building, agriculture trade, and rural development and poverty alleviation.

Establishing effective cooperation among the three countries in merchant shipping and other maritime transport related matters, is another important area for trilateral cooperation. Major areas include, cabotage and inland waterway transport in order to facilitate the movement of cargo and persons among the three countries.

The programme for Trade Facilitation for Standards, Technical Regulations and Conformity Assessment will help develop common procedures and work programmes to implement and establish a mechanism to exchange information and experiences on regulatory issues, organising sector specific seminars and taking steps towards establishing cooperation amongst the Indian, Brazilian and South African regulators and harmonising standards to facilitate trade.

IBSA global merchandise trade which was valued at US $ 300 billion in 2003, has spiralled upwards to reach the current figure of US $ 600 billion. The figure goes up to US $ 720 billion if exchanges in the service sector are included. Intra-IBSA trade increased by 50 per cent by 2004 and 30 per cent by 2005. A target of US$ 10 billion has been set for 2007, which appears eminently achievable given the current levels of trade and its growth rate. From another viewpoint, even if 10 per cent of IBSA's global trade could be achieved as intra-IBSA trade, the figure would be impressive. It is also worth mentioning that India-Mercosur and Mercosur-SACU PTAs are yet to be implemented. The process of widening and deepening these PTAs and moving towards a trilateral FTA arrangement involving India, Mercosur and SACU is also in its incipient stages. The positive spin-off from these multilateral arrangements is bound to have a beneficial impact on improving the intra-IBSA trade levels.

While the progress achieved so far by the IBSA Dialogue Forum is impressive by any standard, it would be prudent to avoid complacency. Connectivity both by air and surface routes needs to be quickly established and reinforced. The deeply entrenched mindset of perceived geographical barriers, which prevents the growth of both trade and tourism, needs to be overcome. Enhanced connectivity has become a pre-requisite to build upon the positive and optimistic atmospherics that surround the IBSA experiment now. Indeed, the challenge would be to operationalise the agreements in the field of maritime transportation and air services. The suggestion from the Brazilian Foreign Minister to invite airline and shipping companies from the three countries to business events in the future is one way of sustaining the momentum.

The possibilities of cooperation in the energy sector have already been identified by the three countries as having promising potential. The challenge of energy security is faced by the rapidly growing economies of all the three countries. The existing technological strengths built by the three countries, in the field of wind and solar energy by India, ethanol by Brazil and liquid fuel by South Africa can be pooled and expertise shared, in order to develop synergies.

While it is incumbent upon the governments to provide initial thrust, at this stage when IBSA is reaching the take-off stage, a considerable responsibility devolves upon the business community of the three countries to take the vision of mutually beneficial trilateral cooperative framework forward. The agreements signed provide the enabling environment for the business communities to come forward and take the task of building economic, commercial and technological links forward in right earnest. The apex business chambers of the three countries have already covered a lot of ground in this direction. It would be desirable to exploit the positive demonstration effect generated by large and high visibility projects, which can act as both focal and disseminating points for the launch of a wide range of joint ventures. The dynamics of the market would, sooner rather than later, ensure that impediments currently being experienced by way of inadequate transport links, banking and insurance infrastructure would be overcome.

The business communities of the three countries would be able to readily identify opportunities in each others countries. Some of the sectors which can benefit from technology transfer, trade, investment and setting up of joint ventures in the three rapidly growing economies of India, Brazil and South Africa include, agriculture, food processing, automotives, pharmaceuticals, retail, engineering, minerals and metals, information technology, petroleum, biotechnology and banking. This list is at best indicative of but at the same time it highlights the wide range of opportunities that are available. The business chambers of the three countries could work together in this joint spirit. Database on these business opportunities can be rapidly created, feasibility studies on the promising projects completed and research and consultancy, as well as handholding functions provided to the enterprising entrepreneurs.

While the governments of the three countries have made a beginning in terms of setting up institutional mechanisms to promote trilateral interaction, in the midst of all the action taking place among the three countries, it is easy to ignore that a matching institutional mechanism needs to be put in place domestically within each of the three countries to bring together the various ministries, departments and other institutions and entities which are working towards making the IBSA experiment a success. It is vital, therefore, to set up an interministerial steering committee which would derive its membership from not only the government but also the business community as well as cultural and other institutions so that an internal ongoing review can be conducted on a regular basis and corrective measures taken to keep the IBSA juggernaut on the right track. Such steering committees could meet at least once a quarter. Additional meetings could take place on need-based principle.

It is of utmost importance that the IBSA initiative catches the imagination of the entrepreneurs, industrialists and businessmen.

To that end, it may be advisable to consider launching trilateral trade events, to be held by rotation in each country. While these events would be multisectoral, it may also be necessary to urge the apex chambers of the three countries to earnestly consider sector-specific exhibitions, which could be mounted on a regular basis in the three countries. Mutual participation in the exhibitions needs to be supplemented by exchange of sector and product-specific delegations. Agriculture and food processing and mining and minerals are two promising areas. Annual business seminars to be held by rotation in each country, which could be addressed at the ministerial level, could keep trilateral business interaction on the fast track.

Important as it may seem, to strengthen ties amongst our business communities, it will eventually be robust people-to-people links which would provide the mainstay for the IBSA initiative. The popular mind needs to become enamoured of the IBSA story. Only with infusion of elements such as tourism and cultural exchanges can the IBSA charisma be built up. Some elements which come readily to mind include popularisation of yoga, exploiting the universal appeal of Indian cuisine, development of tourism packages encompassing the tourist attractions of all three countries, organising cultural festivals in each others countries and building a constituency of students whose university experience encompasses spending at least a semester in the other two countries.

A recent UNCTAD study has brought out both the positive impact of IBSA on the member countries and the inherent untapped potential. The paper emphasises that, if successful, IBSA will not only act as an excellent illustration of South-South cooperation but each IBSA country could act as a hub of growth and development in its respective continent. "The IBSA countries can reinforce each others strength by building on a market of 1.2 billion people, 1.8 trillion dollars of GDP and foreign trade of nearly 600 billion dollars. This would make the IBSA partnership of immense strategic value not only in terms of multilateral trade negotiations but also in terms of shaping the respective roles of IBSA member countries in global economic governance."

Not only commodities but also minerals and metals sector provide opportunities for trade and investment cross-fertilisation. The creation of synergies between petrochemicals and coal sectors of the three countries could be mutually beneficial. Collaboration in development and application of technology for exploration, extraction and processing of natural resources would be another such area. Even in the field of manufacturing, where a common refrain is that the three countries have competing economies, the UNCTAD study suggests that, at a disaggregated economic level, there is considerable scope for intra-industry as well as inter-industry trade and FDI. In the services sector, there is considerable potential, particularly in the area of maritime transport services, infrastructure and commercial services. The paper categorises energy as an 'interesting' area of collaboration where efforts could be focussed on oil shale extraction and processing, as well as clean coal technology. Brazil's expertise in deep-water oil extraction and ethanol could be availed of by the other two members.

The authors of the study conducted a comprehensive tariff liberalisation simulation whose conclusion clearly points to a significant trade potential amongst the IBSA countries. Trade creation gains are recorded in the twin scenarios of partial liberalisation of 50 per cent and full tariff liberalisation of 100 per cent. In the case of full liberalisation in tariffs, the trade can grow by more than 100 per cent. Even in the field of investment where all three IBSA countries are existing destinations for FDI, enhanced IBSA trade interaction is likely to lead to increased investment flows through intra-firm trade and global production networks. The UNCTAD study suggests that an IBSA-wide investment promotion package may add further impetus to the existing favourable investment climate, especially in the mineral, metals and mining sector.

It is instructive to go through the list of suggested measures and guiding principles for action formulated by the UNCTAD study. The establishment of air and maritime connectivity is considered to be important. These transport linkages could be created through an increased volume of trade and more balanced trade flows. The critical elements in the success of IBSA initiative, and in determining where available opportunities can be fully exploited and new opportunities created, would be a utilisation of synergies and value-added element of a truly tripartite arrangement. It would also be important to give a big push so that a critical mass of business exchanges and demonstrable winners can be created. The thrust areas could include non-conventional energy sources, iron and steel, high-tech areas as well as public health. The three economies would also need to undertake accelerated steps through more ambitious trade liberalisation and facilitation. Similarly, more liberal PTA/FTA approaches would help enhance the scope of trade and investment interaction. The UNCTAD paper opines that a 'variable geometry' approach needs to be followed so that areas amenable to trilateral cooperation can be pursued without waiting for creation of a minimum common denominator. Such an 'early harvest' strategy would help maintain momentum in the initial phase following which steps towards more ambitious economic integration can be taken.

If the pre-requisites enumerated above in the form of guiding principles of action can be put in place, India, Brazil and South Africa have all the necessary wherewithal to become 'natural' trade and investment partners. The success of the IBSA initiative would thereby contribute to the emergence of the 'new geography of international trade' and bolstering of South-South cooperation.

The IBSA initiative interconnected as it is by a common vision is rooted in current realities of a rapidly changing world order and the experience of the developing countries in the global multilateral arena as well as in the ambit of South-South cooperation. The initiative, therefore, is not only topical and pragmatic but also eminently practical.

22

India and Africa: a response to African institutionalisation in the 21st century

Gurjit Singh

The African Union

The creation of the African Union (AU) has been described as "an event of great magnitude in the institutional evolution of the Continent." The African heads of State and Government and the Organization of African Unity (OAU) through the Sirte Declaration of September 1999 called for the creation of an African Union to hasten the integration of the Continent so that it would be empowered for a bigger role in the emerging economy of globalisation. Concurrently, the Sirte Declaration sought a more direct approach to deal with the multifarious socioeconomic and political issues which Africa was faced with and which could be accentuated as Africa became a part of the global economy.

The OAU, of which the AU is a successor, was established in 1963 when decolonisation and the fight against apartheid were still the major issues facing Africa. The OAU's objectives were mainly to free the whole continent from the colonisers and from apartheid, to create unity among African countries, to enhance development cooperation and to secure the sovereignty and territorial integrity of its members, besides promoting international cooperation within the framework of the United Nations. As the first pan-African organisation which covered the whole continent, the OAU was an institution to which all African states could belong as soon as they emerged into nationhood much as they were welcomed into the Non-Aligned Movement (NAM) and the United Nations. Thus, the OAU was one of the initial steps to an international identity for emerging African countries.

The OAU provided the first avenue for all African countries to take a comprehensive view of matters which require coordination due to their perceived commonality of interests among all African countries. It also provided an avenue for coordination among African countries while dealing with other international fora and issues. The most sustained coordination, of course, came from the Committee for Liberation of Africa which sought true African unity in creating an international momentum to support the liberation and anti-apartheid movements in Africa.

Thus, during the period of OAU, African countries had already initiated a momentum for economic progress and social development which set the basis on which the African Union could be created. Some of these efforts between 1980 and 2001 took into account the changing realities of the world, particularly the freedom of the whole of Africa from colonisation and apartheid, the emerging opportunities in the globalising world and the changing economic and social requirements of African countries themselves. Some of the important developments were the Lagos Plan of Action (1980) which focussed on self-reliance in development and cooperation for that purpose among African countries; the African Priority Programme for Economic Recovery (APPER) (1985) which was an emergency response to deal with the development crisis in the 1980s which had enhanced the indebtedness of African countries and also required a collective action to deal with the problems of famine and drought which had become endemic in that period; this was followed in 1997 by the African Common Position on Africa's External Debt and in 1991 the Abuja Treaty which established the African Economic Community (AEC) which sought to create a six-phase programme for establishing the African common market using the route of regional economic communities (RECs). The Abuja Committee came into force in 1994.

Similarly, on the political side, the 1990 OAU Declaration on the political and socioeconomic situation in Africa and the fundamental changes taking place in the world emphasised the African resolve to seek its own destiny and directly face the challenges to peace, security and democracy; in the same year the Charter on Popular Participation showed the determination of the member states of the OAU to bring the individual in Africa at the core of development and decisionmaking related to it in an effort to seek participatory democracy. The Algiers Decision of 1999 on Unconstitutional Changes of Government and the Lome Declaration of 2000 on the Framework for an OAU Response to Unconstitutional Changes were important developments to deal with military coups and subversion of democracy and constitutional changes and a reaction to the times. These were supported by the 1981 adoption in Nairobi of the African Charter on Human and Peoples' Right and the Grand Bay Declaration and Plan of Action on Human Rights which ultimately led to the establishment of the African Human Rights Commission located in Banjul, the Gambia.

In trying to deal with peace and security, the OAU adopted in 1993, the Mechanism for Conflict Prevention, Management and Resolution which showed the determination of the African leaders to find solutions within Africa to conflicts and the lack of security and stability. This was supported by the Cairo Agenda for Action in 1995 and the 2000 Solemn Declaration of the Conference on Security, Stability, Development and Cooperation which held establishment of democracy and good governance in Africa as basic principles of the OAU.

All these efforts led to the Constitutive Act of the African Union which was adopted in 2000 at the Lome Summit and the New Partnership for Africa's Development (NEPAD) adopted as a programme of the African Union at the Lusaka Summit in 2001.

Emergence of the African Union

The OAU initiative mentioned above created a path for the emergence of the African Union. In July 1999, the OAU Assembly decided to hasten the process for economic and political integration in Africa and over the next four annual summits the African Union was formally created. At the 1999 Extraordinary Session of the OAU in Sirte, it was decided to establish the African Union and at the Lome Summit in 2000, the Constitutive Act of the Union was adopted. At the Lusaka Summit (2001) a clear procedure for implementing the African Union was adopted and at the Durban Summit (2002) the African Union was formally launched and the first assembly of the Heads of State and Government was convened. Due to these efforts between 1999 and 2001, the AU was born as Africa's principal institution for the promotion of accelerated socioeconomic integration of the Continent which would lead to greater unity and solidarity between African countries and peoples.

The Vision of the AU:

- The AU is Africa's premier institution and principal organisation for the promotion of accelerated socioeconomic integration of the continent, which will lead to greater unity and solidarity between African countries and peoples.

- The AU is based on the common vision of a united and strong Africa and on the need to build a partnership between governments and all segments of civil society, in particular women, youth and the private sector, in order to strengthen solidarity and cohesion amongst the peoples of Africa.

- As a continental organisation, it focusses on the promotion of peace, security and stability on the continent as a prerequisite for the implementation of the development and integration agenda of the Union.

The African Union has an assembly of the Heads of State/ Government and is the supreme organ of the Union. The Executive Council is a ministerial body responsible to the Union and a Commission headed by the Chairperson and nine other elected commissioners including the Deputy Chairperson. The Secretariat is broadly modelled on the Commission of the European Union. There is also a Permanent Representatives Committee, a Peace and

Security Council, a Pan-African Parliament and Economic, Social and Cultural Council, a Court of Justice and the specialised technical committees. Principal financial institutions include, the African Central Bank, the African Monetary Fund and the African Investment Bank. Several of these institutions have not yet fully emerged or protocols for their establishment have not yet been created though substantial progress has been made. The African Union Commission is, however, fully in place with a chairperson, a deputy chairperson, eight commissioners and staff members. The portfolios of the Commission have a direct relevance to the growing engagement of India and the potential that such a collaboration has in the future. These are:

1. Peace and Security (conflict prevention, management and resolution, and combating terrorism).

2. Political Affairs (human rights, democracy, good governance, electoral institutions, civil society organisations, humanitarian affairs, refugees, returnees and internally displaced persons).

3. Infrastructure and Energy (energy, transport, communications, infrastructure and tourism).

4. Social Affairs (health, children, drug control, population, migration, labour and employment, sports and culture).

5. Human Resources, Science and Technology (education, information technology communication, youth, human resources, science and technology).

6. Trade and Industry (trade, industry, customs and immigration matters).

7. Rural Economy and Agriculture (rural economy, agriculture and food security, livestock, environment, water and natural resources and desertification).

8. Economic Affairs (economic integration, monetary affairs, private sector development, investment and resource mobilisation).

The African Union has a rotational head who is the Head of State/Government of a member state of the Union broadly conforming to a regional rotational policy. President Thabo Mbeki of South Africa who was the host of the Durban Summit where the AU was formally launched in 2002, was the first President followed by President Joaquim Alberto Chissano of Mozambique who was the host of the second Summit in 2003. He was succeeded by President Olusegun Obasanjo, of the Federal Republic of Nigeria till 2006. Since then, however, the presidency of the African Union has not been co-terminus with a host and since 2005 it has been decided to have two summits every year instead of one. Normally the January Summit is held at the headquarters of the Union in Addis Ababa, Ethiopia while the mid-year Summit in June/July is rotated among select hosts. The current President of the African Union is President Denis Sassou-Nguesso of the Republic of Congo which has not hosted the summit and represents Central Africa.

NEPAD

The NEPAD strategic framework emerged from the work of five Heads of State of Algeria, Egypt, Nigeria, Senegal and South Africa who were tasked by the OAU to create an integrated socioeconomic development framework for Africa and this was formally adopted in July 2001. NEPAD was designed to focus on the immediate challenges facing Africa including the increasing levels of poverty, the challenge of development and the marginalisation of Africa from a globalising world. The NEPAD leadership was to create a new matrix that could contribute to the renewal of Africa and take into account larger concerns which their trade and development partners had and focus on them to generate a higher degree of confidence and consequently, a more focussed approach to governance and development. The objectives and principles of NEPAD were broadly the same as for the African Union and NEPAD ultimately became an action plan of the African Union. Coordination efforts for NEPAD and the AU Commission continue and the objective is to firmly integrate NEPAD's plans within the AU's working environment.

Regional Economic Communities (RECs)

The AU also has to contend with a large number of regional economic communities (RECs) in Africa which predate the formation of the AU and which often have a multiplicity of membership i.e. some countries belong to more than one regional economic community. While the RECs can be considered as building blocks towards an African economic community under the African Union, in reality many of them work independently and tap the same sources of support that the AU seeks to obtain from donor partners. An intensive effort by the African Union Commission and the Economic Commission for Africa to integrate the regional economic communities is underway. The theme of the July 2006 Banjul Summit of the African Union was "Harmonisation with the RECs." If this is consolidated it will lead to greater coordination and liberate some funding which is being duplicated as well as allow for more clearer harmonisation of regional objectives and creation of regional projects.

The AU at present recognises eight Regional Economic Communities in Africa and these are the: Common Market for Eastern and Southern Africa (COMESA); Southern Africa Development Community (SADC); Economic Community of West African States (ECOWAS); Intergovernmental Authority for Development (IGAD); Economic Community for Central African States (ECCAS), Arab Maghreb Union (UMA); Community of Sahelo-Saharan States (CEN-SAD); and East Africa Community (EAC).

India's engagement with some of these RECs has been consistent. India has MoUs with SADC, EAC and COMESA and discussions with ECOWAS, ECCAS and IGAD are underway. These MoUs have focussed on supporting capacity building within these organisations and to support their objectives and seek enhance India's profile with them and seek political and economic engagement as it emerges. The first Ministerial meeting with SADC took place in Namibia in April 2006 and with ECOWAS in the same period in New Delhi. A similar engagement with other RECs is contemplated. With those

RECs with which India has lower level of interaction efforts to engage them are being expedited. The Indian Ambassadors located at the headquarters of the RECs are normally appointed as India's representative to the respective REC.

Africa development bank group

India joined the Africa Development fund on 6 May, 1982 and the Africa Development Bank Group on 6 December, 1983. It has over 4800 shares in the AfDB with a voting power of nearly 0.25 per cent. A trust fund was placed with the African Development Bank in July 1998, under which India financed 24 studies and projects. In addition, the Exim Bank of India established an African Project Development facility and an African Management Services Company in association with the International Finance Corporation to promote private sector development in Africa. The Indian membership of the African Development Bank has opened opportunities for Indian companies in Bank sponsored infrastructure development projects in Africa and the Trust Fund and the Exim Bank's facilities have started feasibility studies to a small extent. A much larger interface with the Bank and its various windows is required from the Indian side including a close association with its closer coordination with the African Union and the Economic Commission for Africa.

Current issues facing the African Union

The African Union can be described as a fledgling body seeking to find its feet and is trying to come to terms with the problems faced by its member states. At the same time, it has to 'compete' with existing bodies at the regional and national level and the UN agencies and donor agencies which deal particularly with the same issues concerning the continent. Among the many challenges which face the African Union are healthcare and epidemics particularly tuberculosis, malaria and HIV/AIDS which are rampant in Africa. Similarly, it has to confront socioeconomic issues dealing with development, poverty alleviation, education and the environment as well as food security, agricultural development and the prevention of desertification among others. It still has to contend with threats to democracy in individual countries, the civil wars which have afflicted many countries in the Continent including Burundi, DR Congo, Somalia and others and the unsettled decolonisation of Western Sahara whose membership of the African Union under the nomenclature of the Sahrawi Arab Democratic Republic led to the withdrawal of Morocco from the African Union. Thus the challenges which the African continent faces are many and Africa's institutions are not always capable of dealing with these problems and require support from international organisations and donor agencies and countries but due to the lack of firm institutions such assistance is often fragmented and duplicated. One of the challenges of the African Union is, therefore, to try and provide means for coordinating efforts related to development and the maintenance of peace and security and good governance by working with support organisations and regional institutions already on the ground and harmonise and coordinate their objective and functions. This task is neither easy to accept nor to do.

Similarly, while confronting economic issues the African Union has to deal with the fact that Africa as a whole has a GDP of US $ 500 billion and a combined total debt of US $ 200 billion. African countries have barely 2 per cent of the world international trade mainly focussing on commodities and actually provide a large market for the bigger trading countries of the world. The African Economic Community which was envisaged by the AU has to coordinate with several regional bodies. Though the African Union presently recognises 8 RECs there are at least 14 intergovernmental organisations focussing on regional issues and also have several treaties and agreements governing the relationship among their member states. According to the *Assessing Regional Integration in Africa* prepared jointly by the Economic Commission for Africa and the African Union in 2006, out of the 53 member states of the African Union, 26 belong to 2 of the 14 intergovernmental regional organisations, 20 belong to 3 and one country even belongs to 4 regional bodies! No doubt, this proliferation of groups and membership presents its own set of challenges and accentuates the problems of multiplication and duplication of efforts and resources.

India's engagement with the African Union

The Indian response to the changing international environment since the end of the Cold War and the emergence of new countries as well as responding to the challenges and opportunities emerging from India's own economic liberalisation, opened up a wide variety of opportunities across the globe. Interestingly, the end of the Cold War also saw changes occurring within Africa and the movement from the OAU to the AU also took place in the years thereafter. Thus, India and Africa were changing almost at the same time. The new challenges and the response to them including the emergence of new institutions like AU saw a renewed systemic response from India.

Emerging from such engagements was the desire to have a steadfast and incremental relationship transcending the excellent relationship that India enjoyed bilaterally with most African countries. The opportunity came through the visit by President A.P.J. Abdul Kalam to Africa in 2004 when, in an address to the Pan-African Parliament in South Africa, he presented the vision of a Pan-African e-Network.

Pan-African e-Network Project

The proposal for establishing the Pan-African e-Network Project is being implemented in conjunction with the African Union. The offer was examined by the African Union in 2005 and the Advisory Committee to the Chairperson concluded that the project would suit the requirements of Africa in fulfilling the Millennium Development Goals.

The project would use Indian expertise in information technology to bring benefits for healthcare and higher education in Africa, including in remote areas. The network will be connected by a satellite/fibre optical network for tele-medicine, tele-education and VVIP interface. The current project cost is about US $ 100 million, which will be given as a grant by the Government of India. It consists of 5 regional universities, 5 regional super specialty hospitals, 53 learning centres and 53 hospitals in all countries of Africa. These will be linked to 6 universities and 6 super specialty hospitals in India. Each country is required to sign an agreement with the Indian implementing agency, the Telecommunication Consultants India Limited (TCIL).

Based on these consultations, a set of draft agreements, which regional institutions and national implementation authorities are to sign with the Indian side, have been created and circulated in the working languages of the African Union Commission. A decision has been taken to host the hub for the project in Senegal. Fourteen countries have so far signed bilateral agreements from the target of 15 in the initial period of the programme. The bids of Ibadan Hospital in Nigeria and Makerere University in Uganda for hosting regional centres have been approved for consideration. Bids from other regions for hospitals and learning centres are to be obtained.

Under this project, the AU has disseminated information and draft agreements, set up the criteria for selecting regional institutions and decided on the location of the hub. The remainder of the implementation would be undertaken bilaterally with national governments and implementing agencies under the overall umbrella of the AU. The AU-India Steering Committee would continue to provide experience sharing as the project is implemented. It would also look at issues of sustainability of the project, particularly after the grant period is over and provide guidance to countries on implementation and choice of subjects for tele-education and areas of specialist consultation for tele-medicine.

In the future it is expected that closer harmonisation of pharmaceutical pharmacopeias, greater entry of Indian drugs and medicines, closer consultation between India and African doctors and consultants would emerge from the tele-medicine segment of this Project. Continuing medical education would be a significant contribution through the Pan-African e-Network Project at the regional level where five regional super specialty hospitals would come into contact with India's super specialty hospitals. Similarly, where tele-education is concerned, a much wider range of Indian courses from India's elite universities would be available to the African students. This would significantly augment the nearly 15,000 African students who study in India and bring a much larger number of students into the ambit of India's educational experience. This has a significant impact which the general African respect for India's educational prowess and human resource development would welcome. It would create a larger linkage across the Indian Ocean and provide a strong impetus to HRD programmes in Africa.

At present the Indian approach is to further diversify relations with the African Union on a functional basis so that closer interaction through them will allow for more institutional linkages to be established with African partners in such fields. It would also allow India to set a larger role commensurate with its growing socio-economic profile in Africa, in particular. For this, a concerted effort to deal with some of the selected divisions of the African Union is underway.

Trade, industry and investment

The Commissioner for Trade and Industry of the African Union has been sensitised to various developments which bilaterally occur between India and African countries. The true realty is that the engagement that India has bilaterally with many African countries is not entirely reflected in its relationship with the Trade and Industry Division of the African Union mainly because at the macro level Africa mainly is engaged in seeking preferential facilities for its trade. The American Growth and Opportunities Act, the Cotonou Agreement with the European Union and the preferential access granted by China have dominated their agenda. Under consistent engagement the African Union established a task force to look for enhanced partnerships with its 'new partners' like India, China and Brazil. This task force was established in September 2006 and met with the Indian Representative to the African Union. The occasion was one to sensitise the task force of the AU Commission about India's longstanding and deep rooted relationship with Africa and to create a common focus for enhancing that relationship to suit the Pan-African goals which the African Union Commission and its task force were seeking to enlarge. The task force was also invited to the India-Africa Project Partnership Conclave in New Delhi in October 2006.

Trade

India-Africa bilateral trade has risen from $ 967 million in 1991 to $ 9.14 billion in 2005. India's exports to Africa in the same period have increased from $ 394 million to $ 5.4 billion and account for nearly 7 per cent of India's export basket. It is significant to note that with Africa, there is a near balance of trade though this may not be true for every country or region. It is also significant that the impact of growing liberalisation in India has allowed Indian companies to be more competitive and challenge traditional economic partners of African countries. There is also a greater liberalisation accorded to Indian companies to invest overseas and the surge of Indian investment in selected African countries is very visible.

The growing openness of the Indian market and demand for some products, particularly natural resources and agricultural products in India is growing. This allows African countries to tap the Indian market by assuaging the demand for particular products in India. Some countries in Africa run a trade surplus with India by tapping such demand. These include Benin, Cote d'Ivoire, Gabon, Guinea Bissau, Morocco, Senegal, South Africa, Tunisia and Zimbabwe. For instance, in Senegal, there is an Indian investment in a joint venture to produce phosphoric acid from the large deposits of phosphorus in Senegal. The exports from that joint venture to India actually create a trade surplus for Senegal in its trade with India. This example can be emulated by other countries having significant resources which are in demand in India. Where agricultural products are concerned, several countries export such a large amount of cashew-nuts to India that they run a trade surplus with India. Africa is a producer of agricultural products, particularly in horticulture and floriculture but most of these have European destinations in mind and are encouraged by the leverage accorded to them by the Cotonou Agreement. The same enthusiasm can be utilised to turn production towards Indian demands to enhance African exports to India since many of the current agriculture exports from Africa actually compete with Indian exports, e.g. coffee, tea, flowers and the like.

Trade policy in the African context is often governed by available concessions and the directions of African exports often follow such facilities. At the Hong Kong meeting, to take forward the Doha Development Round of the WTO one of the suggestions had been for developed countries to provide greater facilities for LDCs. India is considering such steps keeping in view its own position in the WTO and the involvement of a large number of its population in agriculture. India has provided special access facilities to the LDCs under SAFTA and the concept of providing similar facilities to other LDCs is feasible in the future.

At the same time, there is an undoubted increase in India's exports to Africa as the enhancement of standards and quality, improvement of delivery schedules and the acceptance in Africa of the cost effectiveness of Indian imports has been established. This is particularly true of manufactured products but equally true in other sectors. Thus, pharmaceuticals, chemicals and dyes, engineering products, motor vehicles and rubber and plastic products have acquired a good hold in the African markets. At the same time, sugar, wheat, rice and other basic products also find a market. The Focus Africa Programme of the Ministry of Commerce launched in 2002, provided a greater impetus to focussed trade promotion and the greater participation of Indian companies in African trade fairs has also contributed immensely to brand recognition and enhancement of Indian exports.

Lines of Credit

Many Indian initiatives to enhance economic cooperation with Africa have been through the extension of lines of credit at the bilateral, regional and Pan-African level. India is a member of the African Development Bank and the Afri-EXIM Bank through which an Indian Trust Fund, and an Indian line of credit, respectively operates to achieve developmental goals in Africa. At the present time, nearly $ 2 billion in Indian lines of credit is operating in Africa either through bilateral, regional or Pan-African institutions. At the regional level, India has lines of credit available with the East Africa Development Bank, the PTA Bank for the COMESA region,

BOAD for the West Africa region and most recently, an LOC of $ 250 million to the ECOWAS Development Bank. In order to cover the gap which India has traditionally had with some West African countries, a TEAM-9 approach was created under which US $ 500 million was committed for project partnerships with countries in Central and West Africa. Similarly, there has been a line of credit of US $ 200 million to assist NEPAD under which developmental projects in Angola, Senegal, Mali, the Gambia and the DRC have been approved. At the bilateral level, lines of credit have been extended to Kenya, Tanzania, Mozambique, Zambia, Namibia, Ethiopia and others. In fact, in 2006 Exim Bank, which is the main functionary for Indian lines of credit in Africa, is running 46 lines of credit with various countries and institutions in Africa. Many of these bilateral lines were facilitated by the writing off of the debt owed by several African countries under the HIPC initiative which led to the restructuring of commercial debt in 2003 amounting to $ 20 million. This reflected India's wish to engage with Africa in a new matrix of cooperation.

The lines of credit which have been extended to Africa had a twin impact. First, it helped to strengthen private sector and small and medium enterprises through transfers of technology as well as management and entrepreneurship. This has contributed to the development of the private sector, to the development of entrepreneurship and to the development of employment opportunities in several African countries. Secondly, lines of credit have focussed on project partnerships under which larger projects have been financed and have contributed to the development goals established by several African countries. These have included projects in telecommunications, railways, transport, power and related sectors.

Infrastructure consortium for Africa

As India engages with the African Union indicating its desire to have a wider reach, the opportunities under NEPAD particularly in regional projects which are coordinated by the Infrastructure Consortium for Africa need to be carefully considered. The growing reach of Indian companies, the availability of Indian finance to the tune of approximately $ 1 billion per annum, the ability of the Indian private sector to invest overseas and the growing emphasis on infrastructure development in Africa provide an ambience in which Indian policy needs to respond appropriately. The number of regional projects under the NEPAD umbrella which the Infrastructure Consortium for Africa for instance deals with include regional river basin projects which are multipurpose projects including dams, water resources, irrigation, power generation and attendant transmission substations and distribution segments. Often feasibility studies are conducted by international donor agencies or donor partners. But the projects are often not fully funded. When the projects receive full financing, Indian companies are getting the low end of the project, e.g. transmission lines and the like. In order for Indian companies to get opportunities at a larger level India's approach should be to join with other partners to partially fund segments of regional projects where Indian companies have core competence. Through this, Indian companies would obtain a larger participation in bigger projects in Africa which are on the anvil. Their participation would also open a larger amount of sub-contracting work. Thus, alternating our approach to focus LOCs from bilateral projects to regional projects is envisaged.

Infrastructure

Connected to this has been the greater entry of Indian companies both public and private into Africa. Under the greater understanding achieved by the financing of projects under lines of credit, the ability of Indian companies to provide competent services under internationally funded projects gave them a confidence which has led to a surge of investment of Indian companies in African countries. In Sudan, India has invested in the energy sector to the tune of US $ 1.5 billion while in Ethiopia itself, the growing private sector opportunities have seen more than 180 Indian companies invest in Ethiopia, mainly in the small and medium enterprises and floriculture. The greater freedom accorded to the Indian private sector under the liberal economic norms in India allows Indian companies to reach out and seek new economic opportunities and this brings them to Africa in good measure. Thus, the economic engagement of India with Africa through the terms of lines of credit and investment by private and public sector companies have been important elements in creating a new paradigm of economic cooperation.

The Infrastructure Consortium for Africa at its meeting in 2006 in Addis Ababa, for the first time invited India and a few other partners. India responded to this initiative and established a close relationship with its main participants including the African Development Bank. The representative of the ICA at the Bank was invited to participate in the Conclave in New Delhi, in October 2006 and present the projects to attract Indian participation.

Also, there is a visible transition from bilateral lines of credit to fairly large regional lines as in the case of TEAM-9 and the $ 250 million allocated to the ECOWAS Development Bank. Further, it is to be noted that smaller international lines given to regional institutions like BOAD for West Africa, the PTA Bank for COMESA and the East Africa Development Bank have either focussed on small industry projects or not been utilised. This is often because some of these institutions do not have the capacities to evaluate projects brought to them. In such cases, the availability of projects with feasibility studies established as under the NEPAD/Infrastructure Consortium approach could be a solution. Capacity building with the African financial institutions and a clearer willingness to fund feasibility studies is now more necessary than ever.

Thus, the focus of our lines of credit should clearly shift to a project-linked approach preferably with a large ambit and include in it a regional focus. This will have the benefit of bringing the full range of Indian technology and services in the play, make us participate in large projects possibly with other partners and shift from a trade promotion to a project formulation approach. Similarly, there is also a requirement to move from the generic announcement of lines of credit to a focussed project-linked approach. Lines of credit should be given ideally in situations where feasibility studies have been carried out, project profiles exist and funding requirements for either the entire project or parts of it can be met through an Indian LOC. The advantage of this would be that the annual cap of above $ 1 million which the Finance Ministry places on lending under the LOC scheme can be better utilised if linked to ready projects rather than to generic announcements under which projects often take several years to fructify. The actual effect of such LOCs under these circumstances would be felt more immediately and consistently.

Investment

As a conscious policy, India would like to take the path from trade to investment in its relationship with African countries. In 2002, the Focus Africa programme was used to highlight greater opportunities which Indian companies could tap in Africa and support was granted to Indian commercial institutions who would study such opportunities and enhance their contacts. The programme was initially focussed on eight African countries but the surge of demand from other African countries forces MEA and MOC to convert the programme into an all African one indicating how strong the demand for Indian goods and services had become all over Africa. Keeping this experience in mind, and the experience of the lines of credit extended to African financial institutions, it was decided to launch the India-Africa Project Partnership in which the lead was taken by the Confederation of Indian Industry (CII) and the EXIM Bank of India and supported by the Ministries of External Affairs and Commerce & Industry. The first of these partnerships was in 2005, under the objective of "Expanding Horizons" and in which 160 delegates from 32 African countries participated in a Conclave held in November 2005. Over 70 projects estimated to cost about $ 5 billion were discussed at the Conclave and efforts are underway to bring them to the formulation and implementation stage. The second Conclave in 2006 focussed on "India: A Partner of Choice". Prior to this, there were three regional conclaves in Africa—in Lusaka, Addis Ababa and Accra in April-May 2006, where Indian companies travelled to take forward this project partnership and establish first-hand contacts with African companies in the respective regions. Before the main conclave, similar conclaves were held in major Indian cities like Mumbai, Kolkata, Hyderabad and Pune to sensitise a large number of Indian companies on the emerging opportunities in Africa and bring the results of the regional conclaves to them. The major thrust of these conclaves would be to enhance the possibility for Indian participation in African projects through a public-private partnership and to enhance the impact of India's capacity building and resource mobilisation initiatives to seek greater avenues of direct finance through the use of public and private banks and new financial instruments.

Indian companies have shown immense initiative and strength in bidding for internationally financed projects in several African countries. The rate of success has differed mainly due to local conditions and the scale of projects. In Ethiopia, for instance, in the last few years Indian companies have secured projects worth nearly $ 500 million. These projects have included power transmission lines, rural electrification, electricity substations, telecommunication equipment supply, road construction and consulting and the like. The sources of funding include, the World Bank, the Africa Development Bank, the European Union and other bilateral donors and several Arab funds. This allow Indian companies to make a contribution to the development of local infrastructure at a cost lower than what many of these countries can get from their traditional economic partners. The cost effectiveness and efficiency of Indian companies have been established and allows them to use this as a springboard for projects with a larger spread. Of course, this would require a coordinated approach among Indian companies to work together which is often a difficult thing for them to do.

Indian investment and technology can jointly be tapped for the services sector which can move beyond trade and manufacturing sector investment. For instance, telecommunications, banking, insurance and the like are areas where Indian companies can provide technology and investment. At present, there are 22 Indian banking operations in Africa which include 15 branches and 4 subsidiaries. Indian investment in insurance companies is also useful as it brings about India's successful experience in this sector into joint venture companies. Investments in tourism, hospitals, the transport sector and in education and training are other areas which could be positively considered particularly in a regional and pan-African context.

Among the core strengths of India which can be transferred into close collaboration with African institutions is our financial services sector which could include banking, insurance, stock exchanges, credit rating agencies and commodities exchanges. Indian banks have made a foray into Africa but largely into areas with large NRI/PIO presence. Indian banks have got sufficient experience and clout to move beyond into areas where Indian companies are acquiring assets and opportunities in African countries. Their activities can be threefold: to enhance corresponding relationships with local banks, entry into management contracts with banks and to have joint ventures. An independent assessment by Indian banks of African banks in countries with which India has a strong economic partnership can be assisted by the African Union Commission and should be undertaken as this would allow Indian banks to provide credits to banks in African countries in support of the Indo-African economic partnership. There is little reason for the economic partnership to flourish and Indian banks and insurance companies not taking part in this exercise.

Similarly, the growing number of stock exchanges in Africa reflects local conditions and differences in monetary policy within Africa. With the Economic Division of the African Union Commission, discussions have been held on sharing the Indian experience of the national stock exchanges which provides a multi-floor trading in contrast to the 28 stock exchanges in India. The creation of an African stock exchange is a subject on which India and the African Union Commission can work together. Similarly, the success of the commodities exchanges in India have been studied for setting up a pan-African commodities exchange. This is perhaps even more important than a stock exchange, as commodities are among the largest segment of Africa's trade and any systematic organisation of that can enlarge opportunities by spacing out supply orders and securing a clearer payment system that would greatly assist the farmers and traders in commodities in Africa. Ethiopia has been studying the MCX in Mumbai and a group of South African entrepreneurs along with partners in Botswana have been working on the possibility of a pan-African commodities exchange with the support of the African Union Commission. India will willingly come forward to support this transfer of an IT-linked project into the trade and industry development of Africa.

Similarly, the expertise gathered by the Exim Bank of India can be shared with select countries preferably on a regional basis to create credit—rating agencies and credit—risk management systems. This would require coordination with central banks and the Exim Bank's close relationship over a period of time with African Development Bank will come into use in such an endeavour.

Science and technology

Besides the Pan-African e-Network Project and cooperation in trade and industry, the Science & Technology Division of the African Union Commission has been engaged with the Indian Mission to the AU in Addis Ababa. The AU Commissioner for S&T has been invited for a study visit to India in November 2006 at which time, she is expected to interact with Indian institutions and to explore possibilities of enhanced cooperation with India. The theme of the AU Summit to be held in Addis Ababa in January 2007, is "Science, Technology and Research for African Development" and India has been invited to participate in the Congress of African Scientists and Policy Makers to be held in Alexandria (Egypt) from 26-28 October 2006. The working groups of this Conference would produce recommendations for the 2007 Summit. India has been requested to make a presentation on "Harmonizing Science & Technology for Socioeconomic Development". The other countries are China, Brazil and Finland. A senior officer from India is expected to attend. Given India's strength in science and technology as a basis for economic progress, there is a strong desire within the African Union

Commission to have institutional links with the Indian scientific establishment. To this end, we need, to invigorate our relationship on an institutional basis with the AUC by using a variety of partners.

Defence

Among the various aspects of engagement with the African Union Commission, their requirement for training and capacity building of their nascent standby brigades, which were to be the building blocks of their peacekeeping activities are being discussed.

At the request of the AU Commission, initial discussions on their structures to be developed and capabilities to be enhanced is to be undertaken between an Indian military delegation and the peace and security division of the AU Commission. The aim is to see how the Indian experience can be shared with the AU's efforts to enhance its own capacities for peacekeeping operations in Africa.

Another aspect is the maintenance of peace and security which unfortunately continues to have an important role in the African continent. The scourge of war needs to be removed from our midst and open space for political activity and dialogue needs to be created. There have been several initiatives within Africa itself and the African Union Commission also has spent a lot of time on peace and security. India's position on this has been to support processes where conflict can be ended, peace maintained and space created for political dialogue. Thus, Indian Peacekeeping Forces under the United Nations have acquired a significant role in several African conflicts and I believe that they have been successful in meeting the objectives set for them. The earliest Indian peacekeeping Forces were involved in the Democratic Republic of Congo during the Katanga/Shaba secession and have since played a role in many other African countries. Currently, Indian troops are deployed under the UN flag under UNMEE in Ethiopia and Eritrea; in Sudan and in the eastern part of Democratic Republic of Congo. During the Second AU Summit in Mozambique, the Indian Navy had provided security cover in the Indian Ocean as a symbol of our closeness and support to Africa. Besides this, India has also sent military training teams to countries in peace time to support the professionalisation of military institutions and we have had such training teams in Namibia, in Lesotho, in Tanzania, in Rwanda, in Zambia and Ethiopia at varying times.

Among the activities of the African Union Commission, the Peace and Security Department attracts the maximum attention from its traditional partners and the maximum financial support. This is besides the support provided for operations like in Darfur for the African peacekeeping forces. The main requirements of the Peace and Security Department are to support missions as and when they come up, to create a structure which has been outlined by the creation of five standby brigades in each region which would be available for deployment as and when a crisis emerges. These standby brigades require a common training, logistical arrangements, supply lines and equipment. The EU and other European partners are extremely focussed on this approach and traditionally the UK had led the donor partners in formulating their response to the requirements of the Peace and Security Department. India has a strong tradition of peacekeeping in Africa and its training facilities in India can be well utilised to work with the African Union Commission to create capacities in their structures which would provide harmony in training, logistics and related development activity which will make the standby brigades more effective. Our constant engagement with the African Union Commission in this regard is an objective which could have more far-reaching impact than envisaged in the initial stages.

Capacity building

Capacity building is one of the most significant contributions that India has made to Africa over a period of time. Capacity building has basically been undertaken in three dimensions between India and Africa. First, through the medium of higher education where nearly 15,000 students from Africa study in India either through bilateral scholarships, government sponsorships or on a self-financing basis. Secondly, the exceedingly successful ITEC

Programme which provides a variety of courses to most countries in Africa and thirdly, by the support of Indian investors and those implementing internationally financed projects in Africa which often have a training component inbuilt in them.

India's own success in human resource development has encouraged African students to look at India as an alternative source for education. Under the Indian Technical and Economic Cooperation programme, more than 1000 people from Sub-Saharan Africa received training annually in India and since 1964, India has spent more than US $ 1 billion for such assistance including training, deputation of experts and implementation of projects in African countries. Besides this, many African students go to India either on scholarship or a much larger number on self-financing basis and today, we see nearly 15,000 students from Africa studying in India while Indian professors, doctors, engineers, accountants and other experts are present in several African countries. The entry of private sector IT training companies from India into franchise arrangements in African countries and contributing to the growth of IT-related HRD is a new phenomenon which helps African countries generate trained manpower to grasp global opportunities. Similarly, under the ITEC programme, India has created capacity building institutions in several African countries which are providing regional benefits. The Entrepreneurship, Development and Training Centre in Senegal, IT Training Centre in Ghana, and Plastic Technology Training Centre in Namibia, are some such examples under which training facilities have been created for local needs and have slowly been expanded to cover the development of regional HRD capacities. We believe through these functional contributions, India's capacity-building projects would help to create backward integration with growing industrialisation in many of these countries.

In 2005, India became the first Asian country to be a full member of the African Capacity Building Foundation (ACBF) with a contribution of US $ 1 million to the ACBF mission to building capacity for sustainable development and poverty alleviation in Africa. India has also offered capacity-building support to the African

Union and to regional economic communities with several of whom we have MoUs for cooperation.

India has allocated 10 slots in the year 2006-07 for the Indian Technical and Economic Cooperation (ITEC) programme to the AU Commission personnel. The Commission has already nominated two candidates to attend courses in information technology and more nominations are expected in due course. A greater thrust to supporting capacity building within pan-Africa and regional institutions in Africa and to conducting courses under their ambit would be a useful strategy.

The focus of the ITEC programme has also to be altered, keeping in view the new opportunities that engagement with pan-African and regional organisations in Africa offers. The ITEC has been a successful programme which requires modulation to meet the new requirements. While it has created a large number of courses in India with which African technocrats can be engaged and contribute to human resource development and capacity building, it has to be evaluated afresh. Sometimes institutions in India tend to become captives of a situation and innovative thinking then dissipates.

Keeping in view our willingness to engage with regional projects, lines of credit which are functionally oriented and a thrust on private sector investment we should offer specialised training courses to support ventures on the above lines. For instance, if India is providing a line of credit for a particular sector or a regional project we should bring in an ITEC support of specialised courses in those areas to support capacity building linked to such projects. For instance, if a river basin project is being undertaken there are several specialised courses which could be undertaken to support the project implementation around it. Such courses should have 10 to 15 participants from the participating countries and be specially tailored to that requirement. Similarly, private sector investment projects in particular areas can also be supported by ITEC without making a differentiation between public and private sector engagement. For instance, if private sector investment in floriculture and horticulture is picking up in a particular region of Africa we should offer to support training and capacity building in that sector under ITEC as that will enhance the scope of Indian investment. Thus, a greater linkage of the ITEC training programme with specific objectives set through functional engagement of investment, lines of credit and contracts won under international financing should be focussed. Good beginnings have been made through a training programme carried out with COMESA on drug controllers in COMESA countries in India, in 2005 and earlier a programme for training chief executives of chambers of commerce in selected African countries. More of these kind of programmes need to be done so that the functional advantages of such training can be of direct benefit to areas where India has an abiding relationship with African countries.

Similarly, the ITEC programme needs to become more flexible and functional with regard to implementation of projects overseas on a grand basis which could create support systems for further projects under LOCs or private sector investment. At present the implementation problems of a project decided on are immense and the gestation period of projects to be undertaken under ITEC are long and cumbersome.

In reality, given the ambit which the ITEC programme covers and the opportunities which the growing institutionalisation in Africa, for instance, offers certainly calls for the upgradation of several divisions of MEA into a development cooperation agency which could take holistic views of ideas mentioned in this chapter and provide a coordinated approach for effective implementation.

Framework for cooperation with the African Union for an India-Africa partnership

Since 2003, India and the African Union have been discussing from time to time the possibility of establishing an India-Africa Forum to engage in more substantive discussions and bring an institutional basis to the strong relationship that India has with African countries bilaterally. Such an approach would also recognise India's willingness to deal with Africa on a pan-African institutional basis and bring in its ambit, its strong relationship with the African Development Bank, the Economic Commission for Africa and link it to a coordinated approach with the African Union. In 2004, India presented a draft *Vision Document* to the African Union which did not elicit much response possibly because of the depth and diversity of the relationship with it. The African Union is finding it much easier to deal with more nascent arrangements with South America and the Republic of Korea and to go along with existing institutional arrangement which China had established (the China-Africa Forum) and Japan (the Tokyo International Conference for African Development—TICAD) which meet periodically but had not had an effective follow-up mechanism. The France-Africa Summit, an expansion of the Francophone Summit, meets periodically and is guided by France while the Africa-Europe Summit has not succeeded after the first one mainly due to problems on how to deal with regimes in Africa not acceptable to the EU.

The Indian approach to such an institutional arrangement takes into account the greater depth and diversity in India's relationship with Africa than many of its other partners. The historical legacy with support to political movements in Africa, no stigma of colonialism, the presence of a large diaspora in Africa, the energy of the private sector clearly visible and a sustained programme of capacity building and human resource development as well as technology transfer over the last 60 years gives the Indian relationship with Africa a variety which is overwhelming in its shared vision.

Thus, the approach that India seeks to follow is to further enhance the diversity and bring it into an engagement which would enhance the overall profile of India with Africa. In this, the objectives of the African Union Commission and its growing harmonisation with NEPAD and the regional economic communities would stand us in good stead. Similarly, since 2006, the AU Commission, the African Development Bank and the Economic Commission for Africa are coordinating their activities better. Such synergy would also support the diversity of India's relationship with Africa.

The Indian approach would look at sectoral collaboration to enhance the existing relationship. These could include sectors where

India has core advantages and something new to offer like in healthcare, ICT development, human resource development, financial services and the like. Similarly, we would utilise the growing political engagement between India and African countries to have sectoral ministerial meetings over a period of years so that initiatives in those sectors acquire greater government backing. Similarly, ministerial meetings with selected RECs with whom India has growing interests, need to be consolidated where exist (SADC, ECOWAS) and initiated where absent (COMESA, EAC, ECCAS, IGAD, UMA). On the other hand, a sensitisation of governments with engagement with India through a public-private partnership would become more visible and viable. In due course, India should aim for a summit with Africa provided it has a definite agenda, determined preparation and committed follow up.

This approach is based on the understanding that India enjoys vast political goodwill in Africa. Since the emergence of the African Union, there is a greater recognition of changes in the world and India as a traditional partner of Africa is now seen as a major player in the world both economically and politically. Many African countries see India as their voice in international fora, particularly in the WTO and as a potential permanent member of the UN Security Council. To this end, Africa remains supportive of India.

Conclusion

Africa would remain a continent of challenges and opportunities due to its sheer size, growing population and growing investment in development and infrastructure. These would provide India an opportunity to be a partner and to take advantage of economic prospects. Unlike competitors, India has a collective edge in areas like financial services, human resource development, ICT, healthcare and the like. India's engagement with Africa has been successful and as Africa institutionalises and organises itself through the African Union and related bodies, India should remain abreast of these bodies and their objectives. India would need to reaffirm its traditional support and reorganise its engagement profile and seek the support of pan-African institutions like the African Union, the

African Development Bank and the Economic Commission for Africa, to enhance its engagement and interface. The political advantage of this would be more than commensurate with India's foreign policy objectives. Similarly, the economic fall out of such an engagement would have a strong bearing on the growth of our companies overseas and the establishment of a more diversified and strong economic and technological relationship with Africa.

23

India and Africa: a contemporary perspective

Navdeep Suri

Around mid-summer in 2005, Africa became the focus of the world's attention when the high-powered Blair Commission on Africa submitted its recommendations in May with lofty promises of debt relief and a quantum jump in aid to Africa. Around the same time, Bob Geldof and Sonny Bono were organising the Live-8 concert series that were seen by an estimated 2 billion viewers around the world. The G-8 (+5) met in the salubrious climes of Gleneagles in Scotland in July and endorsed the recommendations of the Blair Commission. The IMF and the World Bank, in their annual meeting in Washington a couple of months later in September, formally put in place a mechanism to reward countries that had demonstrated the requisite fiscal rectitude needed to qualify for debt write-offs under the Highly Indebted Poor Countries (HIPC) programme.

There was an air of optimism, a glimmer of hope that the concentrated efforts of the international community would finally see Africa emerge out of its debilitating cycle of debt and poverty. Optimists were even daring to call 2005, "The Year of Africa".

That was the summer of 2005. Some progress has undoubtedly been registered, but is it enough? I dare say that at this stage, many of the moving spirits behind last year's seminal events are less than sanguine. Prime Minister Blair, in fact, has been forced to revisit the issue in July 2006 by putting in place another high-powered panel. This one is led by Mr. Kofi Annan, President Obasanjo and the indefatigable Bob Geldof and with the financial backing of Bill Gates. The panel's primary job will be to track and monitor progress on promises made at the Gleneagles Summit and to report to the next G-8 Summit. These promises include:

(i)   Increase in aid to Africa by $ 25 billion a year by 2010 and a doubling of aid over six years.

(ii) Full debt cancellation for world's poorest 18 countries.

(iii) Universal access to anti-HIV drugs in Africa by 2010.

(iv) Reform of trade rules.

The panel has its work cut out. Progress at the Doha round of WTO can only be described as glacial, despite the considerable help provided by global warming to speed up the pace of our planet's receding glaciers. LDCs in Africa are crying out for fairer trade even while a number of developed countries continue to distort terms of trade by providing the most egregious subsidies on commodities like cotton and sugar. One wonders if the newly set up panel will actually try to name and shame the more recalcitrant members of the world's most exclusive club.

This is the context in which we can look at India's own record on Africa and take some pride in the fact that we have certainly tried to make the first decade of the new millennium 'our years of Africa'.

So, why this sudden focus on Africa? After all, isn't Africa the continent that is usually viewed through the prism of poverty and famine; civil war and brutal, internecine conflict; AIDS and malaria; and backwardness and corruption. But while each of these attributes is true in part, there is a profound change underway that is beginning to attract the attention of the international community.

Growing political stability

On the political side, the continent is progressively embracing the values of democracy and good governance. These values are enshrined in the New Partnership for Africa's Development (NEPAD) and are reflected in the fact that two-thirds of African

States have successfully held multiparty elections. As many as 24 countries have signed up for the African Peer Review Mechanism (APRM), a unique instrument under which they agree to let a panel of 'wise men' benchmark their performance against 4 broad parameters (and 91 specific indicators) of democracy and good governance. The practice of a two-term limit on the tenure of the head of state is widely gaining currency.

There is also a growing sense that Africa must take charge of its own destiny, and this is reflected in the determination with which the African Union was able to reverse the incipient coup in Togo and in its ongoing efforts to broker a peace deal in Cote d'Ivoire. In the process, the AU is sending out a strong signal of its unwillingness to tolerate the kind of forced regime changes that were so commonplace, until fairly recently.

Equally important is the commitment that several countries are showing to the concept of two limits. We have seen this reflected in peaceful transfer of authority in countries like Tanzania, Ghana and Benin. But most significant is the transformation in Nigeria, frequently wracked by military coups but now preparing for elections as President Obasanjo enters the final months of his second term.

Progressive economic revival

A similar transformation is also underway on the economic side. IMF estimates project real GDP in sub-Saharan Africa to grow at 5.9 per cent in 2006. As many as 20 countries averaged a growth rate of over 5 per cent during the past decade, and a handful have been growing at double digit rates on the back of major oil discoveries and high international prices of oil. A survey by *The Economist* provides additional evidence of robust growth in sizable pockets by revealing that 6 of the 12 fastest growing emerging market economies are in Sub-Saharan Africa!

And while sky-high crude oil prices might provide an explanation for the scorching growth rates in Chad (34 per cent), Equatorial Guinea (23 per cent), Angola (28 per cent) and Sudan (14 per cent), the real story lies in the discipline demonstrated by the steady performers in carrying out radical structural adjustment programmes mandated by the Fund-Bank group to qualify for debt relief under the HIPC initiative. Thirty-two (32) of the 38 countries identified under this initiative lie in sub-Saharan Africa. Nine of them have reached Decision Point and become eligible for immediate debt relief, while as many as 14 have reached the crucial Completion Point where debt relief becomes irrevocable and additional 'topping up' aid is available to mitigate external shocks.

These countries are now poised to reap the rewards for their good economic performance. The 14 countries of sub-Saharan Africa that have reached Completion Point would immediately become eligible for 100 per cent debt relief, saving them $ 42 billion in cumulative debt-service obligations to the World Bank alone. The World Bank estimates that this would bring down the net present value (NPV) of their debt to export ratio from 140 per cent to a more sustainable 52 per cent. Most of the nine countries that have already reached Decision Point are also expected to make the grade to Completion Point within the next year or two, enabling them to break out of the debilitating cycle of unsustainable debt-service obligations and insufficient resources for social sectors. There is a sense of optimism that the resources freed up from debt servicing will now become available for urgent development needs.

Improved credit ratings

A parallel initiative undertaken by UNDP in partnership with Standard & Poor to establish foreign currency sovereign ratings for sub-Saharan countries has also thrown up interesting results. Botswana gets an 'A' rating–the same as several Western countries and, perhaps surprisingly, higher than South Africa which gets a BBB investment grade rating. Equally significant is the case of the B+ rating secured by Ghana, Senegal and Benin, placing them at par with Brazil and a notch above Turkey and Indonesia, who are at the same 'B' level as Burkina Faso, Mali, Mozambique and Madagascar!

These UNDP/S&P ratings for these countries take into account a number of factors including:

- Commitment to macro-economic stabilisation and reform programmes.
- Substantial debt-relief prospects under the HIPC initiative.
- Significant socioeconomic stability.
- Low fiscal deficit and low inflation rates.
- Membership of regional economic groupings like WAEMU in West Africa and CEMAC in Central Africa, where the currency (CFA) is issued by a common central bank, linked to the Euro and has guaranteed convertibility, through the Central Bank of France.

Taken together, the sovereign currency ratings provide a pretty reasonable guide to the improving economic standing of several countries in Africa.

The downside

But despite these positive indicators, it is a fact that much of Africa remains desperately poor. The number of persons living below a per capita income of $1 per day has doubled since 1981 to 314 million; 34 of the poorest countries in the world lie in sub-Saharan Africa, and 24 of the 32 lowest ranked countries on the Human Development Index also lie in this region. HIV/AIDS and malaria do kill 2 million Africans each year, and countries like Zimbabwe, Somalia and Guinea have regressed to negative growth rates. The same IMF study that shows steady economic growth in 20 countries also points out that 16 of the 20 countries with the most difficult business conditions are in sub-Saharan Africa. Political instability and poor law and order situation in several countries, weak institutional capacity and the difficulty of enforcing legal contracts in others are among the key factors that contribute to the political, economic and security risks of doing business in Africa. The old generation 'Big men' continue to dominate in countries like Gabon, Angola and Congo–Brazzaville and ethnic and political disputes continue to fester in Sudan, Cote d'Ivoire and Somalia and between Ethiopia and Eritrea.

Implications for India

So, while statements about the 21st Century being 'Africa's century' and of Africa emerging as the continent whose time has come may smack of irrational exuberance, there is merit in taking the forward-looking view that in a number of countries, democracy and political stability have developed firm roots and economic reforms have become irreversible. Viewed from this perspective, Africa emerges as an important market for our goods and services, a vital element in our quest for energy security, a significant source of minerals and other natural resources for our burgeoning economy and a potentially attractive destination for our farmers. It also offers us an opportunity to review our foreign policy priorities and to refashion our traditional precepts of South-South cooperation in the context of globalisation and other 21st Century phenomena.

This has attendant implications for India's own foreign policy. It would, of course, be a cliché to state that the practice of foreign policy is all about the pursuit of national interest. I would suggest that it is in India's enlightened self-interest to become a strong and reliable partner in Africa's quest for economic development. It is, therefore, a challenge for us to not merely strengthen our ties at the bilateral level but also to develop relationships at the sub-regional and pan-African levels and to create the policy instruments needed to forge a genuine partnership with Africa. In doing so, we do bear in mind that from the political perspective, Africa, with its 53 seats in the United Nations General Assembly and three in the (unreformed) Security Council, will always matter. It is, therefore, useful to look at some of the key political and economic dimensions of our approach towards Africa.

Strengthening bilateral ties

On account of its close association with the decolonisation and anti-apartheid movements in several countries and the contribution of the Indian diaspora in some others, India enjoys enormous goodwill in Africa at the political and popular level. We are seen as a role model on account of our democracy, our robust institutions and our strong economic performance. Leaders of modern India from Mahatma Gandhi and Pandit Nehru to Mrs. Indira Gandhi and Shri Rajiv Gandhi are held in exceptionally high esteem. And as Africa strives to attain its development aspirations, there is a new generation of leaders in Africa who are increasingly looking at India and China to reduce their dependency on former colonial masters. India is now seen as a source of technology and products that are often more affordable and appropriate for African conditions, of managerial skills, and even of concessional finance to bridge the resource gap. This growing interest of Africa in India is clearly reflected in the sustained flow of high-level visits to India. During the first half of 2006, India received such visits from Gabon, Mauritius, Angola, DR Congo, Ghana, Nigeria, Senegal, Benin, Ethiopia, South Africa, Namibia, Zambia, Zimbabwe, Malawi, Mozambique, Eritrea, etc.

India-AU relations

At the pan-African level, India is making a conscious effort to develop an institutional relationship with the AU. Our dialogue with the AU leadership has included discussions on setting up an India-Africa Forum. We aim to expand the scope of this dialogue to include themes like democratisation, UN reform, peace and security, terrorism, trade and investment and energy and infrastructure. We are also looking at a possible relationship with the Pan-African Parliament. We have already demonstrated our strong support for the New Economic Partnership for Africa's Development (NEPAD) through a $ 200 million line of credit. Over the coming months, we also expect to set up an India-Africa Eminent Persons Group and to initiate an India-Africa dialogue focussing on key sectors like energy, education, healthcare, IT, agriculture and small and medium enterprises.

Relations with regional groupings

Africa is a vast continent that comprises as many as 53 independent countries. The five key sub-regions of Africa are progressively working towards greater economic integration. As this trend gathers momentum, it becomes especially important for us to establish an institutional relationship with the key economic and sub-regional groupings. We have taken the first step in this direction through the establishment of an India-SADC Forum that links India with 14 countries from Southern Africa. We propose to do the same with regard to the 15-nation Economic Community of West African States (ECOWAS) and have made a beginning in this direction during the visit of a ministerial delegation from ECOWAS in April 2006. We have also initiated a dialogue with the 11-member Economic Community for Central African States (ECCAS) during the AU Summit in Banjul, in July 2006 and hope to take this process further during the coming months. The first Ministerial Summit with the 20-member COMESA (Common Market for Eastern and Southern African Countries) takes place in New Delhi, on 5-10 October 2006. Our relations with Eastern African Community (EAC) are being similarly activated. We will soon sign a PTA and Comprehensive Economic Partnership Agreement with Mauritius, which will also serve to enhance our economic ties with Africa. Negotiations are also expected to be launched for a PTA with SACU (Southern African Countries Union).

Forging a genuine partnership

India remains committed to developing a genuine partnership with our friends in Africa. There is a growing awareness in Africa that Indian technology is especially relevant to their development requirements and we are seeing India emerge as a preferred source of projects, technical know-how, managerial skills and development finance. We are providing an impetus to this process through capacity-building programmes and bilateral assistance, by providing concessional finances and by developing structures for public-private partnership. It is useful to look at each of these elements individually.

Capacity building

Africa today is the largest recipient of India's technical cooperation programmes and we have so far extended more than

US$ 1 billion worth of such assistance including training, deputation of experts and implementation of projects in African countries. Over 1000 officials from sub-Saharan Africa receive training annually in India under the ITEC programme. In the area of human resource development, India continues to contribute substantially. Annually over 15,000 African students study in India and Indian engineers, doctors, accountants, teachers are widespread in several African countries.

India recognises the African focus on human resource development to overcome the gap for development in indigenous capacities, including the priority being given to the primary and tertiary education sectors. This is also our primary focus of cooperation within SADC framework. Further, India's membership of the African Capacity Building Foundation (ACBF) and through extensive use of the ITEC programme has contributed to the development of capacity building in Africa. The public sector educational consultancy firm EDCIL has MoUs with many countries for secondment of teachers and for determining of school and college curricula.

In this respect, of note is the initiative we have taken with 14-member strong grouping of the Southern African Development Community (SADC) to project India's soft power in areas considered critical to Africa's development, namely, agricultural technologies, bio-tech, seeds technologies; water resources development; entrepreneurship development for growth or SMEs, human resources development including capacity building and training, drugs and pharmaceuticals with special emphasis on HIV/AIDS, ICT, trade, industry, finance, etc.

Bilateral assistance

We have also provided direct assistance to a number of countries in response to humanitarian emergencies or in the context of longer-term development projects. The Ministry's 'Aid to Africa' programme provides the resources for these projects. In the last year or so, we have responded to requests for emergency assistance by sending foodgrains to Chad and Guinea, medical supplies to Cote d'Ivoire,

Guinea, Niger and the Gambia, and pumps, tents and other relief material to Senegal. During 2006 itself, we have provided an agricultural assistance package comprising 60 tractors and associated equipment to Cameroon, Benin and DR Congo and Togo. The IT Park in Mauritius, the Entrepreneurship Training and Development Centre in Senegal, the Kofi Annan Centre for Excellence in IT in Ghana and the machine tools facility in Nigeria are some of the outstanding examples of India's technical and financial collaboration with these countries.

Concessional finance

We acknowledge, however, that directly-aided projects of this nature will only be able to meet a miniscule part of Africa's requirements. We also recognise that without access to affordable financial packages, our offers of transfer of technology and management skills will not be enough. We have, accordingly, placed a special emphasis on creative use of lines of credit and have crafted initiatives that are uniquely relevant to the development priorities of our friends in Africa. In this regard, the TEAM-9 initiative bears special mention. It seeks to foster a closer economic and political partnership between India and nine specific countries from West Africa. A line of credit of $ 500 million provided by us for this programme is producing outstanding results. Projects worth over $ 200 million are already at varying stages of implementation. We are using these lines of credit to finance a diverse range of projects such as irrigation in Senegal, urban transport in Cote d'Ivoire, agricultural machinery in Mali and Burkina Faso, a mini-steel plant and a cotton ginning plant in Chad, and rural electrification and a presidential office complex in Ghana.

We are also providing crucial support for the New Partnership for Africa's Development (NEPAD) through a line of credit of US$ 200 million to assist the NEPAD's objectives. Several projects in Senegal, Mali, the Gambia, DR Congo and Mozambique worth over US$ 100 million are already being implemented within the ambit of this programme. They include coaches and locomotives for the Dakar-Bamako railway line and tractors and other agricultural equipment for the Gambia. In DR Congo, we have supported construction of a cement plant in Kisangani and have provided 250 buses for urban transport in Kinshasa. An agreement for rural electrification project in Mozambique will be signed soon.

A further line of credit of $ 250 million has been extended by EXIM Bank to ECOWAS Bank for Investment and Development. This will support projects throughout the 15-member ECOWAS region, promoting regional integration and creating opportunities for Indian companies to participate in the energy, telecom, railways and other sectors in this region. Similar lines of credit, albeit on a smaller scale, have been extended in the past to other regional institutions such as PTA-COMESA Bank.

We have also provided substantial lines of concessional credit on a bilateral basis to individual countries like Sudan, Ethiopia, Mauritius, Seychelles, etc. and are looking at similar proposals from several other countries. In the process, we have been able to develop lines of credit as an effective instrument for delivering carefully targeted development assistance to a broad range of countries across the African continent.

Public-private partnership

We find that these lines of credit are an excellent example of public-private partnership since they encourage our leading corporate houses to undertake projects in countries where they have hitherto been reluctant to venture. The lines of credit are extended through EXIM Bank after obtaining the concurrence of the Ministry of Finance. The recipient country offers a sovereign guarantee for repayment, and the choice of Indian companies for executing individual projects is left strictly to the recipient government.

We are also strengthening the public-private partnership for Africa's development by working closely with our industry. As an example, the Ministries of External Affairs and Commerce and EXIM Bank cooperated with the Confederation of Indian Industry in organising two highly successful India-Africa Conclaves in New Delhi, in March and November 2005. Each of these events attracted the participation of large numbers of ministers, officials, businessmen and bankers from Africa. They also generated tangible project proposals, some of which are beginning to take concrete shape on account of financing offered under our lines of credit. We have built upon the success of the two Conclaves by organising similar events in different regions of Africa. These have enabled large Indian business delegations to participate in regional conclaves held in Ethiopia, Zambia and Ghana in April and May 2005. In India, the next major conclave is being planned for October 2006.

With the government primarily playing the role of a catalyst and facilitator, these events are creating greater awareness of mutually beneficial business opportunities and provide a platform for business-to-business interaction. Our friends in Africa have responded enthusiastically to these initiatives and several countries have appreciated our efforts to focus on private sector-led trade and investment and reduce dependency on foreign aid.

Promoting trade and investment

The growing trade and investment linkages and our desire to access Africa's energy and mineral resources and participate in the farming sector are important elements of our economic diplomacy in Africa.

Rapid growth in trade, exports

The uptrend in the African economy since the early 1990s also coincides with the acceleration in India's own economic growth since the initiation of economic reforms in 1991 and these trends are reflected in India's bilateral (non-oil) trade with Africa, which has grown almost 10-fold from $ 967 million in 1990-91 to $ 9.14 billion in 2004-05. Exports during this period have increased from a mere $ 394 million to $ 5.4 billion, while imports have risen from $ 573 million to $ 3.8 billion. As a result, Africa's share in India's total exports has trebled from 2.2 per cent to 6.8 per cent while the continent's share of our total imports has also gone up from 2.4 per cent to 3.5 per cent, yielding a substantial balance of trade surplus in the process.

Equally encouraging is the sharp acceleration in our exports in the last couple of years, growing by 23.2 per cent in 2003-04 and by as much as 39.1 per cent in 2004-05. These positive trends have continued during the first quarter of 2005-06, with India's exports to Africa rising by as much as 63 per cent and imports by 35.5 per cent.

South Africa and Nigeria have consistently ranked as our two largest trading markets in Africa, followed by Egypt, Kenya, Sudan, Togo, Mauritius, Algeria, Ghana and Tanzania. Petroleum products have emerged as our largest single item of export to Africa with a 13 per cent share, followed by manufactures of metals (9.6 per cent), drugs and pharmaceuticals (8.4 per cent), machinery and instruments (8.2 per cent), non-*basmati* rice (8.1 per cent), transport equipment (7.8 per cent), cotton-yarn fabrics made-ups (7.4 per cent), and primary and semi-finished iron and steel (5.2 per cent).

In the import basket, gold accounts for as much as 42.3 per cent of our total imports from Africa. It is followed by inorganic chemicals–primarily phosphates from Senegal and Morocco (16.2 per cent), cashew-nuts from Ivory Coast, Guinea Bissau and Tanzania (8.8 per cent), metal ores (6 per cent), wood and wood products (4 per cent) and raw cotton (3 per cent).

Skewed pattern of trade

These encouraging trends in trade with Africa, however, mask some important facts. First, it is only with a dozen or so countries on the continent that we have a significant trading relationship; in a much larger majority, however, we are virtually absent–in economic as well as diplomatic terms.

Second, it is a fact that our current import basket from Africa reflects a fairly neocolonial pattern of importing unprocessed raw materials that may not be sustainable in the context of Africa's own development aspirations. Our private sector is ideally placed to make relatively small investments that enhance our competitiveness, create local value addition and foster a perceived win-win situation. Local manufacturing/packaging of products ranging from pharmaceuticals, detergents, cosmetics and even food products like biscuits and fruit juices can be done at relatively low cost and would compete effectively with imports from Europe.

We are making a beginning through modest investments in countries like South Africa, Mauritius, Tanzania and Kenya in East

Africa and in Nigeria and Ghana in West Africa. Figures released by the Government of Ghana, in fact, indicate that in 2004, India emerged as the largest foreign investor in the country in terms of the number of investment proposals and the second largest after UK in terms of the quantum of FDI. We expect this process to receive a further boost as a result of the concessional lines of credit for which a conscious effort is now being made to promote joint ventures.

Natural resources

We are aware of Africa's enormous wealth of natural resources and the manner in which these resources made Africa the target of rapacious exploitation over the last 150 years. In our own efforts to secure access to some of the resources needed for our growing industries, we must strike a careful balance between our needs and the imperative of respecting Africa's own development priorities and environmental concerns. There is an obligation on us to show that India is different, that we can give back to the local economy more than we take away from it. It is important to establish win-win partnerships that show clear benefits for the African economy and society in return for the mineral resources that we obtain from them.

Energy resources

A similar situation also prevails in the energy sector. Along with Sudan, the countries around the Gulf of Guinea are emerging as major producers of hydrocarbons. We have a very successful collaboration in Sudan where we are already demonstrating the manner in which we can contribute to development of local infrastructure and educational and medical facilities in the areas of our operation. Indian companies are in the process of concluding important agreements in Nigeria and hope to enter the energy sector in other important countries in the region. We recognise the growing importance of Africa to our energy security and it is important that we work closely with our friends in Africa to ensure that while we seek greater access to energy resources, we also contribute handsomely through major development projects in power generation and other infrastructure sectors.

Agriculture

We are also looking at several substantive proposals for collaboration in the agricultural sector. African leaders often bring up the subject of our Green Revolution and our ability to feed a billion people. They have also proposed the creation of mechanisms that enable our farmers to work in mutually productive agricultural projects in Africa, in a manner that contributes to our farmers' well-being and also brings food security to the concerned countries.

Pan-African e-Network

The Pan-African Network is a remarkable new project that attempts to add a fresh dimension to India's partnership with Africa. The initiative for setting up a Pan-African Network was announced by President Kalam, during an address to the Pan-African Parliament in South Africa in September 2004. ISRO and TCIL thereafter worked closely with Rashtrapati Bhawan to prepare a detailed report on the proposed project that would aim to provide proto-types for tele-education and tele-medicine in all 53 members of the African Union. It would also set up a VVIP network providing video conferencing and VOIP facilities to all 53 heads of state/ governments. After an initial presentation on this project to AU Commission Chairman Prof. Alpha Konare and other members of the Commission in Addis Ababa in May, detailed discussions were held with a special consultative committee of the AU in July 2005. The Committee's report formally endorsed the project and paved the way for an MoU that was signed between the Government of India and the AU in October 2005, in New Delhi during the visit of a high-level AU delegation. A technical committee of the AU announced in June 2006 that it has selected Senegal as the country where the satellite hub for the entire project will be located. In parallel, 12 individual countries have already signed memoranda of understanding signalling their desire to participate in the project, and several other countries are in the pipeline. The entire project cost of about $ 100 million, including the cost of running the project for a five year period after initial installation, is proposed to be met through a direct grant by India.

Meanwhile, work on a pilot project in Ethiopia is in full swing and we expect to launch it before the end of 2006. We are also working on a request from the African Union Commission to set up a tele-medicine clinic at the Medical Centre in the AU headquarters in Addis Ababa.

Establishing the institutional framework

We are also trying to put in place an institutional framework that provides the umbrella under which trade and industry can flourish. India has signed Double Taxation Avoidance Agreements and Bilateral Investment Promotion and Protection Agreements with several African States and would endeavour to expand this to other countries and regional and pan-African institutions to provide facilitation and encouragement to greater investment and public-private sector partnerships. In fact, BIPAA with SADC has already been proposed and a SADC-India Business Forum meet will take place in New Delhi before the October 2006 Conclave. In addition, joint commissions and joint trade committees with several African countries, are also working successfully.

Peacekeeping Operations

India recognises that in the absence of peace and security, economic development will continue to remain a mirage in several war-ravaged parts of Africa. From the time of the conflicts in Biafra and Katanga, India has been one of the largest contributors to peacekeeping in Africa. We currently have 4,500 troops in DRC and sizeable contingents in Sudan and in Ethiopia and Eritrea. Our troops are making an impressive contribution to peace and security and to fostering socioeconomic development in the areas of their operations.

The China Factor

Of late, the international media and even sections of the Indian media have started to pay serious attention to China's aggressive diplomatic push into Africa, making a comparison with India virtually unavoidable. Over the last decade, China has used a combination of top-level visits, huge concessional credits and high-visibility projects in an unabashed bid to secure preferential access to Africa's hydrocarbon resources, mineral wealth and timber, as also to Africa's growing markets. In countries ranging from Zimbabwe and Zambia to Angola, Congo-Brazzaville, Gabon and Sudan, Chinese diplomacy has yielded lucrative rewards for its burgeoning economy. At the same time, a wide range of African leaders have been given red-carpet treatment in Beijing over the last few years, paving the way for the diplomatic overdrive of the first decade of the new millennium. Between them, Foreign Minister Li, Premier Wen and President Hu have visited as many as 15 countries in Africa during the first half of this year alone, setting the stage for the first China-Africa Summit in Beijing in November 2006.

India's diplomatic initiatives, in contrast, have been hamstrung by two major constraints. First, with just 6 under-sized diplomatic missions covering 25 countries in West and Central Africa, we compare poorly with China's 22 well-staffed missions in the same regions. Without a larger diplomatic footprint on the ground, we will continue to face serious hurdles in achieving our economic and political objectives. Second, a serious deficit of high-level visits from India to Africa exacerbates the growing asymmetry in high-level political exchanges. Nigeria is a case in point. President Obasanjo is a recipient of the Indira Gandhi Peace Prize and has visited India thrice since he was elected President in 1999. Yet, the last bilateral VVIP visit from India was by Jawaharlal Nehru in 1962! Direct contacts at the highest political level matter more in Africa than in other parts of the world; neglect of major countries like Nigeria and Angola must be addressed on a priority basis.

Having acknowledged these constraints, we must nevertheless pose the question: Should India try to emulate China's Africa Policy? Is it possible? And is it desirable?

I would submit the proposition that it is neither possible nor even desirable for India to emulate China's Africa policy. In purely economic terms, China has a decade's headstart over India. Chinese oil companies routinely outbid ONGC by committing astronomical sums. And while we may highlight that we are extending lines of credit of almost $ 2 billion in Africa, the Chinese have pledged over $ 4 billion each in Angola, Sudan and Nigeria alone. We cannot match China in dollar for dollar spending. Nor do we have the command economy where state-owned entities can be directed to pursue the larger national interest regardless of their own bottom-line.

And even if we could, it is not particularly desirable to follow the Chinese model because some of their policies and practices are clearly beginning to attract a backlash. Discussions with a number of senior African officials and reports in influential sections of the media suggest that:

(i) Chinese companies execute projects on a turnkey basis, relying solely on Chinese manpower and materials and making no effort towards transfer of technology and local personnel.

(ii) While Chinese-built football stadia have sprouted in virtually every African capital, one pensive Foreign Minister called them unviable assets with neither the stadia nor the grandiose presidential palaces and national assembly buildings constructed by China in several countries contributing to capacity building.

(iii) A related development is the mushrooming of Chinatowns in many African capitals. Often populated by project workers who have stayed back illegally, these 'Chinatowns' start to compete in the economic space traditionally occupied by the indigenous trader/shopkeeper. Zambia's opposition leader Michael Sata has threatened to make this a key issue in the forthcoming elections.

(iv) In some of the more developed economies like South Africa, Kenya and Ghana, local producers of textiles, plastics, etc. are being wiped out by ultra low-priced Chinese imports. The growing resentment was manifest during recent Chinese VIP visits to Kenya and South Africa.

(v) In countries like Gabon, concern is being expressed over ecologically damaging practices followed by Chinese logging companies after obtaining large timber concessions.

(vi) At the political level, China's willingness to deal with some of Africa's less popular regimes is seen as a blatant disregard to the principles of democracy and good governance enshrined in NEPAD. Chinese assertions that they follow a policy of non-interference in the affairs of recipients may get plaudits from beleaguered African leaders but does not find much traction amongst the 'reformers' in Africa. The fact that neither Zimbabwe nor Sudan figured in the 15 countries visited by FM Li, Premier Wen and President Hu has been seen in these quarters as a possible sign of Chinese sensitivity to growing criticism.

The Chinese experience does, nevertheless, hold some useful lessons for India. Even as we work towards expanding our diplomatic footprint and planning high-level exchanges, we must consciously build on our areas of strength. We are increasingly seen by Africa as a preferred partner in areas ranging from IT and healthcare to agriculture and SMEs. The challenge for us is to improve our delivery systems for project assistance and to develop policy investments like our lines of credit that galvanise greater private sector participation in key areas of economic development.

The way forward

In sum, we see immense opportunities for mutually beneficial cooperation across a wide range of areas throughout the African continent. At the same time, we must also take note of some of the very real constraints that we face and take urgent measures to address them. It is a fact that since the late 1980s, India lost some momentum and could have done more to build upon its traditional strengths in the continent. At a time when China and other major countries have aggressively expanded their presence in Africa, we have actually closed down our missions in Guinea, DR Congo, Malawi and Burkina Faso. While some of these decisions were clearly prompted by the requirements of cost cutting and austerity that were imperative at that point of time, the long-term impact has been negative. We could also have done more to sustain our relationship with several key countries through active political exchanges.

We are now trying to address this situation on a priority basis. The reopening of our mission in DR Congo in August 2006, is an important first step. It is the third largest country in Africa, and one with which we have traditionally enjoyed very warm and friendly relations. We must sustain this momentum and rapidly expand our diplomatic footprint in the continent. We are, accordingly, moving a proposal to open new diplomatic missions in several key countries that are important from an economic and political standpoint. We are also looking at a number of other proposals that will remove bottlenecks currently faced by Indian companies in establishing joint ventures and other business enterprises in Africa.

Steps have been taken to consolidate our strategic and defence ties with countries which straddle the important sea lanes in the Indian Ocean and are members of IOR-ARC including South Africa, Mauritius, Mozambique, Seychelles, Eritrea, etc.

A programme of visits is being formulated for Minister of Overseas Indian Affairs to tour the region especially with strong diaspora in countries such as South Africa, Mauritius, Kenya, Uganda, Tanzania, etc.

Conclusion

There is no doubt that since the beginning of the new millennium, India has started to emerge as a significant player in the African continent. Our lines of credit are beginning to have a transformational impact in terms of our relationship with individual countries and with regional economic groups like SADC and ECOWAS. It is a sign of India's growing stature that not only an overwhelming majority of the 53 member states but also groups like SADC and ECOWAS have come out with an endorsement of India's candidature for permanent membership of the UN Security Council. At the same time, our consistent support in WTO to matters of vital importance to Africa (such as cotton subsidies) has been widely appreciated across the continent. Initiatives like the TEAM-9 group have been so successful that in barely a couple of years, since it came into existence, we have requests from half a dozen countries that are keen to join it. The Pan-African e-Network project is also being greeted with similar enthusiasm and it can rapidly emerge as a symbol of India's commitment to help Africa bridge the digital divide. We recognise the significance of China's advances in Africa but feel that it is neither possible nor desirable for us to emulate the Chinese approach.

We intend to work steadily to carry this process forward in a manner that India's partnership with Africa becomes a true symbol of South-South cooperation, delivering clear-cut economic and political dividends to both sides of the equation.

Bilateral relations

24

India and Afghanistan

I.P. Khosla

Introduction

In order to develop fully the potential for a mutually beneficial bilateral relationship between India and Afghanistan it is necessary that Afghanistan be enabled to play its due role in the geostrategy of the South Asian region. For that to happen it must develop unity and strength; but there is nothing inevitable about this development of unity and strength. During the half century there have been several cases of nation states that have been unable to sustain these attributes, that have fragmented and faded in strength. In the case of Afghanistan, too, there have been a number of predictions about the inexorable advance to fragmentation; and the tendencies that may lead to such an outcome certainly convey the impression of being unstoppable. At the same time nationalism and the political desire for unity among all the tribes and ethnic groups that inhabit the country have, through its history of the last two and a half centuries, been dominant.

Afghanistan's immediate neighbours, and the more distant powers that could play a role in this matter, have no particular self-interest in ensuring Afghan unity. The latter especially have presided over the breakup of other nations. Their interests in Afghanistan lie in another direction, that of a global geostrategy, and may neither be adversely affected nor benefit from such a breakup. Pakistan, of course, regardless of its protestations, would quietly welcome such an event. But for India it is of prime importance that the unity of Afghanistan is built up for, as mentioned above, without that the full potential of Afghanistan's role in South Asia cannot be realised. In what follows an attempt is made to assess the balance of forces in this regard and put India's policy in perspective.

Topography, climate and national character

In summary it can be asserted that Afghanistan's topography and climate do not encourage the formation of a national character that is easily amenable to discipline or unified endeavour. Afghanistan is part of an arid and semi-desert belt that stretches from the Iranian plateau eastwards. For the most part it is rock and gravel and limestone, with a barren central mountain range, the Hindu Kush which starts from the quadri-junction in the North West Karakorum range where Afghanistan meets Tajikistan, China, and India (Jammu and Kashmir state); then extends south and west across central Afghanistan. Only 12 per cent of the land area is arable, as compared to 54 per cent in India. Of this only two and a half per cent is dry land farmed. Afghanistan is much less densely populated, but has twice as many people per hectare of arable land as India. And it is not fertile: one hectare feeds two people compared to eight in India. This is not due only to technology but also to topography.

Another disincentive to settled farming is the extremes of temperature: very hot summers and cold winters; sharp variations between day and night. Precipitation is low, an average of 13 inches per annum, and in some areas like the southwest only 2 inches. So most of the agriculture is on the very small amount of irrigated land that is available like along the Oxus, the Kabul river and a few others in the east. Settled farming is difficult, but the grass lands in the mountains encourage animal husbandry, large migrations of people in search of summer and winter pastures, and nomadism (there are two million nomads). In terms of sociopolitics it is the nomad, the unsettled population, which is the most difficult to tame, to unify and to discipline. The people of the mountain, through the centuries and across continents, have had certain character traits in common, traits which influence their attitudes as individuals and as members of social and political groups, and which separate them from the people of the plain. Their history, wrote Braudel in his definitive study of the Mediterranean is to remain almost always on the fringe of the great waves of civilisation and this is the nature of the Afghan. They have endurance and strength, the ability to bear hardships which others can not sustain, as can be expected from the meagre livelihood that comes out of hard labour in almost uninhabitable terrain; but socially they have three predominant characteristics: first is vertical organisation, the family and tribe are the units that command loyalty, not horizontal affiliations like caste or language or religion as in India or most of Europe; second there is no landed nobility, since land owning is not important, and a strong democratic egalitarianism—the poor and the rich live in like houses and in a tribal meeting or *jirga* each one expresses views fearlessly, it is often difficult to find out if there is any hierarchy at all; third, honour is prized above all other virtues. There is a three pillar code of honour for the Pashtuns for instance, comprising Pashtunwali or the code by which the Pashtun will conduct community life; melmastia or the code of hospitality; and badla or the code of revenge. It is difficult to subjugate them; they are not easily tempted by the lures of civilisation, and willing to fight for their freedom; centralised political systems generally fail to bring them within the fold. In Afghan society, the attitudes of the people, particularly those of the Pashtuns, are of the mountain. Equally, the Afghans reject centrally imposed religion or dogma. Islam since the Ghazni empire has been accompanied by belief in *shamans* and mystics, by the strength of the Sufi tradition with its saints and songs, by pilgrimage to the graves of holy men, the *pirs* and the *khwajas*. Afghan unity, in other words, is not easy to come by, given the national characteristics of the people.

Tribal and ethnic divisions

The divisions in Afghan society are of two kinds. At the broadest level there is the division between Pashtun and non-Pashtun; and there has always been social fragmentation among the various Pashtun tribes, as also within the different non-Pashtun ethnic groups. Before 1747, the year Ahmad Khan of the Abdali (later Durrani or its Mohammadzai branch) tribe brought together the heads of the different Pashtun tribes as well as of the other ethnic groups, including the Tajiks, the Uzbeks, the Hazaras and Baluchis, to form a united Afghanistan, the Ghilzai (a Pashtun tribe) had been dominant. During the next two centuries the struggle between the Durrani and the Ghilzai continued. They came together when there was an external threat, as during the wars against the British and later against the Soviet Union, then separated and fought against each other when there was no threat. But the Durrani continued to rule the country; though even within this tribe different branches or sub-tribes came together, parted, and fought against each other.

The non-Pashtun ethnic groups are also divided. The largest of them is the Tajik, some four and a half million people inhabiting an area north of Kabul up to Badakhshan and Kunduz on the Tajikistan border. Between the Tajiks of Badakhshan and of Panjsher, for instance, there have been differences for centuries. This was one factor in the problems that emerged between the political leadership of the Jamiat-e-Islami under Burhanuddin Rabbani, a Badakhshani who became President of Afghanistan in June 1992, and the military leadership of the same party under Ahmad Shah Masoud. The Panjsheris still dominate the Tajiks and this has been a cause of some unhappiness among other Tajiks.

The Hazaras, about one and a half million inhabiting central and western Afghanistan, are the third largest ethnic group, and have also been divided. Unified by their deep rooted suspicion and dislike of the Pashtuns (though one of their commanders sided for a short time with the Pashtun dominated Taliban) the Hazaras are divided along religious lines between Shia (the majority), Sunni and Ismaili; between ultra-conservatives, modern radicalists and maoists; and, through the 1980s and early 1990s, between allegiance to different commanders like Ismail Khan in Herat, Abdul Ali Mazari south of Kabul, Karim Khalili along the northern highway and Jaffar Naderi in the north.

The Uzbeks are the fourth largest ethnic group, some one million located in Balkh and Jawzjan provinces along the borders with Uzbekistan and Turkmenistan. The divisions among them were shown most dramatically when the Taliban attacked Mazar-i-Sharif in May 1997. An Uzbek general, Abdul Malik, separated from his leader Abdul Rashid Dostum, to help the Taliban; and then, four days later, turned on the Taliban to drive them out of the city. In general the Uzbeks, however, are less divided than the other major ethnic groups. There are others, in smaller numbers: like the Turkmen, the Baluchis, the Aimaq, the Kirghiz, the Nuristani, which have not played such an important role in recent developments. It is not just tribe and ethnicity that divides the Afghans. At the religious level there is the divide between Sunni and Shia, which, since it broadly corresponds to the ethnic divide between non-Hazara and Hazara, reinforces the latter. There are also divisions among the Sunni, between the Deobandis of the Hanafi sect for instance, which included the Taliban leadership, and those influenced by the Wahhabism of Saudi Arabia. The above examples are not to essentialise the ethnic or tribal or religious divisions in Afghanistan, but to amplify that, recognising such divisions, every neighbour from the British and Tsarist Russia to the Soviet Union and then Pakistan, has consistently followed a policy of sharpening them, of weakening Afghan nationalism through sociopolitical fragmentation.

Global geostrategy

The global geostrategic explanation has generally been given by international affairs commentators most often for the importance of Afghanistan in Asian affairs. After Soviet troops entered Afghanistan in December 1979 this explanation became more pointed; and after 9/11 and the global war on terror, even more so.

This has a long history dating back at least to the invasions of India through Afghanistan. On the map of global geostrategy Afghanistan figured in historical perspective as an area through which India was invaded. From the 4th Century BC raid of Alexander of Macedon to the white Huns of the 6th Century AD, from the Arabs in the 8th Century to Amir Timur in the 14th Century, invaders (in this view), "stormed one after another through the narrow defiles that break through the great rocky barrier and lead into the plains of the interior."[1] To take another example, "at the crossroads of Central Asia, the area that comprises modern Afghanistan has been subjected to constant invasion throughout recorded history."[2] Historians and statesmen have seen Afghanistan's history since that time in terms of its geography, as the provision of a passage to India. Lord Palmerston explained this as the Russian threat, which was so often invoked by the British in India during the remainder of the 19th Century in order to justify their policy of trying to secure the breakup of the country. The same sentiment, in essentials, was echoed by President Carter in his January 1980 State of the Union message: "The region now threatened by Soviet troops in Afghanistan contains more than two-thirds of the world's exportable oil ... The USSR is now attempting to consolidate a strategic position that poses a grave threat to the free movement of Middle East oil", and the theme was repeated often thereafter. As the British Indian and Russian empires moved north-west and south-east respectively in the 19th Century, this essentialisation came to be described differently. Afghanistan became a buffer, a mechanical contrivance set up by the two empires to prevent a direct collision; it "took its modern form as a buffer state between the British and Russian empires in the late nineteenth century."[3] Jawaharlal Nehru puts the matter in the same terms. Writing in 1934, in *Glimpses of World History*, he underlines that for long periods Afghan history was almost a part of Indian history. But "since its separation, and specially during the last 100 years or more, it has been a buffer state between the two great empires of Russia and England." Another, more recent, is the economic explanation. There are Afghanistan's own resources of copper, iron

---

1. Majumdar, R.C., H.C. Raychaudhuri and Kalikinkar Dutta (1967). *An Advanced History of India*, Macmillan, London, p. 5.

2. Economist Intelligence Unit, *Country Profile, Afghanistan 1996-97*, p.52.

3. Rubin, Barnett R. (1997). "Women and Pipelines: Afghanistan's Proxy Wars", *International Affairs*, April, Vol.73, No. 2.   p. 285.

ore, and natural gas among others; and the Soviet invasion (as well as previous attempts to control Afghan territory) is explained in terms of the long-term objective of controlling these. Or, more commonly, there is the use of Afghan territory for access to the resources of Central Asia, which may be summarised in the over used phrase 'crossroads of Asia'. Thirdly, the importance of Afghanistan is explained in terms of the spread of Islamic fundamentalism; in the 1980s by citing the policies of the Mujahideen groups, and from the mid-1990s by citing those of the Taliban and its support to international terrorism as represented by al-Qaeda. Sometimes, the whole world is seen to be threatened and Afghanistan becomes part of a grand international phenomenon: restless Islam asserting itself everywhere in the world against regimes it regards hostile. This view has of course become particularly prominent after 9/11. At others the threat is more localised, against the 'soft underbelly' of the former USSR composed of Islamic states, or against the Middle East, or even to rouse the Muslim minorities resident in West Europe.

Afghan unity

However the real aim of the external powers that Afghanistan has had to face during the two and a half centuries of its history was, in the case of the British, the annexation, or at least subjugation of the country and its breakup if neither was possible; in the case of the Soviet Union during the 10 years that they occupied the country, its breakup and at least partial integration with the neighbouring Soviet republics; and in the case of Pakistan thereafter, its weakening through fragmentation if possible, by other means if not. It was in pursuit of the disintegration policy that the British, launched the Second Afghan War, 1878-1880, and, after entering Afghanistan, formally severed western Afghanistan from the rest of the country, and created a separate entity out of Kandahar province. But by 1881, following a number of military engagements including a decisive defeat at Kandahar, the British withdrew. The new ruler, Abdur Rahman, quickly brought western Afghanistan and Kandahar under control, and set about extending and consolidating his authority by bringing the tribes and ethnic minorities under firmer central rule. Abdur Rahman was not the author of Afghan unity, which in its present general geographical area dates back to 1747. In October of that year a tribal gathering or *loya jirga* assembled in Kandahar. It included representatives from the tribal and ethnic groups now in Afghanistan: the Uzbeks and Hazaras; the Tajiks and Baluchis; Popalzai and Ghilzai and all the major tribes. They agreed on a ruler for the whole country. This was not a nation state in the modern sense (nation states in the modern sense were not known anywhere till about 1880). The central power did not rule over and administer citizens directly; the tribal chiefs remained powerful enough to be the main intermediary in all matters. In the ever shifting conceptual framework of national identification which is typical of all nations, Afghan unity at the time was expressed most categorically in their opposition to any foreign invading power.

His rule, however, gave the name Afghanistan to the area, and he was the first to consolidate the country on modern lines, to create the kind of cohesion of purpose needed to build strength. Abdur Rahman has been criticised for accepting the Durand Line, which was drawn by the British to define the border between India and Afghanistan, for the line dissected the Pashtun tribes and their lands, and arbitrarily included in India territories and peoples which had always been Afghan. But the line, which became a continuing source of friction, was the price he paid to achieve his main task: to make a modern nation state, and to increase his own power over his citizens at the expense of the tribal chiefs. He did this through a full scale ideological campaign, using British aggression to invoke Islam as a basic unifying force, appealing for *jihad* against the unbeliever, and claiming divine sanction for his own rule. Thus he opposed the tribal model of the state, in which the authority of the *amir* or ruler is exercised through the intermediacy of the tribal chiefs, by the use of an Islamic model, in which the 'amir as commander of the faithful' exercises direct authority over his people. He and his successor Habibullah, who ruled till 1919 were also able to co-opt the *ulema* (as the main intermediaries of Divine sanction) into the state apparatus, thus further strengthening the basis for national consolidation.

The Third Afghan War (1919) was initiated by Amanullah because he felt the unity and cohesion of Afghanistan, built by stages over four decades, had reached a level at which he, as ruler, felt confident of challenging the British. Secondly, the spread of Pan-Islamic sentiment across West Asia after Turkey entered the 1914-1918 European war meant that such a challenge would be popular and seen as a *jihad* by the religious leaders. Thirdly, the struggle for independence in India had reached a new phase, the Afghan ruler wanted to support it at a time of British weakness after that war, and in fact one of the proximate incentives was his reaction to the Jallianwala Bagh massacre in Amritsar on 15 April 1919. In early May, Afghan troops crossed the border and occupied a few villages, there was a little fighting, and what became known as the War of Independence ended with Afghanistan gaining complete control of its foreign affairs. Its acceptance of the Durand Line was confirmed. Under Amanullah, with the prestige of victory in the war, a new phase of secular modernisation began, the next step in further consolidating central rule, this time by reducing the position of the Ulema. This nationalism used the concept of the Fatherland, or *Watan*, in which the King played the central guiding role and was the focus of the citizen's loyalty. Though Amanullah took Afghanistan too fast along the road to secular nationalism, and had to abdicate in 1929, his successor Zahir Shah was able successfully to modernise Afghanistan along the same lines. From 1933 to 1973, helped by a small but growing group of modernisers, he gave a nationalist focus to the Afghans. History was rewritten to show that Afghanistan existed as a national entity even before 1747, traditional culture was developed including the printing of old Pashtun and Farsi literature, and above all Islam was more firmly co-opted into the state apparatus.

Soviet policy

However the policies of the external powers to try to divide the Afghans, one from another, continued. By 1973 the gradual modernisation of Afghanistan through expansion of the government apparatus, infrastructure and the economy including the private sector had led to demands for political liberalisation. A growing, but still tiny, urban middle class demanded rapid westernisation, the abandonment of traditional socioreligious practices, and the reduction of religious influence. At the opposite pole, there was an Islamic revival led by scholars educated at Al-Azhar University, or influenced by Maulana Maududi. Traditional Afghan society has been moderate: one of the reasons for the gradual consolidation of internal cohesion was the ability, under the guidance of the successive rulers or kings, of Sunnis and Shias, Pashtun and non-Pashtun, to tackle the problems of sociopolitical development with an accommodating flexibility. There was very little domestic support for leftist or Islamist extremes; the representatives of both were from the newly educated urbanised middle class. But the pressure of external forces pushed Afghanistan's polity into a mounting confrontation between these extremes in which the voices of the moderates were silenced. In July 1973 Mohammad Daoud, a cousin and brother-in-law of King Zahir Shah, with the help of a group of army officers, staged a bloodless coup in which he abolished the monarchy, declared Afghanistan a Republic and proclaimed himself President. The Soviet Union was the first to recognise the new government; the size of the Soviet aid programme was substantially increased, and followed up with a regular exchange of high level visits between Kabul and Moscow, while relations with Washington cooled. The coup brought not only the leftists in the army to power and those officers who had, as the official Soviet history notes, gravitated towards democratic political groups and supported them; but also the People's Democratic Party of Afghanistan (PDPA), some of whose members became ministers. This party, described by the Soviet official media as a vanguard party and the most consistent defenders of the working people's interests, which had split soon after it was founded in January 1965 into a largely Pashtun dominated Khalq group and a more generally non-Pashtun Parcham group, remained divided, and the Soviet officials assigned to look after its interests ensured that roughly equal favours were bestowed on both groups so that it stayed so. As the weight of one branch of politics shifted to the left and to inspiration from the Soviet Union, the Islamists at the other end of the spectrum looked increasingly to Pakistan. By 1975, after a series of uprisings to overthrow the government of President Daoud had failed, several of the more radical of them had taken shelter there, and in stages thereafter even the moderates went into exile. The stage was set for the next step in fragmenting Afghan society.

The Saur Revolution of April 1978 and its second stage in December 1979 took the polarisation of Afghan internal and external politics all the way into open warfare. On April 27, 1978, the PDPA took over power, killed Daoud and proclaimed the birth of the Democratic Republic of Afghanistan. The Khalq group in the Party played the dominant role. In the second stage of the Revolution the Khalq leadership was replaced by the Parcham, Soviet troops entered the country, and for the next decade domestic and external policy was directly controlled from Moscow. At the other extreme the Islamists, fighting a *jihad* against the Soviet occupation of their country, came increasingly under Pakistan's control. Soviet policy during that decade was the same as Lord Lytton's: disintegrate Afghanistan, for a weak political system would be easier to control. Villages, tribes, regions should support the PDPA and the Soviet Union; if not they were counted hostile and attacked. Such policies led to a large exodus of refugees to Pakistan and Iran. Whole villages left; whole tribes who were not trusted left; and apart from creating a man-power pool of nearly three million Afghans in Pakistan and one and a half million in Iran from which Mujahideen under their direct control could be recruited, this enabled the Pakistan authorities, in particular, to tutor a substantial proportion of the Afghan population with its own version of Islam. And, equally important, the polarisation of society, which had so far been confined to the urbanised middle class, was now extended to the people in every region and village of the country.

The pre-1978 policies of promoting cohesion were being reversed in other ways also. The 1985 constitution provided for the creation of administrative units based on national characteristics. By 1988 the PDPA, under Soviet guidance, was actively encouraging the different nationalities such as the Pashtuns and Tajiks, the Hazaras and Uzbeks, to develop distinctive identities by promoting their particular culture. Where previously national *jirgas* or assemblies brought the different nationalities together, now separate *jirgas* were organised for each; and each was offered autonomy within its area, so that the local tribal or national leader would exercise effective power with minimal administrative interference from Kabul.

Devolution of power to the different regions was also encouraged through external contacts. From March 1987 direct discussions between Afghan provinces and neighbouring Soviet Republics on expanding economic, cultural and educational co-operation began. Three Soviet republics, the Turkmen, Uzbek and Tajik, bordered northern Afghanistan's provinces, and the latter were encouraged to, and did, enter into direct cooperation with them. That the provinces had substantial populations of Turkmen, Uzbek or Tajik ethnic origin, and that they were the most highly developed industrially, with gas, fertiliser, power and irrigation projects set up over the years with Soviet assistance, facilitated such co-operation. And as 1988 progressed reports came in that the ethnic divisions were being firmed up, with Hazaras moving out of non-Hazara areas, Uzbeks out of non-Uzbek areas and so on. Abdur Rahman's policy of ensuring an ethnic population mix within each province was being reversed. Where Abdur Rahman had used British subsidies and support to strengthen the central administration, to bring the tribes under better control, Soviet policy from 1979 to 1989 was to divide or disperse (into Pakistan) the Pashtuns, and encourage the non-Pashtun identification of self with ethnicity through concessions and financial inducements, and particularly by developing direct relations with the neighbouring Soviet republics; when the republics became independent in 1991 their own policies of ethnic assertiveness further sharpened the ethnic divisions in Afghanistan.

Pakistan's policy

Pakistan, even more than the Soviet Union, was opposed to a future Afghanistan being united and strong, hence its policy *vis-à-vis* the Mujahideen was precisely complementary to that of the Soviet Union towards the PDPA government. In ensuring that if ever a Mujahideen government came to power the country would be fragmented or at least disunited, Pakistan had two main levers: the supply of arms, money and material to them; and Islam. To Pakistan's Inter-Services Intelligence (ISI), which had been in touch with the leaders for several years, was given the task of coordination, and they decided to support not one, or two, or three, but seven political parties. By agreement with the USA and Saudi Arabia, who were the main foreign suppliers of arms, material and money for the purpose, all such supplies were channelled through the Pakistan authorities, so that all the groups except these seven found their resources drying up, and disappeared. The ISI thereafter ensured by the judicious distribution of arms and other supplies, that none of the seven could become too powerful. Gulbuddin Hekmatyar's Hizb-e-Islami, which at one stage proposed a confederation between Afghanistan and Pakistan, was the only one often (for even he was not always trusted) given more generous treatment. In general while a nominal balance was maintained between such Ghilzai groups and those of the Durrani who supported the return of Zahir Shah, Pakistan consistently favoured the former, and above all the Hizb-e-Islami. Pakistan's basic objective was to weaken the Afghan state through a systematic policy of socio-political fragmentation. Other neighbours had followed the same policy, but Pakistan has stronger compulsions. It needs strategic depth *vis-à-vis* India; it has to try to settle its own Pashtun problem; and, two new factors: if Afghanistan remains in such an unsettled state that there is little prospect of the former Mujahideen returning to peacetime occupations, a large pool of battle-tested persons would become available for use in Jammu and Kashmir as also elsewhere in India; and there was the prospect, however unrealistic, of getting gas and oil from Turkmenistan through Afghanistan.

The consequence of keeping the Pashtuns divided was that the Tajik, Uzbek and Hazara groups, particularly those led by commanders located within Afghanistan, gained in strength, upsetting the traditional balance between Pashtun and non-Pashtun. By 1982 already the differences between the different Mujahideen groups, Shia and Sunni, Pashtun and non-Pashtun, Pashtun and Pashtun, were so deep that at the OIC Foreign Ministers conference of August that year they could not agree on a spokesman. At that conference and at later international gatherings where the same problem arose repeatedly, each side would appeal to the Pakistan leadership, the latter would appeal to them to settle their differences; and the matter would be left at that. There followed clashes in the field between Pashtun and Tajik, between Pashtun and Uzbek, or between different Pashtun groups such as Durrani and Ghilzai, and even within the same group. But the ISI were able to ensure that none of the seven groups was eliminated. The outcome of Pakistan's policy of promoting divisions between one tribal or ethnic group and another was that once the government supported by Moscow fell in 1992 there was no agreement on who should succeed it; the different Mujahideen groups fought with each other and now Pakistan was able to take the lead by sponsoring a new group 'the Taliban' in 1994. By mid-1996 they had taken most of southern and eastern Afghanistan including Kabul. The infighting among the Mujahideen who had fought the Soviet troops had taken such a bad turn that it was actually with some relief that the Taliban were welcomed by people from different parts of the country. The effects of 18 years of war, the destruction of villages, the repeated internal and external migrations, the constant living on the edges of subsistence, were gradually undermining the broader national loyalties of the people, thus providing an opening for external interference, an opening that was used to try further to fragment the country.

Taliban policies

By mid-1997 Taliban controlled most of Afghanistan except the non-Pashtun Northern provinces, and they had issued a series of edicts which, in their rigid interpretation of the Sharia, were intended to antagonise the more liberal-minded minority ethnic groups, and even many of the Pashtuns. There were edicts to forbid the flying of kites, the playing of football or chess; listening to music, dancing or going to the cinema—the cinema halls were reportedly converted to mosques; there was to be no photographing of people or animals, reading of foreign books or magazines; girls schools were closed, women were forbidden from work, and men were compelled to grow beards. In Kabul the 'Department for the Promotion of Good and the Fighting of Evil' had dozens of inspectors constantly on the move, alert for violations of the rules for dress or prayer. Even in Iran or among the Muslim Brotherhood in Egypt, often regarded as the leading representatives of fundamentalist Islam, this rigid interpretation of doctrine was denounced. The Taliban was, in fact, engaged in executing a carefully prepared plan to destroy the Islam of Amir Habibullah: that Islam which brought together Shia and Sunni, Tajik and Uzbek, Hazara and Pashtun to form a unified nation state, the Islam promoted and accepted by an urbanised middle class and which brought increased cohesion to the country. Taliban was signalling to this class that they were no longer acceptable in the country; they were telling potential modernisers and nationalists who wanted consolidation of the state and nation building by incorporation of religion into the state, that now it would be incorporation of the state into religion. This was far from blind fanaticism; knowing that the imposition of rigid rules will lead to social fragmentation, this was a policy with a careful aim pursued at the behest of Pakistan. As they advanced from Kandahar northwards in early 1995 it became clear that, apart from enforcing their version of the religion, they had two things in mind: Pashtun dominance; and ethnic separation. They tried to rouse Pashtun passions, saying that an unholy gang was trying to grab power. The Tajiks, Uzbeks and Shiites had no right to stake claim since political power in Afghanistan had always remained with the Pashtun. And in the areas captured by them, which were largely Pashtun, the non-Pashtuns were often driven out; so that, in a process already set in motion in the 1980s, Uzbek moved to Uzbek majority areas, Tajik to Tajik majority areas, Turkmen to the north east or even to Turkmenistan.

The present situation

Following the terrorist attack on the US on 9/11, the events leading up to the ouster of the Taliban government and the installation of a new government under President Hamid Karzai are well known and do not need recounting here. It is important to note however that after 2001 the determining external influence in terms of Afghanistan's domestic situation is that of the US, and the US is not interested either, on the one hand, in promoting or, on the other, in opposing policies which consolidate the internal unity and strength of Afghanistan unless these policies also help it to achieve its own aims there, which are of quite a different nature.

The biggest problem faced by Afghanistan today is the deteriorating security situation. From the political point of view elections have been successfully held to Parliament and for the Presidency. Hamid Karzai, who was elected President, is acceptable to all Afghans and, indeed it can be said without doubt that he is the only one who would be so acceptable. This augurs well for the future of democracy. But security is another matter.

One of the first questions is how to reduce the power of the regional warlords, many of whom are more powerful than Karzai himself if account be taken of their strength in terms of trained troops. It goes without saying that, the more powerful they are, the more difficult it would be to have a strong central government. A second problem is the growing menace of the drug trade, which ensures that they are well financed. The latest reports suggest that some 200,000 hectares of land are now under poppy cultivation, that farmers are still reluctant to move into cultivating other crops since the income from the poppy is so high. Some 40 to 60 per cent of the Afghan GDP is from the drug growing and trade and in provinces like Helmund, which are hardly under the control of the central government; acreages are expected to grow dramatically. So this is the large source of income for the warlords and each is an independent centre of power. When Karzai tried to control their power and removed the governors in Kandahar, Helmund and Oruzgan provinces, they took all their people along and the security situation deteriorated. This decentralised structure makes it easier for the Taliban/al-Qaeda to move through the country and attack the government and foreign troops. Indeed during the first half of the year 2006 the security situation had in general deteriorated so far that the US had to mount a special operation, "Operation Mountain Thrust" with extensive bombings leading to heavy collateral damage and concern expressed by Karzai, that this should be avoided. Meanwhile, the accretion of forces for Kabul is not progressing well. The Afghan National Army, which was planned to have a strength of 70,000, now plans, more realistically, to aim for 50,000, of which only around 35,000 are in position. The police is virtually non-existent, though a strength of 37,000 is claimed; corruption is reportedly rife, and the competence of the police is yet to be tested. The economy has been seriously damaged by decades of war. Over 80 per cent of the population is engaged in agriculture, mainly subsistence and some commercial. Industry is small-scale and includes textiles, furniture, shoes, hand-woven carpets, natural gas, coal, copper and fertilisers. The main exports are fruits, nuts and carpets. Industrial goods, cement, electronics, food items are the main imports. Pakistan, Iran, Uzbekistan, Tajikistan, India, China, Japan and the EU are the major trading partners. Total revenue in the last fiscal year, 2005, is expected to be US $ 333 million against total budget outlay of US $ 4.75 billion. The deficit will be met by donor contributions. USA, EC, Japan, UK, Germany and India are the major donors in addition to the major multilateral institutions.

US policy

The US has about 18000 troops (one per 1200 per heads of population, less than it has had in any other major conflict zone), largely in the South and East, and the intention was that these will gradually be reduced and replaced by the troops of other NATO members, though it remains to be seen how far this can be put into practice. This comprises the coalition force. The other force is ISAF, mandated by the UN for security in Ḳabul and the North. German, Italian, British, French and Turkish and other NATO members contribute to ISAF (the international security assistance force), which has a total of about 12,000 troops. The US and the West have three main aims: first, the search for and the elimination of al-Qaeda and Taliban remnants; second, stabilising the Karzai government, which leads to a catch-22 situation: the search for al-Qaeda and Taliban means strengthening the local warlords or strongmen, since the US does not have enough troops for large ground operations which are carried out by the latter, which means Karzai cannot control them, which means less stability for Karzai; third, the longer-term interest which has also assumed importance, namely ensuring a military political presence in the Central Asian region as a whole, now more important since Uzbekistan decided to terminate the US military facilities and have the Russians in instead. This connects with great power rivalry with Russia and China and with access to the energy sources of the entire region.

The main problem facing the US is that the insurgency led by Taliban, al-Qaeda and the Hizb-e-Islami of Gulbuddin Hekmatyar has increased, particularly in 2005, and, as mentioned above, the first half of 2006, with more US troops killed than the total since 2001. Insurgent tactics have improved; they set up road blocks and ambushes and retreat into the hills before reinforcements can get there; aerial bombing is not useful since there are enough caves in the mountains. Motor cycle attacks in the cities have increased. Remote controlled roadside bombs have made an appearance as have suicide bombers, especially car bombs rammed into convoys or into buildings. The number of suicide bombings in 2005 doubled compared to 2004. In general, the insurgents have learnt and are following similar tactics to those used in Iraq. There is some indication that there have been contacts between the insurgents in the two theatres, meaning that for the US this may become one war instead of two. The operations undertaken by the US revealed, in any case, that the Taliban and their supporters such as Gulbuddin Hekmatyar and Haqqani are no more a rag tag army but mobile and well organised and armed and divided into a number of different groups, so that the elimination of one does not make much of a difference in the total level of insurgency; in other words their capacity for making trouble is increasing, not decreasing. At one point in 2006 they were able to take control of some parts of Helmund, though not for long. The Taliban and other insurgents have a safe haven in Pakistan, where the governments in the neighbouring provinces of Baluchistan and NWFP are sympathetic as well as Islamic. The 2,400 km border is impossible to seal and Pakistan has not been able to mount operations on its side due to tribal opposition. A second problem is that the US is getting more unpopular due, first, to the general perception among the Afghan populations of its attitude to Islam. In May 2005, as one example, responding to reports that US operatives in Guantanamo Bay detention centre had flushed a copy of the *Koran* down the toilet, there were riots and demonstrations which spread in days to 10 provinces, with "Death to America" slogans, storming of a US convoy and storming of the Pakistan consulate. This included the North where there is no Taliban. Second, there is anger at the US policy of indiscriminate bombings from the air and insensitive house searches including the women's quarters. Karzai's suggestion that this be done only with his approval was rejected. Another incident occurred in May 2006 when a speeding US truck was involved in a fatal accident in Kabul; rioting by the residents in the area followed. But US vehicles have to drive fast since that is the only way to minimise the chances of a terrorist attack and this, in turn, places everyone else in danger.

India and Afghanistan

There are, of course, strong emotional bases for close ties between India and Afghanistan, dating back even to pre-history. The *Mahabharata* mentions many places, rivers and names of tribes and their leaders who took part in the epic battle. And, in that great story Gandhari, the wife of Dhritarashtra, as the name suggests, is a princess from Kandahar. Asoka edicts were found there, too, and it is historically true that Afghanistan was the vehicle for the spread of Buddhism from India to Central Asia and beyond. Apart from the Maurya Empire, which included Afghanistan, the Kushans, who did so much to adapt to Hinduism and in the spread of Buddhism, included large parts of Northern India within their territory. So there is a shared history, not always a very happy one, as the repeated invasions from the north-west testify, but shared enough to have created strong bonds of culture. It is possible to argue that after 1947 realism demanded that India should look at Afghanistan within the South Asian framework, as a country to be bound to us in the closest possible relations, regardless of the state of our relations with Pakistan. However the actual approach taken by successive governments in India has been cautious, a blend of the generalised views held by international commentators and of realpolitik, with the former usually taking prime place. India's cautious approach in dealing with Afghanistan has frequently, and from a broad spectrum of political and media opinion, come under attack, though it can be argued that there was sufficient justification for it.

By the argument of the critics—and working on the principles of realpolitik as enunciated from Kautilya to Machiavelli and Hans Morgenthau—Afghanistan should have been one of our closest friends in the region, deserving our political, economic, moral and military support to ensure its strength and stability. This means, first of all that India should have supported the demand for revision of the Durand Line and (an Afghan demand that has never been precisely spelt out) for the autonomy or independence of all the Pashtuns of the Northwest through a process of self-determination; and those demands that Afghanistan has been making over the years on Pakistan, as a landlocked state. However, two aspects of India's foreign policy intervened here. Firstly, in the early years after Independence India hoped that after the ceasefire in Kashmir relations with Pakistan would enable the continuation and even reinforcement of the historical bonds between the two peoples. Further, setting an example, taking the lead in the way foreign relations should be conducted; India believed historically determined borders like the Durand Line should be respected. It was only later that Pakistan extended support to China when the latter questioned the legality of the McMahon Line. Finally, self-determination for the Pashtuns would imply that Pakistan's demand for the same right to the people of Kashmir was justified. So, although relations were friendly with high level visits, expanding trade, aid projects and facilities for training among other cooperative ventures, there was no support for Afghanistan on the issues it regarded as critical, and the Afghans were disappointed, which they showed in particular by taking an even handed position at the time of the Chinese aggression of 1962 as well as during and after Pakistan's aggression in 1965.

Secondly, for a decade and a half after Independence India's policy concentrated on the promotion of international peace and security. The world had emerged for the second time from a devastating war and was dividing up into hostile blocs which could lead to a third. Independent India under the leadership of Jawaharlal Nehru was in a pivotal role; it should set the example, take the first steps to disarm, work for one world, for a commonwealth of nations. There was little room for the realpolitik needed to conduct relations with neighbours, which were often neglected in the pursuit of world peace and an overall world view framework in determining how policies should be decided, and less for Afghanistan, with which there was no *de facto* border. Nehru himself set a tone, which echoes in today's policy pronouncements. Talking in 1950 about Afghanistan and the demands of the Pashtuns, he said, "the Government of India is intimately interested, but it is a matter for abiding regret to us that we can only be interested from a distance without being able to help in any way." When, during the 1960s and 1970s the Cold War entered Afghanistan through rival Western and Soviet economic and military aid programmes focussed on the southern and northern provinces respectively, India could, or considered it could do little to influence a development it would have regarded as a direct security threat, had it occurred in Nepal or Sri Lanka. So when Soviet forces entered the country in December 1979 India's response was influenced more by the need for continuing good relations with the Soviet Union than by what the future of Afghanistan would mean for the neighbourhood and our security.

Overall, therefore, the global or world view framework prevailed in India's policy. Following the ouster of the Taliban and the establishment of the Interim Administration of Afghanistan in November 2001, our political interaction with the leadership of Afghanistan has been intensive and regular. The focus of our interaction has been to support the Afghan Government and the political process in the country as mandated under the Bonn Agreement of December 2001. India's policy thereafter has been expressed through support for the unity, independence, territorial integrity and sovereignty of Afghanistan, a diplomatic way of saying we would like to have a strong and stable Afghanistan which would naturally, given its geostrategic location and socioeconomic composition, be on very friendly relations with us, hence contribute to peace and security in the region. In consonance with this overall approach there have been several high level visits from and to Afghanistan after 2001. This includes four official visits by President Hamid Karzai: as Chairman of the Afghan Interim Administration, 26-27 February 2002; as President of the Transitional Islamic State of Afghanistan, 5-8 March 2003; as President of the Islamic Republic of Afghanistan, a working visit from 23-25 February 2005; and the fourth on April 9-12, 2006, accompanied not only by senior cabinet members and members of parliament, but also business leaders from Afghanistan, while India pledged another $50 million assistance taking the total committed so far to $650 million. From the Indian side, the External Affairs Minister visited Kabul on 15 February 2005. At the invitation of President Karzai, Prime Dr. Minister Manmohan Singh visited Afghanistan on 28-29 August 2005. During the visit, the two leaders held talks on broad range of bilateral issues as well as regional and international issues of common concern. Prime Minister reaffirmed India's continued commitment towards Afghanistan's reconstruction.

India's aid priorities

In response to the request of President Karzai India has decided to focus on infrastructure, road construction, irrigation and power and water supply, to ensure the foundations for stability and consolidation. Traditional areas in which India has been helping Afghanistan like health and education and culture, would also continue. Indeed India's assistance covers every aspect of life in the country: agriculture, industry and the private sector, education and health, transport and infrastructure, media, IT, security, law, banking and urban development. India is, along with Germany and Japan, the best recognised country for the usefulness of its assistance programmes. Our present commitment towards reconstruction effort in Afghanistan adds up to over US $ 650 million, which is a substantial amount for a non-traditional donor like India.

Then there are emergency food supplies: 1 million tonnes of wheat, which was partially converted — due to transportation problems — to 10,000 tonnes of high protein biscuit for the school feeding programme. We have 5 teams of doctors and paramedics in the major cities. Ninety-five tonnes of medicines, winter clothing, and earthquake relief including blankets have also been sent. Other major projects include the artificial limb centres in Kabul and Mazar-e-Sharif and rehabilitation of the Indira Gandhi Institute of Child Health in Kabul.

Capacity building is another field in which India has always been active. We have sent over a thousand Afghan officials for short and long training courses in India; over 250 policemen have been trained. This includes diplomats, officials of the President's secretariat, policemen, doctors and journalists. English language teachers have been deputed to Afghanistan, and we have supplied educational kits to schools, apart from the above mentioned rehabilitation of Habibia school (at the specific request of Karzai, since this was his old school), setting up of a computer training centre, and computerisation of Afghan Foreign Ministry. It has also been agreed that India would assist in establishing a women's vocational training centre and a common facility and tool room centre at the Industrial Park in Kabul. Prime Minister recently also announced 500 scholarships for Afghan students for University education in India and in addition, 500 short-term training fellowships under the ITEC Programme.

We have also actively participated in all important international efforts aimed at political reconciliation and economic rebuilding of Afghanistan. For instance India had announced, in January 2002 at the Tokyo Conference, an assistance of US $ 100 million for Afghanistan's reconstruction, and is contributing US $ 200,000 per annum to the World Bank managed Afghan Reconstruction Trust Fund. As for agreements, India and Afghanistan have signed a Preferential Trade Agreement on 6 March 2003 in Delhi. India has allowed substantial duty concessions for certain categories of Afghan dry fruits, and Afghanistan in turn has allowed reciprocal concessions for Indian products, including tea, sugar, cement, and pharmaceuticals. Other MoUs/agreements have also been signed. These include an MoU on Small Development Projects, an Agreement on Cooperation in the field of Healthcare and Medicinal Science and an MoU on Cooperation in the field of Agricultural Research and Education. The major obstacle in the implementation and expansion of India's economic ties with and assistance in Afghanistan remains, as it has been for half a century, that Pakistan has not so far allowed India's assistance to go through its territory, except some vehicles. So much of it has to go through Bandar Abbas (4-6 weeks transit time) and other available routes.

Conclusion

The end of the Cold War removed from the family of nations what seemed the major source of conflict; the success of regional cooperation puts in its place a partnership mechanism; and the identification of global issues like the environment seemed to herald the coming together of nations and regions in a common effort for the future of mankind. Concord became, and continues to be today the dominant theme of the times, with inevitable implications for India and its neighbourhood policy. In this context there can be no doubt that Afghanistan's membership of the South Asian Association for Regional Cooperation (SAARC) will be beneficial for bilateral relations between India and Afghanistan as well as for the region as a whole. President Karzai during his April 2006 visit to India has talked of a trilateral structure of cooperation, referring to India, Afghanistan and Pakistan. Going even further afield, the Joint Statement issued at the end of that visit mentioned the two leaders' "vision of Afghanistan regaining its strategic position at the crossroads of Central Asia and the Indian subcontinent." Within this kind of generalised elaboration there are the time-honoured principles: respect for territorial integrity and national sovereignty; settling disputes peacefully; and mutually beneficial cooperation. And there are the new ones, of which three are salient: non-reciprocity, where the smaller neighbours benefit; a stress on non-interference, which implies that this government will go further than its predecessors; and a virtually limitless faith in dialogue. The new ones are as unexceptionable as the others, and fit comfortably into the message of global peace and stability emanating from most capitals. To balance the picture, it is worth recalling the limits within which they can be applied. Because of its size India can afford, and may indeed find its interest served, by selective non-reciprocity in relations with the smaller neighbours. Delinking the Ganga waters sharing from transit through Bangladesh, giving limited unilateral trade concessions, and generosity on visas, not to mention the gestures that are being made to Pakistan on issues such as their claim on the Indian state of Jammu and Kashmir, are steps that fall in this category; they reduce the polemic temperature, encourage people to people contact, and promote the regional spirit. It is dangerous, however, if this spirit persuades us to obscure the line beyond which we will not go, and more dangerous if our neighbours believe that we are so persuaded. For there are matters of vital or important interest to India, including political and territorial differences, which fall beyond that line.

Non-interference, too, perhaps needs a rethink; as a principle it is, of course, unexceptionable, but it does need to be taken off its Panchsheel pedestal and made into a working principle in a globalised world. An economy integrated into the global system benefits, but it cannot escape interference from multilateral organisations, non-governmental actors, and even other governments. A culture exposed to the global media is enriched;

but it cannot escape influences which may weaken, partially disrupt, and even interfere with it. India has played a leading role in championing democratic systems and the respect for human rights, for instance in Myanmar. Despite continuing disagreement in the world community, what is generally acceptable today in these matters would not have been acceptable three decades ago. A policy that uses economic strength and the media to promote India's interests, or that advocates respect for human rights, does not violate the non-interference principle. Going further, aspects of the internal affairs of every one of our neighbours impinge on our interests. The flow of refugees from Bangladesh, the threat of additional refugees from Sri Lanka; Myanmar's lack of control in the border regions and Pakistan's inability or unwillingness to control the spread of terrorism directed against India or the transit of drugs; dissidence in Bhutan or economic hardship in Nepal: these are some of the issues in which our interests are served not by accepting the fallout of all this, but by an active effort to cooperate in finding solutions.

A tireless dialogue, again, needs a framework within which our neighbours see it. It would be counterproductive if, for instance, it gave Pakistan the idea that its aim of territorial aggrandisement has not been categorically rejected; or if it becomes a substitute for action to control South Asian problems like the flow of refugees, the traffic in narcotics and the sponsorship of terrorism. As far as our relations with Afghanistan are concerned we have sometimes to remind ourselves that with the partition of India, a united and strong Afghanistan became a problem for Pakistan; the threat to the British position in India turned into a threat to Pakistan. India's security remained still the biggest stake, but the picture was reversed: it was now Pakistan that wanted a weak and divided neighbour and India for whom a clear regional geostrategic interest was to help strong centralised rule there. In the view of the Afghans also, whatever their political persuasion, it has always been clear that India is the one nation for whom a strong and independent Afghanistan is of overriding interest.

The unity of Afghanistan cannot be undone in a few years of internecine warfare and external attempts to fragment the country. The Afghans today still look upon themselves first as Afghans rather than as Uzbeks or Tajiks or Pashtuns. But, as mentioned in the introduction, there is nothing inevitable about this unity; it is not impossible to undo it in the long run. It is not only desirable but necessary for India's future security and for Afghanistan that we play an active role in countering the current policies of dividing one nationality from another, one tribe from another, and in reasserting the need for the international community to agree on a policy of non-interference, and to ensure the integrity of the country.

25

Distant neighbours: India and Bangladesh

Deb Mukharji

The cool relations between India and Bangladesh is one of the ironies of contemporary South Asia. Issues, whose parameters are known, remain unattended and become progressively politicised. Or, perhaps they remain unattended and unresolved because they are politicised. The media in both countries have become adept in depicting each other as the 'other', with little effort either at understanding or creating understanding. The 'other' is mostly seen through the prism of offended national sentiments. What must make this most puzzling is that the two countries have no conflict of interests, nor claims or expectations from each other much different from neighbours anywhere.

India's involvement in the 1971 war, leading to the surrender of the Pakistan army, is vividly remembered in India. Unfortunately, it is remembered largely in the context of Indo-Pakistan relations, the military victory over Pakistan and the consequent emergence of Bangladesh. There is insufficient appreciation that India's actions in 1971 were motivated, at least in some, if not large, part, by its calculations of national interest and the sheer force of events. It was not an act of altruism—which in no way diminishes Indira Gandhi's courageous defiance of American realpolitik. There is inadequate understanding of the horrors of 1971 for the people of Bangladesh, or the valour against impossible odds displayed by the Bangladeshi freedom fighters. It is also forgotten that gratitude has a very short shelf life and becomes rapidly stale, more so in international relations.

Today, Bangladesh is seen as the source of an unending flow of illegal migrants, as a haven for fundamentalists and terrorists and a sanctuary for Indian insurgents in the north-east. A troublesome, non-cooperative neighbour, most difficult to engage. Those in business know that it is also a substantial market for Indian products.

For Bangladesh, India is a giant neighbour without the attributes of a good neighbour, and hence to be treated with caution. While successful in selling its goods, India is unwilling to accord due trade concessions to facilitate greater exports from Bangladesh. Meanwhile, Bangladesh spends its precious foreign exchange in importing goods from India and in tourism, education and medical treatment. Over the years, the Indians have reduced the flow of waters in the many rivers which sustain life in Bangladesh. Even the 1996 Ganga Waters Treaty is not being honoured either in letter or spirit. The 1974 Mujib-Indira Boundary Agreement remains unratified by India. India has not honoured her commitment on Teen Bigha. India is not averse to encouraging anti-state movements in Bangladesh, as seen after Mujib's death and the support to Shanti Bahini in the Chittagong Hill Tracts. The trigger-happy Border Security Force indiscriminately kills Bangladeshis at the border. The Indians cannot be trusted.

This being the sum of mutual public images, one should look at the significance of each to the other.

Despite its opening to the sea and excellent ports giving access to the outside world, India is a natural partner for Bangladesh. India is a market over one billion and transport costs should be attractive for the import of raw materials for the industry of Bangladesh. Indian investment in Bangladesh could feed not only the local market but Indian and international markets as well. Until such time as these facilities are fully developed in Bangladesh, India provides medical and educational facilities, which are, in fact, already widely availed. Association with the much larger and booming Indian economy could provide a large impetus to that of Bangladesh.

A source of constant concern in Bangladesh is the flow of common rivers. Bangladesh would like shating formulae for all rivers, but except for the Ganga, which has a 30 year sharing formula, making it virtually permanent, no permanent arrangement has been reached. The sharing of the Teesta waters was on an *ad hoc* formula to enable the construction of the Teesta barrage by Bangladesh, and would need revision. There has been little or no progress in the matter and even the Joint Rivers Commission, supposed to meet at the ministerial level every six months, meets only after gaps of years. Starting with the Farakka issue, the river waters question has so permeated the psyche of the people that when there are no floods or droughts, it is attributed to good relations between the two governments, with India not releasing excess waters from her dams to flood the country or not withholding it to cause droughts.

It is in the reality of this bleak framework of fear, suspicion and that most intractable of emotions, prejudice, on both sides, that India has to address specific interests and concerns.

Bangladesh shall remain India's most important foreign policy challenge by virtue of being embedded in the most sensitive part of India. A substantial part of the more than 4000 kilometres land and riverine boundary is along the north-east which has seen, and continues to face, a number of insurgencies. Far from being of assistance, the continuing involvement of Bangladesh government or agencies in providing help to the insurgents is without doubt, and senior political leaders have not been averse to affirming that Bangladesh had a moral duty to assist north-eastern insurgencies seeking independence from India. Pakistan, which believes in bleeding India with a thousand cuts to avenge 1971, has been collaborating with its friends in Bangladesh to assist the insurgents.

Complicating the issue are historical legacies. Bangladesh remembers that when Bengal was partitioned in 1905, the eastern part of the then Bengal presidency included the seven sisters of the north-east Migration from Mymensingh to the Brahmaputra valley in Assam in large numbers dates back to the thirties of the 20th Century and many in Bangladesh believe the area to be the legitimate lebensraum for the land-starved people of Bangladesh.

This possessive attitude of Bangladesh to the north-east lies at the root of the denial of transit facilities to India. Arguments for this vary from time to time, but the objective remains the same. There is also the repeated assertion that India, i.e. mainland India, should not trouble to meet the requirements of the north-east which could be taken care of by Bangladesh, or even that India should invest in Bangladesh so that it could better meet north-eastern requirements for which, indeed, special facilities should be granted by India.

Clearly, the future of the north-east would be determined primarily by how the state of India conducts its business and succeeds in meeting the aspirations of its people. But Bangladeshi intentions have been made abundantly clear and need to be noted with due caution. A favourable response from Dhaka on the transit question would be indicative of some change of mind. Given that Bangladesh has even declined to be a member of the Asian Highway project, lest it confer transit facilities to India, this seems unlikely.

In recent years, the increase of Islamic fundamentalist activities in Bangladesh has been a matter of the deepest concern to the international community including, particularly, India. What is rarely noted is that it has also been a matter of anguished concern to large sections of people in Bangladesh and their media has been agitating on the issue for years. Complicating the matter has been, until recently, government silence, if not complicity. A Pakistani newspaper had commented that the Bangladesh government was "most reluctant to take action against the Islamists as long as they continue to attack Awami League cadres and communists. ... A day will come soon enough when the state of Bangladesh will come under threat from the Islamic warriors it is now empowering through denial".[1]

---

1. Swami, Praveen (2006). "Puppet Masters", *Frontline,* April 22-May 5.

Even if the overt activities of these elements is currently subdued after government action following the countrywide bomb blasts in August, 2005, it is also clear that the vast network of such extreme elements that has been allowed to be created, still remains.

The problem has acquired a serious security dimension for India with the increasing number of Bangladeshi *jihadi* elements arrested in India in recent months, some involved in high profile terrorist activities. The pattern often seems to be training in Pakistan followed by executing bomb blasts in Bangladesh, and now also India. The porous border makes it easy for terrorists to move at will. Bangladesh is also now a transit point for Indian *jihadis* to go across the border and thence for training to Pakistan. As Pakistan engages in a dialogue for normalisation with India, its options are being kept open by using Bangladeshi nationals for subversion and terrorism in India. It would be necessary for India to expose the Bangladeshi connection to *jihadi* terrorism both in bilateral discussion as also internationally. It is a cause not only for India but also for the beleaguered people of Bangladesh whose concerns have so often been ignored, if not rubbished, by the government.

Simply put, the issue of illegal migration is one of people seeking better economic prospects. Migration for advancement is an age old worldwide phenomenon, be it for pastures in ancient times to high quality jobs in the West today. With the lines of 1947 having delineated the boundaries of the states of South Asia, there is no reason why India should be host to large numbers of migrants from Bangladesh. The issue is further complicated by what is termed euphemistically as demographic invasion or imbalance. Translated, this means that the number of Muslims in the districts bordering Bangladesh has shown a rapid and disproportionate rise due to illegal migration. And since the origin of the migrants is Bangladesh, a country with which India has less than a comfortable relationship, their loyalties become suspect.

To see the problem as divorced from the concerns of the state would not lead to solutions. A secular Indian state must discharge its duties to its citizens regardless of religion, but cannot assume responsibility towards the citizens of other states at the expense of its own. Blurring the lines of duty, as seen in Assam, is in fact a disservice to Muslim citizens of India. The primary responsibility for the current state of affairs lies with some major political parties of India who have turned a blind eye to illegal migration with an eye on minority votes and appear only recently to have woken up to its implications.

The absence of any sustained and coordinated policy has led at times to eye-catching activities like sending train loads of Bangladeshi immigrants for deportation. Clearly, if there are large numbers of Bangladeshi migrants in India, and they are now in large numbers even in distant cities and in the fields of Punjab, it is because they fulfil some economic needs of the country. The primary issue is not the work they may do, but the question of citizenship. Resolving this with work permits, which is one option, would require the cooperation of the government in Dhaka who have been in a state of denial. The choice for the government of India would lie in national identity cards, at least in border districts, and a far greater vigil at the border than we have been accustomed to. The barbed-wire fencing, effectively implemented, could go some way in preventing future migration. It is no secret that there are major shortcomings in the management of the border, for which the security forces on both sides are equally responsible. The root of the border problems lies in smuggling, euphemistically described as informal border trade, with an annual quantum estimated to be in excess of one billion dollars. This, in turn, has led to extensive criminalisation of the border.

Water resources are a perennial irritant in Indo-Bangladesh relations. Water is life and no state would concede what it considers to be its rightful share. Karnataka and Tamil Nadu may have gone to war had they not been constituent states of the Indian Union. The long festering issue of sharing the flow of the Ganges at Farakka was resolved by a 30 year treaty made possible by the statesmanship of the Bangladesh leadership, the far-sighted policies of the Indian government and the cooperation of West Bengal. There are 53 other common rivers, six of major concern to Bangladesh. Progress on any of these has been abysmally slow. In essence,

Bangladesh would like to maintain current flows, while India has to consider the needs of her people, as much dependent on these waters. The prevalent attitude of Bangladesh is perhaps best reflected recently by a commentator, "The government of India must see beyond technicalities and their local interests."[2] These 'local' interests involve 300 million people in the Ganges and Brahmaputra basins.

A deltaic country, Bangladesh's concern about waters is both genuine and valid, as is the Bangladesh position that the total availability of water is not of much relevance since the total comprised an annual cycle of floods and droughts. The ecology and navigation of Bangladesh depend on the flow of river waters, as do the livelihood of millions. But the issue ultimately of how to resolve a matter of scarce resources cannot always be resolved by political will, even if that were to be available, as was possible on the Farakka question. And the high decibel level of Bangladeshi complaints even when there is shortage due entirely to natural causes, as in the dry season of 2005, does not encourage rational discourse. From news emanating from Bangladesh, it would also appear that optimum utilisation of waters, even from Farakka, is not being made.

It has to be fully recognised that current flows of rivers to Bangladesh will gradually diminish because of increased upstream uses in India. Nor does India have an unfettered and absolute right to the uses of these flows, even if present international law does not prescribe with precision what fair flows to the lower riparian would mean. Without a frank discussion on these lines a permanent solution will continue to be elusive.

It has to be acknowledged that if there is an unusual level of suspicion in Bangladesh on issues related to water, Indians have contributed to it by not sharing information adequately. Advance information on lean flows or possible floods, which upstream measurements would reveal, has not been conveyed to the necessary extent. Greater openness is required. The grand Indian scheme of linking of rivers of the north and the south, perhaps of

2. Abdul Hye, Hasnat (2006). "Sunday Column", *New Age*, Dhaka, March 26.

great merit, advertised with great fanfare and now apparently in the limbo, was publicly and judicially discussed without any information to Bangladesh, leave alone consultations. This could only arouse the worst suspicions in Dhaka. Indians may counter that when there is an effort to share information on future projects, Dhaka's response is one solely of obstruction. From Dhaka's perspective, the waters of the common rivers are gradually diminishing due to upstream uses leaving Bangladesh with an uncertain future. The dialogue between the two countries have tended to be guided more by the technical expertise of their representatives than by any effort to understand, let alone appreciate, the problem of the other.

Discussions on Ganga waters over two decades have underlined that Dhaka is unwilling to apply itself to any solution of the water question beyond trying to retain existing flows. The needs may indeed be genuine, but the needs of one, be it Bangladesh or India, cannot be *ipso facto* considered superior to those of the other. A rational discourse leading to any long-term solution can only be based on the premise of optimum utilisation, acknowledging mutual requirements. Such discussions as have taken place have been bogged down in the swamp of stated national requirements from particular rivers, without due consideration of possible alternatives.

With requirements increasing with population, however, even the best of bilateral understanding would still necessitate augmentation and a holistic approach to the region's water resources. Nepal would hold the key for reservoirs which would augment the lean season flows. As would the North-Eastern states of India. The flow of the Brahmaputra, which brings in more water than the Ganges at its leanest season has to be considered. There have been reports of its flows being planned to be diverted northwards in Tibet. Bangladesh itself may have to consider whether the waters of the Brahmaputra can be more fruitfully utilised. And all this would have to be done keeping in mind environmental concerns and long term consequences of interfering with nature's natural flow, issues to which we are only now beginning to pay attention. Nations would have to ask themselves searching questions if the present state of management of existing flows are nearly optimum.

Clearly, any future long term management of river waters would need the active cooperation of all regional countries involved. Two decades ago India had agreed to trilateral discussions involving Nepal and Bangladesh, but no progress could be made. If the territories of any, as in the case of Nepal, are used also for the benefit of others, suitable fees would have to be paid. Arriving at solutions acceptable to all would be far from easy, but a beginning needs to be made. Looking at the flow of rivers as a natural phenomenon to which we are entitled in perpetuity may have to be replaced by acknowledgement that as a precious and diminishing commodity, a price may have to be paid. A holistic regional approach seems the only way forward.

The question of trade imbalance has assumed large proportions in the Bangladeshi mind and continues to grow This is not always readily understandable as in today's trade regimes people and countries buy where they think it is profitable. There are no specific Indian regulations that target Bangladesh. Nor is reference to an equally large trade deficit with China heard in Dhaka. Indian concessions under the South Asian Preferential Trade Agreement (SAPTA) in line largely with Bangladeshi demands have made little impact. Indian offer of a bilateral free trade agreement, similar to the one with Sri Lanka, continues to await response. The demand for unilateral duty free imports by India continues. If permissible under WTO rules and assuming it does not have wider ramifications, this is something India could consider. It could help if Bangladesh could focus on specific exports rather than seek duty concessions across a broad spectrum.

Looking at the gamut of Indo-Bangladesh relations and looking at the mindsets that operate, one may be tempted to arrive at the conclusion that Dhaka continues to look at Delhi with the complexes of the Middle Ages when it fought the domination of the Turkic or Mughal rulers of Delhi, oblivious of its status today in the comity of nations. An eminent son of Bangladesh of the highest national and international renown, said recently, "A section of our politicians finds it a very attractive theme to impress on the common people of Bangladesh that India is behind all the terrible things that happen in Bangladesh. If you don't vote for our party, India will turn Bangladesh into her client state."[3] Bangladesh, he suggested, was fortunate in having the India—and China—as neighbours and must use this as an opportunity for faster growth.

The politicisation of relations has led to a vicious circle where those encouraging it also find it difficult to move towards co-operation. A case in point is the proposed gas pipeline from Myanmar to India *via* Bangladesh. Absence of response from Dhaka has forced the Indians to negotiate with Myanmar a direct pipeline to the north-east. A tri-nation pipeline would have provided Bangladesh with substantial revenues in transit fees. Dhaka would have liked two preconditions to be met, reduction in the adverse balance of trade and making electricity available from Nepal and Bhutan. The first is not possible to guarantee for trade would find its own level. The latter is eminently possible with the creation of an energy grid for the eastern region, noting, however, that as of now Nepal has a net shortage of energy which it imports from India. The question of Bangladesh importing electricity would arise only after Nepal and Bhutan signal their ability and willingness to do so. Separately, latest reports from Nepal (May 2006) quote a former prime minister as saying that India's grant of transit facilities by road across the Siliguri corridor in 1997 has not been utilised as the necessary infrastructural facilities are not available in Bangladesh. Since the availability of road connectivity to Nepal has nevertheless been a constant refrain in Bangladesh, one must wonder if the creation of issues is the main priority.

Added to this is the Pakistan factor. Over the years Pakistan has succeede.] in persuading like minded-people in Bangladesh to follow its own path of confrontation with India. And there are also many who would do so of their own convictions. It is significant that following the recent peace initiatives between India and

---

3. Yunus, Muhammad (2006). "Report on Address", *The Daily Star*, Dhaka, February 5.

Pakistan, some Bangladeshis express the view that it may also be time for them to adopt a more cooperative approach towards India. Then there are those who hark back to the theme of parity from the Muslim League's favourite slogan before 1947, unmindful of the fact that parity in sovereignty does not translate into parity in other respects.

Despite the hurdles in promoting closer relations, it still remains important for Delhi to make the effort and go the extra mile whenever possible. Improvement is required in communications where Bangladesh's interests may be involved, as in water resources. Instead of withdrawal, it is necessary to put forward to people the rationale for cooperation and the merits of any particular proposal. A great lacuna has been any clearing house for information. Despite the substantial Indian exports to Bangladesh, a joint Chamber of Commerce has been hibernating for years and has only now been revived. Issues are bound to arise, often due to local aberrations, and these must be addressed and rectified and not allowed to fester. Every unreasonable decision by an individual customs officer must not be allowed to be seen or portrayed as a malafide decision of the Indian government.

It is also necessary to note that if interstate relations have not been productive, many in the civil society of Bangladesh are quite aware of the possibilities that exist and need to be pursued. Unfortunately, in the prevailing political ambience they may not always find it expedient to express their views. The same is true of business and industry, though they, fortunately, have not been deterred from pursuing their interests. In the field of culture, too, there continues increased exchanges and interaction at private levels promoting greater understanding.

As India looks at the future, it would be an error to see Bangladesh in unidimensional terms. Suspicions and vested interests notwithstanding, there does exist at many levels both respect and expectations from India that are not unreasonable. To tap into these sources, a policy of fairness that is transparent is necessary. It also requires reminding that relations between states are based on the pursuit of national interests and Bangladesh cannot expect special considerations from India if it continues to be indifferent to issues like transit, or engages in any collusion with Indian insurgents. As the larger of the two states, India has greater responsibilities even as her primary responsibility remains that of her own citizens. The vertical division in the polity of Bangladesh with associated questions about the basis of its nationhood, which impacts also on its external relations, particularly with India, will have to be decided by the people of Bangladesh. Watertight compartments in relations between a state and its people cannot be made. Nevertheless, as interstate relations between the two countries are guided by reciprocity, every effort must also be made to reach out to the people of Bangladesh with the goodwill that is their due.

26

India and Bhutan

DALIP MEHTA

History

Relations between India and Bhutan go back several centuries. It was the Indian saint, Guru Padmasambhava, who introduced Buddhism to Bhutan in the 8ᵗʰ Century, albeit *via* Tibet, and he was followed by several other Indian sages. Buddhism to this day plays a central role in the lives of the Bhutanese people and has influenced Bhutan's institutions, arts, architecture, literature and social structures, and India is revered as the birthplace of the Buddha by all Bhutanese. The spiritual ties between the two countries therefore form an enduring bond.

Political and trade relations have also existed for centuries, between Bhutan and areas like Cooch Behar. The tails of white yaks so essential a part of court and religious rituals in India were among the much sought after items from Bhutan. More formal relation between the Bhutanese state and India began during the 1770s when Warren Hastings sent a mission to Bhutan following a conflict between Bhutan and Cooch Behar. By 1775 the British East India Company had established its authority throughout northern Bengal and in 1876 it annexed Assam. These developments upset Bhutan's interests in the Duars, accustomed as it was to exact tribute from the area, and disinclined to give up what it considered its traditional rights. Friction continued between the Bhutanese and the people of the plains and came to crisis point when Ashley Eden, of the Bengal Government, arrived uninvited in Bhutan in 1863. The humiliating treatment given to him by the Bhutanese, who allegedly smeared his face with dough, led to war and the subsequent Treaty of Sinchula (1865), which deprived Bhutan of any rights in the Duars, for which an annual monetary compensation was given. Dewangiri, in eastern Bhutan, was also ceded to the British, who established an army cantonment there.

Relations between the Bhutanese and the British improved during the reign of the first king, Ugyen Wangchuck, who provided invaluable assistance to the Younghusband Expedition to Tibet in 1903-04. Improving relations was reflected in the Treaty of Punakha (1910) whereby Bhutan's annual subsidy was generously increased, and in lieu of which that country agreed to be guided by Britain in its foreign relations. The British were primarily interested in safeguarding their Indian possession from any threat from the north and an independent buffer in Bhutan served their interests well.

The modern era

It was during the reign of the third King, Jigme Dorji Wangchuck, that Bhutan finally began to emerge from its policy of self-imposed isolation, coinciding with India gaining independence in 1947. Jigme Dorji Wangchuck was a far-sighted monarch who began the process of modernising political institutions in Bhutan. While the Treaty of Friendship of 1949 institutionalised the formal relations between India and Bhutan, the spirit of the relationship grew from visits of the king to India and Prime Minister Jawaharlal Nehru's to Bhutan in 1958. Nehru, at the age of 69 years, accompanied by Indira Gandhi, undertook the strenuous journey, *via* the Chumbi Valley, riding on yaks and ponies, to reach Paro, in Bhutan, to a tumultuous welcome. It was in Paro that Nehru made his famous speech in which he said, "some may think that since India is a great and powerful country and Bhutan a small one, the former may wish to exercise pressure on Bhutan. It is, therefore, essential that I make it clear to you that our only wish is that you should remain an independent country, choosing your own way of life and taking the path of progress according to your own will." He added that "freedom of both Bhutan and India should be safeguarded so that none from outside can do harm to it."

The king reciprocated when he visited Delhi and noted that: "the ties that bind our two countries is a matter of history. Our spiritual heritage, which we consider our greatest treasure, stems from the teachings of the great son of India, Lord Gautama Buddha. The bonds of understanding and friendship have been further consolidated as a result of the growing economic and technical cooperation between our two countries, and I am fully convinced that nothing can ever shake or destroy our friendship."

The geostrategic dimension of the relations between the two countries however came into sharp focus following the events in Tibet, when the Chinese army entered Lhasa in 1950, forcing the Dalai Lama to eventually flee his homeland in 1959. These events sent shock waves through Bhutan and led the Bhutanese to seal their border with its northern neighbour, a decision that had fundamental implications as prior to 1959 Bhutan's principal trade had been with Tibet. Bhutan and Tibet also shared common religious and cultural ties. Developments in Tibet had their repercussion in India as well. Nehru affirmed in Parliament that India's security frontier lay along the Himalayas and India could not permit that barrier to be penetrated. This assurance was well received by the Bhutanese, and was the genesis of the common security approach of the two countries.

Quite apart from the events in Tibet, Bhutan, situated south of the Himalayas, falls naturally into the subcontinental system as its valleys and rivers run into India. Being landlocked, India's ports and communications network serve Bhutan's trade and commerce well. Work on the road linking Thimphu, Bhutan's capital, *via* Phuntsholing with India was completed in 1961. The significance of this highway that links the two countries lies in the fact that the traditional orientation of Bhutan to the north, both in cultural and commercial terms, was now irrevocably turned southwards.

It is important to remember that the Bhutanese take great pride in the fact their country has remained an independent nation throughout its history. While Nehru's 1958 visit led to Bhutan embarking on a programme of planned development activity, the construction of a network of roads built by India's Border Road Organisation, the arrival in Bhutan of Indian experts in fields such as agriculture, horticulture, health, education, power among others, as well as the creation of Bhutan's army trained and equipped by India, the Bhutanese did not wish to be stifled by an exclusively Indian embrace.

Therefore, with India's active support Bhutan began the process of opening up to the rest of the world. It joined the Colombo Plan (1962), the Universal Postal Union (1969), the United Nations (1971), the Non-Aligned Movement (1973) and various other international bodies over the years, including SAARC (1985). However, it was the membership of the United Nations that was of fundamental importance for Bhutan as it was seen as international recognition of their sovereign status. In 1971 Bhutan established diplomatic relations with Bangladesh and today has diplomatic relations with 22 countries, six resident missions including those to the United Nations in New York and Geneva.

As articulated by the present king, Jigme Singye Wangchuck, Bhutan's foreign policy is threefold: ensuring the peace and security of Bhutan's citizens and the sovereign territorial integrity of the country; achieving economic self-reliance; and preserving the ancient religious and cultural heritage of the country. Specifically regarding India, the king has said that over the years the two countries, "have established and strengthened a mutually beneficial relationship. We have shown to the world that an enlightened and far-sighted leadership can make it possible for a large and powerful country like India to co-exist with a small neighbour like Bhutan in perfect harmony, understanding and friendship."

Economics

In 1961, with the financial support of the Government of India, Bhutan embarked on its first Five Year Plan. India continues to be the major donor for Bhutan's economic development. Eight Five Year Plans have been completed, the first two entirely financed by India. Since the Fourth Plan Bhutan has received financial assistance from sources other than India, both multilateral, from agencies such as UNDP, WHO, IMF, IBRD, ADB, UNICEF, and bilateral from Japan, Denmark, Australia, Switzerland, Austria, the UK among others. During Bhutan's Ninth Plan (2002-2007), Government of India's commitment is to the tune of Rs. 710 crores and covers health, education, power, civil aviation, culture and various other sectors. Following the visit of the King to Delhi in January, 2005 India agreed to prepare detailed project reports for two major hydel projects (Punatshanchhu Stage II and Mangdechhu), the establishment of railway links between bordering towns of India and Bhutan and greater cooperation in the fields of agriculture and allied sectors. Some of the major projects in Bhutan carried out with Indian assistance are Paro Airport, the Bhutan Broadcasting Station, a net-work of roads, microwave links, geological and mineral surveys and mapping, the Chukha (336 MW) and Kurichhu (60 MW) hydro-power projects, the Penden Cement Plant, several hospitals and schools. Due for completion in 2006 is the major Tala Hydropower Project (1020 MW) and the Dungsam Cement Plant in south-eastern Bhutan. The Chukha project alone constitutes 30 per cent of Bhutan's annual revenue and its export to India reached 75 per cent in 1998. India in turn benefits from the electricity generated by the project.

A free trade regime exists between India and Bhutan. The India-Bhutan Trade and Commerce Agreement was renewed in March 1995 and was effective for a 10 year period. The Agreement continues to be operative until proposed amendments by the two countries are agreed upon. The Agreement also provides for duty free transit of Bhutanese produce for trade with third countries. Twelve exit and entry points in India have been identified and four more are to be added shortly.

India continues to be Bhutan's major trading partner, with over 90 per cent of Bhutan's exports and imports being accounted for by India. The major items of export from Bhutan to India are electricity, cement, timber and wood products, minerals, cardamom, fruit products, raw silk and alcoholic beverages. Major imports from India are petroleum products, rice, automobiles and spares, machinery, textiles and pharmaceutical products. During 2004-05 Bhutan's exports totalled Rs. 377 crores and imports from India 225 crores.

Culture

There is close cooperation in the cultural and educational fields. Several scholarships are given to Bhutanese students to study in India and Bhutan's Sherubtse College is affiliated to Delhi University. Cultural exchanges between the two countries are frequent and popular. The Bhutan-India Friendship Association is active in promoting people-to-people contacts. The Bhutan-India Foundation, financed by both governments, was established during the visit of the Crown Prince to Delhi in 2003 to foster educational, cultural, scientific and technical cooperation between the two countries.

The Indian community in Bhutan is estimated to be around 32,000 including those working in India-assisted projects. About 1,500 Indians are employed with the Royal Government and the rest are engaged in professions related to health and education among others.

The present monarch

Jigme Singye Wangchuck, the present king, succeeded his father in 1972, when still not 17 years of age. During his reign Bhutan has witnessed rapid social and economic development as a result of his far-sighted planning. He has taken Bhutan's development process seamlessly into the age of computers and information technology, when 30 odd years ago few knew even how to type. What is especially remarkable is that this transformation has not been achieved at the cost of Bhutan's traditions and culture. Throughout the king has placed emphasis on human development with economic growth not an end in itself, but rather as a means for securing the well-being of his people. He has conceived the philosophy of 'gross national happiness', rather than gross domestic product (GDP), as the guiding principle of his planning.

In the sphere of constitutional reforms the king has shown himself to be bold and innovative with a remarkable ability to anticipate the winds of change. From being an absolute ruler he has gradually introduced decentralisation and democratisation of Bhutan's political institutions, something greatly appreciated in India. A draft written Constitution is presently under discussion with the people of all the 20 districts of Bhutan. It comes into force in 2008 when the king will abdicate in favour of the Crown Prince, and constitutional monarchy will come into being in Bhutan, with a parliament, council of ministers and an independent judiciary.

The king has interacted with almost every prime minister of India, all of whom have held him in the highest esteem. He is in many ways the constant factor in Bhutan's exceptional relations with India, and the architect of continuity and harmony between the two countries. He has never waivered in his belief that friendship with India is the keystone of Bhutan's foreign policy. He believes that an economically and militarily strong India is also in Bhutan's interest.

Indian militants in Bhutan

Over the years militants from Assam and West Bengal, ULFA and Bodo groups, had illegally established camps in Bhutan posing a grave security concern to both India and Bhutan. The presence of these militants posed a threat to Bhutan's sovereignty and security while their activities from Bhutanese soil were a threat to India's territorial integrity. When the process of peaceful dialogue between the Bhutan government and the militants failed, the king had no option but to conduct military operations in December 2003. Their decisive and successful outcome further consolidated relations between Bhutan and India as never before. The king became a hero for the peoples of both countries.

The Nepali question

A matter that has caused concern is regarding the Nepali population of southern Bhutan, or Lhotsampas as they are known. The problem is complicated, has cultural, historical and political dimensions and involves the sensitivities of the indigenous inhabitants, the descendants of the original Nepali immigrants and the more recent migrants from Nepal who have come to Bhutan for economic reasons. The King has all along been deeply committed to bringing the Nepali population into the national mainstream. Various measure to integrate the population were introduced, and all Nepali immigrants resident in Bhutan until December 1958 were granted citizenship. However many Nepalis entered Bhutan illegally, because of the open borders. To tackle the question of non-nationals, the Bhutanese government had to resort to, what was often, harsh measures resulting in an estimated 100,000 persons fleeing to refugee camps in Nepal. Many who fled were in fact legitimate nationals of Bhutan. Various rounds of talks have been held between the governments of Nepal and Bhutan and the UN High Commission for Refugees. Their successful outcome will enable genuine Bhutanese nationals of Nepali origin to return to their homeland.

India's role in this matter has been criticised; the Indian government has treated it as a bilateral problem to be resolved between Bhutan and Nepal, fearing that its intervention would only be seen as being partisan. India of course is greatly concerned that prolonging the stalemate may lead to an influx of the refugees illegally entering India. It is in everybody's interest that this sensitive and complicated matter is resolved at the earliest.

China

China has never recognised India's 'special relations' with Bhutan, nor has it accepted India's right to speak on behalf of Bhutan. This has been China's stated policy ever since the Nehru—Chou-En-lai talks of the early sixties. China has all along insisted on direct talks with Bhutan, especially concerning their border negotiations. As mentioned earlier, the Bhutanese were greatly alarmed at the events in Tibet in the fifties and matters did not improve when Mao, in his book *The Chinese Revolution and the Chinese Communist Party*, claimed Bhutan as one of the fingers of China's palm. Further, China published maps showing tracts claimed by Bhutan as part of Tibet. Some of these maps in fact showed areas deep inside Bhutan, including Tashigang, as part of China as well as territory in north-west Bhutan. Bhutan's 470 km long border with China remains undemarcated and delineated. Disputed areas are in high altitude pasture lands that have been traditionally used for grazing by both Bhutanese and Tibetan herdsmen. In the past the Chinese kept up the pressure by intruding, annually, into areas traditionally claimed by the Bhutanese. This was perhaps intended to force the Bhutanese into a direct dialogue, with the offer of a generous border settlement that would wean Bhutan away from India.

Be that as it may, with time and changed circumstances, Bhutan and China finally started their border discussions. Bhutan sent a team to Beijing for the first round of talks in 1984. Several rounds have since taken place and differences have been considerably narrowed. Bhutan, however, has tread cautiously and while seeking a positive conclusion to the negotiations, maintained its close relations with India. In 1998 Bhutan signed an Agreement of Peace and Tranquility on the Border, which was a step forward of substance, especially as in the Agreement Beijing categorically recognised Bhutan's status as a sovereign and independent country. Along with Bhutan's movement forward on the border issue, has been India's discussions with China on its border with that country. As India's relations with China improve, it is reasonable to assume that the boundary question between Bhutan and China may find an easier solution as various sectors are presently claimed by different parties and which would require an overall political solution. Hopefully these issues will be resolved to the satisfaction of all concerned.

At present Bhutan and China do not have diplomatic relations. Sooner or later they will, not only because China is Bhutan's only other neighbour, but now that China has been given 'observer' status at SAARC, a relationship becomes unavoidable. Both India and Bhutan would need to consult each other closely and craft a relationship with China that does not adversely impact on their own, and there is no reason that it should given the improving relations between the two Asian giants. A relationship should develop between the three countries that is sensitive to each other's concerns and mutually beneficial to all.

Future trends

The 1949 treaty

The substance and manner of Bhutan's relations with India has been exemplary over the decades. More than half a century has elapsed since Bhutan and India signed the Treaty of Perpetual Peace and Friendship in 1949. It is time to review the relevance of this Treaty, whether it best serves the interests of the two countries or has become irrelevant, or worse still a potential irritant between them. The Bhutanese have long regarded certain articles of the Treaty as offensive and incompatible with their status as a sovereign and independent country. For example Article II states that the Government of India "undertakes to exercise no interference in the internal administration of Bhutan. On its part the Government of Bhutan agrees to be guided by the advice of the Government of India in regard to its external relations." This article is taken verbatim from the earlier Treaty of Punakha, of 1910, signed between the British India Government and a Bhutan that had been defeated in war. It was actually a 'standstill' arrangement which may have served its purpose then, but is entirely anachronistic today. No such restriction was placed on Nepal in its Treaty with India of 1950, which states that both Governments agree "mutually to acknowledge and respect the complete sovereignty, territorial integrity and independence of each other." This unambiguous and categoric assertion is conspicuous by its absence from the Treaty with Bhutan.

Understandably today the Bhutanese increasingly regard the 1949 Treaty as one signed between unequal partners. Being discriminatory in nature, they see it as anachronistic, humiliating and obsolete, and an unacceptable aspersion on their sovereign status. The Treaty fails entirely to reflect present day realities, unlike, as mentioned above, the 1998 Agreement of Peace and Tranquility on the Border between China and Bhutan, in which the Chinese have unequivocally acknowledged Bhutan's sovereign and independent status. Today in Bhutan there is a vocal, educated and well informed middle class, proud of its country's past and confident of its future, that will not accept a subservient role to any country. An assertive bureaucracy and vocal parliament is unlikely to tolerate much longer a treaty it regards as an affront to its national dignity. In fact, over the years Bhutanese leaders, and debates in their parliament, have questioned the validity and utility of the 1949 Treaty which limits its independent foreign policy decisionmaking powers. With the King abdicating in 2008, a moderating and soothing influence in our relations will no longer be there. The Government of India will have to deal with a far more complex and diverse political regime in Thimphu, rather than the luxury of a single individual.

On several occasions the Bhutanese have deliberately ignored Article II of the Treaty in a conscious attempt to obtain international recognition of its separate status and to act independently of India in its foreign policy. The first such instance was in 1979 when Bhutan voted differently from India on Kampuchea at the Havana Non-Aligned Summit. There have been others since. In all such cases the Government of India has chosen to react by not reacting and merely ignoring such instances. It is fortunate that both governments have not allowed matters to get out of control and this was because Bhutan's right to run its own foreign policy was never questioned.

And it is not as if the 1949 Treaty has never been amended. Article VIII, which deals with extradition, was amended in 1996 by a fresh Agreement which takes into account the present day requirements of both countries.

A treaty should not be regarded as an end in itself but a means to ensure perceived national interests. For India, as far as Bhutan is concerned, these are those of defence and security. In other words a treaty relationship between the two countries should flow from a mutuality of interests in this regard. It is unrealistic to regard a treaty as sacrosanct simply because it exists without considering whether it is in fact effectively safeguarding the interests for which it is there. It would be preferable to arrive at a fresh understanding that is workable and which reflects the interests of both countries, and being signed by two sovereign countries, will have the political will to ensure its implementation.

Flowing from this, it is suggested that a more pragmatic arrangement would be to modify, better still enter into a fresh treaty, that is workable, entered into willingly for mutual benefit and with realistic obligations and responsibilities. As both India and Bhutan share common security perceptions Article II of the existing Treaty should be amended to stating that India and Bhutan will consult closely on foreign policy and security matters that affect their common interests.

India should take advantage of Article X of the 1949 Treaty which states that it "shall continue in force in perpetuity unless terminated or modified by mutual consent". This gives India the ideal opportunity to show its sensitivity towards Bhutan's national aspirations, for after all it is India that has all along recognised Bhutan's independent status, and was instrumental in assisting Bhutan becoming a member of the United Nations and some other international organisations. It would, in the circumstances, be a gracious gesture on India's part to take the initiative in recasting the Treaty and removing what could become a contentions issue between the two countries, as it has with the 1950 Treaty between Nepal and India. It would earn the Indian Government immense goodwill and gratitude in the long run.

It would also reflect the dynamics of changed times and better succeed in preserving the close relations between Bhutan and India while at the same time removing aspects of the present Treaty which cause deep offence to the Bhutanese people. For an arrangement to be workable it must reflect the concerns and aspirations of both the parties, else it becomes a potential source of discord, needlessly blighting an otherwise unique and remarkable relationship between the two countries which so far have never faltered.

Indian agencies in Bhutan

When first Bhutan began the process of modernisation in the early sixties, its manpower was ill-equipped to take on the formidable task and it was Indian experts who assisted with all aspects of endeavour, from running government departments to implementing various projects. Over the years Bhutan has trained an exceptionally professional cadre of officials, diplomats, engineers, doctors, teachers and others, lessening almost entirely its dependence on outside assistance and expertise. As a result, several government of India agencies which had done pioneering work in the most arduous conditions have over time handed over their responsibilities to their Bhutanese colleagues. The Geological Survey of India handed over their establishment and museum in Samtse, southern Bhutan, as did the Police Advisor in Thimphu. The headquarters of Dantak (the Border Roads Organisation) in Deothang, eastern Bhutan a vast complex reverted to the Royal Bhutan Army and was the command centre for Bhutan's successful military operations against the Indian militants in Bhutan. Dantak is now located in more modest accommodation in Thimphu, commensurate with its reduced workload.

The Indian Military Training Team, IMTRAT, has over the decades trained the Royal Bhutan Army into the fighting force that it is today. IMTRAT has done sterling work in Bhutan, is greatly respected and has excellent relations with the Bhutanese army. However, with the changing times it is necessary that their somewhat larger than life profile also changes. For IMTRAT to continue effectively in Bhutan it needs to be less conspicuous as a foreign military presence so that it becomes more acceptable to the general populace. IMTRAT should also vacate the Dzong in HAA, which is a magnificent heritage building of considerable importance and also houses some of the holiest shrines in Bhutan. Such a gesture would earn it immense goodwill among the local people who have an emotional and religious attachment to the building.

Conclusion

Relations between Bhutan and India are intimate and extensive and a rare example of how a large and powerful country and a comparatively small country have enjoyed a mutually beneficial relationship. Leaders of both countries have shown remarkable understanding towards the sensitivities of the other, which has helped to make the relationship so special. Both India and Bhutan share common security perceptions based on geographical considerations and historical ties. While these factors cannot be taken for granted, nor indeed should they be, they can be capitalised upon for further strengthening relations for the benefit of their peoples. Both countries should be flexible and anticipatory in their approach in keeping with the changing times, which alone will ensure durability in their bilateral relations.

27

India and Myanmar

I.P. Khosla

Introduction

In international relations there is a continuing tension between the ethical and the expedient. No one concerned with the subject over a period of time can avoid it; the academic analyst as much as the diplomatic practitioner has to confront it and decide how to deal with it. Resolving this tension is often difficult and always contextual.

In order to illustrate the point, we may take as sample one of the leading academic schools. We would expect the realists to have the most cogent set of reasons to favour the expedient over the ethical, the pragmatic over the principled. In this school, Hans Morgenthau and Kenneth Waltz are the leaders; they wrote the classics. But both of them got into confusion when dealing with this source of tension.

Morgenthau starts with, "the concept of interest defined in terms of power" as the main signpost to guide you through the subject. But then he inserts the "moral significance of political action" as one of his six principles of political realism; and this leads to "the ineluctable tension between the moral command and the requirements of successful political action." However, this moral or ethical aspect is to be judged by its political consequences: "political ethics judges action by its political consequences," or, in other words, it is moral to follow the signpost of interest defined in terms of power, which is a circular argument.[1]

Waltz recognised the circularity of Morgenthau's argument and tried to escape it by deleting the moral from his systemic framework altogether. But then he came up against the problem of why, when the USA is so powerful, when it was capable of bombing Vietnam back into the stone age, was it defeated there. That, he says, was "a clear illustration of the limits of military force in the world of the present..." But he is unable to explain what sets these limits; it can only be the moral, but that has been ruled out, so now he has to take shelter elsewhere, to say that "success or failure in peripheral places now means less in material terms than it did to previous great powers;" "we have so many means of non-forceful leverage" so why should the US be interested in extending military control over others; and "to refrain from fighting is easier because so little is at stake." But all this does not clarify why the US went to that peripheral place, why nonforceful means of leverage were not used, and why it went at all, when so little was at stake. So this, too, becomes a circular argument.[2]

Practitioners do not find it so difficult to resolve this 'ineluctable tension'; for them most situations demand a practical mix of the ethical and the expedient, and often the two are in harmony. One may quote Jawaharlal Nehru. The 'One World' principle occupied an important place in his thinking. Long before India's independence, he had wanted to work for the building up of a world commonwealth. "It is for this One World that free India will work..." This was a world in which international goodwill, peace and freedom prevail. But he also said, "We may talk about international goodwill and mean what we say. We may talk about peace and freedom and earnestly mean what we say." But "the art of conducting the foreign affairs of a country lies in finding out what is most advantageous to the country."[3]

---

1. Morgenthau, Hans J. (1966). *Politics Among Nations, The Struggle for Power and Peace*, Scientific Book Agency, Calcutta. The quotations are from pp. 5 and 10.

2. Waltz, Kenneth N. (1979). *Theory of International Politics*, Addison-Wesley, Reading, Mass. All the quotes are from p. 190.

3. Broadcast from New Delhi, September 7, 1946, reprinted in Jawaharlal Nehru (1961). *India's Foreign Policy*, Selected Speeches, September 1946-April 1961, The Publications Division, Government of India, p. 2. See also p. 28.

Nehru was fortunate. In his experience, with the exception of China,[4] peace and freedom and what is most advantageous generally went together. A typical example may be given, where he clarified that the ethical and the expedient must go hand in hand. In autumn 1950, there was a confrontation between the King of Nepal and the democratic forces represented by the Nepali Congress, on the one hand, and the ruling oligarchy of Ranas, on the other. The King fled to India and Nehru announced that "we have stood for progressive democracy ... specially so, when one of our neighbouring countries is concerned ... we did not wish to interfere with Nepal in any way, but at the same time realized that, unless some steps were taken in her internal sphere, difficulties might arise;" security was involved, for given developments in China and Tibet, and the nature of the Himalayas, "we cannot allow that barrier to be penetrated, to be crossed or weakened, for it is also the principal barrier to India."[5] So there was no tension between the ethical and the expedient. India had a preference about the kind of democratic political setup desirable in Nepal, helped to bring about that setup and served her security interests at the same time.

Indeed, in framing his policies towards Myanmar also, Nehru did not face this 'ineluctable tension'; his relations with U Nu were a model of successfully blending the ethical and the expedient; and it was only in subsequent years that its resolution became an important focus of India's policy. And at that point the senior diplomat in the External Affairs Ministry told representatives from Myanmar, as India prepared to change direction in 1992 from an exclusive concern with the promotion of democracy there to a more pragmatic policy of promoting self-interest: "We conveyed that our objective was not to interfere in the internal affairs of Myanmar. Our only purpose was to stress the fact that India has always been supportive of democratic principles and democratic institutions."[6]

---

4. Pakistan was not an exception since India's attitude to the military government there and our self-interest were in harmony.

5. Nehru, Jawaharlal. *op. cit.*, pp.28 and 436.

6. Dixit, J.N. (1996). *My South Block Years, Memoirs of a Foreign Secretary*, UBS Publishers, New Delhi, p. 168.

A variant on this is the argument that, in Myanmar, "while India could have maintained a public position supportive of democracy and human rights, it should have taken subtle action to ensure that its strategic concerns were acknowledged."[7]

So we have here the ethical, the promotion of democracy, of human rights and so on; we have the expedient, the promotion of strategic concerns; and we have the strong commitment to non-interference as a basic norm for the conduct of international relations. In what follows, an attempt is made to assess the way these ideas combined in our relations with Myanmar during the period 1948 to the present.

The ties of civilisation and culture

Whenever there is a high level visit from Myanmar to India or *vice versa*, the references to the ties of civilisation and culture between the two countries are profuse. To give one recent example, when the Vice Chairman of the Myanmar State Peace and Development Council (SPDC), the highest decisionmaking body in the country, visited India in November 2000, his host, the Vice President of India, referred in his welcoming speech to the bonds of geography, history and culture, linking the two peoples, and added, "numerous references to our ties can be found in the Indian epics *Ramayana* and *Mahabharata*. For Indians, Myanmar is *Brahmadesh*, or the sacred land of Lord Brahma. Indian sailors, traders and exporters who visited Myanmar centuries ago gave her the name of Swarnabhumi—the land of gold"[8] and then went on to refer to Buddhism and the common struggle against colonialism.

There is in Myanmar a tradition that the Buddha himself sent two merchants to Myanmar, Tapusa and Bhallika, with eight hairs of his head, so that they may spread the faith. The hairs were later enshrined at the top of the Singutara hill, and the Shwedagon

---

7. Malik, P.M.S. (1998). India's Ambassador to Myanmar in the years 1990-92, see his article, "Indo-Myanmar Relations" in *Indian Foreign Policy, Agenda for the 21st century*, Vol.2, Foreign Service Institute, New Delhi, p. 286.

8. For the text see *Strategic Digest of the Institute for Defence Studies and Analyses*, Vol. XXXI, No. 2, February 2001, p. 178.

pagoda was built there. Another tradition has it that it was the Emperor Ashoka who sent two missionaries to Myanmar to spread the faith. The connections go beyond Buddhism. *The Glass Palace Chronicles* compiled in 19th Century Myanmar record that since ancient times the Kings of Myanmar were Kshatriyas and originated in the Ganges valley. They accepted the code of Manu as the prime source of law and the Konbaung dynasty (1752-1885 AD, the last one) compiled a new legal code based on that of Manu. The Kings of the Pyu dynasty (17th Century) gave themselves Indian titles: Surya Vikrama; Hari Vikrama; Jayachandra Varman. Then and later Brahmin priests advised on, supervised and even conducted the royal ceremonies such as coronations and audiences, while marriage to Indian princesses were frequent. Selections from the Hindu pantheon were worshipped: Saraswati was Thayethadi; Siva was *Paramizwa*; there was Vishnu and Indra. When the Court wished to promote an image of pomp and stature for Royalty among the people, drama companies were sent around the countryside to perform the *Ramayana*; early in the 19th Century a separate Ministry of Theatre was created for this purpose.

A more recent historic link is the fact that the last Konbaung King was exiled to Ratnagiri in India and died there, while the last Moghul Emperor, Bahadur Shah Zafar, was exiled to and died in Yangon.

The empathy generated by these cultural and civilisational commonalties was an important ingredient in the closeness with which the freedom movements worked together, though there were two hiccups during the time they did so.

From September 1920, when the Indian National Congress (INC) adopted the famous Non-cooperation resolution, its activities were extended in a systematic way to Myanmar. Gandhi, Nehru, Bose and other political leaders from India started visiting Myanmar on the invitation of one or other of the many political and even religious organisations established by the Indian community there. This included, apart from the INC, the Muslim League, the Arya Samaj and the Hindu Mahasabha, the Akali Dal and the Nattukottai Chettiyars. They interacted with the Myanmar political leaders, while the latter adopted many of their political methods. Tharrawady U Pu, a leader of the non-cooperation movement, was called Gandhi Pu.[9] The Dobama Asiayone was an association of Thakins formally organised in July 1933 to demand complete independence. This was a new generation of young leaders who were actually to lead Myanmar into independence, and they regularly attended sessions of the INC. In 1935, at the first conference of the Asiayone, the INC programme in its entirety was adopted. At the April 1939 conference, held at Moulmein, Aung San and U Nu placed the entire programme of action of the INC before the delegates and they again adopted it in entirety. In March 1940, Aung San led a delegation from the Asiayone to the Ramgarh session and thereafter travelled to Gaya, Varanasi and as far as Peshawar and the Khyber Pass.

The first hiccup was about separation. Myanmar had been placed for all administrative purposes under the government of India in 1886 and the "most important political issue which Burma faced from 1931 to 1936 (when separation was finalized) was whether or not the country should be separated from India..."[10] The demand for separation was voiced strongly by the leaders of the Asiayone, but the Indian settlers in Myanmar opposed it, and under their influence the INC had, in 1927, even passed a resolution that it be rejected, a resolution which was later and wisely reversed.

The second arose more from local resentment of the Indian settlers than from any initiative of the latter. In May 1930, there was two weeks of rioting in the Yangon dockyards between Indian dock labour who had struck work demanding higher wages and local workers who had been recruited to replace them. In December that year, a peasant rebellion broke out in protest against the refusal of the government to reduce taxes following the dramatic drop in world rice prices following the great depression; the violence spread to the districts where Indian landowners and tenants were

---

9. See Pradhan, Swatanter K. (2000). *New Dimensions in Indo-Burmese Relations*, Rajat Publications, New Delhi, p.17.

10. Singh, Uma Shankar (1979). *Burma and India, 1948-1962*, Oxford and IBH Publishing Co., New Delhi, 1979, p. 22.

concentrated and became, in some part, an Indians *versus* Myanmar riot before it was brought under control. Again on July 26, 1938 anti-India rioting led by monks spread through most of Southern and Central Myanmar. "The ostensible cause of the riots was the publication of an anti-Buddhist tract by a Burmese Muslim."[11] In September 1938, there was another outbreak of anti-Indian rioting in Yangon, this one quickly brought under control. The leadership on both sides tried to remove the causes of this violence, but they were too deep to be fully removed, as we shall see.

Nehru and U Nu

The great flowering of India-Myanmar friendship happened during the years that Nehru and U Nu were Prime Ministers. This was between 1948 and 1962, a period of about a dozen years given that U Nu was out of power for some of those years. It was a period of complete understanding and perfect friendship that is today cited not only as a model for this relationship but for any bilateral relationship. Their personal relations were close; they had the same wide international interests and, by and large, similar views on the issues; and they did not allow bilateral differences to disturb their mutual understanding.

After the assassination of Aung San on 19 July 1947 U Nu became Prime Minister and, having steered the Myanmar constitution through the Constituent Assembly, and even before the date of independence (4 January, 1948) arrived in New Delhi on 2 December 1947, his first official visit to India and his first meeting with Nehru. In his autobiography U Nu says he "formed an attachment to Pandit Nehru from the time of that first visit.", and hence "took a special delight in visiting India at least once a year." [12] There was no protocol, no routing of a request for a visit through the foreign office, as was the case with visits to every other country, no fanfare or joint declarations or agreed texts. U Nu would, as he says, "merely write a letter telling Pandit Nehru the

---

11. Taylor, Robert H. (1987). *The State in Burma*, C. Hurst and Co., London, 1987, p. 200.

12. Nu, U. (1975). *Saturday's Son*, Yale University Press, New Haven, 1975, p. 225. The book is throughout in the third person, so that U Nu refers to himself as 'he' or 'U Nu'.

date of his arrival and the mode of travel."[13] And he would always, with the exception of that first visit, stay with Nehru. They would meet and talk as friends do, about the situation in Myanmar, then coping with separatist movements and under insurgent attack, about the peace treaty with Japan, about the international struggle against colonial rule and about their dreams of Asian unity, the Cold War and economic development, world peace and cooperation. U Nu was convinced that Nehru was an incarnation of Ashoka. "Athawka had built the first temple at Sanchi; Nehru was building its replica. The same relics of the disciples Sariputta and Moggalana that Athawka had venerated were being respectfully enshrined by Nehru ...The great love that the people had for Athawka they now showed to Nehru...when Nehru in his previous existence lived as Athawka, he, U Nu, must have been somebody in close association with him."[14] And when Nehru told him he had no religion but was inclined towards Buddhism, this was final confirmation for U Nu that he was, indeed, a reincarnation.

Nehru felt just as close, as his letters to U Nu show. In 1956, the latter announced his decision to resign and go into retreat and Nehru wrote, "Your not being Prime Minister creates a little void for me and, I have no doubt, for many others ..." After the caretaker government of Ne Win, U Nu came back to power in 1960 and one of the things he did was to visit Nehru, who was flowing over with happiness, and greeted him with, "when you come here, you not only bring the perfume of your country but also an air of serenity, of calm, of friendliness ... how you have developed these qualities, I do not know."

Among other things the state of bilateral relations can be gauged from the reaction of the Myanmar press to the signing of the Treaty of Friendship on 7 July 1951, which provided that there shall be everlasting peace and unalterable friendship between the two states: "yet another brilliant chapter has been added to the annals of Burmese history;" "this treaty...highlights the

13. *ibid.*, p. 236.
14. *ibid.*, p. 235.

understanding and mutual sympathy that has existed between the peoples of the two countries from time immemorial ... nearly twenty five centuries ago when Buddhism began to spread."[15]

Bilateral relations were not trouble free, but this closeness made them so.

Myanmar took measures like the Land Nationalization Act of 1948 under which non-cultivators were prohibited from possessing more than 50 acres of land each. Now it was the Chettiyars of India who were the largest number of non-cultivators. They had given loans to the Myanmar owners against land as collateral; under the legal systems established by the British action to take possession was swift and gradually they had come to own a great deal of land. In 1939, out of a total of 11.5 million acres of land cultivated in lower Myanmar, 4.5 million was owned by non-cultivators, and of this two thirds was in the hands of the Chettiyars; they stood to lose almost all the land in their names and they would get little compensation.

When the All Burma India Congress approached Nehru, he replied that: "it is essential and in the interests of both countries to have close and most friendly relations with each other. Even if differences arise, these differences must be looked upon as family differences..."[16]

Subsequently, the Annual Report of the Ministry of External Affairs, 1956-57 stated, "Certain measures taken by the Government of Burma in the sphere of trade and economy have adversely affected Indian interests in that country ... This, however, was not allowed to interfere with the cordial relations existing between the two countries."

The measures continued, but it appears that they were not even taken up with the government of Myanmar. On 25 August 1960, the Deputy Minister of External Affairs told the Parliament the measures were being applied without discrimination and since "there

15. See Desai, W.S. (1954). *India and Burma, A Study*, Orient Longman, Calcutta, pp. 107-108.

16. See the quote in Pradhan, Swatanter K. (1948). *op. cit.* n.9, p. 192, citing *The Statesman*, 30 December.

is no discrimination at all, there is no point in our taking up this matter with the government of Burma." After Nehru it would no longer be possible for any government of India to argue that measures taken by a foreign government which affected Indians generally were not discriminatory and therefore were not being taken up.

The 1960 border agreement concluded by China and Myanmar, too, was not allowed to get in the way of this friendship, though U Nu did seem to hold it up as a model.

He said on April 5, 1960, while addressing the Chamber of Deputies, "I cannot let this opportunity go by without expressing my sincere hope that our great neighbours—China and India—will also be able to arrive at a solution very soon of their border problems, and in the same spirit of amity and compromise ..."[17] And he said similar things when he came to India in November 1960, suggesting that Chou En-lai was sincere, so that the Indian press was critical of him and adverse comments were made in Parliament —did he mean that the Indian side was not sincere? To which Nehru responded, "so far as U Nu is concerned, who is a dear friend of ours, with whom I have the privilege of friendship for many years, to conclude that because he said that Mr. Chou En-Lai was sincere he thought that I was insincere, I submit, is an absurd inference."[18] Nehru even added that the China-Myanmar agreement could be considered helpful since it was signed on the principle of the watershed and the Macmahon line, which was India's view also.

The situation changed with the coup in which U Nu was replaced by a military government led by General Ne Win. Parliament was dissolved; the constitution set aside; all courts abolished.

The impact of colonialism

The role of the armed forces and more about the general attitude in Myanmar to the Indian community living there need to be

---

17. Pakem, B. (1992). *India Burma Relations*, Omsons Publications, New Delhi, p. 98.

18. Quoted from the Lok Sabha debates in B. Pakem, *ibid.*, p. 94.

understood in the context of historical developments to grasp that the counterposing of military rule and democracy may be less important than to project the consequences of Myanmar's possible disintegration; and that attitudes to India are not independent of attitudes to the Indian community.

Many kinds of bonds (other than geography, which should be the starting point) contribute to the sovereign integrity of a state; some are more important, some less. A functioning ruling system, what may be called the state structure, is important; religion could be another, as could language, culture and the many intangibles that make for the unity of a people.

The British had an assessment of the reasons for the strength of the sovereign integrity of Myanmar and the consequent scale and intensity of the nationalist resistance they faced there; even after November 1885, with all of the country ostensibly under control, it took them 10 years to subdue the countryside. Based on this assessment they proceeded to destroy first the state structure, second and at the same time, the religious structure and third, the unity of the people.

The destruction of the state structure started with the exile of King Thibaw to Ratnagiri in India and continued with the dismantling of the entire institutional structure of political and administrative authority. This may be contrasted with their policy in India, where they imposed a superior layer of authority, their own, over the existing state structure which was largely left untouched. In Myanmar the Royal family, the nobility, the whole apparatus down to the village headman was removed, exiled or disempowered.

"The destruction of the headmen's personal authority" started the dismantling of local government systems in favour of direct control of the village units, so that the pre-colonial system was "completely replaced by a system of salaried, appointed headmen who ... were cogs in the wheel of a regularised bureaucratic state...."[19] The Military Police, 4,294 in number in 1941, also referred

---

19. See Robert H. Taylor, *op. cit.*, pp. 83-86.

to as the punitive police since they were the ones to carry out punishment, including of entire villages, for violating the norms of colonial conduct, were composed entirely of Indians, with British and Indian officers seconded from the Indian army. Since the headman as the intermediary between higher authority and the people was now powerless, far more coercion was needed and it was the Military Police which did this, ensuring the effectiveness of direct control in lower Myanmar. The Frontier Force of 10,000, established to carry out the same task in the hill areas, was also composed almost entirely of Indians (7,400) with some from the hill areas of Myanmar. In the urban centres, it was the Indians who largely manned the bureaucratic positions. By the end of the 19th Century the entire Yangon police was Indian. By the 1920s they dominated the PWD, road transport, the railways and the ports. In Yangon itself they comprised over half the population.

For the average person in Myanmar, in village and in town, the face of the alien ruler was the face of the Indian. Second to getting rid of the British came the Myanmar nationalist desire to get rid of the Indians. When the Japanese army entered Myanmar in 1942 it was Aung San and his Burma Independence Army which played a major role in chasing out the Indians; and he himself, passing through Delhi on his way to London for talks on independence, told Nehru that the Indians in Myanmar were not in favour of independence. Years later, his daughter was to write of the Burmese growing "though diffused xenophobia fed by a well justified apprehension that their very existence as a distinct people would be jeopardized" by the racial threat, the threat from Indians and Chinese who "set up homes with Burmese women, striking at the very roots of Burmese manhood and purity."[20]

This is not recent however. A member of the Myanmar Legislative Council had said in the 1920s "the Indians have come into all sorts of corners and wherever they have colonized themselves they have taken into themselves Burmese wives and the

---

20. Kyi, Aung San Suu (1991). *Freedom from Fear and Other Writings*, Penguin Books, New Delhi, 1991, pp. 103-104.

race is impaired."[21] And it persisted. In 1979, Ne Win had this to say: "Today you can see that even people of pure blood are being disloyal to others. If people of pure blood act this way, we must carefully watch people of mixed blood", meaning of course those from Indian or Chinese marriages with local people.[22]

At a subsequent period it was possible to assess that "Myanmar regards India as its potential enemy" due in part to historic causes: Indian migration; Indians staffing the administration setup by the British; staffing the army used to subdue the Burmese; Indian moneylenders to whom many Burmese lost their land.[23]

British rule also undermined religion, seen by them as a social bond that could strengthen nationalism. In the pre-colonial period, the monks, spread through every village, and urban centre, provided direct access to the people from the highest levels through their hierarchy. They ran the educational system and provided cultural cohesion. So the ecclesiastical hierarchy and the head of the *Sangha* were stripped of their power by de-recognition, and Buddhist law, which traditionally maintained discipline and order within the *Sangha*, was ignored or superceded by secular or civil law. Lay persons were appointed to administer the major Buddhist pilgrimage sites and public places of worship. In the result, the discipline of the monks declined, monastic education was neglected, pagodas and shrines were denied adequate maintenance, and the supervised uniformity of a religious institution broke up into segregated enclaves for religious observance or salvation.

As in all sociocultural matters the dividing is more effective than the reuniting. U Nu tried to promote Buddhism as the unifying force it once was. He promulgated a Buddha Sasana Act to promote the religion with state support; created a Ministry of Religious Affairs and a Pali University; convened the Sixth Great Buddhist Council (the fifth was in 1871 under King Mindon); and finally, in

---

21. Cited in B. Pakem, *op. cit.*, p. 142.

22. BBC, Summary of World broadcasts, of 15 December 1979 quoting U Ne Win, Chairman, Burma Socialist Programme Party, speaking on 11 December 1979.

23. Steinberg, David I. (1993). "Myanmar as Nexus: Sino-Indian Rivalries on the Frontier", in *Studies in Conflict and Terrorism*, Vol. 16, No. 3, p. 2.

September 1961, six months before the coup that dislodged him, adopted Buddhism as the state religion. None of these steps helped.

The British effort to undermine or destroy the unity of the people in order to minimise opposition to their rule had four facets: converting geography into ethnicity; giving the ethnic groups thus created distinct characteristics; concretising these through administrative practices; and finally, the groups come to see themselves as different

The geography of Myanmar can conveniently be divided into two: the fertile tropical open plain bounded on the Northwest by the river Chindwin, on the South-East by the river Sittang and with the major river Ayeyarwady flowing north to south through its centre; and the horseshoe of mountains which border this plain on west, north and east. The latter comprises over a third of the total land area but only 20 per cent of the population of the country. The British converted this into ethnicity first by separating the people of the mountain from those of the plain.

In October 1886 Lord Dufferin, Viceroy of India wrote to the secretary of state for India in London, that the "Shans, Kachins and other mountain tribes live under the rule of hereditary Chiefs, whose authority is generally sufficient to preserve order among them. Here, then, we have to deal not with disintegrated masses as in Burma proper..." So all that was needed was to secure the allegiance of the Chiefs.[24]

This was also important for the legitimacy of colonial rule; a proposition taken for granted was that the history of Myanmar was "a coherent story of inherent instability having to do with Burma's geography, ethnic heterogeneity and political history, and poppy and personal corruption... save for a short period under British rule, Burma has *never* known peace or unity " (italics in original).[25]

---

24. Smith, Martin (1999). *Burma: Insurgency and the Politics of Ethnicity*, Zed Books, London, p. 41.

25. Tucker, Shelby (2002). *Burma, The Curse of Independence*, Penguin Books, India, p. 7, 209.

They were also constantly further subdivided in neverending refinements of the process of converting geography into ethnicity. "In the various government censuses and reports there were constant shifts in criteria for what was deemed an ethnic group."[26] Each shift meant an expansion in the number of subdivisions. If the people were asked what was the 'language ordinarily used in the house' there was one set of answers. By changing the question to 'mother tongue' the number of subdivisions increased. In the 1921 census, for instance, everybody in Mergui spoke Burmese; 10 years later they were asked if their language was Merguese, a question never earlier posed. 100,000 did so; a new subdivision had appeared as if by magic. By 1931, the last time an ethnic breakdown was tried in the census, there were 44 ethnic subgroups among the Chins alone, who accounted for only 2 per cent of the population.

Then ethnic groups were given specific characteristics. "These diverse peoples have discrete physical attributes, as shown by the anthropometric data collected by British recruitment officers". Thus, the Karen is darker than the Burmese, the Shan is taller than the people of the hill tribes, "but his chest and legs are not so well developed,"[27] and so on. They were all given discrete physical attributes, character specifications like which one was warlike or loyal or submissive, and separate languages. American missionaries played a role in giving languages to those groups who had no idea till then they had one, inventing a script, starting newspapers and developing a literature. And a separate culture, with descriptions of clan systems, marriage customs, inter-tribal affinities and antagonisms. And, of course, histories: the Shans became identified with the ancient Nanchao kingdom in Yunnan; the Pao with the long lost Pyu or the first proto-Burmans; and, of course, there was no shortage of anthropologists who identified one or other group among the Karens with the lost tribes of Israel, because they too had legends of one God, Y'wa, of a Garden of Creation and of a Golden Book.

---

26. Smith, Martin. *op. cit.*, p. 34.

27. Enriquez, Colin Metcalf Dallas (1933). *The Races of Burma*, Government of India, Manager of Publications, New Delhi, 1933, p. 6, which was actually written as a guide for recruiting the Frontier Force and the Army.

Several methods were used for concretising these differences.

Proselytising by Americans, specially the Baptists, by British and European missionaries, was important. They propagated the idea of an independent Karen state while setting up schools and a college (Judson College) which became the focus for the spread of such ideas to other minorities.

Differences in the administrative structure were more important; as earlier pointed out the powers of the pre-colonial administration were dismantled while in the hill areas they were retained. Recruitment to the armed forces consistently favoured the hill people over those from the plain. In 1939 there were only 472 Burmans in the Army, compared with 1,448 Karens, who had played an important role in suppressing the nationalist uprisings of the 1880s and 1890s, and again were used against the peasant rebellion of the 1930s; 886 Chins; and 881 Kachins. In order to ensure separate treatment a Burma Frontier Service was created to administer the hill areas.

In the years after independence the separatist movements of the hill areas accordingly claimed a legitimacy based on representing nations distinct from the Myanmar of the plain. Thus, in a 1959 statement the Shan State Independence Army said there was "no community of language, culture or interests between the Shans and the Burmese save religion, nor is there any sentiment of unity which is the index of a common national mind." The Karen National Union says, "The Karens are much more than a national minority. We are a nation." And the Arakanese Communist Party claimed in 1962 that the people of Arakan are a "nation which has been annexed into an Empire, if it does not get back its sovereignty, is still under the colonial yoke and is still a colonial nation ..."[28]

The view of the government, by contrast, is that Myanmar is a country where several nations live and have lived throughout history, in harmony and unity. The officially approved history books refer to one identity from which the resistance to colonial

---

28. The quotations are from Martin Smith, *op. cit.*, p. 36.

rule arose, one identity from which the Armed Forces or Tatmadaw come, an identity of which the different races are a part.

When Japanese forces entered Myanmar in 1942 the entire state structure disappeared into India. There had been British officials manning the top positions and Indians the ones at middle and lower levels; all of them left in a large scale exodus which included British and Indian business, professionals, the police, missionaries, half a million people in all; Yangon's population was reduced to a third. One extreme view is that state structure proper did not reappear for 20 years. "Viewed from the perspective of the evolution of the state *qua* state, these twenty years (1942-1962) are better seen as a whole, during which the state, denied the support of the British-Indian empire, and briefly and ineffectually backed by the Japanese empire, disintegrated and was displaced."[29] Another way of putting this is that "Burma at independence faced a weak institutional legacy, a vacuum which the new war-time army was soon able to fill."[30]

After achieving independence in 1948, with neither a state structure nor a religious framework to hold it together, with the dominance of separatism from the colonial years, it was remarkable that Myanmar survived in unified form.

In any case, at independence Myanmar did not have a state in the sense of the ruling institutions that have a monopoly on the use of legitimate force. There was the political leadership and nothing below. Months of civil war followed. Parallel governments run by local warlords called *Bo* emerged. They assumed responsibility for law and order, ran their own administrations, issued their own decrees as law. In March 1948, the communists went underground; by October 1948, the Karen nationalist organisation had taken up arms against the government. By May 1949, Karen insurgents were holding out at Insein, nine miles from Yangon, and held out there through a four-month siege by government forces before pulling back. By then the tide was turning and the armed forces were

29. Taylor, Robert H., *op. cit.*, p. 217.

30. Myint-U, Thant (2001). *The Making of Modern Burma*, Cambridge University Press, p. 254.

regaining control; as they advanced they put in place the kind of administration they thought would be most suitable, and this was led by their own officers. It was in any case beyond the capability of the U Nu government at the centre, riddled by internal dissension, to place a civilian structure in place, so the armed forces continued to regard themselves as the state.

As the years went by U Nu's government continued to show a conspicuous lack of ability to lead the state out of the endless demands of the minorities for greater autonomy. U Nu promised statehood to Arakan, then to the Mons, then the Shan, Kachin and Chin leaders demanded the same; it seemed that what had been gained on the battlefield was going to be given up by politics. By early 1962 it was clear, as one author says, that U Nu's policies "had plunged the country into chaos. He had promised statehood to the Shans, and it was obvious that this had only stimulated similar demands from other minorities... any move to yield to such pressures might dismember the Union of Burma."[31]

The Ne Win years

On March 2, 1962 he was due to make a speech promising, so the reports suggested, equal powers to the constituent states, which presaged the breakup of the Union; he never made that speech for Ne Win took over power that morning.

So today the armed forces believe they are the state and the only cohesive force that can keep the state in being.

For two years after the coup relations between India and Myanmar were somewhat strained; not because of democracy, for Nehru did not make any critical comments on this aspect, but because of two other issues, the same issues, in fact, that had come up during the time of U Nu but were not allowed to come in the way of good relations.

In pursuit of the Burmese Way to Socialism, the official economic policy of the military government, four main objectives were

31. Krishnamurthy, S. (2000). "The Political Role of the Army in Burma and Indonesia", in Verinder Grover, (ed.), *Myanmar, Government and Politics*, Deep and Deep Publications, New Delhi, p. 173.

envisaged: the elimination of foreign control over the economy; a reduction in the dependence on foreign markets; balanced industrial development; and the centralisation of economic power in the hands of the state. The first of these was implemented right away; banks, shops, the import export trade, the rice and tobacco industries, travel agencies, all these were the ones largely owned and run by the Indians. All were nationalised. There was no discrimination. Many and much larger western companies were also nationalised. This included the Burma Oil Company, Anglo-Burma Mines Company, Unilever, oil wells, over 800 private schools, ruby and jade mines and others in which ownership was largely in non-Indian hands, though Indians had some ownership interest, and, more important, were the largest single group of employees.

As a people the Indians were the hardest hit. They were there in the largest numbers as owners and employees: half a million at the time. By 1964, 80,000 had registered for repatriation; by 1967, over 200,000 had left. On nationalisations, India's policy was different, though not radically so. Swaran Singh, the Minister of External Affairs, went to Yangon in September 1964 to try to help attenuate the impact of the drastic measures taken by Myanmar, but came back empty handed and had to tell Parliament so, quite in contrast to Nehru's airy dismissal of such measures as 'family differences', which therefore need not be taken up, though, of course there was an element of harshness in Ne Win's treatment of the expatriates compared with U Nu.

The second issue was the less than astute effort by Ne Win to resolve the India-China border question, after the Colombo Powers had failed. As one example, the joint communiqué between China and Myanmar of February 18, 1964 stated that "The two sides were glad to note that the situation along the Sino-Indian border had ceased. They expressed the hope that China and India would find it possible to enter into direct negotiations on the basis of the Colombo proposals so as to remove progressively the differences between them... "[32]

---

32. Cited in B. Pakem, *op. cit.*, p. 99.

After mid-1964, the India-Myanmar relationship began changing. This was partly because the new Prime Minister of India, Lal Bahadur Shastri, had no personal friendship with U Nu, but largely because of the rift between Myanmar and China, a rift which had its sources in the beginnings of the cultural revolution in China, entailing more overt ideological and material support for the Communist Party of Burma (CPB); and in the warm hearted support which the Soviet Union, seen to be close to India, gave to the military government and its policies. Over the next three years, Myanmar-China relations worsened, almost to a break; as the cultural revolution escalated in China and the Chinese community grew more enamoured of it so the Myanmar government took counter measures and the public reacted in tandem. On 26 June 1967, thousands of demonstrators stormed the Chinese Embassy in Yangon and tore down the official seal, while two days later another group stormed right into the Embassy, killed one official and wounded another. This provoked mass rallies all over China. Ne Win was called the Burmese Chiang Kai-Shek, his government fascist and open proclamations of support for the CPB were increased. Its leaders began to appear at public functions alongside their Chinese comrades for the first time. And Chinese army commanders and Red Guards began helping the CPB prepare a major offensive across the border into the Shan state.

This provided the backdrop for a series of high level visits between Myanmar and India. In February 1965, Ne Win was in Delhi on a state visit. No one on the Indian side mentioned democracy. President Radhakrishnan said to him, "you are drafting a new constitution. I have no doubt that the new constitution will give comfort to the people of your country." In December 1965, Prime Minister Shastri was in Yangon and, in their joint communiqué of 23 December were able to agree that "the aims and ideals of the two governments to create a happier future for their peoples were similar and that they could benefit from each other's experience in the development of their respective economies and social programmes on the basis of socialism." In March 1968, Ne Win came on a week long private visit which provoked Chinese ire. A year later, March 1969, Indira Gandhi was in Yangon and less than a year thereafter, Ne Win was back in Delhi. She had seen, more than the others, how Myanmar's tensions with China could be of advantage for India.

But even after her, the change of government in India in 1977 did not affect these exchanges, nor the tenor of the Indian attitude, despite the fact that India had just come through the most undemocratic period in its entire post-independence history. So when Vajpayee as Minister of External Affairs went to Myanmar his speech at the banquet hosted by his counterpart was fulsome in its praise. "We believe in the individuality of nations and the right of each country to choose its own path for progress, its own form of government, its own way of life" so we watched with "appreciation" Ne Win's "Burmese Way to Socialism, to national integration and economic progress."[33]

The rift with China did gradually heal, of course, specially in the late 1970s and early 1980s, but the next big change in the balance between India and China came with the 1988 crisis.

A quarter century of the Burmese Way to Socialism, of the same leaders just getting older, of isolation from the world, of shops getting emptier, brought Myanmar into the midst of an economic crisis. Growth was painfully sluggish, the debt rose while trade fell. Above all, rice production was down; there had already been food riots in the 1980s. In July 1988, following extended public protest against economic hardship, Ne Win resigned, asked that the five other senior armed forces officers resignations be accepted, declared that the "system as a whole had failed" and that there should now be a referendum on whether Myanmar should adopt multiparty democracy. On learning this, of course, there were renewed demonstrations in the streets, which gradually got larger and larger and spread across the country, often joined by armed forces personnel. The administration in several smaller towns collapsed; *ad hoc* committees set up by the students and monks who

---

33. Quoted from Atal Bihari Vajpayee (1979). *New Dimensions of India's Foreign Policy*, Vision Books, Delhi.

had led the demonstrations in the first place, took over. Then on September 12, General Saw Maung as head of the armed services assumed all powers of the state by proclamation; martial law was imposed, a dusk to dawn curfew enforced and a new ruling group, the State Law and Order Restoration Council set up and multiparty elections announced. When they were held, on May 27, 1990, they were actually free and quite fair. Aung San Suu Kyi's National League for Democracy (NLD) won 392 out of 485 seats; the National Unity Party, which was that of the armed forces, won 10.

This unexpected result led to a prolonged confrontation. At first, this was about what the elections were about. Before the elections the SLORC had made it clear that they were to elect a constituent assembly to draft a constitution, which would then pave the way for the formation of the new democratic government; SLORC would only hand over power to that government. The NLD agreed; but now, seeing the result, it insisted on an immediate transfer of power, while SLORC said the original conditions held. In due course, this became a confrontation between autocracy and democracy; and since most of the NLD leaders who managed to escape headed for the insurgent hideouts, it also became elected leaders plus insurgents *versus* the military. Aung San Suu Kyi was, of course, arrested.

India supports democracy

India took the lead in supporting democracy and the elected leaders, while denouncing SLORC. The Indian Embassy in Yangon gave shelter to students escaping the military and at one point almost became a hospital as those getting away from clashes with the armed forces sought to hide there. At the India-Myanmar border all controls were put in abeyance as hundreds of political activists crossed into Mizoram, Manipur and Nagaland. Authorities provided free food and shelter to them. In the years after 1988 also "the government of the day utilized the RBI to stall trade and economic contacts. Technical assistance was also stopped and contact with SLORC was reduced to the lowest possible level."[34]

---

34. P.M.S. Malik, *op. cit.*, p. 287.

When on November 10, 1990, a former Yangon student, Soe Myint, accompanied by a friend, and using bars of soap, hijacked a Thai Airways flight to Kolkata, both were arrested on arrival there, but released after three months and "no further action was taken by any law court, neither in West Bengal nor in New Delhi."[35]

All India Radio broadcasts were expanded in duration and in the number of frequencies; they were handled by the daughter of U Nu, Daw Than Than Nu and her husband U Aung Nyein, and not only publicised statements by the students and leaders of the democratic movement, but so strongly criticised the SLORC that it became more popular than the BBC and the Voice of America within Myanmar. A "Free Aung San Suu Kyi Committee" was launched in India and held regular meetings at which the transfer of power to the representatives of the people was demanded. This was not official but Members of Parliament often attended, including those from the ruling party. In 1991, Suu Kyi won the Nobel Peace Prize and the Prime Minister of India publicly congratulated her. In November 1992, the Indian Minister for Water Resources was reported saying the military junta was a major threat to peace in the subcontinent.

SLORC replied to all this, describing it as interference in the internal affairs of Myanmar, anti-Myanmar propaganda, and accusing India of providing help to rebels seeking to break up the state.

Principle had scored a total victory over pragmatism and the price paid in terms of India's interests was high.

China's pragmatic policy (Chinese pragmatism)

Paukphaw, translated as fraternal or, better, big brotherly, is the term used by the government and officials in Myanmar (when times are good) to describe the relationship with China. By the mid-1980s and certainly after 1988, it was in widespread use. The turning point came at the sixth summit of the Non-Aligned Movement in Havana, which the Cubans used to promote the idea of the Soviet Union

---

35. Egreteau, Renaud (2003). *Wooing The Generals, India's New Burma Policy*, Authorspress, Delhi. p. 123.

as the 'natural ally' of the non-aligned. Myanmar left the movement in protest and seven weeks later Chinese Foreign Minister Huang Ha was in Yangon to thank the government for its 'just stand'.

The Chinese now tried to arrange peace between the CPB and the Myanmar government; in October 1980 Ne Win was in Beijing on a surprise visit to meet the CPB leaders. He also met Deng Xiaoping and Hua Kuo-feng, but without public comment; the Chinese continued to support the CPB and refuse party to party relations with the BSPP, Ne Win's party. In the mid-1980s this changed. Aid to the CPB slowed and then dried up; by 1989 it had collapsed, riven by weakness and internal dissension. At the same time, the Chinese established party to party relations with the BSPP.

When the 1988 crisis happened, bilateral relations were already on a general upward trend. Then China became the first to recognise and greet SLORC and the trend accelerated. Trade expanded, specially border trade. On 6 August 1988, as large scale violence by the military on civilian demonstrators continued on the streets of Yangon and elsewhere, the Vice Governor of Yunnan signed a border trade agreement with the Myanmar Minister of Trade. The markets of Myanmar were soon filled with Chinese goods. By 1993, China was the second largest exporter to Myanmar.

Economic aid was given: soft loans for the purchase of commodities which the stoppage of Western aid had affected; for an airport at Mandalay; a road to connect Yunnan to Mandalay and beyond; a port at Hanggyi on the Bassein river.

Most of all China became the first and the largest supplier of arms to SLORC. In late 1991, a US $ 1 billion was reported; another worth US $ 400 million in 1994. The supplies included fighters, medium tanks, anti-aircraft guns, howitzers, and naval equipment. The supplies were a major factor in the government's successful campaigns against the insurgents during the 1990s.[36]

China-Myanmar relations would in any case have shown a dramatic improvement after 1988. In the eyes of the West, Myanmar

---

36. For more details of the arms supplies see Langpoklakpam Suraj Singh (2006). *Movement for Democracy in Myanmar*, Akansha Publishing House, New Delhi, pp. 210-211.

was to be abhorred thereafter as an oppressive military dictatorship, responsible for persistent human rights violations. Myanmar was isolated, since constructive engagement was only started in 1992 with ASEAN, and in those four years the Chinese took full advantage of having a wide open door.

Back to realism

But it can be said without doubt that for India the 'ineluctable tension' had most rapidly worsened during those four years, given Myanmar's strategic position.

Myanmar is a node that joins three geocultural regions: India on the West; China on the North; and South-East Asia on the East. It is a large node, geographically bigger than any other country on the mainland of South-East Asia. Its border with India is 1643 km, long and it is with four insurgency infested or potentially troublesome Indian states: Nagaland; Mizoram; Manipur and Arunachal Pradesh. And then there is its coastline, which doesn't quite abut on that of mainland India, but is close enough to the Andaman Islands to cause concern in case there is Chinese naval activity along it.

The then Foreign Secretary, J.N. Dixit, who was involved in the transition from principle to pragmatism in the early 1990s, summarises the geostrategic importance.

"Myanmar abuts on our sensitive North-Eastern states and portions of Bangladesh. It shares an equally significant border with China. Myanmar's northern frontiers also constitute a trijunction of the eastern frontiers of India, China and Myanmar... it is on the rim of the Bay of Bengal and India's south-eastern trade routes ... proximate enough to the Andaman and Nicobar Islands so as to affect our security interests in the Bay of Bengal and the seas around it, washing the shores of ASEAN members ... cooperation to counter drug smuggling, drug crimes, insurgency, and security threats to our North-Eastern states are imperatives for our foreign policy."[37]

---

37. Dixit, J.N. *op. cit.*, p. 167.

It was in 1992, that Myanmar decided to open up internally and to diversify its external relations. Martial law ended, so did curfew, which had been part of daily life for years. The release of political prisoners began with several hundred being released in September including U Nu. Aung San Suu Kyi's husband and children were allowed to visit her not once but, in an unprecedented burst of magnanimity, twice that year.

In September, Myanmar rejoined the Non-Aligned Movement and in December hosted a Colombo plan meeting. Meanwhile a tentative dialogue with ASEAN was started, which the latter took up enthusiastically as the beginning of a constructive engagement that would, by stages, see Myanmar become a full member of the Association by July 1997.

India took the first opportunity to invite a delegation led by the Vice Foreign Minister U Baswe, which arrived in Delhi in August 1992. They made three points as the basis for improving relations: first, that India should not concern itself with Myanmar's internal developments; second, that Myanmar recognised the problems arising out of a long shared border, like smuggling, and was ready to cooperate with India in tackling them; third, that they wished to increase economic and technological cooperation with India across the board. The Indian side replied to the first, this being a transition point, that while "our objective was not to interfere in the internal affairs of Myanmar ... India has always been supportive of democratic principles and democratic institutions." On the other two, India was ready to be "positive and action oriented." [38]

This began the period of transition between the ethical, which had been followed so far, and the expedient, which was the policy of the future.

The next step was the visit of the Foreign Secretary to Myanmar in March 1993, during which a number of agreements were signed or agreed: to control smuggling and illegal trafficking in drugs;

---

38. Dixit, J.N. *op. cit.,* p. 168.

for economic and commercial cooperation; for secretary level visits to discuss mutual problems.

During subsequent years the opening to Myanmar expanded rapidly, though not without a hiccup or two. The first priority was the border. Regular meetings between the civil authorities of the two sides were arranged from 1994; a Myanmar India Joint Drug Control Meeting held its first gathering in December 1994. In May that year, India's Chief of Army Staff visited Myanmar, while the then head of Myanmar intelligence, Lt. Gen. Khin Nyunt, visited India. In April 1995, the military authorities of the two sides were able to launch the 'Golden Bird' operation, a joint operation intended to squeeze insurgent groups in a pincer movement. In the middle of this came the first hiccup: India announced that the Jawaharlal Nehru Award for International Understanding would be conferred on Aung San Suu Kyi. The Myanmar military promptly withdrew, so that a number of Naga and ULFA insurgent cadres were able to cross the border and take shelter there.

Here was a sign of the transition, for Dixit is able to say the Award "has created tensions ... should have been avoided in our larger security and strategic interests", and at the same time that it should not "affect the upward curve in Indo-Myanmar relations ... or erode the policy of constructive interaction with the SLORC regime."[39]

There were other hiccups, like the Indian side using Myanmar rebels from Rakhine (Arakan) to gather intelligence about the facilities given by Myanmar to the Chinese along the coast, which policy was reversed only in 1998; or the raised eyebrows in Yangon when George Fernandes, who had given shelter in his own home to Myanmar dissidents and otherwise whole heartedly supported their cause, became Defence Minister in March 1998. But in general, it can be said that the progress of relations has been along a smooth and exponential upward curve.

A good example of this victory of the pragmatic is the events of mid-2003. On the evening of May 30, 2003 a motorcade carrying

---

39. Dixit, J.N. *op. cit.*, pp. 16 and 169.

Aung San Suu Kyi and members of the NLD to a meeting was attacked by truckloads of men armed with sticks and spears. The military, which had presumably set up the attack, intervened, accused her of disturbing the peace, placed her in custody, the other NLD leaders under house arrest, and closed down the party offices. Amidst a chorus of criticism by the West, including fresh sanctions, and an announcement by Japan that it was freezing new aid, there was no initial Indian reaction; then ASEAN came out with a critical statement and India made a more careful one more or less accepting the official explanation. India could not afford the luxury of moral posturing. Succeeding months saw intensified high-level interaction. The Minister of Commerce, Arun Jaitley, was in Myanmar in July 2003 to launch a Joint Trade Committee; Minister for Communications and IT was there a month later to sign an MoU. In September the Indian Naval Chief was visiting, while the same month the Myanmar Air Chief was in India. In November, the Vice President of India was there on an official visit.

High level visits are now a continuing component of the excellent relationship. Since the year 2000, to take a recent sample period, there were visits by Vice Senior General Maung Aye of the SPDC, counterpart of the Vice President of India, in January 2000 and again in November the same year; Foreign Minister Win Aung in January and July and December 2003, then again in July 2004; other Ministers from Myanmar, of Communications, of Energy, of Railways. And the historic visit of Senior General Than Shwe on the invitation of the President of India in October 2004. The list of visits from the Indian side is equally long and impressive: the External Affairs Minister in February 2001, April 2002; Minister for Commerce and Industry, July 2003; Minister for Communications, August 2003; the Vice President in November 2003. And finally the President in March 2006 for, as the briefing described it, "the highest level visit from India in a long time," "a very significant visit ... a very important visit."[40]

---

40. See the briefing in *Strategic Digest*, Vol. 36, No. 4, April 2006, pp. 417-9.

The agreements finalised during these visits have been wide ranging: to establish a Joint Trade Committee; for cooperation in communications, IT and services; consultation between the two foreign offices on a regular basis; on extending lines of credit for various projects; for cooperation in the field of Non-traditional security issues; energy cooperation, among others. And, of course, cooperation along the border to control crime and insurgent activity, which is now at a much reduced level, continues.

Trade is not large. In the year 2003-04 India exported US$ 108 million and imported $ 361 Million, but business links are expanding. The Confederation of Indian Industry and its Myanmar counterpart have a Memorandum of Understanding of February 2000; there have been trade exhibitions and business seminars, so the ground has been well prepared for a rapid future expansion in bilateral trade.

Indian projects in Myanmar are important. There is first the Tamu-Kelewa-Kalemyo road, completed by the border roads organisation in February 2001, to be maintained by the same organisation for six years. This provides the best direct land access to Myanmar and thence, as Indian spokesmen often say, to ASEAN. There is a Kaladan Multimodal Transport Project linking Kolkata port with Sitwe on the Rakhine coast and then on by river and road into Mizoram, thus providing an alternative access route to the Northeast of India. Equally important, ONGC Videsh and Essar oil are exploring for gas off the Rakhine coast, which would contribute to India's energy security.

Conclusion

The story of relations between India and Myanmar suggests three variants of the balance between the ethical and the expedient, and these three apply to any relationship, the more so with our neighbours.

The first is that of 'ineluctable tension', mildly characterised by the first two years of Ne Win's rule (1962-1964) and much more strongly by the four years from 1988 to 1992. We can see this repeated, if random examples be given, in India's relations with

Bangladesh after the military took over there in 1975 and, more recently, for some months, with Pakistan after the October 1999 coup that brought General Musharraf to power there. There is a strong moral content in this policy, but three points need to be made: the moral content can never be separated from a desire to change the type of government we have to deal with, despite all the protestations of not wishing to interfere in internal affairs that have to be, and are, made, so some element of the pragmatic is present; secondly, there are other, less pragmatic, factors at work in the making of this policy like the force of domestic opinion, a general distrust that prevails in India[41] of military governments and, in the case of Myanmar, the sympathy among all circles for Aung San Suu Kyi; third, and despite the above two, one has constantly to be asking the question at what point, as a famous American diplomat put it, "you could no longer cultivate the luxury of high moral attitudes."[42]

The second is that there is no tension, of which the outstanding example is the years of Nehru and U Nu; but other examples are not difficult to cite: the relationship with Bhutan has from the outset been of this nature; with Sri Lanka during the last decade it has been the same.

The third is a combination of the two. This variant can be of two kinds: an uncertain stalemate in which the day to day political and diplomatic business is conducted normally, trade goes on, but there are some unresolved reservations about the internal or external policies of the government concerned; and the transition period, in which the language of the moral is present, but a decision has already been taken that we can no more cultivate this luxury, such as the period 1992-95 in our relations with Myanmar.

41. As is well known, this is not the case with all democracies; some have a strong liking for military governments and autocracies generally.

42. Kennan, George F. (1962). *Russia and the West under Lenin and Stalin*, Mentor Book, p. 370.

28

India and Nepal
Deb Mukharji

April 2006, has been a defining moment in the history of Nepal. What started with a call for a four-day strike by political parties was transformed into a mass upsurge. The final outcome of the non-violent revolution is yet to emerge. But it is certain that Nepal will never be the same again. As the future takes shape, the Nepali people, at last able to feel themselves part of a composite whole rather than disparate groups owing their nationhood to a long-past feudal conquest, will also undoubtedly wish to take a fresh look at their priorities in internal affairs and external relations. This change need not be revolutionary in character, is indeed unlikely to be so, but it will come. India, bound to Nepal by multiple bonds of people and nature, should also take a look at the future of our relationship. Any assessment at present has to assume that the course set by April, 2006, will not be derailed and Nepal not thrown into a state of indefinite anarchy and bitter confrontation.

Some of the traditional elements of Nepali politics will cease to have their present importance. The Rana elite who solely ruled and represented Nepal till 1950 have continued to be prominent in business, industry, the armed forces and civil services. Their inherent capabilities and inter-connectivity will assure them a role of some consequence, though the challenges will be stiffer. The close relations of the Ranas with the palace will be a diminishing factor in Nepali politics. The king, should he be allowed to continue in a ceremonial role, will have to content himself with staying away from interference in political affairs. This would require a major shift in dealing with Nepal. Effectively the sole arbiter between 1960 and 1990, the king retained an important position even after the establishment of multiparty democracy. It was not a role intended or sanctioned by the new constitution. But some of the anomalies in the constitution, King Birendra's positive personal image, the reverence in which he was held by many and the numerous palace apparatus which had been built up over the years, all contributed to the king playing a role of some importance. The palace also contributed to creating divisions within and between political parties for its presumed advantage. King Gyanendra's overt involvement in politics and his effort to go back to a pre-1990 dispensation has now led to the palace being marginalised.

In looking at the future, it has to be clearly understood that the public denigration of the king and the sense of confidence that the people and politicians have acquired, do not leave room for any future active role for the palace. Thus, any suggestion that the king may continue to be a 'stabilising' factor in the turbulence of Nepali politics would be misplaced. It will be, for all practical purposes, a Nepal with a palace, if at all, greatly diminished.

In Nepal, religion and customs have been a way of life. Even if encouraged by the collaboration between the priestly and the ruling classes over the past few hundred years, the bond between people and faith is genuine. It is not aggressive Hinduism (except for those from the elite or priestly class with a vested interest in promoting the divinity of the king and emphasising the Hindu character of Nepal), but an easy and gentle bonding with beliefs. Concurrently, feudal traditions have taken shelter under the garb of religion. Nepal's spiritual attraction and the easy relationship between man and his faith and between the two major religions, may not diminish, but it will cease to be the Hindu kingdom as portrayed over the past two centuries, even should the king remain.

The political parties have so far played the game according to pre-existing norms and rules. This has largely meant manipulative politics with suspicion and rumours a major ingredient. Intrigue and suspicion has been a staple of Kathmandu politics, as noted by a British Resident in the thirties of the 19th Century. Responding to a cold speech by the host at a banquet hosted for him by late King Mahendra in 1963, Sarvapalli Radhakrishnan recalled seeing a statuette of Narada at an exhibition earlier in the day. Naradamuni, he said, was an expert at carrying tales and causing trouble, and all must beware of such people in our midst. It was a remark that may have seemed out of place, but was proof of the wise man's understanding of Nepali polity. After the events of April 2006, it can be hoped that the civil society of Nepal would keep a more vigilant watch and that the nature of Nepali politics may see a welcome change.

The coming months and years would also challenge India. Until the middle of the 20th Century the people of Nepal had no feelings of animus towards India. At the political level, Nepali leaders went to prison fighting the British in the cause of Indian independence in the conviction that Nepal's release from the thraldom of Rana rule could only come if India were free. But even if India was supportive of democracy in Nepal, and much of the agitation was carried out from Indian soil, the relationship was not entirely smooth. India's efforts in opening up Nepal with roads and airports, building hospitals and infrastructure, engaging in the Koshi and the Gandaki projects did not receive, as India saw it, due acknowledgement. While India approached relations with Nepal with all goodwill, there was also a tinge of paternalism. This error was to continue and was not conducive to building healthy relations and could be used for narrow gains by the political classes without necessarily always benefiting the people. While there has been some welcome change in attitudes, this aspect will continue to demand attention.

Meanwhile, after the royal takeover of 1960, the palace evolved a conscious policy of equating Nepali nationalism with anti-Indianism. India came to be described as a threat to Nepali sovereignty, and the king, by virtue of the conquest of the territory by his ancestors, was the sole guarantor of Nepali independence. Nepal has always been free, it was stressed (unlike India) and this theme has found repetition in recent pronouncements. In sum, power to the palace was necessary to save Nepal from the ugly Indian. In a sense, of course, the argument had merit. The British had made their peace with the Nepali elite and were not concerned with the Nepali people. A democratic India could not be indifferent to the people and, to that extent, did pose a threat to established privileges by simply being there. Unfortunately, even if large sections of people stand disenchanted with the monarchy, suspicion of India ingrained over decades may take time to erase.

At this juncture in Nepal, it would be useful for India to look at the future of Indo-Nepal relations. It is obvious that as states, each will pursue its path as each finds appropriate for its people. There are no issues which divide the two countries. Yet, the kind of mutual trust, confidence and cooperation which could be of mutual benefit are not always in evidence. There is not much that India can do about the disparity in size which may be of subliminal concern to her neighbours, except to act in a spirit of strict fairness. Equally important is openness to try and prevent mis-interpretations. At times, too, India has been excessively touchy, particularly with regard to Nepal's foreign relations. India—and Nepal—have moved a great deal since the fifties when India was disturbed at any kind of foreign interest in Nepal, though it must also be noted in fairness that till then Nepal itself did not encourage foreigners. And this sensitivity on the part of India was most astutely exploited by the palace in the sixties by wooing the Chinese. There was no reason for India to be apoplectic about Chinese presence in Nepal, whether then or two decades later. Firstly, as the world moves on it was unavoidable that Nepal would look to broaden its relations with the outside world and China was an obvious choice. Secondly, the weight of geography would always favour close relations between Nepal and India. It is true that new roads are being built from Tibet to Nepal in the central and eastern sectors and a railway will soon connect Beijing with Lhasa and could eventually move southwards towards Nepal. While these would have to be noted for their possible security connotations, it should also be possible to see them as opportunities to be used by Indian trade for the Tibetan market with Nepal resuming the profitable role of a transit point for trade and intercourse between India and Tibet in historical times. The special and unique relationship between India and Nepal, often mentioned, has not prevented the latter from pursuing policies in the past five decades which have not always been helpful to India. There is no reason to believe that Indian diplomacy would not be able to deal with the policies of a more self-assured Nepal pursuing the interests of its people. It should now be easier for each to project to the other the cost benefit ratio of decisions instead of having to cope with decisions taken for narrow ends and persuasiveness based largely on linkages.

Among the issues which should require careful attention and analysis is the 1950 Treaty of Peace and Friendship. It used to be the favourite instrument for whipping up anti-India sentiments. It was described as unequal and an affront to Nepal's sovereignty. Besides the clauses of the Treaty, the fact of the Indian ambassador having signed it with the Nepali Prime Minister was highlighted as extremely offensive, ignoring the fact that the 1923 Anglo-Nepal Treaty was signed by the Nepali Prime Minister with the British envoy. In November, 2000, the Indian ambassador had said at the Nepal Council for World Affairs in response to criticism of the Treaty, that clause 10 of the Treaty permitted either country to terminate it with an year's notice and Nepal could certainly do so if it found the terms of the Treaty to be injurious or unacceptable. Responding to suggestions for changes in the Treaty at the Foreign Office talks in January, 2001, India had said that it was prepared for all options, namely continuation, termination or renegotiation. The question of the Treaty appears to have been on the back-burner since then. However, since the 40 point demands of the *Maobadis*, who will be in parliament in the proposed Constituent Assembly, includes the demand for the removal of "all unequal stipulations and agreements" from the Treaty, the issue may be resurrected.

As is very well known, treaties are valid only so long as the parties honour it. Their importance often lies in the moment of their signing, underlining immediate mutual concerns. When these concerns fade away, so do the relevance of the treaty. The 1971 Indo-

Soviet Treaty has to be seen in the context of the crisis in East Pakistan and the looming war clouds with unqualified US support for Pakistan. The Indo-Bangladesh Treaty of 1972, reflected the relations at the time and reaffirmed Indian commitment to the sovereignty of Bangladesh even as she, at the time, remained unaccepted by large sections of the international community. It is instructive to recall that with political changes in Bangladesh after 1975, this treaty too was depicted as an Indian design on Bangladesh and continued to be a favourite political slogan until it expired in the fullness of time in 1997. The 1950 Treaty contains no clauses that are detrimental to Nepal's sovereignty. The aspects of security and consultations mentioned in the treaty were perhaps more necessary for Nepal then, with the Chinese having just occupied Tibet, and were no different from the terms of Nepal's 1923 Treaty with Britain. As Nepal grew in self-assurance, these clauses came to be depicted as in some way restricting Nepal's freedom of action, though, in reality, Nepal has very much followed an independent foreign policy including every effort to play the China card and sympathy for Pakistan in 1971. As such, then, the Treaty should be entirely dispensable from the Indian point of view.

The problem in dispensing with the treaty arises with Nepali nationals in India being accorded very largely national treatment, with reciprocal facilities in Nepal for Indians being far more restricted. The need for asymmetry was recognised in the exchange of letters accompanying the treaty and the asymmetry continues. Abrogation of the treaty would thus place the millions of Nepali nationals in India, enjoying in many respects the rights of an Indian citizen, in an impossible legal situation. Even if the present treaty confers no benefits on India, she cannot, and should not, enter into a fresh treaty incorporating only what is of advantage to Nepal. The issue has been skirted by letting the treaty quietly hibernate, and this may still be the best course. However, should the new Nepali dispensation seek to raise the issue, all implications of termination as also the obligations of each state in any new treaty, would need to be most carefully gone through. The only 'unequal stipulation or agreement' in the Treaty is, in fact, in favour of Nepal with regard to national treatment. Prejudices ingrained by sustained propaganda are, however, difficult to eradicate.

The presence of Nepali citizens, referred to as 'gorkhas', in the Indian army is one of the unique features of Indo-Nepal relations and, it could be argued, creates special bonds. The induction of 'gorkhas' served a particular purpose for British imperialism in India. Besides their valour, they were also useful against Indian nationalists. The system was continued, presumably partly out of respect for tradition prevalent in the army, as a means of indirect economic assistance and to retain existing bonds. It has been retained at the expense of several tens of thousands of Indian nationals who would have otherwise filled these posts. It is an arrangement with which the 'gorkhas' do not seem to have any problem and the Indian government seems willing to continue. Obviously, recruitment of 'gorkhas' in the Indian armed forces cannot take place without the consent of the Nepali government. While it certainly does create a body of people with friendly links with India and is also the source of both significant employment and substantial earnings for Nepal, there is insufficient benefit to India for the issue to become an irritant.

It is an astonishing reflection of the inadequacies in Indo-Nepal relations that even after decades there is still very little movement on the development of the water resources of Nepal. After the Koshi and Gandaki projects, the last over 40 years ago, the only significant project has been the Tanakpur barrage. The Mahakali Treaty, signed with great expectations a decade ago, has made little progress in implementation. Essentially, a feeling has remained in Nepal, or has been fostered, that the earlier agreements were in some way detrimental to Nepal. Looking at the balance of benefits to each country, the Nepali feelings appear without justification. Equally, India's record of communications in the vital question of water management, be it with Nepal or Bangladesh, leaves a lot to be desired. The issue is far too important to be entrusted to rigid technological dogmas and requires serious and sustained diplomatic and political input. There needs to be open public discussion of issues involved to alleviate possible apprehensions.

The Himalayan rivers arising in or transiting Nepal have a significant hydroelectric potential of 45,000 MW. In addition, and of no lesser importance, is the possibility of controlling the flows of the rivers for both flood control in the rainy season and augmentation of flows during the dry season. The optimum development of this resource is of the greatest importance for India and for even further lower riparian Bangladesh. Obviously, any future development must take fully into account concerns about displacement and environmental effects. These are issues which have constantly come up in India's internal development of water resources. They have to be meaningfully addressed and the future cannot be tied down to simple economic cost benefit calculations and treaty terms. The absence of openness and the constant politicisation of the issue in Nepal has stymied progress. There has been the unusual spectacle of the party associated with the agreement on the Mahakali Treaty subsequently despatching its cadres to block field investigations. Meanwhile, Nepal has awarded some prize sites for hydropower generation to western companies at development costs higher than what should be the norm, bringing into question their future viability. These issues will undoubtedly be looked into by the new government of Nepal. One hopes that the future would see rapid and meaningful cooperation between India and Nepal for development of this constantly renewable source of energy and the potential of water resources in a holistic manner for the benefit of both. The answers to what needs to be done are well known to experts on both sides. What continues to be absent is the political will and the commitment to go ahead.

If indeed the decade of *Maobadi* insurgency has opened the way to a nation state, some of the problems relating to particular groups of people may recede and disappear. Of direct concern to India would be the future position of 'madhesis', the people inhabiting the terai. The terai had been incorporated in the kingdom two hundred years ago, ceded to the British at Sagauli in 1816 and returned to Nepal in gratitude for help in relieving the siege of Lucknow. In appearance and language, the Madhesis are close to their southern neighbours in Bihar and UP and contribute 31 per cent to Nepal's population. They have been systematically discriminated against in terms of citizenship and job opportunities by the ruling elites and their frustration has been mounting. It is not insignificant that the anti-Indian Hrithik Roshan riots of December 2000 had equally targeted 'Madhesis'. India has kept its distance from the issue as it concerned Nepali citizens, but sooner or later the discontent would assume serious proportions. Hopefully, the new Nepal would be more inclusive in its approach to all its citizens.

The relations between Nepal and India are at multiple layers. The traditional elite of Nepal, the Ranas and the Shahs, have had matrimonial linkages with princely families of India for centuries. The 'madhesis' have similar linkages with Bihar and UP. Millions of hill Nepalis work in India and many have family links with Indian citizens of Nepali origin. Many have fled to India in the recent past from remote villages to avoid being caught by the twin dangers of *Maobadi* demands and army action. The chief of the Royal Nepal Army is an honorary general of the Indian army, an honour reciprocated by Nepal. Nepali 'gorkhas' fight in the Indian army for the cause of India. Each of the elements of this relationship is important, but none represents the whole by itself. To describe the relationship of Nepal and India as unique is an understatement. What this also emphatically underlines is that while relations between states occupies much of our attention and analysis, in the case of Indo-Nepal relations, the many connectivities among people can and do play a significant role.

All neighbours are important in their own way for all countries. Nepal's location adjoining the flat Gangetic plains of India, with China to the north, has clear security implications. India must also recognise that Nepal's geographical location poses for it far greater security concerns. It is all very well to play the China card that preys on the Indian mind. It is quite another to move into any close embrace of Beijing, having had a ringside view of the fate of Tibet. Nor is it necessary for Nepal to consider any such choice. In the recent past, Beijing has not pursued any aggressive moves into Nepal, which it considered not too long ago to be a country fraternal to Tibet, to both of whom China was the father, and has been content to respond to Nepali overtures. As far as India is concerned, contrary to the apprehensions of neighbours, the Indian psyche has neither the attitude nor the ruthlessness to pursue a policy of domination. The best guarantee of India's interests in Nepal is the flourishing of independent Nepali nationalism that is able to look at choices and pursue a course beneficial for the people. And it is the people who are the determining factor, for their genuine welfare cannot be divorced from a cooperative relationship with India.

Security has other elements as well. A disturbed state in Nepal would mean an even larger influx of temporary or permanent refugees into India. There are large numbers of Nepali speaking Indian citizens in Sikkim, West Bengal and in the North-East. Events in Nepal will impact on them. In the past, it was from Indian soil that agitations were carried out against the established order in Nepal, and the nature of the border and the existing connectivities have, and will, make this inevitable if there is repression. The *Maobadi* insurgency is the first that is entirely home-grown and use of Indian territory is only sporadic. Instability or uncertainty in Nepal is, therefore, of very direct consequence to India.

From India's point of view it needs to be recognised that new elements have emerged in Nepal in the past few decades. The movement of people and the reach of the media, particularly the radio, have made people more conscious of the world outside and more conscious of their rights. The *Maobadi* insurgency goes beyond mere ideology or the means to power, for it has focussed on some essential needs and concerns of many and conveyed to people in distant corners that there is a commonality in their problems and aspirations. One could say that the past decade has forged a nation state out of disparate regions. Nepal has irrevocably graduated from being identified with a Hindu monarchy.

A parallel development has been the emergence of an assertive middle class, unknown half a century ago, with no particular emotional association with or attachment to India, and able to look at issues from a nationalist Nepali point of view. This self-assurance is reflected in the remarkably courageous press. They are suspicious of politicians who, despite their creditable fight for democracy before 1990 and again recently, have been immersed in the politics of manoeuvres. They are resentful of what they perceive as India's patronising attitudes. As a former Nepali research scholar in a leading Indian university wrote recently, the Indians "think that we Nepalis are not capable of becoming more than private guards, mercenaries, and servants working in *dhabas*, hotels and restaurants. And they think the king is the lord of a man-power company called Nepal." This sense of hurt to a new pride in the nation has to be recognised and assuaged.

As we look at the future, there are questions that need to be asked. What does India see as its core interests in Nepal? What is the new Nepal that is emerging? Are there ways in which India can influence developments in Nepal? And, how would Nepal see its relations with India? A dispassionate look at these questions is essential for creating a stable and mutually beneficial long-term relationship.

India's core interest in Nepal has to be all round development in Nepal for the advancement of all its people. This will suffice to bring about a far greater level of cooperation than we have seen in the past. A politics not excessively tied down to political slogans and coolly assessing the cost benefit calculations of its actions can only strengthen the nation's security. One may even see movement on the development of water resources, of great importance to the region.

The new Nepal is likely to critically examine its national interests and how they can be best pursued. These interests will be defined in more inclusive terms than before. India can influence the future by tendering assistance, when sought, directed largely at alleviating the harsh life of least developed areas as also continuing assistance in building infrastructure and making it always abundantly clear in words and actions that the welfare of Nepal is, in itself, of primary interest to India and that it has no other agenda.

Nepal's view of India has been mixed. Despite the many personal and institutional links, the state and politics have often taken a negative view for partisan reasons. The emerging middle class has been aggrieved by what has often been seen as a patronising attitude of India and Indians. The new Nepal would be deserving of greater respect from not only India but also the international community. With the remarkable political success the people have achieved, it should be possible for a confident Nepal to also break out of the complexes of the past and accept without reservations, so long as its national interests are promoted, hands of friendship and co-operation.

29

India-Pakistan relations

G. Parthasarathy

The inauguration of a bus service between Amritsar and Lahore on March 24, 2006, emerged as an appropriate occasion for Prime Minister Manmohan Singh to spell out his vision for the future of relations between India and Pakistan to people in India and across the border in neighbouring Pakistan. The establishment of the bus service was an emotional occasion for people in Punjab, who have for long sought easy and unhindered access to visit their shrines in Pakistan. Moreover, memories of the violence and bloodshed that accompanied partition have receded. The easing of travel restrictions and greater people to people contacts have resulted in better human understanding and a desire to promote normal good neighbourly cooperation. Despite this, mutual suspicions and antagonisms continue, particularly because of continuing efforts of the Pakistan establishment and militant groups linked to the military establishment to promote and participate in terrorist activities in Jammu and Kashmir and elsewhere in India. At the diplomatic level, the continuing propensity of the Pakistan establishment to undermine efforts by India on issues like its quest for permanent membership of the UN Security Council and the July 18 Agreement on Nuclear Cooperation between India and the USA, naturally provokes misgivings in India about long-term Pakistani intentions.

Despite these misgivings, Prime Minister Manmohan Singh held out a hand of reconciliation and friendship to Pakistan when he spoke at Amritsar. While expressing optimism about resolving issues like Sir Creek, Siachen and Baglihar, he said: "I am convinced that we can move forward if all concerned are willing to accept ground realities; if all concerned take a long view of history and of our destiny". He also asserted: "I have often said that borders cannot be redrawn, but we can work towards making them irrelevant— towards making them just lines on a map. I also envisage a situation when the two parts of Jammu and Kashmir can with active encouragement of the Governments of India and Pakistan, work out cooperative, consultative mechanisms so as to maximize the gains of cooperation in solving problems of social and economic development of the region." Dr. Manmohan Singh added that his "vision" was to make the peace process culminate in India and Pakistan entering into a "Treaty of Peace, Security and Friendship" to give substance to their quest for "shared goals."

Dr. Manmohan Singh also stated in his Amritsar speech that while General Musharraf had taken some "bold steps" to curb extremism, "more needs to be done in the interest of both India and Pakistan." He spoke of expanding people to people contacts, but warned that it would be a mistake to link normalisation of relations between India and Pakistan, with finding solution to the issue of Jammu and Kashmir, as Pakistan does. The Amritsar speech was a response to repeated calls by President Musharraf that Pakistan felt that any solution to Jammu and Kashmir should contain the following elements: (1) "Demilitarization" of Jammu and Kashmir commencing with a pull out of Indian forces from urban centres in the Kashmir valley like Kupwara, Baramulla and Srinagar. (2) Dividing of Jammu and Kashmir into seven autonomous regions-five on the Indian side of the LOC and two on the Pakistan side of the LOC. (3) Making the LOC in Jammu and Kashmir "irrelevant." (4) "Joint Management" of the entire State of Jammu and Kashmir by India and Pakistan.

The statements made by President Musharraf came in the wake of a process of sustained dialogue between India and Pakistan, ever since the Composite Dialogue Process was revived following discussions between President Musharraf and the then Indian Prime

Minister Atal Bihari Vajpayee at the SAARC Summit in Islamabad in January 2004. The dialogue process was revived in the wake of a categorical assurance on January 6, 2004, by President Musharraf that he would not allow territory under Pakistan's control to be used for terrorism against India. The Composite Dialogue Process was initially agreed upon following discussions between Prime Minister Atal Bihari Vajpayee and Prime Minister Nawaz Sharif in New York in 1998. The "Composite Dialogue Process comprises discussions on the following issues: (1) Peace and security. (2) Jammu and Kashmir. (3) Sir Creek. (4) Siachen. (5) Terrorism and Drug trafficking. (6) Wullar Barrage/Tulbul navigation project. (7) Promotion of friendly exchanges in various fields.

This Composite dialogue has been reinforced by the revival of the Ministerial level India-Pakistan Joint Commission that was established in 1983 and by 'back channel' diplomacy conducted by designated representatives. The representatives in the 'back channel' effort presently are our former High Commissioner to Pakistan, Satinder Lambah and the Secretary General of Pakistan's National Security Council, Tariq Aziz. The former External Affairs Minister, Natwar Singh held talks with his Pakistani counterpart Khurshid Kasuri during the SAARC Foreign Ministers meeting in Islamabad on July 19-23, 2004 and earlier at the sidelines of the Asian Cooperation Dialogue Conference in Qingdao on June 21. There have also been Summit level meetings in New York between President Musharraf and Prime Minister Manmohan Singh and when President Musharraf visited India, ostensibly to watch a One Day International Cricket Match between India and Pakistan in New Delhi in April 2005.

Ever since the Composite Dialogue Process commenced in February 2004, a large number of issues have come up for discussion in order to enhance confidence and promote cooperation and contacts. One of the first steps agreed upon in 2004, was the restoration of the strengths of the High Commissions in the two capitals to 110. India has proposed a number of CBMs during the Composite Dialogue Process, in order to enhance contacts between the armed forces of the two countries. These have included direct links between the Operations Directorates of the Air Forces and Navies of the two countries, strengthening communication links between the Directors General of Military Operations and establishment of links between the coast guards of the two countries. There were also proposals for greater exchanges between military establishments and institutions in the two countries. On the civilian side, India proposed the reopening of Consulates General in Karachi and Mumbai, modalities for early release of fishermen arrested for straying across maritime boundaries, enhancing facilities for visits of pilgrims and promoting tourist, cultural and educational exchanges.

The Composite Dialogue Process also provided Pakistan an opportunity to submit around 20 proposals for discussions. These included calls for a "Strategic Restraint Regime," measures for "nuclear restraint," a balance in conventional armed forces, de-alerting of nuclear weapons and avoidance of operational deployment of ballistic missiles and upgrading existing communication links between the Directors General of Military Operations. More significantly, both India and Pakistan presented CBMs relating to Jammu and Kashmir for the first time. India proposed the reopening of the Srinagar-Muzaffarabad bus route, the opening of the Jammu-Sialkot route and mechanisms for promoting cross-border trade and people to people contacts at selected points on both sides of the LOC. India also suggested greater cultural interaction and cooperation, the joint promotion of tourism and cooperation in areas like environment and forestry. Pakistan suggested that there should be no new development of posts and defence works along the LOC, effective monitoring by the UNMOGIP and a substantial reduction of forces on both sides of the LOC. Both sides agreed that the cease fire that came into effect along the LOC and in the Siachen Region in November 2003, must be sustained. This cease fire has, in fact, been an important factor in reducing tensions along the LOC.

The Composite Dialogue has led to several important measures to promote cooperation. Agreement has been reached on the reopening of Consulates General in Karachi and Mumbai, though difficulties in renting of accommodation for the proposed Pakistan Consulate General in Mumbai have led to delays in the Missions being formally reopened. The rail route across the Khokhrapar-Munnabao border has been reopened after a lapse of over four decades. The recently inaugurated Amritsar-Nankana Sahib bus service provides regular access for Sikh pilgrims desirous of visiting Nankana Sahib. The reopening of the Srinagar-Muzaffarabad bus service was widely welcomed not only in Jammu and Kashmir, but internationally. There are now plans to open other bus route for cross LOC travels like one between Poonch and Rawalkot. India also hopes to secure Pakistan's agreement for opening the Kargil-Skardu route for reestablishing the age-old links between Ladakh and Kargil on the one hand and Gilgit and Skardu on the other. Pakistan's response to CBMs and dialogue that affect the people of the Northern Areas on its side of the LOC has thus far been hesitant and defensive. There are now suggestions for opening the Srinagar-Muzaffarabad route for trade. The climate for dialogue has also improved with a series of meetings in Kathmandu, Jammu, New Delhi and Islamabad between representatives of different walks of life in Jammu and Kashmir, from both sides of the Line of Control. New ideas are emerging to enhance cooperation in areas like education, health and disaster management on both sides of the Line of Control.

It would be incorrect to presume that the dialogue between India and Pakistan can be insulated from trends in the internal developments in both countries, or from the geopolitical situation in the extended neighbourhood of both countries in the Indian Ocean Region. More importantly, the role of major powers like the USA and China inevitably affect developments in India and Pakistan. Within India, the UPA Government has largely followed up on the agreement reached between President Musharraf and Prime Minister Vajpayee on January 6, 2004 in Islamabad. Given the fact that foreign policy in India is generally based on a national consensus, there has been a sense of continuity in Indian Foreign Policy, with new Governments invariably honouring commitments made by their predecessors. In Pakistan, however, there has been no such national consensus. When General Zia-ul-Haq overthrew Prime Minister Zulfiqar Ali Bhutto, he was very averse to explicitly agreeing to abide by the letter and spirit of the Simla Agreement signed by Mr. Bhutto. General Musharraf was similarly very averse to agreeing to abide by the principles and provisions of either the Simla Agreement or the Lahore Declaration (that he labelled as nothing but "hot air"), after he overthrew Mr. Nawaz Sharif. This was evident during the Agra Summit in 2001, when General Musharraf demanded new priorities and formulations that were different from those that emerged in Lahore in February 1999. Moreover, Pakistan has invariably based its approach to relations with India on the basis of the support it expects and receives militarily, economically and diplomatically primarily from the United States and China and secondarily from Islamic countries like Saudi Arabia.

The terrorist attacks on New York and Washington on September 11, 2001 had a profound impact on the directions of Pakistan's foreign policy. General Musharraf did not need much persuasion to join America's 'War on Terrorism.' He quickly saw the prospects of becoming an American ally as the key to getting international legitimacy, apart from American and western military, economic and diplomatic support. Pakistan became the key hub for American operations against the al-Qaeda, led by Osama bin Laden and his Taliban hosts. It needs to be recalled that it was with Pakistani acquiescence and tacit support that Osama bin Laden set up the 'International Islamic Front for Jihad against Jews and Crusaders' in Kandahar, in February 1998. This Front brought together groups like the al-Qaeda and Taliban with radical Islamic groups like the Islamic Movement of Uzbekistan in Central Asia, the Abu Sayyaf in the Philippines and extremist Islamic elements operating in countries like Jordan, Egypt and Algeria, apart from radical Islamic separatists in Chechnya. A number of Pakistani terrorist groups like the Harkat-ul-Mujahideen, the Lashkar-e-Taiba, the Jaish-e-Mohammed and the Harkat-ul-Jihad-ul-Islami (that now operates primarily out of Bangladesh), also joined Bin Laden's

Islamic Front. Afghanistan under the Taliban, thus provided 'strategic depth' for Pakistan in its efforts to wage 'low intensity conflict' in Jammu and Kashmir and elsewhere in India. This was most evident during the hijacking of IC-814 to Kandahar in December 1999, when the Taliban allowed its territory to be used to facilitate the aims and objectives of the Pakistani hijackers, who were members of ISI affiliated groups like the Harkat-ul-Mujahideen.

The ouster of the Taliban from Afghanistan and the assumption of office by representative Government led by Hamid Karzai were to have profound implications for developments within Pakistan. The American led attack on the Taliban in Afghanistan, did not destroy, but dispersed the cadres of the Taliban and its allies in al-Qaeda and other members of Bin Laden's Islamic Front. These cadres melted into Pakistan's towns and cities and many took refuge in North and South Waziristan, in the Federally Administered Tribal Areas (FATA), in Pakistan's North West Frontier Province. In the years that followed, Pakistan adopted the strategy of periodically helping the FBI to capture al-Qaeda leaders like Khalid Sheikh Mohammed and Abu Zubaydah, but looked the other way as Taliban leaders established an almost invisible presence in Baluchistan and the NWFP. The US chose to remain silent initially as it felt that the Taliban was no longer an imminent threat. The capture of frontline al-Qaeda leaders like Osama bin laden and Ayman al Zawahiri remained the highest priority for the Bush Administration. But things started to change by 2004, when the Taliban started regrouping and attacking American, Afghan and coalition forces in Afghanistan. The American Ambassador to Afghanistan Zalmay Khalilzad then joined President Karzai and other Afghan leaders in openly accusing Pakistan of aiding the Taliban on its soil.

The extent of support that the Taliban received in Pakistan became evident in 2005, when the US forces suffered around 125 fatalities in operations in Afghanistan. This was more than the casualties suffered in Afghanistan by the US in the preceding three years. While Pakistan deployed over 80,000 troops in North and South Waziristan in response to US pressure to hunt down Osama bin Laden, not a single Taliban leader has yet been killed or captured in these efforts so far. What has happened instead, is that the tribal population in FATA has made common cause with groups like the Islamic Movement of Uzbekistan and confronted the Pakistan army. This, in turn, has led to a parting of ways between General Musharraf and his erstwhile political allies in the traditionally pro-military right wing Islamic Parties like the Jamat-e-Islami (JI) and the Jamat-Ulema-e-Islam (JUI). Thanks to over two decades of close links with the ISI, both these Parties now head the Provincial Government in the NWFP and wield considerable influence in Baluchistan. While the JI has close links with the Hizb-ul-Mujahideen in Jammu & Kashmir the JUI is linked to both the Harkat-ul-Mujahideen and the Jaish-e-Mohammed. The JUI, however, attaches greater priority and importance to its links with the Taliban, than in supporting the ISI sponsored Jihad in Jammu & Kashmir.

Given the links between the groups like the Lashkar-e-Taiba on the one hand and the Taliban and al-Qaeda on the other, the US finally moved to declare these groups as International Terrorist Organizations, only after the terrorist attacks on 9/11. Pakistan was soon forced to follow suit. But even today, these terrorist groups function quite openly under new names in Pakistan and in POK. Thus, General Musharraf has endeavoured to run with the hare and hunt with the hounds in both Afghanistan and Jammu & Kashmir. While he has banned groups like the Taliban and the Lashkar-e-Taiba, covert links between the ISI and these groups have continued. It is in these circumstances that President Bush minced no words in cautioning Pakistan about its need to act firmly against terrorist groups during his brief visit to Pakistan in March, 2006. General Musharraf, therefore, finds himself in a difficult political situation both domestically and internationally today. Domestically, he has earned the wrath of former allies in the Islamic Parties by backing the American efforts to root out the al-Qaeda in Waziristan. At the same time, his aversion towards former Prime Ministers, Benazir Bhutto and Mr. Nawaz Sharif has created a virtually unbridgeable rift between himself and the military establishment on the one hand and two of the most influential mainstream political parties, the PML (N) led by Nawaz Sharif and the PPP led by Benazir Bhutto, on the other. But, in an ultimate analysis, the United States has little choice but to strive to ensure that Pakistan and its army establishment remain under the control of 'moderate' individuals and political parties. American economic and military assistance to Pakistan will continue as a part of this effort. While lip service may be paid to democracy in Pakistan, the US will back any military ruler, or military dominated government that it regards as being reliable.

While China has urged that India and Pakistan should resolve their differences including on Jammu & Kashmir bilaterally, it has nevertheless provided Pakistan continuing support economically and more importantly, militarily. China's cooperation with Pakistan to help Pakistan to develop nuclear weapons is reported to have commenced in 1976. China has, since then provided Pakistan with new centrifuges and ring magnets for its uranium enrichment programme, apart from actual designs of nuclear weapons. Over the past decade, China has provided Pakistan with assistance to acquire a range of medium range missiles (the Shaheen I and the Shaheen II) to target major urban centres in India. More recently, the Cruise Missiles tested by Pakistan are evidently of Chinese origin. In the conventional military sphere, China is in the process of supplying advanced fighters—the JF-7 and the F-10 to Pakistan. It is providing the Pakistan navy four Frigates and is also helping Pakistan in the production of tanks. In maritime terms, China has sought to give the Pakistan navy strategic depth by extensive assistance to develop the Gwadar port off the Makran coast in Baluchistan. Shortly, after a visit by the then Chinese Prime Minister Zhu Rongji to Pakistan in 2001, General Musharraf announced that he would not hesitate to provide base facilities for China's navy in Gwadar if Pakistan's security was threatened. It is, therefore, apparent that even as India and China seek to improve relations, China will use Pakistan as a strategic ally to strengthen its influence astride the oil rich Persian Gulf and also as a part of a larger policy of 'strategic containment' of India.

In its quest for support on Jammu & Kashmir and 'parity' with India, Pakistan diplomacy has focussed considerable attention on use of the 'Islamic card'. The forums of the OIC are used repeatedly to seek resolutions that condemn India for alleged human rights abuses by India in Jammu & Kashmir. Serious concern was voiced in Pakistan when King Abdullah of Saudi Arabia proposed that India could be associated, like Russia, with the OIC. Pakistani expatriates have been used over the last few years in countries like Saudi Arabia and the UAE to incite Muslims from India to associate themselves with groups like the Lashkar-e-Taiba. All this has been part of a strategy to foment communal violence in India that would threaten the very fabric of India's secular society. Arab countries are constantly reminded by Pakistan of India's ties with Israel and the existence of an alleged 'Hindu-Jewish Axis' that would threaten their security. These efforts by Pakistan are likely to continue and may meet with some sympathy, if not success, in the Islamic world. But, by and large, Indian diplomacy in the Islamic world has met this challenge satisfactorily, though much will depend in the future on our success in maintaining communal harmony within India.

A major factor that has to be borne in mind in assessing the prospects for the future of India-Pakistan relations is the predominant influence of the Pakistan army in the country's national life and particularly on issues pertaining to the country's nuclear programme and its relations with India, Afghanistan and the United States. The bulk of Pakistan's existence as an independent nation state has been under military rule, or military dominance. And, but for brief period after the Bangladesh conflict of 1971, the army has played a domineering role in shaping national policies and priorities. Even though President Musharraf today claims that he has introduced 'genuine democracy' in Pakistan, effective power in the country is wielded not by the civilian rulers or Parliament, but by General Musharraf and his Corps Commanders and Principal Staff Officers. While the civilian bureaucracy was an important partner of the army during military rule under Field Marshal Ayub Khan, General Yahya Khan and General Zia-ul-Haq, the bureaucracy's influence has been relatively limited under General Musharraf, who appears to have greater faith in the Police Service. Army officers today occupy posts ranging from Vice Chancellors of Universities, to Secretaries in Provincial Governments and Ambassadors in important capitals. The army has a huge economic empire within Pakistan, in areas ranging from cement, fertilisers and the sugar industries to real estate, banking, transportation and even school networks. The army is today a state within a state in Pakistan. It will not relinquish these powers easily in the foreseeable future. And a degree of hostility towards India remains a strong *raison d'être* for the army's role in Pakistan.

In these circumstances, President Musharraf has to carry out a delicate balancing act of responding to American and international pressures to end support for terrorism on the one hand and accommodating the army establishment's demands for 'strategic depth' by sustaining the remnants of the Taliban in Afghanistan and 'bleeding India' in Jammu and Kashmir and elsewhere, on the other. His problems have been further compounded by the upsurge of insurgency in Baluchistan where the army establishment has been forced to resort to the use of airpower against its own citizens, as in North and South Waziristan. At the same time, closer links between India and the USA largely spurred by belated American recognition of the resilience of India's democracy and its continuing high rates of economic growth is causing a concern in Islamabad. There does now appear to be an increasing awareness and recognition of these new realities by the elite in Pakistan and a feeling that confrontation with India and an excessive focus on the Kashmir issue have not served the country well.

Whether the army establishment shares such views remains to be seen. But, one can discern some change in stereotype thinking of the past. In Pakistani history books and folklore, Aurangzeb was the greatest Mughal Emperor and Akbar rarely merited charitable references. The permission accorded to screening of the Indian film epic *Mughal e Azam* seems to suggest that there is at least a willingness to look at history in more objective terms. It, however, remains to be seen whether Pakistani history textbooks shed their past communal prejudices. Similarly, the readiness of General Musharraf to put behind constant references to UN Resolutions on Jammu & Kashmir and speak of solutions that do not alter boundaries or borders is a welcome development. At the same time, it remains to be seen whether Pakistan's recent readiness to deal with and talk to political leaders other than its protégés in the Hurriyat Conference is a tactical move given current differences within the Hurriyat, or is a better appreciation of political realities in Jammu & Kashmir. But all this has to be coupled with the fact that despite his assurance of January 6, 2004, that Pakistan will not allow territory under its control to be used for terrorist activities against India, General Musharraf has allowed and indeed collaborated and facilitated the activities of terrorist groups, functioning under new names in both POK and within Pakistan itself.

The present geopolitical situation and the internal developments in Pakistan present new challenges and opportunities for India in dealing with Pakistan. The basic challenges that India faces in dealing with Pakistan arise from two factors. The first arises from Pakistan's use of terrorism as an instrument of state policy in Jammu and Kashmir and elsewhere in India. Addressing the English Speaking Union in Karachi on April 11, 1999, General Musharraf (who was then only the army chief and not the Head of Government in Pakistan) proclaimed that India was a "hegemonic power" and that "low intensity conflict with India would continue even if the Kashmir issue was resolved". His close associate and former Chairman of the Joint Chiefs of Staff Committee, General Aziz Khan, made similar comments a few years later in Rawalkot. Thus, continuing support for "low intensity conflict" within India would remain an unstated policy of the Pakistan military establishment. Secondly, rather than seeking a relationship of 'sovereign equality' with India, the Pakistan elite has an obsession with seeking 'parity' with India.

The first challenge posed by Pakistan has obviously to be met by astute political management within India, with an abiding commitment to the pluralistic and secular values enshrined in the Constitution. It is now recognised that both in Punjab and in Jammu and Kashmir, Pakistan took advantage of our failings and shortsighted policies, like the patently rigged elections of 1987 in Jammu and Kashmir, which promoted alienation and disaffection. Secondly, there is need for aggressive diplomacy in pointing out to the world community, how Pakistan's use of extremist groups to promote terrorism poses a danger not only to India but to the international community as a whole. For example, supporters of the Lashkar-e-Taiba have been arrested in countries ranging from the US and UK to Australia, for involvement in terrorist activities. The diplomatic challenges posed by Pakistan's quest for 'parity' with India can best be met by accelerated economic growth and more active economic engagement, both bilaterally and regionally with countries in India's extended neighbourhood across the entire Indian Ocean Region. In an ultimate analysis, the challenges posed by Pakistan will be best addressed by domestic political stability, enhanced defence modernisation and preparedness and accelerated economic growth within India. There is no room for emotionalism or sentimentalism in dealing with Pakistan. While we should be ready for constructive dialogue, we should also make it clear that we will raise the costs for Pakistan diplomatically and otherwise, if it persists with policies designed to 'bleed India'.

India has also to take a far more proactive approach in its bilateral engagement with Pakistan. It is now clear that even though there may be reservations in the military establishment, the Islamic parties and certain sections of political and media opinion about the present dialogue process, public opinion at large in Pakistan has welcomed moves to ease tensions and promote cooperation. The advent of satellite television has also given Pakistanis a new insight into life in India. But, even today India adopts very restrictive and cumbersome visa procedures. These need to be changed and simplified and irksome requirements of police reporting for visitors from Pakistan, done away with. It is imperative that new schemes be devised for inviting delegations of youth, professionals and businessmen to visit India. We should also seek greater contacts between military establishments. Rather than insisting on reciprocity, unilateral moves on such issues need to be taken by us.

Prime Minister Manmohan Singh's address in Amritsar and the proposals of General Musharraf on "self-governance" and "Joint Management" and agreement by the two leaders that there can be no change of borders or boundaries, along with the commitment that efforts have to be made to make borders "irrelevant," create negotiating space for moving towards greater congruence of viewpoints. It is important that there should be a consensus on both sides of the LOC in Jammu & Kashmir on what self-governance really means. Efforts could be made to see if the degree of self-governance in POK and the Northern Areas could initially be brought to the same levels in Jammu and Kashmir. An intra-Kashmiri dialogue can be initiated to see how the widest possible consensus can be developed on the parameters of self-governance and devolution in Jammu and Kashmir. The Eminent Persons Group set up by SAARC Heads of Government presented a detailed report entitled "SAARC Vision 2020" on how South Asia should move towards becoming an Economic Union by the year 2020. This report has been accepted for adoption by SAARC Heads of Government during the Kathmandu Summit in 2002. Implementation of this report would lead to a situation where borders become irrelevant for trade and investment. If this is coupled with other moves for easy travel across the LOC, we could make the LOC "irrelevant" — "just a line on a map" as envisaged by Dr. Manmohan Singh. Even General Musharraf's proposal for "Joint Management" can be addressed by setting up mechanisms for promoting cross-LOC cooperation in Jammu & Kashmir.

Despite the prevailing optimism about a 'breakthrough' in India-Pakistan relations, there is need for caution and circumspection on dealing with sensitive issues like demilitarisation of Siachen, or indeed within Jammu & Kashmir as a whole. Ever since 1947, Pakistan has not hesitated to use irregular forces in the garb of Mujahideen to seize territory in Jammu & Kashmir. Even today there is a close nexus between the ISI and such Mujahideen groups. New Governments in Pakistan have a tendency of refusing to honour commitments of their predecessors. More importantly, the prospects of long-term stability in Pakistan cannot be guaranteed. In its Report of 2001 entitled "Global Trends 2015," a panel of experts set up by the CIA stated: "Pakistan will not recover easily from decades of political and economic mismanagement, divisive politics and ethnic feuds...In a climate of continuing domestic turmoil, the Central Government's control will probably be reduced to the Punjab heartland and the economic hub of Karachi." The report also held that: "Pakistan will be more fractious, divided and dependent on international financial assistance."

Given the fact that Pakistan today possesses nuclear weapons, the international community will make every effort to see that the country does not become as fractious and dysfunctional as the *Global Trends 2015 Report* predicts. Nuclear weapons in the hands of militant, fundamentalist groups are a nightmare for the entire international community. It does appear that Pakistan will remain an international basket case dependant on foreign assistance for the foreseeable future. The Pakistan army will continue to substantially influence foreign and national security policies. Experience has shown in the past, especially during the 1965 and Kargil conflicts that the Pakistan army feels that every opportunity to strike at India must be availed of, when India's defence capabilities are run down, or vulnerable. There should, therefore, be no compromise on issues like Defence preparedness or on demilitarising any territory controlled by India, unless there are foolproof guarantees that we can act decisively against possible exploitation by Pakistan. In discussing CBMs on conventional force levels, nuclear arsenals and defence spending, it has to be borne in mind that while Pakistan's conventional and nuclear capabilities are 'India specific,' our conventional and nuclear policies have to take into account Chinese capabilities also. Despite this, Pakistani proposals on issues like dealerting of nuclear weapons and separation of nuclear warheads from missiles should be seriously considered.

In the light of the foregoing, it would only be prudent to conclude that while there are now significant possibilities for improving the climate of relations and resolving differences with Pakistan, India also faces serious challenges because of the inherent fault lines in the state system of Pakistan. India cannot wish away the fact that the use of 'militant Islam' and terrorism as instruments of state policy by powerful sections of the Pakistan establishment remains a potent threat. There is also little doubt that the yearning for 'parity' with India is a factor of Pakistani diplomacy and indeed, state policy that drives Pakistan to extreme lengths to upstage and embarrass India on every conceivable occasion. It is only when there is a significant change in the mindset of the Pakistani establishment on these crucial issues that we can expect to have a normal and good neighbourly relationship with Pakistan.

30

India and Sri Lanka: from uncertainty to close proximity

Nagendra Nath Jha

The two great communities, *viz.*, Sinhalas and Tamils have been almost sole inhabitants of Sri Lanka for, approximately, 2,500 years. That they both, originally, hail from India, is proudly acknowledged by them, the Sinhalas from Bihar, Bengal and Orissa, principally, with a fairly liberal sprinkling of Kerala influence and culture on them, and the Tamils from Tamil Nadu.

The advent and impact of Buddhism on the Sinhalas, in fact, drew them even closer to the main cultural and religious ethos of India. The Tamils on the other hand, while also continuing to derive their overall cultural and spiritual inspiration from India (Tamil Nadu), did, however develop in relative isolation on account of the geography of their areas of habitation. They claim, probably with some justification that, for instance, their language is even purer than Tamil spoken in Tamil Nadu and that their distinct cultural evolution, over the centuries, ingrained an even purer form of worship and religious practices.

Actually, however, and very unfortunately the positive interaction between them though inhabiting a small island, has been insufficient. Thus, we have a background denoting minimum contact leading thereby, to a lack of rapport between the two communities, which is an important contributory factor to the unfortunate situation prevailing today.

The advent of the British did not result in any great change in the situation obtaining. While they did unite the country, they did little or nothing to develop the island as a whole, whether the Tamil North-East or the Sinhala South, economically. The Tamils however, benefited in one vital respect. British rule opened up certain classy educational institutions set up by the missionaries. The Tamils, who because of the dry and scrubby nature of the lands they occupy, have consequently, developed a sense of thrift and hard work and were quick to grasp the opportunity provided. Therefore, it came as no surprise to anyone that at the time of Independence, in February 1948, it was the Tamils who occupied most of the senior and middle levels of administration, in fact, quite disproportionate to their numerical presence in the island. This was one of the principal causes of the rapid build up of tension between the two communities in the immediate aftermath of Independence.

It is also important to bear in mind that though a minority, in Sri Lanka, the Tamils have a distinct region, in the island, where they constitute a majority. These are the Northern and Eastern provinces (or at least most of the Eastern province). These have all along been regarded by the Tamils as their 'homeland'. This feeling, always strong, has only been further reinforced in the post-Independence era culminating in the India-Sri Lanka Agreement of July 1987, conferring a degree of autonomy to the North-East province. Very wisely and very understandably, the Agreement refers to the merger (by it) of North and East provinces as "areas of traditional Tamil habitation." The Tamils of Sri Lanka, even the most moderate ones, are unanimous on this issue and resent deeply any attempt to deny or alter this position. They have, therefore, been extremely concerned at what they perceive as post-Independence governments, seeking to disturb the ethnic ratios in the Eastern province, in particular, where a number of irrigation schemes have resulted in a large number of Sinhala colonisers moving there from the Sinhala South of the country. For instance, in 1981, the national census indicated that Tamil population in the Eastern province had declined to 47 per cent from a figure of 82 per cent in 1971. While no doubt this was happening largely because of the land factor at the popular level it was seen as yet another attempt to Sinhalise the entire island.

That is why the earliest Tamil attempts at rectifying the situation were limited to highlighting two issues, namely, the legitimate use of their language in their areas of habitation and controlling the colonisation or resettlement of Sinhala settlers in the east. The reference, here is to the Bandaranaike-Chelvanayakam pact of January 1957 and subsequently to the Senanyake-Chelvanayakam pact of 1965. In fact, it is the considered view of long time Sri Lanka watchers, that the non-implementing of these pact denoted the first golden opportunity lost, something that could have led to a genuine resolution of the problem, at that stage itself.

The first mentioned pact stated that "pending the establishment of regional bodies, state aided colonization will be suspended and that the two provinces would enjoy some kind of regional autonomy as well on the delegation of powers to regional bodies for development oriented subjects." The other major clause in this pact recognised Tamil to be statutorily and administratively the national language of the Tamil speaking people in Ceylon and that Tamil was to be made the language of administration and the courts in the two provinces.

Actually, this was a courageous decision taken, by a Prime Minister who had in his election campaign promised that Sinhala would become the official language of the country within '24 hours' of his assuming office. For this gesture to the Tamils he had to pay with his life. A Buddhist monk shot him dead in the late September, 1959.

Prime Minister Bandaranaike's assassination did not spur the government to honour the settlement. Sinhalese was declared as the official language of the country from 1 January, 1961. The maximum that government would promise was a series of regulations to ensure 'reasonable use' of Tamil language especially in the administration of the Northern and Eastern provinces. All this was looked upon as a major betrayal by the Tamils.

The second pact, the S-C pact, emerged with the advent of a UNP Government supported by the Tamil Party. It was, as expected, a second attempt to gain recognition for the Tamil language and stop colonisation.

It envisaged a moderate degree of devolution at the district council level including on the question of land alienation. It also included a compromise formula in which Tamils were assured priority for allotment, irrespective of whether they were based in the North or the East. On the language issue, Parliament adopted the Tamil Language (special provisions) regulations, 1966. These were approved by Parliament on 11 January, 1966 but after considerable opposition, in the streets, by the Buddhist clergy and the *Maha Sangha*. The subsequent event returned the SLFP back to power in 1970, they went about their goal of drafting a new Constitution which enshrined Sinhala as the official language with special provisions for Buddhism.

At this point it would be useful to make a note of the fact that the psychological conditioning of the two communities played an important role in the evolution of their political thinking and objectives. The Tamils did not regard themselves as being bound by the terms of the settlement at the time of independence. They felt that they should have been extensively consulted and would be secure only in a federal type of arrangement for the country. They felt that they had been conciliatory enough but the Sinhalas were not appreciative of or indifferent to their genuine concerns.

The Sinhalas on the other hand had a total misconception of the word 'federal'. They regarded themselves as living in a state of siege wherein they found themselves surrounded on three sides by Tamils, in their own country, and just across the Palk Straits lived more than 60 million Tamils in Tamil Nadu. In this state of mind it was not at all surprising to note that few, if anybody, made an attempt to probe the other's psyche.

Regarding the word 'federal', unfortunately the Sinhalas were mortally terrified of it equating it with 'secession'. But, at the same time, it must be said to their credit that in well under 60 years they have by and large covered an enormous distance in both understanding its precise meaning and, more importantly, in the evolution of their thinking. In fact, to any long-term observer of the Sri Lanka scene the transformation is nothing short of revolutionary. Similarly, the Tamils, too, have accepted that there are limits; beyond which the Sinhalas will not go and that the urge to safeguard the unity of one's country is a universal phenomenon. Except of course, for the LTTE among them.

It is therefore, worth repeating that a really priceless opportunity was lost in the 1960s to resolve this issue, but unfortunately, the Sinhalas were simply for it.

As if to rub salt on wounds the infamous 'standardisation' of marks for students seeking admission to university's science-based courses was introduced. For example, between 1965-70, the Tamil share, e.g. in medicine was of an average 53 per cent against 41 per cent for the Sinhalas, in engineering it was 50 per cent and 48 per cent, respectively, but now it came down to 33 per cent in medicine and 25 per cent in engineering. As per the new regulations introduced the Sinhalas were given an extra 10 per cent marks added on to their aggregate in order to bring them at par with the Tamil application. Actually, these ratios were even then not bad in relation to their total percentage of population though it was violative of every canon of fair play. In the emotionally charged atmosphere, however, prevailing in the country on account of a whole series of measures taken by the government e.g., the nationalisation of plantations, the prominent position given to the Buddhist religion etc., the Tamils got the impression that they had only a secondary role to play in the affairs of Sri Lanka.

At his stage, it would be useful to try and understand the true nature of the LTTE's thinking. Shortly after its founding, it stated, with absolute candour that the "establishment of a sovereign, socialist democratic peoples, govt." was primary objective employing the only option available to them, *viz.*, the path of revolutionary struggle to liberate the "Tamil homeland." It was also made clear by them that such an armed struggle would, initially, be waged through 'guerrilla warfare' to be gradually and systematically transformed into a genuine people's 'war of liberation later'. Anton Balasingham tried to put their point of view as follows:

"Plunged into the despair of unemployed existence, frustrated without the possibility of higher education, angered by the imposition of an alien language, the Tamil youth realized that the redemption of their plight lay in revolutionary politics, a political that should pave the way for a radical and fundamental transformation of their miserable conditions of existence.

"The only alternative left to the youth, under the conditions of mounting national oppression, the youth rightly perceived, was none other than a revolutionary armed struggle for the total independence of their nation."

On its part, the Sri Lankan government was not indifferent to LTTE posturing and threats. A reference has already been made, earlier, to the very considerable evolution in Sri Lankan (particularly Sinhala) thinking on the issue of federalism. The earliest signs of this were manifest in 1985, itself, more specifically at the Indian sponsored Thimphu talks, which was able to bring face to face, the various Tamil groups/parties to the table apart from the Sri Lankan Government. In fact, the Thimphu talks were noteworthy in more than one way. It was the first time the LTTE were able to articulate, formally and face to face, something that had been hinted at and propagated through the media *viz.*, the recognition of a separate Tamil nation and their right to self-determination. It was also notable for the fact that the leader of the Sri Lanka delegation was able to use, without any acute discomfort, the word 'self-determination' when he stated the right of self-determination in the running of government *viz.*, in the management of one's own affairs.

The Sri Lankan Government, did come up with some suggestion for devolution to ensure a greater sharing of power by the people and their maximum participation in identifying their needs and problems and deciding upon matters vitally affecting their interests. The Tamils, however, were adamant about their recognition as a separate nation and on their right of "self-determination."

In retrospect it can be said that it was a real pity that the Thimphu talks did not succeed. As stated earlier, it was the first time that the Tamils and the Government had come face-to-face and with India's attempted mediation were having an opportunity to discuss their problems frankly. The government showed considerable patience and maturity in the face of particularly, LTTE's intransigence and the latter's starting off from a maxima list which, however, showed poor tactics and understanding of negotiations.

The infructuous nature of these talks also confirmed something that was becoming increasingly apparent, namely, the tenuous hold of the Indian government on the LTTE, especially, despite its best efforts to play the role of an interested and well-meaning mediator.

Lalith Athulathmudali the then National Security Minister, summed it up very succinctly in the Sri Lankan Parliament when he said, on May 20, 1986, that "their (LTTE's) published statements, their private commentaries, their pamphlets, everything show that they are against the ongoing Indian efforts. But strange enough they are not being condemned by India." Thus, we see that a good 15 to 18 months before the induction of the IPKF and its subsequent conflict with the LTTE , it was becoming increasingly obvious that the LTTE, were clearly manipulating the Tamil Nadu factor in domestic Indian politics to exploit the Government of India (GoI) to their utmost capabilities.

The GoI intervened again when the Sri Lankan army was on the verge, for the first time, of scoring a decisive victory over the LTTE in the Vedamarachi region of the north by 'advising' the Sri Lankan government to desist from proceeding with the operation, India, perhaps for one last time, tried to bail the Tamil militants out of a tight military corner. From the Sri Lankan point of view this was, obviously a most undesirable development since they felt that this had deprived them of a golden opportunity to strike a decisive blow and probably end the war for once and for all. In fact, Lalith Athulathmudali never forgave India for depriving him of his moment of glory. But it did have the effect of pushing a somewhat chastened LTTE towards seeking an honourable settlement brokered by India.

The India and Sri Lanka Accord (ISLA) of July 29, 1987, did provide the Tamils with something that they had been agitating for since Independence. It led to the 13th amendment shortly thereafter, which devolved certain powers and functions to the Provincial Councils setup and most vitally for the Tamils, even the most moderate among them brought about most sought after and longed for merger of the Northern and Eastern Provinces to form the North-East Province. It has been widely interpreted as being the most important achievement of the ISLA. In fact, with the benefit of hindsight one can fairly easily pinpoint the flaws in the Agreement. To start with, it should have been signed by the Government of Sri Lanka with the Tamils. After all, it dealt with an entirely domestic matter and for the sake of its greater acceptance it should have kept the GoI as a guarantor only. Then, despite the merger, the Tamils were not satisfied because of the referendum clause in the Agreement. It was laid down that the merger would require to be endorsed through a referendum in the Eastern Province by December 1988. Fortunately, informally, it was agreed that the referendum would be postponed by six months at a time by the president. Actually, this is how the referendum has been avoided so far. The Tamils, however, found this provision objectionable because in the event of a referendum the East would opt out.

To the Sinhalas it looked too much like a dictated document and the incorporation of the second part, *viz.*, a supposedly confidential exchange of Letters between the two governments tended to confirm this view — the latter dealt with the discouragement of the VOA relaying station proposed to be set up and also to the exclusion of foreign military personnel and experts by the Sri Lankan army. The exclusion of foreign companies from Trinconalese was also included.

The LTTE, however, had yet another reason for opposing the ISLA. While it is correct that a High Commission officer had visited Jaffna and the overall impression created was that after the Vedamarachi push by the Sri Lankan army they were a chastened lot, what was overlooked was that Prabhakaran himself had not met the High Commission official. That itself should have helped to anticipate that there were pitfalls ahead.

In this context, it is useful to bear in mind that Prabhakaran felt extremely humiliated at being forced to come to Delhi and kept as a virtual prisoner in the Ashok Hotel. He is reported to have uttered that the humiliation had to be avenged one day. About the ISLA he felt that it was an act of cheating and a betrayal of Tamil interests.

Finally, it is well known that the Prime Minister of Sri Lanka, Premadasa (to be President lesser than two years later) was against the ISLA. What is perhaps less well known is that no attempt was made by the Indian side to keep in regular touch with him with a view to taking him on board. Not only him but even the leaders of friendly parties like SLFP, including Mrs. Bandaranaike and her son Amira were kept totally in the dark about the ISLA.

Unfortunately for Indo-Sri Lankan relations, there was a total absence of the previous personal rapport that existed between Prime Minister Rajiv Gandhi and J.R. Jayawardene, between Rajiv Gandhi and Premdasa. Moreover, the latter was strongly of the view that the strains in the body politics of Sri Lanka were the outcome of years of rule by the elite, both Tamil and Sinhale. He was convinced, therefore, that once the elite were out of the way, since both he and Prabhakaran were from a humble background and class, they would understand each other much better. His belief was reinforced by the fact that he had regularly won his seat to Parliament from the Colombo (Central) constituency which has traditionally been one with large Tamil presence. Therefore, what one witnessed was a ludicrous situation in which the IPKF, dispatched to Sri Lanka, at the invitation of the Sri Lankan government was ridiculed by Tamil Nadu Government who, also, did not hesitate to give a donation of Rs. 4 crores, in Chennai, to the LTTE. In Sri Lanka, on the other hand, the Prime Minister later President, Premadasa supplied, secretly, weapons to the LTTE to fight the Indian army which, after all, had been invited by his government to that country.

Actually, what Premadasa had failed to grasp was that the entire dynamics of the situation had changed. By the time he assumed the Presidency the unfortunate situation had already gathered momentum for over three decades, including over 10 years of LTTE terrorism. However well meaning and well-intentioned, it was well beyond his capabilities to halt the downslide. Put simply, things had gone on for far too long and gone too far.

Premadasa's period was marked by a certain degree of uncertainty. Though the IPKF which had rendered yeoman service to the cause of Sri Lankan unity, something which is now in the process of being appropriately duly recognised by the Sri Lanka Government, had departed that country on 24 March 1990, a collective and residual bitterness remained in his dealings with India, for a mixture of reasons and experiences outlined earlier. He remained suspicious and distrustful of his powerful neighbour, it was felt by most people that these two traits arose out of a feeling of having been belittled and slighted by the Indian leaders. Nevertheless, he remained proud of his Indian cultural links and raised the economic relationship to a higher plain. Simply because he was of the view that Indian products, especially transport equipment, were much cheaper and this would earn him added popularity with the people. He enthusiastically supported the proposal to raise the Joint Committee to the level of Joint Commission, with separate committees for political, economic, cultural and science and technology cooperation.

Premadasa had a phenomenal memory which, among other things he used fairly liberally to enforce professional responsibility on the part of his senior ministers and senior bureaucrats. It could sometimes result in unpleasant and nasty shocks, for the latter, in particular!

India had, obviously, learnt a great deal from its period of intervention (both political and military) and did its utmost to keep itself totally disinvolved in Sri Lankan affairs. In the immediate aftermath of the withdrawal of the IPKF it was felt that, for some time at least, it would be worthwhile to permit things to simmer and let the Sri Lankans get on with themselves. Even when it was crystal clear that Premadasa was making a serious error of judgement by handing over the areas vacated by the IPKF to the LTTE, the GoI desisted from advising him otherwise. But, the GoI responded positively and with alacrity to moves to strengthen cooperation in the economic field. Private sector investments, by both Tatas and Leyland, were already in the pipeline and Ceat tyres also commenced production of tyres at their factory. Privatisation of the management of tea estates, also went to Indian parties from South India and cooperation in dairy sector, with Amul, was first discussed in January 1993. Therefore, it can be that the withdrawal of the IPKF catalysed the commencement, in a big way, of a movement in this vital sector and it is very rewarding to note that, today, it has grown into a healthy tree.

Again, in the investigations following former Prime Minister Rajiv Gandhi's assassination, the Sri Lankan Government extended wholehearted cooperation to the Indian Special Investigation Team (SIT). Not once did the High Commission ever have reason to discern the slightest lack of cooperation on Sri Lanka's part.

But traces of an attitudinal hangover still remained in President Premadasa and which were yet to be completely eliminated. It was precisely in this in-between period when an informal proposal was made to him to test the waters, so as to say. It was made to him on 7 July 1991 a date of some significance in the sense that it was literally a few weeks after the assassination of Shri Rajiv Gandhi. It was quite clearly, yet another opportunity presented and subsequently lost. Something that would have averted a great deal of further blood-letting in that lovely island. It was suggested to him that in order to choke off the LTTE from its sources of weapon supplies, it would be a good idea for the Indian and Sri Lankan navies to jointly patrol the Eastern coast of Sri Lanka which was the principal route taken for the weapon supplies to reach the LTTE. No force in the world can fight without its regular source of weapon supplies being intact. A kind of a blockade of the Eastern coast of Sri Lanka, would ensure that these supplies were virtually reduced to a trickle. Also, in the process, it would not be necessary for Indian forces to either set foot on Sri Lankan soil or enter its territorial waters.

Domestically, in India there would be no public outcry since, the public feeling, against the LTTE was extremely high, particularly in view of the shock waves generated by Rajiv Gandhi's assassination. In subsequent years, the LTTE also accepted they had erred grievously in carrying out the assassination.

Premadasa, however, was not impressed by this line of thinking. In all probability he was still optimistic about the influence wielded by him over Prabhakaran. Thus, it can be stated with great confidence that this was an error of major proportions and yet another historic opportunity lost.

In the post-Premadasa period both Chandrika Kumartunga and Ranil Wickremasinghe have gone to great lengths to accommodate Tamil demands, even the LTTE ones. A cease-fire has been in force since February 2002 and despite the numerous violations and provocations, principally by the LTTE, has held and this too redounds to the credit of the government.

Again to the eternal credit of the Sri Lankan Government both sides at Oslo, in December 2002, agreed to find a solution along federal lines to the Tamil question. But unfortunately for that country the cease-fire, which granted the LTTE *de facto* control of a large part of the North-East, only appears to have further whet their appetite towards a realisation of Eelam. Even on such a humanitarian matter as post-Tsunami relief the LTTE has fused its demand for a virtually independent administrative structure with a demand for control over reconstruction and rehabilitation work in the North-East. This has prolonged the misery of its own fellow Tamils with regard to receiving prompt relief and rehabilitation. But the point to emphasise here is that those who are even slightly familiar with the Sri Lankan situation, would be the first to recognise the momentous significance of this acceptance by the Government of Sri Lanka, of the federal concept. The exact wording of the statement is as follows:

"The parties agreed to explore a solution founded on the principle of internal self determination in areas of historical habitation of the Tamil speaking peoples based on a federal structure within a united Sri Lanka."

Its uniqueness lay in the fact that it was based on a proposal made by the LTTE who thus committed themselves to a federal setup in the country within a united Sri Lanka. A few months down the line at the sixth round held in Japan the two sides reiterated their commitment to this earlier formulation. They also agreed to invite the Forum of Federations, a Canadian based international organisation, to participate as consultants at the seventh session.

A likely reason for the LTTE's climb down to their ostensible acceptance of a mutually satisfactory federal solution within a united Sri Lanka, must lie in the fact that even they would be aware of a changed global environment since 9/11. Thus, Prabhakaran was constrained to state on Heroes Day, in November 2002, that the "LTTE cannot ignore changing global environment and the need to adjust its freedom movement." Furthermore, there is no disputing the fact that the Karuna episode had definitely weakened the LTTE both militarily and politically. Then, they would also be aware that despite their military performance they did not have Jaffna and Palaly with them—were unable to capture them in the so-called Eelam War III.

The biggest challenge to the new President is to somehow maintain the fragile peace of the cease-fire and, at the same time, move towards a reconciliation. But given the nature of his alliances with the JVP and the National Heritage front, and non-dependence on the Tamil parties, he may not have the political space and manoeuvrability to achieve peace with the LTTE. Of course, he has the political maturity and sagacity to get around these problems but he would be well advised to ensure that he retains the goodwill of the moderate Tamil parties and even beyond them of the silent majority among the Tamils, *viz.*, the moderate Tamil public opinion in the country.

His task is not made any easier by the fact that the LTTE is determined not to talk from a position of military weakness and, unfortunately, will not talk whenever militarily confident. Despite paying lip service to viable alternatives to Eelam. His remarks of 1987 resonate loud and clear even today. He said: "I have unrelenting faith in the proposition that only a Tamil Eelam can offer a permanent solution to the problem of the people of Tamil Eelam" and that he would continue to fight for the objective of attaining it. As though this was not enough, the Interim Self-Governing Authority (ISGA), proposed by the LTTE is virtually a call to the Sri Lankan Government to accept a *de facto* Eelam, which would, in probability constitute a final step before the proclamation of an Eelam state. The ISGA proposals to seek to ensure that the LTTE will always enjoy a majority of the appointees on it, its Chairman would be elected by a majority of the ISGA Committees, and he would appoint Chief Administrator for the North East. It and not the government would appoint an independent Election Commission, a Human Rights Commission and that all expenditure in the North East would be under the control of the ISGA and that in the event of any disagreement or dispute between the parties over the interpretation or implementation and in case of disagreement over the appointment of the Chairman of the Arbitration Tribunal the International Court of Justice would be requested to appoint the Chairperson. Obviously, the ISGA represent a set of proposals which no self-respecting nation can accept and the LTTE must be aware of this. Quite clearly, therefore, it is an attempt to move in the direction of separation in the hope that the Sri Lankan government would be compelled to accept it as a *fait accompli*.

Give Prabhakaran's oft-stated views on the subject, the LTTE, would like to go ahead as rapidly as possible to a *de jure* Eelam. A political level acceptance, however by the Government is simply not on. For instance, since 1995 the Jaffna Penninsula has been in the control of the Government, and with 40,000 troops stationed there, it will be next to impossible for the LTTE to dislodge a well entrenched army from there. Secondly, even if it were able to do so, it would still have to hold it in the face of an army onslaught. The third factor coming into play would be the isolation which it faces as not only India but the international community is committed to preserve Sri Lanka's sovereignty and opposition to the creation of Eelam which must always be factored into the calculations. The entire Indian neighbourhood is already highly vitiated and not entirely palatable.

All the same, India cannot maintain a disinvolved posture. Among all our neighbours it is the only country with which India has cordial and warm relations. Despite a period of uncertainty in the 1980s, in particular, the geographical and ethnic proximity and

and basic goodwill that India and Sri Lanka have for each other, have contributed silently but most significantly to the relationship to be able to withstand the shock waves generated by the turbulence of that decade. The reiteration of our commitment to the multiethnic, plural nature of Sri Lankan politics and the strenuous efforts made in that direction, have also been a major factor in the inherent stability of this relationship. The contour of this relationship has, throughout, remained intact and unaffected.

The economic cooperation launched during the Presidency of Premadasa has borne fruits in the subsequent period. The Indo-Sri Lanka economic ties are looked upon as a model relationship and the Free Trade Agreement, signed in December 1998 and implemented from March 2000, is seen as a significant success. The Joint Statement, issued by the two sides, at the conclusion of President Rajapaksa's visit, on 30 December 2005, expressed satisfaction at the "dynamism of the bilateral economic relationship." It also noted "the good progress by the two Governments in building upon the success of the Indian Sri Lanka Free Trade Association by negotiating a comprehensive Economic Partnership Agreement (CEPA)" and expressed confidence that the "finalization of the CEPA on the basis of mutual benefit for both sides, would further unleash the inherent synergies between two countries." As a result of the FTA, the trade between the two countries has increased by 195 per cent with Indian exports going up by 111 per cent and Sri Lanka's by 366 per cent.

India is the largest source of imports into Sri Lanka and, in turn, India has become the third largest export destination for Sri Lankan goods, up from the 22nd spot earlier. A $ 100m credit line has been announced by India, as well as additional credits for a rail link between Colombo and Matara as well as a thermal power plant of 500 MW in Trincomalee. The latter would be in addition to already obtaining on lease 99 oil storage tanks of World War II vintage, for renovation and upgrading.

Thus, there now exists a situation in which India is active on the trade and economic fronts but passively interested in the political field. While there are understandable reasons for the latter stance

—based on domestic political comprehensions—it is a dichotomous situation which may not entirely be possible to sustain in the long run. On the part of Sri Lanka, it would be useful for the new government to recommit itself to the Joint Statement of December 2002, regarding a federal structure and to make the merger permanent. Any retracting from that position would provide just the excuse the LTTE is looking for to convey to the Tamils of the North-East and also to the international community generally, to hold it up as an 'act of perfidy' on the part of the Sinhala majority; irrespective of the fact that their own commitment to a federal structure is no more that perfunctory. Fortunately, however, for Sri Lanka, the new President and his team have displayed great restraint, maturity and patience, even in the face of enormous provocations, such as the recent attempt to assassinate the Army Chief General Forseeka. Another thing the Sri Lankan Government will have to bear in mind is that its position will be much stronger, during negotiations if there is a prior convergence of views between the SLFP and the UNP. Immediately after this it should try and take the two Buddhist parties along, also. Of course, this may turn out to be a more challenging task but once again, with the President's experience, tact and sophistication it may not prove an impossible task. In any event he can always take recourse to a referendum. Given the two decades or more of fratricidal conflict prevailing in their country, one is confident that the people of the island will opt for peace and stand by the formula of December 2002, with whatever adjustments are mutually agreed to by both sides. There is no need for him to disband the Tamil paramilitary forces, as demanded by Prabhakaran, since they are important constituents of the overall forces available to the government. It would be necessary, however, to ensure that they must not be permitted to indulge in reprisal or revenge killings for this would, yet again, provide the LTTE with a convenient handle.

The Indian Government, on its part, must publicly display greater interest. While from the Sri Lankan side there have been any number of visits at the level of the President and the Prime Minister, from the Indian side, however, there appears to have been a paucity of such high level visits. Irrespective of the number and scale of international monitoring efforts in Sri Lanka, India will always occupy the highest position in Sri Lankan minds and perspective. Visits by us of the type suggested, will have a reassuring effect on the people and will help to assure them of India's continued support and goodwill. Furthermore, India should act, as quickly as possible on the Sri Lankan request regarding a Defence Cooperation Agreement with suitable provisions for the unceasing flow of weapons from India as well as enhanced training facilities at our institutions. Then, India should also expand the scope of the FTA to the maximum possible extent including sympathetic consideration to their idea of a tea cartel between the two countries. Additionally, Indian tourist inflow into that country has grown enormously in last few years. This can be further facilitated by Indian tourists being permitted to carry Indian currency (within certain liberal limits) into that country and Sri Lanka providing exchange facilities, if possible at special tourist rates of exchange.

Turning again to the political side, India must continue to attend the cosponsor meeting as an observer, at the least. The fisherman's problems can be resolved by developing an efficient machinery for their verification and prompt release and repatriation.

India's actions will be enormously helpful towards contributing to an early resolution of the problems so that the two highly talented communities of Sri Lanka can contribute their best to making the island an Asian paradise.

31

India-Sri Lanka: new directions

Mohan Kumar

Introduction

Every current inhabitant of Sri Lanka can trace his descent to India in some way. It is therefore no exaggeration to say that Sri Lanka and India are closely linked through geography, history, religion and culture. While the geographical proximity is obvious, the one on history and religion requires careful appreciation of past patterns of emigration from India to Sri Lanka. It is widely believed that the majority community in Sri Lanka i.e., the Sinhalese, went there from present day Bihar and Orissa. The other important minority community, Sri Lankan Tamils (not to be confused with the plantation or the upcountry Tamils) went there from Tamil Nadu several hundred years ago. In contrast, the upcountry or plantation Tamils were taken to Sri Lanka from Tamil Nadu by the British in the 19th Century as indentured labourers to work in the tea plantations. It is good to bear in mind the fact that there is very little in common between these two communities in Sri Lanka, besides the Tamil language. The Sri Lankan Tamils are involved in a bitter ethnic struggle with their Sinhalese brethren; the upcountry or plantation Tamils are involved in an economic struggle! A small word on the Muslims of Sri Lanka. It is only recently that this community has developed a religion-based identity. Otherwise, virtually every Muslim speaks the Tamil language and was part of the Sri Lankan Tamil community. The fact that Muslims of Sri Lanka now seek a religion-based identity rather than one based on ethnicity or language, will be an important factor in the future politics of Sri Lanka.

As for religion, the main one *viz.*, Buddhism went from India and it is interesting that it flourished much more in Sri Lanka than in its country of origin. The religious links between the Sinhalese and places in India such as 'Bodh Gaya' are significant. There are hundreds of Buddhist pilgrims who travel to India every year.

The above links of geography, history and religion obviously lead to an inescapable conclusion: that Indians and Sri Lankans occupy the same cultural space.

Sri Lanka—a fairly advanced South Asian country

The political movement for independence in India was long and the struggle lasted almost a hundred years. In contrast, there was no major 'independence struggle' in Sri Lanka and it is fair to say that independence came to Sri Lanka without much of a struggle! Be that as it may, Sri Lankans enjoyed adult suffrage much before independence even while Indians had to wait till after independence to achieve it.

Sri Lankans often claim that if it was not for the ethnic strife which engulfed the island, it would have been another 'Singapore'. This is no empty boast. If you look at the latest human development indices of Sri Lanka, the country comes out on top in South Asia by a big margin. As is known, the human development index focuses on three measurable dimensions of human development: long and healthy life, being educated and a decent standard of living. It may thus be observed that rather than go by the yardstick of income alone, it includes important indices such as life expectancy, school enrolment and literacy. And as the latest UNDP report for Sri Lanka underlines, Sri Lanka continues to come out on top in South Asia and this despite the heavy toll taken by the ethnic conflict for over two decades now. Life expectancy is something like 74 years, comparing well with some developed countries. Similarly, the literacy level is over 90 per cent, whereas the average for South Asia hovers around 50 per cent. As for access to basic health facilities, 90 per cent of the population have access to some form of basic health care and 100 per cent of the children are immunised. These are very impressive achievements by any standard (let alone South Asian standards) and the fact that this is so despite the ethnic problem makes it truly remarkable.

India's policy towards Sri Lanka

It is clearly not the aim of this chapter to trace the history of how the ethnic issue arose in Sri Lanka. There is enough literature on that, which is easily available. What is nevertheless important for understanding the Indo-Sri Lankan bilateral relations is to dwell at some length on India's motives, interests and security imperatives that determine her policy towards Sri Lanka.

We have already covered the important links of history and culture that exist between Sri Lankans and Indians. With a mere 20 miles separating the two countries, there was special affinity between the Sri Lankan Tamils and the Tamil speaking people of the South Indian state of Tamil Nadu. When the most horrible anti-Tamil riots happened on the streets of Colombo in 1983, it was natural for the Tamils in Sri Lanka to flee to Tamil Nadu and it was entirely understandable for the latter to welcome their Tamil brethren. This affinity based on language and ethnicity is therefore a reality and it continues to this day. Indeed since January this year, the hostilities between the armed forces and the LTTE have led to over 15,000 Tamil refugees from Sri Lanka fleeing to Tamil Nadu. It is therefore correct to surmise that the safety and well-being of Sri Lankan Tamils does matter to the people of Tamil Nadu in particular and to India in general.

A fundamental tenet governing India's policy towards Sri Lanka is its commitment to the unity, sovereignty and territorial integrity of Sri Lanka. This is far more important than it seems at first glance. After all, if one goes back deep into history the inhabitants of Sri Lanka did face repeated invasions by South Indian rulers. In more recent times, in the eighties, India supported the cause of the Tamils, which it still does. But, at no point of time in India's independent history, did she want Sri Lanka's unity, sovereignty and territorial integrity undermined or compromised. Indeed in the Indo-Sri Lankan Agreement (ISLA) of 1987, there is a clear and unambiguous commitment to preserve the unity, sovereignty and territorial integrity of Sri Lanka.

Although the presence of the Indian Peace Keeping Force (IPKF) in Sri Lanka became controversial and it finally quit in 1990, the Sri Lankans today look upon the Indian armed forces as non-threatening and friendly. For instance, when Sri Lanka suffered from floods in 2003, the Indian armed forces including the medical corps provided help and relief to flood stricken victims. Again, when the Tsunami tragedy struck in December 2004, the Indian armed forces were the first to arrive in the island nation for help and relief. The common people of Sri Lanka, thus, have great affection and respect for the armed forces of India. Compared to the early history when invasions used to happen from Southern India into Sri Lanka, the transformation cannot have been more remarkable. From posing a threat to Sri Lanka in the early part of modern history, India is now a friendly neighbour who is committed to protecting Sri Lanka's unity, sovereignty and territorial integrity.

A strong, stable but most of all, a peaceful Sri Lanka is an imperative for India. This is axiomatic, because any trouble in Sri Lanka can and does spill over into India. Sri Lanka can achieve peace and stability only if there is a permanent and enduring settlement to the ethnic issue. India believes that it is only a political and negotiated settlement that can deliver a permanent and enduring solution. Such a solution, while of course safeguarding the unity, sovereignty and territorial integrity of Sri Lanka, must also meet the legitimate aspirations of all sections, including the minorities, of Sri Lankan society. The Indian Constitution, dynamic and flexible such as it is, could provide a useful reference point in such an exercise. India stands more than ready to share her experience and expertise in this regard.

The LTTE, of course, remains proscribed in India. Its top leaders stand convicted of having committed the heinous crime of assassinating former Prime Minister Shri Rajiv Gandhi. The LTTE continues to believe in violence to achieve its goals and aims. Not only is this unacceptable, but so also its claim of being the 'sole representative' of all Sri Lankan Tamils. Given the international opinion against terrorism in the post 9/11 period and the utter futility of its own tactics so far, it can only be hoped that the Tigers will change their stripes!

India has always had an abiding interest in the security of Sri Lanka. The fact that Sri Lanka is so close to India on her southern flank and the fact that it is so strategically located in the Indian Ocean suggests that foreign presence inimical to her interests would pose a problem for India. There is ample testimony to this in the side letters exchanged between the late Prime Minister Shri Rajiv Gandhi and the late President of Sri Lanka, Mr. J.R. Jayawardene. Suffice it to say that the security of Sri Lanka is closely linked to that of India's own security and the two are thus interdependent.

The Indo-Sri Lanka FTA—a role model for the region

The signing of a bilateral Free Trade Agreement (FTA) between India and Sri Lanka in December 1998 was a defining moment in the relationship. To understand the pathbreaking nature of the Agreement, we need to appreciate the differences in size between the two economies, the competitive nature of the basket of exports of both countries and the inherent insecurities of a small country such as Sri Lanka *vis-à-vis* a big one such as India. While it is easy enough to see what was in it for a country such as India, it is Sri Lanka that had to overcome resistance from several domestic actors. A combination of factors led to Sri Lanka deciding to take the plunge. First, Sri Lanka had an impeccable record of a relatively open economy amongst the South Asian countries. In fact, Sri Lanka was the first to embark on economic reforms as far back as 1977, long before any other South Asian country thought of doing so. Second, Sri Lanka was smart to understand that India was a growth opportunity, not a threat to its market. Last but not least, Sri Lanka realised that its future, whether it is tourism or foreign direct investment, lay more with India rather than with far away UK or Australia. The experience so far has vindicated Sri Lanka's motives on embarking upon a FTA with India. For India too, it was a bold step. This was the first FTA that India signed with any country. The Indo-Sri Lankan FTA seeks to establish a free trade area for goods through a phased duty reduction programme subject to negative lists, rules of origin and safeguard measures. The results of the FTA for both countries are more than satisfactory. Between the period 2001 and 2005 (the FTA though signed in December 1998, became operational from March 2000) the FTA prompted a 200 per cent increase in bilateral trade. While India's exports to Sri Lanka increased by 139 per cent, Sri Lankan exports to India registered a whopping increase of 717 per cent during the same period. Most importantly, the trade balance which was totally in favour of India by a ratio of 16 to 1 in 1998, became much more balanced in favour of Sri Lanka in 2005 by a ratio of 2.4 to 1.

The FTA has thus emerged as a good role model for the South Asian region. A global study on economic integration between regions came to the conclusion that leaving aside sub-Saharan Africa, South Asia is the 'least-integrated' region economically. This is because countries of the region have always allowed politics to trump economics. This needs to change and the Indo-Sri Lanka FTA shows the way forward by providing proof, if proof was needed, that economic integration is a win-win scenario for all the countries of the region. The Indo-Lanka FTA was in this sense 'avant-guarde' and the SAFTA (South Asian Free Trade Agreement for SAARC countries) is now trying to accomplish the same for the South Asian region.

The IOC story

One of the biggest Indian investments in Sri Lanka is that of the Indian Oil Corporation. The IOC has a wholly owned subsidiary in Sri Lanka by the name of Lanka Indian Oil Corporation (LIOC). Since its entry in 2003, LIOC has become a major player in the petroleum sector in Sri Lanka. LIOC, at the time of writing, has total investments of over US$ 100 million. The LIOC has taken on long lease and is currently managing and operating the 99 oil tanks in the Trincomalee Oil Tank Farm. LIOC also bought 100 retail petroleum outlets from the state-owned Ceylon Petroleum Company (CPC).

The LIOC story proves that there can be mutually beneficial cooperation in the areas of investment and services between the two countries. It also highlighted the fact that the FTA was confined only to goods and that investment and services were excluded from its scope of operation. This prompted the two governments to set up a Joint Study Group in 2003 with the specific mandate of looking at a Comprehensive Economic Partnership Agreement (CEPA) between the two countries.

Comprehensive Economic Partnership Agreement

As with the FTA, the initiative for a Comprehensive Economic Partnership Agreement (CEPA) came from Sri Lanka. The credit for long-term vision therefore should go to the Government of Sri Lanka at the time. Early in 2003, the then Government of Sri Lanka decided to constitute a Joint Study Group with the clear mandate to submit recommendations for closer economic and commercial partnership between the two countries. The Government of Sri Lanka did so for the following reasons:

- to forge closer economic integration between the Sri Lankan economy and the dynamic states of Southern India;
- to take full advantage of the economic boom in India;
- to include services within the scope of bilateral economic cooperation since Sri Lanka had competitive edge in services, while India had an edge in goods; and
- to seek Indian investment into Sri Lanka.

There was unanimity in the Joint Study Group that both countries stand to benefit by entering into a Comprehensive Economic Partnership Agreement (CEPA). As opposed to the FTA which dealt only with goods, the CEPA was supposed to address issues such as:

- reduction of items under the Negative Lists; (For the uninitiated, negative list refers to the list of products in which the country does not want to make tariff concessions. For instance India has a negative list of 429 items under the FTA while Sri Lanka has a negative list of 1180 items.)
- harmonisation of customs procedures;
- standardisation and trade facilitation;

- inclusion of trade in services; and
- investment and economic cooperation.

If the FTA is to be made meaningful and mutually beneficial, there needs to be significant reduction of the negative lists of both countries. This calls for political will, more than anything else, to fight vested interests.

In any framework such as FTA, the 'rules of origin' play an important role. In order to claim duty-free entry into the Indian market, there is a stipulation in the FTA that there must be domestic value addition of 35 per cent of the FOB of the finished products. While some criteria relating to 'rules of origin' are a must, care must be taken to see that it is not applied irrationally while making sure that it is not abused. Indeed, the Joint Study Group was quite radical in suggesting the doing away with the domestic value addition requirement in some cases.

As noted earlier, one of the basic differences between the FTA and the CEPA was the inclusion of trade in services. It was noted that in service sectors such as IT and knowledge-based services, India had established a presence in the global market and that this could be an area for bilateral cooperation. More importantly, areas where Sri Lanka could benefit are education, healthcare, infrastructure services, transport, railways, aviation, ferry links and power generation. With this in mind, the Joint Study Group urged both countries to enter into negotiations that cover all service sectors and all modes of supply using the WTO General Agreement on Trade in Services (GATS) as the negotiating framework. No cooperation in the vital area of services is possible without free movement of people from country to another. The Joint Study Group rightly laid emphasis on lowering barriers to the movement of people, particularly professionals and businessmen and urged negotiations for the mutual recognition of professional qualifications.

Some new vistas of cooperation

Reference has already been made to the Indian Oil Corporation story in Sri Lanka. In the future, however, both countries have the potential to collaborate in the exploration and production of hydrocarbons in Sri Lanka.

A draft Memorandum of Understanding is currently under consideration between ONGC Videsh Limited and Sri Lanka's Ministry of Petroleum. The scope of the MoU would include:

(a) petroleum exploration and production operations in Sri Lanka;

(b) joint studies and various R&D projects;

(c) exchange of experts; and

(d) training of Sri Lankan nationals in petroleum related fields.

Considering both Sri Lanka and India are oil importing countries, cooperation in this sector will prove critical to the energy security of both countries.

Yet another area of cooperation, hitherto unexplored, lies in exploiting maritime resources in the respective EEZs (Exclusive Economic Zone) as well as in the Continental Shelf. For this to be done, there is an imperative need for both countries to agree on the delineation of the outer limits of the Continental Shelf. There have been three rounds of talks already, but progress needs to be expedited. This is because the maritime resources need to be tapped by both countries for the benefit of the two peoples. Perhaps, it is time these discussions are raised from the 'technical' to the 'political' level. Undue delay will result in both countries losing out.

Full economic integration and total connectivity

This chapter is rightly entitled: "India and Sri Lanka: New Directions". The ultimate destination of the Indo-Sri Lanka bilateral relationship is clear 'full economic integration and total connectivity'. We have spent a lot of time talking about the Comprehensive Economic Partnership Agreement (CEPA) which, if concluded quickly by both countries, will bring the goal of full economic integration a lot closer. But perhaps, one should even dream beyond the CEPA to look at one common currency (to begin with, the Indian currency may be made acceptable in Sri Lanka) and eventually a 'customs union'.

In order for the above dream to come about, there needs to be 'total connectivity' between India and Sri Lanka. Total connectivity implies both real and virtual connectivity. In terms of real connectivity, the one success story we do have is in the area of civil aviation. From 2002, there has been a paradigm shift in the number of flights. By October 2006, there were 116 flights between the two countries in a week! Indeed, Sri Lankan Airlines is the largest foreign carrier (in terms of flights) operating in India.

A direct consequence of the high frequency of flights from India to Sri Lanka and *vice versa*, is that Indians are now the largest number of tourist arrivals in Sri Lanka. In 2006, Indian tourist arrivals in Sri Lanka will exceed well over 100,000, leaving UK a distant second. Here is a concrete example of how some of India's neighbours who complain of trade deficit with India can seek to offset it in other areas. Sri Lanka thus offers lessons for our other neighbours.

There used to be a ferry service between Colombo and Tuticorin. This is something that needs to be restored at an appropriate time. There is no better way to promote people-to-people contacts among ordinary citizens of India and Sri Lanka. There has been a proposal from Sri Lanka for a land bridge (between Talaimannar and Rameshwaram) mirroring the legendary Hanuman bridge. It sounds like an idea whose time is awaited.

Finally, a word on virtual connectivity. Recently, an under the sea submarine optical fibre cable has been installed between Colombo (Sri Lanka) and Tuticorin (India). This is a potentially important development for telecommunications, broadband connectivity and voice/data transmission. It can already be said, with some conviction, that both India and Sri Lanka share the same electronic space!

In conclusion, there are no limits to the level and extent of bilateral cooperation between India and Sri Lanka. Limits to closer bilateral cooperation will only emanate from bad politics. It is for statesmen and right thinking people in both countries to rise to the challenge. Clearly, the future beckons India and Sri Lanka.

32

India and China: long road towards peace and development

C.V. Ranganathan

I

The ancient links which existed between India and China stretching back to the first millennium and beyond have been of seminal importance to both countries. Buddhism from India spread to China and further to its north and east through the first 12 centuries of that millennium and shaped Chinese knowledge of much of India. The enriching intellectual interactions between the rulers and peoples of the two countries went beyond religion to comprehensively encompass two way trade, science, technology, mathematics, literature, linguistics, architecture, medicine, even music. As Dr. Amartya Sen points out in his essay on "China and India" in his book *The Argumentative Indian*: "If China was enriching the material world of India two thousand years ago, India was busy, it appears, exporting Buddhism to China" (p.167)[1]. It would seem that this was a perfect mutual fit of hard and soft power in those early times.

Looking into this past, Dr. Sen also raises a very relevant parallel to the contemporary situation between India and China. Under a subsection of the above essay, titled, "Insularity and Openness",

1. Sen, Amartya (2005). *The Argumentative Indian*, Penguin Books.

he recalls that around the 8th Century C.E. there was vociferous resistance in China to the spread of Indian—particularly Buddhist—influence in the royal court and among the people. Led by some Daoists and Neo-Confucianists, this resistance was infused by a strong sense of intellectual nationalism, a sense of the superiority of Chinese ways and a concern about the maintenance of family and social order. The perceived loss of the central position of China in the order of things in the world was also among their concerns. The Chinese Buddhist response, also affirmed by some Daoists, contributed to opening up and highlighting the universalist ethics underlying Buddhism. In a celebrated piece, Mouzi, a Daoist, made a vigorous defence of Buddhism and of the compatibility of the Buddhist outlook with Chinese ethics. Further, he raised serious doubts as to whether the Chinese could claim to be uniquely central in the world by articulating a strong claim for Buddhist universalism. The contribution of Buddhism to China was to induce a sense that there were sources of wisdom outside China, thereby encouraging Chinese intellectuals to go abroad, particularly to India, in search of truth and enlightenment.

Dr. Sen adds that, in the reverse direction, the celebrated pilgrims from China moderated Indian chauvinism and the sense of civilisational exclusiveness. This comes out starkly in the heated dialogue between Xuan Zhang and his peers at Nalanda when the Indian hosts tried hard to dissuade him from returning to China by referring to China's backwardness. Xuan Zhang left, but with no bitterness, pleading that Buddhist doctrines being of universal relevance must be shared. From all this, Sen comes to the conclusion that "the broadening effects of Buddhist connections on the self-centredness of both Chinese and Indian intellectuals are among the significant secular consequences of those [ancient] linkages."

It was the spirit of the inclusive and universalist ethics shared in pre-imperialist times between the two civilisational states that was invoked by Nehru when India became independent and China was 'liberated' in 1949. The entry of Chinese forces into Tibet in 1950 cast a shadow. However, acknowledgement of the factual, not fictional, status of Tibet, military prudence, a sense of realpolitik to avoid involvement by major Western powers, and the inexorable logic of geography, gave little option, as he saw it, except to place primary reliance for ensuring peace on the borders on a policy of friendship with China. Nehru was committed to building a relationship which would underpin his broader vision of the role of China and India in post-colonial Asia. The resolution of the pending issues relating to Indian-inherited legacies in Tibet resulted in an agreement which incorporated the Panchsheel (Five Principles) in 1954. These are: mutual respect for each other's territorial integrity and sovereignty; mutual non-aggression; mutual non-interference in each other's internal affairs; equality and mutual benefit and peaceful co-existence.

Given the international situation of the early fifties, one would agree with Mira Sinha Bhattacharjea: "1954 [Panchsheel] introduced into the rigid ideologically divided world of that era, different and challenging perceptions of the structure of international relations and its dynamics, as well as of the norms, standards and modalities of state behaviour" (from her essay in Man Singh, 1998).[2] For a few years, India offered a positive fit for Chinese policies to befriend Asians and Africans in the rapidly post-colonising world. However, it seemed that the spirit of Panchsheel which permeated international issues involving China where India played some part (examples, the Korean War, the situation in Indo-China and in the United Nations), was not as visible in the bilateral issues which flared up. The disturbances in Tibet and contradictory views on where the long India-China boundary lies brought to the fore the intense nationalism which Mao Zedong symbolised. Its manifestation was a wholesale rejection of the order surrounding China brought into existence during colonial and imperial times. After the Dalai Lama came to India in 1959, it took a number of years for the Chinese to understand that India's policy of granting him asylum for humanitarian reasons was not to pursue any political agenda *vis-à-vis* Tibet, which was recognised by India as a part of China.

---

2. Man Singh, Surjit, (ed.) (1998). *Indian and Chinese Foreign Policies in Comparative Perspective*, New Delhi.

The tale from 1959 in India-China relations surrounding the boundary dispute was one of misperceptions and lost opportunities, leading to bitterness, armed conflict and a frozen state of hostility which lasted for nearly two decades.[3] This sorry tale has been covered in the book coauthored by C.V. Ranganathan and Ambassador V.C. Khanna, *India and China: The Way Ahead* (second edition, 2004). Briefly, the India-China boundary conflict arose primarily because of the conflicting concepts of both sides with regard to the extent of their territorial sovereignties. The Chinese concept was one of strategic borders which required the regime of the People's Republic of China, established in 1949, to negotiate new borders with all its neighbours, reflecting national acts of present governments rather than the inherited positions of past imperialist regimes. India's concept was one of historic borders. It held that there existed a well-defined customary and traditional boundary with China, marked by the world's most impressive geographical features. It was delimited for a major portion by agreements or treaties and controlled on its side by administrative jurisdiction exercised during pre-British and British times. The Chinese were prepared to back their concept with military and other action such as road building. India's approach was primarily declaratory, and then ineffectively military as the conflict worsened.

Here attention can be drawn to just one aspect covered in that book, namely the domestic circumstances in China from 1959 when Mao Zedong assumed *de facto* paramount authority. Humiliation of prominent Chinese leaders who, he felt, opposed him or questioned his policies marked domestic politics. Stretching into the decade and a half of the Great Proletarian Cultural Revolution unleashed by Mao in the mid-sixties, the Sino-Soviet ideological and interstate dispute came to the forefront. Policies adopted by Khrushchev in the post-Stalinist era convinced Mao that the Soviet Union was headed towards revisionism and that this could infect China too. In international relations Khrushchev's attempted reconciliation with USA was seen as an example of the Soviet Union sacrificing China's interests, for example by reneging on cooperation

---

3.   Ranganathan, C.V. and V.C. Khanna (2004). *India and China: The Way Ahead* (2nd ed.).

to produce nuclear weapons. The Soviet Union's leadership of the then international communist movement was seen as an attempt to split it. Khrushchev's reversal of earlier Soviet policies *vis-à-vis* India and the special role he attached to the improvement of communications and economic and military relations with India came in for special criticism. In an article which appeared in the *People's Daily* in 1963, called "A Mirror for the Revisionists", there was a severe indictment of the Communist Party of India (CPI). Amongst other points related to the pro-Soviet stance of CPI, this article made the improvement of Indo-Soviet relations the symbol of all that was going wrong, in Mao's view, with the Khrushchev-led Soviet Union. In Mao's worldview, India became doubly aligned with USA and Soviet Union, when China's relations with both were at a nadir. Another article, reportedly vetted by Mao, "More on Nehru's Philosophy in the light of the Sino-Indian boundary question" (October 1962), contained a vitriolic personal attack on Nehru and expressed unhappiness with Soviet neutrality as between India and China when armed conflict between the two appeared imminent. Macfarquhar, a reputed teacher and scholar of Harvard University, came to the conclusion that this article on Nehru was consistent with and prefigured China's anti-Soviet policies of 1963-64, "thus making it as a weapon in the ideological struggle with Moscow rather than in its military struggle with India" (pg. 310).[4] The above developments have been recalled only to emphasise the many baneful influences, external and internal, on India-China relations for the two decades after 1959. These happily ceased to exist from the post-Mao Zedong era.

A decade of internal chaos and turmoil followed the unleashing of the Great Proletarian Cultural Revolution from the mid-sixties devastating the Chinese economy. China followed autarchic economic policies at home and was isolated abroad. It had also vastly reduced the cultural, intellectual and living standards of the Chinese people. When Deng Xiaoping assumed the position of paramount leader in 1977, the Chinese set themselves the task of transforming

---

4. MacFarquhar, Roderick (1997). *The Origins of the Cultural Revolution: The Coming of the Cataclysm, 1961-1966*, Oxford University Press, Oxford.

the domestic situation. For this, a drastic transformation of the way Mao Zedong looked at the world needed to take place too. Domestically, the new road for economic growth was through reform and 'opening up'. Externally, the compulsion for the existence of a peaceful international environment surrounding China on all sides, to promote its domestic priority of economic and social development, made China work hard towards attaining this. A peaceful international environment for developing China while using its development to promote friendly and peaceful relations with neighbours and others became the twin mutually reinforcing objectives.

The above broad shift in China's strategy coincided with *détente* between the USA and the former Soviet Union from the eighties. By the mid-eighties, China's difficult relations with the latter were normalised following major initiatives taken by Gorbachev. The end of the Cold War provided a more benign global environment for China's growth. It withstood the impact of the disintegration of the former Soviet Union by hastening the pace of reforms which benefited millions, if not all, the billion-plus of the population. Problems with the United States were contained in the interests of security, access to American markets and flows of investments into China. The 16 characters directive that Deng put out in 1992 to tide over difficulties in the relations between China and the USA, may be recalled here: "Increase trust, reduce trouble, promote cooperation, avoid confrontation" (*zengjia xinren, jianshao mafan, fazhan hezuo, bugao duikang*).

As domestic growth gathered momentum from the mid-nineties, China began its adaptation to the requirements of membership of the World Trade Organization (WTO) Eventually, it used its admission to this body to force through the domestic reforms needed to build up the institutional basis for closer integration with the world economy and to better leverage the process of globalisation. China also normalised relations with almost all other South-East Asian countries through the eighties. India benefited from the vast changes in China's domestic policies and China's changing worldview.

II

In 1988, the former Prime Minister of India, Rajiv Gandhi, visited China. That visit to China by India's Head of Government came after a gap of 34 years since his grandfather, Jawaharlal Nehru's, visit in 1955. This undesirable hiatus in the millennial old India-China relationship was a reflection of much that had gone sour in bilateral relations from the late fifties of the last century.

The several specific achievements of Rajiv Gandhi's visit were:

- This was the first such visit by a Prime Minister of India to China since Nehru's visit in 1954. The symbolism of a highest-level visit from India, in return for the many visits to Delhi by Prime Minister Zhou was very necessary in the Chinese context. It convinced them of India's wish to mitigate, if not solve, old and pending problems, while imparting momentum to an all-round development of relations between the two countries.

- A Joint Working Group (JWG) at the level of Vice Ministers for negotiations on the boundary question and for the maintenance of peace and tranquility along the boundary was formed. The institution of the JWG laid the ground work for avoidance of tensions along the LAC and for drawing-up specific confidence building measures which came in 1993 and 1996.

- Another Joint Working Group was set up to promote trade and investment. This JWG was also meant to meet annually at the level of ministers.

- Discussions were held with Deng Xiaoping and other top state and party leaders including Zhu Rongji, who was then the Prime Minister of China. A common refrain from the Chinese side in these high-level talks was that both India and China needed a peaceful environment. They had the common responsibility of promoting the social and economic development of their vast populations, of safeguarding regional and global peace, and of cooperating in establishing a fair and rational world order. The old Five Principles formulated jointly by the leaders of the two countries in the fifties could still provide the common-sense basis for this.

- An address by Rajiv Gandhi to more than a thousand students of the leading Tsinghua Technical University made a deep impact when he called upon the educated youth of both India and China to contribute to a constructive forward-looking future in India-China relations.

Between 1988 and 2003, there was a brisk exchange of highest level visits by Presidents, Vice Presidents, Premiers, Foreign Ministers and other cabinet rank Ministers between India and China. In addition, in those years, most of the members of the Politburo and its Standing Committee, the principal organs of decision-making of the Chinese Communist Party, visited India. In 1993 and in 1996 when the former Prime Minister of India, the late P.V. Narasimha Rao, visited China and when former President Jiang Zemin visited India respectively, two major agreements related to the India-China boundary were signed. These are the 'Agreement on the Maintenance of Peace and Tranquility along the Line of Actual Control in the India-China Border Areas' (September 7, 1993) and the 'Agreement on Confidence Building Measures in the Military Field along the Line of Actual Control in the India-China border areas' (1996). Taken together, these two agreements reflected the political determination of the leadership of the two countries to ensure peace and stability along the long and disputed border. Important institutional steps to address the boundary dispute were taken in 2003 when Prime Minister A.B. Vajpayee visited China.

That visit came after a temporary hiccup in relations preceding and following the Pokhran II nuclear explosions by India in 1998. Statements by high Indian government leaders describing China as a "threat" and the correspondence between the Indian Prime Minister and President Clinton indirectly pointing to China as a reason for the Indian tests, vitiated the atmosphere of friendship built up assiduously from 1988. Fence-mending exercises at the academic and high government levels ensued in 1999-2000 and in 2002, when the former Chinese Premier Zhu Rongji visited India.

The Indian Prime Minister's visit in 2003 was a very important one for the first ever Joint Declaration to be signed at that level. It contained a road map for a wide range of interactions covering the political, security, economic and social fields. On the bilateral level the two sides agreed to each appoint a special representative to explore "from the political perspective of the overall bilateral relationship the framework of a boundary settlement." The clear indication that both sides were aiming at a pragmatic solution of the boundary dispute based on political considerations was thus signalled.

During his 1988 visit, Rajiv Gandhi had a meeting with the late Deng Xiaoping. At that meeting Deng said: "In recent years there has been comment about the next century being the Asia-Pacific century. I do not agree with this viewpoint. The combined population of the two countries is 1.80 billion. If India and China fail to develop, it cannot be called an Asian century."

Within two decades of Deng's statement, its prophetic importance is beginning to be realised by the Indians, Chinese and the world at large even as India and China have significantly deepened their constructive engagement straddling many diverse fields. There is a broadening of mutual understanding at the highest political levels over where India and China are placed, *vis-à-vis* each other and with respect to the rapidly changing contemporary global and regional situations in Asia which impact on both countries. The implementation of confidence building measures (CBMs) in the military fields to ensure the maintenance of peace and tranquility along the long border, albeit disputed, and an intensification of exchanges at different levels between the armed forces are other welcome developments. A remarkable growth in the two-way trade between India and China has resulted in China and Hong Kong becoming top ranking economic partners of India.

There is a palpable and growing interest on the part of Indian and Chinese entrepreneurs to partner in mutually profitable joint ventures and investments in manufacturing and other service areas. Well-known Indian companies have invested in China in fields as diverse as information technology, telecommunications, energy, pharmaceuticals, chemicals, packaging, and automotives. Improved communication through direct flights between the two countries have led to increasing numbers of exchanges in cultural tourism. The growing spending power of vast sections in each country is an impetus for deep mutual exploration of the myriad 'soft' sectors such as information technology enabled services, human resource development, entertainment, food, fashions, and similar areas. Exchanges between academic scholars and non-governmental civil society organisations either on a bilateral basis or under the aegis of international bodies are burgeoning.

Thus, India is in the process of having a density of interactions with China, which the latter has enjoyed for some years with developed countries. One can discern a palpable self-confidence in India at various levels to strengthen relations. The robust and steady growth of its economy, the rapid adaptation by its industrialists and business entrepreneurs to the challenges of globalisation and to competition from China in areas where India was traditionally strong, add to India's self-perception that India can 'rise' in the global economic order. The capacity of the Indian political system to absorb and represent multiple, at many times opposing views, on the directions of economic and social policies through democratic institutions is a phenomenon which is the pride of Indians and admired universally. The professionalism of India's armed forces, backed by a minimum nuclear deterrent which India will never be the first to use, ensures respect for India's territorial integrity and capacity to undertake voluntary international responsibilities in the cause of peace and stability.

Deng Xiaoping's statement to Rajiv Gandhi is also prophetic in the sense that the sequential rise, first of China and then of India, is not a matter for China and India alone. A noteworthy feature of the early years of this century has been a move from the almost unilinear focus on China to include India. Comparisons between India and China highlighting the strengths and weaknesses of each have almost assumed industry proportions in India, in China and the West. The global impact of the growth in recent years of the political economies of both are much-discussed topics at major international gatherings. The point to emphasise in all this is that there has been a shift in the centre of geopolitical gravity away from the Occident. It is now well-recognised that India and China are drivers of the Asian and international economies. Other major powers and regional groups in Asia such as Japan and the Association of South-East Asian Nations (ASEAN) have recognised this and have strengthened their engagements with India.

International developments since the demise of the former Soviet Union have highlighted anew what nature, geography and man's ingenuity had promoted in ancient and pre-modern historic times, namely, the spread of the intellectual influence and commerce of the two large civilisational states, India and China, over a wide swathe of continental and maritime Asia. In contemporary times, it is more than ever evident that Indian and Chinese interests intersect over a very wide arc extending from West Asia through Central Asia and South Asia to South-East and East Asia. India and China either share immediate borders with countries of this vast region or are near neighbours to them, not separated by big distances. Within this arc from the West of Asia to its East is contained the source of raw materials, particularly energy, required by both. It is also the source of problems caused by unstable governments, unresolved conflicts and violent extremism, which impact on regional peace and stability and which in turn could affect both countries.

During Chinese Premier Wen Jiabao's visit to India in April 2005, several agreements were signed with the Government of India which would serve to consolidate the trend towards friendly relations that was first set in motion during the 1988 visit to China of Rajiv Gandhi. In the Joint Statement signed by the Prime Minister of India and the Chinese Premier, it was decided to establish an "India-China strategic cooperative partnership for peace and prosperity." This phrase is a mutual acknowledgement of the wider significance of India-China relations, going beyond the purely bilateral to encompass regional and global issues of concern to both sides. The partnership is based on the "Five Principles, mutual respect and sensitivity to each other's concerns and aspirations, and equality." These phrases are not mere rhetoric but a mature summing up of the experience of both countries in dealing with each other. They are also meant to guide public perceptions on these relations.

Two important agreements signed on the occasion of Premier Wen's visit, are the 'Political Parameters and Guiding Principles for the Settlement of the Boundary Question' and a 'Protocol on Modalities for the Implementation of Confidence-Building Measures in the Military Field along the Line of Actual Control in the India-China Border Areas'. The Protocol bases itself on operational ground practice of the two armies in keeping the peace following two earlier agreements in 1993 and 1996. The Agreement on the boundary question crystallises in the clearest and mutually acceptable terms the bottom lines that could govern an eventual settlement, which would be based on political (not purely academic) considerations. It closes a yawning gap in public acknowledgement by both parties of a *de facto* situation which came into being after 1962, but which was never formally accepted as something approximating to a reality which both countries could live with. As such, the Agreement should be of immense help in the education and creation of public opinion in the plural society of India and a society such as China, which has seen bursts of strident nationalism. A good augury is that the Boundary Agreement has not been subjected to criticism by the media in India, pointing to the degree of political maturity achieved in the relationship. It represents a quintessential summing-up of the mutual understanding achieved between the two sides based on the experience of discussions over the last decades. India views the boundary question from the long term and strategic perspective of India-China relations, rather than as a mere territorial issue. The mechanism of discussions through special representatives of the two governments for the eventual solution of the question provides an appropriate forum for reaching an agreement which would safeguard the vital interests of both sides.

Viewed in its totality the relationship between India and China has assumed a more wholesome character, where differences are managed imaginatively and where governments act as facilitators for a wide spectrum of activities to be undertaken by diverse sections of the two peoples, within and outside the two governments. In a continuum from 1988, when improvements in India-China relations started, there has been a consensus across the political spectrum on India's China policy, all the more remarkable considering that quite a few changes of governments led by different parties and coalitions took place. An elaborate intergovernmental dialogue architecture has been put in place. These include subjects such as security, strategic issues, policy planning, finance, cooperation on multilateral subjects, such as issues before the UN and WTO, environment, counterterrorism and others of a functional nature. 2006 has been declared by both sides as the "year of India-China friendship" with a series of commemorative events due to take place in both countries.

III

Within a few years of this millennium, India has become well poised in its relations with all the major powers and groupings; USA, European Union (EU) Russia, Japan, China and ASEAN. Each of these compartments of India's relations serve to reinforce a wide spectrum of India's interests in ensuring development, peace and stability. Care must be taken to see that no single compartment of each of India's relations with the major powers and groupings impacts adversely on the other. In the context of China, the Indian Prime Minister gave a clear expression to this in the wake of the recent substantive improvements in Indo-US relations: "The World has enough space to have India and China develop together. I don't believe that having a good relationship with the USA means we are opposed to China." USA enjoys a density of relations with China covering strategic, political, economic, social and other interests, which it is not going to jeopardise by seeking to overtly contain China with India's help.

The 2005 Joint Statement signed by the Chinese and Indian Premiers recognises that both countries share common interests in the maintenance of peace, stability and prosperity in Asia and the world at large, and also that they share the desire to develop a closer and more extensive understanding and cooperation in regional and international affairs. Acknowledging their linked destinies as neighbours and the two largest countries of Asia, both sides have agreed in the statement that they would, together, contribute to the establishment of an atmosphere of mutual understanding, trust and cooperation in Asia and the world at large. Further, they have committed to facilitating efforts to strengthen multilateral coordination mechanisms on security. All this amounts to formal acknowledgement that the good neighbourly diplomacy followed by India and China has been extended from their immediate neighbourhoods to a policy for multilateral regimes in Asia.

As of now, the most visible example of India and China participating and contributing to regional cooperation is in South-East Asia, potentially extending to East Asia. Both India and China look upon the Association of South-East Asia Nations (ASEAN) as the principal driver of Asian economic integration. Prominent leaders among the members of the ASEAN look forward with eagerness to leveraging the rising political and economic status of India and China for the benefit of ASEAN. They warmly welcome the great improvement in India-China relations, which vastly adds to the comfort levels of the member states of ASEAN. Senior statesman and now Minister Mentor of Singapore gave public expression to this sentiment when he said, "The renaissance of China and India in economic, social and cultural fields will shift the world's centre of gravity from the Atlantic to the Pacific and Indian Oceans."[5] Other leaders in South-East Asia look upon the growth of India-China relations and its impact on South-East and East Asia as the latest instance of major power relations in Asia becoming multidimensional, not structured along any single axis as was the case in the last century. This would entail the fashioning of a regional architecture in Asia, which is inclusive of the reasonable interests of all the major and powers and groups—USA, European Union and Russia.

While it is evident that the member states of ASEAN expect India, China, Japan, and the Republic of Korea to play key roles

---

5. Keynote speech by Minister Mentor Lee Kuan Yew at the official opening of the Lee Kuan Yew School of Public Policy on 4 April 2005.

along with ASEAN in working towards closer Asian economic integration, they feel that the coming into being of multiple and overlapping networks is feasible. This is necessary because each of the major Asian countries is in the process of entering into free trade or regional trade agreements, and other types of economic agreement either with ASEAN as a whole or with individual countries. Hence an open regionalism would be necessary, which permits connectivity both amongst regional players and with the rest of the world and with global institutions.

The above broad approach was evident when Prime Minister Dr. Manmohan Singh shared India's vision and long term expectation at the East Asia Summit held in Kuala Lumpur in December 2005. He envisaged an integrated market from the Himalayas to the Pacific Ocean linked by road, rail, air and shipping services. If such a situation came into existence, an Asian community would be constituted as an 'arc of advantage' across which there would be a large scale movement of people, capital, ideas and creativity. For such a vision to be realised, it is necessary for India and China to cooperate along with other South-East and East Asian nations.

It is evident that there is an interconnectedness of security concerns in Asia. Regional stability in terms of security and economic and social development is a concern for both India and China, as threats affecting one part of Asia could impact on neighouring states in Asia. In ASEAN and in the Asian Regional Forum (ARF), China and India are both party to a range of declarations and plans of action against terrorism and other non-traditional security threats. This forms a solid basis for practical cooperation to combat the threats posed by terrorism, piracy and other maritime crimes.

ASEAN is also keen to exploit synergies between India and China in practical ways. This they hope to achieve through political dialogue on the shape and development of the East Asia Summit into an open and inclusive regional architecture. Economic cooperation they hope could be fostered by measures to encourage regional trade and investments and by setting up economic institutions. Environmental cooperation, which could focus on transboundary pollution, water problems, preservation of biodiversity and urban environmental issues, is also proposed. Lastly, in order to enhance the impact on the peoples of Asia, cooperation in education, health, science and technology, media and culture has to be brought on the agenda. The initiatives taken at the academic level by India and some other governments to bring about connectivities in communications, trade and culture between Bangladesh-China-India and Myanmar (BCIM) contain the potential of opening up Eastern India to its South-East Asian neighbourhood. Six meetings of this BCIM group have taken place. From these meetings it became evident that Myanmar is by no means looking upon itself as an exclusive zone of Chinese interest. It strongly invites India and Bangladesh to join in developing infrastructure projects there. The group seeks to open up transborder road and other links between parts of countries, such as in Eastern India and South-Western China, Yunnan province, through Bangladesh and Myanmar. In the broader context of China developing rail transportation links in Tibet and making investments in the western regions of China, the explorations undertaken by the BCIM group would prove useful. India's Look East policy would be incomplete without the realisation of connections between India's eastern regions with South-East Asia and Western China.

The overall situation in North-East Asia contains issues that impact on the region's peace and security. The non-compromising nuclear policy of North Korea is matched by American firmness in not making concessions without adequate guarantees from it. Japan's deep economic interdependence with China is not reflected in political warmth between them. Japan's concern over China's military modernisation is shared by USA whose defence links with Japan intensify. Whether the *status quo* in Taiwan will endure forever depends on the domestic political dynamics of Taiwan and China. There are maritime territorial disputes between China and Japan, and between Japan and the Republic of Korea. With the spread of institutions for regional cooperation in areas East of India to the Pacific, India has become a dialogue partner covering all subjects.

India's evolving position would be watched with keen attention by the Chinese in the context of overall India-China relations. Through the East Asia Summit process, the interdependence of security concerns between South-East and East Asia is something to which all member states who participated in the Summit would have to pay attention. India's interests in East Asia are well served by the *status quo* in the Taiwan Straits, by a peaceful resolution of North Korea's resolve to have nuclear weapons, and by improved political relations between China and Japan.

India has been invited as an observer of the Shanghai Cooperation Organisation. Russia, China and four Central Asian states are members of this regional grouping. Set up to combat terrorism, extreme religious fundamentalism and secessionism, it has grown in acceptance into a regional association to promote security, economic cooperation and cultural relations, and to prevent drug smuggling and transborder crisis. India's link with the group can serve to expand bilateral links with the prominent Central Asian states and to be part of border transregional projects, for example in the field of energy. The declaration adopted in April 2006 when President Putin visited China calling for the setting up of trilateral cooperation between Russia, China and India needs to be taken seriously by India. Its government must give thought on how to give effect to this desirable idea and the appropriate institutional framework for such cooperation.

The logic of geography is unrelenting, and proximity is the most difficult and testing among the diplomatic challenges India faces with respect to its neighbourhood. It is obvious that India's relationship with China, described as one of strategic cooperative partnership, would need to be tested with respect to the commonly shared neighbourhood. It is also self-evident that India's security interests are best served if all our neighbours evolve as viable states with moderate, stable, political and social systems, and with robust economies. A removal of these present deficits would give all our neighbours the confidence to take advantage of India's growing strengths to reap political and economic benefits. The most desirable outcome for India would be if the people and governments of

Pakistan, Nepal, Bangladesh and Sri Lanka take domestic responsibility to remove Indian concerns, since their policies often cause problems for India. Feudal autocracy, militarism, acquiescence and complicity with fundamentalist terrorists and extremists, lack of responsiveness to the legitimate demands of the majority are some of the characteristics which bring insecurities to South Asia.

The principles of respect for sovereignty and non-interference in internal affairs are challenged in situations where states either are not willing or have lost capacities to exercise domestic responsibility with regard to situations which bring harm to neighbours and to the international community. Adoption of more people-oriented policies rather than regime-oriented policies becomes necessary when regimes are not seen to exercise responsibility and control with respect to transborder developments such as terrorism, crime, illegal migration, etc. In the context of improving India-China relations, the time has come for mature and sensitive dialogues between the two countries on similar policies which would favour stability and development in the neighbourhood.

It is logical that in the nature of things as they have evolved over the last few years, India, USA and China share some common interests in South Asia although no common approaches to secure these interests are visible. Absence of the possibility of military conflict, strict control over the spread of technologies related to non-conventional weapons from areas known for proliferation, and prevention of the reemergence of fundamentalist or extremist ideologies leading to international terrorism are some of the common interests. Thus, there is room for dialogue at intergovernmental and academic levels between the three countries on how these common interests can be pursued. The maturity with which Indian and Chinese leaders achieved a strategic consensus should lead to a situation where the accretion of power by India and China does not lead to a display of power politics in India's neighbourhood and elsewhere. In the wise words of a veteran Chinese diplomat who knows South Asia well: "In order to reduce the possibility of any setback [in India-China relations], legitimate interest and concerns of either side need to be kept in mind when the other side takes important steps on sensitive questions."

To conclude, the rise and peaceful development of China would be incomplete without the comprehensive improvement of its relations with India. Conversely, India's success in positioning itself as a global or strategic partner of the major powers—USA, European Union, Russia, Japan—and groups such as ASEAN would not have been achieved without the rapid improvements in India-China relations. Together their mutual determination to work together in strategic, security and economic fields is a harbinger that the two civilisational states would have a beneficial impact on Asia in the first decades of this millennium.

33

India and China: new directions

Sanjay Bhattacharyya

The remarkable economic growth in India and China has captured the attention of the international community as have the relative stability in their political regimes, their closer interaction with the global community and their growing strategic importance. The phenomenon of the parallel growth and development of the two most populous economies is unprecedented in modern times and promises to be an important pillar in the emerging new international order.

The facts that India and China have ancient civilisations, are home to two-fifths of humanity and are confidently emerging from the shadows of poverty and decades of lack of development are now widely recognised. Both chose their own distinct paths of economic resurgence—India embarked on a path of sustainable growth and development while China is experiencing its 'peaceful rise'.[1] The economic growth of such large and populous economies not only spurs the dynamics of domestic growth and consequently an interest and influence in regional and international affairs but also provides economic stimulus to the neighbourhood. The momentum

---

1. The 'peaceful rise' (*heping jueqi*) of China has been under discussion among Chinese scholars for over a decade and is based on the aspiration to acquire great power status. They defined China's growth objectives in the medium and long term after the fruits of reforms and opening up to the outside world started bearing fruit. The use of the expression 'rise' (*jueqi*) has been a cause of some anxiety among China's neighbours in North-East and South-East Asia and certain major powers.

of change of such large entities cannot be ignored. The world is undergoing profound changes and the emerging forces in India and China will also influence it.

This chapter will not deliberate on the 'India *versus* China' debate, but will focus on the 'India and China' thesis as a model for growth and development. It will trace the different patterns of economic growth, which have acted as the engines of change; examine the changing perceptions on how we regard each other; briefly outline the major trends in our bilateral relations; and explore possible responses to emerging global challenges and opportunities, which will provide new directions in our relations.

Growth patterns

Traditionally, the rapid rise in the economic and political power of nations has been attributed to a combination of factors including, sustained high economic growth, expanding military capabilities, active promotion of high technologies and large young populations. This hypothesis is often used to explain the rise of major powers in the industrial era. Indian policy makers have emphasised that growth depends not only on elements of hard and soft development but also on the institutional linkages underpinning the development process. Chinese scholars have advocated the concept of comprehensive national strength,[2] which includes natural resources, manpower, culture, economics, science and technology, military power and political and international influence. The Indian approach lays stress on the welfare of the individual while the Chinese focus on the aggregate power achieved by the nation as a whole. This somewhat different focus in development has also contributed to the variations in our growth paths and in the development of institutional infrastructure, on the one hand, and physical infrastructure, on the other. The complexities of the modern world demand that additional factors such as the spirit of entrepreneurship, access to technology and

---

2. Chinese scholars have done seminal work on this concept and developed elaborate quantitative models using sectoral indices to evaluate not only China's comprehensive national strength but also for its comparison with other powers.

finance, levels of innovation, engagement with the global economy and interaction in politico-strategic issues be also considered as critical elements in the growth process.

The recent economic growth paths in India and China have been spectacular but similar patterns have also been seen in Asia and in other pockets in the developing world. The rise of the Asian tigers (RoK, Taiwan, Hong Kong and Singapore), almost two decades ago, saw accelerated growth rates with significant expansion of manufacturing capacities and integration with the global economy, particularly through trade and capital flows and promoted a surge in growth levels in the ASEAN region.[3] Brazil and Russia[4] are currently experiencing high growth levels and growth is picking up in South Africa and Eastern Europe. There is a sense of optimism and confidence in the developing world that their economic prospects will continue to improve, despite rising energy prices and resource constraints. In the developed world, in Japan, USA and the European Union, there are signs of economic resurgence, albeit at lower levels. However, the growth of India and China stands out, not only for the high growth rates sustained over decades but also for its huge momentum and its increasing leverage. The large populations of the two economies, even when operating at lower per capita income levels, translate into a considerable economic force capable of playing a major role in the global economy.

India has maintained high levels of economic growth and development for over a decade and half after the introduction of the policies of reform and liberalisation. What makes the Indian experience special is that the largest democracy has garnered support from market forces and engineered an endogenous process to shatter the barriers of the 'Hindu rate of growth' and propel an agrarian

---

3. The growth pattern continued till the Asian financial crisis hit the region in July 1997, crippling financial flows and undermining business confidence. China, and India, remained largely immune to its effects.

4. The BRICs (Brazil, Russia, India and China) report expands the enthusiasm regarding India and China to include Brazil and Russia and states that the growth pattern of all the four states is spectacular. It suggests that the growth of these economies will provide traction for economic growth and attract investments, not only in their own economies but also in their respective regions.

economy, dependent on the vagaries of the monsoon, to a service oriented economy, developing high technology and services for an expanding middle class and also for the richest nations in the world. Democracy and market forces have ensured that India not only feeds its large population and provides gainful employment to ever-increasing numbers but also harnesses resources for optimal utilisation and efficiencies. Consequently, even in the manufacturing sector, capital-output ratios tend to be low while energy-efficiency ratios and appropriate technology usage tends to be high. However, slow growth of the infrastructure sector, incomplete reforms in the regulatory environment, legacy of restrictive labour laws, rapid rise in energy consumption levels and relatively weak regional trade linkages act as constraints to our growth objective. The vitality of our economy comes from an entrepreneurial spirit, well developed institutions of market economy, a robust financial sector, global strength and competitiveness in several areas of high-technology, world-class production centres and a strong middle class. Moreover, the emphasis on scientific and technological skills and managerial abilities has provided the basis for the growth of a population that is innovative and adapted for the knowledge economy. India is thus poised to become the fastest growing large economy in the coming decades.

The Chinese growth rates, since the advent of the policy of reform and opening up to the outside world, have been remarkable. China adopted an export-led and investment-driven growth model with the objective of becoming a middle-level developed country by 2050.[5] In order to increase its share in overall world manufacturing output and global trade, China established a number of competitive manufacturing hubs with world-class infrastructure, beginning with the establishments of special economic zones.[6] China took

5. After 1978, when China launched the policy of reform and opening up to the outside world it spelt out its long term economic objective of doubling its GDP roughly every decade to reach the income of a middle level developed country by mid-21st century. China is on track to attain its objectives.

6. The SEZs, started since 1978, opened up the influx of foreign direct investments and technology for the establishment of manufacturing facilities for export markets. They also provided for a relaxed labour regime at low cost to attract foreign and overseas Chinese investors to shift their manufacturing facilities to the mainland. This prototype for spectacular growth was repeated further in the Pearl river delta, the Yangtze dragonhead and then to the hinterland.

advantage of low labour costs, economies of scale, quality control and branding to penetrate global markets at prices that are highly competitive[7] and emerge as the 'factory of the world'.[8] The lure of doing business in China and the preferential policies provided by it have made China the largest recipient of foreign direct investment, with inflows from overseas Chinese as well as multinational corporations, mainly in the export-oriented sector. The State meanwhile encouraged high levels of public spending in infrastructure through administrative fiat at low interest rates. The paucity of market controls however, led to excessive investments and subsequent overheating in the Chinese economy.[9] The Chinese government's efforts to slowdown the economy and/or cool certain errant sectors and regions have had limited success. The other woes in the Chinese economy include, inequality between urban and rural areas, between the rich coastal region and the hinterland, and between different sectors of the economy; decline in the agricultural sector; distress in the financial sector with high levels of non-performing assets; high dependence on large infusions of capital and scarce energy resources; low levels of profitability; limited growth of new entrepreneurship; and, perhaps most seriously, limited domestic demand. Large migration flows, especially from villages and from agriculture, and sometimes, there are instances of social unrest. The other serious casualty has been the environment as the rush for growth often relegates green issues to the background. Economic growth has thus not always translated into development. The Chinese economic juggernaut is expected to keep rolling on, nevertheless, because of the vitality it possesses, the inroads it has made in global markets and the fact that the authorities are aware of the contradictions and problems it faces and are engaged in seeking solutions.

---

7. Chinese export prices tend to be very low. This is attributed to low input costs (labour, capital, energy and raw materials), scale economies in manufacturing, subsidies by local authorities, deep penetration in foreign markets and advantageous exchange rates.

8. The share of China's contribution to world manufacturing output has increased from under 4 per cent in 1980 to over 12 per cent in 2005.

9. The Chinese government is acutely conscious of the contradictions in the process of growth and the Premier's address at the annual session of the National People's Congress lists them out in detail along with measures proposed to address them.

The economic growth of nations as large as India and China has strategic implications, both in the region and beyond. It serves as a magnet for economic activity in the region not only through direct trade and investment links but also through the higher levels of business confidence it generates which encourages extra-regional players to join in. Although some members of the region may feel threatened by the growth of the larger economic powers and may seek the countervailing support of regional or even extra-regional players and some others may feel compelled to adjust their own preferences, the benefits of growth far outweigh the negative aspects. It is also seen that as the economic space of large nations grows, so does its concept of the neighbourhood and this facilitates the inclusion of more countries within the ambit of regional growth and cooperation. In such circumstances, regionalism and multilateralism find greater scope and democratisation is promoted, not only in the economic realm but also on social and political issues. The opportunities for taking advantage of the complementarities thus increase and competition emerges as a healthy input spurring further growth and development.

Perceptions

India and China are among the ancient civilisations of the world. This provides us not only with the wisdom and experiences of the achievements and shortcomings of our past but also a confidence in our aspirations for the future. The latent force of history acts as an inspiration and provides a bonding element for the peoples. The civilisational contacts are not the dominant element in the relations between India and China but they remain a guiding spirit. There is historical evidence of the exchanges of scholars in ancient times between the two countries,[10] which facilitated understanding within the two cultures. The Chinese acknowledge that Buddhism came to China from India and carved out a niche

---

10. Prominent among the scholars from India to China are Kasyapa Matanga and Dharmaratna who lived in Luoyang (67 AD), Kumarajiva who lived in the Xinjang areas and visited Changan (382 AD), and Bodhidharma, a prince from South India who started the Shaolin School in Henan province (520 AD). The most celebrated of the Chinese scholars to visit India are Fa Xian (399-412 AD), Xuanzang who attended Nalanda (in India from 631-645 AD), and I Tsing (671-699 AD).

in their psyche and social life which facilitated the introduction of concepts from Indian religion, philosophy, literature and arts.[11] While the Buddhist influence provides a certain warm feeling among the Chinese for India, there was relatively limited exposure of ancient Chinese civilisational in India and similar feelings among Indians are restricted to the recounting of the experiences of Chinese travellers who visited India in ancient times and the introduction of products brought by Chinese traders.

Interstate relations are based on hard assessments of geo-political realities, economic opportunities and perceptions and how they interact with national priorities. Although perceptions tend to attach higher priority to certain elements of an informal analysis they also contribute to decisionmaking and policy formulation. Interestingly, there is a mirroring of the perceptions of both Indian and Chinese academics and strategic thinkers while reviewing the relations with the other.[12] Both sides take note of history, large populations, political consolidation, recent experience of economic growth and development and the geopolitical situation and then draw similar conclusions about the other.

The Indian perception of China recognises the fact that there are differences in systems and policy approach between the two, but there is a dominant mainstream belief calling for constructive engagement with China. This belief cuts across ideologies and party lines and has remained fairly consistent over time and has provided for a coherent policy approach. The perceptions among the academics and strategic thinkers fall into three main strands:

- Constructive engagement: The proponents believe India and China are both growing powers, there will be benefit for

---

11. Indian Buddhism's spread in China led to a new amalgam enriching Chinese society. Buddhism introduced the pantheon of Indian deities, promoted practice of yoga and supported welfare-oriented governance. Buddhist beliefs adjusted to Chinese practice by allowing relaxations permitting such as luxury in lifestyles and the pursuit of salvation without having to renounce the world. The development of the Chan sect and its manifestation in Chinese literature and arts resulted from Buddhist influence. Even today one comes across Chinese who refer to India as the 'western heaven' (*xitian*), a place where they would aspire to be reincarnated after death.

12. The comparison is based on an examination of published accounts in both countries. An analysis of the available literature displays that scholars on both sides have similar degree of interest in each other leading to wide coverage of developments in both countries.

both in taking advantage of the complementarities in the relationship and both can pursue a policy of constructive engagement in various spheres. They see opportunities not only in bilateral engagement but also in the regional and multilateral arena. They also opine that India needs to be aware of China's future power projection but believe that the relationship can be managed in a manner such that neither side constitutes a threat to the other. In many ways this represents the mainstream view within the academic community.

This approach acknowledges the historical connections, shared experiences, developments in bilateral relations since independence and commonalities in the aspirations underlying the different development paths. The proponents believe that the dialogue and engagement between the two countries in recent times have borne fruit and there is better understanding, including through the conclusion of treaties, which provides a platform for cooperation. It contends that the topmost priority for both nations is to bring about economic development and that this endeavour demands that they not be distracted and that there be a peaceful and stable environment in the neighbourhood. In this effort it calls for closer engagement and accepts the role of various actors, including from business, culture, media and others in bringing about closer people-to-people relations. At the same time, they are also conscious of how China deals with the differences it has with its neighbours in North-East and South-East Asia, its close military and strategic cooperation in India's neighbourhood and the outstanding bilateral issues between India and China and recognise that these issues could potentially become irritants in the future if not managed appropriately. It also recognises that the strategic-geopolitical environment has changed and that the world is in a transitional phase in which the old dogmas of power politics are being replaced by the need for greater consultation and engagement. The strategic cooperative partnership between the two is a natural corollary to the process.

- China threat: The proponents of this hypothesis contend that China poses an immediate and real threat to India. These scholars note that China has a troubled history which includes export of communist ideology to several countries, armed conflicts with its neighbours, tendency to escalate tensions in its neighbourhood, a massive programme of defence modernisation and its wish to use the gains of its economic growth to promote its expansionist policies in the neighbourhood. They cite China's close military and nuclear relations with Pakistan, its tough stand on territorial issues with ASEAN neighbours, its record of missile supplies and its tendency to resort to use of force, as examples. They further contend that Chinese animosity towards India is manifest in its desire to expand its influence in South Asia and to strategically contain India. A fringe within the community of strategic thinkers shares this hypothesis.

- China not a competitor, even in the future: The proponents of this hypothesis subscribe to Chinese pronouncements of seeking a peaceful neighbourhood and suggest that China has no interest in adversarial, or even competitive, relations with India (or with other countries) and will thus never pose a threat. They further state that the two countries share a range of commonalities in policy approach and thus there could be no contractions in the bilateral relations. Apart from repeating the rhetoric, they have neither deliberated on the bilateral relations nor proposed concrete steps to enhance it.

Similarly, current Chinese perceptions of India are also dominated by an appreciation of the changes that have taken place in recent times and the desire to engage in closer contacts, especially in the economic field. The views of the scholars are the outcome of research and discussion between the thinks tanks and policy makers and although there is often an outward projection of unity, certain differences of views can be discerned. Change in perceptions is also noticeable over time. The perceptions of the academics and strategic thinkers can also be classified into three broad strands:

- India is a weak power: Chinese scholars have contended that India is an inferior power that is not a serious rival. They point out that India's economy was stuck in the quagmire of low growth and even when the pace picked up it fell far short of China's growth rates. They mention that democracy in India seeks to accommodate too many diverse interests and thus becomes an inhibiting factor; consequently outcomes are both delayed and restricted. They have also criticised the practice of religion, caste and poverty as factors limiting India's growth potential. They contend that China's socialist system and unified government provide the basis for quick decisions and steady progress while India's system allows too much latitude to disparate forces, which work at cross purposes and thus slow down growth rates. Chinese scholars had established benchmarks for their development levels accruing from the policy of reforms—initially with Japan and then with USA – and they thus felt that comparisons with India were not in the same league. Some scholars even felt it necessary not to applaud India's achievements as it might distract from the greater endeavour of projecting their own growth. This line of argument, which was popular in the published writings of Chinese scholars in the past is less common now.

- India is a threat: Chinese scholars have voiced their concerns about India for decades and many have stated explicitly that India is a threat. Their insecurities stemmed from the differences in ideology between India and China and a suspicion that they would be encircled. They registered their opposition to India's position on Tibet and the Dalai Lama, contending that this was part of an imperialist plot and a colonial legacy against China; criticised India's closer relations with countries in China's periphery, in the years soon after independence, stating that India sought regional hegemony; commented sharply on India's ideological beliefs that contradicted China's communism, particularly in the troubled era of the 1960s and 1970s; and voiced suspicions regarding India's support for multipolarity after the end of the Cold War. Some scholars have taken exception to India's position on the boundary issue complaining that India seeks to deny China its territorial rights on the basis of colonial era documentation.

In recent times, when India's economic growth acquired momentum, some scholars called for an intensification of the efforts to forge closer ties with the countries in India's periphery such that China's countervailing power against India would not be diminished; when it was realised that India had an edge over China in certain high technology sectors they advocated stepping up efforts, including even learning from the Indian experience, to reduce the gap; and when the international media reported on the relative growth paths of India and China and suggested that there was the possibility of competition for economic space, they called for statements that the two were not in a competitive relationship. Chinese scholars were divided in internal debates on the objectives and implications of India's nuclear tests in 1998, with one camp noting that India's test had undermined the improvements in bilateral relations and it was aimed not only at acquiring great power status but also at China and thus should not be accepted, while some others noted that it had to be recognised as a legitimate right of a sovereign state. Some Chinese scholars continue to view India's relations with USA with suspicion, some fear that India may emerge as a rival in the security scenario and some see it as part of a design to contain China. The proponents of the India threat thesis in China have receded from the forefront in recent times when the focus has been on attaining significant improvements in bilateral relations.

• Engagement: There is a growing realisation in China that the sustained growth of India is indeed a reality that cannot be ignored. To some extent, the increasing geopolitical importance of India and the improvement in bilateral relations have spurred the need to have a new look on how to perceive India. Chinese scholars have concluded that India has achieved 'spectacular success' in several areas; that 'besides the five major powers, India is also a major power with great potential for development so far as population and territorial size and regional influence are concerned and it is expected that India will become a newly rising force not to be neglected in the upcoming structure of the Asia-Pacific'; and that 'Indian power will greatly increase, especially after 2010'. Most importantly, in view of China's own priority on domestic economic development it needs a peaceful and stable neighbourhood and the avoidance of hotspots bearing potential for conflict. The new trend notes that there is mutual advantage in engaging India further in several sectors for win-win solutions. Chinese scholars have also been quick to point out that China is ahead of India in the race for development and that the gap is not expected to close for a long time.

In addition to the perceptions of how India and China regard each other, the perceptions of other players in the region and that of the major powers also have a bearing on future developments. Both are engaged in closer economic and strategic contacts with Asian neighbours, with major powers and with other countries. In Asia, ASEAN sees economic and political cooperation with India and China as the pillars of regional stability and prosperity; the East Asia Summit recognises the fundamental role of the two in an emerging Asian architecture; SAARC has forged cooperative relations with China; and SCO has done likewise with India. Similarly, Africa and Latin America have also welcomed stepped up levels of cooperative interaction with both. There is recognition that the economies and geopolitical importance of both India and China are expanding, their domestic markets are attractive to foreign investors and strategic relations are being forged. Partners in the region remain desirous of exploiting the markets, collaborating in business links, utilising the developments in high technology and expanding strategic ties. While there may be some negative sentiments regarding the 'rise' of China and the desire to have countervailing forces, both also have to contend with difficult relations with certain neighbours. The patterns of relations and interaction in Asia are being redrawn to reflect the emerging realities and India and China along with other Asian partners will be required to play their due roles. Major powers including USA, EU and Russia already have extensive contacts with both, which are expected to strengthen further, and they remain positive about further engagement and the development of closer relations.

Trends in bilateral relations

Our relations with China are an important element of our foreign relations not only because we are neighbours but also because our cooperation will positively impact on the peoples of our two countries, the region and the world. We are engaged in the pursuit of a common aspiration of providing a better quality of life to our peoples through economic progress and prosperity, the development of art, culture, literature and sports and the emergence of a plural and multifaceted society that utilises the natural talents and versatility of our peoples to the full. Our relations, characterised by a strategic cooperative partnership for peace and prosperity continues to strengthen and is a strong pillar of the evolving structure of international relations.

The basic trend of our bilateral relations has been a growing maturity in our relationship based not only on mutual benefit but also sensitivity to each other's concerns. Both sides are conscious that ours is a complex relationship with both challenges and opportunities and both sides have displayed the desire to promote understanding and trust. The strong foundation of our relations has been achieved by frequent interaction at the highest political levels. This demonstrates the strong political commitment to strengthen the relationship and to outline the basic principles for its future guidance.

Both sides are aware that there are issues where differences exist and have taken a pragmatic, yet principled, approach in dealing with them. On the complex boundary issue, the two sides are engaged in a structured dialogue through the mechanism of the special representatives appointed by the Prime Ministers to seek a resolution from the political perspective and from the overall context of our bilateral relations. At the same time, other mechanisms are engaged in the implementation of the Peace and Tranquillity Agreement and the Confidence Building Measures Agreement. The framework of negotiations assures us that while we are seeking a resolution of outstanding issues in a responsible manner through peaceful dialogue these differences will not impede the development of relations in other areas.

As growing powers we have also forged relations with other big powers based on principles and our respective national interests. These relationships, which must be seen in conjunction with our independent foreign policies, also provide a template for the interplay of our bilateral relations. The maturity in our relationship also rejects outmoded concepts such as balance of power or of containment. Our growing bilateral relationship also reflects an understanding of our unique responsibilities on regional and international issues. We share the desire for a stable neighbourhood to pursue our goals of growth and development.

An encouraging development in our relations is the rapid growth in our bilateral economic and trade cooperation in recent years, which has provided a new dimension to our relationship. The businessmen have seized investment opportunities and options for joint investments, including in third countries, are being explored. This cooperation acts as a new bridge in our expanding ties. It is admitted, however, that our economic relations though impressive in terms of growth is yet far short of its true potential. The basket of goods and services being traded needs to be expanded such that it generates its own momentum and is sustainable. Although both India and China are members of WTO and also of regional pacts, we need to further promote complementarities in trade and encourage fair trade, which is mutually beneficial. The conclusion of enabling agreements will provide an environment which will give a fillip to economic cooperation. There have been similar positive developments in virtually every other sphere of economic activity and there has been a spurt in people-to-people contacts, which will further promote trust and understanding.

The importance of multilateral cooperation and coordination has led to extensive interaction in a wide range of areas in bilateral, regional and international fora. India and China are active participants in the work of UN and its agencies, and also in organisations such as WTO, ASEAN, SCO, and others. Our dialogue transcends bilateral relations to encompass regional and global issues such as terrorism, security, environment, sustainable development and trade.

Global challenges

The current geopolitical situation is in transition and new relationships are being carved out in different parts of the world. The revolution in transport and communications, globalisation of the market place and expanding aspirations of the people of the world have introduced fresh paradigms to growth and development. The world appears smaller and time has shrunk but transitions are not seamless. There remain impediments in securing benefits from the march of globalisation—some pertain to the distribution of economic and social benefits while others relate to security concerns arising from transnational issues. These include economic issues such as flow of technology, communications, investments, trade, environmental concerns, movement of people and diseases, and also security concerns such as terrorism, narcotics, organised crime and ideologies. Globalisation means new opportunities; it also means shared responsibilities for problems that may arise in the future. There is need to promote the concepts of sustainable economic development; to rouse the world's conscience to the importance of eradicating poverty, promoting education and women and children's rights for a more equal and humane world; and to address the imbalances and inequities in global economic development such that developing countries may secure their rightful place in the new international order. There is need to strengthen the vital role of the United Nations and the international legal system in world peace, stability and development; reform of the multilateral system;

and promoting regional initiatives aimed not only at furthering trade and investment linkages but also at wider economic, political and social interaction. The world needs a new international order in which the old model based on the balance of power and on confrontation is replaced by an approach based on win-win options and coexistence.

In these and the other challenges that we face today, there is the opportunity for greater cooperation and coordination between India and China. We should be cognizant of the fact that not only should we take advantage of the good opportunity we have in our respective paths of development and our bilateral relations today but also that we need to join hands together for common good and as a responsibility for the future of mankind and its heritage. Our response to the global challenges we face will provide new directions in our relationship.

First, the gulf between the developed and developing worlds is not sustainable. The need in the developing world is to focus on rapid growth and development such that the living conditions of the peoples can improve, while the desire of the developed world is to sustain its current high living standards. A cooperative spirit could have achieved both objectives. However, the uneven spread of the benefits of globalisation, the dominance of the interests and leverage of the developed in economic relations and the paucity of options with the developing world ensures that the disparities remain and are often accentuated. In fact, the current regimes of globalisation add to the asymmetries in which the resources that developing countries seek are priced high and remain far short of their needs while they are often compelled to part with their own resources at adverse terms of trade. Ongoing negotiations to correct the imbalances in the regimes for trade, financial and technology flows have shown the doggedness of the developed countries in not conceding ground.

In an interdependent world it is no longer possible to sustain islands of development surrounded by underdevelopment and deprivation. The world needs to recognise this and take corrective measures. The reason why the gulf persists is because a lower level of development often implies a lower proportion of value-addition leading to lower price realisation and consequently lower remuneration for the worker. The economic and social success of India and China shows that it is possible to develop growth models that are a magnet for economic activity and that it is also possible to lift up two-fifths of humanity and make them productive and confident individuals. Moreover, our success also offers hope to many others that they too can come out of poverty and can carve out a niche in the globalised world. Similar progress has been achieved in other parts of the developing world and it is possible through regional arrangements to spread these benefits further. It is thus imperative that we persevere in our own development efforts, continue to cooperate with and assist others in the developing world to enhance capacity building to remedy the inequities. At the same time, we should continue negotiating for improvements in the multilateral regimes such that they are mindful of the needs of the developing world and such that the developed countries recognise that cooperation and accommodation are necessary.

Second, the quest for resources is becoming more intense. Our development pattern is highly dependent on resource use, including energy, raw materials as well as finances and technology. Resources are becoming scarcer and more expensive. Yet, the availability of secure, stable and sustainable resource flows is an imperative for the manufacturing sector. A rush for available resources leads to excess demand situations providing for inflationary trends which will reduce the competitiveness of the manufacturing sector. More importantly, they also add to the costs of development and limit growth. Similarly, financial flows and technology transfers, which are crucial for investments and innovation and hold the key to success in development efforts, are curtailed or priced at exorbitant rates. South-South cooperation has, to date, had marginal success in the creation of appropriate technologies and in obtaining critical technologies and funds from the developed world.

Resource security, particularly energy security, is a pressing requirement. Collaborative efforts between India and China in securing access to resources beyond their frontiers will be critical in being able to maintain the competitive edge. We have witnessed significant advances in new age technologies providing for energy efficiencies through the use of alternative and renewable resources and clean development mechanisms; engineering developments that require lower inputs of scarce resources and use more of man-made composites; and the revolution in communication and information which enable people to conduct business seamlessly and at minimal resource cost. Many of these innovations have been developed in India and China and our scientists have tested many more. The results are encouraging and it will be in our interest to try to make these options more economically viable. We should not only join forces in the quest for securing economic and stable sources of resources but also take the lead in the development and utilisation of new technologies, in the institutionalisation of viable financial markets and in the evolution of technology and standards regimes which will address the needs of the developing world and provide sustainable development.

Third, the central role of the human being in all development efforts has to be emphasised. Despite growth, vast swathes of the population remain outside its ambit and live in depravation. Issues such as poverty, education, health and employment need to be addressed directly as do issues such as rights and freedoms with regard to democracy, religion, equality and welfare such that human capital develops. Human resources are the most critical input in development and adequate investment is necessary to ensure its competitiveness. This means greater attention to the development of a knowledge economy in which productivity, entrepreneurship and innovation are suitably rewarded. Citizens have to feel that they have a stake in the development process and must be able to pursue their dreams in line with national objectives.

Tremendous progress has already been achieved by both India and China to address the basic needs of their vast populations through people-oriented programmes, especially in removing poverty and providing education. Further cooperation in the field of medicine, particularly traditional medicine, will provide local and low-cost solutions to improve health conditions not only in India and China but also in the rest of the developing world. A feature common to both countries is the continuing trend of migration. On the one hand, migration reflects an imbalance of skill levels and of demand-supply functions and is even said to drain away the potential for national development, but on the other hand, it also leads to higher productivity and incomes as well as dispersal of skills to other parts of the country or the world. India and China, which have large overseas populations have realised that such 'brain drain' can also be seen in the positive context to obtain benefits in win-win situations both in terms of national development as also for understanding and leverage in foreign lands. We have to equip our peoples with the wherewithal to be the torchbearers of an innovation-led knowledge economy such that they can be competitive in the future.

Fourth, there is a need to revisit the models of development being practiced. In order to bridge the huge gap in development levels, developing countries feel pressured to place priority on achieving high growth rates. However, a blind pursuit of growth can have disastrous consequences on economic and social systems and environmental conditions and can even lead to collapse and chaos. The trauma of the process of growth and the limits of its potential must be understood while shaping a more sustainable growth model. Sustainability must take regard of the local situation, availability of resources and the capacity to maintain the momentum of growth. In an interdependent world, we can imbibe best practices from elsewhere and adapt them to our use. Respect for the environment is critical such that we do not overexploit our resources and leave an empty heritage for our successors.

India and China, as big countries with large populations, have to be particularly mindful of the levels of usage and the quality of our key environmental resources such as water, air and soil as well as the preservation of our cultural resources including customs and traditions of the minorities and also pluralism in social and political life. These will become vital elements in maintaining the tempo of our vitality in the future. Our experience has been mixed in this regard and while some successes have been achieved in some areas there is a lot more to be done. It is critical that we pass on our heritage to succeeding generations while ensuring that they will have access to resources for their development.

Fifth, there is a need to promote an ideology of holism, which embraces coexistence, plurality and tolerance. There have been great changes in the international scenario in the years after the end of World War II. Several new countries have emerged, new cultures have acquired prominence, new fissures in society and religion have come to the fore, new aspirations have been expressed and new power equations have developed. The hopes of an era of security and stability after the end of the Cold War have not yet been realised. Instead, new political problems and security challenges have emerged, including the growth of fundamentalism and terrorism. The world needs a new international order in which the old model of confrontation is replaced by a new approach that evolves from rule-based legitimacy, consultation and respect for the principles of sovereignty and non-intervention. Thus international relations need not only be to display sensitivity to each other's concerns but also provide space for all to live in peace and prosperity. A future international order based on multipolarity connotes different nodes functioning in harmony and cooperation with one another and provide for economic and social development. The new international order also demands a greater role and restructuring of the UN and multilateral organisations.

India and China have been in the forefront of the momentous changes that are shaping the new international order. The experience of our ancient civilisations, our interaction with different cultures both within the country and in our external relations and our recent period of economic growth and development give us the strength to play a leading role in the shaping of the new international order. The depth of our relations with major powers such as USA, EU and Russia and the close relations we enjoy with partners in the developing world in Asia, Africa and Latin America put us in the unique situation where our counsel is valued and our economic and technical prowess are highly regarded. In the new century, we can embark on a relationship which leverages our advantages to mutual benefit to bring forth an ideology of development emphasising sustainability, equity and welfare while paying attention to social, cultural and environmental considerations; and an ideology of interstate relations based on a holistic approach which puts man at the centre and accords importance to the interplay between man and nature and has consideration for coexistence, plurality and tolerance while cherishing the diversity around us.

34

India and France

Dilip Lahiri

Summary

The Indo-French relationship is now described by both countries as strategic, with a common preference for a multipolar international system, sales and technology transfer of sophisticated defence equipment, and close cooperation in the space and nuclear fields. But the two countries did not have a meaningful and substantive relationship till as late as the 1970s, with the notable exception of a strong French presence in providing defence supplies to India right from the fifties. The trend even since then has been for some apparent impetus to be generated by high level visits, petering off into long periods of stagnation till the next high level visit. Chirac's visit in 1998 is commonly seen as a turning point and, despite some intermediate slackening of pace, its impact has lasted till the present. But it is probably still an open question whether or not Indo-French relations can acquire the broad and stable base and the genuine and proactive involvement and commitment of important governmental, business and cultural personalities and institutions on both sides necessary to enable it to develop a self-sustaining momentum.

History

Almost at the same time as the British founded their East India Company, the French founded one too. Their first factory was set up in 1688, like the British, at Surat. But besides having all the usual difficulties with Indian princes, the French had to fight the British and also the Dutch. Both at land and sea the Dutch beat the French, and drove them again and again out of the factories which they tried to establish.

Eventually the French bought a small piece of land from an Indian prince about a hundred miles south of Madras where they built a fort and town, which they called Pondicherry. But after some years, the Dutch, who were fighting with the French at home, drove them out and occupied Pondicherry. This seemed to signal the end of French power in India. But four years later, peace was signed between the Dutch and the French, and one of the conditions of the treaty was that Pondicherry should be given back to the French.

Then in 1744, the French and British went to war at home and carried the war into their colonies in India. After initial successes under Dupleix, the French Governor of Pondicherry, when they occupied most of Madras and it seemed at one time that the French would prevail in India, they suffered a catastrophic defeat against the British under Clive at the siege of Arcot in 1751. France formally gave up its aspirations for an empire in India as a footnote to the 1763 Treaty, which brought an end to the French and Indian (American) Wars. But desultory French efforts to harry the British in alliance with Indian princes continued. Though pre-revolutionary France under Louis XVI was not much interested in these games, French soldiers were recruited to train Tipu Sultan's army. Napoleon Bonaparte was very interested in resurrecting a French empire in India and saw the road to this ambition leading through Tippu Sultan's Mysore. But Napoleon got bogged down in Egypt on his way to India. A few hundred French mercenaries were recruited in Mauritius for the Mysore army but came to a disastrous end at the battle of Srirangapatnam on May 4, 1799 when Tipu Sultan was killed and French colonial ambitions in India came to a definitive end.

During these years, French citizens worked in various fields for Indian independent states in Mysore, Gwalior, etc. After the Napoleonic Wars, many French soldiers became military or political counselors of Indian states. There is even a now fully Indianised descendent of the French Bourbons settled in Indore. France has inherited a great tradition of research in India, particularly in philosophy and culture. The Oriental Languages School was established in 1795; the first chair in Sanskrit was accredited in 1812 at the College de France. This tradition of studies and research on India was maintained even after the end of French colonial ambitions in India due to its continuing connections through its remaining possessions in Pondicherry, Chandernagore, Mahe, Karaikal and Yanam which were returned to India only in 1954. Pondicherry has an important French community who are mainly descendants of the Indians who opted for French nationality in 1954. The French Institute, the French School of the Far East, an institution of international repute, is an important source of knowledge of India in France, albeit with its focus on the past and Indian exoticism.

Another chapter in relations between India and France—sordid and brutal initially but with a happier denouement—was the transport of poor and helpless Indians from the Madras region and a few from Bihar and Bengal as indentured labour in horrendous conditions to the French sugar islands in the Indian Ocean and the Caribbean, principally under an agreement between Britain and France for about 25 years from 1862 after the abolition of slavery in France. Réunion, Guadeloupe and Martinique are today French metropolitan departments and have French prefects. The people of Indian origin there are all French citizens. Over 25 per cent of the population of Réunion, a little less than 10 per cent in Guadeloupe and much smaller percentage in Martinique are of Indian origin, though there has been much intermarriage in the Caribbean with descendents of African slaves, who incidentally were considered a cut above the 'coolies' from India in the local social hierarchy. The French way in these islands had resulted in substantial cultural deracination, though remnants of the old temples and religious practices were clandestinely preserved, as well as an excellent spiced meat curry which has a place of respect in the local cuisine. Their language is entirely French, with very occasionally a little Tamil. They are well integrated in their societies, with little of the ill feeling between the descendents of Indian indentured labourers and African slaves pervasive in the British Caribbean. With Indian independence and improvement in their own economic and social circumstances, there has been a resurgence of interest in Indian culture and in rediscovering their roots. Several members of the community are prominent in the civil service and politics, both as mayors of municipalities as well as Deputies representing the islands in the French parliament.

Images of each other

Apart from the fascination with which French culture and style is universally regarded, of particular interest for post independence India was France's aggressive assertion of autonomy in foreign policy, despite being a part of the US-led NATO military alliance. There was much admiration and a desire to emulate in India's circumstances the panache and dynamism in the conduct of French foreign policy, and its confident assumption of national grandeur as a *sui generis* Great Power after rising like a Phoenix from the ashes of World War II. Two hundred years of British political and cultural domination has also resulted in the internalisation of many of the earlier anti-French affectations of the English by sections of the Indian elite. This has also led to a lack of sufficient encouragement for developing French language skills and studies. This has been a perennial impediment to the growth of people to people interactions and to genuine depth in Indo-French relations and has to some extent driven the French to look to the UK and later the US for the lead in their understanding and dealings with India. Of course, the French have also been no slouches in contributing to this state of affairs with their linguistic and attitudinal exclusivism.

France also has a fascination with its historical associations with India, reflected in the many Paris street names recalling places and generals featuring from the period when they were vying with the British for an empire in India. Indology remains alive and well in France. But its focus is on Sanskrit and ancient India's brilliant achievements in art, sculpture, literature, philosophy, music and dance, and it coexists uneasily with France's typically European distaste and pity for post independence India's images of poverty, illiteracy and backwardness. Contemporary India lost out to the India of myth and legend. In the fifties and sixties there was also the constant irritation at India's crusading role in decolonisation which impacted heavily on the French who were among the most stubborn in holding on to their overseas possessions.

There were no high level exchanges of visits almost till the eighties. French business was slow to look at opportunities in India. They also made some disastrous mistakes, *inter alia* in their choice of Indian partners and getting involved in acrimonious disputes and litigations. However, great multinationals do not like admitting to their mistakes, and the anecdotal image of India in French business circles is still that it is a difficult place to do business in (not entirely untrue) and that it is an Anglo-Saxon area of influence.

Matters have not been helped by the creeping malaise in French national morale about their place in the world. So the focus has remained on culture, with an increasing popular fascination with Bollywood and Indian kitsch. Over the last few years the Indian image has dramatically improved in France, as it has in the rest of the world. There is a clear realisation in French government and business circles that they have a lot to do in India and that it will be an uphill struggle. On the negative side, the current French phobia about being swamped with Maghrebis is inevitably stoked by the bands of pushy young men from India and Pakistan, presumably illegal entrants, peddling miniature replicas of the Eiffel Tower to strollers and tourists on the Champs de Mars and periodically getting chased off by the police. The modest and increasing expatriate Indian community is left alone and even respected as hardworking and apolitical.

Contemporary organisation of Indo-French relations

No state visit from the French side was made to India between 1944 and 1965. Between 1965 and 1976, two Prime Ministers visited India: Pompidou and Jacques Chirac. Only in January 1980 did a French President, namely, Giscard d'Estiang, visit India. From 1980 onwards, the number of visits by various French Ministers have multiplied. Since then several Head of State/Government visits have been exchanged, President Mitterrand's visits in 1982 and 1989 generated some expectations, particularly due to his personal relations with the Francophile Indira Gandhi. But these did not bear much fruit. Narasimha Rao's 1995 highly successful visit just after Chirac was elected was a tone setter and notable because for the first time India Inc. accompanied an Indian PM to France and the elite of French industry and business, also for the first time, came in droves for interaction with him. President Chirac came to India in January 1998 on a landmark visit which set relations on a fresh trajectory. PM Vajpayee visited France in September 1998 and President Narayanan in April 2000. French Prime Minister Raffarin visited India in 2003. After a gap of a few years in summit level visits Prime Minister Manmohan Singh went to Paris in September 2005 and President Chirac to Delhi in February 2006 when a number of important pending issues were resolved. During this period there were annual visits by foreign ministers, more regularly sustained from the French side than the Indian, as well as frequent visits by ministers of both sides dealing with various areas of functional cooperation.

An elaborate dialogue infrastructure has evolved in the wake of these interactions and provides a framework for regular, structured consultations between France and India on a variety of issues of mutual concern.

Among these are:

Strategic Dialogue: This mechanism has assumed pride of place in our consultative mechanisms and consists of meetings twice a year between personal representatives of the French President and the Indian Prime Minister. In practice, these have been Chirac's Diplomatic Representative on the French side and the National Security Adviser on the Indian side. It has become traditional for the personal representatives to be provided a private meeting with the host HOS/HOG after each dialogue session so that the relationship receives sustained high level attention. It is assumed that the personal representatives speak with authority and that any commitments given would be fulfilled. Set up during Chirac's visit in 1998, the underlying premise was that France would work with its partners, and particularly the P5, to alleviate the restrictions on nuclear trade imposed on India after the 1998 tests with a view to enabling India to obtain the latest generation French nuclear power plants which are the most efficient available. This issue has figured prominently during the dialogues, and indeed these discussions enabled the French to play a helpful role in the background moves that led to the Indo-US nuclear deal. But the dialogue has ranged much wider and has been notable for its spirit of confidence and frankness on sensitive issues. Not least, it has facilitated networking at this privileged level with other important countries.

Foreign Office Consultations: Earlier held annually between the Secretary-General on the French side and the Indian Foreign Secretary, one unfortunate side effect of the Strategic Dialogue has been that this mechanism has fallen into disuse. Effectively, the main bread and butter forum for overseeing bilateral relations has disappeared.

The High Committee for Defence Cooperation: Held once a year, alternately in India and in France, the Indo-French High Committee for Defence Cooperation was set up in 1998. It is co-presided by the ministerial representative of the French Defence Minister and the Defence Secretary in the Indian Ministry of Defence. It comprises three sub-groups on military cooperation, defence industrial cooperation for armaments and strategic issues respectively. The Indian and French Defence Ministers signed a comprehensive defence agreement during Chirac's visit to India in February 2006 setting up a joint committee which would be responsible for defining, organising and coordinating bilateral cooperation agreements in defence sector. These included defence strategic dialogue, professional exchanges, joint exercises, visits and training, cooperation in the field of defence material and transfer of technology, exchange of views on security threats and global terrorism and exchange of experience in peacekeeping operations.

Indo-French Working Group on Terrorism: Held once a year, alternately in India and in France since September 2001. It provides both sides a useful opportunity for exchange of views on current trends of terrorism in various parts of the world and for strengthening bilateral coordination in the fight against international terrorism.

Indo-French Initiative Forum: Held once a year, alternately in India and in France. Launched on the occasion of the state visit of the French President to India in 1998, the Indo-French Initiative Forum is an attempt to associate eminent French and Indian personalities in the development of a stable and lasting partnership. Co-presided by Mr. Jean François-Poncet, a former foreign minister and Mr. M. K Rasgotra, an earlier Indian foreign secretary, it has around 40 personalities representing culture, scientific research, media and the economy. The initiatives taken up by the forum in these different areas are intended for implementation with the support of the public authorities of the two countries. The forum has not fulfilled the expectations of either side, and the level of attendance on the French side has been disappointing. The membership has recently been revamped from both sides and the results remain to be seen.

Joint Commission for Cultural and Scientific Cooperation: Held once a year, alternately in India and in France. This commission provides the forum to examine all projects relating to cooperation in the fields of culture, science and technology and to define new priorities for establishing a lasting and substantial partnership between France and India. Bilateral cooperation in science and technology is regulated under four broad categories: (i) overall umbrella agreements between the two governments; (ii) Indo-French Center for the Promotion of Advanced Research (IFCPAR), also known by its French acronym CEFIPRA, set up in 1987 as a joint and equally funded project with the objective of catalysing and streamlining bilateral cooperation in emerging advanced areas of common research; (iii) Agreement between Indian ministries/organisations and their French counterparts, dealing in specific areas of science and technology; and (iv) institution-to-institution agreements e.g. the Indian Centre for Scientific Research (CSIR) and the French National Centre for Scientific Research (CNRS).

Joint Economic Commission: The joint commission helps to take stock of the progress of the different economic working groups. It is a forum for exchanges on multilateral trade issues, financial cooperation and bilateral relations (level of exchanges, custom duties, and investments). The following Indo-French economic working groups fall under the umbrella of the commission.

1. Working group on energy:

   Set up as a follow-up of the state visit to India of French President Jacques Chirac in January 1998, it involves on the Indian side the Ministry of Petroleum and Natural Gas, Ministry of Coal and Mines, Ministry of Non-Conventional Energy sources as well as the Central Water Authority and the Atomic Energy Commission. This working group meets once a year, alternately in France and in India, and addresses issues related to energy sector policy in both countries. It aims at bilateral cooperation in various fields between French and Indian companies as well as between official organisations from both sides.

2. Working group on Information Technology and Telecommunications:

   Created under the aegis of the Directorate General for Industry, Information Technology and Post (DIGITIP), the Indian Department of Telecommunications (DoT) and the Indian Department of Information Technology, this joint committee addresses institutional issues related to various topics like regulation in the information technology sector, market restrictions, legal issues arising between telecom operators and customers. It also associates representatives of Indian and French companies during one to one business meetings that are organised to coincide with the working group.

3. Working Group on Agriculture:

   Held once a year, alternately in France and in India, the main areas selected for cooperation are business, trade and WTO quality and standardisation, cold chain research and preservation, intellectual property and geographical appellations, rural and forestry development.

4. Working Group on Exploration and Development of Mines:
   Held once a year, alternatively in India and France this Group provides an institutional framework for cooperation in the field of mining. The projects presented from the French side have received a very favourable response from the Indian side. Several projects are being carried out presently,and more are under consideration.

Barring the strategic dialogue, the results from this dense pattern of interaction has been mixed. On the one hand, regular contact at the functional level is generally always to the good. But the tendency has been for these committees and working groups to wake up shortly before a meeting becomes due, to engage in some elegant presentations at which both sides are good, and then to go into hibernation till the next meeting. This is, of course, typical of most bureaucratic institutionalised dialogues. At some stage, however, both sides will need to address the question of whether or not this structured dialogue can be made more result-oriented.

Current status of Indo-French relations

Strategic partnership

The current development and consolidation of Indo-French relations can be traced to the state visit of the President of France to India, from January 24 to 26, 1998, which provided a new impetus to the bilateral relations and allowed the establishment of the foundations of a durable partnership. A significant element of the revived relationship is the strategic dialogue, initiated in October 1998. It was considerably strengthened in the wake the nuclear tests in South Asia when France, contrary to several partners,expressed opposition to international sanctions, according priority to dialogue. priority to dialogue. France also expressed support for India's inclusion as a permanent member in an expanded UN Security Council. Due to this, the convergence of views on Iraq and the shared desire to move towards a multipolar world generally, and the traditional cooperation on defence, civilian nuclear and space matters, France came to be regarded by India as a partner to be counted on and as one of its important strategic interlocutors.

During the exchange of visits by the Indian PM and the French President in September 2005 and February 2006, the two leaders reaffirmed the strategic character of the Indo-French partnership and committed themselves to further strengthening and deepening the relationship. Major deals were finalised regarding submarines and purchase of Airbus aircraft. Several major new agreements and understandings on cooperation in civilian nuclear energy, defence, space, trade promotion and culture were signed, reflecting the broad and diversified nature of the Indo-French engagement.

Economic relations

Trade and investment have traditionally been the weakest link in Indo-French relations and have stubbornly resisted responding to the promotional efforts of both governments. Confidence and comfort at a working level between private industry on both sides have clearly not so far achieved a critical mass. This is not typical only of India. The French economic profile is generally low in Asia. On the other hand, there is a widespread recognition among French business that India is a place that they cannot afford not to be in. There is a theory that substantial Indo-French trade and investment deals are in the pipeline and will automatically get reflected in figures in the coming years. Supporting evidence for this is cited as the large number of French companies, including industry leaders, who are studying the Indian market, establishing offices in India and a market presence.

Be that as it may, current figures are quite dismal. Large percentage increases are cited by vested interests to show that we are on the right road, but these are calculated from such an insignificant base in the early nineties as to be largely meaningless. Total two-way trade today is less than $4 billion annually, around 0.5 per cent of France's total trade. Total investment approvals from France are less than 3.5 per cent of the total. During the February 2006 Summit at Delhi, it was agreed that bilateral trade would be doubled in five years. How this is to be done is not clear. The governmental infrastructure in the form of the Joint Commission and various working groups has run out of steam, and, in any case, the principal actors in this field will have to be private business. This is starting to happen now. In the 2005 Le Bourget show, the private Indian companies placed orders worth €13bn (out of total sales of €43bn at the show), while negotiations with Air India and Indian Airlines had been going on for several years. Though hitherto the French private sector has demonstrated no particular enthusiasm in associating with government led promotional initiatives towards this objective, the attraction of the large Indian market and recent strides in the manufacturing sector to match those in IT, coupled with some disillusionment with China, seem to be finally changing their mindset. One common refrain these days is 'our turnover is larger in China but we make money in India'.

The main industry association from India with an institutional presence in France is the Confederation of Indian Industry (CII) which has an advisor based in Paris. FICCI and ASSOCHAM are also trying to establish niches. The French Employers' Association MEDEF is the main French interlocutor, though there are others. Their promotional activities have become quite stale and generally attract the same group of participants from companies already present in India and are probably not contributing much added value. It is of course different when there are star performers from India. PM Manmohan Singh's meeting with the French business community in September 2005 was a 'power breakfast' with top 30 CEOs from diverse fields who came at short notice.

Defence cooperation

France has traditionally been among the major suppliers of advanced armaments to India, starting from the light AMX tanks, which faced the initial brunt of the Pakistani armoured thrust in 1965. The Indian Air Force was the first foreign customer of Mirage aircraft, having used the Mysteres before that. While the catholic disregard of the French as to the destination of their sales—whether to India, Pakistan or China—was disturbing for India, one comfort was that the French did not interrupt supplies when they were needed most, such as in the event of an Indo-Pakistani conflict. Since Chirac's visit in 1998, the French have apparently made a conscious choice not to supply new advanced weapons systems to Pakistan, though earlier contracts would be implemented and refurbishment of old Mirage stocks by cannibalising from Libya, Australia, etc. would be facilitated.

The French armed forces have close relations with the Indian Air Force, Navy and Army, in that order. Major and sophisticated joint exercises are regularly conducted. The French have much respect for the individual skills and tactical professionalism of Indian armed forces personnel.

Nuclear cooperation

France and India have had a long history of cooperation in the nuclear field that stretches back to 1949, with a joint agreement to extract thorium from monazite sand. This was followed by the exchange of a number of India's nuclear scientists with the French nuclear establishment including Dr. Raja Ramanna, Dr. Homi Sethna and Dr. P.K. Iyengar. During the late 1960s the French were instrumental in helping India set up a heavy water production facility at Baroda and subsequently during the period 1978-79, they were also instrumental in facilitating the construction of the fast breeder test reactor at Kalpakkam. This cooperation over the FBR went ahead in spite of India's nuclear test in 1974. With the understanding of the US, the French undertook to supply enriched uranium fuel for the Tarapur Atomic Power Station after US supplies were cut off, but this supply stopped following France's official accession to the Non-Proliferation Treaty in 1992.

President Jacque Chirac was accompanied during his visit to India in 1998 by a high-level delegation that included the CEO of Framatome, part of the French consortium Areva, specialising in the design and construction of nuclear power plants. This was to form the basis of a 'structured dialogue' that included cooperation in civilian nuclear energy. The principal logic of the dialogue was to arrive at a formulation which would facilitate cooperation in the realm of civilian nuclear power that included the transfer of nuclear know-how along with advanced civilian nuclear technology. Side by side with efforts to resolve the roadblock with the NSG, feasibility studies were started for setting up six 1000 MW pressurised water nuclear power plants for India. While there are many obstacles ahead, there is clear convergence now in the stance of the United States, the United Kingdom and France towards India. All three see India as a responsible nuclear power, well advanced in nuclear technology and each supports an Indian exception to NSG rules, and they remain convinced of persuading the other 41 members of the NSG, should India agree to undertake certain steps. India does have a long history of cooperation with France in the nuclear sphere and clearly has a lot to gain from French cooperation in the development of a civilian nuclear power sector in India.

France sponsored and provided strong support for India's entry as a full member of the EU led International Thermonuclear Experimental Reactor (ITER) project to be set up at Cadarache in France.

Space

The Indo-French cooperation in space sciences with the Indian Space Research Organisation (ISRO) goes back to 1972. France contributed significantly to the launch of the Indian satellite Apple. It also provided India with technology transfer from the rocket engine Viking. From a pure scientific perspective, cooperation started with the visit in 1999 of a delegation of the French space agency, the CNES.

Current active cooperation in space science and technology includes the joint development of the Megha-Tropiques observation satellite for the study of tropical climate. It is expected to be launched in 2008-09. The design, manufacture and launch of this satellite are co-financed by the CNES and ISRO. The heavier range of Indian satellites is still launched by the European Ariane rockets from Kourou in French Guyana.

Science and technology cooperation

These are the most active and robust bilateral cooperation programmes. Fundamental sciences, especially mathematics, astronomy, physics, as well as social sciences are the traditional areas of scientific cooperation between the two countries. However the increasing implication of sciences in industry (information technology, biotechnology, chemistry, etc.), in medicine and in the management of natural resources (satellite observations, atmospheric and oceanic modelling) have created a need for collaborative research in these applied fields of science and technology. Virtually all the premier institutions of both countries are stakeholders in the Indo-French cooperative activities in these fields.

Education and culture

There is considerable cooperation between India and France in the field of culture and education. The Cultural Exchange Programmes (CEPs) promote institutional exchanges between the Maison des Sciences de l'Homme (MSH) on the French side and the Indian Council for Social Sciences Research (ICSSR), the UGC, the Indian Council for Historical Research (ICHR) and Indian Council for Philosophical Research (ICPR) on the Indian side. The current CEP is for the period 2004-2006. A major exhibition of the Gupta period is due to be held in the Grand Palais in 2007. Cultural exchanges enjoy a wide and discerning audience among the French population. The ICCR sponsors a number of Indian practitioners of dance, music and the arts to France, while a significant number of Indian artists also visit France at the initiative of various local cultural associations. Popular Indian cinema has also made inroads into France, in addition to the more traditional art films.

Apart from organising an active cultural promotional programme in India, France offers scholarships for scholars in French literature and for educational sciences, public administration, fine arts, mass communication, etc. Other cooperative programmes in the field include a subsidy to the Ecole to the University Grants Commission. Scholarships are also offered in fields such as French language, hotel management Nationale d'Administration (ENA) by the French to facilitate study tours of trainees from the Indian Institute of Public Administration, long-term courses of ten and half months at the Institut Internationale d'Administration Publique (IIAP) and professional training for Indian archaeologists at the Centre de Recherche et de Restauration des Musees.

Problem areas and prospects for the future

Absence of a foreign policy with respect to the other

The content and potential of Indo-French relations clearly make the building of a strategic partnership appropriate. Despite the rhetoric about the strategic relationship on both sides, the logic of this has not been internalised by either side and the tendency is to deal with mutual relations as a laundry list of the various bilateral interactions.

Lack of common understanding regarding the elements that each side is to put on the table for the strategic relationship

France does not appear naturally on the Indian radar screen, except when we seek their support on a specific issue. For France as well, India does not come immediately to mind as an interlocutor for consultations, except on India centric issues. The strategic relationship envisaged by Chirac in 1998 was a deliberate departure from past habit and practice, and thus involved going against the grain. Both sides accordingly need to put in much more work at nurturing it through frequent exchanges of visits and consultations on regional and international issues at various levels. Interlocutors with line responsibilities on both sides need to adopt the increasing Western practice of close networking by email and telephone and develop personal familiarity and rapport.

The need to guard against unrealistic expectations

It needs to be understood and accepted that the requirements of a strategic relationship does not automatically mean agreement, even on matters which one partner regards as vital for its interests.

Regarding expansion of permanent membership of the UN Security Council, for example, we should recognise that France would be happiest if the *status quo* could safely be left undisturbed. But France feels that, unless Germany was allowed in, its own position could be in jeopardy by calls for a common European seat. Its strong support for the other claimants, including India, results from the realisation that Germany cannot get in alone. If Germany could otherwise be bought off, French support for India on this issue is likely to evaporate.

Similarly, on nuclear non-proliferation, the French position is quite as firm as the acknowledged high priests of the NPT and NSG. However, having been in a similar position to India till 1992, when it ratified the NPT (though it was recognised as a nuclear weapon state in the NPT, unlike India) its understanding of India's predicament, and the idiom it uses, are more palatable to us and helpful. It would however be quite unrealistic to hope to drive a breach between France and the US or NSG on India's account.

The same situation exists in respect of France's advocacy of the lifting of the EU arms embargo against China, its recognition of the need to tackle 'root causes' while combating international terrorism, or its attempts to maintain a balance in its relations with India and Pakistan, despite rhetorical denials.

While both sides will naturally continue to try to convince the other of its positions, they need to keep in mind that the strategic relationship remains valuable despite occasional inability to agree, and to hold back from placing heavier loads on the strategic relationship bridge than it can bear.

The US-France-India triangle

The French perceive a reduction in the Indian interest in and commitment to the strategic relationship with France after the sudden transformation in its relations with the US, though they saw no contradiction between the two. Both sides of course have the correct understanding that, when push comes to shove, the relationship with the US will take priority over the support that either can provide to the other when this goes against the US line. The challenge for both countries is to arrive at the level and nature of the strategic relationship that will add value and leverage to each country's relations with the US.

The European Union

The EU is at the core of French foreign policy. India, on the other hand has no foreign policy towards the EU, and Indo-EU relations are merely the sum total of the admittedly frequent but essentially formalistic Indo-EU functional interactions. On important matters, even on issues on which the EC/EU have competence, the Indian tendency, probably justified at present, has been to deal with London, Berlin or Paris over the heads of the EU. This will become progressively more difficult as the French space to pursue its special relationships with countries becomes increasingly circumscribed by its imperative to retain a leading role in the construction of a united Europe.

35

India and Russia

Anuradha M. Chenoy

The international political system is witnessing shifts that challenge traditional paradigms of hegemony and balance of power. Military prowess and capability as the key to great power status or dominance has been repeatedly challenged at great cost in human and material terms. The concept of great power earlier linked primarily to military and economic capacity now includes human development and human security at par with the preceding two. Regional alliances play an important and proactive role enabling nations to greater roles. Civil society and non-state forces have become acknowledged actors in international politics.

In this arena, India is seeking a greater role for itself in the international system. This aspiration is based on the view that India is a stable democracy with significant human and material resources; it is an increasingly important economic power; it has an established record as a responsible and international law abiding state and it has consistently voiced the concerns of the developing countries as a leader of the Non-Aligned group. Indian foreign policy makers argue that at this stage of 'take off' as a great power India needs to re-invent itself. For this proposed new role India requires new allies and partnerships, including with the dominant superpower. This assumption raises questions about India's traditional partnerships and vision of the international political system. Within this, are the questions of India's relations with Russia and the new alliance systems that are emerging in the region and globally.

Clearly, India in its traditional 'balancing' role would seek partnerships of equality with all powers. However, if India does not show its independence as it has done in history, it can fall into the trap of 'aligning' with one tendency or bloc at a cost to its ambition. It is in this context that it is important to view India's relations with Russia.

India's relations with Russia are a critical aspect of India's role in the international political system and have deep domestic implications for both India and Russia. Indo-Russian relations are embedded in a history of trust, mutual compatibility and interest that makes it difficult to find parallels in bilateral relations. Since history is a guide and indicator of future trends this special relationship is likely to strengthen unless policy makers choose to forget if not reject history. This chapter will review the relations between these two countries in the light of the recent trends in global politics; raise questions on the staying power and direction of this relationship.

The importance of international vision

In their repeatedly stated international vision both Russia and India support the concept of a multipolar world, an idea shared by China and many others.[1] This concept argues that while there is one superpower there can be multiple poles that are important centres of economic and political power that can act as independent actors.[2] This conceptualisation determines policies that work towards the further strengthening and creation of the multipolar world as opposed to an assertion of a unipolar world. This vision supports: the coexistence of multiple powers and possibilities in the international system; a collective security that is inclusive; greater regionalism to foster common regional interest; negotiated settlements; the possibility of independent foreign policy; and that

---

1. This concept is outlined in "The National Security Concept of the Russian Federation", *Nezavisimoye Voennoye Obozreniye*, 17 December 1997; and finds a place in the Indian-Russian strategic Agreements of 2000; also Alexie K. Pushkov, "Modern World Order: The Russian View", unpublished Paper at the Harvard Academy for International and Area Studies, Cambridge, Massachusetts, November 13-15, 1997.

2. Primakov in interview in *Nezavisimaya Gazeta*, 30 December 1997.

international decision be made through bodies like the UN that should be strengthened, democratised and empowered.[3]

The unipolar concept in contrast asserts the domination of a single hegemonic superpower. It is from the vision of a unipolar world that ideas like: 'clash of civilisations'; 'with us or against us'; 'single path of development'; 'military and superpower hegemony'; 'regional hegemony' and 'client states' and other such ideas and threats arise. These ideas provide justification of policies that include: regime change or selective military intervention in specifically chosen states in the name of human rights and democracy initiatives; sanctions outside the ambit of international law and institutions; the creation of regional hegemony based on military force; and road blocks for international law (which is justified on the basis that the international system is anarchic). A foreign policy based on the unipolar idea is bound to lead to military alliances; hegemonic policies and creation of regional hegemony that promotes regional tensions.

Would the two alternate visions of unipolar or multipolar lead to military blocs and revive a politics of Cold War? This is a far fetched idea that attempts to revive Cold War memories and threats and in the present circumstances is not possible because: multi-polarity seeks collective security and a politics of inclusion. It is opposed to any one single ideology—thus for example, the market; liberal; state-guided ideologies are all equally acceptable to it, whereas the unipolar vision argues for only the primacy of the market. The multipolar vision emphasises non-military solutions to international problems; it argues for inclusion of states. (Thus, Iran participated as an observer at the meeting of the Shanghai Cooperation Organisation, rather than be isolated as outcaste.) Multi-polarity thus broadens the concept of security. The powers that advocate a multipolar vision—Russia, India, China and others, can engage seriously with the US and all other powers and seek to strengthen this relation while maintaining an independent foreign policy.

---

3. The Foreign Policy Concept of Russia, 28 June 2000.

Clearly then, as long as India advocates and chooses its policies in accordance to the multipolar concept, it will be able to engage closely with its traditional partners like Russia and the CIS; make new partnerships with China and keep its interest with superpowers like the US without compromising its interests.

Is Russia important for India?

The economic decline of Russia after the Soviet disintegration, its uneasy transition to a market economy, the lack of institutional structures to sustain a healthy market system or vibrant democracy, its open engagement and new friendships and allies including with the US, China, EU and an opening with Pakistan led to the belief that Russia could no longer be a stable partner for India. On the other hand, India with the newly acquired status as a major power, attractive for its economic growth, market, middle class and new aspirations, raises the primary question, is Russia still important for India? And how much can India deepen its alliances with Russia? To address this it would be useful to deconstruct India's linkages with Russia in different sectors.

The strategic advantage

The Russian-Indian relation gives a strategic advantage to both. This calculation is not based on unqualified or speculative futuristic projections (for example: that this relation will make India into a great power), but on time tested and empirically verified conclusions. More than 80 bilateral documents give the necessary politico-legal basis to this relation topped by the Indo-Russian Strategic Agreement of 2001. This Agreement gives India-Russia relations multiple directions and establishes strategic and political sub-systems within a bilateral framework. This is evident from official terminology: "Indo-Russian relations are civilisational and time-tested", and "importance attached to them cuts across party lines in India and is not subject to political vicissitudes".[4] The eulogies and rhetoric India and Russia extend to each other play out in

---

4. "Bilateral Relations between India and the Russian Federation", Ministry of External Affairs (Central and East European Division) 28 November 2002.

military, economic and public relations. In concrete terms the strategic edge that India gets from its relation with Russia are in areas that are critical to Indian interests like Kashmir; energy security; relations with China and Central Asia.

Kashmir and terrorism

Russia's stand on the issue of Kashmir and the terrorism faced by India on account of this dispute has been consistent and unconditional over time or regime change. Every Russian leader from Yeltsin to Putin has reiterated this and it forms the basis for India's trust towards Moscow. Russia has never tried to 'balance' India's interest with Pakistan; India has not been ever put into a position of having to compete with other countries to prove its 'loyalty' by approving all other Russian positions (for example on Iran, Iraq, etc.); Russian defence and strategic support is not balanced with a link to any other Russian partner, including China.

International terrorism is perceived as a threat in the Russian National Security Doctrine, and both India and Russia expressed concern that the international coalition against terrorism has not paid sufficient attention to terrorism in regions like Kashmir, Chechnya, etc. and is focussed entirely in Afghanistan and Iraq. It can thus be judged to be selective and motivated. Russia and India have had reason to combine forces on this issue, resolved to exchange information and set up working groups and will have to address this problem regionally.

Central Asian Republics and the SCO

Strategic interests of India where Russia is the key player are the Central Asian Republics (CARs) and the Asian regional networks like Shanghai Cooperation Organisation (SCO). These two issues are interlinked with other key strategic and material interests of India like energy security; relations with China and regional security.

India has built long term, independent and autonomous relations with the Central Asian Republics. Of these, Kazakhstan, Tajikistan, stand out, while Uzbekistan, Kyrgyzstan and

Turkmenistan have yet to reach the same level. India's interest in the region lies in the vast oil and natural gas reserves in Kazakhstan, Turkmenistan and Uzbekistan. In Tajikistan, India has a geo-strategic interest, since it borders Afghanistan, Pakistan and West Asia. India has negotiated an airbase here. The Central Asian states have attracted much international attention and all great powers have been making an attempt to influence the politics of the region. It was for such geostrategic reasons and access to hydrocarbon resources and pipelines that the US negotiated and built military bases in the Central Asian States (CAS). A decade of ties that were built through the mechanism of the Commonwealth of Independent States (CIS) were violated as the Russians view US bases as an attempt to curb Russian influence in the region.

The effort to bypass the traditional oil and gas pipelines from Russia and Iran and pass through instead regions favoured by the US like Turkey and Georgia, further heightened geostrategic rivalry. (For example the Baku-Tbilisi-Ceyhan-BTC pipeline through Turkey and Georgia.) The Russians argue that they can meet the transportation needs for Caspian Sea oil and gas.[5] The Caspian Sea Basin is the region of major hydrocarbons. India can gain access to this region primarily through Russia. The colour revolutions of 2004-5 that led to regime changes in Ukraine, Georgia, Kyrgyzstan and violent uprisings in Uzbekistan were viewed by the CARs as US intervention who used the 2005 meeting of the SCO to demand a timeline from the US on vacating their troops from the region. The SCO has not been supportive to regime change, gave shelter to Uzbekistan when it was being pressurised by the US and it has discredited the colour revolutions.

India has wisely kept out of the geostrategic rivalries even though it has interests in this region. However, India has a strategic disadvantage since unlike Pakistan and China it does not have direct access to the CARs. In these circumstances it needs Russia that is a long term ally in the region. Russia is linked with the CARs through historic ties manifest in common links that range from

---

5.   May 22 2000, Eurasianet.

transportation and pipeline routes; a 10 million diaspora of ethnic Russians throughout the region; the presence of 20,000 Russian troops in CIS region; share in river, communications and power grids. A slew of formal treaty arrangements besides the SCO like the Collective Security Treaty Organization; CICA, etc., bind Russia with the region as natural and long term allies. India to maintain its link with the region thus has to fortify its relation with the Russians and CARS both independently and through deeper participation in organisations like the SCO where the heads of states of this region meet regularly.[6]

The SCO deals with more than the issue of energy. It is primarily a security organisation favoured by both Russia and China as the key regional organisation for collective security. The 2006 meeting attended by the Presidents Putin and Hu Jintao said that the SCO had a role "in maintaining peace and stability in the zone of its responsibility." The serious role that they envisage for the SCO is evident in what they envisage: "in case of emergency events, jeopardising peace, stability and security in the region, the SCO members states will immediately establish contacts and start consultations on a rapid joint response so as to defend to the utmost extent, the interests of the Organization and its member states."[7] The Chinese President had earlier argued that the SCO would also deal with the 'three evils—terrorism, separatism and extremism'. These concerns are shared by India, Russia and China and the other members and observers and give them opportunity to look for collective solutions for these. The US is wary of the SCO since they believe it can become an alternative to their plans for expansion of influence in the region and for their proposed 'partnership for peace' plan that is part of NATO linkages in the region It would be in US interest that India downgrades its interest in the SCO and there will be pressure on India to do so In this context, it would have done India well if the Prime Minister had himself attended this meeting just as the Presidents of Pakistan and Iran did. None of

6. In the June 2006 SCO meeting in Shanghai, India was represented by Petroleum Minister Mr. Murli Deora.

7. Documents of the Shanghai Cooperation Organisation, 17 June 2006.

the members or observers in the SCO can become full or equal members of NATO and thus need their own organisation. At same time, the SCO does not plan to be a military alliance and focuses on economic, energy and regional security. In fact the Chinese have repeatedly talked of the 'SCO as non-aligned organisation'. In these circumstances, India should make all attempts to become a full member of the SCO.

The Russia-India-China possibilities

The idea of the Russia-India-China triangle floated by Foreign Minister Primakov has been put on the back burner. However two things stand out. One is Russia's deepening engagement with China and second, the improved Sino-Indian relations to the point where the two do not see each other as threats.[8] The Russian and Chinese have moved from a 'constructive partnership' in 1994 to 'strategic partnership' by 1996 and then the important Treaty for Friendship, Alliance and Mutual Assistance of 2001 (Xinhua, 16, July, 2001). This treaty was the first after the 1950 Sino-Soviet Friendship Treaty of 30 years that had formed the base for the Sino-Soviet linkages. This Treaty is comprehensive, touching on all vital issues of Sino-Russian relations; envisages cooperation in energy, military; trade and shares a common vision of international affairs including the need for a multipolar vision and world. It is thus designed to make long lasting commitments and to resolve outstanding problems. The Russians are keen that India take advantage of these relations and again the SCO is a body that can enable this partnership.

Defence

India's relations with Russia are based on structural inter-dependence where both countries are mutually dependant on each other. A key to this is that the Indian military continues to depend on Russia for almost 70 per cent of its military hardware imports. This dependence has gradually been re-inventing itself from a supplier-client relation to one of partnership with joint production of sophisticated weaponry ranging from equipment to the

---

8. Statement of Defence Minister Pranab Mukherjee, *The Hindu*, 13 June 2006.

manufacturing of the indigenous Brahmos missiles. Russian Indian collaboration in space, nuclear power, satellite technology makes Indian military and security apparatuses intertwined with Russian military industrial complexes. During the painful Russian transition, India's imports from Russia helped sustain the economies of the Russian military industrial complex and 800 Russian defence industries kept working on Indian (and Chinese) orders.

India is one of the world's most lucrative arms markets. In 1987, Soviet Union had supplied 44 per cent of global arms export while the US had 29 per cent. By 1997, Russian share of the global market had fallen to just 4 per cent. By 2000, Russia revived its arms sales and is third after the US and Great Britain. Defence orders from India sustain part of the Russian military industrial complex especially in St. Petersburg and Irkutsk that would otherwise have faced closure at the time of transition in the Russian economy. India is the only country with which Russia has a long-term programme of military-technical co-operation, which was signed in 1994, till the year 2000 and renewed for another 10 years. Annual orders from Russian defence industry work out to about $ 2 billion. (China is Russia's only other partner of this scale.) India has a programme for 1 billion dollars with the Russians for the manufacture of the fighter planes: the SU-30KI fighters. India also gets much naval hardware from the Russians and has recently acquired the 636-class submarines. Defence is thus the major component of Indo-Russian relations. It underlies the economic and strategic relations between the two. In fact, it is the most privileged part of the relationship.

Energy

An increasingly strategic area of India-Russia relations is now linked to the energy sector. As an oil importing dependant nation, India imports 80 per cent (70 mm tonnes of crude oil, that comes to 30 billion dollars in 2005-06) of its oil needs. Russia has come to the assistance of India during their oil crisis time and again. The then Indian Petroleum Minister Mani Shankar Aiyer saw this need in October 2004 when he said: "In the half-century of Indian independence, Russia has guaranteed our territorial integrity, and in the second half it may be able to guarantee our energy security.

What I am talking about is the strategic alliance with Russia in energy security, which is becoming for India at least as important as national security."

India is seeking to increase its energy imports from Russia and the Central Asian Republics of Kazakhstan and Turkmenistan in various ways that include partnership and investments in oilfields, however, it needs to be more focussed in this realm. A North South International Transport corridor that is based on a combination of land and sea routes is on the anvil and India needs a collaboration with Iran and Russia in this regard. This is an issue that has been objected to by the US, who support the Turkmenistan-Afghanistan-Pakistan pipeline instead, since that would be under US control. India has a clear interest in Russian hydrocarbon resources as evident from the ONGC investments in Sakhalin I and II. The Russians have invited India to be part of Sakhalin III, shortly after they denied this deal to the US. However, India will have to shrug off US pressure if it wants to ensure its interests in this region.

Russia is important for India's nuclear energy plants and is assisting India in building the Kudunkulam (Tamil Nadu) nuclear plant ($2.6 billion) that is to be operational in 2007. The frequent attempts by the US in blocking Indian indigenous industry in these sectors getting Russian equipment, for example the cryogenic rocket; and nuclear engines for this plant have been bypassed by the Russian firms with backing from the Russian Government. In early 2000 the Glavkosmos firm retained autonomy and was firm on supplying these engines to India despite US pressure on Russia on the basis of the missile technology control regimes (MTCR). Similarly in 2006, India required 60 tonnes of uranium that Russia has undertaken to supply, even before India received the sanction from the nuclear suppliers groups. Under the rules only members of Nuclear Non-proliferation Treaty can acquire this. US opposes this until the Indo-US nuclear agreement comes through.

Trade and economics

A matter of concern to both Russia and India is the small share of Indian capital in investments in the Russian economy and bilateral trade between the two, which reached only $3 billion in 2005-06. This trade that was at an all time high during the Soviet period saw a decline after Soviet disintegration. The privatisation of both economies and the problems with the rupee-ruble exchange rates and the large Indian debt became a roadblock. These glitches have been overcome over the last decade and the Indian rupee debt has been used for investment projects in India and Russia nearing completion. In this context, both sides have agreed to facilitate an increase in trade to US $ 5 billion. India's interest in investing in Russia lies in the fact that the investments by ONGC-Videsh in the gas projects of Sakhalin I and 3 are the largest external investments made by India with investments of almost US $ 3 billion planned.

Russia which had been marked by political instability, economic and financial crisis, high inflation and a lack of economic laws and regulations is a chapter of the past. Russia today has shown consistent increase in GDP by 7 per cent per annum and industrial growth of 3 per cent per annum, and has a favourable trade balance and substantial foreign exchange reserves. Laws regulating the economic and financial system have been put in place and have worked well during the last five years. The high prices for Russian raw material exports, especially oil have played a big role in Russian economic success. The political system has seen regular elections for the Parliament and the President. The federal system has been working and an attempt to stop the autarchy of some regions has been made by centralising the appointment of Governors. Several Russian business tycoons who were seen to have made large profits through illegal means have been indicted for tax evasions and assets of the giant Yukos oil company owned by one such imprisoned oligarch Mikhail Khodorkovsky, have been bought over by companies controlled by the Russian Government.

In such changed circumstances, the agreements signed during the 2005 Putin visit between the State Bank of India, the Canara Bank and several Russian banks that are to open operations in both countries will assist Russian Indian business deals. This is important since trade and economic cooperation depends on the financial mechanisms of implementing deals and projects, and the recognition of bank guarantees. This agreement brings the banks of both countries into each other's markets, conforming to international trade practices. Russia's request that it be given 'market economy' status, which is necessary while they negotiate entry into the World Trading Organization has been supported by India. This status has been given to them by USA, China and the European Union.

The Russian government's intention to diversify trade, joint ventures and economic partnerships is evident with the setting up of the joint working groups on business. India and Russia have in the recent past collaborated on the supercomputer Padma Ru and proposals are being worked on new projects. While the mechanics of all these bilateral ties are regulated by the Russian-Indian Inter-Governmental Commission for Scientific, Technological and Cultural Cooperation that has held 10 sessions till 2006, it is clear that the two countries need to diversify their trade, commercial and cultural relations. Russia-India signed an accord in 2005 on joint development and use of the Russian Global Navigational Satellite system for peaceful purposes. While India has signed a similar agreement with the European Union, the access given by the Russians is at a qualitatively higher level. This plant is supplied equipment by 300 Russian enterprises. Such instances multiply in the history of India-Russia relations.

Several sectors of the two countries are complementary and yet unexplored for example, the services, the small scale and education sectors. These sectors had a history of collaboration during the Soviet period. The intermediate period of transition saw a setback to these, and now both governments need to provide information and sets standards for these structures. Indian students have a great interest in going to medical and engineering schools in Russia. The Russian students would gain from coming to Indian management schools technological and liberal social science institutions. Despite the current drawbacks that range from below standard facilities and the problem of recognition of degrees, thousands of Indian students still attend Russian medical colleges. The Education and Human Resource Ministries of both countries need to look urgently into this aspect, since it remains a sector with unexplored potential.

Conclusion

The balance that Russia wanted to maintain just after the Soviet disintegration gradually gave away due to force of circumstance and became a tilt in favour of India. Witness, for instance, the Foreign Policy Concept of the Russian Federation 1992 that stated in the context of the Indo-Pak conflict that Russian policy should not be seen as 'pro-Indian'. This document proposed that ties with Pakistan be brought up at level with India and those relations with both 'rest on economic stimuli'. By 1996, this argument was dropped and replaced by the multipolar concept where Foreign Minister Primakov gave central place to relations with India. In 2000 the Russian national security doctrine had radical shifts when the authors argued: "Russia's foreign economic interests do not lie with the West; instead Russia must seek markets in the Third World countries."[9] The Foreign Policy Concept of June 2000 spoke of "strengthening traditional partnership with India, including in international affairs" as a crucial direction of Russian foreign policy as proactive engagement with India had been re-initiated. This had resulted in the Strategic Partnership Agreement in 2000; Indo-Russian relations have moved up every year.

9. Current Digest of Post-Soviet Press (2000). "Russian National Security Doctrine", January 10, *Current Digest of Post-Soviet Press*, Vol. 52, No. 4, pp. 19-20.

36

India and the United Kingdom
Krishna V. Rajan

It has taken a good half century after India became independent from British colonial rule, for India and the United Kingdom to fashion a relaxed, stable, forward-looking relationship based on their competitive advantages and complementarities in additions to the shared assets bequeathed to them by history.

British and Indian mindsets arising from the colonial experience have inevitably influenced policies and perceptions in both countries. India's long struggle for independence was bound to leave bitter memories on both sides. Indian leaders recognised the positives of the colonial linkage, and supported arguments for relations with Britain uncluttered by memories of the colonial past. Even before India's independence in 1947, Mahatma Gandhi had made it very clear that he "would cut India off from the British Empire completely; from the British nation not at all ... but it must be a partnership on equal terms." Later, when India's Constituent Assembly was debating membership of the Commonwealth, Jawaharlal Nehru stressed, "India (does) not lack faith in herself, and (is) prepared to cooperate even with those with whom she had been fighting in the past." As the Indo-British relationship continued to decline, Nehru was still pleading eight years later at a banquet in New Delhi in honour of Sir Anthony Eden that: "we should have the capacity to forget what ought to be forgotten and remember what ought to be remembered...that is what wisdom demands."

Clearly, as former Foreign Secretary M. Rasgotra has commented, "this lofty view of Indo-British relations" could not prevail over "lesser mortals" in New Delhi and London, in whose minds "memories of both kinds lingered, influencing their mutual responses and attitudes...and introducing a fair measure of ambivalence in their dealings."

In the perception of some observers, the root of the problem initially was the absence of understanding among British thinkers about India's civilisational and cultural strengths. Prof. Lord Bhikhu Parekh maintains that 19th Century British liberals, such as James Mill, J.S. Mill and McAulay saw India as a "semi-barbaric" country occupying a place half-way between the "African savages" and "civilized Europeans." He recalls the description of William Wilberforce of India as "one grand abominable nation." ("Have you ever met an Indian?" asked Beverly Nichols in *All I Could Never Be*, after travelling the length and breadth of India, suggesting that while it was possible to meet Gujaratis or Bengalis or Tamilians, there was no such thing as an 'Indian'.) This view of India began to change as the talent of Indians and the services they performed for British interests (e.g. in the World Wars) became more widely known, as Indians shed their sense of racial inferiority and stand up for their rights, and as they produced leaders of international stature, especially Mahatma Gandhi—but the abiding image among many Indians of earlier generations is of the British constantly making misassessments based on arrogance or ignorance or both, of Churchill's claim to fame being his description of Gandhi as that "half-naked fakir."

Similarly, Britons find it puzzling that attempts by Indian leaders, right up to the present day, to articulate an objective view of the colonial experience and acknowledge that it was at least in part, helpful in integrating India and preparing it to be a modern democratic state, have invariably stirred controversy at home. As when Prime Minister Manmohan Singh said the following in his acceptance speech of the honorary doctorate at Oxford in 2005:

India's experience with Britain had its beneficial consequences too. Our notions of the rule of law, of a Constitutional government, of a free press, of a professional civil service, of modern universities and research laboratories have all been fashioned in the crucible where an age old civilization of India met the dominant Empire of the day. These are all elements which we still value and cherish. Our judiciary, our legal system, our bureaucracy and our police are all great institutions, derived from British-Indian administration and they have served our country exceedingly well. The idea of India as enshrined in our Constitution, with its emphasis on the principles of secularism, democracy, the rule of law and, above all, the equality of all human beings irrespective of caste, community, language or ethnicity, has deep roots in India's ancient culture and civilization. However, it is undeniable that the founding fathers of our Republic were also greatly influenced by the ideas associated with the age of enlightenment in Europe. Our Constitution remains a testimony to the enduring interplay between what is essentially Indian and what is very British in our intellectual heritage.

Most Indians have tended to resist such assessments of the net benefit to India of the colonial linkage as being overly generous to the ex-colonial power, and would resonate more comfortably with views such as those of, for example, Shashi Tharoor in *India: From Midnight to the Millennium*:

Learned British econometricians have tried to establish that the net result of this experience was neutral—that the British put about as much into India as they took out of it...The negative side of the ledger is easily listed: economic exploitation (often undisguised looting of everything from raw materials to jewels); stunting of indigenous industry (symbolized by the deliberate barbarity with which, on at least two occasions, the British ordered the thumbs of whole communities of Indian weavers chopped off so that they could not compete with the products of Lancashire); the creation of a landless peasantry (through land settlement acts that vested ownership in complaisant zamindars created by the British to maintain rural order; and general poverty, hunger and underdevelopment... British rule gave India a political unity...but also sowed a disunity rooted in sectarianism.

The final parting between Britain and India in 1947 was a remarkably friendly and civilised affair, considering the partition of India, the human suffering it had caused in both India and Pakistan, and suspicion of Britain's responsibility in the tragedy through its policies of 'divide and rule'. Bhikhu Parekh marvels at the fact that Lord Mountbatten, "the man who was responsible for most mismanaging the partition" was invited by India to stay on as Governor-General.

Independent India, especially with Jawaharlal Nehru as Prime Minister felt that it could do with Britain's help in playing its due role in international affairs. It also wanted British goodwill, just as British seemed to need Indian's respect and goodwill despite all that had happened between them in the preceding decades.

But India could hardly ignore the fact that in Britain, while there was goodwill for India and admiration and respect for leaders like Mahatma Gandhi and Jawaharlal Nehru, there was also widespread scepticism about the prospects for India's future stability, peace and democracy, and even its modern identity.

From Britain's viewpoint, India's support for decolonisation, leadership of the Non-Aligned Movement, the tendency of being somewhat permissive in regard to Soviet misadventures (Hungary) while taking the high moral ground on similar Western follies (Suez), created question marks about India's intentions *vis-à-vis* the West.

India's disappointment with Britain was all the more acute because it had problems even when the Labour Party—believed to be more sympathetic towards India, much appreciated for its support in earlier years for India's independence, its stand against racism and discrimination and on Third World issues—was in power. In 1947-48, it was a Labour government that rejected India's request for military aid; in the 1965 Indo-Pakistan War, again it was a Labour Prime Minister, Harold Wilson, who hastily (and wrongly) named India as the aggressor. And later, it was mainly Labour leaders like Gerald Kaufman, Roy Hattersley, Max Madden who took anti-India positions because of pressures from their pro-Pakistan voters.

Britain's attempts to equate India with Pakistan whenever there were serious India-Pakistan tensions (1965, 1971), its support to the US policy of militarising Pakistan, its somewhat unhelpful attitudes on the Kashmir disputes (in India's view), created tensions. Former Foreign Secretary Rasgotra has described the deep concern in India, both under Indira Gandhi as well as Rajiv Gandhi rule, at Britain's apparent unwillingness rather than inability to act firmly against UK-based Indian origin sympathisers of violent extremists in Punjab and Kashmir through the seventies and eighties. An angry Rajiv Gandhi resorted first to a virtual freeze on Indo-British economic relations (1984) and later a "broad-fronted restriction in all Indo-British dealings" (1987), because Britain would not move, despite the assassination on British soil of an Indian diplomat, Ravindra Mhatre in Birmingham, or even after India Gandhi's assassination at the hands of a Sikh militant in her security entourage. For a year and a half, there were no defence or commercial contracts awarded to Britain, no VVIP or VIP visits, British aid offers were bluntly rejected, the British High Commissioner lost his privileged access to senior levels of the Government in New Delhi.

Throughout this period, there was a new developing reality in the Indo-British interaction: the increase in size of the Indian community. In 1947, there were barely 5,000-8,000 Indians in the UK. In the late fifties and early sixties, there was a sudden influx of immigrants from rural Punjab, seeking new opportunities in *vilayat* before the Commonwealth restrictions on immigration came into force. For a decade after the early sixties, there was a steady flow of persons of Indian origin, mostly British passport holders, fleeing discrimination and worse from countries like Uganda. There was also an increase in the number of Indian professionals coming on work permits. This phenomenon of a visible increase in the Indian-origin population in Britain provoked reactions of a racial kind, still remembered through utterances such as Enoch Powell's infamous "rivers of blood" speech. It cast a shadow on the bilateral relationship, even if the official policy of the government of India was not to involve itself with the interests of the Indian diaspora settled in other countries.

In another way, the tendency of British politicians to appease their increasingly important Indian and Pakistani constituents even when they were being pressurised to take anti-India postures in Parliament (e.g. on Khalistan, Kashmir, human rights) and the remarkable insensitivity of the British Government to Indian demands to take stronger action against anti-India militant activity from or indeed on British soil, threatened to make the Indian community in Britain a source of concern rather than an asset in bilateral relations. Despite the excellent rapport that Mrs. Thatcher and Mrs. Indira Gandhi enjoyed at a personal level, they could not prevent a serious deterioration in the bilateral ties, and this was almost entirely due to the differing perceptions on how activities of some sections of the Indian community in the UK should be handled.

Up until the early nineties, given the recurring problems, divergent approaches, conflicting compulsions not to speak of deep-rooted misperceptions on both sides, most observers would have been reconciled to the reality that India and Britain, despite their shared assets and considerable national competitive strengths, were condemned to remain 'friendly' at best, but never 'great friends'.

But by the turn of the nineties, and in subsequent years several things have happened that have completely transformed and significantly upgraded the nature and long term objectives of the bilateral relationship. At the global level, the end of the Cold War signified the emergence of a unipolar world order. India with Narasimha Rao as Prime Minister and Manmohan Singh as Finance Minister launched itself on the route of economic reforms in 1991, opening up a totally new future for economic cooperation with other countries. The Indian community in the UK, at more than a million, was now high profile, successful, active and a source of jobs, wealth, funds and could no longer be ignored either by India or by the UK as a potentially important asset for either country or in their bilateral ties. Their sizeable presence in key marginal constituencies made them a political force; but relations with India outweighed pressure from such constituents for irresponsible politics in Parliament. Most important, there was now acceptance that militant activities against India should be prevented on British soil, in Britain's own interests as much as to satisfy Indian demands. India's demand for an Extradition Treaty, on which the Thatcher Government for some inexplicable reason had dragged its feet, received a favourable response now. Similarly, another long standing Indian grievance, of always equating India and Pakistan, began to be addressed.

These positive developments owed much to John Major, who had succeeded Margaret Thatcher as Prime Minister. Whatever his ratings in Britain may have been, he was an instant hit in India— his admiration for Sachin Tendulkar, passion for Indian curry, relaxed informality, recognition of India as a force for peace and stability in international affairs and respect for India's point of view on a range of issues, won him much affection. India's gesture of inviting him to be the Chief Guest on its Republic Day in January, 1993 was significant in symbolic as well as substantive terms. Heads of State or Government from various countries had until now witnessed the Republic Day Parade on India's national day, but to invite the Prime Minister of Britain, given the colonial background and recurring irritants in the relationship, had hitherto never been considered seriously. Besides, there was always the possibility of the political opposition, of the day, creating a major controversy to embarrass any government trying to honour Britain on India's day of national pride. In the event, the Congress Government of Narasimha Rao consulted the Opposition and obtained its endorsement to inviting Major without difficulty—a clear cross-party expression of support for a more mature, durable relationship based on solid mutual political, trade and economic interests as also a recognition of the more conscious British effort being made under Major to understand Indian concerns, interests and priorities.

Major was accompanied by a powerful business delegation, overruling advisors who felt that this might be inappropriate since the blasts at economic targets in Mumbai in retaliation for the destruction of the Ayodhya mosque took place shortly before the visit—an emphatic assertion of confidence in India which went down very well with Indian public opinion. The Indo-British

Partnership was set up during the visit, and a new chapter was initiated in bilateral relations. While the Labour opposition in Britain felt somewhat marginalised by all this bonhomie, the soundness of the political judgement underpinninig Major's India policies was confirmed a few years later, when Major was replaced by Tony Blair. The latter has gone even further in displaying understanding both of India's sensitivities as well as India's potential and actual importance on the world and its relevance to Britain's present and future interests. The quality of the bilateral relationship today, described as "the best it as ever been", owes much to Blair's vision.

Today, not only are there very frequent high level visits between the two countries, these have been institutionalised. Moreover, there are regular business summits, a security dialogue, a defence consultative group, a joint working group on international terrorism and drug trafficking, and an India-UK consultation on strategic issues. Both countries being vibrant democracies, an important addition to this basket of institutional interactions is the existence of 'Friends of India Groups' within each of the major British parties, in addition to the famous 'Curry Club', the Indo-British Parliamentary Group in London, and the recently established Indo-British Parliamentary Forum in New Delhi.

Both countries have embarked on firming up a 'strategic partnership' which takes into account present as well as likely future issues and priorities at a global, regional and national level. The 'Prime Ministers' Initiative' signed by Tony Blair and Dr. Manmohan Singh on 20 September 2004 identifies the key areas for cooperation:

- foreign and defence policy, including the fight against proliferation of weapons of mass destruction;
- the war against terror;
- combating illegal immigration;
- expanding two-way trade and investment;
- cooperation in science and technology;
- sustainable development, with special focus on environment; and
- further expansion of educational and cultural links.

Interestingly, a report commissioned by the British Foreign and Commonwealth Office identifies a number of strategic international priorities for the UK over the next 5-10 years, among which are:

- making the world safer from global terrorism and weapons of mass destruction;

- reducing the harm to the UK from international crime, including drug trafficking;

- preventing and resolving conflict through a strong international system;

- building an effective and globally competitive EU in a secure neighbourhood;

- promoting sustainable development and poverty reduction under pinned by human rights, democracy and good governance; and

- managing migration and combating illegal immigration.

India is identified as a country with which the UK must seek to build strategic relations in a number of these sectors.

It may be useful at this stage to give a broad brush picture of the extent of cooperation in some of the sectors mentioned above.

Terrorism

Britain, which barely a decade ago was sceptical and unreceptive in regard to Indian pleas for cooperation against terrorism, is now one of India's key partners along with the US in containing this threat. 9/11, and the terrorist attacks inside Britain, have accelerated the change in Britain's approach which was apparent after the mid-nineties. The UK-India Joint Working Group on terrorism meets regularly, operational-level links are strong, and intelligence sharing increasingly effective. British concerns about dealing with extremism and Islamic fundamentalism are areas in which India's inputs could be invaluable, given its long experience in this sector. Given the increasing complexity and possible involvement of 'indigenous Islamic' fundamentalists in terrorist acts in both countries, the challenge will be to bring sanity to the war on terror as much as to fight terror, so that the pluralistic ethos which both countries attach so much importance to is not endangered.

The UK and India are working together to promote in the UN the Comprehensive Convention for the Suppression of International Terrorism.

Trade and investment ties

There has been a steady expansion as well as diversification of trade and investment links. While bilateral trade has increased in both directions, so have investments. India is the third largest foreign investor in the UK just as the UK is the third largest investor in India.

The UK is successful in attracting investment from India because it allows dynamic businesses to grasp new opportunities, technologies and markets through agility and innovation in an open and cost-effective environment. With its strong economy, policy of free trade, international competition and commitment to deregulation, the UK is often the favoured best place in Europe for starting a business. The UK does not only offer its own domestic market, it is a gateway to the massive market of Europe of over 500 million consumers—larger than the US, Canada and Japan combined. The UK has the largest amount of venture capital available in all of Europe. British companies are creating wealth at three times the rate of their European counterparts. The UK also has one of the lowest corporate tax rates in Europe with a top rate of 30 per cent and the top rate of personal tax is one of Europe's lowest (40 per cent). Finally, labour costs in the UK are considerably less than in Germany, the Netherlands and Belgium.

The UK accounts for 3.7 per cent of India's total foreign trade in goods; trade in services has grown by 4.7 per cent, accounting for as much as 25 per cent total of bilateral trade. Two-way trade of goods and services between India and the UK has doubled since 1993; over 2447 new Indo-British joint ventures have been approved by the Government of India since August 1991. The UK is India's fourth largest trading partner. It accounted for 3.7 per cent of India's total foreign trade in goods in 2004-05. Trade in services grew by 4.7 per cent and accounted for 25 per cent of total bilateral trade in 2003. Increasingly, most major British companies consider it 'business critical' to have partnerships in India. These partnerships are vital in developing the competitiveness of British business.

UK is the third biggest inward investor in India (it has the third largest share of new investments approved since 1991—9.5 per cent— well ahead of Germany, Japan and France). Mauritius and USA are the top two investors. In effect, therefore, Britain is next after the US. Top sectors for UK FDI to India include power, oil and gas, telecom and service industries.

Hi-tech sectors, R&D, science and technology

The coming years should see more cooperation in biotech, healthcare, pharmaceuticals, automotive, engineering, ICT and other hi-tech areas.

Indian companies are finding the intellectual capital offered by the UK essential in developing their global presence. There have been major R&D investments by Indian firms in UK, particularly in IT and pharmaceutical sectors.

The UK is experiencing strong interest from Indian ICT and biotech companies, partly because Indian companies recognise the UK's massive investment in the science base, making the UK an ideal place to conduct R&D. This may not be very widely known, but the UK is an R&D world leader—in biotechnology, telecommunications, performance engineering, computing, electronics, satellite design and construction, and alternative energy technologies. It has an innovative culture and high-tech expertise that attracts Indian businesses looking for high skills and technological insights. With 1 per cent of the world's population, the UK conducts 4.5 per cent of the world's science and produces 8 per cent of the world's scientific papers. The UK has been involved in some of the leading innovations of the past 25 years. These include the internet, the cellphone with GSM services, GPRS, dual mode 3G started in the UK, the first programmable computer was invented about 50 years ago in the UK, and the UK created fibre optics.

The UK and India both foresee future economic benefit flowing from scientific and technological breakthroughs. And both governments recognise the value of international collaboration. India has traditional strengths in agricultural science and pure and theoretical sciences, especially chemistry and mathematics and has become a world leader in IT, particularly software development. It has developing strengths in medicine and pharmaceuticals, biotechnology, nuclear technologies, space sciences and energy technologies.

There is growing interest in the UK about what is going on in Indian science, more Indian students are studying in the UK and visits by scientists in both directions are increasing. Investment is also increasing, including the example of AstraZeneca setting up a tuberculosis research facility in Bangalore.

Development cooperation

In the area of aid, India is the largest single recipient of British bilateral aid receiving 200 million pounds in a year. Of late, the focus of aid programmes has shifted to areas like power, water, health and education.

DFID (the British Department for overseas aid) has been implementing programmes to assist the Indian Central and selected State Governments to achieve the poverty reduction objectives of the Government of India's Tenth Plan and the internationally agreed Millennium Development Goals (MDGs).

These national programmes include the District Primary Education Programme (DPEP), health interventions (AIDS, TB, Polio) and direct financial support to the activities of several partner agencies, including the ADB, World Bank and number of UN organisations. These activities are much appreciated in India.

Education

The British Council operation in India is one of the world's largest. It constitutes a real engagement of education, culture, science and technology. Up to 700 scholarship awards are offered to Indians by UK institutions each year. The flow of students to

UK is rising: currently 16,000 students a year go to study in the UK (up from 1000 over the last decade). In addition, increasing numbers of Indian students are studying for UK qualifications in India *via* distance/virtual learning through partnership in India with UK accredited institutions.

Defence

The Indo-UK defence relationship has never been stronger. The modern relationship has been developed through the India-UK Defence Consultative Group (DCG). Established in 1995, the DCG meets annually (the venue alternates between Delhi and London) and is co-chaired by the UK Permanent Under Secretary of State for Defence and his Indian equivalent. It has three sub-groups, covering military to military contacts, defence equipment and research and technology.

The bilateral programme of exercises, exchanges, training courses and high-level visits continues to accelerate. Activity level have tripled since 2002-03. Highlights include an average of five friendship visits per year. Furthermore, the heads of all three services and the British Chief of Defence Staff have visited each other's countries over the last three years.

There is a long-standing bilateral defence equipment relationship, including sales to India of Canberra, Jaguar and Sea Harrier combat aircrafts, ex-RN aircraft carriers, VIP/transport aircraft and Sea King helicopters. More recently (March 2004), a contract (initially worth 795 million to UK) for 66 Hawk Advanced Jet Trainers from BAE Systems was agreed; this is progressing well. Defence equipment cooperation continues, especially with radars, army communications networks, VVIP helicopters, naval support vessels and upgrades to existing equipment.

Financial services

In the area of financial services, the ceilings on FDI in Indian financial institutions are being progressively lifted, with the result that more and more foreign banks are positioning themselves for acquisition and expansion in the Indian capital market. India has a number of advantages as compared with other emerging markets, and its regulatory and policy track record are both well deserved. British banks and financial institutions have traditional links with India and could take advantage of them in the new situation. Similarly, Indian financial institutions will increasingly have a role in the British financial market.

What does the UK expect from the bilateral relationship in the coming years? A British study, "India-Britain 2020" offers the following:

- greater awareness and understanding of India on the part of UK's decision and opinion makers across a range of departments to the "long term significance of developments in the Indian subcontinent" comparable to those in North America, Europe and China;

- enhanced Indo-British cooperation on a number of global concerns, e.g. promoting democracy and stability in South Asia; promoting liberalisation in services and agriculture; combating terrorism and drug trafficking;

- sharp increase in number of Indian student achievers in the UK comparing favourably with those studying in the US;

- major increase in number of Indian companies investing in UK, especially in hi-tech areas such as IT and pharmaceuticals;

- sharp increase in UK investments in India in financial services and infrastructure, as well as energy, tourism, R&D;

- substantive involvement of British engineering and other Companies in India's energy, water and telecom sectors;

- major increase in Indian tourism in Britain and *vice versa*;

- development of medical tourism and cooperation in health-care between the Indian private and public sector health services;

- Emergence of the UK, as an important supplier of India's advanced weapons and training requirements.

One has not seen a similar attempt to identify what India's expectations from Britain would be, but the following would possibly not be far off the mark:

- total cooperation on all terrorist related activity in South Asia;

- respect for Indian sensitivities in regard to relations with difficult neighbours;

- support for India's role on the world stage on par with the major powers;

- easing of visa restrictions for travel to Britain and Europe;

- facilitating higher study in the UK for deserving students from disadvantaged communities;

- intensified cooperation in creating R&D hubs, world-class infrastructure, export-oriented manufacturing units;

- visible results in the search for energy security;

- massive investments in high-tech industries;

- major strides in enhancing Indian capacities in agriculture, rural development, food processing, and

- continued support for and expanded cooperation in the health sector.

It is ironic that just when Britain seems to have discovered the importance of India and its relevance to its own interests, many Indians are not sure about the importance of the British connection for India. It is true that Britain's economic and political weight are unlikely to increase in the medium term, going by present trends. Its projected growth rate will be far more modest as compared to that of the US; its manufacturing base is on the decline; having hitched its wagon to the EU, it will also have to suffer if, as expected, the EU stalemate in the deepening/widening process is a protracted one. It is also possible that some of its current competitive strengths—tolerance of diversity, low labour costs—would come under pressure because of the range of challenges it will have to tackle—containing Islamic extremism without creating anti-Moslem sentiments; adjusting to an ageing demographic profile without creating social tensions; and so on. But the intangible assets which have been the real source of Britain's competitive strength –language and easy communication; superior education systems; great political stability; fair commercial and business practices—will in fact remain, and make Britain even more attractive as a partner in a world of expanding opportunities.

Moreover, the logic of a future strategic relationship goes beyond simple bilateral mutuality in commercial terms. Britain is a world power with considerable influence in a number of key bodies which have a major role in world affairs—the G7, the UN Security Council, to name just two. Britain has taken the lead to invite India to the G7 when it chaired the Summit at Gleneagles in 2005, and has followed it up with a suggestion that India should become a permanent member of that Group. Similarly, Britain has taken the lead in endorsing the Indian bid for permanent membership of the Security Council. The quality of cooperation in other areas, for e.g. in the war against terror can hardly be exaggerated. In areas like R&D, services, education, infrastructre development, co-production arrangements for the global market, the potential is immense.

37

The India-US joint statement of July 18, 2005—a year later

Shyam Saran

It is a little unusual to revisit a Joint Statement agreed upon a year ago. More often than not, Joint Statements recede rapidly from public memory. I can think of very few other Joint Statements that have been dissected in as much detail as this one. What is so special about the July 18 Joint Statement that it warrants an analysis even a year later? Is it in any way a defining document of our contemporary diplomacy? Does it have a significance beyond the subject matter it addresses? Does it depart from our orthodox positions on important issues? The answer is yes to all of the above queries, in greater or lesser measure.

Before we get to the Joint Statement itself, let us spend a little time understanding how we got there in the first place. July 18, 2005 was not an overnight happening. Nor was it conceived in a vacuum. It, in fact, represents a culmination of steps, spanning a number of governments, and made possible as a result of the trust and confidence that had been incrementally built up between the two countries. The broad range of cooperation that it offers reflects a larger engagement over many years between our two societies.

There were six key developments that merged to create the basis for July 18. First and foremost, an India growing at the rate of 8 per cent per annum has led to a very different attitude on the part of the US towards India. This may be stating the obvious, but I am not sure how many of us appreciate its consequences. Ambassador Blackwill's erstwhile description of our trade being "as flat as a *chapatti*" is now a distant memory. Bilateral trade, in fact, has been growing at a healthy 20 per cent plus annually and we are now the fastest growing export market for the US. An India of high growth rates creates new demands for goods, services and technologies that a global trading nation like the US cannot ignore. The experience of companies already operating in India has been positive, as indeed has been their profitability. It has taken us some time, but we have clearly caught America's attention; and not merely as an investment destination. There is recognition that India too can produce world-class companies—in manufacturing as well as in services. India is today being invariably equated with China in terms of potential and possibilities.

A second significant element is that of the new calculus that India is a nuclear weapon power. This has made a compelling case for greater engagement with India. We saw that manifested, for example, in the 'Next Steps in Strategic Partnership' initiative of January 2004. The acknowledgement, on July 18, of India as a country with an impeccable record in non-proliferation of weapons of mass destruction and as a responsible state with advanced nuclear technology is noteworthy.

A third development is the larger strategic canvas that argues in favour of raising the quality of Indo-US ties. As a pluralistic and secular democracy in a world where fundamentalist violence is on the rise, India's emergence as a model of stability, modernisation and predictability, has begun to impact on international consciousness. To this has been added a healthy respect for our capabilities that have been steadily growing across the board. We have become a major interlocutor on key global challenges—from environment and pandemics, to counter-terrorism and disaster relief. The US strategic assessment of India is articulated both in its *National Security Strategy* of March 2006 and the *Quadrennial Defense Review Report* of February 2006. The NSS speaks of India as a major power shouldering global obligations. Similarly, the QDR refers to India, along with China and Russia, as key factors in determining the international security environment for the 21st Century.

A fourth element in the US approach to India has been its awareness of the potential that our partnership holds in respect of the knowledge economy. Interestingly, the majority of our current initiatives, in one form or the other, are strongly knowledge-based— be it S&T, agriculture research, energy issues, space, atomic energy, health or high-technology. We have heard from the highest levels in the US how much importance they attach to cooperating with a society that produces graduates by the millions and engineers, technicians and doctors by the hundreds of thousands. There is growing awareness as well of our demographic advantages. We note this in the US National Intelligence Council's 2020 report on *Mapping the Global Future* that argues that new service sector jobs in India (and China) could exceed availability of similar skills in advanced economies. The report predicts that this would lead to a surge in technology applications, which in turn could lead to new international alignments.

A fifth point to be noted is that these developments are part and parcel of India opening up to the world. The impact of India integrating with the global economy cannot be underestimated, least of all on its leading player, the United States. This is not just in terms of business, services or even connectivity. Indians are making a visible impact on the rest of the world and certainly in the US, this is symbolised by the success of the Indian-American community. Two million Indians have not only established an enviable professional reputation but have a median income 50 per cent more than the national average. Their image, over the years, has helped to shape ours.

As an open society and an open economy, the growth in India's capabilities has been welcomed by the world. Our record and our worldview give no cause for apprehension in any quarter. At the same time, there is no reason to remind us that we have an obligation to the world from which we all draw sustenance. Even in the past, when our resources were less, India has contributed towards addressing global challenges to the best of its ability, including the use of its military forces in UN peacekeeping missions. As the 2004-05 tsunami relief efforts demonstrated, this approach stands reaffirmed with greater capacities at our command. That was why the July 18 Joint Statement envisaged the establishment of a global partnership as part of the transformation of our ties.

The United States is clearly the pre-eminent power of our times. There can be no argument that better relations with the US are in our national interest. It is our largest trade partner, investor and technology source. Equally important, as the pre-eminent power, the US helps shape global sentiment. From the economic perspective, initiatives with the US can advance our development processes and accelerate our growth rate. Technologically, a partnership with the US would enormously benefit a country like India whose future is so tied to the knowledge and service industries. There are strong security convergences between us, be it on terrorism, maritime security or other threats from non-state actors. From the political perspective, stronger ties make themselves positively felt on our relations with third countries. Domestically, India is seeking to leapfrog in its development process. In foreign policy, we require adjustments in the international order so that our aspirations are accommodated. A stronger relationship with the US can offer benefits on both fronts. The challenge to Indian diplomacy, of course, is to maximise the gains while minimising the costs, and create an international environment that is supportive of our developmental goals.

It was with this approach that we embarked on a process that led to the July 18 Joint Statement. In doing so, we sought to synchronise our diplomacy much more closely with the changes that have taken place in India over the last 15 years. Our objective was that India, which was making such strenuous efforts domestically to catch up with the world, should craft a foreign policy that supported and acted as a multiplier on those efforts. Rising expectations are as relevant to diplomacy as they are to impelling an improvement in the quality of life. India's diplomats have to do their share in ensuring, for example, that our energy security was effectively met. It was important that we were not left out of global research initiatives. Or that our access to global natural resources was not hindered in any way. And, that the interests of our industry and our services sector were well served by creating expanding opportunities for our talented professionals worldwide.

July 18, marks our determination to put behind us an era of defensive diplomacy. If India is to become a credible candidate for permanent membership of the Security Council, then we must adjust our traditional positions. Our foreign policy must reflect our national aspirations and express our confidence as an emerging global player. We cannot duck the difficult issues of the day and display an aversion to risk taking. July 18 is, in some ways, an effort to usher in a change in mindset.

The Joint Statement of July 18 covers three clusters of issues: (i) those that directly address our national development goals and reflect the leveraging of Indo-US ties to advance those goals; (ii) the dismantling of the technology denial regimes that constrain Indo-US cooperation and the medium term emergence of India as the leading knowledge-enabled power; and (iii) the key global responsibilities that India and the United States need to address.

The three key constraints on the further growth of the Indian economy are that we are woefully behind in our lack of a modern infrastructure, in agricultural productivity and commerce, and in energy security. These three concerns form the tripod on which the Indo-US developmental agenda currently rests. On July 18, we agreed to set up a CEOs Forum to harness private sector energies and ideas to revitalise our economic cooperation. The very composition of this Forum, that includes 10 key CEOs from each country, reflects how differently we regard each other today. The Forum has presented its report to the Prime Minister and President Bush in March 2006 and its recommendations are currently being examined. Infrastructure modernisation through a dedicated fund is among them, and we should expect to hear more from the planned Investment Summit at the end of the year.

In agriculture, we have embarked on an ambitious knowledge initiative that seeks to revive the traditions of the Green Revolution by linking our educational institutions. We have, worked out a detailed three-year work plan that covers agricultural education and training, biotechnology, water management, and food processing and agro-business.

On energy, our dialogue has catalysed activity across the entire spectrum. As a result of post-July 18 discussions, we have been able to finalise Indian participation in the FutureGen Initiative dealing with clean coal and the Integrated Ocean Drilling Programme, dealing with gas hydrates. A number of energy efficiency activities and programmes have also been initiated. Indian participation in the ITER fusion energy initiative was another important result of the July 18 commitments, catapulting India into a select group of advanced countries, namely the EU, France, Russia, China, Japan and South Korea to collaborate in an area of science of enormous promise for meeting our future energy needs.

The dismantling of the technology denial regimes, led by the US—but imposed by other advanced countries as well—has been a key objective of the Indo-US nuclear deal. For historical reasons, what began as the imposition of limitations on India's access to nuclear technology and equipment after our PNE in 1974, steadily expanded over the ensuing years to cover virtually the entire high-tech field on grounds that most advanced technologies have dual uses. In dismantling these denial regimes and enabling our business and industry to access dual use technologies, the nuclear deal will really be the key that will open this lock. While it may be true that the denial of such technologies has, in some cases, encouraged indigenous innovation and led to outstanding achievements by our scientists, an increasingly globalised and competitive world demands a different response. As the Indian economy matures, and moves towards an ever more sophisticated knowledge and technology driven society, the importance of dismantling these technology denial regimes cannot be underestimated. This will also create opportunities for our scientists and technologists to benefit from regular interaction with their counterparts in the rest of the world and bring to the table their own considerable achievements in several fields.

Even as we seek to put the era of technology denial behind us, parallel initiatives have been undertaken to build a more durable S&T partnership between us. In July 2005, we agreed to sign an S&T framework agreement, which was done that September, along with a protocol that addressed IPR generation issues. By March 2006, we were ready to announce a Bi-National S&T Commission that is now under implementation. We need to nourish exchanges and build capacities that would strengthen technology innovation and applications. India lags far behind in its generation of patents, which is the hallmark of a competitive industrial culture. Participation in international S&T exchanges and initiatives, not only with the US, but other partners as well, will be one of the key priorities for our diplomacy.

Global issues of common concern are an intrinsic aspect of the emerging Indo-US strategic partnership. An important initiative was the promotion of democratic capacities in emerging democracies. India has valuable experience through the ITEC programme in building civic society and contributing to the strengthening of democratic institutions. We have joined the US to launch the UN Democracy Fund last September. Combating terrorism is another important shared goal and we have ongoing exchanges and activities in that direction. Pandemics are yet another common challenge that we have chosen to address and our cooperation on HIV/AIDS and avian flu has yielded beneficial results. We have also agreed upon a disaster relief initiative and a maritime cooperation framework that draws upon the new Defence Framework that we finalised in June 2005.

The nuclear issue has dominated the public discourse on Indo-US relations since July 2005 and in March 2006, we completed discussions with the US Government on a range of issues including supply assurances, that allowed us to finalise the Separation Plan. These discussions were based on a clear understanding that the nuclear deal was about civil nuclear energy cooperation between India and the US and not about India's strategic programme. In pursuing such cooperation, India was, however, willing to provide assurances that what it received as part of international cooperation from the US and other partners would not be diverted to third countries, and would not be diverted to non-civilian uses within India. We reject any limitation on our strategic programme, but we do not expect our partners to, in any way, assist that programme either. Our part of commitments having been delivered upon, the US is now engaged in adjusting its laws to enable full civil nuclear energy cooperation with India.

We are, quite clear that India cannot undertake any obligations going beyond the July 18 Joint Statement and the Separation Plan. India's obligations will only be those that we undertake in the bilateral 123 cooperation agreement and the safeguards arrangement with the IAEA.

It has been asked whether our strategic options are not being restricted as a result of the July 18 commitment to continue our voluntary moratorium. This is not a new commitment, even in a bilateral understanding. In 1998, in the UN General Assembly, we had expressed a willingness not only to continue the moratorium but also to move towards its *de jure* formalisation. The Separation Plan has also been depicted by some analysts as eroding the vigour of our strategic deterrent.

July 18 is a milestone in the road to realise our aspirations. It is something of a departure from the beaten track, but one necessary for the times. Our mission is to realise its full potential, to create new opportunities to advance our national goals.

Edited version of the Address delivered at India Habitat Centre, New Delhi, July 2006.

38

India and USA: new directions

S. Jaishankar

Relations between India and the United States have surged in the last two years. The announcements after Prime Minister Manmohan Singh's talks with President Bush in Washington DC on 18 July 2005 laid out the full extent of the transformation underway in the relationship. Eight months later, President Bush's visit to India in March 2006 provided confirmation that rapid progress was being made in implementing the agreed agenda. Spanning a wide range of economic and trade goals, energy and environment concerns, science and technology collaboration and defence and security cooperation, the strategic partnership between the two countries has clearly moved beyond rhetoric into substance. A convergence of interests in meeting key global challenges has also gained recognition in the process, encouraging the two countries to work more closely together.

It is the nuclear understanding reached in July 2005 that really symbolises this new phase of partnership. If successfully implemented, it would put an end to the era of technology denials and help address India's energy security needs. By expending considerable domestic and international political capital to make an exception for India, the deal also sends a political message about the transformation that this understanding portends for Indo-US relations. The unfolding of the process of building this strategic partnership and forecasting the likely directions of growth are the twin themes of this chapter. Every analysis must have a starting point, but identifying one for a dynamic process is difficult. Therefore, this account walks backwards—beginning with the current state of play and then analysing how we reached there. The framework of the 18 July 2005 and 2 March 2006 Joint Statements, issued after the two summit-level meetings, is the appropriate point to start.

The breadth and intensity of the engagement with the United States contemplated in this framework is unique in terms of India's relations with foreign partners. It could be argued that this is not unnatural, given that the United States is indeed the pre-eminent power in the world today. But then, it has been that for years without apparently making that much of an impact on India. It is also India's largest trade partner, the biggest source of foreign direct investment, the major collaborator in technology and a home for a particularly successful Indian community. None of that is a sudden discovery either. What can be safely said is that the objective conditions for the transformation of Indo-US relations had been created by 2005. But it would be a mistake to attribute to what took place in July that year an inevitable character. The framework we are examining is not a passive one, where structural trends unfolded by themselves. Instead, it is a construct of active initiatives, based on conscious policy choices, of engaging the US across the board. Many of these efforts are specifically targeted, while others are broader in their intent. Some are practical and immediate, others more aspirational and long term. Their cumulative impact, however, brings out the full extent of a strategic relationship that is now taking form.

Since the new phase of Indo-US ties is symbolised by the nuclear understanding of July 2005, this must then be the focus of our analysis. Briefly put, the deal was that despite India remaining outside the NPT and maintaining a strategic programme, the United States was prepared to amend its domestic laws and bring about adjustments in the international regime for the resumption of international cooperation with India in civilian nuclear energy. India was also to be included in key international research initiatives, such as on fusion energy. Obviously, since India continued to maintain a strategic programme, it would have to reassure potential partners that cooperation was not diverted in that direction. To ensure this, India was required to prepare a separation plan of its civilian and military facilities, and place its civilian facilities under the IAEA safeguards. India also agreed to conclude an Additional Protocol with the IAEA that strengthens the effectiveness of the safeguards system. There was also a reasonable expectation that India's export control regime would ensure that there was no risk of technology leakage to third countries. This was done through harmonisation with NSG/MTCR guidelines and the introduction of comprehensive export control legislation. The deal required India to undertake to refrain from transferring enrichment and reprocessing technologies to nations that do not have them and support international efforts to limit their spread. Other commitments made by India were to reiterate the continuation of its unilateral moratorium on nuclear testing and work with the US for the conclusion of a multilateral FMCT. Obviously, the key concept underlying the understanding was the recognition of India as a 'responsible state with advanced nuclear technology'. In plainer English, this meant that India's strategic programme was accepted as a reality and that its behaviour and record made it an acceptable partner in the non-proliferation context for whom an exception could be politically justified.

In retrospect, it seems a little perplexing that the 18 July deal came as such a surprise. After all, Indian and American diplomacy had been grappling with this challenge since 1998. During the Clinton Administration, extensive discussions took place between teams led by Foreign Minister Jaswant Singh and Deputy Secretary Strobe Talbott. In the first Bush Administration, these threads had been picked up, leading eventually to the Next Steps in Strategic Partnership (NSSP) initiative announced in January 2004. The United States had accepted the reality of a nuclear India and was willing to relax some of the particularly stringent export control measures that targeted the Indian industry. Looking back, it would appear that the 18 July understanding was simultaneously a continuity with the past and yet a radical departure from it. The continuity reflected the momentum of earlier initiatives and it would only be fair to acknowledge that that these represented critical confidence building measures. For example, the NSSP provided for end-use verification measures that were finalised in September 2004. It envisaged a comprehensive export control legislation that was passed in May 2005, as well as adherence to NSG and MTCR guidelines. Without them, it is unlikely that the Bush Administration would have made the leap of faith that it did in July 2005. On the other hand, it was equally evident that the earlier initiatives were significantly inhibited by having to function within an orthodox NPT construct. A US participant once described the NSSP as a compromise between those in the US who wanted to do business with nuclear India and those who did not. Till July 2005, it was precisely this halfway house approach that prevented a decisive breakthrough. Any consensus that emerged from a broad process in Washington, particularly a bottom up one, was inevitably a dilute one. A full-blooded approach had to be leadership driven, and that is exactly what happened in the discussions leading up to 18 July 2005. Another complicating factor was a residual belief in an India/Pakistan equivalence, which made it virtually impossible to carve out an exception for India. Conventional Washington remained grudging and half-hearted in its acceptance of nuclear India, leading to an obsession with fissile material production moratorium and 'strategic restraint'. That the solution to the longstanding impasse could be a weapons-neutral one—neither seeking a cap or rollback on India's part nor facilitating an expansion of the strategic programme—was something few had envisaged.

The 18 July understanding broke decisively with the past, willing to revisit fundamentals and discard those orthodoxies that prevented a coming to terms with reality. There was a recognition that an insistence on a fissile material production moratorium or on strategic restraint would only lead to a dead end. On the Indian side too, the understanding required a new boldness and greater self-confidence. Raising the stakes from tactical concessions for temporary fuel supply to comprehensively addressing the challenge of technology denial regimes was not an easy decision to make. The legacy of the past—particularly Tarapur—intruded sharply into the present, even if few actually grasped previous history. Unsuccessful attempts at engagement only strengthened suspicions at the Indian end, putting trust and confidence at a premium. An elite little used to dealing constructively with the United States and consequently unversed in its political processes found it difficult to comprehend an iconoclastic Administration bent on reshaping the world. The diplomatic strategy that produced the 18 July 2005 understanding, however, derived from an analysis of the global situation that envisaged leveraging opportunities that it offered, and a holistic and long-term view of India's national development.

The first reactions to the nuclear understanding when it was announced were undeniably positive, more so in India than perhaps in the United States. There was a broad understanding that the deal represented a goal that Indian diplomacy had been pursuing for years, if not for decades. The obligations of India were also generally perceived to be in conformity with the requirements of maintaining a credible minimum deterrent. Beyond the nuclear issue, it was also appreciated that the understanding signified something special in India's ties with the United States and demonstrated India's arrival on the global scene. For years, the nuclear differences had poisoned the entire well of the relationship. Proponents of better ties felt that it was time that this thorn is removed from its throat. The United States would no longer have to bear the political burden of enforcing a set of rules targeting India. Without that, major initiatives in any field would eventually flounder on this critical difference. The reactions of other nations to the 18 July understanding only confirmed its political significance. Whether they were positive and welcoming, or critical of the exception made, or even arguing for similar treatment for another nation, the fact was that the world stood up and took notice. On the US end, however, the going was considerably tougher. The Administration found itself disadvantaged initially by the lack of consultations with the Congress, understandable given that the 18 July negotiations went down to the wire. The magnitude of the exception for India was a further cause for concern, as the NPT was widely held to be one of the cornerstones of the current global order. While emphasising India's record of nuclear responsibility and restraint, the case had to be made largely in terms of the 'big picture' gains. This, however, got out of hand in the Congressional consideration process when unreasonable expectations were articulated in intemperate language. The battle between the traditional exponents of non-proliferation and the more imaginative advocates of this initiative took the form of a debate on the trade offs between non-proliferation, grand strategy, energy needs and environment. The process challenge that both sides faced was that given their internal divisions, arguments made by proponents of the understanding at one end were cited by the opponents of the deal at the other. Indian assurances on maintaining the integrity of the deterrent mutated into evidence of a weapon-building overdrive when read in Washington. Conversely, the gains for non-proliferation projected in the US Congress were deemed as proof in New Delhi that India's national security stood weakened. The challenges of conducting complicated diplomacy in an era of connectivity were truly daunting.

Difficult questions were raised about different aspects of the nuclear understanding in both countries, as indeed they should be. In India, these focussed on implications for national security and technology autonomy. In the United States, they dwelt on the consequences for the future of the NPT. Since the Indian debate was much more narrowly focussed, it also involved a high degree of detail. The necessity of entering into this understanding with the United States had to be explained in a manner where commendable Indian achievements in the face of technology denial were not diminished. This involved communicating the challenge to our economic, energy and technology growth prospects posed by the continuation of the *status quo*. The fallout of the nuclear technology denial regime on other aspects of dual use technology and high technology were more than evident. Similarly, Indian scientists were being denied an opportunity to participate in global research. Our economic growth required a rapid expansion of our civilian nuclear power programme, which was difficult in these circumstances. The current target for nuclear power was 20,000 MW by 2020, and even this target was only achievable on the assumption that we would import six reactors of 1000 MW each. Without an adjustment to the NSG Guidelines, there was little prospect of securing international cooperation. Even enriched uranium fuel for the US-supplied Tarapur reactors was posing a problem and was eventually secured only in the post-18 July environment. Interestingly, both in India and the US, arguments were made that nuclear power constituted only 3 per cent of the overall energy mix and did not warrant either the attention or the expenditure of political capital. This ignored the reality that nuclear power remained low precisely because of the post-1974 technology denial regimes and that their removal was critical if this percentage was to be raised.

India's growing energy consumption, rising oil prices, the volatility of the hydrocarbon producing region and the emissions implications of fossil fuel use were all strong arguments to revisit nuclear power at this jucture. Indeed, the Indo-US nuclear deal did not happen in isolation from global energy developments. They took place at the very time when key governments, not limited to the United States, were pushing for a revival of their nuclear industry. On India's part too, even from the narrow energy perspective, the nuclear deal happened at a time when India aggressively pursued hydrocarbon interests abroad, invested in clean coal projects, explored gas hydrates and coal bed methane, participated in the Asia Pacific Clean Development Partnership and established Energy Dialogues with the US, EU and other interlocutors.

The dismantling of technology denial regimes goes beyond nuclear energy and pertains directly to the emergence of India as a knowledge power. At a time when the service industry is growing and India is leveraging its population by developing their skills, it cannot remain impervious to technology denials becoming progressively stricter. In a world where terrorism and WMD proliferation are increasingly perceived as co-joint threats, a multiplication of international regimes of a restrictive character is only to be expected. To watch this happen without preparing a countervailing strategy would be the height of irresponsibility. Without a remedy, there will only be more examples of the licence denial of the US made Cray Supercomputer for use in weather modelling and forecasting, because it could also help in nuclear test simulations. A lasting solution for the technological upgradation of the Indian economy has to be found. In a globalised world, where growth is increasingly knowledge and technology driven, the impact of the nuclear deal cannot be underestimated. Its significance to the participation of Indian scientists and engineers in global technology initiatives is immediate. Equally, the lifting of technology restrictions will enable multinational companies, currently unable to undertake cutting-edge research work in India because of these restrictions, to do so.

Concerns about heightening our vulnerability were natural in an area with strong national security connotations. Here, the problem depends very much on how it is defined. On the one hand, India seeks to move on a technology track that would be specific to our national circumstances. On the other, our objective is to expand nuclear power and create a large and varied reservoir of nuclear skills. The import of reactors has always taken place whenever permissible, as reflected in the past import of Tarapur, Rajasthan and Kudankulam reactors over three decades. The 18 July understanding should be regarded as an enabling provision that will lead to the resumption of access to international cooperation. India will have choice once again, and it will be up to us to decide whether we should exercise it or not. It in no way binds us to sourcing technology, supplies or even fuel from a particular nation. Nor would it lead to dependency on a single partner. On the contrary, the supply assurances of the Separation Plan have exactly the hedging provision that guards against market disruptions and capricious supply cutoffs. The deal with US unlocks a larger global cooperation that is otherwise denied to us. In that sense, the US is negotiating not just on its own behalf but for the entire international community. To then evaluate this understanding purely in Indo-US terms would be doing it injustice. The costs of separation of civilian and military facilities have also been raised in the course of the debate. To a considerable degree, the separation should be regarded as a cost-irrelevant exercise. If India, with its strategic programme, was interested in resumption of international cooperation, then we are necessarily required to address the legitimate concerns of our partners that the cooperation provided by them is not diverted to our strategic programme. Curiously enough, similar separation commitments made by China to secure Australian uranium passed largely uncommented. Through appropriate identification of facilities and phasing, the separation can be carried out without incurring high costs or affecting the strategic programme negatively. A cost-benefit analysis should also reasonably factor in the economic gains of our access to international cooperation in civilian nuclear energy as well as the long-term implications of participation in global R&D.

The intrusiveness of the proposed arrangements was also to be considered, particularly as India was committed to moving into the uncharted territory of an Additional Protocol. As a declared nuclear weapon state, India obviously will have to enter into a unique India-specific safeguards arrangement and an Additional Protocol that would take this into account. We have considerable experience of implementing safeguards and will have to ensure that all national security concerns are factored in as we make our decisions. Similarly, any perception that the separation of our programme has diminished our capability to support the deterrent had to be firmly met. India has an undifferentiated programme where civilian facilities also contained strategic elements. Through the separation exercise, we have consolidated our strategic programme, while ensuring that the requisite capabilities to support a credible minimum deterrent are maintained. Ironically, an argument was made that this agreement will place India at a disadvantage *vis-à-vis* a Pakistan that will not have to separate its programme. Clearly, proponents of this view had little knowledge of either programme to even consider making such a comparison. A distorted assessment of our reiteration of the unilateral moratorium on testing also needed to be contested strongly. The 18 July Joint Statement represented the red line for the Indian side. It was, in fact, less forthcoming than a 1998 willingness to convert the moratorium into a *de jure* commitment or indeed to offer to sign the CTBT. In fact, India has not given up the right to test if it so deemed that necessary. Nor did the US draft legislation make that demand of us. If Pakistan really felt that it would be in an advantageous position as a result of the Indo-US understanding, then Pakistan itself would not be asking US for a deal similar to the India-US deal on civilian nuclear energy cooperation. Instead, Pakistani leaders have made a strong and persistent effort to be equated with India and derive the same benefits of civilian nuclear cooperation.

The trust and reliability issue was harder to address. The deal was based on the assumption that the future of Indo-US ties was not a simple extrapolation of the past. India and US had arrived at an agreement after a difficult and painstaking process in which both sides expended considerable political capital. Neither party has an incentive to depart from a cooperative relationship that has been established with such great effort. Indeed, the larger the scope and extent of our cooperation, the more powerful will be the case against disturbing it. While no relationship can be completely free of risk, a judgement could be made that a future US Administration will take into account the totality of our strategic partnership when making a decision that has consequences for a sensitive facet of our ties. The debate here demonstrated that a large segment of our intelligentsia had still to understand that the counter to dependency was inter-dependency and not autarchy. Status was another important even if intangible consideration. The deal did have to meet criticism that India was not 'recognised' as a nuclear weapons state. This ignored the fact that US, however powerful, was only one of the parties to the NPT and did not have a mandate to that effect. Some commentaries also took the benefits and advantage too literally and wanted India to be exactly the same as the P-5—again oblivious to the fact that P-5 themselves had very varying practices. The fact is that India is a nuclear weapon state because India has nuclear weapons. This is not a status that has to be bestowed by others. Through the July 18 understanding, we have not only secured an acceptance of our strategic programme but also ensured that the international community will resume civilian nuclear cooperation without that becoming an obstacle. It is only nuclear weapon states that have such arrangements.

The supply assurances that were negotiated during President Bush's visit to India were a unique feature of the agreement. It was somewhat ironical that in the obsession to benchmark ourselves against the P-5's rights—real or imagined—the significance of this achievement was not fully appreciated. From the energy security perspective, a multi-layered supply assurance that touches upon raw materials likely to be in short supply is a very major step forward. Equally, this was calculated to set the ghosts of Tarapur to rest. In essence, the assurances composed of a US commitment to create necessary conditions for India to obtain full access to the international fuel market, including reliable, uninterrupted and continual access to fuel supplies from firms in several nations. This was additionally supported by the US willing to incorporate supply assurances in the bilateral cooperation with India, negotiating an India-specific fuel supply agreement with the IAEA as well, supporting an Indian effort to develop a strategic reserve of fuel for the lifetime of Indian reactors, and working with other supplier nations to restore fuel supply in the event of disruption. In the light of these understandings and a provision for corrective measures to ensure uninterrupted operation of its civilian reactors, India agreed to safeguards in perpetuity. No non-nuclear weapon state has such a safeguards-supply arrangement in place. Where nuclear weapon states are concerned, their safeguards arrangements vary quite considerably, some of them being significantly more generous in their declaration of civilian facilities. Rather than blindly emulate their practices, we have fashioned a unique arrangement suited to our specific objective of enhancing energy security. It may be noted that China, a nuclear weapon state under NPT, has also entered into a unique arrangement recently with Australia that envisages expansion of safeguards coverage in order to secure access to uranium.

The list of US concerns articulated during the course of the Congressional consideration of legislation and the public debate in the Washington think tanks was almost as long and complicated, but obviously different in its focus and intent. The first charge was that the deal with India undermined the NPT and encouraged Iran and North Korea to be more difficult. This drew the expected counter that India's non-proliferation record justified the exception and that it could not be compared to states that were party to NPT. The Director General of IAEA provided strong support to arguments that the deal represented a net gain for global non-proliferation. The important distinction made by India between supporting non-proliferation and advocating a new global consensus on the one side, and subscribing to the NPT on the other—articulated by its Foreign Secretary in October 2005—impacted positively on this debate. Strenuous attempts were made by some non-proliferation and South Asian specialists to press for a criteria based approach—a euphemism to give Pakistan a similar deal. This continued till March 2006, when President Bush forcefully pointed out in Islamabad that India and Pakistan had different histories. The threat of a Chinese reaction was also invoked to stop the deal, with as little success. The Indian Separation Plan came in for close scrutiny and much was sought to be made of the fact that eight PHWRs remained outside the civilian domain. The Plan itself had brought out that the standard reactor capacity in India was much less than a P-5 reactor. Moreover, considering India's record of restraint and its voluntary decision to go only for a credible minimum deterrent, it made no sense that India would behave differently when it actually had less unsafeguarded reactors. Not concerned that this contradicted their push for more reactors being placed under safeguards, the non-proliferation lobby then charged that the deal would make foreign uranium available to India's safeguarded reactors while freeing up domestic uranium for its weapons programme. It took Secretary of State Rice to rebut this argument firmly, when she pointed out to Congressional Committees that India had actually enough uranium for its strategic programme and that a crunch, if at all, would only be felt in the civilian programme where India was prepared to accept growth limitations if necessary. A strong push was also made for a fissile material production moratorium, which interestingly involved a deliberate obfuscation by leading experts of China's position on the matter.

The entire exercise, still underway as the US Congress moves towards finalising the legislation, generated as much heat as it did light. On the Indian side, objections have taken the form of literal textual analysis to more primitive scare-mongering approaches. Intent on missing the woods for the trees, absurd and often artificial benchmarks were advanced that ignored the reality of India's requirements. Comparisons were often selective, and unwelcome examples like China's uranium agreement with Australia ignored. The very framework of the debate was often distorted with either/ or choices being introduced of energy security and non-proliferation. That the 18 July statement was multidimensional in its nature was given a go by. In its more atavistic form, the criticism of the deal attacked the very concept of separation, insisting that the exercise was as unaffordable as it was dangerous. All through, this kept bumping against the broad common sense of the Indian polity that recognized that 18 July represented a fundamental break-through *vis-à-vis* a technology denial policy in place for three decades. US opposition adopted similarly extreme tactics, with freedom of arguments sometimes extending to facts as well. Some of India's programmes already in the public domain were deliberately demonised. The rhetoric against the nuclear deal reached its nadir with comparisons to the intelligence manipulation preceding the Iraq war. As the smoke cleared, what became apparent was that the US Congress bought into the India relationship overwhelmingly. India's non-proliferation record and democratic credentials gave them the sense of security to approve an India exception. The visible investment of political capital and energies by the US Administration caused even the sceptics to take a second look. The strong bipartisan support generated on the US side also surprised many observers in India. By August 2006, the key hurdle to be crossed on the US side was to ensure that the final legislation passed by the Congress remained within the framework of the 18 July Joint Statement and the Separation Plan. The one complicating factor was that the nature of the American political process allowed policy statements and even policy measures to be attached to the legislation. Political change being a gradual exercise, enough vestiges of past thinking crept back to vitiate the atmosphere. Even as we go to press, the jury remains out on the conformity of the legislation to the framework of 18 July Joint Statement and the Separation Plan. The new directions of Indo-US relations would obviously be significantly influenced by success or failure in that regard.

While the nuclear understanding took most of the political oxygen, Indo-US ties actually moved forward very significantly on a number of other fronts as well. Noteworthy among them was economic cooperation, which was accorded a prominent place in the framework that we are examining. Even before the Prime Minister's July 2005 visit, the Indian side made some decisions that sent a clear message of the importance it attached to the relationship. The Indo-US Economic Dialogue that was established during President Clinton's visit was revitalised through the appointment of the Deputy Chairman of Planning Commission as its Indian Co-Chair. Unlike its earlier format that was an aggregation of its sub-dialogues, the new incarnation focussed on key issues that needed high-level attention. By the time the Prime Minister reached Washington, the long-pending dispute over the Dabhol/Enron project stood resolved, an Open Skies aviation agreement concluded and an understanding reached on partnering with the US Trade Development Authority to facilitate infrastructure investment. Non-US specific steps on patents enforcement and investment diversification also contributed to the climate. The July 2005 visit witnessed the launching of a CEO Forum to harness private sector energy and ideas to deepen the bilateral economic relationship. It was also the occasion to announce the Knowledge Initiative on Agriculture focussed on promoting teaching, research, service and commercial linkages. By the time President Bush came to India, the CEO Forum had produced its report of recommendations and the agriculture initiative a three-year work plan.

The CEO Forum defined six priority areas of cooperation and proposed specific initiatives that it recommended for expeditious implementation. On physical infrastructure development, it encouraged public-private partnerships with speed, efficiency and transparency in infrastructure contracts to attract US companies; partnering with the US to make Mumbai a regional financial centre; establishing a $ 5 billion plus infrastructure fund in the private sector; and setting up large scale special economic zones with world-class infrastructure to serve both domestic and export markets. To enhance energy security, the report recommended power sector reforms; introduction of cost-effective and clean environment technologies, especially for coal, bio-fuels, hydrogen and wind energy; early enactment of the Petroleum and Natural Gas Regulatory Board Bill and the Natural Gas Pipeline Policy; and supporting the opening up of civilian nuclear technology supply from US to India. In human resource development, the CEOs urged establishment of institutions of higher education with leading US institutes; setting up new institutions of higher learning and giving private institutions a freer hand in financial and curriculum areas; and upgrading and setting up additional industrial training institutes. On technology exchanges, the recommendations included relaxation of restrictions on transfer of high technology and accelerated transfers of dual use items; removal of constraints on R&D collaborations and setting up of an R&D centre in India for industrial applications; promoting technology exchange in agriculture and commodity markets including through a dedicated centre; leveraging the capability of US agriculture universities to upgrade Indian institutions; and partnering in biotechnology by jointly developing a regulatory pathway. On industry and trade promotion, the CEOs regarded a US-India Comprehensive Economic Cooperation Agreement as a medium-term objective. They sought reduction of restrictions on foreign investment including retail, insurance and banking; facilitation of movement of business and professional people; encouragement of tourism; negotiating a totalisation agreement; establishing a dispute settlement mechanism; encouraging greater defence industry cooperation with a liberal offset regime and the creation of an Indian Institute of Regulation. The last basket pertained to intellectual property protection with calls for national coordination of IPR enforcement efforts, establishing specialised IPR courts and initiating a national programme to crack down on piracy.

The recommendations of the CEO Forum are currently being processed by the two governments and follow up action is expected to be taken by the Economic Dialogue. These could provide the basis for an Indo-US investment summit in the near future. The high-powered composition of the Forum makes it apparent that this was not a routine exercise. Clearly, the corporate sector in both countries has chosen to invest in the relationship, beginning with the attention and ideas of their leaders. It is obvious that the United States views the growth of the Indian economy in strategic terms and believes that an acceleration in growth rates would have consequences that would benefit both nations. The US economic push into China two decades ago also had a strategic purpose and it remains to be seen whether India can make as good a use of opportunities as China did. At least at a perceptional level, the sharp rise of interest in India on the part of the United States has contributed to India now being talked about in the same breath as China. Given the complexities of this area, the contours of the new directions remain unclear, even though we now have a track record of 15 years of economic reforms. The role of external factors in the modernisation of a society is a debate in itself and it would suffice to note here that some of the dramatic examples of change in Asia—including Japan, ASEAN, South Korea and now China—were all significantly influenced by external inputs.

Prospects for Indo-US cooperation in agriculture rate a special mention, if only because of the tradition of the Green Revolution. It is the one area where the case for leveraging the bilateral relationship to advance Indian growth is compelling. Indian agriculture lags well behind industry and services sector and faces major challenges of productivity, environment, water management, technology application and marketing. Neither is India sufficiently prepared for an era of vigorous internal or external agricultural commerce. Our production statistics are matched by our wastage statistics and food processing remains a sector of unrealised potential. And yet, this was neither reflected in our priorities in the past nor till July 2005, did we really seek solutions for our problems through this relationship and others. The Agriculture Initiative has gathered steam within a year with substantial commitments made by the two sides. Thirty-eight Indian institutions have expressed interest in involving themselves with this endeavour. The four focus areas identified for joint projects are human resource development; water management; food processing and bio-fuels; and biotechnology. The expectation is that the initiative would contribute to the development of Indian agricultural curriculum reform, lead to training and faculty exchanges including in cutting-edge and niche areas, encourage public-private partnership in agriculture development and strengthen institutional building. It is our hope that the Agriculture Initiative would contribute to the rejuvenation of this sector and thereby, to India's national development.

The Indo-US Energy Dialogue, also constituted in 2005, leads the engagement between the public and private sectors of the two countries across the entire energy spectrum. The dialogue has five Working Groups: Coal, Power and Energy Efficiency, New Technologies and Renewable Energy, Oil and Gas, and Civilian Nuclear Technology. The efficient development of coal resources has been a key priority and India became a partner in the US-led international FutureGen near-zero emission power plant research project in April 2006. It is likely that major Indian companies would join as participants in the counterpart commercial initiative of FutureGen. The feasibility of Integrated Gas Combined Cycle power plants is being discussed with the US and corporate collaboration is envisaged on advanced R&D of clean and efficient power generation. Establishing a clearing house for coal-bed methane is a near term objective. The US has also supported Indian private sector efforts at developing CBM resources. Projects designed to improve the power generation infrastructure and enhance the efficiency of power usage are also being taken up between India and the US. On the oil and gas side, the Indo-US partnership is supporting a feasibility study for a national pipeline grid, strengthening the collection of hydrocarbon data, working on safety and inspection issues of offshore oil and gas operations, in addition to encouraging investments by US companies in this sector. The US supported India's participation in the Integrated Ocean Drilling Programme and has provided technical support for the first hydrate drilling offshore in India. In non-conventional energy, the focus has been on the development, deployment and commercialisation of technologies for sustainable and renewable fuels. Hydrogen and biofuels are expected to be important areas of collaboration. In civilian nuclear energy, India joined the ITER fusion energy research project with the support of US and other key partners. These efforts are complemented by the participation of India and the United States—along with Australia, China, Japan and ROK—in the Asia-Pacific Partnership on Clean Development and Climate. This partnership aims to provide technology and market solutions to many of the environmental challenges facing the world today.

Science and technology has been the mainstay of a relationship even when it was going through difficult times. It is natural that it should now begin to flower, deriving strength from the economic underpinnings of the ties. In July 2005, it was decided that an S&T Framework Agreement would be concluded to provide for joint research and training, as well as the establishment of public-private partnerships. This was done in September 2005, along with an IPR protocol. By March 2006, the two governments decided to further upscale their collaboration by creating a Bi-National Science and Technology Commission. It would not only generate more partnerships in S&T but also actively promote industrial R&D. This is currently under implementation. The network between technology institutions of the two countries represents one of the most vibrant elements of the relationship, one that would play an even greater role as India emerges as a knowledge power. New mechanisms of cooperation are emerging, such as projects between Boeing and the Indian Institute of Science, many of which could not even have been contemplated some years ago. High-technology transfers and strategic commerce between the two countries will only accelerate this happening. The High-Technology Cooperation Group that was established in 2003 has emerged as an important hub of activity. It has promoted industry working groups in defence technology, bio-technology and nanotechnology. By systematising verification procedures and liberalising restrictive regimes, an enabling climate has been created for greater Indian access to US high technology products and services. The demands from Indian industry are expected to grow as the economy becomes more mature. The efforts of the last two years have now moved from dismantling control categories to evolving a positive 'White List' of civilian end-users eligible to access US origin high technology. Space cooperation also deserves special mention, having featured prominently in the NSSP as well. The two countries have established a dedicated working group to broaden the ambit of their dialogue. Commerce in space end-items has become much freer and the Indian lunar mission will be carrying US scientific payloads. The conclusion of a commercial space launch agreement is the main outstanding commitment that is being addressed.

India's defence and security cooperation with the United States has also made significant progress over the last decade. While growth has been largely incremental—reflected in the sophistication of exercises and intensity of mil-to-mil cooperation—the conclusion of the New Framework for the India-US Defence Relationship on 28 June 2005 marked a quantum change. This framework articulated the shared security interests of the two nations, including maintaining security and stability, defeating terrorism and violent religious extremism, preventing WMD spread and protecting the free flow of commerce *via* land, air and sea lanes. To that end, it was agreed that Indian and US defence forces would conduct joint and combined exercises and exchanges, collaborate in multinational operations when it is in their common interest, strengthen military capabilities including in counterterrorism, expand their defence trade, provide for technology transfers, collaborations, coproduction and R&D and exchange intelligence. A new Defence Procurement and Production Group was constituted to oversee defence trade, coproduction and technology collaboration. Consequent to this new framework, a Disaster Relief Initiative was finalised in July 2005 and a Maritime Cooperation Framework in March 2006. These developments highlighted the changing security environment in which the cooperation was evolving. It focussed on threats from non-state actors, transnational forces and natural disasters where the United States and India, as nations with deployable capabilities, would be expected to step up and shoulder responsibilities. The international response to the December 2004 tsunami was, in many ways, the unspoken model that guided thinking and planning. The New Defence Framework was subjected to considerable scrutiny and was not entirely without controversy on the Indian side. Many of the judgements passed reflected the assumptions of a past era and did not take into account the changing nature of contemporary threats. Indo-US military to military cooperation has now assumed a structured format, with the Malabar series of naval exercises, the Cope series of air force exercises and the Yudh Abhyas series of Army exercises constituting an annual feature. Assuring US companies of a level playing field in defence procurement has also significantly widened India's technology options. The new directions on defence ties can be judged to be promising but sensitive, in the last analysis, to the overall climate of relations.

The convergence of interests between India and United States in meeting global challenges has also strengthened their bilateral bonds. In the aftermath of 9/11, the focus of global challenges was on combating terrorism. India was clearly a beneficiary of the US policy to remove Taliban from power in Afghanistan. In Indian public perception at least, the expectations of relief from more immediate cross-border terrorism have not been fully met. Counter-terrorism remains an active facet of Indo-US ties. However, global issues go well beyond and it is instructive to note that the key challenges identified by the US National Security Strategy of March 2006 correspond to many of India's own priorities: championing aspirations of human dignity, defeating global terrorism, defusing regional conflicts, combating WMD threats, supporting global growth through free markets and trade, and confronting the challenges of globalisation. This has allowed the two nations to develop an active agenda of global issues where their ability to work together advances their respective national interests. India and the United States are today engaged in addressing security and humanitarian issues through joint and coordinated efforts. This extends to combating a range of transnational challenges—from marine pollution and natural disasters, to piracy and trafficking in persons. In the health sector, expedited USFDA approval processes have added to the Indian capability to contribute in the struggle against HIV/AIDS at a global level. Similarly, the two countries are meeting the challenges of avian flu in a larger international context. Their commitment to fight against illegal trade in wildlife and wildlife parts is another manifestation of their ability to work with each other. Another notable development was the Global Democracy Initiative, aimed at strengthening democratic practices and capacities in emerging democracies. This then led the two countries to help launch the UN Democracy Fund in September 2005.

Many observers find themselves unable to keep pace with developments in Indo-US relations because they are positing the relationship on a static global situation, much of it irrelevant to present day reality. It is essential to appreciate the full consequences of the end of the Cold War, not just in Europe where we tend to focus, but globally as well. For the United States, Europe is increasingly a competitor, as well as a model of alternate lifestyles and values. China's growing influence is a complicated and dynamic element in the calculus, made more uncertain by its unique political ethos. It is a society, in Secretary Rice's words, that needs to be helped to make the right choices. The structural limitations of the US-Russia relationship are also quite evident by now. Further into East Asia, Japan remains inhibited about global responsibilities. ASEAN too is largely preoccupied with its internal dynamics. The US relationship with the nations of West Asia is likely to be difficult in the foreseeable future. It is in this larger global setting that the United States has sought to reach out to India. The arrival of India on the global scene is advantageous to US interests, and an acceleration in this process, even more so. India is a liberal, democratic, secular and pluralistic society with a market economy that has no irreconcilable differences with the United States. Its recent growth rate points to it becoming a major economic power. Its demographic structure and human skills can enable it to emerge as a knowledge power as well. It has a history of stability, of responsibility, and of global contributions. With its immense diaspora, India's soft power is only beginning to be felt by the world. Policy-driven reports like the *National Security Strategy*, the *Quadrennial Defense Review* or the National Intelligence Council's *2020 Report* all look at India, not necessarily where it is today, but where it will be a generation from now. It is this logic that drives the recent US initiative and the bipartisan consensus over the nuclear initiative point to it going beyond the current Administration.

From the Indian perspective, a strengthened relationship with the US has its not inconsiderable merits. It will certainly help in the acceleration of India's economic growth and the development of its technological capacities. It would contribute to a higher international profile and impact positively on third countries as well. As a revisionist power, India seeks a more accommodating global order, and the United States can make a difference in this quest. In the final analysis, the natural behaviour of India and the United States are likely to serve each other's interests. However, a deliberate strategy of dovetailing their efforts will obviously benefit both. The challenge that the relationship faces and will continue to do so for some time is the likelihood of unmet expectations. In both nations, there would always be a trend of opinion that would seek to put the relationship to test. It is inevitable that some such tests would not be passed and one or the other nation is unable to live up to standards that it publicly espouses. The strategic partnership is still at an early stage and for it to mature, it is important that policy makers strive for the optimal rather than the ideal, until such time that comfort and confidence have grown. The new directions of Indo-US relations draw strength from broad economic and political forces that draw the two societies closer. That is likely to go forward in any case. What remains to be determined is whether this coming together can be given a firmer strategic direction through the judicious exercise of policy choices by their decision makers.

39

India and Indonesia

Baladas Ghoshal

The role of Indonesia in India's foreign policy and strategic calculations needs to be viewed within the broader context of India's Look East Policy. While some specific issues that pertain only to bilateral relations between India and Indonesia need to be factored in building cooperative relations that can endure the test of time, the superstructure of that relationship has to be built on an overarching framework.

The changed international environment and the convergence of interests

The changes, which have taken place in the international and regional politico-strategic situation in recent years, have helped to improve markedly the environment for positive developments in India-South-East Asia relations. The end of the Cold War and the breakdown of ideological barriers led to a more pragmatic approach by India. The ground realities in the Asia-Pacific region have similarly changed. The erstwhile foes like ASEAN and Vietnam have now not only become friends but also cooperating actively in the integration of the region. On India's part, she is letting no chance go by, to prove that she wishes to be integrated into the global market and do business with all countries.

While most significant opportunities for cooperation between India and South-East Asian have emerged in the economic field, it is the political and strategic understanding that must form the foundation for working towards a synergy of interests and building up of comprehensive ties. The globalisation and the diffusion of science and technology have further accelerated the reshuffling of power hierarchies. With the disintegration of the erstwhile Soviet Union and the successor state, Russia's decision, by design as well as by its relegation of its economic position, to abdicate its status as a superpower by resiling from its commitment to security overseas and forging a link of active strategic cooperation with the western powers, the United States has emerged as the only superpower in the world. Indeed, it has been acting as one in pursuit of its national interests. The absence of countervailing power against the United States poses a new challenge for the foreign policy of Third World countries like India and that of ASEAN.

While militarily the United States continues to be the only superpower, from economic point of view the world has become multipolar, centring around three major economic regions, i.e., North America dominated by United States, the European Union, Asia and the Pacific dominated by Japan—each competing with the other for the world market, raw materials and political influence. Scholars like Paul Hirst and Grahame Thompson give credence to such assumptions when they claim that the world economy is not truly global but centred in this triad. They present data on trade, foreign direct investment and financial flows to show that globalising activities are concentrated in the developed countries. They still continue to harmonise policy and shape the flow of finance and economic governance in general. Left to its logic, globalisation widens the gap at the national and international level between those equipped to benefit from it and those left on the sidelines. In the developed world, technology and finance are the clear winners of globalisation, while labour, in the traditional sense of the term, is a loser. So the clear challenge is one of wealth distribution.

Again, the global economy, particularly international finance is marked by instantaneous transactions of enormous magnitude manipulated by speculators who can easily upset national economies. This is a theme, which the former Malaysian Prime

Minister Mahathir Mohammad had articulated for a long time that needs attention of the countries, which are vulnerable to such manipulation. Given the potent dynamic of economic globalisation, how can market forces become effectively regulated in the future? As the Seattle conference a few months ago showed, emerging market economies and developing countries are less and less inclined to accept that globalisation should proceed according to the priorities and agenda set only by the United States and Europe. Multilateralism has been used in too many cases to provide a convenient cover or international blessing for actions or initiatives designed with only national interests in mind. A truly multilateral system will have to integrate different regional sensitivities, priorities and interests in a way that makes different countries, regardless of their size or economic mass, feel that they have a good possibility of having their say and expressing their interests. It is in the interests of India and the countries of South-East Asia to coordinate their policies in such a fashion that the emerging economies in Asia, Latin America and Africa be made much more integral parts of the structures and mechanisms for global governance.

As we have noted earlier, there is certain convergence of interests among the triad in regard to security and strategic objectives, i.e., the preservation of the *status quo* and prevention of the rise of new powers, particularly in the Third World. Pressures are being brought to bear on Third World states by a new alliance consisting of both the West and East, including Japan, who have suddenly become overzealous about self-determination in parts of sovereign states and are not hesitant to use their political and economic leverage to interfere in other states' affairs in the name of human rights and good governance. The end of the Cold War, therefore, has increased rather than decreased the relevance of the Non-Aligned Movement's struggle for international peace and equity. From the perspective of the Third World, the struggle for a just and equitable world order in the new international environment can be furthered, however, not through confrontation but through engagement with the developed countries while at the same time fashioning a common approach amongst the developing countries. Indeed the central tenet of both India and ASEAN countries is that South must revive dialogue with the North, while at the same time intensifying South-South cooperation. Both believe that however unsettling and unfair the international political and economic system is, reforming it from within is possible. That is why both actively engage in initiatives to promote North-South dialogue and consultations with the G-7 and within the G-15. That is why India and the countries of South-East Asia have encouraged policies that place great importance to basics: food sufficiency, population planning, debt management and sustainable development. In accordance with their common goal on such issues, India and ASEAN can and do coordinate their activities in this area. Indeed on many other issues in the political, economic, cultural and other fields (environment, human rights, labour standards, etc.), India and ASEAN countries in recent times have been fashioning similar viewpoints to champion their cause in regional and international fora.

Sharing of experience in creating multiethnic societies

It is the shared experience in dealing with multiethnic groups that should provide the imperatives for political cooperation between India and ASEAN. It is here that issues like Kashmir, Mindanao, Aceh and West Irian assume significance in the relationship between the two regions. India has always looked at the ethnic issues in any state including in ASEAN as part of a problem of all multi-ethnic states to integrate the diverse groups into a single political community based on shared identities while at the same time preserving their cultural, social, linguistic and religious diversities. In line with basic approach to ethnic problems, India has consistently supported all ASEAN countries' attempts to integrate their diverse groups within their respective states. It would, therefore, expect the ASEAN countries also to treat India's problems with ethnicity, religious extremism and terrorism supported by a third country, for example in Kashmir, with similar understanding and empathy. India has sought to resolve the Kashmir problem politically and democratically under conditions of a large and dangerous insurgency that has received full support from Pakistan. Kashmir being a Muslim-majority state but with a significant non-

Muslim minority is a test case for India to maintain its secular nationalism. One should not forget the fact that India happens to be the second largest Muslim state in the world, next to Indonesia, and Kashmir's secession from India on the simple argument of its Muslim majority, would have a disastrous effect on the other Muslims in India.[1] To quote M. J. Akbar, a leading journalist in India and a commentator on Kashmir: "Pakistan has no place for Muslims who believed in Pakistan in 1947. But it continues to demand the integration of Kashmiri Muslims who in 1947 did not particularly want to join Pakistan. ... And here is the Paradox. Hindu majority India cannot give up Kashmir precisely because Kashmir has a majority of Muslims. It is the only Muslim-majority State in a country that built its foundations on cultural cohesion instead of religious divide. If India surrenders Kashmir with the indifference it would never show over Gujarat or Rajasthan, then New Delhi's claim to secularism becomes fundamentally flawed. India cannot be the same country if it surrenders Kashmir. This is one reason why Pakistan wants Kashmir so badly."[2]

It is within this background that India would like the ASEAN countries to understand the significance and the complexities of Kashmir, which has often in the past been a major source of misunderstanding between the two regions. A failure by the ASEAN states to understand the complexities of the ethnic issues, the danger posed by armed secessionist movements and trans-border terrorism, and India's efforts to solve the grievances through political dialogue and democratic methods, can only have a deleterious effect on relations between the two regions. Now that some ASEAN countries are themselves the victims of radical Islam and its terror networks, whose breeding ground is universally known to be in the hundreds of 'madrasas' that produce 'Jihadis', they have somewhat changed their views on Kashmir. In any event,

---

1. On the aspect of linkage between Kashmir and India's secularism and the fate of the Indian Muslims, see, Akbar, M.J. (1990). *Kashmir: Behind the Vale*, New Delhi, Penguin Books. Also see his "Elusive Peace," *Far Eastern Economic Review*, 3 December 1998, and Baladas Ghoshal, "Internal Source of Conflict in South Asia," in Kanti P. Bajpai and Stephen P. Cohen (eds.) (1993). *South Asia After the Cold War*, Boulder, Colorado: Westview Press, pp.67-90.

2. M.J. Akbar, *op. cit.*

the political understanding between India and ASEAN would surely depend on what positions some of the ASEAN states adopt on the Kashmir issue and India's territorial integrity.

Growing political and strategic cooperation between India and ASEAN

A major manifestation of the growing understanding and the importance India and the South-East Asia attach to their relations is the number of high level visits that their leaders have undertaken over the last 10 years. A further manifestation of the growing political and economic interaction is ASEAN's decision to confer upon India, first the sectoral dialogue partnership (SDP) in 1992 and then the full dialogue partnership (FDP) in 1995. This has enabled India not only to initiate greater economic interactions with the ASEAN region, but also provided its political leadership opportunity to regularly interact with ASEAN leaders and policy makers and to fashion and build common approaches to many issues of regional and international importance. India had already attended a number of ASEAN Post Ministerial Conferences (PMC), in Jakarta, Kuala Lumpur, Manila and Hanoi, and found them extremely useful in networking and building trust and confidence among the partners. India's participation in the ASEAN Regional Forum (ARF) meeting is equally of great significance, for it allowed her entry into multilateral security deliberations outside the United Nations aegis for the first time and provided New Delhi and its defence establishments both at official and non-official levels, greater access to information, and offered opportunity to develop proximity on strategic and security related issues. During the last 10 years or so, India participated in a number of ARF activities relating to confidence-building measures (CBMs), maritime search and rescue, peacekeeping, non-proliferation, preventive diplomacy and disaster management and found them productive and useful for the facilitation of the introduction of appropriate CBMs among participants. India has vital stake in security in the Asia-Pacific region and the thrust for ensuring peace and disarmament at the ARF discussions was viewed by India as an approach towards genuine pluralistic security order. Beginning with its sectoral dialogue partnership with the ASEAN it has now graduated itself to the status of ASEAN-India summit, at par with ASEAN+3 (China, Japan and South Korea). India also participated in the East Asian Summit (EAS) held in Kuala Lumpur in December 2005, along with Australia, New Zealand, China, Japan, South Korea and the 10 ASEAN countries.

In the post-Cold War period, India and the countries of ASEAN are confronted with new security issues, which have opened up opportunities for cooperation. The end of the Cold War by eliminating the ideological bases of conflict between the two superpowers, the United States and the erstwhile Soviet Union, has lessened the chances of any conflict between the major powers, thereby removing any possible uncertainties in the strategic environment of Europe. This has not happened in the case of Asia-Pacific which is home to some of the largest and key states of the world within its ambit—Japan, China, India, Indonesia, Korea, Russia and the United States; and where exists a series of sovereignty disputes and military issues leading to an uncertain and complex security environment. In Asia-Pacific, the United States is the strongest power in terms of political, economic, technological and military capabilities, but that has not allowed her to determine the economic, political, security and other forms of interaction in the region unilaterally, essentially because of the existence of other powers, like Japan, China, Russia and India who may not have the wherewithal of power at the moment to challenge the supremacy of the United States but can deter its hegemonic role. As other powers develop their economic and military capabilities in course of time and thus their leverage, there is likelihood of a gradual decline of the US predominance and the region moving slowly towards a polycentric system. But the process towards a polycentric system is not going to be smooth while new powers are emerging and the strategic order mobile and shifting. The region, therefore, has to create a new balance of power amidst conditions that are rapidly changing. The strategic imperatives for cooperation arise from these uncertainties in regional security environment. The threat of terrorism both from within and across borders are now confronting both India and ASEAN countries calling for close monitoring, coordination and fashioning a joint approach in combating the scourge. Among other areas where India and ASEAN nations can coordinate their efforts are problems of piracy, environmental pollution, narcotics traffic, illegal migration and other security-related issues, including the safety of the sea-lanes-of-communication (SLOC) vital for the free flow of goods and economic prosperity of the region. Above all, India and ASEAN need to contribute to the maintenance of peace and stability in the region, so that the countries in South-East Asia can pursue their economic development and progress for their people.

Role of Indonesia in India's policies and strategies in ASEAN

Having outlined the broad contours and parameters of India's South-East Asian regional policies and strategies, which will allow India a much more important role and a higher profile, it will be worthwhile to highlight the role Indonesia can play in that strategy. Politically, we are close geographical neighbours who share a maritime boundary with a mutual stake in each other's progress, prosperity, stability and territorial integrity. As pluralistic democracies and developing societies, we face similar challenges. Indonesia is not only the most populous country in the region with the largest Muslim population in the world; it has also immense natural resources and a strategic location, for it controls all or part of the very major waterway between the Pacific and the Indian Ocean. The US pacific command transits these SLOCs in order to support operation in the Gulf. The Japanese need these waterways to transit their oil tankers. More than half of all international shipping trade traverses these waterways. Indonesia is the fulcrum in the South-East and, therefore, holds the key to the stability and security of the region. Indonesia made ASEAN possible. ASEAN's formation was a result of Indonesia's adopting a more cooperative approach to its neighbours. The cohesion among ASEAN countries has added to the stability of the East-Asian region by allowing smaller countries to band together to form a counterweight to larger regional powers. Though by far the largest member of ASEAN, Indonesia has been careful to ensure that ASEAN has remained an organisation of equals. The health of ASEAN is dependent on the health of Indonesia. A blow to Indonesia undermines the integrity of ASEAN as an institution, as well as regional security.

The success of Indonesia, as a pluralistic and democratic state is essential not only to the peace and prosperity of the South-East Asian region, but also to the security of India. As the country with the largest Muslim population in the world, Indonesia has a key role to play in demonstrating the virtues of tolerance and mutual respect in a diverse, multiethnic polity. The ability of so many Muslims to thrive economically and pursue a democratic, just society shows the way forward for Muslim and multireligious societies. Second, Indonesia's success in its current effort at creating a democratic polity and sustaining a secular society in the face of challenges, from communal and reactionary forces that have now risen dangerously to the surface across the country is again vital to the stability and security of India. It is beset with separatist movements, communal violence, some restless soldiers, religious tensions, a static economy and heavy debt. On top of that, it is facing a difficult transition from authoritarianism to democracy in an environment where the civil society is quite weak due to its marginalisation under the Soeharto regime, and it is in dire need of capacity-building support. While the rest of the region has somehow recovered from the great Asian economic crisis, Indonesia is still under economic and political turmoil causing serious concern about the very survival of the country. The future course of the country may be decided by a struggle between the new democratising impulse and the forces of chaos that seek an advantage in provoking the religious, social and separatist tensions.

India's stakes in the success of democracy in Indonesia

If democracy fails in Indonesia, it will not only lead to the revival of the authoritarian forces and the old regime but also the rise of militant Islam in a country that, despite being the largest Muslim country in the world, has tried to preserve a secular society. And the implications of that will not only have an effect on the security and stability of ASEAN but will also have a bearing on India's own polity and security. India, therefore, has a great stake in the success of Indonesia's democracy, and can attain some positive gains in her relations with the latter if only she can help in Indonesia's democratisation efforts through training in capacity and institution building. Here in this chapter we will flag off two areas where India can make effective contribution to the stability and security of South-East Asia by helping the region in capacity building. I would argue in this chapter that India's ability to play a major role in Asia lies not so much in the area of trade and investment of the region, but in her human resource and democracy. The extension of adult franchise and individual freedom to Indians immediately after Independence in 1947 has produced a large middle and professional class and endowed India with a strong human resource base. This has given India a certain comparative advantage over other Asian countries. Knowledge of English language, which has become the most important language in an era of globalisation, is also another advantage.

India can use its soft power, which lies in our strength as the largest democracy in the world. It may be seem disorganised, but it has also shown a lot of creativity in managing a multiracial and multicultural society in place, and in the evolution of people's empowerment. It is in this sphere that India can make an abiding contribution to the process of democratisation and nation building of the region by helping them in human resource development and democratic capacity building. South-East Asian countries are not only multiracial and multicultural, but some of them are also in the process of democratic transformation. The Western model of democracy may not be of direct relevance to these countries, as the societal and historical circumstances are quite different. India's experience in nation building and democratic experiment is much more relevant to them. Helping them in that transformation can also further India's interests in South-East Asia more. To emphasise the importance of democracy in creating the bond between India and Indonesia, Prime Minister Manmohan Singh noted: "We are Asia's largest pluralistic democracies. The focus of governance in democracies is to meet popular aspirations and to ensure that equity and social justice accompany economic growth. Both our countries are engaged in meeting this challenge. In fact, there has been considerable expansion of our trade, economic and investment relations over the past few years." India is fiercely proud of its democracy and there is no doubt that organising elections for a potential constituency of 670 million voters is an incredible undertaking. Indonesia could learn much from the speed and transparency with which votes are tallied and the extensive powers accorded to the Electoral Commission (EC). On paper it could be argued that comparatively Indonesia has a much better chance of making democracy work. It has only one-fifth of India's 1.03 billion population, its literacy rate is 87 per cent and on all the indicators including gross national income, life expectancy and infant morality rates, Indonesia ranks higher. At the same time, Indonesia is also ranked as one of the most corrupt countries in the world.

Former President Wahid and many other Indonesian leaders have great respect for India's ability to practice democracy despite many shortcomings. In my conversations with him in July 2000, President Wahid showed interest particularly in 'Panchayati Raj' and decentralisation mechanism in our Centre-State relations. He wanted to empower the people at the local level through his decentralisation plans, which are now in force from early 2001. While the central government is impatient to implement autonomy hoping that a fairer distribution of national wealth will reduce separatist sentiments and regional violence, there is a complete lack of institutions at local level to absorb such autonomy. Autonomy alone cannot achieve economic justice and community peace unless there are institutions and procedures to operate such decentralisation. This is where India can offer help through its Indian Technical and Economic Cooperation (ITEC) Programme for training in 'Panchayati Raj' and institution building at the grassroots level. With little investment, India can reap rich dividends in terms of both promotion of democracy in a vitally important neighbouring country and goodwill from the Indonesian leadership as well as the people.

India can also take the help of some of our NGOs who are doing a yeoman service in building grassroots democracy in India to help the Indonesian NGOs to build the same in their country. The forces in Indonesia that were pushing for change during the anti-Soeharto agitation, practically all have joined the government leaving the opposition quite weak and confused. This has led to the emergence of outside groups, who are now taking the actual lead in laying down foundation for a civil society capable of pushing for change. Throughout Indonesia, previously uninvolved teachers, workers, journalists, poets and novelists are breaking away from the corporatism of the Soeharto regime and are trying to create a whole range of new institutions. These aim to fight corruption, resist violence and work for human rights. They call them Corruption Watch, Parliament Watch, Military Watch and their numbers are increasing. With all their enthusiasm to lay the foundation for democracy, some of them lack experience in capacity-building activities due to lack of political space during the Soeharto regime, and would be too willing to receive help and support in building the basis for grassroots democracy.

India's potential as the educational hub of Asia

Another area where India can help Indonesia and in which she has a comparative advantage, is in the field of higher education. While answering questions from the editors of *Jakarta Post* during Prime Minister Manmohan Singh's visit to Indonesia in April 2005 at the commemoration of the Bandung Conference on how India planned to follow up the results of the meeting, he declared that India intended to stay engaged by sharing experiences—"gained from our own development process—with nations in Asia." To quote Prime Minister Singh: "Human resource development holds the key to employment and wealth creation, particularly in this age of globalization. This has been our strategy and we have laid particular emphasis on training and skills development as we globalize. We have extended technical assistance valued at about US$ 1 billion. We stand ready to do more." Undoubtedly, Indonesia has been one of the prominent beneficiaries of our technical cooperation programmes meant for fellow developing countries. Around 1000 Indonesian experts as well as officials received training in India under ITEC. India offered more than 1100 scholarships to

Indonesian students to study at Indian universities. In May last year, India opened a US $ 750,000 Vocational Training Centre and it will open another one in Aceh soon. But there are greater potentials for India-Indonesia cooperation in education, which will be of benefit to both the countries. One of the important reasons for the Asian economic crisis of the late nineties was that while there had been a shift in the production line, there was no commensurate development in higher education in most of the Asian NICs to keep pace with such shift.

Culture as a tool of diplomacy

Yet another area that can promote India's soft power in South-East Asia in general and Indonesia in particular, is its culture. Indian culture is an inseparable part of Indonesian customs, and our cultures and values are closely related, bearing in mind the history of the civilisational contacts between India and Indonesia, which span over 2000 years. If carefully pursued, our cultural diplomacy can further cement the bond between the two countries based on our pluralist traditions and our need for maintaining 'unity in diversity', the basic philosophy of our states.

Promotion of tourism as a means of people to people contact can be an important instrument of our cultural diplomacy in Indonesia. Even though Indonesia happens to be the largest Muslim country in the world, its cultural heritages are essentially Hindu-Buddhist in origin, manifesting in temple architectures of Prambanan and Borobudur in Central Java and innumerable Candis scattered all along the area. While their origin might have been from India, Indonesian themselves have contributed quite significantly in improvising and enriching that culture. Indian tourists could be encouraged to travel in larger numbers to those sites to discover the inherent genius of the Indonesian people in preserving that culture and values, and in the process the common bond between the two countries. Similarly, Islamic cultural heritages and monuments are part of our composite Indian civilisation, which need to be presented before the Muslims of Indonesia and Malaysia.

An account of past and present India-Indonesia relations

India-Indonesia relations have passed though ups and downs and have been characterised by both friendship and indifference. During Indonesia's independence struggle against the Dutch, India provided both emotional and material support to her to overcome the Dutch onslaught on her leaders, as well as to seek recognition from the international community. India convened a special conference on Indonesia in 1949, in New Delhi, to condemn the Dutch colonialism and to mobilise international support for its independence. Together with Australia, India championed the cause of Indonesia's freedom in the United Nations, which eventually was able to persuade the Dutch to leave Indonesia. As a recognition of India's role in the freedom struggle, Indonesia conferred the highest title of 'Pahlawan Indonesia' to Jawaharlal Nehru, and to Biju Patnaik, who took great risk in flying a plane to Jogjakarta, the then Republican capital to rescue Sutan Sjahrir and Soekarno. As a consequence of such interactions, India-Indonesia relations in the immediate post-independence period were characterised by friendship and common approach to world issues based on their commitment to non-alignment, anti-colonialism and anti-racialism. Even though India's economic relations with the region was generally weak during the period, yet it was quite substantial with Indonesia. But the friendly relations were quite short-lived, as Indonesia's internal developments together with its changed foreign policy perspectives in the late fifties and early sixties drove the two countries away from each other.

Even though relations became normal during the Soeharto era, but given Indonesia's political and economic orientation and a very pro-American foreign policy, India, with its command economy, a disorganised democracy (as perceived by the Indonesian elite at the time) and its closeness to the erstwhile Soviet Union, was not at all an attractive partner for close cooperation, and *vice versa*. Indian Prime Ministers did not bother to visit Indonesia, the second largest country in East Asia and a strategically important maritime neighbour for 14 years during the past two decades. However, thanks to the end of the Cold War and the onset of India's Look

East, Policy from the early 1990s, perceptions of each other have changed dramatically underlining the need for close cooperation for creating a peaceful and stable order in Asia. During the past six years, every Indonesian President visited India and two successive Indian Prime Ministers, Vajpayee and Manmohan Singh went to Jakarta. Starting with former President Abdurrahman Wahid in 2000 and accelerating under Megawati Sukarnoputri and President Susilo Bambang Yudhoyono administrations, Jakarta moved closer to New Delhi. Prime Minister Manmohan Singh also led a high level delegation to the Asian-African Summit (AAS) in Jakarta, in April 2005. In his desire to further this improved relationship with 'a superpower in information technology and world's fourth largest modern economy' President Yudhoyono visited Bangalore, Agra and New Delhi and agreed with India to establish a 'strategic partnership' to open a new chapter in bilateral relations. The new strategic partnership (NSP) is designed to address the long-term interests of both countries, thorough closer diplomatic coordination, stronger defence relations, enhanced economic relations especially in trade and investment, greater technological cooperation, intensified cultural ties, educational linkages and people to people contacts. By working together and drawing upon each other's strengths, it is hoped that the NSP will enable India and Indonesia to contribute to regional and global peace, prosperity and stability. The NSP is premised on the recognition that "as world's largest democracies, and as independent-minded nations with a long tradition of internationalism, the combined voice of Indonesia and India can make a difference in international affairs." Indonesia strongly supported India's participation in the first East Asian Summit (EAS), which was held in Kuala Lumpur in December 2005. India was also perceived as a balance to China. Indonesia, for example, sought to avoid aligning with China while retaining friendly ties to other powers such as the US, a classic 'hedging' strategy. The participation of India, Australia and New Zealand was seen as ensuring that ASEAN remained at the centre of any emerging East Asian community.

In the context of the NSP, there is now a growing cooperation between the two countries in the field of defence and security. Recognising the important role India and Indonesia are called upon to play in the promotion of regional security by virtue of their being close geographical neighbours with a shared maritime boundary and common security interests, officials of the two countries agreed during President Yudhoyono's visit to an annual India-Indonesia Strategic Dialogue. This was an attempt to further institutionalise the already existing Bilateral Agreement on Cooperative Activities in the field of Defence concluded in 2001, and expands this cooperation. The bilateral MoU on Cooperation to Combat International Terrorism is another important move by the two countries to synchronise their efforts to fight terrorism in a comprehensive and sustained manner. President Yudhoyono welcomed India's offer of cooperation in procurement of defence supplies, defence technologies, joint production and joint projects, met with Minister of Defence, Pranab Mukherjee to talk specifically about cooperating in the defense sector, with a further follow-up to be arranged by officials at the Ministerial level.

Recognising that both countries have large exclusive economic zones and maritime interests, India and Indonesia also agreed to work closely to enhance cooperation in capacity building, technical assistance and information sharing between their respective relevant agencies. Other signed deals include memorandums of understanding (MoUs) on marine and fisheries cooperation and on the establishment of a joint study group to examine the feasibility of a comprehensive economic cooperation agreement. There was also an agreement for cooperation in education and training between the Indonesian Ministry of Foreign Affairs and the Foreign Service Institute of the Ministry of External Affairs.

Besides Susilo's visit, there were several events in 2005 that strengthened bilateral relations between the two countries. In response to the tsunami disaster in Aceh, India, which was also affected by the waves, deployed two naval ships carrying medical teams and US $ 1 million in relief materials. India's then foreign minister Natwar Singh attended the Tsunami Summit in January

2005 and the country announced another US$ 2 million aid to Nias, which was shattered by a deadly earthquake in March 2005. In July 2005, Indian Chief of Naval Staff, Admiral Arun Prakash visited Indonesia to strengthen defence cooperation between the two countries. His visit coincided with the arrival of Indian aircraft carrier *INS Viraat* and four other ships in Jakarta. The arrival of an Indian naval squadron in Tanjung Priok Harbour in Jakarta Bay led by the aircraft carrier *INS Viraat* as its flagship presented "the most impressive display of India's growing maritime strength since the visit of the cruiser *INS Delhi* in June 1950," to quote an editorial of *Jakarta Post*. The editorial went on to suggest that the visit of the aircraft carrier *INS Viraat* with the Indian chief of the naval staff, Adm. Arun Prakash, on board was a substantial event whose significance went well beyond a run-of-the-mill showing-the-flag exercise. "The arrival of such an impressive Indian naval squadron in Indonesian waters while President Susilo Bambang Yudhoyono is visiting the People's Republic of China is surely an indication that, given the interesting geopolitical shifts that are sure to affect the overall balance of power in the Asia-Pacific region, Indonesia must be smart and nimble in formulating and implementing its politico-military strategy so as to further the country's national interests," reported *Jakarta Post*. India and Indonesia began joint naval patrols off the Andaman Islands in the Bay of Bengal to check poaching, smuggling and drug trafficking in 2002. India is also providing an escort for ships passing through the Indian Ocean bound for South-East Asia through the Malacca Strait, between Malaysia and Indonesia.

India's Chief of Army Staff, General J. J. Singh, visiting Indonesia in mid-March this year, met with Indonesia's Defence Minister Juwono Sudarsono and his Indonesian counterpart Gen. Djoko Santoso. During his talks with Sudarsono, in Jakarta, Gen. Singh suggested "a joint exercise [and] joint training, with a United Nations peace-keeping backdrop or a counter-terrorism scenario." It was left to Indonesia to respond to this initiative, he said. Asked about Mr. Sudarsono's comment that India and Indonesia were exploring the possibility of a strategic partnership in the military domain, Gen. Singh said the bilateral dialogue was "not really" focussed on "revolutionary military affairs" despite the emergence of some "strategic dimensions." Sudarsono said, both sides were currently studying possible partnerships, including cooperation between their state-owned weapon industries and that he would coordinate with the ministry for research and technology to assess the sophistication and the price of some defence technology India had offered. He said Indonesia was seeking non-lethal technology defence equipment such as for transportation and logistics.

Cooperation in science and technology

Cooperation Agreement on Scientific and Technical cooperation was signed in 1982. The agreement provided the umbrella for cooperation between India and Indonesia in the field of science and technology, but no notable progress was made for a long time, except in the field of remote sensing. The cooperation between Indian Space Research Organisation (ISRO) and its Indonesian counterpart LAPAN has made considerable progress since the two organisations began cooperation in the beginning of the 1990s. In 1998, Indonesia agreed to open a Telemetry Tracking Command and Network (TTC) ground station in Biak in Papua province for satellites and geostationary launch vehicles. India is building a US$ 900,000 second ground station, an expansion from the previous one, in Biak. In January 2003, during the visit of Prime Minister Vajpayee, a MoU for cooperation in the field of science and technology was signed under which a Joint Committee has been established. The areas of cooperation planned under the MoU are biotechnology, renewable energy sources, medical sciences, science policy, science popularisation, and information technology, agriculture and marine science.

Trade, investment and economic relations

Indonesia is our second largest export market in ASEAN (after Singapore) and one of our leading export destinations among developing countries. During 2004, bilateral trade expanded 36 per cent to reach US $ 3.27 billion. Bilateral trade further increased during 2005 by 20 per cent to US $ 3.93 billion. Indian exports remained steady at US $ 1.05 billion while imports increased by 32.61 per cent in 2005. India is Indonesia's largest buyer of crude palm oil (CPO) and importer of its mining, petroleum, pulp and paper and textile products. India exports refined petroleum products, wheat and rice, sugar, animal feeds and iron and steel products to Indonesia. As Indonesia has emerged from its economic downturn, bilateral trade has surged in the past three years. However, there remains vast untapped potential for further growth. Both countries have set an ambitious target of tripling of bilateral trade to US$ 10 billion by 2010 and Indonesia's Minister of Trade Mari Pangestu visited India twice in August and November 2005. The balance is expected to surpass the US $ 4 billion mark in 2006.

Promising areas of investment include the energy sector like coal mining and gas (both upstream and downstream), manpower and engineering consultancy services for the petroleum industry, power generation, mining industry, non-conventional energy, plantation (particularly CPO), IT, toll roads, ports and railways, telecommunications, pharmaceuticals and healthcare services also Indian companies in oil and natural gas and in the coal-mining sectors.

Conclusions

Political, economic and strategic factors in the post-Cold War period call for expanded cooperation between India and Indonesia. It is essential that all-round ties be steadily deepened and widened so that both emerge stronger not only to face the new challenges in the areas of security, politics and economy, and the problems emanating from deep asymmetry of power in the international system, but also to shape the future of Asia and the world.

40

India and Japan

Aftab Seth

Fifteen hundred years ago there was a meeting of minds, a beating together of hearts, a spiritual union that occurred between India and Japan.

In the era of Shotoku Taishi, the sublime and compassionate message of the Buddha came to the shores of the stunningly beautiful Japanese archipelago. The Japanese people, the elites and the common man alike embraced the teachings of the Buddha and internalised the essence of India's message of brotherhood, love and friendship. Japanese scholars over the centuries continued this intellectual discourse with India and several travelled to China and India for pilgrimage and acquisition of knowledge. Notable among such scholars was Kobo Daishi of Kagawa prefecture whose birth place in Zentsu-ji is commemorated with a beautiful temple set amid a forest of camphor trees. Kobo Daishi travelled to China in 804 and acquired precious Buddhist texts from India, which he brought back with him to Japan.

At the Buddhist University in Nalanda in Eastern India, scholars from the entire Buddhist world, in their thousands, gathered together to build a sense of 'Asian consciousness' of which Japan was an integral part.

Techniques in textile design and manufacture such as 'shibori', 'tie and dye' or 'calico' (sarasa) and the *ikkat* designs of Orissa marked another aspect of the cultural interflow between our two countries.

About 450 years ago, yet another dimension was added to the India-Japan story, by men like Saint Francis Xavier (1506-1552). This Spanish missionary came to the West coast of India and established a centre in Goa. From there, missionaries and traders travelled to Miyazaki and Kagoshima prefectures in Kyushu. Later, Spanish and Dutch and English traders, from their bases in India and the East Indies, travelled to China and Japan. This traffic maintained a constant flow of goods, people and ideas. Tokugawa Ieyasu (1542-1616) wanted to engage the Europeans in trade where the profit for them could be as high as 20 to 30 per cent. Ieyasu, however, was persuaded to change his mind because of the European war, in which the Spanish Habsburgs were fighting the Dutch, who sought their independence. In the event, the Dutch were the winners and were the only Europeans permitted to trade with Japan, though they were confined to Dejima in Nagasaki prefecture. Through the Dutch the exchange of goods between India and Japan continued, although the intellectual discourse was largely suspended.

This situation changed dramatically after the Meiji Restoration in 1868 and the opening up of Japan under new governance. While Japan's political orientation remained essentially western oriented, same important links with India, spiritual and material, were restored.

Tada Motokichi (1829-1896) of Shizuoka prefecture was sent by the Meiji Government to India to learn about black tea production. He travelled to tea gardens in Assam and Darjeeling and visited tea factories in Calcutta. On his return to Japan after a couple of years, he introduced black tea production in Shizuoka prefecture, thus establishing a link which exists till this day.

Sri Jamshed Tata, a leading industrialist of India *en route* to the USA, stopped in Japan and learned much from the rapid industrialisation that he witnessed at the end of the 19th Century.

On the spiritual front, Swami Vivekananda, the great disciple of Rama Krishna, who preached the message of tolerance and universal brotherhood, visited Japan. He went to all the major centres of Buddhist learning and was struck by the piety, cleanliness and patriotism of the Japanese. With the chief priest of Enkaku-ji in Kamakura, Vivekananda travelled to the USA. In Chicago, he and his Japanese friend shared the wisdom of the East with hundreds of intellectuals who had gathered to attend the first World Parliament of Religions in 1893.

Rabindranath Tagore, the Nobel laureate poet, visited Japan three times in the early years of the 20th Century. His Vishwabharati University at Shantiniketan became an important point of contact for Indo-Japanese intellectuals and artists. Okakura Tenshin, Yokoyama Taikan, Arai Kampo were amongst the prominent Japanese who brought back to Japan the art and spiritual heritage of India.

At the political level, the Russo-Japanese War (1904-1905) had a profound impact on the Indian national movement. The Japanese victory over a major European empire, split the Indian National Congress Party between those who wished to follow a constitutional path and those who wished to follow Japan and use military force to gain independence from the British.

It was to Japan again that a national leader Rash Behari Bose fled in the late 1920s and where he was given refuge. He married a Japanese woman, Nakamura Toshiko, and founded the first Indian Restaurant in Japan in Shinjuku, Tokyo.

The relationship between India and Japan until 1939 saw many positive developments. Hundreds of Japanese businessmen lived in India and India was Japan's third largest trade partner after the US and China.

During the Second World War, Subhas Chandra Bose, a national leader, sought Japanese military help to build the Indian National Army (INA) composed of Indian prisoners of war, who had been captured by the Japanese army, when the conquest of South-East Asia was accomplished. Soldiers of the INA fought alongside their Japanese brothers at many battles. Thousands of them died and are buried together with the Japanese in Imphal in Eastern India.

After the war, India made several important gestures of friendship towards Japan. Prime Minister Jawaharlal Nehru refused to sign the San Francisco Treaty, which offended "the dignity of Japan." Instead, India signed a separate Treaty in April 1952 and waived all rights to reparations.

Nehru further encouraged Indian iron ore exporters to supply all Japanese requirements in order to rebuild Japan's Steel industry. Iron ore from Australia and other sources was not readily available to Japan. Deeply moved by the misery of Japanese citizens in the wake of war, Nehru presented a baby elephant to Ueno Zoo in Tokyo in March 1945, as all the animals had either been burned, poisoned or had starved to death, during the war. The elephant named after his daughter Indira, who later also became Prime Minister, brought much cheer to the children of Japan and to their parents.

The Tokyo War Crimes Tribunal had an Indian Justice, Radha Binod Pal, whose dissenting judgement holding the wartime leaders 'not guilty', did much to restore the sense of self-esteem and dignity of the Japanese people. Based on his understanding of International Law, Pal's judgement was published in 1952, after the end of the occupation and lifting of censorship. It reinforced the impression that just as Gandhi wanted a "fair and non-violent" victory against British, Pal wanted a "fair and non-violent" judgement of Japan and its leaders.

Indo-Japanese relations in the 1950s were marked by Japan's decision in 1958 that India would be the first country to receive Japanese official development assistance (ODA).

A breakthrough in the relationship occurred in August 2000, when Prime Minister Mori Yoshiro made a historic visit to India. The establishment of a Global Partnership in the 21st Century was strengthened by the subsequent visit to Japan in December 2001 of Prime Minister Atal Bihari Vajpayee and in April 2005, of Prime Minister Koizumi Junichiro to India. In the last year alone, almost 20 exchanges of cabinet rank ministers have taken place between India and Japan. A major decision has been taken to boost trade and investment and cooperation in science and technology.

A review of Trade, ODA and S&T data would make this wide ranging cooperation evident. Japan's ODA loan to India is about Yen 125 billion per annum.

India ranks 25th in Japan's Exports and 30th in Japan's Imports, while Japan ranks: 8th in India's Exports and 9th in the list of Major Trading Partners of India. The two-way trade is about US $ 5 billion per annum.

Major items exported to Japan from India include Manufactures and Primary commodities like raw wood, iron ore, non-ferrous metal scrap, mineral fuels, coal, chemicals, textiles, non-metallic mineral products and metals and food stuff, power generating machinery, audio and visual apparatus, thermionic values and transistors, electrical measuring instruments, motor vehicles, scientific and optical equipment, wood manufacturers, furniture, travel goods, etc.

Major items imported from Japan to India include chemicals (14%); manufacture goods: metal products, iron and steel products (8%); machinery other than electric: power generating machinery, metal working machinery, pump centrifuges (26%); electrical machinery (15%); transport equipment (8%).

Potential growth areas for India's exports are computer software and IT enabled services; gems and jewellery; processed food, fruit pulps, juices, squashes; dairy products–milk and milk products; cut flowers; fruits like mangoes, grapes and bananas; herbal products like henna, aloe, etc.; textile products; marine products like shrimps and lobsters; beverages like tea and coffee especially ready to drink tea and coffee; Indian handicrafts; leather garments and products. Potential areas for project exports from India include computer software and IT enabled services and skilled manpower.

Potential growth areas for imports by India are chemicals, manufacture goods, industrial machinery, electrical industry, transport equipment and metallurgy.

India-Japan S&T coperation

India considers Japan as a very important country for having cooperation in the field of science and technology. Scientific cooperation between India and Japan is already progressing significantly in most of the pioneering areas under (i) India-Japan Cooperative Science Programme (IJCSP): under the aegis of India-Japan Science Council, (ii) Intergovernmental S&T Programme of Cooperation; under the aegis of Joint Committee on India-Japan Cooperation in S&T.

Under the present programme, following six broad areas for cooperation are underway, namely:

i) Molecular structure, Spectroscopic and Dynamics

ii) New materials

iii) Modern Biology and Biotechnology

iv) Manufacturing Science

v) Astronomy and Astrophysics

vi) Surface and Interface Science including Clusters.

New India-Japan S&T initiative

With a view to provide more focus and purpose to S&T cooperation between the two countries a New Science and Technology Initiative has been included in the Joint Statement that was issued on the occasion of recent Japanese Prime Minister Koizumi's visit to India in April 2005.

Following areas have been included to explore possible substantial collaboration giving due consideration to existing mutual strengths of India and Japan in these areas of research and also keeping in mind the new and upcoming technologies of future:

Modern biology, biotechnology, health and care, agriculture, hydrocarbon fuels, nanoscience and technology, environment, information and communication technology, robotics, alternative sources of energy.

Indian scientific proven capability in almost all the above listed areas of science and technology complements the elaborate S&T needs of Japan giving rise to a tremendous potential for mutually beneficial cooperation between the two countries and can form an important component for mutually agreed 'Japan-India Global Partnership' in the 21st Century.

Cooperation with JST

Cooperation between Japan Science and Technology Agency (JST) and Department of Science and Technology (DST) of India, on science and technology multidisciplinary research and development in different areas including Information and Communication technology is soon going to be finalised. JST is the second largest funding agency of Japan which supports bilateral basic research in the areas of importance.

Signing of an agreement between JAXA and ISRO

An agreement concerning the Consideration of Potential Future Cooperation in the Field of Outer Space, including Satellite Remote Sensing, Satellite Communications and Space Science was signed between Indian Space Research Organisation (ISRO) and Japan Aerospace Exploration Agency (JAXA) during the visit of Secretary, Department of Space.

The Agreement was signed from Indian side by Shri G. Madhavan Nair, Secretary, Department of Space and Chairman, ISRO, and from Japan side by Mr. Keiji Tachikawa, President, JAXA, in October 2005, in Tokyo.

On the academic front it has been agreed by the two Prime Ministers that 10 universities on both sides will establish relations, that 30,000 Indians will learn Japanese every year, that Japanese will be offered as an optional language at all IITs and that Japan will build an IIT of its own. The impact of these decisions on future generations of young Japanese and Indians will be profound.

Since January 2000, when George Fernandes became the first Indian Defence Minister to visit Japan, Ishiba came in May 2003 to India, becoming the first Japanese Defence Minister to visit India. Top military leaders have exchanged visits; a comprehensive security dialogue between Japan-India, involving the civil and military establishments takes place annually, and the navies and coast guards of both counties have regular joint exercises.

At the United Nations (UN), India and Japan are together trying to ensure permanent membership of the UN Security Council (UNSC) for both countries. The G-4 draft resolution of 6 July 2005 (L.64), which generated very wide support in the general membership in the 59th Session of the General Assembly, was resubmitted by Brazil, Germany and India on 5 January, 2006. It is widely recognised that no other model for the reform and expansion of the UNSC has met with a similarly high level of endorsement. A comprehensive reform of the UNSC will bring it in line with contemporary realities and strengthen the UN as a whole. The objective of resubmitting the G-4 resolution is to instil positive dynamics into the process of Security Council reform, which had been emphasised in the Outcome Document of the World Summit held in September 2005.

Brazil, Germany and India will continue the cooperative framework of the G-4 with Japan. All Member States genuinely interested in reform are welcome to discuss the draft resolution. Discussions will be undertaken with an open mind with a view to further broadening the basis of support. The aim of resubmitting the G-4 draft resolution is not to call for a vote in the immediate future, but to further explore the potential of joining hands with all member states supporting structural reform of the Security Council. In this context, the efforts of the African Union are encouraging. The project of the S-5 Group of Countries is also to be noted. Both these initiatives share to a large degree the reform aims of the G-4 draft resolution.

It is also encouraging that the President of the General Assembly has recently noted the need for modernising the Security Council and stressed the continuing willingness of the wider UN membership to pursue this goal.

It is hoped that the tabling of G-4 draft resolution will impart new impetus to Security Council reform, without which the overall reform of the UN will be incomplete, as has been stated on several occasions, including by the UN Secretary General.

Foreign Minister, Taro Aso of Japan on 7 March, called on a group of Tokyo-based envoys from African nations for their support in Japan's efforts to reform the UNSC, "I would like to invite our African friends to cooperate with us in achieving a concrete outcome by the end of the 60th session of the General Assembly of the UN" in September 2006. Japan told Germany that their plans to reform the UNSC must gain the support of the United States and Germany agreed to cooperate on UNSC reform despite differences. Taro Aso in his talk with visiting German foreign Minister said, "We share the perception that UNSC reform is a pending issue and that we will continue cooperating on it."

The US Secretary of State, Condoleezza Rice said on 3 March 2006, "We understand India's aspirations for a Security Council seat, and we support an enlarged, more representative Security Council … that looks like 2005—not 1945." India will continue to work closely with Japan in this important matter.

India and Japan share a common desire to see a multipolar world. We desire multilateral diplomacy, which seeks to enhance the prosperity, stability and security of Asia, and the sea lanes through which our commerce passes. We also wish to strengthen the global mechanisms for ensuring peace in the world at large.

India and Japan are equally committed to the concept of sustainable development which protects the environment of this planet which is our common home. This is in keeping with Hindu-Buddhist-Shinto traditions, and the inclusive ethos of Indian civilisation.

Looking at the future, Japan's relations with India are poised to move forward with a speed and intensity that has not been witnessed so far. The number of business organisations showing an interest in India continues to increase. Japanese investment flows into India's equity markets topped almost $ 4 billion last year. At a recent sale of debt bonds in Japan, India's EXIM (Export and Import) Bank was able to garner 23 billion. These are all signs of the increasing confidence with which Japanese business interests view India. But there is need for Japan to quicken the pace of its movement into India. It has to make up, in a sense, for lost time. Korea and China have expanded trade and investment with India in the last 5 to 10 years at a rate which is several times the Japan-India figures.

As briefly mentioned earlier, the decision of our two Prime Ministers to expand the teaching of Japanese at Indian Institute of Technologies (IITs) and at select high schools, with as many as 30,000 young Indians learning Japanese ever year, will have a profound impact on the future of our relations. With India's demographic advantage being sustained for the next three decades, India will continue to be a young country, with large numbers of skilled young workers being added to the workforce every year. Japan on the other hand, has a declining birth-rate and will therefore be able to make use of these bright young Japanese-speaking Indians, who will be available for work in Japan or with Japanese enterprises in India.

At the political level, and in matters relating to strategic issues, it is worth underlining that both our countries share many vital perceptions. In matters concerning the war on terrorism, the safety of sea lanes, the preservation and strengthening of multilateral organisations and multilateral diplomacy, on the security and stability of Asia and on global problems like HIV/AIDS, Bird Flu and SARS, India and Japan have worked together in the past and will continue to cooperate in the future. Our ancient friendship will reach new heights in the decades and centuries to come.

Figures on 'Trade and ODA' have been kindly furnished by the Embassy of India, in Tokyo.

41

India and South Africa: ties that bind

Harsh Bhasin

South Africa enjoys a unique pride of place in India's national psyche which traces its origins to the era predating India's own Independence. This was because India always linked her own struggle for freedom and Independence with the cause of the oppressed majority of South Africa—a link forged by the Father of the Nation, Mahatma Gandhi, who took up this cause as a mission, and relentlessly fought for 21 years the might of an oppressive regime's overt racial discrimination policies. Later, he applied the same techniques of passive resistance and civil disobedience to successfully bring Independence for his own motherland, India. It came as no surprise, therefore, that when I first met Nelson Mandela, his words to me were: "Remember that India gave us Mohandas Gandhi; South Africa returned him to India as Mahatma Gandhi."[1]

Little wonder, therefore, that India and South Africa have enjoyed a special relationship ever since the advent of majority rule in South Africa in 1994—a relationship that is poised to grow and strengthen further in the decades of the new millennium. In this chapter we will examine the historical sinews of this relationship, how India furrowed a lonely path against the mighty powers through the difficult four decades after her own Independence, never

---

1. The author met Nelson Mandela soon after his release from prison in February 1990, when he visited Botswana. The author was India's envoy in Gaborone at the time.

for once wavering in her belief of the just cause of South Africa's majority people, and how this has laid the firm foundation for a sound relationship between the two 'next-shore' nations who together share the warm waters of the Indian Ocean. Major and multifaceted bilateral developments in the early years of the post-1994 Republic will be examined, together with their impact on the future relationship across a wide spectrum–political, economic, cultural, defence, tourism etc. to name a few. To quote President Mandela again,[2] ours is "a partnership forged in the crucible of history, common cultural attributes and common struggle".

For the purpose of this study, we will consider all these aspects of relations between India and South Africa within the following chronological framework:

    a.   Developments predating India's own Independence in 1947.

    b.   Developments from 1947 until the advent of majority rule in South Africa in 1994.

    c.   Developments from 1994 onwards until the present day.

As is inevitable in any such study, a strict compartmentalisation is not always possible, or even desirable, for many of the events spill over the chronological divide despite efforts to maintain the integrity of the unfolding, fascinating story of the two nations whom destiny, and a congruence of interests, has brought together to face the challenges of the new millennium.

Developments predating India's own Independence in 1947

The dominant element in this period was clearly the Gandhian presence in, and influence upon, the South African political landscape, but before that a word about what brought the budding young barrister, M.K. Gandhi Esq., freshly-minted from the Lincoln's Inn in London, to South Africa, would be in order.

The story begins in the year 1860, when indentured labour from India began to be brought to South Africa to work on the sugarcane fields of Natal by the erstwhile British colonial masters who

---

2. State visit of President Mandela to India in 1995.

controlled both sides of the Indian Ocean. An interesting minute recorded by the then British Governor of the province provided the justification for this urgent need—that Indian workers were more disciplined and conscientious than their native African counterparts and moreover, the latter were highly prone to this peculiar propensity of downing their tools and run for their native villages in the interior just precisely at the time when the cane crop was ideally ripe for harvesting; worse still, the native Africans tended to slash the sugarcane reeds well above the ground, thereby losing the maximum sugar content which is concentrated in the part closest to the ground. The Indian workers, on the other hand, it was argued, patiently cut the cane reed close to the ground, thereby maximising the sugar content (read 'profits').

Several waves of indentured labour followed the (success of the) first. Later, sensing business opportunities, enterprising Gujaratis from the Porbandar coast of western India, famous for their uncanny commercial acumen, made their way to South Africa, albeit in passenger steamships paying their own fares. Thus, in contrast to their low-wage earning fellow-countrymen who preceded them, this relatively better-off and self-sustaining group of immigrants to Natal, came to be known as 'Passenger Indians'. Soon they began running, thriving businesses, catering largely to the non-white populace of Natal province and its environs.

A prominent member of this community, one Mr. Dada Abdullah ran afoul of the strict and racially-biased South African laws and had a case registered against him. This was at a time when South Africa was in the grip of racial discrimination and confident that he would not be able to obtain justice at the hands of any white lawyer, he was on the look out for a lawyer from India. Hearing of this, the young M.K. Gandhi set sail for South Africa in 1893 to defend Dada Abdullah & Co. What eventually happened to this case has become somewhat shrouded in mystery but what it did to Gandhiji has become the stuff of legends and indeed immortalised in Richard Attenborough's classic film epic *Gandhi*.[3]

---

3. And years later through Indian movie director, Shyam Benegal's *In the footsteps of the Mahatma*.

Returning to South Africa in 1896 Gandhiji, appalled at the open discrimination against all non-whites, decided that this was the cause he would adopt and fight for in the larger ends of justice, driven as he was, peculiarly enough, by what he admitted was his training as a lawyer in England which had imbued him with a strong sense of justice and fair play.

The story of Gandhiji being thrown off the train at Pietermaritzburg is too well known to be retold in detail here. Suffice it to say that his sense of justice and morality was totally outraged when he was thrown out of the 'whites only' section of the train in spite of being in possession of a duly purchased first class ticket.[4] From that historic moment onwards Gandhiji decided to launch what eventually came to be the *tour de force* of his struggle for the emancipation of the oppressed, first in South Africa and later, in India.

Before returning to India in 1914, Gandhiji had tried and successfully experimented with passive resistance or *Satyagraha* and civil disobedience to an extent where the South African authorities began to sit up and take notice of his activities. He was detained on several occasions but all these only helped to endear him even further in the eyes of all non-whites — be they black Africans, coloured people or ethnic Indians. His legacy endures in South Africa. He set up the Phoenix settlement near Durban and the Tolstoy Farm outside Johannesburg to propagate his message and mobilise the dispossessed people of South Africa against the oppressive regime in power. Admittedly, Gandhiji got too involved in India's own struggle for Independence after his return from South Africa but the cause of the vast majority of the underprivileged and economically deprived people of South Africa, always remained close to his heart.

The population of indentured labour which had started streaming into South Africa in 1860, together with the succeeding 'passenger Indians' have today grown to a population of well over

---

4. To commemorate the event a plaque is installed at the Pietermaritzburg Railway Station and has almost become a place of pilgrimage for Indian visitors to South Africa.

one million people or 3 per cent of the entire population of South Africa.[5] Keeping in mind the growth of the community of Indian origin, the Indian Government had appointed a High Commissioner to South Africa by the early 1940s, well before India's own independence. Then, at the very first session of the UN General Assembly in 1946, India placed the question of racial discrimination on the agenda of the world body, thereby drawing the attention, and hopefully the conscience, of the entire civilised world, to the abominable practice forced upon the vast majority by the white minority regime. Later India carried the same message, with renewed vigour, in bodies such as the Commonwealth and the Non-Aligned Movement (NAM). The public reaction in India against Asiatic Land Tenure and Indian Representation Act was so strong that the Viceroy's Executive Council felt obliged to recall the Indian High Commissioner to South Africa soon after India lodged the complaint in the UNGA in June 1946. A trade embargo soon followed, even though South Africa accounted for some 5.5 per cent of India's overall exports. Referring to these developments, the well-known President of the ANC in the 1950s, Chief Albert Luthuli, recorded in his autobiography: "The way in which India at the UN has taken up cudgels on behalf of the oppressed South African majority and dragged the whole scandal of apartheid into the open, has heartened us immeasurably."

A few months before India's Independence, in May 1947 Gandhiji appealed to Field Marshal Smuts, as a 'trustee' of Western civilisation, to end the suppression of Africans and Asians in South Africa. Not only did this appeal fall on deaf years, apartheid became so entrenched that it was soon enshrined as an instrument of state policy through a series of discriminatory laws such as the infamous Group Areas Act, the Separate Amenities Act, the Immorality Act and the Population Registration Act, etc.

---

5. According to the well-known historian, Leonard Thompson, by the end of the century, there were more Indians than whites in the province of Natal.

Developments from 1947 until the advent of majority rule in South Africa in 1994

The five decades between India's Independence and the advent of majority rule in South Africa were characterised by a relentless assault on the forces of colonialism, racial discrimination, and oppression all over the globe but particularly in the African continent. Starting with the Asian People's conference in New Delhi in 1947, through the Bandung Conference in Indonesia in 1955, at the Afro-Asian Peoples' Solidarity Organization (AAPSO) in 1958, at all Commonwealth meetings, in NAM and elsewhere, India espoused the cause of bringing an end to minority rule in South Africa. At the UN India kept up relentless pressure for a rapid movement towards decolonisation and self-government. To quote Pandit Nehru: "Where freedom is confined to a minority and the great majority have no share in it and, indeed, are suppressed politically, socially and racially, in defiance of everything that the UN and the world community stand for" was something that could not be tolerated any longer. To give concrete shape to its pronouncements, despite her limited resources, India made whatever contributions it could afford, towards the International Defence and Aid Fund for Southern Africa, UN Trust Fund for Africa, the UN Education and Training Program for South Africa besides other such bodies set up to assist the newly emerging countries on the African continent. India was also in the forefront of vigorous efforts in the British Commonwealth to get the body to take a firm stand against apartheid, which ultimately led to the expulsion of the country from the body in 1961.

The Indian parliament adopted several resolutions condemning the apartheid policies of the white South African regimes. In recognition of the role played by the ANC in bringing an end to apartheid in South Africa, and to provide greater impetus to the goals of the ANC to bring about a just political order in South Africa, India allowed the ANC to establish an informal presence in India in 1960, which was later upgraded to full-fledged resident mission in New Delhi, in 1967. This was an event of great jubilation, attended by representatives of liberation movements in Africa and various peace movements of USA, Europe, Australia, Canada and Latin America. There was widespread popular support for this move in India and especially among student groups, academics, trade unions, political activists, writers and farmer's associations who often held peace marches to draw world attention to the struggle of the majority people of South Africa. Similarly, the Indian parliament adopted several resolutions condemning the apartheid policies of the South African regime. As President Thabo Mbeki was later to say, "India systematically, over a period of many years and long before its own emancipation, became an unshakable ally in the cause of enlightenment in South Africa. Even in our darkest days of repression, despite the economic cost, in the face of insults and taunts flung at its leadership by bigots, India never gave up its role as a key ally in bringing an unjust system crashing down in South Africa. This, of itself, helped to unite us South Africans in our resolve to win the struggle and to share in the fruits of non-racial, non-sexist freedom."

The prestigious Jawaharlal Nehru Award for International Understanding, instituted in 1965 as a tribute to the memory of India's first Prime Minister was conferred on Nelson Mandela in 1979 while he was still in prison. The same year saw the efforts of India and other like-minded countries succeed in designating 1979 as "Anti-apartheid Year" by the UN. Later, Nelson Mandela also received the Gandhi Peace Prize. Meanwhile, intensive and extensive training in different disciplines began to be imparted to substantial numbers of ANC cadres in India, in part to prepare them to take on responsibilities of administration, diplomacy and governance in the long run, but also to meet some of the basic needs of education and training that were denied to them by the apartheid regime in their own homeland.

These efforts received a further boost when, at the Commonwealth Summit in Harare (Zimbabwe) in 1987, India took the lead in the establishment of the AFRICA Fund—the acronym meaningfully doubling up for the very evocative "Action For Resistance to Invasion, Colonialism and Apartheid" (AFRICA). Through contributions to this fund, frontline states bordering South

Africa were given economic assistance to resist the minority regime in South Africa's actions against these economically vulnerable neighbouring countries. While the actual impact of the AFRICA Fund is not always adequately appreciated or acknowledged, it nevertheless did contribute at least a few nails to apartheid's ultimate coffin[6].

International attention to the outrages committed by the white minority government in Sharpeville (1960), District Six (1965) and Soweto (1976), also helped mobilise the worldwide struggle against apartheid. The imprisonment of Nelson Mandela, who was sentenced to 27 years in prison for daring to speak up against the atrocities of the apartheid regime, also shook the conscience of the entire world and calls for his release became more vocal. This led to the regime making half-hearted attempts at reform, such as the ill-fated 'tricameral' experiment in which limited political rights were sought to be given to the coloured and Indian communities, totally ignoring the vast majority of black Africans. Clearly, the experiment was doomed to failure and the Government of India called upon the Indian community in South Africa not to fall victim to the machinations of the white minority government and urged them not to participate in a farcical legislative arrangement in which they had only notional rights and in which the vast majority of their non-white brethren had been excluded. India repeatedly emphasised that there was no room for 'reform' of the abominable system of apartheid. It simply had to be ended and elections based on universal suffrage were the only solution to South Africa's mounting problems—problems arising from unremitting internal unrest and increasing external isolation, not to speak of the mounting opprobrium of the entire civilised world.

India kept a close watch on these emerging developments in South Africa. After vehemently condemning the 'tricameral' experiment of 1984, and with the launch of the AFRICA Fund in 1987, India stepped the pressure on South Africa in various

---

6. Designed to assist vulnerable frontlines in their struggle against South Africa, the moral and material assistance totalled some US $50 million from India alone.

international fora. Attempts by India and other like-minded countries eventually resulted in the imposition of comprehensive and mandatory sanctions by the UN against South Africa. To closely monitor the events in South Africa, a special cell was created in India's foreign office in 1987 and a resident mission was established in Botswana (the geographically closest 'frontline' state to South Africa) for better and more effective liaison and co-ordination with the liberation movements in South Africa. The Natal Indian Congress and the Transvaal Indian Congress (both founded by Mahatma Gandhi during his sojourn in South Africa in 1894 and 1903, respectively) kept in close touch with the Mission and provided useful inputs to hasten the downfall of the apartheid regime.

It was not until the fall from power of the old guard led by the wily P.W. Botha, often referred to as the 'Groot Krokodil' (Great Crocodile) in the late 1980s and his replacement by the pragmatic and forward-looking F.W. de Klerk as President that South Africa began witnessing the first signs of meaningful change on its political landscape. He announced a series of measures, starting with the release of Nelson Mandela, followed by all-Party discussions to chart out a new course for South Africa's future. The talks were centred around drawing up a new constitution in which the rights of all South Africans, irrespective of the colour of their skin, were to be guaranteed—truly a first such momentous event in this troubled land. The road to what ultimately led to South Africa becoming a nonracial Democratic Republic in 1994, however, was not a smooth one. Many bumps—big and small—were encountered on the way during discussions of Codesa-I and Codesa-II (Conference for a Democratic South Africa), and later what became known just as 'Multiparty Talks'. There were strong, sometimes vicious, pressures from the extreme right (among the white minority) and the extreme left (among the more militant liberation movements such as the PAC), but ultimately the middle path taken by the National Party (NP) led by F.W. de Klerk, and the African National Congress (ANC) led by Nelson Mandela, prevailed and elections took place, based on Universal suffrage, in April 1994. The international community recognised the sagacity and statesmanship of both the great architects of this peaceful transformation—Mandela and de Klerk, by jointly conferring the 1993 Nobel Peace Prize on them.

India welcomed Nelson Mandela's release from prison on 11 February 1990, with great joy and unbound enthusiasm. The Prime Minister sent a special envoy to personally extend an invitation for him to visit India, which he did on 15 October 1990. He received an unprecedented welcome and rousing reception wherever he went. In his speeches he referred to India as "a home away from home" and profusely thanked India and her people for standing steadfastly committed to the cause of bringing an end to apartheid in South Africa. Referring to India's leading role in mobilising world opinion against the racist minority white regime, he said, "We would not be talking of victory today if the example set by the young Republic of India had not been followed by the rest of the world". Mandela was conferred India's highest civilian award, the Bharat Ratna (Jewel of India) during this visit.

Mandela requested for India's continued assistance to the ANC during the transition phase as the organisation readied itself to assume the mantle of governance after the first nonracial elections. India responded generously to this request, which included extensive human resources development and training in civilian as well as non-civilian areas, continued moral and material support including notably, the outright purchase of the prestigious Shell House for the use of ANC as its headquarters in a prestigious precinct of downtown Johannesburg.

Developments in India-South Africa relations since the advent of majority rule in 1994

With the successful conclusion of all-Party talks for drawing up a new Constitution, once it became abundantly clear that the movement towards a nonracial democracy in South Africa was clearly becoming a reality, India opened an Indian Cultural Centre in Johannesburg in May 1993, whilst South Africa opened a mission in New Delhi in November 1993, following the visit of Foreign Minister Pik Botha. On 22 November 1993, an agreement establishing full diplomatic relations was signed. In December 1993, the Indian Cultural Centre was upgraded to a Consulate-General.[7] April 1994, saw South Africa establish a Consulate-General in Mumbai and the Indian High Commission in Pretoria was set up soon afterwards. A second Indian Consulate-General was opened in Durban, in April 1994. The pace was clearly reflective of the desire on both sides to brook no further delay in establishing full-fledged relations in every possible field – political, economic, trade and cultural etc.—denied to peoples of both countries for all too many decades.

The first ever free, truly democratic and nonracial, elections held in South Africa in April 1994, which brought the ANC to power with an overwhelming majority and installed Nelson Mandela as the President, brought unprecedented jubilation in India as it was a dream that India had unflinchingly fought for since her own Independence in 1947, come true. It would not be an exaggeration to say that outside of South Africa itself, perhaps no other country witnessed such scenes of joy and celebration as India. The then Vice-President of India, K.R. Narayanan, represented the nation at the inauguration of Nelson Mandela together with a large delegation of prominent dignitaries. The late Prime Minister, Rajiv Gandhi, who was the architect of the AFRICA Fund, was represented by his widow, Sonia. President Mandela broke protocol and went out of the way to honour her presence on the occasion.

Mandela later visited India in January 1995, as the Chief Guest on India's Republic Day celebrations; in March 1997, on a state visit when the Red Fort Declaration[8] was signed and in 2001 for receiving the Gandhi Peace Prize. Thabo Mbeki paid an official visit to India in December 1996 as Deputy President, and then again as President in October 2003. During the latter occasion, he was accompanied by no less than 11 cabinet ministers, and the visit resulted in five

---

7. The author had the unique honour of being both the first (and only) Director of the Indian Cultural Centre and later India's first ever Consul-General in Johannesburg.

8. The Red Fort Declaration reaffirmed the close ties between the two countries, based on a common commitment to economic development, social justice and cooperation for a global order that is marked by peace, security and equity.

agreements being signed in key areas, namely, an Extradition Treaty, a Cultural Exchange Program, an Agreement on Mutual Legal Assistance in Criminal Matters, and Agreements on cooperation in the field of power and in the field of hydrocarbons.[9]

In the other direction, Prime Minister I.K. Gujral became the first Indian Prime Minister to visit South Africa in October 1997. Vice-President Krishan Kant attended the inauguration of President Thabo Mbeki in January 1999. Prime Minister Vajpayee visited South Africa for the NAM Summit in Durban, in September 1998 and for the CHOGM summit in November 1999. Vice-President Bhairon Singh Shekhawat visited South Africa in April 2004. This regular interaction between the leadership of both countries at the highest levels has resulted in the forging of strong, mutually reinforcing ties across a wide spectrum. Providing the necessary lubricant, and indeed serving as an active catalyst for these growing ties are the regular Foreign Office Consultations and the annual Joint Commission meetings, led at the level of Foreign Ministers. These are further reinforced by frequent Ministerial-level meetings from both sides, as well as senior-level business visits and conferences organised with unfailing regularity by CII and FICCI, both of whom have offices in South Africa.

A spate of delegations followed the advent of the new majority government in South Africa, in 1994, both from India's public and private sectors, to take advantage of the unprecedented goodwill that was gushing forth towards each other in both countries, catalysed in no small measure by the million-strong community of Indian origin. Direct flights started between the two countries following an air-services agreement that was concluded in record time. Bilateral trade, non-existent until the advent of the ANC-led majority government in 1994, shot up from zero to well over US $ 2 billion within a decade. These figures do not include India's imports of gold from South Africa. Barring gold imports, the trade

---

9. Also, a Joint Declaration was issued during this visit reaffirming the commitment of the two countries "towards a strategic partnership, based on their shared values: democracy, economic development with social justice, and a just and equitable global order."

is fairly evenly balanced between imports and exports as of now, though this trend may well not hold for too long as South Africa is increasingly emerging as a significant supplier of defence equipment to India.[10]

Besides direct trade, a host of other commercial interactions have emerged with equal vigour. Indian companies find South Africa an attractive destination for investments. Typical areas have so far been pharmaceuticals, textiles, engineering goods, IT, small-scale industries, the transport sector, and more recently sunrise sectors such as IT and communications. To service these activities, the Export-Import Bank of India and the State Bank of India have opened their offices in Johannesburg while the Bank of Baroda has done so in Durban.

In the other direction, South African companies have invested a modest US $ 50 million in India in areas such as diamonds, petrochemicals and breweries—with companies such as De Beers, SASOL and South African Breweries (SAB) in the lead. In the services sector, South African companies have been active in India in fields ranging from highway construction to airport design and upgradation.

Tourism between the countries has recorded a significant rise since 1994, with figures poised to touch the 1 lakh mark within the next few years. Flight connectivity and capacity availability continue to be restraining factors, especially in terms of direct links. Only South African Airways has a direct South Africa-India air link though Air India is reportedly reconsidering the same once its fleet is augmented by 2007-08. South Africa is increasingly becoming a preferred destination for Bollywood film producers who find outdoor locales there ideal for film shoots.

South Africa has been among the major beneficiaries in manpower development under India's ITEC (Indian Technical & Economic Cooperation) programme. Prior to 1994, a large number

---

10. A Defence Cooperation Agreement was signed in September 2000, which also provides for joint production facilities and third country marketing. South Africa Defence personnel are trained at various Indian institutions.

of ANC cadres received training in various disciplines under ITEC. The programme was expanded and extended for South Africa in the post-1994 period. So far, over 500 (?) trainees from South Africa have undergone training under this program in fields ranging from diplomacy (Foreign Service) to community development. South Africa's Minister of Public Service and Administration visited India in November 2005, to identify areas for further cooperation under this programme.

The signing of an Agreement on Reciprocal Promotion and Protection of Investments is reportedly at an advanced stage of discussion between the two countries[11]. Once in place, it could pave the way for some preferential trading arrangement either with South Africa alone, or in a larger regional context with member countries of the Southern African Customs Union (SACU). The India-South Africa Commercial Alliance (ISACA), groups government and private sector on both sides.

Deliberate emphasis has so far been laid on the economic aspect of the bilateral relationship because it is the belief of the author that this will be the engine driving the growth of bilateral relations between India and South Africa. However, the political aspect of the relationship is equally significant as it invariably provides the underpinnings of all other aspects of the relationship.

Fortunately for India and South Africa, both share an abiding commitment to democracy and the rule of law, South-South co-operation, WTO issues on developing countries' priorities and are members of NAM, IOR-ARC, the Commonwealth as well as being partners in initiatives ranging from UN reform to peacekeeping operations in Africa. South Africa is largely supportive of India's quest for permanent membership of the UN Security Council and is trying to work on a consensus in the African Union on the subject, even as it is staking its own claim for an African seat on the UNSC. On Kashmir, again South Africa largely endorses India's position for resolution of the issue within the bilateral framework

---

11. Estimated investment from India in South Africa is around US $ 200 million, while from South Africa in India is estimated at over US $ 50 million.

of the Simla Agreement. Publicly, South Africa denies the export of arms to Pakistan though every now and then there are reports of arms shipments to that country. On terrorism, while South Africa condemns terrorism, it invariably insists on a universally acceptable definition of 'terrorism' and calls for removing the 'root causes' of terrorism.[12]

Besides IOR-ARC, India and South Africa are together involved in two other joint regional initiatives of which mention must be made, namely IBSA and NEPAD.

IBSA: In June 2003, the Foreign Ministers of India, Brazil and South Africa met in Brasilia and agreed to set up a Dialogue Forum for regular consultations on matters of mutual interest. The second meeting of the IBSA Trilateral Ministerial Commission was held in New Delhi, in March 2004. The three Foreign Ministers agreed on a Plan of Action for trilateral cooperation in the fields of Transportation (Civil Aviation and Shipping), Tourism, Trade and Investment, Infrastructure, Job creation through small, medium and micro-enterprises, Science and Technology, Information Society, E-Governance, Capacity Building, Local Content Development, E-Health, Information Society, Health, Energy, Defence and Education. The third Meeting, held in Cape Town (March 2005) added the fields of Culture and Agriculture. The fourth Meeting was held in Rio in March 2006.

NEPAD: India has been strongly supportive of the objectives of New Partnership for Africa's Development (NEPAD) ever since its inception, and as a token of its support, has pledged US $ 200 million so far, to be utilised through credit lines, grants, etc.

Some critics tend to make much out of the misunderstanding caused by South Africa's somewhat hasty reaction to India's nuclear tests in May 1998, and later to Mandela's unintended expression of concern for Kashmir at the NAM summit in Durban, in 1998. Both countries have put these events well behind them and decided

---

12. This sensitivity arises from ANC's own earlier record; during the freedom struggle, the ANC was not averse to, and indeed often resorted to, using terrorist tactics against the white minority regime in response to the ruling government's violent suppression of blacks.

to move forward to forge a strategic partnership[13] with a clear vision for the future.

Conclusion

India-South Africa relations are on a sound upward trajectory, even if, like any trajectory, the angle may vary from time to time. Unflinching support to the struggle against apartheid in the earlier years pre-1990, the moral and material support to the ANC during its darkest days led to an abundance of mutual goodwill on the parts of both governments and their peoples and a common vision for the future. The trade turnover now exceeds two billion dollars (excluding defence sales). South Africa has a million-strong, influential and quite prosperous Indian community who act as vital bridges between the country of their origin and the country they proudly call home today. The Indian private sector has already established a visible presence in South Africa, fully cognizant of its strength as the economic powerhouse of Africa[14] and also its unlimited potential as a gateway to the rest of Africa and to South America, straddling as it does the major international sea routes between the Indian and Atlantic Oceans.

As two major regional powers, India and South Africa have a shared vision of a more just and equitable world order. Both are actively working towards reform of the UN system and each is an aspirant for a seat on the UN Security Council as a permanent member. On economic issues, whether within the framework of WTO or outside, both countries often forge and project a common position for a world order in which the rights of the poorer developing countries are protected. Both countries play an active role within their respective regions—South Africa in AU, SADCC and SACU, and India in SAARC, BIMSTEC and MGC, etc. In a larger global context, both countries enjoy an identical outlook which helps them project the interests of the developing countries. As a founder

---

13. The Joint Declaration signed during President Mbeki's visit in October 2003, clearly states that "The Strategic Partnership between India & South Africa is guided by a common vision of a global order marked by peace, security and equity."

14. South Africa's GDP is larger than the rest of SADC, or of Egypt, Nigeria and Kenya put together.

member of the G-20 and an active member of the G-8, South Africa forcefully projects the interests of the third world along with India. The IBSA initiative, as well as fora such IOR-ARC provide additional platforms enabling frequent consultations between leaders of both countries. Defence supplies have lately added another, rather significant, element in the bilateral relations with the feeling in India that South Africa will always be a reliable and trustworthy supplier, given the history of our past relationship. Underpinning all this, is the strategic partnership which embraces political, security and economic dimensions.

India needs South Africa's diamonds, gold and reliable defence supplies just as much as South Africa needs India's teachers, administrators, managers and Information & Communication technology (ICT) personnel. South Africa is keen to work with India to fulfil its skill gaps in many areas across the board in order to realise its dream of black economic empowerment. The Indian Technical & Economic Cooperation (ITEC) Programme is being re-engineered to meet South Africa's growing skilled manpower needs. There is also considerable scope for collaborative R&D in many areas of industry, science and technology ranging in scope from pharmaceuticals to defence technologies.

The full potential of relations between India and South Africa has not yet been tapped, but there is every reason for optimism that given past history and today the frequent contacts between the leadership of both countries in the public and private sectors, and also given the pace of progress in every field of bilateral endeavours, the future of relations between the two countries are poised to attain even greater heights in the new millennium.

42

India and Brazil—a new dynamic

Hardeep Puri

There is a tide in the affairs of men, which, taken at the flood,
leads on to fortune... on such a full sea are we now afloat and
we must take the current when it serves or lose our ventures.

Shakespeare—*Julius Cesar*

The first decade of the 21st Century is witnessing the
establishment of a unique and multifaceted partnership between
Brazil and India, the newly anointed emerging giants of Latin
America and Asia, respectively. Judging by the range and value of
opportunities being generated and tapped in political and economic
fields, one can discern a 'tide' in the affairs of Brazil and India. It
merits being taken 'at the flood' by policy makers and diplomats,
economic actors and scientists as well as the civil societies in both
countries. It is also equally true that any slacking of interest or
effort on their part would risk jeopardising the 'fortune' that the
partnership already delivers or promises in the future.

But building solid bilateral relations between countries
previously constrained by history, geography and their own
capacities requires more than going with the tide. A clear set of
priorities need to be adopted along with acceptable modalities for
implementation of 'rolling action plans' in different areas. Defined
goals need to converge towards a common vision based on shared
values. In absence of such vision, diplomatic activity is rendered
mere movement without purpose. The management of these

activities may give episodic satisfaction to the dramatist personae involved, without producing sustainable impact.

On the other hand, the contours of a strategic vision should not only be shaped by the ideals of a visionary but also be grounded in objective realities and assessment of what is truly achievable within given circumstances and time frames. In India-Brazil relations some of this envisioning, coupled with hard nosed calculation of prospects has seriously begun at several levels with positive results. There is a coming together of political commitment by both governments with the traction being provided by the business community, development experts and technologists who recognise substantial mutual benefits, now and in the future.

The new depth and momentum that this relationship is acquiring is fuelled essentially by three separate but concomitant processes. Firstly, the scale, scope and audacity of the development enterprise in the two countries fosters natural affinities. Not only do their achievements such as democracy and economic and social progress unite India and Brazil, but this unity is strengthened also by their problems and struggles as post-colonial nation states. There is increasing realisation that they can each draw upon a reservoir of development lessons lived and learnt by the other and thus, adopt best practices to speedily and equitably climb the development ladder. Secondly, on the bilateral track a whole new and expanding universe is opening up for mutually beneficial cooperation. These are in areas ranging from trade, investment, agriculture, manufacturing and services to energy, environment, science and technology. Finally, there is a strong multilateral plank of issues on which Indo-Brazil partnership, if not leadership, is crucial for furtherance of their own interests, that of other developing countries and of the global community in general.

Both Brazil and India stand out among the so-called BRIC, (considered the four developing countries — Brazil, Russia, India and China with most potential for development in the next 50 years) as large democracies and bottom up societies. But both Brazil and India are countries of pronounced inherent contrasts. They have traditionally been viewed by the West in terms of negative stereotypes—notable social and economic disparities, the enormity of the developmental challenges and the need for domestic reform. A more sympathetic and respectful appreciation by the West of the two large open and pluralistic societies based on a strong advocacy of human rights and buoyant economies is a more recent development. There is recognition that both rightfully deserve a place on any high table of responsible democracies and economies that matter.

Hailing the rise of India and Brazil and their categorisation as big competitive markets by developed countries, international financial institutions and multinational companies has led to greater awareness about each other's intrinsic and growing worth. The recognition of India's emergence as a global services provider and Brazil as the world's agriculture supplier has contributed to their self-confidence and mutual esteem. Policy makers and the corporate sector have begun to admit to the regional and global dynamo role of the two economies and hence, believing in the prospects of a quantitative and qualitative leap in trade and investment ties with cascading effect in other areas of the relationship.

The 'vision' of bilateral relations that the two countries share is both remarkable and can serve as a model for other developing countries. This vision comprises several elements; shared developmental challenges; aspirations to raise the standard of living of their respective populations; joint endeavours in two important areas of transformational diplomacy—the G-4 and the India-Brazil-South Africa initiative; and realising the immense potential of bilateral economic relations, particularly through development-oriented science and technology and enlargement of the trade and investment sphere of interaction. The sectors which readily suggest themselves for enhanced cooperation, based both on existing levels of cooperation and potential are: energy—petroleum and ethanol, health, pharma and biotech, agriculture and food processing, ICT, including education, media and entertainment, automotive industries, engineering, infrastructure, and manufacturing of civil aircraft.

The decision by both countries to establish a Joint Commission for the annual comprehensive review of their bilateral relations at foreign ministers level reflects the importance that they attach to their bilateral relations. India's opening up and impressive rates of growth made it an ideal partner, particularly as Brazil experienced a major hike in its relations with the other Asian giant, China. Brazil's immense potential as a partner for cooperation, both in and of itself and as a gateway to Latin America naturally suggested itself to India. This thrust manifested itself in and was born of multiple developments such as sharp increase in bilateral trade, regional trade bloc agreements, science and technology cooperation and environment. As a result, it was deemed fit to create a special organisational support structure in the form of a Joint Commission to carry this momentum further.

The Second Meeting of the Joint Commission at Ministerial level in Brasilia on 2 February 2006, has put in place a framework of cooperation in sectors as diverse as agriculture, defence, energy, health, space science and technology, social development, trade and investment, etc. Governments can only outline a paradigm and framework for cooperation. The commercial arrangements between economic entities in the two countries must necessarily be worked out by themselves through the market. However, the very fact that the newly appointed Minister of State for External Affairs, Shri Anand Sharma travelled to Brazil in February 2006, almost within 48 hours of assuming charge, highlights the commitment at the governmental level. It is equally reassuring that the economic actors are beginning to take full advantage of the opportunities available in both countries.

While it is true that Brazil's potential value to India and of India to Brazil has never been greater than now due to a conjunction of political factors and economic complementarities, the relationship itself goes back to many decades as independent nations but also to centuries as civilisations. The exchanges between South America including Brazil possibly commenced with migration from Asia in the ancient period of our history which contributed to formation of the indigenous people of the Americas. The direct exchanges that took place from the 16th to the 18th Century between the two major pillars of the Portuguese colonial empire, namely, Brazil and the present Indian State of Goa, was responsible for bringing an Asian, more particularly, an Indian component into the early stages of the Brazilian melting pot. This is reflected in the flora and fauna, food and dressing habits and even in folk traditions such as stories of *Panchatantra*, which helped shape the emerging Brazilian cultural identity. Over the years, Indian philosophy and psycho spiritualist currents such as yoga have influenced Brazilian intellectual and cultural life as reflected in the works of philosophers such as Farias Brito and poets, Cruz e Souza and Cecilia Meireles.[1] India and Brazil curiously share many folk traditions such as BoiBumba of the North of Brazil being similar to the Poikal Kudhirai of the South of India and usage of sea shells for sooth saying in the North East of Brazil and Kerala in India. Further research may throw up very interesting findings about such connectivities.

On the political side, India registered its diplomatic presence in Brazil soon after Independence. Brazil's immediate official recognition of India allowed the Indian Embassy being opened in Rio de Janeiro, the former capital on May 3, 1948, which was then shifted to the new capital, Brasilia on August 1, 1971. Acknowledging the growing commercial potential of Indo-Brazilian relations, an Indian Consulate General was opened in 1996 in Brazil's commercial and industrial centre, São Paulo. In addition, there are Honorary Consuls in Belo Horizonte and Rio de Janeiro. Brazil in turn has had an Embassy since 1949, and is scheduled to open its Consulate General in Mumbai, shortly.

Against this background of formal political and people to people relations, it is important to identify the existing and potential complementarities that are changing the face of Indo-Brazilian relations. It is not merely Brazil's size that renders it an ideal partner for special cooperation with India. In 2005, Brazil surpassed Mexico to become the largest economy in Latin America with its GDP at US$ 795 billion and expected to grow at 4 per cent. Further, what

---

1. Prof. Dilip Loundos article on Brazil-India Relations in Stanley Wolpert (ed.) (2005). *Encyclopedia of India*, Farmington Hills (MI/US), Charles Scribner's Sons Reference Books.

distinguishes Brazil, apart from economic weight and its democratic credentials, is the wealth of its natural resources—land, minerals, metals, and freshwater reserves—which, together with the high literacy and entrepreneurial skills of its 180 million population, its strong manufacturing base, and its position as an agricultural powerhouse, endow it with a gravitas which few other countries possess. In fact, Brazil is a BRIC economy on the ascendant. Whilst India and China are likely, as will be discussed below, to confront an imminent scarcity of land on account of their large and growing populations, Brazil has singular advantages.

For India, Brazil's vast land area and its abundant mineral, metal, water and energy resources and agricultural production capacity are a perfect match for its existing and future deficits and exponential needs in these areas. India needs to link up with the Brazilian economy in order to successfully fuel its 8 to 10 per cent economic growth that is being targeted, to reduce poverty, ensure food and energy security as well as access to fresh water for its huge and growing population and provide key inputs to its industry to become a global manufacturing hub.

The importance of Brazil's territorial expanse and land area needs to be fully appreciated in India. Brazil with an area of 5 million sq. kms. has 2.6 times India's land area and only one-sixth of India's population—approximately 180 million. Thus, its population-land ratio is very favourable. Brazil accounts for 20 per cent of world's arable land and nearly, 20 per cent of its fresh water resources.

Agriculture and agribusiness—complementaries and potential

In no sector is the contrast and therefore, the complementarity between India and Brazil more evident than in the area of agriculture and agribusiness. First and foremost it is truly remarkable that Brazil utilises only 47 or 48 million hectares, i.e. 5.7 per cent out of its total area of 851 million hectares. The potential for expanding the area under cultivation is, therefore, immense. Brazil has been a star performer in this sector and over the past 20 years, made spectacular advances not only in raising agricultural productivity but also in transport, storage, distribution and export of agricultural products.

It is already an engine of agricultural development and, by any yardstick, destined to be the agricultural superpower of this century. With virtually unlimited acreage, ideal weather conditions, plentiful water and advanced technology, it is the world's number one exporter in a number of commodities such as beef, coffee and orange juice. It is quickly climbing the charts in other commodities such as sugar, soybeans, soyoil, poultry, cotton and tobacco. Brazilian agriculture exports currently account for over 36 per cent of its total exports. On the other hand, Brazil is also a major agriculture importer with imports in commodities such as wheat and rice where India could position itself to be a supplier of choice, given right kind of policies and partnerships

The policy framework for agribusiness in Brazil has concentrated on removing whatever impediments that might have existed. Outstanding agricultural research by EMBRAPA, the government agricultural research institutes, and others, has led to some leading-edge work. These and other development organisations have ensured consistent improvement in crop productivity and ever-higher yield levels as well as a coordinated national effort to genetically upgrade the livestock, earning Brazil worldwide respect and admiration. A distinguishing factor that puts Brazilian agriculture in the major league is the extent of mechanisation and technology intensity as well as success in commercial agriculture, trade logistics to handle bulk exports, high quality standards related testing, certifying and conformance infrastructure as well as the sophistication and scale of its agroprocessing industry. In all of these areas, India can take a leaf out of the Brazilian book.

By contrast, Indian agriculture is largely of a subsistence nature based on smallholder farming with limited commercialisation, export capacity and orientation. Indian agriculture is also plagued by heavy dependence on weather and irrigation. It suffers from low yields per hectare, volatility in production and wide disparities of productivity over regions and crops. There is a bias towards foodgrains cultivation, distribution and stock piling on account of food security concerns. Although, India is among the leading producers of rice, wheat and sugar, it is not a major exporter of most agricultural commodities. The proportion of agricultural exports to total export has come down to 10.2 per cent in 2004-2005 i.e. US $ 13 billion.

The performance of the agricultural sector which grew at only 2.3 per cent pales in comparison to growth in industry (8.3 per cent and services 9.8 per cent). There is an urgent need to increase agricultural processing from current 2 per cent to 25 per cent and improve its quality. This is necessary not only to save the billions of dollars of food lost every year before it reaches the market but also to upgrade export capacity. Trade logistics for agriculture imports and exports also need to be considerably improved. Policy pronouncements in India, including personally by the Prime Minister, clearly point to the importance that is being attached to reinvigorate the agricultural sector, to improve productivity levels and seek global competitiveness particularly if the WTO negotiations do result in subsidy cuts by the developed countries and liberalisation in agricultural tariffs. In the light of these shortcomings and requirements in India's agricultural development and trade, cooperation with Brazil is a strategic imperative.

In particular, India faces over the next 20 years, a situation where it will not have enough land to grow the food required to feed its growing population whose consumption will in time increase considerably with higher standards of living. By 2030, India's population is expected to be 1.44 billion and by 2050, 1.59 billion. With declining productivity, tightening environmental regulations, irregularity of monsoons and water shortages, shrinking land area available for agriculture due to industrialisation and urbanisation, India will have to import reasonable share of agricultural consumption in non-food security areas as well. It is Brazil which can then be an ideal partner with its plentiful land, high productivity and export surpluses. Acquisition of agricultural assets and investment of capital and human resources by India in Brazil, will pay high dividends both in the immediate and long term. This is something which the Brazilian Government is also encouraging.

Even in areas where India seeks to be a globally competitive exporter such as sugar, cotton and horticulture, Brazil can help in raising productivity and quality. For this, collaboration at the institutional level between designated institutes of agricultural research and standard setting and certification can be enhanced so that both can benefit from shared R&D and embark on a comprehensive programme to improve agricultural productivity in areas where each has strengths. This is already in progress with an MoU for cooperation between Indian Council of Agricultural Research (ICAR) and EMBRAPA. Time has also come for initiating cooperation between Brazilian and Indian agricultural universities. Ways will have to be found, including through link up with major Brazilian food processing companies which represent a world-class industry, to commercially exploit possibilities and upgrade the entire food-processing sector in India.

The sugar sector presents an interesting scenario of similarities and contrasts between the two countries in agriculture. Brazil is the world's largest sugar producer and India is a distant second but that is where the comparison ends. On average, Brazilian households consume twice as much sugar as Indian households. India's large population, however, ensures that India remains the world's largest market with the possibility of it continuing as a net importer. India's smaller size, one third that of Brazil, and six times its population results in cane having to compete heavily with essential food crops. Equally, if not even more importantly, the better use of soil and genetically engineered cane has improved land productivity which is remarkable for a country that unlike India, uses almost no irrigation. Brazil's productivity has been increasing roughly by 1.5 per cent every year for the last 30 years. Its cost of production is lowest in the world as against India's position as medium-cost and US as among the highest-cost producers.

India's rapid eco growth, likely increase in population and land scarcity makes Brazil an ideal candidate for sourcing its requirements of sugar and ethanol to meet food and energy security needs. Cane can be grown on 75 per cent Brazilian land or twice the land area of India. Moreover, since foreigners do not face many restrictions on acquisition of land, time is opportune for Indian investors— agricultural and sugar industry to acquire agricultural, sugar and ethanol assets in Brazil. Such interest is already being evinced but needs to proceed more quickly, particularly since countries like China also seem to be beginning to acquire such assets.

One area where India has made a contribution to Brazil is cattle farming. It is remarkable that the bulk of the Brazilian livestock of cattle, approximately 185 million, is of Indian origin. This grass fed variety 'Zebu', known locally as 'Nelore' was largely imported from Andhra Pradesh where the variety is known as 'Ongole'. 2006 marked the hundredth anniversary of the first cattle being imported from India to North-Eastern Brazil. One of the major preoccupations of the Brazilians is the importation of fresh embryos from India to rejuvenate their stock.

Energy symbiosis

Brazil's energy requirement and management of supply and demand of energy sources are slated to have dramatic influence on its future economic development and on the energy balance of the Western hemisphere. Conversely, India's burgeoning energy needs and its management of supply, demand and use of and access to energy sources will determine its ability to sustain its rapid economic growth and reduction of poverty and affect global energy balance in the medium to long term. Both India and Brazil seek energy security, indeed energy independence as President Kalam, termed it in his 2005 Independence Day Address. However, unlike Brazil which is largely self-sufficient in energy sources and has vast untapped potential of oil and gas, India's dependence on foreign oil and gas is considerably growing.

Hence, the partnership in the energy area with Brazil can be an important element of India's energy security strategy. Both countries seem to be following similar energy strategies that are based on maximising domestic exploration and production of oil and gas, to access conveniently oil and gas resources elsewhere on a secure basis, diversify sources of energy, particularly, renewable energy sources such as solar energy, wind energy, biofuels and nuclear energy. In the oil and gas area, collaboration has already started in terms of trade and investment, but it is also in areas like biofuels that the future of energy cooperation between them is promising.

In April, 2006, ONGC Videsh signed an investment of over US$ 400 million for the acquisition of a stake in an offshore block in South-East Brazil. The Brazilian oil major Petrobras is also eyeing the Indian market. On June 21, GAIL and Petrobras, Brazil's energy giant signed a cooperation and confidentiality agreement. Petrobras has also shown keen interest in partnering GAIL for various exploration projects, including blocks in Iran such as Block 12. This development comes close on the heels of GAIL along with its consortium partners signing the exploration and production sharing agreement (EPSA) with the Sultanate of Oman for Block 56 in Oman. GAIL has 25 per cent participating interest in the Consortium.

In the biofuels sector, Brazil has blazed a trail by developing an ethanol industry far ahead of that in any other country. Brazil's sugarcane industry has also benefited from skyrocketing global demand for ethanol. Many Brazilian cars run on hydrated ethanol; over 70 per cent of cars in production today are 'flexi-fuel', meaning they can run on both ethanol and gasoline. Furthermore, one-fourth of the gasoline mixture in Brazil is anhydrous ethanol, *versus* 5-10 per cent in most countries using biomass fuel. The country's ethanol expertise stems from a market that originated in the 1990s, when Brazil was energy self-sufficient and oil prices were low. Today, because oil prices are so high, the ethanol industry has helped Brazilian consumers and businesses save billions of dollars. The growing economies of scale have made Brazilian ethanol production costs the best in the world.

It is ironic that the links in biofuel sources can trace their origin to the colonial era and the fact that the Portuguese took the Jetropha plant from Brazil to India which today has been identified as the primary plant for biodiesel production in India and Brazilians seek to borrow from the Indian experience in this respect. Contemporary cooperation is, however, centred on the ethanol programme whose origins are more recent. It was the visit in 2003 of the then Indian Minister of Petroleum to Brazil which, inspired by the Brazilian success story, resulted in the introduction of a 5 per cent blending requirement of ethanol in nine of our states. Our inability to implement this effectively, let alone expand this, has been due to the competing demands from the potable alcohol lobby in India. Given a choice between a higher economic returns from potable alcohol, the ethanol programme clearly suffered. The current energy scenario characterised by petroleum prices in the vicinity of US$ 70-80 per barrel with little or no likelihood of restoration of the *status quo ante* at dollars 28 per barrel in the foreseeable future has suddenly refocussed attention on the economic viability of ethanol as a viable cost effective, cleaner alternate fuel that can take some pressure off petroleum. It is no surprise that Indian economic entities are now actively pursuing the acquisition of both greenfield and mature manufacturing assets in both sugar crushing and ethanol production in Brazil.

Sustaining the surge in bilateral trade

Developments in bilateral relations between India and Brazil in the past few years, particularly since 2003, have demonstrated that the constraint of physical distance need not be an impediment to a significant, perhaps even spectacular, strengthening of bilateral relations between India and Brazil. The surge in bilateral trade has electrified the relationship more than anything else in the past 2-3 years. For many decades, Indo-Brazilian trade has been at a modest level and hovered around US $ 200 million till the late 1990s. The breakthrough came between 2003-2004 when it increased appreciably. President Lula's landmark visit to India as Chief Guest for Republic Day in January 2004, ushered in a qualitative transformation in bilateral relations and a quantum jump in economic interaction. 2005 registered a 100 per cent increase in trade over the 2004 figure for two-way trade to reach a figure of US $ 2.5 billion.

According to studies carried out including by organisations such as UNCTAD, based on recessed comparative advantage (RCA) analysis and going by the new trade and investment nexus that is emerging, Indo-Brazil trade can indeed easily reach US$ 10 billion in the next 3 to 5 years. The enabling policy environment and corporate activism is in evidence and the imperatives of cooperation are asserting themselves. It should, therefore, not be difficult to meet these targets in different areas and convert the current surge into an enduring and substantial trade relationship.

There is considerable scope to expand trade in pharmaceuticals in terms of bulk drugs as well as finished formulations since Brazil is the biggest importer of pharmaceuticals in the region. Opportunities are growing in organic and inorganic chemicals, in automobiles and transport equipment. Newer areas like Ayurveda which is now recognised legally as an alternative therapy in Brazil, biotechnology agribusiness and IT can also generate substantial trade flows. Additionally, the avenues for Indian contractors, suppliers and consultants for participating in projects funded by multilateral financial institutions such as the World Bank are many, with 50 projects worth 4 billion committed and a programme of projects worth up to US $ 7.5 billion envisaged over the next four years.

Among the new areas, Indo-Brazil trade and investment in the biotech area have bright prospects India has several comparative advantages in this sector in terms of knowledge, skills, R&D facilities and cost structures and as a consequence, several major global biotech companies are showing increasing interest in developing partnerships with Indian counterparts. India's core competence in biotechnology spreads over human and animal healthcare to agricultural as well as industrial biotechnology and initiatives like the biotechnology policy, biotech parks would only contribute towards realising the high growth potential of this sector. Brazil also has a huge market for biotech related products. The market primarily includes supplies and instruments used in biotech research, biopharmaceuticals, vaccines and human and animal diagnostic tests. India and Brazil can work together towards manufacturing products derived from biotechnology and also as research collaborators. Opportunities exist in manufacturing vaccines, bioactive therapeutic proteins, laboratory supplies and equipment. Bioinformatics is also a prospective area of mutual collaboration. Finally, contract-research in segments of new drug discovery, clinical trials, and bio-informatics related services could strengthen the synergy between the pharmaceutical and biotechnology sectors.[2]

Two points stand out: this increase in trade does not include the big ticket items such as trade and investment in the energy sector-petroleum, purchase and possibly joint production of aircraft and cooperation in the infrastructure sector such as railways, presently under discussion. These figures also do not reflect the India-Brazil trade and investment in sectors like IT and pharmaceuticals, figures for which tend to be reflected in the trade statistics of European countries where the Indian entities are registered rather than in the bilateral trade figures. Equally, if not more importantly, this level of trade, which has the potential of being doubled or even trebled in the short to medium term, has not yet benefited from the India-Mercosur preferential tariff arrangement, which is still to be ratified by the Mercosur countries and is expected to take effect sometime in 2006.

As an important member of Mercosur, Brazil provided valuable assistance to India for signing a Framework Agreement with the bloc, in June 2003, in Asuncion. During President Lula's visit to India, when he was Chief Guest for Republic Day in January 2004, Mercosur signed a Preferential Customs agreement. The accord expands on the framework agreement signed in June 2003. The Customs duty accord is expected to eventually lead to a Free Trade Agreement. During the 10th Anniversary Summit of Mercosur in Brazil in December, 2004, India and Mercosur initialed a trade agreement. The agreement involves 450 products from each side with duty reductions of 10 per cent to 100 per cent. The formal protocol incorporating these annexes to the PTA between India and Mercosur was signed in New Delhi, in March 2005. Efforts are under way to deepen the Indo-Mercosur PTA and to link it under IBSA to SACU as well. The GSTP negotiations for South-South trade liberalisation will create further trade opportunities.

---

2. EXIM Bank's study, *Biotechnology: Emerging Opportunities for India.*

What, then, is the outlook for bilateral trade in the foreseeable future? On a fairly conservative basis, we could have US $ 4-5 billion worth of trade in the next 2-3 years and US $ 10 billion in the next 5 years. Though these figures sound ambitious, they are not unrealistic provided we can ensure that an enabling and facilitative environment is fostered.

Opportunities in infrastructure and manufactures national resources

Brazil possesses extremely rich mineral deposits. It has proven and estimated reserves of iron ore totalling 48 billion tonnes. Identified deposits would be capable of meeting world demand for iron (based on current levels and predictable growth) for the next 500 years! In addition, Brazil has proven deposits of 208 million tonnes of manganese, 2 billion tonnes of bauxite, and 53 million tonnes of nickel with new discoveries which could amount to more than 400 million tonnes. The recent confirmation of the existence of large, high-grade (1.3 per cent) uranium reserves in the states of Minas Gerais and Goiás is of great significance. Brazil has reserves of potassium phosphate, tungsten, cassiterite (the chief source of tin), lead, graphite, chrome, gold, zirconium (a strong ductile metallic element with many industrial uses), and the rare mineral, thorium, a radioactive metallic element. Brazil produces 90 per cent of the world's supply of gems, such as diamonds, aquamarines, topazes, amethysts, tourmalines, and emeralds.

If India is to continue to grow at around 8 per cent or so in the coming decade, its growth and the overall Asian boom will require natural resources to feed it. Brazil not only has these resources but the capacity to continue to supply them over an extended period of time. The synergy is being perceived in both countries. There are opportunities in the area of mining equipment and economically and environmentally sustainable state of the art extraction and processing technologies. The world's second largest economic entity, in the sector of minerals, the Brazilian company, CVRD has already opened an office in New Delhi and Indian public sector majors in this area are also prospecting opportunities.

Brazil being a rich repository of these minerals as well as having highly diversified and competitive industrial base particularly, in natural resource intensive sectors, points to enormous complementarities with India's manufacturing, exports and infrastructure related capacities and ambitions. They also suggest opportunities for acquiring mining and related assets, long-term arrangements for purchase and joint ventures with local enterprises. Collaboration for export to third country markets can also be pursued in areas such as gems and jewellery, automotive sector, mining equipment where India and Brazil have comparative advantages they can bring to collaboration for joint production, transfer of technology and exports to third countries.

Infrastructure is a critical area where major business opportunities beckon for Brazil in India. India is expected to spend approximately $ 50 billion every year for at least the next five years to upgrade its infrastructure. India's current annual spending on infrastructure is only around $ 20 billion or barely a fraction of its GDP of US$ 740 billion, as nominally calculated. China's spending, in contrast, is $ 230 billion or 12 per cent of its GDP. Infrastructure spending in India in the next five years has to rise dramatically. Even the enhanced spending will be inadequate to catch up with the infrastructure available in developed countries. This spending will have to be on CAPEX enhancement, ports, airports, shipping, railways, roads, telecom and power. And this is where the magic of absolute numbers manifests. If, as against the anticipated annual investment of $ 50 billion, only $ 40 billion is spent, even this is equal to two-fifths of the GDP of Philippines.

On its part, Brazil is rated by some to have the best infrastructure among the four BRIC economies.[3] There are also opportunities for economic entities in both countries to collaborate in joint ventures in the infrastructure sector in Latin America and Africa. Brazil has demonstrated rare success in public private partnerships in infrastructure financing and development, which

---

3. Washington Council on International Trade.

could be models for replication in India. Activities to harness these synergies in the infrastructure sector are ongoing.

India can contribute in the rejuvenation of Brazilian infrastructure in the railways sector. There has been a resurgence of interest on the part of the Brazilian government to invest in new passenger trains and routes and by private rail operators to upgrade and repair existing tracks as well as acquire rolling stock, new freight wagons as well as locomotives in a significant up scaling. Indian companies including public sector IRCON and RITES as well as private sector companies such as BESCO can participate in multimillion dollar opportunities for supply of engineering and contracting services in track and bed upgradation, sleepers and signalling equipment and for the refurbishing, manufacture and supply of freight wagons and locomotives. Some beginnings in this area that have been made, need to be followed up in order to compete with US and now China in the Brazilian rail market.

The phenomenal growth of the civil aviation sector in India and demand for aircrafts has generated considerable interest in Embraer, Brazil's successful manufacturer of 50 to 100 seater civil aircraft. India has already purchased a few Legacy aircraft for its VIP squadrons. Fifteen have separately been purchased by a regional airline in the South with more orders in the pipeline. There is no reason why the two countries should not enter into joint production in India for exploiting not only the Indian market but also India's growing links with South and South-East Asia and benefit from Brazil's progress in this area.

Information technology—the India advantage

Brazil has viewed India's emergence as an IT superstar and export performer with admiration, particularly because despite a well-developed IT sector, its export success has been limited. This is an area where Indian IT majors can invest and trade to significant advantage. Brazil accounts for more than half of Latin American IT market with 28 million internet users as against India's 38 million. IT spending is rising rapidly mostly from the financial services segment and there are many opportunities for Indian IT companies to bid for IT contracts with Brazilian banks and insurance companies. For example, US $ 3 billion a year is invested in IT by Brazilian banks alone. Indian IT majors like TCS are viewing Brazil not only as an important market in itself but as a spring board for other parts of Latin America, North America and Africa. This mutually beneficial interaction is resulting in employment generation with TCS scheduled to employ 2000 Brazilians along with concomitant skill upgradation and advantage of India Brand Equity in this sector while India gets new and additional markets and truly global outreach.

The potential investment boom

There is a growing awareness in Brazil that the Indian economy is reasonably competitive and well-positioned after the first generation reforms. Interest rates are generally in line with global trends. Inflation is under control at around 4.5 per cent. The currency is stable and tariffs are slowly but surely approaching global levels.

At the same time, as India has recently surpassed United States as the second most attractive foreign direct investment location in the world, Brazil has regained its place amongst the first 10 in investment destinations.[4] However, Brazil has managed to attract far bigger amounts of FDI in the past–in some good years i.e. 2001 as high as US $ 28 billion a year and more recently, US$ 17 billion in 2004. Its FDI to GDP ratio has touched 5.5 per cent as against India's 0.5 per cent. Brazil's attraction for Indian investors is on account of its market size of 100 million economically active consumers, abundant natural resources, good infrastructure, stable institutions, democratic regime, growth potential and freedom from political unrest and terrorism.

For Brazilian investors in India, the allure is on account of positive demographic changes, a population of 1.1 billion with a working population of 500 million, constituting one of the largest pools of consumers worldwide. Its middle class segment, with

---

4. *FDI Confidence Index*, 2005, Vol-VIII, AT Kearney.

annual income of less than US $ 3000, is set to multiply nine times in the coming decade. There are seven million people entering the 'young spenders' category, i.e., aged between 20 and 34, every year. The consumption spend is estimated to double to US $ 500 billion in five years.

Among developing countries, both India and Brazil are leading the pack in outward FDI. Indian outward investment which is now approaching US $ 11 billion and going beyond traditional destinations in Asia and Africa to Latin America is already targeting Brazil and seeking to utilise its full potential in areas such as agriculture, minerals, petrochemicals and pharmaceuticals. On the other hand, Brazilian corporate sector has also been actively investing abroad. From 1994 through 2004, Brazil's outward investments in the international market jumped from US $ 700 million to US $ 9.5 billion—(an increase of 1,357 per cent) in Latin America and US but also increasingly in Asia and Africa. India's emergence as a top FDI destination should also attract Brazilian investment in areas ranging from food processing, infrastructure, manufacturing, mining, gems and jewellery, etc. Another aspect that will give a fillip to Indo-Brazilian investment is that some mid-size manufacturers and service providers from Brazil have been told by their multinational clients to move to India to strengthen their multinational contacts in areas such as the automotive sector and IT. There is thus, optimism that bilateral FDI flows could grow several fold to 2-3 billion dollars in couple of years riding on the present encouraging trends.

Science and technology

Both Brazil and India have traditionally placed a strong emphasis on science and technology in their respective education systems and can boast one of the most comprehensive R&D infrastructures in the developing world. Brazil is rated to have the largest and most diversified system of science and technology in Latin America with considerable achievements in the last 50 years as demonstrated by its capacity for oil drilling in deep waters, aeronautics, space and nuclear programmes and advances in frontier technologies including nanotechnology and biotechnology.

There is respect in Brazil for India's appearance on the world stage as a knowledge power and an R&D platform for global MNCs. Both countries have demonstrated world-class expertise in several areas of specialisation and have many symbiotic possibilities which are beginning to be realised.

Balancing environment, intellectual property with development needs

Both India and Brazil have been in the forefront of emphasising the important role of environment as a resource-base necessary for sustainable development. They also face serious challenges of protecting their ecosystem and forest cover and in the face of unrelenting demands of economic development. As large ecologically, mega diverse countries, they share a common desire for their populations to benefit from their countries' rich biodiversity and associated traditional knowledge. They have developed a genuine partnership and have acknowledged that they have a responsibility to manage resources wisely in an environmentally sustainable way. They have also emphasised that there has to be a strong prioritisation of the development and poverty reduction concerns. This is evident in how they have worked together in the context of the Kyoto Protocol and post-Kyoto perspective, that is how to confirm assumption of responsibilities to reduce emissions without hobbling the development processes.

On intellectual property protection related issues, India and Brazil have held similar positions for a long time both in terms of domestic policies and legislation as well as international disciplines. Both have emphasised that intellectual property protection is an important requirement for promoting innovation. However, they have argued that the degree of protection should be in keeping with the stage of economic and technological development of a country and fully take into account public interest needs such as access to affordable medicines or food. They have also emphasised the importance of competition policy for ensuring that monopolistic IPR protection and appropriation of patents should not block innovation and endogenous technological capacity and its dissemination and use for development purposes. They have calibrated their intellectual property protection in a way as to provide sufficient policy space for domestic industry to develop innovation capacity just as the developed countries themselves had done in the earlier stages of the development. Today both countries, thanks to this strategic approach, are in line to be owners of more and more patents and copyright worldwide.

In areas where developing countries are repositories and owners of intellectual property such as traditional knowledge, India and Brazil have pushed for international protection of IPRs. This is being pursued in fora like the Convention on Biodiversity and WIPO. However, a main focus of attention in recent years has been the WTO TRIPs Council, where they have co-authored (along with other developing countries, such as Peru) a number of submissions related to the CBD-TRIPS relationship and IPR protection of traditional knowledge. The main concrete suggestion has been the 'disclosure requirement' i.e. in patent applications based on genetic resources and where relevant associated traditional knowledge, the source of the genetic resources and associated traditional knowledge should be disclosed in the patent application. In addition, evidence of prior informed consent and benefit sharing should be disclosed. In the absence of these, the patent should not be granted. Violations discovered after the fact should result in the patent being cancelled. India and Brazil have tabled proposals in the TRIPs Council seeking amendments to reflect this in TRIPs agreement and this effort is gathering support, including from some quarters in the developed world.

One area where the emphasis in positions is slightly different, although by no means opposing, is traditional knowledge databases or registries. In India, large portions of traditional knowledge are codified, notably the traditional medicinal knowledge contained in the Ayurvedic and other ancient texts. This is not the case in Brazil, where more traditional knowledge has not been codified and written down, but rather is held by indigenous communities or members thereof. India has developed a Traditional Knowledge Digital Library (TKDL), which comprises these ancient texts translated and put into a digital format. The TKDL is to be sent to all patent offices to facilitate a more informed search on prior art and thus, prevent the granting of inappropriate patents on processes or products based on Indian traditional medicine. Brazil generally takes a much more cautious approach to the database issue in general, expressing concerns that until an international system of protection of traditional knowledge is in place, TK databases (particularly of TK not in the public domain) could end up facilitating unauthorised use of TK and biopiracy. The country position reflects the concerns expressed by many Brazilian indigenous groups on this issue.

It is tempting for an Ambassador to build high expectations on a relationship where there is evidence of an unprecedented augmentation at a given time. But equally, it is prudent not to pitch the expectations at unrealistic and unrealisable levels. In assessing the achievables, we have to ask a number of fundamental questions. Will this positive trend hold? Will the political and economic actors sustain their focus, interests and efforts sufficiently, for long enough time and in the right way to reap the rich harvest that this promises? Are the countries going to be able to overcome their own developmental shortcomings to be the kind of A-team partners they seem destined for? Is there substance and genuine complementarity in their respective success stories? A positive evolution has been that these questions are beginning to be asked and responded to not only among select elites but by broader constituencies in both countries without any preconceived notions or prejudices.

A broad cross-section of Indians including in the media, are taking note that Brazil's achievements as a developing country are impressive by any standards. It has a per capita income fivefold that of India. Tight monetary policy designed to hold the inflation rate which is primarily responsible for high interest rates and relatively slow growth in recent years notwithstanding, Brazil is expected to grow by 4 per cent this year. With interest rates expected to slowly come down, there is no reason why Brazil should not be a leading BRIC economy. In fact, some analysts posit that it could even outperform the other BRIC economies. It has the institutional framework required, immense natural resources and an educated and entrepreneurial population. There is among Indians who have interacted with Brazil, an echo of what a Swedish businessman commented recently:

"Everything you imagine about Brazil—soccer, carnival, pretty women, caipirinha—is true. But there is much more. There is a sophisticated society, an excellent professional standard, great companies."[5]

On the other side, India's remarkable success in the last two years and the very favourable world press that we have been receiving as a result of growth rates in the vicinity of 8 per cent have already registered in the mindset of the Brazilian elite. The question most frequently asked in decisionmaking circles, both private and government, is: what is it that India has done that Brazil needs to emulate? This new-found interest is reflected in cover issues of prestigious weekly magazines of Brazil. *EXAME*, circulation 200,000, carried a cover issue on India, the dominant theme of which was "Economy". The *VEJA*, (circulation 1.1 million, second largest selling magazine in the world) cover issue carried 19 pages on the new and vibrant India.

Not to be outdone, the Brazilian version of 'Playboy' magazine has carried an article on 13 reasons why Indians are smarter than Brazilians and 5 reasons why the Brazilians are more successful than Indians. Among the first 13 reasons, Indian's command over English language, greater competitive spirit because of the need to fight for space and food unlike Brazilians, special mathematical, scientific and engineering and entrepreneurial abilities, creativity in overcoming structural barriers, high quality educational systems, faith in their Gods to find a way out for them, ability to shift and evolve an economic model most suited for themselves through calibrated reforms and most importantly, a wave of optimism and self-esteem, that Indians have never felt before, among Indians today that India can become a significant economic power. On the other hand, five reasons that puts India at a disadvantage *vis-à-vis* Brazil include large scale deprivation—more than 250 million people below poverty line without economic and social safety nets, poor

---

5. In flight magazine of Brazilian Airline, TAM.

infrastructure, high illiteracy, conservative elites and corruption, worse than in Brazil. Some of these may be impressionistic assessments of the writer, but they largely reflect popular perceptions of the relative merits of the India-Brazil equation as well.

Multilateralism—common endeavours

Brazil and India have been 'soulmates' in the multilateral arena at least for three decades and sometimes this dimension has tended to dominate the relationship. Both have placed high priority on strengthening multilateralism and democratising institutions of global governance with greater role for developing countries. They have also tried to influence political, security, economic, social and environmental discourse at the multilateral level. This has been in the direction of establishing a level-playing field for developing countries, giving them greater voice in shaping international rules and disciplines, so that they are in keeping with their size, capacity and level of development and can better serve their needs and interests. They have also sought to assume greater responsibility and progressively increase their contribution to global public good in keeping with their augmented capacity while arguing for requisite development policy space and flexibility where necessary.

Indo-Brazil cooperation in the multilateral field encompasses most UN and other organisations ranging from, (a) working together in the UNGA in the context of UN reform, (b) pushing the development, public interest and transfer technology agenda *vis-à-vis* intellectual property rights protection generally and in the World Intellectual Property Organization particularly, (c) conceptualising environment as a resource-base necessary for sustainable development and the principle of differential responsibility in various environment related fora, multilateral environment agreements (MEAs) and in trade and environment related negotiations in the WTO, (d) working for the promotion and protection of human rights at home and in the world as forward-looking pluralistic democracies, (e) seeking greater role and participation of developing countries in decisionmaking in IFIs including through the G-24 mechanism and (f) influence negotiations and promote implementation of the first international public health treaty in the world—the WHO Framework Convention on Tobacco Control (WHO FCTC), 27 February 2005.

However, there are two areas, which now stand out for particularly close coordination in international fora, namely, multilateral trade negotiations (MTNs) in the WTO and attempts to expand the permanent membership of UN Security Council to include countries like India and Brazil. Their cooperation in the area of trade policy goes back many years and they have been 'comrades in arms' on behalf of developing countries, particularly since the Uruguay round of trade negotiations in 1980s and 1990s with a strong say in inserting the development dimension in the creation of the present WTO. They have sought an open-rule based, predictable, non-discriminatory and equitable trading system which is responsive to developing country's needs and interests. In the on-going Doha negotiations in the WTO, both have assumed a leadership role through developing country, issue based coalitions such as the G-20 in agriculture and G-11 in NAMA whilst earning a place at the core decisionmaking level through participation in the so-called five most interested parties or FIPs along with US, EU, Australia and more recently G-6, replacing in some senses the traditional QUAD of developed countries—US, EU, Japan and Canada. They have learnt to leverage their growing economic clout and their large and rapidly expanding market to get the best deal for themselves and the developing world.

The aspirations of both countries to be permanent members of the Security Council constitutes another important plank of multilateral cooperation. It reflects a reality of contemporary, political, security and economic architecture that is emerging on the ground. Both have rightly argued that the Security Council of the 21st Century will not be properly equipped or have the necessary legitimacy without incorporating the largest and pre-eminent democracies and economies from the developing continents of Asia and Latin America such as India and Brazil, that too with significant global engagement and outreach in all spheres. This quest and its achievement, however difficult, will indeed continue to animate Indo-Brazilian relations for years to come.

Overcoming impediments

The United Nations Conference on Trade and Development (UNCTAD) prior to its Eleventh Session in São Paulo, Brazil from 13-18 June 2004 had organised a Forum on Regionalism and South-South Cooperation in Rio de Janeiro on June 9, 2004 and had looked at the case of India and Mercosur. It concluded that bilateral trade between India and Mercosur is inhibited by various factors, including (a) lack of information on the part of all partners on the potential, policies and import regulations of other partners; (b) poor air and sea transportation links; (c) trade restrictions; (d) inadequate banking and insurance facilities; (e) high transaction costs; and (f) language problems. If these problems are addressed, then bilateral trade between India and Mercosur could grow 16-fold in both directions, reaching US $ 13 billion.

Of the factors mentioned above, in relation to India-Mercosur, remedial action at least in so far as Brazil is concerned has been taken to correct the information deficit on the 'potential, policies and import regulations'. Intergovernmental awareness has worked to bridge the information and perception gap whilst cooperative networking amongst Chambers of Commerce of India and Brazil have also made the necessary efforts. EXIM Bank's publication such as *Indo-LAC Business* aims to facilitate business information between and LAC region including Brazil and provide a platform for business communities to ventilate their concerns as well as indicate opportunities.

The information and connectivity gap also arises from the language gap. Brazil's English speaking population is extremely limited and India's Portuguese speaking population even so. There is need on both sides to help create more linguistic bridge building assets.

The constraints imposed by 'trade restrictions' will be rectified in due course when the India-Mercosur PTA take effect and liberalisation under the GSTP negotiations also come on stream. Steps are already underway to improve the banking and insurance facilities. There is need for India and Brazil to act as the engine of the 3rd round of GSTP negotiations so that their bilateral trade liberalisation as well as South-South trade liberalisation is effectively promoted to best effect.

Trade and investment financing links between Brazil and India have many gaps. On the Indian side, the EXIM Bank has been active in entering into line of credit financing mechanisms with two commercial banks of Brazil—Banco Bredesco and Unibanco of Brazil and has supported Indian companies in their export and investment ventures in Brazil in sectors such as bauxite mining, home textile furnishing, power transmission and pharmaceutical, chemical and petrochemical products, etc. The proposed opening of a branch of Bank Itau in New Delhi, is an indicator that the Brazilian economic elite has begun to take note of the growing opportunities for business in India. There is an urgent requirement for the Indian financial sector—banks and insurance companies to be actively present in Brazil to provide the financial backing to the expended trade and investment that is on the horizon. Given sufficient commitment, the 'language' problems as indeed of 'high transaction costs' can be corrected. What clearly stands out as the most important impediment are the 'poor air and sea transportation links'.

On October 14, 2004, Finance Minister Shri P. Chidambaram announced that the Government of India has given its approval for signing of an air services agreement between India and Brazil. Under the new arrangement, which was initialised in May 2004, an IBSA civil aviation agreement was also initialised in July 2005, both countries shall have the right to designate one or more airlines for operating the services. The new agreements signify an important landmark in civil aviation relations between India and Brazil and between India, Brazil and South Africa. However, implementing this agreement is going to be a challenge, given the problems their national airlines are facing. However, in the new liberalised context of the civil aviation sector in India and already open civil aviation regime in Brazil, other airlines could be found for operating the services, should Air India and VARIG not find it possible to operate the services as foreseen.

But this is where the good news ends. Unless connectivity, both by air and surface routes is quickly established and reinforced, this positive and optimistic 'take off' paradigm could be severely undermined. According to FICCI, it takes 28 days, for goods to be shipped between India and Brazil with a six-day waiting period at a transhipment port. In addition, the traditionally Eurocentric mindsets of the travelling elites in both countries has resulted in a situation of geographical absurdity in that instead of direct air links through South Africa, people find it more convenient to connect *via* European points like London and Frankfurt. There is some basis for optimism given that in both civil aviation and shipping, there is acknowledgement that a critical mass in bilateral economic relations has already been attained and that operators in these two sectors... therefore cash in on the market logic of significantly and profitably augmenting services between India and Brazil/Latin America.

The quantum of bilateral trade between India and Brazil alone would appear to justify direct shipping links between Latin America and India. Adding in existing exports from Argentina to India of soya and existing and potential trade with other Latin American countries, it appears that we are beyond the critical mass required. Since trade and shipping appear to follow each other, it should not be difficult to now put in place direct shipping links. There are good reasons for optimism. A large Indian steel producing entity, Jindals, has just made a US$ 2 billion plus investment in iron ore assets in Bolivia, a landlocked country. This investment makes economic sense only if the iron ore is used to produce steel with the gas readily available in Bolivia for consumption in the larger economies of Asia. This will necessitate the use of Brazilian ports.

The picture in respect of civil aviation is similarly encouraging. São Paulo is not only the commercial hub of Brazil, accounting for nearly 45 per cent of its GDP, but is also the commercial nerve centre for the whole of Latin America. The air routes from São Paulo to Johannesburg and from São Paulo to different European points are profitable and coveted. The fact that Lufthansa flies twice daily between Frankfurt and São Paulo and other major European airlines at least once daily from São Paulo to different European cities is indicative of both existing and potential traffic. South African Airways flies daily between Johannesburg and São Paulo and between Johannesburg and Mumbai and soon between Johannesburg and New Delhi. A direct flight between India and São Paulo, with a stopover in Johannesburg not only makes commercial sense but would cut flying time by as much as 7 to 8 hours. It would reduce total flying time to about 17 hours, the time that it presently takes to fly to New York from India. Similarly, a Delhi/Frankfurt/São Paulo flight would again be an attractive commercial proposition apart from providing the much-required connectivity between India and Brazil.

Experience has shown that while impediments such as the lack of adequate connectivity both in shipping and air transportation links can have a constraining impact, the enhanced economic interaction, especially when it reaches critical mass can, in turn, overcome the impediments. This process now seems to be in evidence. The marketplace has the ability to ensure that transportation links, the required infrastructure for insurance and banking quickly establish themselves as business opportunities, become evident.

Any discussion on 'overcoming impediments' in the context of Brazil-India corridor would be incomplete without at least a mention of the more obvious factors–bureaucracy, red tape and corruption, lack or inadequate infrastructure or the so-called 'Brazil cost' of transactions and uncertainties and delays in terms of policies in India. It is not that these factors are unimportant. On the contrary, their importance should not be underestimated. If India can have an annual bilateral trade of US $ 20 billion with China and Brazil of US $ 12 billion, all that is being suggested is that a quantum jump can be registered, these 'impediments' notwithstanding. In any case, most of these impediments are encountered and need to be overcome even when China, for example, trades with Brazil.

Development experience—lessons learnt

An entire volume can be written on the unique development experience that both countries have registered individually and collectively and on the very many lessons that they have drawn from each other's development experiences. Many of these have already been outlined. Areas of mutual learning could relate to (a) the pace, sequencing and manner of economic reform and liberalisation of various sectors of the economy and policies and measures that have or have not worked; (b) social policies including those for ensuring distributive justice, for poverty reduction, provision of food, housing, employment to the poor, social safety net schemes, labour policy; (c) infrastructure development models including for public-private partnership and universal access to essential services; (d) renewable energy development; (e) genetically modified crops (GMO)—advantages and risks; (f) environment and natural resource management.

One point that needs to be stressed is that Brazil and India had different trajectories of development. While Brazil had its nationalistic days when import substitution was in vogue, it did not prevent Brazil from developing western style retail, real estate management, cosmetics, cold storage, consumer oriented technologies such as ATMs, parking systems, building materials, etc. which are very well developed and opening up to foreign investment in a fairly comprehensive way. India's import substitution also to an extent meant a non-consumption, investment oriented approach that eschewed potato chips but welcomed computer chips. India has been ahead in some sectors of education, medicine and pharmaceuticals and satellite technology. India can draw upon many urban transportation and infrastructure models including tolling systems, parking systems, state of the art construction materials and methods which are much more developed in Brazil.

With a combined GDP of over US $ 1.6 trillion, calculated using the nominal currency method or US $ 5.27 trillion (India 3.7 and Brazil 1.57), based on purchasing power parity, and a combined market of 1.3 billion people, the avenues for mutually beneficial cooperation between Brazil and India are broad and deep. That they are able to pursue their developmental aspirations domestically within the framework of open, democratic societies is creditable. Their developmental experience, presents empirically sound, experiential knowledge that can be accessed and, with suitable modifications, applied in other developing countries of the world. Brazil and India, offer alternate development models for developing countries rather than the 'one size fits all' prescriptions.

The fact that the most spectacular economic success stories of the emerging economies until recently were under totalitarian regimes whether in Korea or China or Chile had largely undermined the possibility of an alternate, non-Western role model for other developing countries. Development among emerging societies was always seen as a mutually exclusive choice between sociopolitical values and economic success.

The developed West was thus seen as the only place, whether due to the Weberian thesis on the Protestant ethic or some other mysterious reason where individual freedom and success could go together. Developing countries had to fundamentally change themselves to approximate western societies if they have to be successful and free societies. This has also led to many regions of the world such as the Middle East with a rich and proud history to mistrust the entire democracy—capitalism bandwagon as a vested interest project to challenge their cultures and so lose out on the benefits of these social forms and mechanisms.

Brazil and India could yet be the best hopes to provide developing countries with an alternate, benign and successful development paradigm that borrows from the developed West but retains the individual identities of their societies. The fact that they come from two different continents and have had different historical tracks will be useful to generalise learnings from their success beyond the specifics of their culture and/or historical anomalies, thus providing the first serious challenge to an almost exclusively developed West-entric model of human development. Only when such models produce the ability and confidence to solve emerging market problems through mutual collaboration and learning, without necessarily depending on the developed West is empirically demonstrated and across corridors such as India and Brazil or in an expanded forum like IBSA, will a larger wave be generated.

43

India and Canada

Prem K. Budhwar

Over the last nearly 60 years, since India's Independence in 1947, India-Canada relations have been something of a roller coaster ride. Starting with a phase of 'special relationship' to the emergence of certain irritants, to harsh language and accusations of 'betrayal' following India's Pokhran I in 1974, to a near freeze bordering on indifference, to the injections of mutual suspicion in the 1980s when India was rocked by militancy, to the rediscovery of India by the mid-nineties, to a renewed setback in 1998 in the aftermath of India's Pokhran II, to, hopefully the final realisation that if put and kept on a mature course these relations can and should realise their full potential. This has been, in brief, the story of India-Canada relations in the last six decades.

In the immediate aftermath of World War II, India-Canada relations got off to a happy start indeed. As an active participant in war on the Allied side, Canada emerged as a major member of the Western world, ranking only after the USA and Britain. France was as yet recovering from the pangs of capitulation in the war. Germany and Italy were still licking the wounds of their defeat and destruction. So was Japan in the Far East. Canada, alongside the USA and Britain, was a natural choice as a major Western player on the world scene. And, it took on that role happily and enthusiastically.

At the other end of the world, marking the beginning of the end of colonialism was the emergence of India as an independent nation and a major one at that. Jawaharlal Nehru, independent India's first Prime Minister, was an acknowledged and respected leader of not only India but of the fast emerging so called Third World. Nehru's vision and idealism inspired many and earned him international respect and recognition. In his very first visit to Canada in 1949 Nehru hit off extremely well with the then Canadian leadership of Prime Minister Louis St. Laurent and Foreign Minister Lester Pearson. Immediately preceding this visit Nehru was in the USA where he encountered different vibes, notably with the then US Secretary of State, Dean Acheson. The Canadian leadership by contrast gave Nehru the respect that was his due, remained modest about projecting Canada. Altogether the chemistries of the two sides jelled well. This was to mark the beginning of what commonly got labelled as a special relationship' between India and Canada.

This happy phase in these bilateral relations witnessed several positive outcomes. India and Canada cooperated actively on the international scene, including peacekeeping. Spurred on by the 1954 Colombo Conference India emerged as a major recipient of Canadian economic and technical assistance. Canada also became the first Western country to assist India on the nuclear energy front. The two countries had regular high level exchanges. Canada succeeded in ensuring, through its compromise formula, that India stayed in the Commonwealth even after declaring itself a Republic in January, 1950. This was a period when both India and Canada took each other seriously. Understood each other well and cooperated actively. Happy times indeed.

But, the atmospherics of the Cold War started catching up. The Geneva Conference of 1954 on Indochina had set up three International Control Commissions for Indo-China with India as the Chairman (perceived as neutral) and Canada and Poland as members, each representing the Western and Communist Block respectively. The subsequent warming up of Indo-Soviet relations (1955 onwards in particular) and the developing strains in Indo-US relations (1954 US military aid agreement with Pakistan) were developments that were to gradually sully India-Canada relations. Canada increasingly felt, rightly or wrongly, that India as the

Chairman of the ICCs for Indochina was tilting things in favour of the Communist Block. India often felt that Canada was acting as the West's Trojan horse in these international bodies. These mutual suspicions not only kept growing but very often turned into bilateral irritants. Outwardly mutual cooperation in various fields, carefully founded on the first phase of this relationship, continued. But the undercurrent of distrust, even occasional acrimony was hard to miss. During the 18 years of existence of these Commissions (1954-1972), because of a rapid turn over policy (Indochina was considered a hardship posting for Canadians) close to 300 Canadian diplomats, at different levels, served in Indochina on the three Control Commissions for Indochina. Many amongst them probably did not go back with happy or pleasant memories of their official dealings with their Indian colleagues on these Control Commissions. This sizeable chunk was to man the Canadian Foreign Office in the years to come. Their unfriendly, if not hostile, view of India had to cause a negative fallout on India-Canada relations. An invisible irritant had got injected into this relationship that, sadly enough, did no good.

Both India and Canada were barely coming out of this phase when a major blow was struck. This time it was India's first nuclear test of May, 1974 with Canada viewing it as a serious breach of its nuclear cooperation with India. The then Canadian Prime Minister, Pierre Trudeau, was in no mood to mince words and publicly accused the then Indian Prime Minister, Indira Gandhi, of 'betrayal'. Canada unplugged all nuclear cooperation with India. Relations in other fields also consquently suffered. They went into a near freeze mode. At best they could be described as routine.

This was the kind of backdrop to India-Canada relations as we stepped into the eighties. It was to be a difficult decade for India. Militancy in Punjab was picking up momentum in the name of the so called 'Khalistan'. Canada with its large Sikh immigrant population got sucked into this problem. Constituting an important vote bank the extremist Sikh elements in Canada, however small in number, found that country to be a convenient and safe base for their anti-Indian activities. Indian interests in Canada came under the shadow of serious threat. This included India's diplomatic missions and offices, besides other Indian establishments. The blowing up in June, 1985 of the Air India Flight 'Kanishka' from Montreal to London killing all 300 plus on board was possibly the lowest point in India-Canada relations. It was commonly believed to be the work of Sikh extremists based in and operating from Canada. It was attributed to a serious security lapse on the part of the concerned Canadian agencies. The impression to emerge in several quarters was that it was Canada's tolerance, if not encouragement, of extremist elements on its soil that was to blame for such a dastardly act of terrorism resulting in the loss of so many innocent lives. Canadian pleas of their liberal laws failed to cut much ice. If anything things only got worse in subsequent years. Anti-Indian propaganda and activities became a common thing on Canadian soil, necessitating the provision of special protection to Indian establishments there. Canadian expressions of concern for human rights caused more irritation than anything else. There was a growing feeling on the Indian side that Canada was not unable but unwilling to check, if not stop altogether, this anti-Indian tirade on its soil. The days of 'special relationship' looked like distant history.

It was only the nineties that once again were to witness an upswing in India-Canada relations. Feeling somewhat uncomfortable with its over dependence on just the next door US market, Canada was looking for fresh opportunities. Its growing ties with China and other countries of the Asia-Pacific region were beginning to bring rich dividends. Asia was widely recognised as the region of rapid growth in the future. Its size and population were a promising market. Asia was a favoured destination for developed and industrialised countries, be it for trade, investments or other vital inputs into their own economies. The realization was finally dawning on Canadian policy makers that they could not continue to ignore or remain indifferent towards a country of the size and potential of India. The opening up of the Indian economy and the visible steps towards its liberalisation from 1991 onwards was not going unnoticed in Canada. Its other Western friends and partners, the USA included, were already moving in fast. Was Canada to remain stuck in the past and miss out on this opportunity. The bringing out of a special report "Focus India" by the Canadian Foreign Office in June 1994 was the first clear signal of changed thinking in the pipeline. Things picked up momentum fast. The frequency of high level visits increased. Broad smiles started replacing the earlier frowns. The climax came in January, 1996 when the then Canadian Prime Minister, Jean Chrétien, came on an official visit to India leading a 'Team Canada' of nearly three hundred captains of industry and trade besides some Federal Ministers and Premiers of most provinces. It was after a little over a quarter century that a Prime Minister level visit from Canada to India was taking place. And, that too in a big way, literally two plane loads full. Canada was the flavour of the month in India; long lists of agreements and MOUs, extensive write ups, etc. Prime Minister Chrétien reflected this changed mood and atmosphere in his famous one-liner: "Canada is back in India and is here to stay."

For a while at least, the lows of the past were almost forgotten. The focus was now on the future. If Canada was ready and willing, so was India with matching enthusiasm. Bilateral trade picked up. The atmosphere changed for the better for economic and technical cooperation. India was no longer viewed as the object of Canada's assistance but as a partner, in mutually beneficial relations, virtually in all fields. There were hints that even the sensitive nuclear cooperation could resume once a few technical hurdles are overcome. This is where India-Canada relations stood in 1997 as India celebrated 50 years of its Independence. It almost looked like a swing back to the good old days of a 'Special Relationship'.

But sadly dark clouds appeared once again over this relationship otherwise so carefully and consciously nursed particularly over the previous five years. India's nuclear tests of May 1998 and formally declaring itself to be a nuclear weapons State, overnight, put the clock back. Canada was virulent in its criticism of India. Sanctions imposed. There was talk of 'punishing' India. All meaningful interaction with India was suspended. Even invitations to some senior Indian Ministers to visit Canada were unceremoniously withdrawn. And, Canada was not alone in this. The USA, Western Europe, Japan, even down under Australia and New Zealand were equally strident in their criticism of India.

But India stood firm. The scene had changed over the last nearly quarter century since India's first nuclear test. Here was now a nation of a billion strong, with an economy registering an annual GDP growth rate of around six per cent. An economy figuring amongst the worlds' top 10 in terms of purchasing power parity. A country with a thriving and expanding middle class of 300 million. Having one of the worlds' largest pools of technical manpower and an acknowledged leader in the IT sector. A country self-sufficient in food and with a rapidly expanding industrial sector. A recognised regional power, with considerable military muscle and raring to play its due role globally. India at the start of the 21st Century was too big and important to be simply ignored or wished away. Ever since the opening up and liberalisation of its economy it was too large and tempting a pie in terms of commercial, economic and investment opportunities to be overlooked. There was every sign that the 21st Century was going to witness maximum growth in Asia, of which India constituted a vital and important component. India was willing and ready to sit it out, strong criticism from certain international quarters notwithstanding. That is what it did, with the inevitable beginning to happen soon. One by one its critics, Canada included, relented. They saw and accepted the reality of things and started coming back. This time India did not have to wait for decades. Canada, along with the rest, was back in business, perhaps even sooner than was expected. High level contacts resumed just as relations in most other areas were sought to be restored to normalcy. It had all the appearances of an early damage control exercise.

It is often asked, why is it that despite so many commonalities, India-Canada relations keep running into roadblocks? Both are large countries endowed with rich natural and human resources, though in terms of population India far outstrips Canada. Both are members of the Commonwealth, have a federal structure and are vibrant parliamentary democracies with an acknowledged firm commitment to preserving liberty and protecting human rights. Both are open and transparent societies with a free and independent media. Both have been and continue to be active players on the international scene invariably acting in tandem. Both have a similar legal and judicial system. Both are very much English speaking countries and have basically only goodwill towards each other. Both are multicultural and multiracial societies committed to a mosaic culture. India thrives on its unity with diversity because of the way it has evolved as a nation over the centuries resulting in a civilisational unity. Canada, a very young nation by contrast, is the product essentially of immigrants rendering its mosaic culture a necessity. And, neither India nor Canada have any direct clash of security interests nor do they pose a threat to each other. Why then, these commonalities notwithstanding, are the two countries at loggerheads from time to time? A searching question indeed but to which a satisfactory answer need not be hard to find.

In my considered opinion, over the last 60 years, India-Canada relations have suffered, at least from time to time, due to several factors. If their full potential has not always been exploited I think the fault lies on both sides. Call it inadequate care and attention. Call it a failure to understand or appreciate each others concerns. The fact is that there has been something amiss somewhere and it is for both sides to be concerned about it and address the problem adequately.

Take India first. In the average Indian mindset, North America and the USA are almost synonymous. One is not even contemplating a comparison between the USA and Canada. The former is today the sole superpower in the world. It has the largest economy and a frontrunner in science and modern technology. But all that and more need not be allowed to overshadow what Canada is. It is not merely a vast country (the second largest in geographic size in the world) but an acknowledged world leader in vital areas like mining, oil and gas exploration, energy including hydroelectric and nuclear, telecommunications, environment, agriculture, food storage and agro processing, electric power generation, transmission and distribution, satellite and data communications, advanced materials, biotechnology, packaging and processing machinery, to highlight some main ones only. All these are areas of vital interest to India as it forges ahead in its economic growth and development. Canada deserves to be viewed as a vital and potential partner. Lack of adequate attention, be it at the hands of concerned departments of the government or the captains of private industry and commerce, in India, is a constant Canadian refrain, and, I think, not always without justification. Often in its dealings with North America, Indians tend to be too US centric. This can be understood up to a point. But it should not be allowed to overlook or ignore the Canadian option. Here is after all a country highly advanced with a very developed system of education, research, health services and ensuring a quality of life to its people which has qualified Canada for several years running now as the number one country in the world, on the UN scale, to live in. Incidentally, the same scale ranks the USA at somewhere around number eight. Canada is both fortunate and unfortunate to be living in the shadow of its next door colossus, the USA. But it is not just a case of the melting pot culture of the USA against Canada's mosaic pattern. Canada is, and proud to be, quite different from the USA. Even its leadership likes to market, from time to time, the concept that while dealing with Canada you have the advantage of doing your business with North America without having to deal with the USA. This sensitivity of the Canadians certainly has not received the attention at India's hands that, in my view, it deserves. And this does not have to be out of any sense of charity. Certainly not, the guiding consideration should be mutuality of interest and benefit.

But the ball lies in the Canadian court as well. Easy access to the vast US market next door has perhaps made things a little too easy for Canadian entrepreneurs and manufacturers. In the process they have not been aggressive and determined enough to penetrate the far off markets and destinations. They have to realise that each country has its own work culture that need not always be tailor-made to suit the Canadian style. It is an increasingly competitive world, but one is not always sure if the Canadians are equipped to face the hurly burly scenario of the new emerging markets where other players are far more aggressive and motivated. This realisation appears to be slowly dawning upon the Canadian business circles, and I see no reason why they cannot take on these challenges. Their greatest strength being the high quality of their product.

But the political leadership of Canada also needs to introspect. In my view, they have not always been sensitive enough towards India's sense of self-esteem, and even more importantly, its genuine security concerns. Canada is fortunate in sharing its land border, albeit a very long one, with just one country, *viz*: the USA. A country with which for almost two centuries now it has enjoyed very friendly and tension free relations. Can that be said of India? Here is a country sharing unsettled borders with many, surrounded by open hostility, constant acrimony, and suspicion with all these elements often escalating into tense borders and open wars. If India expresses serious security concerns and pumps vast sums into maintaining a reasonably modern military machine, it has good reasons for doing so. Its indifference towards defence preparedness in the early years following independence cost it dearly. The same logic can be extended to justify India's refusal to sign the NPT, the CTBT and finally to go ahead and proclaim itself to be a nuclear power in May, 1998. India has a powerful neighbour to the north with whom it has still to have a settled border. A country with a vast, modern and expanding military machine besides being an impressive nuclear power with a well developed delivery system. India also has a neighbour to its west that was not only sitting on a basement nuclear bomb but was also happily spreading nuclear proliferation. Further west there is an aspiring nuclear power. The USA has part of its nuclear arsenal based in the Indian Ocean. Which country with a responsible attitude towards its national security could forever remain indifferent towards building up its own credible nuclear deterrent? That is precisely what India did in May, 1998. It had had enough of pious platitudes of the other nuclear powers. Its pleas for global nuclear disarmament had been falling on deaf ears. Clearly there was no choice left for India but to join the ranks of nuclear powers.

But one regrets to note that Canada just refused to look at these harsh realities from India's point of view. If Canada were to at least imagine itself to be similarly placed as India, a virtual island surrounded by a hostile or unfriendly sea, it would very likely see things in a different perspective. But it refused to do so in 1974 and the story was repeated in 1998. If India's security scenario were the same as Canada's I am sure, it would have viewed things differently—the nuclear option included. Canada virtually faces no external threat, more so with the end of the Cold War and the demise of the USSR. But India has in the past and continues to face serious threats to its national security. This ground reality has unfortunately not been understood or accepted by Canada. And, this has possibly emerged as the single largest factor complicating India-Canada relations. Surely on this aspect Canada could have at least realistically agreed to disagree with India without exposing the fundamentals of this otherwise promising relationship to unnecessary pressures and setbacks. All this naturally does not go down well with Indian policy makers who feel, and not without justification, that Canada has been insensitive towards India's genuine security concerns. The Canadian political leadership, no matter of which hue, would do well to ponder over this seriously if India-Canada relations in the future are to be immunised against setbacks of the type which have already overshadowed them twice within a span of a quarter century-1974 and again 1998. They need to break out of this syndrome.

A related aspect, which has often in the past at least been an irritant, is Canada's somewhat Pak-centric approach to the overall South Asian scenario. May be Canada hoped that this way it will manage to carve out for itself a greater role in conflict resolution in South Asia. Clearly this has not happened. Canada's tendency to, over the years, deal even handedly with India and Pakistan could not be appreciated by India. Let Canada deal with the reality of Pakistan as it is. Let it help Pakistan economically. Let it push and promote the cause of genuine democracy in Pakistan. India would only welcome it. For, India has a vital stake in a peaceful, friendly, stable, economically secure and progressive Pakistan. Why only

Pakistan, all its neighbours in South Asia. Peaceful surroundings mean only good for India. But if instead one notices a tendency to equate when there is no justification for it. To privately express understanding for India's concerns but publicly sing a different tune; the net outcome cannot always be a happy one. Here again, I think Canada needs to seriously ponder over this. One even gets the impression that it is slowly abandoning this attitude. If so, it is a welcome sign. Deal with Pakistan as it is. Deal with India for what it is. The two are not the same. This reality ought to be accepted and respected.

A major complicating factor in India-Canada relations to emerge from the 1980s was militancy and terrorism. While extending proforma support and understanding for India the widespread feeling in India remained that Canada was not doing enough. That it could and should do more. That if not actively encouraging, it was at least tolerating open anti-Indian activities on its soil. Activities ranging from, collections of funds, to training and arming of militants, to open insults and threats to India and its establishments, to virulent anti-Indian tirades and propaganda in the Canadian media. Canadian pleas of near helplessness, its taking shelter behind its liberal laws and other such explanations failed to carry much conviction with India. Whether Canada was succumbing to the pressures of its own votebank politics, or did not care much as long as these elements on its soil did not pose a direct threat to it, can be debated and speculated. But the reality to emerge was not pleasant. Canada just did not appear to be doing enough.

In fact, this tendency was noticeable generally in the case of the West. As long as militancy and terrorism were not hitting them directly they could afford to be smug. Turbulence, violence, death and destruction, loss of innocent lives in far off lands was not a matter of such serious concern. A few expressions of dismay placed on record, a message of sympathy sent, seemed to suffice.

In that respect, 9/11 in the USA in 2001 was the first wake up call. Madrid and London did not take long to follow. Finally, the harsh reality emerged that by tolerating, if not actually nurturing, the Frankenstein monster of terrorism and fundamentalism, you were not necessarily or for long keeping it from hitting you directly. Double speak of the past, pleas of helplessness in the face of their so called liberal system and laws, were soon to be replaced by the by now famous battle cry; "global war against terrorism." Finally, awareness had come that this menace was indeed global and it respected no borders. Its reach was truly worldwide. And, the only way to tackle it effectively was to act in concert with others, sincerely and actively rather than to evade the issue and be indifferent while others were being bled. Hopefully this changed mindset will serve India-Canada relations well in the future.

Now, a few words on some of the elements of India-Canada relations which could and should play a much more helpful and positive role in the future. First of all, the Indo-Canadian community. This sizeable chunk, of Canada's total population and spread all over this vast country, should take on the challenge of acting as a bridge of understanding and closer and friendlier relations between India and Canada. They have not only numbers on their side but a growing clout within Canada. It makes one proud to see how the Indo-Canadian community has progressed from the sad days of the Komagata Maru episode in 1914 when more than 350 Indians were stopped from landing at Vancouver and finally sent back after two months. Since the conferring of franchise in April 1947, following Nehru's vigorous intervention, by the Canadian Province of British Colombia, to Indian immigrants, the Indo-Canadian community has come a long way indeed. Today many amongst them are occupying leading positions in Canada in fields as varied as commerce, medicine, academics, banking and finance, communications and sophisticated electronics, to name a few only. But perhaps even more interesting and significant has been the inroads made by Indo-Canadians into the Canadian political landscape, both at the provincial and national levels. They are today elected representatives in several provincial assemblies. For the first time, the 1993 general election brought three Indo-Canadians as popularly elected members of Parliament in the Canadian House of Commons (the Lower House of Parliament).

The latest general election held in January, 2006 has raised this number to eight. An Indo-Canadian has been a Federal Minister. While one even rose to be the Premier of the Province of British Colombia. The same British Colombia that had once denied entry to the first batch of Indian immigrants in 1914. Whichever way one looks at it, the Indo-Canadian community has been a unique success story indeed.

Admittedly they have their constraints. They are part of the Canadian mainstream now. They have their local political interests and constituencies to serve. It is the familiar story of votebank politics. But if they were to finally put down the baggage of the past they could and should be highly instrumental in serving as a bridge of understanding between India and Canada. A bridge across which should only lie greener pastures and mutual benefits. I think this realisation is gradually dawning upon the Indo-Canadian community. The recent decision by India to grant dual citizenship should help this process further. For, it is time the large and increasingly influential Indo-Canadian community takes upon itself and seriously the task of further strengthening and expanding India- Canada relations in the overall context. They can and should contribute substantially towards this highly desirable objective. This would indeed be my plea to them.

Another India-Canada link which dates back to 1968, the Shastri Indo-Canadian Institute (SICI), has as yet to fully realise its potential. Particularly when it comes to academic exchanges and linked activities. If any two countries have to understand and appreciate each other better, interaction at the academic level can play a crucial role. Academics constitute one of the significant opinion makers in any country, more so when the two countries involved believe in academic and intellectual freedom of thought and expression. SICI has indeed made substantial progress over the years. It is not perhaps widely known today that over 20 Canadian universities are its active members. It is perhaps even less widely known that India has as many as 13 centres for Canadian studies spread across the country. Possibly one of the largest academic exchange programmes that India has with any foreign country. That is saying a lot, but its potential needs to be further and fully exploited by way of building bridges between India and Canada.

A closely related development in recent years has been the growing number of Indian students going to Canada for higher studies and specialisation. Canada has a fine and world-class system of university education. And, studying in Canada costs almost half of what it would in the USA with the standard of education in the former being as high as in the latter, if not a shade better. This growing trend is to be welcomed as a long-term investment in a better understanding of Canada by India.

Media on both sides can and should also play a crucial role. Regrettably this has not happened so far. India figures fairly well in terms of coverage in the Canadian media, print, visual and audio. But not always in a helpful context. Disaster news, violence and death, corruption and nepotism, poverty and shortages, these themes appear to capture the imagination of the Canadian media much more than India's success stories of which there is no dearth. But they are not considered news worthy or making a good story. In the process an average Canadian reader, viewer or listener gets a somewhat distorted picture of India. India's direct publicity efforts help to an extent, but an average Canadian is understandably inclined to believe more what his 'independent' media reports. Not even remotely is it to suggest that the Canadian media should gloss over negative news from India. All that is expected is balanced reporting, the good with the bad, objective and not biased versions.

It is time for the Indian media also to wake up to the reality of Canada which, as of now, figures very little in the Indian media. If the Canadian side is largely guilty of commission then the Indian side is guilty of omission. Media representatives on both sides need to rectify this. Interact a lot more with each other. Both India and Canada have an independent and vibrant media. Both sides should feel more responsible towards promoting a better understanding between these two countries, and more importantly the peoples of India and Canada.

As someone who was directly and intimately involved for five years in the working of India-Canada relations, I have great faith in their future. I see immense potential that has largely remained untapped. There is basic goodwill on both sides that is waiting to be converted into a mature, enduring and mutually beneficial relationship, nay partnership, between India and Canada. I hope my prognosis is correct.

National security and foreign relations

44

Changes in the international security environment and India's response

K. Subrahmanyam

"What this agreement says is things change, times change, that leadership can make a difference and telling the world, sending the world a different message from that which is what used to exist in people's minds." This was President George Bush's reply on March 2, 2006 during a press briefing at Hyderabad House in New Delhi when a US correspondent questioned the wisdom of rewarding India by exceptionalising it from the Non-Proliferation Treaty even as it violated the Treaty by conducting nuclear tests in 1998.

That the Bush Administration had come to conclude that there are irreversible changes under way in the international security environment today was highlighted by Dr. Condoleezza Rice, the Secretary of State in an article "The Promise of Democratic Peace" in the *Washington Post* on December 11, 2005. She wrote, "...in times of unprecedented change the traditional diplomacy of crisis management is insufficient. Instead, we must transcend the doctrines and debates of the past and transform volatile *status quos* that no longer serve our interests. What is needed is a realistic statecraft for a transformed world."

She described the transformed world in the following terms: "For the first time since the Peace of Westphalia in 1648, the prospect of violent conflict between Great Powers is becoming ever more unthinkable. Major states are increasingly competing in peace and not preparing for war. To advance this remarkable trend the United States is transforming our partnership with nations such as Japan and Russia, with the European Union, and especially with China and India. We are building a more lasting and durable form of global stability: a balance of power that favors freedom."

These are not the views of the US leadership alone. Similar views are held by the Indian Prime Minister, Dr. Manmohan Singh. On 20th October 2005 addressing the Combined Commanders Conference he said, "The end of the Cold War, increasing global inter-dependence and the global nature of many threats have made strategic concepts developed in a bipolar world irrelevant. The United States has emerged as the dominant economic, military, technological and cultural power. However, the European Union, Russia, China, Japan and India will consolidate their individual position and will be required to play a global role. We must evolve a new paradigm of security cooperation relevant to an emerging multipolar world in which global threats will require global response."

He further added, "It is clear that each of the major powers will seek normal and mutually beneficial relations with the United States. They will also seek to improve bilateral relations with each other, independent of their relations with the US. Our strategic policy must orient itself to this new complexity. We must shed our Cold War *shibboleths*, rework our relationships with all major powers and emerging economies and improve our relations with all our economic partners and neighbours."

This perception of the international security environment is vastly different from the conventional and widely prevalent one, which views the world as totally dominated by the sole superpower—the United States—and which seriously considers the possibility of a containment strategy by the US *vis-à-vis* China. Dr. Rice, in the *Washington Post* article cited earlier, said, "Today however, we have seen that these assumptions no longer hold and as a result the greatest threats to our security are defined more by the dynamics within weak and failing states than by the borders between strong and aggressive ones. The phenomenon of weak and failing states is not new, but the danger they now pose is unparalleled. When people, goods and information traverse the globe, as fast as they do today, transnational threats such as disease or terrorism can inflict damage comparable to the standing armies of nation states. Weak and failing states serve as global pathways that facilitate the spread of pandemics, movement of criminals and terrorists, the proliferation of the world's most dangerous weapons."

A month earlier, speaking at the 40th anniversary commemoration of Institute for Defence Studies and Analyses on 11th November 2005, Prime Minister Manmohan Singh said, "The danger of a number of failed states emerging in our neighbourhood has far-reaching consequences for our region and our people. The impact includes crises which generate an influx of refugees and by destabilization of our border areas."

The traditional view in our country is to trace our security problems primarily to Pakistan and China. In the light of this new interpretation of the international security paradigm, the threat from Pakistan is one emanating from a failing state that is part of a global problem. With respect to China, "the game of nations is one of competition and cooperation. Therefore the Cold War logic of projecting nations in terms of ideological antagonisms is obsolete," to quote Prime Minister Manmohan Singh at the Combined Commanders Conference. While it is true that major nations who constitute balances of power are not likely to engage in direct wars with each other, one cannot rule out the possibility of a major power using a failing state as a conduit for weapons of mass destruction as has happened in the case of the China-Pakistan proliferation axis and through it to other weak and failing states such as Iran, North Korea and Libya. In this context it is relevant to quote Dr. Rice: "Our experience of this worldview leads us to conclude that the fundamental character of regimes matters more today than the international distribution of power." Dr. Manmohan Singh in his speech of 20th October, was explicit in elaborating the threat to India. He said, "... yet threats to security remain from terrorism, from anachronistic ideologies, parochialisms of various kinds and obsolete ideas about wars, as exhibited by Pakistan in Kargil. We cannot also ignore the strategic cooperation that Pakistan has secured from China in many ways. We cannot rule out the desire of some countries to keep us engaged in low intensity conflict with some of our neighbours as a means of getting India bogged down in a low level equilibrium."

He explained this development further in his speech: "While the international community has made some progress in evolving a rule-based order for managing the economic and trade dimensions of globalisation, the absence of an effective rule-based order is actually felt in addressing contemporary security threats, especially with regard to terrorism and the proliferation of weapons of mass destruction."

While at the leadership level there is clear recognition of the radical changes that have taken place in the international security environment and the consequent need to adjust our responses to it, in popular discourse there is very wide prevalence of the conventional perception of the last 60 years of a world dominated by antagonistic powers, a possibility of violent conflict among major powers and the need to pursue a strategy of non-alignment. The rise in India's power and stature in the international system is acknowledged more outside the country than within. Since the concept of a multi-member balance of power is new to India and the country was not familiar with it ever since it became independent, there is an insufficient understanding of the dynamics of the current international situation and the diplomacy of the balance of power.

But today's balance of power is not the same as the one that prevailed in Europe between the Congress of Vienna and the outbreak of the First World War, during the period of Pax Brittanica. Although there was no repetition of all-European wars of the type of the French revolutionary Napoleonic Wars during this period, there were a number of other limited wars: the Crimean War, the Austro-Prussian War, the Franco-Prussian War, the War of Italian Independence, the Balkan War, etc. Now because of the existence of missiles and nuclear weapons, the "prospects of violent conflict among the major powers is becoming ever more unthinkable," as

Dr. Rice points out. The balance of power does not mean that all powers should be of equal military capability. Even during the 19th Century the results of wars showed that Germany was militarily more powerful than either Austria or France. It only means that each power is capable of acting relatively autonomously and has sufficient military, political, economic and other capabilities to count significantly in the international system.

In a sense, the bipolar world too was one of balance of power. No doubt there was no equality in endowments between the US and the Soviet Union. However the Soviet Union had adequate conventional military, missile and nuclear capabilities to deter the United States' far superior power in all spheres—military, economic, technological, agricultural and soft power. The non-alignment adopted by Jawaharlal Nehru as a strategy was in fact an exercise in balance of power in the bipolar world, where the two powers were precluded from going to war with each other because of nuclear deterrence. India did not choose to be neutral, even though many Western scholars, including Americans, could not distinguish between neutrality and non-alignment. Neutrality would dictate that a country stayed out of all disputes and did not offer an opinion on any of them. Non-alignment, on the other hand, involved judgment on merits and on the basis of the country's national interests in each case of dispute between the antagonists. Even if India happened to vote in the majority of cases in the UN against the US, it was not a foregone conclusion. Even when India refrained from public criticism of the Soviet Union with respect to Hungary, Czechoslovakia and Afghanistan, it did convey its disapproval in private to the Soviet leadership. India refused to endorse the Brezhnev's anti-Chinese Asian Security plan. Therefore for India, non-alignment was a strategy of balance of power in a bipolar world. That is also the reason why India never favoured the conversion of the Non-Aligned Movement into a third force, wanting instead for it to retain its independence of judgment. While the Non-Aligned Movement was strongly in favour of the Non-Proliferation Treaty, India was determined to become an autonomous nuclear weapon power.

The Cold War international system was bipolar because the major powers that felt threatened by Soviet power and the international communism it espoused lined up behind the leadership of the US to contain the Soviet Union. Even China, an earlier ally of the Soviet Union, which gradually developed deep hostility towards it, switched sides and re-enforced the US containment strategy *vis-à-vis* the Soviet Union.

Once the Cold War came to an end with the Paris treaty on Conventional Forces in Europe and the subsequent collapse of the Soviet Union, because of its own internal contradictions, bipolarity ceased to exist, and the major nations which had lined up with the US due to their perception of the Soviet threat started asserting their autonomy. The international economy became globalised. The European Union expanded taking in an increasing number of Eastern European countries, including many former members of the Warsaw Pact. Communism as an ideology collapsed all over the world including in Russia, China, the former republics of Soviet Union and Eastern Europe. NATO developed a Foundation Act on Mutual Relations, Cooperation and Security with Russia and Partnership for Peace treaty with other former constituent republics of the Soviet Union—now sovereign states. All of Europe, including Russia, came under the Organization of Security and Co-operation in Europe (OSCE), an umbrella security organisation. Russia posted a permanent liaison officer to NATO. Presidents Bush and Gorbachev signed the START I treaty which reduced the nuclear arsenals on both sides significantly. Concurrently, there were significant reductions in tactical nuclear weapons carried out unilaterally by both countries. There were subsequent confidence building measures, the setting up of risk reduction centres and cooperative efforts to manage fissile material rendered surplus by disarmament. The NATO action in the Balkans first in support of Bosnian Muslims and subsequently in favour of Muslim Kosovans, though disapproved of by Russia, did not evoke any strong reaction.

The Soviet Union was also permissive of the actions of the US-headed alliance against Iraq during the first Gulf War in 1991. The US was able to shift its forces from Western Europe to the Gulf area on the basis of Soviet assurances that the US could do so without any adverse consequences. Following the Paris agreement, there were steady cutbacks in the defence expenditures of almost all NATO member countries. There were also drastic cuts in the defence spending of Russia and the East European countries with the dissolution of the Warsaw Pact. The US, however, continued to maintain its high level of defence spending, while making significant changes in its defence posture. While conscription had been abolished and US forces were consequently reduced in numbers, the US made a conscious attempt to keep up its lead in military technology and have an armed force that would be unchallengeable by any single or combination of powers. The result of this policy was seen in Iraq. The US is able to defeat any other military force, but has problems in keeping even a medium-sized country under occupation. Therefore, it is compelled to look to friends and allies to contribute manpower for sustaining an occupation and carry out nation building.

There were similar radical changes in the Russian-Chinese relationship following the end of the Cold War. The long time border dispute between the two was resolved. Russia and China were able to conclude a 'no first use' agreement with respect to nuclear weapons. Sino-Russian trade expanded rapidly and Russia once again became a major supplier of armaments to China. In 1996, China joined Russia, Kyrgyzstan, Tajikistan and Kazakhstan to establish a group called the Shanghai Cooperation Organisation for confidence building and fighting international terrorism. This was expanded to six with the inclusion of Uzbekistan and Mongolia, Iran, Pakistan and India were admitted as observers. Though there is a belief that this was a move to counter US missile defence and growing US influence in the Central Asian republics, the real significance of the group's creation was the end of Russo-Chinese animosity and the beginning of an era of cooperation between the two Asian giants.

Therefore the five major powers—the US, Russia, China, European Union and Japan—who were involved in adversarial relationships for decades, today maintain cordial relationships. The policy of containment has ended and there is a normal trade relationship between the US and Russia. The two are partners in the international space station project. Russia was invited to join the G-7 group of leading industrial powers to make it the G-8. Moscow is hoping to join the WTO as soon as it completes its domestic structural adjustments to become eligible. Russian pipelines have become a major supplier of oil and gas to Central and Western Europe. Further expansion in oil and gas resources is expected to make Russia a major energy supplier to the world rivalling Saudi Arabia. The globalisation phenomenon has stepped up trade all over the world and increased the economic interdependence among the major nations. China's trade is 1.42 trillion dollars. Foreign investment in China reached 60.3 billion dollars in 2005. China today holds the highest foreign exchange reserves overtaking Japan. These are among the primary indicators of China's integration with the rest of the world. In such circumstances it is absurd to talk of US attempts to contain China, as is done by some pro-China ideologues in India.

This is a kind of new world order, unprecedented in history, in which Dr. Condoleezza Rice says the prospects of violent conflict among major powers is becoming ever more unthinkable. That, however, does not mean that there will be no wars at all. Within the last five years, wars have been fought between US-led alliances in Afghanistan and Iraq. Before that in 1999, Pakistan launched an assault on India in the Kargil sector. It is, therefore, not possible to rule out wars between two medium powers, or between a medium or small power and a major power. The former type of war can normally be halted by the UN Security Council, unless there are divisions among major powers and serious conflicts of interests among them. A war among the two medium powers may get converted into a proxy war—as happened in the case of the Iran-Iraq war of the 1980s. In today's globalised balance of power system that possibility appears to be remote. The war between a small or medium power and a major power can become a prolonged one as wars in Vietnam, Afghanistan and Iraq have demonstrated. While it is possible for a major power to occupy the territory of a medium or small power, it is very difficult to keep it under occupation for a prolonged period at an affordable cost. Therefore, even that type of war is not likely to occur frequently though miscalculations of the kind the US made with respect to Iraq cannot be completely ruled out.

Small and medium powers are not normally in a position to stockpile adequate quantities of weapons and ammunition to fight prolonged wars. In the absence of ideological animosities among the five permanent members, the Security Council is not likely to be deadlocked in taking effective action under Chapter 7 of the UN Charter and invoke sanctions against the two antagonists of medium or low capability thus bringing the war to an end. Indo-Pakistan wars fall into this category.

During the period of the Cold War, the US and USSR were in a position to confront each other without taking into account the much smaller arsenals of other weapon powers. Today, the smaller nuclear weapon powers, particularly Pakistan and India are not in a position to consider resorting to nuclear weapons without giving due consideration to the possible reactions of major nuclear weapon powers. In other words, while a nuclear confrontation between the US and Russia would have been a two person game, other nuclear confrontations do not fall into that category. For instance, Pakistan cannot think of using its nuclear arsenal *vis-à-vis* India without calculating not only certain Indian retaliation but possible punishments of various kinds by other powers like the US. Pakistan getting away with a nuclear strike would severely damage the United States' national security and interests. Pakistan should also take into account that it is under continuous surveillance by the US super secret ECHELON system and it cannot rule out a pre-emptive strike by the US if it were to think of a nuclear strike on India. Therefore even with respect to Indo-Pakistani nuclear confrontation, it is necessary to think beyond a two-person game. The Indian no-first-use and credible-minimum-deterrent doctrines take these considerations into account.

The most important change that India has to take note of in its security environment is the US declaration of its intention to help India build itself into a world-class power in the 21st Century. The US is doing this in its own national interests. However, US *bona fides* in this respect have not been deemed adequately credible among different sections of this country. Most of India's security problems *vis-à-vis* Pakistan could be traced back to the United States' tilt towards Pakistan at the expense of India during the Cold War. There is an extrapolation from the past history of US-Pakistan relations that the US would continue to favour Pakistan at the expense of India. This is substantiated by the continued US military assistance to Pakistan and the muted criticism of Pakistan's role in sustaining its campaign of cross-border terrorism against India. The US strategy appears to be to help India to become a major power, including in the military field, even while sustaining its hold on Pakistan's military leadership and using it to the maximum extent possible in its war against al-Qaeda and the Taliban. The Pakistanis, at the same time, are acutely aware that the US would lose interest in them if the wars against al-Qaeda and the Taliban are successfully concluded. They have, therefore, no interest in enabling the US to succeed completely in that war. At the same time, they have to demonstrate that the US gains certain minimum military benefits through its alignment with Pakistan. They are also able to blackmail the US with implied threats of a nuclear Pakistan falling into the hands of Islamic *jihadi* elements. In this game of sophisticated blackmail the Pakistani military leadership has so far been successful. This is a matter of grave concern for India.

However, there is a difference between the situation before 2005 and now. Unlike in the earlier period, the US is willing to sell India armaments that are more sophisticated than those made available to Pakistan. While this policy no doubt benefits US armament manufacturers, it is no reason why India should not try to equip itself adequately to deter Pakistan. Secondly, unlike in the earlier period when there was no clash of national security interests between the US and Pakistan, there is now a major fundamental contradiction in security interests. Pakistan is the epicentre of the *jihadi* terrorist cult. The US is the primary enemy of the Islamic *jihadists*. So long as Pakistan continues to be the home of *jihadism*, the US cannot feel secure. Most attempted and successful terrorist attacks, including 9/11, have had some Pakistani connection. Therefore, the US is interested in a cultural change within Pakistan in which the dominant aspects of the extremist cult are replaced by a more moderate Islam. To bring that about, the support given by the military and political establishment of Pakistan to Islamic extremism will have to be weakened and eventually eliminated. That means the Pakistani state has to undergo a radical transformation. The US believes that General Musharraf and other generals like him are likely to bring about this change over a period of time. The US has been guilty of wrong assessments on Pakistan and the Taliban in the 1980s and 1990s and may therefore well be indulging in similar gross misjudgments. 9/11 was the price the US paid for its folly on Pakistan and the Taliban.

Kargil was perhaps the last attempt by Pakistan to use its army, albeit covertly, to alter the *status quo* in Kashmir. It found that it no longer had the support of the US or even China for its efforts to alter the *status quo* in Kashmir with armed force. The Pakistani leadership has since changed its Kashmir strategy. It has dropped its demand for a UN-sponsored plebiscite, but is now proposing autonomy for ethnically demarcated regions in the former princely state of Jammu & Kashmir, demilitarisation, and some form of joint control over some of the regions. The proposals are deliberately vague and appear to be meant, essentially, to keep the Kashmir issue alive. The lack of seriousness of Pakistan is evident from its not conferring full citizenship rights to the population of the Northern areas and the absence of free and fair elections in Pakistan-occupied Kashmir.

General Musharraf has not kept the promises he made to the international community in his broadcast on 12 January 2002 about cracking down on terrorist organisations. Groups which have been banned have just changed their names and continue to function. Most of the leaders of these banned organisations are free and active. The Pakistani terrorist organisation Lashkar-e-Taiba is now reported to have taken over the mantle of al-Qaeda in this part of the world. Though the peace process initiated by Prime Minister Vajpayee in

January 2004 has been sustained and has made some progress with respect to train and bus routes and increased travel between the two countries, Pakistan is still refusing to honour its commitments under the SAFTA (South Asian Free Trade Area agreement arrived at in SAARC), and extend a most favoured nation treatment to India. Pakistan has shown no signs of wanting to end its attitude of hostility. Meanwhile, the cross-border infiltration of terrorists continues and terrorist acts are perpetrated in Jammu and Kashmir and rest of India under directions from sources in Pakistan, as monitored telephonic intercepts have revealed.

The Pakistani strategy towards India was based on the assumption that Indian unity was vulnerable and Pakistan would be able to disintegrate India through its campaign of terrorism and by triggering off communal tensions. While this has been the long term Pakistani strategy towards India, recent developments in the Indo-US relationship are likely to further reinforce the Pakistani resolve to pursue a strategy of disrupting India. From its creation in 1947 on the basis of the two-nation theory, Pakistan had entertained an attitude of sibling rivalry towards India. Irrespective of enormous disparities in sizes, populations, endowments and capabilities, Pakistan has tried to project itself as an equal to India. This it tried to do during the Cold War years in the military sphere with help from the US. From the 1980s onwards, it has mostly depended on China to obtain its nuclear weapon and missile technologies and thereby flaunt its equalisers with India. Since the July 18 Indo-US Agreement, Pakistan has demanded nuclear exceptionalisation from the United States on the lines extended to India. The US President publicly rejected this demand, highlighting that the two countries had different histories. Pakistan has made no secret of its deep resentment of India's rapid economic growth and the increasing international recognition India is gaining. One must therefore expect that elements of the Pakistani military establishment, particularly the Inter Services Intelligence wing and Islamic *jihadi* elements, will attempt to make use of the asymmetric strategy of terror against India to dissuade foreign investments from coming in, to create communal tensions and disrupt social peace and tranquility. They may also target major infrastructure projects for their terroristic attacks. India has been a victim of Pakistan's proxy war and terror campaign for well over 20 years. As long as Pakistan is dominated by Islamic *jihadi* elements in its intelligence, armed forces and in various apostate religious militias posing as Islamic it will remain a threat primarily to India and to the rest of the world as well. This is a threat from a failing state that India and the international community have to be prepared to deal with.

The US is aware of the threat arising from Pakistan. The US legislation following the 9/11 Commission report specifically focuses attention on Pakistan and the need for making it a moderate Islamic state. The US *Quadrennial Defense Review* deals with possible threats arising from states with weapons of mass destruction (WMD) losing control over them. There is little doubt that this is a reference to Pakistan. Of late there is increasing articulation in the US about the inadequacy in cooperation from Pakistan in dealing with Taliban operations against Afghan and Allied forces in Afghanistan, many of which are launched from Pakistani soil. The US is also aware of the proliferation activities of Pakistan to Iran, North Korea and Libya. In spite of all these factors establishing Pakistan's involvement in terrorism and proliferation, the US has deliberately chosen to accept the Pakistani offer of cooperation in the war on terrorism and as a *quid pro quo* has been extending Pakistan both economic and military assistance.

The US logic appears to be on the following lines. When faced with the US ultimatum, Pakistan agreed to cooperate in the war against its own client regime, the Taliban in Afghanistan, and made available all necessary bases and facilities to the US. The US, therefore, cannot afford to antagonise Pakistan in addition to Iraq and Iran. Other than Indonesia, Malaysia, Lebanon,Turkey and Bangladesh, Pakistan is one of the few Islamic countries with some familiarity with democracy. It also has a sizeable middle class with a stake in democracy. Pakistan has nuclear weapons and also a record of proliferation. In US calculations, Pakistan's armed forces are, relatively speaking, still more in contact with the realities of the rest of the world and are less fanatical than certain other sections of the Pakistani polity. For these reasons, the US appears to have decided to engage with Pakistan and particularly with the Pakistani armed forces' leadership. The United States' biggest worry concerns Pakistani proliferation and Pakistan losing control over its weapons. In the light of these concerns, the US feels that they will have to have a presence in Pakistan to be in a position to monitor developments and to take preventive and pre-emptive action if necessary.

The Pakistani army leadership is fully aware of the United States' concerns and exploiting these concerns to its advantage. The US involvement in West Asia is likely to be of a long-term nature, and consequently the US stake in Pakistan too is likely to be long term. In fact as long as Pakistan has nuclear weapons and poses a threat of proliferation, the US cannot afford to disengage itself from Pakistan. Economic engagement with Pakistan is necessary to cultivate the Pakistani middle class. Military assistance to Pakistan needs to be kept up to maintain links with the Pakistani military. Besides these considerations, the US is also likely to be swayed by the possibilities of China converting Pakistan into their client state. Under these circumstances, the US is to some extent in the position of a hostage to Pakistan.

Unlike in the Cold War era when the US tilted in favour of Pakistan and did not mind Pakistan gaining at the expense of India, the US, at present, has developed high stakes in India. Therefore the US decision to permit arms exports to India of a qualitatively superior nature to what it transfers to Pakistan and a new framework for the US-India defence relationship has been signed. The US hopes to contain Pakistan on both sides and to work for a change in the orientation of the Pakistani state through its present and succeeding leaderships. There is no alternative to this strategy except to permit Pakistan to become an un-tethered nuclear-armed terrorism-sponsoring state. But it is difficult to predict how long it would take US to persuade the Pakistani leadership to give up sponsoring *jihadi* terrorism.

Therefore, the Indian security assessment has to be on the basis that this country is likely to face a prolonged period of terrorism directed by sources in Pakistan. The Indian security apparatus must, therefore, gear itself up for a war of attrition on the terrorist front. There is considerable disillusionment in India on the US continuing its aid to Pakistan in spite of its proven record of terrorism. On that account, there are many advocates of a policy of maintaining a distance from the US and not improving Indo-US defence cooperation. That would be a wrong approach and would serve Pakistan's purpose. The right approach will be to increase cooperation with the US and try to develop a common strategy *vis-à-vis* Pakistan to contain and convert Pakistan into a moderate Islamic state. One can draw an analogy with George Kennan's strategy of containment, which brought about the desired results 40 years later. No doubt six decades of American tilt towards Pakistan and estrangement from India still leaves vast gaps in mutual confidence between the American and Indian bureaucracies. The change of direction in the US strategy is still top driven and adequate cooperation in intelligence is still to develop between the two countries, even though they share a common objective *vis-à-vis* Pakistan. The solution is not to maintain a distance from the US but to step up cooperation and achieve a degree of mutual confidence when a cooperative strategy *vis-à-vis* Pakistan becomes possible.

Pakistan has been able to use the territories of Bangladesh and Nepal as transit points for infiltrating terrorists into India. There has been a certain amount of permissiveness on the part of the governments of these two countries in allowing the terrorists to use their soil as safe havens. Things are likely to change for the better in Nepal. But Bangladesh needs more than the pressure from India to deny transit facilities for Pakistani *jihadists*. Here a common anti-terror strategy with the United States and European Union and combined pressure on Bangladesh would be more effective.

India also has to modernise its armed forces if it is to play the role of a balancer of power in the international system. It should be in a position to provide security to the international community when called for. Till now, the Indian armed forces have been designed to defend the Indian territory from external aggression.

It should now acquire capabilities to be able to operate on UN peacekeeping and peace enforcement missions with full logistic capabilities. It should also be able to provide security for sea-lanes in the waters of the Indian Ocean. Above all, given the likelihood of Pakistan's continued hostile intent towards this country, the Indian armed forces should be built up to be a credible deterrent in terms of conventional capability. Since Pakistan will continue to have access to US arms, India should equip itself appropriately with more sophisticated arms so that Pakistan does not indulge in any adventurism using its US-manufactured equipment. Here India will have to avail itself of the US offer to provide India with more sophisticated weaponry than Pakistan, and enter into co-production arrangements. Unlike during the Cold War period, India is now financially in a position to afford to import its choice of defence equipment based on merits. The balance of power system demands that India should be in a position to deter the challenges posed by neighbouring failing states. In this respect defence cooperation with Russia, the US and the European Union provides India with optimum advantages. Cooperation with one major power need not be at the expense of another power, since they are not adversaries of one other.

India's interests and security are affected by developments in West Asia, the ongoing war in Iraq, tensions between the US and Iran, the Israeli occupation of Palestine and the ongoing terrorist campaign by the *jihadi* extremists. India derives a significant portion of its energy resources from this region. Millions of Indian labourers are earning their livelihood in the countries of this region and are sending billions of dollars of remittances back to India. All the major powers of the world are vitally interested in this area since China, Japan, the US and the European Union derive their energy resources from these countries, and the region adjoins the 'near abroad' of Russia. *Jihadi* extremists have waged a campaign of terrorism in Russia and had supported the separatists in the war of Chechen secessionism. Therefore this region will continue to be the focus of attention of all major powers, particularly the US, in the indefinite future as it has been since the end of the Second World

War. The situation in Iraq will not end with a US withdrawal as predicted by some observers.

Among the major powers, the US has adopted an aggressive policy towards the region, combined with soft policies towards Pakistan and Saudi Arabia, while the others have gone along with the US, either actively or passively. Not even Russia or China has been inclined to oppose US policies vigorously. France and Germany disagreed with the US on Iraq but have been going along with the US on the Iranian nuclear enrichment issue. China and Russia differed with the US on Iraq and on the nature of sanctions on Iran, but have gone along in principle with possible punitive action against Iran if it does not suspend uranium enrichment. It is therefore difficult to consider the entire West Asia as a single problem. The Islamic world is highly divided. There is the Sunni-Shia divide threatening to split Iraq. The *jihadi* extremists are in conflict with the orthodox clergy. There is popular resentment against unrepresentative regimes. Therefore India should consider its position on the various issues arising in the West Asian region on their merits, as the other major powers do, and not in the framework of a clash of civilisations, as the Islamic *jihadists* propagate. There is general unanimity of views on the need to fight *jihadi* terrorism, though the US continues to be soft on certain groups of Pakistani *jihadis*. That calls for a sophisticated strategy on the part of India. India has to fight its own battle against Pakistani terrorism, without counting on US help in this battle, even while attempting to benefit in overall terms through a general enhancement of relations, such as a defence relationship with the US. Though India may not have active US support in fighting Pakistani terrorism, it would be counterproductive to alienate the US. That would serve to help the Pakistani *jihadis* in their vicious objectives against this country. India has not allowed China's active assistance to Pakistan in its nuclear and missile programmes come in the way of advancing its relationship with China. Similarly, India should not allow the US softness towards Pakistani *jihadis* come in the way of its enhancement of relationship with the US.

India's relationship with the South-East Asian countries has improved, even as Indo-US relations started to get better. India's relations with South-East Asia were very intimate in the 1950s and up to the mid-1960s. At this time, the South-East Asian countries supported the US during the Vietnam War and consequently drifted away from India. However, India is now a member of the ASEAN regional forum and is developing free trade relations with ASEAN. India has a legitimate interest in the security of the Malacca Straits and in the oil shipping lanes traversing the Indian Ocean. This calls for an adequate bluewater naval capability befitting one of the six balancers of power in the international system.

China and Russia along with Kazakhstan, Uzbekistan, Tajikistan and Kyrgyzstan have established the Shanghai Cooperation Organisation (SCO) with India, Pakistan, Mongolia and Iran as observers. In some quarters this organisation is viewed as a countervailer to US power and influence. Some ideologues in India even advocate India aligning itself with this organisation. In this era of balance of power and globalisation, it is extremely unlikely that major powers will bind themselves in fixed alignments. There could be greater bilateral or regional cooperation among nations for their collective benefits, but a fixed alignment to hard balance the pre-eminent power is counterproductive. Russia, as a rising energy supplier to the international community, is attempting to develop its relations not only with China, but also with Japan and the European Union. It is unlikely that Russia, which considers itself a European nation, would play the second fiddle in a formal alignment with China. Therefore while there is no harm in India associating itself with the Shanghai Cooperation Organisation, there can be no alignment with China and Russia any more than an alignment with any other major power. At present, India has strategic partnerships with the US, the European Union and Russia, and strategic dialogues with China and Japan, which it hopes to convert into strategic partnerships in due course.

The key to the new role India is to play is an 8-10 per cent economic growth. That would necessitate increased interaction with the rest of the international system in terms of trade, technology transfers, and foreign direct investment, and as a preferred destination for BPO and R&D outsourcing. This is no longer an era in which missiles and nuclear warheads are the currency of power. Rather, this century will have knowledge as the currency of power. India's unique advantage is that in the next 30 to 40 years it will have the largest population with the youngest age profile in the world among the major powers. This large, youthful population can be educated to make India a knowledge power. This likely development has been better recognised abroad than in India. We see sections of our political class still harking back to slogans of the Cold War, non-alignment and the permit licence-quota *raj*. Though the Prime Minister has emphasised the inevitability of globalisation, the opportunities for fast growth provided by the current international environment, and the balance of power international security system, these concepts are still to become accepted wisdom even in our own mainstream political parties. The foreign office bureaucracy, the intelligence services, the media and academia are still to adjust themselves to this new international environment. Changing the conventional orientation of a nation is no doubt a leadership function and it takes time to carry it through. In that sense India has only just now started to respond to the challenges of the new millennium. It will take quite some time before this response can mature.

45

Aerospace challenge to India

Jasjit Singh

There is a vital aspect of our foreign policy that has not received the attention that it deserves. India has tended to view air power purely in terms of defence and the theme of air power in the foreign policy of nations might appear to be strange. The roots of this concept lie in the basic precept that military power is an instrument of the state and must (when properly employed) serve a rational political purpose. Clausewitz had argued that war—an activity undertaken by military forces—is an instrument of politics by other means. If the essential role of military power is to serve rational political goals, then those goals will need to be viewed under the heading of defence of the State, its sovereignty and territorial integrity at one level, and to support the country's foreign policy to safeguard and sustain national interests through international relations, at another. The last is undoubtedly pursued through diplomacy. But diplomacy gains in strength and substance when it can rely on the availability of usable credible force which may or may not be actually employed. Most modern nation-states normally treat military power as part of the total diplomatic package available for the pursuit of foreign policy.

An examination of the subject of foreign policy of nations would indicate that its primary objectives are the pursuit and servicing of national interest. These interests can be broadly categorised under two themes: those related to economic interests, and/or, those concerning the security and safety of the country. The first aspect, of pursuit of economic and trade interests as a major component of foreign policy, has been assuming greater salience in recent decades largely due to the globalisation processes going on in the world. Many countries, in fact, name their foreign policy establishments as 'foreign and trade' departments. Geoeconomics has always been a key component of the foreign policy of nations. Colonial empires were established across the world with military power in search of economic resources and the right to exploit them for national good. Interestingly, it was military power that was used to expand and control the empires in order to draw the maximum economic benefit and control material and human resources to serve national security interests of the imperial powers. The problem has been that India has tended to look at military power almost completely in the context of military goals, roles and missions, and not paid enough attention to the foreign policy linkage that military power and its employment has with it. This is, in spite of the fact that military power, especially air power, has actually played a crucial role in support of foreign policy goals and objectives over the past six decades.

For example, take the case of UN peacekeeping operations across the world, since the Korean War five decades ago. India has firmly believed that promotion of international peace and security, and peaceful resolution of conflicts, wherever they take place, is in India's national interests. The result has been that India has been involved in perhaps the maximum number of UN peacekeeping missions and continues to be so. It has also paid a heavy price in the shape of precious lives lost in the process of peacekeeping. The consistently high levels of performance of Indian peacekeeping contingents have contributed to India's standing in the world as a responsible power, as well as increasing the demand for its military to help stabilise difficult situations in numerous countries and regions. More importantly UN Peacekeeping has contributed in no small measure to our foreign policy goals of supporting international peace and security at one level and opposing separatism on ethno-communal basis.

More and more UN peacekeeping operations now include, air power components, making it more effective and efficient, especially in developing countries and regions where transportation infrastructure is far from satisfactory. The classical case of UN peace-keeping operations, including combat air power in the early years was the operation in Congo in 1961-62. We have also undertaken peacekeeping under bilateral framework at the request of legitimate governments threatened by separatism and other challenges. The case of Maldives in 1988, stands out besides the operations in Sri Lanka in 1971 and once again in 1987-1990.

Instrument of national power

Foreign policy of nations requires that all instruments and components of national power be employed in an optimal way and synergised to pursue national interests. Historically, there are a number of elements that go to make up a country's total national power: size, population, economy, geography, military power, etc. It is inevitable, therefore, that each and all of them would have an influence and role in the optimisation of the foreign policy of nations. Military power today is composed of many components, depending largely, though not entirely, on technological strength and the competitive advantage it confers on the nation, and the reach of the military. The greater the reach, the greater is its ability to influence events farther away from homeland. This is the reason why the United States maintains a military capability that has a global reach in keeping with its definition of its global strategic and national interests.

It is not surprising, therefore, that the US air power and space capabilities play a crucial role in supporting US foreign policy goals with combat as well as non-combat operations. Military training, arms transfers, and arms control are all employed in support of national interests. The UN as well as the North Atlantic Treaty Organisation (NATO) leadership are clear that availability of US air power assets would remain critical to any humanitarian mission and peace-keeping operations across the world since no other country maintains capabilities at that level even though it would need the capability in pursuit of its interests. This, in turn, creates a dependency on the US even by its close allies, thus, influencing their foreign policy to remain aligned to that of (if not dependent on) the US.

Technological changes in recent decades have led to the situation where air power (and space capabilities) has become the prime instrument of military power. This thinking is deeply embedded in US's policy and performance. But this is not limited to the US and China has started to increasingly rely on air power capabilities in the paradigm of its Comprehensive National Power. The Chinese Central Military Commission, the ultimate authority for employment of military power, for example, has concluded that air power and precision strike are now the primary means of conducting warfare, with ground operations remaining secondary.[1] For the first time in its history, it has included the Commander of the Air Force in its Central Military Commission. It is inevitable, therefore, that the comprehensive national power of nations would give increasing importance to building and using air power and space capabilities in the coming years.

A classical case of our air power being employed in support of our foreign policy goals without firing a shot was the strategic airlift from the Middle East in 1990-91. Nearly 300,000 Indian citizens living and working in Iraq/Kuwait suddenly became hostage to the 1990-91 War in Kuwait and the Gulf region. It was obvious that our national interest required that at least all those who were willing to be evacuated could be transported by road to Jordan and accommodated in refugee camps while a massive airlift plan for their evacuation was put into place. In the three-odd weeks, during which the airlift operation was going on, 113,824 Indian citizens were airlifted in our transport fleet without a single incident. This was perhaps the biggest strategic airlift since World War II. More important, it demonstrated that India could airlift such a large number of its citizens from a very difficult war zone in an extremely

---

1. The PRC's Central Military Commission concluded in December 1995, that the ground battle was now secondary to the air battle. See Mark Stokes, "China's Missile, Space, and Conventional Theatre Missile Development Implications for Security in the Taiwan Strait," in Susan M. Puska ed., *People's Liberation Army After Next* (Carlisle Barracks, Pa: Strategic Studies Institute, US Army War College, 2000), p. 109. This, however, may not necessarily apply to other threats.

efficient manner with indigenous capabilities. Not surprisingly, this attracted more attention in the West than in India! There is also an obvious role for air power that becomes critical for foreign policy: access to landlocked counties like Afghanistan. For most of the six decades, the only physical contact to pursue bilateral relations between Afghanistan and India has been by air. The main method of contact between the Central Asian states and India continues to rely on aircraft, some of which have been gifted by the Indian government to Afghanistan for the purpose. Air power, of course, played a crucial role in the defeat and eviction of Taliban by the United States, launching air strikes from continental America, on one side and aircraft carriers in the Indian Ocean, on the other. But our own air power has played a crucial role in the post-war stabilisation of Afghanistan.

There are also negative sides which actually prove the rule. Intelligence in all its diverse dimensions, constitutes a key foundation for all foreign policy measures. In the recent past, we have witnessed the impact of intelligence failures with respect to the Iraq War severely complicating the British and American foreign policy goals of stabilising the country after the war since the intelligence failures had deprived them of any legitimacy for having launched the war in the first place. Much of the national intelligence relies heavily on air power and space assets.

Air power as a coercive instrument

There are numerous occasions and requirements when foreign policy goals may require coercion to be applied as an instrument of state policy. And very often air power becomes the prime instrument of coercion because it has some unique attributes that allow it to play a major role in three salient areas, contributing to successful coercion: (i) achieving escalation dominance, (ii) defeating the adversary's military strategy, and (iii) magnifying third party threats. Its classical example is the 'no-fly-zone' imposed on two-thirds of Iraq, after the 1991 Gulf War where 300,000 operational sorties were flown by the US-led coalition during 1998-2003 till the eve of the Iraq War in March 2003, in conjunction with economic sanctions.

India has itself used air power to coerce another country in pursuit of its foreign policy goals even if we have not studied it adequately. As the *Enterprise* Task Force was sailing toward the Bay of Bengal, it was obvious that the US would ultimately seek to land forces inside East Pakistan, and this required adequate operationally available runways. Normally, IAF would not have needed to attack airfields in East Pakistan after the solitary fighter squadron of Pakistan Air Force was destroyed in the first 36 hours. But the IAF engaged in heavy attacks on all airfields in East Pakistan throughout the remaining days of the war to make sure they would remain unfit for possible use for landing US (or Chinese) forces which would have complicated India's policy choices. These airfields were heavily defended by anti-aircraft weapons and the IAF suffered substantive losses in this process. But air power deterred any plan to land forces inside East Pakistan.

The air strikes by a formation of MiG-21 aircraft at the residence of the governor of East Pakistan in Dhaka just when he was chairing a crucial meeting to discuss the current situation during the 1971 War, is another case of coercive compellence. The highly successful strike led to an immediate decision by the governor to surrender and not only saved precious lives, shortened the war, but also provided the most potent instrument to achieve our foreign policy goals.

Sixteen years later, the escalating ethnic conflict in Sri Lanka had led to a situation where the Sri Lankan forces had practically laid a siege to Jaffna in the north and the people, a large proportion of them Indian citizens among the majority Tamil population, had started to suffer heavily due to food shortages and lack of other essential commodities like medicines caused by a virtual economic blockade by Sri Lankan military. Relief supplies were despatched by a flotilla of the Indian Coast Guard. But its progress was blocked by the Sri Lankan Navy narrowing the Indian option where a direct military conflict with Sri Lanka was not in our interest. Finally, rice and other supplies were dropped from the air by An-32 transport aircraft escorted by Mirage 2000 fighters, in June 1987 in an operation that came to be known as the 'rice bombing' of Jaffna.

This led directly to the July 1987 Indo-Sri Lanka Accords and the withdrawal of the Sri Lankan Army from the northern region and Jaffna.

Air power has been invaluable in emergencies, whether man-made or triggered by natural disasters, requiring rapid response both within the country as well as outside it. India has pursued a foreign policy to support legitimate friendly countries and to provide assistance to eliminate threats to the sovereignty, integrity and viability of legitimate governments. One of the incidents which led to define the framework of future bilateral relations is the now almost forgotten incident arising out of the Ranas' revolt in Nepal in the late 1940s. The king of Nepal sought Indian assistance when things became untenable for him in 1950 and even his life was in danger. A single DC-3 Dakota transport aircraft of Indian Air Force was despatched to evacuate the king which was done successfully and peacefully, even though there were some tense moments during the process. The revolt died down and the king was restored to his throne. Therein lies the genesis of the Indo-Nepalese Treaty of Friendship which has guided the bilateral relations and foreign policy of the two countries since then. The immediate support to the Maldives in 1988, in restoring the rule of the legitimate government threatened by terrorist groups, is another example.

Air power and deterrence

Our national interests demand that we accord the highest priority to human development of our people and improve the quality of their lives. This requires a sustained environment of durable peace. In turn, this leads to the obvious conclusion that our national policy goals should seek to prevent a war and/or armed conflict being imposed on us. This, in turn, can be achieved primarily through building cooperative relations with other countries. But this also requires us to ensure a high degree of credible deterrence, conventional and nuclear, against any potential adversary who might be tempted to undertake aggression. In order to ensure the requisite credibility, those capabilities must naturally also cater for deterrence failure, in which case we should be able to achieve our objectives at the earliest, at minimum costs.

Deterrence has operated for centuries, and it has been an implicit as well as an explicit factor in the creation of military power as well as in the relationship between states. There is nothing new here. Nuclear weapons have added one unique dimension because of the very destructive power that can be unleashed with them. Essentially, deterrence is of two kinds. One is achieved through 'denial' of victory, or even of the ability to wage war, by conveying to the adversary that the costs of his actions would far outweigh any perceived benefits that he might be seeking by resort to war. Most of the time in history, deterrence has functioned through the denial process. The other dimension of deterrence operates through the promise of 'punishment' where we hold out a threat, stated or not-stated, implicit or not so implicit, that there will be a level of punishment imposed where the adversary could lose much more, if it were to pursue a certain course of action which is hostile to our interests.

Each component of military power has different capabilities for deterrence. For example, land forces are the core military power for providing deterrence through denial; but land forces cannot punish independently of denial, for the simple reason that land forces will be engaged by land forces. The moment you are engaged with land forces, they must win, lose or accept a ceasefire through a negotiated settlement. Land forces do not possess any capability to punish except through the direct cost imposed on the enemy's land forces. In that case, the chances are that you would need to destroy, partially or totally, his military capability. Land forces can engage with the other land forces and then fight through, to impose a cost. Once engaged, it is difficult for them to disengage without a definite result being obtained. But they do not possess any independent capability of punishment. Naval forces have the ability for deterrence through denial, but to an extent, also through punishment since they do not have to remain engaged in armed conflict all the time. Once naval guns started to provide a certain minimum range, naval ships could open fire at even the land targets and yet retain the capability to withdraw at will. This is what gave rise to the term 'gunboat diplomacy'.

Air power, which delivered the atomic bombs on Hiroshima and Nagasaki, is acquiring increasing capabilities for both discrete strikes with precision weapons at long ranges as well as for a variety of roles, merging with space on one side and the expanding role of unmanned air vehicles (UAVs) on the other. Air power has an inherent capability to provide deterrence through punishment. But the increasing capabilities of air power to make a stronger contribution to war-fighting are also boosting its attributes for deterrence through denial, functioning as a force multiplier, in this regard. The revolution in military affairs as well as the new concept of network-centric warfare and their technologies mostly revolve around air power.

Deterrence failure

While air power plays an increasingly crucial role in defence through deterrence, it is equally important in case of deterrence failure when war becomes inevitable. In almost every war that we had to fight, air power tilted the balance of success between victory and loss in our favour in all, except one. Our land forces (and naval forces in 1971) have performed admirably in wars often against severe odds. But we need to recognise that air power played a key role in each and every one of them, mostly providing the critical factor that created the opportunities for land forces to defeat the aims of the enemy. This reality is often ignored even by the air force itself. In most cases, this role was performed not so much by combat air power, but by airlift. For our defence, airlift at crucial periods of history has been more significant than the Berlin Airlift for its strategic implications.

Combat air power came to play a key role in the 1947-48 war in Jammu & Kashmir Its use does not seem to have been seen as escalatory or in any way inviting adverse reactions from any quarters.[2] One can even argue that unless we look for it, the use

---

2. The role of combat air power in the war appears to have been consciously curtailed by the British commander-in-chief of the IAF working in consonance with his British counterpart in Pakistan and the British government rather than the Indian government. This neutralised the advantage that the IAF had over the Pakistan Air Force. See *C. Dasgupta, War and Diplomacy in Kashmir 1947-48* (New Delhi: Sage Publications).

of combat air power in that longest war that we fought might even go unnoticed! And our so-called 'official' histories only bring greater confusion, through ignorance, to bear on history.[3]

Very often, we need to look at failures to arrive at valid reasons for future policy. During the 1962 Sino-Indian War, we used air power only for transportation of troops and logistics and the very small helicopter capability for casualty evacuation. Combat air power was not employed in the war. The actual reasons have not been easy to discern. But one thing is clear: a major factor for not employing combat air power was the concern that our cities could not be defended (due to paucity of air defence capabilities) in case China used its air power. The realities of the limitations on the Chinese Air Force due to the need for operating from airfields on the Tibetan plateau, the limited payload that the short range combat aircraft of their air force could carry, etc. do not seem to have received the type of attention they deserved. Overall failure of the higher defence system to cope with the dynamics of the war added to the problems where the fighting men paid for the failures of planning and higher direction of war. In substance, India was self-deterred by the assumed air power of China and failed to use available capabilities to at least reduce the negative impact of Chinese use of force. It is worth recalling that the White House intelligence summary at that time had concluded that while Indian ground forces would face serious setbacks due to logistics deficiencies, the use of combat air power by India would make a significant impact on the outcome of the war.

What emerges from the study of the history of air power is that it makes a definitive contribution to the foreign policy of nations, though in negative terms in some cases, where it has not been employed appropriately. For far too long we have focussed almost entirely on the kinetic shock effect of air power to the detriment of a better understanding of its psychological shock effect. Kinetic effect

---

3. The official history of the 1962 War, as available on *The Times of India's* website informs us that a jet engine had been fitted on the "tail" of the Packet aircraft! Hunter and Mystere aircraft are depicted as "bombings" and no mention of Canberra light bombers is made in such listings. Official history of the 1965 War, compares attrition in relation to the inventory of aircraft rather than the number of sorties flown which is the traditionally accepted global norm.

is unquestionably crucial. Without it, the political psychological shock effect itself would lose much of its impact since it provides the physical evidence of the impact. Management of the public information system and embedded media may enhance the psychological impact, but if the kinetic effect is at very low levels, it would be difficult to create the impressions merely by manipulating information.

It needs to be noted that the above has to be situated in the ongoing trends where the very nature of war and diplomacy has undergone fundamental change. Perhaps, the best way to express this is to look back in history when the soldiers and diplomats had very distinctly, different almost mutually exclusive roles, so much so that when the diplomats failed, the soldiers were called in. And when the soldiers failed—or succeeded, the diplomats again took over. It is therefore, natural that air power plays its appropriate role in our foreign policy in future, as indeed it has done in the past.

Challenges for India

As the Indian Air Force enters its 75th year, it is time we looked ahead to what IAF would and should be? The air force has been facing severe combat aircraft shortages, essentially because we have ignored modernisation during the past nearly two decades. The most visible impact has been that the combat force level, authorised at 37 squadrons (35 approved before 1962 as interim force against a requirement of 50) including two sanctioned as temporary establishment (in 1982) has already dropped by 6 squadrons and another 5 may become non-operational by end 2007, due to lack of aircraft.[4]

The decline in combat force level has to be seen in the context of increasingly adverse conventional aerospace balance in the region that IAF would be expected to cope with in the coming decades. A massive military modernisation going on in China for a quarter century (and that in Pakistan, since 1999, when it realised that it

---

4. Air Marshal V.K. Bhatia and Air Marshal B.K. Pandey, "IAF's Edge Analysed", *SP's Aviation*, Issue No. 2/2006, pp 10-19.

was handicapped in providing support to its army in Kargil because of the increasing obsolescence of its air force) has already changed the aerospace scenario; and threatens to make it worse.

We may or may not face the prospect of a two-front war. But what we are already facing is a two-front aerospace power modernisation of unprecedented scale and technological dimensions. The strategic nexus between the two at nuclear and conventional military level has to be factored into our thinking. The short answer that emerges is that in another five years or so, China would be operating 400-odd Su-30/27 class and another 200-odd J-10 multi-role combat aircraft supported by AWACS (Airborne Warning and Control System) so crucial across the Himalayan terrain, and aerial refuelling systems, not to talk of modern air-launched missiles with precision strike capability against air and ground targets. All this would be operationally supported by a rapidly expanding space capability to support air operations. At the same time, the railway line to Lhasa opened on July 1, 2006, has altered the dynamics of logistics for the PLA in the crucial region of Tibet.

The air force would have to contest dominance in the air against a technologically capable large force on one side and a professional increasingly high-technology air force on the western sector. IAF would no doubt be able to handle this. But the mere contest for air superiority would take away air effort from our ability to support the army leaving it vulnerable to hostile air power. We could also land up with the situation of 1965, when the air force had to battle a technologically superior force and was accused of inadequate close support to the army.

There are three core challenges that need attention and which are not easily manageable. The first is how to restore the force level at least to the authorised level? The very process of acquiring new aircraft takes time and money; and acquiring new types and absorbing them in service takes even longer. The process of acquiring 126 multirole combat aircraft had started a long time ago. By any calculation, it would take another 5-7 years for suitable aircraft to be evaluated and selected and another 5-15 years for the supply of the numbers required. Meanwhile, more aircraft would have finished their design life with a negative impact on force levels which would be difficult to compensate with currently known acquisition (like the Su-30 manufacture). For example, 7-8 squadrons of the upgraded MiG-21 squadrons would require replacement in another 10-15 years while the LCA would barely enter service by that time.

One solution is to acquire more of the types of combat aircraft already in service which may not be the ideal solution, but which would serve the purpose of helping restore the force level earlier by cutting down the time for acquisition. The obvious choice would fall on MiG-29 and Mirage 2000 types. Acquiring what in the automobile sector has come to be known as 'pre-owned' aircraft would need to be explored on priority. This is what IAF had done when its force level had to be increased rapidly in early 1960s. The second aspect is to focus on the long-term force level required in the context of the changes taking place across the borders and the tasks and missions of the air force having increased manifold. At the minimum, this would require building up to 50-odd combat squadrons at the earliest, knowing that earliest could be 20 years or more away. Except that decisions would have to be made now.

Last, but the most important issue is the question of funding modernisation of the air force. The overall defence budget has been reducing as a percentage of GDP over the past two decades. Given the trends, it is unlikely that defence budgets would increase markedly from the average levels of the past 15 years, that is, around 2.3 per cent of GDP. There is no doubt that we must keep defence expenditure at the lowest level possible; but if that level does not provide credible defence, the investment in defence can become counter-productive by providing incentive for aggression as indeed happened in 1999, in Kargil. We will, therefore, have to place a special emphasis on air power modernisation.

46

Managing India's nuclear security environment: challenges and policy options

Mani Singh Mamik

India's nuclear environment has been influenced by many changes including the evolution of a new unipolar global power structure, the rise of China and fast-paced globalisation leading to interdependencies. India has an important place in the information revolution. The shrinking of distance and free flows of ideas, capital, goods and services are growth enablers but also have negative connotations in respect of security of states and people, including nuclear security.

India's nuclear environment

The Indian perceptions of threats in current international milieu are: long-term nuclear technological and material denial; access to nuclear and weapons of mass destruction (WMD) to terrorists, non-state actors, groups, organisations, individuals sometimes aided by hostile states; state to state threats; unauthorised or accidental use of nuclear weapons, mishaps and the probability of loss, theft, tampering or natural calamities causing a crisis situation; and regime collapse that can happen in any of the nuclear capable (state with nuclear material) or weapon state with consequences of nuclear material or weapons falling into wrong hands.

State to state threats have generally been on the decline since the end of the Cold War. This is due to the reduction in readiness/

deployment and non-targeting policy, cuts in size of arsenals following bilateral accords on arms control, dismantling of surplus excess delivery vehicles and removal of fissile material from launchers.

Besides nuclear technology and material denial, nuclear threats to India in the past have been many, both overt and covert. The documented ones are the nuclear coercion by the US in 1971 and on a countless number of occasions, threats veiled or otherwise emanating from Pakistan during Kargil War in 1999 and the most recent in 2004. Pakistan continues to test ever-increasing range ballistic missiles despite a plethora of CBMs being put in place. On the Chinese side, there is increasing shift to mobile systems which can be brought up to Tibet especially with the new rail link to Lhasa and its likely extension to Xighatse (near the Sikkim border).This makes India vulnerable all through its length and breadth, whereas India still lacks a 3500 km+ missile to strike the industrially advanced coastal cities in China in retaliation, if required. With the US, moving additional nuclear missile firing submarines to the Pacific to address the China (now, North Korea too) factor, and also deploying an Anti-Missile Defence system in North-East Asia, there is bound to be a quantitative and qualitative enhancement of Chinese capabilities.

One man command and control system in Pakistan, complicates the India targeted doctrine of "strike India no matter who strikes you" as enunciated by Gen. Mirza Afzal Beg of Pakistan.

India's response to nuclear threats

India, as a nation, has been a significant participant in the global system and always respected its international obligations in all bilateral, regional, multilateral and global accords. However, despite its professed and continuous policy of non-alignment, it has made accords and agreements to enhance its security and strategic options in pursuance of its supreme national interest when survival or future wellbeing is at stake.

India and the Soviet Union formalised their strategic equations by signing the Indo-Soviet Treaty of Peace, Friendship and Cooperation, on 7 August 1971. It was one of the best kept secrets in Indo-Soviet relations. Articles 8 and 11 of this treaty provided for defence cooperation and mutual defence assistance in case of either party being subjected to threats to their territorial integrity and security. The treaty acted as a leverage and did deliver on its assumptions and raised India's strategic position in the region as well on a global basis but it severely came to test in 1979-80, when the Soviet Union intervened in Afghanistan. India could not support intervention in a non-aligned country situated in its neighbourhood.

Recent developments

The 1998 tests initially pushed US towards insistence on freeze, non-deployment or weaponisation and then rollback of India's nuclear programme. This policy changed after the Bush Administration took over in 2001 and the thrust shifted to accommodation. The dialogue continued despite the change in India's ruling parties and leaders and moved towards a mutually acceptable solution for India getting technology access and the US getting non-proliferation assurances. In mid-March 2005, Secretary of State, Rice visited New Delhi on a path-breaking visit to dramatically redefine US strategic interests in Asia. The US was keen on a whole new security architecture in the region, a goal that was written into a 10-year military pact signed by the two defence establishments, in June 2006. Philip Zelikow, policy advisor in the State Department, summed up the tectonic shift in US policy in the following words: "(The US) goal is to help India become a major world power in the 21st Century. We understand fully the implications, including military implications, of that statement."

The rationale for the move to get India on board seems to have come from a continous and calibrated upgrading of ties through the NNRSP programme. The impetus could also have come from a project study called "Universal Compliance" (2004-05 study by the Carnegie Endowment for International Peace), which based the new US strategy on six fundamental premises. These are:

1. To dissuade or prevent China from competing harmfully with it, the United States must mobilise states on China's periphery to balance Chinese power.

2. The United States should cultivate a partnership with India and enhance India's international power. A more powerful and collegial India will balance China's power in Asia.

3. To win over India, the United States should change national and international laws and rules that bar technology cooperation with India due to India's nuclear weapons and ballistic missile programmes.

4. India will have to increase its use of nuclear energy in order to fuel economic growth and reduce its rate of greenhouse gas emissions.

5. India never has been a threat to the United States or the liberal international system. India's possession of nuclear weapons breaks no international treaty. India's exclusion as an accepted nuclear-weapons power is a historical anomaly that should be corrected.

6. The established global non-proliferation regime is predicated on rules that do not sufficiently discriminate between bad actors and good actors.

Imperatives for India

For India, there was a need to find greater energy resources for growth and clean nuclear power was one answer. Despite India building 16 power reactors on its own, India needed larger reactors and knowhow available with the Nuclear Supplier's Group led by the US. India and the US engaged in quiet diplomacy to find a way out, post the 1998 nuclear tests.

With the July 2005 Indo-US Civil Nuclear Cooperation Agreement, India has shown that it wants to by and large go along with the global system and share its responsibilities towards non-proliferation and access to nuclear fuel and technology. The plan for separation of nuclear installations between civil and military installations to facilitate this agreement was finalised during the visit of President Bush to New Delhi, on 2 March 2006.

With this agreement, India attempted to manage three transitions in its nuclear environment in one stroke. First, its right to have a nuclear weapons programme was accepted (but not the demand to be a nuclear weapon state). Second, by separating its military and civilian nuclear facilities and putting civilian ones on IAEA safeguards in a phased manner, India moved from a nuclear pariah of prolonged technology denial to an access regime for its civilian nuclear programme. The third objective was to achieve energy assurance whilst meeting global concerns of non-proliferation over which India has a meticulous record of controls for over 50 years. Energy security was sought by getting assurances of continuous supply of fuel (even to stockpile) for those reactors that were to be placed under safeguards (which presently numbered 14 and 8 others were to be designated as military). Further, fast breeder reactors were to be kept outside the scope of inspections. However, the agreement is in the process of ratification by the US Congress. It has passed muster through the two House Committees after considerable deliberation The bill received overwhelming support in the US House of Representatives, in July 2006 with some amendments and awaits approval by the US Senate scheduled for November 2006. However, the fate of the deal has been complicated after North Korea's nuclear test, on 9 October 2006.

The scientific community in India has indicated its unhappiness with the deal and called for comprehensive nuclear and energy security with greater exploitation of indigenous resources.

The present state of play

Despite this path-breaking feat, there was continual criticism in the United States whether this deal made a dent into US's NPT commitments and legitimised Indian movement to weaponise. *The New York Times* in its editorial, on 1 March 2006, called it an unnecessary agreement which should be killed (even before it was signed).

These objections and fears in the US pertained to the following issues:

(a) India would be encouraged to increase its bombmaking capacity with the military reactors.

(b) India should agree to a bilateral agreement not to test any device and the cooperation would cease if it does.

(c) India should declare the size of its minimal nuclear deterrent and it should be capped there.

(d) India should first work out safeguards with the IAEA and then only can the legislation be brought to the house.

(e) NSG members like Australia and Germany would not change their stand on cooperation till India signs the NPT.

(f) The NPT regime so painfully established would suffer a body blow especially in regard to dealing with Iran, North Korea, etc.

During the negotiations with the US, India wanted the status of a nuclear weapon state (NWS) which was denied. This has been a continued US position of always ensuring that despite concern for safety and security of nuclear arsenals, nothing was to be conveyed or seem to be conveyed to India or Pakistan that they were legitimate nuclear weapon states. The US demanded that all civilian reactors be under safeguards in perpetuity which is not done for nuclear weapon states. Thus, one of the tenets of the July 18, 2005, agreement was broken. Consequent to this, India was asked to approach the IAEA for India-specific safeguards as part of the implementation as safeguards for NWS were not applicable.

It seems that the IAEA has already refused to apply safeguards applicable to nuclear weapon states and is insisting on application of safeguards applicable to non-nuclear weapon states. It could be possible that India may not agree to these safeguards wholly or partly after the 123 Agreement is signed.

During the negotiations, non-proliferation and capping India's military capacity was one of the prime US objectives. Almost all the points listed in the Glenn-Symington Amendment of 1998, have been incorporated in 2005 Agreement (restraint on non-testing of long range Agni III missile shows that it is true). There was an all-round feeling in India that the US was shifting its goal posts and insisting on concessions that were never envisaged in the original agreement. India's expectations from the agreement include that US should give India full access to technology and lift all restrictions on dual-use technology. India is also sensitive to restrictions on India's foreign policy, like was evident on the issue of Iran. India is sensitive to subliminal signals articulated in the form of Sense of House, Presidential reporting, or Congressional oversight portion of the US Bill. India would also like the bilateral Indo-US 123 Agreement to be signed before considering IAEA safeguards in order to ensure that there is no further arm twisting. India expects firm guarantee of optimum fuel supply and has reservations about the House of Representatives Bill referring to opposing of fuel supply by US in NSG, if US cuts off supply of fuel. India would also be averse to any US inspection and would like an India-specific protocol rather than an additional protocol as per IAEA standard with modifications. Last but not least, India would prefer to work towards an FMCT and for nuclear disarmament of all nuclear weapons states (as per Delhi Declaration).

Challenges and options

The instruments available for environment shaping are treaties and agreements as also Track II diplomacy. There is a need for a viable development strategy for peaceful uses and sharing of technology and energy security, strategies and deterrent capability and decisionmaking as also counter terrorism to meet the challenges. The challenges that can be foreseen in the short , medium and long-term are briefly stated below:

(a) Making a national 20 and 50-Year Energy Assurance plan with nuclear contribution based on the outcome of the Indo-US Cooperation Agreement and NSG inputs keeping in mind own capabilities and fuel availability with enhanced mining as suggested.

(b) Setting up of a separate SPV for formation of a new entity to build new reactors with foreign assistance under safeguards.

(c) Developing a cooperative regime with the nuclear suppliers's group to lift all restrictions smoothly.

(d) Set up a agreed system of safeguards with the IAEA that does not impede or place restrictions on our freedom of choices in the long term.

(e) In this respect, while not deserting the unilateral moratorium on nuclear testing, clarify and propagate that it will not hesitate to do so if required to for its supreme national interest.

(f) Measures to combat nuclear terrorism should be undertaken through a global agreement with states bound by convention to prevent such activities at all costs.

(g) Restrictive regimes of CTBT and FMCT should be looked at and addressed multilaterally and India should not give any bilateral undertakings in this respect.

(h) Our policies and postures should strive to make state to state threats not only a thing of the past but also such as to penalise the threatener in a manner that will prevent recurrence.

(i) The credibility and capability of our deterrent should never be compromised in any manner keeping in mind the uncertainty in the international system.

(j) Continue leading and maintaining a relentless pressure and participation in the global war on terror and also sensitise the international system to India's vulnerability and its stress on human rights and justice.

(k) In the long term, India should be a leading nuclear power and exporter in terms of domestic installed capacity, its unique technologies like fast breeder reactors and thorium fuel cycle.

(l) The foreign policy should have inherent capacity and capability to ensure multiplicity of options so that deterrence does not fail or seem to fail under any circumstances.

The first necessity of avoiding state to state threats is ensuring credible deterrence through proven, effective, capable weapons and delivery systems, besides demonstrated will and resolve to use them.

The efficacy of the arsenal and assurance of its performance needs to be improved to ensure there are no duds in the inventory. Institutionalisation of decisionmaking is desirable. Decisionmaking under stress and time compression in the current political system with the present heterogeneous demographics has become difficult. The aim is to reduce misperception, or a miscalculation of intentions and capabilities, and uncontrolled escalation, through CBMs and have a feedback mechanism to cross-check reassurance. Besides threat reduction measures, technology should be effectively used to obviate any accidental or unauthorised use by having safer, less sensitive nuclear weapons. India should be prepared for a disaster in our neighbourhood and have mechanism of communication and cooperation to act in the best interest of humanity. Examine Cooperative Threat Reduction programme of the US to secure weapons and facilities. Even though the US does not permit any cooperation with states outside the NPT, Pakistan has received assistance from the US. In order not to be cowed down by threats that Pakistan keeps making, it is necessary to deter it from taking the first step as retaliation may not be guaranteed by circumstances. Hence, a war fighting stance and consequence management approach needs to be examined and kept as an option.

Nuclear terrorism

No greater surprise can come about but from some deviant individual or group with radioactive material or even a small crude device threatening to have placed it at a key location or threatens to explode it or actually does it (including himself). Internationally, our foreign policy focus should be to continually educate and sensitise the world community of the evil designs of rogue elements and also their supporters through hard impeccable evidence at frequent intervals. One of the key steps in fighting nuclear terrorism is denying access to the terrorist or his agents from any nuclear material or weapons or facilities and key personnel who are vital to protect stowage, codes and operations as well as custody of material. In a globalised world, commerce and flow of finished goods, raw material, investments and information cannot be impeded. The speed of delivery and supply chain assurance are crucial for competitiveness whilst it is an enabling factor for the economy, it is an opportunity for the terrorist to act against nuclear installations or use radioactive material illegitimately. While port security has been one of the action agenda points, difficulty in speedily scanning containers, railway wagons (like India-Pak rail exchanges) and trucks (going across the LOC) will be a Herculean task. Anti-money laundering laws need to be enforced and the close monitoring of cash flows in and out of the country without impeding FII and FDI in real business transactions should be vigorously pursued along with cooperation from other states and financial institutions.

Conclusion

Nuclear threats are changing in both the content and context of targets and those targeting them. From physical state-owned instruments of terror they have descended to greater probabilities of use in crude form or RDDs by terrorist groups. These dissatisfied extremist individuals are highly motivated and technologically more advanced to adapt crude devices into forceful explosives. India has faced state to state threats ranging from technological denial and deprivation of nuclear material to coercion and outright threat of a nuclear strike. The highlight of India's unique strategic situation is requirement for deterrence against two simultaneous nuclear adversaries, which takes into account new weapon capable states that are emerging or likely to emerge in the region, a contingency India has to face and be prepared for in terms of resources, deployment and protection. Pakistan presents India multipronged threats. Its India-centric nuclear disposition to hit India no matter who attempts to take out Pakistani nukes, together with it being the nexus of terrorism coupled with a *jihadi* posture over a boundary dispute, makes it a serious threat.

The geography and short time of flight also add to problems of crisis response and civil defence. Even with the construction of metros in leading cities there is little or no protection in most cities. In addition to threat reduction measures including CBMs like hot lines, it is time to reorient our 'no first use', protection, deployment and readiness policy. In such time-urgent situations, previous methods of dealing with these, with downright ignorance or sequenced mobilisation and deployment as also forming alliances would be rather too late.

The 1971 Indo-Soviet Treaty delivered to India, strategic space and insulation to achieve its objectives and when reciprocity was demanded it gave visible support at some cost to its credibility to the erstwhile Soviet Union. The rising global price for oil and necessity for reduction of global pollution and warming made it necessary for India to seek cooperation with the United States, on July 18, 2005, to end a 32-year denial of nuclear material and technology and open a new possibility of energy assurance.

Despite this history, after the July 18, 2005 accord, India did vote along with the US for referring Iran to the Security Council on two occasions in November 2005 and February 2006, much against its domestic compulsions. It has also played its regional role in democracy building and contribution to reconstruction in Afghanistan, stabilised the difficult political situation in Nepal and continues to remain engaged in bringing about a reduction in the scale and level of violence in Sri Lanka.

No matter what the economic imperatives may be, India's strategic capability needs to remain intact and progressively improved along with strong security, vigilance, citizen participation and proactive intelligence to meet both state to state and non-state nuclear threats. The nation cannot afford to let down its guard, especially in regard to nuclear facilities and remain ever vigilant. India has to harness nuclear energy both for its development and also, its protection with or without others.

47

Maritime strategy and securing national resources

Raja Menon

Background

Indian maritime security during the British days was the responsibility of the British C-in-C of the Far East Fleet, based in Singapore. The analogy was similar to pre-Independent India not having a foreign service, and therefore a foreign policy. Unlike the Indian Army, which was responsible for both the territorial integrity of the British Indian Empire as well as the expansion of the British empire into external territories, the British Royal Navy saw the fledgling Indian Navy as a strategic competitor. Since navies operate in the external environment, the British attitude to the Indian Army and Navy was entirely different. As a result, there was no heritage of strategic maritime thinking in Delhi in 1947 and for many years to come thereafter. In the early years the maritime thinking in Delhi was fostered in the tradition of British strategic thought, heavily dependent as it was on trade, maritime supremacy and the preservation of the sea lines of communication (SLOC). Joint Commonwealth exercises fostered the British tradition of protecting commerce and commerce raiding until the 1962 war with China and the 1965 war with Pakistan. Both these wars, deeply continental in origin and of a relatively short duration, suddenly brought home the truth that short continental wars would make it difficult to identify useful strategic roles for a commerce protection navy.

The shift to Soviet origin ships from 1967 onwards, with their shorter endurance and heavier armament made it possible to make a smashing impact in the 1971 war, where the isolation of East Pakistan made General Niazi's surrender a foregone conclusion. The missile attack on Karachi with missile boats not built for the purpose showed that Indian maritime forces had absorbed new lessons on the conduct of naval war, under South Asian conditions. Subsequent to 1971 some lessons were learnt in geopolitics in a roundabout way, with the move of the *USS Enterprise* into the Bay of Bengal and the ceding of the British territory of Diego Garcia to the Americans.

These lessons were that:

- Maritime freedom gave a world power unlimited and legal access to any part of the globe for power projection.

- Geography could be changed catastrophically in a favourable or unfavourable manner by the granting of basing rights by littoral powers to major extra-regional powers.

The presence of Soviet submarines in the Indian Ocean to counter the *USS Enterprise*, the Indo-Soviet treaty of friendship and the US naval presence in Diego Garcia placed Indian maritime interests at variance with the USA's world interests for the duration of the Cold War. Apprehensions about Sri Lankan intentions on granting basing rights at Trincomalee to a foreign power led the Indian defence forces to eventually intervene in the Sri Lankan civil war with operation Pawan. Although the Navy made it possible for the Army to operate in Sri Lanka successfully, the maritime isolation of Sri Lanka was never seen as an Indian strategic objective. As a result, Prabhakaran and the LTTE maintained a steady logistic supply from South-East Asia and fought the Sri Lankan Army to a standstill. In many ways, the failure to stop Prabhakaran was the first grand strategic failure of Indian maritime policymaking. The failure indicated the weaknesses of mechanisms in Delhi to identify clear geopolitical objectives in cooperation between the defence and external affairs ministries and the armed forces. Part of the failure arose from the unfamiliarity of Indian decision makers to deal with security interests *outside* India and its territory.

Geopolitics of the Indian Ocean and sources of conflict

Purely maritime issues can lead to conflict, but man's presence on land requires that one also examines conflicts based on unresolved continental disputes. A geopolitical study of the Indian Ocean to assess the possibilities of conflict must necessarily look at hostility between states that have a certain *gravitas*, whether those issues originate on land or sea. The following section lists issues recognised as disputes. Many of them are active and possibly dangerous, while others are long dormant like inactive volcanoes, which have the capacity to erupt on unpredictable occasions.

Territorial disputes

- Ownership of Abu Musa Sini and Tunb Islands—Iran and UAE.
- India-China boundary question.
- Bassas da India dispute between France and Madagascar.
- Djibouti claimed by Somalia.
- Harrar Islands disputed by Bahrain and Qatar.
- Juba strip claimed by Kenya and Somalia.
- Pakistan raising Jammu & Kashmir issue.
- Iraq's claim on Kuwait.
- Mayotte claimed by France.
- Neutral Zone dispute between Dubai and Abu Dhabi.
- The Ogaden claimed by Ethiopia and Somalia.
- Qaruh and Umm-al-Muradin Islands claimed by Kuwait and Saudi Arabia.
- Swani occupied region claimed by Swaziland.
- Tromelin Island claimed by France, Madagascar, Mauritius and Seychelles.
- Ownership claims related to Spratlys and Paracels.

The disputes listed here are in some cases dormant, with no evidence of the dispute visible in the territories. Others are hotspots where low intensity infiltration, terrorism and criminal activity are all present. Of these, very few disputes are large enough to feed the fires of national hostility, leading to open war. Many of the others are claims that disputants cannot renounce for fear of a domestic backlash, but which do not form part of the current political fabric of that society. Even the larger disputes could be quiescent, but are in the temporary limelight owing to one or another of the disputants having given it priority for political reasons outside the dispute. If at all a generalisation can be made, it is that none of these disputes are so forceful and urgent, as to cause imminent war, except in the near term perhaps for Kashmir. However, in the medium to long term, many other disputes can turn ugly with rapidity, depending upon geopolitical developments, concerns and clash of strategies.

Boundary disputes

Listed below are some boundary disputes in the Indian Ocean littoral, both land and maritime.

- Durand Line between Afghanistan and Pakistan;
- The Thai-Cambodia and Cambodia-Vietnam border;
- The Sudan-Kenya border;
- The Ethiopia-Eritrea border;
- The Saudi Arabia, Yemen, UAE borders;
- The India-Bangladesh and India-Pakistan maritime boundaries;
- The Thailand, Cambodia, Vietnam maritime boundary;
- The Bahrain-Qatar maritime boundary;
- The Sino-India boundary question.

The disputes listed here are essentially quarrels based on the alignment of the boundaries, many of them remnants of settlements during the colonial era when the territory on both sides of the boundaries were all part of the semi-colonial possession. When looked at in isolation, none of these boundary disputes has the weight to be a source of conflict, by itself, although India and China have fought a war over their boundary problem. That dispute has now cooled down considerably under measures taken by both sides to build CBMs and prevent conflict. At stake in the other disputes is much less territory and other national interests and therefore, although the list is a long one, none of these disputes are seen as an impending *causus belli*.

Non-traditional threats to security

If the territorial and boundary disputes by themselves are unlikely to induce any of the concerned nations into conflict, then what can? It is difficult to answer this question without going deeply into the sources of conflict. But the importance of listing these political trouble spots is this. When a state's internal dynamics go out of balance, most usually through bad governance, then pressure builds up on foreign policy that is otherwise better left alone. But the factors that compel governments to seek outlets to relieve domestic pressure arise from a number of factors that need deeper analysis. In many ways, population pressures lie at the heart of many if not all problems of governance in Asia. Population projections are a useful tool to predict instabilities that may take myriad other forms.

The movement of labour and capital repatriation

As the world gets 'smaller', one of the phenomena to note is that labour has begun to travel to fulfil a demand, in the same way that goods do. It is often said that one day, the flow of labour will be stopped when the numbers increase to unmanageable levels. This belief sounds dangerous, as by then, the economic dependence on the huge amounts that are repatriated by the labour would have grown to such an extent that their being turned off could cause an economic slump if not a collapse. It is estimated that the total amount of money earned around the Indian Ocean littoral and repatriated back to the parent country is about $ 73 billion and is second only to the cost of oil exports in the region. In the Indian

Ocean region, the great labour suppliers are the Indians, Pakistanis and Bangladeshis.

It is still daunting to note that in the Indian Ocean region alone, there are 8,992,368 persons of Indian origin and Indian nationals combined. Of these, about 60 per cent are persons of Indian origin, the largest numbers being concentrated in Malaysia (1.6 million), Mauritius (700,000), Myanmar (250,000), Réunion (200,000), Australia (160,000) and Yemen (100,000). These numbers of PIOs do not include the 3.5 million Indian citizens in the Gulf. Obviously, the PIOs are emigrants while the Indian citizens are to be treated as labour flow. The interest that any other country might take extra-territorially to protect their people would largely depend on the ability of the parent country to do something concrete. All South Asian neighbours have tried to woo the Gulf countries to continue to grant visas to their workforce to work in ever larger numbers. Conversely, the host states have a lever with the labour supplying nations that they use quite often to gain advantages in international relations. With such large numbers of Indians abroad contingency maritime planning for their safety is a necessity.

Terrorism

The activities of the al-Qaeda are too well known to merit repetition. However, it is necessary to look at the future objectives of this organisation. During the last year the geographic location of Osama bin Laden has been fairly well established, but that cannot be said of his deputy Zawahiri nor of the new crop of leaders who have come up during the last five years. From the Indian stand-point it is necessary that any activity at the strategic level against world terrorism must attempt to isolate the al-Qaeda from the Jemmah Islamiah (JI) and the Lashkar-e-Taiba. The post- Jakarta bombing investigation has revealed that the JI had its target list 'approved' by the al-Qaeda on the basis of which funds were made available by the al-Qaeda to the JI. India and the US have conducted many conferences to assess the possibility of interdicting the links in cyberspace and this is an ongoing effort. The geographical space that links them is the Indian Ocean and it is clear that only the

Indian Navy has the resources to map the activities in this ocean, albeit with some force accretions. The recent activities of the LeT in peninsula India is a confirmation that their objectives are not confined to changing Kashmir's status but aim at a grand but vague objectives of establishing a Caliphate.

South-East Asia

In South-East Asia, the equivalent of the al-Qaeda, is the Jemmah Islamiah (JI) which is the holding company for a clutch of terrorist organisations. Although this region is reputed to have a gentler brand of Islam and the levels of fundamentalism is markedly lower than the version pushed out by the Saudi Wahhabi, the JI is potentially dangerous because it has politically dangerous ambitions. Its overtly stated goal is the establishing of the *Daulah Islammiah Raya*, an Islamic state to include Indonesia, Malaysia, Borneo, Southern Thailand and Southern Philippines. The origin of this political objective remains murky, but Abu Bakar Bashir is reputed to be one of the two founders of the confederation with Hambali from Malaysia as its number Two. During the Suharto regime, Bashir lived outside Indonesia in fear, but has now returned. In an extraordinary act of political courage Megawati had charges framed against Bashir and imprisoned him for four years. The other members of the leadership, besides Hambali, also recently arrested, are Isamuddin (wanted by the Indonesian police), and Iqbal Rehman currently in Malaysian police custody. The difference between the al-Qaeda and the JI is that many of the JI's functionaries are middle class professionals. Coming under the JI's holding power are a bigger group of terrorist organisations that include the Abu Sayyaf in Southern Philippines, the Moro Islamic Liberation Front, and the Free Aceh Movement. Indonesia has yet two more splinter groups known as the Laskar Jihad and the Islamic Defenders Front. It is not very clear whether the Malaysian terrorist organisation the KMM is another holding company like the JI or its subordinate.

Geographically speaking, the remarkable fact about the al-Qaeda and the JI is that they are separated by the Indian Ocean. Ever since many of the countries in the region improved their airport security, much of the travel between the Western and Eastern branch of terror has been by sea. The most notorious of these movements were the escape of the al-Qaeda members in the Meccah, a country craft which conveyed about 50 al-Qaeda members from Karachi to Chittagong, and later from Chittagong to Aceh.

Arms flows supporting terrorism

For a number of years there has been a constant flow of arms, drugs and people originating in South-East Asia, travelling east to the Philippines, north along the East Andaman Sea to Chittagong and west to Sri Lanka. To take the Sri Lankan insurgency first, captures made by the Indian and Sri Lankan navies have indicated that the shipments originate on the Indian Ocean portion of the Thai Coast, but the arms themselves often seem to be identical with those issued to the Thai Army. There is little doubt that the failure to isolate Sri Lanka from the sea, despite it being an island was one of the chief causes of the LTTE's ability to wage a long war against the Sri Lankan state. Similarly, the arms to the Moro Liberation Front and the Abu Sayyaf seem to originate on the East Coast of Malaysia and are carried by sea to the Philippines. There is a continuous counter movement of illegal Philipino people travelling without legal papers in the opposite direction. The northward movement along the East Andaman Sea had the Myanmarese dissidents and the Indian insurgents as their customers. Arms for them seem to originate along the Indian Ocean coast of Thailand, although the gang leaders may be located in Malaysia or Thailand. Arms meant for India are unloaded south of Chittagong and conveyed overland, as are the arms for the Myanmarese insurgents. Quite often drugs from the Shan and Karen areas of Myanmar flow back to South-East Asia on the same route. The fact that sea routes used by criminals are often used for political purposes have been demonstrated by the use of the Dubai gold smuggling route to India being used for transporting seven tonnes of RDX for the Bombay blasts.

Weapons of mass destruction (WMD) proliferation and the proliferation security institute (PSI)

This subject, an offshoot of what might be termed anti-terrorist activity has wider implications for India in the post Bush-Manmohan Nuclear Deal era. It must be accepted that the present implementation of the NPT has not really inhibited the breakout by rogue states and the threat of non-state actors armed with WMD. Therefore other initiatives built 'around' the NPT must be looked at, and the foremost example of a non-NPT initiative is the PSI, in which India has a special interest, with a proliferator as a neighbour. India's concern of not joining the PSI as a non-core member has been taken care of by dismantling the core group. On the other hand, early Indian mistaken apprehensions of the PSI being a unilateralist approach and violative of international maritime laws has not yet been corrected. This needs to be done. Article 1540 provides enough justification for nations to enact legislation to legalise the PSI. A careful reading of the clauses of the PSI will show that there are provisions dealing with the sensitivity of entering territorial waters. India as an emerging power has to differentiate and enlarge its vision from those acceptable in the mid-19th Century when interdicting international shipping was legal only against slavery, mutiny and piracy.

The maritime boundary

India has delineated its maritime boundaries with Sri Lanka, Myanmar, Thailand, Indonesia and Malaysia. Boundaries with Pakistan and Bangladesh are outstanding with the former creating a perennial problem with captured fishermen being incarcerated for months at a time. The maritime boundary settlement (MB) is ostensibly held up owing to the difficulty of determining the terminus of the land boundary and hence the alleged start of the maritime boundary. The problem goes back to the 19th Century when the Rao of Saurashtra and the Governor of Sindh (British) delineated the boundary along Sir Creek. The creek has now shifted and Pakistan contends that the terminus should stand where it originally did. India's stand is that the centre of the current Creek mouth should be the terminus.

Eventually the effects of the Sir Creek dispute are marginal on the land question, but would have a greater effect on the maritime boundary, since it runs for 200 nautical miles to seaward. However, even the effect on the maritime boundary is so marginal that the settlement of the dispute appears to be held hostage more to political considerations than technical.

The maritime boundary delineation has held hostage an even bigger issue and that is the right of both countries to claim the extension of the continental shelf as an exclusive area of resource exploitation of the seabed. The UN permits countries whose continental shelvers are within the 350 NM limit to claim exclusive rights beyond the EEZ provided they lodge watertight claims by 2006. India and Pakistan are unable to do this because they have not determined the trijunction point at which their continental shelf zone and the two EEZs meet. They cannot determine this point until the terminus of the maritime boundary is mutually agreed upon.

Preserving the sea lines of communication(SLOC)

Trade preserves and increases the wealth of nations. Despite the great increase of the trade in knowledge goods the volume of international trade that goes by sea is still about 90 per cent. In terms of value the sea-borne trade has reduced to just above 70 per cent, but the sea-lines of communications are still the great arteries of the wealth of nations. The most heavily travelled choke point in the world is the Malacca Strait.

This strait alone has a traffic density of 200 ships a day. But the bigger ships already use the Sunda and Lombok straits because of the depth restrictions of the Malacca route. The Makassar-Lombok route sees about 3,500 ships per year while the Sunda has another 3,500 transiting through per year. But, of equal significance are the straits of Hormuz where almost 90 per cent of the traffic consists of oil and gas carries of some kind. These straits see a flow of 60 ships per day. This density and volume of traffic makes the Indian ocean a vital link in the trade pattern of the world. India with its unique position and capability can ensure, along with the US, the safety of these critical sea lanes round the year. As the Chinese economy grows, their Indian Ocean trade volume will increase. However, in the foreseeable future the Indian Navy is the only littoral navy that has the capability to ensure the broad surveillance and policing capability of the Indian Ocean trade routes.

The maritime effects of large naval forces on the geostrategy of India

During peacetime the presence of foreign warships are often referred to, to indicate the level of tension in a region. Most people may be unaware of why this statistic is of importance. It is normally assumed that geostrategy is a permanent factor, which everyone is well aware of. This assessment is made on the basis that the locations of countries are fixed and geographical boundaries are almost permanent. The inferrence from all this is that the quantum and direction of a potential threat are well-known and unlikely to change. For instance, a potentially hostile country may have a strategic airbase 200 miles from a major Indian city. But that airbase remains a fixed geographical entity and doesn't move. Large naval forces, however, can change the geostrategical picture for a littoral nation.

As the weapon power of ships continues to increase, the ships are not merely concerned with attacking other ships but with destroying targets on land. It has been estimated that the economy of a medium-sized nation can be set back by 20 years by attacking its economic targets with a few hundred precision guided missiles. So it is important to know where 'foreign' warships are in large numbers, because they constitute a potential neighbour in terms of a military threat. Those warships have a legal right to operate outside the territorial waters for indefinite periods, the only restriction being the ban on collecting scientific data in the EEZ.

In times of tension, there is certain amount of jockeying for position if foreign warships are in the Indian areas of interest. It would be impossible for India to renounce the right to maintain a superiority of sea control in the approaches to the Peninsula.

China in the Indian Ocean?

China is an essentially Pacific Ocean rim power. It is not an Indian Ocean power. However all world powers have a world presence and it is the legal and free use of the sea that confers upon a world power, its world presence. In that sense, the USA is the most powerful nation in the Indian Ocean, more powerful than any of the littoral powers. One day it is possible that China may become a world power too, but that is unlikely before 2050. Once that happens a Chinese presence in the Indian Ocean cannot be contested, but there is a great degree of turbulence to be transited before that happens, particularly if the Chinese presence in the Indian Ocean is not confined to peaceful trade only. Unfortunately the nuclear arming of Pakistan, the supply of the M9 strategic missile factory to Pakistan, the cooperation between China and Pakistan in the development of an India-specific cruise missile, makes it necessary for India to look at the Gwadar Port developments with disquiet. The development of Gwadar Port must also be seen in conjunction with the alleged presence of the Chinese in the development of Myanmar ports and the presence of Chinese on Coco Island, which can only be an attempt to monitor the Indian missile ranges operating from Balasore and Sriharikota. If the rise of China is to be peaceful and maritime forces of the USA, China and India are to coexist, the constant attempt to bolster Pakistan's offensive capability will need an explanation from China. Failing this, India will have to fortify its maritime defences.

For all these reasons, further Chinese attempts to enter the Indian Ocean with naval ships and nuclear submarines cannot be ruled out. The routes that the Chinese must take passes through one of the three straits—the Malacca, the Sunda or the Lombok. The ownership of all these straits are with Indonesia and that makes the cooperation of Jakarta a vital matter for Indian maritime security in the ocean. The importance of pre-emption in these matters cannot be overstated. In the long years of peace, the constant use of certain bases like Gwadar could well turn into a decisive advantage if crises develop. During crises, the fact that India had not taken any action to contest certain developments could be mistakenly construed to mean acquiescence. Once a unit enters the ocean, it can disappear in the vast distances of the seas and hence, a strong surveillance capability at the mouth of the Malacca Strait is a definite Indian strategic requirement of the future.

Securing India's energy sources and routes

The year 2003 saw a conference on the concept of Peak Oil, the point at which consumption begins to outstrip production. Generally it is believed that Peak Oil would come about between 2007 and 2010. Indian reserves are expected to run out about 2020, in which year the reserves of China, Latin America, Indonesia and Western Europe would also have run out. The only major source then will be the USA, Russia, the Middle East and Africa. But the amount of hydrocarbon reserves in these areas tell another story. The reserves in the Saudi peninsula will be 10 times larger than those in Africa and 20 times larger than the American reserves. Hence, the movement of hydrocarbons well emanate solely out of the Saudi peninsula from about 2020 onwards. Obviously this shortage is not going to occur suddenly in 2020, but there is going to be a period of great turbulence approaching 2020, as the growth rates of China and India expand hugely and China's hydrocarbon consumption overtakes the EU's. How will nations meet the challenges of this turbulent period? It is virtually impossible to predict. For instance, oil is actually brought out of the ground by oil companies. Would these companies sell at OPEC prices plus, to the highest bidder or to 'friendly' countries whose bids are not the highest, or to nations that create credible military threats, or to the neediest nations on the basis of some friendship and charity? It is currently impossible to tell.

However, it seems apparent that nations are moving or inching closer to the Saudi peninsula as 2020 approaches. This movement may be militarily by land, by sea or both. The most dramatic demonstration of this movement is by China which has obtained a foot-hold on the Makran Coast, through the ostensible 'development' of Gwadar.

It is clear by looking at the energy figures that China will face the resources problem at least 5 or 10 years earlier than India. By 2015 China's consumption would be more than double that of India's, while its own resources will be running out. Therefore, in the geopolitics of oil, would the two leading Asian countries end up in a rivalry that turns unpleasant? Looking at all these factors, maritime interests in the protection of resources leads us into considering the following issues.

- Traditional SLOC protection of hydrocarbon shipments.
- Securing the overseas oil fields that have been acquired during the turbulent phase of declining oil.
- How may the new set of giant gas pipelines be secured?

Traditional SLOC protection

Of all the commodities the interruption of which could cause national disaster, oil is the foremost one. India's economy demands the unloading of three tanker a day every day 365 days in the year. Most refineries are on the coast and there is no hydrocarbon crude pipeline that can shift crude oil. A preponderance of production assets on the North-West coast also makes it necessary that seaward defence occurs well out towards the Pakistan coast. For these reasons, Bombay High will need protection well to seaward and all oil traffic wells have to the marshalled to inward convoying points and brought in under escort. With the introduction of sea-to-land missiles, some of the more prominent refineries that provide strong electromagnetic return echoes will need fixed and mobile defences.

Securing the overseas oilfields

Clearly some oilfields like the Sakhalin are too far to attract Indian protection. On the other hand, they are also immune to the disturbances of the subcontinent. To-date no country has evolved any procedures for the defence of overseas oilfields, but in areas where turbulence is in evidence, a defensive plan either independently or in consonance with other powers might be in order, particularly in areas such as the Sudan.

Defence of pipelines

The major difference between a pipeline and a SLOC is that the latter needs only transient protection. Ships travelling the high seas cannot be interdicted in a permanent manner. A pipeline on the other hand, is a far more reliable way of transporting the commodity in peacetime. When the pipeline is cut, the entire supply is however lost. Today the threat to pipelines may well come from non-state actors. For this reason, a capability to monitor pipelines overseas will always be a defence priority.

Maritime warfare: littoral warfare

The last decade and a half has seen a revolutionary change in the nature of warfare, including maritime warfare. Not surprisingly, the change has been dubbed the revolution in military affairs (RMA). The phenomenon of an RMA is not new, as the world has seen RMAs in the past in the form of disciplined Greek manoeuvring infantry and cavalry, the speed of movement of Genghis Khan and the army system of Napoleon. This time the RMA is technology led and, as in some previous RMAs, like the one introduced by Genghis Khan, it is driven by the speed of warfare. By speed is not meant the speed of weapons or weapon platforms, but the speed of sequencing tactical actions in such a way that the enemy Commander becomes paralysed, being unable to react relevantly. The technology that has led to this revolution has been made possible by vastly increased sensor capability, the passing of extensive video information through wide band connectivity, and hence the speeding up of the command process. As a result of the RMA, the balance in maritime warfare has shifted in favour of the 'fleet'. By this is meant that there has been a long and historic conflict for superiority between the 'fleet' and the 'shore' over two centuries with sometimes one side dominating and sometimes the other. The present RMA has made it possible to 'decapitate' the command process of the shore, because the shore assets (sensors) are fixed and can be located precisely with GPS and attacked with PGMs. This is not so with the moving assets of the fleet, which cannot be targeted unless it is in real time.

For these reasons the prevalent strategy in the ocean is littoral warfare. A nation can either do it or have it done to them. An adjunct of the war in the littoral is the increase in joint operations and the effects of maritime operations on land warfare. As a result, in future wars the battle between ships is only the early phase of the ultimate battle which will be to affect the course of the land war. The passing of the tactical picture through wide band connectivity, is normally called network-centric warfare, an aspect of war for which the Indian Navy is readying for. Much of this strategy has already taken into account that future conventional wars may be fought between nuclear armed nations. Hence the strategies will have to be modified, but the tool of conventional war will not be given up, nor can it be, particularly to discourage states from providing support to non-state actors. It may well be that war duration could be curtailed, in which case, shorter wars fought at greater speed fits in with the overall strategy.

Power projection

Oceanic power projection is a culmination of political resolve through sustained allocation of resources in assets and infrastructure, the creation of diplomatic space for international manoeuvre, and the convergence of strategic, economic and political interests of the parties concerned. It can only be effective if intelligence leverages the reach and firepower of assault operations. Power projection capability in future will be a combination of a reduction in the quantity of weapons but a great increase in endurance of the fleet to maintain its presence in distant waters. The great powers, in their future force projection doctrines, will factor in the need for large 'conventional' formations for attaining these politico-military objectives. Therefore all great powers, as also a few regional powers, continue to acquire a credible force projection capability.

Role of allies in force projection

Since the capability for force projection would always be limited and tailored to react to emergency situations in far off places, it is invariably linked to the role of allies and coalition partners. Thus it depends also on the power and cooperation of allies where force is to be projected, whether European partners under NATO, or pro-

US states in the Indian Ocean region. The 'front line' must be able to absorb the shock of initial aggression as also provide facilities that would enable reinforcements to accumulate safely. Thus, on-the-spot presence as also access to bases and base facilities help force projection. Over the years, the United States is being increasingly denied political-military support in the Gulf, and therefore might have to plan for military operations even in a hostile environment. The US Navy is increasingly discussing the concept of sea-basing as a future doctrine. The Indian Navy found it difficult to maintain the UN patrol off Somalia in 1992-1995 without access to bases. The fuel offtake arrangement with Singapore will be of great assistance to operate in South-East Asia.

Power projection and related operations

Strategic objectives behind power projection, to a large extent, determine the nature of the capability required to attain those objectives. Power projection capability is determined by multiple factors. The most important of them is the objective. It is often intended only as an instrument of coercion or as gunboat diplomacy. To be credible it must be effective at least as a means of punishment without escalating the conflict to attrition and ground-based warfare. Earlier, the means employed were gunboats for shore bombardment and blockade. Now, air power and long-range missiles with PGMs launched from the sea or air platforms have extended the range at which force can be projected.

The other intermediate method of power projection, is to employ air and sea-based power, without entering into ground-based operations, to attain the political objectives. India came close to using power projection during Operation Parakram, albeit with limited resources. Finally, power projection becomes the means to fight a war i.e. use of ground forces, to attain the stated political objectives. During the post-Cold War era, this was illustrated by operations to liberate Kuwait in 1991, Operation Enduring Freedom in 2001-02, and operations in Iraq in 2003 to overthrow the Baath regime of President Saddam Hussein.

The nature of maritime power projection has to be analysed under two broad heads: control (positive) and denial (negative).

In the first case, power is projected across the seas while in the other case the adversary is denied the power to deploy or use such force. In view of the fact that weapons and systems employed for both types of power projection have increased in range, those who seek to control the space employed for power projection and those who seek to deny it to the adversary are both keen to extend the range of their operations. China's strategy is a good illustration of a power augmenting its 'denial' capability as also to extend the range of its operations to neutralise American power projection capability. In the Indian Ocean, Australia and India have that capability. Others, including Pakistan or Iran, have only a limited denial capability along their coastal belt.

Assessment of combat power of regional navies

Combat power is essentially the effectiveness of a navy in combat. Too often is it confused with ordnance delivery capability. Today, the factors that influence combat power of a navy are much too diverse and include ordnance delivery capability, situational awareness (sensors), command and control (networking), relevance of a navy's platforms for the country's security strategy and the effort made to synchronise the navy's strategy with world strategic trends. The factors used in this study to assess the combat capability of Indian Ocean navies are set out in the succeeding paragraphs.

- platforms with ocean capability;
- the presence of force multipliers for REACH;
- maritime air;
- littoral sea denial;
- amphibious capability and power projection, oceanic and regional;
- connectivity and the RMA; and
- other combat power parameters.

To avoid tedious repetition of the characteristics of each navy it might be more profitable to put the above parameters into four groups, as follows:

Types	Characteristics
Backyard navies—with a limited blue water capability	Navies that can exert a sea-denial capability close to their littoral. Their strategy is essentially defensive, but in articulating that strategy, the force structure exhibits varying degrees of efficiencies resulting in a strong or weak local sea-denial Navy.
Blue-water navies	Navies that have synthesised their strategic objective and force structures into producing blue water forces in varying efficiency. The commitment to blue water operation is often diluted by inadequate stress on force multipliers, surveillance, networking and as is common in the Indian Ocean area, an ambivalent posture regarding investment on blue water and local sea-denial.
Blue-water navies with overseas power projection capability	Although there is only one true blue-water navy with power projection capability—the US Navy—the weakness of many navies in the region gives a few regional navies a marginal overseas power projection capability.
Token navies	A number of navies have merely got their foot in the door of establishing a naval force, which are so small as to have no defining characteristic.

Backyard navies

Almost all navies in the Indian Ocean region are about 50 years old and are a post colonial phenomena. Being adjuncts of newly independent countries, the overarching strategy of these navies has been subordinated to the national preoccupation of 'preserving' their new found independence. Threats to independence have invariably been seen as territorial although all these very countries had only recently been released from colonisation by overseas powers. Nevertheless, the structure and role of their navies quite often are appendices of a larger strategy of territorial defence.

In fairness to some of these navies, they have attempted to go beyond a mere backyard capability, by integrating elements of their air forces into an overall maritime strategy. This takes their maritime strategy into what might be called a fortress type of defence. Notable examples are Singapore and Pakistan. In Singapore's case, the entire air force strike formations are well equipped and worked up to perform maritime strikes. Supporting this air element is an efficient Hawkeye Squadron which extends the maritime search task to well beyond the coast. Similarly, Pakistan's one squadron of Mirage Vs, based at Masroor, operating in conjunction with their maritime reconnaissance squadrons extend the sea denial capability of the Pakistan Navy to well beyond their shores. The remaining backyard navies all have one thing in common—their preoccupation with the surface-to-surface missile fitted in small combatants as the main armament. This weapon and the inability of these navies to carry the weapon far out to sea gives an indication that their strategy is to fight a defensive battle off their coastal waters.

Blue-water navies

There is, in the real definition of the term, only one blue-water navy in the region and that is the Australian Navy. The force mix of the Australian Navy has been configured after the revolutionary Dibbs Committee Report in the mid-eighties which predicated no threat to Australia for 20 years, and a two-year gap before any threat could be built up. The Australian naval infrastructure is very deep and extremely expensive, with the country fielding a navy half the size of the Indian Navy, on a similar budget. The more expensive 'tail' of the Australian Navy consists of better workshops, logistics, software and tactics support organisations, a much larger maritime strike aircraft component—possibly of the same standard as the American F-18 Hornets. Its tanker to warship ratio is the highest in the IOR, it has 68 x F-18 Hornets to compensate for the loss of its single aircraft carrier—but most impressively it has the equivalent of the naval tactical data system of the Americans which links all the ships and aircraft. This capability, which amounts to networking, gives the Australians a situational awareness approaching that of the US Navy, minus the National Technical Means (NTM) based on satellites.

Three other navies have some kind of oceangoing capability and these are the South African, the Saudi Arabian and the Indian navies. The South African Navy has run into severe financial difficulties and may find it increasingly difficult to maintain an oceangoing capability. There may also be no need to maintain one in the coming years owing to changes in the geopolitical scene. On the other hand, the defence arrangements in the South Africa region require that South African troops may be needed to act in a stabilising role in the entire region. This would not require an ocean going capability but more of logistics and lift rather than amphibious ships. The South African Navy is already moving in this direction and in the next 20 years South Africa may cease to have an ocean going navy.

Saudi Arabia is a more interesting case in that, by spending huge amounts of money the Saudi Navy has some impressive capabilities on paper. Although the Arab sailing tradition is an old and competent one, this tradition has not been carried forward in the Saudi Navy which rarely operates for more than 5-6 days at a time, at sea. The navy has acquired almost 30 LCACs capable of lifting a battalion minus, but have deployed only a few of these and that too, on supporting oil rigs. So while the Saudi Navy is the only one with the ability to fund an oceangoing navy, numerous other problems seem to be an obstacle to their achieving a blue-water status.

The Indian Navy, mentally and intellectually is a blue-water force, but this mental aspiration has not yet translated into the force structure. The historical reason for this is the transition made from low weapon density, long-legged British origin ships acquired in the fifties to high weapon density, short endurance Soviet ships in the seventies and eighties. The naval leadership of India has recognised the problem, but the long lead time needed to correct ship design and ship acquisitions has to play out the time lead. One method of calculating the undue weight given to brown-water operations is to arrive at the ratio of main armament weapons fitted in oceangoing ships compared to the number of similar weapons fitted in coastal operations ships. The main armament in the Indian Navy is undoubtedly the surface-to-surface missile. The ratio of surface-to-surface launchers in large ships *versus* small ships puts it at roughly 6:5 today and exactly 1:1 about five years ago indicating that the ratio is improving in favour of a blue-water navy. However, roughly 50 per cent of the Indian Navy's main armament is still fitted on brown-water ships and this is the factor that leads to the mismatch between ideas and practice. The other parameters of a blue-water force are better. They are the MPA to major combatant ratio, the major combatant to tanker ratio and the effectiveness of networking. The last factor is the simplest to deal with and since data linking doesn't exist in any form, not even between MPAs and major combatants, this is a serious setback to situational awareness of the Indian Navy, and detracts from its ordnance delivering capability.

48

International terrorism:
the Indian response

Afsir Karim

Preamble

The contours of international terrorism have been changing rapidly and a new strategic vision is required to meet the challenges of postmodern terrorism. The lines between external and internal aggression are being gradually blurred by the new strategies of international terrorist groups though they still depend largely on stealth, infiltration and subversion with frequent thrusts to attack selected targets. Besides destructive attacks on selected targets, the focus of international terrorist groups is on degrading the industrial, economic and military assets of a targeted adversary by a gradual process of attrition or by coercive strategies that include mass casualty attacks. International terrorist groups acting through their surrogates now pose serious threats to many nations of the world and India is one of their major targets.

Understanding the nature of international terrorism is necessary to formulate effective counter-terrorist strategies. Defining terrorism presents serious problems at the very outset. Divergent national and strategic interests of various countries, communities and ethnic groups frustrate all attempts of defining terrorism in precise terms. In the present environments it has not been possible to find a universally acceptable definition of terrorism. It is also not been easy to identify terrorism because it comes in various shapes and forms that defy attempts of forming a coherent picture of its complex nature. Terrorism has lately taken the form of a specialised and highly organised politico-military activity that unleashes recurring violence on its victims with specific political goals and motives. Terrorism that is launched across international boundaries with predetermined political objectives generally employs inordinate force and violence against non-combatants. Assassinations of high-profile leaders, massacre of innocent people, engineering incidents with the aim of creating inter-religious and ethnic conflicts and fomenting socioeconomic unrest, form an important part of the strategy of international terrorist groups. International terrorist organisations based in several countries have acquired the wherewithal to generate low-intensity conflicts in targeted countries and pose a serious threat to their integrity and economic well-being.

Reorganisation of counter-terrorist infrastructures and reorientation of conventional methods of combating terrorism have acquired certain urgency in India, due to rise in activities of the international terrorist groups. A combined effort by all instruments of state power and international support is essential for achieving long-term goals of eliminating terrorists and defeating terrorism.

The threats and challenges of international terrorism have become gradually more daunting with the increasing availability of sophisticated weapons and new technologies to the terrorist groups. Possibility of acquisition of Chemical-Biological-Radiological and Nuclear (CBRN) weapons by terrorist groups has gradually increased and this poses the most serous security challenge to the entire international community. Bioterrorism is emerging as an imminent threat as the knowledge of breeding various pathogens and turning them into weapons is fairly widespread.

Terrorism may be sponsored or instigated by a country or a group of countries or international terrorist groups to intimidate and overawe a targeted country or an entire region for achieving long-term political and military objectives. Terrorism is a new face of modern warfare that may be launched to present an asymmetrical sociomilitary challenge to more powerful adversaries. Terrorist groups operating across international borders employ diverse strategies that defy attempts of understanding the pattern of their operations, there are, however, certain features common to all types of terrorism. Terrorism, unlike other conflicts deliberately employs brutal force and catastrophic attacks against civilians calculated to influence a larger audience, to undermine their morale, spread despondency and erode their will to resist. As terrorist groups rapidly change their target areas and operational techniques, their activities do not generally come on the radar screen of intelligence agencies until they have acquired menacing proportions.

Pakistan has been supporting and encouraging multiple forms of terrorist-oriented conflicts in India with the aim of fomenting ethnic, communal and political conflicts. Most of these conflicts have been aggravated because of support from Pakistan-trained groups which have been infiltrated for gaining political support in chosen areas. These groups instigate and assist local terrorist and separatist organisations in enlarging the conflicts with the aim of undermining the sociopolitical cohesion and damaging the economic infrastructure in targeted areas. It seems India's focus has remained mainly on preventing terrorist attacks rather than taking an overarching view of the larger Pakistani designs of sponsoring or abetting terrorism in various parts of India.

The ultimate nature and shape of terrorist operations in India, including conflicts instigated by international terrorist groups, will depend on how India responds to the covert methods, subversion and catastrophic terrorism employed by international terrorist organisations. The challenges of internal destabilisation, subversion, creation of administrative and economic chaos to drive a wedge between the people and the government, engineering horizontal and vertical cleavages among diverse sociopolitical and ethnic groups to destabilise the country cannot be met by conventional responses.

Although the basic equation between application of physical force and power remains unaltered, combat power alone cannot defeat a shadowy enemy that does not offer a worthwhile target and uses civilians as a shield. Conventional methods are unlikely to create an environment that is essential for a burnout of grassroots support of terrorism. An entirely new kind of politico-strategic response is required to neutralise the threat of international terrorism. India has so far shown no firm strategy to deal with the terrorist bases in its immediate neighbourhood from where transnational terrorism is being launched. An armed response against trans-border terrorism that is confined to our own territory suffers from serious limitations and restricting the use of force within our own borders is proving increasingly unproductive.

The organisation and the *modus operandi* of international terrorist groups operating in our neighbourhood have undergone a radical change since 9/11 and the subsequent military action by the US against al-Qaeda and its satellite groups in Afghanistan-Pakistan belt. A reassessment of the developing situation, the new strategies, weapon systems and sources of finance of various terrorist organisations operating across international borders is required.

International groups of various hues, operating at the global level, have now joined hands with the regional terrorist outfits to form amorphous groups without a central organisation that can be targeted. Besides fomenting unrest and strife in the country, narcotic trafficking, smuggling of arms and explosives, subversion of democratic institutions form part of their operations. A multi-pronged offensive of this kind can pose a serious threat to the security and integrity of any country in the world.

India has to take special notice of emergence of the Islamic terrorist groups in its extended neighbourhood because of its vulnerability, given a highly complex mosaic of Muslim and non-Muslim populations in the region. Porous international borders and ethnic affinities between various countries of the region facilitate infiltration and operations of fundamentalist forces in India.

Infiltration of armed Islamist groups from Pakistan continues unabated in Jammu & Kashmir. The elected representatives, government establishments and non-cooperative civilians are their main targets, besides the security forces. The sponsored and domestic terrorist groups supported by fundamentalist organisations within Jammu & Kashmir continue to foment trouble and blood of many innocents is still being shed. Lack of cooperation among political parties and absence of any political movement within Jammu & Kashmir, to counter terrorism creates an environment in which terrorist groups are able to operate with impunity. The political, ethnic and religious polarisation is not being addressed with the urgency it deserves.

Pakistan is following a dual policy of continuing the dialogue with India and supporting fundamentalist groups, which carry out terrorist activities. Pakistan's policy makers still seem to believe that unless pressure is maintained on India through terrorist attacks it will put negotiations on Jammu & Kashmir on the back burner. Fundamentalist groups in Pakistan who believe that *jihad* must be waged to wrest Kashmir away from India are not seeking a peaceful solution of the Jammu & Kashmir problem. Although Pakistan, as well as India are under considerable pressure from the international community to reach an amicable solution of the Jammu & Kashmir problem, the situation is not likely to change in the intermediate time frame despite the peace initiatives. The growing influence of the fundamentalist groups in Pakistan and their potential of starting a war between India and Pakistan, which may turn into a nuclear confrontation, cannot be ignored.

It is important to determine whether counter-terrorist institutions and policies in India are primarily oriented to meet the direct and indirect challenges of international terrorism. It is necessary to define the coordinating agencies at national and local levels, the resources required to implement crisis management schemes and the political fallout of terrorist strikes against sensitive targets in the country. In a democratic setup governments and policies change periodically, long-term policies based on national consensus should emerge to meet threats posed by various types of terrorism.

Defining terrorism

A definition of terrorism that has universal acceptance has yet to be found. The United Nations, while attempting a comprehensive definition of terrorism merely described some broad characteristics of terrorism:

"Terrorism is, in most cases, essentially a political act. It is meant to inflict dramatic and deadly injury on civilians and to create an atmosphere of fear, generally for a political or ideological (whether security or religious) purpose. Terrorism is a criminal act. But it is more than mere criminality. To overcome the problem of terrorism it is necessary to understand its political nature as well as its basic criminality and psychology."

Terrorism has also been defined as, "the substance of application of violence or threatened violence intended to sow panic in the society, to weaken even overthrow the incumbents, and to bring about political change." Walter Laqueur notes that the current definitions of terrorism fail to capture the magnitude of the problem worldwide.[1]

Yehezkel Dror observes, "Terrorism causes or reinforces analogous processes in international relations, breaking some of the few restrictions on 'permissible' modes of violence and adding to the barbarization of the global system."[2]

One of the definitions of terrorism by Rand Corporation states, "Terrorism is violence, or threat of violence, calculated to create an atmosphere of fear and alarm, through acts designed to coerce others into actions they would not otherwise undertake or into refraining from actions that they desired to take."[3]

The National Memorial Institute for the Prevention of Terrorism uses the definition set forth in statute by the United States Federal Government, according to them:

"The term 'terrorism' means premeditated, politically motivated violence perpetrated against non-combatant targets by sub-national groups or clandestine agents, usually intended to influence an audience."

The term 'international terrorism' has been described by them as, "terrorism that involves citizens or the territory of more than

---

1. Laqueur, Walter (2002). *The War on Terror*, A Council on Foreign Relations Book, Foreign Affairs, New York, pp. 1-2.

2. Dror, Yehezkel (1993). *Terrorism as a Challenge to the Democratic Capacity to Govern*, Wesleyan University, pp. 73-74.

3. Rand Corporation MIPT Terrorism Knowledge Base Glossary, RAND-MIPT Terrorism Incident Database Project, *www.rand.org/ise/projects/terrorismdatabase/*.

one country". The term 'terrorist group' means any group practicing, or that has significant subgroups that practice, international terrorism.[4]

More than a score of definitions have been in circulation over the years, however, these definitions serve little purpose because of variations in international perspectives and the rapidly changing patterns of terrorism. It may be better to ignore the semantic debates and focus on the nature and characteristics of terrorism in all its manifestations with a view to initiate counter measures. Terrorism can form part of guerrilla warfare, insurgency and turmoil of various shades; it has been frequently used as an instrument of subversive warfare launched against occupation forces. However, a terrorist is neither a "guerrilla fighter nor an insurgent soldier", a terrorist makes no distinction between combatants and non-combatants, and his main brief does not go beyond disruption or destruction of a targeted entity.[5]

Facets of international terror

Terrorists violate all normative values, they believe "more horrible the act the better to affect the targeted entity." No rules of human conduct are respected as long as the act of terror serves the purpose of the perpetrators. The abnormal intensity of force used by the terrorists against civilians and soft targets, sets it apart from all other categories of violence.[6] Acts of wanton killing of innocent citizens during wars are well known but killing of civilians as symbolic acts to spread terror in peacetime is peculiar to terrorism.

Terrorism has been unable to bring about a political change in any part of the world because the chaos and sociopolitical confusion it causes by wanton destruction of human and material resources does not promote any political process. In the recent past, terrorist groups generally functioned with the covert political backing of

4. The National Memorial Institute for the Prevention of Terrorism. *http://www.mipt.org/terrorism defined.asp.*

5. Karim, Afsir (2005). "Terrorism and Indian Response", *Emerging India Security and Foreign Policy Perspectives*, pp. 328-329.

6. Hanle, Donald J. (1989). *Terrorism: The Newest Face of Warfare*, pp. 184-186.

one country or the other, but several international terrorist organisations have now become stateless political entities, though they still require temporary bases on the soil of the states where safe haven is available and the political climate and location is favourable for carrying out their activities. The transnational terrorist groups operating against India have support bases in Pakistan, Bangladesh and Nepal; the Islamic militants organisations based in these countries comprise fundamentalist religious segments of various hues recruited from several parts of Asia and Africa.

Islamic terrorist attacks of a vicious kind have been witnessed in the recent past, in different parts of India because it has now become a target of global *jihadi* terrorism that is capable of causing massive destruction by employing new techniques and sophisticated weapons to penetrate seemingly well-sanitised areas. The suicide squads of the *jihadi* organisations who carry concealed explosives on persons or vehicles, merely represent one facet of the phenomenon.

The rank and file of the global Islamist groups, like al-Qaeda and its satellites, are primarily motivated to avenge perceived assault on Islamic values by the western world, in their worldview, the US emerges as the senior member of a "Zionist-Crusader Alliance dedicated to subjugating Muslims, killing them, and, most important, destroying Islam."[7] 'Hindu India' is now considered as the third partner in the alliance and therefore, a legitimate target of attack.

After 9/11, it has been proved that no part of the world can be considered safe from catastrophic terrorism, India is particularly vulnerable to terrorism that is linked to Islamic fundamentalism because of the demographic complex of the region combined with economic disparities and separatist tendencies found in many parts of the country. A variety of terrorist groups receiving aid and sustenance from global *jihadi* network threaten political stability of India by indulging in wanton destruction of human and material assets in several parts of the country.[8]

---

7. Doran, Michael Scott (2002). *Somebody Else's Civil War, The War on Terror,* A Council on Foreign Relations Book, Foreign Affairs, New York, pp. 44-45.

8. *op. cit.* 5.

Whether terrorism is a passing phenomenon or a facet of catastrophic warfare that may last long, is yet to be determined. Yehezkel Dror aptly observes, "We do not know whether terrorism is a temporary curse sure to weaken or whether over the long run it will develop into a major catastrophe."[9]

Hylke Tromp, an eminent political scientist says that surrogate terrorism is actually "A Third World War, which has assumed the completely unexpected form of 'protracted' warfare by terrorist methods."[10]

The threat

The pattern of operations and *modus operandi* of the terrorist organisations must be assessed realistically and accurately, to identify the nature of terrorist threats which have the potential to escalate and spread. Sponsored terrorism poses the most serious threat to the integrity of the country as it involves well-entrenched forces assisted by indigenous elements and mercenaries who use massacre of innocent people as a weapon for creating fear and spreading chaos calculated to undermine confidence of the people in the government's ability to control the menace. Both material and human targets of high symbolic value are attacked for generating fear and creating suspicion between various castes and communities. Porous borders between countries of South Asia provide favourable conditions for free flow of fundamentalist ideas and armed infiltrators across international borders, consequently, domestic and international terrorism aid and abet each other.

Specific threats posed by international terrorism to destabilise India by encouraging internal strife, turmoil and terrorism may be summarised as under:

- Spreading lawlessness in large parts of the country to bring crucial economic and political activities to a standstill.
- Planned disruption and sabotage of trade and industry.

---

9. *op. cit.* 2.

10. Tromp, Hylke (1978). *Politiek Terrorisme: De Derde Wereldoorlog in een Vol-Strekt Onverwachte Vorm?* Universiteitskrant, Groningen, p. 11.

- Supplying sophisticated weapons and explosives to separatists and armed micro-political groups to fuel internal conflicts and terrorism.
- Promotion of ethnic and religious strife by engineering provocative communal incidents.
- Attacking or subverting of country's financial institutions, banks and stock exchanges.
- Smuggling of drugs for funding terrorist operations.
- Poisoning of food supply and water storage and distribution systems.
- Penetration of sensitive organisations to undermine national security.
- Attacks on civil and military establishments and infrastructures.
- Catastrophic terrorism to cause mass casualties.
- Cyber or electronic pulse attacks may be mounted on communication and command and control centres, transportation system and vital industrial installations.[11]

Catastrophic terrorism or mass casualty terrorism through weapons of mass destruction is now a real and present danger; terrorists operating against India may acquire fissile nuclear materials, nuclear devices of several varieties, and chemical and biological weapons from global terrorist network. Energy sources, transportation, public health and economic infrastructure can be targets of attack deep in Indian territory; in these circumstances the protection and security of civil institutions and the industrial infrastructure has to be given top priority.

The spectre of mass casualty terrorism looms larger because of the growing danger of religious and fundamentalist-motivated terrorism in our immediate nieghbourhood. The death toll in the overcrowded urban centres in India could be a matter of tens of thousands, resulting in large-scale carnage leading to the collapse

---

11. *op. cit.* 5.

of the administration and industrial infrastructure. *Jihadi* groups are targeting political, social and economic institutions, on which the society is based, for expanding their political base in the subcontinent. They believe these institutions and the state machinery will eventually collapse under the onslaught of terrorism and internal turmoil, if ethnic and communal tensions are brought to a boiling point.

Availability of new technologies to the terrorists will enhance their capabilities and give them power of greater destruction. Progress and industrialisation, better and faster means of communication are likely to facilitate terrorist attacks; wide media coverage of events will increase the dramatic impact of terrorism and encourage daring attacks by the terrorist groups. Counter-terrorist policies must address the future threats taking these factors into account.

Sponsored terror

Most armed groups operating in India depend directly or indirectly on the assistance of Pakistan for training, safe houses and financial support; it is not possible to counter Pakistan-supported terrorism effectively without severing the link between these groups and their sponsors in Pakistan. India has yet to formulate an effective policy to get over this problem. Indications are that Pakistan will continue to assist trans-border terrorism regardless of the peace process now underway. The operations of Pakistan-sponsored terrorist groups now extend beyond Jammu & Kashmir in many other parts of India. Sponsored terrorism is being used by Pakistan as the main instrument to destabilise and weaken India.

Pakistan is using sponsored terrorism in conjunction with insurgency in Jammu & Kashmir to wage a low-intensity conflict, in which its own nationals, *jihadi* war veterans from several countries, specially recruited and well-trained irregular forces are employed. The armed forces of Pakistan are not directly involved but they provide logistic and fire support to infiltrating columns. Terrorist groups have also established bases in remote areas within Jammu & Kashmir to launch lethal attacks against civilians and soft-military targets from these hideouts. Pakistan-sponsored terrorist organisations in Jammu & Kashmir are employing highly motivated foreign terrorists, with specific instructions to massacre or drive away minorities as a part of ethnic cleansing in specified areas. Some other groups are specially tasked to attack places of worship to damage India's secular image and disturb communal harmony in various parts of the country.

The main features of Pakistan-sponsored terrorism in India are:

- Terrorism and violence through mercenary-*jihadi* groups, with the aim of destabilising the state of Jammu & Kashmir, they have been suitably armed and trained to confront the armed forces of India.

- Arming and assisting domestic terrorist groups operating in various parts of India.

- Assisting Naxalites and other allied groups to generate violence by attacking, police, paramilitary personnel and economic infrastructure in return for supply of weapons, provision of safe bases and financial assistance.

- Supplying arms and providing training facilities to insurgent and separatist groups operating in Northeast India.

- Spreading disorder by generating communal violence to divert material and human resources away from constructive socioeconomic activities.

- Destabilising provincial governments in sensitive areas to create political and administrative chaos.

- Creating conditions for caste, ethnic and religious strife to spread disorder and lawlessness in large parts of rural India.

- Exploiting sensitive issues such as, Gujarat riots and Babri Masjid-Mandir dispute, to widen communal divides.[12]

A brief on international terrorist groups based in Pakistan

The US State Department listed, Lashkar-e-Taiba (LT), and Jaish-e-Mohammed (JEM), as foreign terrorist organisations after the

---

12. *ibid.*

December 2001 attack on the Indian Parliament. Harakat ul-Mujahedeen (HUM) was named earlier, Pakistan has banned these groups, but they continue their usual activities by changing their names, al-Qanoon or Lashkar-e-Omar, Khuddam-ul-Islam (KUI) and Jamaat-ul-Furqan (JUF) are some of the assumed names of Jaish-e-Mohammed, Lashkar-e-Taiba, and other Pakistan-based terrorist groups. Hizb-ul-Mujahidin, is the largest Kashmiri militant group operating from Pakistan, and Pakistan Occupied Kashmir.

All the terrorist groups based in Pakistan and Pakistan Occupied Kashmir are manned mostly by Pakistani nationals, besides ethnic Kashmiris, Afghans and Arab veterans of the Afghan war.

The financial support for these terrorist groups comes mainly from various West Asian countries and Pakistan. Their fund raising is still not constrained in Pakistan, despite the government freezing their assets.

Harakat-ul-Mujahideen (HUM)

An Islamic militant group based in Pakistan that operates primarily in Kashmir. It has conducted a number of operations against military and civilian targets in Kashmir and other parts of India. HUM was responsible for the hijacking of an Indian airliner on 24 December 1999, it demanded and succeeded in getting Masood Azhar, a leader of former Harkat-ul-Ansar and Omar Sheik released. Omar Sheik was later convicted of the abduction/murder of US journalist Daniel Pearl.

Jaish-e-Mohammed (JEM)

The Jaish-e-Mohammed is an Islamic extremist group that was formed by Masood Azhar in early 2000. Based in Peshawar and Muzaffarabad, it is politically aligned with Pakistan's Jamiat Ulema-i-Islam of Fazlur Rehman faction (JUI-F). The new name of JEM is, Khuddam-ul-Islam, and it continues to function in Pakistan with impunity, despite the ban.

On 1 October 2001, the JEM claimed responsibility for a suicide attack on the Jammu and Kashmir Legislative Assembly but later it denied the claim. India publicly named JEM and Lashkar-e-Taiba

(LT) for the 13 December 2001, attack on the Indian Parliament. Pakistani authorities suspect that perpetrators of anti-Christian attacks in Islamabad, Murree, and Taxila, during 2002 were affiliated with the JEM.

Most of the JEM's cadre and material resources have been drawn from the militant groups, Harakat-ul-Jihad-al-Islami (HUJI) and the Harakat-ul-Mujahedeen (HUM). The JEM maintains close ties with the Taliban and al-Qaeda.

Lashkar-e-Taiba (LT)

The LT is the armed wing of the Pakistan-based religious organisation, Markaz-ud-Dawa-wal-Irshad (MDI)—an ultra-radical organisation formed in 1989. The LT is one of the best-trained terrorist groups operating in Kashmir. LT has adopted a new name after the ban—Jamaat-ud-Dawa.

The LT has conducted a number of operations against military and civilian targets in Kashmir since 1993. The LT claimed responsibility for numerous attacks in 2001, including an attack on Srinagar airport, an attack on a police station in Srinagar; and an attack on a post of Indian Border Security force. It was involved in the attack on the family quarters of an army base in Kaluchak, in Jammu, and the 13 December attack on the Indian Parliament building.

Senior al-Qaeda leader Abu Zubaydah was arrested from an LT safe house in Faisalabad in March 2002; this confirmed the suspicion that LT was facilitating the al-Qaeda movement in Pakistan.

Hizb-ul-Mujahidin (HM)

Hizb-ul-Mujahidin, is the largest Kashmiri militant group operating from Pakistan, and Pakistan Occupied Kashmir, it was founded in 1989 and supports the liberation of Kashmir. The group is one of the militant wings affiliated to Pakistan's largest Islamic political party, the Jamaat-i-Islami, the faction, led by Syed Salahuddin is made up primarily of ethnic Kashmiris from both sides of the Line of Control in Jammu & Kashmir.[13]

---

13. Excerpts: *Pattern of Global Terrorism-2002-2005*, released by the Office of the Coordinator for Counterterrorism: Background Information on Designated Foreign Terrorist Organisations.

Counter-terrorism: national policy and counter-terrorist infrastructure

It is necessary to survey the entire landscape surrounding international and transnational terrorism for formulating appropriate counter-terrorist strategies. The planning has to commence after a comprehensive assessment of counter-terrorist effort, a policy statement must issue from the highest authority encompassing all counter-terrorist measures, clearly defining the long-term goals that have to be achieved and counter-terrorist infrastructure that must be established to achieve the goals.

The most effective counter-terrorist efforts are ultimately those that create a backlash against the terrorists; a vigorous psychological campaign along with 'incremental and pragmatic' offensive action must be put into motion to counter-terrorist designs. It is, however, not easy to raise the costs for the terrorists, since they only need a few brutal attacks to reassert their presence. They can raise the ante by engineering incidents in which innocent civilians are gunned down by the security forces either in crossfire or due to mistaken identity. It is also easy for terrorists to attack few sensitive soft targets to demonstrate that the security forces are not winning, a conventional armed response does not therefore prove very effective for conducting operations against insurgent- terrorism. Counter-terrorist operations generally prove to be a frustrating exercise for the armed forces, more so, if they tend to be reactive. Successful tackling of terrorism requires extraordinary foresight combined with speedy action because the threats of terrorism mutate much more quickly compared to the response of the counter-terrorist forces. A hurried assembling of counter-terrorist forces, taking *ad hoc* actions against hijackers, hostage takers, sponsors of attacks on crowded market places generally end in failures that boost terrorist morale.

Some counter-terrorist policies merely shift the threat from one form or one place to another, seemingly successful operations, may just be forcing terrorists to develop innovative methods that cause greater damage and more destruction. The bomb blasts in various parts of India and the advent of suicide bombers to kill ordinary civilians are examples of dangerous mutation of threats after tight security measures were instituted to protect targets of high symbolic value.

So, far India's response to terrorism has been primarily focussed on law enforcement related to specific acts of terrorism. The laws have often been misused to serve a political purpose of the government or of particular parties with negative impact on counter-terrorist operations, certain laws affected innocent persons more than the terrorists. On the other hand downplaying the criminal justice and security aspects and focussing on favoured political processes can be equally damaging. It is crucial that authorities do not undermine public confidence in the rule of law, and adopt a course that puts equal emphasis on law enforcing measures and political and socioeconomic reforms to combat terrorism.

The use of military force, to attack terrorists' assets, is seen by many people as the only way of effectively preempting terrorist designs. It is vitally important to attack the terrorist infrastructure with speed as this can act as an effective deterrence on terrorist activities, and reassure the public at the same time that the government is not a helpless spectator in the face of terrorist threats. Experience shows that the overemphasis on use of security forces is rarely successful in defeating terrorism in the long run; it can on the other hand, result in alienating people and increasing support and sympathy for the terrorists and their objectives.

Military force can be used with greater affect against terrorist bases and essential infrastructure across national frontiers. Terrorist groups are, however, becoming increasingly amorphous, and rely less and less upon traditional organisational structures, thus presenting few worthwhile military targets. Terrorist are also adept in using civilians as a human shield to protect themselves, in such environments it becomes increasingly difficult to identify their bases or to pinpoint targets against which the military can retaliate. The perception that the war against terrorism can be won with traditional military tactics is a dangerous illusion that undermines other more essential counter-terrorism efforts. Military power should be used as a part of a multifaceted campaign that combines social, economic, legal, diplomatic and political measures.

Harsh police action without appropriate political initiatives and a just approach, generally aggravates the situation and gives a fillip to terrorism, at least in medium future span. Ethnic or religious discrimination invariably leads to escalation of terrorism, as the confrontation between religious fundamentalism and secular ethos leads to political polarisation.

It may be a matter of time before some terrorists groups acquire and use chemical, biological, radiological devices to cause mass casualties, acquiring tactical nuclear weapons from rogue states or their scientists is also in the realm of possibility now. Counter-terrorist policies must assess the dangers of mass casualty weapons realistically, and take appropriate damage control and other necessary measures without delay.

To formulate affective strategies to combat transnational terrorism and reduce the capability of trans-border terrorist groups, it will be necessary to accurately determine and detect the following:

- Political influence in targeted areas, reach and collaboration with the terrorist groups operating in various parts of our country.
- The supply routes and the sources of weapons systems, financial support.
- Organisation and international affiliations of various terrorist groups.
- Sponsoring organisations and their political aims.
- Local support bases and front organisations and institutions.

Sharing information about terrorists groups at regional and global levels will be required to get reliable intelligence of terrorist organisations, locations and the possible plans of attacks. Acquisition of appropriate technologies can greatly assist in warding off terrorist attacks, keep terrorist organisations off balance and interfere with their command, control and communication systems. Security forces can play a limited role in attacking and destroying terrorist hideouts but only a multidimensional task force can provide the capability and organisational skills required to defeat terrorism. Terrorism can be managed more effectively if there is better cooperation between the intelligence, law enforcement and judicial agencies. If the counter-terrorist policies are undermined by local political, ethnic or religious considerations, terrorist threats cannot be met effectively.

The increase in ethnic and religious tensions has a direct relationship with group mobilisation that is essential to promote terrorism. The chaos and panic created by repeated terrorist strikes are designed to fuel communal conflicts and create political polarisation, a situation in which terrorists and their sponsors gain maximum advantage because it narrows down viable options available to the government. To counter international terrorist groups it will be necessary to strengthen all the components of the state and form them into a composite force to act against terrorist organisations and their sponsors both inside and outside the country. Denial of use of foreign bases available to the terrorists close at hand for initiating and conducting terrorist attacks across international borders must be given priority. If military force cannot be used for blocking external assistance and isolating terrorists from their sponsors, deft diplomatic, political and paramilitary initiatives would be necessary.

Counter-terrorist operations should not be limited to 'search and destroy operations', other measures such as, ensuring security of the people, protection of industrial infrastructure and political and administrative institutions should be given equal importance. The critical aspect of winning 'hearts and minds' of the people should receive much greater attention than is generally the case. Experience shows that socioeconomic programmes are extremely effective in eroding the grassroots support of terrorism in the long-term perspective. Involving large segments of people in the development and welfare programmes can wean away local populace and potential recruits from joining terrorist network.

An apex body at the national level will be required to formulate and oversee counter-terrorist strategies besides ensuring close coordination between various agencies in the country. This establishment will require professional and multidisciplined experts and resources to implement plans for deterring, preempting and preventing domestic and international terrorist attacks. It will also formulate, response and preparedness programmes and plan professional intelligence inputs. The apex organisation will require some of the following components:

- Special research centres.
- Terrorist-specific intelligence cells to obtain real time intelligence.
- A special organisation for formulating strategies for winning the battle of hearts and minds.
- Covert counter-terrorism planning groups.
- Special response units.
- Information technology group.
- Foreign cooperation cells.

The apex body should be capable of rendering advice to the government on positioning of assets for appropriate responses to terrorist strikes in any part of the country. It would also coordinate programmes of crisis and consequence management, infrastructure security plans, functioning of terrorist tracking cells; blocking of terrorist-financing and weapon, supply channels.

Concluding observations

Terrorism across international borders by Pakistan-based groups was not countered vigorously in the initial stages by India and consequently, it took the shape of a prolonged shadow war. Generally, no solid evidence can be mustered against a state that is sponsoring terrorism as it uses proxies and mercenaries instead of employing its own armed forces, Pakistan, therefore, continued its covert operations against India for a long time without any fear of being indicted by the international community. Assistance and cooperation of international community is important to deter the threat posed by international terrorism, whether state-sponsored or otherwise, and it is a difficult task for any one country to deter terrorist attacks without international cooperation.

The fundamentalist organisations in Pakistan, with the tacit support of the armed forces, gradually mobilised vast resources of manpower, arms and finances, to carry out trans-border operations against India. Countering sponsored-terrorism is a far more complex task than an ordinary military operation, especially in an environment where the terrorists operate in small groups from safe bases provided by a neighbouring country.

Pakistani Islamists, a conglomerate of several radical groups, aim to bring the entire subcontinent under their sway; fundamentalism and terror serve their purpose of gaining political space. Religious extremists and terrorists are being employed extensively to provoke communal and ethnic conflicts with the aim of destabilising and weakening India. Transnational terrorism continues to be the favoured form of warfare by Pakistan, since it is comparatively risk free; however, one of the possible dangers of continued Pakistani support to *jihadi* terrorism is that it can once again bring India and Pakistan to the brink of a war. As both the countries have nuclear weapons even a nuclear confrontation cannot be ruled out.

In Jammu & Kashmir, the disruptive and violent phase of *jihadi* terrorism remained unchecked for a long time because its destructive potential was neither foreseen nor countered effectively by India. Terrorists exploited religious sentiments and their ability to merge with the local population helped. Religious sensitivities of the people were used by the *jihadi* groups to muster local support, this campaign was not countered at the political level, as a result religion-based political institutions continued preaching hatred unchecked. The political causes of the growing fundamentalist mindset and socio-economic factors responsible for it must be addressed on priority. Media can play an important role in countering fundamentalist propaganda.

The efforts of Pakistan for curbing trans-border terrorism, despite various assurances by President Musharraf himself, are not particularly encouraging. Trans-border terrorism has set entirely new norms and it seems no part of India can now be considered entirely safe from surprise attacks. It is virtually impossible to defend all the targets all the time, however, strong counter-terrorist measures can make trans-border attacks more difficult to mount and greatly reduce the damage.

Compartmentalisation of counter-terrorist efforts militate against well thought-out and coordinated planning and actions. Terrorist-specific regional intelligence cells provided with appropriate technology to detect sleeper cells, watch terrorist movements to anticipate their plans are necessary. Crisis management schemes, indicating focal points for national and state-level resources for combating terrorism are required to be coordinated at the highest level. India is not yet fully prepared or equipped to take on global *jihadi* terrorism and its support systems in South Asia.

Indiscriminate use of force can lead to escalation of terrorist activities. Comparative studies regarding relationship between harsh measures and escalation of conflicts show that there is need of evolving methods of using force in a manner that cause minimum collateral damage. Political, economic, social and military measures have to be enmeshed suitably for countering terrorism without hurting the common man. India has managed to control the fallout of terrorist attacks fairly well but has not been able to curb terrorism in its various other manifestations.

The present trends indicate that new technologies may enhance destructive capabilities of the terrorist groups and give them power of greater coercion. Rapid transportation facilities and better means of communication systems may facilitate catastrophic attacks.

"This phenomenon known as international terrorism may prove to be the most formidable foe ever known to the free world. It is rooted in Islamic extremism, fueled predominately by a primitive desire to vanquish all infidels, beginning with Israel and ending with much of the free world."[14]

---

14. Williams, J.B. (2006). "Are We Winning the War Against International Terrorism?", *The American Daily Analysis with Political and Social Commentary*, Phoenix, Arizona, Friday, March 24.

"It's army is bigger than most will let on, scattered to all corners of the earth, operating largely below radar in more than 60 countries, employing the most brutal tactics known to mankind, usually against soft civilian targets with the intent of consuming the hearts and minds of innocent people all over the globe with fear. Even the most powerful military on earth can't win a war its people won't allow it to fight."[15]

Accurate prediction of the future shape of terrorism is not possible, because it depends on several dynamic variables. If a short span is taken into account and the ongoing war against international terrorism is correlated to terrorist activities in various parts of the globe, a hazy picture of future shape and form of terrorism may emerge, whether terrorism is a facet of a new kind of warfare that may last long, is yet not clear.

---

15. *ibid.*

Nuclear energy and disarmament

49

Disarmament and India's nuclear diplomacy: evolution of a 'reluctant' nuclear weapon state

Arundhati Ghose

On the 11th of May 1998, India conducted three nuclear tests followed almost immediately, on the 13th of May, with two more and a declaration of nuclear weapon state status. Apart from the expected negative reactions of almost all governments, an unintended and yet inevitable consequence of these events was a proliferation of articles, theses and books on the origins of India's nuclear programme and the apparent contradiction between India's nuclear policy and diplomacy, particularly since the tests came after decades of India's vociferous advocacy of nuclear disarmament and the need for a nuclear weapon-free world. Many of these commentators, mainly from the disarmament lobbies and non-Indian sources, presented narratives which posited the assumption that the tests were a straightforward case of India's hypocrisy and deviousness; there was a sense of betrayal leading to vicious attacks on India's policies and actions, alleging that India had been all along pursuing a clandestine weapons policy to achieve an international status she otherwise lacked, while cynically using a smokescreen of the cause of nuclear disarmament. Others, analysts mainly of Indian origin, approvingly (or disapprovingly, in a few cases) claimed that India had at last thrown off the burden of years of rhetoric and unrealistic idealistic posturing and had adopted a 'realistic' and 'enlightened' view of the world. Neither group felt that there was any case for a genuine commitment to disarmament and a nuclear-free world. One can hardly fault either school, given that almost exactly 10 years earlier, in 1988, on the occasion of the presentation by Prime Minister Rajiv Gandhi of an Action Plan for a Nuclear-Free World to a Special Session of the UN General Assembly on Disarmament, the Ministry of External Affairs published an anthology of selected writings and speeches by India's leaders, past and present, on *India and Disarmament*. This publication contains selected pieces which strongly promote the objective of the total elimination of nuclear weapons and, according to the then Foreign Minister of India, P.V. Narasimha Rao, indicated that: "India has remained steadfast in her policy through the past decades. If humanity is still haunted by the spectre of a nuclear holocaust, it is not for lack of adequate effort on the part of India and other like-minded countries. The impassioned advocacy of disarmament by our national leaders has influenced world public opinion even if it has fallen far short of the ultimate objective."[1] It was inevitable, then, that 'world public opinion' would react sharply and in fury to the developments of 1998.

The facts are incontrovertible: India was a passionate advocate of disarmament—in the UN and other forums and had launched many initiatives which were aimed at the elimination of all nuclear weapons. India was a part of the disarmament lobby. It is equally true that after Independence, India pursued a policy of building her weapons capability without, however, actually building a nuclear arsenal—at least, according to all reports, till the late 1980s. If one is therefore, to contest the charges made by the critics, as this essay will seek to do, some basic questions will have to be debated: one, why did India push so strongly for nuclear disarmament? Two, if indeed she was intent on weaponisation, why did she not take action to build an arsenal earlier? India has been called a 'reluctant' nuclear weapon state. What made India 'reluctant'? Was India's diplomacy able to deal with these intricate and complex issues and

---

1. Rao, P.V. Narasimha (1988). "Foreword" in *India and Disarmament*, External Publicity Division, Ministry of External Affairs.

what Rajesh Rajagopalan has called a 'distracted' policy?[2] How does a 'reluctant' Nuclear Weapon State deal with emerging challenges?

India's diplomacy to project and protect India's options and interests from the fifties to Pokhran II may supply some indicators as to how India, now a Nuclear Weapon State, might confront the challenges of the future.

Before turning to what can best be only an outline of the evolution of India's nuclear policy, some general comments would seem to be in order. Firstly, it is necessary to note that most commentaries and even research on the subject has tended to be, to use Rajagopalan's word, 'intuitive' or inferential,[3] as it is widely agreed that there are very few written sources which could throw light on the process of nuclear decisionmaking: most of the available literature is in the form of speeches by leaders, correspondence and recollections and recalled interviews. Secondly, decisionmaking on nuclear issues remained confined to a very few, particularly in the early years. According to Perkovich, " Indian nuclear policy making has been highly personalized and concentrated in a handful of political leaders and scientists."[4] In the fifties and sixties, decisions on the directions of India's nuclear programme remained almost exclusively in the hands of Nehru and Homi Bhabha. The fundamentals and future contours of the programme were moulded by these two personalities, and it would be inevitable that their personal approaches and prejudices would leave an impact on these policies. There was, indeed, public debate, which bolstered the anti-nuclear inclinations of Nehru; it says much of the force of Bhabha's influence when one considers that India's nuclear weapons capability was begun under his tutelage. Tracing the rationale and evolution of India's nuclear policy and diplomacy in this period, depends heavily on pronouncements by Nehru, who was his own Foreign Minister and Minister-in-charge of Atomic Energy. (This pattern

2. Rajagopalan, Rajesh. unpublished article "Explaining Indian Nuclear Weapons Policy".

3. *ibid.*

4. Perkovich, George (1999). *India's Nuclear Bomb: The Impact on Global Proliferation,* New Delhi, OUP, p. 9.

was, and has been followed by the majority of India's Prime Ministers.) Interpretations and emphases are bound to differ but, at a level, one would have to take Nehru's statements at face value that he was ardently in favour of nuclear disarmament, yet reluctantly, gave permission and indeed, encouraged, according to Karnad, the development of atomic energy in the full knowledge of its dual use applications.[5] As early as 1948, in a letter to the Defence Minister, Baldev Singh, he wrote, "The future belongs to those who produce atomic energy. This is going to be the chief national power of the future. Of course, defence is intimately concerned with this. Even the political consequences are worthwhile"[6] (Chengappa, p. 71). Even after Nehru, the nuts and bolts of the nuclear issue remained restricted to the Prime Minister and his/her close advisers and to senior scientists in the Department of Atomic Energy and BARC. Finally, India's diplomacy in this period remained constant on the issue of nuclear disarmament; India's security interests were rarely directly articulated in this context, though the inference appears fairly clear, as will gradually become evident.

The birth of the atomic age with the bombings of Hiroshima and Nagasaki coincided with the final push for India's independence from colonial rule. It was inevitable, therefore, that the political leaders who saw the achievement of freedom as victory both in political and moral terms—not only political independence from foreign rule, but a moral victory, given the uniqueness of the means of attaining the ultimate goal—should view the use of nuclear weapons in both political and moral terms. The aversion to nuclear weapons, so clear from the statements of Gandhi and Nehru, launched India on her campaign for the elimination of nuclear weapons. It would be simplistic to locate the opposition to nuclear weapons solely in the moral or ethical sphere, however. In 1954, Nehru, reacting to a US nuclear test, wrote in *The National Herald*,

---

5. Karnad, Bharat (2002). *Nuclear Weapons and India's Security-The Realist Foundations of Strategy,* New Delhi, Macmillan India, p. 181.

6. Chengappa, Raj (2000). *Weapons of Peace-The Secret Story of India's Quest to be a Nuclear Power,* New Delhi, HarperCollins India, p. 71.

commenting on the fear that these weapons inspired, "... fear would grow and grip nations and people and each would try frantically to get this new weapon or some adequate protection from it."[7] In the same year, speaking at a Conference of Scientists on the Development of Atomic Energy for peaceful purposes, he noted that: "A dominating factor in the modern world is the prospect of these terrible weapons suddenly coming into use before which our normal weapons are completely useless."[8] Both these trends appear simultaneously in Nehru's, and India's nuclear policy in the future. At the diplomatic level, Nehru and his successors maintained that the world's, and by inclusion, India's, security was safer in a nuclear-free world; at ground level, enamoured as he was with the development potential of nuclear energy, capacity was slowly being built to meet a situation when the weapons may suddenly come into use, "before which our normal weapons (would be) completely useless."[9] Nehru recognised that India, as perhaps other (weak) states might "frantically" try to acquire these weapons or "adequate protection from (them)." Nehru appeared to be quite clear that India should not be frantic in her search for security. He had been convinced by Bhabha that the peaceful use of atomic power could help solve India's acute developmental needs; he was equally conscious of the dual-use quality of nuclear technology. Seeking protection from an outside power would have been unwelcome to a newly independent country, though, as we shall see later, Nehru himself was forced to seek such help in the wake of the Chinese attack in 1962. According to Perkovich, one of the commentators I have referred to earlier, "India took a stance (in rejecting the Baruch Plan for global control of fissile material) that would characterize its nuclear diplomacy for decades; it supported the principle of ensuring that nuclear material and capabilities would be used only for peaceful purposes, but it resisted any measures that would allow some states to retain nuclear weapons while denying others the

7. Nehru, Jawaharlal (1954). "The Death Dealer", *The National Herald*, April 2; *India and Disarmament* (*op. cit.*).

8. *ibid.*

9. *ibid.*

full freedom to exploit their resources as they saw fit. India was and would remain fiercely jealous of its sovereignty, resistant to any inequalities and inequities, wary of any semblance of colonialism, and righteous in its demands for disarmament."[10]

An elaboration of this analysis, based on the dilemma facing India, could have suggested to Nehru an alternative policy, one that nicely coincided with the moral repugnance Nehru felt for nuclear weapons. This would entail working assiduously, with other newly independent states, for the elimination of these weapons, which were possessed only by the 'old' powers, as they were seen as a threat to India's and to international security. The objective of Nehru's disarmament diplomacy was not as far-fetched or naïve as it may appear today, nor, in my view, was it a devious screen behind which he secretly authorised a nuclear weapon programme. After all, of the three global objectives Nehru had set for Indian diplomacy, decolonisation was in the process of being achieved (and by the end of the sixties was almost complete), and development was beginning to be accepted as a major item on the international agenda. There was no reason why, with sufficient international pressure, similar successes could not be achieved in disarmament.

Had disarmament not become embroiled in Cold War politics, and had it succeeded, India and other weak states concentrating on the enormous economic challenges facing them would not have to divert resources and attention towards the acquisition of these weapons; if, however, disarmament failed, and the weapon states refused to give up their weapons, India would have to be ready to acquire these weapons "before which our normal weapons are completely useless."[11] This explanation of the seeming dichotomy in Nehru's approach to nuclear weapons is supported by an eminent biographer of Nehru, Dr. S. Gopal, and mentioned by Chengappa. According to the latter, when Bhabha was keen on signing the proposal to set up a regulatory body for fissile material, Nehru noted, on file," This is a political decision not to be taken by nuclear

---

10. Perkovich, George, *op. cit.*, p. 21.

11. Nehru, Jawaharlal, *op. cit.*

scientists."[12] Chengappa quotes Dr. Gopal as saying: "It is not generally known that Nehru wrote to Bhabha that he was against outlawing of atomic weapons. His policy was never to use it but to have it because we can't completely abjure from it. Whereas Bhabha wanted to outlaw it completely in line with Nehru's public speeches. Nehru said: 'No! No! Don't go that far'."[13]

India's nuclear diplomacy was, therefore faced with a delicate task; to push for the elimination of nuclear weapons, which if achieved would obviate the need for India to weaponise her developing nuclear technology, bearing in mind not only economic but moral costs; simultaneously, India's option to weaponise had to be a feasible option—as a country generally sensitive to the binding nature of international agreements, especially on weaker states, India had to manoeuvre for space to achieve her national security goals. This was the basic thrust of India's diplomacy for several decades, through the Chinese aggression of 1962, China's first nuclear weapon test in 1964 , through to the implicit threat to India from the nuclear armed *USS Enterprise*, during the last stages of the Bangladesh War in 1971. Frequently the delicate balance was itself threatened, especially when individual Prime Ministers were themselves personally against the bomb, on Gandhian grounds.

It is not my intention to detail the evolution of India's nuclear programme through the years. More competent and more knowledgeable persons have written at length on the subject. It is, however, necessary to identify some significant moments in the narrative to assess how India's nuclear diplomacy had to adapt and adjust itself to emerging realities on the ground.

The first of these critical periods determining India's approach to nuclear weapons occurred in the early sixties; 'defeated by an expansionist China', India and annexed part of Indian territory in 1962. In October 1964, China conducted its first nuclear weapon test. There was an outcry in the Indian Parliament, and, even in

12. Chengappa, Raj, *op. cit.*, p.83.

13. *ibid.*

1962, a demand from the opposition Jana Sangh for immediate weaponisation of India's nuclear technology. Nehru responded that India had called for the nuclear powers to renounce their nuclear tests. India could not now "go in for doing the very thing which we have asked other powers not to do to justify the minor psychological advantages that nuclear status would confer. We have often said from the very first day we started the reactor in Bombay, that we on no account would manufacture nuclear weapons... I hold to that."[14] Almost as though to bolster his commitment to a world free of nuclear weapons, Nehru, at this time of national crisis, not only entered into an Agreement for Cooperation with the United States concerning the civil uses of atomic energy, which entered into force in 1963, but was one of the first world leaders to sign a Treaty he had wholeheartedly supported, the Partial Test Ban Treaty which banned nuclear testing in the atmosphere, saying that it would "take us towards disarmament and peace."[15] Yet he had already received information from the US that China was on the verge of conducting a nuclear test.

It is a moot point why Nehru refused to exercise the nuclear weapon option at this point in time, whether it was the lack of technology or material, or a conviction that an attack by conventional weapons should not lead to a nuclear arms race, what is clear is that India's nuclear diplomacy, her disarmament diplomacy, became even stronger, even while Nehru unsuccessfully sought 'protection' from the US and UK from Chinese aggression. By the time China carried out its first nuclear test, Nehru was dead and Prime Minister Shastri was faced with intense pressure, in Parliament from the Opposition and from his own party. At a session of the All India Congress Committee held in Guntur, Andhra Pradesh, the Parliamentary General Secretary stated, "If we do not decide today to make the bomb, events will force us after some time to do so. If suddenly China attacks us, we will have to seek the help of the USA or Russia. This should not be. We must have our

14. Statement by Nehru in Shyam Bhatia (1979). *India's Nuclear Bomb,* Ghaziabad, Vikas, p. 121.

15. Nehru quoted in G.G. Mirchandani (1968). *India's Nuclear Dilemma,* New Delhi, Popular Book Services, p. 240.

own bomb."[16] This view was reiterated at the Durgapur meeting of the AICC the following year.

At the diplomatic level, India condemned the test. Sardar Swaran Singh, the then Foreign Minister, speaking in the UN General Assembly on 14 December 1964, said, "India cannot but condemn the nuclear test conducted by the People's Republic of China. This action of China is fraught with dangerous consequences. It may well start a fresh nuclear race among countries which admittedly possess nuclear capability at the present time."[17] India also asked for the inscription of an item on non-proliferation on the agenda of the current session of the UN General Assembly and sought nuclear guarantees from the recognised nuclear weapon states. At home, in Parliament, he said, "It is a matter of grave concern for the world and also it is a matter of importance that the principal nuclear powers...should find some answer to the situation that has been developed by new countries coming into possession of nuclear devices. Therefore, the non-nuclear world should have the assurance, should have the satisfaction, should have the sense of security and safety that by their adherence to the policy of non-proliferation they do not expose themselves to the danger that is inherent in the proliferation of nuclear weapons...We are not asking for any nuclear shield from any particular country ..."[18] India tried to get the international community to put pressure on China to desist from nuclearisation, while maintaining her own position against building nuclear weapons.

Prime Minister Shastri, whose Gandhian approach to nuclear weapons was more instinctive than Nehru's, was firm that India would not respond to the Chinese test by entering into an arms race. Speaking to Parliament on 8 November 1964, he said, "We will try to eliminate the threat and terror of nuclear weapons rather than enter into competition with other countries to make or produce

---

16. Quoted in Shyam Bhatia, *op. cit.*, pp. 110-111 and G.G. Mirchandani, *ibid.*, p. 28.

17. Statement by Sardar Swaran Singh to UN General Assembly on 14 December 1964, *Documents on India's Nuclear Disarmament Policy*, Vol. II, Gopal Singh and S.K. Sharma (eds.), New Delhi, Anamika, 2000, p. 576.

18. *ibid.*, p. 576.

atom bombs here."[19] Even Defence Minister Y.B. Chavan claimed that the Chinese nuclear test would "not have a significant impact on China's military strength since the short term threat to India remained China's conventional forces."[20] Dr. Homi Bhabha, supposedly an advocate for the bomb, who had, soon after the Chinese test said that Indian scientists could if they wanted produce a nuclear bomb in 18 months, spoke of the cost of a nuclear weapon in a radio broadcast, and concluded by calling for the United Nations and the "great powers" to pursue nuclear disarmament so that "states like India that have voluntarily refrained from developing weapons will not have to do so in future."[21] However, while maintaining the anti-nuclear weapon option stand at home and abroad, Shastri did agree to permit the Department of Atomic Energy to start work on a Study on Nuclear Explosions for Peaceful Purposes (SNEPP), a study to make nuclear devices for peaceful purposes such as blasting tunnels and flattening the land for development work. It needs to be pointed out here, that 'peaceful nuclear explosions' (PNEs) were on the agenda of the International Atomic Energy Commission, and the US had, in 1964, conducted an international Plowshare Symposium to increase interest in PNEs for large-scale engineering projects. In addition, following Nehru's example, he, Shastri, appealed, unsuccessfully, to the US and UK for some form of 'protection' from China's nuclear threat.

Before turning to a critique of India's responses to the first major international crisis faced by the nation since independence, it is necessary to briefly refer to the fact that India's economy, in the sixties was in a parlous state; in 1962 she suffered military reverses at the hands of expansionist China, in 1964, that same country exploded its first nuclear device, in 1965, there was a brief war with Pakistan, to which China pledged support, though it did not in fact demonstrate it in any concrete way, and in 1966 India saw the

---

19. Statement by Prime Minister Shastri to All India Congress Committee on 8 September 1964, quoted in Shyam Bhatia: *op. cit.*, p. 111; G.G. Mirchandani, *op. cit.*, p. 29.

20. Statement by Defence Minister Y.B. Chavan in G.G. Mirchandani, *ibid.*, p. 26.

21. Homi Bhabha, All India Radio address, 24 October 1964, in Jain, J.P. (1974). *Nuclear India*, Vol. 2, New Delhi, Radiant Publishers, pp. 159-161.

great famine in Bihar. India was always short of funds and was becoming dependent on aid, including food aid from the developed countries. The paucity of resources in the national exchequer may have determined much of India's reluctance to go in for weaponisation at that point in time. According to interviews held by Chengappa with senior nuclear scientists, including Raja Ramanna and Homi Sethna, it would appear that the technology and material for weaponisation were not available.[22] In fact, India produced her first weapons-grade plutonium from the CIRUS reactor, only in 1964.

It is clear that both Nehru and Shastri remained committed to the importance of disarmament, even to meet India's security needs; India was reluctant to take a decision on weaponisation, unless her international efforts failed. To that extent, the 'balance' introduced in India's nuclear diplomacy remained intact, though there was a momentary disjunction when a purely pacifist Prime Minister initially refused to contemplate India as a nuclear weapon state. It was the Chinese test of 1964 that brought into the open the implicit understanding formulated by Nehru that India had an option (to weaponise), which could be exercised if the circumstances so warranted. It would be fruitless to speculate how Nehru would have responded to the Chinese test as it severely tested his belief in the power of the international community, which he believed, in the ultimate analysis, would be responsible and fair. Critics have argued that there was a degree of naivete in Nehru's analysis of the compulsions and constraints of power, that he did not in fact, comprehend the complexities of power in international relations. Given his political background and his firmly held beliefs, Nehru would probably have agreed with this view. His approach certainly gave him international stature—but it did so for India, too. Whether India could have been served better in nuclear diplomacy, is a question also open to debate.. At the international level, India's ideas found acceptance, though not perhaps in the way in which she would have preferred. Issues she fought eloquently for as a

---

22. Chengappa, Raj, *op. cit.*, p. 112.

means of restraining an emerging and hostile China, non-proliferation of nuclear devices and technology, assurances to non-nuclear states by nuclear weapon states of safety and security, the voluntary abjuring of nuclear weapons by non-nuclear weapon states, were seeds which later found expression in the Nuclear Non-Proliferation Treaty (NPT), a Treaty which ironically accepted a belligerent China as a recognised nuclear weapon state.

A major development in India's nuclear diplomacy came with the adoption of the NPT in 1968—it came into force only in 1970. During the negotiations, India's nuclear diplomacy was established for several decades, as her approach and objectives were concretely spelt out for the first time. It appears necessary therefore, to describe, in some detail, the Indian negotiating positions during the debate, and the Indian policy responses to the evolving situation on the ground.

At the UN Disarmament Commission held early in 1965, discussions turned to a consideration of a treaty or convention to prevent the proliferation of nuclear weapons. While the Indian representative to the Commission spelt out the principles that should, in India's view inform any proposed treaty, shortly thereafter, in the Eighteen Nation Disarmament Committee (ENDC) Ambassador Trivedi clarified India's interpretation of the concept of proliferation. At the Commission, Ambassador B.N.Chakraborty presented a 'comprehensive proposal' based on five principles that introduced the concept of 'balance' as the basis of any future treaty. The nuclear weapon powers were to undertake:

- not to transfer nuclear weapons or nuclear weapons technology to others;
- nuclear powers should agree not to use nuclear weapons against countries that did not possess them;
- the UN must safeguard the security of countries which may be threatened by nuclear weapon states or states near to possessing nuclear weapons;
- there should be tangible progress toward disarmament, including a comprehensive test ban treaty, a complete freeze

on the production of nuclear weapons and means of delivery as well as substantial reduction in the existing stocks; and

- it should be a Treaty committing non-nuclear powers not to acquire or manufacture nuclear weapons.

Clearly, the Indian focus was on China and the Chinese threat. India had once more turned to the United Nations for succour and support when faced with a threat to her national security. According to Perkovich, "Assuming that such a treaty were to be completed soon with China's adherence, China would not be able to build and deploy a nuclear arsenal capable of threatening India militarily. Security guarantees would then reassure India against any residual Chinese nuclear capability or blackmail. If, on the other hand, China did not join the non-proliferation treaty, the recommended security guarantees would augment India's protection against blackmail or aggression by India. The security guarantees formulated in India's proposed treaty pointed to the United Nations, not to the United States and the Soviet Union, as guarantors."[23] Notwithstanding this understanding, Perkovich goes on to identify that the, "American and Indian visions of an effective non-proliferation treaty formed the parameters of debate, with the other nations in between."[24] The consternation felt in India would have been considerable, given her assumption that as a democratic friendly country she would have received more understanding from the US against Communist China, rather than battling against the US on what was, to her, a matter of national security.

As battle was joined, Ambassador Trivedi speaking at the ENDC on 12 August 1965, clarified India's understanding of proliferation. He said, "When we are talking, therefore, of non-proliferation, the fundamental problem we have to consider is that of the proliferation that has already taken place...we are talking of proliferation of nuclear weapons not of the proliferation of a so-called closed club...A non-proliferation agreement is, therefore, basically an agreement to be entered into by the nuclear powers not to proliferate

23. Perkovich, George, *op. cit.*, p. 103.
24. *ibid.*

nuclear weapons... A prohibition to proliferate applies firstly to those who are in a position to proliferate or reproduce themselves and only secondarily to those who may subsequently be in such a position."[25] For India, the NPT was to be a disarmament treaty, with the current interpretation of non-proliferation as an adjunct. He added that it would be unrealistic and irrational "to impose obligations only on non-nuclear powers", while the nuclear weapon states continued to hold and increase their arsenals.[26]

On the basis of the five principles spelt out at the Disarmament Commission, Trivedi proposed a two-stage treaty—the first part relating to the obligations of the nuclear powers, and the second, those on non-nuclear states. This was a refinement of a proposal already made by Italy, which had proposed that non-nuclear states might agree to renounce unilaterally, acquiring nuclear weapons, but only for a specified period of time: if the nuclear powers made no progress towards disarmament, the non-nuclear countries "would resume their freedom of action." These proposals were rejected by the nuclear states, and India made her position clear: "An opposition to the concept of nuclear monopoly or privileged club membership is thus our fundamental response in any examination of a draft treaty or convention on non-proliferation."[27]

India was not alone in her efforts to mould the proposed treaty to encompass disarmament. On 15 September, along with seven other neutral or non-aligned countries presented a memorandum to the ENDC and then to the UN General Assembly. (The other seven countries were Brazil, Burma, Ethiopia, Mexico, Nigeria, Sweden and the United Arab Republic (Egypt), presaging later similar group initiatives, especially during Rajiv Gandhi's Prime Ministership.) The memorandum stated that, "measures to prohibit the spread of nuclear weapons should be coupled with, or followed by, tangible steps to halt the nuclear arms race and to limit, reduce and eliminate

---

25. Statement by Ambassador V.C. Trivedi to the Eighteen Nation Disarmament Committee (ENDC) on 12 August 1965, *Documents on India's Nuclear Disarmament Policy*, Vol. II, p. 590.

26. *ibid.*, p. 589.

27. *ibid.*, p. 594.

the stocks of nuclear weapons and their means of delivery."[28] It was not, therefore, a lonely battle fought by India against the US or even all the nuclear weapon states. At least, the battle had not become a lonely one yet. At the UN General Assembly, India worked hard for the adoption of resolution 2028(XX), which mandated the ENDC to negotiate "an international treaty to prevent the proliferation of nuclear weapons." The Resolution laid down five main principles to be followed, of which the most important were:

"a) The Treaty should be void of any loopholes which might permit nuclear or non-nuclear powers to proliferate, directly or indirectly, nuclear weapons in any form; b)The Treaty should embody an acceptable balance of mutual responsibilities and obligations of the nuclear and non-nuclear powers."[29] The resolution was adopted with no votes against and only five abstentions.

The same General Assembly called, by its Resolution 2032(XX) for the suspension of nuclear and thermonuclear tests, and requested the ENDC to continue "with a sense of urgency" its work on a comprehensive test ban treaty and on arrangements to ban effectively all nuclear weapon tests in all environments."[30] At least at the international level, India had secured support for her point of view, though these resolutions were to be implemented, if at all, when the very same nuclear weapon states were ready to do so, and in forms determined by them.

As already noted, for India, these measures were China focussed. At a time when she was facing severe drought at home, leading to acute dependency on imports of food through the US PL 480 programme, and the external threat from repeated Chinese tests, India had to use her diplomacy to try and cope with the situation and get some breathing space. During the negotiations, India made

---

28. *ibid.*, p. 602.

29. Resolution 2028(XX) adopted by the UN General Assembly on 19 November 1965, on Non-Proliferation of Nuclear Weapons, *Documents in India's Nuclear Disarmament Policy,* Vol. II. pp. 606-608.

30. Resolution 2032(XX) adopted by the UN General Assembly on 3 December 1965, on Suspension of Nuclear and Thermonuclear Tests, *Documents on India's Nuclear Disarmament Policy,* Vol. II, p. 610.

her objectives quite clear. At the ENDC, Ambassador Trivedi, speaking on the issue of banning of tests through the Partial Test Ban Treaty and the proposed comprehensive treaty, did not mince words: "...yet one country, in its arrogance and recalcitrance, in its utter disregard of the will and welfare of humanity, not only refused to subscribe to the PTBT, but even glorified in its refusal and in its defiance. The refusal of the People's Republic of China to subscribe to the Moscow Treaty and its flamboyant explosion of atomic devices, not once but twice, is a much more serious problem than the lack of progress on reaching agreement on prohibition of underground tests...It is, therefore urgent and vital for the international community to examine what steps should be taken to ensure the universality of this very partial Moscow Test Ban Treaty...The Indian delegation is particularly distressed to find that many people talk in terms of accepting the 'fait accompli' or accepting the evil. We must reject (this) unequivocally."[31]

India's second priority area was to ensure the proposed treaty was a 'balanced' one, that it was not discriminatory against the non-nuclear weapon powers. The emphasis on non-discrimination was neither an ethical issue nor a symptom of India's colonial past. There is no doubt, the demand for equality among all states in the nuclear field kept open the option for nuclear capable countries to weaponise if the nuclear weapon powers did not disarm. Referring to principle (b) of UN General Assemble Resolution 2028(XX), Ambassador Trivedi said in the ENDC: "It is not merely a question of sovereign nations rejecting treaties imposed by powerful nations on weak nations. It is not merely a question of rejection of unequal and discriminatory treaties...The main emphasis of this principle is, of course, on the balance of mutual responsibilities and obligations of the nuclear and non-nuclear powers."[32] Interestingly, India did not, at this point in time, stress nor attempt to introduce into the discussions, its earlier request for security guarantees for non-nuclear states. This was pursued bilaterally.

---

31. Statement by Ambassador V.C. Trivedi to the ENDC on 15 February 1966, *Documents on India's Nuclear Disarmament Policy*, Vol II, p. 617.

32. *ibid.*, p. 624.

On May 9, 1966, China conducted its third test, claiming it was a thermonuclear test. Responding to this event, Defence Minister Swaran Singh, speaking in the Lok Sabha said, "...We have made a careful assessment of the situation in consultation with our Service Chiefs and Atomic Energy experts...Government feel that the interests of world peace and our own security are better achieved by giving all support to the efforts for world nuclear disarmament than by building our own nuclear weapons."[33] This assertion was made despite many members of Parliament calling for a change in government's policy. The anti-nuclear forces within India were, however considerably strengthened, firstly, by the appointment of the pacifist Vikram Sarabhai, to head the Atomic Energy Commission (he had said in a press interview that "an atomic bomb explosion (was) not going to help our security"[34] and that the economic costs of weaponisation were unaffordable by India), and secondly, by a majority of MPs signing a memorandum in support of restricting nuclear technology only to peaceful uses. Sarabhai even stopped all work on the study authorised by Shastri on nuclear explosions for peaceful purposes. However, the issue of PNEs (peaceful nuclear explosions) remained on the international agenda. At the UN General Assembly, India argued that PNEs should be legally permitted within the scope of the evolving Treaty, but to be conducted under international safeguards and after the state concerned announced its intentions. In the ENDC, India reiterated the importance of permitting access by developing countries to nuclear science and technology.

By early 1967, however, it became clear that neither India's concerns nor those of other non-nuclear non-aligned nations were being taken into account. The issue of security assurances were not in the ambit of the Treaty, the 'balance of responsibilities and obligations' was also being lost as the debate focussed more on the need to control horizontal proliferation, i.e. the spread of nuclear weapons to more countries, than on vertical proliferation i.e. the

---

33. Statement made by Defence Minister Sardar Swaran Singh to the Lok Sabha on 10 May 1966, on the Chinese thermonuclear test: *Documents on India's Nuclear Disarmament Policy*, Vol. II, p. 637.

34. Sarabhai, Vikram (1966). "Press Conference", June 1, in Jain, J.P., *op. cit.*, p. 179.

increase in the size of existing arsenals of the nuclear weapon states The US and the USSR, which had earlier presented two separate drafts of a non-proliferation treaty at the same time as the Eight Nation memorandum, decided to negotiate among themselves the text of a single draft, and India's apprehensions increased. Ambassador Trivedi, speaking at the ENDC said, "Even apart from measures of disarmament, however, the very facts of political life of today demand that nations, and particularly a nation like India, which is exposed to nuclear blackmail, take full account of the needs of national security...the great powers have (held) that they cannot accept this or that proposal of nuclear restraint or reduction because it would adversely affect their security. But when they address themselves to non-nuclear powers, the nuclear weapon powers argue that nuclear weapons provide no security and that the best way the non-nuclear nations can safeguard their security is to sign a discriminatory treaty—a treaty which will at the same time give unfettered license to five powers to proliferate."[35] In a clear reference to China, he added, "It is a matter of vital concern to India, that one of the lesser nuclear powers, in particular, is feverishly building up its arsenal of weapons and developing its delivery capability."[36]

The issue of security guarantees was not explicitly proposed, though at about the same time, in May 1967, Mrs. Gandhi sent her Principal Advisor, L.K. Jha and Vikram Sarabhai to Paris, London, Moscow and Washington, to sound out these countries on the feasibility of security guarantees. In fact, they, unsuccessfully as it happened, proposed security guarantees for non-nuclear weapon states as an alternative to a nuclear non-proliferation treaty. During the Washington visit, Jha apparently informed the US Secretary of Defense that India was reluctant to sign the NPT as it was emerging, as she was concerned about her security in regard to China, and because India was apprehensive about the potential

---

35. Statement by Ambassador V.C. Trivedi to the ENDC on 23 May 1967, *Documents on India's Nuclear Disarmament Policy*, Vol. II, pp. 696-697.

36. *ibid*.

curtailment of the development of her indigenous nuclear technology programme.[37]

In the final stages of the negotiations, which were being conducted on the basis of the US-USSR draft, the UK proposed that some kind of security guarantees for non-nuclear weapon states could be appended as a protocol to the Treaty. This was clearly found unsatisfactory by India. Spelling out, in the UN General Assembly, India's objections to the Treaty that had emerged, Ambassador Azim Hussain concentrated on the lack of balance in the Treaty and referred in detail to the threat from a nuclear armed China and the inadequacy of the draft in containing China's ambitions. He said that the Treaty did not "provide a more direct juridical and compulsive link with measures of nuclear disarmament." He also objected to "the one-sided prohibitions on non-nuclear weapon states in respect of peaceful utilisation of nuclear energy. It prevents them from conducting nuclear explosions for peaceful purposes...Nations everywhere should be free to acquire the knowledge (of the peaceful uses of the atom) and to have the freedom to use such knowledge." He also expressed India's dissatisfaction at the absence of security assurances in the body of the Treaty, as had been mandated by the General Assembly in Resolution 2028(XX). He said, "Any security assurances that may be offered by nuclear weapon states should not be regarded as a *quid pro quo* for the signature of a non-proliferation treaty...(a similar tactic was employed by the nuclear weapon states at the time of the indefinite extension of the NPT in 1995, with more success)...the threat of nuclear weapons to non-nuclear weapon states arises from the possession of such weapons by certain states...the threat has existed in the past and will remain, even after a non-proliferation treaty has been concluded, until such time as the nuclear menace has been eliminated altogether."[38]

---

37. US Defense Department memorandum of conversation between L.K. Jha and US Secretary of Defense in Perkovich, George, *op.cit.*, p. 136.

38. Statement by Ambassador Azim Hussain to the Political Committee of the UN General Assembly on 14 May 1968, *Documents on India's Nuclear Disarmament Policy*, Vol. II, pp. 749-759.

India had decided to reject the Treaty. In the Lok Sabha, Prime Minister Indira Gandhi said that, in rejecting the Treaty, "we shall be guided entirely by our enlightened self-interest and the considerations of national security...the issue before us is essentially a political one. And it also has serious implications as regards security matters." The Prime Minister reiterated India's commitment not to manufacture nuclear weapons herself, but added, that the consequences of non-signature "may mean the stoppage of aid...may involve sacrifice and hardship, (yet) it will be the first step towards building the real strength of this country."[39] The ambiguity of these words, and the fact that the decision not to sign was taken when India was still dependent on foreign aid, might indicate that an attempt was being made by Mrs. Gandhi to restore the balance in India's nuclear policy that had been lost after Nehru's death. Yet Mrs. Gandhi also emphasised, during the same speech, that India was not going to manufacture nuclear weapons and that India remained committed to nuclear disarmament. On the other hand, it could just as well been a declaration that India would resist any external pressures which might be imposed on her to sign the Treaty. Whatever the explanation, there is no doubt that the NPT negotiations were, for India a steep learning curve on the exercise of power in international relations. As Perkovich says, "India may have had logic, principle and the 1965 negotiating mandate on her side, but the United States and the other nuclear powers had power on their side."[40]

By this time, China had conducted seven nuclear tests, including a thermonuclear one, as well as tested a missile with a nuclear warhead. India, on the other hand, was wracked by economic problems that had made her seem vulnerable not only to foreign pressures, but, as a democracy, to strong anti-nuclear weapon sentiment, both in Parliament and in the establishment, including in the services. Even after her experience on the Kashmir issue, she had turned to the UN and to the international community for help

---

39. Statement of Prime Minister Indira Gandhi to the Lok Sabha on 5 April 1968, *Documents on India's Nuclear Disarmament Policy*, Vol. II, p. 740.

40. Perkovich, George, *op. cit.*, p. 127.

in facing the Chinese threat. This had been slightly at variance with Nehru's policy. During the NPT discussions, the effort was, given the cultural aversion to nuclear weapons and the other external factors, not to turn to weaponisation at the first challenge, but to try and ensure through her nuclear diplomacy, international action to help India cope with the situation. In the event of the failure of this effort, which it spectacularly did, India's indigenous technology was to continue to be developed, but now also in her security interests.

To assume that during the two years or more in the UN and the ENDC, India was indulging in pure subterfuge as she was secretly developing her weapons capability, or that the effort at the diplomatic level were mere exercises in rhetoric, is too simplistic. There is no doubt that the stand taken in New York and Geneva were authorised from headquarters, and the constraints faced by the government at home would have determined the brief. The failure to achieve a satisfactory solution to its security problem clearly spurred India's decision to move more surely down the road to weaponisation, though the actual decision to do so may have come much later.

While India signalled her independence from the NPT, the Treaty text essentially became the centre of the current non-proliferation regime, and in the succeeding Review Conferences, was never again revisited on the issues India had pursued; the original mandate was forgotten and the regime, which was over subsequent years tightened considerably, became a vehicle for the control of non-nuclear weapon states. Nuclear proliferation is today taken to mean only horizontal proliferation and disarmament or the reduction and elimination of existing arsenals gradually lost its primacy as a cause of concern. Several non-nuclear weapon states members of the NPT and India, have indeed, tried to keep the issue of disarmament at the forefront, but the question of revising the NPT has never arisen.

The next two decades saw India continue her efforts to keep disarmament in focus in international forums, through the Bangladesh War of 1971 when India was sought to be coerced by the nuclear might, not of China, but of the United States, through her own solitary peaceful nuclear explosion in 1974, through the internal emergency of the mid-1970s, through reports of Pakistan's acquisition of nuclear weapons and Sino-Pak collaboration in the latter's efforts to build up an arsenal, and Mrs. Gandhi's assassination in 1984. Through all these significant developments, India maintained her anti-manufacture of nuclear weapon stance, though some have asserted that a decision to weaponise was taken in 1980, by Mrs. Gandhi after receiving information about Pakistan's nuclear weapon programme in 1979. This is corroborated by an account given by Chengappa of an aborted attempt to test in 1982.[41] Others assert that the 1974 test was only a technology demonstrator, a signal to China and the Soviet Union, emphasising India's independence after the dependence on the latter during the Bangaldesh War.[42] As already noted, India had raised the issue of freedom of non-nuclear powers to carry out PNEs in the UN. India's disarmament diplomacy after 1974, saw a period of intense activity. India had supported the UN declaration of the 1970s as a Disarmament Decade, and reiterated her commitment to the non-manufacture of nuclear weapons, particularly after the PNE. On 15 June, 1974, Ambassador Rikhi Jaipal, speaking to the IAEA Board of Governors, said: "In carrying out the underground nuclear experiment last month, India did not violate any international treaty or agreement. The Prime Minister of India reaffirmed India's opposition to nuclear weapons and their use, and to the application of nuclear energy for military purposes, and reiterated that India had no intention of manufacturing nuclear weapons..."[43]

Notwithstanding her protestations, sanctions were imposed on India, which effectively cut off her access to nuclear and dual-use high technology. This affected not only her nuclear industry but also other technology dependent programmes, such as space. India's PNE of 1974, made a lasting impact on the non-proliferation regime

41. Chengappa, Raj, *op. cit.*, p. 258 Also see the Chapter "Do you want our skulls cracked?".

42. Air Commodore Jasjit Singh (retd.) in discussion with author.

43. Statement by Ambassador Rikhi Jaipal to the IAEA Board of Governors on 15 June 1974, *Documents on India's Nuclear Disarmament Policy*, Vol. II, p. 876.

and its supporters. Soon after, a group of countries called the London Club was set up to regulate the flow of technology and materiel to all non-nuclear countries, but particularly India, which was also monitored by the Sanger Committee. The London Club eventually evolved into the Nuclear Suppliers Group (NSG). Into the disarmament debate, therefore, India introduced a new element, and began an unremitting campaign against *ad hoc* export control groups which arbitrarily decided on access of developing countries to civilian technologies. India insisted on the difference between weapons technology and that developed for peaceful purposes. These developments became a part of India's overall approach, not only to the issue of nuclear weapons and disarmament, but also to the international order that had been established.

India participated in the first UN General Assembly Special Session on Disarmament, held in 1978, at the level of Prime Minister Morarji Desai, who, at a personal level, was strongly anti-nuclear weapons. In his speech on the occasion, he outlined four urgent steps that needed to be taken, particularly by the nuclear weapon states, for international peace and security. These were:

(i)   a declaration outlawing utilisation of nuclear technology for military purposes;

(ii) qualitative and quantitative limitations on nuclear armament and a freeze of present stockpiles, under international safeguards;

(iii) a reduction of stockpiles within a time-bound programme, not extending a decade, to achieve total elimination of nuclear weapons; and

(iv) a comprehensive, universal and non-discriminatory test ban treaty, under international inspection.[44]

Some reflection of these proposals found place in the Final Declaration of the Session, which also established the Conference on Disarmament (CD) to succeed the ENDC. The Declaration still

---

44. Speech by Prime Minister Morarji Desai to the First Special Session of the UN General Assembly on Disarmament, 9 June 1978, *Documents on India's Nuclear Disarmament Policy*, Vol. II, p. 945.

forms, in the view of the non-aligned countries, the major reference point for the agenda of the CD.

This position was maintained by India through to the Second Special Session on Disarmament in 1982. India was represented by her Foreign Minister, Mr. P.V. Narasimha Rao, who added to the list, the need for a "binding convention on the non-use of nuclear weapons."[45]

Once more, India was taking on the powerful nuclear weapon states, once more with little success. Once more, India had to disassociate herself from the conclusions adopted by a majority, this time on the grounds that the positions had been so diluted as to render them ineffective. By 1979, information had become available to India that Pakistan had started a nuclear weapons programme; shortly thereafter, it was learnt that China, which had politically though not militarily supported Pakistan during the 1965 and 1971 wars, had begun to collaborate with the latter in its nuclear and missile programmes. During this period, too, there were reports in the West that India herself was preparing for a second test, a decision which was inexplicably aborted. In this background, India's hyperactive disarmament diplomacy is striking. The old question was raised: was India using international forums to buy time before she could produce enough fuel to enable her to test again? (It has been held, by Chengappa among others, that the 1974 test had not been followed by others as India had run short of plutonium.)[46] Or was her belief in the efficacy of international pressure still intact, that some of the 'collateral' disarmament measures might just succeed, thereby meeting the demands of her moral and ethical conviction of the inherent evil of nuclear weapons on the one hand, and her security needs on the other? Or, had external pressures been successful in restraining her from an action that might have led to wider less controllable consequences? If indeed India had the ability to test in 1982, and did not do so for whatever reasons, this

---

45. Statement by Foreign Minister P.V. Narasimha Rao to the Second Special Session of the UN General Assembly on Disarmament, 11 June 1982, *Documents on India's Nuclear Disarmament Policy,* Vol. II, p. 983.

46. Chengappa, Raj, *op. cit.*, p. 112.

might explain her enthusiasm for disarmament at the international level. It was not till 1988, the year Rajiv Gandhi presented his Action Plan for a nuclear weapon-free world only to have it rejected, that India is supposed to have taken the decision to weaponise her nuclear technology.

Rajiv Gandhi's activism on disarmament issues, *inter alia*, through the Six Nation Five Continent Initiative on Peace and Disarmament (the other countries were Argentina, Greece, Mexico, Sweden and Tanzania), culminating in the Action Plan, were in a sense, a response both to his own personal convictions and to the pressures being brought on India to constrain her nuclear programme through the proposed seven nation meeting to discuss the India-Pakistan nuclear programmes, an initiative not favourably viewed by India. The Action Plan was, India felt, a "diplomatically credible response to the US[47] in that India (and other threshold countries) would also assume responsibilities if the nuclear weapon states assumed theirs. This was a variation of the approach proposed by India in 1965 and during the NPT negotiations. In fact, the Action Plan proposed the negotiation of a 'new Treaty' which "would replace the NPT."

The Action Plan, while it covered all areas of disarmament, including space weapons, conventional arms, chemical and biological weapons, concentrated on nuclear disarmament. It detailed measures to be implemented within a time-bound framework (within 22 years) which included, in stages, the reduction of existing nuclear arsenals, cessation of production of nuclear weapons and fissionable material by the nuclear weapon states, and a moratorium on testing followed by a comprehensive test ban treaty. While the major steps were to be taken by the nuclear weapon states, non-nuclear weapon states undertook "not to cross the threshold into the acquisition of nuclear weapons" as a measure collateral to nuclear disarmament. Other collateral measures included a convention on non-use and the conclusion of a new treaty eliminating all nuclear weapons by 2010. In an impassioned speech at the third Special Session on

---

47. Muchkund Dubey in discussion with author.

Disarmament, while presenting the Action Plan, Rajiv Gandhi, after making a strong plea for nuclear disarmament asked a significant and revealing question: "Left to ourselves, we would not want to touch nuclear weapons. But when, in the passing play of great powers rivalries, tactical considerations are allowed to take precedence over the imperatives of nuclear non-proliferation, with what leeway are we left?"[48] Unfortunately for nuclear disarmament and non-proliferation, and not unexpectedly, the nuclear weapon states, particularly the US, dismissed the Action Plan as unrealistic and refused even to consider it.

By 1988, Pakistan's nuclear weapons programme was placing a great deal of stress on India's stated decision not to manufacture nuclear weapons. On the same day that Rajiv Gandhi presented the Plan to the General Assembly, he was interviewed by CNN: "We've had the means for almost 14 years now" to make nuclear weapons, he said, "but we'll do our best not to do so... It's very obvious that they (Pakistan) have a nuclear weapons programme...based on well smuggled or stolen technologies. And its pretty obvious to the world where these technologies are being stolen from."[49] According to Chengappa, Rajiv Gandhi based his decision on grounds spelt out in a memorandum submitted to him by his main advisers, which included the rejection of the Action Plan by the nuclear weapon states, vulnerability to China in the event of a (likely) US tilt to that country, Pakistan's bomb programme and India's readiness in terms of materiel and delivery systems. Gandhi is reported to have said in reaction to the memorandum, "I am most reluctant to exercise the option but I can't sacrifice national security."[50] India's belief in the efficacy of international pressure to help her face her security challenges was finally snapped.

---

48. Speech by Prime Minister Rajiv Gandhi to the Third Special Session of the UN General Assembly on Disarmament June 9 1988, *Documents on India's Nuclear Disarmament Policy,* Vol. III, þ. 1156.

49. Prime Minister Rajiv Gandhi to CNN quoted by Gene Kramer: "Gandhi says, 'we will do our best' not to build nuclear weapons", Associated Press, June 9, 1988.

50. Chengappa, Raj, *op. cit.,* p. 332.

After 1988, India did not take any major disarmament initiatives—the road to Pokhran II was one in which India was reactive, to the tightening of the non-proliferation regime after the end of the Cold War in the early nineties, the indefinite extension of the NPT in 1995 and the almost surreally reminiscent of the NPT negotiations, negotiations on the Comprehensive Test Ban Treaty. India still called for a commitment by the nuclear weapon powers to a time-bound programme for disarmament, but she also linked this to her security needs. India's articulation on this occasion was markedly different. She said: "Countries around us continue their weapon programmes, either openly or in a clandestine manner. In such an environment, India cannot accept any constraints on its capability if other countries remain unwilling to accept the obligation to eliminate their nuclear weapons."[51]

Pokhran II had become inevitable, and India's disarmament diplomacy, maintained at a high level of tension, suffered a tremor when she declared herself a nuclear weapon state.

On 27 May 1998, Prime Minister Vajpayee, speaking in the Lok Sabha said: "At a global level, we see no evidence on the part of the nuclear weapon states to take decisive and irreversible steps in moving towards a nuclear weapon free world...The touchstone that has guided us in making the correct choice (to conduct the tests) was national security...we had taken a number of initiatives in the past. We regret that these proposals did not receive a positive response. In fact, had their response been positive, we need not have gone in for our current testing programme. We have been and will continue to be in the forefront of the calls for opening negotiations for a nuclear weapon convention."[52] India announced a voluntary moratorium on further testing, declared her intention to participate in a Fissile Material Cut-off Treaty (FMCT) in the CD, undertook to institute stringent export controls on nuclear and missile related technology and announced a 'no-first-use, doctrine.

---

51. Statement by Ambassador Arundhati Ghose to the Conference on Disarmament on 20 June 1996, *Documents on India's Nuclear Disarmament Policy,* Vol. III. p. 1387.

52. Statement by Prime Minister Atal Behari Vajpayee to the Lok Sabha on 27 May 1998, *Documents on India's Nuclear Disarmament Policy,* Vol. III, p. 1472.

Today, India has weathered the storm created by the 1998 tests, and that largely due to the bilateral diplomacy conducted with major countries. Her multilateral disarmament diplomacy has been more muted and low profile. It is clear, though, that India was and continues to be a 'reluctant' nuclear weapon state. Rajesh Rajagopalan is less than complimentary about India's responses to the several security crises that she encountered on the way to weaponisation. Commenting in an unpublished article on the 'distracted' trajectory of India's weapons programme, he says: "The broad conclusion is that though domestic-level variables have been noteworthy (in the decisionmaking process), on balance it does appear that the more important driving force behind the Indian nuclear programme was fear of Chinese and Pakistani nuclear capabilities. Indian decision makers did not respond well to these fears, and considerations such as economic developmental worries, the cost of a nuclear arsenal, intense ethical dislike of nuclear weapons and the odd hope that the international community had a responsibility to protect India, all ensured that the Indian nuclear weapons programme was far slower and more uncertain than most observers thought possible."[53] However, it does not appear that India thought that weaponisation was inevitable; there is sufficient evidence to prove that the very constraints placed on the weapons programme was coupled with a worldview that did see India's security as part of international security. Failure does not necessarily determine the correctness or otherwise of choices made on the basis of a cultural and historically-based conviction.

India appears to have retained some smatterings of idealism within its new-found 'realist' worldview. It has adopted a doctrine of retaining a 'credible minimum deterrent' and a 'no first-use' policy. She continues to support efforts to discuss nuclear disarmament in the CD and has stated her willingness to participate in any negotiation to limit and reduce nuclear weapons, at the appropriate time. However, challenges lie ahead. Can this policy effectively face them? With Chinese conventional superiority, can India today afford

---

53. Rajagopalan, Rajesh, *op. cit.*

a nuclear weapon-free world? Will the elimination of nuclear weapons increase international peace and security in view of the enormous technology gaps which exist? Already India's disarmament diplomacy appears to have adapted to new realities— in addition to nuclear disarmament, India today is less allergic to the substance of the NPT and appears to accept that the dangers from proliferation are more immediate. In the process of implementing the Indo-US nuclear energy deal of 2005, India is bringing her own policies closer to those of the *ad hoc* export control groups she had long castigated. In the event a universal, verifiable FMCT ever comes into being, India has expressed her willingness to support it—presumably as a nuclear weapon state.

"Disarmament today is a concept at a discount"[54] may be an extreme interpretation of the current situation. Yet, it is a fact that there is little movement towards the delegitimisation of nuclear weapons in the policies of the nuclear powers, including India, as nuclear weapons continue to play an important role in their strategic doctrines. There is no doubt that other non-nuclear countries will also aspire for the security nuclear weapons are seen to give; non-proliferation cannot succeed without disarmament. Yet, sadly, in this situation, it appears unlikely that India will take any major initiative on disarmament—it is more likely that we will see a prolonged period of quietude.

---

54. K.S. Subhramanyam in discussion with author.

50

Nuclear non-proliferation and international security—an Indian perspective

Shyam Saran

India's commitment to nuclear non-proliferation is not new. Indeed, this is an area where we can truly claim to be among the founding fathers! The Indian leadership, particularly Jawaharlal Nehru,. was among the first in the world to appreciate the dangers that nuclear weapons posed to humanity. As with the rest of the world, our understanding of the complexities of the challenges posed by nuclear weapons developed over time. Initially, Hiroshima and Nagasaki were responsible for a strong sense of moral outrage at a weapon of mass destruction. It took the Bikini Atoll tests and the fate of the Japanese vessel 'The Fortunate Dragon' to dramatise the dangers of radioactivity. As the number of nuclear weapon powers increased, and their rivalry acquired an increasingly adversarial character, there was a growing realisation of the political, military and eventually even existential nature of the problem. At the same time, nuclear technology offered a promise of development that could not be ignored, least of all by a society emerging from colonial rule and seeking to leapfrog in its development process. Bilateral cooperation programmes and the Atoms for Peace contributed to the spread of nuclear technology and its increasing application for power generation and other civil purposes. These two competing trends created the dilemma of how the benefits of the technology could be best harnessed without adding to the security challenges inherent in that spread. That is an issue that still confronts the international community and is one that is not confined to nuclear technology alone.

The initial debate about the control of nuclear weapons and technology, focussed on four issues: cessation of nuclear testing, creation of nuclear-free zones, the problem of sharing nuclear weapons particularly within alliance structures, and the possibility of renunciation of nuclear weapons by nations that had not yet produced them. India took a position on each one of these issues, arguing strongly in favour of restricting both the spread and quantum of nuclear weaponry. Pandit Nehru's call in 1954, for a 'standstill' to nuclear weapons tests and then for a test ban, began a process that eventually led to the 1963 Partial Test Ban Treaty. *En route*, this debate also produced the 1959 Antarctica Treaty that created a nuclear-free zone on that continent. The application of a nuclear-free zone in other areas was not deemed viable by India given the proximate location of nuclear weapon powers, a position that continues to this day. The sharing of nuclear weapons, a prospect that seems so ludicrous today, was a serious possibility in the 1950s and 1960s, and sharing of weapon technologies had actually taken place. India's position was one of firm opposition, and this eventually became a global norm. It was the renunciation of nuclear weapons that became the most contentious issue in the non-proliferation proposal debate.

In 1956, India proposed the international control of military reactors and then co-sponsored the non-proliferation proposal in the United Nations. Nehru prophetically warned the world as far back as 1957, not only of nuclear proliferation but of connected dangers of terrorism. But from being an early and enthusiastic supporter of this concept, Indian reservations deepened as it watched the evolution of an international treaty conspicuously lacking, despite its strong urging, in a mutuality of obligations between the weapon states and non-weapon states. Finally, as you are all aware, India chose not to be a party to the NPT, precisely because of its inherently discriminatory nature.

As a responsible nuclear weapon state, we are even more conscious of our obligations to the international community on the control of WMD technologies and their delivery systems. This appreciation has guided many of the policy initiatives undertaken in recent days, but this may be an opportune occasion to spell out India's current approach to global non-proliferation and international security, particularly as it has evolved since India's emergence as a Nuclear Weapon State in May 1998. The key components of this approach are:

(i) While India is a Nuclear Weapon State, it remains committed to the goal of complete elimination of nuclear weapons. The model that could be followed in this regard is the Chemical Weapons Convention, which is both multilateral as well as non-discriminatory in the rights enjoyed by, and obligations it imposes, on parties to the Convention. We continue to believe that the best and most effective nuclear non-proliferation measure would be a credible and time-bound commitment to eliminate nuclear weapons from existing arsenals, including India's own nuclear weapons. We have no desire to perpetuate the division between nuclear-have and have-nots.

(ii) A new global consensus on non-proliferation is called for, taking into account the new challenges that have emerged since the Nuclear Non-Proliferation Treaty was concluded. Clearly, some NPT members, both Nuclear Weapon States and non-Nuclear Weapon States, have not adhered to the provisions of the Treaty and this requires global norms that go beyond the NPT. For example, India has agreed in the Indo-US Joint Statement of July 18, that it would not transfer reprocessing and enrichment technologies and would support international efforts to limit their spread. We have accepted that a new global consensus would have to be based on new and more rigorous standards being observed in export controls on sensitive technologies. India has signalled its willingness to be part of this consensus by adopting a very comprehensive WMD export control legislation and harmonising our export control lists with those incorporated in the Nuclear Suppliers Group (NSG) and Missile Technology Control Regime (MTCR) guidelines. This has enabled us to fulfil the obligations prescribed in the UNSC Resolution 1540.

(iii) We believe that states should adhere to the commitments that they have made under international treaties and instruments and must be transparent in fulfilling their commitments. We are unable to accept as legitimate the pursuit of clandestine activities in respect to WMD related technologies. Our own security interests have been seriously undermined by the clandestine nuclear weapons programmes in our neighbourhood aided and abetted, or at the least, selectively ignored by some NPT signatories themselves. In seeking clarity on such clandestine activities, the international community must focus not merely on recipient states but on supplier states as well; otherwise our global non-proliferation effort would be undermined by charges of motivated selectivity and discrimination. With respect to the Iran nuclear issue, we welcome Iran's cooperation with the IAEA in accounting for previously undeclared activities, but it is important that remaining issues which involve the Pakistan-based A.Q. Khan network are satisfactorily clarified as well. We see no reason why there should be an insistence on personal interviews with Iranian scientists but an exception granted to a man who has been accused of running a global 'nuclear Wal-Mart'. These aspects must surely be considered for an objective assessment on this question.

(iv) For the future, we believe we have the responsibility and the capability to participate fully and actively in global R&D efforts to evolve proliferation-resistant nuclear technologies, which enable us to derive the full benefit of nuclear energy, minimising the risk of diversion to military uses. There are two critically important projects in which some key countries with advanced nuclear technology are members. One is the International Thermonuclear Energy Research (ITER) project, which is aimed at development of energy through nuclear fusion. The EU, US, Russia, China, Japan and South Korea are partner countries, and India is likely to be invited soon to join as a full partner. The other is the US-led Generation IV initiative, which aims at creating reactor prototypes that are not prone to proliferation. India looks forward to join this cutting-edge effort as well. In both cases, India's participation is welcomed not only in recognition of its advanced capabilities but also its record as a responsible nuclear state.

If you look at India's recent actions against the backdrop of this approach, then a great deal of the apprehension and negative perception about India's nuclear policy, would appear misplaced.

- Firstly, there is a continuity and consistency in our approach that may sometimes be masked by the particularities of a specific decision.

- Secondly, what appears to some observers as inordinate external influence over our decisionmaking in sensitive areas is, in fact, rooted in our own well-considered and independent judgement of where our best interests lie. This is in keeping with our tradition of non-alignment.

- Thirdly, we must adjust to change; change inherent in our emergence as a Nuclear Weapon State, change inherent in the sustained dynamism and technological sophistication of the Indian economy, and, as a consequence, change in global expectations of India as an increasingly influential actor on the international stage.

Since 1998, a key challenge to India's foreign policy has been to seek global recognition and understanding of its impeccable record on non-proliferation, despite its decision to acquire nuclear weapons. This recognition is important, though some may not see it that way. We live in an increasingly globalised world and as India's economy shifts towards greater technological sophistication, it will need access to cutting-edge technologies in virtually all fields. In each of the recent initiatives India has taken, whether the NSSP, the July 18 Indo-US Joint Statement, the applications to participate in ITER and Generation IV, Glonass and Galileo Satellite Navigation Systems, the Indo-US Space Launch Agreement, and several others, this technological compulsion has been a major consideration. These would not have been possible, and India could have remained in a technological strait-jacket had it not backed up its commitment to non-proliferation with the adoption of global norms as has been done by other states with advanced nuclear technology. The cumulative results of the steps we have taken, such as enactment of the WMD Bill, the upgradation of the national export control lists so as to harmonise them with those of the NSG and MTCR, the proposed separation of our civilian and military nuclear facilities and the negotiation of an additional protocol with the IAEA, is to increase the confidence of the international community in the robustness and effectiveness of our export control systems making us a more viable destination of advanced dual-use technologies. With the US, there is already a more liberal and predictable licensing of dual-use technology for Indian industry.

Indeed, we have a situation today where the government has created a favourable enabling environment and it is our end-users who should display greater vigour in taking advantage of resultant opportunities. China, with a much less favourable licensing regime, imports 10 times the dual technology that we do from the United States. For our space and nuclear industries, the completion of NSSP resulted in the removal of many of our organisations from the Entity List, with consequent licensing benefits. Some organisations remain listed and we continue to work for their removal. The 'NSG plus' and 'MTCR plus' restrictions that were in place were also done away with. The space industry today is permitted direct cooperation for developing, producing, marketing and operating US commercial satellites and those of third nations that contain US origin components. It created the basis for discussions that we have currently on the conclusion of a bilateral space launch agreement with the US. It has also contributed to a useful dialogue on the subject of missile defence.

What does the international community gain in making an exception to the current regulations for India? How do we answer the proponents of the current global non-proliferation regime, who see the exception being made for India as the unravelling of this regime?

The exception for India is rooted precisely in its record on non-proliferation, even though it is not formally a member of the NPT. It is significant to note that the Indo-US understanding in civilian nuclear cooperation is prefaced by President Bush conveying his appreciation for India's strong commitment to preventing WMD proliferation. He has acknowledged India as a responsible state with advanced nuclear technology. There is today no other state, which has this record of responsibility and is still denied non-discriminatory access to civilian nuclear technology.

Secondly, our export controls are today at global standards and our policy of non-transfer of re-processing and enrichment technologies, in fact, put us in an 'NPT plus' category.

Thirdly, in considering its approach towards the resumption of full civil nuclear energy cooperation with India, the international community has to ask itself whether India is a partner or a target for the global non-proliferation regime. It clearly cannot be both at the same time. Our view is that India's commitment and India's record points to it being a partner. Technology-denial regimes that treat India as a target must, therefore, be abandoned.

Fourthly, the international community also needs to ask whether the global non-proliferation regime is better with India inside the tent or outside. As a corollary, will civil nuclear cooperation with India strengthen the non-proliferation system or weaken it? Obviously, we cannot be inside the tent if we do not measure up to the required norms. We, of course, are convinced that we do, for the reasons that I have already enumerated.

India is today a rapidly expanding industrial economy with a wide array of technologies that are relevant to proliferation. That in itself makes a case why our export controls and their effective implementation will matter more and more for global non-proliferation efforts. As a nuclear weapon state, our support for international norms is critical for their success. But it is not only in our controls and restraint that we can make a difference. The time when NPT was regarded as self-enforcing is long past. The spread of technologies cannot be controlled by cartelisation alone. There are enough examples to show that commercial and political incentives can defeat that. The challenge that the world currently faces requires more active endeavours. This is particularly so as the dangers of non-state actors acquiring nuclear weapons have given the WMD threat an added dimension. UNSC Resolution 1540, is one example of the global community's response. There are others, among them a combination of national and transnational efforts. The Container Security Initiative and Proliferation Security Initiative are two such examples. Advocates of non-proliferation must seriously examine whether the support of India towards global efforts is to their advantage. That support is difficult to muster if India perceives itself as unfairly treated despite its demonstrated commitment to a rule bound system.

A word about separation of our civilian and military nuclear facilities. Some non-proliferation advocates contend that since it is India which will determine what is civilian and what is military, this would open the door for flouting non-proliferation norms. This betrays a lack of understanding of the July 18 Joint Statement. The Indo-US Agreement is not about India's nuclear weapon programme. It is about civilian nuclear energy cooperation. The objective of the Agreement is to advance India's energy security through full civilian nuclear energy cooperation. It is legitimate for our partners to expect that such cooperation will not provide any advantage to our strategic programme and hence, the need to separate it from our civilian nuclear sector. But it makes no sense for India to deliberately keep some of its civilian facilities out of its declaration for safeguards purposes, if it is really interested in obtaining international cooperation on as wide a scale as possible. This would be quite illogical.

India is poised today to enter a new phase in its foreign policy. We aspire to be a permanent member of the Security Council. We are demonstrating a growing capability to shoulder regional and global responsibilities. Our focus is increasingly on transnational issues that today constitute the priority challenges—whether it is terrorism or proliferation, pandemics or disaster relief. We cannot sit out the debates on the big issues of our times. Our interests demand a vigorous and articulate diplomatic effort that explains our positions and advances our interests. Non-proliferation is one area where we have a record to be proud of, and I would conclude by emphasising that it has been and will remain one of our principal contributions to international security.

Edited version of the Address delivered at India Habitat Centre, New Delhi in October 2005.

51

The evolution of India's nuclear doctrine

C. Raja Mohan

Introduction

The decade and a half that followed the end of the Cold War and the collapse of the Soviet Union has been a momentous one for India. It is a period in which India had rapidly adapted to a new global circumstance and recast its economic and foreign policies. Under simultaneous pressure to cope with the new wave of economic globalisation as well as the emergence of a unipolar world, India had to discard many traditional assumptions about the framework of its economic developmental strategy as well as the national security strategy. As India embarked on this fundamental transformation, its approach to nuclear weapons and related policies came under extraordinary stress. While its decision to conduct five nuclear tests during May 1998 was emblematic of the new approach to nuclear weapons, the last years of the 20th Century and the first decade of the 21st became a period of fast nuclear learning for the nation as a whole. These years turned out to be decisive in the evolution of India's nuclear doctrine, the strategy to achieve its nuclear objectives and the nuclear diplomacy. The broad national consensus on nuclear policy that was forged in the decades that preceded the end of the Cold War had to be reorganised on an entirely different basis. These included premises about the nature of nuclear weapons, the relationship between nuclear weapons and national security, the organisation of civilian and military nuclear programmes and the approach to constructing a secure nuclear order.

Forging a nuclear doctrine for India has not been easy. Here I use the word doctrine in the broadest sense and not merely to describe the military/political organisation of nuclear weapons, their deployment and a doctrine for their employment. I include the full range of political—internal as well as external—as well as military issues that were thrown open by India's decision to become a nuclear weapon power in 1998. The forging of a credible nuclear doctrine, in that sense, became a testing ground for the resolution of the tension between the old and new ideas about the nature and place of India in the world and the role of nuclear weapons in the nation's larger strategy. Since the early 1990s, the international pressure on India's nuclear programme steadily mounted and New Delhi could no longer avoid making choices—one way or another—on issues relating to nuclear weapons. Nuclear ambiguity no longer served India's purposes. In the middle of 2006, few in the world doubt that India has successfully managed to resolve many of its nuclear dilemmas and overcome the political and diplomatic costs of making the transition from nuclear ambiguity. The chapter is an attempt to distill the essence of the imperatives for this nuclear transformation, the diplomacy that engineered it, and the nuclear doctrine that India managed to construct since the early 1990s.

Unsustainable ambiguity

For far too long, India had refused to define the nature of its nuclear posture. New Delhi's prolonged indecision—from the time its northern neighbour China tested its nuclear weapons in 1964 October—meant India was neither a 'nuclear fish' nor a 'non-nuclear fowl'. India was caught in the limbo of nuclear ambiguity, unwilling to choose between being a nuclear weapon power and a non-nuclear state. The only answer it had for global nuclear problems was to call for a complete elimination of nuclear weapons; yet it would not give up its own nuclear weapon capability. By the mid-1990s, India had a significant stockpile of fissionable material to manufacture nuclear weapons. It had conducted one nuclear test in 1974 and had continued work on the design of nuclear weapons since then. It had delivery systems—aircraft and short range missiles—capable of reaching Pakistan. It had tested the longer range Agni missile that could give it a deterrent capability against China. Yet all this did not add up to a credible deterrent force. Clear cut political and organisational decisions to bring these threads together into an operational nuclear weapons system seemed to elude India.

In avoiding the final political decisions on its nuclear security policy, India had paid a heavy price in terms of tensions with the great powers over nuclear issues, increasing burden of technology sanctions, and instability in relations with her neighbours. So long as India failed to come to terms with its nuclear option, the international system tried to roll it back. As non-proliferation concerns topped international agenda after the 1991 Gulf War, India's nuclear and missile policies took the centre stage in its relations with all the major powers. The US took the lead in demanding an immediate cap on India's nuclear and missile capabilities, with a view to rolling back these over a period of time. India in the early 1990s was forced to discuss this agenda with the United States as well as all the other great powers in bilateral engagement. The government of Mr. P.V. Narasimha Rao and those of H.D. Deve Gowda and Inder Kumar Gujral that followed it ducked and dodged these pressures and often tried to finesse the question of the future direction of India's nuclear policy.

But it was virtually impossible to resolve the nuclear differences with the great powers. And the nuclear tensions with them became an albatross on the neck of India as it desperately sought to rework its relations with all the major powers. Meanwhile, India was recognising the costs of its nuclear ambiguity in terms of its isolation from the flows of advanced technologies in the world. It could not find any nation in the world that was in a position to transfer technology to India in a number of key sectors from the nuclear energy to advanced information technology. Cumulatively, these sanctions began to severely hurt India's hopes of mastering modern technologies. They also came in the way of ensuring India's energy security and developing a modern competitive economy in a range of sectors.

The unresolved nuclear status of India also began to complicate the regional dynamic with Pakistan in the 1990s. From the late 1980s, when Pakistan completed its acquisition of a nuclear weapon capability, new boldness crept up into its policy on Kashmir. Having successfully neutralised India's conventional superiority, Pakistan unleashed massive campaign of terror and destabilisation in Jammu & Kashmir with the confidence that New Delhi was no longer in a position to hit back. India was then forced to face up to a double jeopardy—a nuclear asymmetry as well as the vulnerability to a proxy war by Pakistan that it could not retaliate against. More fundamentally, Pakistan saw itself as a nuclear weapon power and the control of the Pak Army over the nuclear weapons meant an effective integration of nuclear weapons into the overall strategic approach of Pakistan towards India. New Delhi, on the other hand, even though it was probably in the possession of nuclear weapons by the early 1990s, it was unwilling to formalise its possession of nuclear weapons either internally or externally. At a more basic level, the policy of nuclear ambiguity prevented India from making the world understand the massive security challenges it was facing from Pakistan's aggressive policy on Kashmir.

India's nuclear asymmetry *vis-à-vis* China, meanwhile, was creating a different set of challenges *vis-à-vis* China. No one can question the basic fact that India's own nuclear debate began in 1964 when China first conducted its first nuclear test, months after the border conflict of 1962. The All India Congress Committee in fact demanded in 1965 that the government move quickly towards building nuclear weapons. Yet, the inherited idealism from the national movement prevented India from moving decisively forward on acquiring a nuclear weapons capability. It was only Pakistan's nuclearisation with Chinese assistance in the 1980s that eventually forced an Indian decision to build nuclear weapons. An equally important concern for India has been the rapid economic advancement of China in the 1970s and 1980s, which steadily expanded the difference between India and China in most of the basic indicators of power. By the 1990s, India was increasingly concerned about its relative decline *vis-à-vis* China and recognised the importance of bridging the divide. India was deeply aware that without an attempt to catch up with India, it would be marginal in the future strategic calculus of Asia. Most of the nations in South and East Asia were now looking to China for regional leadership. India, which had originally led the movement for Asian solidarity, was now irrelevant on both economic and security points of view. The growing gap between Indian and Chinese potentials created a profound complex in New Delhi that prevented it from realising the full potential of Sino-Indian relations and embarking on a confident effort to resolve the long-standing boundary dispute.

Crossing the rubicon

India's marginalisation on the global scene and its growing nuclear isolation raised some fundamental challenges to Indian nuclear policy by the mid-1990s. The indefinite and unconditional extension of the Nuclear Non-Proliferation Treaty in the summer of 1995 removed whatever illusions there were in New Delhi regarding the total elimination of nuclear weapons. The debate in Geneva on the drafting of the Comprehensive Test Ban Treaty suggested that India's future nuclear weapon options were now being closed. Meanwhile, there was no respite from the United States on high technology related sanctions. All these developments raised a fundamental question. If India was paying a high price for its nuclear ambiguity, was it not sensible to cross the nuclear rubicon become an overt nuclear weapon power and absorb the additional costs that would come in the wake of its nuclear tests? While the philosophical answer seemed easy and was in the affirmative across the national security establishment, the problem was one of managing the immediate consequences of an Indian defiance of the international system. At the end of 1995, when India came close to testing, the political leadership pulled back from the nuclear brink. It was assessed that the immediate costs of testing—international sanctions and opprobrium—outweigh the potential benefits. By 1998, another leadership then in charge decided otherwise. That it was indeed possible to overcome the costs of nuclear testing and that it was not possible to isolate India for too long.

The decision to cut the nuclear Gordian knot in May 1998 turned out to be a bold one. Somewhat counter-intuitively, the decision allowed the creation of a new framework to transform relations with all the major powers including the United States and China. Prime Minister Atal Bihari Vajpayee was roundly criticised for dragging of China into the articulation of the case for India's tests in his letter to the world leaders after May 11, 1998. For those favouring a normalisation of relations with China which had begun in 1988, Vajpayee's letter to President Bill Clinton and others was a big tactical blunder. But by raising these issues in a letter to President Clinton, India has not gained anything. India's decision to cite the China threat might have been motivated by the expectation that the argument might sell in the United States, and that Washington might ultimately accept nuclear India as a valuable partner. The immediate outcome was completely the opposite. The Clinton Administration shared the letter Vajpayee had written with the Chinese and together Clinton and Chinese President Jiang Zemin came down heavily against India during the former's visit to China during June 1998. To Vajpayee's critics, India's nuclear tests and the reference to China in its justification had brought Washington and Beijing only closer and seemed to threaten the Sino-Indian entente since 1988.

By the middle of the first decade of the 21st Century, the idea that India and the US could be partners in constructing a stable balance of power is no longer fanciful. India's diplomatic engagement with both the US and China since Pokharan II has seen extraordinary successes. After the initial castigation of India, both the US and China have sought to build strategic partnerships with India. If one of the principal objectives of nuclear testing was to restore India's strategic autonomy in the world, Pokharan II and the diplomacy that followed generated these gains in an ample measure. Many other nations, including Japan, had to adjust to the changed international perception of India after Pokharan II and unilaterally end the sanctions imposed on India after May 1998. Pokharan II has positioned India to become an indispensable element of Asian and global balance of power.

Pokharan II also allowed India to better manage the regional dynamic with China and Pakistan. The new sense of self-confidence *vis-à-vis* China and the prospect of an inevitable strategic parity with Beijing allowed New Delhi to approach its bilateral problems with China in a more practical manner. Without Pokharan II, it was entirely unlikely that India would have agreed to find a political solution to the boundary dispute with China as it did during Vajpayee's visit to Beijing in June 2003. After its initial mismanagement of relations with Pakistan, India chose to reach out to Pakistan in early 1999 when Vajpayee visited Lahore. Although the initiative failed amidst the outbreak of the Kargil War in the summer of 1999, India's mature response during the crisis laid the foundation for a transformation of the framework of engagement with Pakistan. The renewed confrontation in 2002 forced the international community to put pressure on Pakistan to stop cross-border terrorism. The formalisation of its nuclear weapons status through Pokharan-II also allowed India to consider the first negotiations since the Shimla Agreement on the contentious question of Jammu and Kashmir. The nuclearisation of the subcontinent and the military tensions reinforced the reality that borders in the region cannot be altered by force. This opened the door for some creative approaches to the resolution of the Kashmir question transcending the territorial approach.

Despite the widespread international condemnation of its nuclear tests, Indian diplomacy managed to take the edge off the international criticism within a short period of time. By showing a willingness to find accommodation with the global nuclear order and by demonstrating responsible nuclear behaviour in its conflict with Pakistan after the nuclear tests, India has reinforced its claim to be accepted as a legitimate nuclear weapon power. Although India is not formally seeking the *de jure* status of a nuclear weapon power, it was determined to remove the many restrictions on technology transfer that apply to non-nuclear states. While India's negotiations with the US on this question did not make much progress during the Clinton Administration, the Bush years began to produce different outcomes. Success eventually came India's way at the beginning of the second term of the Bush Administration. The Joint Statement signed by Prime Minister Manmohan Singh and President George W. Bush on July 18, 2005 finally opened the doors for full civilian nuclear cooperation between India and the international community. Although the implementation of the agreement remains to be finished as of mid-2006, considerable progress has already been made. But in reaching the long awaited objective of removing the major nuclear discrimination against it, India had to make considerable adjustments to its own nuclear posture both in the military and civilian domains since 1998. The following sections identify the new elements of the Indian nuclear doctrine that emerged since May 1998.

Nuclear soft speak

Nuclear weapons bring with them enormous responsibility to the nations that possess them. This simple truth was not so evident to Indian leaders in the immediate wake of Pokharan II when India declared itself a nuclear weapon power. It took a while for India to recognise that when the nuclear voice is gentle, it gets greater respect and appreciation from the world. A series of statements from the highest level in New Delhi following Pokharan-II quickly raised the political temperature in the region and invited adverse reaction from the US and elsewhere. The Prime Minister, Atal Behari Vajpayee's statement about India having the 'big bomb' and his reference to using the nuclear weapons in 'self-defence' sent entirely wrong signals about India's nuclear intentions. Aggravating the situation, the Home Minister, L.K. Advani, talked tough against Pakistan and referred to the changed geopolitical situation in the subcontinent after India's five nuclear tests. The Scientific Adviser to the Defence Minister who later went on to become the President of India, Abdul Kalam declared grandly that the nuclear threat against India has been vacated. These statements drew a hostile response from the top leaders of Pakistan and it elicited a strong international condemnation of India for escalating political tension in the region.

The needlessly provocative statements by the Indian government created a huge political opening for Pakistan to campaign against an 'aggressive India' and paint its own nuclear tests as 'a defensive reaction' to India's tests. Islamabad succeeded in this diplomatic effort and gathered political sympathy in many key capitals of the world. While India's decision to test was seen as a 'surprising defiance' of the world, the Pakistani move was seen as "a helpless response" against India's hostile move. By the time of the Kargil War and later in the military confrontation with Pakistan after the December 13, 2001 attacks on the Indian Parliament, New Delhi had a much better grip on the art of nuclear signalling and proved more adept at managing the international perceptions of a nuclear risk in the subcontinent. By demonstrating restraint on the one hand and suggesting the possibility of nuclear escalation, India managed to get the international community to intervene in both the conflicts to put pressure on Pakistan. In the first case, the signals from India that it cannot fight on the Kargil heights with one hand tied behind its back produced relentless US pressure on Pakistan to vacate its aggression unconditionally. And during 2002, the implicit Indian threat to go to war after a full scale military mobilisation, the international community got the Pakistan President, Gen. Pervez Musharraf, to offer for the first time promises on ending cross-border terrorism.

A credible minimum deterrent

Beyond the immediate tensions with Pakistan that preoccupied India after Pokharan II, India had the important task of articulating a nuclear doctrine that its own people, the national security establishment and the international community clearly understood. At home the challenge, after decades of avoiding a public debate on the nuclear doctrine, was to educate its own public opinion about nuclear weapons. The message that nuclear weapons were not weapons of war but weapons of mass destruction that were not really useable was not an easy one. The principal purpose of acquiring these weapons, the government suggested, was to prevent other great powers from trying to blackmail India. The central theme of the draft nuclear doctrine that was unveiled in August 1999 was simple: that the only function of nuclear weapons was to deter the use of similar weapons against the nation by others and stop the prospects of coercive nuclear diplomacy against India. Internationally the message from the nuclear doctrine was that India would pursue a responsible nuclear posture that will minimise the dangers that arise from the possession of nuclear weapons.

The other task before New Delhi was to communicate to the world that India is considering a nuclear deterrent force that is modest in size and will be guided by a doctrine that is responsible. India, it was suggested, had no need to embark on an open-ended construction of a large nuclear force or imitate the Western doctrines of nuclear security. The Indian objective to build a small but credible nuclear deterrent that can survive an adversary's attack and impose a reasonable punishment on the attacker is all that India really needs and can afford. Although the doctrine was called a draft, it reflected the broad contours of official policy. Even more important was the fact that the ideas embedded in the draft nuclear doctrine had been thoroughly debated in the late 1980s by a small group of nuclear experts that Prime Minister Rajiv Gandhi had assembled. That debate had produced two essential concepts—credible minimum deterrence and no first use. These two ideas were also the key to the draft nuclear doctrine.

The Indian emphasis on these two concepts were greeted with scepticism both at home and the world. The doctrine's suggestion that India could do with a small nuclear arsenal were challenged by critics who contended that small nuclear arsenals were vulnerable to a pre-emptive attack and therefore cannot credibly deter a nuclear armed adversary. The demand from super hawks at home was for a large arsenal and outside critics insisted that India will end up with a large arsenal and an arms race any way. But, India's nuclear doctrine pursued a different logic. India neither needs nor can it afford a massive nuclear weapons programme. The Indian doctrine argued that credible deterrence does not lie in large numbers but in the ability to respond to a nuclear attack. India also emulated the Chinese nuclear experience, where a small nuclear arsenal of 400 managed to deter both the United States and the Soviet Union, with whom it had adversarial relations at one point of time or another. India also assessed that there is no way an attacker can expect to wipe out the entire nuclear arsenal of an adversary. The 1991 Gulf War has shown that despite the massive military and air superiority enjoyed by the United States and its allies, and the thousands of air sorties they ran over the small geographic space of Iraq, they could not wipe out the missiles of Saddam Hussein. Is China or Pakistan or even the United States in a position to believe that they can 'take out' a dispersed Indian nuclear arsenal?

India also had little time for the superpower nuclear strategy with its large arsenals that were deployed in different modes and demanded an expensive command and control system. India believed that dispersal of its nuclear assets, and the creation of a capacity to bring them together at one's choosing, the problems of survivability, retaliation and tight command over the forces could be resolved. That India's emphasis on a credible minimum deterrent and no first use were not mere slogans but of operational significance has been revealed by its unhurried approach to expansion of either fissile material capabilities or the production of delivery systems. This has helped avoid an arms race with either Pakistan or China, while providing an essential nuclear insurance to Indian security.

From disarmament to arms control

New Delhi has had a basic difficulty in the past on articulating its nuclear policy in terms—balance of power and arms control—that are intelligible to the rest of the world. The founding fathers of the Indian Republic and the succeeding leaders have always shunned the notion of balance of power. Power politics, they said, was passé in the second half of the 20th Century. Instead, India expressed its foreign policy objectives in the framework of liberal internationalism and the idea of 'one world'. It emphasised the need to redefine the old rules of international politics to ensure a more peaceful and cooperative international society. Despite the continuous compulsions on India to adapt to the real world, the formal and public discourse on India's foreign policy remained rooted in the moral and the normative universe. Having declared itself a nuclear weapon power, after years of vacillation, India has begun to make a few basic transitions in its approach to the world—from the normative to the pragmatic, from ideas of collective security to those of balance of power, and from the notion of disarmament to arms control. The Indian Government has not in any way suggested since 1998 that it was discarding its historical emphasis on global nuclear disarmament, in particular the total elimination of nuclear weapons within a reasonable time frame. Yet, the salience of disarmament as an objective in Indian foreign policy has steadily declined since 1998.

The idea of disarmament demands total abolition of nuclear weapons. The notion of arms control in contrast focuses on reducing the nuclear threat in the short term. India tended to reject in the past arms control arrangements as temporary palliatives to the problem of the very existence of weapons of mass destruction. More often than not, India argued, arms control only ends up as a cover for the pursuit of arms races by the major powers. Although the idea of nuclear disarmament became a *mantra* for Indian diplomacy by the late 1980s, it never was seen in such obsessive terms by Jawaharlal Nehru. India's first prime minister, after all, was a great champion of the Comprehensive Test Ban Treaty and the Fissile Materials Cut-off Treaty from the 1950s. Even more important, Nehru was the first to sign the Partial Test Ban Treaty of 1963, despite the fact that the treaty did not prohibit underground nuclear testing and was also prevented India from future tests of its nuclear weapons in the atmosphere.

In the early 1990s, India found that supporting the CTBT and the FMCT talks gave it a way out of the American pressures to accept nuclear arms control in a bilateral framework with Pakistan. When it found that the CTBT was taking away India's option to test nuclear weapons forever, it chose to oppose it in 1996. But in the immediate wake of Pokharan II, India announced a unilateral moratorium on nuclear testing and sought to leverage its potential signature on the CTBT as a way to get the US to lift all nuclear sanctions against India. That manoeuvre had come to a halt when the US Senate itself had refused to ratify the CTBT in 1999. But India's willingness to negotiate on its CTBT signature reflected an important change in approach on New Delhi's part. Until May 11, 1998 the Indian diplomatic objective was to create and sustain the option to make nuclear weapons when needed. In defence of this option, India was careful not to accept any restraints. Since Pokharan II, however, the task has been to defend India's nuclear deterrent, reduce the political and economic costs of exercising India's nuclear option, and eventually gain international acceptance of its new status. This in turn demanded greater flexibility in the Indian approach to arms control, including potential restraints on India's own nuclear capabilities.

The bargain between what India can offer in terms of arms control, whether it is in relation to nuclear testing or fissile material production and what it could gain in return for such limits has been a continuing theme in India's nuclear diplomacy since May 1998. The reference to the voluntary moratorium on nuclear testing and the commitment to negotiate an FMCT have been among the major reciprocal gestures that India had made in the July 18, 2005 statement in return for full nuclear energy cooperation with the international community. This was part of a practical recognition of the fact that the campaign for nuclear disarmament that it has conducted in the past has lost much of the earlier momentum on the world stage. New Delhi has also sensed that the pursuit of the goal of total nuclear disarmament can at best be longer term 'normative' and not a 'policy objective' in the near-term. Since declaring itself a nuclear weapon power, India has rightly placed greater emphasis on finding a pragmatic accommodation with the global nuclear order.

Supporting non-proliferation

Nothing illustrates the significant changes in India's nuclear mindset after May 1998 than its one hundred eighty degree turn on the NPT. After years of lambasting the treaty, which had become the veritable symbol of a discriminatory order for India, New Delhi has since 1998 has come to endorse explicitly the basic objectives of the treaty. For nearly three decades, India, ambiguous about its own nuclear posture, whined and complained about the inequities and unfairness of the NPT. Despite the fact that much of the world came to accept the NPT, India kept up its demonisation of the treaty. But having acquired nuclear weapons itself, and recognising the importance of preventing the further proliferation of weapons of mass destruction, India now takes a more objective and relaxed view of the treaty system. Even as it recognised that the NPT system will not be able to confer the status of a nuclear weapon state on India, New Delhi is confident enough to extend political support to the NPT and its objectives. During the NPT review conferences of 2000 and 2005, India, at the level of foreign ministers, endorsed the objectives of the treaty and proclaimed that it was in full compliance with the obligations of the Treaty that accrue to a nuclear weapon state. Similarly, India also started supporting various nuclear free zone agreements in the world after years of denouncing the proposal for a South Asia nuclear weapon free zone. Implicit in its support for the free zones was also the commitment that India is ready to offer 'negative security assurances' or no first use commitments to key neighbouring regions.

Besides warming up to some of the traditional nuclear arms control measures, India also sought find ways to cooperate with the new ideas on non-proliferation that began to emerge under the Bush Administration. When President Bush announced a sweeping seven-point agenda that went beyond the NPT structure, for constraining nuclear proliferation in 2003, India's reacted in a measured manner. Contrary to the traditional argumentation in India about the discriminatory nature of the global nuclear order, the government actually welcomed the initiative and called for cooperative international action to stem the new tide of global proliferation of weapons of mass destruction. These included such controversial proposals such as the Proliferation Security Initiative, which demanded military action against illicit traffic in WMD materials and the denial of plutonium reprocessing and uranium enrichment technologies to non-nuclear states. In the July 18 statement India committed itself to the former and promised to join the former.

The underlying premise of the Indian response to Bush proposals was that India, as a responsible nuclear weapon power is determined to contribute to the construction of a new global nuclear order. Amidst the stereotyping of the Indian nuclear responses in the 1970s and 1980s, the original approach of India to non-proliferation has often been forgotten. It was India in fact that launched the global debate on non-proliferation four decades ago. Shocked by China's first nuclear weapon test in October 1964, India initiated the international debate on non-proliferation. But the outcome of that negotiation, the Nuclear Non-Proliferation Treaty (NPT), did not address India's concerns and New Delhi has remained an outsider. India was never impressed with the NPT. But India is not gloating today over its crisis since it always shared the objective of non-proliferation. As the global debate on the NPT enters a new phase, India, as a self-declared nuclear weapon power, has begun to respond with some sophistication to the new international initiatives on non-proliferation. Part of Indian motivations also relate to the importance of differentiating New Delhi from the cavalier nuclear and missile export policies of China and the nuclear black-market operated by Pakistan's A.Q. Khan. A central theme articulated by India since May 1998 has been its impeccable record on nuclear non-proliferation and the importance of treating it as a "responsible nuclear weapon power". One consequence of this has been the controversial Indian decision to vote against Iran at the International Atomic Energy Agency during 2005-06. Despite its good relations with Iran, India was prepared to acknowledge that it will not support proliferation by any country.

Codifying national restraint

It was one thing to support global non-proliferation measures as part of India's post Pokharan II nuclear strategy; it was entirely another, when it came to accepting binding legal restraints on India's own WMD programmes. The first steps of national restraint came after Pokharan II as part of the nuclear dialogue with the Clinton Administration during 1998-2000. During that dialogue India accepted export controls as an important benchmark and in meeting it New Delhi began to upgrade and tighten its controls over exports of sensitive materials and technologies relating to WMD programmes. In the past, India had dismissed these export control norms as an attempt by the North to control technological flows to the South. But now, recognising the danger of proliferation of

WMD India was converting its long-standing commitments on preventing others from acquiring nuclear weapons into formal legal commitments.

The second set of moves on national restraint came in the negotiation of the so called 'Next Steps in the Strategic Partnership' during the first term of the Bush Administration. The NSSP marked an important shift in the nuclear dialogue between India and the United States. It provided a basis for ending the long-standing nuclear disputes between the two nations since 1999 and open the door for reciprocal gestures—on non-proliferation from India and loosening advanced technology transfers from the United States. The NSSP involved the further upgradation of controls over the flow of high technologies out of India and stringent end use verifications on the transfers of materials and technologies to India's civilian sectors. The former was about 'outward proliferation' and the latter about providing assurances to the US that there would be no 'internal proliferation'. India accepted these constraints in return for the US loosening controls over high technology exports. As part of this effort, India also established a strong domestic legal basis for non-proliferation by passing the WMD Act of 2005 that defined the terms for ensuring punishment for individuals and entities for proliferation.

The mother of all national restraints adopted by India was surely the commitment to separate its civilian and military nuclear facilities and place the former under international safeguards. This was the principal obligation India undertook in the July 18, 2005 statement. This was in return for full civilian nuclear energy cooperation. What was a historic burden for India—a military programme embedded in a civilian nuclear programme—became the principal lever for gaining access to global nuclear energy markets. Unlike most other nuclear weapon powers, India did not set up a dedicated military nuclear programme. Instead it sought to pursue the weapons option as part of a larger civilian nuclear programme. There was huge bureaucratic resistance in the Indian Department of Atomic Energy to whether and how to separate the two components of the programme, which in turn became a grist to the mill of those opposed to the Indo-US nuclear deal of July 18. In the end though the DAE came up with a separation plan just before President Bush came to India on March 1, 2006. Separation of the two elements of the programme had always a value of its own, irrespective of external demands. Nuclear separation allows more efficient pursuit of both the civilian and military objectives of India's nuclear programme, assures those who cooperate with India that imported technology and material will not be used for nuclear weapons, and brings as much as 65 per cent of current Indian nuclear capacity under international safeguards.

Avoiding regional war

The nuclear rhetoric of the government in the wake of Pokharan II had heightened tensions with both Pakistan and China. Since then, New Delhi has embarked on a formal nuclear and military dialogue with both countries. The nuclearsiation of the subcontinent, India has come to accept, demands a sustained engagement with both its nuclear neighbours. Prevention of an intended or accidental nuclear war with Pakistan and China has become one of India's highest national security objectives. In the past, India was so preoccupied with the criticism of the global non-proliferation order that it did not accept regional arms control as a necessary and legitimate political objective. Since Pokharan II, the approach has involved a conscious pursuit of nuclear stabilisation measures with its neighbours. Not only do nuclear weapons demand a greater responsibility from a nation that gets them but they also increase that nation's stake in the sobriety of the nuclear adversary's policy. In other words, deterrence locks adversaries into a common search for stability.

And, stability between nuclear adversaries can only be achieved through a sustained dialogue on military confidence building and the reduction of the nuclear threat. India attempted to initiate this during Vajpayee's Lahore visit in early 1999 by signing an MoU on military and nuclear CBMs. The process of implementing these was held up by the Kargil War and could be resumed only in mid 2004 when the peace process was revived on the basis of a new framework. Since then, a series of agreements on avoiding accidental nuclear war and prior notification of ballistic missile launches were negotiated. Pakistan, however, had some fundamental reservations about CBMs in general. It suspected that the focus on CBMs would take attention away from what it considers the core issue of Jammu and Kashmir. Pakistan also seemed hesitant to facilitate simple CBMs of contact and communication between the two military establishments.

While Indian policy evolved from the past opposition to CBMs to considerable enthusiasm, New Delhi discovered that CBMs alone are not enough to bring stability to the Indo-Pak relationship. Although nuclear CBMs of the kind the US and Soviet Union had implemented during the Cold War have some value in the context of Indo-Pak nuclear relations, the threat to stability in the region has come from an entirely different source. It was Pakistan's support to cross-border terrorism in India. Recognising that India did not have too many conventional military options against it, the Pak Army has found it easy to pursue a sub-conventional low-intensity conflict against India. While international pressures after September 11, 2001 and the Indo-Pak military confrontation in the summer of 2002 have forced a verbal change in Pakistan's approach to cross-border terrorism, there is no basic change in Islamabad's strategy of destabilising India. Dealing with this challenge remains a huge unfinished agenda in India's nuclear and national security strategy. The creation of a new strategy might involve a complex mix of different options, including the pursuit of missile defence, the development of new strategy that focuses on special forces and the use of the revolution in military affairs, and trans-border conventional military options, and the capacity to pursue a limited war under the shadow of nuclear weapons. Ironically, the biggest consequence of the nuclearisation of the subcontinent has been the renewed urgency of transforming the conventional military doctrine and strategy.

Shunning xenophobia

India's post Pokharan policy has seen some dramatic shifts in some of India's most dearly held nuclear, diplomatic and political positions over the decades. Given the rapid and tumultuous adaptation of Indian positions, it was inevitable that a noisy domestic debate would ensue. India's public nuclear debate since Pokharan II has often turned shrill, jingoistic and internally divisive. For some in India, nuclear weapons have become an end in themselves. Instead of seeing nuclear weapons as an instrument of policy, they are being turned into a fetish. Nuclear 'autonomy' has been converted into emotive slogan, when the central consequences of nuclear weapons is an extraordinary interdependence with the nuclear adversaries. India's necessary search for an accommodation with the global nuclear order are being challenges on the basis of old premises, originally invented to defend India's nuclear option. Despite the fact that India defied the world in 1998, it successfully withstood international sanctions and is close to being accepted as a full fledged nuclear weapon power—pressures have been mounted against the government for initiating reasonable compromises with the international community. Ironically the very xenophobia that grew out of India's long nuclear isolation, is now coming in the way of a long over due reconciliation between India and the global nuclear order.

Generating a new national consensus on nuclear diplomacy and doctrine has been a high domestic priority for the Indian political class after May 1998; but it has remained elusive. The NDA government sought to take the entire credit for the nuclear tests of May 1998 despite the fact that it was many Congress governments that laid the foundation for a nuclear weapons programme. The UPA government, in turn, failed to bring the NDA on board as it embarked on a major initiative to elevate India's standing in the global nuclear order. The NDA, which started these negotiations with the US has turned out to be an opportunistic opponent. Beyond the level of the political parties, there has been a vigorous dissent within the Indian intelligentsia against Pokharan II and the subsequent nuclear diplomacy. Opposition to nuclear weapons has a long lineage in India deriving its strength from the ideas of non-violence. Socialists, communists, and liberals in this country have long opposed the bomb as both immoral and dangerous. Many

Indian economists have long argued against nuclear weapons as a useless diversion from the task of economic development. On the Left, there has been a long tradition of opposing all engagement with the United States in the name of anti-imperialism. On the Right the bomb was always popular. But the nativists and conservatives have found it difficult to accept the post-Pokharan imperatives towards the US, China and Pakistan.

Criticism and dissent are healthy and have long been part of the Indian democratic tradition. Informed intellectual dissent generates pressure on the government to continually impart a reality check to its nuclear policies, prevents an excessive reliance on the views of the official scientific establishment, and forces a useful public debate on the direction of India's nuclear policy. This should be welcome rather than being branded as "anti-national". Although there has been a noisy nuclear debate in the country since May 1998, it is yet to reach a stage of maturity where many unresolved questions of India's nuclear policy are put to public scrutiny. Getting to that next stage is the collective national challenge that now faces India. Overcoming the past xenophobia is the key to the consolidation of India as nuclear weapon state with rising influence on the international stage.

Foreign economic policy

52

Economic diplomacy and its significance for foreign policy

Abid Hussain

Introductory remarks

To put in the words of Joseph Nye, who said in a different context, "diplomacy is the ability to affect the outcome you want and, if necessary, change the behaviour of others to make it happen i.e. getting others to do what you want." Diplomacy influences the decisionmaking of others as also influences policymaking at home. It seeks to restrict such actions of others that may hurt the country's national interest and induce such intentions and actions that would benefit one's country. Diplomacy, by itself, is more about the method and less about the substance of policy though it rests heavily on it. It is true that state policies are manifested by diplomatic actions. Good diplomacy could win friends but remains barren unless it is put in pursuit of a (national) cause. Diplomacy at its best, acts like a bee which picks up nectar from flowers without ruffling the petals or preventing the flower from growing into a fruit.

Diplomacy works to achieve the objectives set by the state. Objectives could be varied. These could be territorial, religious, ideological, economic, etc. Of late, countries are no more desirous of annexing territories or interested in creation of ideological state. In economic success, they see their gains. There is acceptance that economy is central to foreign policy and should be the key guiding factor for diplomacy. A clear preference is being given to geo-economics over geopolitics.

From politics to economics

Till recently, diplomacy was packaged to achieve politics objective like making and transforming power structures, making balance-of-power arrangements work, creating and maintaining balance in military terms and handling strategic options concerning security, etc. In recent times, countries prefer to extend their economic clout by entering into trade agreements rather than by launching trade wars. Economic diplomacy has become the common choice of countries and, in some respects, has replaced political diplomacy. It is now increasingly cast in the framework of geoeconomy.

The reasons for the shift are not far to seek. The 1980s and 1990s ushered in certain significant changes that have enhanced the claims of economic diplomacy. Traditionally, the power of political diplomacy was imbedded in 'strength for war'. With wars becoming costly and the results of war remaining inconclusive, states had to opt in favour of economic diplomacy, since this switch was found advantageous to them. As Richard Rosecrance writes: "In the past, it was cheaper to seize another State's territory by force than to develop sophisticated economic and trading apparatus needed to derive benefit from commercial exchange with it." Now it is no longer so, which enhances the validity of pursuing economic diplomacy.

Yet another factor, which gave primacy to economic over political diplomacy, is the advent of mind boggling technological revolution. It made creation and accumulation of wealth, through application of newer technologies, much more remunerative, easier and faster in comparison to creation of wealth through traditional and indigenous forms of technology. Disadvantages of cutting oneself away from the sources of new technology became obvious. With this, therefore, followed a change in conviction within the countries that they should give up strategies of insular development and find peaceful means and commercial ways of linking themselves to such of those countries, which were technologically advanced.

In doing so, economic diplomacy had a clear edge over other forms of diplomacy. A paradigm shift in this regard compelled the foreign policy of a country to follow a path which would ensure and heighten international flows of knowledge, investment, goods and services from other advanced and better placed countries to accelerate the domestic growth processes, which was fundamental to the development of people. And, this had to be reflected in the context of foreign policy.

Additionally, the end of the Cold War, the demise of Soviet Union and disenchantment with ideological battles also combined to mark the ascendancy of economic diplomacy over geopolitics. Peaceful and non-military economic developmental measures ensured better results, which led to sprouting of newer forms of economic diplomacy.

From confrontation to cooperation

All over the world , a new realisation dawned that a country's interests are best served not by playing the game of cold blooded power politics but by taking recourse to economic diplomacy, thereby achieving its objectives through negotiations and enriching the country by application of better technologies obtained from abroad. A stream of windows for instance, got opened when countries opted in favour of free trade and an open economy. Best results followed by focus upon relations which ensure reduction in tariff and other forms of trade eliminating discriminatory treatment in international commerce, finance, technology, etc. The world witnessed a shift in favour of strategies which helped to forge greater economic connectivity among countries and greater inter-exchanges amongst them. Pulls of political diplomacy, on the other hand, fail to find adequate and solid answers to common problems.

Political confrontation, antagonism and differences with other countries had to be replaced by economic cooperation and dialogue. Political diplomacy, which usually operated with implied military threats and hegemonic assertions, yielded place to policy of dialogue, discourse and negotiations. Foot soldiers and guns were replaced by economic players and economic diplomacy.

It is the function of economic diplomacy to bring on board the high commercial and financial benefits, which were earlier foregone due to rigid ideological position taken by governments. Once the political and ideological beliefs got largely defused, economic diplomacy became the main interest of foreign policy.

Best international practices of economy were harnessed and arrangements worked out to achieve mutual trust and confidence. Considerable significance was attached to commerce, democracy and law. They assumed respectability and reverence.

Some of the policy instruments used to advance a country's economic interests, are: trade, taxes, subsidies, export-import, quota, voluntary export reservations and import expansions, etc. These set targets for negotiations with foreign countries. Enabling arrangements were also envisaged to ensure constant and abiding flows of investment technology, etc. Negotiations and other mechanisms like dispute settlement arrangement, etc. are used to extract gains from other nations and sometimes even to drive hard bargains.

Economic reforms in India and its diplomacy

India could not remain immune to the changes of 1980s and 1990s. India undertook bold initiatives in its policies as a response to the evolving circumstances. Initially, India's foreign policy was driven by political objectives. Its economic segment was small and not very significant. Its best diplomats mostly conducted activities to advance India's political agenda. It was much later that economic issues started to move from the periphery to centre stage. Though Non-alignment and Panchsheel remained firm pillars of its international architecture, the matters of economics slowly started to assume equal, if not greater, importance. Subsequently, economic diplomacy started to run parallel to and, at times to overwhelm political diplomacy. Gradually, economic diplomacy has led to internationalisation of its domestic policy and the consequent domesticisation on the external front.

India's foreign policy and its diplomacy have now become more economic-centric than before. Not that foreign policy was earlier totally devoid of any economic content but it remained constrained and insulated. India had long remained committed to a closed economic regime, which being averse to outside flows, was given to export pessimism, import restrictions, etc., that had little need to forge closer relations with other countries. Foreign economic relations, at best, remained either frozen or confined to socialist countries and to countries that believed in the virtues of such economies. Domestic economic requirements did not exercise any strong pressure on foreign policy to seek trade relationship with other countries. Later, with a paradigm shift, an open economy came to the centre stage and conferred centrality to the imperative to knit viable networks of relationship with foreign countries for foreign investment and markets.

Further, with rising domestic aspirations, higher economic growth became an objective of national interest. Growth was considered indispensable for eradication of poverty in the country. It exercised a larger claim on policymaking. Economic policies started moving in the direction of liberalisation, which favoured a free and open market regime. As a consequence, foreign policy had to be reoriented to serve these requirements by building a new structure of relationships with outside countries. Since foreign policy is an extension of domestic policy, changes in the latter became a key to nuanced shifts in India's foreign policy with economic diplomacy emerging as the leading factor.

One of; the pre-requisites of a good economic policy is to have a good domestic economic regime, since there is an inescapable connection between the two. One cannot have a good economic foreign policy with a weak domestic economy. Growth provides the sinews of confidence. A strong domestic economic base is essential for launching a successful economic foreign policy. This explains how India's economic reforms of nineties made a difference and made it possible for its foreign policy to forge ahead with economic diplomacy, which had earlier remained moribund.

Success of economic diplomacy also rests on a country holding a few bargaining chips in the shape of certain economic assets and abilities, which are most eagerly needed by other countries. They serve as bait to catch big fishes and make a country negotiate from a position of strength. For some, oil is such a bait, for some others, it is industrial might, and for still some others, it is precious minerals, metals and technology. In the case of India, its large growing consumer market, its entrepreneurial middle class, its brainpower and technological outfit, etc. are the assets, which can be used diplomatically as bargaining chips. Like in the game of poker one who holds strong cards wins, so also in economic matters. Arewin Bevan, Labour Minister in the Attlee Government in the early fifties, had said, "Let me have 1,00,000 tonnes of coal and I can give you a strong foreign policy." In other words, reciprocal benefit accrues on the basis of assets, which are coveted by others.

To be effective internationally, the objectives of economic diplomacy have to be worked out very clearly and translated into specific proposals bearing in mind principles of reciprocity, etc. A framework for negotiation with other markets has also to be in place. A lot of preparatory homework has to be done at highly efficient level to make diplomatic moves in this respect; operational to clinch economic and commercial deals.

Regional integration

Cooperation and integration at regional and global levels are also to be nurtured and effectively implemented. With globalisation, economies have become more integrated through cross-border flows of trade, investment, technology and finance, etc., transcending narrow nationalism. Transnational pipelines, cross-border trade arrangements, multinational manufacturing alliances, large scale outsourcing, migration of labour, multistate financial combinations and technological collaborations are the new networks binding many countries into economic relationships. While no country can afford to be outside these arrangements, they, at the same time, would not like their sovereignty to be abridged by these arrangements. Economic diplomacy has to secure these twin objectives of ensuing global tie-ups without hurting the national sovereignty.

The potency of global market forces involves establishment of regional and global organisations, entailing certain transfers of sovereignty by the state for the sake of promoting the nation's trade. The needs of economy and process of technology lead to interdependence of economy. Foreign policy has to play an important role in making it happen.

Globalisation and international relation

International relations have gone through a radical transformation of unmaking power structure with which we had lived so far. Since the end of the Cold War and emergence of global information age, there is a vast paradigm shift in the forms of international relationships. The world has become interdependent and no state, however strong it may be, can prosper in isolation. Unipolarity has short life. Countries, big or small have to get on with network arrangements of bilateral, regional and global nature. Seeing the historical shift, some countries have moved ahead of others, mounting initiatives to adjust with new realities. Their foreign policy has concentrated on building a string of new alliances to reap the harvest of new developments.

New institutional arrangements of cooperation with other countries have also come about. For instance, SAFTA is a step in the evolution of SAARC as a regional trade block. Once a country decides to become part of global economy, it cannot get involved in the given transformation. Regional blocks are the building blocks for global trade. Regional arrangements have now become the order of the day, so has a country to participate in multilateral arrangements. One cannot but be a part of the regional arrangements and also remain connected with global arrangements. At present, there are about 200 regional trade agreements in operation. In formation of the regional group and joining the global arrangements, there is always a fear of a state being coerced into subordinating its national sovereignty to accomplish regional and global harmony.

Care has to be taken to see that joining regional or global arrangements would not adversely affect the national interest and ideals. A former French Prime Minister has said, "Making of Europe, without unmaking France, is my ambition." So should be the approach of other countries. The regional interest will have to include the national interest.

Though the advantages of regional arrangements are well known, these could also hinder multilateral trade liberalisation processes. Regional arrangements should not become a patchwork quilt of trading arrangements, which could prove harmful. There is also a 'convoy problem', whereby the pace of progress is held back by the least willing member. The foreign policy should see to it that such eventualities are ably handled through economic diplomacy. Cooperation and integration at the regional level has to be handled wisely so that moves in the direction of regional arrangement facilitate and not hinder multilateral liberalisation. The foreign policy, while supporting the moves towards regionalisation and globalisation, should see to it that the reversal of policies by the developed countries that are adversarial to the interests of the weak and marginal countries, is prevented from causing harm to their economy. Economic diplomacy should be vigilant in this regard and checkmate it. It should be exercised by patience, subtlety and imagination. Recognising the limited influence that some of the countries can exercise in the global multilateral arena, they have to strengthen their position through alliances, which play an importance role in making economic diplomacy more effective at regional and global levels.

Need for alliance is not confined to small emergent economies. It has its uses for developed country too. However strong and big a country may be, it needs support from others to be effective in multilateral deals and affairs. It also requires to defuse tensions between the countries. Complexities of alliances arise from the fact that the same country may not have the same interest in respect of several other issues. Alliances are interest based. As interests vary, a chain of different interests call for different alliances. It is not necessary that a country should be a partner of the same country in all transactions.

Economic diplomacy and political diplomacy

Economic diplomacy cannot be devoid of political diplomacy. Role of politics is not to be underestimated. It would be wrong to believe that politics is dead. Primacy of economics does not mean the end of politics. In fact, politics remains the arena through which trade opportunities are evaluated and choices made. One cannot opt out of politics. At times, it is the political power equation that puts restraints on countries, which would otherwise have malign intent in mind. Politics could defuse tensions and help in formulating a better framework for political and economic cooperation. Sometimes, what cannot be achieved through economic arrangements, could be achieved with the help of political intervention. Economic diplomacy could use political opportunity to attain its aims. For instance, America's concern to have peace in the Pacific offers India an opportunity to use this to its economic advantage.

Similarly, there are countries, which for their own political reasons would like to help in the eradication of poverty, illiteracy, etc. Diplomacy must take advantage of these and convert such possibilities to the country's benefit. Sometimes domestic politics has a way of confounding economic projections, hinder economic growth and, thereby, present a sharp dilemma. Here again, the economy diplomacy must find ways of countering and neutralising political suspicions to clear the ground for satisfactory progress. Sometimes, economic agreements should not be looked upon merely from the economic point of view. For instance, there would be cases when free trade is used as an instrument of political arm-twisting.

Economic diplomacy also needs to get over political enmities. It will have to overcome narrow political nationalism. Historical baggage, which is inherited from the past, has got to be discarded. There is ample evidence to convince us that old estrangements have been overcome through economic diplomacy and not through political one-upmanship. In fact, economic leverage has been used to obtain such results.

Economic sanctions are also used to achieve political goals, though in some cases it failed to yield the desired results. Deft handling of problems wins friends and confers political legitimacy to economic deals. Long seen as a political and military threat, China of late, by using economic diplomacy, capitalising on its economic dynamism, has won more friends from Asia to Africa and Latin America than when it talked of revolution coming out of the barrel of the gun. Timely and intelligent purchase policy or discrete operations and markets could also amend politically adverse situations. Economic diplomacy can help to transform political relations. India's relations with China are getting normalised mostly due to economic moves and economic diplomacy.

Today we hear less of China *versus* India and more of China plus India. Since the two countries are getting closer in economic arena, the political differences are no longer acrimonious. Purchase of Boeings or opening of arms trade have also brought the business lobbies in America closer to the business interests in China and India. The use of oil diplomacy is another instance to prove how the economic interest influences political arrangements. Our economic diplomacy should also forge relations with such of those countries, which are politically committed to removal of poverty, etc. Economic diplomacy should take advantage of such internationally supported environment which helps the less fortunate countries in raising their level of development and improving the quality of life of their citizens.

The military dimensions

Though the relative weight of military dimensions is reduced yet its power to influence decisions cannot be overlooked. It remains true that military strength does give an edge to a country to enforce decisions, including economic decisions. There continues to be an inescapable connection between the two. It will be for the foreign policy to intertwine the legitimate roles of the two. Geopolitics and security interests cannot be overlooked. Moreover, good fences help to make good friends.

Need for professionalism

Economic policy issues have become so complex that these call for handling of economic matters by trained and experienced professionals. Scholarly advice and professional excellence would be needed to formulate the country's policies. Foreign office and embassies have to recast their role to strengthen their professional capabilities to handle the stream of new situations. At present, they are too meagre. These must be augmented. Entry of professional economists to handle some of these matters is also found to be useful. As advisers to the administration and diplomats, they proved to be of much help. But there have been occasions when their influx has proved to hinder or deter diplomacy from adopting the right course. It is necessary, that their advice is subjected to reality check by the market agents, administrators and diplomats. The 'Shock Therapy' of Jeffrey Sachs bedeviled economies and went wrong in Russia. This is in no way to denigrate the role economists or experts play but is a warning against leaving things to be conducted by experts alone. Diplomacy cannot indeed be confined to diplomats alone nor can diplomats be left out of shaping the policy.

Professionals could give different scenarios of things to come and suggest ways to handle them. But it is for the diplomats to sell the ones that suit the situation. Those who play cards do know how a good hand may lose if these are not played correctly. The need for role of diplomats lies there. Economic diplomacy also calls for a different mindset than the one which had concentrated on political diplomacy so far. The new situations calls for diplomats to have a new mindset. But to change convictions is not easy. Those who had remained convinced of the virtues of closed economy cannot find it easy to see the benefits of moving away from the conventionally accepted position. Blatant disregard of the pride of petty bureaucrats cannot be ignored either. This can become a roadblock too.

It is becoming evident that with many new agents and actors emerging on economic international scene, one cannot handle issues only through the government representatives. The various lobbies and interest groups cannot be ignored and have to be cultivated. Their participation in policymaking through track two diplomacy and their role in implementation have important implications for the success of economic diplomacy. The Presidents and the Prime

Ministers of several countries travelling abroad always take along with them businessmen, academicians and lobbyists. Their inclusion speaks of their importance in shaping the economic diplomacy, and contribution in framing and implementing economic projects.

There are also large-scale reversals, transgressions and rollbacks of international policies relating to free trade, etc. These require to be carefully countered and provided with suitable solutions to restore the legitimacy of agreed international policies. This might call for a series of dialogues and exchanges to prevent the applecart from being upset.

It is also imperative that a country sets up sound national and international think tank arrangements to facilitate examination of developing situations both adversarial and advantageous. Experts of think tanks can provide countervailing ideas to handle unhelpful developments and also suggest ways and means of taking advantage of new opportunities arising. In India, there is a dearth of such institutions and it is urgently necessary to make good this deficiency. Institutional policy parameters could be formulated with their help and the state could use their inputs in working out alternative policy syndrome. There have also to be other relevant ancillary institutions to meet the requirements of the tasks involved.

India should also take active part in summits and secure preferential access for itself and for other developing countries. Its endeavour should be to become a part of a general move, to raise the level of economic development in pursuit of social justice.

Conclusion

As India becomes economically strong, it will have to use its growing power in a benign manner. Success of its economic diplomacy lies in India becoming a responsible stakeholder in the international system. This would mean that she will have to be more than a member of the international system and make moves which would strengthen the international system to help the lot of less privileged countries. Such a response, from a position of economic strength, would not be out of narrow parochial self-interest but would show concern for others and will be prepared to pay a price which comes from becoming a global power. There will always be the temptation to act tough, high and mighty with other countries. India, will have to resist it and adopt the middle path of cooperation and non-confrontation.

It should be the endeavour of Indian diplomacy to use the economic card to work out, lines of cooperation with rising China and enter into strategic relationship with America, the two powers with which we had a chequered past of interactions.

No diplomacy, much less economic diplomacy, can succeed in achieving its final goal unless its economic success is intimately concerned with promoting high moral principles. We should not be looked upon as predators or bullies.

It is reasonable to anticipate a bright future for India as an economic power, contributing to the sterling values of a just and rule-based world order, pursuing norms that will permit working with others to create stability, economic growth and democratic values. Once that happens, human rights and freedoms will become an integral part of the world order, radiating love and the power of ideas.

53

India rising: strategic issues in the international trading system

Lakshmi Puri

> Trade, having for its purpose, the acquisition of things not possessed, and preservation of things possessed and bestowal of things augmented on worthy recipients.
>
> — Kautilya, *Arthashastra*

> History balances the frustration of how far we have to go with the satisfaction of how far we have come.
>
> — Louis F. Powel

As India entered the 21st Century, it seemed transformed in the first five years from a reluctant debutante in international trade into an emerging powerhouse with a will to trade and invest. Many in the trade and development community had foreseen, especially since the 1990s that at some point in India's trade and development endeavour, a critical mass would be reached for such a transformation. It also confirmes India's intrinsic worth as a large, well-diversified and strategically globalising economy. The unfolding of India's trade success story is a prominent part of the 'India rising' or 'emerging giant' phenomenon today, sweeping across government policy corridors, corporate boardrooms, strategic think tanks and media networks globally. To apply the concept developed by Raúl Prebisch, founding Secretary-General of United Nations Conference on Trade and Development (UNCTAD), India seems to be at last moving from the 'periphery' of international trade and development towards its 'centre'.[1]

It is evident that India's trajectory of economic growth and development, including through an enhanced trade and investment performance, has come to matter more vitally for the world. It is welcoming India as the 'stealth miracle economy' and a formidable trading power in the making. There is recognition of what India has done right in its development strategies, trade liberalisation and economic reforms as there used to be of India having 'missed the bus'. India's emerging 'knowledge power' status and its human resource reservoir is seen in conjunction with images of a 'population bomb' and the literacy gap. Its being able to pull more people out of poverty since its independence than ever before (58 per cent in 1947 to 25 per cent presently) and its 350 million middle class consumers constituting the nucleus of 'India rising' are being hailed alongwith concerns about millions of people living in abject poverty.[2]

The result of this India rising related positive and more balanced assessment has spawned a novel trade and development discourse framed by a number of 'extreme choices'. Over the next 15 years, as we approach the perfect vision of 2020, these choices will get even more starkly posed. There will be little quarter given to India for mediocrity in trade and development performance and its destiny would either be to succeed spectacularly or fail disappointingly. Most important of these choices would relate to whether it could be a regional and global growth and trade dynamo on the scale and level of Japan and China, using trade for driving into developed country status beyond 2020 or remain a relatively modest player.

---

1. Dr. Raúl Prebisch was Secretary-General of UNCTAD from 1964 to 1969. In his writings, he articulated a development paradigm wherein the issue of development strategy was placed within the context of a centre-periphery view of the world in which there were rich, technologically advanced, dynamic and fast growing industrial countries at the centre and poor, technologically backward, slow paced developing economies at the periphery. He believed that the central question of global development and positive sum interdependence was how to integrate the peripheral countries into the growth dynamics of the centre.

2. Planning Commission of India's Tenth Plan targets to reduce poverty to 19.3 per cent by 2007.

India could be a real magnet for the world's investible surpluses and attract FDI flows commensurate with its needs and potential or it could continue its anaemic record. India could become a leader of globalisation by pursuing a bold strategy on outward FDI to acquire critical assets in other countries and best leverage its assets of manpower, skills and entrepreneurship or it could be overtaken by proactive countries like China. It could become an innovator and generator of technologies and patents in its own right or be content with an R&D subcontracting role for MNCs. It could make up the enormous infrastructure handicap and inadequacies in agricultural productivity whilst speeding up to secure a manufacturing advantage to match its growing and variegated services one. Alternately, its shortcomings in infrastructure could pull its performance down in all three areas.

Other critical questions include whether it will use its own trade and investment policies as well as global governance frameworks to exploit its comparative advantages while serving critical energy, food, land, demographic, technological and ecological security needs. Is India going to 'green its growth' or march relentlessly towards an ecological wasteland that many fear? Will it capitalise on its rich and unique cultural heritage and marry it with its growing mastery over telecommunication and audio-visual media to be an influential cultural power, defining idioms of contemporary global culture or will its own culture be overwhelmed by that of the West? Will political democracy have the necessary wherewithal of good governance and sound institutional backstopping to deliver on economic democracy and social equity or will the world's largest free market democracy' fail to provide broad based prosperity, equity and poverty eradication that this model must, to confirm its triumph in the world.

It is necessary to do a reality check and answer these questions in a systematic way. We must trace the progress of India's trade and investment policies and achievements over the years up to the present and assess the prospects and the targets for the future. Further, the rapidly changing international trading system and the rules of the game have to be assessed particularly in terms of India having to operate under it and to help shape it in its own short and long term interests. Deriving from this scenario, policy responses to the strategic challenges and opportunities for Indian diplomacy-both bilateral and multilateral will have to be fashioned.

Historical overview of economic development strategy

For many years after Indian independence, the historical memory of the British East India Company coming to India to trade and staying on to establish a colonial empire for 190 years, coloured the perception of the Indian polity and people to keep the role of foreign trade and investment in India's economic development and planning process minimal. Further, the influence of the Gandhian concept of 'swadeshi' lingered on until the 1990s and militated against an import culture in particular and a foreign trade orientation in general.

The emphasis was on building up self-sustaining capacity in agriculture, industry and science and technology as part of the Nehruvian vision for India's development. Policies, therefore, reflected import substitution and not export led growth, emphasised food security and self-sufficiency and the need to build up a large and comprehensive manufacturing base for everything from a needle to a spacecraft. The public sector was positioned to occupy the 'commanding heights' of the national economy, whilst the private sector was given space in a strategic way with encouragement to 'national champions'.

A conscious industrial policy was used to diversify the country's production capacity to increase its value added and productivity. This and private sector ownership of 70 per cent of domestic industry provided a strong and experienced entrepreneurial foundation for the Indian economy and its dynamic participation in international trade and investment in later years. Most of India's productive sector has relied on public resources and domestic private sector investment during this phase. However because of relatively low gross domestic savings to GDP and low gross capital formation as well as the fact that public resources including the limited FDI were insufficient to meet ever growing needs, there have been critical resource gaps in domestic productive investment and serious deficits especially in social and physical infrastructure.[3] Making up these deficits may now hold the key to India achieving a virtuous circle of trade, FDI and development.

Evolution of Indian trade policy

India's post Independence share of world exports stood at 2.2 per cent in 1948. This progressively fell to 1.3 per cent in 1953 and 0.5 per cent in 1983. Post the economic reform of 1990s, this share rose to 0.6 per cent in 1993, 0.8 per cent in 2002 and 1.5 of global trade in 2004-05. Over the past 20 years, India's foreign trade has grown by over 600 per cent, with the most impressive period beginning post 2000. Between 1990 and 2003 the value of Indian exports and imports doubled. In 2004-05 alone, India's total external trade, including goods and services, grew by 44.2 per cent to US$ 268 billion. India's total trade to GDP has increased from 16 per cent in 1990 to 32 per cent in 2005. Trade in services grew faster than merchandise trade. In 2004-05, growth in services trade was 78.6 per cent, compared to 33.6 per cent in merchandise trade.[4] This growth path is related to changes in India's trade and investment policies and to the coming on stream of comparative advantages built up over previous decades.

Indian development strategies required the use of the infant industry protection and seeking preferential market access to help Indian exports catch up in competitiveness with developed countries. State trading was the norm, with an elaborate import licensing system and a complex import tariff structure. Imports of raw material, intermediates as well as capital goods were controlled and those of consumer goods were generally banned or subject to restrictive conditions.

An external debt crisis and dipping of foreign exchange reserves down to a level which could finance only two weeks imports in 1991, forced the government onto a path of liberalisation and

---

3. In 1950-51, total gross domestic savings of GDP was only 8.9 per cent (1993-94 prices) and so was the gross capital formation. The savings and capital formation ratio went up to 11.6 per cent and 12.7 per cent respectively in 1960-61. (See, *Economic Survey of India 2005-06*.)

4. See, *Economic Survey of India 2005-06*.

deregulation. This irreversibly changed the contours of India's trade and FDI policy. Manufacturing and services sectors were opened up to foreign trade and investment, though the agriculture sector remained relatively protected. Greater market and export orientation were brought in. Competition within the domestic market as well as through opening up to imports in a strategic way became the thrust. Import controls were withdrawn in 1991-92 on virtually all goods. Substantial elimination of quotas on imports was introduced by 2001. Currently, a robust $ 150 billion foreign exchange reserves position had a positive impact on trade and investment liberalisation, which in turn contributed to its augmentation. Moves to seek optimal integration into the international trading system imparted competitive efficiency.

This calibrated evolution in India's trade policy can best be observed when one considers tariff levels on account of these changes. Tariff peaks fell from 300 per cent in 1990-91 to 28 per cent in 2004. Weighted average import duty rates in India for all goods came down from 72.5 per cent in 1991-92 to 35.1 per cent in 2001-2002.[5] India's trade weighted average tariff applied has come down to 10 per cent, though bound rates remain high. Dependence of government revenues on tariffs came down from 25 per cent to 19 per cent in 2000 and in 2006 is to be even lower. Export controls and subsidy programmes with exceptions are being eliminated.

There is a very clear export orientation in India's economic and trade policy today with various measures are being taken for stimulating India's exports like the SEZs and the India Brand Equity Fund.[6]

---

5. The corresponding level in East Asia for the same period was 14.35 per cent for Indonesia, 7.0 per cent for Korea, 9.4 per cent for Malaysia while that for China for the same year was 18.5 per cent and fell further as a result of China's WTO accession. See, Hoda, A. (2002). *India: Trade Policy and Domestic Constraints*, April, Evian Group, Policy Brief, *http://www.eviangroup.org/p/63.pdf*.

6. The new EXIM policy attempted to make the Export Promotion Capital Goods (EPCG) and the Duty Free Replenishment Certificate (DFRC) more exporter-friendly. Furthermore, a National Export Insurance Account is being created for Export Credit Guarantee Corporation (ECGC) to underwrite high value projects implemented by Indian companies. The new EXIM policy emphasises the need to stimulate special economic zones (SEZs) and the technology and employment orientation of exporting sectors. An India Brand Equity Fund is seeking, quite successfully to spread the gospel of India's economic rise and global role in trade and investment.

Transformation in FDI perspectives

FDI inflows into India have been negligible by any standards —whether per capita percentage of GDP, total volume and value or its development and competitiveness impact. UNCTAD data on FDI inflows as percentage of GDP show that the value was 0.04 per cent during 1970s, only picking up in 2003 but still remaining at a modest 0.72 per cent.[7] In 2006, FDI is expected to be US $ 7 billion to India as opposed to US $ 36 billion for China and US $ 17 billion for Brazil. The relatively miniscule role of FDI in India's economic growth can be assessed from the fact that FDI accounts for only 0.5 per cent of its GDP as against 5 per cent for China and 5.5 per cent for Brazil. However, the numbers mask the catalytic value of FDI in connecting Indian agriculture, manufacture and services to world standards and markets in the last few years. The trade-investment nexus is becoming ever more compelling in the 'India Rising' phenomenon and increasingly, investors come to India not only for its market size and tariff jumping reasons, but in search of cost quality competitiveness and high-scale returns. As AT Kearney in its latest report points out, India is on the cusp of an FDI boom.

Until the initiation of new economic reform policies in 1991, FDI policy was strictly controlled and government approach cautious. Foreign capital and investors were 'progressively Indianised' and their development impact sought to be increased. This was through performance enhancing requirements for shedding foreign equity, having Indian joint venture partners, controls on repatriation of profits and outflow of foreign exchange as well as local content, export performance and transfer of technology.

A key driver of change during 1990s has been the close synergy between trade and foreign investment policy. The imperative of becoming part of global production chains and even leading them, has given FDI a crucial role. This transformation in perception and

---

7. Latest Reserve Bank of India (RBI) data of 2004-05 shows the total foreign investment in India is US$ 14.44 billion, of which US$ 5.53 billion is direct investment and US$ 8.90 billion is portfolio investment. (See, RBI website.)

policy from 'red tape to red carpet' with a sector by sector opening up to privatisation and FDI. Policies have depended on perceived development gains, domestic opinion and opportunities provided by the global market. The limits and conditions on FDI are gradually (and in some cases rapidly) disappearing.

Today India is considered the second most attractive destination for FDI, ranking just below China and above US, surpassing other Asian competitors such as Singapore, South Korea, Hong Kong, and Thailand.[8] While the focus of FDI interest in India is the services sectors, primarily IT and software services including IT enabled services—BPO phenomenon, other sectors are catching up including the manufacturing sector where too India is ranked second in the AT Kearney FDI confidence index.[9] Investors range from the top Fortune 500 companies to SMEs from all continents or countries—developed and developing. A welcome trend is for NRIs to significantly invest in manufacturing and services sectors in India though these are nowhere near the levels of investment poured in by overseas Chinese into China.

Attracting FDI in infrastructure and leveraging public resources including World Bank and other donor funding with private flows is a major priority. At present, China spends seven times more than India. India has planned to increase its spending on infrastructure with a commitment of US $ 191.51 billion of investments over the next five years. This would require substantial FDI into physical, social and trade-related infrastructure and fruitful public-private partnerships.

Growth and policy changes have possibly been the most dramatic in services sector-enabled FDI. It is opening up, enabling domestic industry to compete and providing sufficient entry incentive to foreign suppliers. Telecommunications sector has in the last 10 years undergone a sea change with far-reaching privatisation and participation of foreign operators. This has had a positive knock-

---

8. *FDI Confidence Index*, 2005, Global Business Policy Council, AT Kearney.

9. Specific areas in the manufacturing sector that attract investor interest include the automotive, pharmaceutical, chemical, biotech, textiles and garments, gems and jewellery, minerals & steel, electronics and telecom.

on effect on the ICT sector, which is fast becoming the locus of inward and more recently outward FDI. In financial services, a wave of liberalisation, restructuring and regulatory reform has encouraged private sector participation and India has moved from the fourth to the second most attractive FDI destination. Similar liberalisation has swept across in key infrastructure sectors such as energy, transportation and construction. In previously strategic areas such as mining and oil and gas, opening up has been significant. FDI in tourism and the hospitality is being particularly encouraged. To date, the employment and poverty sensitive retail sector remains one of the last bastions for liberalisation and foreign investment. However, FDI in India is still plagued by certain debilitating factors which will be need to be addressed to convert investor interest into actual commitment.

Notably, India is becoming a serious capital exporter and occupying top positions in some developed and developing country markets. This symbolises the internationalisation of Indian companies, their coming of age and competitiveness amid growing confidence. Easing of controls on outward investment and positive encouragement by government have also helped. FDI from India in 2004 stood at USD 2.2 billion as compared to China, which stood at USD 1.8 billion for the same period.[10] In 2006, outward FDI from India is expected to cross US$ 10 billion mark, exceeding inward FDI. Up to 2000 more than half of this FDI arose from the manufacturing sector. Since 2001-02 non-financial services seem to be the thrust of outward investment.[11]

Prospects for India as a regional and global growth pole

Whilst India's economic growth and recent trade and investment performance has been impressive and put India in the league of the dynamic BRIC (Brazil, Russia, India and China) economies and large, diversified and 'advanced developing economies', we need to

---

10. UNCTAD *World Investment Report*, 2005.

11. Some notable instance of outward investment have been the operation of Indian or Indian owned companies such as Tatas, Infosys, Ranbaxy, Reliance, OVL. Destination countries for outward investment are not just developed countries in the EC, the US, Canada, and other developing countries in South and East Asia, Africa, the CIS countries, and further afield in Latin America.

put this progress in perspective. Never in human history has a democracy with over 200 million people sustained annual real GDP growth of 5.9 per cent over a 23-year period.[12] But it is still below China's current high growth rate and that of tiger Asian economies in the past. Similarly, Indian trade performance is dwarfed by that of China and overtaken even by countries like Thailand and Korea.[13]

However, it is evident that India is undeniably emerging as a regional and global dynamo of economic growth and trade and may soon surpass the performance of some of its developing country competitors except China. If we look at long-term growth projections, India seems to win the race ahead of Brazil, China and Russia among the BRIC economies.[14] Further income gaps within India are declining and are already low compared to other BRICs. Recent figures indicate that Gini coefficient is about 32.50 per cent in India, 44.7 per cent in China and 57.9 per cent in Brazil.[15] It is estimated that India's rapid and sustained growth potential was more than of other BRICs. These are predicated on democracy holding social tensions being managed, cultural influence increasing, and poverty reducing to 15 per cent by 2020.

India has the potential to transform the world economy in the next two decades. The size of India's GDP in 2010 could surpass that of certain OECD countries such as Spain, Korea, Canada and equal Japan's by 2025.[16] By 2020, India may contribute 12.2 per cent to the global economic growth.[17] Together India, China and the

---

12. P.K. Basu—Robust Economic Analysis Pte. Ltd.

13. In 2005 China's merchandise exports were US$764 billion *versus* US$96 billion for India, lower than that of Korea's exports which stood at US$290 billion and Thailand's which stood at US$ 110 billion. Roughly 91 per cent of China's exports were manufactured goods *versus* 75 per cent for India. While India is better known for its exports of services, here too China leads with US$ 62 billion *versus* US$ 40 billion for India. On the other hand, 60 per cent of China's service exports were travel and transportation services while in India the figure was 22 per cent. A large share of India's service exports were related to information technology and IT enabled services. See Deloitte Research—*China and India: The Reality Beyond the Hype*, 2005.

14. Sachs, Goldman (2003). "Dreaming With BRICs: The Path to 2050", *Global Economics Paper* No. 99.

15. The World Bank 2006.

16. Addressing a session on *India: The New Paradigm*, World Economic Forum India Economic Summit, November 2005.

17. "Foresight 2020" a study conducted by Economist Intelligence Unit (EIU) and sponsored by Cisco Systems, June 2006.

US will contribute USD 1 trillion to the global economy. Further, India's share in global GDP is expected to rise from 6.2 per cent in 2005 to 8.8 per cent in 2020 and it is expected to create 142 million new jobs. While the US will remain the biggest consumer market, China and India will substantially expand both their consumer base and their consumer spending per person.

With India being regarded as the fast rising global service provider and taking strides towards becoming a manufacturing hub, the prospects of its achieving its full potential in international trade to reach as much as US $ 700 billion in the next few years are bright. Studies, including by the IMF indicated that India undertrades by at least 60 per cent and this translates into approximately US $ 700 billion, bringing it closer to Chinese trade performance than before. A similar analysis can be extrapolated for FDI of US $ 20 billion, given that India is currently ranked second in FDI attractiveness. But, India still has a long way to go in order to achieve both FDI and trade flows that China has and adequacy of infrastructure could be a decisive factor. The need for FDI, particularly in infrastructure is tremendous and India has to compete for global investible surpluses, in an environment characterised by a 'race to the bottom' by host countries. Similarly, it has to contend with competitive Asian, Latin American and even African countries in areas of its strength in merchandise trade and overcome production and supply capacity constraints.

Overall, going by the current wisdom on international trade competitiveness, time and circumstances are propitious for India's success. Henceforth, in the international trade competitiveness game, a country needs to either rely on skills and institutions that promote cutting edge technological innovation i.e. hi-tech or the knowledge economy, or, alternatively, to rely on the low wage economy based on widely available technology with lowest cost labour.[18] India seems poised to win this competitiveness game because it has, alongwith China, perhaps the unique advantage of

---

18. Garrett, Jeffrey (2004). "Globalization's Missing Middle", *Foreign Affairs*, November/December, 83(6): 72-83.

being able to compete on both counts. Add to this, the outward orientation and trade and investment thrust being accelerated, as well as a reservoir of tradable human resources being built up at all skill levels and India's ambition to be a global trading power in the next 10 to 15 years may be realised sooner rather than later.

Sectoral strategies for India's trade dynamism

Against this background of India's trade policy and prospects, it is necessary to assess how India's comparative advantages in agriculture, manufacturing and services are going to pan out in the next 15 years and how trade is going to play a role in achieving key developmental targets, including UN's millennium development goals.[19] A continuing trend has been for India to diversify from commodity exports into manufactures in the seventies and into services in 1990s and 2000 onwards. Today the relative shares in India's export basket of agricultural commodities, manufactures and services is approximately 10 per cent, 39 per cent and 51 per cent respectively. The sectoral strategies for India's trade should aim at upgrading the performance of agricultural exports, becoming a global manufacturing hub and fulfilling India's recognised potential as a global services powerhouse.

Agriculture

Given that over 60 per cent of India's population is employed in the agricultural sector, it is of vital opportunity and concern for food security, rural livelihood and development and secondarily for export earnings. Agricultural trade policies of India have largely been shaped by the limitations of subsistence small holder farming and the need to hold the food price line for essential commodities for poorer rural and urban consumers. However while this policy has been successful in specific regions and aspects, it has been beset with costs, leakages and inefficiencies reflected in the declining share of the agricultural sector in India's GDP from 33 per cent in 1979-1980 to 21.1 per cent in 2004.[20] Moreover quotas, state trading, and

---

19. For further details on UN Millennium Development Goals, see *http://www.un.org/millenniumgoals*.

20. See *Economic Survey of India* and Asian Development Bank database.

very high tariffs have characterised a defensive agricultural trade policy.

Commercial agriculture and export orientation including through agro processing should and has recently become a priority. Government's realisation of the importance of the agricultural sector primarily as a means to bridge the urban-rural divide, generation of employment, and its encouragement of agricultural reform and private sector participation, deserve continuance. Apart from traditional areas like tea, rice, spices, marine products, nuts, and fruits, emerging areas within the agricultural sector include horticulture, floriculture, organic farming, genetic engineering and biotechnology and agro based and food processing industries. These areas, provided they are matched with sufficient agricultural infrastructural and facilitative investments, can result in much needed growth, employment and export boost. Major investment needs to be made in the handling and logistics for agricultural exports as well as in standard setting, conformance and certification infrastructure to meet increasingly stringent health, food safety and environmental requirements in global markets. FDI and trade can inject funds, technology and best practices.

In terms of the external environment for stimulating agricultural exports, liberalisation and reform of internal and international agricultural markets is an important prerequisite, particularly through the WTO. Linking up with global distribution networks and supply chains will at once bulk up and qualitatively improve supply capacity and provide necessary market penetration and India Brand Equity. Active participation in international standard setting including bodies like Codex Alimentarius is another imperative.

Food security dictates that minimum viable domestic production be pursued. However, increasing population and food consumption coupled with land scarcity could in the medium term require cheap and assured imports of food. At the same time, these very factors compel India towards acquisition of overseas agricultural land and captive assets through outward investment and agro-tech, R&D, human resource export related and other cooperation agreements. Equally, in order to support minimum viable production and export capacity, the Indian farmer would have to be provided a level playing field and remunerative returns in domestic and international markets. This is particularly so in relation to their heavily subsidised US and European counterparts.

Manufactures

Manufactures have long been the mainstay of India's trade. Traditional manufacturing strengths in exports have been in areas like textile and clothing, leather, ores and minerals, gems and jewellery, machine tools and parts aluminium, steel and steel products followed in the 1980s and 1990s by the automobiles and pharmaceutical boom. More recently not only is the government and Indian industry speaking of India as a manufacturing hub, but global corporates are demonstrating through their choice of sourcing of manufactures from India and location of manufacturing facilities here that they recognise the India advantage in a big way.

At the same time, Indian companies are making successful forays in the global market. There is product diversification into electronics, chemicals, engineering goods, fast moving consumer goods, power transmission and distribution equipments and components, automation products, telecom equipment, circuit breakers, power, automotive and medical electronics and industrial designs. The scales are much bigger though not anywhere near China's in some of these sectors. Apart from assembly and component production activities, Indian manufacturing has moved into higher value added and high-tech realms and is slowly but surely developing its own global brand equity.

However, this manufacturing success can only be sustained if some of the infrastructure bottlenecks and deficits in areas such as roads, railways, airports, ports, electricity and water can be removed and the cost of trade related infrastructure including finance and electricity can be brought down. Also, the interest in India as a manufacturing destination and source is on account of the lower cost and high quality of skilled and increasingly sophisticated manpower alongwith high quality entrepreneurship. In order to sustain and increase global cost and productivity advantages on account of this 'brainpower', engineering and science and technology education has to be augmented in a significant way. Also scaling up production to make India a candidate for significant global sourcing and entrepreneurial agility to adapt to changing global market requirements, will be crucial for India's acquisition of manufacturing brawn as well.

Services

India ranks among the top 12 developing countries in global trade in services. The recent dramatic spurt in India's trade is on account of the phenomenal growth and qualitative leap in services sector. Indian services exports grew by 17 per cent p.a. in 1990s, and 2004-05 services export earnings was $ 46 billion short of goods exports of $ 80 billion. Further, India is one of the largest recipients of inward remittances among developing countries, with projections of $ 30 billion in 2006.[21]

In 2005-06, India's BPO exports grew at 50-60 per cent per annum standing at $ 6.3 billion; they are projected to rise to $ 20 billion by 2007[22] and $ 25 billion by 2008.[23] Three positive trends need to be followed up. Firstly, there is movement up the value chain to knowledge process outsourcing including analytical work, research and development, consultancy and management. The second trend is reverse outsourcing by Indian companies to other countries such as Mauritius, Bangladesh, Uruguay, Hungary, China, UK and US including in order to supply to global markets. Job creation is rapid and gender positive.

---

21. Services exports are biased towards IT software: 20-30 per cent is business services, communications and banks, hotels and community services. India has captured 65 per cent of the global offshore IT market and 45 per cent of the BPO market. In 2003, India's exports of commercial services other than travel, transportation, and finance amounted to US$ 18.9 billion. The figure for China for the same year was US$ 20.6 billion. Services account for 51 per cent of India's GDP as compared to the 32 per cent share of the services sector in China's GDP. India's success in the services sector has largely been due to IT and IT-enabled services and more recently business process outsourcing.

22. Chanda, Rupa (2006). "Implications of Business Services for Development: Lessons for the GATS Negotiations", UNCTAD-OECD Workshop on Services, June.

23. The major segments of BPO and ITES markets in India are customer care, finance and accounting, human resource management, payment and administrative services, content development, engineering services, sales and legal services.

While India's greatest advantage is its large and ever increasing pool of English language skills, its disadvantage is that literacy rate is only 61 per cent. Beyond the Anglo-Saxon market, to tap the rich seams of French, Spanish, German, Portuguese, Japanese, Chinese, Russian and Arabic speaking markets, the considerable natural linguistic talent that Indians boast of must be cultivated consciously. Language training in some of these commercially important languages is a must, if India is to expand its services advantage especially into West Asia, Latin America and European Union and become a truly global services presence.

To ensure that its 'services success' is sustained and has broader social and economic impact, India would need to follow a four-fold policy. Firstly, basic services such as education, health, water, electricity and housing, etc. should be universally available. The second is to consider how it can build up supply capacity in other services sectors as is beginning to happen in the professional and financial services to some extent but also in the high potential tourism, audiovisual, education and health services sectors. In this regard, apart from the traditional modes of temporary movement of natural persons to deliver services abroad (Mode 4 of GATS) and more recently discovered strengths in Mode 1 (i.e., cross border supply of services or outsourcing), India could make better use of Mode 2 i.e., supplying services to visiting consumers as in health, education and tourism services and Mode 3, i.e., supply of services through investment abroad. The third is to deepen its comparative advantage in existing services sectors such as ICT so as to sustain its services export growth. This includes, aggressively using its cultural cache and status as the second biggest producer of films as well as programme software for TV to market its cultural services. The fourth aspect is to explore and deepen the interlinkages between the manufacturing and services sectors and ride on the synergies between the two.

Fostering a new geography of international trade

It is clear that any 2020 strategic vision for development of India's trade has to be based on reinforcing presence in major markets alongwith geographical diversification into new markets. This would in turn call for strengthening of old alliances and forging new ones. This does not mean taking the eyes off the ball in US and EU markets. They will remain global engines of trade and investment for some decades to come and India's complementarity with these economies will only grow. But there is slowing growth in these markets and stagnation in demand, ageing populations, fierce competition from other countries and new equations arising from India's larger *avatara* as a key importer and exporter of choice. This calls for India's strategic vision encompassing what has been termed the 'new geography of international trade'.[24]

For India, this means riding on the crest of a big new wave of South-South trade and investment flows, both regional and now increasingly interregional. Developing countries are beginning to individually and collectively carry more weight in each other's trade and investment calculus than ever before. UNCTAD studies show that intra developing country trade now accounts for 43 per cent of their total trade. Moreover, this new geography is also on account of developing countries becoming prime target markets and sources of imports for developed countries. In major developed country markets like USA and Japan, developing countries account for over 40 per cent of imports and exports, representing the fastest growing segment of trade in most areas. Though the picture is not the same in FDI flows, these too have begun to mimic trends in trade flows and the South as a home country for FDI is beginning to contribute to this new geoeconomics.

It is true that this phenomenon has been led by the trade dynamism of China—both as a importer and exporter with transcontinental outreach. But increasingly, India is seen as a key driver of the new geography with extant and potential value for both the Southern and Northern economies. The importance of this

---

24. In UNCTAD XI Conference, a segment was organised on "New Geography of International Trade: South-South Cooperation in an Increasingly Interdependent World", see TD/404, 4 June 2004 Eleventh Session, São Paulo, 13–18 June 2004. It was underscored that a new geography of trade is emerging, in which the South is moving steadily away from the periphery of the world economy and trade, reflecting changes in the traditional pattern of the international division of labour. This augurs well for trade to be able to play the role of a genuine locomotive for sustained economic growth, diversification, employment generation and poverty reduction in developing countries.

new geoeconomics is also reflected in the recalibration of India's trade priorities and performance and identification of thrust markets for the present and future.

India has reached a stage in its own trade and development trajectory that permits longstanding commitments to cooperation with the neighbourhood such as SAFTA being realised, along with initiatives with Central and West Asia. Since the 1990s, India invested considerable political capital in launching and implementing a successful 'Look East policy' targeting East and South-East Asian countries. Initiatives have included the Indo-ASEAN dialogue partnership, the East Asia Summit participation, BIMSTEC-FTA, Indo-Thai FTA and signing of India-Singapore FTA. With Japan, the upswing is expected to be sustained and with South Korea, there has been dramatic augmentation in trade and investment with even better prospects in the future. Australia and New Zealand are also potential trade and investment partners.

India's complementary approach to China in trade and investment is crucial, including from a futuristic perspective. Though often seen as a BRIC competitor for natural resources, markets and FDI, the 30-fold increase in trade in the past 10 years to reach over US $ 10 billion, shows that there is enough symbiosis. The trend towards increased cross border investment is also promising in areas ranging from electronics and consumer goods to IT, software and R&D.

Among the BRIC economies, Russia and Brazil have the necessary natural resources and capacity to fuel the growth and dynamism of the other two BRIC economies—China and India and provide the much needed raw materials for food, energy, water, building infrastructure and their continuing industrial revolution. Hence, fashioning strategic geopolitical and business arrangements with Russia and Brazil with renewed vigour, would be integral to India's ambitious 2020 trade and development mission. These two countries would also be crucial for technological collaboration and optimal absorption of Indian human resources, goods and services.

India has recognised the importance of further exploring the trade complementarity-competitiveness-continuum with Africa and

Latin America. Beyond slogans of Afro-Asian and Indo-African solidarity, Africa is emerging for India as a vital new frontier for trade and development symbiosis. India has rightly taken initiatives like cooperation with regional PTAs and economic integration groupings of Africa and Latin America and packages offering unilateral preferential access to African LDCs. Promotion of tri-continental cooperation like IBSA, among India, South Africa and Brazil and India-Mercosur-SACU FTA projects are positive steps. Pursuing interregional South-South trade through GSTP-driven trade liberalisation auspices will give a boost.[25] Crucial aspect of India-Africa and India-Latin America trade and investments links is the development of transport and shipping links and infrastructure.

India has a solid base to build its trade and investment relationship with Africa. India is Cameroon's biggest export destination for cotton and absorbs Senegal's entire phosphates output.[26] In Senegal, Indian investor Tata International has set up units for assembling buses for use and sale in domestic and regional markets. Further India is one of the United Republic of Tanzania's top five sources of imports, which includes pharmaceuticals, transport machinery, consumer goods, construction materials, textiles and iron and steel. India's biggest trade partner is South Africa and its trade links are growing with big economies like Nigeria as well with smaller ones in all parts of Africa.

By 2002 Indian enterprises had investments of $ 330 million in 43 projects in Egypt alone. Indian companies have chemical ventures in Morocco and Tanzania, copper mining in Zambia, oil in Mauritius and Madagascar and telecommunications and textiles in Malawi. India is also the third largest source of foreign direct investment in Uganda. In 2003, ONGC investments in Sudan amounted to US$ 1.6 billion and a US$ 1 billion investment in Ivory Coast's oil sector

---

25. The third round of GSTP trade negotiations were launched by G77 ministers and China in São Paulo, under UNCTAD auspices. See "Developing Countries Launch New Round of Trade Negotiations", UNCTAD/PRESS/PR/SPA/2004/010.

26. Reisen, Helmut (2005). "Asia's Growing Presence in the Global Economy: What's in it for Africa", prepared for the workshop *China and World Economic Development: A View from Latin America and Other Emerging Markets*, held at the ABCDE Conference on 23 May.

has been announced. In the pharmaceutical sector, given high HIV infected populations in both countries Indian companies are working with South African pharmaceutical firms to supply cheap anti-retroviral medicines.

In spite of various constraints, India's trade with the Latin American region during the last few years has been growing rapidly. It increased from US$ 560 million in 1993-94 to US$ 3 billion in 2003-04, registering an increase of more than 430 per cent in 10 years.[27] In the Latin-American relationship, Brazil is the centrepiece with Indo-Brazil trade estimated to be US$ 3 billion this year and major investments in petroleum, transport, IT, sugar and pharmaceutical sectors being announced. The India- Mercosur PTA will provide a further impetus.

Diversifying into new and dynamic sectors of trade

India faces stiff competition from developed and developing countries in global markets in respect of its traditional agricultural, manufacturing and services exports. It faces a fallacy of composition and decreasing returns. India, therefore, needs to continually adopt strategies and policies to build supply capacity and competitiveness and seek enhanced market access to move into what UNCTAD calls new and dynamic sectors of international trade.[28] These are sectors and product groups growing faster than average and including both the most dynamic and high value and volume products as well as new, niche products growing at a fast pace. India is among the top 20 developing countries active in new and dynamic sectors and product groups. Those with considerable potential for India are categories of textiles and garments including tech-textiles, electronics, medical and diagnostic equipments, marine products, horticultural and organic products, renewable energy equipments and biodiversity and traditional knowledge products. More focussed

---

27. Website of the Ministry of Commerce, India.

28. In UNCTAD XI Conference in June 2004 a key policy issue discussed was 'strengthening participation of developing countries in dynamic and new sectors of world trade: Trends, issues and policies'. This has since become an important component of UNCTAD's work programme. See TD/396, 17 May 2004, Eleventh Session, São Paulo, 13–18 June 2004.

attention to horizontal, vertical and diagonal product diversification to increase returns to scale through product differentiation, value addition and technological edge is required in trade strategies.

Capitalising on human resources and skills build-up

For India, developing and gainfully absorbing its enormous human capital, is a strategic trade and development priority. These are linked to the vital goals of demographic management, educational and training capacity building, poverty eradication, employment generation and gender equity. India currently accounts for 16 per cent of the global population, it may run the risk of being the most populous country in the world with the working population peaking in 2020. The youthful profile of its population (60 per cent between the ages of 15-40 years) poses both a challenge and an opportunity depending on how the quantity and low effective cost of labour is turned into quality in terms of education and skills acquisition. Vocational, specialised and technical training including through trade and investment will help equip the abundant labour force with necessary skill sets and in turn give a competitive edge.

Again, this educated labour force would need to find employment either within the country or outside.[29] India's growth rate itself is not sufficient to ensure jobs for its youthful population. This will require that India receive FDI in labour intensive, educational skill building and job creating sectors. Opening up of foreign markets for Indian workers and for its labour intensive exports of goods and services will also be critical.

Becoming an innovation node

To sustain any kind of trade growth, it is important for a country to have a strong science and technology base from which to work and innovate. Whereas India does have a reasonably strong educational and technology base, it needs to be further developed

---

29. In the period 1993 to 2004 unemployment rates increased from 5.6 per cent to 9 per cent in rural areas and from 6.7 per cent to 8.1 per cent in urban areas. However, the bulk of the employment is still generated by the informal sector. A 10 per cent growth across the board is needed to create the 50 million jobs that India requires.

and expanded. India has one of the largest and most diversified networks of state supported R&D institutions and centres of excellence. Every year, 12 million people graduate, out of which 25,000 are Ph.D. degree holders. But considering the size of its population and needs, this is a small fraction and if India is to be a skills, R&D and innovation platform in the global economy and trade, there has to be a significant ramping up of this capacity.

There are three kinds of technologies that India will have to cultivate and master urgently to be ahead in the trade and development race. The first category of commercially viable industrial technology needs to be updated for application in industries such as pharmaceuticals, textiles, chemicals, agroprocessing, heavy machinery and power generation. Secondly, frontier technologies such as biotechnology, nanotechnology, space and satellites, robotics, etc. would give India the desired innovation edge in many sectors and applications of these can earn ever higher returns from product specialisation, upgradation and royalties from patents and transfer of technology. Thirdly, a more basic kind of 'living technology' such as those providing simple but effective solutions for problems on a large or small scale for rural or poorer areas of the country and the developing world at large, like solar electrification, water pumps and purifiers would have a multiplier effect in terms of improving the quality of the life of the poor people and open up the vast 'markets of the poor'[30] in India and elsewhere. An investment will have to be made in providing access to such technologies and research facilities in rural areas so that those who face problems are better motivated and equipped to provide solutions. Given the geographical size and differences, as well as the lack of capital and to some extent political will in the past, the third kind of technology essential for grassroots development has to be given due importance in any far sighted technology, as well as trade and FDI policy.

---

30. Prahalad, C.K. (2005). *The Fortune at the Bottom of the Pyramid: Eradicating Poverty through Profits,* Wharton School Publishing.

Given that innovation is as labour intensive as it was in the past if not more, and the quality of labour inputs in India has improved, India is well placed to partner foreign capital in its search for cost quality competitive and integrated R&D resource platforms. Today India, is considered globally as an important source of R&D capacity, particularly by US and European MNCs which have set up R&D operations in India. The spin offs of such offshoring of R&D to India can be significant. But it is also equally important to develop endogenous R&D and technological wealth. Ways will also have to be found to increase access to either government held or commercially held dual use technologies, some of which are presently out of bounds for India. Becoming part of major developed country government financed multinational R&D projects is another important avenue for building innovation capacity and accessing state of the art technologies. The bargaining power of Indian R&D labour force in sharing the fruits of innovation is increasing due to the advantages they provide and the democratisation of enabling technologies such as IT. Participation in the global 24-hour knowledge factories provides another opportunity to marry India's manpower with its brainpower for maximum trade and investment benefit.

Powering the economy and trade—search for energy security

For India, access to cheap and regular energy sources is of paramount importance, not only for economic progress and trade growth but sheer survival. The choice is between crippling dependency and energy security. As one of the largest and fastest growing economies and populations, its energy needs are burgeoning and its access to affordable energy sources through trade and investment is essential not only to sustain economic growth but also to provide universal access to certain essential services such as electricity and water. Industrialisation has pushed up energy demand, placing India on par with China among the biggest energy guzzlers in the world. This in addition to political and other factors, has pushed up world energy prices and intensified the scramble for conventional energy sources like oil and gas, thus making it all the more important to secure energy sources for the future.

India has to follow a multipronged energy strategy, which includes FDI in oil and gas exploration, intensifying search and tapping domestic sources, including in the ocean. The second is acquiring oil and gas assets abroad in Africa, Asia, Latin America, and Russia through investments in foreign oil companies or entering into long-term arrangements. A third aspect of this multipronged approach has to be the development and commercialisation of new, alternative and renewable energy sources such as solar energy, biofuels, water and hydroelectricity. The strategy has therefore to be a mix of trade, FDI and transfer of technology instruments and policies and the international trading system has to be conducive to its pursuit.

Greening of growth through trade and investment

Another sustainability issue for India, given its geographical, wildlife and vegetation diversity and population pressure on natural resources is how to meet both economic and environmental objectives in the context of its agriculture and manufacturing practices and development strategies. India has to incorporate environmentally friendly trade and investment practices without compromising on its essential economic growth. In this regard, both China and India have raised anxieties on the environment front. These relate to water, air and soil pollution, carbon dioxide emission and climate change, deforestation and desertification as well as environmental concerns that arise from demographic growth and urbanisation.

Whilst switching to environment friendly production and trade is a challenge for India, it can also provide trade and investment opportunities arising from their global and long term impact. Whilst India encourages FDI and joint ventures with global companies in order to achieve commercialisation, scale and scope and transfer of technology, it would have to institute systems to ensure that these activities are environmentally compatible and serve both commercial and sustainable development objectives.

India will require to import environmental goods, services and technology for conversion to environmental friendly production processes and practices in agriculture and manufacturing. Further, it can tap into the export business opportunity in environmental friendly and environmentally preferable products and services such as renewable energy products, solar energy devices, windmills, biofuels as well as natural and organic products, which are experiencing greater acceptance and demand in international markets. In addition, there is a need to explore international environmental agreements to determine how they can be best used to India's advantage, as for example the Clean Development Mechanism, under the Kyoto Protocol on Climate Change.

India and the multilateral trading system

Achieving ambitious targets for a country recognised as one of the largest, fastest growing and rapidly liberalising markets would involve a complex interplay of domestic policies and measures as much as strategic and catalytic intervention in the international trading regime. It is, therefore, necessary to identify the main features of the evolving international trading system (ITS), in terms of current and potential strategic interests and the 'new age economic diplomacy' that India will have to pursue in order to realise its objectives.

The ITS consists of the GATT/WTO based multilateral trading system (MTS) and over 300 RTAs and BTAs that now cover over 50 per cent of world trade. The centrepiece of the ITS for India is, and will probably remain, for sometime, the MTS. Firmly anchored in the MTS with most favoured nation (MFN) treatment as its hallmark, India has been a founder member of both GATT (1948) and WTO (1995). It is only recently that India has converted to negotiating some RTAs/FTAs mainly in Asia, in the face of layers of preferentiality against it in most markets.

Considering that a number of important Asian, Latin American and African economies are queuing to sign FTAs with US and EU, India's main platform for regulating its trade with these economies will remain the WTO unless it too seeks special trading arrangements with these two trading giants. The main objective of any FTA with them should not be duty and quota free treatment. Instead, the prime consideration would be to get a resolution on the NTBs that Indian exporters and producers face in these markets, as well as significant and preferential market access for its human resources exports, mutual recognition of degrees and qualifications of scientists and professionals and substantial cooperation in trade related infrastructure building, including standard setting and conformance.

India's role in shaping the trade liberalisation and rule making agenda has progressively grown over the eight rounds of multilateral trade negotiations (MTNs) of GATT/WTO. Beginning with token representation in the first few rounds and modest engagement in the Tokyo Round in 1977-1979, it has been a long road to an active role in the formative period before and during the Uruguay Round (1981-1994) and a decisive, 'high table' role in the Doha Round from 2000 onwards. This progression mirrors the incremental growth in India's trade related capacities and interests and the deepening and widening of the trading regime itself. Even before India's true trade potential was recognised, it tended to play a leadership role on behalf of developing countries and exercise influence beyond its actual trade weight.

Its limited engagement in the earlier phase of MTNs was due to three factors. Firstly, as a relatively small trading entity it had nothing much at stake. Secondly, its relatively closed import substitution model of trade and development policy meant that India was keen to maintain as much protection for its agriculture industry and services sectors as possible and shelter them from reciprocal demands in the request–offer process of MTNs. At the same time, India sought to get preferential market access, particularly for its manufactured exports into developed country markets through other means. Thirdly, US, UK, France and other major trading nations typically took the lead in driving the GATT/WTO agenda, letting developing countries be relatively passive members with lesser commitments but also lesser voice and benefits from the regime. This put even countries like India in a reactive and defensive mode for much of the time, being able to push their 'positive agenda' forward in the negotiations only some of the time.

However, India's activism both in UNCTAD and GATT led to the adoption of certain principles and legal instruments that contributed to the conceptual mainstreaming of the development dimension in the MTS. India worked hard during the Second UNCTAD Conference in New Delhi in 1968 to get the basic principles of preferential market access and treatment to developing countries accepted. This led in 1979 to the adoption of the enabling clause (EC) permitting developed countries to derogate from the MFN principle and grant differential and more favourable treatment to developing countries (DMFT or S&D). The generalised system of preferences (GSP) based on the principles of non-reciprocity, non-discrimination, generalised and unconditional nature was instituted. India has been among the principal beneficiaries of GSP schemes.

The EC also provided what to India has been an article of faith, namely, that DMFT should 'respond positively' to the development, financial and trade needs of developing countries. Further, it was clarified that developed countries shall not seek or require developing countries to make concessions that are inconsistent with the latter's trade, development and financial needs. This translated into non-reciprocity and growth of policy space or flexibilities to developing countries in the form of exemptions, longer transition periods and even freedom to join an agreement or not. Also special consideration was given to South-South preferential liberalisation and to measures directed towards LDCs. All these variations of the DMFT/S&D provisions have been used by India at different stages.

Up to the Uruguay Round, the GATT disciplines encompassed border measures—tariffs and quotas on goods, alongwith some codes such as subsidies. Agriculture, textiles and clothing represented derogations or carve outs from GATT disciplines at the insistence of developed countries. An attempt was made by India in the Uruguay Round to end the discriminatory textile quota regime against developing countries and only a 10-year back loaded phase out process could be won. On agriculture, scant progress was made on the issue of phasing out trade distorting subsidies but it remained an unfinished business to be taken up both as a pretext and a *raison d'être* of the Doha Round. India with its defensive agriculture agenda was not so engaged on this issue. It was content to contribute moderately to tariff liberalisation in agriculture and manufactures.

On services, after strongly resisting in the beginning, India worked to evolve a General Agreement on Trade in Services (GATS) architecture which would provide for 'progressive liberalisation', with countries having the option of scheduling as many services sectors for liberalisation with as many conditions as they wished. Whilst the US and EU as major *demandeurs* obtained some concessions from developing countries on financial and telecommunication services and in defining the three main modes of delivery of services, it was India, alongwith some other developing countries that managed to introduce Mode 4, i.e., temporary movement of natural persons to supply services, into the GATS market access framework. This remains India's main 'positive agenda' in GATS negotiations.

The creation of the WTO as a 'single undertaking' with some 23 multilateral trade agreements covering not only border measures but also 'within the border issues' marked a systemic departure point. Frameworks for services sector liberalisation and work and disciplines in new areas such as Trade Related Intellectual Property Rights (TRIPS), Trade Related Investment Measures (TRIMs) and trade related environmental issues along with a slew of updated and strengthened rules in areas such as customs valuation, anti-dumping, subsidies, sanitary and phyto-sanitary (SPS) measures, technical barriers to trade (TBT) and dispute settlement were instituted.

This has meant that WTO norms now have an unprecedented say in India's domestic economic policy choices. These include what and how Indian industry, agriculture and services sectors produce, how investment, technology, environment and public interest issues interface with production and trade and in what ways the government can and cannot support and protect domestic operators from outside competition and act in public interest. On dispute settlement, India has made good use of the strengthened DSM but it had also had to be a defendant in some crucial cases.

Particularly noteworthy has been India's resistance to the comprehensive and high standards intellectual property protection regime that TRIPs brought in, on grounds of transfer and diffusion of technology and public interest. Apart from getting some flexibility reflected in clauses relating to government use, compulsory licensing and 'best endeavour' on transfer of technology, India had to content itself with winning a 10-year transition period for protection of product patents in pharmaceuticals which allowed a competitive generic medicine industry to flourish and thus ensure access to affordable medicines for its citizens. This cause was, however, later followed up by India in the Doha negotiations with a declaration on TRIPS and Public Health in 2000 and the recent amendment to TRIPS Agreement in 2005-06.

In the Doha negotiations, which India reluctantly joined in launching in 2000, apart from the market access agenda in relation to agriculture, industrial tariffs and services, there is the unfinished business of reform of agricultural trade, principally through the reduction and elimination of all trade distorting subsidies by developed countries, particularly the EU and US. There was a conditional agreement to explore disciplines on the so-called Singapore issues of trade facilitation, investment, competition policy and government procurement. After successive ministerial meetings, only trade facilitation agenda remains from the Singapore issues and the focus has been mainly on agriculture trade reform and liberalisation, non-agriculture market access (NAMA) and services liberalisation and rule making, and in some respects on more effective and operational S&D treatment.

The fate of the Doha negotiations hangs on a balance principally on account of the refusal of the major participants to take the necessary steps in the agriculture area. However, from India's pespective, even the existing body of rules, the progress in liberalisation, and institutional security represented by the WTO are important. India's key interest in the WTO can best be described as upholding an open, non-discriminatory, predictable, rule based and equitable multilateral trading system. It needs openness not only in its traditional developed country markets but also in relation to its 'new geography partners'. Its main market access interests are in markets where its agricultural and manufactured products face high tariffs, tariff escalation and peaks. However, with progressive global reduction in tariffs, non-tariff measures such as stringent and frequently changing and unilaterally imposed product standards and technical barriers and regulations as well as anti-competitive practices have become front stage barriers that need to be addressed in any future negotiations.[31]

In services, India now has a very strong positive agenda particularly in regard to synergistic export of both labour intensive and knowledge intensive services. For this, the Doha Round and its successors must deliver significant opening up in Mode 4 and Mode 1. This would provide full opportunity to reap development gains from the marriage between the range of skills India has to offer with requirements of the global, agricultural, industrial and services economy, the 24-hour 'knowledge factory' and science and technology related global public good. In terms of its cultural services exports too, it should seek better market access through all Modes of delivery, whilst protecting the intellectual property of its traditional knowledge, like yoga, ayurveda and biodiversity products, cuisine, music, dance, arts and crafts etc., and reaping commercial benefits from them.

Obviously, there is expectation that India would in turn also open up its own markets since it is regarded as one of most protected yet attractive ones. In agriculture, India is likely to need to be somewhat protective in selective sensitive product areas for sometime and insistent that developed country trade distorting subsidisation should end. But in the medium term, its own food security related import requirements and need to develop export competitiveness in selected agro industrial areas may impel opening up to foreign trade and investment and global distribution/retail networks and

---

31. See for instance, UNCTAD (2005) *Report of the Expert Meeting on Methodologies, Classification, Quantification and Development Impacts of Non-Tariff Barriers*, TD/B/COM.1/EM.27/3.

supply chains. In manufactures, India is already moving towards rationalised and much lower tariffs. In services too, autonomous liberalisation is moving apace and it is a question of locking this in to multilateral commitments.

Overall, India may benefit from linking up its economic reform, autonomous liberalisation to the WTO processes. WTO disciplines could catalyse the domestic reform agenda and in turn, economic reform imperatives inspire India's shaping of these disciplines, while helping the accrual of credits and reciprocal concessions from other trading partners. Moreover, firms and import sectors affected by own liberalisation will need to be enabled to adjust with minimum socioeconomic costs and dislocation through well targeted and financed adjustment schemes.

A major challenge for Indian economic and trade diplomacy in the context of growing trade and investment capacity, profile and ambition is, how to reposition India in the spectrum of WTOs framework of rights and obligations and its future agenda. On one hand India is being asked to assume more obligations on par with OECD countries, on the grounds that its size, diversified supply capacity and large volume and value of trade, put in the category of 'advanced developing country' with little need for preferential treatment and policy space. On the other hand, its low per capita income, high levels of poverty and continued need to take measures towards public provisioning of goods and services to the poor and foster particular regions, communities and sectors that require retaining development policy flexibility and preferential access.

There are similar dilemmas with regard to exploiting India's growing technology stature and R&D capabilities. Its requirements for reaping rewards through intellectual property protection of technologies and audiovisual works, and extending such protection to traditional knowledge are well recognised. However, such protections have to be balanced with the need for continuing innovation through reengineering and wider technology diffusion especially for the masses. Its own IPR laws have to reflect this balance but in fora like the WTO and WIPO too, India will have to carefully articulate the interests of an increasingly R&D and technology capable developing economy with vast needs of 'technology immersion'.

Another challenge for Indian trade diplomacy will be to combat the scare scenarios coming up in major markets about the 'manpower threat', the spectre of 'job switching' and the 'outsourcing bogeyman' connected with India's perceived human resources and 'knowledge power' related success. The fear among some developed countries is that not only is India soaking up blue collar and some lower end, white-collar jobs but is also capturing the high-tech and high-skilled jobs from their developed country counterparts. In addition, security provides an ubiquitous and unchallengeable excuse for erecting barriers against both outsourcing of services to India and allowing Indian labour to move even temporarily to deliver services in developed markets. Efforts, therefore, will have to be deployed to pursue Mode 4 liberalisation in WTO and through bilateral deals, when necessary. India should also try to keep the so-called trade related labour standards agenda of the WTO legislative calendar. Otherwise, it could well block Indian objective to get further recognition for labour factor mobility in the context of freer, fairer and more equitable multilateral trading system.

Considering that India is aggressively exporting capital for acquisition of energy, mineral and agricultural assets, it would be important to reassess the need for a multilateral agreement on investment in the WTO as a complement to BIPAs with target countries. There may also be need for disciplines on anti-competitive practices of global enterprises such as abuse of dominance of market power, cartels, and transfer pricing in own markets and those faced by Indian enterprises and investors in export markets to ensure 'true' contestability of markets. Whilst the latest competition legislation adopted in India will help, the right kind of disciplines in the WTO on anti-competitive practices could also benefit India. India's bidding for international, publicly-financed projects, including in ICT area, would also call for WTO norms on transparency, fairness and increased market access to be revisited.

The proliferation of quality, technical, health, safety and environmental standards on the whole range of goods, and procedural, visa, technical and qualification requirements for services exported by developing countries like India are both a competitive challenge and an opportunity. Since India is mainly a standard-taker and not a standard-maker, it is vulnerable to the vagaries of developed country governments and big buyers dictating specifications of what is to be supplied irrespective of its necessity or validity. Such non-tariff barriers have the effect of negating tariff liberalisation and trade openness, are discriminatory and render the trading system more unpredictable and iniquitous. If on the other hand, India can increasingly involve itself in international standard setting and network of mutual recognition agreements, work for further clarifying the rather loose disciplines in SPS and TBT and GATS Agreements of WTO, it would be a big winner. Building credible and comprehensive conformity assessment, testing and certification systems, and seeking removal of procedural and technical bottlenecks for services exports are other pre-requisites.

Conclusion

Building on the positives of its economic achievements and policy evolution, India is indeed poised to live up to its own ambitions and the expectations of the world, in assuming its due place in the front rank of trading nations. The challenges are many. However, the arrows that it has in its trade and development quiver are many and potent as well and can help India hit the target. Indian policy makers and economic actors will have to increasingly realise that domestic policies can no longer be made in isolation from global opportunities, constraints and systemic requirements. Indian diplomacy will have to be front footed in seeking and cultivating every new opportunity and market to push and develop dynamically, India's comparative advantages. Whilst strengthening and strongly influencing the WTO in the light of its short and long-term interests, India may need to selectively enter into special trade and investment alliances—formal or informal with major and emerging partners. The make or break issues for India's trade and development success are human resources development and absorption, mastery and diffusion of technology, infrastructure sufficiency and upgradation, regional and social equity and most importantly energy and food security. Conversely, foreign trade, investment and transfer of technology alongwith the rules of the game set in WTO and elsewhere, can be crucial for achieving these goals. This synergy represents a vital task for Indian foreign policy calling for a creative and sustained endeavour to reach the perfect vision of 2020.

54

Oil diplomacy for India's energy security

Talmiz Ahmad

Energy is the fuel that drives the economy and provides nations with the annual growth rates essential for their economic development. This stark fact has led most countries to attach the greatest importance to 'energy security': this simply means the assured and, where possible, exclusive access to energy resources at affordable prices to obtain sustainable economic growth rates and national economic development.

Most of the world's energy comes from hydrocarbons (oil and gas) which account for 65 per cent of the world's energy requirements. While oil accounts for 42 per cent in the global energy mix, the other sources of global energy are: coal (24 per cent), natural gas (22 per cent), nuclear energy (6 per cent) and renewable and non-conventional sources (7 per cent). World energy demand increased by 95 per cent over the last 30 years and is expected to rise by 60 per cent over the next 20 years. During this period, the demand for oil will increase by 42 per cent while the demand for gas will increase by 97 per cent.

In recent years, the most significant development in the consumption of hydrocarbon fuels is the increase in Asian demand: over the last few decades, between 1970-1994, Asian energy demand increased by 400 per cent, with demand for oil increasing by 274 per cent, world demand growth during this period was only 63 per cent. Now, Asian requirement of oil is expected to increase from 30 million barrels per day currently to 130 million barrels per day in 2020.

The bulk of this increase will be accounted for by China and India, together responsible for 35 per cent in the world's incremental consumption of energy. China's consumption has been increasing at the rate of 5 per cent per annum. A country, which was self-sufficient in hydrocarbons till 1993, will be importing 40 per cent of its requirements by 2010; 10 years later, in 2020, its consumption of oil will be 9.5 million barrels per day, with import dependency being well over 60 per cent. Today, China is the world's second largest energy consumer, while India ranks sixth.

Global oil scenario

Let us take a look at the supply side. World oil reserves are estimated at 1.35 trillion barrels; they are 2.3 trillion barrels if oil sands and shales are taken into account. The Gulf provides the bulk of the world's oil: just five countries of the Gulf (Saudi Arabia, Iraq, Iran, Kuwait and the UAE) have about 70 per cent of the world's reserves. By 2020, this region will produce 55.5 million barrels per day, a two-and-a-half times increase over 1991. The share of Gulf oil exports in world export will increase from 42 per cent in 1995 to 59 per cent in 2020. Not surprisingly, world dependence on Gulf oil is likely to increase significantly. This is particularly true in respect of Asia: Asian countries already depend upon the Gulf for 75-80 per cent of their requirements. China, which got 53 per cent of its oil from the Gulf in 2000, will obtain 80 per cent in 2010.

The other significant sources of international oil are the Caspian Sea region and Western and Central Africa. The Caspian region came to international attention in the context of hydrocarbons only after the break-up of the Soviet Union. In the early 1990s, US reports had dramatically suggested that the Caspian basin reserves were around 200 billion barrels and, with appropriate investment and exploitation, this region could even rival the Gulf. However, as the 1990s progressed, more moderate assessments emerged. The IEA suggests that proven Caspian oil reserves are between 15-40 billion barrels, while possible reserves are between 70-150 billion barrels.

Thus, this region is not expected to provide production beyond 5 per cent of world demand in 2020.

Similarly, Sub-Saharan Africa, with Nigeria as the traditional producer and with new discoveries in Angola, Sudan, Ivory Coast, Chad, Equatorial Guinea and Ghana, accounts for 12 per cent of world production but has just 8.3 per cent of world reserves. Sub-Saharan output is expected to increase from 3.8 million barrels per day to 6.8 million barrels per day in 2008, and to 9 million barrels per day in 2030.

Natural gas

Natural gas, being a 'clean' fuel, is increasingly seen as the fuel of the 21st Century. Between 1980 and 2003, the share of gas in the world energy mix rose from 18 per cent to 22 per cent. The demand for gas is expected to increase at 2.4 per cent per annum till 2020, when it will constitute 25 per cent of the world energy mix and consolidate its position as the number two fuel in the world's energy mix. Since 1980, proven world gas reserves have increased at 3.6 per cent per annum, with volume tripling from 77 trillion cm to 179 trillion cm in 2004.

Over the next 25 years, the energy requirements of Asia are expected to increase two-and-a-half times, an increase of an additional 2-2.5 billion tonnes oil equivalent (toe). Gas will have a significant place in this scenario. At present, Asia has much less share in gas demand than the world average, (6 per cent *versus* 12 per cent). Hence, to meet Asia's rapidly increasing energy requirements, consumption of gas will have to increase; the expectation is that it will do so from 210 M toe in 1997, through 600 M toe in 2020, to 800-900 M toe in 2030. In short, natural gas demand growth in Asia will be between 5-10 per cent per annum, depending on the state of the economy, about double the growth in oil demand.

The principal sources of global gas also lie in Asia. The Asian area of Russia has 27 per cent of the world's proven reserves, followed by Iran (15 per cent) and Qatar (14 per cent). In fact, North and Central Asia and the Gulf between them have over 70 per cent of world reserves. As against this, the principal consumers of Asia-China, Japan, Republic of Korea and India—together have less than 2 per cent of global reserves, with Japan and Korea having no reserves at all. At the same time, in 2004, the latter two countries imported just over 100 billion cubic metres of gas as LNG as against a total global LNG trade of 178 billion cubic metres. The principal supplier to Western Europe is Russia: Russia is already the largest supplier of gas to Europe; by 2030, it will meet 50 per cent of Europe's needs.

On the supply side, the prognosis relating to gas is quite comfortable: present resources can meet current demand for 60 years. With new discoveries, reserves could meet demand for 150 years at present rate of consumption.

Today, out of the total gas production of 2691 billion cu. m., only 25 per cent is internationally traded, 19 per cent being transported through transnational pipelines and 6 per cent as LNG. Europe is the principal importer of gas by pipeline (320 billion cu. m. p.a.), followed by USA(102 billion cu. m., from Canada). Japan is the principal importer of LNG (76.95 billion cu. m.), followed by Europe (40 billion cu. m.), Republic of Korea (30 billion cu. m) and USA (19 billion cu. m.). According to industry forecasts, international trade in natural gas is expected to increase significantly in coming years, accounting for one-third of world output, by 2020. This increased trade will cover both LNG and piped gas. International trade in LNG is expected to grow by 7 per cent p.a. till it becomes 38 per cent of gas trade by 2020.

The USA is expected to emerge as a major buyer of LNG, with terminal capacity reaching 140 billion cu. m. after the completion of 10 new terminals. Piped gas carried by transnational pipelines will grow to become 50 per cent of international trade by 2020.

The problem pertaining to gas is not with the reserves; it has to do with the need for fresh investments over the medium-term to develop new fields, albeit in the traditional areas where production in the old fields is declining. It is estimated that investments of about $ 1-1.2 trillion would be required over the next 10 years to develop the potential to meet global requirements.

The Indian hydrocarbon scene

The *Hydrocarbon Vision 2025*, published by the Government of India in February 2000, set out in stark terms India's energy security predicament: its crude oil self-sufficiency declined from 63 per cent in 1989-90 to 30 per cent in 2000-01. The situation is only likely to get worse in the future: India's demand for oil is expected to increase from 122 million tonnes in 2001-02 to 196 million tonnes in 2011-2012, and 364 million tonnes in 2024-25. Domestic production during this period would increase from 26 million tonnes to 52 million tonnes in 2011-12, and to 80 million tonnes in 2024-25. In 2024-25, crude oil self-sufficiency would be a mere 15 per cent.

The situation relating to gas is equally grim. From 49 billion cu. m. in 2006-07, India's demand for gas is expected to rise to 125 billion cu. m. in 2024-25. As against this, production from existing fields and discoveries is 52 billion cu. m., leaving a gap of 75 billion cu. m. to be filled through new domestic discoveries and from imports.

Nuclear power in India's energy security

One of the important aspects of the recent Indo-US nuclear agreement is the emphasis it has placed on the development of nuclear energy to generate power in India. Many commentators have rightly pointed out that nuclear energy has the potential to meet India's energy requirements over the long term: indeed, after 2050, if all goes well, India could generate so much electric power from nuclear energy that its dependence on other energy sources would significantly come down.

Unfortunately, this enthusiasm for nuclear energy has led to some degree of confusion with regard to the actual place of nuclear energy in our power generation scenario over the next 25 years. The Kirit Parikh Report has set out the issues quite clearly: India needs sustained growth of 8 per cent p.a. up to 2031 to pull increasing numbers of its people out of the poverty trap. To achieve this, its primary energy supply has to increase 3-4 times, and electricity supply has to increase nearly seven times, i.e., power generation would have to increase from 123,015 MW today to 778, 095 MW in 2031-32. The report again correctly states that in order to achieve these ambitious targets, India would need to pursue all available fuel options and energy forms, both conventional and non-conventional.

Let us take a look at the global scene. In 2003, nuclear power plants provided 16 per cent of world electricity production. Countries with a share of nuclear power of over 40 per cent of total power produced are: France 78 per cent; Belgium 55 per cent; Sweden 50 per cent; and Republic of Korea 40 per cent. In the United States, nuclear power stations' share in total electricity production is 20 per cent.

Globally, in 2030, fossil fuels (coal, oil and gas) will dominate the energy mix to the extent of 72 per cent. Their share is expected to come down slightly in 2050, to 55 per cent, with an anticipated increase in the share of biomass and other renewables (35 per cent). The share of nuclear energy, 5.2 per cent in 2030, will increase to only 11 per cent in 2050.

Today, India's energy mix is: coal 50 per cent; oil and gas 45 per cent; hydropower 2 per cent; and nuclear 1.5 per cent. In 2022, fossil fuels will continue to dominate India's energy mix to the extent of 75 per cent, with hydropower providing 14 per cent, and nuclear power 6.5 per cent. Even robust votaries of nuclear power in India have noted that, most optimistically, nuclear energy will provide only 8.8 per cent in India's energy mix in 2032, as against 76 per cent for fossil fuels, and 12 per cent for hydropower. In 2052, when nuclear energy is likely to be 16.4 per cent of our energy mix, coal is expected to be 40 per cent; hydrocarbons 35 per cent; and hydropower 5.1 per cent.

It is important to note that the significant increase in the share of nuclear power in our energy mix from 2032 to 2052 is premised on the successful implementation of the three-stage nuclear power programme of the Atomic Energy Commission (AEC). First conceived in 1958, so far only the first stage has been completed, with the second stage (involving the development of Fast Breeder Reactors) having commenced in October, last year.

The importance of the recent nuclear agreement lies in the fact that India would partner the principal nuclear energy producing countries in the development of a frontier technology to obtain renewable energy on long-term basis. Nuclear power technology will become technologically and commercially viable only after 2030. During this period, we will have to grapple with complex issues pertaining to: availability of raw materials of the desired quality, quantity and price; technologies relating to reactors and ancillary equipment; and safety and waste-disposal issues.

For the next 25 years at least, fossil fuels will dominate our energy requirements. In an otherwise unpropitious domestic and international environment, we will have to ensure that our energy security interests are fully safeguarded so that we can achieve the projected growth rates to pull millions of our people out of poverty. How this can be done is central to India's 'oil diplomacy'.

India's oil diplomacy

To meet the challenge of energy security, the *Vision 2025* document has set out an elaborate action plan for the acquisition of hydrocarbon resources required by the country to meet its economic requirements. It provides for a robust effort to expand domestic production of oil and gas through the liberalisation of the oil sector, encouragement to the entry of private Indian and foreign companies, investments in technology and R&D, and so on.

An important component of this effort is the external dimension which constitutes the area of India's 'oil diplomacy': this consists of substantial, robust and multifaceted engagements across the world to promote India's energy security interests. These overseas engagements are aimed at promoting the following:

a) Significant enhancement of domestic resources and capabilities by bringing in state-of-the-art foreign technology and expanding the national knowledge-base.

b) Acquisition of assets abroad; these are of two types:

    i) equity participation in producing fields; and

    ii) exploration and production (E&P) contracts in different parts of the world, both onshore and offshore.

c) Participation in downstream projects (refineries and petrochemicals) in producer and consumer countries on the basis of criss-cross investments.

d) Finalisation of long-term LNG contracts.

e) Setting up of transnational gas pipelines.

The contemporary international hydrocarbon environment is highly competitive, pitting corporations and nations against each other in ruthless contention, and involving billions of dollars of financial flows and, on occasion, even extra-legal skulduggery. At the same time, this is also a period of unprecedented opportunity, with high oil prices opening up exploration and production prospects and compelling producer and consumer countries to pursue investments in the downstream sector. India's long-term interests lie in putting together alliances and partnerships that would bring together different capabilities in joint proposals.

The Petroleum Ministry, over the last year, has engaged across the globe carrying the message of partnership and synergy in place of wasteful and unnecessary contention. Some of its significant interactions have been with the Gulf countries, particularly Saudi Arabia; Russia; the Central Asian countries of Kazakhstan, Uzbekistan and Azerbaijan; and Turkey and Romania, that constitute a link between Central Asia and Europe. Other engagements have included: Norway, Nigeria, Angola, some Latin American countries, and most recently, China. These diplomatic engagements have confirmed that the countries concerned are anxious to cooperate and that they see in India a worthy partner, given its human, capital and technical capabilities.

The proposed cooperation ranges across the hydrocarbon value chain, and includes prospecting in each other's territories, as also exchanges in regard to R&D, technology, safety norms and training.

Beyond the bilateral aspect, it includes the possibility of Indian and foreign national companies working together on specific projects in third countries, particularly in the Gulf, the Caspian area, Africa and Latin America.

Interactions with China, Saudi Arabia, Norway, Nigeria and some other countries illustrate the range and depth of India's bilateral hydrocarbon engagements.

The Petroleum Minister's visit to China in January 2006, was the result of preparations over one year. During the Round Table of Asian Oil Ministers, the Chinese delegate had spoken of the "great potential of cooperation" among Asian countries "in terms of increasing oil supply capacity and safeguarding regional oil security." In April 2005, the Indian and Chinese Prime Ministers stated in their Joint Statement that the two countries would "cooperate in the field of energy security and conservation" and that the organisations of the two countries would also "engage in the survey and exploration of petroleum and natural gas resources in third countries."

During his visit, the Indian Petroleum Minister stated:

We look upon China not as a strategic competitor but as a strategic partner. I am struck at the virtual similarity, indeed identity of our respective national requirements in the hydrocarbons sector as also the similarity, indeed virtual identity, in our national approaches towards finding practical solutions to the emerging energy demands of our fast-growing economies, which are among the fastest growing of the major economies of the world.

The two sides identified the following specific areas for bilateral cooperation:

i) upstream exploration and production, including seismic surveys, IOR and EOR, and joint ventures in E&P;

ii) refining and petrochemicals and the marketing of petroleum products and petrochemicals;

iii) transmission and city distribution of gas, including CNG;

iv) the laying of national and transnational oil and gas pipelines;

v) frontier and cutting-edge research and development in hydrocarbons;

vi) invigorating technological innovation and induction;

vii) software and other information technology applications in the hydrocarbon sector;

viii) energy efficiency and energy conservation programmes, and promotion of environment friendly fuels; and,

ix) unconventional hydrocarbon sources, including:

- coal bed methane;
- underground coal gasification;
- shale oil and shale gas;
- commercialising the production of gas hydrates;
- the hydrogen economy.

Since the visit, bilateral exchanges between Indian and Chinese companies have been intensified and joint bids for assets acquisition in third countries are being actively explored.

Saudi Arabia is India's largest supplier of crude oil, meeting 25 per cent of its annual requirements. Following the visit to India of King Abdul bin Aziz in January, 2006, the two countries have agreed to transform their present commercial ties into a "strategic energy partnership". This partnership is to be concretised through investments in each others' downstream and petrochemicals projects, as also through India's participation in Saudi Arabia's upstream proposals in the gas sector. Noting that Saudi Arabia is the world's principal oil producer and India is a major hydrocarbon importer, the two countries "affirmed the importance of stability in the oil market for the world economy." The Indian side praised Saudi Arabia as a "trusted and reliable source of oil supplies to international markets in general and the Indian market in particular."

India's cooperation with Nigeria, one of the world's principal oil producers is novel in that it is based on leveraging its hydrocarbon potential to promote domestic economic development projects: the MoU concluded by the ONGC-Mittal joint venture,

OMEL, with the Nigerian Ministry of Energy provides for OMEL to set up a refinery, power projects and railway-lines and equipment in exchange for two oil blocks on nomination basis, a long-term contract for supply of oil, and access to gas once the LNG facilities have been set up. This pioneering approach to bilateral cooperation, could serve as a model for India's interaction with other African countries which have a rich hydrocarbon potential even as they need considerable inputs of capital for their economic and infrastructure development.

Four countries, i.e., Russia, Norway, Japan and Republic of Korea have emerged as important partners for Indian companies for the development of domestic resources and capabilities, covering issues such as: increased oil recovery (IOR) and enhanced oil recovery (EOR); commercial and strategic storage; promotion of conservation and of environmental friendly fuels; training; health and safety; development of unconventional energy resources such as coal bed methane, underground coal gasification and gas hydrates; and, above all, pursuing equity participation and E&P proposals in third countries.

These proposed engagements emerging from India's 'oil diplomacy' involve refreshing traditional relationships with a new hydrocarbon-related content such as the proposed links with Russia and Romania, or replacing old suspicions with the new building blocks of cooperation, understanding and friendship with countries such as Pakistan, Bangladesh and China. It also has the potential of expanding India's diplomatic penetration across continents to new areas such as Norway, Latin America and countries of North and West Africa, that have traditionally been at the margins of India's diplomatic consciousness, and imbuing them with a new importance and urgency.

Indian oil diplomacy has already begun to yield concrete results. We have a 25 per cent equity participation in an oil producing field in Sudan, which provides India with three million tonnes per annum. Other producing fields in which India has equity states are in: Russia (Sakhalin I), Vietnam and Myanmar. We have also secured E&P contracts in Iran, Egypt, Qatar, Nigeria, Libya, Syria and Cuba.

As noted above, India's external hydrocarbon strategy is being implemented in a highly competitive international environment which is made up of international and national oil majors contending vigorously for assets in the few new areas in which they are available, i.e., in the Caspian, in Western and Central Africa, and in some parts of Latin America, while consolidating their presence in the Gulf. Again, this effort is currently being mounted in an oil market that has seen prices reach new heights, which has generated a frenzied environment, with international companies offering billions of dollars for assets that have acquired an enhanced and even undue value because of the high oil prices.

Taking into account the geopolitical situation and the competitive edge that informs the global hydrocarbon scenario, some of the major future challenges to Indian oil diplomacy are examined in the following paragraphs.

Clearly, the Gulf region has and will continue to have a central position in India's quest for energy security. However, the hydrocarbon resources of this region will be sought not just by India but also by other Asian and even European countries. The USA too will import a substantial portion of its requirements from the Gulf, even though it has been attempting to diversify its sources to Latin America, Africa and Europe.

The Gulf region has also unfortunately been in the vortex of considerable instability and insecurity for more than 25 years, witnessing the eight-year Iran-Iraq war in the 1980s; the first Gulf war in 1991; the prolonged period of sanctions, no-fly zones and inspections against Iraq, all through the 1990s; and, finally, the fallout of September 11 and the US-led war on Iraq in 2003. In spite of this environment of instability and violence, the region has generally been able to maintain the oil and gas supplies required by the world. However, from a geopolitical perspective, we cannot discount the possibility of large scale violence which could seriously disrupt supplies. This also raises questions relating not only to the security of the hydrocarbon facilities and the regimes that control them but also the safety of maritime carriers and the freedom of the sea lanes, and of the Straits of Hormuz, the Suez Canal and Bab-al-Mandab.

Hence, even though the Gulf will continue to be the principal supplier of hydrocarbon resources to India, prudent energy security policies require that sources of supply be diversified. In this context, it is noteworthy that Nigeria has now emerged as the number two supplier of oil to India, though these supplies are mainly based on spot purchases, rather than term contracts as is the case with supplies from the Gulf. On these lines, India is also actively looking for assets, both in terms of equity participation and E&P contracts, in Central Asia, West and Central Africa and Latin America. We have had some modest success in acquiring stakes in blocks in Nigeria, and are pursuing proposals in Angola, Kazakhstan, Cuba and Venezuela.

India is an active player in the LNG market. So far, two agreements for supply of five million tonnes of LNG have been finalised with Qatar and Iran. However, given India's huge requirements and proposals to set up additional LNG terminals along both the West and East coasts, India has already conveyed to both these countries and to other suppliers its need for increased supplies.

Transnational oil and gas pipelines

Transnational oil and gas pipelines are not only able to transport large quantities of hydrocarbons across hundreds, and even thousands, of kilometres, but, given their reach and range and the terrain they traverse, they also have significant geopolitical implications and even the ability to influence bilateral relationships and regional cooperation scenarios. For instance, the recently completed Baku-Tblisi-Ceyhan (BTC) oil pipeline seems to be an attempt to exclude Russia and Iran from the Central Asian hydrocarbon calculus. However, this policy is unlikely to succeed over the medium-term as Central Asian countries can be expected to make every effort to reach the lucrative markets of Asia through pipelines across Russia and Iran.

Kazakhstan on its part had already indicated its interest in utilising its hydrocarbon potential to firm up engagements with all its neighbours: if it has pleased the Americans by participating in the BTC pipeline, it has also participated with the Russians in the Aktau-Novorossisk oil pipeline, and with the Chinese in the 2000 km long Kazakhstan-China oil pipeline. The outlet for Kazakh oil to the Gulf, through Iran, was the first project considered by the Kazakhs, in the late 1990s, and had to be put on the backburner under US influence. This project could be revived, this time as a gas pipeline project, to take advantage of the huge market for Kazakh gas in South Asia.

Already, transnational oil pipelines are having certain curious implications for India's quest to diversify its sources. Thus, the BTC pipeline, intended to carry Caspian oil to Europe, has also raised the possibility of Caspian oil being shipped to India from Ceyhan, either through the Suez Canal (in case of small-shipments) or through the newly revived Ashkelon-Eilat pipeline in Israel (which has a two-way flow capability) which, through a double shipment arrangement by crude carriers from Ceyhan to Ashkelon and then from Eilat to India, has for the first time made Caspian oil available to India.

Again, in case the plan for a sub-sea pipeline from Ceyhan to Israel *via* Turkish Cyprus is realised, then India and other Asian countries would be able to obtain Caspian oil at Eilat on the Red Sea. Similarly, when the proposed pipeline from Alexandria to the Red Sea is completed, India would be able to access oil from North Africa, particularly Algeria and Libya, which today can reach India only by going round most of the African continent.

In order to meet its gas requirements, India is vigorously pursuing transnational gas pipeline projects both on its eastern and western land frontiers. The Iran-Pakistan-India pipeline is expected to bring to India nearly 90 MMCMD of gas which will be utilised to fuel power and fertiliser projects in North and North-Western India. India has been invited to participate in the Turkmenistan-Afghanistan-Pakistan pipeline, as a full partner. This will give us access to Central Asian gas resources and augment the supplies received from Iran. In the East, the Myanmar-India pipeline will not only bring Myanmar gas, but would also enable us to monetise Tripura gas, and promote power and industrial projects in our North-East and Eastern regions.

There is no doubt that transnational pipelines are difficult and complex ventures since:

(i) they involve different countries with differing interests;

(ii) being transnational in character, and involving neighbouring countries, they frequently bring on board a substantial and complex political baggage of disharmony and discord; and,

(iii) the projects are beset with serious technical and financial difficulties, requiring the mobilisation of huge resources from domestic and international sources in a environment of mutual trust and confidence.

These problems are particularly daunting in an Asian environment which has been the theatre of considerable intra-continental discord and conflict, and has relatively few success stories in regard to regional and continental cooperation. It is also true that some of the issues that divide Asian countries, particularly neighbours, are fairly complex and are unlikely to be resolved in the near future.

At the same time, it should be noted that the international community, over the last 35 years during which thousands of kilometres of oil and gas pipelines have been laid across all our continents, has developed laws, rules, norms and practices that ensure that pipelines can be insulated to a considerable extent from the vagaries of day-to-day politics and made 'safe and secure' on the basis of international best practice. Not surprisingly, today 130 transcontinental pipeline projects, valued at dollars 200 billion, are at various stages of implementation in Europe, Africa, North and Latin America, and above all, Asia.

While the challenges involved in the implementation of transnational pipeline projects are serious, what gives them impetus is the common interest of oil and gas producers to have stable markets for their products and for Asian consumers to have assured supplies to maintain their economic development programmes. Though Asia has relatively little experience of transnational oil and gas pipelines, the availability of abundant hydrocarbons within the continent, as also the overwhelming demand for this resource, ensures that concerns of national security and energy security can and should coalesce.

Complementary interests in energy security of producers and consumers constitute the strongest factor in enabling policy makers to replace contemporary political discord with energy-based cooperation. The proposed Asian gas grid, which is merely a vision at present, could in time become the best manifestation of this approach.

The Asian gas grid

While the world's gas map depicts numerous pipelines moving across thousands of kilometres from Russia, Central Asia and the North Sea to Western Europe, hardly any pipelines move Eastwards and Southwards. This is now set to change due to two important developments:

(i) the increasing Asian demand for gas; and

(ii) the ability of Asia to transport gas economically from producers to consuming centres.

The Asian gas grid envisages the setting up of a series of pipelines that will carry natural gas in North and Central Asia and the Gulf to the various consumption centres in East and South Asia. Some of the principal pipelines in the proposed grid are:

i)   the Russia-Kazakhstan-Iran pipeline to the Gulf,

ii) the Myanmar-China pipeline,

iii) the Sakhalin-Nakhodka-ROK-China pipeline,

iv) the Uzbekistan-Turkmenistan-Azerbaijan pipeline,

v)   the extension of the BTC pipeline from Ceyhan through Syria and Jordan to Egypt,

vi) the Iran-Pakistan-India pipeline, and

vii) the Turkmenistan-Afghanistan-Pakistan-India pipeline.

According to current estimates, the additional pipelines required to realise the Asian gas grid would be about 22,500 km, costing about 22 billion dollars. The Asian continent, particularly Russia, the principal Asian consuming countries, and the major producing countries of the Gulf are readily able to provide the financial and technological resources for the project.

Besides contributing significantly to the growth and prosperity of the continent as a whole, the project would have other benefits such as developing the electricity, petrochemical and fertiliser industries; promoting transcontinental cooperation in trade and industry; upgrading local skills and expanding employment opportunities; and, above all, generating the resources that would enable Asian governments to fund their poverty alleviation and other welfare programmes.

In simple financial terms, there would be very obvious advantages for all the countries involved in the grid, the producers, the consumers and the transit nations. According to an energy consultant, total financial benefits in the first year of the project (2006) would be dollars 1.5 billion. Over the next few years, the benefits would increase significantly every year, amounting to dollars 55 billion in 2025.

Regional cooperation

In recent years, energy think tanks have engaged in a debate on whether the global supply of hydrocarbons has 'peaked' so that the next few years will see a steady decline in supplies, with consequent implications for prices, economic development programmes and heightened political contentions. However, the emerging view is that hydrocarbon resources are available to meet demand over the next 30-50 years. Historically, though predictions of 'peak oil' have been made from time to time, global production has regularly increased to meet demand. As Daniel Yergin has pointed out, new technologies have made it possible for oil companies to find new sources of oil and extract oil from old sources. According to a survey released by him recently, between 2004-2010 world oil supplies will increase by 16 million barrels a day, well over the likely demand increase.

However, there is no room for complacency since new oil will be available in physically challenging areas such as the deep sea or frozen terrain or environmentally sensitive locations. Again, it will require huge investments for its extraction, amounting cumulatively to about $ 5 trillion up to 2030, at the rate of $ 20 billion per annum.

Meeting the global demand for oil and obtaining the financial resources to ensure supplies requires the rejection of political contentions based on narrow national considerations and, in its place, calls for an integrated regional and global effort to pool together the world's human, financial and technological resources in a spirit of cooperation for mutual benefit.

India took the first significant step in promoting this cooperation at regional level by convening a Round Table, in New Delhi, in January 2005, of the four principal Asian oil-consuming countries—China, Japan, Republic of Korea and India—getting into dialogue with the principal oil-producing countries of West Asia and South-East Asia. The 11 assembled Ministers agreed on the importance of this first dialogue between Asian consumers and producers and, in a consensual statement, identified substantial commonality of interests as also specific areas of cooperation.

Separately, to complement the earlier Round Table, India again took the initiative to bring together the four principal Asian oil-consuming countries in dialogue with oil-producers of North and Central Asia, including Russia, Kazakhstan, Uzbekistan, Azerbaijan, Turkmenistan and Turkey, in November 2005.

These two regional Round Tables have thrown up a number of specific areas for cooperation. These include: reform of the Asian oil markets, promotion of criss-cross investments in hydrocarbons between producers and consumers, development of strategic reserves, development and transfer of R&D and technology, and development of capabilities to promote energy conservation and efficiency and environment-friendly fuels.

At the second Round Table, the assembled dignitaries approved a consensual document committing themselves to regional cooperation in the Asian oil and gas economy. Specifically, they agreed to study: "the promotion of developing gas and oil interconnections through LNG and through transnational oil and gas pipelines within the Asian region for integrating energy markets as well as improving the transportation infrastructure." The studies to be undertaken will focus on "the exploration of alternative linkages by land and sea throughout Asia."

The Ministers recognised that, for these interests of Asian consumers and producers to be pursued effectively, the knowledge-base of Asian countries would have to be expanded in those areas where the interests of producers and consumers coalesce. The Ministers agreed to meet annually to pursue their consensual plan of action.

Energy security for India

Given the central role that energy security plays in the national development of a country, it has to be seen as an integral part of the national security of the country concerned. However, energy security has attributes that distinguish it from other aspects of national security: first, while various aspects of national security are generally *status quoist*, in that they protect and sustain the existing order, be it national borders, national political structures or national values, energy security is a dynamic concept in that it enhances a nation's economic and, therefore, political status by providing it with the resources to pull its people out of poverty and pursue national growth and development.

Secondly, while national security has at its core the maintenance of a country's national interest, energy security cannot be attained on a purely national basis; it is inherently cooperative in character and is founded on engagements with other countries — given that hydrocarbon resources will continue to dominate the global energy mix (and, hence, the energy mix of most countries) for at least the next 25 years if not longer, for the world's energy resources to be harnessed efficiently, a cooperative approach at bilateral, regional and international levels is both inevitable and urgent.

This cooperative approach logically emerges from the realities of the contemporary global hydrocarbon scenario. As noted above, a major mobilisation of the world's capabilities and resources has to be mounted to explore and develop the world's hydrocarbon potential which is available in diminishing quantities, individual discoveries finds are generally smaller than before and are increasingly difficult to access. In response, the oil industry is already integrating in significant ways: major companies are merging to pool together their financial resources and technological capabilities. Again, there is a clear trend in favour of national oil companies integrating across the hydrocarbon value-chain, from exploration to production, to transportation, to refining and petrochemicals. E&P contracts in developing producer countries are increasingly being linked to refinery proposals and, on occasion, even to other infrastructure development proposals such as roads, railways, power, mining and port development projects.

Above all, the surge in oil prices over the last one year, even as it has adversely affected economies in different parts of the world, has called for greater scrutiny of the organisation and functioning of the world's oil markets—their non-transparent and non-rational foundations and procedures, with attendant calls for reform, particularly from developing countries that are seeing their hard-earned resources wither away and their development programmes in jeopardy.

India has just commenced a constructive engagement at bilateral, regional and global levels. It is increasingly being seen as a significant player in the international energy economy and as a valued partner in the world's quest for energy security. However, these are early days and only the first steps have been taken. The task before us is to understand the importance and impact of the contemporary global developments set out above and effect the required adjustments in our politics and policies and, above all, in our mindset, in order to effectively respond to these global challenges.

This is a thoroughly revised and expanded version of an article by the author that had appeared in *Seminar* (November 2005).

Heritage, culture and diplomacy

55

Indians around the world

J.C. Sharma

Introduction

The role played by the Chinese diaspora in modernisation and economic development of China and the Jewish diaspora in mobilising political support for Israel has brought the role of overseas communities into sharp focus. All the countries with large overseas communities are engaging in developing policy framework and mechanism to leverage this important resource in pursuit of their national interests. The end of the cold war and the process of globalization and economic liberalisation have given a further impetus to this phenomenon. East European countries and the Baltic Republics are making a determined effort to leverage their diaspora for the transformation of their societies. Valdas Adamkus an American of Lithuanian origin in Chicago returned to Lithuania to become the President of the country. In a reversal of its earlier policy, Vietnam is also making determined efforts to involve her diaspora in accelerating the economic development. Ireland is a major success story of economic resurgence by leveraging the resources of her diaspora. With over $ 22 billion per year, India is the largest recipient of remittances in the world. Besides investments and remittances, the transfer of knowhow and skills is being accorded a very high priority by most of the countries.

The communication revolution and the global reach of the media are creating a major change in the nature of relationship between the diasporas and their countries of origin. Because of the presence of large overseas communities, many internal political developments quickly acquire an external dimension. Diaspora takes keen interest in the electoral process and also fund political parties and candidates. Some non-resident Indians (NRIs) have even returned to contest elections.

A number of separatist movements the world over draw sustenance, particularly financial support, from the diasporic communities. The terrorist organisations often try to tap the diasporic network in planning and execution of designs. India has directly experienced the implications of diaspora's involvement in the separatist movement in Punjab. The Liberation Tigers of Tamil Eelam (LTTE) also has a strong support base among the sections of Tamil diaspora around the world. Inter Service Intelligence (ISI) has actively cultivated some segments of the Indian diaspora. Because of major security implications and important role of diaspora in the development process, particularly technology transfer, the strategic communities have also started paying attention to the study of diaspora.

The presence of large overseas communities has become one of the important factors in bilateral relations between various countries. The overseas communities no doubt, are also emerging as an important market for the products and services from the countries of their origin.

The Indian diaspora

The role of the Indian diaspora in India's fight for independence from British rule deserves special attention. The independence movement received substantial support from the overseas Indian communities. Mahatma Gandhi evolved his basic strategy for India's independence movement in his long years in South Africa. The Congress Party had established relationship with Indian communities in several countries. India League in UK and the Gadar Party in North America played an important tool in mobilising support for our independence movement. The India League in the UK and the Gadar Party in North America were prominent in mobilising support for our fight for freedom. Netaji Subhash Chandra Bose's Indian National Army (INA) attracted numerous recruits and received valuable support from our diaspora in South-East Asia. Gandhiji returned permanently to India after a long sojourn in apartheid South Africa where he had perfected the art of non-violent struggle against racism of the worst kind. He applied the same principles of truth and non-violence to lead the millions of Indians in their successful fight for freedom. The Indian independence movement in turn, greatly influenced our diaspora throughout the world and inspired them to take an active part in the freedom movements in their respective countries.

The Indian diaspora spans the globe and stretches across all the oceans and continents. Indian diaspora is so widespread that it has been said, perhaps in a lighter vein, that: "the sun never sets on the Indian diaspora." It is estimated to be about 20 million strong. There are about 10,000 or more overseas Indians in 48 countries. In 11 countries, there are more than half a million persons of Indian descent and they represent a significant proportion of the population of those countries. They speak different languages and are engaged in different vocations. Their industry, enterprise, economic strength, educational standards and professional skills are widely acknowledged. What gives them their common identity is their Indian origin, their consciousness of their cultural heritage and their deep attachment to India.

Driven by the economic compulsions generated by colonialism, people of Indian origin began to migrate overseas in significant numbers only in the 19th Century. In a uniquely diverse pattern that has not been replicated by any other diaspora, except perhaps the Chinese, Indians spread initially to the countries of Africa, Caribbean, South-East Asia and Fiji. They migrated in small numbers to the West Coast of Canada and the US. It was succeeded in the second half of the 20th Century, by a steady outflow of some of India's best professionals to the developed countries of the West. In the wake of oil boom in 1970s, India's skilled and semi-skilled labour moved to West Asia and the Gulf. Sri Lanka and Nepal also have large population of persons of Indian origin, including people who are not citizens of these countries. These communities are a class apart because of the policy of open borders with Nepal and historical reasons and political complexities in Sri Lanka.

There are three major categories of overseas Indians. The first category consists of Indian citizens staying abroad for an indefinite period for whatever purpose. They have been classified as NRIs in the Foreign Exchange Regulation Act 1973. An overwhelming number of NRIs are in the Gulf countries. However, significant numbers are also present both in the developed world and in South-East Asia. This category of overseas Indians (OIs) is a comparatively recent, mid-20th Century phenomenon. It was an entirely voluntary response to the demand for labour to fuel faster development, initially in the post-World War II Europe and later, in oil-rich Gulf countries. A person ceases to be an NRI as soon as he becomes a citizen of the country of his residence.

The second category of OIs is Persons of Indian origin (PIOs) who have become citizens of the countries of their settlement. It includes the descendents of the migrants who were recruited as indentured labour by the British, French, Dutch and Portuguese colonial masters and the Indians who have migrated from former British colonies in various parts of the world.

There is also a category of PIOs who are legally and technically branded as Stateless Persons of Indian Origin (SPIOs). They have no documents to substantiate their Indian origin. There is reluctance, and in some cases outright refusal to accept them in countries of their permanent domicile. Lack of any tangible evidence also disqualifies them for Indian citizenship. Fortunately, now SPIOs primarily remains in Sri Lanka and Myanmar.

Migration under colonial rule

In ancient times, migration of Indians to other parts of the globe was driven by both the spirit of adventure and trade in spices and precious metals such as gold and silver. It was peaceful and not a product of military conquest and thus, Indian culture and civilisation left an indelible mark on these regions.

The abolition of slavery in the British, French and Dutch colonies in 1834, 1846 and 1873, respectively, created extreme shortages of labour in the plantation economies of their colonies. A large number of Indians were recruited as indentured labour and transported to various parts of the Empire.

The majority of the migrants under the indenture system were induced or encouraged to leave India by painting a rosy picture of the life ahead. The contracts were not only unethical but also illegal because most Indians were innocent of the provisions. In many cases, they were not even correctly told the names of the countries to which they were transported. A number of workers did not survive the arduous voyage. Mortality rate was high because of the inhuman conditions of their camps and the cruelty of their employers. Indentured labour was, therefore, nothing but a euphemism for slavery. The extraordinary achievements of Indian workers in the face of these heavy odds is best described by Vishwamitra Ganga Aashutosh, a Mauritian poet:

No Gold did they find
Underneath any stone they
Touched and turned
Yet
Every stone they touched
Into solid gold they turned

In the first phase, beginning in 1834 the majority of emigrants were recruited in the 'hill coolie' district of Chota Nagpur division and Bankura, Birbhum and Burdwan districts of the Bengal Presidency. Soon the recruiting areas were pushed westward into the Hindi speaking zones and most of the indentured labour was hired from Eastern and Central UP, Western Bihar and later, from the Madras Presidency. They left India by ships from Calcutta and Madras. Subsequently, Indian labour was taken to Sri Lanka and Malaysia under the *Kangani* (a foreman acting as recruiter) system and to Burma (Myanmar) under the *Maistry* (labour supervisor responsible for recruiting) system. France sent labour from its colonies in Pondicherry and neighbouring areas to Réunion,

Martinique and Guadeloupe. Holland recruited indentured Indians for its colony in Suriname. Portuguese also recruited Indians from their possessions in Goa, Daman & Diu for their colonies in Africa and Macao. In the early phase of this migration, the overwhelming majority of migrants were males. It was only in the later period that special efforts were made to recruit females. The indenture system came to an end in 1917. But, traders and other enterprising people who voluntarily followed these migrants at their own expense in search of greener pastures continued to come under the 'free passage system'.

Indian emigration to what were once the East African Community (Kenya, Uganda and Tanzania), as well as the then Northern and Southern Rhodesia (Zambia/Zimbabwe) was necessitated in the 19th Century by the extension of the British colonial empire to Africa. Eastern African Railways was constructed through the sweat and blood of Indians. Four workers died for each mile of the railway line laid. Indians introduced organised commerce in East Africa replacing the barter system they established regular shops and were known as *Dukawala* (shopkeepers).

Migration of Indians to North America began in mid-1903 when Sikh male immigrants from Punjab settled in Vancouver, British Columbia to work in lumbering, agriculture and the railroads. Most of these migrants had served in the British Army or in the lower echelons of bureaucracy. As there was a steady increase in the number of Indian workers, the Canadian Government passed several laws to limit their entry into Canada. The *Komagata Maru* (a Japanese ship) incident of 1914 brought into sharp focus the fortitude of Indian immigrants and the blatantly discriminatory and racist attitude of the Canadian authorities.

Some of these workers radiated southwards to California and the neighbouring areas as US had till then not passed discriminatory legislation. A small number of students who had come to pursue higher education chose to stay back in the US. As a result of lobbying by Indians, the Congress passed an Act in 1946, which gave Indians the right to naturalisation and allowed a token quota of 100 immigrants. This act enabled Dalip Singh Saundh, who had come as a student, to become the first Asian member of the US Congress in 1956.

The *Raj* connection led to the emergence of an Indian community in UK. Some Parsis and Bengalis settled down in UK in the 18th and 19th centuries as professionals. The number further increased, as many soldiers of the British Indian Army settled down in Britain. Dadabhai Naoroji was elected the liberal member to the House of Commons in as early as 1892.

The migration of labour under indenture system led to the emergence of large overseas Indian communities in Mauritius and Reunion Islands; South and East Africa; Guyana, Trinidad and Tobago, Suriname, Guadeloupe and Martinique in the Caribbean region and Fiji in the Pacific.

The independence of above mentioned colonies did not end the trials and tribulations of the Indian settlers in spite of the fact that they had played an important role in the struggle for independence. Except in Mauritius and to some extent South Africa, everywhere else they were branded as 'outsiders' and subjected to discriminatory treatment. They were denied their due share in the important organs of the state, particularly armed forces, police and bureaucracy. In Fiji, they were denied the land rights. Here, envy of their economic status and political activism prompted several anti-Indian coups. In Africa, their prosperity and lifestyle generated some resentment among the local population. The Indians, however, continue the struggle for political power. Cheddi Jagan, Bharat Jagdeo, Basdeo Panday and Mahendra Chowdhary did succeed in attaining highest political offices. Jaggernath Lachmon became the longest serving speaker of Suriname. Because of poor representation in vital organs of state, their hold on power remains tenuous.

The blatantly discriminatory treatment coupled with the problems of safety and security led to migrations to the developed world. In East Africa, Idi Amin's brutal treatment and expulsion of Asians led them to migrate to UK, Canada, US and Australia. A large number of Indo-Caribbeans migrated to UK, Canada, US and Holland. The coups in Fiji against leaders of Indian origin led to the migration of many educated Indians to Australia, New Zealand and Canada.

However, the resilience and sheer grit of the Indian community enabled them to overcome these crises. Their professional skills and business acumen earned them special place in the economic, social and developmental activities in the countries of their settlement. Anand Satyanand, an Indo-Fijian has been nominated to take over as the Governor General of New Zealand. Shridath Ramphal had a long innings as the Secretary-General of Commonwealth.

With a population of more than 700,000 PIO, Mauritius is the only country where Indians constitute 70 per cent of the total population. This coupled with their stewardship of independence movement under the leadership of Sir Shibsagar Ramgulam, has enabled them to achieve political pre-eminence and have a major share of power since independence. The economic power, however still remains in the hands of French companies.

The Indian communities in Réunion Islands, Guadeloupe and Martinique were granted full French citizenship giving them a prominent position in civic and political life. They are trying to recapture their cultural heritage which had got diluted because of the policies of the colonial rulers and conversions in earlier stages of migration.

1.2 million strong Indian community has a long history of political activism and struggle against apartheid in South Africa. Recognising this, both President Nelson Mandela and President Mbeki appointed Indians to prominent positions. The affirmative action policies have however created a sense of vulnerability among some sections of the Indian community. The future of the Indian community will depend on its ability to play a positive role in the South African reconstruction and renaissance. The Indians play an important role in the economy as well as in professions in East Africa.

The colonial connection also led to settlement of large number of Indians in Sri Lanka, Myanmar, Malaysia and Singapore. Majority of them worked in plantations. However, a number of them were involved in services like police, railways, education, law and medicine. Indian migrants in Malaysia suffered under the Bhumiputra policy. 1.6 million Indian community here, has per capita income lower than the national average. In Burma, Indians suffered heavily as a result of the policy of Burmanisation (replacing English with Burmese in all teaching establishments and in government administration). This led professionals and educated Indians to migrate from 1962-1964. The present day community lags behind in education and professions, the areas they dominated till independence.

The Indian community constitutes approximately 9.7 per cent of Singapore's population. The current President S.R. Nathan is of Indian origin. There are about 85,000 Indians in Thailand, 55,000 in Indonesia, 38,000 in the Philippines and 7600 in Brunei.

Migration after Independence

A steady flow of migration took place after Independence that included skilled, unskilled and high-qualified professionals who went to UK, and other countries of the West to meet the shortages of labour in the wake of the Second World War. Indian healthcare professionals became the backbone of the National Health Care Service of UK. Post-independence migration to USA and Canada was primarily education driven. The Immigration Act of 1965 in US and the regulations introduced in Canada in 1967, paved the way for the settlement of a large number of professionals in both these countries. The term 'brain drain' was coined primarily because of the migration of highly qualified professionals from India to the United States. Indian community in US, UK, Canada, Australia and New Zealand constitutes primary migrants from India and secondary migrants of Indian origin from Africa and the Caribbean. There is however limited interaction among the two. There are 50,000 Indians in Hong Kong. In Europe, Indian communities are also present in Netherlands, Portugal, France, Germany, Italy and Greece. Spain and Canary Islands have prosperous Sindhi communities. The Gujarati community in Antwerp plays a major role in diamond trade.

The 45,000 strong Indian community in Israel is unique, as its members have not migrated because of any persecution or discrimination. The members of the community are keen to maintain their links with India.

From their humble beginnings in the industrial and retail sectors, Indians have risen to become one of the highest earning and best-educated groups in UK. They have made a mark in politics with 6 elected MPs and 14 members in the House of Lords, including Lord Meghnad Desai, eminent economist, and two Baronesses. Businessmen, like steel magnate Lakshmi N. Mittal, S.P. Hinduja, Lord Swaraj Paul, Lord R.K. Bagri. Gujaratis and celebrity authors like Nobel Laureate Sir Vidya Naipaul, Salman Rushdie, Amitava Ghosh are counted among Britain's Who's Who. Gujratis, who migrated from East Africa as 'free passengers', enjoy an enviable status as successful entrepreneurs. Indian food is so relished among the locals, that chicken tikka is jokingly referred to as the national dish of Britain. No doubt, Indian community has emerged as the most influential ethnic minority in UK.

The Indian community in the US has emerged as the largest and fastest growing constituent of the diaspora. Due to their rich contributions in the fields of medicine, engineering, knowledge-based industries, agriculture, education, finance, medicine, management and particularly, information technology, its members have created a special niche for themselves. High levels of education have enabled Indo-Americans to become a very productive segment of the US population and to contribute to the unprecedented economic boom of the nineties. The Patels, a sub-community of Gujaratis, occupy such a dominant position in the hotel industry that sometimes 'Motels' are jokingly called 'Potels'. The per capita income of the community is higher compared to the average per capita income of US. These achievements have given Indians the confidence to take greater interest in the affairs of the mainstream community. They have become politically more active.

Overseas Indians in Canada lay great emphasis on education and are highly regarded in the fields of medicine, academia, management and engineering. Herb Dhaliwal's appointment as

Federal Cabinet Minister and Ujjal Dosanjh's election as first non-white Premier of British Columbia are important landmarks in the political arena. There are eight Indo-Canadian MPs in the Canadian Parliament. Indo-Canadians enjoy great respect in Canadian society.

The hi-tech and education-driven migration is contributing to the growth of Indian community in Australia. Both Australia and New Zealand have a sizeable presence of Indo-Fijians.

The oil boom of the seventies opened vast opportunities in the Gulf region. Even though Indian blue-collar workers and professionals constitute the single largest expatriate workforce in the Gulf Cooperation Council (GCC) countries, but they have no prospect of acquiring local citizenship. They are preferred because of their diligence and high qualifications. Their presence has no adverse effect on the local society. The Indians in the gulf contribute over 40 per cent of the total remittances. A study by the Centre for Development Studies (1972-2000), showed that remittances formed 22 per cent of the Kerela State's income in the nineties. They made the largest purchase of Resurgent India Bonds and Millennium Bonds.

In response to serious complaints of exploitation by agents and the employers in the gulf, Indian Government has taken many steps to safeguard the interest of migrant workers in the Gulf. The Emigration Act of 1983, was enacted to provide a regulatory framework. Welfare officers have been posted in all the Indian missions. Although, there has been some improvement over the years, but a lot still needs to be done.

Religious and socio-cultural attitudes

The entire Indian diaspora shares one common feature. It takes great pride in its civilisation and cultural heritage. Religion plays an important role in the affairs of the Indian community. The scriptures of Indian epic *Ramayana*, *Hanuman Chalisa* and *Bhagvad Gita* have sustained them spiritually and given them required strength to tide over adversaries. It has enabled them to cope with the stresses and strains caused by an alien environment. They have constructed numerous temples, gurudwaras, mosques and some churches. The Swami Narayan temple, on the outskirts of London is one of the finest examples of Indian architecture. In Mauritius, they have even created a huge lake called *Ganga talaab* (lake). Water from the Ganges and all other sacred rivers of India was put in this lake at the consecration ceremony.

Indian music and dance remain popular with the diaspora. Bollywood has an all pervasive influence and is an important medium of maintaining ties with India. While the dress of the host country is adopted for day to day work, traditional costumes of India are popular on all festive occasions. In fact, most Indian women maintain two wardrobes. Indian cuisine remains their favourite, no doubt with local modifications.

The Indian community has formed a number of social, cultural, political and religious organisations. They have also maintained a tradition of philanthropy benefiting both locals and Indians. Overseas Indians, particularly the post-independence migrants, take active interest in political and social developments in India. In times of national crises or natural calamities, the community associations raise generous contributions for relief and rehabilitation of the victims in India.

Conscious of the debt they owe to the country of their origin in terms of the value systems that have helped them rise meteorically among the Indo-Americans. This has led to a strong desire in them to give back something to India. Inspired by the American tradition, many Indians, particularly IIT graduates, have established Chairs and schools in their institutions. Some Indo-Americans have also helped establish Chairs in Indian studies in the US universities. The community has a number of NGOs engaged in projects in the fields of education, healthcare and rural development.

Official policy

The complaints about the cruelty and exploitation of Indian indentured labour, forced Government of India to take direct interest in the subject. Inspired by Lord Macaulay, Act V of 1837 was enacted for the welfare of overseas Indian workers. The Office of the

Protectorate-General of Emigrants was created to protect the interests of the immigrant workers.

Government of India appointed a Commission of Enquiry which had the Indian Russomoy Dutt as one of the members. In 1859, a system of writing annual reports was introduced for the first time. Ingnoring the appalling conditions of indentured labour, the Government of India allowed the French and the Dutch to recruit from India. Alan Octavian Hume suggested to the Governor-General Lord Lytton in 1877, that indentured labour be banned as it had antagonised the Indian public opinion. Disregarding the advice, it allowed migration to Uganda for building the East African Railways. The British Government was finally forced to bring indenture to an end in 1917.

The Indian National Congress took keen interest in the issue and discussed it in several Congress sessions. There were three main schools of thought in the party among the nationalists. One group believed in an Indian colony abroad to serve as an outlet for surplus population. The second group stressed the right of the Indians overseas to equality of status and treatment throughout the British Empire. The third group accorded primacy to the interests of local indigenous majority. Nehru was also influenced by the third group and a reflection was his decision to dissolve the Ministry of Overseas Indians in 1947.

The reverberations of the Indian independence movement were felt in all the colonies across the world and particularly, in the British colonies. The PIOs took active part in most of these independence movements. In many cases, they created the political consciousness among other fellow citizens of the country. Mahatma Gandhi's role in arousing political awareness in South Africa is very well known.

Indians played an important role in the political awakening in East Africa. In Fiji, they first promoted the idea of independence. Chhedi Jagan played a leading role in the independence of Guyana.

The Government of India under Pandit Jawaharlal Nehru extended strong support to these movements. The situation however, became complex after these countries attained independence. The aggressive nationalism in the wake of independence often worked to the disadvantage of Indians. They faced expulsion from Myanmar (Burma). The cruelty of Idi Amin is too well known to be repeated. The Indians in Caribbean also had faced a very difficult time. The Government of India faced a policy dilemma. Nehru had always advocated that the PIOs should identify themselves with the countries of their settlement. As a champion of the anti-colonial movement and a strong opponent of apartheid, he could only advocate a peaceful and amicable co-existence. It was felt that Nehru's policies failed to sufficiently protect the legitimate interests of the PIOs. His successor, Prime Minister Shastri worked out the Shastri-Sirimavo Agreement with Sri Lanka for settling the question of Indians in Sri Lanka.

The Indian government did whatever it could to provide some succour to the hapless victims of Idi Amin's cruelty. It strongly lobbied with the Government of the United Kingdom (UK) to take responsibility for British subjects of Indian origin. It allowed them to stay in India till they had made alternative arrangements. The Indian communities in Myanmar, East Africa and Caribbean definitely felt that the Indian Government had not done enough for them during their hour of need.

Nehru did take up the question of citizenship rights of Indians with the Canadian leaders and discussed their welfare with other leaders of the Commonwealth. The Indian government, within the constraints of the prevailing political situation and India's economic limitations, tried to do whatever it could for the welfare of overseas Indians. India extended generous assistance in the field of education and healthcare. A number of overseas Indians were given scholarships to study in India. The assistance was provided to the overseas community to maintain and strengthen their cultural and civilisation heritage.

The military coups in Fiji brought into sharp focus the vulnerability of some of the large overseas Indian communities. Once again, there were somewhat unrealistic expectations from the Indian Government. India led at strong lobbying effort in all international forums and even succeeded to a certain extent as international sanctions were imposed.

The Indians in Guyana and Trinidad have faced similar problems. Chhedi Jagan was kept out of power by intrigue and unfair means. There have been reports of threats of violence and intimidation of Indian voters. President Bharat Jugdev's government in Guyana remains under constant threat. In Trinidad and Guyana, the bureaucracy, the army and the police are heavily dominated by the blacks while the Indians are not given their due share in these vital organs of the state. In the early years after Independence, Cold War politics had its own impact on inter-racial relations in Caribbean countries. The Indian Government has generally followed a policy of restraint, ensuring that it is not accused of interference in the internal affairs of the countries concerned.

Political engagement of the diaspora

The strong reaction to political developments in India in the 1970s by the diaspora in US and UK, made Government of India develop a policy of engagement towards the communities in the developed world. It led to the efforts by major political parties to mobilise the overseas Indian communities in their favour. Indian missions were asked to develop close rapport with the communities. The need to counteract the active support and funding to the Khalistan movement by certain sections of the Sikh community, gave a further impetus to this process of engagement. The global organisation of PIO was formed in 1989.

Because of their extraordinary achievements, the first generation migrants acquired the confidence to take part in the activities of the mainstream society in US, Canada and UK. The affluent Indians started making contribution to the election funds. In US, several organisations were formed to actively lobby for promoting India's interests and counteract anti-India forces. The community is playing a major role in mobilising support for Indo-US Nuclear Co-operation agreement. Political activism has led to keen interest in India's internal political developments including electoral politics. Various religious and ethnic groups lobby for causes of their respective communities leading to divisions in the community. These have been exploited by the intelligence agencies of the countries inimical to India's interests. Several parliamentarians from UK, US and Canada take more than usual interest in various internal political issues in India because of the presence of large Indian communities in their constituencies. Various groups in India also make use of the diaspora for promoting their interests.

Political Implications: The presence of significant numbers of overseas Indians is an important factor in bilateral relations with countries of their settlement. The impact can be both positive and negative. UK Government's attitude towards PIOs with British passports from East Africa was a subject of constant negotiations between India and UK. The activities of the Khalistani separatists were a major irritant in India's relationship with Canada for nearly two decades. The ouster of Bawadra and Mahendra Chowdhary Government had a major adverse impact on Indo-Fijian relations. Differences in approach to post-1987 coups developments in Fiji cast a shadow on India's relations with Australia. Presence of diaspora in Iraq and Kuwait heavily influenced India's policy towards Saddam regime in 1991. India had to pay a heavy price for this policy. Maltreatment of Indian IT professionals in Malaysia created an outrage in Indian media. The plight of Indian workers in the Gulf has an impact on Indian public opinion.

Social issues

Emergence of large overseas communities has generated several issues with serious legal and consular implications. The issues of abandoned brides and related matters, like child custody, maintenance and property have acquired serious proportions. On their part NRIs have complained of harassment under dowry laws. Suitable mechanism would have to be evolved to deal with these issues.

Role of diaspora

The relationship between India and her diaspora is closely interlinked. The diaspora has maintained emotional bond with India and the network of about 20 million Indians settled abroad is a potential forum to showcase India on the World stage. They can play a very constructive role in the development of India and contribute towards mutually beneficial relations with the country of their residence.

Political Role: The diaspora can supplement the efforts of the government. Some influential members of the diaspora have access to the highest level of decision makers. They can facilitate contacts and sensitise the senior leaders on issues of vital concern to India. The diaspora members in democratic countries play an important role in briefing elected representatives on India related subjects. They can also facilitate their visits to India. No doubt they play a very useful role in providing access to parliamentarians and opinion makers. Many Indians now occupy important positions in the media. This can help in creating better awareness about India related matters. They can also facilitate access to the editorial board and staff. The Indian academics can also help in creating better awareness about India amongst fellow academics and student community. Senior academics had helped arrange my talks in leading American Universities in the wake of India's nuclear tests. Some leading academics of Indian origin are also consulted by the government of their respective countries. They can also help arrange dialogue with leading intellectuals. The political organisations of the diaspora also act as influential lobbying groups. The young Indians working in US Congressional offices are a great asset for both the countries.

Economic Development, Commerce and Trade: The liberalisation of Indian economy since 1991, has opened up opportunities for accelerating the development process and investments in India. The diaspora can help increase bilateral trade and commercial relationship with a number of countries. The overseas Indians can be major catalysts in the development of quality infrastructure. They can facilitate the entry of venture capital funds and participate in various financial schemes like deposits in banks, bonds, shares, mutual funds and others. Israel has a well-organised system of raising billions of dollars every year through Israel bonds with the help of Jewish diaspora. The finance professionals can help to make Mumbai an international financial centre. High-quality result oriented business outsourcing is yet another field of participation by the diaspora.

Indian diaspora is an asset as a customer. They are the link to the flourishing markets across international borders. They make personal use of daily consumables from India, enjoy Indian movies, music and buy ornamental goods like art and craft. This not only opens up the Indian market abroad but also provides a platform for cross-country selling and trade.

Besides being customers, members of Indian diaspora can be successful suppliers of their businesses and trade in India. The senior professionals in multinationals can motivate their corporations to invest in India and make it their manufacturing and R&D base. This opens up a world of opportunity for India to have hands on to hi-grade technology, working skills, management and material. The diaspora can also make a significant contribution to the growth of tourism and its infrastructure in India.

Science and Technology and Knowledge-based industries: There is a large reservoir of highly trained experts and scientists in knowledge-based industries, such as, information technology, biotechnology and nanotechnology. They can play an important part in developing India as an R&D centre. Taiwan and Israel have leveraged their diaspora very effectively for R&D and technology transfer.

Healthcare: The pioneering role and the success of institutions like Apollo, Escorts and Prasad Eye Institute, clearly demonstrates the part that diaspora can play in secondary and tertiary healthcare in India. They can be a major asset in promoting India as a healthcare destination. The diaspora can effectively contribute towards the expansion and growth of pharmaceutical industry. Indian doctors can facilitate tie-ups for clinical trials and medical outsourcing. Overseas Indians can be a major resource in popularising Ayurveda abroad.

Education and Culture: These are the other two areas where diaspora can play an important role in strengthening linkages between India and countries of their residence. They can help to revamp education sector and establish world class institutions in the country. India Business School, Hyderabad is a fine example of the role of diaspora in developing management studies. The proposed Institute of Public Health would be yet another model of partnership with diaspora. Similarly, they can facilitate setting up of Indian academic institutions abroad. The diaspora can facilitate academic exchanges, collaborations and twining arrangements between Indian and foreign institutions.

Philanthropy: The Indian diaspora has been eager to donate generously for worthy development causes in India. Major diaspora organisations and forums are actively involved in the promotion of education, healthcare, rural development and micro-financing making a vital difference in the areas of their adoption and thus, to India as a whole. Some diaspora volunteers also share their expertise in various fields.

Initiatives since the nineties

The achievements of India and her diaspora created the right climate for opening a new chapter in their relationship. Recognising the importance of overseas Indians in the wake of liberalisation and globalisation, the government took new initiatives to engage the diaspora. The PIO Cards Scheme covering all segments of the diaspora was launched in 1999.

A high level committee

A high level committee was appointed by the Government of India in August 2000, under the chairmanship of Dr. L.M. Singhvi, a distinguished Member of Parliament who had been India's High Commissioner in the United Kingdom. The other members were R.L. Bhatia, MP, a former Minister of State in the Ministry of External Affairs and currently, Governor of the State of Kerala, J.R. Hiremath, former diplomat and special envoy of PM for Africa fund, Baleshwar Agarwal, Secretary General of the Antar Rashtriya Sahayog Parishad (ARSP), which has been involved with matters concerning our diaspora for several decades. The author was the member secretary. The terms of reference for the HLC required it to make a comprehensive study of the Indian diaspora; identify whatever problems it had been encountering and make detailed recommendations for resolving those problems. The Committee travelled to 21 countries and interacted with a wide cross-section of the Indian diaspora. It commissioned studies and received expert group reports from several ministries and organisations like FICCI and CII.

This report is the first most exhaustive study on the Indian diaspora and its relationship with India. The Committee also examined the diaspora's expectations from India. All segment of diaspora want assistance from the mother country to maintain their cultural and civilisational heritage and pass it on to the coming generations. The diaspora in developing countries, particularly in the countries where they feel economically vulnerable, is keen to avail of higher education facilities in India. They want assistance in equipping them with qualifications which would ensure economic security and upward social mobility. No doubt all sections of diaspora would like to have an enabling environment to facilitate their commercial and economical interaction in India. The report provided a blue print for leveraging the strengths of India and her diaspora to their mutual advantage.

The Committee made three interim recommendations:

a. Improvement in PIO Card Scheme and reduction of fee.

b. To declare January 9 as Pravasi Bharatiya Divas (PBD).

c. Institute Pravasi Bharatiya Samman Awards.

All the three interim recommendations were accepted by the government. Other recommendations have also received favourable consideration and a number of them have been implemented.

Dual citizenship

The Committee suggested that dual citizenship should be permitted for members of the Indian diaspora who satisfy the conditions and criteria laid down in the legislation to be enacted to amend the relevant sections of the Citizenship Act, 1955. It did not recommend the grant of political rights and employment in government services. The Committee did not favour the automatic grant of dual citizenship and suggested that specific applications be made for the purpose. In a nutshell, the Committee suggested a new class of citizenship called Overseas Citizen of India.

The government accepted the Committee's recommendation and the Parliament passed a bill granting dual citizenship in March 2003. This facility was to be granted to OIs only in those countries which clearly accepted the concept of dual citizenship.

Dual citizenship is a complex issue and granting it has generated a degree of resentment among sections of PIOs in countries like Trinidad, Guyana, Fiji and South Africa. There is some misunderstanding on this subject. The primary objective of dual citizenship laws of the countries like Trinidad and Guyana is to make enabling provisions for maintaining linkages with their citizens who are settled in US, Canada and UK. These provisions were not meant to enable 51 per cent Indo-Guyanese or 40 per cent Indo-Trinidadians to take up the citizenship of India. Most critics have also not understood the political sensitivities and complexities in these countries. The provision of dual citizenship would make them more vulnerable and provide ammunition to their critics who have maintained that Indians were outsiders in these countries. It is doubtful that Indians from East Africa would have been able to settle down in UK, Canada, US and Australia in such large numbers, if they had dual citizenship of India. Dual citizenship is an evolving process which would raise many legal and consular issues of jurisdiction. It could be refined as some experience is gained over a period of time. The government must develop expertise in the field of private international law to safeguard its interests.

Pravasi Bharatiya Divas (PBD)

The government declared on the 9th of January as the Pravasi Bharatiya Divas (Indian Diaspora Day). The day was chosen because Mahatma Gandhi had returned to India on January 9, 1915, after spending 21 years in South Africa. It symbolises the commitment and attachment to the cause of India by overseas Indians.

The Prime Minister inaugurated the first PBD on January 9, 2003. Around 2000 overseas Indians from 62 countries attended the event. It witnessed an unprecedented enthusiasm in India for fostering a relationship with the overseas Indians. The five-plenary and nine-parallel sessions were devoted to discussing cooperation between India and the diaspora in knowledge-based industries, investments, healthcare, voluntary sector, ethnic media. The entertainment programme showed the extraordinary popularity of Bollywood among all segments of the diaspora and the role it plays in connecting diaspora to India.

The External Affairs Minister in his address clearly stated that India has shed the inhibitions to engage the diaspora. The event was a milestone in India's relationship with its diaspora. It raised the feeling of collective diasporic consciousness and the Global Indian Family and was a major step in development of a web like relationship between India and all the constituents of its diaspora.

The Second Pravasi Bharatiya Divas held in Delhi from 9-11 January 2004, was also an outstanding success. One of the highlights was an internship programme for 25 youths of the diaspora from across the world. The Prime Minister announced the decision to establish Pravasi Bharatiya Kendra (Indian Diaspora Centre) in Delhi. The Government would give an initial corpus of 250 million rupees and suitable land in a prestigious location.

Ministry for overseas indians affairs

The UPA government carried the process further for strengthening the ties with the diaspora and established a separate Ministry of Overseas Indian Affairs. They continued the policy of celebrating the PBD and the third PBD was held in Mumbai, from 7-9 January, 2005. In his inaugural address, the Prime Minister announced further liberalisation of the policy for dual citizenship. The President conferred the Pravasi Bharatiya Samman Awards.

The fourth PBD was celebrated in Hyderabad. The Prime Minister handed over Overseas Indian citizenship cards to first two recipients. A programme for developing diaspora knowledge network was announced. A scheme was also launched in partnership with UTI bank for facilitating remittances. The government also declared its intent to favourably consider the demand for voting rights for

NRIs. A bill is being drafted for this purpose. The grant of voting rights to Indians in the foreign countries, in general and the Gulf in particular deserve a very thorough study and debate as it has far reaching implications for our national interests. In any case, such a right should be first extended to the voters living in various parts of the India outside their own constituency.

All the four PBDs have had a special session on the Gulf. The discussions in these sessions have resulted in several initiatives like establishment of a Pravasi Bima Yojna, granting of educational facilities to the children of blue-collar workers, 24-hour help lines and introduction of direct flights. The Overseas Indian Ministry is also taking steps to control the activities of unscrupulous agents.

The PBD has emerged as an important forum for interaction with diaspora. It also provides an opportunity for intra-diaspora dialogue on issues of concern to them. During the second PBD, leading industrialist Mukesh Ambani had told the author that this event has the potential to become the Davos of Indian diaspora. It must however, be organised in a very professional manner and the venue must be announced a year in advance.

Conclusion

The destinies of India and its diaspora are intertwined. It is best illustrated by the achievements of both since the 1990s. It was during this period that India registered it's most impressive economic performance and became a full-fledged nuclear power. Synergies between India and Indo-Americans in the information technologies sector provided impetus to the development of a mutually beneficial relationship. These developments enhanced the prestige of both India and her diaspora. It cannot be a mere coincidence that it was during the 1990s that persons of Indian origin became Presidents, Prime Ministers and Ministers in a number of countries. They also attained the highest positions in academia and in the corporate world.

The diaspora is poised to play an important role in accelerating the development process worldwide. This process needs to be nurtured. India would have to create enabling environment for investments and hassle-free mechanism for technology transfer. The Ministry of Overseas Indians must have a system for regular interactions with eminent personalities and organisations of the diaspora from different parts of the worlds. Greater attention need to be paid to the non-English speaking overseas communities. The High Level Committee's recommendations for establishment of a data bank and Pravasi Bhartiya Kendra must be implemented without delay. The Kendra must emerge as a focal point of diaspora related activities throughout the year. It must have an excellent library and a permanent exhibition on evolution of the Indian diaspora in various parts of the world. India can learn a lot from the experience of other countries with large diasporas. The Kendra and some other dedicated think tanks should provide facilities for research for this purpose.

A special emphasis must be given to engaging the younger generation of the diaspora by expanding youth exchange, internship and India study programmes. A good beginning has been made however, it needs to be substantially expanded. A good example is the MASA (journey) programme of Israel. MASA's vision is that every year young Jews from around the world will start their journey with a semester or year in Israel, exploring the land, experiencing its culture, growing and learning together as they enter the global community. It is a partnership between the Government of Israel and Jewish Agency both contributing US$ 50 million each. Under a similar programme, the Indian universities should be encouraged to start India study programmes of different durations for diaspora youth. The Ministry of Overseas Indians can partner such programmes with various diaspora organisations.

To conclude, a new chapter has been opened in India's relations with its diaspora, including relations among the Indian diasporic communities worldwide. Overseas Indians are invaluable in India becoming a knowledge superpower and becoming a developed country by 2020.

56

Culture as an instrument of diplomacy

Pavan K. Varma

The coinage Cultural Diplomacy is fairly new but if we think back, this idea is as old as history. All accounts of our past, show how cultural negotiations—the gifting of gems and jewellery, art objects and artefacts, the sharing of court poets, dancers, musicians, painters, sculptors, even cooks, craftspeople, weavers and so on, presenting rare plants and animals of one's country to another, are records of how political issues have been resolved, or at least restrained, with help from things which are part of the cultural composite of a nation. Trade opened new avenues of approach to each other. Markets opened up and aided this process. All exchanges, economic and otherwise, closed in distances and brought communities together. They cemented a friendship that had beneficial long-term effects. This was cultural diplomacy at play.

Now we are looking afresh at this idea because its value is not lost to us. We know that governments are made up of people, and they work for and with the people. Any policy matter, therefore, is intricately joined at the core with people. Culture takes root in people directly, because all of us understand and connect to matters of culture—music, dance, drama, food, dress, films. The list is inexhaustible. We may, or may not, make sense of foreign policy, but a song touches us directly even if the words make no sense. Images, from a film or a play, evoke memories in us instantly. They mirror our lives, our experiences. They force us to face the reality that, ultimately, we are essentially the same, subjects to the same emotions, feelings and desires. No matter how many borders separate us, no matter how many boundaries we have between us, there are many indivisible aspects to us.

Cultural activity is very often a part of our daily lives. But when it is consciously given a shape, it succeeds in spreading those aspects of ourselves that truly and essentially characterise us as a community and as a nation. Sharing, sensitivity and respect for our own culture, and for those of others, forms the core of cultural diplomacy. This thought also forms the core of Indian philosophy— all that is noble must be allowed to flow in. This belief allows a continuous interaction between cultures, one that is constructive and lays the foundation for an onward journey between one human being with another, cutting across borders and boundaries, moving beyond barriers and boardrooms.

When we listen to someone singing, we go through a range of emotions. And the same happens whether we watch a dance performance, or a play, or look at a painting. In case, the lyrics remain foreign, it is the music which touches us, which connects us to the singer. If the words make sense, they transport us to feelings above the ordinary. For example, a Sufi song by Abida Parveen lifts us up to feelings completely removed from those of land and boundaries. There is, at that moment, no thought of which country she comes from. We connect instantly to the Great One and His is the spirit that fills us. Even in the case of a modern rock performance, where the sentiments may be far removed from a spiritual experience, and the lyrics may seem to resonate with modern angst, we react to the words which probably force us to face the truth of a lonely, rootless, deprived life. Even to those of us who may not take well to modern music, we never dismiss a song or a singer because of her or his nationality, rather we do so on the grounds that the words are too depressing, or the music too loud, and so on.

The same holds true for any of the art forms. A play, written in one country and re-adapted in another, connects at a level deeper than the verbal. *The Ramayana* is one epic, but its story is told with variations by different nations. The Malaysian version has numerous shades which may not be seen in the Indonesian one. In spite of its shades, it remains the story of the victory of good over evil, a universal narrative that would relate across the globe. Shakespeare's plays, whether reinterpreted in Mizoram or made into films—such as *Ran* in Japanese or *Maqbool* and *Omkara* in Hindi—play again upon universal themes which we respond to as people, not as Indians or of other nationalities. We look to such means of cultural sharing with gratitude. Such exchanges bring us far closer to each other than other logical, well-thought arguments ever can.

Today, we have once again become aware of the importance of cultural diplomacy. This consciousness can be seen across the globe. Institutes of cultural diplomacy have come up, which impart training for what is seen as an indispensable subject of study and practice today. The British foreign secretary now presides over a board on cultural diplomacy. The British Council and the BBC are two of its other participants. The Alliance Française, the cultural extension of the Government of France, much like the British Council and the Indian Council for Cultural Relations (ICCR), is being given renewed importance wherever it exists. Even today, Russia has over 80 active cultural centres in various parts of the world, of which there are 5 in India; the erstwhile Soviet Union had maintained over 150 such Centres abroad. Notably, the US Secretary of State, Condoleezza Rice, stated in great detail in her testimony to the Senate on the eve of her confirmation to the post, that her focus is on the "soft power" of America, and how it could be leveraged in the interests of that country. According to a recent edition of the *Newsweek*, China is the latest entrant to this field. China's focus on cultural diplomacy will be aggressive; by the year 2010 it intends to spend 10 billion dollars, an astounding amount, to set up 100 centres abroad. These centres, in keeping with its spirit of antiquity and history, will be named, interestingly enough, after Confucius.

The challenge for India, in the face of such figures, is great. We are emerging slowly as an important face in the areas of politics, economics and the military. In the field of culture, however, we have always been a superpower, given our civilisational depth and antiquity. It was this realisation of our cultural force that led to the conceptualisation and creation of the ICCR as far back as 1950. Maulana Abul Kalam Azad founded the Institution, and his vision was fully shared by Pandit Jawaharlal Nehru, our first Prime Minister. India stands today at the threshold of being accepted as a new global cultural ambassador, a perception no doubt modulated by the fact that we are emerging as a significant global power in other arenas as well. The interest in what we have to offer culturally has always been there, but today it is seen in a new light. The world wants to know what makes us tick; they want to study our history and our roots; they wish to understand our age-old tradition and wisdom; and they want to understand what makes us respect and retain our diversity. Perhaps, the most important question they have is how such a multilayered country, with such a large number of the poor, has managed to become the world's largest democracy, and is now poised to become a major economic power. The world wants, in short, to understand India's past, not only for its antiquity, but to link that heritage to the changes of the present and the promise of the future.

In this scenario, India has an opportunity to project our strengths. We are a democratic and secular nation; we are a plural society that respects and draws sustenance from its diversity; we have a rich and ancient heritage; we are a multilingual, multi-religious and multiethnic people who have managed to preserve our individual essence and national character.

Such strengths of our country are reflected in our foreign policy objectives and further reinforced through our diplomacy. To my mind, politics and culture are complementary, two sides of the same coin. In fact, cultural diplomacy itself is an intensely political matter, while politics can't do without cultural interventions. The practice of culture within a country, and by extension the practice of sharing cultures across borders, helps to lay the foundations of and reinforce political diplomacy.

The ICCR already runs 20 cultural centres abroad and supports 24 Chairs of Indian studies in universities around the world. It plans to open some new cultural centres abroad, which includes one in Washington. We hope this centre will come up at the earliest possible. Plans are already underway to open centres in Kabul, Kathmandu, Dhaka, Paris, Tokyo, Bangkok, and one in West Asia, among other parts of the world. In August 2005, during his official visit to Afghanistan, Prime Minister Manmohan Singh announced 500 scholarships for Afghan students to pursue undergraduate and postgraduate studies in India. The ICCR has been mandated to administer this special scheme, which includes courses in the Arts, Sciences, Engineering, Commerce, Business Administration and Law. The response to this offer has been overwhelming. The Centre in Kabul will help to service these 500 scholarships for Afghan students. The ICCR currently offers 1200 scholarships every year to foreign students to pursue undergraduate, postgraduate and Ph.D. courses in India. The grant of scholarships to Afghan students, which is in addition to the general scholarships already offered by the ICCR, is a positive step toward strengthening and promoting Indian cultural ties with other nations.

Overall, the ICCR has increased the pace of its activities tremendously. This can be seen in the number of activities that have been organised, both in India and abroad. In February 2006, a very successful Conference, "Continents of Creation: Legacy, Identity, Assertion," was held in New Delhi and Neemrana. This brought together 45 writers from 20 countries of Africa and Asia to converse on matters of international consequence that impact us all today. An important forthcoming event later this year is the Festival of India for the European Union in Brussels; work is on for a proposed Festival of India in Japan in 2007, which marks the 60th anniversary of our Independence. In Mumbai, at the Jinnah House, plans are underway to set-up a South Asian Centre for Arts and Culture which will become a vibrant focus for South Asian cultural activities—Art, Music, Theatre, Films, Dance. After all, it is we in India who share Urdu with Pakistan, Nepali with Nepal, Bangla with Bangladesh, Tamil with Sri Lanka and English with the rest of the world!

Indians, in my view, are specially blessed as model cultural ambassadors. The composition of our country is such that we live a cultural medley every moment of our lives. India is made up of numerous states, each a tiny nation in itself. We have an array of languages; in most cases, we speak a different dialect every few kilometres. Communication is an art, one that most of us begin to learn and appreciate the moment our senses come alive. We are a multireligious country. Our respect for the faith that we subscribe to individually, extends to what others practice as well. This sensitivity and respect for each other's beliefs is enshrined in the Constitution of the country making us a secular nation. Our legal systems reflect this double combine very well. They keep the secular nature of the country in view while at the same time keeping religious sentiments protected as far as possible.

As Indians we live a life of convergence and divergence, which orchestrates beautifully. We share food habits, yet we nurture flavours and aromas peculiar to us. We share dress codes and yet are aware of the slight differences which set us apart. Our fabrics are very similar and yet we are alert to the slight shifts in the regions they come from by that one small motif or colour used. Our architecture varies from state to state and yet the sharing is so obvious. Our places of worship are structured in ways that we can read our philosophies in them. Hundreds of such examples are available. And it is these lived instances which record the cultural negotiations that we are part of every minute as Indians.

Cultural diplomacy is, therefore, an integral aspect of our vocabulary. As Indians, we have understood in innate ways that we must retain our individual traits as well as draw from our community bank. We know that it is the exchange of 'culture' between ourselves that draws us closer and makes us stronger. We are able to perceive the universal in the individual precisely, and *vice versa*, because we live this fact. For us, therefore, as a nation, to extend this idea to the political front on an international level is not really a difficult task.

Culture is an enormous source of power. It has the potential to shape, alter and impact the ideas and opinions of public communities. From a wide ranging perspective, culture has the capability to resolve tensions and prejudices—ethnic, religious, communal, national and international. It can create a climate of tolerance, respect and understanding among nations, religions and entire regions. It is thus, an essential medium for peaceful and tolerant contact and communication. From a more political point of view, culture is both a diplomatic tool and a crucial bridge. It leads us to understand each other with the help of what gives us, to a large extent, our identities. A theatrical evening, a film show, a painting exhibition, a *qawwali* performance sets the mood for an instant connection between peoples which can further lead to other areas of cooperation. Cultural exchanges can take away the formality which may be seen in an across-the-table negotiation. The feelings of comfort and ease that cultural interactions can bring will add to other forms of diplomacy.

The success of cultural diplomacy relies on intercultural dialogue and mutual respect. It is an active and planned process, unlike what many see as a random series of events. It is actually a projection of our identities, our philosophies, our values, the unique personality and essence of a nation, on an international platform, and the willingness to expose ourselves to cultural assets of other nations. In its implementation it requires the support and active involvement of a country's peoples, its artists, its non-governmental organisations, corporate entities and all others who give that country its individual character and mood. Cultural diplomacy cannot be practiced in a vacuum. It must be a multifaceted interaction, one that holds the power to join each of us to a larger world, one which will teach us respect, appreciation and sensitivity to ourselves and to others.

57

Media and diplomacy
Navtej Sarna

I had heard somewhere that Hermes is the God of Diplomacy. When I looked up the ancient deity on Google (surely the greatest invention since scotch tape) I found that he was also the God of several other things—shepherds, merchants, athletics, thieves and liars, to name a few. Somewhat bemused, I wondered if the connection of diplomacy to some of the other dubious categories to whom Hermes played God was due perhaps to the presumption that diplomacy also involves a certain amount of shrewdness and cunning. But then, on reading more, the penny suddenly dropped. Hermes is, most importantly, the messenger of the God to the humans—carrying and explaining messages, crossing boundaries between the different worlds and guiding lost souls. In other words, he is an envoy and a communicator—some sort of mix of a modern day diplomat and media person.

In fact, the ability to communicate is an essential prerequisite common to the media person and the diplomat. Diplomatic communication among the ancient Greek city-states depended on direct and oral exchanges and face-to-face contacts between representatives. Envoys were chosen for their oratorial skills; Pericles and Demosthenes were often entrusted with delicate diplomatic missions. Harold Nicholson recalls that Sri Krishna, an envoy of an ancient Indian ruler, would say before embarking on a mission: "I will go to convey the matter of my master, the ruler, in the most eloquent manner... I will persuade the men of their court to accede to his demands. Then, if I fail and war erupts, the world will see how we were right and how they were wrong... and the world will not judge us wrongly."

The ability to communicate effectively as well as correct use of language, information gathering skills and incisive analysis should have ensured that media and diplomacy were sister worlds. Perhaps, they are, but often it seems that they are stepsisters. The reason is not far to find. A very fundamental difference seems to outweigh the commonalities. Diplomacy among nation states in the modern sense has been practiced, for the large part, in secret despite Woodrow Wilson's call in 1918 for "open covenants, open arrived at". Secret messages, cipher telegrams, confidential exchanges are the bread and butter of traditional diplomatic practitioners. This is not the place to go into the necessity of various levels of secrecy; suffice it to say that this approach very often governs the mindset of the practicing diplomat. A journalist, on the other hand is guided only by one motivation—that he has to find a story and once he has found it, he has to tell. Given these two antithetical approaches, it is only natural that the relationship between diplomacy and media begins on a somewhat uncomfortable basis. Nevertheless, for at least two crucial reasons, diplomats have no alternative but to successfully manage this relationship. First, the media has a growing and undeniable impact on how foreign policy initiatives are projected and perceived; secondly, the media is the main vehicle that makes the image of a country. Individuals or countries who manage the diplomacy-media relationship better than others run away with a tremendous advantage.

In the Indian context, one can discern several changes in the recent past that make proper management of this relationship imperative as well as complicated:

- Exponential growth in communication technology over the last 15 years or so has changed the way diplomats and media persons work. In the 16th Century it took four months for a Hapsburg diplomat to travel to Moscow and in the 17th Century it took 11 days to send a courier from Paris to Madrid. By the end of the 18th Century, a US President could write a memorandum to his Secretary of State, lamenting the fact that the ambassador in Spain had not been heard from for two years. "If we do not hear from him this year," he added, "let us write him a letter." In my own experience as a young diplomat in East Europe in political turmoil in the mid-eighties, I recall that it was fairly safe to send letters by diplomatic bag regarding demonstrations and protests, the only competitor being the BBC World Service radio. The diplomat no longer enjoys such luxury; in fact, he no longer even enjoys the luxury of merely reporting events. The CNN factor, first witnessed in hotel lobbies in Delhi during the 1991 Gulf War, has changed all that. Given the instant communications, it would be futile for a diplomat to report, as in the past, the fact of a protest or a demonstration. He must presume that before he reports the facts, they are already known or in fact, they have been seen on the screen by those who matter. The diplomat's role, therefore, becomes that of an analyst rather than a mere reporter and he has to ensure that he has added enough value to what he is sending back home if it is to have any impact beyond what the TV channels have already registered. Instant television has, therefore, changed the role of a diplomat from information gatherer to information analyst. The media person too is increasingly unwilling to be far away from the scene of action and relying on agency copy. An ever-larger number of media organisations want their people on the spot sending back special dispatches in print, and more important, on camera.

- In the comfortable old days—again, we need to look no further then 15 years ago—the world of diplomacy in India was covered by a set of about 20 erudite, polite gentlemen of the press and the dutiful Doordarshan and All India Radio. Briefings were comfortable, friendly and somewhat leisurely affairs, full of intellectual wit and repartee. The media persons would gather what they could before turning to the *chai, samosa* and *gulab jaman* and thereafter find, their way back to their offices to tap out the stories for the rest of the evening. Today we have to deal with not only a hugely expanded print media but also more than 30, 24-hour TV news channels, several news agencies and even on-line journals. More than 70 Indian correspondents are now on the MEA beat, not to mention the more than 200 foreign correspondents based in Delhi (the number of foreign media representation could probably cross 500, if one were to include Indian nationals writing for foreign media organisations). Its not only that the numbers have changed, the timelines have shrunk. Twenty years ago the Official Spokesman's briefing at 4:30 pm would usually wait to be carried the next morning, and perhaps in the Doordarshan and AIR bulletins in the evening. Nowadays, the briefing is often on the air even before the Spokesman has returned to his room, and the quest for clarifications has already begun as the story develops further. And 4:30 pm is no longer the sacrosanct hour of the briefing anymore, again a reflection of changing media demands. If a story breaks at 7 am in the morning, as stories have a way of doing, it is difficult to tell an aggressive TV journalist, already under pressure from competition, that he or she should wait till 4:30 pm for a reaction. Polite, erudite gentlemen of the press definitely still cover foreign policy but so do several young, confident enthusiastic TV reporters who will give you three sentences between commercial breaks to capture the nuance of a diplomatic situation. The diplomat involved therefore, has to be prepared to react at all times and has to choose his idiom accordingly. Should he respond with a byte, bit or book?

- A very high level of media interest in foreign policy issues is thus today, a reality. But, this interest level is not uniformly distributed over global issues. The unfortunate reality is that a story on India-Pakistan or India-US relations, will usually overcome any space or time constraints but the same cannot be said about stories concerning India's relations with the rest of the world. In the areas in which it is interested, our media is not content simply to report events. Very often, the media is almost a third player, with a view of its own, wanting to set or influence agendas. This is only to be expected in a free democratic environment and nowhere has this been truer than in the case of India-Pak relations. In recent years, media engagements at the summits in Lahore (1999), Agra (2000), Islamabad (2004) and Delhi (2005), has been at unprecedented huge levels and added its own volatile charge to the bilateral discussions. Availability of spokesmen, alacrity of response, depth and range of briefings, have played a critical role in determining how the issues under discussion, have been perceived by the public. There are several other incidents in recent times, when media interest has brought issues which would normally have been the subject of negotiations between foreign offices and embassies out into the street. The hijacking of IC-814 to Kandahar, the kidnapping and fortunate release of three Indian truck drivers in Iraq and the recent evacuation of Indians from Lebanon are obvious examples.

The short point behind detailing the above trends is that diplomats have to realise that the media dimension of any foreign policy initiative, development or crisis has to be considered and addressed. It is sometimes useful, if not very charitable, to imagine the media industry as a many-headed behemoth, each head representing a TV channel or a newspaper. The behemoth needs to be fed with information at regular intervals. It cannot go hungry. If one party does not feed it, the other will.

It would be somewhat presumptuous for this writer to lay down any prescribed modalities as to how media has to be engaged. These modalities vary with each particular situation and a certain amount of flexibility in one's method is not only necessary but desirable. It would also depend upon the nature of the issues involved, the scale of the media present and the desired objective. Press conferences, small briefings, background briefings, interviews, written briefs are among the various options that can be deployed. For instance, over the last few years, technology has enabled us to refine the methodology of MEA briefings. Today, depending on the nature of the news of the day, the full scale on camera briefing is varied with electronic issue of briefing points and postings on the website.

Having said that, a few general comments which would be applicable to any diplomat who has to interact with the media whether at headquarters or in missions abroad would perhaps not be out of place. The first prerequisite is an open and positive mindset which projects a willingness to engage the media and not to regard it as an adversarial party. Media persons like diplomats have a job to do and appreciate those interlocutors who help them to perform their job successfully and effectively. That is not to imply that the diplomat has to breach any rules of his job. Media persons are aware that there are things which diplomats can discuss and there are things which must remain confidential; for the most part, they are willing to respect this distinction. Press officers also need to know that media persons work under time pressure. They appreciate straight answers. If you don't have the information or cannot divulge it, then it is best to tell them so and allow them to move on to other sources. Ground realities for conversations and briefings should be clearly set and once set, they are usually respected. Media persons appreciate background briefings. It helps them to understand the context of an issue and if they are foreigners then the broader political, social or cultural ramifications which would help their story into perspective. George Merlis in his book *How to make the most of every media appearance* lays down five commandments, which are worth repeating:

1. Thou shalt be prepared.
2. Thou shalt know to whom thou art speaking.
3. Thou shalt be quoteworthy.
4. Thou shalt be practiced.
5. Thous shalt not lie, evade or adopt an attitude.

For press officers in Mission, it is essential to understand the requirements and the methods of working of the local media and respond to them accordingly. For instance, in Washington DC senior editors and correspondents would rarely be available to respond if called cold on the telephone. In fact, more often than not, the telephones are on voicemail mode. However, a courteous message either by voicemail or by email is almost always responded to and appreciated. Similarly, they would expect their email or voicemail queries to be responded to by the end of the day. Focussed, early morning breakfasts are considered more productive than backslapping, long and boozy dinners. Forthrightness and candour go further than obvious spin. Up-to-date, concise briefing material (not spam) is always appreciated. The rules of the game may be completely different in capitals like Moscow, Cairo or Islamabad.

I would like to end by quoting two incidents which are still fresh in my memory because of the two gems of wisdom that they left with me. First, I remember a hard drinking one-time war correspondent telling me over a Burmese lunch in a small restaurant in Washington DC, "In the media make your friends when you don't need them." And when I first took over the job of the Official Spokesman, a lady of considerable experience warned me, "Don't be overconfident with the press—they can be ruthless."

That about sums it up.